The Official Guide to
U.S. Law
Schools

FROM THE PRODUCERS OF THE LSAT

yale
Harvard
Fordham

Bantam Doubleday Dell

Published by
Bantam Doubleday Dell Publishing Group, Inc.
1540 Broadway
New York, New York 10036

ISBN: 0-385-31297-0

ISSN: 0886-3342

Manufactured in the United States of America
Published simultaneously in Canada

June 1994

10 9 8 7 6 5 4 3 2 1

Table of Contents

How to Use This Book

The Official Guide to U.S. Law Schools is both a resource book for individuals seeking broad information about law school in general, and an up-to-date, detailed guide to the 176 ABA-approved law schools.

In the school profiles section, which comprises the bulk of this book, you will find several pages of information on each of the ABA-approved law schools in the United States. This information is provided by the individual schools each fall and includes current data on the school's admission process, programs of study, enrollment and student body, faculty, library and physical facilities, career services, financial aid, and more. A new chapter this year features a visual geographic guide to law schools across the country. We provide information on school and city populations on these pages as well. Most schools also provide an admission profile grid displaying information on the number of applicants and admitted students grouped by their LSAT scores and GPA numbers.

The first 13 chapters of the *Official Guide* are geared toward answering your questions if you are:

- considering a law school education after graduation from college

- preparing to enter law school in the near future

- thinking about law as a possible career choice

- contemplating a change from your current career

The *Guide* gives answers to the most commonly asked questions regarding law as a career, preparation for and application to law school, the choice of a school to attend, and the financing of a law school education. Additionally, the *Guide* addresses the important issue of opportunities in law for minority men and women. Information can be found both within the individual school descriptions and, more specifically, in Chapter 7. This book also contains recent information regarding admission to the bar and job prospects, including useful statistics based on the experiences of 1992 law school graduates.

No guidebook on legal education can rightly claim to be a final authority on the many questions that the law school applicant will encounter. Whether you are choosing a school, selecting courses or other activities, or investigating career opportunities, you will be faced with decisions that, in the final analysis, will be yours alone to make. As you seek counsel from those who have been to law school, those who teach law school, those who admit students to law school, and those who successfully practice law, you are likely to meet strongly divergent viewpoints on the numerous points that concern you. Regarding various aspects of legal education, there is no single school of thought, but rather ongoing, vigorous discussion of numerous important issues. Your research will help you to make **informed** choices, which will increase your chances of success in meeting your own goals. We urge you to review carefully the information in this book and understand its limitations. Additionally, you should seek information from as many sources as possible, particularly from the law schools themselves. The information provided in this volume is one way to start.

Chapter 1: Being a Lawyer

Lawyers and Their Skills

Law practice is so diverse that it is not possible to describe the so-called typical lawyer. Each lawyer works with different clients and different legal problems. Ordinarily, certain basic legal skills are required of all lawyers. They must know:

- how to **analyze** legal issues in light of the existing state of the law, the direction in which the law is headed, and relevant policy considerations;

- how to **synthesize** material in light of the fact that many issues are multifaceted and require the combination of diverse elements into a coherent whole;

- how to **advocate** the views of groups and individuals within the context of the legal system;

- how to give intelligent **counsel** on the law's requirements;

- how to **write** and **speak** clearly; and

- how to **negotiate** effectively.

■ Analyzing

Lawyers must be able to determine the fundamental elements of problems. They spend much time discerning the nature and significance of the many issues in a particular problem. In every issue, the lawyer must study the relationship between each element in order to arrive at an answer, result, or solution.

■ Synthesizing

Lawyers must learn that because of the complexities of many issues and the number of laws either directly or tangentially relevant, they must be able to pull together in a meaningful, focused, cogent manner often large amounts of material.

■ Advocating

As an advocate, the lawyer's role is to represent his or her client's particular point of view and interests as vig-

orously as possible. The American judicial system assumes that equitable solutions will emerge from the clash of opposing interests. The success of this adversarial system of American law depends upon the talents and training of the lawyers who work as advocates within it. Lawyers must be able to use their advocacy skills to marshal evidence and present arguments as to why a particular outcome is desirable.

■ Counseling

Lawyers also spend a good deal of their time giving clients legal advice. Few ventures in the modern world can be undertaken without some understanding of the law. Through their knowledge of what the law involves, lawyers advise clients about partnerships, decisions, actions, and many other subjects. In many cases, the lawyer's role as a counselor serves as much to prevent litigation as to support it.

■ Writing and Speaking

Whether in the courtroom or the law office, lawyers must be effective communicators. If lawyers could not translate thoughts and opinions into clear and precise English, it would be difficult for the law to serve society. After all, the law is embodied in words, and many of the disputes that give birth to laws begin with language—its meaning, use, and interpretation. Litigation leads to written judicial opinions; congressional enactments are recorded as printed statutes; and even economic transactions must be expressed as formal, written contracts.

■ Negotiating

One of the lawyer's primary roles is reconciling divergent interests and opinions. When the parties to a proposed transaction disagree, the lawyer, acting as a facilitator, may be able to help them negotiate to a common ground. Although the client's interests are a lawyer's first priority, often those interests are served best after compromise and conciliation have paved the way to an equitable settlement. Because lawyers are trained to see the implications of alternative courses of action, they are often able to break an impasse.

Fields of Law

Lawyers are central figures in the life of a democratic country. They may deal with major courtroom cases or minor traffic disputes, complex corporate mergers or straightforward real estate transactions. Lawyers may work for giant industries, small businesses, government agencies, international organizations, public interest groups, legal aid offices, and universities—or they may work for themselves. They represent both the impoverished and the wealthy, the helpless and the powerful. Lawyers may work solo, in a small group, or in a large law firm.

About 71.9 percent of American lawyers are in private practice, most in small, one-person offices and some in large firms. Roughly 10.7 percent of the profession works for government agencies, 9.8 percent works for private industries and associations as salaried lawyers or as managers, and one percent is in legal education. Many lawyers develop expertise in a particular field of law. Large law firms that provide a full range of legal services tend to employ more specialists. The sole practitioner, who must handle a variety of problems alone, may have greater opportunity to work in several areas.

Of course, there are lawyers in large firms who maintain general practices, and lawyers in one-person offices who concentrate on a particular legal issue. Both specialized and general practice can be rewarding. One offers the satisfaction of mastering a particular legal discipline, and the other the challenge of exploring new fields. Following are brief descriptions of selected areas of specialization, though there are many areas of the law that can rightly fall into more than one category:

■ Corporate Law

The corporate lawyer helps clients conduct their business affairs in a manner that is efficient and consistent with the law. The responsibilities of a corporate lawyer can range from preparing the initial articles of incorporation and by-laws for a new enterprise to handling a corporate reorganization under the provisions of federal bankruptcy law. Examples of other areas of corporate law practice include (but are not limited to) contract, intellectual property, legislative compliance, and liability matters.

■ Criminal Law

Criminal defense lawyers represent clients accused of crimes. Their public counterparts are the prosecutors and district attorneys who represent the interests of the state in the prosecution of those accused of crimes. Both types of criminal lawyers deal with fundamental issues of the law and personal liberty. They defend many of the basic rights considered crucial to the preservation of a free and just society.

■ Environmental Law

Environmental law is a relatively new area that was born out of widespread public and professional concern about the fate of our natural resources. Lawyers in this field may tackle legal and regulatory issues relating to air and water quality, hazardous waste practice, natural gas transportation, oil and gas exploration and development, electric power licensing, water rights, toxic torts, public land use, marine resources, and energy trade regulation. They may work directly for governmental agencies that address environmental problems or represent corporations, public interest groups, and other entities concerned about protecting the environment.

■ Family Law

Family, or domestic relations, law is concerned with relationships between individuals in the context of the family. Many lawyers who practice this kind of law are members of small law firms or are sole practitioners. They specialize in solving problems that arise among family members and in creating or dissolving personal relationships through such means as adoption or divorce.

■ Intellectual Property Law

Intellectual property law is concerned with the protection of inventors' rights in their discoveries, authors' rights in their creations, and businesses' rights in their identifying marks. Often, an intellectual property lawyer will specialize in a particular area of the law. For example, for those attorneys with a technical background, patent law is a way to combine one's scientific and legal background into one practice. A copyright attorney counsels authors, composers, and artists on the scope of their rights in their writings, music, sculpture, and even personal identities, negotiates contracts which will protect these rights, and litigates in court to enforce these rights. Additionally, in today's global economy, intellectual property issues are at the forefront of international trade negotiations and environmental treaties.

■ International Law

International law has grown significantly as a field of practice, reflecting the increasing interdependence of nations and economies. Public international law provides a limited range of job opportunities, particularly with national governments or international institutions or with public interest bodies. Immigration and refugee law also assumes increasing importance as more people move more frequently across national boundaries for business, tourism, or permanent resettlement. Private international law may offer more extensive employment opportunities, either through law firms or for corporations, banks, or telecommunications firms. Fluency in another language or familiarity with another culture can be a decided advantage for law school graduates who seek to practice in the international arena.

■ Securities Law

Securities law is an extremely complex area that almost always requires the services of a specialist. In the past, lawyers who acquired this specialty were involved with the formation, organization, and financing of corporations through securities such as stock. However, in recent years, such lawyers also have become involved in mergers, acquisitions, and corporate takeovers.

■ Tax Law

In the past 50 years, the importance and complexity of federal, state, and local taxes have necessitated a specialty in this field of law. It is one area of the law where change is constant. The federal Internal Revenue Code and its associated regulations is now several thousand pages in length. New statutes, court decisions, and administrative rulings are issued frequently, and the tax lawyer must be alert to these changes. Economic planning usually includes attention to taxes, and the tax lawyer often assists clients in understanding and minimizing their tax liabilities.

Chapter 2: Becoming a Lawyer

A legal education is both challenging and rewarding. You will develop your analytical, synthesizing, creative, and logical thinking skills, and you will strengthen your reading and debating abilities. A legal education is necessary to become a lawyer in the United States, but it is also excel-lent preparation for many other careers, both because of the framework for organizing knowledge it provides and the analytical approach it brings to problems. Many teachers, business people, and writers first obtained a legal education before pursuing careers other than law.

Juris Doctor Degree

ABA-approved law schools generally require three years of full-time study to earn the Juris Doctor (J.D.) degree. Schools with part-time programs require four years of part-time study to earn the J.D. degree. Most law schools share a common approach to training lawyers. However, they differ in the emphasis they give to certain subjects and teaching methods, such as opportunities for independent study, legal internships, participation in clinical programs, and involvement with governmental affairs.

Law school can be an intense, competitive environment. Students have little time for other interests, especially during the first year of law school. The ABA requires that no full-time student hold an outside job for more than 20 hours a week. Most schools encourage their students to become totally immersed in reading, discussing, and thinking about the law.

■ The First Year

The newness of the first year of law school is exciting for many and anxiety-provoking for almost all. Professors expect you to be prepared in class, but in most courses, grades will be determined primarily from examinations administered at the end of the semester or, at some schools, the end of the year. The professor may give little feedback until the final examination.

■ The Case Method Approach

The "case method" is what first-year law students are likely to find least familiar. By focusing on the underlying principles that shape the law's approach to different situations, you will learn to distinguish among subtly different legal results and to identify the critical factors that determine a particular outcome. Once these distinctions are mastered, you should be able to apply this knowledge to new situations.

The case method involves the detailed examination of a number of related judicial opinions that describe an area of law. You will also learn to apply the same critical analysis to legislative materials and scholarly articles. The role of the law professor is to provoke and stimulate. For a particular case, he or she may ask questions designed to explore the facts presented, to determine the legal principles applied in reaching a decision, and to analyze the method of reasoning used. In this way, the professor encourages you to relate the case to others and to distinguish it from those with similar but inapplicable precedents. In order to encourage you to learn to defend your reasoning, the professor may adopt a position contrary to the holding of the case.

Because this process places much of the burden of learning on the student, classroom discussions can be exciting. They are also demanding. However uninformed, unprepared, or puzzled you may be, you will be required to participate in these discussions.

■ The Ability to Think

The case method reflects the general belief that the primary purpose of law school is not to teach substantive law but to teach you to think like a lawyer. Teachers of law are less concerned about rules and technicalities than are their counterparts in many other disciplines. Although the memorization of specifics may be useful to you, the ability to be analytical and literate is considerably more important than the power of total recall. One reason for this approach to legal education is that in our common-law tradition, the law is constantly evolving and changing; thus, specific rules may quickly lose their relevance.

Law is more an art than a science. The reality lawyers seek in analyzing a case is not always well-defined. Legal study, therefore, requires an attentive mind and a tolerance for ambiguity. Because many people believe incorrectly that the study of law involves the memorization of rules in books and principles dictated by learned professors, law schools often attract those people who especially value structure, authority, and order. The study of law does **not** involve this kind of certainty, however; complex legal questions do not have simple legal solutions. Law professors rarely have the answers and they prefer to encourage students to develop their own responses to legal issues.

■ The Curriculum

As a first-year law student in an ABA-approved law school, you will follow a designated course of study that may cover many of the following subjects:

- **Civil procedure**—the process of adjudication in the United States; i.e., jurisdiction and standing to sue, motions and pleadings, pretrial procedure, the structure of a lawsuit, and appellate review of trial results.

- **Constitutional law**—the legislative powers of the federal and state governments, and questions of civil liberties and constitutional history, including detailed study of the Bill of Rights and constitutional freedoms.

- **Contracts**—the nature of enforceable promises and rules for determining appropriate remedies in case of nonperformance.

- **Criminal law and criminal procedure**—bases of criminal responsibility, the rules and policies for enforcing sanctions against individuals accused of committing offenses against the public order and well-being, and the rights guaranteed to those charged with criminal violations.

- **Legal method**—students' introduction to the organization of the American legal system and its processes.

- **Legal writing**—research and writing component of most first-year programs; requires students to research and write memoranda dealing with various legal problems.

- **Property law**—concepts, uses, and historical developments in the treatment of land, buildings, natural resources, and personal objects.

- **Torts**—private wrongs, such as acts of negligence, assault, and defamation, that violate obligations of the law.

In addition to attending classes, you may be required to participate in a moot court exercise in which you take responsibility for arguing a hypothetical court case.

After the first year, you will probably have the opportunity to select from a broad range of courses. Generally, you will take courses in administrative law, evidence, civil litigation, corporations, taxation, wills and trusts, commercial law, and family law before completing your degree. These universal courses are basic to legal education. Every law school supplements this basic curriculum with additional courses, such as international law, environmental law, conflict of laws, labor law, criminal procedure, and jurisprudence.

■ Opportunities to Practice What Is Learned

Legal education is primarily academic, in that students devote most of their time to mastering general concepts and principles that shape the law. Most schools offer a variety of professional skills courses as well. Law schools place less emphasis on matters such as legal drafting and law office management than on legal principles. However, a number of schools have programs designed to offer students direct experience in legal practice. These programs allow second- and third-year students to participate in court trials and appeals, render counseling, undertake legislative drafting, and do other legal work for academic credit. Schools differ in the range and variety of practical education they offer, but the trend toward integrating this experience with theoretical study continues to grow.

■ Extracurricular Activities

Student organizations greatly supplement classroom learning. Typically, these organizations are dedicated to advancing the interests of particular groups of law students, such as black, women, or Hispanic students; or to promoting greater understanding of specific legal fields, such as environmental or international law; or to providing opportunities for involvement in professional, social, and sports activities.

A unique feature of American law schools is that law students manage and edit most of the legal profession's principal scholarly journals. Membership on the editorial staffs of these journals, also called law reviews, is considered to be a mark of academic distinction. Selection is ordinarily based on outstanding academic performance, writing ability, or both, as discussed on page 19 of this book.

Bar Associations

Bar associations are membership organizations designed to raise the standards of the legal profession and to encourage professional unity. Each state has its own bar association. There are also a variety of national, state, local, and special-interest bar associations.

The largest national organization of attorneys in the United States is the American Bar Association (ABA), which sponsors a number of programs dealing with legal education, law reform, judicial selection, and professional responsibility. The ABA publishes the *Model Rules of Professional Conduct*, a set of regulations governing ethical standards in the practice of law. Attorneys who violate the standards are subject to censure, suspension, or disbarment.

Many bar associations sponsor programs intended to broaden the availability of legal services and to familiarize the public with the legal profession. They also conduct extensive continuing legal education programs to help members update their skills and their knowledge of the law.

■ Admission to the Bar

To practice law in the United States, every lawyer must be admitted to a state bar. Standards for admission to state bars are regulated by each state and differ from state to state. In order to be admitted to the bar, most states require that candidates:

- Possess a law degree from an ABA-approved law school;

- Pass state examinations that test their knowledge of the law, skill in reasoning, and understanding of legal ethics and professional responsibility; and

- Show evidence of fitness to practice law, understanding of legal ethics, and sound character.

Lawyers may practice only in the state or states where they are members of the bar in good standing. However, many states will admit a lawyer to its bar if the lawyer has been admitted to the bar of another state and has practiced law actively for a certain number of years. This is known as reciprocity. States usually grant temporary bar admission for particular cases.

Many states have student practice rules that, in conjunction with students' academic programs, admit advanced law students who are under the close supervision of an admitted lawyer. A few states require law students to register with the board of bar examiners before graduation or, in some cases, soon after they're enrolled in law school, if they intend to practice in those states. So, if you're planning to attend law school, you should check the bar admission requirements for those states in which you may wish to practice after graduation.

Federal courts set their own standards for admission. The most basic requirement for federal district court admission is that the lawyer be admitted to the bar in the state in which the federal district is located.

A good source of information regarding bar admission requirements is the latest edition of the ABA's *Comprehensive Guide to Bar Admission Requirements*, which should be available in any law school library.

Bar Approval and School Selection

A number of law schools have not been approved by the American Bar Association. Some states permit graduates of these schools to take the bar examination or will admit to their bars one who has been admitted to the bar of another state (even though he or she graduated from a school not approved by the ABA), but most do not. Before you enroll in a law school not approved by the ABA, consider the limitations that result from obtaining a degree from these programs.

A few institutions offer correspondence courses purporting to provide a legal education. The ABA expressly disapproves of correspondence law courses. Correspondence law school graduates are not eligible to take the bar examination in any state except California, and even there only under special conditions.

Legal Education and Bar Admission Statistics

Year	Total J.D. Enrollment*	Total J.D. Women Enrollment*	First Year Enrollment*	Total LSAT Administrations	Est. ABA Applicants†	J.D. or LL.B Awarded*	New Admissions to the Bar*
1981-82	120,879	43,245	42,521	119,291	72,912	35,598	42,382
1982-83	121,791	45,539	42,034	112,125	71,755	34,846	42,905
1983-84	121,201	46,361	41,159	105,076	63,801	36,389	41,684
1984-85	119,847	46,897	40,747	95,563	60,338	36,687	42,630
1985-86	118,700	47,486	40,796	91,848	61,304	36,829	42,450
1986-87	117,813	47,920	40,195	101,235	65,145	36,121	40,247**
1987-88	117,997	48,920	41,055	115,988	74,938	35,478	39,918**
1988-89	120,694	50,932	42,860	137,088	82,741	35,701	46,528***
1989-90	124,471	53,113	43,826	138,865	88,303	35,520	47,147
1990-91	127,261	54,097	44,104	152,685	94,026	36,385	43,286††
1991-92	129,580	55,110	44,050	145,567	91,954†††	38,800	N/A
1992-93	128,212	54,644	42,793	140,054	86,530	42,037	N/A
1993-94	127,792	55,132	43,644	N/A	N/A	40,263	N/A

* Sources for these figures include ABA's *A Review of Legal Education in the United States*, Fall 1992.
** No data were available from New York state in this year; therefore, this figure is lower than in prior years.
*** Represents 45,999 admitted by examination, plus 529 admitted by diploma privilege. It does not include admissions on motion by a jurisdiction of attorneys from other jurisdictions, which totaled 8,209.
† Numbers noted in this column include only current-year applicants.
†† No data were available from Puerto Rico and the Virgin Islands in this year. Includes 416 admitted by diploma privilege. It does not include admissions on motion by a jurisdiction of attorneys from other jurisdictions, which totaled 5,418.
††† Revised

Chapter 3: Preparing for Law School

Acquire a Well-Balanced Education

Students interested in legal study should get the most from their undergraduate education. A college education should stand on its own merits as preparation for a lifetime of active involvement in a diverse and changing society.

Admission committees are usually impressed by applicants who can convincingly demonstrate that they've challenged their thinking and reasoning skills in a diverse course of undergraduate study. While no single curricular path is the ideal preparation for law school, you should choose courses that sharpen analytical reasoning and writing skills. Law schools prefer students who can think, read, and write well, and who have some understanding of what shapes human experience. This understanding includes an appreciation for the wide variety of value systems that underlie that experience. You can acquire these attributes in any number of college courses, whether in the humanities, the social sciences, philosophy, or the natural sciences. It's not so much a matter of what you study as it is a matter of selecting courses that interest you, challenge you, and require you to use researching and writing skills. Because a lawyer's work involves most aspects of our complex society, a broad liberal arts curriculum is the preferred preparation for law school.

Maintain a Rigorous Course Load

High academic standards are important when selecting your undergraduate courses. The range of acceptable majors is broad; the quality of the education you receive is most important. You should acquire skills that enable you to think critically, reason logically, and speak and write effectively. Undergraduate programs should reveal your capacity to perform well at an academically rigorous level. An undergraduate career that is narrow, unchallenging, or vocationally oriented is not the best preparation for law school.

Law school admission committees want to see how the courses you chose relate to one another, and they want a sense of how you rise to intellectual challenge, whether in the sciences, the liberal arts, the business curriculum, or elsewhere. In assessing how favorably a law school will view your application, you should examine your courses. Try to fit them into this sort of overview. To what extent can they be seen as part of a whole, and to what extent do the parts seem to coalesce intellectually?

The Pros and Cons of a "Prelaw" Major

Unlike the premedical curriculum that contains specific courses, some obligatory, there is no recommended set of prelaw courses. Law schools prefer that you reserve your legal study for law school and fill your undergraduate curriculum with broad, diverse, and challenging courses. Prelaw courses that introduce you to broad legal principles may present you with enough information to decide whether you want to continue with a legal education, but they are rarely taught with the same depth and rigor as actual law school courses. A prelaw curriculum that is designed to encompass a broad array of liberal arts courses, however, can be excellent preparation for law school. Be sure you know precisely what is meant by "prelaw" when choosing your undergraduate course of study.

Prelaw Advisors

Prelaw advisors at undergraduate institutions are a good source of information before and during the law school admission process. If you are considering law school, you should introduce yourself to a prelaw advisor as soon as possible. The advisor knows his or her school's course offerings quite well and will be able to direct you to courses that will better prepare you for law school. The prelaw advisor should also be quite helpful during the law school application process. Advisors have the latest information on the Law School Admission Test (LSAT), the Law School Data Assembly Service (LSDAS), and even on many law school requirements. In addition, they may be able to point you toward law schools that would be particularly well suited to your needs and interests.

If you are considering law school but are not currently enrolled in a university, you may be able to obtain counsel from the undergraduate prelaw advisor at the college from which you graduated. Most prelaw advisors will be happy to answer any questions you may have.

Chapter 4: LSAT and Other Criteria for Admission

How Law Schools Select Applicants

Almost everyone admitted to law school graduates. In fact, on average, less than 5 percent of law students drop out of school for academic reasons.

No concrete principles exist for predicting who will perform well in law school, so admission committees seek the most qualified from the pool of applicants. In order to be fair, schools rely heavily upon selection criteria that bear on expected performance in law school and can be applied objectively to all candidates. Law schools consider a variety of factors in admitting their students, and no single qualification will independently guarantee acceptance or rejection. However, the two factors that usually outweigh the rest are prior academic performance and the Law School Admission Test score.

The most difficult admission decisions are those regarding candidates who are neither so well qualified nor so deficient as to present a clear-cut case for acceptance or rejection. These applicants constitute the majority of the applicant pool at many law schools and are the candidates that most law schools spend the bulk of their time reviewing.

■ Criteria that May Be Considered by Law School Admission Committees

- LSAT score
- Undergraduate grade-point average
- Undergraduate course of study
- College attended
- Improvement in grades and grade distribution
- College curricular and extracurricular activities
- Ethnic background
- Individual character and personality
- Letters of recommendation
- Written personal statement on the application
- Personal interview
- Work experience or other postundergraduate experiences
- Motivation to study and reasons for deciding to study law
- State of residency
- Difficulties that you have overcome
- Precollege preparation
- Anything else that stands out in an application

The Law School Admission Test (LSAT)

All American Bar Association (ABA)-approved law schools and many non-ABA-approved law schools require that you take the LSAT. (On rare occasions, exceptions may be made for people with certain disabilities.)

The test consists of five 35-minute sections of multiple-choice questions, in three different item types. A 30-minute writing sample is administered at the end of the test. Four of the five sections contribute to the test taker's score. The fifth section typically is used to pretest new test items and to preequate new test forms. Law Services does not score the writing sample. Copies of the writing sample are sent to all law schools to which you apply.

Some schools place greater weight than others on the LSAT; still, low LSAT scores will hamper your chances for admission, particularly at the most competitive schools. Most law schools do make a genuine effort to evaluate your full credentials.

■ What the Test Measures

The LSAT is designed to measure skills that are considered essential for success in law school: the reading and comprehension of complex texts with accuracy and insight; the organization and management of information and the ability to draw reasonable inferences from it; the ability to reason critically; and the analysis and evaluation of the reasoning and argument of others.

The three item types in the LSAT are:

Reading Comprehension Questions
These questions measure your ability to read, with understanding and insight, examples of lengthy and complex materials similar to those commonly encountered in law school work. The reading comprehension items consist of passages of approximately 450 words, each followed by five to eight questions that test reading and reasoning abilities.

Analytical Reasoning Questions
These questions are designed to measure your ability to understand a structure of relationships and to draw conclusions about that structure. The examinee is asked to make deductions from a set of statements, rules, or conditions that describe relationships among entities such as persons, places, things, or events. They simulate the kinds of detailed analyses of relationships that a law student must perform in solving legal problems.

Logical Reasoning Questions

These questions are designed to evaluate your aptitude for understanding, analyzing, criticizing, and completing a variety of arguments. Each logical reasoning question requires the examinee to read and comprehend a short passage, then answer one or two questions about it. The questions test a variety of abilities involved in reasoning logically and critically.

■ Your Score as a Predictor of Law School Performance

The LSAT, like any aptitude test, is not a perfect predictor of law school performance. The predictive power of an admission test is limited by many factors, such as the complexity of the skills the test is designed to measure and the unmeasurable factors that can affect students' performances, such as motivation, physical and mental health, or work and family responsibilities. In spite of these factors, the LSAT compares very favorably with admission tests used in other graduate and professional fields of study. (For additional information about the predictive value of LSAT scores, refer to Appendix G in the 1994-95 edition of the *LSAT/LSDAS Registration and Information Book*.)

■ Test Preparation

Most law school applicants familiarize themselves with test mechanics and question types, practice on sample tests, and study the information available on test-taking techniques and strategies. Though it is difficult to say when examinees are sufficiently prepared, very few people achieve their full potential without some preparation.

Law Services publishes a variety of materials to help you prepare for the LSAT.

The Official LSAT PrepTest

Each *Official LSAT PrepTest* contains a previously administered LSAT, an answer key, and a conversion table that helps you compute your score. The PrepTest allows you to prepare for the LSAT by simulating actual test conditions and checking your answers to see which question types you might need to practice. The disclosed tests are made available approximately six weeks after they are administered. *PrepTest I* (the June 1991 test) is distributed free of charge by Law Services along with the *LSAT/LSDAS Registration and Information Book.*These books are available through the mail from Law Services, or at law school admission offices, undergraduate schools, and testing and counseling centers.

The Official LSAT PrepKit

The PrepKit will help you to maximize your mastery of the three LSAT question types. This boxed set of test preparation tools includes: an introductory booklet with instructions and general test preparation information; three complete practice tests (PrepTests II, IV, V), including writing samples and answer keys; and three interactive workbooks. Each workbook contains practice test questions and answers, with explanations for both correct and incorrect answers. The workbooks help you understand how to work on each item type; the PrepTests allow you to work on timing and test-taking instructions.

LSAT: The Official TriplePrep

Three PrepTests provide more practice than one, and buying three together in one book costs less than buying them separately. *TriplePrep—Volume 1* contains PrepTests II (October 1991 LSAT), IV (February 1992 LSAT), and V (June 1992 LSAT). *TriplePrep—Volume 2* contains PrepTests III (December 1991 LSAT), VI (October 1992 LSAT), and VII (February 1993 LSAT). *TriplePrep—Volume 3* contains PrepTests VIII, IX, and X. *TriplePrep—Volume 4* contains PrepTests XI, XII, and XIII. *TriplePrep* contains answer keys, writing samples, and score-conversion tables for all three PrepTests. (**Note:** PrepTests II, IV, and V are also included in *The Official LSAT PrepKit.*)

Candidates may order publications directly from Law Services by mail, or by telephone using a Visa or MasterCard. For further information, or to order publications, contact:

Law Services
Box 2400
661 Penn Street
Newtown, PA 18940-0977
215.968.1314

For further information about your LSAT score and on the question of taking the test more than one time, please refer to your *LSAT/LSDAS Registration and Information Book.*

Academic Record

Undergraduate performance is generally an important indicator of how someone is likely to perform in law school. Hence, many law schools look closely at college grades when considering individual applications.

Course selection also can make a difference in admission evaluations. Applicants who have taken difficult or advanced courses in their undergraduate study often are evaluated in a more favorable light than students who have concentrated on easier or less advanced subjects.

Many law schools consider undergraduate-performance trends along with a student's numerical average. Thus, they may discount a slow start in a student's undergraduate career if he or she performs exceptionally well in the later school years. Similarly, admission committees may see an undergraduate's strong start followed by a mediocre finish as an indication of less potential to do well in law school. Candidates are advised to comment on irregular grade trends in the personal statement section of the application.

Grade Conversion Table

LSDAS Conversion 4.0 Scale	Grades as Reported on Transcripts				
	A to F	1 to 5	100-0*	Four Passing Grades	Three Passing Grades
4.33	A+	1+	98-100	Highest Passing Grade (4.0)	Highest Passing Grade (4.0)
4.00	A	1	93-97		
3.67	A-	1-	90-92		
3.50	AB				
3.33	B+	2+	87-89	Second Highest Passing Grade (3.0)	Middle Passing Grade (3.0)
3.00	B	2	83-86		
2.67	B-	2-	80-82		
2.50	BC				
2.33	C+	3+	77-79	Third Highest Passing Grade (2.0)	Lowest Passing Grade (2.0)
2.00	C	3	73-76		
1.67	C-	3-	70-72		
1.50	CD				
1.33	D+	4+	67-69	Lowest Passing Grade (1.0)	
1.00	D	4	63-66		
0.67	D-	4-	60-62		
0.50	DE or DF				
0.00	E and F	5	Below 60	Failure (0.0)	Failure (0.0)

*In some instances, a school's numeric grading scale might be converted differently than shown here.

Additional Admission Decision Factors

Most law schools consider more than academic records and LSAT scores when evaluating applicants. These factors are particularly significant after the preliminary review of an application.

Letters of Recommendation

The most effective letters of recommendation are those from professors who have known you well enough to write with candor, detail, and objectivity about your academic and personal achievements and potential. Work supervisors also can write in support of your application.

tion. Letters that compare you to your academic peers are often considered the most useful. Most schools do not consider general, unreservedly praiseworthy letters helpful. Some schools do not require letters at all, and some schools will not read letters of recommendation if they receive them.

Work Experience

Law schools want diverse, interesting classes, representative of a variety of backgrounds. A candidate who applies to law school several years after completing his or her undergraduate education, and who has demonstrated an ability to succeed in a nonacademic environment, is sometimes more motivated than one who continues his or her education without a break. In fact, only about 40 percent of law students enter directly from college.

Interviews

In general, evaluative interviews are not a part of the law school admission process. However, some schools use interviews as a way for admission committees to select from a group of candidates who all appear very similar on paper. In such cases, the school will contact you to set a time for the interview. Occasionally, a school will grant an applicant's request for an interview. If you would like additional information regarding a particular law school, or if you believe an interview might raise your chance for admission, contact the law school directly. Some schools do not grant interviews under any circumstances.

Graduate or Professional Study

Prior success or failure in other graduate or professional school work, including other law schools, may also be a factor in the admission committee's decision. In any case, you are required to report such work to any law school to which you apply.

Minority Applicants

Almost all law schools have active recruitment programs for students who are members of minority groups to help ensure greater minority representation in the legal profession. Law schools strongly encourage minority applicants. (See Chapter 7 for further details on minority recruitment and enrollment.)

Your Personal Essay

Always remember that there is something special— something interesting—about you. Maybe you've had some experience, some training, or some dream that sets you apart from others. Law schools want to recruit men and women who are qualified for reasons beyond grades and scores. The essay or personal statement in your application is the place to tell the committee why you are special. **Your application is definitely not the place to be falsely modest.**

In general, your evaluation of actual experiences has more value to the committee than speculation about future accomplishments. Also, if you have overcome a serious obstacle in your life to get where you are today, by all means let the admission committee know about it. Any noteworthy personal experience or accomplishment may be an appropriate subject for your essay, as long as it is meaningful and interesting. Be sure to do more than just state it; describe the thing you are talking about briefly but concretely, and why it had value to you, whether it is a job, your family, or your upbringing. You are simultaneously trying to add information and create structure. **Be brief, be factual, be comprehensive, and be organized.**

You are a storyteller here. You want a living person— **you**—to emerge. The statement is your opportunity to become vivid and alive to the reader, and it is an opportunity to demonstrate your ability to write and present a prose sample in a professional manner.

Assessing Yourself Realistically

When selecting law schools to which you will apply, the general philosophy is that you should have a threefold plan: dream a little, be realistic, and be safe. Most applicants have no trouble selecting dream schools—those that are almost, but not quite, beyond their grasp—or safe schools—those for which admission is virtually certain. Applicants often have difficulty being realistic about their qualifications and their chances of being accepted at particular law schools.

Unquestionably, **the number one strategic error in law school admission is a candidate's failure to evaluate realistically his or her own credentials.**

■ Use Admission Profile Grids in this Book

Check your qualifications against the admission profile of the law schools to which you aspire. Most schools publish detailed statistics on how many applicants with a certain LSAT score and GPA are accepted. You can also find LSAT/GPA data grids, charts, and statistics in this book. You may use these data to help you determine where you should apply. Apply to those law schools whose student body profiles most closely match your personal profile. Those schools will be as anxious to accept you as you are to be admitted.

The school profiles contained in this volume should provide you with some of the information you'll need to help you make this decision. You should make your final decision only after reading the informational materials available directly from law schools.

■ Research Specific Law Schools that Interest You

Other sources of information include:

- **The school's admission office.** This is a good source for general information about your chances for admission . Do not hesitate to request admission counseling. Be sure to obtain current catalogs from each law school you are considering.

- **Your college or university prelaw advisor.** Your prelaw advisor can often provide you with reliable information about which law schools fit your personal profile. He or she may also be able to tell you which law schools have accepted students from your school in the past and provide you with an overview of the admitted students' credentials. This is not to say that you should narrow your focus to only those law schools where others from your undergraduate school have been admitted.

- **Law School Forums.** The Law School Forums, organized by the Law School Admission Council, are excellent opportunities to talk with law school representatives from around the country in one central, urban location—usually a hotel exhibit hall. Recent forums have been held in Atlanta, Boston, Chicago, Houston, Los Angeles, and New York City. In 1993, 154 of the 176 ABA-approved law schools participated in the forums, and 16,855 people registered as attendees. Because the costs of traveling to a number of law schools can be expensive, many prospective law students find the forums to be the most productive means of gathering information and making school contacts. Approximately 20.9 percent of the forum attendees traveled over 100 miles to get to a forum. Forum admission is free; for dates, times, and locations of 1994 Law School Forums, see the list toward the end of this book.

- **School representatives and alumni.** Take advantage of opportunities to talk with law school representatives and alumni. When you talk with alumni, remember that law schools sometimes change fairly quickly. Try to talk to a recent graduate or to one who is active in alumni affairs and therefore knowledgeable about the school as it is today.

- **School visits.** You can learn a surprising amount about a school from talks with students and faculty members. Many law schools have formal programs in which a currently enrolled student will take you on a tour of the campus and answer your questions. Such a first-hand experience can be quite valuable in assessing how you would fit into the school.

■ Keep Your Options Open

Flexibility is a key word in the law school admission process. Keep your options open. Even during the early stages of the admission process, you should continually reevaluate your prospects and prepare alternative plans. For example, don't set your sights on only one law school and one plan of action. You could severely limit your potential and your chance to practice law.

Chapter 5: Applying to Law School

Working With Law Services: Registering for the LSAT, Subscribing to the LSDAS

Law Services administers the LSAT and serves as a liaison for much of the communication between you and the law schools. You are expected to send your individual law school application **directly to each law school** to which you apply; however, your test scores, transcripts, and other academic information and biographical data are sent to the law schools through the Law School Data Assembly Service (LSDAS).

Comprehensive information about LSAT registration and LSDAS subscription is set forth in complete detail in the *LSAT/LSDAS Registration and Information Book*, published annually. This publication is available at no charge through Law Services or at any of 1,500 national distribution sites located on undergraduate campuses (principally prelaw advising offices and career centers) and at law schools. (Law Services operators will provide a list of distribution locations nearest your zip code; call 215.968.1001.)

You need not subscribe to the LSDAS at the same time you register for the LSAT, but doing so will simplify the process. Application deadlines for the law schools to which you apply dictate when you should subscribe to the LSDAS.

■ Planning Ahead for Law School Deadlines

You may wish to use the Request for Information postcards included in the back of this book to obtain materials from law schools. Most law schools have a variety of application requirements and deadlines that you **must** meet to be considered for admission. If you are applying to a number of schools, the various deadlines and requirements can be confusing. It probably will be helpful if you set up a detailed calendar that will remind you of when and what you must do to complete an application.

You will also want to be sure you can make an LSAT score available to a law school before its application deadline. In registering for the LSAT, be sure to give yourself enough time to select a convenient testing location and prepare for the actual test.

Below is a chart listing all scheduled test administrations, including alternate dates for Saturday Sabbath observers, along with corresponding deadlines and fees.

LSAT Dates, Deadlines, and Fees (1994-1995)

All scheduled administrations of the LSAT, both for regular test takers and test takers who are Saturday Sabbath observers, are listed below along with their corresponding deadlines and fees.

Test Dates

■ **Regular**	Monday, June 13, 1994	Saturday, Oct. 1, 1994	Saturday, Dec. 3, 1994	Saturday, Feb. 11, 1995	
■ **Saturday Sabbath Observers**		Monday, Oct. 3, 1994 Nondisclosed*	Monday, Dec. 5, 1994 Nondisclosed*	Monday, Feb. 13, 1995 Nondisclosed*	
■ **Score Report mailed (approx.)**	July 25, 1994	Nov. 14, 1994	Jan. 16, 1995	March 27, 1995	

Deadlines	Postmarked by	Postmarked by	Postmarked by	Postmarked by	Fees
■ **Regular Registration** US/Canada/Puerto Rico Foreign	May 10, 1994 April 29, 1994	Aug. 30, 1994 Aug. 19, 1994	Nov. 1, 1994 Oct. 21, 1994	Jan. 10, 1995 Dec. 30, 1994	$76
■ **Late Registration by Mail** US/Canada/Puerto Rico	May 11-20 1994	Aug. 31-Sept. 9, 1994	Nov. 2-11, 1994	Jan. 11-20, 1995	$76 plus $44 late registration fee
■ **Late Registration by Telephone** (215) 968-5710	May 23-27, 1994	Sept. 12-16, 1994	Nov. 14-18, 1994	Jan. 23-27, 1995	$76 plus $44 late registration fee (Visa or MasterCard only for telephone requests)
■ **LSAT Registration Refunds** (partial only)	June 20, 1994	Oct. 10, 1994	Dec. 12, 1994	Feb. 20, 1995	$33

* A nondisclosed test is one where the test taker receives only his or her score. The credited answers, the test questions, and a copy of the test taker's answer sheet are not released to the test taker.

The Law School Data Assembly Service (LSDAS)

Nearly all LSAC-member law schools in the United States require applicants to subscribe to the LSDAS. Many nonmember law schools require this as well.

The LSDAS provides a means of centralizing and standardizing undergraduate academic records to simplify the law school admission process. The service organizes, analyzes, and summarizes biographical and academic information for law school applicants and subsequently prepares an LSDAS Law School Report to be sent within two weeks to all law schools from which a report request has been received.

If you subscribe to the LSDAS, every undergraduate, graduate, and professional school you have attended—including law school—must send an official transcript to Law Services. An official transcript is one that is signed, sealed, and sent by the registrar to Law Services. Do not send your own transcripts directly to Law Services; these will be returned to you unprocessed.

You may subscribe to LSDAS by using the same registration form you use to register for the LSAT in the *Registration and Information Book*. This book also provides complete information on transcripts, LSDAS Law School Reports, and other LSDAS subscription information.

You will make the processes of registering for the LSAT and subscribing to the LSDAS much smoother if you take the time to read and understand all the information in your *Registration and Information Book*. Many applicants delay the processing of their registration forms because they have not followed all directions and have not filled out the forms correctly.

Information on LSDAS fees is as follows:

- **LSDAS subscription fee**   **$77**
  12 months of service (includes reporting to one law school requiring LSDAS)

- **LSDAS Law School Reports**   **$7 each**
  (ordered when you subscribe to LSDAS and pay the $77 LSDAS subscription fee)

- **Additional LSDAS Law School**   **$9 each**
  Reports (ordered after you subscribe to LSDAS initially)

- **LSDAS subscription renewal**   **$44**

■ Fee Waivers for Law Services

Fee waivers are available for the LSAT, LSDAS, and Prep-Kit (see the *Registration and Information Book*). Fee waivers can be authorized **only** by LSAC member law schools, which are listed in the *Registration and Information Book*. Fee waivers cannot be granted by Law Services, financial aid offices of undergraduate institutions, or any organization other than a member law school. See the *Registration and Information Book* or contact a law school admission office for details.

The Admission Process

Law school applicants can expect that the admission process will be quite competitive. Most law schools receive more than enough applications from highly qualified candidates, many of whom would be perfectly capable of completing a law school education. The dilemma for admission committees is that limited space and resources mandate the denial of admission to many of these candidates.

■ The Importance of Complete Files

Remember that law schools require complete files before making their decisions. A law school will consider your file complete when it has received your application form; LSDAS Law School Report (or LSAT Law School Report if the law school does not require LSDAS); letters of recommendation (if required); any requirements unique to the particular school; and application fee.

■ Rolling Admission

Many law schools operate what is known as a rolling admission process: the school evaluates applications and informs candidates of admission decisions on a continuous basis over several months, usually beginning in late fall and extending to midsummer for waiting-list admissions.

At such schools, it is especially important for you to apply at the earliest possible date. The earlier you apply, the more places the school will have available. Most schools try to make comparable decisions throughout the admission season, even those that practice rolling admission. Still, it is disadvantageous to be one of the last applicants to complete a file. Furthermore, the more decisions you receive from law schools early in the process, the better able you will be to make your own decisions, such as whether to apply to more law schools or whether to accept a particular school's offer.

■ Applying to More than One School

The average applicant applies to 4.7 law schools. You should be sure to place your applications at schools representing a range of admission standards. Even if you have top qualifications, you should apply to at least one safety school where you are almost certain of being admitted. This is your insurance policy. If you apply to a safety school in November, and are accepted in January or February, you may be disappointed but not panicked if you are later rejected by your top choices.

■ The Preliminary Review of an Application

Applicants whose qualifications more than fulfill the school's admission standards are usually accepted during the first round of decisions. With some exceptions, candidates whose credentials fall below the school's standards are usually rejected. Full admission committees may never even get to examine these files.

Most applications are not decided upon immediately. They are usually reviewed in depth by a full committee that bases its admission decision on many facets of each application (see "How Law Schools Select Applicants," page 7). The length of time it takes the committee to review an application varies; consult the individual law schools to which you apply.

■ Waiting Lists

If you have strong qualifications, but you do not quite meet the competition of those currently being admitted at a particular law school, you may be placed on a waiting list for possible admission at a later date. The law school will send you a letter notifying you of its decision as early as April or as late as July.

It is up to you whether you wish to wait for a decision from a school that has put you on a waiting list or accept an offer from a school that accepted you at an earlier date.

Most schools rank students who are on the waiting list. Some law schools will tell you your rank. If a law school doesn't tell you, you might ask the admission office how many students have been placed on the waiting list.

■ Seat Deposits

Many law schools use seat deposits to help keep track of their new classes. For example, a school may require an initial acceptance fee of $100, which is credited to your first-term tuition if you actually register at the school; if you don't register, the deposit may be forfeited or returned partially. A school may require a larger deposit around July 1, which is also credited to tuition. If you decline the offer of admission after you've paid your deposit, a portion of the money may be refunded, depending on the date you actually decline the offer. At some schools, you may not be refunded any of the deposit.

The official position of the Law School Admission Council is:

> Except under early decision plans, law schools should permit applicants to choose among offers of admission as well as offers of scholarships, grants, and loans without penalty until April 1. Admitted applicants who have submitted a timely financial aid application should not be required to commit to enroll until notified of financial aid awards that are within the control of the law school.

Misconduct and Irregularities in the Admission Process

The Law School Admission Council has established procedures for dealing with instances of possible candidate misconduct or irregularities on the LSAT or in the law school admission process. Misconduct or irregularity is a serious offense with serious consequences. Misconduct or irregularity is the submission, as part of the law school admission process, of any information that is false or misleading. A finding of misconduct or irregularity does not require a finding of intent. Examples of misconduct and irregularities include, but are not limited to: submission of an altered or a nonauthentic transcript; submission of an application containing false or misleading information; submission of a fraudulent letter of recommendation; falsification of records for the purpose of applying to another law school; impersonation of another in taking the LSAT; switching of LSAT answer sheets with another; taking the LSAT for purposes other than law school admission; copying on, or other forms of cheating on, the LSAT; obtaining advance access to test materials; theft of test materials; submission of false information to the Law School Data Assembly Service (LSDAS); false statements or omissions of information requested on the LSAT/LSDAS Registration Form or on individual law school application forms; or falsification of transcript information, school attendance, honors, awards, or employment. A charge of misconduct or irregularity may be made prior to a candidate's admission to law school, after matriculation at a law school, or after admission to practice.

When alleged misconduct or irregularity brings into question the validity of data about a candidate, the school may be notified of possible data error, and transmission of LSAT scores and LSDAS reports will be withheld until the matter has been resolved by the Law School Admission Council's Misconduct and Irregularities in the Admission Process Panel. The Council and/or Law Services will investigate all instances of alleged misconduct or irregularities in the admission process in accordance with the LSAC Rules Governing Misconduct and Irregularities in the Admission Process.

A panel representative will determine whether misconduct or an irregularity has occurred. If the panel representative determines that a preponderance of the evidence shows misconduct or irregularity, then a report of the determination is sent to all law schools to which the individual has applied, subsequently applies, or has matriculated. Such reports are retained indefinitely. In appropriate cases, state and national bar authorities and other affected persons and institutions may also receive notification. Individual law schools and bar authorities determine what action, if any, they will take in response to a finding of misconduct or irregularity. Such action may include the closing of an admission file, revocation of an offer of admission, dismissal from law school through a school's internal disciplinary channels, or disbarment. Thus, a finding of misconduct or irregularity is a very serious matter. More information regarding misconduct and irregularity procedures may be obtained by contacting Law Services.

Chapter 6: Choosing a Law School

For some people, the choice of which law school to attend is an easy one. The most outstanding students will probably be able to go anywhere, and they will select the schools they perceive to be the most prestigious or which offer a program of particular interest. Others who need to stay in a particular area, perhaps because they have a family or a job they don't want to leave, will choose nearby schools and schools with part-time programs.

However, the majority of applicants will have to weigh a variety of personal and academic factors to come up with a list of potential schools. Then, once they have a list, and more than one acceptance letter, they will have to choose a school. Applicants should consider carefully the offerings of each law school before making a decision. The quality of a law school is certainly a major consideration; however, estimations of quality are very subjective. Factors such as the campus atmosphere, the school's devotion to teaching and learning, and the applicant's enthusiasm for the school also are very important. Remember that the law school is going to be your home for three years. Adjusting to law school and the general attitudes of a professional school is difficult enough without the additional hardship of culture shock. Don't choose a law school in New York City if you can't bear subway commutes, noise, and the fast pace. And, if you've lived your entire life in New York, can you face the change you will experience in Kentucky? You also may want to

ask yourself if you are already set in an unshakable lifestyle or if you are eager for a new environment.

■ Applicants With Disabilities

All schools receiving federal funds—and this includes nearly all colleges and universities—are legally obligated to provide accommodations that make programs accessible to qualified persons who have disabilities. Most schools, especially large state universities, are generally well equipped to handle a variety of needs. **If you are a student with a disability, you need not permit your disability to govern choices of where to further your education.** You should decide which schools you are interested in attending, based on your interests and qualifications, regardless of disability.

Schools also acknowledge the importance of representation of persons with disabilities in the legal profession; the schools welcome your viewpoints and perspectives. Often law schools give weight to the fact that an applicant has successfully overcome obstacles to build a solid record of academic and professional performance. By law, schools are not permitted to ask about an applicant's disability status; thus whether or not you disclose on your application that you have a disability is entirely up to you.

The HEATH Resource Center can help you throughout the admission process. For more information on how to contact this organization, see page 37.

Ranking Law Schools

■ Law Schools and Reputation

Many people will tell you to apply to the schools that take students in your GPA and LSAT ranges, and then enroll in the best one that accepts you. Law school quality can be assessed in a number of ways.

There is a hierarchy of law schools based on reputation, job placement success, strength of faculty, and the prestige of the parent institution (if there is one). In fact, a study done at one university suggests that undergraduate students perceive schools not only in terms of a hierarchy but also in terms of hierarchical clusters. In other words, certain schools are grouped together in terms of equivalent quality and prestige. Also, there are books or magazine articles that assign law schools purported numerical quality rankings. According to the ABA:

No rating of law schools beyond the simple statement of their accreditation status is attempted or advocated by the official organizations in legal education. Qualities that make one kind of school good for one student may not be as important to another. The American Bar Association and its Section of Legal Education and Admissions to the Bar have issued disclaimers of any law school rating system.

Prospective law students should consider a variety of factors in making their choice among schools.[1]

Since there is no official ranking authority, you should be cautious in using such rankings. The factors that make up a law school's reputation—strength of curriculum, faculty, career services, ability of students, quality of library facilities, and the like—don't lend themselves to quantification. Even if the rankings were more or less accurate, the school's reputation is only one factor among many for you to consider.

■ What's in a Name?

While going to a "name" school may mean that you will have an easier time finding your first job, it doesn't necessarily mean that you will get a better legal education than if you go to a lesser-known law school. Some schools that were at their peaks years ago are still riding on the wave of that earlier reputation. Others have greatly improved their programs and have recruited talented faculty, but have not yet made a "name" for themselves. Of course, schools already considered excellent have a stake in maintaining their status.

Once admitted, many applicants elect to attend "name" schools. However, in making this decision you should consider a variety of factors, such as the contacts you may acquire at a school in the area where you hope to practice, the size of the school, and cost. The substantive differences between schools should be your focus when making this important choice rather than the school's reputed ranking.

The Parent University

About 90 percent of ABA-approved law schools are part of a larger university. The reputation of an undergraduate school may influence the reputation of the law school so you might want to investigate the college before committing to the law school.

In addition, there may be some advantages to attending a law school that is part of a university. Such law schools may have more options for joint-degree programs or for taking a nonlaw school course or two. They also may have more academic and social activities, campus theater groups, sports teams, and everything else that comes with university life. Perhaps most important, the university can act as a support system for the law school by providing a wealth of facilities, including student housing and support for career services.

National, Regional, and Local Schools

A **national** school will generally have an applicant population and a student body that draws almost indistinguishably from the nation as a whole and will have many international students as well. National schools also have the most information about employment opportunities across the United States. A **regional** school is likely to have a population that is primarily from the geographic region of its location, though many regional schools have students from all over the country as well; a number of regional schools draw heavily from a particular geographical area, yet graduates may find jobs all over the country. Generally speaking, a **local** school is drawing primarily on applicants who either come from or want to practice in the proximate area in which the school is located. Many local law schools have excellent reputations and compete with the national schools in faculty salaries, in research-supporting activities, and in resources generally. Check the school's catalog or talk with the admission and placement staff to get a clear breakdown on where their students come from and where they are finding jobs.

[1] The American Bar Association. *Policies of the Council of the Section of Legal Education and Admissions to the Bar and of the Accreditation Committee.* Indianapolis, IN: 1987, Statement 20, p. 18.

Evaluating Law Schools

The best advice on how to select a law school is to choose the school that is **best for you**. The law schools invest substantial time and effort in evaluating prospective students, and applicants should evaluate law schools with equivalent care. The following are some features to keep in mind as you systematically evaluate law schools. (Costs and other financial criteria are not included below; they are discussed in Chapter 8.)

Each listing in this *Guide* provides school-specific information in the following categories as well.

Enrollment/Student Body

The academic qualifications of the student body are important to consider. It's a good idea to select a law school where you will be challenged by your classmates. Use the admission profile grids in this book to check the LSAT scores and GPAs for the previous year's entering class. Try to select a school where your averages will not be significantly different from those of your fellow law students. This is especially true for those with high scores and high GPAs, who would do well at any law school. Because of the important role of student participation in law school classes, your legal education might not be as rewarding as it could be if you are not challenged by your classmates.

You might also inquire about the diversity of the student body. Are a majority of the students the same age, race, sex, and so on? Remember, differences among students will expose you to various points of view; this will be an important aspect of your law school education.

Find out how many students are in a typical class. Much of the learning in law school depends on the quality of class discussion. Small classes provide essential interaction; large classes and the Socratic method provide diversity, challenge, and a good mix of reactions, opinions, and criticism.

It is also important to find out the total number of students enrolled at the school. Not surprisingly, the larger law schools tend to offer a larger selection of courses. Of course, more doesn't always mean better, and no one student has time to take all the courses offered at a large school. However, if you think you want to sample a wide range of courses, you are apt to have more opportunity to do so at a law school with a large faculty.

Part of the law school learning experience takes place after class with fellow students and with members of the faculty. Check to see whether faculty and students are on campus for a substantial part of the day.

Larger schools may also offer more extracurricular programs, greater student services, and a larger library. However, faculties at smaller schools may be able to give students more attention, and students at smaller schools may experience greater camaraderie. The size of a school is a personal consideration. Some students thrive in large schools; others prefer a smaller student community. Ask yourself which kind of student you are.

■ Faculty

You will undoubtedly wish to assess the faculties of the law schools you are considering. School catalogs will give you some idea of the backgrounds of the full-time faculty—where they went to school, what specialties they have, and what they have published. If the catalog tells you only where degrees were earned, ask for more information. You may also want to check the latest edition of the AALS's *Directory of Law Teachers* available at local law libraries. It may help you to know that some of the faculty have interests similar to your own.

- **Is the faculty relatively diverse with respect to race, ethnic background, gender, degrees in other fields, and breadth of experience?** A faculty with diverse backgrounds will have various points of view and experiences. This diversity will enrich your legal education, broaden your own point of view, and help prepare you for the variety of clients you will work with after law school.

- **How many full-time professors teach how many students—that is, what is the faculty/student ratio?** Although some of the most prestigious law schools are famous for their large sections in the introductory courses, they also provide smaller classes, clinics, simulations, and seminars in advanced subjects. According to the ABA's *Standards and Interpretations*, it is not favorable to have a full-time faculty to full-time student ratio of 30 to one or more. (The ABA, for purposes of its calculations only, counts as "full-time" those teachers who are employed as full-time teachers on the tenure track or an equivalent, and who do not hold an administrative office. In addition, the ABA considers three part-time students equivalent to two full-time students.)

- **Are some of the teachers recognized as authorities in their respective fields through their writings and professional activities?** Law school catalogs vary widely regarding information about faculty. Some merely list each faculty member's name along with schools attended and degrees earned. Others may provide details about publications, professional activities, and noteworthy achievements, particularly when an individual is an authority in his or her field.

- **Are there visiting professors, distinguished lecturers and visitors, symposiums and the like at the schools you are considering?** Law school lectureship programs are a good means of presenting the knowledge and views of academics outside of the particular law school you attend.

■ The Library and Other Physical Facilities

Chances are you will spend more time in the library than anywhere else, so take stock of the place before you get there. There are five factors to consider when assessing a law school library: the quality of its holdings, cataloging methods, staff, and facilities; and the hours the library remains open.

Whether a library has 250,000 volumes or 2.5 million volumes tells you little about the actual usefulness of the library. It may have an unfathomable number of volumes, but many of them may be outdated, irrelevant, or not readily available to students. All ABA-approved law schools must maintain a library that has the research materials considered essential for the study of law. Beyond that, find out if the school has any special collections and whether it subscribes to a computerized legal research service such as LEXIS or WESTLAW. Also, find out how many copies of essential materials are available, particularly for large classes.

Even if the library has all the materials you need, you won't be able to get your hands on those materials if the cataloging is years behind. Find out about the quality of the library's professional staff. Is there an adequate number of reference librarians for the number of students and faculty being served? Is the staff helpful?

Be sure the library has an adequate number of comfortable seats with at least enough carrels to accommodate a reasonable number of students at any given time. There should also be conference rooms that students may use for group discussions.

Because you will need to spend much of your time in the library, make sure its hours will accommodate just about any schedule you might have. It should open its doors by the start of classes and remain open well into the night, with a professional library staff available to assist students.

■ Curriculum

The range and quality of academic programs is one of the most important factors to consider when choosing a law school.

Almost all law schools follow the traditional first-year core curricula of civil procedure, criminal law, contracts, torts, and property (see Chapter 2). Do not assume that all law schools have programs that suit your personal needs and special interests. If you don't have any specific interests in mind—and many beginning students don't—try to make sure the school offers a wide range of electives so that you will have many options. A thorough grounding in basic legal theory will enable you to apply the principles learned to any area of law to which they pertain.

In fact, you shouldn't overemphasize your search for specialties; most law students are not specialists when they graduate, nor do they need to be. Generally speaking, new lawyers begin to find their specialties only in the second to fifth years of their careers. A well-rounded legal education from a respected law school is the best preparation for almost any career path you take. The schools' catalogs and the descriptions in this book will tell you a good deal about academic programs. You may also wish to ask school representatives questions such as: Does the school offer a variety of courses, or is it especially strong in certain areas; what sizes are the classes; are seminars and small-group classroom experiences available; and are there ample opportunities for developing writing, researching, and drafting skills?

Beyond the content of law school courses, other academic program considerations may be of interest to you as a prospective law student.

■ Special Programs and Academic Activities

Joint-degree Programs

Joint-degree programs allow you to pursue law school and graduate degrees simultaneously. Almost every combination is available at some institutions. Among the more popular degrees are the J.D./M.B.A. and the J.D./M.A. in such areas as economics or political science. For details, check individual school catalogs and Chapter 12 in this book (Key Facts About ABA-Approved Law Schools).

Master of Laws (LL.M.) Programs and Special-Degree Programs

Many law schools offer advanced degrees that allow students to take graduate-level law courses. The LL.M. degree is quite common and usually is tailored to individual interests. Some schools offer master of laws degrees with particular concentrations, such as a master of laws in taxation and master of comparative law. Students may enroll in LL.M. programs only after having received the J.D. degree.

A few schools also offer very specific, special-degree programs. Some of these specialties include a Doctorate in Civil Law, Doctor of Juridical Science, and Doctor of Jurisprudence and Social Policy. Finding out what types of advanced degrees a law school offers may help you determine the emphases of the school.

Part-Time and Evening Programs

Part-time programs may be offered either in the evening or the day. For the past 10 years, approximately 17 percent of law students have been enrolled in part-time programs. The conventional wisdom is that if you are financially able to attend law school full-time, you ought to do so.

Part-time programs generally take four years to complete instead of three years. If you wish to enroll in such a program, you may be limiting your options somewhat since less than half of the law schools offer part-time programs.

Clinical Programs and Moot Court Competition

Many law schools offer students authentic experiences as lawyers by involving them with clients and providing opportunities to rehearse trial advocacy in moot court competitions. It is important that students become adept at using interviewing, counseling, negotiating, and investigating skills.

The best clinical programs involve students in actual legal situations, simulations of such situations, or a combination of both, either at the school itself or in the community. Clinical programs at some schools offer a team-teaching approach; practical, professional skills are taught along with traditional classroom theory. In this manner, faculty can advise and work closely with students.

Law Reviews

Most law schools have a law review—a journal of scholarly articles and commentaries on the law. Writing for the law review of a school can be important to both your legal education and your career in law. Thus, evaluating the law review at a particular law school may be worthwhile when trying to choose the right school to attend.

Traditionally, student law review editors are chosen on the basis of academic standing—usually from the top 10 percent of the class—but writing ability may also be a criterion. Today, a growing number of schools select law review editors by holding a competition in which students submit a previously assigned writing sample to the current editorial board of the review. If you are on the law review, employers may assume you are either one of the brightest in your class, or an outstanding writer—or both.

If possible, check the law reviews of the schools you are considering. The character of the review may be a reflection of the character of the institution that supports it.

Order of the Coif

Many law schools have a chapter of the Order of the Coif, a national honor society for outstanding students. Students are elected to Coif on the basis of scholarship and character. Check to see if the schools you are considering include such a chapter.

Academic Support Programs

Programs for students who need or who are expected to need assistance with legal analysis and writing are offered by most law schools. Students are invited to participate in these programs on the basis of either their entering credentials or their demonstrated academic performance. This assistance may be offered in the summer prior to beginning law school, during the academic year, or both. The aim of academic support programs is to ensure that students have an equal opportunity to compete in law school. For further information about academic assistance programs, consult the admission office at the law school.

■ Student Organizations

You can also tell something about a law school's intellectual resources and its students by the number and range of student associations and organizations sponsored on campus. Many schools have chapters of the American Bar Association—Law Student Division; a student bar association; associations for minority groups, such as the Asian, Black, Hispanic, and Native American Law Student Associations; and associations based on religious affiliations. Some, but not all, schools sponsor an environmental law society, a gay and lesbian law student society, a legal assistance society, a postconviction assistance project, an ACLU group, a federalist society, a volunteer income-tax assistance program, a law student spouses' club, an international law society, a law and technology society, or a client-counseling society. Determine which associations are important to you and check individual law school catalogs to see which law schools offer what you need.

■ Career Services and Employment

One of the tests of a good law school is the effort the institution makes to help its students and graduates understand their career options and find satisfying employment. Planning a career in law requires students to integrate their legal education and personal goals in the context of the employment marketplace. Some students begin law school with a clear idea of how they expect to use their legal education (although they may change their minds along the way). Others are uncertain, or see a number of tempting possibilities. The career services office, faculty, and alumni/ae of the school are valuable resources in the process of understanding and selecting among the many opportunities available to lawyers.

The first role of the career services office is to educate students about career opportunities in all sectors, including government and public service, law firms of all sizes and specialties, corporations, and so forth. To accomplish such a task, a law school may arrange panel presentations, meetings with practicing lawyers in different fields, and a library of career information materials. Career services professionals also teach students job-search strategies, such as effective interviewing skills and employment research, and discuss students' individual interests, options, and presentation.

One of the most visible career services provided by many law schools is the opportunity to interview with employers on campus for summer and full-time jobs.

Ideally, the recruiters should represent a broad range of legal options (small and large firms, government agencies, public interest groups, corporate law departments) and sufficient geographic diversity to meet your needs. Be aware that the number of recruiters at the law school does not necessarily reflect the range of options open to students.

In most schools, only a small percentage of the class gets jobs through on-campus interviewing. Therefore, it is important to investigate the additional support provided by the career services staff and the experiences of the school's students and graduates in finding jobs.

Career services offices are concerned about all students, not just those at the top of the class rankings. Most spend a great deal of time and effort working with students individually and marketing the school to potential employers in order to increase students' options.

Here are some questions you may want to ask about a school's career services:

- What programs does the school offer to introduce students to career options? Do they seem interesting, relevant, and timely?

- Are the career-counseling professionals accessible, respected, well-qualified, and supportive?

- Are the school's faculty and graduates involved in educating students about their career options?

- What types of employers, and how many, recruit on-campus each year? What are the average number of interviews and offers per student? What percentage of students obtain jobs through the on-campus interviewing process?

- What positions have graduates taken in recent years? What work do students do during the summers? In what locales do students and graduates work? Are these employment profiles changing?

- What are the average or median salaries for the school's graduates?

- What percentage of students have accepted positions by graduation; within six months of graduation?

- Does the school offer career counseling and information for its graduates?

Chapter 7: Opportunities in Law for Minority Men and Women

A Career in Law for Minority Group Members

The legal profession is cognizant of the minority exclusion and underrepresentation that has historically pervaded American society. The legal system, which greatly values and benefits from multicultural perspectives, acknowledges the importance of diverse legal representation.

Many minority men and women seek a career in law as a way to address social and political issues. A law career provides a singular opportunity to effect change both on an individual level—by representing the interests of a client—

and on a global level—by setting policy or establishing a precedent in the governmental or business arenas.

Although minority participation in law school and the legal profession is increasing every year, more can and is being done to attract minority men and women to the profession. Outreach efforts by the legal system can and do counteract the shortage of minority lawyers. So does the realization on the part of minority men and women that law can be a rewarding and fulfilling career.

Acquiring a Legal Education

Individual law schools and legal organizations have worked hard to assure continued progress toward alleviating the historic shortage of minority lawyers. For example, the Law School Admission Council established a Minority Affairs Committee and appropriated $1.2 million to be used for projects designed to increase the number of minority men and women who attend law schools. The American Bar Association adopted a law school standard calling for specific commitments to provide full opportunities for members of minority groups.

The Association of American Law Schools also requires that member schools provide full opportunities in legal education for minorities and has programs to increase the number of minority faculty.

A legal education can provide you with considerable opportunity. You will have spent approximately three years thinking critically, reading broadly, and debating forcefully, and these skills are worthwhile in most everything you do.

Admission to Law School

Admission to law school is competitive—sometimes very competitive. However, getting into law school may be less difficult than you expect. Because there are many law schools and varied admission standards, it is advisable for you to do sufficient research and be selective.

- Read and reread the information in this book and study law school catalogs.

- The recently published *Thinking About Law School: A Minority Guide* offers realistic tips on how to assess your chances for admission, select the right law school, and finance your legal education. It also includes personal accounts by law school graduates who represent the kind of ethnic diversity law schools seek to achieve. (The book is published by and available from Law Services.)

- Get advice from a prelaw advisor, an academic counselor, a minority affairs advisor, or a practicing lawyer.

- Find out more about the regional summer institutes sponsored by the Council on Legal Education Opportunity (CLEO). Contact information for CLEO can be found on page 37 of this book.

Let the law schools you have selected know that you are interested. Often a school will have a specific program, a minority organization, designated personnel, or a law student to provide assistance for minority applicants.

Don't be intimidated by the law school admission process. Many minority men and women have been surprised by how well their credentials served them in getting into law school. The schools take all aspects of candidates' applications into account when they evaluate them. Personal, social, and ethnic background are considered, as are undergraduate records, LSAT scores, and letters of recommendation. Interesting life experiences, as well as past employment experiences, also count.

For information on the number and percentages of specific minority students and specific minority faculty at ABA-approved law schools, consult Key Facts for Minority Law School Applicants on the following pages.

Once You Are in Law School

Once you are in law school, you will encounter a difficult but manageable academic program. Very often minority student groups will advise, assist, and support newcomers. Most minority students perform successfully in law school; they are also able to make effective use of their law degrees, whether practicing law or following other career avenues.

Key Facts for Minority Law School Applicants

The chart that follows is based on figures supplied by the majority of Law School Admission Council-member law schools in the fall of 1993. Not all schools use the same classifications for minority groups; as a compromise we are using the classifications defined at the end of this chart.

This information was reported by the schools in Fall 1993, thus the figures may have changed.	Total No. of Students	Number and Percentage of Minority Students						Total No. of Faculty	Number and Percentage of Minority Faculty						Total No. of full-time Visiting Minority Faculty	No. of Part-time Minority Faculty	% of Minority Students Receiving Scholarships or Grants	Average Amount Per Scholarship or Grant
		AI/AN	A/PI	B/A-A	H/L	Other	Total No. of Minority Students		AI/AN	A/PI	B/A-A	H/L	Other	Total No. and % of Minority Faculty				
University of Akron School of Law	605	1 0.2%	24 4%	33 5.5%	7 1.2%	-	65 10.7%	45	-	-	3 6.7%	-	-	3 6.7%	-	-	-	-
Albany Law School	798	3 0.4%	49 6.1%	24 3%	14 1.8%	-	90 11.3%	78	-	1 1.3%	5 6.4%	-	-	6 7.7%	-	-	68	$10,300
American University—Washington College of Law	1170	15 1.3%	102 8.7%	72 6.2%	72 6.2%	-	261 22.3%	47	-	-	3 6.4%	1 2.1%	-	4 8.5%	-	10	40	$8,000
University of Arizona College of Law	480	15 3.1%	24 5%	22 4.6%	69 14.4%	-	130 27.1%	56	1 1.8%	-	1 1.8%	3 5.4%	-	5 8.9%	-	2	57	$3,721
Arizona State University College of Law	512	26 5.1%	35 6.8%	32 6.3%	62 12.1%	-	155 30.3%	40	-	-	-	2 5%	-	2 5%	1	-	61	$4,766
University of Arkansas School of Law—Fayetteville	419	11 2.6%	2 0.5%	21 5%	3 0.7%	-	37 8.8%	40	-	-	2 5%	-	-	2 5%	-	-	57	$4,667
University of Arkansas at Little Rock School of Law	421	5 1.2%	7 1.7%	39 9.3%	11 2.6%	-	62 14.7%	45	1 2.2%	1 2.2%	3 6.7%	-	-	5 11.1%	-	2	13	$6,000
University of Baltimore School of Law	1054	21 2%	16 1.5%	144 13.7%	13 1.2%	-	194 18.4%	44	-	1 2.3%	4 9.1%	-	-	5 11.4%	1	3	80	$1,000
Baylor University School of Law	409	4 1%	9 2.2%	9 2.2%	43 10.5%	3 0.7%	68 16.6%	44	-	-	1 2.3%	-	-	1 2.3%	-	-	75	$1,200
Boston College Law School	835	4 0.5%	54 6.5%	56 6.7%	48 5.7%	-	162 19.4%	42	-	2 4.8%	3 7.1%	1 2.4%	-	6 14.3%	-	3	82	-
Boston University School of Law	1182	9 0.8%	99 8.4%	76 6.4%	59 5%	-	243 20.6%	128	-	2 1.6%	3 2.3%	3 2.3%	-	8 6.3%	-	5	58	$7,000
Brigham Young University—J. Reuben Clark Law School	475	6 1.3%	36 7.6%	6 1.3%	27 5.7%	4 0.8%	79 16.6%	48	-	-	1 2.1%	1 2.1%	-	2 4.2%	1	-	90	$2,500
Brooklyn Law School	1441	8 0.6%	89 6.2%	57 4%	71 4.9%	-	225 15.6%	107	-	1 0.9%	6 5.6%	2 1.9%	-	9 8.4%	-	4	62	$5,126
University at Buffalo, State University of New York School of Law	781	6 0.8%	33 4.2%	54 6.9%	38 4.9%	-	131 16.8%	71	1 1.4%	-	4 5.6%	-	-	5 7%	-	2	30	$10,000
University of California at Berkeley School of Law (Boalt Hall)	780	9 1.2%	109 14%	57 7.3%	104 13.3%	-	279 35.8%	102	-	2 2%	8 7.8%	3 2.9%	-	13 12.7%	3	2	85	$1,300
School of Law, University of California—Davis	478	10 2.1%	76 15.9%	17 3.6%	36 7.5%	2 0.4%	141 29.5%	31	-	-	1 3.2%	2 6.5%	1 3.2%	4 12.9%	-	-	69	$2,857
University of California—Hastings College of the Law	1264	16 1.3%	159 12.6%	93 7.4%	129 10.2%	8 0.6%	405 32%	114	-	2 1.8%	2 1.8%	2 1.8%	1 0.9%	7 6.1%	-	7	74	$1,820

School																	
School of Law, University of California, Los Angeles	978	11 / 1.1%	152 / 15.5%	84 / 8.6%	138 / 14.1%	-	385 / 39.4%	96	5 / 5.2%	6 / 6.3%	6 / 5.2%	-	16 / 16.7%	-	5	-	-
California Western School of Law	860	5 / 0.6%	49 / 5.7%	15 / 1.7%	51 / 5.9%	14 / 1.6%	134 / 15.6%	80	1 / 1.3%	4 / 5%	2 / 2.5%	-	7 / 8.8%	-	-	37	$15,700
Capital University Law & Graduate Center	790	3 / 0.4%	10 / 1.3%	34 / 4.3%	10 / 1.3%	-	57 / 7.2%	31	-	4 / 12.9%	-	-	4 / 12.9%	-	-	75	$3,000 to $4,000
Benjamin N. Cardozo School of Law Yeshiva University	920	-	41 / 4.5%	35 / 3.8%	24 / 2.6%	-	100 / 10.9%	47	-	2 / 4.3%	-	-	2 / 4.3%	-	-	90	$2,000 to $4,000
Case Western Reserve University School of Law	638	-	22 / 3.4%	43 / 6.7%	3 / 0.5%	-	68 / 10.7%	76	-	1 / 1.3%	-	-	1 / 1.3%	-	-	96	$6,090
Catholic University of America—Columbus School of Law	945	2 / 0.2%	34 / 3.6%	59 / 6.2%	52 / 5.5%	2 / 0.2%	149 / 15.8%	124	-	7 / 5.6%	2 / 1.6%	-	9 / 7.3%	-	2	-	-
Chicago-Kent College of Law—Illinois Institute of Technology	1237	1 / 0.1%	75 / 6.1%	85 / 6.9%	37 / 3%	8 / 0.6%	206 / 16.7%	62	2 / 3.2%	3 / 4.8%	2 / 3.2%	-	7 / 11.3%	-	3	41	up to $16,540
University of Chicago Law School	530	3 / 0.6%	31 / 5.8%	45 / 8.5%	32 / 6%	-	111 / 20.9%	61	-	3 / 4.9%	-	-	3 / 4.9%	1	5	75	-
University of Cincinnati College of Law	394	-	13 / 3.3%	38 / 9.6%	8 / 2%	3 / 0.8%	62 / 15.7%	25	-	1 / 4%	1 / 4%	-	2 / 8%	-	1	68	$3,783
Cleveland State University—Cleveland-Marshall College of Law	1006	4 / 0.4%	29 / 2.9%	78 / 7.8%	23 / 2.3%	5 / 0.5%	139 / 13.8%	41	1 / 2.4%	3 / 7.3%	-	-	4 / 9.8%	1	1	32	$2,400
University of Colorado School of Law	476	14 / 2.9%	8 / 1.7%	22 / 4.6%	53 / 11.1%	-	97 / 20.4%	62	1 / 1.6%	1 / 1.6%	5 / 8.1%	1 / 1.6%	8 / 12.9%	-	3	84	$4,041
Columbia University School of Law	1053	5 / 0.5%	104 / 9.9%	94 / 8.9%	81 / 7.7%	-	284 / 27%	101	2 / 2%	5 / 5%	1 / 1%	-	8 / 7.9%	1	2	52	8548
University of Connecticut School of Law	655	1 / 0.2%	30 / 4.6%	39 / 6%	32 / 4.9%	-	102 / 15.6%	95	-	3 / 3.2%	1 / 1.1%	-	4 / 4.2%	1	1	-	-
Cornell University Law School	568	7 / 1.2%	50 / 8.8%	32 / 5.6%	34 / 6%	2 / 0.4%	125 / 22%	56	1 / 1.8%	2 / 3.6%	-	1 / 1.8%	4 / 7.1%	-	1	60	-
Creighton University School of Law	559	-	2 / 0.4%	16 / 2.9%	20 / 3.6%	-	38 / 6.8%	51	-	2 / 3.9%	-	-	2 / 3.9%	-	1	71	$9,755
Cumberland School of Law—Samford University	627	1 / 0.2%	4 / 0.6%	29 / 4.6%	4 / 0.6%	-	38 / 6.1%	58	1 / 1.7%	1 / 1.7%	-	-	2 / 3.4%	-	2	67	$11,350
University of Dayton School of Law	491	1 / 0.2%	13 / 2.6%	24 / 4.9%	11 / 2.2%	5 / 1%	54 / 11%	55	-	2 / 3.6%	1 / 1.8%	-	3 / 5.5%	-	1	60	$4,560
University of Denver College of Law	1080	12 / 1.1%	39 / 3.6%	30 / 2.8%	68 / 6.3%	-	149 / 13.8%	49	1 / 2%	1 / 2%	2 / 4.1%	-	4 / 8.2%	-	1	52	$4,722
DePaul University College of Law	984	3 / 0.3%	41 / 4.2%	55 / 5.6%	67 / 6.8%	-	166 / 16.9%	109	-	5 / 4.6%	3 / 2.8%	-	8 / 7.3%	-	3	-	-
University of Detroit—Mercy School of Law	914	1 / 0.1%	10 / 1.1%	47 / 5.1%	6 / 0.7%	-	64 / 7%	56	1 / 1.8%	2 / 3.6%	-	-	3 / 5.4%	1	2	85	$7,500
Detroit College of Law	756	1 / 0.1%	10 / 1.3%	49 / 6.5%	9 / 1.2%	-	69 / 9.1%	60	-	8 / 13.3%	1 / 1.7%	-	9 / 15%	-	6	74	$5,000
Dickinson School of Law	523	1 / 0.2%	12 / 2.3%	11 / 2.1%	8 / 1.5%	-	32 / 6.1%	61	1 / 3.3%	2 / 3.3%	-	-	2 / 3.3%	-	-	47	$6,013
District of Columbia School of Law	284	2 / 0.7%	7 / 2.5%	107 / 37.7%	17 / 6%	6 / 2.1%	139 / 48.9%	35	-	14 / 40%	2 / 5.7%	-	16 / 45.7%	1	4	70	$2,267

School (This information was reported by the schools in Fall 1993, thus the figures may have changed.)	Total No. of Students	Minority Students AI/AN	A/PI	B/A-A	H/L	Other	Total No. of Minority Students	Total No. of Faculty	Minority Faculty AI/AN	A/PI	B/A-A	H/L	Other	Total No. and % of Minority Faculty	Total No. of full-time Visiting Minority Faculty	No. of Part-time Minority Faculty	% of Minority Students Receiving Scholarships or Grants	Average Amount Per Scholarship or Grant
Drake University Law School	553	1 / 0.2%	12 / 2.2%	19 / 3.4%	15 / 2.7%	1 / 0.2%	48 / 8.7%	65	-	-	1 / 1.5%	2 / 3.1%	-	3 / 4.6%	-	2	73	$10,298
Duke University School of Law	595	1 / 0.2%	20 / 3.4%	45 / 7.6%	8 / 1.3%	-	74 / 12.4%	82	-	1 / 1.2%	3 / 3.7%	-	-	4 / 4.9%	-	2	-	-
Duquesne University School of Law	644	1 / 0.2%	5 / 0.8%	38 / 5.9%	2 / 0.3%	-	46 / 7.1%	58	-	2 / 3.4%	2 / 3.4%	1 / 1.7%	-	5 / 8.6%	-	1	60	$6,000
Emory University School of Law	740	-	30 / 4.1%	84 / 11.4%	15 / 2%	12 / 1.6%	141 / 19.1%	78	-	1 / 1.3%	4 / 5.1%	-	-	5 / 6.4%	1	1	60	$8,140
University of Florida College of Law	1150	3 / 0.3%	23 / 2%	130 / 11.3%	49 / 4.3%	-	205 / 17.8%	68	-	1 / 1.5%	5 / 7.4%	1 / 1.5%	-	7 / 10.3%	-	-	35	$5,000
The Florida State University College of Law	600	2 / 0.3%	10 / 1.7%	81 / 13.5%	55 / 9.2%	-	148 / 24.7%	58	-	-	4 / 6.9%	2 / 3.4%	-	6 / 10.3%	-	-	42	$5,000
Fordham University School of Law	1503	4 / 0.3%	100 / 6.7%	102 / 6.8%	98 / 6.5%	-	304 / 20.2%	187	-	1 / 0.5%	3 / 1.6%	-	-	4 / 2.1%	-	6	54	$5,000
Franklin Pierce Law Center	394	-	10 / 2.5%	3 / 0.8%	-	-	13 / 3.3%	51	-	-	-	-	-	-	-	-	5	$12,100
George Mason University School of Law	687	2 / 0.3%	22 / 3.2%	48 / 7%	12 / 1.7%	-	84 / 12.2%	50	-	2 / 4%	4 / 8%	-	-	6 / 12%	-	2	31	up to $6,500
George Washington University National Law Center	1464	2 / 0.1%	97 / 6.6%	120 / 8.2%	63 / 4.3%	-	282 / 19.3%	75	-	1 / 1.3%	5 / 6.7%	4 / 5.3%	-	10 / 13.3%	-	5	73	$6,000
Georgetown University Law Center	2051	9 / 0.4%	164 / 8%	235 / 11.5%	144 / 7%	8 / 0.4%	560 / 27.3%	84	-	1 / 1.2%	9 / 10.7%	1 / 1.2%	-	11 / 13.1%	1	9	-	up to $12,100
University of Georgia School of Law	641	-	11 / 1.7%	49 / 7.6%	5 / 0.8%	-	65 / 10.1%	39	1 / 2.6%	-	3 / 7.7%	-	-	4 / 10.3%	-	4	71	$3,500
Georgia State University College of Law	622	2 / 0.3%	25 / 4%	82 / 13.2%	20 / 3.2%	3 / 0.5%	132 / 21.2%	41	1 / 2.4%	1 / 2.4%	3 / 7.3%	-	-	5 / 12.2%	-	2	16	$2,500
Golden Gate University School of Law	740	9 / 1.2%	106 / 14.3%	22 / 3%	52 / 7%	-	189 / 25.5%	109	-	6 / 5.5%	3 / 2.8%	3 / 2.8%	-	12 / 11%	1	8	20	$10,000
Gonzaga University School of Law	556	6 / 1.1%	20 / 3.6%	2 / 0.4%	10 / 1.8%	-	38 / 6.8%	43	-	-	-	-	-	-	-	-	10	up to $2,500
Hamline University School of Law	603	2 / 0.3%	19 / 3.2%	25 / 4.1%	10 / 1.7%	2 / 0.3%	58 / 9.6%	73	2 / 2.7%	-	7 / 9.6%	1 / 1.4%	-	10 / 13.7%	-	9	41	half or full
Harvard University Law School	1616	5 / 0.3%	147 / 9.1%	182 / 11.3%	80 / 5%	25 / 1.5%	439 / 27.2%	113	-	3 / 2.7%	6 / 5.3%	2 / 1.8%	-	11 / 9.7%	2	3	36	$6,500
University of Hawaii at Manoa—William S. Richardson School of Law	240	5 / 2.1%	163 / 67.9%	2 / 0.8%	3 / 1.3%	-	173 / 72.1%	36	-	13 / 36.1%	2 / 5.6%	-	-	15 / 41.7%	1	10	-	-
Hofstra University School of Law	832	-	28 / 3.4%	68 / 8.2%	50 / 6%	-	146 / 17.5%	42	-	-	2 / 4.8%	-	-	2 / 4.8%	-	-	69	$5,823
University of Houston Law Center	1170	6 / 0.5%	42 / 3.6%	58 / 5%	98 / 8.4%	18 / 1.5%	222 / 19%	48	-	-	3 / 6.3%	4 / 8.3%	-	7 / 14.6%	-	10	60	$1,800

School	Total	(2)	(3)	(4)	(5)	(6)	(7)	(8)	(9)	(10)	(11)	(12)	(13)	(14)	Amount
Howard University School of Law	463	3 / 0.6%	15 / 3.2%	375 / 81%	16 / 3.5%	-	409 / 88.3%	42	1 / 2.4%	-	31 / 73.8%	32 / 76.2%	16	60	$7,500
University of Idaho College of Law	293	3 / 1%	13 / 4.4%	1 / 0.3%	16 / 5.5%	4 / 1.4%	37 / 12.6%	22	1 / 4.5%	-	-	1 / 4.5%	-	-	N/A
University of Illinois College of Law	626	-	36 / 5.8%	73 / 11.7%	29 / 4.6%	-	138 / 22%	65	-	-	3 / 4.6%	3 / 4.6%	-	35	$6,500
Indiana University School of Law—Bloomington	619	1 / 0.2%	33 / 5.3%	60 / 9.7%	30 / 4.8%	-	124 / 20%	54	-	-	2 / 3.7%	2 / 3.7%	-	58	$4,000
Indiana University School of Law—Indianapolis	823	3 / 0.4%	25 / 3%	67 / 8.1%	16 / 1.9%	6 / 0.7%	117 / 14.2%	63	-	1 / 1.6%	4 / 6.3%	6 / 9.5%	4	75	varies
University of Iowa College of Law	660	11 / 1.7%	37 / 5.6%	67 / 10.2%	34 / 5.2%	-	149 / 22.6%	54	1 / 1.9%	-	3 / 5.6%	6 / 11.1%	-	76	$5,570
The John Marshall School of Law	1202	5 / 0.4%	37 / 3.1%	48 / 4%	42 / 3.5%	-	132 / 11%	54	1 / 1.9%	-	3 / 5.6%	5 / 9.3%	-	-	varies
University of Kansas School of Law	525	7 / 1.3%	8 / 1.5%	22 / 4.2%	25 / 4.8%	-	62 / 11.8%	39	-	2 / 5.1%	1 / 2.6%	3 / 7.7%	-	81	up to $7,500
Lewis and Clark, Northwestern School of Law	698	12 / 1.7%	55 / 7.9%	14 / 2%	22 / 3.2%	-	103 / 14.8%	100	-	-	1 / 1%	1 / 1%	-	23	$4,083
University of Louisville School of Law	532	2 / 0.4%	8 / 1.5%	14 / 2.6%	9 / 1.7%	-	33 / 6.2%	29	-	1 / 3.4%	3 / 10.3%	4 / 13.8%	-	100	$3,956
Loyola Law School, Los Angeles, Loyola Marymount University	1361	7 / 0.5%	226 / 16.6%	59 / 4.3%	120 / 8.8%	-	412 / 30.3%	96	3 / 3.1%	-	6 / 6.3%	12 / 12.5%	6	33	$3,060
Loyola University Chicago School of Law	687	2 / 0.3%	47 / 6.8%	24 / 3.5%	27 / 3.9%	16 / 2.3%	116 / 16.9%	34	-	1 / 2.9%	3 / 8.8%	4 / 11.8%	2	34	$2,350
Loyola University School of Law—New Orleans	795	5 / 0.6%	12 / 1.5%	109 / 13.7%	43 / 5.4%	6 / 0.8%	175 / 22%	31	1 / 3.2%	-	4 / 12.9%	5 / 16.1%	5	40	$150—full
University of Maine School of Law	267	3 / 1.1%	7 / 2.6%	4 / 1.5%	2 / 0.7%	-	16 / 6%	23	-	-	-	-	-	63	$10,000
Marquette University Law School	495	3 / 0.6%	15 / 3%	16 / 3.2%	10 / 2%	-	44 / 8.9%	21	-	2 / 9.5%	1 / 4.8%	4 / 19%	2	90	$2,000 to full tuition
University of Maryland School of Law	856	2 / 0.2%	52 / 6.1%	195 / 22.8%	14 / 1.6%	-	263 / 30.8%	50	1 / 2%	-	6 / 12%	7 / 14%	-	72	$1,000 to full tuition
McGeorge School of Law, University of the Pacific	1259	9 / 0.7%	99 / 7.9%	22 / 1.7%	53 / 4.2%	-	183 / 14.5%	88	4 / 4.5%	-	3 / 3.4%	11 / 12.5%	3	46	$3,000 to full tuition
Memphis State University—Cecil C. Humphreys School of Law	423	-	-	28 / 6.6%	-	-	28 / 6.6%	41	1 / 2.4%	-	1 / 2.4%	1 / 2.4%	-	100	$8,000
Mercer University—Walter F. George School of Law	409	-	4 / 1%	39 / 9.5%	24 / 5.9%	1 / 0.2%	68 / 16.6%	30	-	2 / 6.7%	2 / 6.7%	2 / 6.7%	1	71	$7,964
University of Michigan Law School	1147	19 / 1.7%	57 / 5%	103 / 9%	72 / 6.3%	-	251 / 21.9%	97	2 / 2.1%	-	2 / 2.1%	6 / 6.2%	-	46	$500-full tuition
University of Minnesota Law School	810	18 / 2.2%	48 / 5.9%	30 / 3.7%	20 / 2.5%	-	116 / 14.3%	128	1 / 0.8%	-	5 / 3.9%	8 / 6.3%	-	50	full tuition
The University of Mississippi School of Law	510	12 / 2.4%	7 / 1.4%	27 / 5.3%	6 / 1.2%	-	52 / 10.2%	32	-	2 / 6.3%	2 / 6.3%	3 / 9.4%	-	100	full tuition
Mississippi College School of Law	376	1 / 0.3%	4 / 1.1%	23 / 6.1%	7 / 1.9%	1 / 0.3%	36 / 9.6%	35	-	1 / 2.9%	1 / 2.9%	1 / 2.9%	-	18	$7,279

This information was reported by the schools in Fall 1993, thus the figures may have changed.

School	Total No. of Students	AI AN	A PI	B A-A	H L	Other	Total No. of Minority Students	Total No. of Faculty	(Faculty) AI AN	A PI	B A-A	H L	Other	Total No. and % of Minority Faculty	Total No. of full-time Visiting Minority Faculty	No. of Part-time Minority Faculty	% of Minority Students Receiving Scholarships or Grants	Average Amount Per Scholarship or Grant
University of Missouri—Columbia School of Law	455	2 0.4%	-	33 7.3%	2 0.4%	-	37 8.1%	36	-	-	1 2.8%	-	-	1 2.8%	-	-	94	$4,000
University of Missouri—Kansas City School of Law	460	1 0.2%	4 0.9%	14 3%	9 2%	-	28 6.1%	28	-	-	2 7.1%	-	-	2 7.1%		-	43	$3,600–$13,000
University of Montana School of Law	229	9 3.9%	-	-	-	-	9 3.9%	27	1 3.7%	-	-	-	-	1 3.7%	-	-	78	$10,082
University of Nebraska College of Law	469	5 1.1%	14 3%	22 4.7%	13 2.8%	-	54 11.5%	56	-	1 1.8%	3 5.4%	-	-	4 7.1%	-	2	87	varies
New England School of Law	1129	5 0.4%	22 1.9%	10 0.9%	21 1.9%	-	58 5.1%	103	-	1 1%	3 2.9%	-	-	4 3.9%	-	2	36	$4,683
University of New Mexico School of Law	343	28 8.2%	13 3.8%	13 3.8%	103 30%	-	157 45.8%	29	-	-	2 6.9%	4 13.8%	-	6 20.7%	2	2	30	$2,466
City University of New York School of Law at Queens College	450	3 0.7%	22 4.9%	66 14.7%	33 7.3%	-	124 27.6%	55	-	5 9.1%	8 14.5%	5 9.1%	1 1.8%	19 34.5%	-	1	70	$2,300
New York Law School	1369	2 0.1%	93 6.8%	119 8.7%	89 6.5%	-	303 22.1%	49	-	2 4.1%	2 4.1%	3 6.1%	-	7 14.3%	-	5	37	$4,792
New York University School of Law	1299	2 0.2%	125 9.6%	86 6.6%	89 6.9%	-	302 23.2%	204	1 0.5%	3 1.5%	9 4.4%	-	-	13 6.4%	-	4	-	-
University of North Carolina School of Law	704	7 1%	11 1.6%	76 10.8%	11 1.6%	-	105 14.9%	42	-	-	4 9.5%	-	-	4 9.5%	1	1	49	$1,973
North Carolina Central University School of Law	306	3 1%	1 0.3%	165 53.9%		-	169 55.2%	25	-	-	14 56%	-	-	14 56%	4	3	-	varies
University of North Dakota School of Law	243	4 1.6%	3 1.2%	1 0.4%	2 0.8%	-	10 4.1%	26	-	-	-	-	-	-	-	3	-	-
Northeastern University School of Law	603	2 0.3%	61 10.1%	36 6%	27 4.5%	-	126 20.9%	55	-	2 3.6%	7 12.7%	2 3.6%	-	11 20%	-	4	-	varies
Northern Illinois University College of Law	308	1 0.3%	4 1.3%	33 10.7%	31 10.1%	6 1.9%	75 24.4%	38	-	-	3 7.9%	1 2.6%	-	4 10.5%	1	1	33	$3,076
Northern Kentucky University—Salmon P. Chase College of Law	446	-	9 2%	34 7.6%	3 0.7%	-	46 10.3%	47	-	-	3 6.4%	-	-	3 6.4%	-	1	22	varies
Northwestern University School of Law	612	2 0.3%	69 11.3%	54 8.8%	27 4.4%	-	152 24.8%	111	-	1 0.9%	7 6.3%	2 1.8%	-	10 9%	-	5	76	varies
Nova University—Shepard Broad Law Center	859	5 0.6%	8 0.9%	103 12%	81 9.4%	-	197 22.9%	86	-	1 1.2%	3 3.5%	5 5.8%	-	9 10.5%	1	2	35	$4,696
Ohio Northern University—Claude W. Pettit College of Law	397	2 0.5%	2 0.5%	22 5.5%	7 1.8%	-	33 8.3%	41	-	-	-	-	-	-	-	-	53	$7,000
The Ohio State University College of Law	660	3 0.5%	27 4.1%	78 11.8%	15 2.3%	-	123 18.6%	57	-	1 1.8%	6 10.5%	-	-	7 12.3%	-	1	80	varies

School	(1)	(2)	(3)	(4)	(5)	(6)	(7)	(8)	(9)	(10)	(11)	(12)	(13)	(14)	(15)	(16)	(17)	(18)
University of Oklahoma College of Law	670	28 / 4.2%	15 / 2.2%	12 / 1.8%	14 / 2.1%	-	69 / 10.3%	40	1 / 2.5%	1 / 2.5%	-	-	-	2 / 5%	1	-	90	$3,000
Oklahoma City University School of Law	658	19 / 2.9%	10 / 1.5%	17 / 2.6%	15 / 2.3%	-	61 / 9.3%	47	1 / 2.1%	2 / 4.3%	-	1 / 2.5%	-	3 / 6.4%	-	1	-	$6,033
University of Oregon School of Law	410	12 / 2.9%	16 / 3.9%	16 / 3.9%	12 / 2.9%	-	56 / 13.7%	40	-	2 / 5%	1 / 2.5%	1 / 2.5%	-	4 / 10%	-	-	80	$3,370
Pace University School of Law	794	1 / 0.1%	31 / 3.9%	46 / 5.8%	52 / 6.5%	-	130 / 16.4%	-	-	-	-	-	-	-	-	-	-	-
University of Pennsylvania Law School	710	2 / 0.3%	40 / 5.6%	76 / 10.7%	30 / 4.2%	-	148 / 20.8%	93	1 / 1.1%	3 / 3.2%	-	1 / 3.2%	-	4 / 4.3%	-	4	-	-
Pepperdine University School of Law	714	5 / 0.7%	37 / 5.2%	24 / 3.4%	61 / 8.5%	-	127 / 17.8%	46	-	1 / 2.2%	-	1 / 2.2%	-	2 / 4.3%	-	1	100	$6,000
University of Pittsburgh School of Law	697	-	20 / 2.9%	54 / 7.7%	8 / 1.1%	4 / 0.6%	86 / 12.3%	63	-	3 / 4.8%	1 / 1.6%	-	-	4 / 6.3%	-	-	90	$4,500
Puget Sound/Seattle University School of Law	867	13 / 1.5%	61 / 7%	23 / 2.7%	23 / 2.7%	9 / 1%	129 / 14.9%	40	-	-	2 / 5%	1 / 2.5%	-	3 / 7.5%	-	-	26	$5,308
Quinnipiac College School of Law	708	3 / 0.4%	28 / 4%	15 / 2.1%	23 / 3.2%	-	69 / 9.7%	65	-	3 / 4.6%	1 / 1.5%	1 / 1.5%	-	5 / 7.7%	-	-	-	-
University of Richmond—T.C. Williams School of Law	456	3 / 0.7%	36 / 7.9%	41 / 9%	12 / 2.6%	9 / 2%	101 / 22.1%	87	-	7 / 8%	2 / 2.3%	-	1 / 1.1%	10 / 11.5%	-	7	82	$5,000
Rutgers—The State University—School of Law—Camden	721	-	83 / 11.5%	76 / 10.5%	50 / 6.9%	-	209 / 29%	37	-	2 / 5.4%	2 / 5.4%	1 / 2.7%	-	5 / 13.5%	-	3	29	varies
Rutgers University School of Law—Newark	774	2 / 0.3%	51 / 6.6%	108 / 14%	80 / 10.3%	-	241 / 31.1%	80	-	4 / 5%	1 / 1.3%	-	-	5 / 6.3%	-	3	40	$2,000
St. John's University School of Law	1179	1 / 0.1%	43 / 3.6%	54 / 4.6%	56 / 4.7%	7 / 0.6%	161 / 13.7%	50	1 / 2%	5 / 10%	-	1 / 2%	-	7 / 14%	-	3	31	varies
Saint Louis University School of Law	826	-	18 / 2.2%	69 / 8.4%	24 / 2.9%	1 / 0.1%	112 / 13.6%	44	-	3 / 6.8%	1 / 2.3%	-	-	4 / 9.1%	-	-	90	$4,500
St. Mary's University School of Law	746	7 / 0.9%	16 / 2.1%	16 / 2.1%	142 / 19%	-	181 / 24.3%	69	-	1 / 1.4%	-	3 / 4.3%	-	4 / 5.8%	-	5	35	varies
St. Thomas University School of Law	478	2 / 0.4%	6 / 1.3%	32 / 6.7%	112 / 23.4%	-	152 / 31.8%	60	-	5 / 8.3%	1 / 1.7%	5 / 8.3%	-	11 / 18.3%	-	4	35	$6,057
University of San Diego School of Law	1072	19 / 1.8%	73 / 6.8%	24 / 2.2%	74 / 6.9%	-	190 / 17.7%	114	-	3 / 2.6%	2 / 1.8%	4 / 3.5%	-	9 / 7.9%	-	1	46	up to full tuition
University of San Francisco School of Law	659	2 / 0.3%	98 / 14.9%	31 / 4.7%	30 / 4.6%	6 / 0.9%	167 / 25.3%	91	-	6 / 6.6%	4 / 4.4%	3 / 3.3%	-	13 / 14.3%	3	5	-	$5,000
Santa Clara University School of Law	883	4 / 0.5%	134 / 15.2%	47 / 5.3%	78 / 8.8%	30 / 3.4%	293 / 33.2%	53	-	3 / 5.7%	2 / 3.8%	1 / 1.9%	1 / 0.7%	6 / 11.3%	1	-	70	$1,000 to $15,540
Seton Hall University School of Law	1375	7 / 0.5%	47 / 3.4%	138 / 10%	77 / 5.6%	-	269 / 19.6%	148	-	7 / 4.7%	2 / 1.4%	6 / 4.1%	-	16 / 10.8%	-	8	67	$2,800
University of South Carolina School of Law	765	-	4 / 0.5%	62 / 8.1%	4 / 0.5%	-	70 / 9.2%	44	-	3 / 6.8%	-	-	-	3 / 6.8%	-	-	37	$1,500
University of South Dakota School of Law	218	3 / 1.4%	1 / 0.5%	2 / 0.9%	-	-	6 / 2.8%	16	-	-	-	-	-	-	-	-	50	$1,000
South Texas College of Law	1316	1 / 0.1%	69 / 5.2%	68 / 5.2%	99 / 7.5%	-	237 / 18%	89	-	3 / 3.4%	1 / 1.1%	1 / 1.1%	-	5 / 5.6%	-	2	41	$5,413

This information was reported by the schools in Fall 1993, thus the figures may have changed.	Total No. of Students	Number and Percentage of Minority Students						Total No. of Faculty	Number and Percentage of Minority Faculty						Total No. of full-time Visiting Minority Faculty	No. of Part-time Minority Faculty	% of Minority Students Receiving Scholarships or Grants	Average Amount Per Scholarship or Grant
		AI AN	A PI	B A-A	H L	Other	Total No. of Minority Students		AI AN	A PI	B A-A	H L	Other	Total No. and % of Minority Faculty				
University of Southern California Law Center	600	8 1.3%	63 10.5%	60 10%	46 7.7%	-	177 29.5%	76	-	2 2.6%	3 3.9%	-	-	5 6.6%	1	3	70	$7,000
Southern Illinois University School of Law	344	-	6 1.7%	22 6.4%	9 2.6%	-	37 10.8%	33	-	-	2 6.1%	1 3%	-	3 9.1%	-	-	67	$1,800 plus tuition waiver
Southern Methodist University School of Law	749	2 0.3%	45 6%	41 5.5%	63 8.4%	-	151 20.2%	41	-	1 2.4%	3 7.3%	2 4.9%	-	6 14.6%	-	-	43	$8,000
Southern University Law Center	339	-	-	198 58.4%	-	-	198 58.4%	37	-	-	24 64.9%	-	-	24 64.9%	-	7	15	$4,000/year
Southwestern University School of Law	1149	5 0.4%	143 12.4%	51 4.4%	72 6.3%	-	271 23.6%	78	-	2 2.6%	4 5.1%	6 7.7%	-	12 15.4%	-	6	38	$7,115
Stanford University Law School	536	24 4.5%	59 11%	44 8.2%	66 12.3%	-	193 36%	45	-	1 2.2%	3 6.7%	2 4.4%	-	6 13.3%	1	-	50	up to full tuition
Stetson University College of Law	648	3 0.5%	18 2.8%	34 5.2%	45 6.9%	12 1.9%	112 17.3%	83	2 2.4%	-	1 1.2%	1 1.2%	-	4 4.8%	-	-	68	$2,000
Suffolk University Law School	1700	6 0.4%	74 4.4%	74 4.4%	50 2.9%	-	204 12%	130	-	-	4 3.1%	1 0.8%	-	5 3.8%	-	3	18	$2,100
Syracuse University College of Law	810	3 0.4%	107 13.2%	81 10%	52 6.4%	-	243 30%	41	-	1 2.4%	3 7.3%	-	-	4 9.8%	2	-	50	$4,085
Temple University School of Law	1274	2 0.2%	72 5.7%	116 9.1%	45 3.5%	-	235 18.4%	190	-	3 1.6%	25 13.2%	3 1.6%	-	31 16.3%	-	20	59	$2,000
University of Tennessee College of Law	472	4 0.8%	4 0.8%	39 8.3%	2 0.4%	-	49 10.4%	36	-	-	3 8.3%	-	-	3 8.3%	-	-	80	$8,875
The University of Texas School of Law	1487	5 0.3%	63 4.2%	104 7%	170 11.4%	8 0.5%	350 23.5%	153	-	1 0.7%	4 2.6%	5 3.3%	1 0.7%	11 7.2%	1	7	86	$3,638
Texas Southern University—Thurgood Marshall School of Law	650	7 1.1%	14 2.2%	337 51.8%	144 22.2%	-	502 77.2%	45	-	-	24 53.3%	4 8.9%	-	28 62.2%	2	10	20	$1,000
Texas Tech University School of Law	627	5 0.8%	13 2.1%	13 2.1%	74 11.8%	-	105 16.7%	36	-	-	1 2.8%	3 8.3%	1 2.8%	5 13.9%	-	-	97	$2,035
The University of Toledo College of Law	630	3 0.5%	7 1.1%	34 5.4%	16 2.5%	-	60 9.5%	58	-	-	2 3.4%	-	-	2 3.4%	-	1	60	$5,800
Touro College—Jacob D. Fuchsberg Law Center	864	-	40 4.6%	86 10%	63 7.3%	4 0.5%	193 22.3%	41	-	-	3 7.3%	-	-	3 7.3%	-	-	70	FT $7,085 p/y; PT $2,868 p/y
Tulane University Law School	1000	3 0.3%	42 4.2%	110 11%	57 5.7%	12 1.2%	224 22.4%	48	-	1 2.1%	5 10.4%	-	-	6 12.5%	-	1	56	$8,350
University of Tulsa College of Law	628	41 6.5%	9 1.4%	11 1.8%	11 1.8%	3 0.5%	75 11.9%	37	1 2.7%	1 2.7%	2 5.4%	2 5.4%	-	6 16.2%	-	-	23	$7,862
University of Utah College of Law	366	9 2.5%	21 5.7%	6 1.6%	16 4.4%	-	52 14.2%	27	1 3.7%	-	-	3 11.1%	-	4 14.8%	-	2	58	50% of res. tuition
Valparaiso University School of Law	539	-	12 2.2%	16 3%	11 2%	7 1.3%	46 8.5%	25	-	-	2 8%	-	-	2 8%	-	-	62	$4,600

School	Enrollment	AI/AN	A/PI	B/A-A	H/L	Other	Total Minority	Faculty	Fac AI/AN	Fac (cat)	Fac Total Min	(#)	(#)	Amount
Vanderbilt University School of Law	540	-	54 10%	56 10.4%	5 0.9%	-	115 21.3%	32	-	2 6.3%	2 6.3%	2	80	$8,000
University of Virginia School of Law	1148	3 0.3%	33 2.9%	114 9.9%	11 1%	-	161 14%	55	1 1.8%	3 5.5%	4 7.3%	-	62	$7,429
Wake Forest University School of Law	465	3 0.6%	3 0.6%	25 5.4%	1 0.2%	2 0.4%	34 7.3%	34	-	2 5.9%	2 5.9%	2	2	$7,150
Washburn University School of Law	425	2 0.5%	23 5.4%	21 4.9%	23 5.4%	-	69 16.2%	59	2 3.4%	2 3.4%	6 10.2%	1	83	$3,700
University of Washington School of Law	474	22 4.6%	83 17.5%	33 7%	43 9.1%	2 0.4%	183 38.6%	44	1 2.3%	3 6.8%	4 9.1%	-	50	$2,000
Washington and Lee University School of Law	360	1 0.3%	10 2.8%	36 10%	9 2.5%	-	56 15.6%	48	1 2.1%	1 2.1%	2 4.2%	-	-	-
Washington University School of Law	650	4 0.6%	25 3.8%	42 6.5%	11 1.7%	-	82 12.6%	86	-	2 2.3%	2 2.3%	6	90	$8,000
Wayne State University Law School	700	5 0.7%	2 0.3%	66 9.4%	21 3%	-	94 13.4%	66	-	2 3%	2 3%	3	90	$1,000 to $15,000
West Virginia University College of Law	452	1 0.2%	8 1.8%	27 6%	1 0.2%	-	37 8.2%	50	-	1 2%	1 2%	-	17	$500 to $17,000
Western New England College School of Law	775	3 0.4%	11 1.4%	26 3.4%	18 2.3%	-	58 7.5%	59	-	3 5.1%	3 5.1%	2	10	$4,242
Widener University School of Law	2193	2 0.1%	44 2%	66 3%	33 1.5%	22 1%	167 7.6%	97	-	5 5.2%	5 5.2%	4	13	$5,300-$14,150
Willamette University College of Law	484	6 1.2%	32 6.6%	9 1.9%	9 1.9%	1 0.2%	57 11.8%	39	-	1 2.6%	1 2.6%	-	46	$6,923
College of William and Mary—Marshall-Wythe School of Law	564	1 0.2%	16 2.8%	57 10.1%	3 0.5%	-	77 13.7%	50	1 2%	4 8%	5 10%	1	62	$1,424
William Mitchell College of Law	1130	13 1.2%	35 3.1%	56 5%	22 1.9%	-	126 11.2%	35	2 5.7%	1 2.9%	3 8.6%	4	65	$1,667
University of Wisconsin Law School	919	15 1.6%	27 2.9%	57 6.2%	49 5.3%	-	148 16.1%	47	1 2.1%	4 8.5%	7 14.9%	-	65	$5,300
University of Wyoming College of Law	222	3 1.4%	1 0.5%	1 0.5%	8 3.6%	-	13 5.9%	17	-	-	-	-	46	$1,800
Yale Law School	617	6 1%	71 11.5%	59 9.6%	38 6.2%	-	174 28.2%	46	3 6.5%	3 6.5%	6 13%	6	-	-

Minority Key Facts

AI/AN American Indian / Alaskan Native
A/PI   Asian/Pacific Islander (i.e., Chinese, Japanese, Korean, Vietnamese, etc.)
B/A-A Black/ African American
H/L   Hispanic/Latino (i.e., Mexican American, Chicano, Puerto Rican, etc.)
Other

Note: Enrollment figures listed in this Minority Key Facts chart may not directly correspond to figures listed on the preceding Key Facts chart. The discrepancies are due to differences in enrollment definitions used by schools. For example, some schools include part-time as well as full-time students in their totals; others do not. Several schools included LL.M. candidates, dual-degree students, or other graduate students in their totals on one chart but not the other. For the most up-to-date and accurate figures, contact individual schools directly.

Chapter 8: Financing Your Legal Education

The Cost of a Legal Education

The cost of attending law school is a figure that includes tuition, fees, books, housing, and other living expenses for the academic year. It can vary significantly from one school to another. Tuition alone can range from a few thousand dollars a year to almost $20,000 per year. After adding in housing, food, books, and personal expenses, the figure may go well beyond $75,000 for a three-year law school education.

The cost of attending a particular law school is only one of the many factors you should consider in making your choice.

Financial Aid: A Student's Responsibilities

The first step in applying for financial aid for law school is to complete the Free Application for Federal Student Aid (FAFSA), available from your college or university financial aid office or from the law school to which you are applying. The FAFSA is a need analysis tool developed by the U.S. Government, Department of Education. It asks for information about your income, assets, and other financial resources. The information you provide on the financial aid form will be used to compute how much you and your family should contribute toward your legal education. Many schools also require copies of annual federal tax returns to verify financial information; some schools also require students to fill out a supplemental form to be considered for institutional aid. Once the analysis is completed, the financial aid officer at the school can determine what types of aid you will need—such as scholarships, grants, loans, or work-study—to pay your law school expenses.

For complete and individualized information on financing your law school education, contact the financial aid office at the individual law school(s) to which you apply.

Determining How You Will Pay

There are three basic types of financial aid:

- **Scholarships, Grants, and Fellowships**—These types of awards, which do not have to be repaid, are given according to need and/or merit. *Their availability is quite limited*, and they are usually awarded by the law schools themselves. The law school's financial aid office can give you more information.

- **Federal College Work-Study**—This federal student aid program allows educational institutions to hire students to work either on- or off-campus for the institution or other eligible employers. Work-study placement is usually awarded to second- and third-year students, since you are expected to concentrate fully on your school work during your first year. Sometimes a student may be able to combine earned income for educational expenses with useful job experience, such as working in a legal aid office.

- **Loans**—Education loans may be awarded directly by the school or through other private agencies. The largest student loan programs are funded or guaranteed by the federal government. Some are awarded on a need basis, while others are not need-based. Some types of loans will require a credit check. Student loans are usually offered at interest rates lower than consumer loans, and the repayment of principal and interest usually begins after the end of your educational program.

Debt Management

Approximately 75 percent of law school students rely on education loans as their primary source of financial aid for law school. An education loan is a serious financial obligation that must be repaid. Dealing with this long-term financial obligation can be made easier through the implementation of sound debt management practices—both while you are in law school and following your graduation.

■ Credit History

It is very important that you have a good credit history. In today's society, most students have already established a credit history through their repayment records as reported by financial institutions and major retail stores to national credit bureaus. Lenders refer to these credit bureau records to determine your credit worthiness. The credit bureaus report the amounts you borrowed or charged, your outstanding balances, and the promptness by which payments have been made. Failure to pay your financial obligations in a prompt and timely manner will jeopardize your eligibility for some education loans.

If you have been denied credit in the past—or if you even suspect a problem with your credit history—it is wise to get a copy of your credit report. Usually, you can obtain it from a credit bureau in your area. Contact the bureau in writing, giving your name, address, and social security number. You can expect to pay a nominal fee unless you have been denied credit recently, in which case the report may be free. Review your report carefully and clear up any problems you can. Keep in mind that it takes time—possibly months—to clear up errors or other problems, so do not wait until the last minute.

■ Loan Default or Delinquency

These two terms are often confused: **delinquency** occurs when you have begun repayment on a loan or other obligation and have missed one or more payment dates; **default** generally occurs when a delinquency goes beyond 150-180 days.

Delinquencies appear on credit records and may hinder you from qualifying for an education loan that requires a credit check. Defaults are even more serious and are likely to prevent you from successfully applying for federal financial aid as well as disqualifying you for most other educational loans. If you are in a default status, you must take steps to change your status if you wish to apply for a federally guaranteed loan for law school. Contact the servicer of your loan(s) for more information on this subject.

■ Planning Ahead: Repayment of Your Loan

Your income after law school is an important factor in determining what constitutes manageable payments on your education loans. Although it may be difficult to predict what kind of job you will get (or want) after law school, or exactly what kind of salary you will receive, it is important that you make **some** assessment of your goals for the purpose of sound debt management. In addition to assessing expected income, you must also create a realistic picture of how much you can afford to pay back on a monthly basis and maintain the lifestyle that you desire. You may have to adjust your thinking about how quickly you can pay your loans back, or how much money you can afford to borrow, or just how extravagantly you expect to live in the years following your graduation from law school.

Your education loan debts represent a serious financial commitment which must be repaid. A default on any loan engenders serious consequences, including possible legal action against you by the lender and/or the government.

There are alternatives available to you to lessen the burden of repayment following law school, including the federal loan consolidation program. The financial aid office at your law school can advise you about repayment issues.

Chapter 9: Finding a Job

Employment Prospects

Because the number of practicing lawyers in the United States continues to increase, it may become more difficult for recent graduates to find jobs in some fields and in certain parts of the country. Opportunities will vary from locality to locality and among legal disciplines. Future lawyers may have to devote considerable time and energy to secure a first job that they consider acceptable. Competition for certain positions will continue to be intense, while opportunities in other fields may expand.

Future demand for people with legal training is almost impossible to predict. Demand for legal services is substantially influenced by the state of the economy. Rising caseloads in the nation's courts and continuing federal and state regulation suggest that the need for lawyers is growing. Whether this expanding need will match or fall short of the parallel growth in the number of practicing lawyers is a question no one can answer with certainty. Lawyers with outstanding academic credentials will continue to obtain desirable positions.

The legal profession itself may adapt to changing job markets by encouraging the entry of lawyers into relatively new fields of law, such as environmental law, intellectual property law, immigration law, and other fields. In addition, certain parts of the country are underrepresented by lawyers.

■ Career Satisfaction

A job search strategy requires careful self-assessment in much the same way as a school search strategy does. A legal career should meet the interests, abilities, capacities, and priorities of the individual lawyer. Career satisfaction is a result of doing what you like to do, and being continually challenged by it. It is up to you to determine what skills you are comfortable using, and to discern which skills are required in the specialties or types of practice you are considering.

■ Gathering Information

Take advantage of any programs and workshops offered by the career services office at your law school. (See page 20 for more on the role of the career services office.) Place your name on file in the office, and be sure to maintain contact with the staff even after you leave school.

The National Association for Law Placement (NALP) is an important source of information (see page 38 for details). This chapter includes a number of charts and graphs compiled by NALP that provide current information relating to employment of law school graduates.

■ Nonlegal Careers for Lawyers

Law-trained individuals pursue a wide variety of careers, and the skills discussed in the first section of this chapter provide excellent training for law school graduates who pursue directions outside the practice of law itself. Lawyers work in the media; as teachers of college, graduate school, and law school; and in law enforcement, public relations, foreign service, politics, and administration.

National Association for Law Placement (NALP) Employment Report and Salary Survey

■ Types of Employment

Data collected on employer types help us understand how new graduates are absorbed into various sectors of the economy. As in all prior years that NALP has collected data, the most common employment setting was that of private practice within a law firm. Of graduates known to be employed, 59 percent obtained their first job in a law firm. This represents a decline from the 60.8 percent for the Class of 1991 and the fourth year in a row that this percentage has declined from the high of 64.3 percent for the Class of 1988.

The second most frequent employment setting, accounting for 28.2 percent of employed graduates, was in public service. This total consisted of government (including the military) at 13.4 percent, judicial clerkships at 12.4 percent, and public interest at 2.4 percent; all are virtually unchanged from 1991. Conversely, business and industry, accounting for 8.9 percent of jobs, showed a notable increase from the 1991 figure of 7.5 percent.

**Types of Employment
Class of 1992*
(Six Months Post-J.D.)**

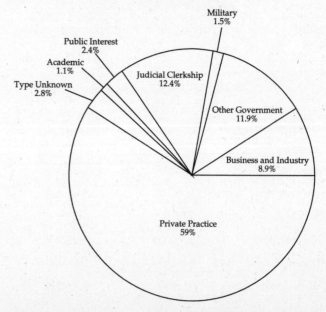

*Represents 72.1% of survey respondents

Eighteen-year Comparison of Employment (by Field) of New J.D. Graduates

Employment Field	1975	1976	1977	1978	1979	1980	1981	1982	1983	1984	1985	1986	1987	1988	1989	1990	1991	1992
Private Practice	51.0	52.4	53.0	53.0	54.0	55.1	57.9	59.6	60.4	57.4	60.2	61.6	63.5	64.3	62.4	62.9	60.8	59.0
Public Interest	5.6	5.0	5.3	5.9	5.4	4.3	3.4	3.0	3.1	3.3	3.3	3.0	3.0	3.1	3.4	2.1	2.3	2.4
Business	9.6	10.0	10.0	10.6	10.5	11.0	11.3	10.8	10.8	10.8	10.4	9.2	7.9	6.9	5.8	6.9	7.5	8.9
Government	17.6	17.5	16.7	15.5	14.7	14.0	12.0	10.9	11.5	10.9	12.7	12.0	12.1	12.0	11.4	13.7	13.4	13.4
Judicial Clerkships	9.6	9.1	8.9	8.9	9.8	10.1	10.4	11.0	11.7	10.1	11.9	12.5	12.5	12.7	12.2	12.7	12.4	12.4
Academic	3.4	3.4	3.3	3.5	3.0	3.1	3.1	3.1	1.5	1.8	1.5	1.7	1.0	1.0	1.0	0.8	1.0	1.1

Charts, tables, and copy adapted with permission from the National Association for Law Placement's Class of 1992 Employment Report and Salary Survey

The table above illustrates the distribution of employer types since 1975. It is important to note, when examining this table, that prior to 1990 public defender positions were categorized as public interest employment; beginning in 1990, these positions were reclassified as government employment. In addition, prior to 1983, the academic category included those pursuing an advanced degree full-time.

■ Salary as an Employment Factor

The average starting salary for the class of 1992 was $42,000, and the median starting salary for the class of 1992 was $36,000. The latter figure, which represents a decrease from the previous year, does not indicate that employers actually cut salaries. Instead, the decline resulted from graduates obtaining relatively more jobs in smaller firms where base salaries are generally lower.

Full-Time Salary Median By Employer Type*

General Category	Legal Jobs Only	Non-Legal Jobs Only
Academic	$30,000	$38,000
Business/Industry	$40,500	$40,000
Clerkship	$32,000	n/a
Government	$31,000	$39,500
Private Practice	$47,500	$36,000
Public Interest	$26,000	$30,000

*Based on 1992 Salary Data

Median Starting Salaries* In:

	Private Practice	Business & Industry	Government
Atlanta	$56,000	$43,500	$32,700
Boston	$66,000	$42,000	$30,000
Chicago	$68,000	$42,000	$30,000
Houston	$53,000	$45,000	$34,000
Los Angeles	$68,000	$40,000	$41,000
Minneapolis/ St. Paul	$51,000	$38,500	$32,900
New York City	$82,000	$50,000	$33,000
Philadelphia	$55,000	$39,350	$31,000
San Francisco	$65,000	$36,000	$33,700
Washington, DC	$69,000	$40,000	$32,500

*Full-time jobs only

■ Geography as an Employment Factor

Geographic considerations provide yet another perspective on the placement of new law graduates.

Jobs by City

The 20 cities with the largest number of jobs reported accounted for 41 percent of all jobs with a known location. These top 20 cities, listed in the table, correspond fairly closely to the top 20 cities in terms of population except that this list includes St. Louis, Indianapolis, and Columbus and excludes Cleveland, Denver, and Phoenix. Not surprisingly, New York City accounts for the largest number of jobs, just under 8 percent of the total.

Jobs by State

States vary widely in the number of jobs each provides, again reflecting the distribution of the total population. However, the top 10 states in terms of total reported jobs taken have remained the same over the past six years, with New York and California consistently ranked first and second. Other states have fluctuated to varying degrees in their ranking. Prior to 1991, Washington, DC moved up steadily in the ranking; since then it has retreated to fifth place.

Jobs by Region

The distribution by region of jobs taken by law graduates reflects the overall distribution of population. Four regions, Mid-Atlantic, South Atlantic, Pacific, and East North Central, dominate the job market, continuing to account for 70 percent of the jobs for which a location was reported. The East South Central and Mountain states continue to provide the fewest jobs.

Place of Work versus Place of School

Comparing the locations of graduates' law school training with the location of their first job offers some insight into the way each geographic market attracts and absorbs graduates within that market. Some of the underlying factors at work are the supply and demand for new law graduates in each market, the perceived attractiveness of each market, and individual preferences.

Nationally, about three-quarters of graduates accepted jobs within the region where they attended law school. Only three regions, Mid-Atlantic, South Atlantic, and Mountain, were below this average: 58.8 percent of jobs in the Mountain region were taken by graduates from that region and just over 70 percent of jobs in the Mid- and South Atlantic regions went to regional graduates. In contrast, 86.4 percent of jobs in the West North Central region were obtained by regional graduates.

The percentage of graduates staying in a state is often correlated with the relationship between the supply of graduates in that state and the demand for graduates, measured by the number of jobs in that state. Other factors include the proportion of graduates who are state residents and the presence of national versus regional law schools in the state.

Cities With the Largest Number of Jobs Reported

	City	Number of Jobs
1.	New York City	1,900
2.	Washington, DC	1,301
3.	Chicago	952
4.	Los Angeles	742
5.	Houston	522
6.	Boston	509
7.	Philadelphia	505
8.	Minneapolis/St. Paul	378
9.	San Francisco	364
10.	Atlanta	340
11.	Dallas/Fort Worth	334
12.	Pittsburgh	271
13.	Miami	259
14.	San Diego	235
15.	St. Louis	224
16.	Baltimore	203
17.	Indianapolis	192
18.	Detroit	183
19.	Columbus	180
20.	Seattle	177

Top Ten States With Largest Number of Jobs Per State
1987-1992

Rank	1987	1988	1989	1990	1991	1992
1.	New York	New York	New York	New York	New York	New York
2.	California	California	California	California	California	California
3.	Texas	Illinois	Illinois	Wash DC	Illinois	Pennsylvania
4.	Illinois	Wash DC	Wash DC	Illinois	Wash DC	Illinois
5.	Pennsylvania	Texas	Pennsylvania	Texas	Pennsylvania	Wash DC
6.	Florida	Pennsylvania	Massachusetts	Pennsylvania	Texas	Texas
7.	Wash DC	Massachusetts	Florida	Florida	New Jersey	Massachusetts
8.	Massachusetts	Ohio	Ohio	Massachusetts	Massachusetts	Florida
9.	Ohio	Florida	Texas	New Jersey	Florida	New Jersey
10.	New Jersey	New Jersey	New Jersey	Ohio	Ohio	Ohio

Jobs and Graduates by Region*

Region	Graduates with Known Emp. Status	Graduates with Known Job Location	Jobs Reported in Region	Graduates Staying in Region	Percentage of Jobs to Region Graduates	Percentage of Grads Staying in Region
New England	2,991	2,430	1,699	1,387	81.6%	57.1%
Mid-Atlantic	5,597	4,508	5,371	3,828	71.3%	84.9%
East North Central	4,877	3,752	3,434	2,870	83.6%	76.5%
West North Central	2,184	1,786	1,519	1,312	86.4%	73.5%
South Atlantic	6,048	4,701	4,649	3,359	72.3%	71.5%
East South Central	1,325	1,155	987	812	82.3%	70.3%
West South Central	2,337	1,875	1,939	1,588	81.9%	84.7%
Mountain	844	679	948	557	58.8%	82.0%
Pacific	4,138	2,916	3,256	2,474	76.0%	84.8%
Total	30,341	23,802	23,802	18,187	76.4%	76.4%

*U.S. Census Bureau Regions

	Region	States Included
1.	New England	CT, ME, MA, NH, RI, VT
2.	Mid-Atlantic	NJ, NY, PA
3.	East North Central	IL, IN, MI, OH, WI
4.	West North Central	IA, KS, MN, MO, NE, ND, SD
5.	South Atlantic	DE, DC FL, GA, MD, NC, SC, VA WV
6.	East South Central	AL, KY, MS, TN
7.	West South Central	AR, LA, OK, TX
8.	Mountain	AZ, CO, ID, MT, NV, NM, UT, WY
9.	Pacific	AK, CA, HI, OR, WA

Chapter 10: Organizations You Should Know About

You may have questions concerning a variety of issues while you are applying to law school, once you are in law school, and even after you have your degree.

The following organizations may provide you with the answers you need.

American Association of Law Libraries (AALL)

The American Association of Law Libraries exists to provide leadership in the field of legal information, to foster the professional growth of law librarians, to develop the profession of law librarianship, and to enhance the value of law libraries to the legal community and to the public. AALL members come from all sizes and types of libraries: the Library of Congress, legislative libraries, academic law libraries, law firm libraries, bar association libraries, county law libraries, court libraries, and law libraries in business and industry. The association

publishes a scholarly journal, a monthly magazine (*AALL Newsletter*), and an annual directory and handbook, as well as a minority law librarians directory.

For more information, contact:

American Association of Law Libraries
53 W. Jackson Blvd., Suite 940
Chicago, IL 60604
312.939.4764

American Bar Association (ABA)

The American Bar Association is the national organization of the legal profession. It is composed principally of practicing lawyers; judges; court administrators; law teachers; public service attorneys; many nonpracticing lawyers who are business executives, government officials and so forth; and law students. Although the ABA does not have the power to discipline attorneys or enforce rules, the association leads by serving as the national voice of the profession.

The ABA, with about 385,000 members and over 28,000 law student members, is the world's largest voluntary professional association. It serves a dual role as advocate for the profession and for the public. During the past decade, the association has initiated hundreds of programs addressing a wide range of public concerns. Response to these concerns is made possible by thousands of volunteers who contribute both time and money.

The Council of the Section of Legal Education and Admissions to the Bar of the ABA is identified by the US

Department of Education as the "nationally recognized accrediting agency for professional schools of law." The role that the American Bar Association plays as a central accrediting body has allowed accreditation to become national in scope rather than fragmented among the 50 states, District of Columbia, the Commonwealth of Puerto Rico, and other territories. Most admitting jurisdictions require applicants for admission to be graduates of law schools approved by the American Bar Association.

The ABA may be contacted for information on the accreditation of law schools and the role of lawyers in the legal profession:

Office of the Consultant on Legal Education
American Bar Association
Indiana University
550 West North Street, Third Floor
Indianapolis, IN 46202
317.264.8340

Association of American Law Schools (AALS)

The Association of American Law Schools was founded for "the improvement of the legal profession through legal education." It is an association of law schools that serves as the law teachers' learned society. The association requires quality teaching and scholarship of its 159 member schools.

The organization provides a range of services to law schools. Among them are professional development workshops and conferences for law faculty, facilitation of law faculty recruitment, publication of the *AALS Directory of Law Teachers*, and interpretation of the mission and needs of legal education as the principal repre-

sentative to other national higher education organizations, the federal government, and learned societies.

The AALS may be contacted for specific information about the role of legal education in the profession:

Association of American Law Schools
1201 Connecticut Ave., NW
Suite 800
Washington, DC 20036-2605
202.296.8851

Council on Legal Education Opportunity (CLEO)

The Council on Legal Education Opportunity is a federally funded program designed to increase the number of attorneys from educationally and economically disadvantaged backgrounds. CLEO implements its goals by conducting academic summer institutes for prospective law students and providing annual fellowships. Each year CLEO accepts a number of students to attend regional summer institutes around the United States. Students who successfully complete CLEO have an increased probability for admission to law schools around the country. The organization is sponsored by the American Bar Association, the Association of American Law Schools, the Hispanic National Bar Association, the National Asian Pacific American Bar Association, the Law School Admission Council, and the National Bar Association.

CLEO may be contacted for information on preparation for, and financing of, legal education for disadvantaged persons:

Council on Legal Education Opportunity
1800 M Street, NW
Suite 160, South Lobby
Washington, DC 20036
202.785.4840

HEATH Resource Center

The American Council on Education operates the HEATH Resource Center, the national clearinghouse on postsecondary education for individuals with disabilities. HEATH can provide information about requesting disability-related accommodations, ascertaining the level of physical and programmatic access available at law schools, and thinking through disability issues surrounding the application process. A reprint of "Students with Disabilities and Law School" from the HEATH newsletter is available free by request.

For more information, contact:

HEATH Resource Center
One Dupont Circle, NW
Suite 800
Washington, DC 20036-1193
202.939.9320 (in Washington)
800.54.HEATH (outside DC)
(Both numbers are Voice/TDD.)

Law School Admission Council/Law School Admission Services

The Law School Admission Council (LSAC) is an association of law schools in the United States and Canada. It was founded in 1947 to coordinate, facilitate, and enhance the law school admission process. The organization also provides programs and services related to legal education. All law schools approved by the American Bar Association (ABA) are LSAC members. Canadian common-law law schools with programs of study that fulfill the requirements of the Federation of Law Societies of Canada (FLSC) also are included in the voting membership of the Council. Both LSAC and its operating organization, Law School Admission Services (Law Services), are nonprofit corporations.

The services provided by Law Services include: The Law School Admission Test (LSAT); the Law School Data Assembly Service (LSDAS); the Candidate Referral Service (CRS); and various publications and LSAT preparation tools. The LSAT, LSDAS, and CRS are provided to assist law schools in serving and evaluating applicants. Law Services does not engage in assessing an applicant's chances for admission to any law school; all admission decisions are made by individual law schools.

The LSAC and Law Services exist to serve both the law schools and the candidates for admission. Last year, Law Services administered about 140,000 tests, supported roughly 456,000 law school applications, and processed 188,000 transcripts.

For more information on the LSAT, LSDAS, and law school admission, write or call:

Law Services
Box 2000
661 Penn Street
Newtown, PA 18940-0998
215.968.1001

For information on minority opportunities in law, write or call:

Law Services
Minority Opportunities in Law
Box 40
661 Penn Street
Newtown, PA 18940-0040
215.968.1338

National Association for Law Placement (NALP)

The National Association for Law Placement is a professional organization of law schools and legal employers. NALP's mission is to provide information, coordination, and standards for fair recruiting for all of the participants in the legal recruiting process. NALP provides a forum for discussion of recruiting trends and problems among school and employer representatives; provides professional education and resources for law school career services professionals and legal employers, recruiting directors, and hiring attorneys; and conducts research on legal employment.

NALP publishes resource materials that assist students in making informed career choices. All publications are available through the law school's career services office. However, NALP is not an employment agency, and does not offer specific job listings or maintain comprehensive employment statistics on attorneys other than recent graduates.

NALP believes that each law school offers unique programs and opportunities and, like the American Bar Association and the Law School Admission Council, does not rate law school or career services offices.

For further information, contact:

**National Association for Law Placement
Suite 450
1666 Connecticut Avenue, NW
Washington, DC 20009-1039
202.667.1666**

Chapter 11: Prelaw Readings: Books of Interest

The following list of prelaw readings offers prospective law students an overview of selected classics and current titles in certain subjects: law school and legal education, the legal profession, biography, and jurisprudence and legal issues. This year we've added a new section on financing law school. Some of these publications list sources for financial aid, but students will need to call or write the individual organizations for the most up-to-date information.

This list should not be construed as the official bibliography of Law School Admission Council/Law School Admission Services; it is beyond the scope of this publication to provide any sort of definitive catalog of prelaw readings.

Some of these books have already withstood the test of time, and are as relevant today as when they were first written and published, generations ago. Examples are: Richard Kluger's *Simple Justice*—a rare glimpse into the private workings and deliberations of the Supreme Court; and Karl Llewellyn's *The Bramble Bush*—a classic study of how legal education shapes our legal institutions.

Some titles simply reflect the most current writing on the subjects listed above and are not necessarily recommended simply because they appear on this list. It will be up to you to search out the titles that pique your interest and make your own determination of their worth. The aim of our list is merely to give you a head start. We hope that those interested in pursuing legal studies will find the issues raised and the ideas discussed in these works helpful in making the decision to choose law as a career.

■ Law School and Legal Education

Barber, David H. *Winning in Law School: Stress Reduction.* 2d ed. Dillon, CO: Spectra, 1986.

Bay, Monica. *Careers in Civil Litigation.* Chicago: American Bar Association/Law Student Division, 1990.

Bell, Susan J. *Full Disclosure: Do You Really Want to Be a Lawyer?* Princeton, NJ: Peterson's Guides, 1989.

Bell, Susan J. *Interviewing for Success and Satisfaction.* Chicago: American Bar Association/Young Lawyers Division, 1989.

Calamari, John D. and **Joseph M. Perillo,** eds. *How to Thrive in Law School.* Pelham Manor, NY: Hook Mountain Press, 1984.

Carter, Lief H. *Reason in Law.* Boston: Little, Brown and Company, 1988.

Chase, William C. *The American Law School and the Rise of Administrative Government.* Madison, WI: University of Wisconsin Press, 1982.

Curry, Boykin, ed. *Essays That Worked for Law Schools: 35 Essays from Successful Applications to the Nation's Top Law Schools.* New York: Fawcett Book Group, 1991.

Deaver, Jeff. *The Complete Law School Companion: How to Excel at America's Most Demanding Post-Graduate Curriculum.* New York: John Wiley & Sons, 1992.

Delaney, John. *How to Do Your Best on Law School Exams.* 2d ed. Bogota, NJ: John Delaney Publications, 1988.

Directory of Law School Joint Degree Programs. 2d ed. Washington, DC: Federal Reports, Inc., 1991.

Dutile, Fernand N., ed. *Legal Education and Lawyer Competency: Curricula for Change.* Notre Dame, IN: University of Notre Dame Press, 1981.

Dworkin, Elizabeth, Jack Himmelstein, and **Howard Lesnick.** *Becoming a Lawyer: A Humanistic Perspective on Legal Education and Professionalism.* St. Paul, MN: West Publishing, 1989.

Farnsworth, Edward A. *An Introduction to the Legal System of the United States.* 2d ed. Dobbs Ferry, NY: Oceana Publications, 1983.

Gillers, Stephen, ed. *Looking at Law School: A Student Guide from the Society of American Law Teachers.* 3d ed. NAL/Dutton, 1990.

Goldfarb, Sally F. *Inside the Law Schools: A Guide by Students for Students.* 6th ed. New York: Plume, 1993.

Goodrich, Chris. *Anarchy and Elegance: Confessions of a Journalist at Yale Law School.* Boston: Little, Brown and Company, 1991.

Hegland, Kenney F. *Introduction to the Study and Practice of Law in a Nutshell.* St. Paul, MN: West Publishing, 1983.

Kaplin, William A. *The Concepts and Methods of Constitutional Law.* Durham, NC: Carolina Academic Press, forthcoming.

Kelman, Mark. *A Guide to Critical Legal Studies.* Cambridge, MA: Harvard University Press, 1987.

Legal Education and Professional Development — An Educational Continuum. Report of The Task Force on Law Schools and the Profession: Narrowing the Gap. Chicago: American Bar Association, Section of Legal Education and Admissions to the Bar, July 1992.

Llewellyn, Karl N. *The Bramble Bush: On Our Law and its Study.* rev. ed. Dobbs Ferry, NY: Oceana Publications, 1981.

Margulies, Sheldon and **Kenneth Lasson.** *Learning Law: The Mastery of Legal Logic.* Durham, NC: Carolina Academic Press, 1993.

Martinson, Thomas H., J.D., and **David P. Waldherr, J.D.** *Getting Into Law School: Strategies for the 90s.* New York: Prentice Hall, 1992.

Mayfield, Craig K. *Reading Skills for Law Students.* Charlottesville, VA: Michie Co., 1980.

Moliterno, James E. and **Fredric Lederer.** *An Introduction to Law, Law Study, and the Lawyer's Role.* Durham, NC: Carolina Academic Press, 1991.

Re, Edward D., and **Joseph R. Re.** *Law Students' Manual on Legal Writing and Oral Argument.* Dobbs Ferry, NY: Oceana Publications, 1991.

Roth, George. *Slaying the Law School Dragon: How to Survive—and Thrive—in First-Year Law School.* 2d ed. New York: John Wiley & Sons, 1991.

So You Want to be a Lawyer: A Practical Guide. Newtown, PA: Law School Admission Services, Inc., 1993

Stevens, Robert. Law School: *Legal Education in America from the 1850s to the 1980s.* Chapel Hill, NC: University of North Carolina Press, 1983.

Stover, Robert V. *Making It and Breaking It: The Fate of Public Interest Commitment During Law School.* Urbana, IL: University of Illinois Press, 1989.

Swygert, Michael I., and **Robert Batey**, eds. *Maximizing the Law School Experience: A Collection of Essays.* St. Petersburg, FL: Stetson University College of Law, 1983.

Turow, Scott. *One L.: An Inside Account of Life in the First Year at Harvard Law School.* New York: Penguin Books, 1978.

Vanderbilt, Arthur T. *Law School: Briefing for a Legal Education.* New York: Penguin Books, 1981.

Williams, Glanville. *Learning the Law: A Book for the Guidance of the Law Student.* 11th ed. London: Stevens, 1982.

Wydick, Richard C. *Plain English for Lawyers.* 2d ed. Durham, NC: Carolina Academic Press, 1985.

■ Legal Profession

Abel, Richard L. *American Lawyers.* New York: Oxford University Press, 1989.

Arron, Deborah. *Running From the Law: Why Good Lawyers Are Getting Out of the Legal Profession.* Berkeley, CA: Ten Speed Press, 1991.

Arron, Deborah. *What Can You Do With a Law Degree? A Lawyer's Guide to Career Alternatives Inside, Outside, and Around the Law.* Seattle: Niche Press, 1992.

Bailey, F. Lee. *To Be A Trial Lawyer.* New York: John Wiley & Sons, 1985.

Caplan, Lincoln. *Skadden: Inside the Business of Law in America.* New York: Farrar, Strauss & Giroux, 1993.

Carey, William T. *Law Students: How to Get a Job When There Aren't Any.* Durham, NC: Carolina Academic Press, 1986.

Couric, Emily. *The Trial Lawyers: The Nation's Top Litigators Tell How They Win.* New York: St. Martin's Press, 1988.

Delaney, John. *Learning Legal Reasoning: Briefing, Analysis and Theory,* rev. ed. Bogota, NJ: John Delaney Publications, 1987.

Epstein, Cynthia Fuchs. *Women in Law.* 2d ed. Urbana, IL: University of Illinois Press, 1993.

Foonberg, Jay G. *How to Start and Build a Law Practice.* 3d ed. Chicago: American Bar Association/Law Student Division, 1991.

Galanter, Marc, and **Thomas Palay**. *Tournament of Lawyers: The Transformation of the Big Law Firm.* Chicago: University of Chicago Press, 1991.

Greene, Robert Michael. *Making Partner: A Guide for Law Firm Associates.* Chicago: American Bar Association, Section of Law Practice Management, 1992.

Harrington, Mona. *Women Lawyers: Rewriting the Rules.* New York: Alfred A. Knopf, 1994.

Henslee, William D. *Careers in Entertainment Law.* Chicago: American Bar Association/Law Student Division, 1990.

López, Gerald P. *Rebellious Lawyering: One Chicano's Vision of Progressive Law Practice.* Boulder, CO: Westview Press, 1992.

Luney, Percy R., Jr. *Careers in Natural Resources and Environmental Law.* Chicago: American Bar Association/Law Student Division, 1987.

Mayer, Martin. *The Lawyers.* Westport, CT: Greenwood Press, 1980.

Moll, Richard W. *The Lure of the Law: Why People Become Lawyers, and What the Profession Does to Them.* New York: Penguin Books, 1990.

Munneke, Gary A. *The Legal Career Guide: From Law Student to Lawyer.* Chicago: American Bar Association Career Series, 1992.

O'Neill, Suzanne B. and **Catherine Gerhauser Sparkman**. *From Law School to Law Practice: The New Associate's Guide.* Philadelphia: American Law Institute/American Bar Association Committee on Continuing Professional Education, 1989.

Shaffer, Thomas L. with **Mary M. Shaffer**. *American Lawyers and Their Communities: Ethics in the Legal Profession.* Notre Dame, IN: University of Notre Dame Press, 1991.

Shropshire, Kenneth. *Careers in Sports Law.* Chicago: American Bar Association/Law Student Division, 1990.

Speiser, Stuart M. *Lawyers and the American Dream.* New York: M. Evan and Co., 1993.

Stewart, James B. *The Partners.* New York: Simon & Schuster, 1983.

Thorner, Abbie Willard, ed. *Now Hiring: Government Jobs for Lawyers (1990-1991 edition).* Chicago: American Bar Association/Law Student Division, 1990.

Utley, Frances, with **Gary A. Munneke**. *Nonlegal Careers for Lawyers: In the Private Sector.* 2d ed. Chicago: American Bar Association/Law Student Division, 1991.

Walsh, Michael. *Insider's Guide to Law Firms.* Boulder, CO: Insider's Guide to Law Firms, 1993.

Wayne, Ellen. *Careers in Labor Law.* Chicago: American Bar Association/Law Student Division, 1985.

■ Biography

Auchincloss, Louis. *Life, Law and Letters: Essays and Sketches*. Boston: Houghton Mifflin Co., 1979.

Baker, Leonard. *John Marshall: A Life in Law*. New York: Macmillan, 1974.

Barth, Alan. *Prophets with Honor: Great Dissents and Great Dissenters in the Supreme Court*. New York: Vintage Books, 1975.

Darrow, Clarence. *The Story of My Life*. New York: Charles Scribner's Sons, 1932.

Davis, Deane C. *Justice in the Mountains: Stories & Tales by a Vermont Country Lawyer*. Shelburne, VT: New England Press, 1980.

Davis, Lenwood G. *I Have a Dream: The Life and Times of Martin Luther King*. Westport, CT: Negro Universities Press, 1973.

Davis, Michael D. and **Hunter R. Clark**. *Thurgood Marshall: Warrior at the Bar, Rebel on the Bench*. New York: Birch Lane Press/Carol Publishing Group, 1993.

Douglas, William O. *Go East Young Man: The Early Years*. New York: Random House, 1974.

Douglas, William O. *Court Years, 1939-1975: The Autobiography of William O. Douglas*. New York: Random House, 1980.

Dunne, Gerald T. *Hugo Black and the Judicial Revolution*. New York: Simon & Schuster, 1977.

Frankfurter, Felix. *Felix Frankfurter Reminisces*. New York: Reynal & Co., 1960.

Griffith, Kathryn. *Judge Learned Hand and the Role of the Federal Judiciary*. Norman: University of Oklahoma Press, 1973.

Griswold, Erwin N. *Ould Fields, New Corne: The Personal Memoirs of a Twentieth Century Lawyer*. St. Paul, MN: West Publishing, 1992.

Howe, Mark deWolfe. *Justice Oliver Wendell Holmes*. Cambridge, MA: Harvard University Press, 1957 (vol. 1), 1963 (vol. 2).

Kahlenberg, Richard D. *Broken Contract: A Memoir of Harvard Law School*. New York: Farrar, Straus & Giroux, 1992.

Lynn, Conrad J. *There is a Foundation: The Autobiography of a Civil Rights Lawyer*. Westport, CN: Hill & Company, 1978.

Marke, Julius J. *The Holmes Reader*. Dobbs Ferry, NY: Oceana Publications, 1964.

Mason, Alpheus. *Harlan Fiske Stone: Pillar of the Law*. New York: Viking Press, 1956.

Murphy, Bruce Allen. *The Brandeis/Frankfurter Connection: The Secret Political Activities of Two Supreme Court Justices*. New York: Oxford University Press, 1982.

Nizer, Louis. *Reflections Without Mirrors: An Autobiography of the Mind*. New York: Doubleday, 1978.

Noonan, John T. , Jr. *Persons and Masks of the Law: Cardozo, Holmes, Jefferson, and Wythe as Makers of the Masks*. New York: Farrar, Straus & Giroux, 1976.

Pusey, Merlo J. *Charles Evans Hughes*. New York: Macmillan, 1951.

Rowan, Carl T. *Dream Makers, Dream Breakers. The World of Justice Thurgood Marshall*. Boston: Little Brown & Company, 1993.

Schwartz, Bernard. *Super Chief, Earl Warren and His Supreme Court—A Judicial Biography*. New York: New York University Press, 1983.

Simon, James F. *Independent Journey: The Life of William O. Douglas*. New York: Harper & Row, 1980.

Thomas, Evan. *The Man to See: Edward Bennett Williams, Ultimate Insider; Legendary Trial Lawyer*. New York: Simon & Schuster, 1991.

Urofsky, Melvin I. *Louis D. Brandeis and the Progressive Tradition*. Boston: Little, Brown and Company, 1981.

Westin, Alan F. *Autobiography of the Supreme Court: Off-the-Bench Commentary by the Justices*. Westport, CT: Greenwood Press, 1978.

White, G. Edward. *Earl Warren: A Public Life*. New York: Oxford University Press, 1982.

White, G. Edward. *Justice Oliver Wendell Holmes: Law and the Inner Self*. Oxford University Press, 1993.

Wigdor, David. *Roscoe Pound: Philosopher of Law*. Westport, CT: Greenwood Press, 1974.

■ Jurisprudence and Legal Issues

Ball, Milner S. *The Word and the Law.* Chicago: University of Chicago Press, 1993.

Bickel, Alexander M. *The Least Dangerous Branch: The Supreme Court at the Bar of Politics.* 2d ed. New Haven: Yale University Press, 1986.

Bickel, Alexander M. *The Morality of Consent.* New Haven: Yale University Press, 1975.

Bodenhamer, David J. and **James E. Ely, Jr.**, eds. *The Bill of Rights in Modern America.* Bloomington and Indianapolis: Indiana University Press, 1993.

Burns, James MacGregor, and **Stewart Burns**. *The People's Charter: Pursuing Rights in America.* New York: Alfred A. Knopf, 1991.

Cahn, Edmond. *The Moral Decision: Right and Wrong in the Light of American Law.* Bloomington, IN: Indiana University Press, 1955.

Cardozo, Benjamin N. *The Nature of the Judicial Process.* New Haven: Yale University Press, 1921.

Dershowitz, Alan M. *The Best Defense.* New York: Random House, 1982.

Dershowitz, Alan M. *Taking Liberties: A Decade of Hard Cases, Bad Laws, and Bum Raps.* Chicago: Contemporary Books, 1988.

Finkel, Norman J. *Insanity on Trial.* New York: Plenum, 1988.

Howard, A.E. Dick. *The Road from Runnymeade: Magna Carta and Constitutionalism in America.* Charlottesville, VA: University of Virginia, 1968.

Irons, Peter. *The Courage of their Convictions: Sixteen Americans Who Fought Their Way to the Supreme Court.* New York: Penguin, 1990.

Irons, Peter and **Stephanie Guitton**, eds. *May It Please the Court: The Most Significant Oral Arguments Made Before the Supreme Court Since 1955* [audiocassette]. New York: New Press, 1993.

Kairys, David, ed. *The Politics of Law: A Progressive Critique.* New York: Pantheon Books, 1982.

Kirk, Russell. *The Roots of American Order.* Malibu, CA: Pepperdine University Press, 1981.

Kluger, Richard. *Simple Justice: The History of Brown vs. Board of Education and Black America's Struggle for Equality.* New York: Alfred A. Knopf, 1976.

Konefsky, Samuel J. *The Legacy of Holmes and Brandeis: A Study in the Influence of Ideas.* New York: DeCapo Press, 1974.

Lee, Rex E. *A Lawyer Looks at the Constitution.* Provo, UT: Brigham Young University Press, 1981.

Lewis, Anthony. *Gideon's Trumpet.* New York: Random House, 1964.

Lewis, Anthony. *Make No Law: The Sullivan Case and the First Amendment.* New York: Random House, 1991.

MacKinnon, Catharine A. *Only Words.* Cambridge, MA: Harvard University Press, 1993.

Pfeffer, Leo. *Religion, State and the Burger Court.* Buffalo, NY: Prometheus Books, 1984.

Pound, Roscoe. *Law and Morals.* South Hackensack, NJ: Rothman Reprints, 1969.

Rehnquist, William H. *The Supreme Court: How It Was, How It Is.* New York: Quill Press, 1987.

Rosenberg, Gerald N. *The Hollow Hope: Can Courts Bring About Social Change?* Chicago: University of Chicago Press, 1991.

Savage, David. *Turning Right: The Making of the Rehnquist Supreme Court.* New York: John Wiley & Sons, 1992.

Schwartz, Bernard. *A History of the Supreme Court.* New York: Oxford University Press, 1992.

Shapiro, Fred R. *The Oxford Dictionary of American Legal Quotations.* New York: Oxford University Press, 1993.

Shapiro, Joseph P. *No Pity: People with Disabilities Forging a New Civil Rights Movement.* New York: Random House, 1993.

Simon, James F. *The Antagonists: Hugo Black, Felix Frankfurter and Civil Liberties in Modern America.* New York: Simon & Schuster, 1989.

Sobol, Richard B. *Bending the Law: The Story of the Dalkon Shield Bankruptcy.* Chicago: University of Chicago Press, 1991.

Spence, Gerry. *With Justice for None.* New York: Penguin, 1990.

Stone, Geoffrey R., Richard Epstein, and **Cass R.Sunstein**, eds. *The Bill of Rights in the Modern State.* Chicago: University of Chicago Press, 1992.

Sunstein, Cass R. *Democracy and the Problem of Free Speech.* New York: The Free Press, 1993.

Treanor, Richard Bryant. *We Overcame: The Story of Civil Rights for Disabled People.* Falls Church, VA: Regal Direct Publishing, 1993.

Tribe, Laurence H. *God Save This Honorable Court: How the Choice of Supreme Court Justices Shapes Our History.* New York: Penguin/Mentor, 1986.

Unger, Roberto M. *Knowledge and Politics.* New York: The Free Press, 1984.

van den Haag, Ernest, and **John P. Conrad**. *The Death Penalty: A Debate.* New York: Plenum, 1983.

Westin, Alan F. *The Anatomy of a Constitutional Law Case: Youngstown Sheet & Tube Co. v. Sawyer.* New York: Columbia University Press, 1990.

Williams, Patricia J. *The Alchemy of Race and Rights.* Cambridge, MA: Harvard University Press, 1991.

Wishman, Seymour. *Anatomy of a Jury.* New York: Penguin, 1987.

■ Financing Law School

Cantrell, Karen and **Denise Wallen**. *Funding for Law: Legal Education, Research and Study*. Phoenix, AZ: Oryx Press, 1991.

Cassidy, Daniel. *The Graduate Scholarship Book: The Complete Guide to Scholarships, Fellowships, Grants, and Loans for Graduate and Professional Study*. 2nd ed. National Scholarship Reference Service, Prentice-Hall, 1990.

Cronin, Joseph Marr, and **Sylvia Quarles Simmons** (eds.). *Student Loans: Risks and Realities*. Dover, MA: Auburn House Publishing Co., 1987.

Johnson, Willis L. *Directory of Special Programs for Minority Group Members: Career Information Services, Employment Skills Banks, Financial Aid Sources* (5th edition). Garrett Park, MD: Garrett Park Press, 1990.

Financial Aid for Minorities in Business and Law. Garrett Park, MD: Garrett Park Press, 1994.

Kirby, Deborah M. (ed.) *Scholarships, Fellowships, and Loans: 1994-1995* (10th edition). Detroit: Gale Research, Inc.

The Loan Repayment Assistance Report. Washington, DC: National Association for Public Interest Law, 1993.

McWade, Patricia. *Financing Graduate School*. Princeton, NJ: Peterson's Guides, 1993.

Schlachter, Gail Ann. *Financial Aid for the Disabled and Their Families, 1994-96*. San Carlos, CA: Reference Service Press.

Schlachter, Gail Ann. *Directory of Financial Aids for Minorities, 1993-95*. San Carlos, CA: . Reference Service Press.

Schlachter, Gail Ann. *Directory of Financial Aids for Veterans, Military Personnel, and Their Dependents, 1993-95*. San Carlos, CA: Reference Service Press.

Schlachter, Gail Ann. *Directory of Financial Aids for Women, 1993-95*. San Carlos, CA:. Reference Service Press.

Williams, Franklin A. and **Mark Fischer**. *The Law Student's Guide to Scholarships and Grants*. New York: Scovill, Paterson, Inc., 1994.

Chapter 12: Key Facts About ABA-Approved Law Schools

This information was reported by the schools in Fall 1993, thus the figures may have changed. The reader is cautioned against making direct comparisons of complex information limited to chart form. Be sure to go beyond the table, indeed beyond the two-page descriptions that follow, if you wish to inform yourself adequately about a particular school. Symbols and footnotes are explained on the last page of this chart.

School	Enroll. Full-time	Enroll. Part-time	% Women	% Minority	Faculty Full-time	Faculty Part-time	Day	Evenings	Required credits	Total credits for J.D.	Joint degrees offered	Graduate law study available	Evening division	Transferable summer courses offered	Summer matriculation for 1st-yr	Midyear matriculation for 1st-yr	Academic Support Programs offered	Library full-time staff	Volumes and equivalents	Tuition in-state, full-time	Tuition out-of-state, full-time	Tuition in-state, part-time	Tuition out-of-state, part-time	Application fee	Application deadline for fall	Financial aid application deadline	Official Guide page	Grid included
ALABAMA																												
University of Alabama School of Law	559	-	38	10	25	19	•		43	90			•			•	•	13	259,000	$2,938y	$6,190y		-	$25	3/1	3/1	66	
Cumberland School of Law—Samford University	627		39	6.4	32	26	•		53	90	•		•	•	•	•	•	11	210,000	$13,850	$13,850			$40	5/1	3/1	132	•
ARIZONA																												
University of Arizona College of Law	480	-	45	27	28	28	•		39	85	•	•		•			•	14	332,200	$2,844	$8,350			$35	3/1	3/1	72	•
Arizona State University College of Law	512	-	41	30	30	10	•		40	87	•			•			•	15	311,000	$2,844	$8,350			$35	2/15	3/1	74	•
ARKANSAS																												
University of Arkansas School of Law—Fayetteville	419	-	36	9	33	7	•		44	90	•	•		•				6	220,000	$2,876	$6,020			-	4/1	5/1	76	•
University of Arkansas at Little Rock School of Law	276	145	48	15	25	20	•	•	50	87	•		•	•	•		•	13	230,000	$1,356	$2,928	$113h	$244h	$40	4/1	5/1	78	•
CALIFORNIA																												
University of California at Berkeley (Boalt Hall) School of Law	780	-	46	36	80	22	•		34	81	•	•					•	12	600,000	$4,414	$12,113			$40	2/1	3/2	94	•
University of California—Davis	478	-	48	30	31	7	•		33	88	•	•					•	16	370,154	$4,359	$12,058			$40	2/1	3/1	96	•
University of California—Hastings College of the Law	1264	-	49.5	32	51	63	•		34	88	•			•			•	8	541,315	$4,349	$12,048			$40	2/15	2/15	98	•
University of California, Los Angeles School of Law	978	-	42	39	72	24	•		35	87	•	•				•	•	25	469,108	$4,503y	$12,202y			$40	1/15	-	100	•
California Western School of Law	860	-	43	16	46	34	•		43	89	•			•		•	•	12	207,582	$15,700	$15,700			$45	5/1	3/4	102	•
Golden Gate University School of Law	527	213	50	26	29	80	•	•	60	86	•	•	•	•			•	12	200,000	$14,554	$14,554	$10,109	$10,109	$40	4/15	3/1	174	•
Loyola Law School Los Angeles, Loyola Marymount University	1025	336	44	30	57	39	•	•	43	87	•		•				•	32	340,456	$16,604	-	$11,102	-	$50	2/1	3/2	216	•
McGeorge School of Law, University of the Pacific	858	401	44	15	50	38	•	•	62	88	•	•	•	•			•	19	385,000	$15,114	$15,114	$8,952	$8,952	$40	5/1	none	226	•
Pepperdine University School of Law	714	-	44	18	37	9	•		57	88	•						•	30	235,000	$17,800	-			$40	3/1	4/15	292	•
University of San Diego School of Law	757	315	42	18	67	47	•	•	48	85	•	•	•	•			•	19	320,000	$16,480	$16,480	$11,690	$11,690	$35	2/1	3/1	320	•
University of San Francisco School of Law	529	130	50	25	26	65	•	•	10-15d / 9-11e	86	•	•	•	•			•	12	246,962	$15,800	$15,800	$567u	$567u	$40	4/1	3/1	322	•

This page is a continuation of a multi-column reference table of U.S. law schools (no column headers appear on this page). The columns, read from the school-name column rightward, are: school, and a series of admissions/enrollment, program (•), student-faculty ratio, library volumes, tuition, application-fee, deadline, and financial-aid columns.

School	C1	C2	C3	C4	C5	C6	•	C8	C9	•	•	•	•	•	Ratio	Library	Res. tuition	Nonres. tuition	PT res.	PT nonres.	Fee	Deadline	Deadline	•	No.
Santa Clara University School of Law	678	205	50	33	34	19	•	45	86	•			•	•	17	209,624	$15,540	$15,540	$11,298	$11,298	$40	3/1	3/1	•	324
University of Southern California Law Center	600	-	42	36	48	28	•	34	88	•			•	•	19	330,000	$19,156	$19,156	-	-	$60	2/1	2/15	•	334
Southwestern University School of Law	811	338	50	24	48	30	•	55	87	•		•	•	•	18	340,000	$16,240	$16,240	$10,322	$10,322	$50	6/30	6/1	•	342
Stanford University Law School	536	-	47	36	45	59	•	26	86	•			•	•	9	414,000	$20,186	-	$10,322	-	$65	3/1	3/15	•	344
Whittier College School of Law	429	240	40	28	28	12	•	38	87	•			•	•	7	230,000	$15,960	$15,960	$9,576	-	$50	3/15	6/1F	•	400
COLORADO																									
University of Colorado School of Law	476	-	45	20	31	31	•	45	89	•		•		•	8	280,000	$4,063	$12,537	-	-	$40	2/15	asap	•	122
University of Denver College of Law	800	280	44	11	49	34	•	47	90	•		•		•	7	259,243	$15,221	$15,221	$9,820	$9,820	$45	3/1	2/15	•	136
CONNECTICUT																									
University of Connecticut School of Law	433	222	50	16	42	53	•	42	86	•		•	•	•	16	382,752	$8,552	$18,036	$298c	$629c	$30/$45	3/1	3/1	•	126
Quinnipiac College School of Law	531	177	32	9.7	35	30	•	53	86	•		•	•	•	6	278,000	$13,200	$13,200	$550	$550	$40	rolling	4/1	•	302
Yale Law School	617	-	41	28	46	54	•	24	82	•		•	•	•	47	850,000	$19,780	$19,780	-	-	$60	2/15	3/15	•	414
DELAWARE																									
Widener University School of Law	1505	688	41	8	96	110	•	51	87	•	•	•	•	•	17	480,500	$14,200	$14,200	$10,650	$10,650	$60	5/15	4/15	•	402
DISTRICT OF COLUMBIA																									
American University—Washington College of Law	858	312	49	22	47	89	•	34	86	•		•	•	•	18	328,897	$17,566	$17,566	$651ch	$651ch	$55	3/1	2/15	•	70
Catholic University of America—Columbus School of Law	670	275	47	16	47	77	•	33	84	•		•	•	•	15	220,000	$17,690	$17,690	$635ch	$635ch	$55	3/1	3/1	•	112
District of Columbia School of Law	284	-	50	49	26	9	•	56	85	•		•	•	•	9	172,000	$2,900	$9,500	-	-	$35	4/1	5/30	•	146
George Washington University National Law Center	1196	268	40	19	75	121	•	32	84	•		•	•	•	29	402,766	$18,400	$18,400	$650c	$650c	$55	301	N/A	•	166
Georgetown University Law Center	1547	504	46.6	27.3	84	161	•	31	83	•		•	•	•	67	727,709	$9,498s	$9,498s	$650c	$650c	$60	2/1 FT 3/1e	3/1	•	168
Howard University School of Law	463	-	54	88	24	18	•	30	88	•		•	•	•	12	240,000	$9,625	$9,625	-	-	$60	4/30	4/1	•	188
FLORIDA																									
University of Florida College of Law	1150	-	40	18	68	4	•	37	88	•		•	•	•	8	530,000	$121ch	$384ch	-	-	$20	2/1F 5/15S	3/1F 7/1S	•	156
The Florida State University College of Law	600	-	47	25	42	9	•	35	88	•			•	•	7	345,425	$3,590	$11,233	-	-	$20	2/15	3/1	•	158
University of Miami School of Law	1223	185	42.4	23	53	85	•	76	88	•		•	•	•	43	391,284	$17,062	$17,062	$12,782	$12,782	$40	3/7	3/1	•	232
Nova University—Shepard Broad Law Center	834	25	40	22.9	39	47	•	28	84	•		•	•	•	8	261,307	$15,410	$15,410	$12,960	$12,960	$45	3/1	4/1	•	276
St. Thomas University School of Law	478	-	36	31	29	31	•	47	90	•		•	•	•	17	213,489	$13,550	$13,550	-	-	$40	4/30	3/1	•	318
Stetson University College of Law	648	-	52	17	35	48	•	55	88	•		•	•	•	15	316,000	$16,585	$16,585	-	-	$40	3/1	4/1	•	346
GEORGIA																									
Emory University School of Law	740	-	43	19	40	38	•	39	88	•		•	•	•	21	260,000	$17,000	$17,000	-	-	$45	3/1	3/1	•	154
University of Georgia School of Law	641	-	43	15	39	13	•	33	88	•		•	•	•	20	456,000	$2,677	$7,221	-	-	$30	3/1	3/1	•	170
Georgia State University College of Law	378	244	50	21.2	37	4	•	44	90	•		•	•	•	6	220,327	$2,632	$7,500	$1,710	$4,734	$10	4/1	5/1	•	172
Mercer University—Walter F. George School of Law	409	1	41	17	29	20	•	53	88	•		•	•	•	13	252,000	$13,800	$13,800	-	-	$35	4/1	5/1	•	230

This information was reported by the schools in Fall 1993, thus the figures may have changed. The reader is cautioned against making direct comparisons of complex information limited to chart form. Be sure to go beyond the two-page descriptions that follow, if you wish to inform yourself adequately about a particular school. Symbols and footnotes are explained on the last page of this chart.

School	FT enroll	PT enroll	% Women	% Minority	Faculty FT	Faculty PT	Day	Evenings	Required credits	Total credits J.D.	Joint degrees	Grad law study	Evening division	Transferable summer courses	Summer matric.	Midyear matric.	Acad. Support	Library FT staff	Volumes & equivalents	Tuition IS full-time	OOS full-time	IS part-time	OOS part-time	Application fee	App. deadline fall	Fin. aid deadline	Official Guide page	Grid
HAWAII																												
University of Hawaii at Manoa—William S. Richardson School of Law	240	-	48	72	16	20	•		42	89	•						•	9	230,593	$2,400	$7,820	-	-	-	2/16	3/1	182	•
IDAHO																												
University of Idaho College of Law	293	-	33	13	20	2	•		33	88							•	8	146,000	$2,300	$6,810	-	-	$30	2/1	2/14	190	•
ILLINOIS																												
Chicago-Kent College of Law—Illinois Institute of Technology	868	369	48	17	62	64	•	•	39	84	•	•	•				•	22	430,000	$16,540	$16,540	$11,815	$11,815	$40	4/1	4/15	114	•
University of Chicago Law School	530	-	42	21	40	21	•		40	105	•	•					•	24	555,000	$19,095	$19,095	-	-	$45	-	3/15	116	•
DePaul University College of Law	730	254	48	17	43	66	•	•	40	86	•	•	•	•			•	25	312,000	$14,115	$14,115	$9,018	$9,018	$40	4/1	3/1	138	•
University of Illinois College of Law	626	-	42	22	30	35	•		38	90	•	•					•	6	593,000	$4,166	$11,778	-	-	$30	3/15	3/15	192	•
The John Marshall School of Law	609	372	39	20	54	136	•	•	41	90	•		•	•			•	20	291,000	$13,200	$13,200	$7,920	$7,920	$40	4/1	-	202	•
Loyola University Chicago School of Law	511	176	55	17.5	33	80	•	•	43	86	•	•	•	•			•	7	270,218	$13,950	$13,950	$10,460	$10,460	$40	4/1	3/1	214	•
Northern Illinois University College of Law	308	-	41	24	25	10	•		38	85	•			•			•	12	200,000	$4,207	$6,511	-	-	$35	5/1	3/1	268	•
Northwestern University School of Law	612	-	42	25	54	57	•		32	86	•	•		•			•	31	556,743	$18,170	-	-	-	$60	2/1	3/16	272	•
Southern Illinois University School of Law	344	-	41	11	25	8	•		47	90	•			•			•	19	301,526	$2,796y	$8,388y	-	-	$25	-	-	336	•
INDIANA																												
Indiana University School of Law—Bloomington	614	5	44	20	35	19	•		38	86	•			•	•		•	9	510,000	$4,413	$12,140	$142c	$391c	$35	-	3/1	194	•
Indiana University School of Law—Indianapolis	525	298	41	13	38	25	•	•	53	90	•		•	•	•		•	23	410,000	$4,453	$11,588	$3,017	$7,850	$35	3/1	N/A	196	•
University of Notre Dame Law School	583	-	41	21	35	25	•		63	90	•			•			•	20	340,000	$16,400	$16,400	-	$7,610	$45	4/1	4/1	274	•
Valparaiso University School of Law	501	38	45	8.5	25	17	•		49	90	•			•			•	8	214,600	$13,710	$13,710	$7,610	-	$30	4/15	4/1	374	•
IOWA																												
Drake University Law School	553	25	41	9	23	43	•		45	90	•			•	•		•	5	240,000	$13,780	$13,780	$460	$460	$35	3/1	3/1	148	•
University of Iowa College of Law	660	-	43	23	52	2	•		35	90	•			•	•		•	24	727,308	$3,624	$10,190	-	-	$20	2/1	3/1	200	•
KANSAS																												
University of Kansas School of Law	525	-	43	12	29	10	•		45	90	•			•	•		•	9	325,000	$2,928	$6,996	-	-	$40	3/15	3/1	204	•
Washburn University School of Law	425	-	44	16	27	32	•		34	90	•			•		•	•	17	250,467	$4,844	$7,000	$173ch	$250ch	$30	3/15	3/15	386	•

KENTUCKY																				
University of Kentucky College of Law	413	4	40	6	28	20	•	34	90	• •	13	328,730	$3,280	$9,420	-	-	$25	3/1	4/1	206
University of Louisville School of Law	426	106	45	6	29	10	•	44	90	• •	12	236,032	$3,490	$9,630	$2,342	$6,438	$30	2/15	4/1	212
Northern Kentucky University—Salmon P. Chase College of Law	275	171	47	10	20	27	•	64-66	90	• •	6	233,526	$1,750	$4,820	$147sh	$403sh	$25	3/1	2/1	270
LOUISIANA																				
Louisiana State University Law Center	743	-	43	7	36	11	•	39 hr	97	• • •	9	539,287	$1,937	$4,247	-	-	$25	2/1	3/1	210
Loyola University School of Law—New Orleans	551	244	48	22	31	30	•	70	90	• • •	17	230,000	$14,663	$14,663	$9,933	$9,933	$20		-	218
Southern University Law Center	339	-	38	58	22	11	•	75	96	• • •	14	339,763	$30,884	$62,884	-	-	-	3/31	4/15	340
Tulane University Law School	1001	-	42.5	22.4	48	48	•	31	88	• • •	19	470,000	$17,575	$17,575	-	-	$45	5/1	2/15	368
MAINE																				
University of Maine School of Law	263	4	49	6	16	7	•	35	89	•	12	280,000	$6,840	$13,560	-	-	$25	2/15	2/14	220
MARYLAND																				
University of Baltimore School of Law	636	418	45	15	44	57	•	55	90	• •	17	230,000	$2,645	$4,785	$221h	$375h	$35	4/5	4/1	80
University of Maryland School of Law	604	250	50	30	50	53	•	38-39	85	• •	25	325,000	$6,921	$12,664	$5,187	$9,493	$40	2/15	2/15	224
MASSACHUSETTS																				
Boston College Law School	835	-	47.5	19.4	42	36	•	39	85	• •	20	320,000	$17,720	$17,720	-	-	$50	3/1	3/1	84
Boston University School of Law	1182	-	42	21	58	70	•	29	84	• •	25	464,000	$17,630	$17,750	-	-	$50	3/1	4/1	86
Harvard University Law School	1620	-	40	27	80	33	•	30	82	• • • •	95	1,745,000	$17,750	-	$8,250	-	$65	2/1	3/1	180
New England School of Law	640	489	42	5	40	63	•	42	84	• •	16	242,000	$11,000	-	-	-	$45	3/15	4/15	250
Northeastern University School of Law	603	-	56	21	31	24	•	48	99	• •	14	164,880	$16,860	$16,860	-	-	$55	3/1	3/1	266
Suffolk University Law School	990	650	52	13	70	60	•	58	84	• •	10	300,000	$14,340	-	$10,756	-	$50	3/1	3/4	348
Western New England College School of Law	482	293	48	8	29	30	•	42	88	• •	7	301,000	$11,775	$11,775	$8,830	$8,830	$35	3/1	4/1	398
MICHIGAN																				
Detroit College of Law	418	338	35.7	9.1	28	32	•	60	85	•	6	200,000	$12,000	$12,000	$9,000	$9,000	$35	4/15F 10/15Ja	3/15	140
University of Detroit—Mercy School of Law	914	-	44	9	28	28	•	45	86	•	10	190,000	$12,000	$12,000	-	-	$50	4/15	3/1	142
University of Michigan Law School	1186	1513	43	22	82	15	•	31	83	• •	40	750,000	$12,475	$19,575	-	-	$70	2/15	-	234
Thomas M. Cooley Law School	110	-	30	8	-	-	•	72	90	• •	19	305,000	$425c	$425c	$425c	-	$100	2/15	3/15	362
Wayne State University Law School	510	190	48.1	13.3	32	34	•	35	86	• •	12	416,000	$5,750	$12,440	$3,132	$6,700	$20	3/15	4/23	394
MINNESOTA																				
Hamline University School of Law	603	-	45	10	29	44	•	31	88	• •	10	204,000	$12,560	$12,560	-	-	$30	5/15	-	178
University of Minnesota Law School	810	-	41	15	54	38	•	32	88	• •	28	800,000	$6,624	$12,544	-	-	$30	3/1	3/15	236
William Mitchell College of Law	508	622	47	11.6	35	65	•	56	86	•	17	200,000	$12,870	$12,870	$9,340	$9,340	$35	5/1	-	408
MISSISSIPPI																				
The University of Mississippi School of Law	507	3	33	10	24	8	•	55-58	90	•	13	260,000	$3,006y	$6,268y	-	-	$20	3/1	3/1	238
Mississippi College School of Law	376	-	38	9.8	17	18	•	54	88	•	5	220,000	$10,050	$10,050	-	-	$20	5/1	5/1	240

This information was reported by the schools in Fall 1993, thus the figures may have changed. The reader is cautioned against making direct comparisons of complex information limited to chart form. Be sure to go beyond the table, indeed beyond the two-page descriptions that follow, if you wish to inform yourself adequately about a particular school. Symbols and footnotes are explained on the last page of this chart.

School	Full-time	Part-time	% Women	% Minority	Faculty Total full-time	Faculty Total part-time	Day	Evenings	Required credits	Total credits to obtain J.D.	Joint degrees offered	Graduate law study available	Evening division	Transferable summer courses offered	Summer matriculation for first-year students	Midyear matriculation for first-year students	Academic Support Programs offered	Library full-time staff	Number of volumes and equivalents	In-state, full-time	Out-of-state, full-time	In-state, part-time	Out-of-state, part-time	Application fee	Application deadline for fall admission	Financial aid application deadline	Official Guide page number	Grid included
MISSOURI																												
University of Missouri—Columbia School of Law	455	-	42	8	31	5	•		57	89	•			•			•	15	275,000	$6,060	$11,945	-		$25	-	3/1	242	•
University of Missouri—Kansas City School of Law	460	-	42	6	28	29	•		52	91	•	•	•	•			•	5	245,000	$6,281	$12,133	-	-	$25	-	-	244	•
Saint Louis University School of Law	559	267	40.1	13.6	44	15	•	•	36	88	•	•	•	•			•	8	400,000	$13,520	$13,520	$10,100	$10,100	$30	3/1	4/1	314	•
Washington University School of Law	656	-	42	13	38	48	•		39	85	•	•		•			•	17	475,544	$17,750	-	-		$50	3/1	3/1	392	
MONTANA																												
University of Montana School of Law	229	-	38	4	18	9	•		69	90	•						•	11	123,853	$4,591	$9,292	-	-	$60	3/15	3/1	246	
NEBRASKA																												
Creighton University School of Law	541	18	43	7	23	28	•		39	94	•			•			•	13	197,402	$12,056	$12,056	$400ch	$400ch	$40	5/1	4/1	130	•
University of Nebraska College of Law	467	2	43	11	26	30	•		45	96	•	•		•			•	11	303,748	$3,024	$7,758	-	-	$25	3/1	3/1	248	•
NEW HAMPSHIRE																												
Franklin Pierce Law Center	394	-	39	3	24	27	•		39	84		•		•			•	8	186,000	$12,100	$12,100	-		$45	4/1		162	•
NEW JERSEY																												
Rutgers—The State University—School of Law—Camden	584	137	45	30	37	60	•	•	36	84	•			•			•	21	450,000	$6,388	$9,792	$264	$407	$40	3/1	3/1	308	•
Rutgers University School of Law—Newark	527	247	46	31	35	45	•	•	31	84	•			•			•	9	392,796	$6,388	$9,792	$264c	$407c	$40	3/1	3/1	310	•
Seton Hall University School of Law	996	379	45	20	51	97	•	•	46-48	85	•			•			•	26	315,595	$15,870	$15,870	$11,638	$11,638	$45	4/1	5/15	326	•
NEW MEXICO																												
University of New Mexico School of Law	343	-	56	46	29	19	•		42	86	•			•			•	18	350,000	$2,466	$8,274	-		$30	2/1	3/1	252	•
NEW YORK																												
Albany Law School	772	26	46	11.3	41	37	•		35	87	•			•			•	17	424,000	$16,275	$16,275	$13,020	$13,020	$50	3/15	-	68	•
Brooklyn Law School	1025	416	39.7	15.6	70	46	•	•	34	86	•			•			•	10	415,251	$16,800		$12,600		$50	none	3/1	90	•
University at Buffalo State University of New York School of Law	781	-	43	17	39	32	•		34	82	•			•	•	•	•	20	310,000	$5,000	$9,650	-		$50	2/1	3/1	92	
Benjamin N. Cardozo School of Law Yeshiva University	920	-	47	10	47	25	•		34-35	84	•			•	•	•	•	7	352,200	$16,375	$16,375	-	-	$50	12/1Ja 4/1 MaSe	12/15Ja 4/15 MaSe	108	•

School	•	Pg	Deadline	Deadline	Fee	$	$	$	$	#	#	f	f	f	%	Range/#	#	#	#	#	Enroll
Columbia University School of Law	•	124	3/1	2/15	$65	—	—	$19,200	$20,000	1,420,000	38	•	•		83	32	37	64	27	41	1053
Cornell University Law School	•	128	3/15	2/1	$60	$19,200	$19,200	$19,200	$19,200	507,221	22	•	•		84	32	23	33	22	37	568
Fordham University School of Law	•	160	3/1	3/1	$55	$13,425	$13,425	$17,900	$17,900	410,690	10	•	•		83	45	135	52	21	40	1131
Hofstra University School of Law	•	184	5/15	4/15	$50	—	—	$16,380	$16,380	395,000	21	•	•		85	45	25	42	17	40	832
City University of New York School of Law at Queens College	•	254	7/1	3/14	$35	$300c	$196c	$3,887	$2,647	210,620	16	•	•		92	58	16	39	28	50	438
New York Law School	•	256	—	4/1	$50	$12,500	$12,500	$16,670	$16,670	377,124	22	•	•		86	34	101	49	22	39.5	890
New York University School of Law	•	258	5/1	2/1	$65	—	—	—	$19,740	888,000	60	•	•		82	37	97	105	23.2	44	1299
Pace University School of Law	•	288	2/1	3/15	$50	—	$12,160	—	$16,180	266,085	8	•	•		90	40	29	49	16.3	46	460
St. John's University School of Law	•	312	4/1	3/1	$50	—	$11,650	$15,500	$15,500	408,738	7	•	•		85	61	13	50	14	40	867
Syracuse University College of Law	•	350	3/1	4/1	$40	$739ch	$739ch	$16,900	$16,900	318,772	16	•	•		87	40	34	41	30	43	797
Touro College—Jacob D. Fuchsberg Law Center	•	366	6/1	5/1	$40	—	$11,770	—	$14,470	310,000	22	•	•	•	87	41	24	41	22	42	539
NORTH CAROLINA																					
Campbell University—Norman Adrian Wiggins School of Law	•	104	—	3/15	$30	—	—	$11,750	$11,750	146,000	7	•	•		90	70	15	20	3	40	310
Duke University School of Law	•	150	1/15	1/15	$60	—	—	$18,600	$18,600	450,000	23	•	•	•	86	30	49	33	12	40	595
University of North Carolina School of Law	•	260	3/1	2/1	$55	—	—	$10,328	$1,512	360,000	21	•	•	•	86	39	11	31	14.9	44.6	704
North Carolina Central University	•	262	3/15	4/15	$15	$8,928	$1,340	$8,969	$1,381	101,649	10	•	•		88	65	5	20	55	57	224
Wake Forest University School of Law	•	384	5/1	3/15	$50	—	—	$14,200	$14,200	250,000	13	•	•		89	41	33	34	8	39	465
NORTH DAKOTA																					
University of North Dakota School of Law	•	264	5/1	4/1	$35	—	—	$3,367	$1,359	250,000	9	•	•	•	90	33	13	13	4	37	243
OHIO																					
University of Akron School of Law	•	64	—	—	$35	$4,870	$2,741	$8,117	$4,568	216,000	11	•	•		87	44	22	23	11	36	384
Capital University Law & Graduate Center	•	106	4/1	5/1	$35	$7,923	$7,923	$12,927	$12,927	215,000	11	•	•		86	42	46	31	7	42	479
Case Western Reserve University School of Law	•	110	3/1	4/1	$40	$658ch	$658ch	$16,600	$16,600	304,331	28	•	•		88	33	30	46	10.8	44.8	628
University of Cincinnati College of Law	•	118	3/1	4/1	$35	—	$186sh	$11,268	$5,796	338,358	24	•	•		88	35	26	25	16	44	394
Cleveland State University—Cleveland-Marshall College of Law	•	120	3/1	3/1	$35	$372sh	—	$9,652	$4,826	290,000	—	•	•	•	87	46-56	31	41	17	41	620
University of Dayton School of Law	•	134	3/1	5/1	$40	—	—	$13,384	$13,384	208,000	11	•	•		87	36	28	27	11	40	491
Ohio Northern University—Claude W. Pettit College of Law	•	278	—	—	$40	—	—	$16,960	$16,960	225,000	10	•	•		87	54	15	26	9	30	397
The Ohio State University College of Law	•	280	3/1	3/15	$30	—	—	$12,200	$4,950	590,000	20	•	•		88	39	20	37	18.6	45	660
The University of Toledo College of Law	•	364	4/1	3/15	$30	$7,709	$4,012	$10,280	$5,350	260,000	14	•	•		87	40	22	36	10	39	447
OKLAHOMA																					
University of Oklahoma College of Law	•	282	3/1	3/15	$25	—	—	$9,198	$3,160	261,277	16	•	•		90	40	8	32	10	40	670
Oklahoma City University School of Law	•	284	3/1	—	$35	$7,000	$7,000	$10,850	$10,850	215,455	11	•	•		90	43	21	27	9.3	35	418
University of Tulsa College of Law	•	370	—	—	$30	$8,715	$8,715	$12,450	$12,450	260,000	13	•	•		88	42-44	19	37	12	35	456

This information was reported by the schools in Fall 1993, thus the figures may have changed. The reader is cautioned against making direct comparisons of complex information limited to chart form. Be sure to go beyond the two-page descriptions that follow, if you wish to inform yourself adequately about a particular school. Symbols and footnotes are explained on the last page of this chart.

School	Full-time	Part-time	% Women	% Minority	Faculty full-time	Faculty part-time	Day	Evenings	Required credits	Total credits for J.D.	Joint degrees	Graduate law study	Evening division	Transferable summer courses	Summer matric.	Midyear matric.	Academic Support	Library staff	Volumes & equivalents	Tuition in-state FT	Tuition out-of-state FT	Tuition in-state PT	Tuition out-of-state PT	Application fee	Application deadline	Financial aid deadline	Official Guide page	Grid
OREGON																												
Lewis and Clark Northwestern School of Law	473	216	42	15	39	61	•	•	35–40	86	•	•	•	•			•	-	-	$13,900	$13,900	$9,600	$9,600	$45	3/15	2/15	208	•
University of Oregon School of Law	410	-	44	13.7	29	11	•		40	85	•			•			•	12	325,000	$6,964y	$12,680y			$50	401	3/1	286	•
Willamette University College of Law	484	-	38	12	29	10	•		37	88	•			•			•	10	290,400	$12,800	$12,800			$40	4/1	2/1	404	
PENNSYLVANIA																			244,000									
Dickinson School of Law	520	3	49	6	26	35	•	•	41	88	•	•	•				•	13	325,000	$12,200	$12,200	$425h	$425h	$50	2/15	2/15	144	•
Duquesne University School of Law	290	354	43	7	21	37	•	•	64	86	•		•					16	192,000	$10,353	$10,353	$7,798	$7,798	$40	4/1d	5/1e	152	•
University of Pennsylvania Law School	710	-	40	21	39	54	•		34	89	•	•					•	80	540,000	$18,460	$18,460			$60	2/1	-	290	
University of Pittsburgh School of Law	684	13	46	12	35	28	•		53	88	•						•	17	265,000	$9,608	$14,802	$9,608	$14,802	$40	3/1	3/1	294	•
Temple University School of Law	883	391	44	18	59	131	•	•	38	83	•	•	•				•	11	438,743	$7,178	$13,300	$5,742	$10,640	$50	3/1	4/1	352	•
Villanova University School of Law	675	-	47	15	37	37	•		34	87	•						•	22	420,000	$15,620	$15,620	$15,620	$15,620	$75	1/31	3/1	380	•
Widener University School of Law (see Delaware)																												
PUERTO RICO																												
Inter American University School of Law	312	296	44	0	20	18	•	•	62	-		•	•	•			•	-	160,098	$3,225		$2,365		-	-		198	
Pontifical Catholic University of Puerto Rico, School of Law	251	164	48	0	19	10	•	•	82	94	•		•	•			•	5	152,305					$25	5/15	9/24Se 01/29Ja	296	•
University of Puerto Rico School of Law	253	204	47	0	33	23	•		70	92	•			•			•	41	210,628	$2,623		$1,713		$15	2/16	4/15	298	•
SOUTH CAROLINA																												
University of South Carolina School of Law	765	-	39	10	44	25	•		45–47	91	•			•			•	5	326,000	$4,970	$10,546	$206ch	$434ch	$25	2/15	4/15	328	•
SOUTH DAKOTA																												
University of South Dakota School of Law	218	-	41	3	16	2	•		44	90	•			•			•	7	155,717	$66ch	$135ch			$15	3/1	3/1	330	•
TENNESSEE																												
Memphis State University—Cecil C. Humphreys School of Law	399	24	39	7	21	20	•	•	56	90	•			•			•	12	245,334	$2,962	$7,504	$127h	$324h	$10	2/1	4/1	228	•
University of Tennessee College of Law	472	-	44	10	36	28	•		45	89	•			•			•	15	345,000	$3,092	$7,716			$15	2/1	2/14	354	•
Vanderbilt University School of Law	550	-	39	21.3	-	-	•		33	88	•			•			•	18	329,060	$17,750	$17,750			$50	2/1	3/1	376	•

This page is a continuation of the "Key Facts" reference table for law schools (states Texas through Wyoming). The column headings do not appear on this page. Values are transcribed below in reading order; several additional yes/no (•) indicator columns appear between the numeric columns.

School	Enr.	Enr.2	c3	c4	c5	c6	a	b	Min.	Endowment	Tuition A	Tuition B	Tuition C	Tuition D	Fee	Deadline	Deadline	Page
TEXAS																		
Baylor University School of Law	409	-	41	17	22	22	76	120	4	157,250	-	-	-	-	$35	3/1	5/31	82
University of Houston Law Center	817	353	44	19	48	65	33	88	15	420,000	$4,800	$7,300	$4,682	$7,832	$50	2/1	-	186
St. Mary's University School of Law	746	-	47	24	35	34	47	90	-	267,600	$420h	$12,000	-	-	$45	3/1	4/1	316
South Texas College of Law	854	462	40	18	54	35	41	90	14	290,000	$12,000	$12,000	$8,000	$8,000	$40	3/15	5/1	332
Southern Methodist University School of Law	749	-	43	20	39	2	33	90	24	440,199	$17,372	$17,372	-	-	$45	3/1	5/1	338
The University of Texas School of Law	1487	-	42	23.5	62	91	39	86	46	850,000	$4,440	$8,640	-	-	$50	2/1	3/1	356
Texas Southern University—Thurgood Marshall School of Law	650	-	43	77.2	31	14	68	90	9	300,000	$1,800	$3,150	-	-	$40	rolling	5/1	358
Texas Tech University School of Law	627	-	37.4	17	23	13	55	90	16	250,000	$120	$210	-	-	$40	2/1	-	360
UTAH																		
Brigham Young University—J. Reuben Clark Law School	475	-	35	18	29	19	32	90	13	330,000	$4,200	$6,300	-	-	$30	2/15	5/1	88
University of Utah College of Law	366	-	43	14	27	28	66	88	11	264,000	$3,853	$8,529	-	-	$25	2/1	2/15	372
VERMONT																		
Vermont Law School	483	-	49	9	31	22	42	84	12	175,000	$15,039	$15,039	-	-	$50	2/15	2/15	378
VIRGINIA																		
George Mason University School of Law	349	338	42	12	29	21	v	87-92	10	260,000	$6,384	$16,212	$228sh	$579sh	$20	4/1	3/1	164
Regent University School of Law	325	-	27	5	13	12	60	90	9	280,000	$10,000	$10,000	$695ch	$695ch	$30	4/1	7/15	304
University of Richmond—T.C. Williams School of Law	456	1	50	22	23	64	35	86	13	215,320	$14,040	$14,040	-	-	$35	1/15	2/25	306
University of Virginia School of Law	1148	-	38	15	55	52	27	86	27	700,000	$7,570	$15,678	-	-	$40	1/15	2/1	382
Washington and Lee University School of Law	360	-	40	16	36	12	38	85	25	297,000	$13,600	$13,600	-	-	$40	2/1	3/1	390
College of William and Mary—Marshall-Wythe School of Law	564	-	43	14	27	23	44	90	15	300,000	$5,340	$13,530	-	-	$30	3/1	2/1	406
WASHINGTON																		
Gonzaga University School of Law	541	15	38	7	33	10	58	90	11	196,150	$425c / $13,175y	$425c	$425c	$425c	$30	3/15	5/31	176
Puget Sound/Seattle University School of Law	719	148	46	15	40	25	45	90	18	300,258	$13,800	$13,800	$13,800	$13,800	$50	4/1	3/1	300
University of Washington School of Law	478	-	46	39	44	24	84q	135q	32	450,000	$4,000	$10,000	-	-	$50	1/15	2/28	388
WEST VIRGINIA																		
West Virginia University College of Law	452	16	46	8	26	12	49	90	11	198,400	$3,384	$8,354	-	-	$40	2/15	3/1	396
WISCONSIN																		
Marquette University Law School	495	-	44	11	21	30	46	90	18	220,000	$12,600	$12,600	$182c	$473c	$35	3/15	3/1	222
University of Wisconsin Law School	869	50	44	16	47	-	60	90	10	400,000	$4,348	$11,334	-	-	$35	2/1	3/1	410
WYOMING																		
University of Wyoming College of Law	222	-	45	6	14	3	52	88	6	174,000	$3,328	$7,396	-	-	$35	4/1	2/15	412

Key Facts Abbreviations and Footnotes

• yes	s per semester	e evening(s)	Ja January	asap as soon as possible	q per quarter credits
c per credit	sh per semester hour	d day(s)	Ma May	hr hour(s)	v varies
h per hour	u per unit	F Fall semester	Se September	r resident	
ch per credit hour	y per year	S Spring semester	- not available	nr non-resident	

Chapter 13: Geographic Guide to Law Schools in the United States (by region)*

New England

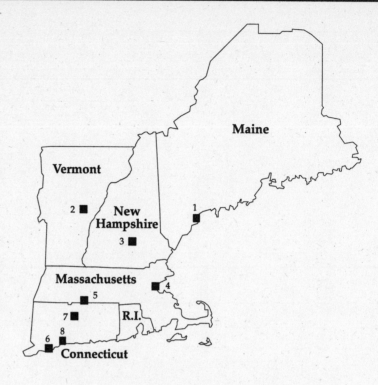

Maine
1. Portland—Population: 64,358
   University of Maine—Enrollment: 263/4

Vermont
2. South Royalton—Population: 23,089
   Vermont Law School—Enrollment: 483/NA

New Hampshire
3. Concord—Population: 36,006
   Franklin Pierce—Enrollment: 394/NA

Massachusetts
4. Boston—Population: 574,283
   Boston College—Enrollment: 835/NA
   Boston University—Enrollment: 1,182/NA
   Harvard (Cambridge, MA)—Enrollment: 1,620/NA
   New England—Enrollment: 640/489
   Northeastern—Enrollment: 603/NA
   Suffolk—Enrollment: 990/650
5. Springfield—Population: 156,983
   Western New England College—
   Enrollment: 482/293

Connecticut
6. Bridgeport—Population: 141,686
   Quinnipiac—Enrollment: 531/177
7. Hartford—Population: 139,739
   University of Connecticut—Enrollment: 433/222
8. New Haven—Population: 130,474
   Yale—Enrollment: 617/NA

"Enrollment" represents the numbers of total full-time/total part-time students. NA stands for "Not Applicable."

*Population information is derived from the U.S. Bureau of the Census, Population Division, Washington, DC. Data is accurate as of the 1990 Census. City populations reflect the number of people residing in the city proper, not the metropolitan area which would include outlying suburbs as well. Donald P. Racheter, director of the prelaw program at Central University of Iowa, also contributed data for these regional maps.

Northeast

New York
1. **Albany—Population: 101,082**
   Albany—Enrollment: 772/26
2. **New York City—Population: 7,322,564**
   Benjamin N. Cardozo—Enrollment: 920/NA
   Brooklyn—Enrollment: 1,025/416
   Columbia—Enrollment: 1,053/NA
   Fordham—Enrollment: 1,131/372
   City University of New York—Enrollment: 446/8
   The New York Law School—Enrollment: 890/479
   New York University—Enrollment: 1,299/NA
   St. John's University (Jamaica, NY)—
   Enrollment: 867/312
3. **Ithaca—Population: 29,541**
   Cornell—Enrollment: 568/NA
4. **Buffalo—Population: 328,123**
   University at Buffalo—Enrollment: 781/NA
5. **White Plains—Population: 48,718**
   Pace—Enrollment: 460/334
6. **Syracuse—Population: 163,860**
   Syracuse—Enrollment: 797/13
7. **Hempstead—Population: 725,639**
   Hofstra—Enrollment: 832/NA
8. **Huntington—Population: 18,243**
   Touro—Enrollment: 539/325

New Jersey
9. **Camden—Population: 87,492**
   Rutgers–Camden—Enrollment: 584/137
10. **Newark—Population: 275,221**
    Rutgers–Newark—Enrollment: 527/247
    Seton Hall—Enrollment: 996/379

Pennsylvania
11. **Carlisle—Population: 18,419**
    Dickinson—Enrollment: 520/3
12. **Pittsburgh—Population: 369,879**
    Duquesne—Enrollment: 290/354
    University of Pittsburgh—Enrollment: 684/13
13. **Philadelphia—Population: 1,585,577**
    University of Pennsylvania—Enrollment: 710/NA
    Temple—Enrollment: 883/391
    Villanova (Villanova, PA)—Enrollment: 675/NA
14. **Harrisburg—Population: 52,376**
    Widener—(see Delaware—Midsouth region)

Midsouth

Kentucky*
1. **Lexington—Population: 225,366**
   University of Kentucky—Enrollment: 413/4
2. **Louisville—Population: 269,063**
   University of Louisville—Enrollment: 426/106

West Virginia
3. **Morgantown—Population: 25,879**
   West Virginia—Enrollment: 452/16

Virginia
4. **Arlington—Population: 170,936**
   George Mason—Enrollment: 349/338
5. **Virginia Beach—Population: 393,069**
   Regent—Enrollment: 325/0
6. **Richmond—Population: 203,056**
   University of Richmond—Enrollment: 456/1
7. **Charlottesville—Population: 40,341**
   University of Virginia—Enrollment: 1,148/NA
8. **Lexington—Population: 6,959**
   Washington and Lee—Enrollment: 360/NA
9. **Williamsburg—Population: 11,530**
   College of William and Mary—Enrollment: 564/NA

Maryland
10. **Baltimore—Population: 736,014**
    University of Baltimore—Enrollment: 636/418
    University of Maryland—Enrollment: 604/250

District of Columbia
11. **Washington, DC—Population: 606,900**
    American—Enrollment: 858/312
    Catholic University of America—
    Enrollment: 670/275
    District of Columbia—Enrollment: 284/NA
    Georgetown—Enrollment: 1,547/504
    George Washington—Enrollment: 1,196/268
    Howard—Enrollment: 463/NA

Delaware
12. **Wilmington—Population: 71,529**
    Widener—Enrollment: 1,505/688

Tennessee
13. **Memphis—Population: 610,337**
    Memphis State—Enrollment: 399/24
14. **Knoxville—Population: 165,121**
    University of Tennessee—Enrollment: 472/NA
15. **Nashville—Population: 488,374**
    Vanderbilt—Enrollment: 550/NA

North Carolina
16. **Buies Creek—Population: 2,085**
    Campbell—Enrollment: 310/NA
17. **Durham—Population: 136,611**
    Duke—Enrollment: 595/NA
    North Carolina Central—Enrollment: 224/82
18. **Chapel Hill—Population: 38,719**
    University of North Carolina—Enrollment: 704/NA
19. **Winston-Salem—Population: 143,485**
    Wake Forest—Enrollment: 465/NA

*   Northern Kentucky University—see Cincinnati,
    Ohio (Great Lakes region)

Southeast

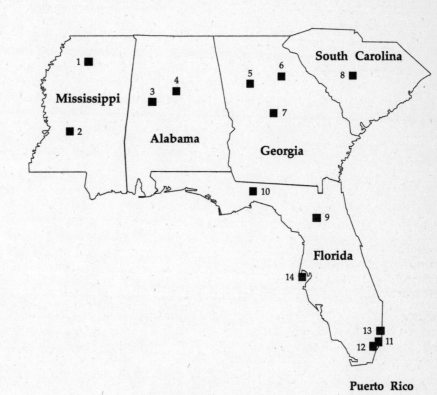

Mississippi
1. **Oxford—Population: 9,984**
   University of Mississippi—Enrollment: 507/3
2. **Jackson—Population: 196,637**
   Mississippi College—Enrollment: 376/NA

Alabama
3. **Tuscaloosa—Population: 77,759**
   University of Alabama—Enrollment: 559/NA
4. **Birmingham—Population: 265,968**
   Cumberland School of Law–Samford University—
   Enrollment: 627/NA

Georgia
5. **Atlanta—Population: 394,017**
   Emory—Enrollment: 740/NA
   Georgia State—Enrollment: 378/244
6. **Athens—Population: 45,734**
   University of Georgia—Enrollment: 641/NA
7. **Macon—Population: 106,612**
   Mercer—Enrollment: 409/1

South Carolina
8. **Columbia—Population: 98,052**
   University of South Carolina—Enrollment: 765/NA

Florida
9. **Gainesville—Population: 84,770**
   University of Florida—Enrollment: 1,150/0
10. **Tallahassee—Population: 124,773**
    Florida State—Enrollment: 600/NA
11. **Miami—Population: 358,548**
    St. Thomas—Enrollment: 478/NA
12. **Coral Gables—Population: 40,091**
    University of Miami—Enrollment: 1,223/185
13. **Ft. Lauderdale—Population: 149,377**
    Nova—Enrollment: 834/25
14. **St. Petersburg—Population: 238,629**
    Stetson—Enrollment: 648/NA

Puerto Rico
15. **San Juan—Population: 437,745**
    Inter American—Enrollment: 312/296
    University of Puerto Rico—Enrollment: 253/204
16. **Ponce—Population: 187,749**
    Pontifical Catholic University—
    Enrollment: 251/164

South Central

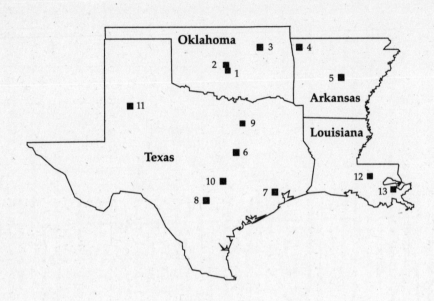

Oklahoma

1. **Norman—Population: 80,171**
   University of Oklahoma—Enrollment: 670/NA
2. **Oklahoma City—Population: 444,719**
   Oklahoma City—Enrollment: 418/240
3. **Tulsa—Population: 367,302**
   University of Tulsa—Enrollment: 456/172

Arkansas

4. **Fayetteville—Population: 42,099**
   University of Arkansas–Fayetteville—
   Enrollment: 419/NA
5. **Little Rock—Population: 175,795**
   University of Arkansas–Little Rock—
   Enrollment: 276/145

Texas

6. **Waco—Population: 103,590**
   Baylor—Enrollment: 409/NA
7. **Houston—Population: 1,630,553**
   South Texas—Enrollment: 854/462
   University of Houston—Enrollment: 817/353
   Texas Southern—Enrollment: 650/NA

8. **San Antonio—Population: 935,933**
   St. Mary's—Enrollment: 746/NA
9. **Dallas—Population: 1,006,877**
   Southern Methodist—Enrollment: 749/NA
10. **Austin—Population: 465,622**
    University of Texas–Austin—Enrollment: 1,487/NA
11. **Lubbock—Population: 186,206**
    Texas Tech—Enrollment: 627/NA

Louisiana

12. **Baton Rouge—Population: 219,531**
    Louisiana State—Enrollment: 743/NA
    Southern—Enrollment: 339/NA
13. **New Orleans—Population: 496,938**
    Loyola–New Orleans—Enrollment: 551/244
    Tulane—Enrollment: 1,001/NA

Mountain West

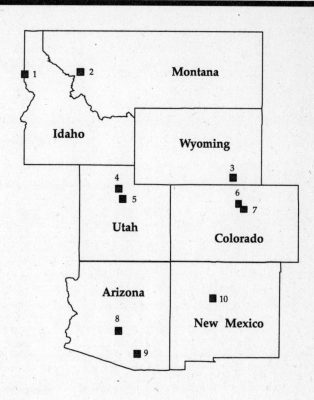

Idaho
1. **Moscow—Population: 18,519**
   University of Idaho—Enrollment: 293/NA

Montana
2. **Missoula—Population: 42,918**
   University of Montana—Enrollment: 229/NA

Wyoming
3. **Laramie—Population: 26,687**
   University of Wyoming—Enrollment: 222/NA

Utah
4. **Salt Lake City—Population: 159,936**
   University of Utah—Enrollment: 366/NA
5. **Provo—Population: 86,835**
   Brigham Young—Enrollment: 475/NA

Colorado
6. **Boulder—Population: 83,312**
   University of Colorado—Enrollment: 476/NA
7. **Denver—Population: 467,610**
   University of Denver—Enrollment: 800/280

Arizona
8. **Tempe—Population: 141,865**
   Arizona State—Enrollment: 512/NA
9. **Tucson—Population: 405,390**
   University of Arizona—Enrollment: 480/NA

New Mexico
10. **Albuquerque—Population: 384,736**
    University of New Mexico—Enrollment: 343/NA

Far West

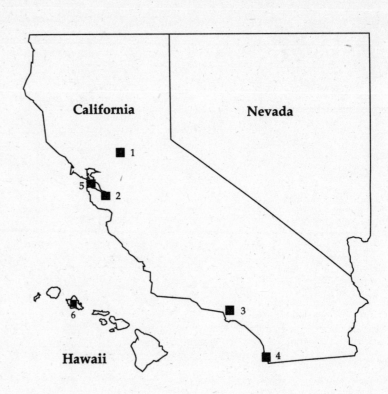

California
1. **Sacramento—Population: 369,365**
   University of California–Davis (Davis, CA)—
   Enrollment: 478/NA
   McGeorge—Enrollment: 858/401
2. **Santa Clara—Population: 93,613**
   Santa Clara—Enrollment: 678/205
3. **Los Angeles—Population: 3,485,398**
   University of California–Los Angeles—
   Enrollment: 978/NA
   Loyola–Los Angeles—Enrollment: 1,025/336
   Pepperdine—Enrollment: 714/NA
   University of Southern California—
   Enrollment: 600/NA
   Southwestern—Enrollment: 811/338
   Whittier—Enrollment: 429/240

4. **San Diego—Population: 1,110,549**
   California Western—Enrollment: 860/NA
   University of San Diego—Enrollment: 757/315
5. **San Francisco—Population: 723,959**
   University of California–Berkeley (Berkeley, CA)—
   Enrollment: 780/NA
   University of California–Hastings—
   Enrollment: 1,264/NA
   Golden Gate—Enrollment: 527/213
   University of San Francisco—Enrollment: 529/130
   Stanford (Stanford, CA)—Enrollment: 536/NA

Hawaii
6. **Honolulu—Population: 365,272**
   University of Hawaii—Enrollment: 240/NA

Northwest

Washington

Oregon

Washington
Seattle—Population: 516,259
    University of Washington—Enrollment: 478/NA
Spokane—Population: 177,196
    Gonzaga—Enrollment: 541/15
Tacoma—Population: 176,664
    University of Puget Sound—Enrollment: 719/148

Oregon
Portland—Population: 437,319
    Lewis & Clark—Enrollment: 473/216
Salem—Population: 107,786
    Willamette—Enrollment: 484/NA
Eugene—Population: 112,669
    University of Oregon—Enrollment: 410/NA

Midwest

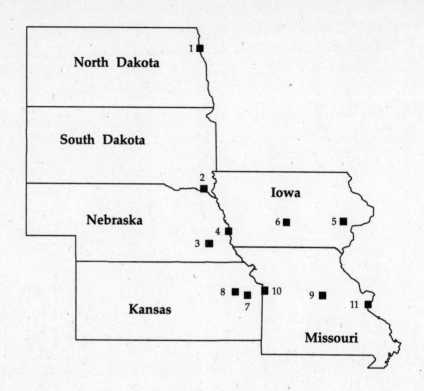

North Dakota
1. **Grand Forks—Population: 49,425**
   University of North Dakota—Enrollment: 243/NA

South Dakota
2. **Vermillion—Population: 10,034**
   University of South Dakota—Enrollment: 218/NA

Nebraska
3. **Lincoln—Population: 191,972**
   University of Nebraska—Enrollment: 467/2
4. **Omaha—Population: 335,795**
   Creighton—Enrollment: 541/18

Iowa
5. **Iowa City—Population: 59,738**
   University of Iowa—Enrollment: 660/NA
6. **Des Moines—Population: 193,187**
   Drake—Enrollment: 553/25

Kansas
7. **Lawrence —Population: 65,808**
   University of Kansas—Enrollment: 525/NA
8. **Topeka—Population: 119,883**
   Washburn—Enrollment: 425/NA

Missouri
9. **Columbia—Population: 69,101**
   University of Missouri–Columbia—
   Enrollment: 455/NA
10. **Kansas City—Population: 435,146**
    University of Missouri–Kansas City—
    Enrollment: 460/0
11. **St. Louis—Population: 396,685**
    St. Louis—Enrollment: 559/267
    Washington—Enrollment: 656/NA

Great Lakes

Minnesota
1. **Minneapolis—Population: 368,383**
   University of Minnesota—Enrollment: 810/NA
   William Mitchell—Enrollment: 508/622
2. **St. Paul—Population: 272,235**
   Hamline—Enrollment: 603/NA

Wisconsin
3. **Madison—Population: 191,262**
   University of Wisconsin—Enrollment: 869/50
4. **Milwaukee—Population: 628,088**
   Marquette—Enrollment: 495/0

Michigan
5. **Lansing—Population: 127,321**
   Thomas M. Cooley —Enrollment: 110/1,513
6. **Detroit—Population: 1,027,974**
   Detroit College of Law—Enrollment: 418/338
   University of Detroit, Mercy—Enrollment: 914/NA
   Wayne State—Enrollment: 510/190
7. **Ann Arbor—Population: 109,592**
   University of Michigan—Enrollment: 1,186/NA

Illinois
8. **Chicago—Population: 2,783,726**
   University of Chicago—Enrollment: 530/NA
   Chicago-Kent—Enrollment: 868/369
   DePaul—Enrollment: 730/254
   John Marshall—Enrollment: 609/372
   Loyola–Chicago—Enrollment: 511/176
   Northwestern—Enrollment: 612/NA
9. **DeKalb—Population: 34,925**
   Northern Illinois—Enrollment: 308/NA
10. **Champaign—Population: 63,502**
    University of Illinois—Enrollment: 626/NA
11. **Carbondale—Population: 27,033**
    Southern Illinois—Enrollment: 344/NA

Indiana
12. **South Bend—Population: 105,511**
    Notre Dame—Enrollment: 583/NA
13. **Valparaiso—Population: 24,414**
    Valparaiso—Enrollment: 501/38
14. **Indianapolis—Population: 731,327**
    Indiana–Indianapolis—Enrollment: 525/298
15. **Bloomington—Population: 60,633**
    Indiana–Bloomington—Enrollment: 614/5

Ohio

16. **Toledo—Population: 332,943**
University of Toledo—Enrollment: 447/183
17. **Cleveland—Population: 505,616**
Case Western Reserve—Enrollment: 628/10
Cleveland State—Enrollment: 620/386
18. **Akron—Population: 223,019**
University of Akron—Enrollment: 384/199
19. **Ada—Population: 5,413**
Ohio Northern—Enrollment: 397/NA
20. **Columbus—Population: 632,910**
Capital—Enrollment: 479/311
Ohio State—Enrollment: 660/NA
21. **Dayton—Population: 182,044**
University of Dayton—Enrollment: 491/0
22. **Cincinnati—Population: 364,040**
University of Cincinnati—Enrollment: 394/0
University of Northern Kentucky—
Enrollment: 275/171 (Highland Heights, KY)

Chapter 14: ABA-Approved Law School Descriptions

The descriptions that follow were prepared by each law school under editorial and formatting guidelines provided by Law Services. The schools were encouraged to use the bulleted lead-ins to each section for quantitative data that did not require a narrative explanation, and to use the descriptive text to provide details on the unique features of the school. Most schools also include admission profiles that illustrate admission prospects based on a combination of LSAT score and GPA.

The purpose of this book is to provide a brief introduction to the programs, facilities, and admission requirements of each ABA-approved law school. For a balanced view of each law school, it is important not only to look at all of the elements included in each school's description on these pages, but also to obtain the catalog and admission materials of each school that interests you. For your convenience, Request for Information cards that may be sent to the law schools are included in the back of this book. The data in the school descriptions and admission profiles are for the 1993-94 academic year unless otherwise noted, and represent full-time, day programs unless otherwise noted.

There are factors that may not predict law school performance but may otherwise affect an admission decision. Many law schools give special admission consideration to members of minority and disadvantaged groups because traditionally they have been underrepresented in the legal profession. Footnotes to the admission grids generally will note any special information about the composition of the applicant pool.

Please Note:

- Unless otherwise indicated, bulleted details in the school descriptions under the heading "Enrollment/Student Body" refer to the 1993 first-year class. The rest of the details under this category refer to the total student body of the law school.

- **Full-time** students are those registered for the number of units that would constitute a full-time load to complete the J.D. in the normal three-year period.

- **Part-time** is anything less than the above.

- **Range of first-year class size** is the range from the smallest first-year class section to the largest. This differs from the size of the entire first-year class.

- **Total full-time faculty** represents permanent faculty appointments on a tenure track, teaching full time.

- **Total part-time faculty** represents part-time and adjunct appointments.

- **Required credits** are nonelective courses needed to obtain the J.D.

- **Total credits required** to obtain the J.D. degree are the number of credits needed to complete the degree.

University of Akron School of Law

Akron, OH 44325-2901

■ Introduction

The law is both a field of study and a practical profession. The University of Akron School of Law appreciates this dichotomy. The School of Law is devoted to affording students not only a sound academic legal education, but also the opportunity to develop the skills necessary to the practicing attorney. The school's location, physical facility, library, curriculum, and extracurricular activities all contribute to the enhancement of the academic and clinical study of law.

■ Enrollment/Student Body

➤ 1,837 applicants   ➤ 724 admitted first-year class 1993
➤ 210 enrolled first-year class 1993
➤ 384 total full-time 1992   ➤ 199 total part-time 1992
➤ 11% minority 1992   ➤ 36% women 1992
➤ 22 states & foreign countries represented 1993
➤ 94 undergraduate schools represented 1993

■ Faculty

➤ 45 total 1992   ➤ 23 full-time 1992
➤ 22 part-time or adjunct 1992   ➤ 18 women
➤ 3 minority 1992

■ Library and Physical Facility

➤ 216,000 volumes & equivalents   ➤ library hours: Mon.-Fri., 8:00 A.M.-11:00 P.M.; Sat., 9:00 A.M.-6:00 P.M.; Sun., NOON-11:00 P.M.   ➤ LEXIS   ➤ NEXIS
➤ WESTLAW   ➤ DIALOG   ➤ 4 full-time librarians
➤ library seats 213

The School of Law is housed in the modern C. Blake McDowell Law Center, dedicated in 1973. The School of Law Library has materials for conducting research on federal law and the law of all 50 states. The library is a federal government depository. The library contains a laboratory for computer-based education, with microcomputers for student use.

■ Location

The University of Akron is a major university with over 28,000 students. The university is coeducational and state supported. The School of Law is located on campus near federal and state courts, which affords students the opportunity, through clinical programs, to gain first-hand experience in the law.

■ Curriculum

➤ Academic Support Program   ➤ 87 credits required to graduate   ➤ 76 courses available   ➤ J.D./M.B.A; J.D./M. Tax; J.D./M.U.S.; J.D./M.P.A.   ➤ semesters, start in Aug.   ➤ range of first-year class size—45-55

The school is fully accredited by the American Bar Association and is a member of the Association of American Law Schools. Graduates are eligible to take the bar examination in every state.

Day students pursue a full-time, three-year course of study. Evening students acquire their degree in four years, including one summer. Eighty-seven semester credit hours are required for the J.D. degree.

Like most law schools, we require students to take a number of courses that are basic to an understanding of the law. These classes are comparatively small, with 40 to 60 students each, encouraging a high level of active participation. Thus, during the first (and probably most important) year of law school, our students are taught in a personalized atmosphere.

We are also committed to training our students in the skills necessary to function as competent attorneys. The required legal writing program is rigorous. Elective courses in trial and appellate advocacy attract large numbers of students. Clinical seminars are available in which students handle civil and criminal cases under the supervision of practicing attorneys. The legal clinic provides further opportunity for students to serve actual clients and grapple with real-life problems. Full-time faculty members bring a great deal of practical experience to these skills-oriented courses, as well as into the classroom.

Our program includes the opportunity to concentrate in certain areas of the law, including trial practice, business, and tax. Students interested in other fields such as labor/employment and criminal law have similar opportunities to specialize.

■ Student Activities

Seventeen student organizations afford an opportunity to assume responsibility and develop skills in practice and leadership and also encourage the formation of friendships. Examples are: *Akron Law Review*, a high-quality national publication produced by student editors; *Akron Tax Journal*, a yearly publication that discusses recent developments in tax law and tax policy issues; Bracton's Inn, which provides opportunities for intramural, regional, and national student competitions; the Law Association for Women's Rights, which is active in supporting and educating others in women's interests; and the Black Law Students Association, which provides social and political support for minority students.

■ Admission

➤ Bachelor's degree required   ➤ no application deadline, rolling admission   ➤ LSAT, LSDAS required
➤ application fee—$35

Candidates for admission must have a baccalaureate degree from a regionally accredited college or university. The school is seeking law students of demonstrated academic ability as evidenced in part by LSAT scores and the undergraduate grade-point average (GPA). The school will be looking beyond the LSAT and GPA for special qualities in applicants for the total of approximately 200 day and evening division openings.

■ Expenses and Financial Aid

➡ *tuition & fees—full-time resident, $4,690; part-time resident, $2,827; full-time nonresident, $8,340; part-time nonresident, $4,956* ➡ *estimated additional expenses—lab fees, $200; books, $350; room (10 months), $2,350* ➡ *scholarships available—merit and diversification of class* ➡ *financial aid available; FAF needed as early as possible*

■ Housing

Limited on-campus housing is available for law students. Contact the Housing Office, 216.972.7800. Contact the University Off-Campus Housing Referral for information about graduate/professional housing off campus. Phone: 216.972.6936.

■ Career Services

The School of Law administers a placement office located in the school to assist students in the career-planning and job-search process.

■ Correspondence

Inquiries concerning the School of Law should be addressed to the School of Law, Admissions Director, The University of Akron, Akron, OH 44325-2901. Phone: 216.972.7331.

Applicant Group for the 1993–1994 Academic Year

University of Akron School of Law
This grid includes only applicants who earned 120-180 LSAT scores under standard administrations.

LSAT Score	3.75 +		3.50 -3.74		3.25 - 3.49		3.00 - 3.24		2.75 - 2.99		2.50 - 2.74		2.25 - 2.49		2.00 - 2.24		Below 2.00		No GPA		Total	
	Apps	Adm	Apps	Adm	Apps	Adm	Apps	Adm	Apps	Adm	Apps	Adm	Apps	Adm	Apps	Adm	Apps	Adm	Apps	Adm	Apps	Adm
175 - 180	0	0	0	0	0	0	0	0	0	0	0	0	0	0	0	0	0	0	0	0	0	0
170 - 174	0	0	0	0	0	0	0	0	0	0	0	0	0	0	2	2	0	0	0	0	2	2
165 - 169	1	1	2	2	2	2	5	5	2	2	2	2	4	3	0	0	0	0	0	0	18	17
160 - 164	5	5	10	10	7	6	12	12	17	17	10	10	13	13	0	0	1	0	0	0	75	73
155 - 159	9	8	11	10	41	39	37	35	51	47	40	39	23	14	3	2	3	0	3	2	221	196
150 - 154	17	16	50	42	81	66	129	100	135	88	78	21	48	9	15	2	0	0	4	2	557	346
145 - 149	7	4	28	6	70	9	117	14	117	12	56	3	35	3	13	2	2	0	6	2	451	55
140 - 144	4	0	15	0	30	1	49	2	43	2	46	0	30	4	16	0	2	0	10	1	245	10
135 - 139	1	0	5	0	7	0	15	0	25	0	25	0	14	0	17	0	2	0	5	0	116	0
130 - 134	0	0	1	0	0	0	4	0	4	0	5	0	10	0	6	0	2	0	5	0	37	0
125 - 129	0	0	0	0	1	0	1	0	3	0	1	0	0	0	1	0	0	0	1	0	8	0
120 - 124	0	0	0	0	0	0	0	0	0	0	0	0	1	0	1	0	0	0	0	0	2	0
Total	44	34	122	70	239	123	369	168	397	168	263	75	178	46	74	8	12	0	34	7	1732	699

Apps = Number of Applicants
Adm = Number Admitted
Reflects 94% of the total applicant pool.

The University of Alabama School of Law

Box 870382
Tuscaloosa, AL 35487-0382

Phone: 205.348.5440

■ Introduction

The University of Alabama School of Law is located on the main university campus at Tuscaloosa. Founded in 1872, the law school has served the state and the nation as the training ground for leaders of the legal profession, business, and government. The curriculum is traditional but broad, with Alabama law emphasized only in a few elective courses. The school has a national reputation for excellence in teaching although the faculty is also committed to scholarly research and writing. The school is accredited by the ABA and AALS.

■ Enrollment/Student Body

➡ *1,218 applicants*   ➡ *298 admitted first-year class 1993*
➡ *202 enrolled first-year class 1993*   ➡ *559 total full-time*
➡ *10% minority*   ➡ *38% women*
➡ *47 states & foreign countries represented*
➡ *317 undergraduate schools represented*

■ Faculty

➡ *44 total*   ➡ *25 full-time*   ➡ *19 part-time or adjunct*
➡ *11 women*   ➡ *4 minority*

■ Library and Physical Facilities

➡ *259,000 volumes & equivalents*   ➡ *library hours: week-days, 7:30 A.M.-MIDNIGHT; Sat., 9:00 A.M.-10:00 P.M.; Sun., 10:00 A.M.-MIDNIGHT; varies during holidays*   ➡ *LEXIS*
➡ *NEXIS*   ➡ *WESTLAW*   ➡ *DIALOG*   ➡ *OCLC*
➡ *7 full-time librarians*   ➡ *library seats 406*

In January 1978, the school moved into the new Law Center building, a spacious structure located on a 27-acre tract on the east side of the campus. The building has been acclaimed as one of the nation's finest educational facilities. The Law Center has a large library, containing approximately 57,005 microfilm documents.

■ Curriculum

➡ *Academic Support Program*   ➡ *90 credits required to graduate*   ➡ *degrees available: J.D.; J.D./M.B.A.; M.C.L.*
➡ *semesters, start in Aug.*
➡ *first-year class size—101 per section*

■ Special Programs

The clinical program, under the supervision of the faculty, enables law students to gain valuable practical experience in interviewing clients, preparing cases, and participating in courtroom presentations. The joint degree program enables students to earn the J.D./M.B.A. (Master of Business Administration). The LL.M. in taxation is awarded to qualified graduates of accredited law schools upon completion of 24 graduate hours. The M.C.L. (Master of Comparative Law) degree is offered to a limited number of international lawyers.

■ Admission

➡ *Bachelor's degree required*   ➡ *application deadline—March 1*   ➡ *LSAT, LSDAS required*
➡ *median GPA—3.50*   ➡ *median LSAT score—160*
➡ *application fee—$25*

A student must obtain a bachelor's degree at an accredited institution before enrolling but may apply during the senior year. Applicants must register for and take the LSAT, preferably no later than the December before enrollment, and subscribe to LSDAS for transcript analysis. Transcripts must show all schools attended and include at least three-fourths of the hours needed for graduation. Students are admitted only for the next immediate fall semester and only for full-time study. Application materials are available in September each year. Students are encouraged to submit applications early. The committee considers all information available about an applicant; however, the LSAT score and undergraduate GPA are by far the most important. Other factors considered include honors, activities, work experience, difficulty of undergraduate course of study, trends in academic performance, leadership ability, writing ability, and the applicant's personal statement. Admission decisions will also be influenced by the law school's commitment to racial, ethnic, cultural, economic, and geographic diversity. Special programs and support are available to members of minority and other diversity groups. Written letters of recommendation are not required. Personal interviews are usually not recommended.

Summer school is open to students who have completed the first year of law school (including students in good standing at other law schools), and graduation can be accelerated one semester by summer course work. The full-time faculty of 25 is comprised of graduates of leading American law schools.

■ Student Organizations

Student organizations represent diverse interests. They include: Black Law Students Association, Environmental Law Society, Trial Advocacy Association, Association for Women and the Law, International Law Society, American Civil Liberties Union Tuscaloosa/University Chapter, and Christian Legal Society.

■ Activities

A broad range of student activities adds to the students' law school experience. *The Alabama Law Review*, published three times a year and edited by students, devotes substantial space to national issues as well as issues of relevance to Alabama. Three additional publications involve student participation: *The Journal of the Legal Profession*; the *Law and Psychology Review*; and the *American Journal of Tax Policy* (American College of Tax Fellows). The law school's moot court, international moot court, and trial advocacy teams have won national honors in recent years. The Student Bar Association (SBA) provides several student services and sponsors a variety of academic and social activities.

■ Expenses and Financial Aid

➡ *tuition & fees—resident per semester, $1,469; nonresident per semester, $3,095* ➡ *estimated additional expenses— $500 books, first-year* ➡ *scholarships available* ➡ *minority scholarships available* ➡ *financial aid available—Family Financial Statement required; March 1 priority deadline*

The great majority of the students enrolled in the School of Law finance their legal education through loans, savings, earnings, and/or contributions from their families. Scholarships are awarded to approximately 25 percent of the first-year students. Scholarship recipients are identified on the basis of their applications for admission, and scholarship applications are unnecessary. Scholarships are sometimes renewable during the second and third years, often depending upon funding availability, the student's need, and whether the recipients maintain stated levels of academic achievement. Limited law school scholarship funds are available to assist extremely needy students. Applicants who have been admitted to the first-year class and who believe they qualify for these need-based scholarships should apply, using the form supplied by the School of Law and available upon request, not later than May 1 pre-

ceding the anticipated enrollment. Scholarship applications are generally required for renewal of law school scholarships. Aid is also available for law students from the university's Financial Aid Office. Further information can be obtained by writing to Director of Student Financial Services, The University of Alabama, Box 870162, Tuscaloosa, AL 35487-0162. Phone: 205.348.6756.

■ Career Services Program

The Career Services Program is designed to assist all students in their efforts to find employment. Extensive on-campus interviewing occurs.

The office has an excellent Career Resource Library. Seminars are presented on résumé writing, interviewing techniques, and job-search techniques to help students refine their job-search skills. Panel discussions are scheduled, and job fairs are supported as part of the Career Services Program.

■ Housing

The university maintains residence halls and apartment units for students. Off-campus housing is also available. For information, students may write to the Office of Housing and Residential Life, The University of Alabama, Box 870399, Tuscaloosa, AL 35487-0399.

Admission Profile Not Available

Albany Law School

80 New Scotland Avenue
Albany, NY 12208

Phone: 518.445.2326

◼ Introduction

Albany Law School, founded in 1851, is one of the nation's oldest law schools. The Law School is part of Union University, which includes Union College, Albany Medical College, and Albany College of Pharmacy. The Law School, while part of the university, has its own governing board.

Albany Law School, a member of the AALS, is fully accredited by the ABA and the Department of Education of the State of New York. The policies of the school are in full compliance with Title IX of the 1972 Education Amendments.

The City of Albany is located 150 miles from New York City and 160 miles from Boston. Albany is an exceptional laboratory for the study of law. Long established here are the agencies of state government, the legislature, the executive, and the state's highest court, the Court of Appeals. Through programs at the Law School and positions available in state government, the Albany Law School student has the opportunity to participate in those processes.

◼ Enrollment/Student Body

➟ 1,998 applicants   ➟ 920 admitted first-year class 1993
➟ 277 enrolled first-year class 1993   ➟ 772 total full-time
➟ 26 total part-time   ➟ 11% minority   ➟ 46% women
➟ 23 states & foreign countries represented
➟ 196 undergraduate schools represented

Albany Law School is considered a midsize law school. Nearly 20 percent of our students completed their undergraduate studies five or more years before starting their legal education, and almost half of our students graduated from college at least one year prior to entering law school.

◼ Faculty

➟ 78 total   ➟ 41 full-time   ➟ 37 part-time

Diversity characterizes the Albany Law School faculty. The 41 full-time professors, clinical and legal research and writing instructors possess law degrees from 24 different law schools, including Harvard, Yale, Columbia, Stanford, New York University, Northwestern, St. John's, Howard, and Georgetown. In addition, 37 adjunct professors enrich the curriculum with their expertise in specific practical areas of the law.

◼ Library and Physical Facilities

➟ 424,000 volumes & equivalents   ➟ library hours: Mon.-Thurs., 8:00 A.M.-MIDNIGHT; Fri., 8:00 A.M.-10:00 P.M.; Sat., 9:00 A.M.-9:00 P.M.;Sun., 10:00 A.M.-MIDNIGHT
➟ LEXIS   ➟ NEXIS   ➟ WESTLAW
➟ DIALOG   ➟ VU/TEXT   ➟ WILSONLINE
➟ 7 full-time librarians   ➟ library seats 492
➟ 45 personal computers available for student use

In 1986 the Schaffer Law Library, one of the finest law libraries in the country, was added to the Albany Law School Complex. In addition to lecture halls and seminar rooms, the complex features a new moot courtroom, a gymnasium, and student lounge. An open-air courtyard connects the complex and is the scene of many informal gatherings.

◼ Curriculum

➟ Academic Support Program   ➟ 87 units/credits required to graduate   ➟ 115 courses available
➟ 15 clinical options including a wide range of externships
➟ degrees offered: J.D./M.B.A.; J.D./M.P.A.; J.D.
➟ terms start in Aug. only
➟ range of first-year class size—250-275

Students may select electives after the first year from a variety of areas including business organizations, constitutional law, environmental law, family law, government administration and regulation, international law, intellectual property, labor law, and taxation.

◼ Special Programs

Clinical Legal Studies provides opportunities for upperclassmen to work and study for credit. They offer students a chance to view the legal system first hand and to begin participating in that system as professionals. Students may choose to participate in the AIDS Law Clinic, Disabilities Law Clinic, Family Violence Litigation Clinic, the Litigation Clinic, or the Placement Clinic which includes Albany County District Attorney's Office, Environmental Protection Bureau, US District Court, US Court of Appeals, NYS Supreme Court, Legal Aid Society, NYS Assembly, Prisoner's Legal Services and the US Attorney's Office. Additionally, students may choose an externship. There are over 30 public law offices in which to work and study as externs.

The Government Law Center (GLC) was established in 1978 to facilitate multidisciplinary study and research in government and the problems facing the government; to introduce students to policy analysis and to public service; and to provide a resource to government in the resolution of specific problems.

The GLC has sponsored conferences and symposia on a wide range of topics. Additionally, the GLC sponsors a series of seminars annually for students on employment opportunities in the government and public-interest sectors. Students are employed each year to assist in research projects undertaken by the GLC.

◼ Admission

➟ Bachelor's degree required   ➟ application deadline—March 15   ➟ applicants encouraged to apply early
➟ decision notification after January 31   ➟ LSAT, LSDAS required   ➟ median GPA—3.25   ➟ median LSAT score—155   ➟ application fee—$50   ➟ students with exceptional academic credentials may apply if 90 semester hours are successfully completed in a regionally accredited institution

An Admissions Committee, consisting of four full-time faculty members, reviews all parts of all applications. Albany Law School does not participate in any type of screening process whereby applicants are automatically accepted or denied. The Committee attempts to select a highly qualified and diverse student body and, therefore, takes many factors into consideration, including LSAT scores, previous scholastic achievement, employment experience, socioeconomic status, minority status, recommendations, and any exceptional circumstances pertaining to the applicant. Evaluative interviews are not part of the admissions process. Rather, applicants are encouraged to submit a written statement detailing all information that might be relevant for an admissions decision.

A small number of transfer students are usually admitted to the second-year class based on superior academic performance.

Student Activities

Students at Albany Law School are provided with opportunities to participate in educational, as well as social, activities. *Albany Law Review* is published four times a year. The *Albany Law Journal of Science & Technology* is a student publication dedicated to the development of the law as it relates to the sciences and the effect technology has upon society. Nationwide moot court competitions help students develop their legal research and advocacy skills. In addition, students can become involved in numerous organizations. The recently renovated gymnasium also provides students with an opportunity to participate in a variety of organized intramural athletic programs.

Expenses and Financial Aid

➡ *tuition & fees—$16,370, full-time; $13,115, part-time*
➡ *merit scholarships awarded on the basis of UGPA and LSAT score* ➡ *diversity scholarships awarded to students with unusual backgrounds including minorities*
➡ *need-based grants from $2,800 to $5,200 per year*

Part-time employment is available. More than 80 percent of the students receive federal, state, or law school monies. Financial aid applicants must submit the FAFSA form and Albany Law School Request for Financial Assistance, a copy of their 1993 Federal Income Tax form, and financial aid transcripts from all postsecondary institutions attended. Prospective students should file the FAFSA as soon after January 1 as possible regardless of whether or not an admissions decision has been received. Accepted applicants with a FAFSA on file in the Financial Aid Office will receive an estimate of their eligibility for all types of aid.

Most students live off-campus in moderately priced, privately owned housing. The Admissions Office maintains a listing of available accommodations. Additionally, a dormitory houses 84 law students in single rooms.

Career Services

The Career Planning Office provides career information and assistance to all students and alumni. Panels, workshops, and individual consultations are offered. Students can participate in on-campus and off-campus recruitment programs. Statistics from the past few years show an employment rate of over 92 percent for graduates.

Applicant Group for the 1993–1994 Academic Year

Albany Law School
This grid includes only applicants who earned 120-180 LSAT scores. If multiple LSAT scores are earned, placement on the grid is determined by the highest score.

LSAT Score	3.75 +		3.50 -3.74		3.25 - 3.49		3.00 - 3.24		2.75 - 2.99		2.50 - 2.74		2.25 - 2.49		2.00 - 2.24		Below 2.00		No GPA		Total	
	Apps	Adm	Apps	Adm	Apps	Adm	Apps	Adm	Apps	Adm	Apps	Adm	Apps	Adm	Apps	Adm	Apps	Adm	Apps	Adm	Apps	Adm
175 - 180	0	0	0	0	0	0	0	0	0	0	0	0	0	0	0	0	0	0	0	0	0	0
170 - 174	0	0	5	5	1	1	4	4	1	1	0	0	1	0	0	0	0	0	1	1	13	12
165 - 169	4	4	8	7	15	15	19	19	11	10	4	1	7	4	0	0	0	0	0	0	68	60
160 - 164	17	17	26	26	47	47	50	49	34	27	16	7	12	2	3	0	0	0	1	1	206	176
155 - 159	20	20	67	66	131	129	122	111	87	38	52	8	20	0	7	1	1	0	0	0	507	373
150 - 154	21	17	66	57	113	74	136	52	100	18	49	2	26	0	8	0	1	0	6	1	526	221
145 - 149	13	7	30	8	57	10	72	7	80	5	36	3	20	0	7	0	1	0	6	5	322	45
140 - 144	6	3	17	2	24	3	41	1	32	0	32	2	28	0	9	0	1	0	3	0	193	11
135 - 139	1	0	2	0	7	0	15	0	13	0	11	0	13	0	5	0	3	0	1	0	71	0
130 - 134	0	0	1	0	1	0	0	0	5	0	3	0	3	0	5	0	0	0	0	0	19	0
125 - 129	0	0	0	0	0	0	1	0	2	0	1	0	0	0	0	0	0	0	0	0	4	0
120 - 124	0	0	0	0	0	0	0	0	0	0	0	0	1	0	0	0	0	0	1	0	2	0
Total	82	68	222	171	396	279	460	243	365	99	204	23	131	6	44	1	8	0	19	8	1931	898

Apps = Number of Applicants
Adm = Number Admitted

American University—Washington College of Law

4400 Massachusetts Avenue, N.W.
Washington, DC 20016

Phone: 202.885.2606

■ Introduction

The American University's Washington College of Law offers opportunity for the study of law in the center of the nation's legal institutions. The law school is minutes from downtown Washington, but at the same time offers the facilities and ambiance of a true campus environment in one of the city's most beautiful residential neighborhoods.

Founded in 1896 by two women, the law school is national in character. It is committed to the development of the intellectual abilities and practical skills required to prepare lawyers to practice in an increasingly complex and transnational world. The school is noted for the accessibility of faculty and administration to its students.

■ Enrollment/Student Body (First-Year Class)

➠ 6,155 applicants ➠ 1,600 admitted ➠ 370 enrolled
➠ 277 total full-time ➠ 93 total part-time
➠ 32% minority ➠ 53% women
➠ 41 states & 8 foreign countries represented
➠ 180 undergraduate schools represented

■ Faculty

➠ 136 total ➠ 47 full-time ➠ 89 part-time
➠ 42 women ➠ 14 minority

■ Library and Physical Facilities

➠ 328,897 volumes & equivalents ➠ library hours: Mon.-Fri., 8:00 A.M.-MIDNIGHT; Sat., 9:00 A.M.-MIDNIGHT; Sun., 10:00 A.M.-MIDNIGHT ➠ LEXIS ➠ WESTLAW
➠ 8 full-time librarians ➠ library seats 377

The school is located on the university's 78-acre campus in northwest Washington, DC. Key features of the Alvina Reckman Meyers Law Library collection include the European Community and U.S. Government depositories and the Baxter Collection in International Law. The library was recently designated as the repository for the National Equal Justice Library, which will be an archive of primary and unique source materials dealing with legal services and public-defender programs. Students also have access to the university's library, the Library of Congress, specialized agency libraries, and other area law libraries to which the school is electronically linked. Other facilities include the John Sherman Myers law school building housing faculty offices and classrooms, and the Cassell Center complex which contains the Practicing Law Center, the admissions and career services offices, and other student offices. A new law school building is planned for opening within the next two years.

■ Curriculum

The law school offers full-time and part-time programs leading to the J.D. degree, which is awarded after satisfactory completion of 86 credit hours, 34 of which are prescribed. All degree candidates must also fulfill an upper-level writing requirement. The Socratic method is the basic form of instruction in the first year. Its purpose is to develop the skills of critical analysis, provide perspectives on the law and lawyering, and deepen understanding of fundamental legal principals. In the Legal Method program, basic legal research and writing skills are taught to groups of 14 students by practicing attorneys and upper-level assistants. In the second and third years, students elect a course of study drawing from advanced courses, seminars, independent research, externships, and clinical programs. Students are exposed to a variety of teaching processes by the law school's distinguished full-time faculty of 47. Other specialized courses are taught by eminent Washington lawyers widely recognized as experts in their fields in the private and public sectors.

■ Special Programs

While many of the advanced courses take place in a traditional classroom setting, a variety of other innovative teaching modes is available to enhance research skills and provide professional training. The Washington College of Law Practicing Law Center enjoys a national reputation for clinical education. Second-year students may participate in the Public Interest Law Clinic; third-year students may develop their lawyering abilities in the Criminal Justice Clinic, the DC Civil Litigation Clinic, the International Human Rights Clinic, the Tax Clinic, or the Appellate Clinic. The Women and the Law Program includes a clinical component in which students represent indigent women in the District of Columbia courts. This program also offers several public-education projects each year, and is designed to integrate women's legal studies into the overall curriculum and to heighten awareness about legal issues affecting women.

Complementing its outstanding curriculum in International Law, the university offers a combined J.D./M.A. in International Affairs with the School of International Service. Combined-degree programs also include a J.D./M.S. with the School of Justice, and a J.D./M.B.A. with the Kogod College of Business Administration. Graduate study is available leading to the LL.M. degree in International Legal Studies.

The externship program places upper-level students in many regulatory and administrative agencies in the city. Field components, taken simultaneously with a seminar, include such areas as security and commodities markets regulation. The Program for Advanced Studies in the Federal Regulatory Process, offered each summer, provides an intensive analysis of the federal regulatory process through lectures and optional field placements in a myriad of federal agencies and nonprofit organizations.

Admission

➤ *Bachelor's degree from accredited college or university required*   ➤ *application deadline—March 1*
➤ *rolling admission, early application preferred*
➤ *LSAT, LSDAS required*   ➤ *application fee—$55*

Applicants to the law school are admitted on the strength of their entire academic and related records. The faculty admission committee gives primary emphasis to the undergraduate record, LSAT scores, and other major accomplishments and achievements, whether academic, work-related, or extracurricular. The benefits the school derives from racial, ethnic, cultural, and geographical diversity among its students are considered in admission decisions. Members of disadvantaged and minority groups are encouraged to apply. Admission to the law school is highly competitive, and operates on a rolling admission basis, so early application is strongly encouraged.

Student Activities

The *Law Review*, the *Journal of International Law and Policy*, the *Administrative Law Journal*, and the *Journal of Gender and the Law* are edited and published by students selected on the basis of scholarship and creative research. The Moot Court Board sponsors intraschool competitions for first-year and upper-level students, and selects representatives for a number of interschool competitions, including the National Moot Court Competition. Other student activities include active

chapters of the Black Law Students Association, the Women's Law Association, the Environmental Law Society, the Hispanic Law Student Association, the Asian Pacific American Law Student Association, the National Lawyers Guild, the Federalist Society, the Lambda Law Students Association, and many other student groups.

Expenses and Financial Aid

➤ *tuition & fees—$17,566; part-time, $651/credit*
➤ *fees—full-time, $320; part-time, $224*
➤ *estimated additional expenses—$8,300 (room, board, books)*
➤ *need-based scholarships available*
➤ *GAPSFAS form due to GAPSFAS by Feb. 15 for scholarships*

Career Services

The Office of Career Services provides individual assistance to students on career counseling and the techniques of job searching. The office arranges for both on- and off-campus recruitment for summer and permanent legal positions, and participates in a variety of hiring consortia. Graduates from 1992 report employment in the following areas of practice: private practice, 45 percent; business and industry, 9.5 percent; government, 16.6 percent; judicial clerkships, 20 percent; public interest, 4 percent; other, 4 percent. A majority of the law school's alumni practice in the Washington, DC metropolitan area; however, its graduates can be found in every state and many foreign countries.

Applicant Group for the 1993–1994 Academic Year

American University—Washington College of Law
This grid includes only applicants who earned 120-180 LSAT scores under standard administrations.

LSAT Score	GPA																				
	3.75 +		3.50 -3.74		3.25 - 3.49		3.00 - 3.24		2.75 - 2.99		2.50 - 2.74		2.25 - 2.49		2.00 - 2.24		Below 2.00		No GPA		Total	
	Apps	Adm	Apps	Adm	Apps	Adm	Apps	Adm	Apps	Adm	Apps	Adm	Apps	Adm	Apps	Adm	Apps	Adm	Apps	Adm	Apps	Adm
175 - 180	0	0	1	1	1	1	0	0	2	2	1	0	0	0	0	0	0	0	0	0	5	4
170 - 174	4	3	10	9	21	21	19	16	15	10	9	8	3	2	0	0	0	0	1	0	82	69
165 - 169	21	21	44	41	86	81	98	89	64	31	34	15	15	3	1	0	0	0	3	0	366	281
160 - 164	62	58	153	138	296	217	274	117	136	30	64	6	42	5	9	1	1	0	10	3	1047	575
155 - 159	87	67	242	104	466	121	395	51	236	25	111	13	55	3	17	1	2	0	17	2	1628	387
150 - 154	46	16	181	32	296	35	316	45	202	20	103	2	67	2	24	1	2	0	15	2	1252	155
145 - 149	19	6	69	13	157	21	177	22	154	6	121	8	44	0	23	1	4	0	12	1	780	78
140 - 144	7	2	24	5	57	7	81	8	98	1	80	2	45	0	20	1	6	0	14	0	432	26
135 - 139	2	0	4	1	18	0	35	0	31	0	47	1	32	1	11	0	5	0	7	0	192	3
130 - 134	0	0	3	0	1	0	8	0	14	0	15	0	18	0	10	0	3	0	4	0	76	0
125 - 129	0	0	0	0	0	0	2	0	3	0	2	0	4	0	1	0	1	0	0	0	13	0
120 - 124	0	0	0	0	0	0	0	0	1	0	0	0	0	0	0	0	0	0	0	0	1	0
Total	248	173	731	344	1399	504	1405	348	956	125	587	55	325	16	116	5	24	0	83	8	5874	1578

Apps = Number of Applicants
Adm = Number Admitted
Reflects 96% of the total applicant pool.

University of Arizona College of Law

Tucson, AZ 85721

Phone: 602.621.3477, 621.7666 Assistant Dean Admissions

■ Introduction

The University of Arizona College of Law was founded in 1915, is the oldest law school in Arizona, and has a rich and distinguished history. The college is an integral part of the University of Arizona, one of the nation's leading research institutions. The College of Law has a national reputation for providing its students a high quality education in a collegial, friendly, and intellectually challenging atmosphere. The College of Law is located in Tucson, an environmentally beautiful and culturally rich city, which is home to an active legal and judicial community. The college is approved by the ABA, and has been a member of the AALS since 1931.

■ Enrollment/Student Body

➡ 2,333 applicants   ➡ 354 admitted first-year class 1993
➡ 150 enrolled first-year class 1993   ➡ 480 total full-time
➡ 27% minority ·   ➡ 45% women   ➡ 30 states & foreign countries represented   ➡ 85 undergraduate schools represented   ➡ 3% persons with disabilities

The students of the College of Law bring varied work and life experiences to the College. The average age of students entering in the fall of 1993 was 27; with 21 percent of the class age 30 or above, and 18 percent of the class holding graduate degrees.

■ Faculty

➡ 56 total   ➡ 28 full-time   ➡ 28 part-time or adjunct
➡ 15 women   ➡ 5 minority

With a ratio of 16 to 1, the college has one of the most favorable student-faculty ratios of any American law school. Many members of the faculty are nationally recognized legal scholars. Five members of the faculty hold endowed chairs. Five faculty members with national and international reputations hold joint appointments in other colleges within the university.

■ Library and Physical Facilities

➡ 332,200 volumes & equivalents   ➡ library hours: Mon.-Thurs., 7:00 A.M.-11:45 P.M.; Fri., 7:00 A.M.-10:00 P.M.; Sat., 8:00 A.M.-8:00 P.M.; Sun., 9:00 A.M.-11:45 P.M.   ➡ LEXIS
➡ NEXIS   ➡ WESTLAW   ➡ OCLC   ➡ DIALOG
➡ 7 full-time librarians   ➡ library seats 353

The College of Law occupies a modern building, which is fully wheelchair accessible, with outstanding classroom, library, and conference facilities. The Arizona State Supreme Court convenes annually at the college and hears arguments on a variety of cases. The library, housing a major research facility, is one of the foremost legal research facilities in the Southwest. There is an expanding foreign law collection emphasizing Latin American law and an International Commercial Law Center within the library. The library houses computer terminals and a student computer laboratory equipped with the most modern technology.

■ Curriculum

➡ Academic Support Program   ➡ BRIDGE (a week-long prelaw program for minority and disabled enrollees)
➡ 85 credits required to graduate   ➡ 80 courses available
➡ degrees available: J.D.; J.D./Ph.D.; J.D./M.A.; J.D./M.B.A.; J.D./M.P.A.   ➡ semesters, start in Aug.

The college has committed substantial faculty resources to the development of research and writing skills. Each first-year student meets in a section of approximately 25 students in one of the first-semester courses. In addition to the substantive course material, the student receives rigorous instruction in legal research and writing. Students must also complete a special writing seminar during the second or third year.

After completing the first-year requirements, students have considerable flexibility in considering second- and third-year course work. The college offers a rich variety of courses taught by nationally recognized faculty, including courses in Business and Corporate Law, Employment Law, Criminal Law, Constitutional Law, Remedies, International Law, Tax, Health Law and Medical Ethics, Indian Law, Environmental Law, Legal History, Water Law, and a wealth of Trial Advocacy offerings.

Students may choose clinical courses offered in criminal and civil law, participating in classroom instruction and field placements in a variety of settings.

In addition, the college sponsors several Congressional and state legislative internships and internship programs with the Navajo, Pascua Yaqui, White Mountain Apache, and Tohono O'Odham tribal governments.

The course of study leading to the J.D. degree is normally completed in six semesters of resident study; a cumulative average of 2.0 (C) is required to graduate.

■ Admission

➡ Bachelor's degree required   ➡ application deadline—March 1, rolling admission Dec. through May, early application preferred   ➡ LSAT, LSDAS required
➡ median GPA—3.38   ➡ median LSAT score—162
➡ application fee—$35

Admission to the College of Law is very selective. There are two ways to be admitted to the College: through the Presumptive Admission process and through the Admission Committee. In the Presumptive process, all applicants are initially ranked according to an index score combining undergraduate grade-point average and LSAT score in a formula. Some applicants are then admitted primarily based upon their index rankings.

In the Admission Committee process, a portion of those students who are not admitted on the basis of their index score in the presumptive process are selected for further consideration by the Admission Committee. In making decisions, the Admission Committee considers all relevant personal information, including graduate education; nature of undergraduate experience; distinctive ethnic or cultural backgrounds; unusual work and travel experience; unique talents, interests, accomplishments; special personal goals; extracurricular activities; or other circumstances such as personal or family responsibilities. The college is very committed to enrolling students who bring diverse perspectives to the college and the legal profession and encourages applications from minority, disadvantaged, and disabled candidates. Students begin their studies in the fall only and must have completed an undergraduate degree from an accredited four-year college. The deadline for completed applications, including transcripts, LSAT scores and two letters of recommendation is March 1. Applicants must take the LSAT no later than the December prior to the year of expected enrollment. A waiver of the fee is available when requested and explained in writing.

Student Activities

The *Arizona Law Review* and *The Arizona Journal of International and Comparative Law* are well-known, student-operated and student-edited scholarly journals on current legal problems. The law school newspaper, *The Arizona Advocate*, serves as a voice for student and faculty opinions on a variety of issues. The students in

the moot court program participate in national and state appellate advocacy competitions.

The student body is self-governing through the Student Bar Association. Students also participate in making law school policy by serving as voting members of student-faculty committees. There is a variety of law student organizations and outstanding scholarship is recognized by membership in the Order of the Coif.

Special Programs

The College of Law cooperates with other colleges at the University of Arizona and offers joint J.D./Ph.D. programs in Philosophy, Psychology, or Economics; a J.D./M.A. program in Economics; a J.D./M.B.A. program; and a J.D./M.P.A. Other concurrent degree programs are available by special arrangement.

Expenses and Financial Aid

➤ *tuition & fees—full-time residents, $2,844; nonresidents, $8,350* ➤ *estimated additional expenses—$9,000 (room, board, travel, books, misc.)* ➤ *scholarships available: need-based & merit-based; tuition waivers* ➤ *minority scholarships available: Graduate Minority Fellowships, Cordova Scholarships, cash awards* ➤ *financial aid available* ➤*USAF preferred—due March 1*

The cost of living in Tucson is relatively modest.

Applicant Group for the 1993–1994 Academic Year

University of Arizona College of Law
This grid includes only applicants who earned 120-180 LSAT scores under standard administrations.

LSAT Score	GPA																					
	3.75 +		3.50 -3.74		3.25 - 3.49		3.00 - 3.24		2.75 - 2.99		2.50 - 2.74		2.25 - 2.49		2.00 - 2.24		Below 2.00		No GPA		Total	
	Apps	Adm	Apps	Adm	Apps	Adm	Apps	Adm	Apps	Adm	Apps	Adm	Apps	Adm	Apps	Adm	Apps	Adm	Apps	Adm	Apps	Adm
175 - 180	1	1	0	0	1	1	0	0	0	0	0	0	0	0	0	0	0	0	0	0	2	2
170 - 174	5	5	1	1	6	6	3	3	0	0	2	0	0	0	1	0	0	0	0	0	18	15
165 - 169	11	11	26	25	29	25	17	10	24	8	14	5	5	0	1	0	0	0	1	0	128	84
160 - 164	45	30	69	28	100	38	85	18	55	5	36	4	11	1	2	0	1	0	2	2	406	126
155 - 159	43	7	117	17	138	16	146	6	85	5	44	3	19	2	11	0	0	0	7	1	610	57
150 - 154	29	2	72	3	124	10	120	7	98	6	45	2	25	1	6	0	0	0	0	0	519	31
145 - 149	12	0	28	3	63	3	71	3	66	1	43	3	24	1	10	0	4	0	6	0	327	14
140 - 144	1	0	10	0	22	0	31	0	23	0	24	0	26	0	16	0	2	0	2	0	157	0
135 - 139	1	0	3	0	5	0	13	0	11	0	9	0	7	0	5	0	2	0	3	0	59	0
130 - 134	0	0	1	0	2	0	2	0	4	0	5	0	3	0	4	0	0	0	1	0	22	0
125 - 129	0	0	0	0	0	0	0	0	2	0	2	0	3	0	0	0	0	0	1	0	8	0
120 - 124	0	0	0	0	0	0	0	0	0	0	0	0	0	0	0	0	0	0	0	0	0	0
Total	148	56	327	77	490	99	488	47	368	25	224	17	123	5	56	0	9	0	23	3	2256	329

Apps = Number of Applicants
Adm = Number Admitted
Reflects 96% of the total applicant pool.
This application profile does not include 10 admits whose offers of admission were deferred until the fall of 1994.

Arizona State University College of Law

Tempe, AZ 85287-7906   Phone: 602.965.7896

■ Introduction

The College of Law is located on the campus of the Arizona State University in Tempe, a suburb of Phoenix. Established in 1966, the law school was accredited by the AALS and ABA in 1969. In the fall of 1992 the college celebrated its 25th anniversary and the accomplishments it has achieved in a relatively short time.

■ Enrollment/Student Body

→ 2,282 applicants → 359 admitted first-year class 1993
→ 156 enrolled first-year class 1993 → 512 total full-time
→ 30% minority → 41% women
→ 23 states & foreign countries represented
→ 71 undergraduate schools represented
→ 1993 entering class, 71% resident, 29% nonresident

■ Faculty

→ 40 total → 30 full-time → 10 part-time or adjunct
→ 10 women → 2 minority

■ Library and Physical Facilities

→ 311,000 volumes & equivalents → library hours: Mon.-Thurs., 7:00 A.M.-MIDNIGHT; Fri. 7:00 A.M.-10:00 P.M.; Sat., 8:00 A.M.-10:00 P.M.; Sun., 10:00 A.M.-MIDNIGHT
→ LEXIS → WESTLAW → 6 full-time librarians
→ library seats 590

Armstrong Hall, a modern, air-conditioned structure, is architecturally designed for the special functions of legal education. Among its features are classrooms with seating on elevated tiers to facilitate dialogue between professors and students; the Willard H. Pedrick Great Hall, seating 400, which serves not only as a courtroom, but also as a location for campus events; and a trial courtroom which is equipped to permit videotaping of trials and other advocacy exercises to facilitate instruction in litigation techniques. Armstrong Hall houses a legal clinic, providing easy access for law student interns.

The John J. Ross—William C. Blakley Law Library is housed in a dramatic and functional new building that opened in August 1993. The collection includes growing special collections in the areas of international law, Indian law, Mexican law, and law and technology. The library has a thirty station computer lab, as well as LEXIS and WESTLAW rooms each containing ten stations, 27 meeting and study rooms and a microforms facility.

■ Curriculum

→ Academic Support Program → Law School Clinic, Prosecutor Clinic, Externship Programs → 87 units/credits required to graduate → 85 courses available → degrees available: J.D.; J.D./M.B.A.; J.D./M.H.S.A.; J.D./Ph.D. Justice Studies → fall semester starts in Aug., spring semester starts in Jan. → range of first-year class size—35-140

The College of Law awards the J.D. degree following a three-year course of study. The first year consists of a required curriculum. In the following years, the student selects from a wide number of legal courses, including small-group seminars, clinic internships, independent and interdisciplinary study, and a trial practice program. Many students also choose to enhance their theoretical classroom knowledge with the practical experience of an externship. The college offers a variety of externship opportunities with agencies and governmental offices.

■ Center for the Study of Law, Science, and Technology

The Center for the Study of Law, Science, and Technology was established in 1984 in response to the increasing number of social and legal questions arising out of new scientific and technological development in areas such as computers, communications, medicine, genetics, space technology, and nuclear power.

The center conducts research, engages in curricular development, sponsors papers and conferences, and brings visiting scholars to the law school. The College of Law co-edits the Jurimetrics Journal, a quarterly journal of the ABA Section of Science and Technology.

■ Clinical Programs

The College of Law offers a variety of clinical courses. In the Law School Clinic students gain experience in interviewing, legal research and writing, fact investigation, discovery, pretrial procedure, and oral advocacy in the courtroom. Students may be assigned to a variety of civil matters. Prosecutor Clinic interns prosecute misdemeanor charges in city courts in Tempe and neighboring communities.

■ Indian Legal Program

The Indian Legal Program (ILP) at the Arizona State University College of Law actively recruits Native American students and promotes Indian legal education in the course curriculum. The ILP also seeks to provide public service to Native American tribes and tribal governments.

The ASU College of Law student body currently includes students from 21 different Native American tribes.

■ Student Activities

The Student Bar Association sponsors numerous activities including lectures and social events. Second- and third-year students publish a professional law review, Arizona State Law Journal. Students also direct the moot court program and participate in national and international moot court competitions. In addition, law students publish a newspaper, Devil's Advocate, and have formed such independent organizations as Women's Law Student Association, Chicano/Latino Law Students Association, American Indian Law Students, Asian Law

Students Association, legal fraternities, and a chapter of the Black Law Students Association. Many students participate in pro bono activities including the Volunteer Income Tax Assistance program and the Homeless Legal Assistance Project. Students also serve as voting members of several College of Law committees.

■ Admission

➡ *Bachelor's degree required from an accredited institution*
➡ *application deadline—Feb. 15* ➡ *LSAT, LSDAS required*
➡ *median GPA—3.40* ➡ *median LSAT score—161*
➡ *application fee—$35*

With approximately 14 applicants for each place in the first-year class, admission to the College of Law is highly selective. Such varied factors as the undergraduate education, LSAT score, trend of college grades, course-selection patterns, quality and grading patterns of undergraduate institutions, work or other nonacademic experience, and cultural or socioeconomic background are considered in the admission decision.

First-year students are admitted only for the fall semester. The deadline to submit an application is February 15. The deadline for completed applications, including an LSDAS report and a personal statement, is March 15. Applicants must take the LSAT no later than December. Transcript evaluation by LSDAS is required.

Transfer applications will be considered on a space-available basis for students with excellent records.

Students who are members of minority groups are encouraged to apply. The College of Law has a vital diversity admission policy, a policy to which the college is enthusiastically committed. Students from diverse cultural, ethnic, and racial backgrounds enrich the educational experience of all students and faculty and ultimately increase the number of minority lawyers in the country.

■ Expenses and Financial Aid

➡ *tuition & fees—full-time resident, $2,844 per year; nonresident, $8,350 per year* ➡ *estimated additional expenses—$7,000 (living expenses, books/9-month academic year)*
➡ *scholarships available: merit & need-based*
➡ *minority scholarships available* ➡ *financial aid available*

■ Placement

The law school Placement Office provides assistance to students and alumni seeking employment. Placement services include a computerized job line and bulletin board of job openings, a resource library, an alumni mentor program and workshops on résumé writing, interviewing and research techniques. Special-interest workshops are offered on various topics such as clerkship positions and public interest law opportunities. The Placement Office also arranges for on-campus interviews with law firms and governmental agencies.

Applicant Group for the 1993–1994 Academic Year

Arizona State University College of Law

LSAT Score	GPA									
	3.75 +	3.50 - 3.74	3.25 - 3.49	3.00 - 3.24	2.75 - 2.99	2.50 - 2.74	2.25 - 2.49	2.00 - 2.24	Below 2.00	NoGPA
175-180										
170-174										
165-169										
160-164										
155-159										
150-154										
145-149										
140-144										
135-139										
130-134										
125-129										
120-124										

■ Good Possibility   ■ Possible   □ Unlikely

University of Arkansas School of Law—Fayetteville

Robert A. Leflar Law Center
Fayetteville, AR 72701

Phone: 501.575.3102

■ Introduction

The University of Arkansas School of Law is located on the main university campus at Fayetteville, a city of 42,000 in Northwest Arkansas. The School of Law was established in 1924 and has continuously sought to provide high quality legal education in a university community. In 1926 the School of Law was approved by the ABA, and in 1927 the school became a member of the AALS.

■ Enrollment/Student Body

➡ 1,028 applicants   ➡ 358 admitted first-year class 1993
➡ 151 enrolled first-year class 1993   ➡ 419 total full-time
➡ 9% minority   ➡ 36% women
➡ 31 states & foreign countries represented
➡ 110 undergraduate schools represented

Although 80 percent of the students are Arkansas residents, others are from every part of the United States. Since the school has no undergraduate course prerequisites, the academic backgrounds and nonacademic experiences of students are varied.

■ Faculty

➡ 40 total   ➡ 33 full-time   ➡ 7 part-time or adjunct
➡ 9 women   ➡ 2 minority

■ Library and Physical Facilities

➡ 220,000 volumes & equivalents   ➡ library hours: Mon.-Thurs., 7:00 A.M.-MIDNIGHT; Fri., 7:00 A.M.-10:00 P.M.; Sat., 9:00 A.M.-10:00 P.M.; Sun., 1:00 P.M.-MIDNIGHT; 107 total hours
➡ LEXIS   ➡ WESTLAW   ➡ Legislate
➡ 6 full-time librarians   ➡ library seats 346

The library is expanding at a rate of over 10,000 volumes a year. Students are trained in the techniques of computer-assisted legal research as well as in the traditional research methods. The law library is a federal and state depository for government documents.

■ Curriculum

➡ 90 credits required to graduate   ➡ 102 courses available
➡ degrees available: J.D.; J.D./M.B.A.   ➡ semesters, start in Aug.   ➡ range of first-year class size—30-75

The primary function of the University of Arkansas School of Law is to prepare lawyers who will render the highest quality of professional service to their clients, who are interested in and capable of furthering legal process and reform, and who are prepared to fill the vital role of the lawyer as a community leader. The school offers a full-time, three-year program leading to the J.D. degree. The degree is conferred upon satisfactory completion of 90 semester hours, including 44 hours of required courses. The first-year curriculum is required. A broad selection of elective second- and third-year courses is available. Students who have completed the first year of law school may earn up to 12 semester hours

of credit in summer school, and graduation can be accelerated one semester by summer course work. The School of Law offers a joint J.D./M.B.A. program with the College of Business Administration. If a student is accepted into both programs, a maximum of six hours of approved upper-level elective law courses may be used on duplicative credit toward the M.B.A. degree and a maximum of six hours of approved graduate courses in business administration may be used as duplicative credit toward the J.D. degree. The Graduate Program in Agricultural Law provides opportunities for advanced study, creative research, and specialized professional training in this rapidly developing area of law. The program is designed to prepare a small number of carefully selected attorneys as specialists in the legal problems of agricultural production, distribution, and marketing. Applicants for admission as candidates for the Master of Laws (LL.M.) in Agricultural Law must have earned a J.D. or LL.B. degree from a fully accredited law school. The applicant must have demonstrated a high degree of academic excellence as evidenced by high academic standing, law review membership, or other educational or professional achievement indicating potential for success in graduate study.

■ Admission

➡ B.A. required   ➡ application deadline—April 1, rolling admission, early application preferred
➡ LSAT, LSDAS required   ➡ median GPA—3.16
➡ median LSAT score—155

First-year students are admitted in the fall and only for full-time study. Prior to enrolling in the School of Law, applicants must have completed all requirements for an undergraduate degree from an accredited four-year college. Admission is based on the applicant's LSAT score and undergraduate GPA. In a small percentage of cases involving Arkansas residents only, additional criteria such as vocational or professional experience, graduate work, and progressive improvement in college work are considered by a faculty admissions committee. Black applicants who are Arkansas residents should contact the Admissions Office concerning a minority admissions program. A preference is given to Arkansas residents; for the current status of this preference, contact the school. A nonrefundable tuition deposit is required of all admitted candidates. The law school's application deadline is April 1 of the year in which admission is sought; however, applicants are requested to apply by January 1 to expedite the selection and notification process. Applicants must take the LSAT no later than February. Applications completed after April 1 will be considered only on a space-available basis.

■ Housing

Housing for single students is available in campus dormitories; apartments are also available for married students. Applicants should write to the Housing Office, University of Arkansas, Fayetteville, AR 72701. A variety of private off-campus housing is available in Fayetteville and surrounding communities, within easy commuting distance of the law school.

■ Student Activities

The *Arkansas Law Review* is a legal periodical published quarterly by the students of the School of Law in cooperation with the Arkansas Bar Association. Candidates for the *Review* are selected on the basis of scholarship and writing ability. Students in their second and third years are encouraged to compete in an intramural moot court competition, and Arkansas students participate in national moot court competitions. The University of Arkansas School of Law also participates in the ABA Law Student Division Client Counseling Competition. The law school operates a legal aid clinic providing counseling and representation for university students and indigent persons seeking legal assistance. An Arkansas Supreme Court Rule permits senior law students, upon certification and under supervision, to appear in court on a no-fee basis. The Student Bar Association sponsors a variety of academic and social activities. All students are also eligible for membership in the Law Student Division of the Arkansas Bar Association. Three of the largest national legal fraternities, Delta Theta Phi, Phi Alpha Delta, and Phi Delta Phi, maintain active chapters at the school. The Women's Law Student Association was organized to provide an opportunity for women to discuss and work with common professional interests and problems. Members of the Arkansas Chapter of Black Law Students Association work as a collective body to inform black students of the

availability and advantages of a legal education, to promote the academic success of black law students at Arkansas, and to increase the awareness and commitment of the legal profession to the black community.

■ Expenses and Financial Aid

➡ *tuition & fees—full-time resident, $2,876; nonresident, $6,020*   ➡ *scholarships available*
➡ *minority scholarships available*

Students are expected to make sufficient financial arrangements for the first year of study without the necessity of seeking employment. All law students are required to be full-time students. All financial aid in the form of Perkins Loans (formerly NDSL), higher education loans, and work-study grants is processed by the University of Arkansas Office of Student Financial Aid, University of Arkansas, Fayetteville, AR 72701. A limited number of law school-administered scholarships are available to entering students. Applications are distributed following fall registration in August.

■ Career Services

The University of Arkansas School of Law feels a definite obligation to assist its graduates in securing suitable employment and maintains an active placement program on a year-round basis. Representatives of law firms of all sizes, banks, business organizations, and governmental agencies visit the school annually and interview third-year students for permanent employment and second-year students for summer positions. A degree from the University of Arkansas School of Law will qualify students to seek admission to the bar in every state. And, each year, a number of Arkansas graduates accept employment in other states.

Applicant Group for the 1993–1994 Academic Year

University of Arkansas School of Law—Fayetteville
This grid includes only applicants who earned 120-180 LSAT scores under standard administrations.

LSAT Score	3.75 +		3.50 -3.74		3.25 - 3.49		3.00 - 3.24		2.75 - 2.99		2.50 - 2.74		2.25 - 2.49		2.00 - 2.24		Below 2.00		No GPA		Total	
	Apps	Adm	Apps	Adm	Apps	Adm	Apps	Adm	Apps	Adm	Apps	Adm	Apps	Adm	Apps	Adm	Apps	Adm	Apps	Adm	Apps	Adm
175-180	0	0	0	0	0	0	0	0	0	0	0	0	0	0	0	0	0	0	0	0	0	0
170-174	0	0	1	1	1	1	0	0	0	0	0	0	0	0	0	0	0	0	0	0	2	2
165-169	1	1	1	1	3	3	1	1	3	3	2	1	0	0	0	0	0	0	0	0	11	10
160-164	9	7	5	5	4	4	13	13	10	9	10	10	5	3	3	0	1	0	0	0	60	51
155-159	11	11	15	12	22	21	32	31	24	20	22	10	17	7	3	1	0	0	5	0	151	113
150-154	11	10	25	24	50	34	58	27	41	12	34	6	18	2	11	0	0	0	5	0	253	115
145-149	7	6	19	10	35	9	52	9	45	3	41	1	22	0	9	0	3	0	4	1	237	39
140-144	3	2	7	1	20	1	21	2	27	0	33	0	24	2	9	2	4	0	8	0	156	10
135-139	0	0	2	0	3	0	10	1	7	0	14	1	5	0	5	1	2	0	7	0	55	3
130-134	0	0	0	0	1	0	0	0	4	1	6	0	6	1	1	0	4	0	1	0	23	2
125-129	0	0	0	0	0	0	4	0	1	0	4	0	0	0	0	0	0	0	1	0	10	0
120-124	0	0	0	0	0	0	0	0	0	0	0	0	0	0	1	0	0	0	0	0	1	0
Total	42	37	75	54	139	73	191	84	162	48	166	29	97	15	42	4	14	0	31	1	959	345

Apps = Number of Applicants
Adm = Number Admitted
Reflects 94% of the total applicant pool.

University of Arkansas at Little Rock School of Law

1201 McAlmont St.
Little Rock, AR 72202-5142

Phone: 501.324.9439

■ Introduction

The School of Law is one of seven colleges and schools that form the University of Arkansas at Little Rock. The School of Law is located in the heart of metropolitan Little Rock, approximately six miles from the main campus of the university. The law school enrolls 421 students out of a total UALR enrollment of 12,070.

UALR is fully accredited by the North Central Association of Colleges and Schools. The law school is approved by the ABA and is a member of the AALS.

■ Enrollment/Student Body

➤ *654 applicants*   ➤ *245 admitted first-year class 1993*
➤ *149 enrolled first-year class 1993*   ➤ *276 total full-time*
➤ *145 total part-time*   ➤ *15% minority*
➤ *48% women*   ➤ *22 states & foreign countries represented*
➤ *125 undergraduate schools represented*

■ Faculty

➤ *45 total*   ➤ *25 full-time*   ➤ *20 part-time or adjunct*
➤ *11 women*   ➤ *5 minority*

■ Library and Physical Facilities

➤ *230,000 volumes & equivalents*   ➤ *98 library hours/week*   ➤ *LEXIS*   ➤ *NEXIS*   ➤ *WESTLAW*
➤ *DIALOG*   ➤ *Case-Base*   ➤ *5 full-time librarians*
➤ *library seats 378*

In August 1992, the School of Law moved to the new law center building. This 140,000-square-foot building is next to MacArthur Park, a 40-acre expanse of greenery, ponds, and gazebos. The five-story atrium library houses conference rooms, open and private carrels, and a reading room, as well as computer labs offering word processing, instructional software, legal research databases, and interactive video.

■ Curriculum

➤ *Academic Support Program*   ➤ *87 credits required to graduate*   ➤ *101 courses available*   ➤ *degrees available: J.D.; J.D./M.B.A.*   ➤ *semesters, start in Aug.*
➤ *range of first-year class size—47-99*

The School of Law offers a program of legal education in both day and evening divisions. The day division operates a full-time program, with an average course load per semester of 15 hours. A full-time student will normally complete the course of study in three years. The average course load per semester in the part-time evening program is 10 hours; the maximum load is 11 hours. The part-time course of study is normally completed in four years. The first-year curriculum is prescribed.

■ Special Programs

The School of Law is noted for its practice skills programs in the upper years. All students are required to enroll in a course in trial advocacy conducted in the law school's trial courtroom. Additionally, students may enroll in other classroom courses with a clinical emphasis and participate in the school's legal clinic. An Arkansas Supreme Court Rule permits senior law students, upon certification and under supervision, to represent clients in civil and criminal cases. Students enrolled in the clinic represent indigent clients under the supervision of law school faculty members. The School of Law offers a joint J.D./M.B.A. degree with the UALR College of Business Administration.

■ Admission

➤ *Bachelor's degree required*   ➤ *application deadline— April 1 (strictly enforced)*   ➤ *LSAT, LSDAS required*
➤ *median GPA—3.12*   ➤ *median LSAT score—152*
➤ *application fee—$40*
➤*rolling admission, early application preferred*

The School of Law enrolls 130 to 150 students each year. At least 80 percent of the entering students are Arkansas residents. The majority are selected on the basis of LSAT scores and undergraduate GPAs, while approximately 40 percent are selected by using additional criteria, such as letters of recommendation, work experience, graduate education, extracurricular activities, evidence of strong motivation and maturity, ethnicity disadvantages, underrepresentation of minorities in the legal profession, and diversity of backgrounds. Nonresident students are selected on the basis of LSAT scores and undergraduate GPAs.

A specific prelaw curriculum is not required. The School of Law subscribes to the comments found in the introduction to this handbook. Each applicant must hold a degree from an accredited college or university. Prospective applicants should contact the Admissions Office as early as possible for details about admission requirements. Students are enrolled only in the fall. Application for admission should be made as early as possible during the school year preceding the date of desired admission and must be completed by April 1 of the calendar year of desired admission.

■ Housing

UALR does not maintain student residence halls for law students; however, numerous private quarters are located within easy commuting distance of the law school.

■ Activities

Law students participate in the many activities generally available at larger law schools. The *UALR Law Journal*, a scholarly publication edited by students at the law school, publishes student notes and comments as well as articles by noted legal educators, judges, and practicing attorneys. A special feature is the Annual Survey of Arkansas Law. A number of prominent speakers are brought to the School of Law each year. The School of Law participates in the national trial advocacy competitions and several appellate moot court competitions. All students may become members of an active student bar association, and advanced students are eligible for membership in the Law Student Division of the Arkansas Bar Association. The Arkansas Bar Association and the School of Law were among the first such institutions in the country to establish this type of student-practitioner relationship. Membership is also available in the Law Student Division of the ABA. Students are represented on some faculty committees and are represented by elected students, who have a vote, at all general faculty meetings. The School of Law has many other student organizations, including the Black Law Students Association, Federalist Society, National Lawyers Guild, Christian Legal Society, Environmental Law Society, and units of Phi Alpha Delta, Delta Theta Phi, and Phi Delta Phi legal fraternities.

■ Expenses and Financial Aid

➡ *full-time tuition—resident, $1,356/semester; nonresident, $2,928/semester* ➡ *estimated additional expenses— $332/semester (books, $250; activity, $10; facility, $40; library $2/credit hour)* ➡ *part-time tuition—resident, $113/hr.; nonresident, $244/hr.* ➡ *scholarships available* ➡ *financial aid available* ➡ *due May 1: application for Federal Student Aid, UALR Financial Aid Student Data Form*

A growing number of scholarships are available to second- and third-year students who demonstrate financial need and possess a strong academic record. The School of Law participates in the Perkins Loan (formerly NDSL), Federal Guaranteed Bank Loan, LEEP, and College Workstudy programs. Short-term student loans are also available. The School of Law requires that applicants for financial aid complete the Free Application for Federal Student Aid, and applicants anticipating financial aid should complete this form. Requests for financial assistance should be addressed to Director of Student Aid, UALR, 2801 South University, Little Rock, AR 72204. Phone: 501.569.3130.

■ Career Services

The Law School maintains an active placement office with the goal of maximizing employment opportunities for both students and alumni. The placement office arranges for on-campus interviews by employers, maintains an up-to-date file of employment opportunities, provides a résumé service whereby students' résumés are forwarded to distant employers of their choice, offers employment counseling, and makes available a number of books and publications concerning legal employment.

Applicant Group for the 1993–1994 Academic Year

University of Arkansas at Little Rock School of Law
This grid includes only applicants who earned 120-180 LSAT scores under standard administrations.

LSAT Score	3.75 + Apps	Adm	3.50 -3.74 Apps	Adm	3.25 - 3.49 Apps	Adm	3.00 - 3.24 Apps	Adm	2.75 - 2.99 Apps	Adm	2.50 - 2.74 Apps	Adm	2.25 - 2.49 Apps	Adm	2.00 - 2.24 Apps	Adm	Below 2.00 Apps	Adm	No GPA Apps	Adm	Total Apps	Adm
175 - 180	0	0	0	0	0	0	0	0	0	0	0	0	0	0	0	0	0	0	0	0	0	0
170 - 174	0	0	1	1	0	0	0	0	1	0	0	0	0	0	0	0	0	0	0	0	2	1
165 - 169	0	0	1	1	2	2	2	2	1	0	2	0	1	1	0	0	0	0	0	0	9	6
160 - 164	4	4	5	4	3	3	8	7	8	5	6	5	1	0	0	0	1	1	0	0	35	29
155 - 159	6	6	13	13	18	17	19	16	14	8	10	3	9	4	2	1	1	1	3	2	95	71
150 - 154	9	7	19	14	24	14	34	15	21	10	22	4	13	4	4	2	1	0	2	1	147	71
145 - 149	7	4	12	6	22	5	22	5	31	8	22	4	12	2	8	1	4	0	0	0	139	35
140 - 144	3	1	7	2	10	1	20	3	19	3	19	2	11	4	6	0	3	0	6	0	104	16
135 - 139	0	0	1	0	4	0	13	0	4	0	13	0	5	0	6	0	1	0	5	0	52	0
130 - 134	0	0	1	0	0	0	1	0	2	0	3	0	5	0	1	0	3	0	0	0	16	0
125 - 129	0	0	0	0	1	0	1	0	1	0	4	0	0	0	1	0	1	0	3	0	11	0
120 - 124	0	0	0	0	0	0	0	0	0	0	0	0	0	0	0	0	0	0	1	0	1	0
Total	29	22	60	41	84	42	120	48	102	34	101	18	57	15	28	4	15	2	20	3	611	229

Apps = Number of Applicants
Adm = Number Admitted
Reflects 93% of the total applicant pool.

University of Baltimore School of Law

1420 North Charles Street
Baltimore, MD 21201-5779

Phone: 410.837.4459, Fax: 410.837.4450

■ Introduction

The University of Baltimore is one of eleven institutions that comprise the University of Maryland System. It offers upper-division, graduate, and professional academic programs through the Yale Gordon College of Liberal Arts, the Robert G. Merrick School of Business, and the School of Law. Among its resources devoted to public-interest research and analysis of contemporary issues are the Hoffberger Center for Professional Ethics, the Center for Business and Economic Studies, and the Schaefer Center for Public Policy. The School of Law is accredited by the American Bar Association and is a member of the Association of American Law Schools. It is located in Baltimore, approximately one mile from state and federal courts, the attractions of the Inner Harbor, and Oriole Park at Camden Yards.

■ Enrollment/Student Body

➡ *2,892 applicants*   ➡ *790 admitted first-year class 1993*
➡ *322 enrolled first-year class 1993*   ➡ *195 full-time first-year class 1993*   ➡ *127 part-time first-year class 1993*
➡ *15% total minority*   ➡ *45% total women*
➡ *15 states & Washington, DC represented*
➡ *114 undergraduate schools represented*

■ Faculty

➡ *101 total*   ➡ *44 full-time*   ➡ *57 part-time or adjunct*
➡ *34 women*   ➡ *9 minority*

■ Library and Physical Facilities

➡ *230,000 volumes & equivalents*   ➡ *library hours: Mon.-Fri., 8:00 A.M.-MIDNIGHT; Sat. & Sun., 9:00 A.M.-MIDNIGHT*
➡ *LEXIS*   ➡ *WESTLAW*   ➡ *CARL (electronic card catalogue servicing the University of Maryland library system as well as the university libraries of California, Colorado, and Hawaii)*   ➡ *17 staff members*   ➡ *library seats 150*

Ten dedicated terminals for computer-assisted legal research systems are available for use by law students and faculty, and library staff members provide training in the use of LEXIS and WESTLAW. In addition, the library's computer lab is open to law students during library hours.

■ Curriculum

➡ *Academic Support Program*   ➡ *90 credits required to graduate*   ➡ *105 courses available*   ➡ *degrees available: J.D.; J.D./M.B.A.; J.D./M.P.A.; J.D./M.S. in Criminal Justice; LL.M. in Taxation; J.D./LL.M.; J.D./Ph.D. in Policy Sciences*
➡ *semesters, start in Aug.*

■ Special Programs

The School of Law sponsors many interschool advocacy competition teams. U of B teams have argued successfully in regional and national competitions, including: ATLA Trial Advocacy; Client Counseling Competition; Client Negotiation Competition; International Moot Court; Labor Law Moot Court; National Appellate Advocacy; National Intellectual Property Moot Court; National Moot Court; Pace National Environmental Law Moot Court; Tax Moot Court; and Trial Advocacy.

Working under the direct supervision of attorneys, U of B law students undertake the representation of real clients and perform all of the tasks necessary for proper representation. Students in the Appellate Advocacy Clinic prepare an entire appellate case, including oral argument in the Court of Special Appeals. The Civil Clinic represents indigent clients before courts and administrative agencies in a variety of civil matters, such as housing, consumer, and selected public benefits cases. Participants in the Criminal Practice Clinic are assigned to the office of either a state's attorney or a public defender to handle criminal cases. In the Family Law Clinic, low-income clients receive legal representation in cases involving child custody, support, divorce, and protection from domestic violence. Students in the Community Legal Education Project teach "street law" to students in a public high school.

The Internship Program combines practical legal experience with a seminar component focusing on the transition from classroom to practice. Internship placement supervisors include attorneys in the private sector (e.g., private law firms, in-house corporate counsel, nonprofit organizations); attorneys in the public sector at the federal, state, and local levels; and federal and state trial and appellate judges.

International Educational Programs—A summer abroad program in comparative law is taught by faculty members from the University of Baltimore and University of Maryland law schools in conjunction with faculty of the University of Aberdeen Law School in Scotland. The School of Law also has established a cooperative faculty exchange with the University of Vilnius in Lithuania and is working with the American Bar Association in providing research opportunities for faculty and students to meet emerging legal needs in the Ukrainian city of Odessa.

Special Programs in Intellectual Property and Taxation—The school's location in the Baltimore-Washington metropolitan area facilitated the development of an extensive program in intellectual property law. In addition to course offerings in patent, trademark and technology law, students have participated on the Intellectual Property Moot Court Team, the *Intellectual Property Law Journal* and in organizing and hosting the National Conference on Industrial Design Law and Practice.

■ Student Activities

The Student Bar Association serves as a principal channel of communication among students, faculty, and administration. Representatives of the SBA serve on all faculty committees. The Black Law Students' Association, Women's Bar Association, Environmental Law Society, International Law Society, and numerous other student organizations bring distinguished guest lecturers to campus to speak on law-related issues.

Law reviews, journals, and other periodicals give students an opportunity to hone their skills in research, analysis, and writing. *The University of Baltimore Law Review*, *The Journal of Environmental Law* and *The Intellectual Property Law Journal* are scholarly publications offering indepth analyses of relevant legal issues of current concern to practitioners and judges. *The Law Forum* specializes in articles that trace developing trends in the law.

■ Admission

➡ *baccalaureate degree required* ➡ *application deadline—April 5* ➡ *rolling admission, complete files before April 5 advised* ➡ *LSAT, LSDAS required* ➡ *median GPA—3.12* ➡ *median LSAT score—155* ➡ *application fee—$35* ➡ *LSAT score must be no more than 3 years old*

The School of Law has established an admission policy designed to obtain a diverse and well-qualified student body. In evaluating applicant files, the Admission Committee places primary emphasis on the Law School Admission Test score and the cumulative undergraduate grade-point average; in most cases, a combination of these elements will be sufficient for the admission decision.

The committee also considers, in close cases, nontraditional factors that may be relevant in determining an applicant's ability to succeed in law school. It seeks to include persons of diverse racial, ethnic, and cultural backgrounds. It considers such factors as the difficulty of the undergraduate field of study, graduate degrees, and other indicators not susceptible to measurement by traditional academic criteria, such as demonstrated ability to overcome adversity, individual achievement, motivation, work experience and character. Applicants should discuss fully in a personal statement any such factors they wish the

committee to consider in evaluating their applications. Interviews are not part of the process; however, frequent group information sessions are scheduled throughout the year.

■ Expenses and Financial Aid

➡ *tuition & fees—full-time resident, $2,645; full-time nonresident, $4,785; part-time resident, $221/credit hour; part-time nonresident, $375/credit hour* ➡ *additional expenses for fees at registration range between $200 and $425 each semester, depending upon number of credits and division* ➡ *eligibility for limited scholarship aid based on merit and need*

The Office of Financial Assistance administers federal, state, and institutional loan programs. First-year students and transfer students seeking financial assistance should apply for financial aid when they submit the application for admission, but no later than April 1 for the fall term.

■ Housing

The university's Student Activities Office assists students in locating suitable accommodations near the university and offers a roommate referral service for interested students.

■ Career Services

The Career Services Center offers a range of traditional and innovative services and programs designed to facilitate the career planning efforts of our students and to maximize their potential for employment.

A survey of the 1992 graduating class discloses that approximately 81 percent of those responding to the survey were employed or continuing their education within six months of graduation.

Applicant Group for the 1993–1994 Academic Year

University of Baltimore School of Law
This grid includes only applicants who earned 120-180 LSAT scores under standard administrations.

LSAT Score	3.75 +		3.50 -3.74		3.25 - 3.49		3.00 - 3.24		2.75 - 2.99		2.50 - 2.74		2.25 - 2.49		2.00 - 2.24		Below 2.00		No GPA		Total	
	Apps	Adm	Apps	Adm	Apps	Adm	Apps	Adm	Apps	Adm	Apps	Adm	Apps	Adm	Apps	Adm	Apps	Adm	Apps	Adm	Apps	Adm
175 - 180	0	0	0	0	0	0	0	0	1	1	0	0	0	0	0	0	0	0	0	0	1	1
170 - 174	0	0	1	1	1	1	4	3	1	1	1	0	2	1	0	0	0	0	0	0	10	7
165 - 169	6	3	3	3	5	5	16	14	12	8	13	5	5	2	0	0	0	0	0	0	60	40
160 - 164	13	10	16	13	31	28	48	39	41	21	25	8	16	4	3	0	0	0	0	0	193	123
155 - 159	12	8	43	36	99	76	151	111	124	41	80	14	31	3	11	0	1	0	2	2	554	291
150 - 154	17	9	70	34	131	51	214	48	154	21	98	4	52	1	18	4	5	0	7	3	766	175
145 - 149	9	2	38	4	102	6	142	11	120	9	79	10	55	2	22	0	3	0	4	0	574	44
140 - 144	3	1	15	3	34	4	59	8	63	5	67	6	51	4	23	0	4	0	8	0	327	31
135 - 139	2	0	5	1	11	0	25	1	28	1	33	0	24	0	15	0	9	0	3	0	155	3
130 - 134	0	0	4	0	2	0	5	0	13	0	18	0	17	0	14	0	3	0	1	0	77	0
125 - 129	0	0	0	0	0	0	1	0	6	0	2	0	4	0	1	0	1	0	1	0	16	0
120 - 124	0	0	0	0	0	0	0	0	0	0	1	0	0	0	0	0	0	0	0	0	1	0
Total	62	33	195	95	416	171	665	235	563	108	417	47	257	17	107	4	26	0	26	5	2734	715

Apps = Number of Applicants
Adm = Number Admitted
Reflects 95% of the total applicant pool.

Baylor University School of Law

P.O. Box 97288
Waco, TX 76798

Phone: 817.755.1911

■ Introduction

Baylor University School of Law, formally organized in 1857, is the oldest law school in Texas. The School of Law is in Waco, on the campus of Baylor University, an institution affiliated with the Baptist General Convention of Texas. Waco is a city of 103,000 located in central Texas midway between Dallas and Austin. Baylor law school's course of study is designed to provide a well-rounded legal education, including training in all facets of the law, including theoretical analysis; practical application; ethics; legal writing; and advocacy, negotiation, and counseling skills, while also giving students the opportunity to focus their studies in an area of interest.

■ Enrollment/Student Body

➡ *920 applicants* ➡ *257 admitted first-year class 1993*
➡ *70 enrolled first-year class 1993* ➡ *409 total full-time*
➡ *17% minority* ➡ *41% women*
➡ *32 states & foreign countries represented*
➡ *112 undergraduate schools represented*

■ Faculty

➡ *44 total* ➡ *22 full-time* ➡ *22 part-time or adjunct*
➡ *9 women* ➡ *1 minority*

Faculty members hold degrees from law schools, colleges, and universities throughout the United States. An emphasis has been placed on recruiting faculty with a strong dedication to teaching and scholarship, along with significant practical experience. Faculty members have an average experience in teaching of over 13 years, and an average experience in the full-time active practice of law, aside from teaching, of over 5 years. A faculty member's quality of teaching is of central importance in the granting of tenure. At the same time, the faculty has produced a significant amount of legal scholarship that has caused a high demand for their services as speakers and lecturers at legal institutes and civic functions.

■ Library and Physical Facilities

➡ *157,250 volumes & equivalents* ➡ *library hours: Mon.-Fri., 7:30 A.M.-MIDNIGHT; Sat., 8:00 A.M.-MIDNIGHT; Sun., 1:00 P.M.-MIDNIGHT* ➡ *LEXIS* ➡ *NEXIS*
➡ *WESTLAW* ➡ *DIALOG* ➡ *OCLC*
➡ *automated on-line card catalog*
➡ *3 full-time librarians* ➡ *library seats 285*

The law school is located in Morrison Constitution Hall. The facilities are devoted to classrooms, several courtrooms, the library, faculty offices, administrative offices, career services, student offices, and lounges. Four courtrooms are located in the Advocacy Wing of the Law School. These courtrooms are used primarily by third-year students in simulating trial advocacy exercises as part of the mandatory Practice Court Program. Two of the courtrooms have complete audio and video capabili-

ties, allowing students to record and later review their trial-advocacy exercises.

The M.C. and Mattie Caston Law Library is designed to provide ample small rooms and areas for study. The Sam and Helen M. Pessarra Computer Lab and Legal Research Center, and M.D. Anderson Foundation/Watson Wise Foundation Computer Lab and Research Center located in the library, serve student and faculty research and word processing. All the personal computers are networked to high quality laser printers.

■ Curriculum

➡ *Academic Support Program* ➡ *120 credits required to graduate* ➡ *84 courses available* ➡ *degrees available: J.D. and joint J.D./M.B.A. and J.D./M.Tax* ➡ *quarters, start in Aug., Nov., Feb., & May* ➡ *range of first-year class size—15-70* ➡ *6 areas of concentration*

Students interested in a more specialized course of study during the second and third years may choose from six areas of concentration—civil litigation, business litigation, business planning, estate and probate, criminal practice, and health care. Reflecting the quality of the education they have received, Baylor graduates continue to pass the Texas bar exam with record success.

■ Individual Attention

Baylor Law School has a target student population of 410. This smaller size allows for all students to be active participants in class. There is room for each student to participate in extracurricular activities, including moot court, mock trial, negotiation, and client counseling competitions at the intraschool and interscholastic level. The legal research and writing program is designed to give students intensive, small-group instruction with generous feedback.

One of the distinctive features of the school is that professors maintain unrestricted hours for student consultation. They are actively involved in all intraschool and interscholastic competitions. Every professor is available for lending advice and guidance in all academic and other matters of concern to students.

■ Flexible Calendar

The school year at Baylor is divided into four quarters. Entering classes are accepted three times a year into the fall (August), spring (February), and summer (May) quarters. A full curriculum is offered during each quarter, enabling a student to graduate in as little as 27 months. After completing the first three quarters, students generally may elect at any time during the year to take time off from their legal studies to pursue a clerkship, internship, or other program to allow the student to apply the principles and skills developed in school. Full-time study is required. Evening classes are not offered.

■ Admission

➡ *fall application deadline—March 1*   ➡ *spring application deadline—Nov. 1*   ➡ *summer application deadline—Feb. 1*   ➡ *LSAT, LSDAS required*   ➡ *median GPA—3.66*   ➡ *median LSAT score—160*   ➡ *application fee—$35*   ➡ *reapplication fee—$10*

■ Student Activities

Each year, Baylor student teams enter several interscholastic mock trial, moot court, negotiation, and counseling competitions. A number of regional and national championships have been won in recent years by Baylor.

The *Baylor Law Review* gives outstanding students selected for academic performance or through a writing competition an opportunity to develop legal-writing ability. The Student Bar Association is the student government in the law school. Three national legal fraternities have active chapters at Baylor and sponsor an array of activities. The Environmental Law Society, the International Law Society and the Christian Legal Society offer opportunities to students to fulfill special interests. The smaller size allows for all students to be active participants in class and in extracurricular activities.

■ Expenses and Financial Aid

➡ *academic merit scholarships available (ranging from amounts equal to 1/3 to full tuition)*   ➡ *minority scholarships available (ranging from amounts equal to 1/3 to full tuition)*   ➡ *financial aid available: Texas Tuition Equalization Grant, Perkins Loans, Baylor Revolving Loans, Stafford Loans, Law Access loans, supplemental loans, and College Access Loans*

■ Career Services

The law school maintains a Career Services Office which acts as a liaison between employers and law students. In addition, the facilities of the University Career Services Office are available to law students. Employment interviews are conducted by prospective employers throughout the year, although most interviewing takes place during the fall. Law firms, corporations, courts and other employers normally visit the law school each year for the purpose of hiring both full-time associate positions and law clerkships or other temporary employment.

Applicant Group for the 1993–1994 Academic Year

Baylor University School of Law
This grid includes only applicants who earned 120-180 LSAT scores under standard administrations.

LSAT Score	GPA 3.75 +		3.50 -3.74		3.25 - 3.49		3.00 - 3.24		2.75 - 2.99		2.50 - 2.74		2.25 - 2.49		2.00 - 2.24		Below 2.00		No GPA		Total	
	Apps	Adm	Apps	Adm	Apps	Adm	Apps	Adm	Apps	Adm	Apps	Adm	Apps	Adm	Apps	Adm	Apps	Adm	Apps	Adm	Apps	Adm
175 - 180	1	1	1	1	0	0	0	0	0	0	0	0	0	0	0	0	0	0	0	0	2	2
170 - 174	3	3	0	0	4	4	2	2	1	1	1	0	0	0	0	0	0	0	0	0	11	10
165 - 169	14	14	4	4	13	13	14	10	6	4	4	1	1	0	1	0	0	0	0	0	57	46
160 - 164	35	34	40	40	30	26	31	19	22	7	7	3	5	0	0	0	0	0	0	0	170	129
155 - 159	42	41	87	63	66	17	47	12	29	6	18	4	8	0	1	0	0	0	1	0	299	143
150 - 154	23	11	48	13	61	10	65	9	40	4	31	4	11	0	4	0	1	0	1	0	285	51
145 - 149	8	1	18	0	25	2	34	2	22	1	23	1	5	0	11	0	2	0	0	0	148	7
140 - 144	3	0	9	0	17	0	26	0	14	0	20	0	4	0	3	0	1	0	2	0	99	0
135 - 139	0	0	1	0	2	0	3	0	4	0	6	0	3	0	4	0	0	0	3	0	26	0
130 - 134	0	0	1	0	1	0	1	0	3	0	0	0	2	0	2	0	1	0	0	0	11	0
125 - 129	0	0	0	0	0	0	0	0	1	0	1	0	1	0	0	0	0	0	1	0	4	0
120 - S124	0	0	0	0	0	0	0	0	0	0	0	0	0	0	0	0	0	0	0	0	0	0
Total	129	105	209	121	219	72	223	54	142	23	111	13	40	0	26	0	5	0	8	0	1112	388

Apps = Number of Applicants
Adm = Number Admitted
Reflects 95% of the total applicant pool.

Boston College Law School

Office of Admissions
885 Centre Street
Newton, MA 02159

Phone: 617.552.4350

■ Introduction

Since its founding in 1929, Boston College Law School has earned a national reputation for educational excellence and the highest standards of professionalism while fostering a unique spirit of community among its students, faculty, and staff. The diverse curriculum is designed to help students develop the skills and knowledge needed to adapt successfully to changes in society and the legal profession. Boston College Law School is located on an attractive 40-acre campus in Newton, Massachusetts, just minutes from downtown Boston. It is fully accredited by both the American Bar Association and the Association of American Law Schools, and has a chapter of Order of the Coif, the prestigious national law school honorary society.

■ Enrollment/Student Body

➡ *5,760 applicants* ➡ *1,069 admitted first-year class 1993*
➡ *269 enrolled first-year class 1993* ➡ *20% minority*
➡ *48% women* ➡ *40 states & foreign countries represented*
➡ *208 undergraduate schools represented*

■ Faculty

➡ *78 total* ➡ *42 full-time* ➡ *36 part-time or adjunct*
➡ *20 women* ➡ *9 minority*

■ Library and Physical Facilities

➡ *320,000 volumes & equivalents* ➡ *library hours: Mon.-Thurs., 8:00 A.M.-MIDNIGHT; Fri., 8:00 A.M.-11:00 P.M.; Sat., 9:00 A.M.-10:00 P.M.; Sun., 10:00 A.M.-MIDNIGHT*
➡ *LEXIS* ➡ *NEXIS* ➡ *WESTLAW* ➡ *DIALOG*
➡ *20 full-time librarians* ➡ *library seats 550*
➡ *Member, New England Law Library Consortium*

All academic, administrative, library and service facilities, including a 25-unit Macintosh computer center, are accessible to disabled persons.

■ Curriculum

➡ *Academic Support Program* ➡ *85 credits required to graduate* ➡ *110 courses available* ➡ *degrees available: J.D.; J.D./M.B.A.; J.D./M.S.W.* ➡ *semesters, begin in the fall* ➡ *range of first-year class size—30-145*
➡ *Semester Abroad at the University of London*

The faculty of Boston College Law School strongly believes in the importance of a general legal education designed to enable graduates to adapt to the changing demands of law practice. Areas of particular focus include constitutional law, business law, dispute resolution, environmental law, family law, international law, sports and entertainment law, and clinical programs.

In the first year, all students take traditional courses including Civil Procedure, Constitutional Law, Contracts, Property and Torts, as well as Legal Research and Writing and an innovative skills course titled Introduction to Lawyering and Professional Responsibility. More than 100 courses offered in the second and third years are elective.

■ Clinical Courses

The Law School is committed to making clinical experiences available to all students who desire them. Present clinical programs offer a variety of subject matter and experiential opportunity. The **Urban Legal Laboratory** is an externship program of individually designed placements with judges, government agencies, public-interest organizations, and law firms in the greater Boston area. At the **Boston College Legal Assistance Bureau** (LAB), students assume responsibility for representation of indigent clients in civil cases.

Criminal Process offers the opportunity to prosecute or defend criminal cases in state court. The **Attorney General Law Clinic** provides a placement in the Massachusetts Attorney General's office and the **Judicial Process** course includes clinical placement with a specific Superior Court justice.

■ Student Activities

Selected students may participate in the following writing programs: *Boston College Law Review; Boston College Environmental Affairs Law Review; Boston College International and Comparative Law Review; Boston College Third World Law Journal;* and the *Uniform Commercial Code Reporter-Digest.*

Boston College Law School supports several annual competitions that help students develop writing, courtroom-advocacy, and client-counseling skills. Over the years, Boston College has performed extremely well in the regional and national competitions, which are judged by faculty, state and federal judges, and practicing attorneys.

The Law School also has a number of student groups reflecting both personal and professional concerns.

■ Admission

➡ *Bachelor's degree from accredited college or university required* ➡ *application deadline—March 1* ➡ *LSAT, LSDAS required* ➡ *application fee—$50*
➡ *rolling admission* ➡ *median GPA (admitted students)—3.55* ➡ *median LSAT score (admitted students)—165*

The Law School has no minimum cutoff either for GPA or LSAT. Academic achievement and LSAT scores are extremely significant, but work and professional experience, college extracurricular activities, the quality of recommendations, and the personal statement also play an important role in decision-making.

In evaluating GPA, class rank as well as courses taken are considered. If the LSAT has been taken more than once, scores are averaged unless a compelling reason is presented for considering a particular score. Less weight is given to the LSAT if the applicant has a history of poor standardized testing.

The personal statement is reviewed with the objective of finding diverse, well-rounded individuals. When an applicant is accepted, a tuition deposit is required, the details of which accompany the acceptance letter.

■ Minorities and Affirmative Action

Boston College Law School strongly encourages applications from qualified minority, disabled, or other students who have been socially, economically, or culturally disadvantaged. A special admissions subcommittee evaluates each applicant in an effort to ensure that all relevant credentials are favorably considered. The Law School has been very successful both in admitting minority and special students, and in retaining them to graduation. Both academic support and minority student mentor programs are available.

■ Expenses and Financial Aid

➡ *full-time tuition & fees—$17,720*   ➡ *estimated additional expenses—$10,000 (room, board, books, health insurance)*   ➡ *need-based financial aid available*   ➡ *FAFSA and Law School Form*

All financial aid is processed through the university's Office of Financial Aid and the Law School Admissions Office. The Financial Aid Office administers federal and private loan programs, the College Work-Study program, and the major Presidential and Law School Scholarship programs. The Law School has also developed a Public Interest Loan Assistance program providing financial assistance to graduates taking lower-paying positions in government, nonprofit corporations, and legal services programs.

All applicants wishing to be considered for financial aid must submit the processed FAFSA (Free Application for Federal Student Aid) and a Boston College Financial Aid Form (sent with the acceptance letter) to the Boston College Office of Financial Aid, Lyons Hall 201, Chestnut Hill, MA 02167 by March 1.

■ Housing

Housing assistance is provided through the university's Office of Off-Campus Housing. Applicants seeking resident assistantships should write the University Housing Office, Boston College, Chestnut Hill, MA 02167.

■ Career Services

The Office of Career Services is dedicated to helping students make the transition from law student to employed professional. Both students and alumni may avail themselves of a wide range of career planning services.

The range of opportunities for graduates spans virtually the entire spectrum of legal practice. Each year more than 1,000 prospective employers solicit applications from Boston College law students. In 1992-93, government agencies, corporations, and public-interest organizations from 26 states visited the campus. More than 93 percent of graduates are employed either prior to or within several months of graduation. The nearly 8,500 alumni are presently practicing in 48 states and a number of foreign countries.

Applicant Group for the 1993–1994 Academic Year

Boston College Law School
This grid includes only applicants who earned 120-180 LSAT scores under standard administrations.

LSAT Score	3.75 +		3.50 -3.74		3.25 - 3.49		3.00 - 3.24		2.75 - 2.99		Below 2.75		No GPA		Total	
	Apps	Adm	Apps	Adm	Apps	Adm	Apps	Adm	Apps	Adm	Apps	Adm	Apps	Adm	Apps	Adm
175 - 180	10	9	4	4	13	9	8	2	1	1	0	0	0	0	36	25
170 - 174	21	20	36	29	52	43	39	11	13	3	11	0	0	0	172	106
165 - 169	75	66	166	133	184	104	129	19	60	2	28	0	11	2	653	326
160 - 164	134	84	342	168	404	81	244	13	102	4	57	1	10	0	1293	351
150 - 159	175	22	501	29	616	24	473	28	242	10	220	3	31	3	2258	119
140 - 149	40	4	99	9	182	5	195	8	174	3	192	2	18	0	900	31
Below 140	1	0	3	0	13	0	39	0	24	0	88	0	7	0	175	0
Total	456	205	1151	372	1464	266	1127	81	616	23	596	6	77	5	5487	958

Apps = Number of Applicants
Adm = Number Admitted
Reflects 95% of the total applicant pool.

Boston University School of Law

765 Commonwealth Avenue
Boston, MA 02215

Phone: 617.353.3100

■ Introduction

Located in Boston, Massachusetts, overlooking a beautiful stretch of the Charles River, Boston University School of Law boasts a 125-year history of outstanding legal education. The school is committed to giving its students the broadest possible exposure to the practice and theory of law. Students graduate with a deep understanding of legal rules and principles, enriched by insights from related disciplines such as economics, philosophy, and history, and with strong analytical and practical skills that lay the foundation for a challenging and satisfying legal career. Boston University School of Law is located in one of the country's most vital intellectual and cultural centers. As a result, the school offers students a wide range of opportunities both inside and outside of class that make for a memorable law school experience.

■ Enrollment/Student Body

➡ *5,300 applicants*   ➡ *1,700 admitted first-year class 1993*
➡ *381 enrolled first-year class 1993*
➡ *1,182 total full-time*   ➡ *21% minority*
➡ *42% women*   ➡ *59 states & foreign countries represented*
➡ *257 undergraduate schools represented*

■ Faculty

➡ *128 total*   ➡ *58 full-time*   ➡ *70 part-time or adjunct*
➡ *41 women*   ➡ *8 minority*

■ Library and Physical Facilities

➡ *470,000 volumes & equivalents*   ➡ *library hours: Mon.-Thurs., 8:00 A.M.-11:30 P.M.; Fri., 8:00 A.M.-9:00 P.M.; Sat., 9:00 A.M.-9:00 P.M.; Sun., 10:00 A.M.-11:30 P.M.*   ➡ *LEXIS*
➡ *NEXIS*   ➡ *WESTLAW*   ➡ *DIALOG*
➡ *5 full-time librarians*   ➡ *library seats 843*

■ Curriculum

➡ *Academic Support Program*   ➡ *84 credits required to graduate*   ➡ *172 courses available*   ➡ *degrees available: J.D.; J.D./M.B.A. (Law & Management & Health Care Management); J.D./M.P.H.; J.D./M.S. (Law & Mass Communications); J.D./M.A. (Law & Preservation Studies; International Relations); LL.M. (American Banking Law, International Banking Law, Taxation)*
➡ *semesters, start in Aug. or early Sep.*
➡ *range of first-year class size—65-105*

During the first week, minority and first-year orientations introduce law students to the study of law. Most of the first-year curriculum is required. Constitutional Law is required in the second year. In the second and third years, the school offers a wide variety of courses and seminars in advanced areas. Legal ethics is taught throughout the curriculum and in a special intensive program.

■ Law, Technology, and Innovation

Situated in an important high-technology area, the school offers a rich array of courses in the rapidly growing area of law, technology, and innovation, including offerings in patent law, copyright, trademark, computer law, communication law, art law, entertainment law, and environmental regulation and toxic torts. In addition, the school offers concentration in intellectual property and a dual J.D./M.S. degree in Mass Communication, and houses the Center for Law and Technology, which explores the frontier of current technology issues.

■ Health Law

Home of the Center for Law and Health Sciences and the American Society of Law and Medicine, the school is well-known for its strong health law curriculum, distinguished health law faculty, a concentration in health care law and two health-related dual degree programs. The school's extremely broad selection of courses, together with health-related offerings in the School of Public Health, comprise one of the most comprehensive health law curricula in the country. In addition, those students who qualify have an opportunity during their second and third years to work for the internationally prestigious *American Journal of Law and Medicine*.

■ International Law, Environmental Law, and Clinical Programs

The School of Law also has special strengths in international and environmental law. The school offers a strong, and rapidly expanding, curriculum in each of these two areas, study abroad programs with Université Jean Moulin in Lyon, France and Oxford University, England as well as a dual J.D./M.A. degree in International Relations.

The school is known for some of the finest clinical offerings in the country. The student can choose from among nine different programs covering practice in the civil, criminal, and alternative dispute resolution areas. With ties to Greater Boston Legal Services and other organizations, these programs offer actual practice experience under the close supervision of a dedicated and highly accomplished group of full-time clinical faculty.

■ Admission

➡ *Bachelor's degree required for admission*
➡ *application deadline—March 1*   ➡ *LSAT, LSDAS required*
➡ *median GPA—3.42*   ➡ *median LSAT score—163*
➡ *application fee—$50*

The Admissions Committee places primary emphasis on an applicant's cumulative undergraduate grade-point average and score on the LSAT. The committee also takes into account other factors, such as marked and sustained improvement in undergraduate grades, outstanding leadership ability, significant postgraduate experience, and motivation for law study. Letters of recommendation also can be very important.

■ Student Activities

Approximately one-third of upper-division students have an opportunity for professional writing experience by participating in one of six law journals. These include: *Boston University Law Review*, *Annual Review of Banking Law*, the *American Journal of Law and Medicine*, *Boston University International Law Journal*, the *Public Interest Law Journal*, and *Probate Law Journal*.

The School of Law also encourages students to become active in student organizations. Reflecting our students' diverse interests and backgrounds, there are a number of active student organizations, including: The American Bar Association/Law Student Division; the Asian American Law Students Association; American Inns of Court; the Black Law Students Association; the Battered Women's Advocacy Project; the Civil Liberties Union; the Communication, Entertainment, and Sports Law Society; the Environmental Law Society; the Film Society; the Gay, Lesbian, and Bisexual Caucus; the Hispanic American Law Students Association; the International Law Society; the Japanese Law Society; the Jewish Law Students Association; Law and Business Society; Legal Follies; the Married Law Students Association; Phi Alpha Delta Legal Fraternity; Public Interest Project; South Asian Law Students Association; Student Bar Association; SBA Yearbook; the Technology, Engineering, and Science Law Association; Voice for Choice; and Women's Law Association, as well as various sports clubs.

Upper-class students may participate in the intramural appellate moot court competition. Teams also compete in the National Moot Court, National Appellate Advocacy, Jessup International Law, Benton Information and Privacy Law, Wagner Labor Law, and Kaufman Securities Law moot court competitions.

■ Expenses and Financial Aid

➡ *tuition & fees—$17,630* ➡ *estimated additional expenses—$11,300* ➡ *tuition grants available, primarily need-based* ➡ *minority scholarships: Martin Luther King Fellowships include tuition, fees, living expenses* ➡ *financial aid available; FAF, federal form, & school of law financial aid application due April 1, parental data required*

■ Career Services

The Office of Career Planning and Placement actively assists students and alumni/ae in securing employment. Each year more than 500 law firms, government agencies, public-interest organizations, and corporations from all regions of the United States recruit law students for summer and permanent positions through visiting, non-visiting, off-campus, and Massachusetts Law School Consortium recruitment programs. The office maintains a comprehensive career resource library, provides career counseling and job listings, and sponsors career panels and interview workshops.

Over the past three years, approximately 80 percent of graduates reporting employment have secured positions or enrolled in an advanced-degree program within six to nine months of graduation. First-year and second-year law students have been similarly successful in securing summer employment.

Applicant Group for the 1993–1994 Academic Year

Boston University School of Law
This grid includes only applicants who earned 120-180 LSAT scores under standard administrations.

LSAT Score	GPA																					
	3.75 +		3.50 -3.74		3.25 - 3.49		3.00 - 3.24		2.75 - 2.99		2.50 - 2.74		2.25 - 2.49		2.00 - 2.24		Below 2.00		No GPA		Total	
	Apps	Adm	Apps	Adm	Apps	Adm	Apps	Adm	Apps	Adm	Apps	Adm	Apps	Adm	Apps	Adm	Apps	Adm	Apps	Adm	Apps	Adm
175 - 180	6	5	3	3	12	12	4	3	0	0	1	0	0	0	0	0	0	0	0	0	26	23
170 - 174	8	8	30	29	36	35	33	32	17	15	6	2	3	0	0	0	0	0	1	1	134	122
165 - 169	46	45	113	107	149	140	121	110	58	38	16	6	7	2	1	0	0	0	9	9	520	457
160 - 164	94	88	250	223	354	230	262	121	99	16	44	4	15	2	3	0	1	0	11	5	1133	689
155 - 159	92	42	273	54	384	30	278	24	133	8	57	2	27	1	7	0	1	0	10	3	1262	164
150 - 154	40	4	150	10	222	20	224	30	118	10	69	5	23	3	8	0	3	0	11	0	868	82
145 - 149	14	2	51	4	112	5	120	8	80	2	51	0	20	0	9	0	1	0	15	2	473	23
140 - 144	10	0	24	0	41	0	63	2	67	0	46	0	30	0	6	0	1	0	15	0	303	2
135 - 139	2	0	4	0	8	0	24	0	16	0	14	0	9	0	5	0	1	0	9	0	92	0
130 - 134	0	0	1	0	3	0	7	0	4	0	7	0	8	0	4	0	0	0	2	0	36	0
125 - 129	1	0	1	0	0	0	2	0	0	0	3	0	0	0	2	0	1	0	0	0	10	0
120 - 124	0	0	0	0	0	0	0	0	0	0	0	0	0	0	0	0	0	0	0	0	0	0
Total	313	194	900	430	1321	472	1138	330	592	89	314	19	142	8	45	0	9	0	83	20	4857	1562

Apps = Number of Applicants
Adm = Number Admitted
Reflects 95% of the total applicant pool.

Brigham Young University—J. Reuben Clark Law School

340 JRCB
Provo, UT 84602

Phone: 801.378.4277

■ Introduction

Brigham Young University, J. Reuben Clark Law School, located in Provo, Utah (about 50 miles south of Salt Lake City), is an integral part of the largest private university in the United States on the basis of full-time student enrollment. Brigham Young University is sponsored by The Church of Jesus Christ of Latter-day Saints (Mormon Church) and has a present enrollment of 27,000 students from all 50 states and more than 70 foreign countries. The Law School is fully accredited by the American Bar Association and is a member of the Association of American Law Schools.

■ Enrollment/Student Body

➤ *656 applicants*   ➤ *227 admitted first-year class 1993*
➤ *153 enrolled first-year class 1993*   ➤ *475 total full-time*
➤ *17% minority*   ➤ *35% women*   ➤ *37 states & foreign countries represented*   ➤ *38 undergraduate schools represented*

■ Faculty

➤ *48 total*   ➤ *29 full-time*   ➤ *19 part-time or adjunct*
➤ *6 women*   ➤ *2 minority*

■ Library and Physical Facilities

➤ *330,000 volumes & equivalents*   ➤ *library hours: Mon.-Fri., 7:30 A.M.-9:30 P.M.; Sat., 8:00 A.M.-11:00 P.M.*
➤ *LEXIS*   ➤ *NEXIS*   ➤ *WESTLAW*   ➤ *RLIN & Nortis*   ➤ *8 full-time librarians*   ➤ *library seats 550*

The law building is designed to accommodate 150 entering students each year. In addition to the law library facilities, the law building contains nine classrooms, three seminar rooms, rooms for group study, a four room interviewing complex, a television studio, a student commons area, and ample space for student organizations and activities.

The law library provides public access by computer terminal to over 150 other institutions' card catalogs on the Research Library Information Network (RLIN) and is equipped with both WESTLAW and LEXIS, computer-assisted legal research databases, which are available for student access. There are personal computers and related printers located in the library that are exclusively for student use. The personal computers are interfaced with the Law School's main computer and are capable of the full range of computer applications from word processing to legal research and data management.

■ Curriculum

➤ *Academic Support Program*   ➤ *Tutorials; Legal Writing Class*   ➤ *90 credits required to graduate*   ➤ *92 courses available*   ➤ *degrees and combined degrees available: J.D.; J.D./M.B.A.; J.D./M.P.A.; J.D./M.A.C.C.; J.D./Ed.D.; J.D./M.O.B.*

The Law School is operated on a semester basis. The fall semester runs from approximately the third week in August until the week before Christmas. Winter semester begins the first week in January and runs until the fourth week in April. The first-year course of study is prescribed and consists of approximately 15 hours per semester. A broad selection of elective courses and seminars is available in the second and third years. The law school offers a tutorial program for all students at no cost.

■ Special Programs

The Law School, in combination with the graduate school of the university, offers joint J.D./M.B.A., Master of Public Administration, Master of Accountancy, and Master of Organizational Behavior degrees. The Law School provides clinical opportunities for students by means of well-developed simulated clinical programs in both civil and criminal matters and by extensive pro bono and externship experience with government and other not-for-profit agencies. A number of innovative curricular and cocurricular programs are being used by the faculty and students: Family Law Society, Natural Resources Law Forum, Government and Politics Legal Society, the International and Comparative Law Society, Negotiations Forum, and American Trial Lawyers Association.

■ Admission

➤ *Bachelor's degree required*   ➤ *application deadline—Feb. 15*   ➤ *LSAT, LSDAS required*   ➤ *median GPA—3.60*
➤ *median LSAT score—162*   ➤ *application fee—$30*

Students are admitted only in the fall semester and only for full-time study. Applications, which are processed on the basis of college work completed to date, may be made at any time after the beginning of the fall semester of the year preceding admission. College grades and the LSAT score are significant but not exclusive determinants of admissibility. The required written recommendations are of significant influence.

■ Student Activities

Law schools have traditionally offered important additional training to a limited number of students through participation on a law review. The objective of the cocurricular programs offered at the J. Reuben Clark Law School is to make law review-quality experience available to a much larger number of students by extending its principles to more categories of activity. Comparable standards of excellence in research, writing, and editing are presently offered in four activities: *Journal of Public Law*, Board of Advocates, *Brigham Young University Education and Law Journal*, and the *Brigham Young University Law Review*.

■ Expenses and Financial Aid

➡ *tuition & fees—full-time, $4,200 and $6,300; part-time, $233* ➡ *estimated additional expenses—$8,930 (room & board, textbooks and supplies, personal expenses, transportation)* ➡ *scholarships available* ➡ *merit and need-based minority scholarships available* ➡ *financial aid available: Federal Student Financial Aid, within 30 days of acceptance to the BYU Law School*

■ Career Services

Placement is regarded by the faculty as a matter of highest priority. A full-time law career services director, a full-time assistant, a full-time secretary, and one part-time employee are assigned to work with students and alumni in finding permanent and part-time employment in the legal profession and summer clerkships. Over 120 law firms, government offices, and businesses recruit regularly at the law school. Types of employment by the 1992 graduating class include private practice (31 percent), business (22 percent), government including judicial clerkships (30 percent), and other areas (17 percent). Job locations include Intermountain West (52 percent); East, South, and Midwest (28 percent); Pacific Coast and Hawaii (20 percent).

Applicant Group for the 1993–1994 Academic Year

Brigham Young University—J. Reuben Clark Law School

LSAT Score	GPA								
	3.75 +	3.50 - 3.74	3.25 - 3.49	3.00 - 3.24	2.75 - 2.99	2.50 - 2.74	2.25 - 2.49	2.00 - 2.24	Below 2.00
175 - 180	Good	Good	Good	Good	Good	Unlikely	Unlikely	Unlikely	Unlikely
170 - 174	Good	Good	Good	Good	Possible	Unlikely	Unlikely	Unlikely	Unlikely
165 - 169	Good	Good	Good	Good	Possible	Unlikely	Unlikely	Unlikely	Unlikely
160 - 164	Good	Good	Good	Possible	Unlikely	Unlikely	Unlikely	Unlikely	Unlikely
155 - 159	Good	Possible	Good	Possible	Unlikely	Unlikely	Unlikely	Unlikely	Unlikely
150 - 154	Possible	Possible	Possible	Unlikely	Unlikely	Unlikely	Unlikely	Unlikely	Unlikely
145 - 149	Possible	Unlikely	Unlikely	Unlikely	Unlikely	Unlikely	Unlikely	Unlikely	Unlikely
140 - 144	Unlikely	Unlikely	Unlikely	Unlikely	Unlikely	Unlikely	Unlikely	Unlikely	Unlikely
135 - 139	Unlikely	Unlikely	Unlikely	Unlikely	Unlikely	Unlikely	Unlikely	Unlikely	Unlikely
130 - 134	Unlikely	Unlikely	Unlikely	Unlikely	Unlikely	Unlikely	Unlikely	Unlikely	Unlikely
125 - 129	Unlikely	Unlikely	Unlikely	Unlikely	Unlikely	Unlikely	Unlikely	Unlikely	Unlikely
120 - 124	Unlikely	Unlikely	Unlikely	Unlikely	Unlikely	Unlikely	Unlikely	Unlikely	Unlikely

Legend: ■ Good Possibility   □ Possible   ▨ Unlikely

Brooklyn Law School

250 Joralemon Street
Brooklyn, NY 11201

Phone: 718.780.7906

■ An Environment for Learning

Brooklyn Law School, a private, independent institution established in 1901, is flanked by the Brooklyn Heights Historic District and the Brooklyn Civic Center. Built up with grand mansions, stately rowhouses, diminutive carriage houses, and handsome educational and religious institutions, the Heights reflects what our city was like at the turn of the century. Lush gardens and almost-secret mews and tree-lined back streets make the Heights one of the most tranquil and beautiful neighborhoods of New York City. The school itself looks out over the U.S. District Court, the New York State Appellate Division Court, the State Supreme and Family Courts, and the City Civil and Criminal Courts. Within easy walking distance are the U.S. Attorney's Office, Kings County District Attorney's Office, Legal Aid Society, and numerous city, state, and federal governmental agencies. Just a few minutes away are Wall Street and its array of financial, legal and corporate institutions.

■ Enrollment/Student Body

➡ 465 enrolled first-year class 1993 (298 full-time, 167 part-time) ➡ 1,025 total full-time ➡ 416 total part-time
➡ 16% minority (first-year) ➡ 37% women (first-year)
➡ 24 states, the District of Columbia, U.S. Virgin Islands, 3 foreign countries represented ➡ 147 colleges and universities represented ➡ 54 majors

■ Faculty

➡ 70 full-time, almost 30% female ➡ 46 part-time
➡ 21/1 student/faculty ratio

A recent survey of law school faculty scholarship ranked Brooklyn Law School among the top 50 U.S. law schools for scholarly productivity.

Recently, two of our professors were appointed by the American Law Institute, one to serve as Reporter for the Restatement of the Law of Suretyship, the other as Co-Reporter for the Restatement of the Law of Torts (Third): Products Liability; they are among the very few faculty members from outside the ranks of the most highly rated national law schools to be so honored. Yet another professor has been named Reporter to the Advisory Committee on Federal Rules of Evidence.

■ Library and Physical Facilities

➡ over 400,000 ➡ 899,700 microforms ➡ 975 periodicals
➡ LEXIS ➡ NEXIS ➡ WESTLAW ➡ DIALOG
➡ 10 full-time librarians ➡ library seats 550 (approximately)

Fall 1993 saw the opening of an 85,000-square-foot addition to our main building, enough room for a 50 percent expansion of our library, including 3 reading rooms, 25 study rooms, 6 conference rooms, 2 computer research centers, a computer training/word processing center, and wired carrels and tables to accommodate laptop computers. Also housed in the building are multiuse classrooms wired for computer-assisted instruction, a new student center and dining room, a conference/reception center, and increased space for faculty and student organization offices.

■ Curriculum

➡ nearly 150 electives in 10 clusters, including criminal law, litigation, economic regulation, international law, and public interest law ➡ 6 joint-degree programs
➡ range of first-year class size—15-125

The core of the first-year curriculum is a Seminar Section Program that provides every full-time student with a small-class (30-32 students) experience in a major required course during the first semester. This allows professors to depart from the standard lecture/Socratic dialogue format and to build a substantial skills training component into the course. This program is augmented by our first-year Legal Writing Program, which is taught by 10 full-time instructors.

Our Professional Skills Program consists of an extensive array of extern and in-house clinics and simulation courses; so much so that in a recent article we were hailed as "a leader in the field." **Extern Clinics** include: **Judicial Clinic** (which last year placed over 160 students, including 46 at the Federal level); **Civil Clinic** (students assigned to assist attorneys in a variety of settings in federal, state and city agencies. Past placement include the S.E.C., U.S. Attorney's Office for both the Southern and Eastern District, and the New York State Attorney General's Office, as well as Legal Aid Society and Legal Services offices); **Criminal Law Clinic** (students work in the office of either of the U.S. Attorneys, one of the District Attorneys, Victim Services Agency, or the Legal Aid Society); and **Dispute Resolution Clinic** (the conceptual framework, range of application and normative constraints on nonjudicial processes: negotiation, mediation, and arbitration). **In-house clinics** include our **Big Apple Clinic** (students handle cases brought by and against the City of New York); **Criminal Appeals Clinic** (students write briefs on behalf of indigent criminal defendants, which are used in argument before the Appellate Division); **Elderlaw Clinic** (students represent aged clients in connection with a variety of legal problems, including benefits, health and consumer matters); **Family Law Clinic** (students represent individuals seeking to establish, modify, or enforce child support orders); **Federal Litigation Clinic** (students represent clients in federal court); **Landlord-Tenant Clinic** (students represent the indigent in housing matters) and **Prosecutor's Clinic** (students prosecute misdemeanor cases in Brooklyn Criminal Court). In the newest of these clinics, **Legislation and Law Reform**, students research, develop, and implement legislative initiatives for the New York State Law Revision Commission. By graduation, nearly 60 percent of all students, perhaps 75 percent of full-time students, take advantage of one or more of these offerings. Our nine

simulation courses focus on discrete skills or on the application of certain skills to a particular area of practice, all in the context of prepared problems and case files.

■ Special Programs

The school's Center for the Study of International Business Law trains lawyers to function in a global environment, shaping international law and business policy. Our curriculum offers over 20 courses in the business law field, several of which focus on international and comparative law. The center sponsors a Fellowship Program and, with the cosponsorship of Queen Mary & Westfield College of the University of London, biennially hosts a symposium in London and New York on international business issues.

In 1985, Brooklyn Law School established the Edward V. Sparer Public Interest Fellowship Program which has provided substantial stipends to students who have served as legal interns in more than 50 public interest law offices nationwide. It also sponsors forums that bring prominent scholars, lawyers, and public policy advocates to the school to discuss current issues in public-interest law.

An effective approach to maximizing our students' learning potential is a comprehensive Academic Support Program offered during the first year. The program consists of an early-start summer legal process course and a series of outreach programs conducted during the first two semesters.

■ Admission

➨ *Bachelor's degree required* ➨ *fall semester admission for entering class* ➨ *no application deadline; rolling admission favors early filing* ➨ *LSAT, LSDAS required* ➨ *application fee—$50* ➨ *1,239 admitted out of 4,169 applicants, first-year class 1993*

■ Housing

Brooklyn Law School has six residence halls in Historic Brooklyn Heights, offering affordable housing just a few blocks from the Law School for a limited number of students.

■ Placement and Career Services

One of the two largest placement offices in the metropolitan area, and the only one with five full-time professionals who are all attorneys, staff size enables the office to devote approximately one-third of its time each week to job development; i.e. opening new markets and opportunities to our students, without any diminution in day-to-day operations. The linchpin of the office's services is its emphasis on individualized counseling. During the 1992-93 academic year, over 1,600 on-campus interview appointments between students and prospective employers were conducted.

Over the last several years, classwide placement rates have been very high, with the graduating classes of 1986-89 reporting average employment rates of 97 percent, and the classes of 1990-92 reporting average rates of 88 percent, despite a nationwide economic downturn.

Applicant Group for the 1993–1994 Academic Year

Brooklyn Law School
This grid includes only applicants who earned 120-180 LSAT scores under standard administrations.

LSAT Score	3.75 +		3.50 - 3.74		3.25 - 3.49		3.00 - 3.24		2.75 - 2.99		2.50 - 2.74		2.25 - 2.49		2.00 - 2.24		Below 2.00		No GPA		Total	
	Apps	Adm	Apps	Adm	Apps	Adm	Apps	Adm	Apps	Adm	Apps	Adm	Apps	Adm	Apps	Adm	Apps	Adm	Apps	Adm	Apps	Adm
175 - 180	2	2	0	0	1	1	1	1	1	1	1	1	0	0	0	0	0	0	0	0	6	6
170 - 174	3	3	4	4	5	5	11	11	2	2	1	1	2	2	1	1	1	1	0	0	30	30
165 - 169	13	12	13	12	26	26	20	20	19	19	16	14	4	4	3	2	1	0	0	0	115	109
160 - 164	18	16	46	45	87	86	88	85	47	45	47	46	21	18	4	4	1	0	4	3	363	348
155 - 159	31	28	90	71	180	120	170	75	130	48	80	27	41	13	19	4	3	0	15	7	759	393
150 - 154	29	14	83	45	193	94	270	49	178	16	131	11	61	3	26	2	2	0	13	3	986	237
145 - 149	24	5	73	12	116	15	174	8	174	8	108	1	67	2	34	0	7	0	16	0	793	51
140 - 144	8	0	29	0	49	0	101	0	102	1	102	0	74	0	30	0	7	0	19	0	521	1
135 - 139	3	0	10	0	23	0	40	0	55	0	51	0	47	0	29	0	8	0	9	0	275	0
130 - 134	1	0	0	0	6	0	11	0	15	0	17	0	25	0	20	0	7	1	6	0	108	1
125 - 129	0	0	1	0	0	0	2	0	5	0	7	0	5	0	2	0	1	0	3	0	26	0
120 - 124	0	0	0	0	0	0	0	0	0	0	0	0	2	0	0	0	1	0	0	0	3	0
Total	132	80	349	189	686	347	888	249	728	140	561	101	349	42	168	13	39	2	85	13	3985	1176

Apps = Number of Applicants
Adm = Number Admitted

University at Buffalo, State University of New York School of Law

Admissions Office
O'Brian Hall, Amherst Campus
Buffalo, NY 14260

Phone: 716.645.2061

■ Introduction

The State University of New York (SUNY) at Buffalo School of Law is the only law school in the SUNY system. The school provides a comprehensive curriculum similar to that of other major state law schools, while at the same time affording students a broad range of curricular options and special programs. The Buffalo model of legal education emphasizes the study of law in its social context, and a large number of interdisciplinary courses and programs support this emphasis. Close connections are maintained with other departments in the university, and dual and joint-degree programs are encouraged and supervised through the Baldy Center for Law and Social Policy.

■ Library and Physical Facilities

➡ *310,000 volumes & equivalents*   ➡ *LEXIS*
➡ *NEXIS*   ➡ *WESTLAW*   ➡ *DIALOG*
➡ *LRS*   ➡ *QL*

The school is housed in John Lord O'Brian Hall, a seven-story building completed in 1973. O'Brian Hall is located on the Amherst Campus of SUNY at Buffalo, which is one of the four university centers of the SUNY system. The classrooms, library, offices, and study space for the law school are in carpeted rooms which provide bright and comfortable work places. The library contains a major collection of periodicals and public documents; has an extensive collection of microfilms, audiovisual equipment, and materials; and is a depository for US government publications.

The Amherst Campus provides recreational and cultural space including two theaters, chamber music, and concert halls, a ceramics and art center, and athletic facilities in a new 10,000-seat fieldhouse.

■ Curriculum

➡ *Academic Support Program*   ➡ *82 credits required to graduate*   ➡ *two semesters and summer session*

Instruction is offered in two semesters from late August to May and in a summer session from mid-May to mid-July. Six full-time semesters, or five full-time semesters plus two summer sessions, are required for graduation. A part-time program allows students to spread their work over eight semesters.

The first-year program includes instruction in civil procedure, contracts, constitutional law, criminal law, legal research and writing, property, and torts (civil wrongs). These are the standard subjects in the first year of all American law schools. In addition, the first year affords an introduction to aspects of the social and economic context of the legal system and to legal institutions and processes.

Beyond the first year, students are required to complete 54 semester credit hours of work. One course is required (federal taxation, three credit hours), and each student must complete one seminar or other approved writing course (three credit hours). The balance of the upper-division program is elective, and students may choose from a full spectrum of survey and advanced courses covering the main fields of public and private law, from a very rich selection of seminars and small group courses in special or emerging areas of law study and research, and from clinics and simulations devoted to professional skills training.

■ Special Programs

The school offers special programs emphasizing interdisciplinary study and applications of law. The clinical program is distinguished in that the skills training is coordinated with substantive law courses to give students theoretical understanding of practical issues. The program allows students to serve clients and conduct research and fieldwork in such areas as economic development, mental health law, occupational safety and health law, school and education law, and international protection of human rights.

The school also has an extensive joint-degree program, which permits students to earn credit toward a master's or Ph.D. degree and the J.D. In recent years, the most active joint-degree programs have been with political science, management, philosophy, sociology, and economics. Special programs can be arranged with other departments. The interdisciplinary programs of the school are administered by the Baldy Center for Law and Social Policy. The center provides fellowship awards for outstanding J.D./Ph.D. students, offers advice and assistance to all joint-degree candidates, and supports interdisciplinary research and curriculum development.

The Legal Methods Program is a first-year program for students who are educationally disadvantaged. Based on the recognition that quantitative measurements of success in law school are not infallibly reliable predictors, the Admissions Committee reviews these applications for other signs of achievement that portend success in law school. Tutorial assistance in substantive courses is provided as well as intensive writing assignments given in the LMP and in the research and writing course. Correspondence regarding the program should be directed to Aundra Newell, Associate Dean for Student Services.

■ Admission

➡ *application deadline—Feb. 1*
➡ *LSAT, LSDAS required*

The school has no specific undergraduate course prerequisites. The school admits first-year students only in the fall semester (late August); application materials are available the preceding September.

Transfer with advanced standing is open to students who have successfully completed one year of work in an ABA-accredited law school.

■ Student Activities

Law student extracurricular activities are managed by law students through an elected representative body, the Student Bar Association. SBA-sponsored activities include lectures and special education programs, coordination of student participation in law school governance, and social events for students and faculty. Other student organizations include the Moot Court Board, which sponsors mock appellate practice competitions; *The Opinion*, the student newspaper; the *Buffalo Law Review*, a professional journal edited by students; and special interest groups such as the Asian Law Students Association (ALSA), the Latin American Law Students Association (LALSA), the Black Law Students Association (BLSA), the Native American Law Students Association (NALSA), the Association of Women Law Students, and the National Lawyers Guild.

■ Expenses and Financial Aid

➡ *tuition & fees—resident, $5,000; nonresident, $9,650*
➡ *estimated additional expenses—$4,000-5,000*

New York state residents are eligible for the Tuition Assistance Program (TAP) and State University Supplemental Tuition Awards (SUSTA). Students are eligible for Perkins (formerly NDSL) and federally insured loans offered through the New York State Higher Education Assistance Corporation (NYSHEAC). TAP and SUSTA are based on need.

For more information, write to the Financial Aid Office, 232 Capen Hall, North Campus, Buffalo, NY 14260.

■ Housing

Limited housing for single students is available in the new dormitory complex. A wide range of private apartments is available. Write to the University Housing Office, Richmond Quadrangle, SUNY, Amherst Campus, Buffalo, NY 14261.

■ Career Services

The school's Placement Office guides students in career selection and serves as a liaison between students and prospective employers.

In addition to providing services for third-year students, the Placement Office also aids first- and second-year law students in conducting their summer job search.

In recent years, over 90 percent of the eligible graduates in a class have been employed in legal work within nine months of graduation. New York and the northeastern states, as well as Washington, DC, are the most common locations for SUNY at Buffalo graduates. The southeastern, midwestern, and western states have also attracted graduates to such cities as Chicago, Miami, Detroit, and Los Angeles.

To obtain additional information, please contact Director of Placement, School of Law, O'Brian Hall, Amherst Campus, Buffalo, NY 14260.

Applicant Group for the 1993–1994 Academic Year

University at Buffalo, State University of New York School of Law
This grid includes only applicants who earned 120-180 LSAT scores under standard administrations.

LSAT Score	3.75 +		3.50 - 3.74		3.25 - 3.49		3.00 - 3.24		2.75 - 2.99		2.50 - 2.74		2.25 - 2.49		2.00 - 2.24		Below 2.00		No GPA		Total	
	Apps	Adm	Apps	Adm	Apps	Adm	Apps	Adm	Apps	Adm	Apps	Adm	Apps	Adm	Apps	Adm	Apps	Adm	Apps	Adm	Apps	Adm
175 - 180	0	0	0	0	0	0	1	0	1	0	0	0	0	0	0	0	0	0	0	0	2	0
170 - 174	3	0	3	0	2	0	4	2	5	1	0	0	1	0	0	0	0	0	2	1	20	4
165 - 169	7	3	14	3	18	9	19	7	12	3	2	1	4	2	0	0	0	0	0	0	76	28
160 - 164	14	2	34	8	32	6	34	7	12	2	9	4	5	4	0	0	0	0	6	4	146	37
155 - 159	23	9	53	24	60	26	29	14	11	6	10	5	2	2	0	0	0	0	1	0	189	86
150 - 154	8	6	31	15	29	12	16	7	11	7	6	3	6	3	0	0	0	0	3	3	110	56
145 - 149	2	1	12	6	10	4	7	1	11	7	2	2	4	2	0	0	0	0	2	1	50	24
140 - 144	0	0	2	2	3	1	6	3	9	7	2	1	1	1	0	0	0	0	2	2	25	17
135 - 139	1	1	1	1	1	0	2	0	1	1	0	0	0	0	0	0	0	0	0	0	6	3
130 - 134	0	0	0	0	1	1	0	0	0	0	0	0	0	0	0	0	0	0	0	0	1	1
Total	58	22	150	59	156	59	118	41	73	34	31	16	23	14	0	0	0	0	16	11	625	256

Apps = Number of Applicants
Adm = Number Admitted

University of California at Berkeley School of Law (Boalt Hall)

220 Boalt Hall
U.C. Berkeley, CA 94720

Phone: 510.642.2274

■ Introduction

Boalt Hall is located on the campus of the University of California at Berkeley. The campus is surrounded by wooded, rolling hills, and the city of Berkeley, which has a long history as one of America's most lively, culturally diverse, and politically adventurous cities. The surrounding San Francisco Bay Area offers culture, entertainment, and natural beauty without rival, much of which is accessible by BART (the Bay Area Rapid Transit system). All of Northern California, with its great variety of cultural and recreational opportunities, is within easy reach. Boalt Hall is one of the world's leading institutions of legal education and research. The school is a member of AALS and is approved by the ABA.

■ Enrollment/Student Body

➡ *5,240 applicants*   ➡ *809 admitted first-year class 1993*
➡ *269 enrolled first-year class 1993*   ➡ *780 total full-time (no part-time)*   ➡ *36% minority*   ➡ *46% women*
➡ *90 undergraduate schools represented*
➡ *more than 50 states & foreign countries represented*

The academic backgrounds and nonacademic experiences of Boalt Hall students are varied, and there is a substantial representation of various graduate and professional degrees. An advanced graduate (LL.M.) program admits 20-25 students annually from foreign countries.

■ Faculty

➡ *80 full-time*   ➡ *22 part-time or adjunct*
➡ *23 women*   ➡ *13 minority*

■ Library and Physical Facilities

➡ *600,000 volumes & equivalents*   ➡ *12 full-time librarians*
➡ *LEXIS*   ➡ *NEXIS*   ➡ *WESTLAW*
➡ *INNOPAC*   ➡ *MELVYL*

The law library's collection includes the Robbins Collection of Ancient, Canon, and Ecclesiastical Law, and extensive special collections on comparative and international law, natural resources, and the environment. The law library is linked by computer to the collections at other national law schools and to the combined university library holdings that number more than 7 million volumes. The late Chief Justice Earl Warren, an alumnus of the school, designated the law library as a depository for U.S. Supreme Court records and briefs, and it is also a selective official depository of U.S. government documents. The library maintains a photocopying service and IBM and MacIntosh PCs for student word-processing.

Adjacent to the law school is a dormitory reserved for law students. The university also maintains limited housing for students who are married or who have children. Most law students live in rented apartments or houses in the area.

■ Admission

➡ *Bachelor's degree required*   ➡ *application deadline—Feb. 1, early application strongly preferred*   ➡ *LSAT, LSDAS required*   ➡ *median GPA—3.70*   ➡ *median LSAT score—167*   ➡ *application fee—$40, fall admission only*

Applications are evaluated primarily in terms of undergraduate academic work and LSAT score. Academic and other references, exceptional accomplishments, prior employment, graduate study, and other activities are also considered. Applicants are advised to submit two letters of recommendation with their application. December is the last acceptable test date to meet the February application deadline, and repeated LSAT scores are averaged. Admission is highly selective; approximately 20 applications are received annually for each place in the first-year class. When necessary, disadvantaged students may be given special consideration in admission in order to achieve diversity in the entering class. Some decisions are made as early as January, and the bulk of decision letters are mailed by May. Early application is advised.

■ Student Activities

Students edit and publish nine legal periodicals: the *African-American Law and Policy Report*, the *Asian Law Journal*, the *Berkeley Journal of Employment and Labor Law*, the *California Law Review, Ecology Law Quarterly, High Technology Law Journal*, the *International Tax and Business Lawyer, Berkeley Women's Law Journal*, and *La Raza Law Journal*.

Participation in moot court is compulsory for first-year students; advanced students may participate in voluntary moot court and in honors competitions. Other activities include the Boalt Hall Student Association; the Boalt Hall Women's Association; the Berkeley Law Foundation; International Law Society, National Lawyers' Guild; and many student cultural and affinity groups.

Student activities and educational programs are enriched by the activities of the Earl Warren Legal Institute, an interdisciplinary law-related research and public service unit of the university.

■ Curriculum

➡ *Academic Support Program*   ➡ *85 credits required to graduate*   ➡ *more than 175 courses available*
➡ *semesters, begin in Aug.*
➡ *range of first-year class size—30-100*

An orientation program introduces new law students to the school and to legal learning at the beginning of the fall term. The first-year curriculum is prescribed. Upon completion of the first year, simulation-based courses are available in legal interviewing, legal counseling, legal accounting, and legal document drafting and are taught by teams of lawyers from large Bay Area law firms. Boalt Hall also offers the following clinical programs that are integrated with substantive courses: Disability Rights;

Immigration and Asylum Appeals; Domestic Violence; and The Berkeley Community Law Center. Interested students may be placed for a full semester as law clerks to federal and state judges or with public-interest, government, and private lawyers.

■ Special Programs

Concurrent-degree programs that allow students to earn the J.D. and a master's degree in another field in four years have been established with the following departments of the university: Asian studies, business administration, city planning, economics, journalism, public policy, and social welfare, as well as doctoral programs in economics and legal history. In addition, students may arrange concurrent programs with other campus departments.

Combined-degree programs are available with The Fletcher School of Law and Diplomacy at Tufts University or with the John F. Kennedy School of Government at Harvard University. Unique among American law schools is the Graduate Program in Jurisprudence and Social Policy, an interdisciplinary legal studies program leading to the Ph.D. that requires no prior legal training, and which also may be earned concurrently with a J.D.

Boalt Hall's concentration programs include Criminal Justice and Public Policy; Environmental Law; International and Comparative Legal Studies; Law and Technology/Intellectual Property; and Traditionally Disadvantaged Groups.

■ Expenses and Financial Aid

➧ *tuition & fees—full-time resident, $4,414, nonresident $12,112* ➧ *estimated additional expenses—$9,700* ➧ *need-based financial aid available* ➧ *FAFSA form for need analysis due* ➧ *deadline for priority consideration— March 2*

The university is normally able to cover most or all of the financial need of applicants eligible to receive funds. All financial aid is need-based and each package consists of grants-in-aid, Perkins and Stafford loans, and work-study funds for continuing students. Nonresidents may become residents after one year if appropriate steps are taken and if certain eligibility requirements are met. All fees are subject to change without notice.

■ Career Services

The Boalt Hall Career Services Office serves as a resource for Boalt Hall students, alumni, and prospective employers. It operates one of the largest on-campus recruitment programs in the country; provides opportunities for part-time, summer, and full-time legal positions; and maintains extensive files on a wide variety of positions available throughout the nation. The career services staff provides career counseling, résumé workshops, and programs on opportunities for traditional and nontraditional law careers.

Applicant Group for the 1993–1994 Academic Year

University of California at Berkeley School of Law (Boalt Hall)
This grid includes only applicants who earned 120-180 LSAT scores under standard administrations.

LSAT Score	3.75 +		3.50 -3.74		3.25 - 3.49		3.00 - 3.24		2.75 - 2.99		2.50 - 2.74		2.25 - 2.49		2.00 - 2.24		Below 2.00		No GPA		Total	
	Apps	Adm	Apps	Adm	Apps	Adm	Apps	Adm	Apps	Adm	Apps	Adm	Apps	Adm	Apps	Adm	Apps	Adm	Apps	Adm	Apps	Adm
175 - 180	51	50	42	40	30	13	14	2	2	0	2	0	3	0	0	0	0	0	1	0	145	105
170 - 174	105	100	143	96	89	12	50	7	9	0	6	0	5	0	2	0	0	0	4	3	413	218
165 - 169	219	118	305	44	214	10	133	7	43	1	22	0	5	0	3	0	0	0	14	5	958	185
160 - 164	229	44	354	38	282	20	143	8	62	2	34	0	12	0	3	0	0	0	21	0	1140	112
155 - 159	110	11	220	10	212	22	126	2	65	3	36	0	20	0	5	0	0	0	24	1	818	49
150 - 154	50	3	110	10	124	10	140	3	90	0	46	0	20	0	8	0	2	0	29	1	619	27
145 - 149	16	1	38	1	88	0	76	0	65	0	46	0	34	0	9	0	2	0	22	0	396	1
140 - 144	9	0	21	0	29	0	40	0	46	0	40	0	21	0	8	0	3	0	16	0	233	1
135 - 139	1	0	3	0	16	0	14	0	15	0	16	0	14	0	3	0	1	0	6	0	89	0
130 - 134	0	0	0	0	2	0	4	0	6	0	4	0	6	0	3	0	2	0	2	0	29	0
125 - 129	0	0	0	0	0	0	0	0	1	0	5	0	2	0	1	0	0	0	1	0	10	0
120 - 124	0	0	0	0	0	0	0	0	0	0	1	0	0	0	0	0	0	0	0	0	1	0
Total	790	326	1236	239	1086	87	740	29	404	7	258	0	142	0	45	0	10	0	140	10	4851	698

Apps = Number of Applicants
Adm = Number Admitted
Reflects 92% of the total applicant pool.

School of Law, University of California—Davis

Admissions Office
Davis, CA 95616-5201

Phone: 916.752.6477

■ Introduction

The School of Law at the University of California, Davis, was founded in 1965. It is accredited by the American Bar Association and is a member of the Association of American Law Schools. The school has a chapter of the Order of the Coif, the national honor society. The law building, King Hall, was named for Dr. Martin Luther King, Jr., in recognition of his efforts to bring social and political justice to disadvantaged peoples.

The Davis campus is 20 minutes from Sacramento and an hour and a half from San Francisco, within easy reach of the major recreational areas of the Sierra Nevada, Lake Tahoe, and the Mother Lode. The campus occupies 3,600 acres within the college town of Davis, where the small-town, friendly atmosphere is a welcome change from the distractions and stress usually associated with more urban environments.

The close proximity to the state capitol and the Bay Area provide both social and political stimulus necessary for a well-rounded educational experience. The campus also offers a full range of graduate and professional programs.

■ Enrollment/Student Body

- 3,372 applicants
- 693 admitted first-year class 1993
- 160 enrolled first-year class 1993
- 478 total full-time
- 30% minority
- 48% women
- 183 undergraduate schools represented

■ Faculty

- 38 total
- 31 full-time
- 7 part-time
- 7 women
- 4 minority
- 1:17 faculty student ratio (full-time faculty only)

■ Library and Physical Facilities

- 370,154 volumes & equivalents
- library hours: Mon.-Thurs., 8:00 A.M.-10:00 P.M.; Fri., 8:00 A.M.-5:00 P.M.; Sat., NOON-5:00 P.M.; Sun., NOON-10:00 P.M.
- LEXIS
- NEXIS
- WESTLAW
- MELVYL
- 4 full-time librarians
- library seats 285

The law school and library are housed in the same building, one of the more modern on campus. It has moot courtrooms, a pretrial skills laboratory, an instructional computer laboratory, study carrels, *Law Review* quarters, lounges, an infant care co-op, offices for student organizations, and is comfortably accessible to disabled students. Every law student has a key to the building and may use the facilities around the clock.

The law library has an open-stack system. All students are assigned to carrels, and books can be charged to carrels. Areas of specialization include: international law, comparative law, environmental law, agricultural law, water law, and space law. The library is a federal and California documents depository and has an extensive collection of California and federal government documents.

■ Curriculum

- *Academic Support Program*
- *88 units required to graduate*
- *108 courses available*
- *degrees available: J.D., J.D./M.B.A.; J.D./M.A.*
- *semesters, start in Aug.*
- *range of first-year class size—30-70*

During the first year at King Hall, students study six basic areas of the law: civil procedure, constitutional law, contracts, crimes, property, and torts. In a major departure from tradition, one of these courses is taught in small sections of approximately 30 students. The first year also includes a week-long introductory course and courses in legal research and writing. Second- and third-year programs are elective, except for a course on professional responsibility and a legal writing requirement. Courses may be selected within broad areas of concentration such as administration of criminal justice, business and taxation, civil litigation, estate planning and taxation, labor and employment law, environmental law, public interest law, and transnational studies.

■ Special Programs

Second- and third-year students have the opportunity to work under the supervision of practicing lawyers in clinicals in immigration law, environmental law, disability rights, tax law, employment relations, administrative law, public interest law, prison law, and criminal justice administration.

King Hall has an integrated civil rights curriculum including a substantive course in civil rights law, a civil rights litigation skills seminar, and a clinic representing indigent persons in civil rights cases. Students participating in the King Hall Civil Rights Clinic are certified to appear in federal court where they provide representation to people who would otherwise have no counsel and gain first-hand experience in constitutional litigation.

First-year students engage in oral argument as a part of the required legal research and writing course. This provides basic preparation for participation in the formal Moot Court program which emphasizes appellate advocacy skills. The program includes an honors competition and a series of regional, national, and international competitions.

Our moot court and trial competition teams have each advanced to the final rounds of the National Moot Court Competition and the National Mock Trial Competition in the last three years. We have also won other state, regional and national competitions.

Skills courses cover the major elements of both litigation and non-litigation practice. These include pretrial skills (interviewing, counseling, document drafting) negotiation and alternative dispute resolution, as well as introductory and advanced trial practice courses.

Students in the Public Interest Law Program receive a special certificate after completing 150 hours of public interest legal service. They take a selection of specialized courses and devote 25 hours to enhancing public-interest law programs.

■ Admission

➡ *Bachelor's degree or equivalent from college or university of approved standing required* ➡ *application deadline—Feb. 1*
➡ *rolling admission, early application encouraged*
➡ *LSAT, LSDAS required* ➡ *median GPA—3.45*
➡ *median LSAT score—164*
➡ *application fee—$40 (waivers available)*

Undergraduate grades and LSAT score form the foundation of the admission evaluation. The Admission Committee seeks students of diverse backgrounds. Consideration is given to ethnic and economic factors, advanced studies, significant work experience, and extracurricular and community activities. An applicant's maturity, capacity to grow, and commitment to law study are also major considerations. Multiple LSAT scores will be averaged. Admission Information Sessions are held at King Hall in November, December, and January. Law student guided tours can be arranged by contacting the Admission Office.

■ Cocurricular Activities

The student-run *Law Review* publishes four issues, including a single-topic symposium issue. The members of the *Law Review* are selected through a writing competition open to all.

The Law Student Association coordinates law student activities. Students sit on the student-faculty Educational Policy, Faculty Appointments, and Admission Committees. Other active organizations include the International Law Society, Environmental Law Society, Student Lawyers for the Arts, Women's Caucus, and Asian, Black, Christian, Jewish, La Raza, Native American, and Filipino Law Student Associations.

■ Expenses and Financial Aid

➡ *tuition & fees—residents, $4,359; nonresidents, $12,058*
➡ *estimated additional expenses—$7,129 (room, board, books)*
➡ *some need-based scholarships available*

Although grant monies are very limited, the School of Law Financial Aid Office administers all nationally recognized aid programs, such as Stafford Loans, Perkins Loans, and Work Study. University student loans and grants are also available. Financial aid applications must be submitted by March 1 of the year in which admission is sought. Applications are accepted after that date, but are considered after timely applications.

■ Housing

A wide variety of housing is available but it is advisable to begin seeking preferred accommodations early. The university maintains on-campus apartments for married students and Leach Hall for single graduate students. Students desiring on-campus housing should apply well in advance of the April deadline.

■ Career Services

The Law School maintains an active Career Services Office to help students secure permanent positions and summer work, as well as part-time or temporary employment during the academic year. Career counseling and résumé consultation are available to all students. Approximately 135 employers use the facilities of the office to interview Davis law students on campus. Special career workshops are scheduled throughout the year to provide students with employment information and to help them develop techniques useful in their job search.

Applicant Group for the 1993–1994 Academic Year

School of Law, University of California—Davis
This grid includes only applicants who earned 120-180 LSAT scores under standard administrations (95% of the total applicant pool).

LSAT Score	3.75 +		3.50 -3.74		3.25 - 3.49		3.00 - 3.24		2.75 - 2.99		2.50 - 2.74		2.25 - 2.49		2.00 - 2.24		Below 2.00		No GPA		Total	
	Apps	Adm	Apps	Adm	Apps	Adm	Apps	Adm	Apps	Adm	Apps	Adm	Apps	Adm	Apps	Adm	Apps	Adm	Apps	Adm	Apps	Adm
175 - 180	5	5	3	3	2	2	3	3	4	4	0	0	1	1	0	0	0	0	0	0	18	18
179 - 174	16	16	17	17	19	19	13	12	6	4	2	1	4	0	1	0	0	0	1	1	79	70
165 - 169	42	40	87	76	86	68	67	31	38	7	12	1	4	0	1	0	0	0	6	5	345	228
160 - 164	82	65	183	82	215	66	143	14	68	7	38	1	10	3	2	0	0	0	9	3	750	241
155 - 159	73	21	186	15	220	21	141	10	86	6	34	0	13	0	9	0	1	0	15	0	778	73
150 - 154	32	3	111	11	143	4	136	12	98	2	59	0	29	1	5	0	2	0	13	1	628	34
145 - 149	8	0	33	0	64	4	70	1	55	0	38	0	30	0	6	0	0	0	12	0	316	3
140 - 144	4	0	13	0	26	1	38	0	39	0	29	0	27	0	6	0	0	0	7	0	189	0
135 - 139	0	0	2	0	8	0	12	0	11	0	11	0	12	0	3	0	1	0	6	0	66	0
130 - 134	0	0	0	0	1	0	7	0	4	0	3	0	4	0	3	0	2	0	0	0	24	0
125 - 129	0	0	0	0	0	0	0	0	1	0	2	0	1	0	1	0	0	0	0	0	5	0
120 - 124	0	0	0	0	0	0	0	0	0	0	0	0	0	0	0	0	0	0	0	0	0	0
Total	262	150	635	204	784	181	630	83	410	30	228	5	137	5	37	0	6	0	69	10	3198	667

Apps = Number of Applicants
Adm = Number Admitted

University of California—Hastings College of the Law

200 McAllister Street
San Francisco, CA 94102

Phone: 415.565.4623

■ Introduction

Since its founding in 1878 as the University of California's first school of law, Hastings College of the Law has been at the center of the legal community in the West. In addition to legal practice that covers the entire spectrum of law, Hastings graduates sit as judges on the California bench by a 3-to-1 margin over any other law school.

Located in San Francisco's Civic Center, students have unparalleled access to the legal community. The California Supreme Court, California Court of Appeals, and the U.S. Court of Appeals for the Ninth Circuit are nearby. Two blocks away is City Hall, offices of the superior and municipal courts. With its central location and strong community links to many of the Bay Area's multicultural neighborhoods, Hastings offers students an educational experience that is virtually unlimited in its breadth and diversity.

■ Enrollment/Student Body

➡ *5,423 applicants*   ➡ *1,348 admitted first-year class 1993*
➡ *419 enrolled first-year class 1993*
➡ *1,264 total full-time*   ➡ *32% minority*
➡ *50% women*   ➡ *56 states & foreign countries represented*
➡ *112 undergraduate schools represented*

Hastings has one of the highest minority-student enrollments of any American Bar Association–approved law school in the nation. Many students come to Hastings from other career experiences. Though student ages range from 21-51, there are a significant number of students over 30; the average age of Hastings students is 27.

■ Faculty

➡ *114 total*   ➡ *51 full-time*   ➡ *63 part-time or adjunct*
➡ *33 women*   ➡ *7 minority*

■ Library and Physical Facilities

➡ *541,315 volumes & equivalents*   ➡ *library hours: Mon.-Fri., 8:00 A.M.-11:00 P.M.; Sat., 9:00 A.M.-10:00 P.M.; Sun., 9:00 A.M.-11:00 P.M.*   ➡ *LEXIS*   ➡ *NEXIS*
➡ *WESTLAW*   ➡ *DIALOG*   ➡ *VUTEXT*
➡ *INFOTRAC*   ➡ *DATATIMES*   ➡ *LEGITECH*
➡ *FIRST SEARCH*   ➡ *EPIC*   ➡ *8 full-time librarians*
➡ *library seats 1,295*   ➡ *computer lab*

The Legal Information Center houses an extensive collection of federal and California documents for which Hastings is an official depository. The breadth and depth of the center's collection, and its state-of-the-art computer-assisted research capabilities draw local attorneys, court personnel, and government agency employees to use the center's resources.

■ Curriculum

➡ *Academic Support Program*   ➡ *Clinical Instruction Program*   ➡ *scholarly publications*   ➡ *88 units/credits required to graduate*   ➡ *303 courses available*   ➡ *selected*

concurrent masters degree programs with U.C. Berkeley
➡ *semesters, begin in Aug.*
➡ *range of first-year class size—16-85*

The Hastings curriculum offers a broad spectrum of courses, from those that are fundamental to all forms of practice to those that reflect increased specialization. After three years of successful study, the student will receive a Juris Doctor degree, conferred by the Regents of the University of California.

Students must complete six semesters in residence, earn 88 semester units, pass all required courses, and earn a cumulative G.P.A. of at least C (2.00). The program is designed for full-time students; new students are admitted only at the beginning of the fall semester.

■ Special Programs

Legal Education Opportunity Programs—Initiated in 1969, the Legal Education Opportunity Program (LEOP) was designed to assist each student in excelling academically at Hastings. Students admitted through LEOP are offered a number of academic support services throughout their three years of study, beginning with orientation for incoming students and ending with a supplemental bar review course.

To be eligible for LEOP, applicants meet faculty established criteria of overcoming a disadvantaged background. This may include, but is not limited to disadvantages suffered as a result of cultural, economic, educational, familial, geographic, linguistic, physical, or social backgrounds.

Institutes and Exchanges Program—As part of the second- and third-year course of study, students at Hastings have the opportunity to participate in student-exchange programs involving Nihon University, Japan, Leiden University, Netherlands; the University of British Columbia, and Vermont Law School, as well as the Land Conservation Institute, the Public Law Research Institute, and the Public Interest Clearinghouse.

■ Admission

➡ *B.A. or equivalent required*   ➡ *application deadline—Feb. 15*   ➡ *admission decisions made early Jan. to mid-May*   ➡ *LSAT, LSDAS required*
➡ *median GPA—3.55*   ➡ *median LSAT score—163*
➡ *application fee—$40*

Students are admitted only in the fall. Although the selection process is highly competitive, each application is read with sincere deliberation. Therefore, candidates are encouraged to provide a complete and candid picture of themselves.

The committee assesses the relative strength of each applicant's academic achievements; LSAT score; professional experience, community, volunteer and extracurricular activities; letters of recommendation and works of written expression.

Student Activities

Hastings publishes more journals that offer credit than most other U.S. law schools. Second- and third-year students may earn academic credit by working on one of five law journals: *Hastings Communications and Entertainment Law Journal*, *Hastings Constitutional Law Quarterly*, *Hastings International and Comparative Law Review*, *Hastings Law Journal*, and *Hastings Women's Law Journal*.

Beyond the first-year moot court requirement, Hastings offers Appellate Advocacy as a second-year elective. Students write a brief and present oral arguments based on the record of an actual case pending in the California or the United States Supreme Court. Second- and third-year students represent Hastings in a number of state, national, and international competitions.

Civil Justice Clinic, Criminal Practice Clinic, Worker's Rights Clinics, Environmental Law Clinic, and Civil Practice Clinic offer students valuable experiences in criminal and civil practice under the supervision of practicing attorneys.

The governing organization of the student body is the Associated Students of Hastings. Additionally, students participate in approximately 40 different social and political groups.

Expenses and Financial Aid

➡ *full-time tuition & fees—residents, $4,779; nonresidents, $12,478* ➡ *limited number of scholarships available* ➡ *FAFSA and Entering Student Financial Aid Supplement required for financial aid; due by Feb. 1*

Typically, some 70 percent of Hastings students receive financial assistance from college-administered sources.

Scholarship awards are made to recognize and encourage the achievement, service, and professional promise of students.

Housing

On-campus housing is available at McAllister Tower, a 24-story building located on the same block as the college. The 250 apartments include efficiencies, studios, one-bedroom, and a few two-bedroom apartments. Students with families are clustered together to provide mutual support and companionship. The Off-Campus Housing Office provides current listings in San Francisco and the Bay Area as well as sample leases and other helpful publications.

Career Services

As part of its commitment to students and alumni, Hastings offers one of the most comprehensive law career services offices in Northern California. Students are provided assistance with law-related résumés, job-search strategies, interviewing techniques, and salary-negotiation skills. A complete set of resource aids, organized in an easy-to-use manner, are available for summer, part-time, and full-time job searches in the legal field.

Hastings annually lists 1,400-1,500 part-time and summer jobs for current students.

Through the fall and spring, approximately 200 employers visit the campus to interview students for both second-year summer associate positions and permanent post-graduation employment. An additional 200-300 employers from throughout the nation participate in the recruit-by-mail program.

Applicant Group for the 1993–1994 Academic Year

University of California—Hastings College of the Law
This grid includes only applicants whose files were complete and reviewed by the Admissions Committee, and who earned 120-180 LSAT scores.

LSAT Score	GPA 3.75 +		3.50 - 3.74		3.25 - 3.49		3.00 - 3.24		2.75 - 2.99		2.50 - 2.74		Below 2.50		No GPA		Total	
	Apps	Adm	Apps	Adm	Apps	Adm	Apps	Adm	Apps	Adm	Apps	Adm	Apps	Adm	Apps	Adm	Apps	Adm
175 - 180	10	8	12	12	11	8	10	6	5	0	2	0	2	1	0	0	52	35
170 - 174	31	29	50	48	50	40	45	23	10	1	6	1	5	0	2	1	199	143
165 - 169	87	78	164	133	173	84	135	23	60	2	29	2	11	0	6	6	665	328
160 - 164	131	116	307	208	342	110	244	33	105	6	60	7	32	3	9	3	1230	486
155 - 159	88	29	258	37	291	44	233	26	138	11	70	7	49	3	19	0	1146	157
150 - 154	40	11	137	20	198	21	204	23	157	12	80	2	63	5	24	2	903	96
145 - 149	14	3	47	10	110	8	110	3	93	4	75	6	60	0	16	0	525	34
140 - 144	5	0	20	0	33	1	49	0	70	1	36	0	45	0	8	0	266	2
Below 140	2	0	5	0	9	0	25	0	23	0	30	0	32	0	5	0	131	0
Total	408	274	1000	468	1217	316	1055	137	661	37	388	25	299	12	89	12	5117	1281

Apps = Number of Applicants
Adm = Number Admitted

School of Law, University of California, Los Angeles

Admissions Office, 71 Dodd Hall
405 Hilgard Avenue
Los Angeles, CA 90024-1445

Phone: 310.825.4041

■ Introduction

The School of Law of the University of California Los Angeles is located on the university campus in the foothills of the Santa Monica Mountains in the Westwood section of the city.

■ Enrollment/Student Body

➦ 5,226 applicants ➦ 1,219 admitted first-year class 1993 ➦ 350 enrolled first-year class 1993 ➦ 978 total full-time ➦ 39% minority ➦ 42% women ➦ over 100 undergraduate schools represented

The student body is a diverse group of whom approximately 25 percent come from outside California.

■ Faculty

➦ 96 total ➦ 72 full-time ➦ 24 part-time or adjunct ➦ 27 women ➦ 16 minority ➦ 6 emeritus professors recalled to teach

■ Library and Physical Facilities

➦ 469,108 volumes & equivalents ➦ library hours: Mon.-Thurs., 8:00 A.M.-MIDNIGHT; Fri., 8:00 A.M.-9:00 P.M.; Sat., 9:00 A.M.-6:00 P.M.; Sun., 1:00 P.M.-MIDNIGHT ➦ LEXIS ➦ NEXIS ➦ WESTLAW ➦ 9 full-time librarians ➦ library seats 417

Documents and computerized systems are available. Students also have access to the university library system of over three million volumes.

■ Curriculum

➦ Academic Support Program ➦ 87 credits required to graduate ➦ degrees available: J.D.; LL.M.; J.D./M.B.A.; J.D./M.A. (Urban Planning)

The law school awards the J.D. degree to students who satisfactorily complete their law study over three years of residence. Only a full-time day program is offered. Second- and third-year students choose from a wide variety of courses, seminars, clinical programs, and independent studies. Outstanding programs in the traditional fields of legal study as well as a broad range of imaginative clinical offerings are made possible because of the school's large, distinguished, innovative faculty, and a new clinical study facility.

■ Special Programs

UCLA offers a wide variety of innovative programs. Joint-degree programs may be undertaken with the Graduate School of Management (J.D./M.B.A.), and the School of Architecture and Urban Planning (J.D./M.A.).

The law school offers a substantial number of clinical programs designed to provide students with experience in performing a wide range of lawyering tasks in a variety of substantive law settings. Students participate in simulated exercises, live client casework, and part-time work in local agencies. The law school also offers an externship program. Students learn matters that cannot be taught in the classroom, such as how agencies make policy, how judges make decisions, how to investigate facts, and how strategy is developed for dealing with legal issues.

As many as 100 students a year have participated in the externship program. Past placements have included, for example, federal district and appellate courts, and public interest and government agencies.

One of the most outstanding features of the curriculum is its flexibility. By careful selection, students are able to build their own course of study, which can lead to either a broad sample of the legal spectrum or a highly specialized and concentrated development of expertise within a particular field.

■ Admission

➦ Baccalaureate degree required ➦ application deadline—Jan. 15 ➦ LSAT, LSDAS required ➦ median GPA—3.57 ➦ median LSAT score—165 ➦ application fee—$40

All applicants must have a baccalaureate degree and take the LSAT no later than December 1993. Any LSAT taken prior to December 1989 is not valid. There are no specific undergraduate course or major requirements. Students are admitted in the fall term only.

Admission is based primarily on proven academic and intellectual ability measured largely by the LSAT and the quality of undergraduate education as determined by not only the GPA, but also by such factors as the breadth, depth, and rigor of the undergraduate educational program. In appropriate cases, the admissions committee may also consider additional factors such as substantial career achievements, ethnicity, disadvantages overcome, diverse backgrounds, and other information relevant to the successful study and practice of law. Because of the large applicant pool, applicants are strongly urged to apply early.

UCLA accepts transfer students. Transfer applications are available after June 1st.

■ Minority Recruitment

In recognition of the underrepresentation of minority members in the legal profession and to diversify the law school's educational program and outlook, the law school in 1967 initiated efforts to increase significantly its minority student enrollment. Since then well over 3,100 minority students have been admitted. UCLA remains committed to maintaining a student body that reflects the diversity of American society. For information, students should contact the Admissions Office.

■ Student Activities

Diverse student interests are represented through various student organizations. Students edit and publish the

UCLA Law Review. The National Black Law Journal, the Chicano/Latino Law Review, and the Asian Pacific Island Law Journal are also published at UCLA, as are the Entertainment Law Review, the Pacific Basin Law Journal, the UCLA Journal of Environmental Law and Policy, and the UCLA Women's Law Journal. The Moot Court Honors Program operates a large and effective program of mock appellate advocacy. There is a very active Student Bar Association. There is a wide variety of other social and political groups. Students publish a law school newspaper and present an annual student-faculty musical.

■ Expenses and Financial Aid

➡ tuition & fees—resident, $4,503; nonresident, $12,202
➡ scholarships available   ➡ financial aid available
➡ admitted applicants will be sent required forms

Loans and some grants are available to students. There is no participation in GAPSFAS.

■ Career Services

The Career Services Office provides opportunities for part-time, summer, and full-time legal positions. It arranges interviews with employers from many parts of the country and maintains extensive files on a wide variety of positions available all over the nation. It also provides excellent career counseling services. The staff conducts individual and group counseling. They also call upon alumni, faculty, and other members of the bar for career counseling, and regularly sponsor career-related programs.

Applicant Group for the 1993–1994 Academic Year

School of Law, University of California, Los Angeles
This grid includes only applicants who earned 120-180 LSAT scores under standard administrations.

LSAT Score	3.75 +		3.50 -3.74		3.25 - 3.49		3.00 - 3.24		2.75 - 2.99		2.50 - 2.74		2.25 - 2.49		2.00 - 2.24		Below 2.00		No GPA		Total	
	Apps	Adm	Apps	Adm	Apps	Adm	Apps	Adm	Apps	Adm	Apps	Adm	Apps	Adm	Apps	Adm	Apps	Adm	Apps	Adm	Apps	Adm
175 - 180	18	18	20	19	16	13	8	7	4	0	1	0	2	0	0	0	0	0	1	0	70	57
170 - 174	46	46	67	65	65	48	33	12	15	1	4	0	4	0	2	0	0	0	2	0	238	172
165 - 169	114	110	221	187	186	95	116	17	39	1	17	0	4	0	1	0	1	0	7	1	706	411
160 - 164	168	130	344	143	304	46	160	9	75	1	37	0	13	0	5	1	0	0	11	0	1117	330
155 - 159	120	14	237	13	262	35	179	19	96	10	56	2	21	1	10	0	0	0	19	0	1000	94
150 - 154	52	4	132	12	166	20	189	20	123	6	72	1	36	0	6	0	2	0	24	0	802	63
145 - 149	10	1	64	0	109	0	112	0	79	0	69	0	40	0	15	0	0	0	20	0	518	1
140 - 144	7	0	17	0	43	0	59	0	65	0	47	0	30	0	8	0	1	0	18	0	295	0
135 - 139	2	0	5	0	9	0	18	0	23	0	25	0	20	0	4	0	2	0	8	0	116	0
130 - 134	0	0	2	0	3	0	6	0	6	0	7	0	8	0	5	0	1	0	2	0	40	0
125-129	0	0	1	0	0	0	0	0	1	0	3	0	1	0	0	0	0	0	1	0	7	0
120-124	0	0	0	0	0	0	0	0	1	0	0	0	1	0	0	0	0	0	0	0	2	0
Total	537	323	1110	439	1163	257	880	84	527	19	338	3	180	1	56	1	7	0	113	1	4911	1128

Apps = Number of Applicants
Adm = Number Admitted
Reflects 94% of the total applicant pool.

California Western School of Law

225 Cedar Street
San Diego, CA 92101   Phone: 619.239.0391, 800.255.4252 (admissions); or 619.525.7082 (bulletin requests)

■ Introduction

California Western is the oldest fully accredited law school in San Diego. Located in one of the most beautiful cities in the world, the law school has a history of providing contemporary legal education. The school is located downtown in a historically designated building. The new campus center houses the bookstore, campus deli, conference rooms, and offices, allowing for expansion of current library and classroom facilities.

■ Enrollment/Student Body

➡ *2,960 applicants*   ➡ *1,400 admitted first-year class 1993*
➡ *375 enrolled first-year class 1993*   ➡ *860 total full-time*
➡ *16% minority*   ➡ *43% women*
➡ *42 states & foreign countries represented*
➡ *153 undergraduate schools represented*

■ Faculty

➡ *80 total*   ➡ *46 full-time*   ➡ *31 full/part-time women*
➡ *7 minority*

A young vibrant faculty are leading contributors to innovative research and practical legal education. The quality of our faculty is evidenced by their legal training at some of the finest law schools in the country, significant scholarly writings, participation in professional associations, and involvement in public service.

"We teach people how to be lawyers as well as how to think like them," says Professor Bill Lynch. "Students learn the practical side of becoming an attorney so that when they graduate they can practice the profession immediately and competently."

■ Library and Physical Facilities

➡ *207,582 volumes & equivalents*   ➡ *library hours:*
7:00 A.M.-MIDNIGHT   ➡ *LEXIS*   ➡ *NEXIS*
➡ *WESTLAW*   ➡ *DIALOG*   ➡ *7 full-time librarians*
➡ *library seats 458*   ➡ *student computer center*
➡ *laptop computer room*

■ Curriculum

➡ *Academic Support Program*   ➡ *89 credits required to graduate*   ➡ *117 courses available*   ➡ *degrees available: J.D. & M.C.L. (Master in Comparative Law for foreign attorneys)*   ➡ *trimesters, start in Aug.*   ➡ *first-year class size—fall, 270; spring, 60*   ➡ *fall class divided into three sections*   ➡ *mid-year class starts spring trimester (January)*

Under the flexible trimester system, students may choose to graduate in two, two-and-one-half, or three years.

■ International Legal Studies Program

Publishing the third oldest *International Law Journal* in the United States, California Western also has one of the best collections of international, comparative, and foreign law resource materials in the Southwest.

"Each year, attorneys from all over the world present papers at the law school," says International Legal Studies Director, Professor John Noyes. "Students have the opportunity to interact with outstanding scholars on an academic and social level."

■ Clinical Internship Program

Our nationally recognized program trains students in lawyering skills and provides the opportunity to put their academic skills into practice immediately. "Over 60 percent of our students participate in the program," according to Professor Janet Weinstein, director of the program. "Students consider their internship experience to be one of the highlights of their education."

■ Graduate Courses

Many students take advantage of our affiliation agreement with San Diego State University, choosing graduate-level courses from such areas as social work, psychology, or business to enhance their legal education.

■ Specialty Courses and Programs

Programs include the Telecommunications Law Institute, the Interdisciplinary Training Program in Child Abuse, and the Institute for Criminal Defense Advocacy. Specialty courses include biotechnology and the law, environmental natural resources, sports, and entertainment law.

■ Admission Standards

➡ *Bachelor's degree required*
➡ *application deadline—fall class, May 1; spring class, November 1*   ➡ *LSAT, LSDAS required*
➡ *median GPA—3.20*   ➡ *median LSAT score—156*
➡ *application fee—$45*

"Admission is competitive," according to Assistant Dean for Admissions Nancy Ramsayer, "but applicants receive full consideration by reviewing each file carefully." Performance on the LSAT and the academic record are the most important factors. However, substantial consideration is given to other factors such as work experience, personal achievements, and volunteer service.

■ Commitment to Ethnic and Cultural Diversity

California Western actively recruits students from current underrepresented groups in the legal profession. According to Assistant Dean for Minority Affairs Jonnie Estell, "Our institutional commitment to diversity resulted in 16 percent ethnic representation in the Fall '93 class."

Student organizations include Black Law (BLSA), Pan-Asian Bar, La Raza, and the Multi-Cultural Associations.

The academic support program includes 1) a two-week, skills-oriented class 2) tutorials offered throughout the first year via small group and individual sessions, and 3) academic counseling.

Housing

"Our Housing Office works closely with students to locate attractive, convenient housing, assist with roommates, and offer information on services associated with relocation," states Housing Coordinator Charlene Chatham. "We provide a full range of assistance to the student and his/her family to make the transition to San Diego and law school a smooth one."

Student Activities

➻ *Publications include: Law Review (top 10%), International Law Journal, and Telecommunications Law Journal*

Specialty student organizations include Pacific Rim Law Society, Institute for Public Interest Law, Environmental Law Society, Family Law Society, International Law Society, Lambda Alpha International Student Association, and Sports, and Entertainment Law Society.

Students share a spirit of cooperation. Study groups, the center of academic and emotional support, are common. Students are actively involved in a wide variety of activities through many student organizations.

Students who relish the challenge of competition will find ample opportunity through appellate advocacy or trial competitions. Our teams consistently place in regional and national competitions.

Expenses and Financial Aid

➻ *tuition & fees—full-time, $15,700* ➻ *estimated additional expenses—books, $662; rent, utilities, food, $6,964; transporta-* tion, $1,900; personal/misc., $3,095 ➻ *scholarships available: Academic Scholars Program, Deans Scholarships for Ethnic & Cultural Diversity, Career Transition Scholarship, J.D. Scholarship for Librarians* ➻ *financial aid available* ➻ *CSS/FAF and FAFSA need forms required* ➻ *FWS, Perkins, Stafford, SLS, and private loans available*

"Being a free-standing law school is a real advantage for us," says Financial Aid Director Kyle Poston. "Law students are our only priority."

Career Services

The Office of Career Services informs students about the many career options available to law graduates through individual counseling. Workshop programs include the Pro Bono, Minority Career Development, and Alumni Career Advisor Network, as well as on- and off-campus recruitment and a monthly newsletter.

The Director of Career Services, Lisa Kellogg, states that "the practical training received by our students makes California Western very popular with a broad range of legal employers."

Alumni

California Western has nearly 5,000 alumni located throughout the world, including a former U.S. ambassador; lawyers in the American embassies in France, Germany, and Belgium; and scores of judges and senior attorneys throughout the United States.

Applicant Group for the 1993–1994 Academic Year

California Western School of Law

LSAT Score	GPA 3.76 +		3.50 - 3.75		3.25 - 3.49		3.00 - 3.24		2.75 - 2.99		2.50 - 2.74		2.25 - 2.49		2.00 - 2.24		1.99 -		LSAT Totals	
	Apps	Adm	Apps	Adm	Apps	Adm	Apps	Adm	Apps	Adm	Apps	Adm	Apps	Adm	Apps	Adm	Apps	Adm	Apps	Adm
175 - 180	0	0	0	0	0	0	0	0	0	0	0	0	1	1	0	0	0	0	1	1
170 - 174	0	0	0	0	0	0	0	0	0	0	4	2	0	0	0	0	0	0	4	2
165 - 169	2	2	4	4	16	16	9	9	11	11	10	10	3	3	1	1	1	0	57	56
160 - 164	12	10	17	10	38	30	55	40	50	41	31	21	25	13	8	2	0	0	236	167
155 - 159	13	12	54	52	96	94	153	150	101	91	80	54	52	27	19	3	1	0	569	483
150 - 154	12	12	68	63	148	135	204	152	216	97	135	45	74	8	23	0	6	0	886	512
145 - 149	5	4	35	23	89	34	158	16	130	4	110	5	60	0	28	0	1	0	616	86
140 - 144	0	0	20	2	21	0	58	1	83	2	52	0	44	0	17	0	4	0	299	5
135 - 139	0	0	2	0	10	0	15	0	26	0	26	0	17	0	8	0	3	0	107	0
130 - 134	0	0	0	0	1	0	7	0	5	0	6	0	4	0	3	0	1	0	27	0
125 - 129	0	0	0	0	0	0	0	0	3	0	1	0	3	0	0	0	0	0	7	0
120 - 124	0	0	0	0	1	0	0	0	0	0	0	0	0	0	0	0	0	0	1	0
GPA Totals	44	40	200	154	420	309	659	368	625	246	455	137	283	52	107	6	17	0	2810	1312

Apps = Number of Applicants
Adm = Number Admitted
Applicants with 120-180 LSAT scores earned under standard administrations 2,810
Applicants with only 10-48 scores earned under standard administrations (not in grid) . . . . 79 (not in grid)
Miscellaneous applicants with no LSAT, nonstandard administration, transfers, or visiting . 70 (not in grid)
TOTAL 2,959

Campbell University—Norman Adrian Wiggins School of Law

P.O. Box 158
Buies Creek, NC 27506

Phone: 919.893.2772 or 1.800.334.4111

■ Introduction

Campbell University, Norman Adrian Wiggins School of Law admitted its charter class in August 1976. The school of law was accredited by the North Carolina State Bar in 1978 and the American Bar Association in 1979.

Campbell University is located in the rural village of Buies Creek, 30 miles south of Raleigh, the state capital, and 30 miles north of Fayetteville—two of the most rapidly growing urban areas in the nation. Founded in 1887, the university's 1,450-acre campus offers programs for approximately 1,800 undergraduate and 800 graduate students.

While Campbell is a Southern Baptist university and establishment of the school of law was conceived as a Christian mission, neither the school of law nor the university, which also maintains a campus in Kuala Lumpur, Malaysia, is sectarian in the narrow sense of the word.

■ Enrollment/Student Body

➡ *900 applicants*   ➡ *187 admitted first-year class 1993*
➡ *119 enrolled first-year class 1993*   ➡ *310 total full-time*
➡ *1% minority*   ➡ *40% women*

■ Faculty

➡ *35 total*   ➡ *20 full-time*   ➡ *15 part-time or adjunct*
➡ *5 women*

■ Library and Physical Facilities

➡ *146,390 volumes & equivalents*   ➡ *library hours: Mon.-Thurs., 7:00 A.M.-MIDNIGHT; Fri., 7:00 A.M.-11:00 P.M.; Sat., 8:00 A.M.-6:00 P.M.; Sun., NOON-MIDNIGHT*   ➡ *LEXIS*
➡ *NEXIS*   ➡ *WESTLAW*   ➡ *1 full-time librarian*
➡ *library seats 414*

The school of law is located in historic Kivett Hall in the center of the Campbell campus. A 35,000-square-foot addition is currently under construction, which will provide additional library space, classrooms, a second courtroom, computer facilities, and student offices.

■ Curriculum

➡ *90 credits required to graduate*   ➡ *degrees available: J.D./M.B.A.*   ➡ *semesters, begin in Aug.*

The law school conducts a seven-week summer session and does not operate a part-time program. A majority of the total hours of study consists of required courses. A broad range of electives, usually including several seminars of 10 or fewer students, is available. The curriculum has been carefully planned to coalesce the practical and theoretical. Jurisprudence is a required subject, and one-third of the third-year curriculum is devoted to an innovative advocacy and practice course designed to bridge the gap between law school and law practice. Fulfillment of an advanced writing requirement and completion of one of several planning courses are also prerequisites for graduation.

■ Special Programs

Campbell's first-year program is designed to maximize the opportunity for success in law school and law practice. Over one-half of the first-year classes are sectioned, insuring an average size of 45 to 50 students in most classes, with each student participating in one section of only 25 students. Legal research and writing clinics of nine or ten students each are directed by teaching assistants under the supervision of faculty members.

The North Carolina State Bar's rule allows Campbell's second-year students to prosecute misdemeanors in state courts in conjunction with required criminal procedure and introductory trial advocacy courses.

Students also have the option of pursuing a J.D. and M.B.A. degree concurrently through a special arrangement with the Lundy-Fetterman School of Business at Campbell University.

In 1986, Campbell won the American College of Trial Lawyer's Emil Gumpert Award for the most outstanding trial advocacy program in the nation.

■ Admission

➡ *B.A./B.S. required*   ➡ *rolling admission*
➡ *LSAT, LSDAS required*   ➡ *median GPA—3.2*
➡ *median LSAT score—156*   ➡ *application fee—$30*

Admission to the School of Law is granted on the basis of the faculty Admission Committee's evaluation of the probable contributions of the applicant to society and the legal profession. In an attempt to select objectively those who most possess traits essential for success in the practice of law, Campbell utilizes a comprehensive application questionnaire, including the LSAT/LSDAS reports and writing sample, and requires a personal interview as a prerequisite to admission.

While there is no formal deadline for applications, all initial invitations have usually been extended and a waiting list established by the end of April. Although a baccalaureate degree is generally required, students who have completed three-fourths of the work acceptable for the baccalaureate are also eligible to apply.

Each year, approximately 300 of those in the pool of qualified applicants are granted personal interviews. About 80 percent of those invited for interviews are selected on the basis of grade-point averages and LSAT scores, the balance primarily because of nonquantifiable factors. In past years, from 40 to 54 percent of those interviewed have been extended invitations for admission. Factors considered by the Admission Committee include the applicant's GPA, LSAT score, work experience, maturity, intellectual honesty, innovativeness, leadership, self-reliance, ability to overcome obstacles, pleasantness of personality, demonstrated moral and physical courage, sophistication in the sense of being able to function in varied contexts, and potential for unusual contributions to society.

■ Performance-based Admission Program

Since 1977, the school of law has conducted a performance-based admission program during its summer session. Approximately 70 applicants take two regular law school courses for a total of six credit hours in the seven-week session. Students making a superior grade in each of the two courses are guaranteed positions in the first-year class in the fall. Students not making superior grades, but achieving a satisfactory average, are placed on a waiting list with qualified applicants not participating in the program. Performance in the program is a factor considered by the Admission Committee in filling vacancies from the waiting list.

■ Minority Admissions

The school of law actively recruits minority students. Campbell's personalized admission and educational programs, equally available to minority and nonminority applicants and students, have resulted in the admission of minority students whose academic achievements have far surpassed projected class standing based solely on the LSAT/GPA statistics.

■ Student Activities

A chief goal in structuring a small law school was to afford every student an opportunity for meaningful participation in cocurricular activities. The student-edited *Campbell Law Review* was established in 1978. Students also publish the *Campbell Law Observer*, the nation's only student-edited newspaper for the legal profession, the circulation of which includes 10,000 North Carolina lawyers. The school has a full program of moot court activities, and students participate in re-

gional and national moot court and trial court competitions. Delta Theta Phi and Phi Alpha Delta legal fraternities have established chapters at Campbell, as have Women in Law, the Law Students Civil Rights Research Council, and the Christian Legal Society. The Student Bar Association maintains an extensive speakers program and coordinates student participation in law school activities. Law Partners is an organization composed of spouses of law students. The law school maintains an active intramural program, running its own basketball league and participating in university leagues in other sports. Golf tournaments are held on the campus at Keith Hills Golf Club, one of North Carolina's outstanding golf courses.

■ Expenses and Financial Aid

➡ *full-time tuition & fees—$11,750* ➡ *10 full-tuition scholarships, partial scholarships, research and teaching assistantships available* ➡ *minority scholarships available* ➡ *extensive financial aid program, including work study, Law Student Assured Access, and National Director Student Loans*

The cost of living in Buies Creek and the surrounding communities is low by national and urban standards.

■ Career Services

The placement office corresponds with over 1,800 employers. About 98 percent of all Campbell Law School alumni have passed at least one state bar examination. Approximately 10 to 20 alumni are admitted to the U.S. Supreme Court Bar yearly.

Admission Profile Not Available

Capital University Law & Graduate Center

665 S. High Street
Columbus, OH 43215

Phone: 614.445.8836, fax: 614.445.7125

■ Introduction

Capital University Law & Graduate Center is located adjacent to downtown Columbus, Ohio, a growing, major metropolitan area of over one million inhabitants. Columbus is the capital of Ohio, and all of the state judicial, legal, and governmental offices are readily available to law students. The metropolitan location provides various cultural opportunities, including a symphony, ballet, numerous resident theaters, touring shows, and extensive collegiate athletics.

The law school is a member of AALS, is fully accredited by the ABA, and is a charter member of the League of Ohio Law Schools. The university is an institution of the Lutheran Church of America and includes three undergraduate colleges, a Graduate School of Administration, and the law school. Total student population is about 3,450.

■ Enrollment/Student Body

➡ *1,455 applicants*   ➡ *644 admitted first-year class 1993*
➡ *262 enrolled first-year class 1993*   ➡ *479 total full-time*
➡ *311 total part-time*   ➡ *7% minority*   ➡ *42% women*
➡ *40 states & foreign countries represented*
➡ *150 undergraduate schools represented*

The law school actively encourages applications from minority students, women, and students with disabilities, and admits without regard to race, creed, national origin, or sex. Approximately 55 percent of all incoming, full-time students reside outside of Ohio.

■ Faculty

➡ *31 total*   ➡ *46 part-time or adjunct*   ➡ *7 women*
➡ *4 minority*

■ Library and Physical Facilities

➡ *215,000 volumes & equivalents*   ➡ *24-hour access to law library*   ➡ *LEXIS*   ➡ *NEXIS*   ➡ *WESTLAW*
➡ *INFOTRAC*   ➡ *5 full-time librarians*

Located in the historic German Village district of Columbus, the school is two blocks from the Franklin County Hall of Justice and within seven blocks of the state capitol and Supreme Court.

■ Curriculum

➡ *Academic Success Program*   ➡ *86 credits required to graduate*   ➡ *approx. 150 courses available*   ➡ *degrees available: J.D.; J.D./M.B.A.; J.D./Masters of Sports Administration; Combined J.D./LL.M. in Taxation; LL.M. in Business & Taxation; M.T. in Taxation*   ➡ *semesters, start in Aug.*   ➡ *170-180 first-year day students (2 sections of 85-90 students), 85-90 first-year evening students (1 section)*

Three regular academic years are required in the full-time day division. In the evening division, the part-time course of study requires four years, including two nine-week summer sessions. All students receive a J.D. degree upon graduation. Students may accelerate graduation by one semester through summer school attendance. Numerous elective courses are available which enable a student to pursue a general practice curriculum, a public law curriculum, and a business curriculum, as well as specialties too numerous to include in this description.

The law school has the only ABA-approved postgraduate tax law program for lawyers and accountants in Ohio.

For further details and specific course offerings, please consult the law school viewbook available upon request from the school.

■ Multicultural Affairs

Capital University makes a significant effort to recruit, admit, and enroll minority students. Capital has many programs to aid in the retention of minority students; these include the presence of minority faculty, availability of financial resources, and academic and nonacademic support, as well as placement opportunities through the minority clerkship program. Capital is constantly striving to create a more culturally diverse academic environment within the law school community.

■ Special Programs

The law school's outstanding clinical program, under supervision of faculty members, gives the student hands-on experience working in the legal system. It integrates poverty law, interviewing and counseling, professional responsibility, trial advocacy, advanced evidence, and taxation.

The Law Institutes Program at Capital includes the Capital University Law School Center for Dispute Resolution; the Institute for Citizen Education; the Ethics Institute; the Institute for International Legal Education; and the Summer Program of Comparative and International Law.

In 1993, the innovative Summer Program of Comparative and International Law offered courses from four distinguished legal educators from Israel, Brazil, Venezuela, and Lebanon. They taught classes in the following areas: Transnational Taxation, International Trade and Investment, International Water Rights, and Protection of Minorities under International Law.

Capital University offers the three following joint-degree programs:

In order to offer a joint **J.D./Master of Sports Administration/Facility Management Degree**, Capital University has entered into agreement with Ohio University, one of the pioneers in the field of sports administration. This program allows a student to participate in one of the nation's most reputable sports administration programs while earning a law degree.

The law school and the Graduate School of Administration cooperatively offer a joint **J.D./Master of Business Administration**. The curriculum allows simultaneous enrollment in both schools, and reduces by 18 hours the total hours of credit required for separate J.D. and M.B.A. degrees.

Under the combined **J.D./LL.M. in Taxation**, a student who has had Federal Personal Income Tax (FPIT) may take twelve hours in advanced tax courses while pursuing a J.D. degree. Upon graduation the student would matriculate into the LL.M. program and complete the LL.M. degree in one semester of full-time study (12 credit hours).

■ Admission

➤ *Bachelor's degree required for admission*
➤ *application deadline—May 1*   ➤ *LSAT, LSDAS required*
➤ *median GPA—3.25*   ➤ *median LSAT score—154*
➤ *application fee—$35*

The law school seeks applicants who ranked in the upper half of their undergraduate class and achieved an LSAT score above the 60th percentile. Other factors used in evaluation include the competitiveness and difficulty of the candidate's undergraduate school and course of study, any graduate coursework, employment history, writing ability, and general background.

■ Expenses and Financial Aid

➤ *tuition & fees—first-year full-time, $12,927; first-year part-time, $7,923*   ➤ *estimated additional expenses—$9,500 (includes books and living expenses)*   ➤ *merit-based scholarships; need- & merit-based grants available*
➤ *minority scholarships available (see viewbook)*
➤ *other financial aid available: work-study, student loans, research assistants and teaching assistants*
➤ *graduate FAF required; forms are available after Jan. 1*

■ Student Activities

Numerous cocurricular and extracurricular activities are offered by Capital. These include the Night Prosecutors Program, an award-winning project for resolving minor disputes. Students receive extensive training in crisis counseling and mediation techniques as well as involvement in the criminal justice system.

Capital University Law Review is a student-edited, general review which publishes four journals annually on significant topics of current, social concern. Recent symposia have dealt with ethics and the law, intercollegiate athletics, obscenity, religion and the law, disposal of hazardous waste, sexual harassment, professional responsibility, and product liability.

Extensive programs in appellate and trial advocacy and client counseling are available. In addition to offering courses in these subjects, the law school encourages students to participate in intra- and interscholastic counseling and advocacy competitions each year.

Student organizations include the American Trial Lawyers Association, Black Law Students Association, Capital Public Interest Law Foundation, Christian Legal Society, Delta Theta Phi Fraternity, Environmental Law Group, Hispanic Law Students Association, International Law Society, Law Partners, Law Review, Moot Court Board, Jewish Law Students Association, Phi Delta Phi Fraternity, Phi Alpha Delta Fraternity, a student newspaper, Student Bar Association, Volunteer Income Tax Association, and Women Law Students Association.

■ Career Services

Capital University Law School maintains a full-time career services staff which offers assistance to students and alumni. The Career Services Office assists students in achieving their career goals by providing individual career counseling; serving as an information clearinghouse for job postings and resource materials; presenting a variety of workshops on career options, résumé writing, interviewing, and job search strategies; developing the on-campus interview program; and promoting off-campus interview conferences.

Admission Profile Not Available

Benjamin N. Cardozo School of Law Yeshiva University

55 Fifth Avenue
New York, NY 10003

Phone: 212.790.0274

■ Introduction

The Benjamin N. Cardozo School of Law is a dynamic institution that provides classical legal training within a framework of clinical programs and seminars offering debate on critical issues of our time. Cardozo combines traditional coursework with other disciplines such as history, literature, and philosophy, resulting in a broad program of legal education.

Cardozo is located in historic Greenwich Village in the heart of Manhattan with proximity to New York City's financial and business districts; federal, state, and municipal courts and agencies; and museums, theaters, and concert halls.

■ Enrollment/Student Body

➥ *2,472 applicants*   ➥ *255 enrolled in Sept.; 44 in Jan.; 40 in May*   ➥ *920 total full-time*   ➥ *10% minority*
➥ *47% women*   ➥ *122 undergraduate schools represented by first-year students*

Cardozo's student body parallels the diverse population that is unique to New York City. There is a broad geographical distribution, a strong ethnic focus, and a range of ages. Cardozo offers the Accelerated Entry Plan (AEP), which provides a way for motivated students to begin legal studies in either January or May. AEP students complete six semesters in two-and-one-half years.

■ Faculty

➥ *72 total*   ➥ *47 full-time*   ➥ *25 adjunct*
➥ *13 women*

Cardozo's outstanding faculty are drawn from the leading ranks of America's legal community. Cardozo has been included among the top 20 law schools for faculty scholarship in a recent survey.

■ Library and Physical Facilities

➥ *352,200 volumes & equivalents*   ➥ *integrated automated library system*   ➥ *LEXIS*   ➥ *NEXIS*   ➥ *WESTLAW*
➥ *OCLC*   ➥ *7 full-time librarians*   ➥ *library seats 500*

■ Curriculum

➥ *84 credits required to graduate*   ➥ *139 courses available*
➥ *J.D. degree*   ➥ *first-year section size—50*

First-year students take a series of required courses; the second- and third-year programs are elective, with the exception of required courses in professional responsibility, upper-level legal writing, and advanced legal research.

■ Clinical/Externship Opportunities

Cardozo clinics provide students with practical experience to augment the theoretical training occurring in the classroom. The **Jacob Burns Institute for Advanced Legal**

Studies sponsors academic research and major symposia, and underwrites student scholarships. Under the **Alexander Judicial Fellows Program**, 25 students each year clerk for a federal judge. The **Samuel and Ronnie Heyman Center on Corporate Governance** sponsors conferences in the area of corporate law and society. The **Program in International Law and Human Rights** combines coursework with clinical placements in the United States and overseas with organizations such as Amnesty International and Lawyers for Human Rights. Cardozo's **International Institutes** offer summer programs in Moscow, Budapest, and Israel, focusing on the role of law in a time of international transformation and transition. In the **Appellate Externship Program**, students work in the Appeals Unit of the New York City Department of Law. The **Summer Institute for Placement and Career Development** offers seminars linked to related field placements in specialty areas such as international trade law, bankruptcy, environmental law, entertainment law, and litigation practice. The **Cardozo Public Interest Summer Stipend Program** funds students in summer placements at government agencies and public interest organizations such as the U.S. Attorney's Office, District Attorneys' Offices, and the ACLU.

Students in the **Criminal Law Clinic** work in the Manhattan Criminal Court, representing the criminally accused. The **Criminal Appeals Clinic** allows students to represent indigent appellants before the First Department of the Appellate Division of the New York State Supreme Court. In the **Prosecutor Practicum**, students work in the Manhattan District Attorney's Office. Cardozo's renowned **Intensive Trial Advocacy Program** trains students in advanced courtroom techniques.

Cardozo's **Bet Tzedek Legal Services Clinic** represents indigent elderly and disabled individuals in cases involving entitlement to government benefits. The **Mediation Clinic** enables students to practice arbitration in situations involving personal and social conflict. In the **Tax Court Clinic**, students represent *pro se* taxpayers in cases pending before the United States Tax Court. The **Immigration Law Clinic** allows students to work on all aspects of the immigration process, including political asylum cases.

■ Admission

➥ *Bachelor's degree required*   ➥ *application deadlines—Dec. 1 for Jan. admission; April 1 for May and Sept. admission*
➥ *LSAT, LSDAS required*   ➥ *median GPA—3.30*
➥ *median LSAT score—160*   ➥ *application fee—$50*

Each applicant's LSAT score; undergraduate and graduate records; letters of recommendation; and materials reflecting character, academic achievements, and aptitude for law study are carefully considered. Transfer students may enter in September or January.

Cardozo law school is a nonsectarian school and operates in accordance with the laws of New York State and the

United States. The Association of American Law Schools, which, along with the American Bar Association, accredits the school, has established as one of its standards for accreditation the following: "A member school shall provide equality of legal education for all persons, including faculty and employees, with respect to hiring, continuation, promotion and tenure, applicants for admission, enrolled students, and graduates, without discrimination or segregation on the ground of race, color, religion, national origin, sex, age, handicap or disability, or sexual orientation."

■ Student Activities

Cardozo sponsors four student publications and one faculty journal. *Cardozo Studies in Law and Literature* is a professional journal edited by a senior member of the faculty. The *Law Review, Arts and Entertainment Journal, Moot Court Board, New Europe Law Review,* and the *Cardozo Women's Law Journal* select students on the basis of scholarship and writing ability. Student groups include the Student Bar Association; the Black, Asian, and Latino Law Student Associations; and organizations devoted to specific areass, e.g., Environmental Law, Computer Law, Law and Politics, etc.

■ Expenses And Financial Aid

➡ *tuition & fees—$16,545*   ➡ *merit & need-based scholarships available*   ➡ *financial aid available; FAFSA due April 15*

The major component of the financial aid program is the Cardozo Law School Loan Fund. Students with financial need are expected to obtain loans from state or federally subsidized or insured sources.

The Jacob Burns Scholarship and the H. Bert and Ruth Mack Scholarship programs provide merit scholarships to entering students on the basis of academic excellence and leadership ability. Some additional scholarship funds are also available.

■ Housing

Housing is available in the immediate vicinity of Cardozo as well as other neighborhoods easily accessible by public transportation.

■ Placement

The Center for Professional Development is committed to helping students determine and achieve their career goals. The center offers a full range of placement services, including career counseling, panel discussions, workshops on résumé-writing and interviewing techniques, videotaping of mock interviews, and assistance for alumni seeking new positions. It organizes extensive on-campus recruiting; maintains a special job listing service that includes permanent, part-time, and summer employment; and provides an active alumni referral system.

■ Correspondence

Office of Admissions, Cardozo School of Law, 55 Fifth Avenue, New York, NY 10003. Phone: 212.790.0274.

Applicant Group for the 1993–1994 Academic Year

Benjamin N. Cardozo School of Law Yeshiva University
This grid includes only applicants who earned 120-180 LSAT scores under standard administrations.

LSAT Score	3.75 +		3.50 -3.74		3.25 - 3.49		3.00 - 3.24		2.75 - 2.99		2.50 - 2.74		2.25 - 2.49		2.00 - 2.24		Below 2.00		No GPA		Total	
	Apps	Adm	Apps	Adm	Apps	Adm	Apps	Adm	Apps	Adm	Apps	Adm	Apps	Adm	Apps	Adm	Apps	Adm	Apps	Adm	Apps	Adm
175 - 180	0	0	0	0	0	0	1	1	1	1	0	0	0	0	0	0	0	0	0	0	2	2
170 - 174	6	6	2	2	5	5	7	7	2	2	1	0	2	2	1	1	1	1	0	0	27	26
165 - 169	19	19	20	19	26	26	10	10	16	15	8	6	1	0	1	1	0	0	0	0	101	96
160 - 164	19	17	52	51	81	78	79	77	36	34	24	18	8	6	4	3	0	0	1	1	304	285
155 - 159	34	33	93	66	129	78	123	74	97	53	36	15	16	3	3	2	3	1	8	6	542	331
150 - 154	27	8	71	22	129	20	128	22	95	15	52	3	27	4	6	0	3	0	12	2	550	96
145 - 149	10	1	40	11	75	3	82	6	75	5	48	1	26	2	11	1	2	0	7	2	376	32
140 - 144	2	1	19	0	29	0	55	1	53	1	29	0	23	0	10	0	2	0	3	0	225	3
135 - 139	1	0	3	0	17	0	18	0	14	0	20	0	25	0	7	0	4	0	5	0	114	0
130 - 134	0	0	0	0	2	0	1	0	4	0	10	0	13	0	8	0	1	0	2	0	41	0
125 - 129	0	0	1	0	0	0	0	0	2	0	4	0	0	0	1	0	0	0	4	0	12	0
120 - 124	0	0	0	0	0	0	0	0	0	0	0	0	0	0	0	0	1	0	1	0	2	0
Total	118	85	301	171	493	210	504	198	395	126	232	43	141	17	52	8	17	2	43	11	2296	871

Apps = Number of Applicants
Adm = Number Admitted
Reflects 95% of the total applicant pool.

Case Western Reserve University School of Law

11075 East Boulevard
Cleveland, OH 44106

Phone: 216.368.3600

■ Introduction

The law school, located in Cleveland's beautiful University Circle, offers a nationally recognized legal education at a major comprehensive university in a city that is one of the nation's leading law centers. Founded in 1892, the school became a charter member of the AALS and was among the first schools accredited by the ABA. Today we have about 695 students who come from all over the country for our J.D. and LL.M. programs, and about 7,000 alumni living in virtually every state.

■ Enrollment/Student Body

➡ *2,015 applicants* ➡ *220 enrolled first-year class 1993*
➡ *11% students of color* ➡ *45% women* ➡ *32 states & foreign countries represented first-year class* ➡ *121 undergraduate schools represented first-year class* ➡ *51% outside Ohio*

■ Faculty

Our student-to-faculty ratio, including all faculty, is 18 to 1.

■ Library and Physical Facilities

➡ *304,331 volumes & equivalents* ➡ *LEXIS*
➡ *NEXIS* ➡ *WESTLAW* ➡ *CD-ROMs available on campus network: CIS Masterfile, WilsonDisc Index, LEGAL TRAC, West CDROMS* ➡ *access to 700 electronic services and library catalogs through DIALOG, CWRUnet, OCLC-EPIC, USENET, CLARINET, FREENET, DATA-TIMES, INTERNET, RLIN, HOLLIS, Can/Law, VU-TEXT, CLL CAT, Dow Jones, Hannah Legislative Svc., CUY CTY PL CAT, QL (Quiclaw), NEWSNET, CPL, OCLC*
➡ *9 full-time librarians*

The award-winning law school building is handsome, contemporary, and comfortable. The law school is located in the heart of University Circle, one of the largest and richest cultural and education centers in the nation, just 20 minutes away from downtown. The library's collection includes an extensive British collection and special collections in taxation, labor law, foreign investments, law-medicine, and international law. The library's professional and support staff places a heavy emphasis on assisting those who use the facilities. If we don't have what students need, we will get it. We have focused on the integration of modern technology with traditional research methods. Students benefit from the exciting advances in our computer technology that have enabled students to dial into our computer lab from their homes.

■ Curriculum

➡ *142 courses available* ➡ *joint degrees available: J.D./M.B.A. (Management); J.D./M.S.S.A. (Social Work); J.D./M.N.O. (Nonprofit Management); J.D./M.A. (Legal History)* ➡ *range of first-year class size—16-110*

The first year consists of required courses, including the Research, Analysis, and Writing (RAW) program, which is staffed by full-time instructors, all experienced lawyers. Each RAW section meets in a small group. Additionally, every first-year student will have a small section for one other course. After the first year every student must take Professional Responsibility and a course with a substantial writing requirement. An array of elective courses allows students (if they wish) to concentrate in special areas.

■ The Law Medicine Center

Our long-established Law-Medicine Center focuses on the whole range of legal, social, economic, scientific, and ethical issues in which law and medicine are interrelated. The center also sponsors lectures, major conferences, and smaller forums, and is involved in the journal *Health Matrix* (see below).

■ International Law Program

We expect to prepare our students for a global practice in the 21st century. Our recently endowed Gund Foundation International Law Center has enabled us to strengthen even further our international law curriculum, sponsor visiting scholars from around the world, and provide study and work abroad opportunities for our students. The *Journal of International Law* is student-edited (see below). In addition, the Canada-U.S. Law Institute, sponsored with the law school of the University of Western Ontario, offers courses, cocurricular programs, and student exchanges, and has an affiliated journal.

■ Professional Skills Programs

Besides the traditional classes in substantive law, our law school offers professional skills courses of which we are especially proud, such as Evidence for Litigators and Trial Tactics. Our moot courtroom is a first-rate litigation laboratory, equipped with state-of-the-art taping and editing equipment. We offer a simulation course, called The Lawyering Process, in which students practice interviewing, counseling, and negotiation. In addition, our Law School Clinic allows third-year students to represent actual clients in both civil and criminal cases, earning academic credit while providing a community service. Student interns have the guidance of our full-time clinic faculty, all experienced practitioners.

■ Graduate Law Study

Our **LL.M. in United States Legal Studies** provides graduates from foreign law schools the opportunity to study the U.S. legal system and institutions. Students will have weekly seminars on international business transactions with area practitioners and will be paired with a student mentor and a practitioner mentor from a Cleveland firm or corporation.

The **LL.M. in Taxation** is designed as a part- or full-time program for practicing professionals who wish to gain a thorough understanding of the nation's increasingly complex tax laws and be better able to advise clients, particularly those involved in complicated transactions.

■ Student Activities

The school sponsors four student-edited scholarly journals: the *Case Western Reserve Law Review*; the *Journal of International Law*; the *Canada-U.S. Law Journal*; and *Health Matrix: The Journal of Law-Medicine*. Our student Moot Court Board sponsors an intramural competition and three interscholastic competitions: National, Niagara, and Craven. A fourth moot court competition, the Jessup Competition, is administered by the Society of International Law Students. Our intramural Client Counseling Competition involves about 100 students each year. Finally, we have an intramural/extramural mock trial program. Other activities include the Student Bar Association; Black Law Students Association; Women's Law Association; International Law Society; Law School Academy (a weekly speakers series); National Lawyers Guild; Student Public Interest Law Fellowship; Lesbian and Gay Law Alliance; Second Career Students; Student International Law Society; Environmental Law Society; Jewish Law Students Association, and several legal fraternities.

■ Admission

➤ *Bachelor's degree required* ➤ *application deadline—April 1* ➤ *LSAT, LSDAS required*
➤ *median GPA—3.30* ➤ *median LSAT score—160*
➤ *application fee—$40*

Our admission process is selective (and, as a result, the attrition rate is negligible). We weigh not only grade-point averages and LSAT scores, but also nonquantitative factors. Our standards are rigorous, but not rigid. We accept applications as early as October for admission in the following fall; our deadline is April 1, although early applicants have the best chance for admission and scholarships. As decisions are made, candidates are notified; most decisions are made between January 1 and May 15.

■ Expenses And Financial Aid

➤ *tuition & fees—full-time, $16,680; part-time/credit unit, $692* ➤ *estimated additional expenses—$2,755/semester (books, room & board, living expenses)* ➤ *scholarships available: merit-based scholarships & diversity grants* ➤ *financial aid available; FAF due March 1*

In addition to participating in government financial aid programs, we have our own scholarship funds. Around one quarter of each entering class receives grants. Every year 10 exceptional entering students receive full-tuition scholarships. Every applicant with an outstanding record is automatically considered for scholarship award. In addition, we offer diversity grants.

■ Career Services

Our office offers a full range of services to students and alumni. Our graduates find placement throughout the country, including every major metropolitan area. Each year, employers from around the country visit our campus to interview students. We have an extremely effective network of alumni who live and practice across the United States. Hundreds serve as career counselors, meeting individually with students and hosting luncheons and receptions that help students form important connections.

Applicant Group for the 1993-1994 Academic Year

Case Western Reserve University School of Law
This grid includes only applicants who earned 120-180 LSAT scores in the 1992-1993 testing year.

LSAT Score	3.75+ Apps	Adm	3.50-3.74 Apps	Adm	3.25-3.49 Apps	Adm	3.00-3.24 Apps	Adm	2.75-2.99 Apps	Adm	2.50-2.74 Apps	Adm	Below 2.50 Apps	Adm	No GPA Apps	Adm	Total Apps	Adm
175-180	0	0	1	1	2	2	3	3	0	0	0	0	1	0	0	0	7	6
170-174	7	7	4	4	5	5	7	7	1	1	1	1	4	4	0	0	29	29
165-169	18	18	22	22	19	19	32	31	22	22	6	4	2	1	0	0	121	117
160-164	29	29	53	52	66	65	63	61	37	24	30	14	9	0	0	0	287	245
155-159	25	23	93	84	124	72	114	26	65	5	60	0	22	1	6	2	479	213
150-154	21	14	69	19	88	7	96	4	69	0	26	0	29	0	3	0	401	44
145-149	9	1	28	0	42	1	52	1	40	0	26	1	13	0	5	2	215	6
140-144	3	0	3	0	18	1	19	0	26	0	12	0	20	0	4	0	105	1
Below 140	0	0	0	0	3	0	12	1	9	0	12	1	8	0	8	0	52	2
Total	112	91	273	172	367	157	398	119	269	47	143	21	108	6	26	4	1696	665

Apps = Number of Applicants
Adm = Number Admitted
Reflects 83% of the total applicant pool, including those applicants deferred from 1992.
This grid is to be used solely as a general guide in assessing the possibility of admittance based on quantitative factors. Nonquantitative factors are evaluated in all admission decisions. In cases where an applicant presented multiple LSAT scores, the average was used.

The Catholic University of America—Columbus School of Law

Office of Admissions
Washington, DC 20064

Phone: 202.319.5151

■ Introduction

Founded in 1898, the Columbus School of Law is located on the 154-acre campus of the university. Students and faculty have access to unique legal resources: the Supreme Court, the Congress, the United States and District of Columbia courts, and federal, executive, and administrative departments. Yet, while offering the advantages of the nation's capital, the campus is located in a pleasant, non-commercial area, and offers the scenic atmosphere of a suburban school. Classes are small and personal.

The school is nonsectarian and welcomes students of all religious backgrounds to a program that emphasizes a commitment to community service and the ethical practice of law. The school has been a member of the AALS since 1921, and approved by the ABA since 1925.

■ Enrollment/Student Body

→ *3,200 applicants* → *1,000 admitted first-year class 1993* → *290 enrolled first-year class 1993* → *670 total full-time* → *275 total part-time* → *16% minority* → *47% women* → *50 states & foreign countries represented* → *300 undergraduate schools represented* → *fewer than 50% of students enter directly from college*

The first-year day and evening classes are sectioned in such a way that individual courses have 32 to 65 students. Upper-class courses range from 10 to 70 students. Individual faculty members are available for informal sessions, thus providing a personalized education.

■ Faculty

→ *124 total* → *42 full-time* → *77 part-time or adjunct* → *32 women* → *9 minority* → *5 full-time instructors*

The faculty brings a broad range of interests and experience to the academic setting. The adjunct faculty and professorial lecturers are selected from among local judges and practitioners for their expertise in given areas of law.

■ Library and Physical Facilities

→ *220,000 volumes & equivalents* → *library hours: Mon.-Fri., 7:00 A.M.-MIDNIGHT; Sat. & Sun., 9:00 A.M.-MIDNIGHT* → *LEXIS* → *NEXIS* → *WESTLAW* → *DIALOG* → *computer lab* → *3 VCR playback rooms* → *8 full-time librarians* → *library seats 500*

The Library of Congress and specialized law collections throughout the city complement the law school's legal collections. A new law school facility, completed in 1994, houses all components of the law school. It combines contemporary style with the rich architectural history of the campus. Law students have full access to other campus facilities, including a 40-acre athletic complex with pool, Nautilus equipment, sauna, tennis courts, and track.

■ Curriculum

→ *Academic Support Program* → *Law and Public Policy Program* → *84 credits required to graduate* → *151 courses available* → *degrees available: J.D.; J.D./M.L.S.; J.D./M.S.W.; J.D./M.A.* → *semesters, start in Aug.* → *range of first-year class size—32-65* → *Comparative and International Law Institute* → *Institute for Communications Law Studies*

The prescribed first-year curriculum, materials, and method of teaching are designed to develop the basic analytical skills that characterize the able lawyer and to give the student familiarity with the major substantive areas of law. While lawyers traditionally have been heavily involved with the commercial interests of private or corporate clients, law is becoming increasingly responsible to problems that affect the public interest. The law school curriculum is designed to provide students with the basic knowledge to become effective lawyers in a changing legal environment.

■ Special Programs

The Institute for Communications Law Studies offers a unique opportunity for specialized training in communications law. The Institute currently offers nine courses and related internships to students who will receive the J.D. degree and a certificate from the Institute.

The Comparative and International Law Institute gives students the opportunity to plan a concentration of courses in the public and private areas of international law. Internships and paid employment are also available in these areas. The institute also offers a six-week Summer Abroad Program at the Jagiellonian University in Cracow, Poland.

The Law and Public Policy Program uniquely combines classroom studies in legislative and administrative processes with externships in government agencies and advocacy organizations that affect national public policy.

■ Clinical Programs

The law school offers eight clinical programs, including five that emphasize client representation, case planning, and trial and administrative advocacy. The other three clinical offerings are: The Law and Public Policy Program, the Securities and Exchange Commission Training Program, and the Legal Externship Program.

■ Admission

→ *Bachelor's degree from an accredited college or university required* → *application deadline—Mar. 1* → *LSAT, LSDAS required* → *median GPA—3.20* → *median LSAT score—158* → *application fee—$55* → *admission decisions are made beginning in Dec., and continue until the class is filled*

Applications are sought from all parts of the country and from all racial, religious, and ethnic backgrounds. While heavy consideration is given to the applicant's grade-point average and LSAT scores, decisions are influenced by such other factors as leadership qualities, rank in class, improving performance, academic standards of the undergraduate school, the curriculum, relevant work experience, and evidence of factors that adversely affected the student's grades. Special consideration is given to applicants from disadvantaged groups.

The Preface Program, a three-week summer program, is offered to entering students whose credentials indicate that an intensive introduction to law school would be especially beneficial.

■ Student Activities

The *Catholic University Law Review*, the *Journal of Contemporary Health Law* and *COMMLAW CONSPECTUS: Journal of Communications Law and Policy* are scholarly law journals staffed by outstanding students. The Moot Court Board conducts five major competitions and a number of intraschool competitions each academic year. The Honor Board administers the student-created honor code of ethical standards of personal and professional conduct. The Student Bar Association provides a channel for student opinion and selects representatives to participate as voting members of faculty committees. Other activities include the Thurgood Marshall American Inn of Court, Black Law Students Association, Women's Organization, Latin American Law Students Association, Jewish Law Students Association, Asian-Pacific American Law Students Association, and many other student-interest groups.

■ Expenses and Financial Aid

➡ *tuition & fees—full-time, $18,105; part-time, $13,555* ➡ *estimated additional expenses (room, board, books, transportation)—$11,377* ➡ *scholarships available* ➡ *performance and need-based minority scholarships available* ➡ *financial aid available* ➡ *performance and need-based scholarships are available* ➡ *registration with GAPSFAS and FAFSA is required*

Financial aid decisions are made beginning in March.

■ Career Services

The Office of Legal Career Services actively supports students and graduates in their search for employment by providing counseling as well as activities that facilitate direct placement. On-campus interviews are provided. The school's small size permits individual counseling for each student desiring assistance. Our admissions brochure lists employment statistics, including distribution by type of practice and by geographic location.

■ Housing

A limited amount of graduate housing is available on campus. A variety of apartments and private rooms are within easy traveling distance. The Admissions Office assists students in locating apartments and roommates. Our location is convenient to public transportation, including the metrorail system.

Applicant Group for the 1993–1994 Academic Year

The Catholic University of America—Columbus School of Law
This grid includes only applicants who earned 120-180 LSAT scores under standard administrations.

LSAT Score	GPA																	
	3.75 +		3.50 -3.74		3.25 - 3.49		3.00 - 3.24		2.75 - 2.99		2.50 - 2.74		2.25 - 2.49		2.00 - 2.24		Below 2.00		No GPA
	Apps	Adm	Apps	Adm	Apps	Adm	Apps	Adm	Apps	Adm	Apps	Adm	Apps	Adm	Apps	Adm	Apps	Adm	Apps	Adm
165 - 180	5	5	6	6	12	12	21	20	26	19	18	11	11	5	0	0	0	0	2	1
160 - 164	15	15	30	30	61	58	80	74	68	46	39	16	17	8	8	1	1	0	0	0
155 - 159	23	20	78	67	149	120	192	115	124	47	74	17	40	4	19	3	3	0	9	3
150 - 154	21	10	91	40	156	47	191	37	146	15	95	5	48	1	20	1	2	0	7	1
140 - 149	15	2	55	5	117	11	179	20	191	18	141	5	78	5	46	3	9	0	9	0
120 - 139	1	0	8	0	17	0	25	0	35	0	47	0	56	0	31	0	5	0	3	0

Apps = Number of Applicants
Adm = Number Admitted
Reflects 94% of the total applicant pool.
This grid should be used only as a general guide as many non-numerical factors are alos considered in admission decisions.

Chicago-Kent College of Law—Illinois Institute of Technology

Office of Admissions
565 West Adams Street
Chicago, IL 60661-3691

Phone: 312.906.5020 or 312.906.5230 (TDD)

■ Introduction

Chicago-Kent College of Law, Illinois Institute of Technology is nationally acclaimed for its innovative approaches to traditional legal education and its specialized programs within the law school curriculum.

The law school's unique affiliation with the Illinois Institute of Technology, one of the nation's largest scientific research centers, provides support for interdisciplinary programs including the Center for Law and Computers, the certificate program in Environmental and Energy Law and the Intellectual Property program.

Chicago-Kent is located in downtown Chicago, the heart of the city's commercial and legal communities. The new law school building, completed in 1992, is equipped with the latest technology and includes a four-story library and a complete courtroom. The college is fully accredited by the ABA and the AALS and is a member of the Order of the Coif.

■ Enrollment and Student Body

➡ *3,000 applicants* ➡ *1,200 admitted first-year class 1993* ➡ *868 total full-time* ➡ *369 total part-time* ➡ *17% minority* ➡ *48% women* ➡ *44 states & foreign countries represented* ➡ *308 enrolled first-year class 1993, day division* ➡ *98 enrolled first-year class 1993, evening division* ➡ *44% out-of-state in most recent entering class*

■ Faculty

➡ *126 total* ➡ *62 full-time* ➡ *64 part-time or adjunct* ➡ *30 women* ➡ *7 minority*

■ Library and Physical Facilities

➡ *430,000 volumes & equivalents* ➡ *library hours: Mon.-Tues., 7:45 A.M.-11:00 P.M.; Wed.-Thur., 7:45 A.M.-MIDNIGHT; Fri., 7:45 A.M.-6:00 P.M.; Sat., 9:00 A.M.-6:00 P.M.; Sun., 10:30 A.M.-11:00 P.M.* ➡ *LEXIS* ➡ *NEXIS* ➡ *WESTLAW* ➡ *DIALOG* ➡ *10 full-time librarians* ➡ *library seats 557*

The law library is among the largest national libraries. The collection includes the Library of International Relations and a wealth of material in environmental and energy law, intellectual property, international trade, and labor law.

An essential educational feature of the library and the classrooms is the extensive computer network in the building. Seats in selected classrooms, many library carrels and numerous locations throughout the building are tied to the computer network, enabling students with their own laptop computers to connect into the network and the many legal databases. There are three computer laboratories with more than 75 personal computers reserved for student use. Students can also access the network through their home computers by using modems.

The new Marovitz Courtroom integrates design features from the best courtroom and trial advocacy training facilities in the nation.

■ Curriculum

➡ *Academic Support Program* ➡ *84 units/credits required to graduate* ➡ *over 100 courses offered each academic year* ➡ *degrees available: J.D.; J.D./M.B.A.;J.D./LL.M. in Taxation; J.D./M.S. in Financial Markets & Trading; LL.M. in Taxation; LL.M. in Financial Services Law; LL.M. in International and Comparative Law* ➡ *range of first-year class size—30-100*

Day students usually complete the J.D. degree in three years. Evening students usually finish in four years. Students can transfer between divisions after completing their required courses in the division in which they originally enrolled.

■ Special Programs

Legal Research and Writing—Chicago-Kent has the most comprehensive legal research and writing program in the country. The three-year, five-course curriculum teaches students to analyze a wide range of legal problems and to write about them persuasively.

Law and Computers—Chicago-Kent was among the first law schools to recognize technology's impact on legal education and the profession. Students have access to a wide range of law-specific software and 24-hour access to LEXIS and WESTLAW.

Environmental and Energy Law—The certificate program's interdisciplinary approach to the problems of environmental regulation and natural resources allocation prepares students for practice through a series of courses in law, economic and public policy analysis, and in the scientific aspects of environmental problems.

Clinical Education—The Law Offices of Chicago-Kent, one of the largest in-house clinical education programs in the country, offers six clinical education programs that include civil, tax, and criminal law and externships with government agencies and federal judges.

Trial Skills/Litigation and Dispute Resolution—The law school offers a two-semester sequence in trial advocacy and an intensive course. The courses are taught by skilled judges and experienced practitioners. There is a certificate program in litigation and dispute resolution studies.

International and Comparative Law—The broad curriculum of the certificate program in International and Comparative Law is enhanced by the Library of International Relations, one of few official depositories for United Nations and European Community documents and the largest public research collection in the Midwest.

■ Admission

➡ *B.A. or B.S. required for admission* ➡ *suggested application deadline—April 1* ➡ *LSAT, LSDAS required* ➡ *median GPA—3.20* ➡ *median LSAT score—159* ➡ *application fee—$40* ➡ *rolling admission; early application preferred*

Admission is highly selective. Decisions are based on a range of factors including quantitative and qualitative criteria. Each application is individually reviewed; there is no cut-off. Although the GPA and LSAT are important threshold criteria, consideration also is given to non-numerical factors such as the nature and rigor of the undergraduate curriculum, writing ability, graduate work and professional experience, extracurricular activities, diversity, and the personal statement. The admission requirements for the full- and part-time divisions are the same. Entering classes begin only in the fall. The law school is committed to attracting and retaining students from a variety of racial, ethnic, economic, geographic, and educational backgrounds.

■ Student Activities

The *Chicago-Kent Law Review* is published in symposium format by student editors and staff, in association with a faculty editor. Moot Court and Trial Advocacy teams successfully compete in local, regional, and national competitions every year, providing numerous opportunities to develop litigation expertise. Diverse student interests are represented in a wide variety of social, political, and professional student groups, including the Student Bar Association, Women in Law, and organizations for Asian, black, and Hispanic students.

■ Expenses and Financial Aid

➠ *tuition & fees—full-time, $16,540; part-time, $11,815*
➠ *estimated additional expenses—$550*
➠ *scholarships available* ➠ *minority scholarships available*
➠ *FAFSA, Chicago-Kent Application for Financial Aid, and financial aid transcripts from previous schools required for financial aid; priority deadline—April 15*

The Kent Legal Scholars Program provides full-tuition, renewable scholarships, research assistantships, and special seminars to a select group of students who demonstrate exceptional academic and leadership ability, regardless of need. Substantial scholarship assistance is offered to entering and continuing students based on need and merit. Federal and other loans and minority-student grants are available. A loan-repayment program helps graduates who choose public-interest careers.

■ Career Services

More than 89 percent of recent graduates found professional employment within three months of being licensed to practice.

The Office of Career Services, with four full-time staff members, sponsors fall and spring on-campus interview programs and offers individual counseling on résumé-writing, interview techniques, and job-search strategies.

■ Housing

Affordable on- and off-campus housing is available. The Law Floor in the graduate dormitories on the IIT Main Campus is reserved for law students. The law school is close to all public transportation.

Admission Profile Not Available

University of Chicago Law School

1111 E. 60th Street
Chicago, IL 60637

Phone: 312.702.9484

■ Introduction

Legal education at the University of Chicago has long stressed the interdependence of legal and social studies in the training of lawyers. The school's program combines an emphasis on technical legal knowledge and professional skills with a concern for illuminating the connections between law and the social forces with which it interacts. Contributing to the first objective are opportunities for the application of formal knowledge to specific professional tasks. The school's model court facility provides students the opportunity to take part in moot trials and appellate arguments and to observe actual court sessions. A significant fraction of the faculty represents disciplines other than law, including economics, history, sociology, philosophy, and political science. The curriculum also devotes substantial attention to relevant aspects of political theory, economics, legal history, comparative law, psychiatry, statistics, and other social science methodology. In addition to the student-edited University of Chicago *Law Review*, the University of Chicago *Legal Forum*, and the University of Chicago *Roundtable* the school is the home of four scholarly journals: *Supreme Court Review*; *Journal of Law and Economics*; *Journal of Legal Studies*; and *Crime and Justice: An Annual Review of Research*. It is also the home of the Center for Studies in Criminal Justice, the Legal History Program, the Law and Government Program, the Center for Constitutionalism in Eastern Europe, and the Law-Economics Program. The school is a charter member of the AALS and is on the approved list of the ABA.

■ Enrollment/Student Body

➡ *3,260 applicants*   ➡ *178 enrolled first-year class 1993*
➡ *530 total full-time J.D.*   ➡ *35 graduate students*
➡ *21% minority*   ➡ *42% women*
➡ *44 states & 19 foreign countries represented*
➡ *173 undergraduate schools represented*

■ Faculty

➡ *40 full-time*   ➡ *21 part-time*   ➡ *5 minority*

■ Library and Physical Facilities

➡ *555,000 volumes & equivalents*
➡ *24 full-time library staff*

The Law School is located on the 165-acre, tree-lined campus of the university in Hyde Park, a residential community on the shore of Lake Michigan 15 minutes south of Chicago's business and cultural center. Most of the university's faculty as well as its student body of 8,000 live in this community. The law quadrangle, designed by Eero Saarinen, consists of four connecting buildings surrounding an open court and reflecting pool. The six-story, glass-center structure contains the library, lounge, study areas, and offices. The library's collections of monographs, foreign law materials, and briefs and records in American appellate cases are outstanding. Offices and study areas are distributed around the library's open stacks, facilitating contact between students and faculty.

■ Curriculum

➡ *Academic Support Program*   ➡ *quarters, begin in Sept.*
➡ *105 credits required to graduate*   ➡ *joint degrees offered*

The basic program of study involves three years (nine quarters) of full-time study leading to the J.D. degree. Recesses between quarters occur in mid-December and mid-March. In addition to course work, first-year students perform individual assignments under the direction of a tutor. The tutorial work emphasizes training in research, preparation of legal documents, and oral argument. Second- and third-year students are encouraged to substitute seminar work and individual research under faculty supervision for courses. Students may take a limited number of relevant courses in other departments of the university for credit toward the J.D. degree.

■ Special Programs

In cooperation with the Graduate School of Business, the Law School offers a joint program leading to the J.D. and M.B.A. degrees in four years. Joint programs in history, international relations, and economics are also available. The university's School of Public Policy Studies, which includes several Law School faculty members, offers a one-year program leading to the Master of Arts degree in public policy.

■ Admission

➡ *applications not received before mid-Jan. or not completed by mid-Feb. will not be considered before late spring or early summer*   ➡ *LSAT, LSDAS required*
➡ *application fee—$45*   ➡ *use evaluative interviews*

Admission to the Law School is based upon a careful review of each application by one or more members of the admissions committee. The committee considers all evidence that may indicate academic and professional promise. No automatic quantitative criteria are applied, although academic achievement as reflected in the college record and the evidence of intellectual ability provided by the LSAT are necessarily major determinants. The committee generally considers only a candidate's first LSAT score when multiple scores are presented unless a later score is substantially higher. Each year the Law School conducts evaluative interviews, by invitation, as part of the admissions process. One-year deferred admission will be granted to all admitted applicants who request it prior to June 15.

The admissions committee makes special efforts to ensure that each entering class contains students from a variety of geographic, educational, racial, and ethnic backgrounds, and is particularly interested in receiving applications from women and minority candidates, two groups that have traditionally been underrepresented in the profession.

■ **Student Activities**

About 40 percent of the members of the second- and third-year classes in the Law School serve on one of the three student journals. They are selected on the basis of either academic achievement in the first year or performance in a writing competition open to all students and conducted each year. Approximately 80 second- and third-year students work each year in The Mandel Legal Aid Clinic. The Hinton Moot Court Committee conducts a two-year program in appellate advocacy open to all second- and third-year students. Other student organizations include a local chapter of the Black Law Students Association, Environmental Law Society, the Law Women's Caucus, the Law School Film Society, the Federalist Society, International Comparative Law Society, National Lawyers Guild, the Law School Show, the Gay/Lesbian Law Students Association, Hispanic Law Students Association, and the Asian American Law Students Association.

■ **Expenses and Financial Aid**

➡ *full-time tuition & fees—$19,392*
➡ *estimated additional expenses—$11,900 (living expenses)*

Through scholarship and loan funds, the Law School provides assistance to students who demonstrate financial need. Applicants for aid must register with GAPSFAS. The Law School also offers a number of merit

scholarships which provide up to full tuition to a limited number of exceptional students.

■ **Housing**

A new graduate residence hall, located two blocks from the Law School, is available for 140 graduate students from all areas of the university. Every first-year law student who wishes to do so, usually between 80 to 100 students, will live in this facility, which has mostly single rooms with private baths. The university has sufficient single and married student housing in Hyde Park to meet the needs of all students who request it. Campus buses run frequently during the day and evening between these buildings and the Law School.

■ **Career Services**

A full-time placement office assists students in obtaining permanent, summer, and part-time employment. During the 1992-93 academic year, 350 employers scheduled interviews at the Law School. The distribution of employers by region was Midwest (30 percent), Northeast (37 percent), West (25 percent), and South (8 percent). At the time of graduation, 97 percent of the Class of 1993 was employed; 70 percent joined law firms, 25 percent obtained judicial clerkships, and the remainder were with government or legal services employers. Eight graduates of the Law School will clerk for justices on the United States Supreme Court during the 1993-94 term. Ninety-nine percent of the Class of 1994 and 92 percent of the Class of 1995 had law-related positions during the summer of 1993.

Applicant Group for the 1993–1994 Academic Year

The median LSAT score of all applicants admitted for the 1993 entering class was in the 98th percentile. Of all the applicants who had LSAT scores at or above the 98th percentile, 56 percent were offered admission. The comparable percentages of applicants offered admission with other LSAT scores: 95th-97th percentile, 22 percent; 91st-94th percentile, 13 percent; 85th-90th percentile, 6

percent; below the 85th percentile, 2 percent. The median GPA of all applicants admitted for the 1993 entering class was 3.75. Of all the applicants who had a GPA above 3.7, 40 percent were offered admission. The comparable percentages of applicants offered admission with other GPAs: 3.7-3.5, 25 percent; 3.5-3.3, 9 percent; 3.3-3.1, 5 percent; below 3.1, 2 percent.

University of Cincinnati College of Law

Clifton Avenue and Calhoun Street
Cincinnati, OH 45221-0040

Phone: 513.556.6805

■ Introduction

The College of Law at the University of Cincinnati was established in 1833. America's fourth-oldest law school, the college today is a national public law school serving an enrollment of 400 students—approximately 135 per class. The College of Law is a cornerstone on the University of Cincinnati campus in historic Clifton. This central location approximately 10 minutes north of the city's downtown area provides easy access to state, county, and federal courts, including the U.S. Court of Appeals for the Sixth Circuit. A charter member of the AALS, the University of Cincinnati was one of the first law schools to have a chapter of the Order of the Coif and to be approved by the ABA.

■ Enrollment/Student Body

Report on first-year class 1993:
- *1,401 applicants* - *362 admitted* - *134 enrolled*
- *13% minority* - *40% women* - *22 states & foreign countries represented* - *68 undergraduate schools represented*
- *38 majors represented* - *average age—26*
- *15% of class age 30+ upon entrance* - *62% state residents*

■ Faculty

- *51 total* - *25 full-time* - *26 adjuncts*
- *7 women* - *2 minority*

The law school has doubled the size of the faculty and constructed a new law building and library in the last 15 years. The resulting student-to-faculty ratio is one of the best nationally.

■ Library and Physical Facilities

- *338,358 volumes & equivalents* - *library hours: Mon.-Fri., 7:45 A.M.-11:00 P.M.; Sat.-Sun., 10:00 A.M.-11:00 P.M.*
- *LEXIS* - *NEXIS* - *WESTLAW*
- *UCLIO* - *OHIOLINK* - *OCLC* - *DIALOG*
- *EPIC* - *DATATIMES* - *7 full-time librarians*
- *library seats 385*

The College of Law is one of the few law libraries large enough to seat its entire student body, if necessary. The new student computer lab, completed in 1991, offers an excellent array of computer-assisted research aids and laser printers.

■ Curriculum

- *88 credits required to graduate* - *60-80 courses available*
- *degrees available: J.D./M.B.A.; J.D./M.C.P.*
- *semesters, Aug.-Dec., Jan.-May*
- *range of first-year class size—135*

The College of Law has well developed academic traditions in all major areas of the law. Especially strong programs exist in the areas of corporate and tax law, international law, and human rights.

■ Special Programs

The College of Law recognizes that a lawyer needs both a firm grasp of subject matter and expertise in professional skills. The college has developed an extensive legal research and writing program that not only encompasses the first year, but upper-level courses as well. To involve students directly in the legal system, the Judge In Residence Program brings actual trials to the law school courtroom so that students can observe a visiting judge. The Extern Program and Center for Dispute Resolution provide students with client-representation experience and the opportunity to work with practicing attorneys in public agencies. The Urban Morgan Institute for Human Rights was founded at the College in 1979. Dedicated to drawing attention of the legal and scholarly communities to this new area of the law, the Morgan Institute conducts seminars and conferences, is building a major research library, and edits the *Human Rights Quarterly* (Johns Hopkins University Press), *Pennsylvania Studies in Human Rights* (University of Pennsylvania Press), and the *Amnesty International Legal Support Network Newsletter*. The institute offers fellowships and opportunities to work with international human rights organizations worldwide.

■ Admission Standards

- *Bachelor's degree required*
- *application deadline—April 1* - *LSAT, LSDAS required*
- *median GPA—3.37* - *median LSAT score—162 (89th percentile)* - *application fee—$35*

Applicants must have a baccalaureate degree from an accredited institution prior to enrollment. A valid LSAT score and the LSDAS subscription are required. Applications should be submitted before April 1. Admission to the college is based upon a selective review of each candidate's file. Although the admissions committee relies on the grade-point average and LSAT score to determine the applicant's academic potential, other nonquantitative factors believed to be relevant to success in law school are considered; i.e., the quality of the applicant's education, participation in community service, employment experience, graduate work, and letters of recommendation. The educational philosophy of the college reflects a belief that a quality legal education is enhanced by having a heterogeneous student body. The committee, therefore, also considers race, cultural background, unusual personal circumstances, and age. Admission decisions are made on a rolling basis. Special consideration is given to competitive applications from members of minority groups who have been economically and culturally disadvantaged. Particular effort is made to provide adequate financial assistance.

Student Activities

The University of Cincinnati Law Review was founded in 1927 and was the first law review published by an Ohio law school. Edited quarterly by student editors, *Law Review* members are selected on the basis of both scholastic achievement and writing ability. The College's Moot Court Program participates in all national intercollegiate competitions and annually hosts the National Product Liabilities Competition. The Student Bar Association and Student Legal Education Committee participate in governance of the college, providing student members for law school committees. Additionally, the Volunteer Lawyers for the Poor (VLP) organization was founded in 1991. VLP had approximately 50 students working on public-interest law projects last year.

Expenses and Financial Aid

➡ *tuition & fees—resident,$5,796; nonresident, $11,268*
➡ *scholarships available*
➡ *FAFSA required, March 1 deadline*

Living expenses are estimated at $9,310 for independent students. Scholarships are awarded to approximately 60 percent of the entering class on the basis of academic merit alone or on the basis of merit and financial need. Deadline for receipt of the Scholarship Information Sheet form is March 1. The University Financial Aid Office assists students in obtaining Perkins Loans.

Placement

The college maintains an active Career Planning and Placement Center with a professional staff available to counsel students seeking permanent, summer, and part-time employment. The Career Planning and Placement Office provides an on-campus recruiting program with over 75 law firms and agencies, businesses, corporations, and financial institutions participating. In recent years, over 90 percent of each graduating class has accepted employment within six months of graduation. Typically, 60 percent of a graduating class will enter private practice; 15 percent, judicial clerkships; 10 percent, business/corporations; 13 percent, government; and 2 percent, public interest. While 75 percent of graduates accept employment in the Midwest, an increasing number have accepted positions nationally. Graduates are employed in 48 states, the District of Columbia, and numerous foreign countries. The average salary for the class of 1992 was $37,538.

Applicant Group for the 1993–1994 Academic Year

University of Cincinnati College of Law
This grid includes only applicants who earned 120-180 LSAT scores under standard administrations.

LSAT Score	3.75 +		3.50 -3.74		3.25 - 3.49		3.00 - 3.24		2.75 - 2.99		2.50 - 2.74		2.25 - 2.49		2.00 - 2.24		Below 2.00		No GPA		Total	
	Apps	Adm	Apps	Adm	Apps	Adm	Apps	Adm	Apps	Adm	Apps	Adm	Apps	Adm	Apps	Adm	Apps	Adm	Apps	Adm	Apps	Adm
175 - 180	0	0	1	1	1	1	0	0	0	0	0	0	0	0	0	0	0	0	0	0	2	2
170 - 174	6	6	1	1	5	5	2	2	5	4	0	0	1	1	0	0	0	0	0	0	20	19
165 - 169	7	7	8	8	17	16	13	13	9	9	4	4	2	2	0	0	0	0	0	0	60	59
160 - 164	18	18	30	29	39	34	39	21	23	13	13	5	6	0	1	0	0	0	0	0	169	120
155 - 159	15	10	50	34	71	15	48	6	45	3	25	0	11	1	0	0	2	0	2	0	269	69
150 - 154	21	11	48	8	72	9	75	4	44	1	25	3	18	3	8	0	1	0	4	2	316	41
145 - 149	7	3	22	3	35	4	54	2	45	4	29	4	17	0	7	0	3	1	3	0	222	21
140 - 144	2	0	7	1	11	0	32	0	17	1	33	0	15	0	7	0	0	0	1	0	125	2
135 - 139	1	0	2	0	6	0	9	0	3	0	8	0	9	0	6	0	1	0	1	0	46	0
130 - 134	0	0	1	0	0	0	2	0	3	0	5	0	2	0	3	0	0	0	1	0	17	0
125 - 129	1	0	0	0	0	0	1	0	1	0	0	0	0	0	0	0	0	0	0	0	3	0
120 - 124	0	0	0	0	0	0	0	0	0	0	0	0	0	0	0	0	0	0	0	0	0	0
Total	78	55	170	85	257	84	275	48	195	35	142	16	81	7	32	0	7	1	12	2	1249	333

Apps = Number of Applicants
Adm = Number Admitted
Reflects 96% of the total applicant pool.

Cleveland State University—Cleveland-Marshall College of Law

Cleveland, OH 44115   Phone: 216.687.2304

■ Introduction

The Cleveland State University College of Law, located on the university's new urban campus in downtown Cleveland, is the largest law school in Ohio. It has been training lawyers since its forerunners, the Cleveland Law School and John Marshall Law School, were established in 1887 and 1916, respectively. Since becoming part of the state university system in 1969, the Cleveland-Marshall College of Law has maintained and enhanced its long-standing reputation for training attorneys dedicated to the service of their communities. The college operates a full-time day and part-time evening program, preparing students for practice in any jurisdiction. It is a member of AALS and the League of Ohio Law Schools and is approved by the ABA. Located on Lake Erie, Cleveland is an active cultural center, nationally renowned for its parks, libraries, and museums. The Cleveland Symphony Orchestra is one of the finest in the world. Cleveland is also a major industrial center and headquarters for many large corporations. An excellent rapid transportation system links downtown Cleveland and Cleveland State University to the eastern and western suburbs of the city.

■ Enrollment/Student Body

➤ *684 admitted first-year class 1992* ➤ *300 enrolled first-year class 1992* ➤ *620 total full-time* ➤ *386 total part-time* ➤ *13.8% minority* ➤ *41% women (first-year class)* ➤ *25 states & foreign countries represented* ➤ *150 undergraduate schools represented*

From 15 to 20 percent of each entering class is likely to be over 30 years old, with as many as 15 percent earning advanced degrees before beginning the study of law. From 20 to 25 percent of each class comes to Cleveland State from outside Ohio. Students of color and women are actively recruited and are encouraged to apply.

■ Faculty

➤ *72 total* ➤ *41 full-time* ➤ *31 part-time or adjunct*

■ Library and Physical Facilities

➤ *290,000 volumes & equivalents* ➤ *LEXIS* ➤ *NEXIS* ➤ *WESTLAW*

The university library, with over 800,000 volumes, is readily accessible to law students. Other university facilities, including a bookstore, cafeterias, and modern gymnasium, are also available to law students and are within walking distance.

■ Curriculum

➤ *87 credits required to graduate*
➤ *degrees available: J.D.; J.D./M.B.A.; J.D./M.P.A.*

In both day and evening programs, the core curriculum and most elective courses are taught by full-time faculty.

The adjunct faculty, consisting of prominent judges and lawyers, teach in highly specialized areas. Typically, the J.D. program is completed by full-time day students in three academic years and by part-time evening students in four academic years and two summers. Full-time students may also attend summer sessions to accelerate their study.

■ Special Programs

The urban setting of the college offers unusual opportunities to bring challenging legal experiences to students. Externship programs take the student out of the classroom and into the courtroom. A Street Law Program allows students to earn course credit while teaching law in area high schools. A more specialized clinical opportunity is afforded the students who participate in these programs. The Fair Employment Practices Clinic provides credit for participation in litigation dealing with employment discrimination. The Judicial Externship Program offers upper-level students opportunities to work with state appellate and federal court judges. A joint program with the College of Business permits interested students to earn both the J.D. and M.B.A. degrees in four years. A new program, the J.D./M.P.A. degree program, has been introduced this year. This program is being offered jointly by the College of Urban Studies and the College of Law. Each year lawyers, judges, and legal scholars of national renown are invited to the College of Law as Cleveland-Marshall Fund lecturers. Each of these distinguished visitors delivers a major address and spends two days at the College of Law meeting informally with students and faculty and conducting class sessions.

■ Admission

➤ *fall admission only* ➤ *LSAT, LSDAS required*

Applicants are admitted by the Dean upon the recommendation of an Admissions Committee composed of faculty members and students. Criteria for admission are identical for the full-time and part-time programs. Each applicant must have received a bachelor's level degree from a college or university accredited at the time of the applicant's graduation. Applicants are urged to take the LSAT no later than December of the year in which application is made. Experience has shown that undergraduate grade-point averages and LSAT scores are generally the most reliable measures available for predicting success in law school. For this reason, most students are admitted primarily upon an index combining grades and test scores. However, under the Legal Careers Opportunity Program (LCOP), instituted by the law faculty in 1970, the admissions committee may consider many other factors in an effort to identify students who have faced adversity in the pursuit of their educational opportunities or who have accomplishments and experiences suggesting that they do have the ability to succeed in law school if given the opportunity. These factors include length of time since graduation from college, achievement after college, racial and ethnic status, economic disadvantage, and extracurricular activity. LCOP applicants are required to submit a writing sample, three letters of recommendation, and a personal statement in addition to an LSDAS report. LCOP students are required to attend a summer program prior to fall admission. The application deadline is March 1

Student Activities

The *Cleveland State Law Review* is edited and published by an editorial board consisting entirely of students of high academic standing and superior writing ability. The law review publishes articles by students and legal scholars for the practicing bar and for use in scholarly research. The *Journal of Law and Health* is an interdisciplinary publication that explores ideas in health law and policy. A Moot Court Program is offered to give students an understanding of the appellate process and of the work performed by lawyers at the appellate level. An extensive intramural competition is conducted each year, and outstanding students represent the college in nationwide competitions. All students are members of the Student Bar Association, an affiliate of the Law Student Division of the ABA. Phi Alpha Delta, Delta Theta Phi, and Tau Epsilon Rho, national legal fraternities, have active chapters on campus. Other student organizations include the Black Law Students Association, the Na-tional Lawyers Guild, and the Women's Caucus. In addition, students of the College of Law publish a student newspaper, *The Gavel.*

Expenses and Financial Aid

➡ *tuition & fees—full-time Ohio resident, $5,404; part-time, $2,702* ➡ *full-time nonresident, $10,808; part-time, $5,404* ➡ *financial aid available* ➡ *GAPSFAS due March 1*

The financial aid program at the college utilizes combinations of tuition grants, work-study employment awards, scholarships, and loans. Awards are made primarily on the basis of need, and the college is able to meet a high proportion of the need of all students applying for aid.

Career Services

A full-time placement director provides placement services for students and alumni. Each year employers from law firms, corporations, business, government, legal services, and public interest groups interview students at the Cleveland-Marshall College of Law for part-time, summer, and full-time employment. It is estimated that approximately 50 percent of the attorneys practicing in greater Cleveland are graduates of Cleveland State and its predecessors. Our graduates continue to be highly visible on the northern Ohio bench, in business and industry, public service, government, and private practice.

Applicant Group for the 1993–1994 Academic Year

Cleveland State University—Cleveland-Marshall College of Law
This grid includes only applicants who earned 120-180 LSAT scores under standard administrations.

LSAT Score	3.75+		3.50 - 3.74		3.25 - 3.49		3.00 - 3.24		2.75 - 2.99		2.50 - 2.74		2.25 - 2.49		2.00 - 2.24		Below 2.00		Total	
	Apps	Adm	Apps	Adm	Apps	Adm	Apps	Adm	Apps	Adm	Apps	Adm	Apps	Adm	Apps	Adm	Apps	Adm	Apps	Adm
175 - 180	0	0	0	0	0	0	1	1	0	0	0	0	1	1	0	0	0	0	2	2
170 - 174	0	0	0	0	0	0	1	1	0	0	2	2	2	2	1	1	0	0	6	6
165 - 169	2	2	4	4	4	4	6	6	4	4	3	3	12	5	0	0	0	0	35	28
160 - 164	8	8	8	8	15	15	15	15	14	12	14	14	21	1	4	2	0	0	99	75
155 - 159	5	5	33	33	46	45	59	57	67	60	43	22	50	2	8	0	2	0	311	224
150 - 154	15	15	41	41	83	77	116	66	128	27	75	4	47	2	12	1	2	0	517	233
145 - 149	11	9	18	10	51	20	103	15	83	9	73	7	47	0	21	0	5	0	407	70
140 -144	5	1	7	0	33	7	43	4	53	3	52	0	30	0	16	0	7	0	239	15
135 - 139	1	0	6	2	4	1	14	1	22	0	29	0	8	0	15	0	4	0	89	4
130 - 134	0	0	2	1	3	0	5	0	6	0	8	0	3	0	8	0	1	0	35	1
125 - 129	0	0	0	0	1	0	1	0	2	0	2	0	0	0	4	0	3	0	10	0
120 - 124	0	0	0	0	0	0	0	0	0	0	0	0	0	0	0	0	0	0	0	0
Total	46	40	99	99	240	164	364	166	379	111	301	52	221	13	89	4	24	0	1774	658

Apps = Number of Applicants
Adm = Number Admitted

University of Colorado School of Law

Fleming Law Building
Campus Box 403
Boulder, CO 80309-0403

Phone: 303.492.7203

■ Introduction

The entire School of Law is contained within the Fleming Law Building located on the Boulder campus of the University of Colorado. High admission standards, combined with a relatively small student body and a favorable faculty-to-student ratio, assure a stimulating and challenging academic environment that encourages in-class participation and informal consultations with faculty. The school is a charter member of the AALS and is ABA approved.

■ Enrollment/Student Body

➡ *first-year class 1993—2,746 applicants, 487 admitted, 167 enrolled, 92 undergraduate schools and 28 states represented*
➡ *476 total full-time*   ➡ *20% total minority*
➡ *45% total women*

■ Faculty

➡ *62 total*   ➡ *31 full-time*   ➡ *31 part-time or adjunct*
➡ *15 women*   ➡ *8 minority*

■ Library and Physical Facilities

➡ *280,000 volumes & equivalents*   ➡ *LEXIS*
➡ *NEXIS*   ➡ *WESTLAW*   ➡ *LEGISLATE*
➡ *7.5 full-time librarians*
➡ *library seats 407 (plus lounge seating)*

The University of Colorado Law Library's collection includes statutes and cases from all 50 states, the federal government, and many foreign jurisdictions. The law library is a selective depository for federal government publications. Professional librarians are available to assist students between 10:00 A.M. and 7:00 P.M. The university maintains a computer lab in the library. Students may elect to access computer services from their homes via modem. All computer resources are offered to law students at no charge.

■ Curriculum

➡ *Academic Support Program*   ➡ *89 credits required to graduate*   ➡ *100 courses available*   ➡ *degrees available: J.D.; J.D./M.B.A.; J.D./M.P.A. (plus other joint degrees)*
➡ *semesters, start in Aug.*
➡ *range of first-year class size—24-80*

First semester runs from late August to mid-December and second semester from mid-January to mid-May. An eight-week summer session is offered in June and July for students with advanced standing at any accredited law school. With a limited number of additional hours, a certificate in tax or environmental policy is attainable. The first-year curriculum is required of all students. During the second and third years, coursework may emphasize such areas as natural resources and environmental law, criminal law, commercial law, constitutional law, taxation, and public law.

■ Special Programs

The Natural Resources Law Center has three major areas of activity: research and publication, legal education, and the distinguished visitors and fellows program.

The National Wildlife Federation's Natural Resources Litigation Clinic involves students in complex administrative and judicial environmental litigation. Students work with expert witnesses and staff counsel on a variety of public lands, energy, and water-rights cases, most of which reach the state supreme court or federal appellate court level. A number of student-assisted clinic cases have set precedents and have been published in environmental law texts.

The Legal Aid and Defender Program allows students to represent low-income clients in actual civil and criminal cases in Colorado courts under the supervision of full-time faculty who are experienced trial attorneys.

The Indian Law Clinic provides students the opportunity to work with our native Americans on their unique legal problems.

■ Admission

➡ *Bachelor's degree from an accredited school required*
➡ *application deadline—Feb. 15 (earlier is recommended)*
➡ *rolling admission (first letters go out about Feb. 1; class is usually full about May/June; admission thereafter from the waiting list is limited)*   ➡ *LSAT, LSDAS required*
➡ *median GPA—3.31*   ➡ *median LSAT score—164*
➡ *application fee—$40*   ➡ *new students matriculate in Aug.*

Though admissions decisions are based heavily on the LSAT and undergraduate grades, other factors are also important because they may indicate special qualities of motivation or diversity. These other factors include variety in economic, social, or cultural backgrounds; variety in undergraduate or graduate programs or institutions; unusual employment or other experience; demonstrated and unusual qualities of leadership; special achievement in overcoming personal handicaps or disadvantages; and the ability to contribute the perspectives of racial or ethnic minority or other distinctive communities. In its efforts to offer equal opportunity for obtaining a legal education, the school will take race into account affirmatively as an important factor in the competitive weighing of individual applications.

An introductory summer program, available by invitation only, is offered to those admitted persons whose qualifications suggest that additional academic support may be particularly helpful for successful law study.

Very few transfer students are accepted each year; admission is based on law school performance in addition to the factors noted for beginning students.

■ Housing

The university has dormitories for single students and apartments for married students. Inquiries should be sent to University Residence Halls, Room 80 Hallett,

Boulder, CO 80310 or to Family Housing, 1350 20th Street, Boulder, CO 80302. Most law students live in private housing; students are advised to seek housing early.

■ Student Activities

The Rothgerber Moot Court Competition offers students an opportunity to develop skills in appellate brief writing and oral argument before panels of distinguished judges and lawyers. The Jessup International Law Moot Court Competition and two Trial Practice Competitions also provide students with valuable experience in written and oral advocacy.

The *University of Colorado Law Review*, a professional journal edited entirely by students, publishes scholarly articles and comments on matters of national and state concern. The *Colorado Journal of International Environmental Law* is one of only two such journals in the nation.

Over 20 student organizations invite participation in projects, programs, and social activities. New organizations are created as needs are identified.

■ Expenses and Financial Aid

➡ *tuition & fees—full-time resident, $4,063; full-time nonresident, $12,537* ➡ *estimated additional expenses—$9,400 (all living costs)* ➡ *scholarships available (limited state & private funds)* ➡ *minority scholarships available (some tuition assistance)*

Grants-in-aid are available on a limited basis to eligible resident students and are awarded on the basis of need. Nonresident students may not be awarded grants from state funds under present state policy but may be considered for Federal Perkins Loans and scholarships from private funds. Students may not be employed during their first year, but limited outside employment may be compatible with second- and third-year schedules. Students applying for financial aid, including grants and Perkins Loans, must file the Free Application for Federal Student Aid. This form is available from all local high schools, colleges, and universities, and will be processed at no charge. For the best possible financial aid package, early filing (as soon after January 1 as the applicant's tax information is available) is strongly recommended.

■ Career Services

The School of Law has an active Office of Career Services providing a broad range of employment and career-counseling services. Liaison is maintained with law firms, government agencies, courts, businesses, and other employers who seek the services of students and graduates. The following data are typical of those collected from graduates in recent years.

With 94 percent of the members of the class of 1992 responding, within six months after graduation more than 75 percent were employed. Approximately 46 percent were in full-time positions with law firms, 17 percent were clerking for judges, and 12 percent were employed by governments on local, state, and federal levels. The remainder were occupied in business and industry or legal services and other public interest careers. The information supplied showed that the beginning average salary for a 1992 graduate was $38,343 per year. About two-thirds of graduates remain in Colorado, but graduates of the law school have located throughout the United States and Canada.

Applicant Group for the 1993–1994 Academic Year

University of Colorado School of Law
This grid includes only applicants who earned 120-180 LSAT scores under standard administrations.

LSAT Score	3.75 +		3.50 -3.74		3.25 - 3.49		3.00 - 3.24		2.75 - 2.99		2.50 - 2.74		2.25 - 2.49		2.00 - 2.24		Below 2.00		No GPA		Total	
	Apps	Adm	Apps	Adm	Apps	Adm	Apps	Adm	Apps	Adm	Apps	Adm	Apps	Adm	Apps	Adm	Apps	Adm	Apps	Adm	Apps	Adm
175 - 180	1	1	2	2	3	3	3	3	2	2	1	0	0	0	0	0	0	0	0	0	12	11
170 - 174	9	9	9	9	14	13	17	15	5	4	4	3	2	0	1	0	0	0	1	1	62	54
165 - 169	20	20	49	47	65	63	58	52	39	26	19	10	9	3	2	0	2	0	3	2	266	223
160 - 164	49	18	122	32	147	22	146	17	73	5	33	4	10	1	4	0	1	0	1	1	586	100
155 - 159	47	5	126	8	169	11	169	7	99	1	47	5	21	0	7	0	0	0	11	0	696	37
150 - 154	27	1	75	0	102	6	115	4	93	4	52	2	30	1	6	0	1	0	3	0	504	18
145 - 149	14	2	16	0	52	3	65	2	49	3	38	1	13	0	11	0	0	0	4	0	262	11
140 - 144	0	0	9	0	20	1	23	1	33	0	20	0	17	1	6	0	5	0	1	0	134	3
135 - 139	0	0	1	0	4	0	8	0	10	0	11	0	12	0	6	0	0	0	1	0	53	0
130 - 134	0	0	1	0	1	0	1	0	2	0	2	0	0	0	1	0	0	0	1	0	9	0
125 - 129	0	0	0	0	0	0	0	0	1	0	2	0	2	0	0	0	0	0	0	0	5	0
120 - 124	0	0	0	0	0	0	0	0	0	0	1	0	0	0	0	0	0	0	0	0	1	0
Total	167	56	410	98	577	122	605	101	406	45	230	25	116	6	44	0	9	0	26	4	2590	457

Apps = Number of Applicants
Adm = Number Admitted
Reflects 94% of the total applicant pool.

Columbia University School of Law

435 West 116th Street
New York, NY 10027

Phone: 212.854.2670 and 854.2678

■ Introduction

Columbia law school, in the City of New York, is distinguished, perhaps uniquely among leading American law schools, as an international center of legal education that stimulates its students to consider the full dimensions of the possibility of the law—as an intellectual pursuit, as a career, and as an instrument of human progress. The character of academic and social life at Columbia, like that of New York City, is fiercely democratic, dynamic, creative, and innovative. The law school is especially committed to educating students of differing perspectives, from diverse backgrounds, and with varied life experiences. Men and women choosing to study law at Columbia hail from the small towns, farms, and suburbs of the West, Midwest, and South; the industrial corridors and Ivy halls of the Northeast; the inner cities of every major American metropolis; and the international centers of Europe, Asia, Africa, and Latin America.

Through our admissions program, we seek to enroll an entering class that reflects the broad range of economic, ethnic, and cultural strains found in America. From around the world, we welcome students who will enrich learning at Columbia and thereafter advance the developing legal cultures of their homelands.

Professional prospects for Columbia law graduates are quite extraordinary. Not surprisingly, many of our graduates proceed to productive careers in every conceivable arena of private practice. But, it should be emphasized that while Columbia-trained attorneys are especially well-regarded for their work in corporate law and finance, an unusually high number also serve as state and federal judges, prosecutors, civil and human rights advocates, legal scholars, public defenders, business executives, elected officials, and national and international leaders. Noteworthy also is the fact that many Columbia law alumnae/i contribute significantly to the shaping of American culture at large. Currently, our graduates serve in leadership roles across the fields of art, music, film, publishing, science, professional athletics, philanthropy, and higher education. With an exceptionally talented student body and faculty, and a strong tradition of encouraging students with specialized interests to develop those interests in depth, Columbia law school provides a legal education that gives our students a singular capacity for imagination, originality, and high responsibility in their professional lives.

■ J.D. Enrollment/Student Body

➡ 6,140 applicants 1993   ➡ 16% of applicants admitted
➡ 345 enrolled first-year class   ➡ 1,053 total full-time students
➡ 27% minority   ➡ 41% women
➡ 48 states, 18 foreign countries, and 194 undergraduate schools represented in student body   ➡ 14% earned at least one other graduate or professional degree

■ Faculty

➡ 101 total   ➡ 64 full-time   ➡ 37 part-time or adjunct
➡ 18 women   ➡ 8 minority

■ Library Resources and Research Facilities

➡ 735,000 library volumes   ➡ 685,000 equivalents
➡ LEXIS   ➡ NEXIS   ➡ WESTLAW   ➡ DIALOG

The second largest law collection in this country, Columbia's library is especially rich in American law and legal history, international law, comparative law, Roman law, and the legal literature of the major European countries, China, and Japan. CD-ROMs are also used to support research, not just in American law, but in German, Argentine, and Australian law as well. In addition, the many libraries of the university, containing more than five million volumes, are available to law student.

The law library's on-line catalog provides access to the collection and acts as an index to the major legal serials, as well as providing access to the on-line catalogs of several other major law school libraries. Columbia provides its law students with, what we believe to be, the most extensive and sophisticated computer support of any law school in the nation. The law school's computer network includes a computer lab in the library which is used for instruction, research, and writing. The network is also available through modems to students working in their dorms or homes. The law library provides facilities for visually impaired students.

■ Curriculum

➡ Academic Support Program   ➡ 83 total units required to graduate   ➡ 158 courses available
➡ joint programs with Columbia University's Arts and Sciences (M.A., M.Phil., Ph.D.); Business (M.B.A.); International and Public Affairs (M.I.A.); Journalism (M.S.); Teachers College (M.Ed.); Theatre Arts (M.F.A.); Social Work (M.S.W.); Architecture, Planning and Preservation (M.S.); and with Princeton University's Woodrow Wilson School of Public and International Affairs (M.I.A.)

The foundation of the Juris Doctor (J.D.) program consists of legal method, law and economics, contracts, torts, constitutional law, civil procedure, property, criminal law, foundations of the regulatory state, and perspectives on legal thought. The upper-class program is entirely elective, except for three research and writing requirements, a course in professional responsibility, and a pro bono service requirement. There are approximately 90 seminars (normally limited to 18 students). In these small classes, students engage in intensive study and individualized instruction.

Columbia has a special commitment to clinical education, which places the student in the role of a lawyer doing a lawyer's actual work under intensive faculty supervision. Some examples of clinical opportunities are Family Advocacy, Fair Housing, Law and the Arts, and

Alternative Dispute Resolution: Mediation Clinic. Also available is a summer program which places 60-70 students in Civil Rights and Human Rights Internships in law firms and organizations throughout this country and around the world.

Especially distinguished are Columbia's offerings in international, foreign, and comparative law; constitutional law and theory; corporate and securities law; and human rights.

■ Special Programs

The school is well situated for developing a broad urban affairs program, since New York City is the home of an extraordinary variety of private and government agencies concerned with urban problems, ranging from legal service agencies to community development projects. In all, some 25 courses and seminars are offered in urban law, civil rights and liberties, and criminal law. A variety of legal training opportunities include the Morningside Heights Legal Services, federal and criminal court clerkships, the student legal assistance committee, and placement with urban agencies.

In the fields of international, comparative, and foreign law, Columbia offers approximately 40 courses and specialized seminars. In addition, Columbia is the home of the Parker School of Foreign and Cómparative Law, a center for scholarly activity in foreign and comparative law that sponsors courses, publications, conferences and scholarships.

Columbia's longstanding leadership in international law has been strengthened greatly in the last decade by the establishment of its Center for Chinese Legal Studies, its Center for Japanese Legal Studies, and a joint degree program with the University of Paris.

Columbia is especially strong in the areas of constitutional law. Over 15 different members of the faculty teach at least one course or seminar in constitutional law or constitutional theory.

Other special Columbia programs, serving as catalysts for scholarly work, curricular development, and student enrichment include: the Center for Law and the Arts; the Center for Law and Economic Studies; the Human Rights Internship Program; the Jaffin Program in Law and Social Responsibility; the Legislative Drafting Research Fund; the Samuel Rubin Program, advancing civil rights and civil liberties; the Julius Silver program in Law, Science, and Technology; and the Feminism and Legal Theory Project.

■ Admission

➡ *LSAT, LSDAS required* ➡ *median GPA—3.60*
➡ *median LSAT score—168* ➡ *application fee—$65*

All first-year students enter in late August. Candidates applying for regular admission should apply after September 1 of the year preceding their desired matriculation, but before February 15, the application deadline. Early Decision candidates must complete their applications by December 1 and are notified in late December.

■ Expenses and Financial Aid

➡ *tuition & fees—$20,518/1993-94* ➡ *estimated room, board, and personal expenses—$11,430*
➡ *1993-94 average grant value—approximately $8,000*
➡ *need-based scholarship program*
➡ *GAPSFAS application required—March 1 deadline*
➡ *Public Interest Loan Forgiveness Program (LRAP) available*

Applicant Group for the 1993–1994 Academic Year

Columbia University School of Law
This grid includes only applicants who earned 120-180 LSAT scores under standard administrations.

LSAT Score	3.75 +		3.50 -3.74		3.25 - 3.49		3.00 - 3.24		2.75 - 2.99		2.50 - 2.74		Below 2.50		No GPA		Total	
	Apps	Adm	Apps	Adm	Apps	Adm	Apps	Adm	Apps	Adm	Apps	Adm	Apps	Adm	Apps	Adm	Apps	Adm
175 - 180	60	49	50	43	39	21	13	3	2	0	0	0	0	0	1	1	165	117
170 - 174	123	97	187	146	135	64	62	14	12	1	4	0	3	0	3	1	529	323
165 - 169	331	154	521	141	362	39	124	11	30	1	15	0	7	1	15	6	1405	353
160 - 164	259	48	405	33	321	26	154	17	39	1	28	0	7	0	18	1	1231	126
155 - 159	141	8	253	10	286	14	148	10	73	3	23	0	24	0	26	1	974	46
Below 155	101	3	215	7	306	4	338	1	225	1	146	0	135	0	70	1	1536	17
Total	1015	359	1631	380	1449	168	839	56	381	7	216	0	176	1	133	11	5840	982

Apps = Number of Applicants
Adm = Number Admitted
Reflects 94% of the total applicant pool.

University of Connecticut School of Law

55 Elizabeth Street
Hartford, CT 06105-2296

Phone: 203.241.4696

■ Introduction

Through several decades of sustained and continuing intellectual growth, the University of Connecticut School of Law has emerged as one of the leading public law schools in the country. An excellent student-faculty ratio, small classes, a rich curriculum, student organizations active across the spectrum of legal and social concerns, a regular flow of guest speakers, a committed body of graduates—all of these combine to make Connecticut a strong school and an exciting place to study.

■ Enrollment/Student Body

➡ *1,565 day applicants*　➡ *672 evening applicants*
➡ *383 admitted first-year day class 1993*　➡ *138 admitted first-year evening class*　➡ *133 enrolled first-year day class 1993*　➡ *68 enrolled first-year evening class*
➡ *433 total full-time*　➡ *222 total part-time*
➡ *16% minority*　➡ *50% women*
➡ *16 states & foreign countries represented in first-year class*
➡ *183 undergraduate schools represented*
➡ *46 undergraduate majors represented in first-year class*
➡ *12 foreign colleges & universities represented*

Our students constitute an eclectic and intellectually ambitious community. The class that entered in the fall of 1993 includes 18 percent from ethnic and racial minority groups, 54 percent women, and 14 percent admitted under our Special Admissions Program.

■ Faculty

➡ *95 total*　➡ *42 full-time*　➡ *53 part-time or adjunct*
➡ *11 women*　➡ *12 part-time women*
➡ *4 full-time minority*　➡ *1 part-time minority*
➡ *1 visiting full-time minority*

■ Library and Physical Facilities

➡ *382,752 volumes & equivalents*　➡ *library hours: Mon.-Fri., 8:30 A.M.-11:00 P.M.; Sat., 9:00 A.M.-7:00 P.M.; Sun., 10:00 A.M.-11:00 P.M.*　➡ *LEXIS*　➡ *NEXIS*　➡ *WESTLAW*
➡ *DIALOG*　➡　➡ *8 full-time librarians*
➡ *library seats 223*　➡ *on-line catalog of all library holdings*
➡ *member of New England Law Libraries Consortium, RLG*

With its immediate neighbors—the Hartford Seminary, the Hartford College for Women, and the Connecticut Historical Society—the school is part of an academic enclave in a turn-of-the-century residential neighborhood. Nearby bookstores, pubs, and coffeehouses add to campus life.

Although the school has no dormitories, most students live within walking distance of the campus. Housing is plentiful and varied, ranging from studio apartments that start at around $400 per month to two- and three-bedroom apartments at around $750, to entire houses. The School maintains a comprehensive housing list, with information about accessibility for students with special physical requirements.

■ Curriculum

➡ *Academic Support Program*　➡ *86 credits required to graduate*　➡ *150 courses available*　➡ *degrees available: J.D.; J.D./M.P.H.; J.D./M.S.W.; J.D./M.B.A.; J.D./M.P.A.; J.D./M.A. in Public Policy (Trinity College); J.D./M.L.S. with Southern Connecticut State University*

■ Special Programs

Connecticut was a pioneer in clinical legal education, and our clinics continue to be a distinguishing strength of the school. Students interested in law and economics, feminist legal thought, and legal philosophy will find courses and specialists to meet their needs. Extensive offerings in environmental law are supplemented by a semester exchange program with the Environmental Law Center at Vermont. International law occupies an increasingly prominent place in the curriculum, reinforced by the student-edited *Journal of International Law*. Student-faculty exchange programs with Leiden (Netherlands), Exeter (U.K.), the University of Puerto Rico, the University of International Business and Economics (Beijing), additional programs now being developed with schools in Central Europe, and a new LL.M. Program for foreign lawyers (scheduled to begin in 1994) all provide opportunities for our students to learn from and study with peers trained in different legal systems.

■ Disabled Student Services

The Disabled Student Services Liaison (DSSL) at the School of Law works with disabled students in the development and implementation of reasonable accommodations to allow access to both its physical facilities and its educational and extracurricular programs. Associate Dean Peter Lane and Associate Dean Laurie Werling serve as liaisons. Their office hours are Mon.-Wed., 8:30 A.M.-6:30 P.M., and Thurs.-Fri., 8:30 A.M.-4:30 P.M.

Students with mobility impairments considering applying or admitted to the School of Law are invited to tour the campus. If assistance is required, please contact the DSSL. Students with other disabilities may contact the DSSL for discussion of accommodations.

■ Academic Support Program

Each year, the School of Law offers an Academic Support Program to entering first-year students who requested special admissions consideration, or whose admissions files suggest that they would benefit from individual attention. The program is designed to promote the academic success of those who participate, as well as to demonstrate the School of Law's commitment to ensuring that all admitted students have a full opportunity to maximize their academic potential.

The program consists of a summer session and an academic-year tutorial program. The summer session is conducted during the week immediately prior to the beginning of classes.

■ Admission

➡ *Bachelor's degree required (or foreign equivalent)*
➡ *application deadline—March 1; rolling admissions; early fall applications preferred* ➡ *LSAT, LSDAS required*
➡ *median GPA (day)—3.29* ➡ *median GPA (evening)—3.23* ➡ *median LSAT score (day)—160*
➡ *median LSAT score (evening)—159* ➡ *application fee (day or evening)—$30; (day and evening)—$45*

■ Student Activities

The *Connecticut Law Review*, now in its twenty-sixth volume, publishes approximately 1,000 pages of critical legal discussion each year. The *Law Review* is managed entirely by a student Board of Editors.

The *Connecticut Journal of International Law*, now in its ninth volume, publishes up to three issues per year on topics concerning both public and private international law. Circulated internationally, the *Journal* is wholly student-managed and edited. The *Journal* also sponsors an international legal symposium each year; last year a team of *Journal* members and faculty professors traveled to Budapest, Hungary, where the *Journal* presented a symposium on emerging Human Rights Law in Eastern Europe. In addition, the *Journal* sponsors a number of campus lectures, panel discussions, and social events open to the entire law school community each semester.

The **Connecticut Moot Court Board** provides students with the opportunity to practice oral advocacy in the challenging setting of intramural and interscholastic competitions.

The **Student Bar Association** is the representative student government of the school. It manages an annual budget consisting of funds derived from the Student Activities Fee and the university tuition to support the various student organizations, and to enhance generally the quality of student life.

In addition, a large number of organizations have active chapters on campus.

■ Expenses and Financial Aid

➡ *tuition & fees—full-time resident, $8,552; full-time RI, MA, NH, VT residents, $12,828, full-time all other state residents, $18,036* ➡ *part-time resident, $298/credit hour; part-time RI, MA, NH, VT residents $447/credit hour; part-time all other state residents $629/credit hour* ➡ *additional expenses—$11,147 (living expenses); $1,000 (books & materials)* ➡ *minority scholarship available; Travelers Company Scholarship (includes tuition, fees, and books, for three years, plus living stipend and job with Travelers after first year)* ➡ *financial aid available; Tuition Remission Grant, opportunity scholarship, Stafford Loan, SLS Loan* ➡ *law school financial aid application required by March 1*

■ Career Services

Connecticut operates a comprehensive career services office for the benefit of students and alumni/ae. The school offers a large and geographically diverse on-campus interviewing program, extensive individual and group counseling, a resource library, job listings, mentor programs, employment information sessions, newsletters, and job bulletins.

Applicant Group for the 1993–1994 Academic Year

University of Connecticut School of Law
This grid includes only applicants with 120-180 LSAT scores and a GPA (approximately 95% of all full-time, day-division applications).

LSAT Score	3.75 - 4.00		3.50 - 3.74		3.25 - 3.49		3.00 - 3.24		2.75 - 2.99		2.50 - 2.74		2.25 - 2.49		2.00 - 2.24		Below 2.00		Total	
	Apps	Adm	Apps	Adm	Apps	Adm	Apps	Adm	Apps	Adm	Apps	Adm	Apps	Adm	Apps	Adm	Apps	Adm	Apps	Adm
175 - 180	0	0	1	1	0	0	2	2	0	0	0	0	1	0	0	0	0	0	4	3
170 - 174	1	1	3	3	6	3	11	7	5	2	2	0	1	1	0	0	0	0	29	17
165 - 169	13	10	17	17	29	24	25	20	13	4	9	2	2	0	1	0	0	0	109	77
160 - 164	17	16	46	43	72	57	68	31	29	8	19	4	13	1	1	1	1	0	266	161
155 - 159	23	10	58	21	91	19	79	8	49	4	25	3	10	0	1	0	1	0	337	65
150 - 154	13	2	42	3	72	5	81	6	73	3	21	3	22	0	10	0	2	0	336	22
145 - 149	1	1	19	3	42	1	51	3	43	3	27	1	14	0	8	0	1	0	206	12
140 - 144	2	0	5	0	19	2	28	2	37	0	17	0	9	0	9	0	2	0	128	4
135 - 139	0	0	4	0	5	0	10	0	10	0	8	0	9	0	2	0	1	0	49	0
130 - 134	0	0	1	0	0	0	1	0	2	0	4	0	3	0	2	0	0	0	13	0
125 - 129	0	0	0	0	1	0	2	0	0	0	2	0	0	0	0	0	0	0	5	0
120 - 124	0	0	0	0	0	0	0	0	0	0	0	0	0	0	0	0	1	0	1	0
Total	70	40	196	91	337	111	358	79	261	24	134	13	84	2	34	1	9	0	1483	361

Apps = Number of Applicants
Adm = Number Admitted

Cornell University Law School

Ithaca, NY 14853

■ Introduction

Cornell is a national center of learning located in Ithaca, New York, the heart of the Finger Lakes region of New York State. The law school's small classes, broad curriculum and distinguished faculty, combined with the advantages of being part of one of the world's leading research universities, make it ideal for those who see legal study as a way to make meaningful contributions at all levels of society. Students find Ithaca to be a safe and nonstressful, yet culturally rich, environment in which to pursue legal studies.

■ Enrollment/Student Body

➡ *4,200 applicants*   ➡ *191 enrolled first-year class 1993*
➡ *568 total full-time*   ➡ *22% minority*   ➡ *37% women*
➡ *58 states & foreign countries represented*
➡ *250 undergraduate schools represented*

Over half of Cornell's entering students have taken one or more years between completion of their undergraduate degree and enrollment in law school. Selective admissions standards, combined with an emphasis on applicants' unique records and achievements, ensure that the student body is made up of people with wide-ranging interests, skills, concerns, and backgrounds.

■ Faculty

➡ *56 total*   ➡ *33 full-time*   ➡ *23 part-time, clinical or adjunct*   ➡ *13 women*   ➡ *4 minority*

Cornell's faculty includes tenured and tenure-track faculty who teach and produce scholarship in their area of law; clinical faculty who run client-focused and simulation courses centered around legal aid and several specialty clinics; and a large number of visitors, associated faculty from other university divisions, and adjunct faculty who teach at the school each year. Many of the latter group are legal scholars and professors from other countries who teach in the law school's large and active international program.

■ Library and Physical Facilities

➡ *400,000 volumes & 380,000 microforms*   ➡ *library hours: Mon.-Thurs., 8:00 A.M.-11:00 P.M.; Fri., 8:00 A.M.-7:00 P.M.; Sat., 9:00 A.M.-5:00 P.M.; Sun., NOON-11:00 P.M.*
➡ *LEXIS*   ➡ *NEXIS*   ➡ *WESTLAW*   ➡ *DIALOG*
➡ *7 full-time librarians*   ➡ *library seats 443*

The law school is located in the newly renovated and expanded Myron Taylor Hall, at the heart of the scenic 740 acre Cornell University campus. Hughes Hall, the law school dormitory, is adjacent to the main law school building and contains single rooms for about 80 students and a dining facility for breakfast and lunch.

Cornell is one of the nation's leaders in the development and support of computer-assisted legal research and writing. Students have access to the full array of In-

ternet services, including sophisticated electronic mail. The law school's multiple-node network and computer terminals are available to students for word-processing, legal research, statistical analysis, and database management. Students also have access to any of the 17 satellite computer clusters and mainframe facilities located on the university campus.

■ Curriculum

➡ *Academic Support Program*   ➡ *84 semester credit hours required*   ➡ *degrees and joint/combined programs: J.D.; J.D. with specialization in international legal studies; LL.M.; J.S.D.; J.D./M.B.A.; J.D./M.P.A.; J.D./M.I.L.R.; J.D./M.R.P.; J.D./M.A.; J.D./Ph.D.*   ➡ *semesters, begin in late Aug.*
➡ *first-year class size—27; other class ranges—70-100; first-year intensive writing classes average—15*

Cornell offers a national law curriculum leading to the J.D. degree. First-year students take a group of required courses and an intensive Practice Training course stressing a variety of legal research, writing, and advocacy techniques. After the first year, students may choose from a wide range of elective courses, including many seminars and problem courses. Optional concentrations are offered in four areas—advocacy, public law, business law and regulation, and general practice.

■ Clinical Studies

The Cornell Legal Aid Clinic, offering legal services to individuals financially unable to employ an attorney, provides students with the chance to engage in the supervised practice of law under the direction of experienced attorneys. Clinical faculty also conduct a variety of other specialized clinics and skills courses within the regular curriculum.

■ International Legal Studies

The Berger International Legal Studies Program is one of the country's oldest and most distinguished programs in international legal education. It starts from the premise that to be truly meaningful, international legal studies should be wide-ranging in approach so that students are able to place legal concepts and mechanisms in their proper historical, political, economic, and cultural contexts. Cornell's comprehensive program features a unique J.D. specialization opportunity, a J.D./LL.M. degree in International and Comparative Law, a joint summer program with the University of Paris I (Panthéon-Sorbonne), a comprehensive speaker series, a large number of visiting foreign professors and scholars, a weekly luncheon discussion series, and a leading journal of international and comparative law edited by students.

■ Admission

➡ *Bachelor's degree from accredited college or university required*   ➡ *application deadline—Feb. 1*   ➡ *LSAT, LSDAS required*   ➡ *application fee—$60*

Admission is highly competitive. The admissions committee bases its decisions on such nonquantifiable factors as extracurricular and community activities, life experience, and work background. They also consider factors such as the LSAT score, undergraduate grades, graduate work and recommendations. Minority background is considered a positive factor in an applicant's file and members of traditionally underrepresented minority groups are encouraged to submit a separate statement describing their ethnic, cultural, and linguistic backgrounds.

Student Activities

Student-edited law journals include the *Cornell Law Review* (published continuously since 1916), the *Cornell International Law Journal* (established in 1967), and the newly established *Cornell Journal of Law and Public Policy*.

Student organizations and activities include: American Indian Law Students Association; Asian American Law Students Association; Black Law Students Association; Herbert W. Briggs Society of International Law; Cornell Christian Legal Society; Cornell Criminal Justice Society; Cornell Law Community Volunteer Program; Cornell Law Student Association; Cornell Prison Project; Corporate Law Society; *Dicta*; Entertainment and Sports Law Union; Environmental Law Society; Federalist Society; James R. Withrow, Jr., Program on Legal Ethics; Jewish Law Student Association; Lambda Law Students; Latino American Law Students Association; Law Partners' Association; Moot Court Program; National Lawyer's Guild; Phi Alpha Delta; Phi Delta Phi; Public Interest Law Union; Women's Law Coalition.

Expenses and Financial Aid

➡ tuition & fees—$19,200   ➡ estimated additional expenses—$6,650 room & meals; $740 books & supplies; $3,680 personal expenses   ➡ need-based scholarships offered   ➡ GAPSFAS required no later than March 15

Cornell offers a very supportive need-based financial aid program. An average of 50 percent of students receive scholarship aid, with a higher percentage receiving government-backed loans. Minority and/or economically disadvantaged students are eligible for enhanced scholarship awards.

Career Services

The Career Planning and Placement Office provides employment counseling to students and serves as a liaison with legal employers. Cornell's students continue to be among the most recruited in the country. Every fall, hundreds of employers from across the country visit the law school and conduct employment interviews. Employers also participate in law school-sponsored job fairs in cities such as Boston, Los Angeles, New York, San Francisco, and Washington, DC. The school's public-interest placement coordinator serves as a resource for students interested in public service employment. A generous Public Interest Low Income Protection Plan assists those choosing public-interest law jobs through the use of a moderated loan repayment plan and loan forgiveness.

Applicant Group for the 1993–1994 Academic Year

Cornell University Law School
This grid includes only applicants who earned 120-180 LSAT scores under standard administrations and with reported GPAs.

LSAT Score	3.75 + Apps	Adm	3.50 -3.74 Apps	Adm	3.25 - 3.49 Apps	Adm	3.00 - 3.24 Apps	Adm	Below 3.00 Apps	Adm
175 - 180	13	13	11	10	18	15	9	7	1	0
170 - 174	50	47	71	63	63	48	46	13	23	0
165 - 169	158	115	266	195	197	85	96	15	583	4
160 - 164	223	76	365	75	279	33	134	6	71	3
155 - 159	109	6	220	12	207	16	129	11	100	4
Below 155	56	2	171	4	206	11	190	9	329	1

Apps = Number of Applicants
Adm = Number Admitted

Creighton University School of Law

2500 California Plaza
Omaha, NE 68178

Phone: 402.280.2872

■ Introduction

Creighton University, a privately endowed and supported Jesuit University, was founded in 1878. Creighton is the most diverse educational institution of its size in the nation. In addition to the School of Law, Creighton has a Medical School, Dental School, School of Pharmacy and Allied Health, School of Nursing, School of Business Administration, College of Arts and Sciences, and a Graduate School, making it the center of professional education in the Midwest. The university is located just blocks from downtown Omaha, a metropolitan area with a population of more than 600,000. Known as the River City, Omaha is the heart of the Midlands and the largest metroplex between Chicago and Denver.

■ The School of Law

The School of Law was established in 1904, has been a member of the AALS since 1907 and approved by the ABA for more than 55 years. Alumni from the law school are practicing in all 50 states and in more than 5 foreign countries. The law school's current enrollment is 559 students from over 43 states and more than 195 undergraduate institutions. Twenty-three full-time professors, 75 percent with advanced law degrees, and a group of part-time specialists chosen from the bench and bar comprise the faculty.

■ Enrollment/Student Body

➡ *1,265 applicants*   ➡ *588 admitted first-year class 1993*
➡ *188 enrolled first-year class 1993*   ➡ *541 total full-time*
➡ *18 total part-time*   ➡ *7% minority*   ➡ *43% women*
➡ *49 states & foreign countries represented*   ➡ *195 undergraduate schools represented*

■ Faculty

➡ *51 total*   ➡ *23 full-time*   ➡ *28 part-time or adjunct*
➡ *10 women*   ➡ *2 minority*

■ Library and Physical Facilities

➡ *197,402 volumes & equivalents*   ➡ *library hours: Mon.-Thurs., 7:00 A.M.-MIDNIGHT; Fri., 7:00 A.M.-8:00 P.M.; Sat., 9:00 A.M.-8:00 P.M.; Sun., NOON-MIDNIGHT*   ➡ *LEXIS*
➡ *NEXIS*   ➡ *WESTLAW*   ➡ *6 full-time librarians*
➡ *library seats 325*

■ Curriculum

➡ *Academic Support Program*   ➡ *94 credits required to graduate*   ➡ *135 courses available*   ➡ *degrees available: J.D.; J.D./M.B.A.*   ➡ *semesters, start in Aug.*
➡ *range of first-year class size—10-90*

The first-year curriculum, required of all students, consists of Constitutional Law, Contracts, Torts, and Legal Research during the first semester and Property, Jurisprudence, Professional Responsibility, Civil Procedure I, and Legal Writing during the second semester. Other than Civil Procedure II and advanced legal writing, required of all second-year students, second- and third-year students design their own program of studies from the numerous electives and seminars offered. The curriculum prepares students for the practice of law in any state.

■ Clinic and Internships

Third-year students selected to work in the Legal Clinic provide pro bono legal assistance to indigent citizens of Omaha. The School of Law also offers judicial and clinical internships in a number of city, county, federal, and Legal Aid offices.

■ Student Activities

The Student Bar Association is the student government of the law school. The purposes of the organization are to make law students aware of the obligations and opportunities existing for lawyers through Bar Association activities, promote a consciousness of professional responsibility, and provide a forum for student activities.

The school has chapters of the American Trial Lawyers Association and Phi Alpha Delta and Phi Delta Phi legal fraternities. Other student groups include the Black Law Students Association, the Latino Law Students Association, the Society of International Law, the Environmental Law Society, the Law Partners Association, Federalist Society, ACLU Chapter, Public Interest Forum, the Rutherford Institute, and the Women Law Students Association.

The *Creighton Law Review*, edited and managed by students, is a scholarly legal journal that is circulated nationally and internationally. The *Review* publishes articles contributed by prominent legal scholars, in addition to notes and comments written by students. Appellate brief writing and oral argument begins in the first-year Legal Writing program. During the second year, intraschool tournaments culminate in the selection of students for the domestic and international Moot Court Boards and the selection of teams to compete in regional and national Moot Court tournaments and the Philip C. Jessup International Law Moot Court program. The Client Counseling program promotes student knowledge and interest in the counseling and interviewing functions of law practice. An intraschool competition is held annually and culminates in students being selected for the Client Counseling Board and to represent Creighton in the national competition sponsored by the ABA's Law Student Division.

■ Admission

➡ *Bachelor's degree from accredited college or university required*   ➡ *application deadline—May 1, rolling admission, early application preferred*   ➡ *LSAT, LSDAS required*
➡ *median GPA—3.20*   ➡ *median LSAT score—154*
➡ *application fee—$40*

The applicant's LSAT score and undergraduate GPA are the prime factors in determining acceptance. Applicants with an LSAT percentile of 82-99 and a GPA range of 2.8 or higher have a very good chance of being admitted. Applicants with an LSAT percentile of 56-81 and a GPA of 3.1 or higher have a good chance of being admitted. Applicants with an LSAT percentile of 45 to 55 and a GPA of 3.25 or higher are also considered. Other factors that are considered by the Admissions Committee include the personal statement, demonstrated leadership ability, employment and other experience, and graduate degrees. Two letters of reference are required.

■ Expenses and Financial Aid

➠ *tuition & fees—full-time, $12,376; part-time (per credit hour), $400* ➠ *estimated additional expenses—$10,230* ➠ *merit & merit/need-based scholarships available* ➠ *minority scholarships available* ➠ *financial aid available* ➠ *FAFSA form for need analysis*

Although most scholarships are awarded on the basis of need, academic achievement, and LSAT scores, a limited number of scholarships are awarded solely on the basis of superior academic achievement and LSAT scores. Continuation of scholarship aid after the first year is normally contingent upon financial need and academic

achievement. Once an applicant has been accepted, scholarship applications may be requested from the Law School Admissions Office. Scholarship applications must be received by the School of Law no later than April 1. Long-term, low-interest loans under federal programs, as well as Law Access Loans and LAWLOANS through NORWEST Bank are available. Those seeking loans and scholarship aid must use the FAFSA form. Additional information about scholarships and financial aid is available through the law school's Admissions Office.

■ Minority Scholarship Program

The School of Law actively recruits minority students and has a substantial minority scholarship program. Students from the Black Law Students Association and the Latino Law Students Association are members of the Minority Scholarship Committee.

■ Career Services

The law school's Office of Career Service is committed to providing professional placement services for students and alumni. In addition to seminars and personal counseling, the office hosts prospective employers for on-campus interviews and posts notices for job openings throughout the year.

Applicant Group for the 1993–1994 Academic Year

Creighton University School of Law
This grid includes only applicants who earned 120-180 LSAT scores under standard administrations in the 1992-1993 testing year.

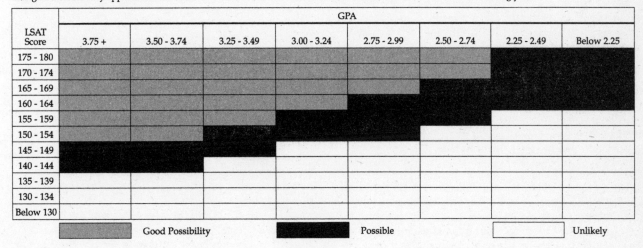

Cumberland School of Law—Samford University

800 Lakeshore Drive
Birmingham, AL 35229

Phone: 205.870.2702, 800.888.7213

◼ Introduction

The Cumberland School of Law, established in 1847 as a part of Cumberland University in Lebanon, Tennessee, is one of the oldest law schools in the country. The school was acquired by Samford University in 1961 and is now known as the Cumberland School of Law, Samford University. The beautiful campus is located in the suburban area of Birmingham, Alabama's largest city, as well as the state's industrial, business, and cultural center. The Cumberland School of Law is a member of the AALS and is approved by the ABA.

◼ Enrollment/Student Body

➦ 1,700 applicants ➦ 235 enrolled first-year class 1993
➦ 6.1% minority ➦ 39% women ➦ 19 states
represented ➦ 93 undergraduate schools represented
➦ 60% of 1993 first-year class from outside Alabama
➦ fall semester enrollment only

Since more than half of the entering class comes from other states, the Student Bar Association (SBA) actively assists each student who desires help in relocating to Birmingham by providing a number of services. For example, students may join the Phoenix Organization for a one-time fee of $30, thereby being relieved of paying deposits to local utility companies.

◼ Faculty

➦ 58 total ➦ 32 full-time ➦ 26 part-time or adjunct
➦ 7 women ➦ 2 minority

A strength of the law school, the 32 full-time faculty members hail from 21 law schools. The academic credentials, scholarly achievements, and publications of each faculty member are highlighted in the *Admissions Prospectus*.

◼ Library and Physical Facilities

➦ 210,000 volumes & equivalents ➦ library hours:
Mon.-Fri., 8:00 A.M.-MIDNIGHT; Sat., 9:00 A.M.-10:00 P.M.;
Sun., 1:00 P.M.-MIDNIGHT ➦ LEXIS ➦ NEXIS
➦ WESTLAW ➦ LEGALTRAC CD-ROM ➦ 11 full-
time librarians ➦ library seats 331 ➦ 23 IBM personal
computers linked to laser printers

Construction began in the fall of 1993 on a new $8.2 million law library. Related construction has already been completed—a new parking deck located directly across the street from the new library site is for law students only.

More than tripling the existing library square footage, the three and one-half story, 60,300 square-foot building will enhance the law library significantly with the following features: a new computer room, providing additional WESTLAW and LEXIS terminals; 10 conference rooms; a 24-seat, 807 square-foot audiovisual room; 4 photocopy rooms; shelf space for an additional 60,000 volumes; 5,000 volumes on compact shelving; microform

room increased in size by 5 times; and an increase in seating by 138.

◼ Curriculum

➦ Academic Support Program ➦ 90 credit hours required
to graduate ➦ 140 courses offered ➦ degrees available:
J.D.; J.D./M.A.E.; J.D./M.B.A.; J.D./M.P.H ➦ range of
first-year class size—5 to 74

First-year students report to school a week earlier than do second- and third-year students for a Legal Research and Writing Workshop. This highly successful program is serving as a prototype for a number of other law schools across the country.

◼ International Law

Cumberland School of Law, Samford University conducts ABA-approved international summer programs in three locations: Heidelberg University, Heidelberg, Germany; University of Kent, Canterbury, England; and, University of Victoria, Victoria, British Columbia. These locations allow the curriculum to focus on the two growth regions in international law: Europe and the Pacific Rim. Each program is designed to combine academic, geopolitical, and cultural experiences for the participants.

◼ Special Programs

During the past decade, Cumberland trial advocacy teams have won national titles in both the National Mock Trial Competition sponsored by the ABA, and the National Trial Competition sponsored by the National Trial Lawyers Association.

An extensive clinical education program is available for the Cumberland student. Qualified students are certified under the Alabama Supreme Court Student Internship Rule, enabling them to practice law under the direct supervision of a licensed practicing attorney.

Legal Internships are available in offices of county attorneys, district attorneys, the state attorney general, Legal Aid, U.S. Probation Officers, and the IRS.

Judicial clerkships are available through a program in which students are assigned to circuit judges. The Corporate Clerkship Program assigns students to legal departments of hospitals, banks, corporations, institutions, or similar offices.

"PALS" (Partnership between Alumni and Law Students) is a special program designed to match up law students with practicing alumni in the Birmingham area who serve as mentors.

The National Alumni Association of Cumberland sponsors a Distinguished Lecturer Series, bringing to the campus outstanding legal scholars. The association seeks to provide a forum in which students and faculty can exchange ideas with distinguished members of the legal community.

■ Admission

➡ *Bachelor's degree from accredited college or university required* ➡ *applications accepted starting Oct. 1* ➡ *rolling admission* ➡ *application deadline—priority, Feb. 28; final, May. 1* ➡ *LSAT, LSDAS required* ➡ *median GPA—3.10* ➡ *median LSAT score—156* ➡ *application fee—$40* ➡ *reactivation fee—$40*

Cumberland School of Law, Samford University does not use a number index system or formula when choosing from the applicant pool those who will be admitted. Every file is thoroughly reviewed by the Faculty Admissions Committee. In addition to the LSAT score and undergraduate GPA, other important factors considered are: undergraduate school grade trend and difficulty of major; activities and leadership qualities; personal statement; graduate work; employment experience; recommendation letters; maturity, discipline, and character.

Admitted applicants are required to pay a nonrefundable $400 seat deposit which is credited toward tuition. The first installment of $150 is due April 1; the final installment is due June 15.

■ Student Activities

Student-run publications include *Cumberland Law Review*; *American Journal of Trial Advocacy*; and *Pro Confesso*. Numerous and varied student organizations are represented on campus.

■ Expenses and Financial Aid

➡ *tuition & fees—$13,850* ➡ *estimated additional expenses—$10 locker rental; $10 parking decal* ➡ *Guaranteed Student Loan Program available through the Office of Financial Aid* ➡ *priority deadline for financial aid—March 1*

All admitted applicants are automatically considered for merit and recruiting scholarship awards. Various other scholarships are available to outstanding students who distinguish themselves academically, or who make outstanding contributions through leadership in the law school's programs.

■ Career Services

Through the Career Services Office, the School of Law (a member of the National Association for Law Placement) assists all law students in locating part-time employment, summer clerkships, and permanent employment upon graduation. Off-campus recruiting programs are available to employers unable to interview at the law school. Cumberland regularly attends the following recruiting conferences: the Southeastern Law Placement Consortium; the Southeastern Minority Job Fair; the Mid-South Law Placement Consortium; and the National Health Law Career Conference.

Applicant Group for the 1993–1994 Academic Year

Cumberland School of Law—Samford University
This grid includes only applicants who earned 120-180 LSAT scores under standard administrations in the 1992-1993 testing year.

LSAT Score	GPA								
	3.75 +	3.50 - 3.74	3.25 - 3.49	3.00 - 3.24	2.75 - 2.99	2.50 - 2.74	2.25 - 2.49	2.00 - 2.24	Below 2.00
175 - 180									
170 - 174									
165 - 169									
160 - 164									
155 - 159									
150 - 154									
145 - 149									
140 - 144									
135 - 139									
130 - 134									
125 - 129									
120 - 124									

■ Good Possibility ☐ Possible ▨ Unlikely

University of Dayton School of Law

300 College Park
Dayton, OH 45469-1320

Phone: 513.229.3555

■ Overview

The University of Dayton School of Law offers a single division, full-time program of studies in a supportive and value-centered environment. The curriculum combines both traditional and innovative teaching methods, and it is designed to prepare graduates for the practice of law or for law-related careers nationwide. A private law school of 485 students, the University of Dayton School of Law continues to build a national reputation as alumni of the law school find employment in a variety of settings throughout the country. The School of Law is approved by the ABA and is a member of the AALS and the League of Ohio Law Schools.

■ Mission

The mission of the University of Dayton School of Law is to enroll a diverse group of men and women who are intellectually curious, who possess self-discipline, and who are well motivated, and to rigorously train them in the substantive and procedural principles of public and private law. Faculty expect that graduates will become highly qualified and competent practicing attorneys who will uphold the highest professional standards.

■ Enrollment/Student Body

➡ *185 enrolled first-year class 1993* ➡ *11% minority students in first-year class* ➡ *43/57 female/male ratio in first-year class* ➡ *107 undergraduate colleges represented in first-year class 1993* ➡ *60% of first-year class from 24 states other than Ohio* ➡ *12% of the first-year class had undergraduate major in engineering and the sciences*

■ Environment for Studying Law

Law School—The School of Law is located in Albert Emanuel Hall and includes class and seminar rooms, a courtroom complex, faculty and student organization offices, formal reception area, and student lounge. The law building and law library are located in the central part of the university campus, within a short walk of university facilities and services.

The University—Founded in 1850, the University of Dayton today is the largest private university in Ohio and the eighth-largest Catholic university in the nation. More than 6,500 undergraduate students and 3,500 graduate students are enrolled at the university. The 80-acre campus is located in a residential neighborhood minutes from the city's center and includes a variety of student services, such as health care, on-campus housing, child care, meal plans, and banking.

The City—Law students have special opportunities available because the metropolitan area (population of 942,000) is home to a sizeable judicial and legal community. Municipal courts, the Montgomery County Court of Common Pleas, the Second Ohio District Court of Appeals, and the U.S. District Court for the Southern District of Ohio are all located nearby. In addition, law students may find part-time employment with a number of the area's several Fortune 500 companies and their divisions (NCR, Standard Register, Mead, and Mead Data Central).

■ Law Library

➡ *208,000 volumes & equivalents* ➡ *more than 5,500 legal serials* ➡ *LEXIS* ➡ *WESTLAW* ➡ *computer center for word processing and database management* ➡ *11 full-time staff*

■ Faculty

➡ *27 full-time* ➡ *28 adjunct*

Student and alumni evaluations consistently give high marks to faculty of the law school. Faculty members are noted for being accessible to students, and it is this commitment that creates an environment which fosters faculty-student interaction. Faculty members at the School of Law bring a breadth of experience and research interests to the classroom.

■ Special Programs

Program in Law and Technology—The Program in Law and Technology allows upper-level students the opportunity to enroll in a number of specialized courses covering patent law, copyright law, trademark law, trade secrets, and transfers of technology and licensing. Additionally, qualified students may be placed as interns with area legal departments and law firms.

Joint Degree Programs—The School of Law offers joint degrees in conjunction with two graduate programs at the University of Dayton. The joint-degree programs are: J.D./Master of Business Administration, and J.D./Master of Science in Educational Administration. Each program is an integrated program of study that results in the conferral of both degrees at the time of graduation.

Law Clinic—The School of Law operates a law clinic which functions as a "typical" small, general-practice law office. Located within the law building, the clinic provides third-year students with the opportunity to represent actual clients, usually in cases involving civil matters.

Judicial Externships—Second- and third-year law students may participate in the law school's externship program offering the opportunity to clerk with area municipal, county, and federal judges. Externs undertake research for case decisions, thereby further developing research and writing skills, as well as gaining more direct knowledge of the judicial system.

Professional Skills Courses—Development of professional skills is offered through a variety of courses at the University of Dayton. These courses emphasize roles, situations, and problems that are commonly encountered by practicing attorneys. Professional skills courses include the three-semester Legal Profession course series, Negotiation and Mediation, Civil Trial Practice and

Criminal Trial Practice, Mock Trial, Complex Litigation, and Land Use Planning.

Academic Excellence Program—The Academic Excellence Program includes a three-day orientation program prior to the start of the academic year, and a weekly tutorial session during both the first and second semesters. Entering students who are from economically or educationally disadvantaged backgrounds are especially encouraged to take part in the Academic Excellence Program.

■ Alumni and Placement Information

Graduates of the School of Law find success in a variety of career endeavors across the United States. A full-time placement director assists students and alumni in career planning and employment search activities. Counseling, career reference materials, position postings for direct contacts, and coordination of on and off-campus interviews are provided as appropriate for those seeking clerkships, part-time and summer employment, further legal education, or permanent positions. Alumni of the School of Law include 2,200 men and women who are using their legal training in a variety of settings throughout the United States.

■ Activities

Student activities include the University of Dayton Law Review, Moot Court Board, Volunteer Income Tax Assis-

tance, Student Bar Association, Women's Caucus, Black Law Students Association, Delta Theta Phi, Phi Alpha Delta, Phi Delta Phi, Society of International Law, Association of Trial Lawyers of America, *Equitable Relief* newspaper, *Fiat Justia* yearbook, Law and Medicine Society, the Law and Technology Society, Christian Legal Society, and the Jewish Student Union.

■ Admission

➡ *Priority deadline for applications—May 1* ➡ *candidates wishing to be considered for full or partial scholarships should submit admission materials by Mar. 1*

■ Expenses and Financial Aid

➡ *full-time tuition—$$13,384 annually* ➡ *35 scholarship awards per year available (based on past academic performance and performance on the LSAT—ranging from full tuition to $2,500)* ➡ *loan programs available* ➡ *part-time employment available for upper-level students*

■ Questions Regarding the School of Law

Prospective students are invited to contact the School of Law Office of Admission with questions and concerns. The Office of Admission hours are Monday through Friday, 8:30 A.M. to 4:30 P.M. (Phone requests for admission materials may be made anytime throughout the week.)

Applicant Group for the 1993–1994 Academic Year

University of Dayton School of Law
This grid includes only applicants who earned 120-180 LSAT scores under standard administrations.

LSAT Score	3.75 +		3.50-3.74		3.25-3.49		3.00-3.24		2.75-2.99		2.50-2.74		2.25-2.49		2.00-2.24		Below 2.00		No GPA		Total	
	Apps	Adm	Apps	Adm	Apps	Adm	Apps	Adm	Apps	Adm	Apps	Adm	Apps	Adm	Apps	Adm	Apps	Adm	Apps	Adm	Apps	Adm
165-180	3	3	6	6	5	5	11	11	2	2	3	3	2	2	1	0	0	0	0	0	33	32
160-164	9	9	19	18	16	16	29	28	20	20	23	22	11	9	4	3	1	1	0	0	132	126
155-159	13	13	39	39	55	53	80	62	74	52	69	38	37	15	10	3	2	0	1	1	380	276
150-154	20	18	76	63	111	64	127	15	122	8	79	4	41	0	21	2	0	0	2	1	599	175
145-149	19	17	47	20	94	33	124	11	126	6	82	4	43	1	19	0	5	0	4	1	563	93
140-144	3	0	19	3	49	13	60	2	52	1	55	2	45	0	19	0	5	0	6	0	313	21
Below 140	1	0	5	1	9	0	27	0	36	1	44	0	43	0	15	0	6	0	8	0	194	2
Total	68	60	211	150	339	184	458	129	432	90	355	73	222	27	89	8	19	1	21	3	2214	725

Apps = Number of Applicants
Adm = Number Admitted
Reflects 97% of the total applicant pool.

University of Denver College of Law

7039 E. 18th Avenue
Denver, CO 80220

Phone: 303.871.6135

■ Introduction

The University of Denver College of Law, a private institution, is located on a 33-acre site which is 15 minutes from downtown Denver. The Law Center, built in 1984, provides more than "state-of-the-art" library, classroom, and student facilities; it also reflects the tradition of the Inns of Court, where students learn the law in the company of members of the bench and bar. The campus is home to the National Center for Preventive Law, the Rocky Mountain Mineral Law Foundation, and other organizations which enhance the academic atmosphere.

■ Enrollment/Student Body

➽ *3,025 applicants*   ➽ *1,180 admitted first-year class 1993*
➽ *341 enrolled first-year class 1993*   ➽ *771 total full-time*
➽ *287 total part-time*   ➽ *14% minority*
➽ *44% women*   ➽ *55 states & foreign countries represented*
➽ *159 undergraduate schools represented*

■ Faculty

➽ *83 total*   ➽ *49 full-time*   ➽ *38 part-time or adjunct*
➽ *17 women*   ➽ *5 minority*

■ Library and Physical Facilities

➽ *274,284 volumes & equivalents*   ➽ *library hours: Mon.-Thurs., 7:30 A.M-MIDNIGHT; Fri., 7:30 A.M.-10:00 P.M.; Sat., 8:00 A.M.-10:00 P.M.; Sun., 9:00 A.M.-MIDNIGHT*   ➽ *LEXIS*   ➽ *NEXIS*   ➽ *WESTLAW*   ➽ *DIALOG*   ➽ *INFOTRAC*
➽ *7.5 full-time librarians*   ➽ *library seats 565*

■ Curriculum

➽ *Academic Support Program*   ➽ *90 credits required to graduate*   ➽ *117 total courses available*   ➽ *degrees available: J.D.; J.D./M.B.A.; J.D. dual degree in International Studies, International Management, Psychology, History, Social Work, Sociology, and Mineral Economics*
➽ *semesters, start in Aug.*
➽ *range of first-year class size—20-84*

Lawyering Process Course—The first-year curriculum includes an innovative Lawyering Process Course which offers students, in small group law firm settings, experience with the standard operations and skills of the lawyer's craft in interviewing, counseling, negotiation, decision making, and litigation. The small groups replicate law firms and reinforce cooperative work. Course work in legal research and writing is taught in the context of simulated client problems.

■ Special Programs

Drawing upon its location in one of the nation's natural resources and energy capitals, the University of Denver College of Law offers a rich program in natural resources and environmental law. Students can choose from a variety of courses. There are also abundant opportunities for independent research and internships in the local energy, environment, and natural resource community.

The International Legal Studies program is designed for students interested in international comparative law, international organization, or transnational business. Students in the program may work on the *Denver Journal of International Law and Policy* as staff members and editors. The International Law Society sponsors a rich schedule of outside speakers and an annual conference with invited guests from many organizations.

Denver University has the only comprehensive program in transportation law in the United States. The program offers a unique opportunity to study the legal, regulatory, economic, and political developments in transportation. The basic course in Transportational Law offers an overview of all aspects of economic regulation of each of the domestic transport modes and also provides a survey of liability issues of the government's role in providing transport services. Students concentrating in Transportation Law are eligible for special scholarships that are awarded separately from other law scholarships.

The Business and Commercial Law program not only trains students to work with business entities but also prepares them for the specific needs of the corporate attorney. The program culminates in specialized seminars in business and commercial law. Corporate internships, highly prized one-semester assignments with large local corporations, are a valuable supplement to the course work.

The Lawyering Skills program focuses on "what lawyers do." Courses in the regular curriculum are supplemented by the practical experience gained through public service legal work in the Student Law Office or through several internships or externships. The capstone of the program is the Student Law Office (Basic Civil Representation, Basic Criminal Representation, Advanced Public Interest Clinic) where students represent needy clients at all levels of the dispute resolution process. If the case reaches the litigation phase, the student handles all aspects of pretrial, trial preparation, and the trial itself—under faculty supervision. Focusing on one-to-one teaching and student responsibility, the program offers a rare opportunity to acquire lawyering skills.

■ Admission

➽ *Bachelor's degree required for admission*
➽ *application deadline—March 1*   ➽ *rolling admission, application preferred Nov.-Jan.*   ➽ *LSAT, LSDAS required*
➽ *median GPA—3.20*   ➽ *median LSAT score—158*
➽ *application fee—$45*

Applications should reach the College of Law between November and February to receive maximum consideration for admission the following August. Students may begin law study only in August. Applicants must take the LSAT and subscribe to LSDAS. A baccalaureate degree from an approved college or university is required prior to registration. LSAT scores and records of academic performances are individually evaluated in the admission process. Of equal importance, however, are the applicant's work experience, significant personal accomplishments, interests, goals, and reasons for seeking admission to law school.

Student Activities

Student activities are sponsored by the Student Bar Association to which most students belong. The University of Denver's Moot Court program is designed to promote the necessary development of students' oral and written skills. D.U.'s law students have the opportunity to participate in six different Moot Court competitions. The Moot Court Board is comprised of students who have demonstrated merit in D.U.'s Moot Court program and have displayed a commitment to improving the oral and written skills of the student body. With faculty integrated support, the Moot Court Board organizes and runs D.U.'s Moot Court program.

Three scholarly journals are edited at the College of Law allowing students to participate in scholarly research in varied fields. Academic credit is awarded for work in the *Law Review, Journal of International Law and Policy*, and *Transportation Law Journal*. Many special interest organizations on campus are officially recognized by the Student Bar Association. Among those groups are the Asian American Law Students Association, the Black Law Students Association, the Entertainment Law Society, the Hispanic Law Students Association, the Native American Law Students Association, the Public Interest Law Group, the Student Trial Lawyers Association, and the Women's Law Caucus/Children's Legal Issues in Perspective.

Expenses and Financial Aid

➻ *tuition & fees—$full-time,$15,221; part-time,$9,820*
➻ *estimated additional expenses—$9,044 (health insurance, books, room and board, transportation)* ➻ *merit- and need-based scholarships available* ➻ *minority scholarships available* ➻ *FAFSA and GAPSFAS form due Feb. 1*

The Chancellor's Scholarship Program provides a unique educational experience to a limited number of motivated and qualified students committed to public service through law. These scholarships are awarded through open competition to entering first-year students. The annual scholarships are renewed for successive years based on satisfactory academic performance and full participation in all the activities of the program.

Career Services

The law school maintains a placement office staffed by a full-time director and a full-time assistant who aid both students and alumni in securing employment. The Placement Office offers direct referral to part-time, full-time, summer, and career positions; arrangement of on-campus interviews each fall for second- and third-year students with law firms, governmental agencies, and corporations; and career counseling. The Placement Office emphasizes its policy against discriminatory practices in the interviewing and hiring of its students and graduates.

Applicant Group for the 1993–1994 Academic Year

University of Denver College of Law
This grid includes only applicants who earned 120-180 LSAT scores under standard administrations.

LSAT Score	3.75 +		3.50 -3.74		3.25 - 3.49		3.00 - 3.24		2.75 - 2.99		2.50 - 2.74		2.25 - 2.49		2.00 - 2.24		Below 2.00		No GPA		Total	
	Apps	Adm	Apps	Adm	Apps	Adm	Apps	Adm	Apps	Adm	Apps	Adm	Apps	Adm	Apps	Adm	Apps	Adm	Apps	Adm	Apps	Adm
175 - 180	0	0	0	0	1	1	1	1	0	0	0	0	0	0	0	0	0	0	0	0	2	2
170 - 174	1	1	1	1	4	4	4	4	1	1	0	0	1	1	1	1	0	0	0	0	13	13
165 - 169	3	3	11	10	17	17	14	12	23	22	11	9	6	3	1	0	2	0	2	0	90	76
160 - 164	21	21	41	40	69	65	92	86	64	50	44	27	26	7	5	1	1	0	2	2	365	299
155 - 159	25	23	83	79	144	127	180	119	131	47	82	17	46	10	10	0	1	0	15	5	717	427
150 - 154	28	23	73	45	122	35	188	33	152	22	106	7	50	2	21	1	3	0	8	1	751	169
145 - 149	13	4	29	6	78	9	94	8	106	6	75	6	40	2	17	1	2	0	14	0	468	42
140 - 144	3	0	18	2	25	2	41	2	50	4	43	2	43	0	11	0	4	0	11	0	249	12
135 - 139	0	0	5	0	10	0	17	0	22	0	25	0	19	0	5	0	1	0	8	0	112	0
130 - 134	0	0	0	0	3	0	4	0	6	0	4	0	7	0	6	0	1	0	5	0	36	0
125 - 129	0	0	0	0	0	0	0	0	1	0	0	0	0	0	1	0	0	0	1	0	4	0
120 - 124	0	0	0	0	0	0	0	0	0	0	0	0	1	0	0	0	0	0	0	0	1	0
Total	94	75	261	183	473	260	635	265	556	152	390	68	240	25	78	4	15	0	66	8	2808	1040

Apps = Number of Applicants
Adm = Number Admitted
Reflects 93% of the total applicant pool.

DePaul University College of Law

25 East Jackson Boulevard
Chicago, IL 60604

Phone: 312.362.6831, toll-free: 1.800.428.7453

■ Introduction

DePaul University is the second largest private university in Illinois and enjoys the advantages of education conducted in a vibrant urban setting. Located in the heart of Chicago's business and legal communities, the College of Law is just a short walk from the Harold Washington Library, the largest municipal library in the world. Proximity to courts, government offices, and many law firms affords extensive contact with Chicago's legal community. Alumni include the Mayor of Chicago, state and federal judges, and managing partners of several Chicago law firms. The college offers full-time, part-time, and summer programs. DePaul is fully accredited by the ABA, is a member of AALS, and has an Order of the Coif chapter. The College of Law has embarked on an ambitious $13 million fund-raising campaign to enhance its endowment and programs, including $6 million targeted for a complete renovation and expansion of its physical plant.

■ Enrollment/Student Body

➡ *3,029 applicants*   ➡ *1,177 admitted first-year class 1993*
➡ *373 enrolled first-year class 1993 (285 day, 88 evening)*
➡ *730 total full-time*   ➡ *254 total part-time*
➡ *17% minority*   ➡ *48% women*
➡ *43 states & foreign countries represented*
➡ *123 undergraduate schools represented in 1993 class*

The college has an increasingly national enrollment—49 percent of 1993 entering full-time students are from places other than Illinois. Each entering class brings a rich diversity in age, ethnicity, education and career experience. For example, 32 students in the 1993 entering class had earned graduate and professional degrees. The average age of full-time day students and part-time evening students is 25 and 29, respectively. DePaul's bar passage rate has consistently exceeded the state average.

■ Faculty

➡ *109 total*   ➡ *43 full-time*   ➡ *66 part-time*
➡ *26 women*   ➡ *8 minority*

DePaul faculty are recognized scholars who represent a variety of professional backgrounds and interests as diverse as the curriculum. Many have advanced degrees in fields such as biology, political science, business, psychology, archeology, theatre, public health, and philosophy.

■ Expenses and Financial Aid

➡ *tuition & fees—full-time, $14,115; part-time, $9,018*
➡ *additional expenses—$9,500 min. (room, board, books)*
➡ *performance & need-based scholarships available*
➡ *Free Application for Federal Student Aid due March 1*

■ Curriculum

➡ *Academic Support Program*   ➡ *86 units required to graduate*   ➡ *144 courses available*   ➡ *degrees available:*

J.D. & J.D./M.B.A.   ➡ *semesters, start in early Aug.*
➡ *range of first-year class size—18-85*

■ Library and Physical Facilities

➡ *312,000 volumes & equivalents*   ➡ *library hours: Mon.-Fri., 8:00 A.M.-11:00 P.M.; Sat., 8:00 A.M.-6:00 P.M.; Sun., NOON-10:00 P.M.*   ➡ *LEXIS*   ➡ *NEXIS*
➡ *WESTLAW*   ➡ *DIALOG*   ➡ *7 full-time librarians*
➡ *library seats 600*

Holding extensive tax, health, and constitutional law collections, the library is also designated as an official government depository. Fully networked word processing and data management facilities include 95 personal computers. Extensive video holdings include lawyering-skills interactive videos. The college occupies six floors in both the 17-story Lewis Center and adjoining 15-story O'Malley Place in Chicago's Loop. Expanded facilities include a new, state-of-the-art Lawyering Skills Center. Completely video equipped rooms enable faculty to record student performances and create simulated jury trials, mediation, negotiations, and appellate arguments.

■ Special Programs

Legal Clinic—An in-house component of the college, the legal clinic has a full-time staff of eight, including four clinical professors. Students serve clients from the initial interview through trial, and acquire extensive experience.

Externships—Providing students with academic credit through supervised field work, externships are offered by federal and state judges, various municipal agencies, and a number of not-for-profit organizations.

International Human Rights Law Institute—This research institute offers exciting student-faculty collaboration. It sponsors conferences, engages in scholarly work, and cooperates with other human rights organizations and international bodies.

Center for Church/State Studies—An academic, non-denominational research institute, the center directs studies of the legal structures of American religious organizations. It offers forums on church/state issues and has initiated a number of innovative community programs.

Health Law Institute—This research institute sponsors national conferences on health law issues and works with community organizations on health policy and legislation. The centerpiece of the Institute is the monthly student-edited *Journal of Health and Hospital Law*.

Study Abroad—DePaul and the University College Dublin have initiated a student-exchange program whereby a small number of second-year students from both law schools undertake legal studies abroad for a semester. In addition, visiting faculty participate as guest lecturers.

J.D./M.B.A.—DePaul grants the combined Juris Doctor and Master of Business Administration degree.

Graduate Studies—The first United States law school to offer courses toward the LL.M. in Health Law, DePaul educates about 35 graduate students each year. The college also offers the LL.M. in Taxation program, which is one of the five largest graduate tax programs in the United States.

Professional Skills—DePaul is committed to education in professional skills. Among courses offered in dispute resolution are Arbitration, Mediation, Advanced Mediation, Interviewing, Counseling and Negotiation. Courses in litigation skills include Pretrial Civil and Criminal Strategies, Trial Advocacy, Advanced Trial Advocacy, Complex Litigation, and Appellate Technique.

■ Admission

➡ *Bachelor's degree from accredited college or university required*
➡ *application deadline—April 1* ➡ *rolling admissions*
(first letters sent about March 1) ➡ *LSAT, LSDAS required*
➡ *median GPA—3.27* ➡ *median LSAT score—158*
➡ *application fee—$40*
➡ *tuition deposit required prior to matriculation*

DePaul adheres to a policy of nondiscrimination and encourages applications from traditionally underrepresented minority groups. A faculty committee reviews applications. Undergraduate GPA and LSAT score are highly significant admission criteria. When the LSAT is repeated, the average score is used. For the 1993-94 academic year, 2,448 candidates applied for admission to the full-time (day) division; 581 candidates applied to the part-time (evening) division.

■ Student Activities

In addition to legal writing and research and senior research seminar courses, four student-edited law journals provide students with intensive legal research and writing training. The journals are *The DePaul Law Review*, the *Journal of Health and Hospital Law*, the *DePaul Business Law Journal*, and the *Journal of Art and Entertainment Law*. The Student Bar Association sponsors lectures and social functions and coordinates community involvement for its members. Through the Student Bar Association and student-faculty committees, students participate in the decision process of the college. Among student organizations are the Moot Court Society; Women's Law Caucus; the Black, Latino, and Asian law student associations; Public Interest Law Association; DePaul chapter of the ACLU; International Law Society; Decalogue Society; National Lawyers Guild; Computer Law Society; Federalist Society; and Environmental Law Society.

■ Career Services

Alumni, faculty, and students contribute to an active and aggressive career services network. The teaching and publishing reputations of the faculty and the largest alumni/ae bench and bar network in the Chicago area complement three full-time DePaul career services officers.

Applicant Group for the 1993–1994 Academic Year

DePaul University College of Law
This grid includes all full-time applicants who earned 120-180 LSAT scores under standard administrations and whose admission files were complete and reviewed by the faculty admission committee.

GPA	120-139		140-149		150-154		155-159		160-164		165-169		170-174		175-180		Total	
	Apps	Adm	Apps	Adm	Apps	Adm	Apps	Adm	Apps	Adm	Apps	Adm	Apps	Adm	Apps	Adm	Apps	Adm
3.75 +	0	0	14	3	19	12	24	24	19	19	2	2	1	1	0	0	79	61
3.50-3.74	2	0	34	4	67	34	79	78	34	34	10	10	1	1	1	1	228	162
3.25-3.49	10	0	91	5	136	45	151	147	50	50	12	12	3	3	0	0	453	262
3.00-3.24	14	0	142	8	170	20	187	144	73	72	22	21	2	2	1	1	611	268
2.75-2.99	21	0	104	5	104	12	113	41	45	36	18	15	0	0	0	0	405	109
2.50-2.74	22	0	81	3	57	10	39	4	20	8	7	4	2	0	0	0	228	29
2.25-2.49	22	0	43	0	34	5	13	2	7	1	4	1	1	1	0	0	124	10
2.00-2.24	13	0	18	0	7	0	11	1	1	0	1	0	0	0	0	0	51	1
Below 2.00	3	0	0	0	0	0	3	0	1	0	0	0	0	0	0	0	7	0
Total	107	0	527	28	594	138	620	441	250	220	76	65	10	8	2	2	2186	902

This chart is to be used as a general guide only.
Apps = Number of Completed Applicants
Adm = Number Admitted

Detroit College of Law

130 East Elizabeth Street
Detroit, MI 48201

Phone: 313.226.0169

■ Introduction

Founded in 1891, Detroit College of Law was the first law school established in Detroit. The college is a privately controlled and endowed coeducational institution devoted exclusively to professional education in law. For 100 years it has continued to provide superior educational opportunities to qualified and ambitious men and women. Many of the most eminent lawyers, judges, public officials, and business executives in Detroit and Michigan are graduates of this famous law school; four of the last six federal judges appointed to the bench of the United States District Court for the Eastern District of Michigan are alumni of the college. One of these four federal judges was recently elevated to the bench of the United States Court of Appeals for the Eastern District of Michigan.

A unique advantage of Detroit College of Law is that it is not a department of a university or similar institution. Institutional and academic policies of the school are established and executed solely in accord with the best interests of the law school and its students, without the need to conform to the policies or practices of the parent institution.

Detroit College of Law is fully accredited and approved by the American Bar Association (ABA) and is a member of the Association of American Law Schools (AALS).

■ Enrollment/Student Body

➡ 1,362 applicants ➡ 146 enrolled first-year class 1993
➡ 418 total full-time ➡ 338 total part-time
➡ 9% minority ➡ 36% women
➡ 150 undergraduate schools represented

The students of the Detroit College of Law represent a wide diversity of educational backgrounds, experiences and national origin. DCL students are undergoing a legal education in the theory and purpose of the law, along with its practical application, thus equipping them to fulfill unique and complicated demands in and outside of the legal profession.

■ Faculty

➡ 60 total ➡ 28 full-time ➡ 32 part-time or adjunct
➡ 15 women ➡ 9 minority

The faculty is composed of resident professors who are devoted, on a full-time basis, to the teaching of law; legal research instructors; and a cadre of adjunct faculty members and practicing attorneys who are specialists with extensive experience in the field of law they teach. By utilizing the talents of both the professional teacher and the practicing attorney, the academic viewpoint of the former is blended with the practical approach of the latter into a sound, well-balanced education in both theory and practice of the legal system.

■ Library and Physical Facilities

➡ 200,000 volumes & equivalents ➡ LEXIS
➡ NEXIS ➡ WESTLAW ➡ OCLC
➡ 6 full-time librarians

The library collection is designed to meet the educational needs of law students. This major research collection includes the statutes of the 50 states, the United States, and Canada, as well as collections of numerous decisions, legal periodicals, and treatises. The library houses a computer lab for students and provides unlimited access to online academic research, as well as word processing programs.

DCL is located in downtown Detroit. The self-contained facilities include the library, classrooms, various faculty and administrative offices, and a newly remodeled moot courtroom equipped with state-of-the-art video technology.

■ Curriculum

➡ 85 units/credits required to graduate ➡ over 125 courses available ➡ J.D. degree ➡ first-year entry in Jan. or Aug. semester ➡ 3-year day and 4-year evening
➡ 8-week summer session for both day and evening divisions
➡ curriculum-related programs offered: Law Review, Moot Court, Externships, International and Comparative Law, Taxation, Lawyering Skills

■ Special Programs

International and Comparative Law—DCL students who wish to develop expertise in this field have the opportunity to study a wide variety of international legal issues. Some of the extensive course offerings include Admiralty, Chinese Law, Comparative Law, Immigration Law, International Business Transactions, International Criminal Law, Nuclear Weapons Doctrine: Arms Control and International Human Rights, International Litigation in US Courts, International Taxation, International Wildlife and Environmental Law, Law of the European Community, Socialist Legal Systems, Transnational Legal Research, and US-Canadian Taxation.

Center for Canadian-United States Law—The Center offers specific courses on Canadian law and Canadian-American legal relations within Detroit College of Law's already extensive international law program. The Center also sponsors the Canadian Summer Law Internship Program which is available to DCL students and guest students from other ABA-accredited law schools.

Taxation—The college has extensive offerings in Taxation designed to provide interested students with the opportunity to develop an expertise in Taxation. Some of the courses include Basic Income Taxation, Estate and Gift Taxation, Partnership Taxation, Business Income Taxation, US-Canadian Taxation, and International Taxation.

Lawyering Skills—Every substantive course develops legal analysis and reasoning; most of them develop other skills as well. DCL offers the following courses that focus directly on the development of lawyering skills beyond legal analysis and reasoning: Advanced Problems in Environmental Law, Advocacy I & II, Arbitration, Business Securities and Tax Planning, Contract Drafting, Counseling, Discovery and Trial Preparation, Transnational Legal Research, and Trial Advocacy and Litigation Seminar.

■ Admission

➟ *Bachelor's degree from an accredited college or university required*   ➟ *application deadline—Aug. entry, April 15; Jan. entry, Oct. 15*   ➟ *rolling admissions*
➟ *LSAT, LSDAS required*   ➟ *median GPA—3.00*
➟ *median LSAT score—155*   ➟ *application fee—$35*

An admission decision is more complex than a mere ranking of applicants on the basis of a numerical formula. Detroit College of Law is committed to a broad inquiry into the role and function of law in society and seeks a diverse student body as an integral part of its educational program. Accordingly, for purposes of discretionary admission, DCL will consider other subjective criteria in addition to an applicant's undergraduate grade-point average and LSAT score.

■ Curricular Activities

The *Detroit College of Law Review* is a legal periodical, published by law students, in which recognized legal scholars contribute book reviews and articles of keen interest to the legal community. The college also publishes the *Journal of International Law & Practice*.

Moot Court at DCL is an extensive program of advocacy training in a competitive framework, permitting students to develop skills beyond those acquired in the first-year Research, Writing, and Advocacy course. The Moot Court Program participates in several national competitions, with teams researching a complex legal problem, writing and submitting a brief and then orally arguing before benches selected from judges and practitioners expert in the field.

Externship Programs are available in the Federal Defender's Office, County Circuit Courts, US Attorney's Office, US Department of Justice, US District Court, US Magistrate's Office, and County Prosecutor's Offices.

■ Student Activities

➟ *Student Senate*   ➟ *Wolverine Student Bar Association*
➟ *Federalist Society*   ➟ *Detroit Bar Association*
➟ *Women's Law Caucus*   ➟ *International Law Society*
➟ *Environmental Law Society*   ➟ *Phi Alpha Delta*
➟ *ABA Student Division*   ➟ *Delta Theta Phi*
➟ *Hands On Detroit*   ➟ *Entertainment & Sports Law Society*

Applicant Group for the 1993–1994 Academic Year

Detroit College of Law

LSAT Score	GPA								
	3.75 +	3.50 - 3.74	3.25 - 3.49	3.00 - 3.24	2.75 - 2.99	2.50 - 2.74	2.25 - 2.49	2.00 - 2.24	Below 2.00
175 - 180	▨	▨	▨	▨	■	■			
170 - 174	▨	▨	▨	▨	■	■			
165 - 169	▨	▨	▨	▨	■	■			
160 - 164	▨	▨	▨	▨	■	■			
155 - 159	▨	▨	▨	▨	■				
150 - 154	▨	▨	▨	▨	■				
145 - 149									
140 - 144									
135 - 139									
130 - 134									
125 - 129									
120 - 124									

▨ Good Possibility   ■ Possible   ☐ Unlikely

University of Detroit—Mercy School of Law

Office of Admissions
651 E. Jefferson Avenue
Detroit, MI 48226

Phone: 313.596.0200

■ Introduction

Founded in 1912, the University of Detroit—Mercy School of Law is a well-established private school located opposite the new Renaissance Center in a downtown Detroit riverfront complex of cultural, sports, convention, and residential facilities. The school is within walking distance of federal and state courts and downtown law firms, and Windsor, Canada, is a five-minute drive across the river. A traditionally rich cultural center, with such renowned institutions as the Detroit Symphony and the Detroit Institute of Arts, the Detroit metropolitan area also provides a unique laboratory for the study of contemporary legal problems associated with urban and industrial redevelopment.

As a national law school, with a faculty drawn from throughout the country, the school offers a broad curriculum and seeks to attract a geographically diverse student body. The school is a member of the AALS and is accredited by the ABA.

■ Student Body

➥ 914 total students   ➥ 9% minority first-year class 1993
➥ 44% women first-year class 1993

The student body is drawn from diverse geographical, ethnic, and religious backgrounds. Two-thirds of the students in the entering class are in the full-time day program. Academic attrition among first-year students is traditionally about 9 percent.

The school offers a special summer program for disadvantaged applicants who do not meet minimum standards for the entering class but nevertheless show potential for the study of law. Successful completion of the summer program permits admission as a regular student in the fall semester.

■ Faculty

➥ 28 full-time   ➥ 28 part-time

■ Library and Physical Facilities

➥ 190,000 volumes & equivalents   ➥ NEXIS
➥ WESTLAW

In 1976, the school completed a $7 million construction and renovation project, which included an architectural-prize-winning library building and a striking three-story interior atrium that serves as an unusually spacious student lounge.

The library is carpeted, air-conditioned, and contains comfortable reading areas, typing and audiovisual rooms, and group study rooms, as well as individual study carrels.

Dowling Hall, a Detroit landmark, contains attractive classrooms, offices, and a bookstore; the atrium and adjoining cafeteria provide a congenial setting for informal student-faculty discussions.

■ Curriculum

➥ 86 credits required to graduate   ➥ degrees available: J.D.; J.D./M.B.A.   ➥ semesters system

The school offers a three-year, full-time day program and a four-year, part-time evening program, both leading to the J.D. degree; academic standards in the two programs are identical. Basic courses in civil procedure, contracts, property, criminal law, torts, constitutional law, taxation, evidence, legal research and writing, and professional responsibility are required, and students must take at least one seminar in their final year. The remainder of the curriculum is elective. The academic year is divided into two semesters and a summer session. Students may accelerate by enrolling in the summer session.

■ Special Programs

The school's commitment to the concept of quality legal education as an approach to urban problems is reflected in opportunities to represent indigent clients under close faculty guidance and a variety of externship placements available through the Urban Law Clinic.

To refine research and writing skills, students may undertake independent research under the direction of a faculty member. The school also provides an opportunity for qualified students to pursue a four-year joint J.D./M.B.A. degree.

Additionally, the law school has a special J.D. degree program for Canadian lawyers, a cross-registration program with the University of Windsor, an exchange program with a French university, and continuing legal education programs for lawyers and other professionals.

Further, the law school conducts a London-based International Law Program which enables eligible students to study at least one semester abroad.

■ Admission

➥ undergraduate degree from accredited institution required
➥ application deadline—Apr. 15   ➥ fall admission only
➥ LSAT, LSDAS required   ➥ median GPA—3.30
➥ median LSAT score—155   ➥ application fee—$50

The school does not require a specific prelaw curriculum and agrees with the recommendations set forth in the introduction to this guide.

While the admissions committee considers the LSAT and undergraduate grades as the most important determinants of admission, it also considers factors such as letters of recommendation, evidence of maturity and leadership, graduate work, and work experience. Two letters of recommendation are required.

Applications are reviewed on a continuous basis and decisions communicated as early as possible. Interviews, though not required, may be granted upon request. A $150 nonrefundable deposit is required of all admitted applicants and credited toward the first semester's tuition. A second deposit may be required. In general, transfer students must have a 3.0 GPA or be in the upper quarter of their law class.

The law school has nondiscrimination and affirmative action policies.

■ Housing

Dormitory facilities are available for single students at the main campus of the university, about six miles from the law school. Married students seeking housing should write to the University Housing Office, 4001 W. McNichols Rd., Detroit, MI 48221. Pleasant apartments are within walking distance of the law school.

■ Activities

The *Law Review* is edited entirely by a student editorial board. Students at the school also edit the Journals of the Corporation and Tax Sections of the Michigan State Bar. A student moot court board helps to supervise the required appellate advocacy program and administers the school's Gallagher competition, as well as participation by students in regional and national competitions.

The Student Bar Association, affiliated with the Law Student Division of the ABA, plays a significant role in student affairs and program development. A student newspaper, *In Brief*, is published for the law school community. Other student organizations include the Black Law Students Alliance; the Latin American Students Organization; and the Women's Caucus; the Justice Frank Murphy Honor Society; a chapter of the National Lawyers Guild; the International Law Society; and chapters of three coeducational legal fraternities.

■ Expenses and Financial Aid

➠ *tuition—$400/credit hour* ➠ *estimated additional expenses—$6,500 (room, board, personal expenses)*
➠ *academic accomplishment scholarships available*

Students who are Michigan residents may apply to the Michigan Board of Higher Education for tuition grants. Loans are available through the Federal Perkins Loan (formerly NDSL) and Michigan Guaranteed Loan Programs and through the state of Michigan. Work-study positions are also available.

■ Placement

A Dean of Placement actively encourages law firms and other prospective employers to interview at the school and counsels and assists students in acquiring both temporary and full-time employment.

Applicant Group for the 1993–1994 Academic Year

University of Detroit—Mercy School of Law
This grid includes only applicants who earned 120-180 LSAT scores under standard administrations.

LSAT Score	3.75 +		3.50 -3.74		3.25 - 3.49		3.00 - 3.24		2.75 - 2.99		2.50 - 2.74		2.25 - 2.49		2.00 - 2.24		Below 2.00		No GPA		Total	
	Apps	Adm	Apps	Adm	Apps	Adm	Apps	Adm	Apps	Adm	Apps	Adm	Apps	Adm	Apps	Adm	Apps	Adm	Apps	Adm	Apps	Adm
175 - 180	0	0	0	0	0	0	0	0	0	0	0	0	0	0	0	0	0	0	0	0	0	0
170 - 174	0	0	0	0	0	0	0	0	2	2	0	0	0	0	0	0	0	0	0	0	2	2
165 - 169	3	3	1	1	4	4	3	3	3	3	2	1	2	1	1	1	0	0	0	0	19	17
160 - 164	2	2	5	5	17	16	13	12	11	7	5	1	6	2	1	0	1	0	3	1	64	46
155 - 159	7	6	24	23	39	38	48	45	42	23	28	7	11	1	4	0	0	0	1	1	204	144
150 - 154	12	11	28	26	59	50	101	76	66	21	45	7	22	1	5	1	2	0	5	1	345	194
145 - 149	9	8	13	11	61	41	63	27	60	10	45	8	26	3	6	1	1	1	5	1	289	111
140 - 144	4	1	8	4	29	9	33	7	42	4	38	6	16	2	16	0	2	0	7	0	195	33
135 - 139	0	0	3	0	6	0	14	0	17	0	13	0	24	2	13	0	5	1	8	2	103	5
130 - 134	0	0	0	0	0	0	4	0	5	0	7	0	6	0	5	0	3	0	2	0	32	0
125 - 129	0	0	0	0	0	0	1	0	2	0	0	0	4	0	1	0	1	0	4	0	13	0
120 - 124	0	0	0	0	0	0	0	0	1	0	0	0	1	0	1	0	1	0	1	0	5	0
Total	37	31	82	70	215	158	280	170	251	70	183	30	118	12	53	3	16	2	36	6	1271	552

Apps = Number of Applicants
Adm = Number Admitted
Reflects 94% of the total applicant pool.

144

Dickinson School of Law

150 South College Street
Carlisle, PA 17013

Phone: 717.240.5207

■ Introduction

The Dickinson School of Law, founded in 1834, is the oldest independent law school in the United States. Its location in historic Carlisle, Pennsylvania enables students to pursue their education in a friendly, safe environment with easy access to Pittsburgh, Philadelphia, New York, Washington, DC, and Baltimore. Located less than 20 miles from the state capital of Harrisburg, the school affords ample opportunities for part-time work in state government agencies and private law firms during the school year and in the summer. The campus is adjacent to Dickinson College, a separate, unrelated undergraduate school that offers law students access to its library, food service, and cultural activities.

■ Enrollment/Student Body

➨ 1,718 applicants   ➨ 177 enrolled first-year class 1993
➨ 520 total full-time   ➨ 6% minority   ➨ 49% women
➨ 28 states & 6 foreign countries represented
➨ 185 undergraduate schools represented

■ Faculty

➨ 61 total   ➨ 26 full-time   ➨ 35 part-time or adjunct
➨ 12 women   ➨ 2 minority

■ Library and Physical Facilities

➨ 325,000 volumes & equivalents   ➨ hours (public use): Mon.-Thurs., 8:00 A.M.-11:00 P.M.; Fri., 8:00 A.M.-5:00 P.M.; students have 24-hour access   ➨ LEXIS   ➨ NEXIS ➨ WESTLAW   ➨ OCLA, RLIN, EPIC   ➨ 6 full-time librarians   ➨ library seats 514

Trickett Hall, the main academic/administration building, is attached to the Sheely-Lee Law Library, a modern research center. The Library/Advocacy Center and Center for Advanced Legal Education provide additional library space. LEXIS and WESTLAW computerized legal research terminals and IBM personal computers are available to students for instruction, research, and word processing.

The school recently acquired a building in Carlisle's downtown area to house its Community Law Clinics. The facility includes an 1,800-square-foot law library for use by student lawyers in the Disability and Family law clinics and the Mediation Center.

Some accommodations for single students are available in the Levinson Curtilage, a dormitory quadrangle.

Reasonably priced off-campus housing is readily available.

■ Programs of Study/Degree Requirements

Dickinson School of Law graduates receive both a broad-based theoretical and practical legal education that prepares them to practice law anywhere in the United States.

Dickinson provides electives and seminars in developing areas of the law as the profession adjusts to meet the changing needs of society. The curriculum includes more than 100 courses in the J.D. program. Skills preparation in trial and appellate advocacy, client counseling, mediation, and legal writing complement the standard course work. With several national interscholastic moot court championships to its credit, Dickinson's advocacy program has been recognized for excellence by the American College of Trial Lawyers. Since 1967, 45 Dickinson teams have finished first or second or have otherwise distinguished themselves in interscholastic advocacy competitions.

Foreign lawyers who have a law degree not founded substantially on the English Common Law curriculum may apply for admission to the Master of Laws in Comparative Law degree program, which requires successful completion of an academic year in residence. The foreign law school attended must have a standing comparable to AALS- and ABA-approved schools.

■ Summer Sessions Abroad

In the early 1980s, Dickinson became one of the first fully accredited law schools to establish an overseas comparative law program for American students. Dickinson offers two, four-week summer credit programs, one in Florence, Italy, the other in Vienna, Austria and Strasbourg, France. In Florence, Dickinson professors collaborate with University of Florence Law School faculty and distinguished lecturers from the Italian legal and business communities. The Vienna/Strasbourg program is held in cooperation with the Economic University of Vienna, the Universities of Vienna and Strasbourg law schools, and legal personnel from the United Nations Commission on International Trade Law and the Council of Europe.

■ Special Programs and Activities

Dickinson was also a pioneer in providing hands-on, clinical experiences to assist students in developing the skills necessary to counsel clients effectively. Through the years, the law school has developed many internal and outplacement clinic programs. These programs include the Family Law Clinic, which handles matters involving divorce, child custody, visitation, protection from abuse, and other family law-related cases; the Disability Law Clinic, which handles disability-related cases; and the Mediation Center, in which specially trained students help to settle conflicts among neighbors, landlords, and tenants, as well as between merchants and consumers and other disputants. Students in the Prison Clinic represent inmates in two Pennsylvania correctional facilities. Students in the Art, Sports, and Entertainment Law Clinic, one of only several in the nation, are exposed to the unique problems and needs of artists, athletes, entertainers and others engaged in art-related vocations. There are also many outplacement opportunities in offices of Legal Services, public defender and district attorneys' offices, judicial clerkships, and legal departments of state government agencies.

■ Admission

➡ *Bachelor's degree required*   ➡ *application deadline—Feb. 15*   ➡ *LSAT, LSDAS required*   ➡ *median GPA—3.40*   ➡ *median LSAT score—156*   ➡ *application fee—$50*

Prior to enrollment, applicants must have completed work for an undergraduate degree from an accredited college or university, as required by accreditation rules of the AALS and the ABA, and must have submitted all college transcripts and scores on the LSAT. All relevant factors will be considered by the admissions committee to identify those applicants who are most likely to make a substantial and constructive contribution to the law school and to the legal profession.

Dickinson participates in the Council on Legal Education Opportunity program and other minority group programs and has hosted the CLEO regional institute five times within the past decade. Historically, Dickinson's minority enrollment has been small. However, more aggressive recruiting efforts and an increased sensitivity to the needs of minority students once they arrive on campus are beginning to have a positive effect.

Personal interviews are not part of the admission process, but applicants are invited to visit the campus and attend a class, preferably in the fall.

Students with an outstanding first-year performance at another AALS school may be considered for admission as second-year students. Transfer applications must be received on or before June 15. No action will be taken on these applications until first-year grades and class standing are received.

The Dickinson School of Law does not discriminate on the grounds of race, religion, color, national origin, sex, age, sexual orientation, or handicap in the administration of any of its educational programs or activities or with respect to admissions or employment.

■ Cocurricular Activities

Founded in 1897, the quarterly *Dickinson Law Review* ranks as one of the oldest law school publications in the country. *The Dickinson Journal of International Law* publishes articles on private and public international law. *The Dickinson Journal of Environmental Law & Policy* is a forum for articles that treat aspects of environmental law.

The Student Bar Association promotes the interests of the school and the students. Other student organizations include International Law Society, Phi Alpha Delta, Delta Theta Phi International, Women's Law Caucus, Minority Law Students Association, Jewish Law Students Association, Christian Legal Society, Amnesty International, Environmental Law Society, Public Interest Law Fund, Federalist Society, and Saint Thomas More Society.

■ Expenses and Financial Aid

Dickinson is one of the best buys in legal education. The current annual tuition is $12,200. The current annual cost per student varies from $19,100-21,000 per academic year. Tuition and fees are subject to change. Grants and scholarships are awarded primarily on the basis of established need with due consideration for academic achievement and potential. Students seeking financial assistance must register with GAPSFAS by February 15.

Applicant Group for the 1993–1994 Academic Year

Dickinson School of Law

								LSAT Score												
	Below 148		148 - 150		151 - 153		154 - 156		157 - 159		160 - 163		164 - 167		168 - 180		No LSAT		Total	
GPA	Apps	Adm	Apps	Adm	Apps	Adm	Apps	Adm	Apps	Adm	Apps	Adm	Apps	Adm	Apps	Adm	Apps	Adm	Apps	Adm
3.75+	10	3	9	1	21	19	20	20	14	13	17	17	5	5	1	1	0	0	97	79
3.50 - 3.74	38	5	33	11	46	39	54	52	27	26	31	31	15	15	3	3	0	0	247	182
3.25 - 3.49	64	6	61	4	72	26	92	61	49	47	32	32	9	8	5	5	1	0	385	189
3.00 - 3.24	82	2	53	0	72	6	69	4	47	31	36	28	17	16	5	5	2	0	383	92
2.75 - 2.99	66	0	40	4	55	2	42	0	33	5	19	9	13	5	1	0	0	0	269	25
2.50 - 2.74	53	1	25	2	33	1	20	0	19	0	17	0	8	2	0	0	0	0	175	6
Below 2.50	65	1	23	0	22	1	14	0	7	0	9	0	3	1	3	2	0	0	146	5
No GPA	0	0	4	0	1	0	0	0	0	0	0	0	0	0	0	0	14	0	19	0
Total	379	18	248	22	321	94	311	137	196	122	161	117	70	52	18	16	17	0	1721	578

Apps = Number of Applicants
Adm = Number Admitted
Reflects 100% of the total applicant pool.

District of Columbia School of Law

719 13th Street, N.W.
Washington, DC 20005

Phone: 202.727.5232

■ Introduction

In 1986, the City Council of the District of Columbia authorized the establishment of the District of Columbia School of Law. The founding class was admitted in 1988. The Council created a dual mission for the School of Law and charged its Board of Governors with a special mandate to recruit and enroll, to the degree feasible, students from ethnic, racial, or other population groups that in the past have been underrepresented among persons admitted to the bar. It also charged the Board with representing the legal needs of low-income persons, particularly those who reside in the District of Columbia.

The DC School of Law is the only publicly funded law school in Washington, DC. It is a free-standing school, not affiliated with any college or university.

■ Enrollment/Student Body

➡ *111 enrolled first-year class 1993*   ➡ *49% minority*
➡ *50% women*   ➡ *average age—30*
➡ *48% DC residents*   ➡ *28 states represented*
➡ *159 undergraduate schools represented*

The School of Law prides itself in attracting an extraordinary student body now totaling about 280. Our student body is a culturally and ethnically diverse group.

■ Faculty

➡ *35 total*   ➡ *26 full-time*   ➡ *9 part-time*
➡ *15 women*   ➡ *16 minority*

■ Library and Physical Facilities

➡ *172,000 volumes & equivalents*   ➡ *LEXIS*
➡ *WESTLAW*   ➡ *DIALOG*   ➡ *6 full-time librarians*
➡ *library seats 200*

The School of Law occupies a six-floor building located in the heart of downtown Washington, DC. The law school building has three large classrooms, two seminar rooms, a student lounge, and several small student conference rooms and work areas.

The administrative offices of the School of Law, including Student Services, are located on the third floor. The fourth and fifth floors and two-thirds of the sixth floor are devoted to the library collection.

In addition to the regular law volumes and volume equivalents, the library supports the Clinical Program by maintaining a small collection of clinical practice material and other material pertinent to each of the clinics.

The Computer Center features computer terminals for student research, word processing, and computer-assisted tutorials in core subjects.

■ Curriculum

➡ *Academic Support Program*   ➡ *85 credits required to graduate*   ➡ *10 required courses*   ➡ *3 semesters of clinical work required*   ➡ *6 clinics available*   ➡ *40 total courses available*   ➡ *J.D. degree*   ➡ *semesters, start in mid-Aug.*

Consistent with DC Law School's mission, the basic program is designed to equip students with the professional skills of practicing lawyers as well as the traditional substantive knowledge of law.

Orientation is a one-week program introducing first-year students to the study of law and the School of Law community. During orientation, students take Lawyering Process I to learn basic legal analysis, and they meet administration, faculty, and continuing students. There is a dean's reception for first-year students in the first week of the regular fall semester. There are also other events planned by student organizations.

In the first year, second semester, students begin their clinical experience by taking Clinic One. The clinics offered in the 1993-94 academic year are Housing/Consumer, Public Entitlements, HIV/AIDS, Juvenile, Legislation, and Government Accountability Project (GAP).

Including the clinic course, the first-year curriculum is prescribed and consists entirely of required courses. After the first year, students also must take Evidence, Constitutional Law, Property, and Professional Responsibility.

The School of Law offers a limited number of summer courses; it does not allow acceleration (early graduation). Students normally complete the program in three calendar years.

DCSL considers academic support to be an integral part of its course of study. Students in academic difficulty at the end of their first semester may apply to be in the enhanced program, which may involve adjusting course loads, counseling, and group and individual tutoring. In addition, faculty members hold extra review sessions during the semester in required courses and provide sample examination questions with model answers. During the first two weeks at the law school, students are given two diagnostic tests, one in reading and one in writing. Test results may be used to help students improve their skills.

The emphasis of the school is on public-interest law; the overall curriculum—clinic and classroom—is designed to support that orientation. In addition, DCSL's goals are consistent with the objectives of legal education proposed by the Long-Range Planning Committee of the American Bar Association. These objectives include "training for [lawyering] competence...[and]...training in professional responsibility."

■ Internship Program

➡ *one semester internship, 8 credits*
➡ *internship seminar, 2 credits*

In addition to the clinic program, students in the second semester, second year, or third year may elect to do an internship in which they work 30 hours a week outside the law school in judicial, legislative, or Congressional offices, or in public interest legal organizations. Faculty members monitor each placement, and students must attend a weekly Internship Seminar at the school. The School of Law emphasizes the importance of supervision, educational merit, and public service in each internship.

■ The Writing Program

Each DCSL student is required to produce significant pieces of writing each of the three years of study. In the first year students satisfy the writing requirement in the Lawyering Process course. In the second and third years, students may satisfy the legal writing requirement as part of a seminar, elective course, clinical practice, or independent study.

■ Admission

➼ *Bachelor's degree from accredited college or university required*   ➼ *application deadline—April 1*
➼ *rolling admission, early application preferred*
➼ *LSAT, LSDAS required*   ➼ *application fee—$35*
➼ *fall admission, full-time, day*

Admission is based upon academic and nonacademic achievements and professional promise. Because the LSAT does not measure the skills, determination, and personal commitment that are vital to competence and success as a legal practitioner, DCSL looks at an applicant's LSAT scores and grades in tandem with other criteria that we believe may provide a more accurate measure of a candidate's potential for success in the study of law. This approach means that our Admissions Committee considers all submitted application material. It reviews closely the application essays and other information supplied with the application, including support documents and recommendations.

■ Student Activities

The first issue of the biannual *The District of Columbia Law Review* was published in 1992. *The Side-Bar* is the student newspaper which is published every month. Students participate in many of the decision processes of the law school. Student organizations include DCSL Student Bar Association, Black Law Students Association, Law Review, Asian Pacific Law Students Association, Voices Juridicas Latinos, The National Lawyers Guild, International Law Students Association, Gay and Lesbian Association of Students, Moot Court Association, and the Women's Law Society.

■ Expenses and Financial Aid

➼ *tuition and fees—DC residents, $2990; nonresidents, $9590*
➼ *additional expenses—$15,205 (room, board, books)*
➼ *need- & merit-based scholarships available*   ➼ *FAFSA for need analysis due Apr. 30; GAPSFAS due by May 30*

■ Career Services

The Career Services Office provides employment information and career services to the School of Law's student body and graduates. The office maintains listings of permanent job openings, fellowships, summer clerkships, and part-time opportunities. The office also coordinates potential internship sites and invites employers to conduct on-campus interviews. The office provides resources for career planning, counseling sessions to assist students in developing their career goals, résumé workshops, and other relevant seminars.

Admission Profile Not Available

Drake University Law School

2507 University Avenue
Des Moines, IA 50311

Phone: 800.44.DRAKE, ex. 2782 or 515.271.2782

■ Introduction

Drake University Law School, a charter member of the AALS, is one of the 25 oldest law schools in the nation, tracing its history to 1865. Accredited by the ABA, the Law School became affiliated with Drake University, a private, independent institution of higher learning, at its founding in 1881.

Drake Law School is located in the urban setting of Iowa's capital, Des Moines, providing law students the opportunity to get hands-on experience with the executive, judicial, and legislative branches of government, the federal courts, administrative agencies, and a wide array of law firms and businesses.

■ Enrollment/Student Body

➡ *1,200 applicants*   ➡ *572 admitted first-year class 1993*
➡ *234 enrolled first-year class 1993*   ➡ *553 total full-time*
➡ *25 total part-time*   ➡ *9% minority*   ➡ *41% women*
➡ *38 states & 3 foreign countries represented*
➡ *184 undergraduate schools represented*

■ Faculty

➡ *65 total*   ➡ *23 full-time*   ➡ *43 part-time or adjunct*
➡ *19 women*   ➡ *3 minority*

■ Library and Physical Facilities

➡ *240,000 volumes & equivalents*   ➡ *library hours: Mon.-Thurs., 7:00 A.M.-MIDNIGHT; Fri., 7:00 A.M.-10:30 P.M.; Sat., 9:00 A.M.-10:30 P.M.; Sun., 9:00 A.M.-MIDNIGHT*   ➡ *LEXIS*
➡ *NEXIS*   ➡ *WESTLAW*   ➡ *4 full-time librarians*
➡ *library seats 700 (new facility in 1993)*

The Dwight D. Opperman Hall and Law Library, dedicated in early 1993 by U.S. Supreme Court Justice Anthony Kennedy, has approximately 70,000 square feet and provides Drake Law students with a state-of-the-art facility for legal research, class seminars and studying. Opperman Hall is wired for computers and is equipped with both on-line legal research training centers.

■ Legal Clinic

The Neal and Bea Smith Law Center, dedicated in 1987 by former Chief of the United States Supreme Court, Warren Burger, houses the Drake Law School Legal Clinic. The center is a state-of-the-art law office, with each student having access to the latest in dictating equipment and computer technology. The Center was selected as the national training and resource institute for public service attorneys. The $1.75 million addition, to be dedicated in early 1994 by U.S. Attorney General Janet Reno, includes a fully computerized courtroom and training facilities for Drake law students.

■ Curriculum

➡ *Academic Support Program*   ➡ *Tutorial Supplement Program of Instruction*   ➡ *90 credits required to graduate*
➡ *96 courses available*   ➡ *additional summer agricultural law program courses which vary annually are also offered*
➡ *degrees available: J.D.; J.D./M.B.A.; J.D./M.P.A.; J.D./M.S. (Economics/Iowa State); J.D./M.A. (Pol. Sci./Iowa State); J.D./M.A. (Journalism/(Economics/Iowa State); J.D./M.A. (Pol. Sci./Iowa State); J.D./M.A. (Journalism/Mass Commun./Iowa State)*   ➡ *semesters, start in Aug.*
➡ *range of first-year class size—15-90*

Educational excellence has long been achieved at Drake Law School through a balance of theory and practice that recognizes the need for both in a quality legal education. The J.D. curriculum at Drake is national in scope and emphasis. A 24:1 student-to-faculty ratio assures on-going, individualized attention.

Summer school is available for both incoming and continuing students, and may accelerate graduation.

■ Special Programs

Trial Practice and Advocacy Skills Programs—Drake students can refine their litigation and lawyering skills by participating in a variety of programs and courses. Students can render meaningful public service by providing lawyering services to low-income and elderly clients through Drake's client representation program. The Neal and Bea Smith Law Center houses the Law School's client representation and judicial clerkship programs, and serves as a center for other professional skills courses and programs.

Students receive academic credit for internships with state and federal judges at either the trial or appellate levels, with state or federal administrative agencies, the state legislature, and state prosecutors. Students may also develop lawyering skills and earn academic credit for participation on Drake's moot court, mock trial, or lawyering skills teams. Third-year students also participate as members in two American Inns of Court Chapters that have been formed by lawyers and judges in Des Moines.

Constitutional Law Programs—Drake is home to the Constitutional Law Resource Center, which was made possible through the United States Congress' selection of Drake Law School to receive one of four endowment appropriations awarded nationally. The center sponsors a lecture series and an annual symposium featuring nationally recognized constitutional scholars.

Another annual lecture, the Dwight D. Opperman Lecture in Constitutional law, emphasizes the significance of constitutional study and the Law School's commitment to it. The Opperman Lecture has been given by Justices of the United States Supreme Court, who have also met with students and participated in the intellectual life of the Law School.

Agricultural Law—Drake has one of the few programs in the nation addressing the timely and important issues in American and international agricultural law and policy. The Agricultural Law Center hosts an annual Summer Agricultural Law Institute and conference, and students write and edit an agricultural law reporter.

■ Admission

➡ *Bachelor's degree required*   ➡ *priority application deadline—March 1*   ➡ *rolling admissions*
➡ *LSAT, LSDAS required*   ➡ *median GPA—3.23*
➡ *median LSAT score—155*   ➡ *application fee—$35*

The Law School is committed to attending, enrolling, retaining, and graduating an academically strong and diverse student body.

All applications are reviewed by a faculty admission committee. Admission to Drake Law School is based upon an evaluation of an applicant's LSAT scores, undergraduate GPA, undergraduate institution attended, coursework, grade trend, writing skills as demonstrated in the LSAT writing sample and personal statement, community extracurricular involvement, graduate school record, relevant work experience, and letters of recommendation. The Law School also offers a summer conditional admission program to a limited number of selected applicants, which provides an opportunity for admission through demonstrated performance in law school courses.

■ Student Activities

Law students participate in many student organizations and cocurricular activities. *The Drake Law Review*, a student edited journal, is published quarterly. Students also publish a law school newspaper. Drake moot court teams consistently win regional competitions and finish strong in national competitions. The Student Bar Association, Legal Research Service, and honorary societies provide students with leadership, public-service, and learning opportunities. Drake students have also formed a variety of organizations around their special interests, including the Drake Law Women, Black Law Students Association, Latino Law Society, Asian-Pacific Islander Association, International Law Society, Christian Legal Society, Environmental Law Society, Federalist Society, National Lawyers Guild and the Law Student Division of the American Bar Association.

■ Expenses and Financial Aid

➡ *tuition & fees—full-time, $13,780; part-time, $460/credit*
➡ *estimated additional expenses—$8,325 (room and board $4,725; personal expenses $2,400; books $800; transportation $400)*   ➡ *scholarships available: Law General (need & merit); Law Opportunity (disadvantaged); Merit Awards; Dean's Awards*   ➡ *minority scholarships: Law Opportunity; Patricia Roberts Harris Fellowships*
➡ *financial aid available; FAFSA, all other forms are accepted*
➡ *priority deadline for scholarships and financial aid—March 1*

■ Career Services

The Law School Career Services Office offers career-planning and counseling services, assistance in résumé preparation, salary and geographical employment statistics, on-campus interviews, nationwide job postings, and state bar examination information. More than 85 percent of Drake Law School graduates are employed in legal positions within 9 months of graduation. Approximately 35 percent of recent graduating classes secured employment in more than 20 states. Law School alumni practice in all 50 states and six foreign countries.

Applicant Group for the 1993–1994 Academic Year

Drake University School of Law
This grid includes only applicants who earned 120-180 LSAT scores under standard administrations.

LSAT Score	3.75 +		3.50 -3.74		3.25 - 3.49		3.00 - 3.24		2.75 - 2.99		2.50 - 2.74		Below 2.50		No GPA		Total	
	Apps	Adm	Apps	Adm	Apps	Adm	Apps	Adm	Apps	Adm	Apps	Adm	Apps	Adm	Apps	Adm	Apps	Adm
175 - 180	0	0	0	0	0	0	0	0	0	0	0	0	0	0	0	0	0	0
170 - 174	0	0	0	0	3	3	0	0	0	0	0	0	0	0	0	0	3	3
165 - 169	2	2	1	1	1	1	4	4	0	0	0	0	6	3	0	0	14	11
160 - 164	3	3	5	5	17	17	12	12	7	7	8	8	1	1	1	1	54	54
155 - 159	11	11	23	23	48	48	53	48	32	29	42	35	20	9	3	3	232	206
150 - 154	6	6	35	33	69	63	86	64	64	27	31	7	36	5	6	1	333	206
145 - 149	12	9	26	15	44	17	68	13	55	9	35	4	23	1	3	1	266	69
Below 145	5	1	4	2	24	2	40	4	47	2	52	4	47	3	12	1	231	19
Total	39	32	94	79	206	151	263	145	205	74	168	58	133	22	25	7	1133	568

Apps = Number of Applicants
Adm = Number Admitted
Reflects 95% of the total applicant pool.

Duke University School of Law

3101 Petty Road Suite 207
Durham, NC 27707-7105

Phone: 919.489.0556

■ Introduction

Duke University, a private institution in Durham, North Carolina, is one of a select group of truly national law schools. Students come to Duke Law School from virtually every state in the country. Duke offers its students a legal education focused on the broad principles that inform the work of judges and lawyers rather than the principles of any particular jurisdiction. Through limiting the size of its entering class to under 200, the law school maintains a particularly supportive and congenial learning environment. The school is accredited by the American Bar Association and the Association of American Law Schools.

■ Enrollment/Student Body

➡ *3,707 applicants*   ➡ *808 admitted first-year class 1993*
➡ *196 enrolled first-year class 1993*   ➡ *595 total full-time*
➡ *12% minority*   ➡ *40% women*   ➡ *45 states &*
26 foreign countries represented   ➡ *178 undergraduate*
schools represented   ➡ *44 foreign LL.M. students in 1993*
entering class

Approximately 36 percent of the 1993 entering class is from the Northeast, 35 percent from the South, 11 percent from the Midwest, and 17 percent from the West. Each year, the law school also enrolls 35-40 LL.M. students and several S.J.D. (doctoral) students from countries outside the United States.

■ Faculty

➡ *82 total*   ➡ *33 full-time*   ➡ *49 part-time or adjunct*
➡ *20 women*   ➡ *4 minority*

The faculty members at Duke are its greatest asset. They are productive scholars whose interests range from federal banking regulation and corporate takeovers to ethnic conflict and feminist legal theory. Duke faculty are dedicated teachers and are actively involved in public service.

■ Library and Physical Facilities

➡ *450,000 volumes & equivalents*   ➡ *library hours:*
24 hours a day   ➡ *LEXIS*   ➡ *NEXIS*   ➡ *WESTLAW*
➡ *First Search, Uncover, DIALOG*   ➡ *Student Research*
Network   ➡ *9 full-time librarians*   ➡ *library seats 397*

Duke law library's outstanding collection of materials is particularly accessible to students. The computer-based Student Research Network, available to all law students, is an MS-DOS based local area network providing access to word-processing software, legal-research databases, computer-assisted instruction exercises, grammar and cite checking software, and the on-line catalog of all library materials and Internet. Through the use of 33 student terminals in the library, students may work with books and computer-based resources, create documents, and print them all from a single location. Students who

have their own PCs and modems also may access the network from home. An additional 20 terminals are dedicated to LEXIS and WESTLAW use.

The law school will complete a new wing in Spring 1994. The addition will increase the library's size by almost 40 percent and will result in expanded space for student organizations and meetings. Students are encouraged to take advantage of the resources of Duke University. With impressive Gothic architecture, 20 acres of formal and informal gardens, and 7,700 acres of undeveloped forest, the beauty of the Duke campus is unsurpassed.

■ Curriculum

➡ *86 units/credits required to graduate*   ➡ *121 courses*
available   ➡ *degrees available: J.D.; J.D./LL.M.;*
J.D./M.B.A.; J.D./M.E.M.; J.D./M.P.P.; J.D./Ph.D. (Pol. Sci.);
J.D./M.A.; J.D./M.D.   ➡ *semesters, start in Aug. (with the*
exception of joint-degree programs)   ➡ *range of first-year*
class size—21-152

All first-year students are required to take the same program of study including a writing tutorial. The second- and third-year programs are entirely elective. Approximately half of the advanced courses and seminars have fewer than 25 students. Upper-class students are permitted to take some courses in other divisions of the university.

■ Special Programs

J.D./LL.M. in International and Comparative Legal Studies. Duke law school offers students enrolled in the J.D. program a unique opportunity to study concurrently for the Master of Laws (LL.M.) in Comparative and International Legal Studies. Duke is the only U.S. law school that makes it possible to earn these two degrees by extending legal study by only two summers. J.D./LL.M. students enroll at Duke during the summer preceding the first year of school, and spend four weeks during the following summer at Duke's Institute of Transnational Law in Brussels.

J.D./M.A. or M.S. Programs. Based on the idea that society will be best served by lawyers with diverse educations, training, and backgrounds, Duke offers accelerated joint-degree programs through which students may obtain a J.D. and a master's degree in any of the following disciplines: Public Policy, Environmental Studies, Political Science, Economics, History, English, Philosophy, Humanities, Cultural Anthropology, Romance Studies, or Mechanical Engineering. The only additional time necessary to obtain both degrees is the summer that precedes the first year of school. In addition to the accelerated programs, Duke offers four-year, joint-degree programs combining law and Public Policy, Environmental Management, or Business Administration.

■ Admission

➡ *Bachelor's degree required* ➡ *suggested application deadline—Jan. 15* ➡ *LSAT, LSDAS required* ➡ *median GPA—3.70* ➡ *median LSAT score—169* ➡ *application fee—$60* ➡ *students are encouraged to take the LSAT no later than December*

Admission to the law school is determined after careful consideration of all information presented in the application. All applications are reviewed by at least one member of the Admission Office staff and by the Assistant Dean for Admissions. The final admission decision is made by the Faculty Admissions Committee. The committee begins review of completed applications around January 15 and applicants are notified of decisions as they are made.

Undergraduate grades, undergraduate institution, and LSAT scores are among the most important criteria in admission decisions. The committee also weighs heavily: demonstrated leadership, community service, graduate study in another discipline, work experience, and other information indicating academic or professional potential. Letters of recommendation play a critical role in the decision-making process. Admission interviews are not customarily granted. Students are encouraged to visit the school during the spring semester.

■ Career Services

The full-time staff of the Career Services office assists students in obtaining summer and permanent employment. In the fall of 1993, almost 350 firms will come to Duke to interview second- and third-year students. An additional group of over 800 employers will request résumés of students. While the majority of graduates begin their legal careers in private law firms, the office provides information on judicial clerkships, opportunities in the federal government, and public-service organizations. Students receive individualized assistance with preparing résumés and cover letters and interviewing skills.

In August 1993, 90 percent of the Class of 1993 was employed; 62 percent in private practice, 24 percent in judicial clerkships (including 2 clerkships in the U.S. Supreme Court), and the remainder in public service, government, or business, or academic positions

■ Cocurricular Activities

The law school publishes four scholarly journals, *Duke Law Journal, Law and Contemporary Problems, Alaska Law Review,* and the *Duke Journal of Comparative and International Law,* as well as two annuals, *Duke Women's Journal of Law & Public Policy* and the *Duke Environmental Law & Policy Forum.* Particularly popular with students is the Pro Bono Project, an organization through which students provide volunteer legal service in individual areas of interest. Other active student organizations include the Dean's Advisory Council, Duke Bar Association, Environmental Law Society, the Black Law Students Association, Women Law Students Association, Moot Court Board, International Law Society, and Prisoners Rights Project.

■ Expenses and Financial Aid

➡ *full-time tuition & fees—$19,016* ➡ *estimated additional expenses—$11,056 (rent, food, health insurance, books, travel, misc.)* ➡ *merit and need-based scholarships available* ➡ *minority scholarships available* ➡ *financial aid available; GAPSFAS need analysis form due in Jan.*

Applicant Group for the 1993-94 Academic Year

Duke University School of Law
This grid includes only applicants who earned 120-180 LSAT scores under standard administrations.

LSAT Score	3.75 +		3.50 -3.74		3.25 - 3.49		3.00 - 3.24		2.75 - 2.99		2.50 - 2.74		2.25 - 2.49		2.00 - 2.24		Below 2.00		No GPA		Total	
	Apps	Adm	Apps	Adm	Apps	Adm	Apps	Adm	Apps	Adm	Apps	Adm	Apps	Adm	Apps	Adm	Apps	Adm	Apps	Adm	Apps	Adm
175 - 180	31	30	21	21	21	18	12	9	2	0	2	0	0	0	0	0	0	0	0	0	89	78
170 - 174	85	83	91	87	69	53	29	9	11	2	1	0	1	0	0	0	0	0	2	0	289	234
165 - 169	206	151	289	125	204	27	87	3	30	1	13	1	5	1	1	0	1	0	2	0	838	309
160 - 164	239	48	302	27	221	13	95	5	33	1	17	1	5	0	2	0	1	0	4	0	919	95
155 - 159	100	6	173	8	144	15	88	4	38	0	18	0	10	0	1	0	1	0	8	0	581	33
150 - 154	34	0	74	0	65	1	75	2	37	1	19	0	13	0	4	0	0	0	8	1	329	5
145 - 149	13	0	43	0	42	0	31	0	42	0	21	0	13	0	4	0	2	0	2	0	213	0
140 - 144	8	0	19	0	21	1	17	0	25	0	14	0	8	0	6	0	2	0	9	0	129	1
135 - 139	7	0	4	0	5	0	8	0	14	0	11	0	10	0	2	0	1	0	1	0	63	0
130 - 134	0	0	0	0	2	0	3	0	2	0	3	0	3	0	2	0	0	0	1	0	16	0
125 - 129	0	0	1	0	0	0	1	0	0	0	3	0	2	0	1	0	0	0	1	0	9	0
120 - 124	0	0	0	0	0	0	0	0	0	0	0	0	0	0	0	0	0	0	0	0	0	0
Total	723	318	1017	268	794	128	446	32	234	5	122	2	70	1	23	0	8	0	38	1	3475	755

Apps = Number of Applicants
Adm = Number Admitted
Reflects 94% of the total applicant pool.

Duquesne University School of Law

217 Hanley Hall
900 Locust Street Pittsburgh, PA 15282

Phone: 412.396.6296

■ Introduction

The Duquesne University School of Law has been in existence since 1911 and is the only multiple-division law school in Western Pennsylvania. Admission requirements, instruction, and the nature and scope of the work required of students are identical for both the full-time day division and the part-time evening division. The School of Law is approved by the ABA and is a member of the AALS.

Duquesne's 39-acre campus is uniquely situated, affording access, within walking distance, to the downtown legal, business, and government communities, and state and federal courts.

■ Enrollment/Student Body

➥ *first-year class enrollment—day, 100; evening, 100*
➥ *290 total full-time*   ➥ *354 total part-time*
➥ *7% minority*   ➥ *43% women*
➥ *28 states & foreign countries represented*
➥ *185 undergraduate schools represented*

The Duquesne University School of Law does not discriminate on the basis of race, creed, color, sex, national or ethnic origin, handicap, or age, nor in the administration of its admission and educational policies. The law school seeks diversity in the student body and encourages members of minority groups and others who have been underrepresented in the legal profession to apply. Out-of-state students typically comprise 30 percent of the full-time entering class.

■ Faculty

➥ *58 total*   ➥ *21 full-time*   ➥ *37 part-time or adjunct*
➥ *4 women*   ➥ *5 minority*

■ Library and Physical Facilities

➥ *192,000 volumes & equivalents*   ➥ *library hours: Mon.-Thurs., 8:00 A.M.-MIDNIGHT; Fri., 8:00 A.M.-10:00 P.M.; Sat., 9:00 A.M.-9:00 P.M.; Sun., 1:00 P.M.-MIDNIGHT*   ➥ *LEXIS*
➥ *WESTLAW*   ➥ *5 full-time librarians*
➥ *library seats 325*

In 1982, the law school moved into the newly completed Edward J. Hanley Hall. This modern facility houses all classrooms, faculty offices, and study rooms for the Law School, including the James P. McArdle Moot Court Room and the John E. Laughlin Memorial Library. The library contains group-study rooms, individual study carrels, and the law school's computer lab. All first-year students are trained on computer-assisted legal research.

■ Curriculum

➥ *BLSA (student-run tutoring program) offered*
➥ *86 credits required to graduate*   ➥ *112 courses available*
➥ *degrees available: J.D.; J.D./M.B.A.; J.D./M. Div.*
➥ *semesters, start in Sept.*
➥ *range of first-year class size—20-100*

The course of study offered at the School of Law is sufficiently broad to prepare students for practice in all states. Three years are required for completion of the course of study in the day division, four years in the evening division.

Electives are offered after the first year of study in such developing areas as products and the consumer, environmental law, law and psychiatry, controlling medical therapy and experimentation, sex discrimination and the law, and legal medicine. An endowed chair in Law and Economics provides students with the opportunity to develop a knowledge of the application of economic principles to the study of law. These elective courses allow students to explore the more contemporary problems of law and society.

■ Special Programs

Students are afforded an opportunity to participate in numerous educational and professional activities, including moot court competitions and a wide variety of clinical programs.

■ Admission

➥ *Bachelor's degree required*   ➥ *application deadlines—day, April 1; eve. May 1*   ➥ *rolling admission*
➥ *LSAT, LSDAS required*   ➥ *application fee—$40*

All candidates for admission must take the LSAT, subscribe to LSDAS, and be graduates of an accredited college or university before enrolling in the law school. Personal interviews by members of the Admissions Committee are not granted, but applicants are encouraged to schedule an appointment to visit the school for an individual information session and/or a tour of the facilities.

The large number of applications received makes the admission process very selective. Most applicants apply well in advance of the deadlines. Students are admitted only for the fall semester.

In evaluating applications, the complete academic record is reviewed with consideration given to the competitiveness of the undergraduate institution, the college major, rank in class, and the overall academic performance. The LSAT is considered to be an important factor in assessing an applicant's ability to succeed in legal study. Graduate study, extracurricular activities, and recommendations also contribute to the committee's assessment. Work experience is considered when an applicant has been employed full-time for a significant length of time.

■ Student Activities

The Student Bar Association maintains a liaison between students and faculty and sponsors social and professional activities for the student body.

Membership in the *Duquesne Law Review* is based on the demonstrated academic ability of the student as well as his or her interest in becoming active in this publication.

Juris, the law school news magazine, is an ABA-award-winning publication containing articles of current interest to the entire legal community.

There are also active chapters of the following organizations available to law students: Phi Alpha Delta legal fraternity; the Women Law Association (WLA); Black Law Students Association (BLSA); ABA/LSD American Bar Association/Law Student Division; International Law Society; Sports and Entertainment Law, Association of Trial Lawyers of America, Environmental Law Association, Health Care Law Society, and Association for Public Interest Law.

■ Expenses and Financial Aid

➡ *tuition & fees—full time, $10,353; part-time, $7798*
➡ *estimated additional expenses—$6,000 (books, room & board)*   ➡ *need- and merit-based scholarships available*
➡ *minority scholarships available (need- and merit-based)*
➡ *financial aid available*
➡ *Duquesne Financial Aid application due May 31*
➡ *PHEAA, FAF, and GAPSFAS accepted*

By maintaining a very competitive tuition rate, Duquesne consistently strives to ensure that the outstanding private legal education provided by the law school is within the reach of all qualified students. A limited number of merit scholarships are awarded to the most outstanding day-division applicants each year. Law School grants-in-aid are awarded primarily on the basis of need. A number of loans sponsored by the state and federal government are available to law students.

For further information write to the Financial Aid Office, Duquesne University, Pittsburgh, PA 15282.

■ Housing

Accommodations are available for law students in the university dormitories. For on-campus residence information write to the Office of Residence Life, Duquesne University, Pittsburgh, PA 15282. Off-campus accommodations are also available nearby.

■ Career Services

The law school's Career Services Office staff offers assistance to students and alumni who are interested in obtaining full-time, part-time, and summer employment. The Career Services Office offers a fall and spring on-campus interview program in which law firms, government agencies, corporations, and accounting firms conduct individual interviews.

Duquesne University School of Law is a member of the National Association for Law Placement, the National Association for Public Interest Law Publication Network, and the Allegheny County Bar Association Minority Job Fair.

Graduates of the law school have consistently passed the Pennsylvania bar examination at a rate that well exceeds the statewide average. The law school has nearly 5,000 alumni throughout the United States and in several foreign countries, with the majority practicing in Pennsylvania and the northeastern United States.

Applicant Group for the 1993–1994 Academic Year

The Law School recognizes the different strengths presented by our day and evening division students and acknowledges that the diversity in the groups cannot be accurately or completely represented in a single grid of average undergraduate GPA and LSAT scores. Graduate degrees and extensive employment experience predominate in the evening division and these factors are considered crucial to an individual assessment of admissibility. Day-division applications are also reviewed individually and factors such as leadership experience, community service and other nonacademic experiences are considered. Applicants should contact the Admissions Office for specific information on the current year's class—Phone: 412.396.6296.

Emory University School of Law

Gambrell Hall
Atlanta, GA 30322

Phone: 404.727.6801

■ Introduction

Emory's location in Atlanta, a national business and legal center, gives Emory law students the opportunity to take advanced classes from, and work with, some of the leading judges and lawyers in the United States. Atlanta is one of America's most beautiful and most livable cities.

The law school also benefits from the strength of Emory University, which was founded in 1836. Emory University School of Law is accredited by the American Bar Association, is a member of the Association of American Law Schools, and has a chapter of Order of the Coif.

■ Enrollment/Student Body

➡ *3,657 applicants* ➡ *1,023 admitted first-year class 1993*
➡ *236 enrolled first-year class 1993* ➡ *740 total full-time*
➡ *19% minority* ➡ *43% women*
➡ *42 states & foreign countries represented*
➡ *over 150 undergraduate schools represented*

■ Faculty

➡ *78 total* ➡ *40 full-time* ➡ *38 part-time*
➡ *70 women* ➡ *5 minority*

■ Library & Physical Facilities

➡ *260,000+ volumes & equivalents* ➡ *library hours:*
Mon.-Fri., 8:00 A.M.-MIDNIGHT; Sat., 9:00 A.M.-MIDNIGHT;
Sun., 10:00 A.M.-MIDNIGHT ➡ *LEXIS* ➡ *NEXIS*
➡ *WESTLAW* ➡ *DOBIS* ➡ *6 full-time librarians*
➡ *library seats 343*

Our modern, air-conditioned building, Gambrell Hall, is a part of Emory's 630-acre campus in Druid Hills, six miles northeast of downtown Atlanta.

Gambrell Hall, constructed in 1972, contains the classrooms, faculty offices, library, student-organization facilities, and auditorium for the law school. The Elbert Tuttle Courtroom was constructed in 1982 and contains a complete television studio equipped for four-camera operation. The library is open-stack with spacious, open reading and study areas. LEXIS and WESTLAW terminals are in the library, and students learn both the techniques of computer-assisted legal research and traditional research methods. Students also have access to the library's computer lab, which offers Apple Macintosh Plus microcomputers for student word processing and other computer needs. A library expansion is planned to take place over the next three years.

■ Curriculum

➡ *88 credits required to graduate* ➡ *180 courses available*
➡ *degrees available: J.D.; J.D./M.B.A.; J.D./M.Div.; J.D./M.T.S.*
➡ *semesters, start in Aug.*
➡ *range of first-year class size—30-60*

The basic program of study involves three years of full-time study leading to the J.D. degree. The fall semester runs from late August to mid-December; the spring semester begins in mid-January and ends in mid-May.

The program of courses for the first year is prescribed. The program of courses for the second and third years is primarily elective. Students can sample a broad spectrum of courses and/or concentrate on a particular area of law.

All first-year courses and the basic second- and third-year courses are taught by full-time faculty members. A distinguished group of judges and practicing attorneys offer specialized courses.

■ Special Programs

The law school believes that its program of trial training is special. Emory's program uses as instructors many lawyers and judges from around the United States. For a two-week period, each second-year student works full-time with these lawyers and judges on each stage of the litigation of a simulated case.

Emory's affiliation with the Carter Center for Public Policy and its location in a city that is fast becoming an international legal center provide some unique opportunities in international law. Visiting international law professors from the former Soviet Union, Yugoslavia, and South Africa greatly enrich course offerings in that area.

The law school offers joint-degree programs with Emory's School of Business Administration and with the School of Theology.

■ Admission

➡ *Bachelor's degree from an accredited college or university required* ➡ *application deadline—Mar. 1*
➡ *modified rolling admission, early application preferred*
➡ *LSAT, LSDAS required* ➡ *median GPA—3.40*
➡ *median LSAT score—163* ➡ *application fee—$45*
➡ *modified rolling admission, early application preferred*

The law school accepts beginning students for the fall term only. Prior to enrollment, a student must have earned a bachelor's degree from an approved institution.

Applications for admission must be received by Emory no later than March 1. Early applications are both encouraged and appreciated.

Many factors are considered in making admissions decisions. Of particular importance are academic accomplishments and LSAT scores. Extracurricular activities, work experience, level of quality and difficulty of undergraduate courses, performance in graduate school, and letters of recommendation are also considered. Special consideration is given to members of minority groups, and members of such groups are encouraged to apply and to provide the Director of Admissions with any specific information about their background or accomplishments that would be of particular interest.

Applicants are encouraged to visit the law school. Upon acceptance, applicants are required to submit a nonrefundable $250 tuition deposit to reserve a space in the entering class.

■ Student Activities

A wide variety of organizations and activities are available to students. As there are three law reviews at Emory, *Emory Law Journal*, *Bankruptcy Developments Journal*, and *Emory International Law Review*, more than 30 percent of the second- and third-year students are involved in law review research, writing, and editing. Candidates for the reviews are selected from second- and third-year classes by the student editorial boards on the basis of scholarship and writing ability.

Students also participate in moot court. Each first-year student prepares a brief and presents an oral argument. In addition, many second- and third-year students compete in intramural and national moot court competitions.

There are numerous special interest and social groups and a very active Student Bar Association.

■ Expenses and Financial Aid

➡ *full-time tuition & fees—$17,170* ➡ *estimated additional expenses—$9,000 (room, board & books)* ➡ *scholarships available: Robert W. Woodruff Fellowships (merit-based) & other merit/need* ➡ *minority scholarships available (merit and need)* ➡ *FAF form due to the College Scholarship Service in early Feb. for financial aid*

■ Career Services

The law school regards placement as a matter of highest priority. A full-time career services office assists students in obtaining permanent, summer, and part-time employment. It arranges interviews with employers from many parts of the country and maintains extensive files on a wide variety of professional opportunities all over the United States. The great majority of Emory graduates join private law firms after graduation. Others work as judicial clerks, enter government service, or work for banks, corporations, or legal aid agencies. Still others pursue a teaching career, but usually after working as a judicial clerk or engaging in the practice of law.

Emory School of Law provides a full range of career planning and placement services. The class of 1992 reported 90 percent employment within six months after graduation in the following fields: 60 percent in private practice; 3 percent in corporations; 17 percent in government; 10 percent in judicial clerkships; and 9 percent in legal services/public interest, academic, and other fields. The geographic distribution reflected by these figures was as follows: Atlanta, 41 percent; Southeast (excluding Atlanta), 19 percent; Northeast, 30 percent; Midwest, 3 percent; West, 6 percent.

Applicant Group for the 1993–1994 Academic Year

Emory University School of Law
This grid includes only applicants who earned 120-180 LSAT scores under standard administrations.

LSAT Score	GPA																					
	3.75 +		3.50 -3.74		3.25 - 3.49		3.00 - 3.24		2.75 - 2.99		2.50 - 2.74		2.25 - 2.49		2.00 - 2.24		Below 2.00		No GPA		Total	
	Apps	Adm	Apps	Adm	Apps	Adm	Apps	Adm	Apps	Adm	Apps	Adm	Apps	Adm	Apps	Adm	Apps	Adm	Apps	Adm	Apps	Adm
175 - 180	3	3	1	1	3	3	6	6	0	0	1	1	1	0	0	0	0	0	0	0	15	14
170 - 174	8	7	17	17	17	17	20	19	6	4	3	0	1	0	1	0	0	0	0	0	73	64
165 - 169	38	38	63	62	83	78	77	70	34	8	9	2	4	0	1	0	0	0	0	0	309	258
160 - 164	77	76	147	123	239	159	165	41	66	4	41	3	15	1	0	0	0	0	4	2	754	409
155 - 159	70	31	183	52	245	25	202	14	80	6	46	2	24	0	4	0	1	0	3	0	858	130
150 - 154	44	7	110	12	132	11	131	22	88	9	50	1	23	0	10	1	0	0	6	0	594	63
145 - 149	15	6	45	14	64	11	77	3	66	0	56	0	35	0	9	0	1	0	7	2	375	36
140 - 144	7	2	17	0	36	0	47	1	58	0	46	1	32	0	25	0	1	0	6	0	275	4
135 - 139	0	0	5	0	13	0	23	0	28	0	25	0	22	0	13	0	4	0	0	0	133	0
130 - 134	0	0	5	0	4	0	4	0	8	0	8	0	10	0	10	0	2	0	2	0	53	0
125 - 129	0	0	1	0	1	0	2	0	1	0	1	0	1	0	0	0	2	0	0	0	9	0
120 - 124	0	0	0	0	0	0	0	0	0	0	0	0	2	0	2	0	0	0	1	0	5	0
Total	262	170	594	281	837	304	754	176	435	31	286	10	170	1	75	1	11	0	29	4	3453	978

Apps = Number of Applicants
Adm = Number Admitted
Reflects 96% of the total applicant pool.

University of Florida College of Law

Assistant Dean for Admissions
Gainesville, FL 32611-2038

Phone: 904.392.2087, Fax: 904.392.8727

■ Introduction

The University of Florida College of Law offers a three-year post-baccalaureate curriculum leading to the degree of Juris Doctor (J.D.), a number of joint-degree programs, and a post-J.D. program leading to the degree of Master of Laws in Taxation (LL.M.). The study of law at the University of Florida prepares students for creative problem solving, dispute resolution, planning and counseling, and policy-making roles in contemporary society. With a student body consistently ranked among the nation's finest, the college is known for graduating leaders for Florida's legal, political, business, and educational sectors, and its faculty and alumni are recognized at the national and international level.

The University of Florida, occupying 2,000 acres mostly within Gainesville's 85,000-population urban area, is a member of the prestigious Association of American Universities and is recognized as one of the nation's leading research universities by the Carnegie Commission on Higher Education. Gainesville, with extensive educational, cultural, and recreational offerings, is consistently ranked among the best places to live in America.

■ History of the College of Law

➡ *founded in 1909*   ➡ *Association of American Law Schools membership since 1920*
➡ *New York State Regents accreditation since 1917*
➡ *American Bar Association approval since 1925*

■ Enrollment/Student Body

➡ *3,100 applicants*   ➡ *480 admitted fall 1993*
➡ *200 enrolled fall 1993*   ➡ *1,150 total full-time*
➡ *18% minority*   ➡ *40% women*   ➡ *70 undergraduate schools represented*   ➡ *280 admitted spring 1994*
➡ *200 enrolled spring 1994*

■ Faculty

➡ *68 full-time*   ➡ *4 part-time*   ➡ *22 women*
➡ *7 minority*

■ Library and Physical Facilities

➡ *530,000 volumes & equivalents*   ➡ *library hours: Mon.-Fri., 7:30 A.M.-11:00 P.M.; Sat., 9:00 A.M.-5:00 P.M.; Sun., 11:00 A.M.-11:00 P.M.*   ➡ *LEXIS*   ➡ *WESTLAW*
➡ *DIALOG, PLATO*   ➡ *8 full-time librarians*
➡ *library seats 875*

The College of Law is housed in two adjacent buildings on the University of Florida campus in North Central Florida. The Legal Information Center's extensive holdings rank it among the two largest law libraries in the Southeastern United States. The library long has been a national leader in audiovisual and microform services and computerized legal research. The library also offers IBM PCs for student use.

■ Curriculum

➡ *88 semester-credits required to graduate*
➡ *over 100 courses & seminars available*   ➡ *degrees available: J.D.; J.D./M.B.A.; J.D./M.A.; & J.D./Ph.D.*
➡ *semesters, start in Aug., Jan., and May (8-week term)*

The College of Law curriculum includes traditional courses on law and legal analysis, skills training courses, international law offerings, and seminars on contemporary legal issues. Students generally are required to complete the first-year curriculum in sequence, and spring entrants are required to attend the first summer term. All students must complete a major research and writing project in the senior year.

Joint-degree programs in accounting, business administration, mass communications, history, political science and public administration, sociology, and urban and regional planning are available to students who meet the requirements of both the College of Law and the Graduate School.

■ Special Programs

The college is home to a nationally acclaimed Graduate Tax Program, leading to the degree LL.M. in Taxation. The program publishes the *Florida Tax Review*, which utilizes LL.M. student assistants.

Clinical programs provide J.D. students with the opportunity to represent actual clients in civil and criminal court cases. The college's Center for Governmental Responsibility provides students with an opportunity to conduct public-interest and environmental research with staff attorneys.

■ Admission

➡ *Bachelor's degree from accredited college or university required*
➡ *application deadline—fall, Feb. 1; spring, May 15*
➡ *rolling admissions, early application preferred*
➡ *LSAT, LSDAS required*   ➡ *application fee—$20*
➡ *median GPA—fall, 3.53; spring, 3.38*
➡ *median LSAT score—fall, 162; spring, 160*

The College of Law enrolls only full-time students in the fall and spring. Approximately 95 percent of those entering successfully complete the first two semesters. The college subscribes to the suggestions on prelaw study included in this guide. In addition to the bulleted requirements above, the College of Law requests that each applicant provide a personal statement and three letters of evaluation. Admission standards are significantly higher for non-Florida residents.

Approximately 50 percent of admission decisions are based primarily on the undergraduate grade-point average and LSAT score. The remainder of each class is selected on the basis of both quantitative and nonquantitative criteria. Applications cannot be processed more than one year in advance of the intended month of entry. However, early completion of applications is strongly recommended. Applicants must take the LSAT prior to application deadlines.

Students may transfer in August, January, or May from ABA/AALS law schools, but the Admissions Committee usually accepts only those transfer applicants who will have completed their first year of law school before enrolling at the University of Florida. Candidates must be in the upper one-third of their class to be considered. A letter of good standing from the dean is required. No more than 28 semester hours or 42 quarter hours will be transferred.

The University of Florida and the College of Law actively recruit minority students. Scholarships and grants are available for qualified minority students. Inquiries should be addressed to the Assistant Dean for Student and Minority Affairs, University of Florida College of Law, Gainesville, FL 32611-2038.

■ Student/Extracurricular Activities

Student activities include the *Florida Law Review, Florida Journal of International Law*, Moot Court and Trial Team. More than 20 extracurricular organizations provide additional opportunities for student involvement.

■ Expenses and Financial Aid

➡ *tuition & fees—Florida residents, $121 per semester hour; nonresidents $385 per semester hour*
➡ *estimated additional expenses—$7,500 room, board, books*
➡ *performance & need-based scholarships available*
➡ *deadlines—March 1 for fall applicants; July 1 for spring applicants (FAFSA and College of Law financial aid application)*

In addition to scholarships and awards, the College of Law provides short- and long-term loans to qualified students. Students applying for College of Law financial aid must have an undergraduate GPA of at least 3.2 and a single or average LSAT score of 158 or higher, and must submit the FAFSA. GPA and LSAT figures used are those reported by LSDAS. For information concerning federal, state, and Law Access loans, write to: Director of Financial Aid, College of Law, 164 Holland Hall, Gainesville, FL 32611-2038.

■ Housing

Housing is available for single students in university dormitories and for families in university apartments adjacent to the law school. Off-campus housing is also available. For more information, write to the Director of Housing, University of Florida, Gainesville, FL 32611.

■ Career Services

The Career Planning and Placement Office assists students in finding employment or clerkships. Approximately 250 employers recruit on campus each year. Approximately 85-90 percent of recent College of Law graduates seeking employment have jobs after taking the bar.

Applicant Group for the 1993–1994 Academic Year

University of Florida College of Law
This grid includes only applicants who earned 120-180 LSAT scores under standard administrations.

LSAT Score	3.75 +		3.50 -3.74		3.25 - 3.49		3.00 - 3.24		2.75 - 2.99		2.50 - 2.74		2.25 - 2.49		2.00 - 2.24		Below 2.00		No GPA		Total	
	Apps	Adm	Apps	Adm	Apps	Adm	Apps	Adm	Apps	Adm	Apps	Adm	Apps	Adm	Apps	Adm	Apps	Adm	Apps	Adm	Apps	Adm
175 - 180	1	1	1	1	6	6	0	0	0	0	0	0	1	1	0	0	0	0	0	0	9	9
170 - 174	2	2	4	3	6	5	8	7	1	1	8	4	0	0	0	0	0	0	2	1	31	23
165 - 169	17	14	36	31	51	38	41	23	14	2	10	2	7	2	0	0	0	0	1	1	177	113
160 - 164	29	22	99	73	108	44	86	19	50	5	39	4	12	2	2	0	1	0	4	1	430	170
155 - 159	42	22	102	23	142	16	134	3	82	2	52	2	26	0	7	0	1	0	7	1	595	69
150 - 154	35	12	85	10	109	5	99	3	92	7	52	2	21	1	10	0	1	0	10	0	514	40
145 - 149	15	2	33	2	51	1	56	7	60	4	42	2	26	3	15	1	2	0	9	0	309	22
140 - 144	7	3	15	3	30	1	36	0	38	3	23	1	25	0	14	0	2	0	7	0	197	11
135 - 139	2	1	4	0	5	1	10	0	18	1	23	0	12	0	9	0	0	0	4	0	87	3
130 - 134	0	0	0	0	0	0	5	0	4	0	7	0	12	0	4	0	0	0	4	0	36	0
125 - 129	0	0	0	0	1	0	2	0	0	0	1	0	2	0	3	0	0	0	1	0	10	0
120 - 124	0	0	0	0	0	0	0	0	0	0	0	0	0	0	0	0	0	0	0	0	0	0
Total	150	79	379	146	509	117	477	62	359	25	257	17	144	9	64	1	7	0	49	4	2395	460

Apps = Number of Applicants
Adm = Number Admitted
Reflects 95% of the total applicant pool.

The Florida State University College of Law

College of Law
Tallahassee, FL 32306-1034

Phone: 904.644.3787

■ Introduction

Florida State University was founded in 1851 as a public seminary for women, and became a coeducational institution in 1948. In 1965, the legislature authorized the establishment of a college of law. The college admitted its first class in 1966. In 1971, it moved into a modern building next to the state capitol and within one block of the Florida Supreme Court Building, the state library, and the state archives. The main university buildings are only a few blocks away. The college is a member of the Association of American Law Schools (AALS) and is ABA-approved.

■ Enrollment/Student Body

→ 2,645 applicants   → 540 admitted first-year class 1993
→ 204 enrolled first-year class 1993   → 600 total full-time
→ 24% minority   → 47% women
→ 76 undergraduate schools represented entering 1993 class

■ Faculty

→ 58 total   → 42 full-time   → 9 adjunct
→ 13 women   → 6 minority

■ Library and Physical Facilities

→ 345,425 volumes & equivalents   → library hours: Mon.-Thurs., 7:30 A.M.-MIDNIGHT; Fri., 7:30 A.M.-10:00 P.M.; Sat., 9:00 A.M.-10:00 P.M.; Sun., 10:00 A.M.-MIDNIGHT
→ LEXIS   → NEXIS   → WESTLAW
→ 7 full-time librarians   → library seats 460

The physical facilities of the College of Law consist of B.K. Roberts Hall opened in 1971; a separate, connected law library building opened in 1983; and the Village Green, completed in 1988.

Roberts Hall houses faculty, staff and student offices, lounges, classrooms, seminar rooms, and a practice courtroom making extensive use of state-of-the-art video technology. The College of Law has been designated a downlink site by the American Law Institute-American Bar Association. Both Roberts Hall and the law library comply with all architectural regulations facilitating use by the handicapped.

The law library's volumes and microform volume equivalents are all cataloged in the Florida State University libraries on-line database, accessible through computer terminals located throughout the library and also available for remote access using computers with modems. Serial subscriptions exceed 5,800; holdings include a wide range of audiovisual materials. Individual and group study, video viewing, microform reading, and computer use and instruction are accommodated within the law library.

■ Curriculum

→ Academic Support Program   → 88 credits required to graduate   → 105 courses available   → degrees available: J.D.; J.D./M.B.A.; J.D./M.P.A.; J.D./International Affairs; J.D./Urban & Regional Planning; J.D./Economics
→ range of first-year class size—30-70

The school operates on the semester basis. The first-year curriculum is mandatory. Current catalogs indicate the range of electives available. While the general curriculum is national in focus, some courses especially relevant to the Florida bar and Florida practice are offered.

■ Special Programs

The college's location in the state capitol provides students with a variety of externship opportunities. Judicial externships are available with the state trial and appellate courts, including the Florida Supreme Court as well as the federal courts. Externships with government agencies, and commissions as well as legal services, state attorney and public defender programs are also available. The college also has a Children's Advocacy Clinic through which enrolled students, under the supervision of clinic faculty, represent the interests of children in a variety of legal settings.

The college also sponsors two summer law programs abroad, one at Oxford University, England and the other at the University of West Indies in Barbados. Faculty from Florida State and the host institutions participate in the programs which are open to students who have completed the first year of law school.

The college also houses the Florida Dispute Resolution Center which was established in conjunction with the Florida Supreme Court. Its purpose is to study and encourage the use of a variety of alternative dispute resolution methods.

The college has a public service fellowship program through which students receive a fellowship in return for a commitment to engage in a variety of public service activities.

■ Admission Standards

→ Bachelor's degree from accredited college or university required   → application deadline—Feb. 15
→ early application preferred   → LSAT, LSDAS required
→ average GPA—3.3   → average LSAT score—158
→ application fee—$20

More than 2,500 applications are expected this year for the 175 places in the entering class.

Files are reviewed by a faculty committee which uses a formula combining GPA and LSAT scores. The LSAT is weighted slightly more than the college grade-point average, but both are significant. The committee considers the pattern of undergraduate performance from year to year as well as the school and coursework pursued by the applicant. Also, it weighs a number of other factors, including institutional interest in maintaining a student body as diverse as possible in the categories of age, sex, and educational background.

Transfer applicants may be admitted to any term after completion of the first year. Transcripts showing a full year's work and a dean's letter indicating the student's class rank and stating that the student is in good academic standing and eligible to return must be provided. Applicants must be enrolled in an ABA-approved law school. Applicants must be in the top 25 percent of their first-year class to be eligible for transfer.

■ Student Activities

One of the most attractive aspects of Florida State University's academic climate is the wide variety of educational and professional opportunities available outside the traditional classroom. The College of Law sponsors *Law Review*, the *Journal of Land Use and Environmental Law*, the *Journal of Transnational Law*, a nationally recognized moot court and trial advocacy program, and a variety of social and professional organizations. The college boasts active ACLU, NLG, and STLA chapters, a Women's Law Society, a Black Law Students Association chapter, a Christian Legal Society, an Entertainment, Arts and Sports Law Society, a Federalist Society, an International Law Society, a Lawyers for Animal Welfare chapter, an Environmental Law Society, a Spanish-American Law Students Association chapter, and Law Partners, a law students' spouse and significant others support group. Both Phi Delta Phi and Phi Alpha Delta

legal honoraries maintain a chapter on campus. F.S.U. was granted a chapter of Order of the Coif in 1979. The Student Bar Association serves an active student government role and coordinates such services as the roommate referral program, a co-op bookstore, and coordination of many law school-sponsored social activities.

■ Expenses and Financial Aid

➡ *tuition & fees—full-time, in-state, $3,590; full-time, out-of-state, $11,400* ➡ *estimated additional expenses—$7,850 (room, board, books)* ➡ *scholarships available (academic and need-based)* ➡ *minority scholarships available* ➡ *financial aid available; Federal Free Form (FAFSA) analysis due by March 1*

■ Housing

Housing is available for single and married students in university dormitories. Three private apartment complexes are located across the street from the College of Law building. Information may be obtained from the Director of Housing, 106 Cawthon Hall, Florida State University, Tallahassee, FL 32306.

■ Career Services

The College of Law is staffed with a full-time director of Career Planning & Placement, who assists both students and alumni in obtaining positions and also helps students find part-time and summer jobs. Students have many opportunities to make their talents known before graduation in both clinical programs and part-time work for state agencies, legislators, and law offices.

Applicant Group for the 1993–1994 Academic Year

Florida State University College of Law
This grid includes only applicants who earned 120-180 LSAT scores under standard administrations.

LSAT Score	3.75 +		3.50 -3.74		3.25 - 3.49		3.00 - 3.24		2.75 - 2.99		2.50 - 2.74		2.25 - 2.49		2.00 - 2.24		Below 2.00		No GPA		Total	
	Apps	Adm	Apps	Adm	Apps	Adm	Apps	Adm	Apps	Adm	Apps	Adm	Apps	Adm	Apps	Adm	Apps	Adm	Apps	Adm	Apps	Adm
175 - 180	0	0	1	1	1	1	0	0	0	0	0	0	2	0	0	0	0	0	0	0	4	2
170 - 174	1	1	0	0	2	2	2	1	1	1	8	7	1	0	0	0	0	0	0	0	15	12
165 - 169	3	3	9	9	18	18	22	19	11	8	8	4	6	2	1	0	1	0	2	0	81	63
160 - 164	26	25	44	43	62	53	68	46	36	10	40	3	18	0	3	0	3	0	5	2	305	182
155 - 159	39	37	85	61	120	47	143	25	96	4	64	2	29	1	8	0	2	0	4	0	590	177
150 - 154	38	14	69	9	130	11	131	7	108	9	65	1	37	1	21	0	1	0	5	0	605	52
145 - 149	20	1	48	5	74	2	90	6	91	3	64	2	31	0	16	1	2	0	10	0	446	20
140 - 144	8	3	26	2	43	3	55	3	58	0	35	1	36	0	12	0	3	0	8	0	284	12
135 - 139	1	0	6	0	15	0	15	0	31	0	34	0	21	0	12	0	3	0	5	0	143	0
130 - 134	0	0	4	0	2	0	4	0	9	0	11	0	11	0	2	0	0	0	4	0	47	0
125 - 129	0	0	0	0	2	0	1	0	1	0	3	0	3	0	1	0	0	0	0	0	11	0
120 - 124	0	0	0	0	0	0	0	0	0	0	0	0	0	0	1	0	0	0	0	0	1	0
Total	136	84	292	130	469	137	531	107	442	35	332	20	195	4	77	1	15	0	43	2	2532	520

Apps = Number of Applicants
Adm = Number Admitted
Reflects 95% of the total applicant pool.

Fordham University School of Law

140 West 62nd Street
New York, NY 10023

Phone: 212.636.6810

■ Introduction

Founded in 1841, Fordham University is a private institution, located in New York City, with an enrollment of some 13,000 students. The law school campus is immediately adjacent to Lincoln Center for the Performing Arts, in the heart of Manhattan. Fordham School of Law, founded in 1905, has been a member of the AALS since 1936 and is fully approved by the ABA.

■ Enrollment/Student Body

➡ *4,852 applicants*   ➡ *1,412 admitted first-year class 1993*
➡ *547 enrolled first-year class 1993 (409 full-time, 138 part-time)*   ➡ *1,131 total full-time*   ➡ *372 total part-time*
➡ *20% minority (26% minority first-year class)*
➡ *40% women (40% women first-year class)*
➡ *27 states, the District of Columbia & 4 foreign countries represented*   ➡ *177 colleges and universities represented*

■ Faculty

➡ *187 total*   ➡ *52 full-time*   ➡ *135 part-time or adjunct*   ➡ *12 women full-time, 25 women part-time*
➡ *4 minority full-time, 6 minority part-time*

■ Library and Physical Facilities

➡ *410,690 volumes & equivalents*   ➡ *library hours: Mon.-Fri., 7:00 A.M.-1:00 A.M.; Sat., 8:00 A.M.-1:00 A.M.; Sun., 8:00 A.M.-1:00 A.M.*   ➡ *LEXIS*   ➡ *NEXIS*   ➡ *WESTLAW*
➡ *DIALOG*   ➡ *10 full-time librarians*   ➡ *library seats 510*

In addition to classroom, faculty, and administrative office space, the law school contains a large amphitheater, an atrium for special events and gatherings, a formal moot courtroom, a student lounge, a spacious cafeteria, and a library. The computer center contains 34 DOS-based 386 SX PCs emulated to both LEXIS and WESTLAW, and supported by laser printers and various word processing packages. These PCs run on the law school's LAN and will eventually allow access, through INTERNET, to global information resources, in addition to the law libraries of several New York area law schools. Law students also have access to the University Computing Center, located within steps of the law school building, which contains nearly 100 DOS-based and Apple PCs, in addition to VAX mainframe terminals which run SPSS statistical and other sophisticated mainframe software packages.

■ Curriculum

➡ *Academic Support Program*   ➡ *83 credits required to graduate, of which 45 credits are required courses*
➡ *190 courses available*   ➡ *degrees available: J.D.; J.D./M.B.A.; LL.M.*   ➡ *semesters, start in Aug.*
➡ *range of first-year class size—18-122*

■ Special Programs

An extensive and growing clinical component is offered which includes a Trial Advocacy Program and clinics in litigation, mediation, and prosecution. Externships in federal, state, and city judges' offices, prosecutors' offices, the Legal Aid Society, the ACLU, the Children's Defense Fund, and many other public service settings throughout the city are also offered. A pilot program on lawyering skills introduces first-year students to a broad range of law practice skills, including negotiating, dispute resolution, client counseling, and witness interviewing. The Moot Court Program, considered by faculty to be one of the more important aspects of the student's law training, provides students with opportunities to participate in several intramural competitions as well as a variety of interschool competitions throughout the country.

Fordham Public Service Programs—Fordham's commitment to producing graduates who will devote themselves to the public interest has resulted in the establishment of the Public Interest Resource Center, an administrative support base for the three public interest organizations in operation: The Fordham Law Community Service Project, The Fordham Student Sponsored Fellowship, and Fordham Pro Bono Students. The Stein Institute on Law And Ethics sponsors lectures and seminars throughout the year. The Stein Center for Ethics and Public Interest Law sponsors an annual symposium on current ethical issues; roundtable discussions among practitioners, scholars, and students engaged in public interest law; and the Stein Scholars Program, a three-year program for specially selected law students who will work in public interest law settings and undertake specialized academic work in legal ethics.

The Fordham Center on European Community Law and International Antitrust provides a teaching and resource facility devoted to two overlapping areas of international law: European Community and international antitrust.

Fordham also has a Law School Public Service Loan Forgiveness Program.

■ Admission

➡ *Bachelor's degree from accredited college or university required*
➡ *application deadline—March 1*
➡ *LSAT, LSDAS required*   ➡ *median GPA—3.30*
➡ *median LSAT score—163*   ➡ *application fee—$55*

The selection of students is handled primarily by eight full-time faculty members, the Assistant Dean of Admissions, the Assistant Dean/Registrar, and the Director of Admissions, who together constitute the Admissions Committee. The Admissions Committee determines admissions criteria based on an evaluation of the applicant pool, comparison to the qualifications of recently admitted classes, and the first-year law school performance of the three most recently admitted classes as revealed in first-year performance validity/correlation studies. For the majority of applicants numeric indicators (LSAT score and UGPA) are the principal criteria relied upon, and the majority of admitted students present an LSAT score above the 92nd percentile and a UGPA above a 3.30. Qualitative factors including prior employment, student activities, service to the community, leadership ability, propensity for public service, and communication skills are also considered in selecting the incoming class. The law school makes an aggressive effort to identify and enroll applicants from the African-American, Asian-American, Latino, and Native-American communities, in addition to applicants who are culturally, socially, or economically disadvantaged. Over the past five years the law school has received an average of 5,000 applications annually for approximately 450 seats, and its acceptance rate has ranged from 13.9 percent to 22.9 percent.

■ Student Activities

Students publish five scholarly journals: the *Fordham Law Review*; the *Fordham Urban Law Journal*; the *Fordham International Law Journal*; the *Fordham Environmental Law Journal*; and the *Fordham Intellectual Property, Media, & Entertainment Law Journal*. Each contains lead articles by distinguished members of the profession as well as student notes and comments. These journals are cited in appellate court opinions throughout the country. Other activities and organizations include the American Bar Association, Law Student Division; Amnesty International; Asian-American Law Students Association; Black Law Students Association; Christian Law Students; the Crowley Labor Guild; Fordham Democratic Law Students Association; Fordham Federalist Society; Fordham Follies; Gay and Lesbian Law

Association; Jewish Law Students; Fordham Law Women; Older Law Students Association; Fordham Republican Law Students Association; Latin American Law Students Association; National Lawyers Guild; Phi Alpha Delta Law Fraternity; the *Advocate*; and the yearbook.

■ Expenses and Financial Aid

➼ *tuition & fees—full-time, $17,900; part-time, $13,425*
➼ *almost all aid is need-based, though a small number of donor scholarships are awarded on the basis of merit*
➼ *GAPSFAS and FAFSA required; due early Feb.*

A twenty-story dormitory, with several hundred beds (in two- and three-bedroom apartments) set aside for law students, and located on the Lincoln Center campus, opened in the summer of 1993. Rates for 1993-94 ranged from $5,685 to $6,900 per person, per academic year (single vs. double occupancy bedroom).

■ Career Services

The School of Law maintains a professionally staffed Career Planning Center which assists all students and alumni/ae in determining their career directions and opportunities and in developing effective employment search skills and strategies. Hundreds of law firms, governmental and public service agencies, and corporations interview at the law school each year. Applications are solicited by employers from almost every state. Employment trends for recent graduates have been about as follows: private practice, 68 percent; government and public interest, 11 percent; corporations, 11 percent; judicial clerkships, 9 percent; and academic, 1 percent.

Applicant Group for the 1993–1994 Academic Year

Fordham University School of Law
This grid includes only applicants who earned 120-180 LSAT scores (90% of total applicants).

LSAT Score	Undergraduate GPA									
	2.00 - 2.49		2.50 - 2.99		3.00 - 3.49		3.50 - 4.33		Totals	
	Adm	Apps	Adm	Apps	Adm	Apps	Adm	Apps	Adm	Apps
176 - 180	0	0	5	5	5	5	3	3	13	13
172 - 175	1	1	7	7	26	27	13	13	47	48
168 - 171	5	8	22	27	71	71	36	36	134	142
164 - 167	7	9	66	75	229	229	126	127	428	440
160 - 163	2	23	49	121	229	381	139	200	419	725
156 - 159	5	36	31	181	47	406	11	207	94	830
152 - 155	5	42	39	189	43	337	12	148	99	716
148 - 151	3	54	21	169	28	264	5	91	57	578
120 - 147	1	185	4	312	1	278	3	88	9	863
Total	29	358	244	1086	679	1998	348	913	1300	4355

Apps = Applications Received
Adm = Applications Accepted

Franklin Pierce Law Center

Admissions Office
2 White Street
Concord, NH 03301

Phone: 603.228.9217

■ Introduction

Franklin Pierce Law Center is a private, ABA-approved national law school. Established in 1973 to encourage innovation in legal education, it remains the only law school in New Hampshire.

The Law Center's commitment to innovation in legal education is reflected in its emphasis on individually tailored legal education; a broad range of learning settings including lectures and seminars; real-client clinics, independent study and externships with lawyers and judges; a community spirit of caring and compassion; and, a close working relationship between students and faculty. Self-reliant students who know their own strengths and objectives thrive at Franklin Pierce and find the focus on personal pride and responsibility more motivating than fear, competition, or class rank.

The Law Center is one of the smallest private law schools in the United States. Each entering class numbers approximately 130 students. Classes tend to be small, especially after the first year. Thirty-five of the 50 elective courses enroll 35 or fewer students.

Located in New Hampshire's capital city of Concord (40,000 population), the Law Center is 25 minutes from Manchester, New Hampshire's largest city, and approximately one hour from Boston, the Atlantic seacoast, the state's lake region and the White Mountains.

■ Enrollment/Student Body

➡ *1,769 applicants* ➡ *430 admitted first-year class 1993*
➡ *134 enrolled first-year class 1993* ➡ *394 total full-time*
➡ *3% minority* ➡ *39% women*
➡ *35 states & 4 foreign countries represented*
➡ *201 undergraduate schools represented*

■ Faculty

➡ *51 total* ➡ *24 full-time* ➡ *27 part-time or adjunct*
➡ *12 women*

■ Library and Physical Facilities

➡ *186,000 volumes & equivalents* ➡ *library hours: Mon.-Thurs., 8:00 A.M.-MIDNIGHT; Fri., 8:00 A.M.-10:00 P.M.; Sat., 10:00 A.M.-10:00 P.M.; Sun., 10:00 A.M.-MIDNIGHT*
➡ *LEXIS* ➡ *NEXIS* ➡ *WESTLAW* ➡ *DIALOG*
➡ *4 full-time librarians* ➡ *library seats 200*

It is the largest law library in the state with special strength in intellectual property.

■ Curriculum

➡ *84 credits required to graduate* ➡ *90 courses available*
➡ *degrees available: J.D./Master of Intellectual Property*
➡ *semesters, start in Aug.*
➡ *range of first-year class size—27-134*

■ Special Programs

Intellectual Property—The internationally recognized intellectual and industrial property (patents, licensing, technology transfer, trade secrets, trademarks, and copyrights) specialization is supported by five full-time faculty members who are intellectual property lawyers. The patent specialty, for those with a technological degree or equivalent, exposes students to patent claim drafting, patent application preparation, and U.S. Patent and Trademark Office procedures. These students are prepared for patent practice immediately upon receiving their J.D. degree. Many will have passed the patent bar examination prior to graduation and gained practical intellectual property experience through externships as well as part-time and summer jobs with law firms, corporations, and the U.S. Court of Appeals for the Federal Circuit in Washington, D.C.

Public Interest—The public interest coordinator works with students to tailor the curriculum (coursework, clinical work, and externships) to fit individual interests and assists students with finding summer and full-time employment.

Civil Practice Clinic—The clinic provides an opportunity within the Law Center to acquire skills in relating effectively with clients and advocating their interests in court. Each year approximately 35 second- and third-year students provide legal assistance to county residents who come to the clinic with problems such as divorce, neglect and abuse of children, child support, housing, and debt collection.

Criminal Law—The Appellate Defender Program, housed at the Law Center, gives students the opportunity to prepare briefs for the New Hampshire Supreme Court in criminal cases ranging from disorderly conduct to first-degree murder. Through the Criminal Practice Clinic students represent clients charged with misdemeanor and juvenile offenses in Concord District Court. In addition, many students work closely with trial attorneys in the statewide Public Defender Program as part of externships and summer jobs.

The Institute for Health, Law and Ethics— is a professional collaboration comprised of faculty members from Franklin Pierce Law Center, Dartmouth Medical School, and the University of New Hampshire. In its ongoing effort to encourage understanding and cooperation among the separate disciplines, the Institute provides students with externships, independent study and employment opportunities, working alongside policymakers in provider and legislative settings. Current projects include: development of model policies addressing issues of concern to hospital ethics committees; compilation of a booklet designed to assist guardians state-wide; sponsorship of an expert conference to study the ethical issues raised by the Human Genome Project; Chair to the Institute for Disability Health Care Reform Task

Force; and, exploration of the viability of Alternative Dispute Resolution in the medical malpractice setting.

■ Admission

➡ *B.A. or B.S. degree required* ➡ *application deadline—April 1* ➡ *rolling admissions*
➡ *LSAT, LSDAS required* ➡ *median GPA—3.0*
➡ *median LSAT score—154* ➡ *application fee—$45*

While LSAT scores and grade-point average are, of course, factors that must be considered in the decision-making process, neither alone is determinative.

Our Admissions Committee is composed of members of the faculty, student body, and the Director of Admissions. The committee utilizes the collective wisdom of affording each application a thorough and thoughtful review. The candidate's personal statement, letters of recommendation, and résumé are evaluated along with the "numbers." Community service, employment during college, and other nonacademic accomplishments are given weight to the extent that they reflect initiative, social responsibility, maturity, and other qualities. Franklin Pierce does not discriminate on the basis of age, sex, race, color, religion, national origin, marital status, sexual orientation, or disability, and encourages members of groups underrepresented in the legal profession to seek admission.

■ Student Activities

Students prepare notes and comments for *IDEA: the Journal of Law and Technology*, published by the Center's Patent, Trademark and Copyright Research Foundation; *Risk Issues in Health & Safety*; and *Annual Survey of New Hampshire Law*; an annual publication consisting of six articles focusing principally on recent NH Supreme Court opinions. Articles are written by second-year and edited by third-year students. Student organizations include: the Law Student Cooperative, Public Interest Coalition, Women's Law Caucus, the Environmental Law Society, the International Law Society, In-house Lawyering and BiGALLA (Bisexual, Gay and Lesbian Alliance), SIPLA (Student Intellectual Property Law Association), as well as chapters of the American Trial Lawyers Association, National Lawyers Guild, Phi Alpha Delta Fraternity, and the American Bar Association/Law Students Division.

■ Expenses and Financial Aid

➡ *tuition & fees—$12,100* ➡ *estimated additional expenses—books $600, living expenses $11,200*
➡ *scholarships available; Franklin Pierce Law Center Scholarships, based on need* ➡ *diversity scholarships available—five full-time tuition scholarships for members of underrepresented groups* ➡ *FPLC Financial Aid Application, GAPSFAS required for financial aid—no specific deadline but the later applied for, the less money available*

■ Career Services

The Career Services Center works with students and alumni to find the best match between their skills and interests and changing legal markets. The center provides extensive individual counseling and guidance, brings attorneys to campus to provide first-hand information about the practice of law, advises students of all resources through weekly publications and job boards, coordinates the efforts of faculty, staff and student groups to provide information about and opportunities to gain experience, and conducts outreach to employers about the high quality of students and the practical learning of the Franklin Pierce legal education.

Applicant Group for the 1993–1994 Academic Year

Franklin Pierce Law Center

LSAT Score	GPA								
	3.75 +	3.50 - 3.74	3.25 - 3.49	3.00 - 3.24	2.75 - 2.99	2.50 - 2.74	2.25 - 2.49	2.00 - 2.24	Below 2.00
175 - 180									
170 - 174									
165 - 169									
160 - 164									
155 - 159									
150 - 154									
145 - 149									
140 - 144									
135 - 139									
130 - 134									
125 - 129									
120 - 124									

Good Possibility   Possible   Unlikely

Note: This chart is to be used as a general guide in determining the chances for admittance. Nonnumerical factors are strongly considered for applicants in all three categories.

George Mason University School of Law

3401 N. Fairfax Drive
Arlington, VA 22201-4498

Phone: 703.993.8000

■ Introduction

George Mason University School of Law was established by authority of the Virginia General Assembly in 1979. It is fully accredited by the ABA, and is a member of the AALS.

Recently, GMUSL has been recognized for its pioneering changes in legal education geared to the increasingly specialized and complex fields of practice that now characterize the legal profession.

■ Enrollment/Student Body

➤ *3,200 applicants*   ➤ *824 admitted first-year class 1993*
➤ *251 enrolled first-year class 1993*   ➤ *349 total full-time*
➤ *338 total part-time*   ➤ *12% minority*
➤ *42% women*   ➤ *28 states & foreign countries represented*
➤ *111 undergraduate schools represented*

George Mason University is an Equal Opportunity/Affirmative Action institution.

■ Faculty

➤ *50 total*   ➤ *29 full-time*   ➤ *21 part-time or adjunct*
➤ *7 women*   ➤ *6 minority*

■ Library and Physical Facilities

➤ *260,000 volumes & equivalents*   ➤ *library hours:*
Mon.-Fri., 7:00 A.M.-11:00 P.M.; Sat.-Sun., 8:00 A.M.-10:00 P.M.
➤ *LEXIS*   ➤ *NEXIS*   ➤ *WESTLAW*
➤ *10 full-time librarians*   ➤ *library seats 600*

The school is a member of the library network of the Consortium for Continuing Higher Education in Northern Virginia, affording access to general university and public library collections.

■ Curriculum

➤ *Academic Support Program*   ➤ *87 credits required to graduate*   ➤ *150 courses available*   ➤ *degree available: J.D.*   ➤ *semesters, start in Aug.*

GMUSL has developed five specialized J.D. programs that give our graduates a competitive edge in today's job market. Four are offered in the three-year day division and one is offered in the four-year evening program. In addition, GMUSL offers a standard law school program in both the day and evening division. More than half the student body elects the standard program.

In each program, "Quantitative Methods for Lawyers" is required of all first-year students and provides the methodological and technical tools necessary to handle complex legal problems by offering a concise primer of economics, accounting, and finance needed for modern law practice.

The legal writing, research, and analysis program reflects the law school's emphasis on the development of legal writing skills. Three years of legal writing courses are required in small classes of 15 students.

■ Special Programs

The Corporate and Securities Law Track prepares students to work in a variety of fields related to corporate law and financial markets. By developing a thorough understanding of both law and underlying theory, students are prepared to deal with rapidly changing business and legal environments. This track requires 90 credits for graduation.

The Financial and Real Estate Law Track gives students extensive preparation for practice in the financial services and real estate industries, and a well-rounded general law curriculum. This track curriculum is designed to give students not only the special legal skills appropriate to the field, but also a thorough understanding of the economics of banking and credit creation and the political factors affecting these institutions. Approximately one-third of a student's courses are specialized. This track requires 91 credits.

The International Business Transactions Track prepares students for practice in the rapidly changing global business community, and provides them with a well-rounded legal education emphasizing analytical and writing skills. This track requires 90 credits.

The Litigation Law Track provides an academic program for students interested in litigation and other dispute-resolution processes. This is not a clinical training program. The track curriculum provides an integrated course of study that will prepare lawyers for successful careers in dispute resolution. This track requires 92 credits.

The Patent Law Track is designed for students having a degree in engineering or one of the physical or biological sciences who may want to consider specializing in patent law. The track is a four-year evening division program providing students with a level of expertise usually found only in attorneys with post-J.D. study or several years of experience. This track requires 89 credits.

■ Admission

➤ *Bachelor's degree required*   ➤ *applicatiom deadline—April 1*   ➤ *LSAT, LSDAS required*
➤ *median GPA—3.27*   ➤ *median LSAT score—160*
➤ *application fee—$20*

Admission selection is based primarily upon the applicant's academic background and LSAT score. Also given consideration are the LSAT writing sample, extracurricular activities, employment and professional experience, a personal statement, letters of recommendation, grades from graduate school, and any other information in the file.

■ Student Activities

George Mason University provides many services to enhance the law school experience and enable students to take full advantage of the university's educational and personal enrichment opportunities.

Student activities include the *George Mason University Law Review*, the *George Mason Independent Law Review*, *Civil Rights Law Journal*, a newspaper, a yearbook, and numerous law-related organizations.

Because of the location of the School of Law, students have an unparalleled opportunity to gain experience in such varied settings as the Office of the US Attorney for both the District of Columbia and the Eastern District of Virginia, as well as federal courts and agencies, local governments, and private firms. GMU's Work-Study Program provides eligible students with on-campus jobs. Eligibility is based partly on need.

The Admissions Office and the Student Bar Association maintain information on available housing each summer to acquaint first-year students with housing opportunities.

Minority Student Services, Disability Support Services, and the Office of Veterans Services both provide specialized assistance, as does the Counseling Center, where a staff of professionals helps students to reach personal, social, and academic goals.

The Patriot Center, a 10,000-seat arena, is home to GMU sports events and community programs. The Harris Theater and Center for Performing Arts provide world-class dance, music, and theater performances. The Sports and Recreation Complex offers indoor and outdoor tracks and playing fields, weight room, sauna, and other facilities.

■ Expenses and Financial Aid

➡ *tuition & fees—full-time resident, $6,384; full-time nonresident, $16,212; part-time resident, $228/semester hour; part-time nonresident, $579/semester hour*
➡ *estimated additional expenses—$8,000 minimum*
➡ *merit-based scholarships available up to $6,500*
➡ *Minority Fellowships—$1,000-$6,500*
➡ *financial aid available: FAF; institutional forms; need analysis done on a one-to-one basis*

Law students can apply for Stafford Loans through participating banks and credit unions. Students may also apply for Perkins Loans which are need-based and depend upon eligibility and availability of funds.

A number of fellowships paying up to $6,500 per year are available for students entering the first year. Primary emphasis is on recruiting members of minorities. These fellowships are awarded competitively to students with academic promise.

■ Career Services

The Office of Career Services aids students and alumni in finding permanent, part-time, and summer jobs by serving as a clearinghouse for information on available positions. It also advises on résumé and interview preparation, and coordinates on-campus interviews. The office focuses on providing resources for career planning and development. As many as 150 firms, businesses, and government agencies interview on campus each year. Graduates find employment in the legal profession throughout the country.

Admission Profile Not Available

George Washington University National Law Center

Washington, DC 20052

Phone: 202.994.7230

■ Introduction

Four blocks from the White House and minutes away from Congress, the U.S. Supreme Court, and various federal departments and agencies, the National Law Center offers its students a special opportunity to study and observe lawmaking at its primary source. The National Law Center, established in 1865, is the oldest law school in the District of Columbia. It is a charter member of the AALS and is fully accredited.

The Law Center is part of George Washington University and is located on its campus in downtown Washington. The university, established in 1821, is a private, nonsectarian institution.

■ Enrollment/Student Body

➡ *7,778 applicants* ➡ *1,896 admitted first-year class 1993*
➡ *475 enrolled first-year class 1993* ➡ *1,196 total full-time*
➡ *19% minority* ➡ *40% women*
➡ *86 states & foreign countries represented*
➡ *273 undergraduate schools represented*

The student body of approximately 1,600 is a varied and interesting group. It represents 50 states and numerous foreign countries. In the last few years, the number of women and minorities seeking a law school education has increased greatly; in the 1993 entering class women constitute 42 percent and minorities 21 percent of the enrollment.

George Washington University does not discriminate against any person on the basis of race, color, religion, sex, national origin, age, handicap, or veteran status. This policy covers all programs, services, policies, and procedures of the university, including admission to educational programs and employment. The university is subject to the District of Columbia Human Rights Law.

Inquiries concerning the application of this policy and federal laws and regulations concerning discrimination in education or employment programs and activities may be addressed to Susan B. Kaplan, Special Assistant to the President, George Washington University, Rice Hall, Washington, DC 20052, phone: 202.994.6500, or to the Assistant Secretary for Civil Rights of the Department of Education.

■ Faculty

➡ *196 total* ➡ *75 full-time* ➡ *121 part-time or adjunct*
➡ *42 women* ➡ *14 minority*

The 75 full-time instructors teach all the basic courses in the law school. In addition, there are 121 adjunct instructors, many of whom are eminent government officials and highly regarded experienced practitioners.

■ Library and Physical Facilities

➡ *402,766 volumes & equivalents* ➡ *library hours: Mon.-Fri., 8:00 A.M.-11:45 P.M.; Sat.-Sun., 9:00 A.M.-11:45 P.M.*
➡ *LEXIS* ➡ *NEXIS* ➡ *WESTLAW* ➡ *DIALOG, VUTEXT, ALADIN* ➡ *12 full-time librarians*
➡ *library seats 674*

In the fall of 1984, the Law Center completed a $16.7 million expansion of its physical plant to substantially improve the facilities for future students. The development included an expansion of the Jacob Burns Law Library and the construction of a new classroom building. Its new facilities provide ample room for study, research, and offices. Stockton and Lerner Halls provide classrooms and offices.

■ Curriculum

➡ *Academic Support Program* ➡ *84 credits required to graduate* ➡ *208 courses available* ➡ *degrees available: J.D.; J.D./M.A.; J.D./M.B.A.; J.D./M.P.H.; J.D./M.H.S.A.; J.D./M.P.A.; LL.M.; LL.M./M.P.H.; S.J.D.* ➡ *semesters, start in Aug. & Jan.* ➡ *range of first-year class size—85-110*

The Law Center is one of the largest law schools in the country and offers many courses and programs. A wide variety of courses are offered in public law as well as in the traditional fields of law. Normally, several sections are offered for all required and basic courses. In addition, a large number of advanced and specialized courses in areas of primary interest are scheduled.

The center awards the J.D. degree upon the satisfactory completion of 84 semester hours. This requirement is normally satisfied in three academic years of full-time study. In some cases, summer school offerings permit a student to accelerate by one semester. In addition to the full-time division, admitted applicants may choose to attend the Law Center in a part-time program which normally requires four academic years and one summer session to complete.

■ Special Programs

The National Law Center offers an unusually strong program leading to the J.D. degree and also to the graduate degrees of Master of Law and Doctor of Juridical Science. A unique concentration of courses is available to students in the areas of patent, tax, and government procurement law; international and comparative law; economic regulation, labor, and corporate law; land-use management, and environmental law. All graduate courses are available to qualified J.D. candidates.

The National Law Center also offers a number of courses structured around such contemporary problems as consumer protection and environmental policies. In many courses, students participate actively in the investigation and resolution of legal disputes in addition to reading about them. The Community Legal Clinic, Institute of Law and Aging, Legal Aid Bureau, and Law

Students in Court are examples of these programs. In the Law Students in Court program, third-year students represent clients in both civil and criminal cases under the District of Columbia's third-year practice rule. Students may also take a number of credit hours of clinical work under the close supervision of a faculty member.

■ Admission

➡ *Bachelor's degree required for admission*
➡ *application deadline—Mar. 1*   ➡ *rolling admission*
➡ *LSAT, LSDAS required*   ➡ *median GPA—3.51*
➡ *median LSAT score—163*   ➡ *application fee—$55*

The National Law Center receives approximately 8,000 applications per year for the entering class. The majority of these applicants are undoubtedly qualified for law study, but space limitations compel the Admissions Committee to be highly selective. No inflexible standards are set; rather, the committee seeks to choose those whose undergraduate records and LSAT scores indicate probable success in law study. Other factors considered include the undergraduate school and major, the personal statement of the applicant, and letters of recommendation, if submitted. In addition to the above, the Admissions Committee makes a positive effort to choose those applicants who will bring as broad a diversity of background as possible to the entering class. The committee begins to review completed applications in mid-January and makes decisions on a rolling basis. Decisions are reported to the applicants immediately, whether the decision is to admit, deny, or take no action and hold the applicant's file for later review.

All applicants must receive an undergraduate degree from an accredited school prior to registration. They must take the LSAT and subscribe to LSDAS. Beginning students are admitted only in September.

■ Student Activities

The *George Washington Law Review* is edited and managed by students of the National Law Center. Published five times a year, the Law Review is devoted exclusively to state and federal public law. In addition, a student board publishes the *Journal of Law and Economic Development*.

The law school newspaper, *The Advocate*, is written and published by students. The Legal Aid Bureau, also student run, is particularly active in offering students opportunities to participate in investigation, research, and litigation.

The Student Bar Association, to which all students belong, is represented on committees overseeing the curriculum, library, and other areas. The association sponsors many activities such as the Van Vleck Case Club Competition, special lectures, a book exchange, and social events.

Applicant Group for the 1993–1994 Academic Year

George Washington University National Law Center

GPA	0 - 10		11 - 20		21 - 30		31 - 40		41 - 50		51 - 60		61 - 70		71 - 80		81 - 90		91 - 99	
	Apps	Adm	Apps	Adm	Apps	Adm	Apps	Adm	Apps	Adm	Apps	Adm	Apps	Adm	Apps	Adm	Apps	Adm	Apps	Adm
3.75 - 4.00	3	0	2	0	8	0	8	1	21	2	41	1	17	2	119	43	186	157	113	106
3.50 - 3.74	7	0	12	0	29	0	29	2	71	4	166	13	51	0	308	50	415	338	255	243
3.25 - 3.49	16	0	26	0	52	1	48	3	124	10	230	19	93	5	424	40	536	272	369	314
3.00 - 3.24	35	0	44	0	44	0	45	1	118	16	237	22	67	3	325	19	353	45	271	99
2.75 - 2.99	36	0	58	0	50	0	55	0	100	5	138	11	39	3	153	12	150	7	125	13
2.50 - 2.74	28	0	50	0	58	0	43	1	63	5	78	7	20	2	87	4	61	4	51	3
2.25 - 2.49	37	0	29	0	29	0	22	0	30	2	51	1	7	0	32	0	36	1	19	0
2.00 - 2.24	17	0	10	0	18	0	9	0	13	0	13	0	3	0	8	0	4	0	3	0
Pass/Fail	7	0	10	0	10	0	5	0	9	0	16	0	5	0	14	0	8	0	5	0

LSAT Percentiles

Apps = Number of Applicants
Adm = Number Admitted

Georgetown University Law Center

600 New Jersey Avenue, N.W.
Washington, DC 20001

Phone: 202.662.9010

■ Introduction

The Law Center is ideally situated to take advantage of
the extensive legal resources of Washington. Its proximity to the courts, Congress, government departments,
and administrative agencies provides the Georgetown
student with an atmosphere for creative thought and
learning. The Supreme Court, the District of Columbia's
Judiciary Square, the U.S. Capitol, and the House and
Senate Office buildings are a short walk from the Law
Center. The excellent research facilities of the Library of
Congress are easily accessible. One of the nation's largest
law schools, Georgetown has been a member of the
AALS since 1902 and was approved by the ABA in 1924.

■ Enrollment/Student Body

➧ *8,950 applicants* ➧ *2,040 admitted first-year class 1993*
➧ *643 enrolled first-year class 1993* ➧ *1,547 total full-
time* ➧ *504 total part-time* ➧ *27% minority*
➧ *47% women* ➧ *52 states & foreign countries
represented* ➧ *233 undergraduate schools represented*

Georgetown is proud of the diversity of its student body
and maintains that diversity by actively recruiting
women and those from diverse ethnic, racial, economic,
and educational backgrounds.

■ Faculty

➧ *245 total* ➧ *84 full-time* ➧ *161 part-time or adjunct*
➧ *48 women* ➧ *20 minority*

■ Library and Physical Facilities

➧ *727,709 volumes & equivalents* ➧ *library hours: Mon.-
Fri., 8:00 A.M.-MIDNIGHT; Sat., 9:00 A.M.-10:00 P.M.; Sun.,
10:00 A.M.-MIDNIGHT, extended hours during exams; Reading
Room open until 2:00 A.M.; 24-hours during exams*
➧ *LEXIS* ➧ *NEXIS* ➧ *WESTLAW* ➧ *DIALOG*
➧ *21 full-time librarians* ➧ *library seats 1,270*

The library combines modern information delivery systems with the book collection of a major research library.
Among its volumes are the reported decisions of all federal and state courts as well as federal administrative
tribunals, all federal and state statutes, subscriptions to
over 8,000 serial titles, and a growing collection of treatises. Special collections include a large collection of
microforms with all available Congressional publications, records and briefs of the U.S. Supreme Court and
several other courts, and United Nations documents.

  McDonough Hall, with its lecture halls, seminar rooms,
faculty offices, bookstore and student dining area and
lounges is the academic center of the campus. The Law
Center is accessible to students with disabilities.

■ Curriculum

➧ *Academic Support Program* ➧ *83 credits required to
graduate* ➧ *281 courses available* ➧ *degrees available:
J.D.; J.D./M.B.A.; J.D./M.S.F.S.; J.D./M.P.H.; J.D./Phil.*
➧ *range of first-year class size—20-130*
➧ *100+ graduate courses available to J.D. students*

Day and evening programs are offered leading to the J.D.
degree. Entry to both programs is in the fall. During the
first year, students are enrolled in either the "A" or "B" curriculum. Students in the "A" curriculum begin their
studies with seven courses. The "B" curriculum, available
to one section of full-time students, requires eight different
courses which emphasize the sources of law in history, philosophy, political theory, and economics. It also seeks to
reflect the increasingly public nature of contemporary law.
Electives satisfy the remaining degree requirements. A residency of six semesters is required for full-time students,
eight semesters for part-time.

■ Tutorial Program

The tutorial program is structured to assist first-year
students in analyzing fact patterns, identifying relevant legal issues, briefing cases, and taking class notes. First-year
students who fall within guidelines for participation set by
the faculty are invited to participate in the program. Other
students may be admitted to the program for special reasons upon permission of the Dean. Tutorial groups are
established for each of the five first-year sections. Each
group is coordinated by an upperclass tutor who meets
with participants at least once a week for two hours. Any
unusual learning problem revealed by this process is then
given individual attention.

■ The Writing Center

The Writing Center provides J.D. and graduate students
with assistance on their written work. Senior Writing Fellows at the center provide feedback on making the
transition from another field of expertise, approaching
scholarly writing, using computer technology and word
processing to improve legal research and writing, paying
proper attention to legal citation form and footnotes, and
mastering English grammar.

■ Special Programs

Georgetown Law Center, a pioneer in clinical legal education, offers an unmatched clinical program. Clinical
programs are divided into two categories: (1) actual client representation programs that permit students to
represent people in court or in administrative hearings
and (2) other programs that allow students to participate
in a nontrial context in federal and local agencies,
schools, and other institutions. The Law Center also offers a Public Interest Law Scholars Program that gives
special encouragement, in the form of enriched educa-

tional opportunities, career counseling, and a limited number of summer employment stipends to students who are committed to practice law in the public interest.

■ Admissions

➨ *B.A. or B.S. degree required* ➨ *application deadline—day, Feb. 1; eve., Mar. 1* ➨ *rolling admission, early application encouraged* ➨ *LSAT, LSDAS required* ➨ *median GPA—3.52* ➨ *median LSAT score—166* ➨ *application fee—$60*

Graduation from an accredited college is generally a prerequisite to admission, but mature students with compelling personal circumstances may be admitted after three years of college. Candidates are evaluated on two scales, academic or objective criteria and personal or subjective criteria. Academic information includes undergraduate records and LSAT scores. Personal factors include extracurricular activities, recommendations, work experience, and diversity of background. Other information giving insight into a candidate's potential for successful performance is also considered. Although Georgetown does not use numerical cutoffs, only candidates with strong objective and subjective credentials are encouraged to apply. Upon acceptance, a prospective student must submit a nonrefundable deposit of $100 by April 15.

■ Student Housing

The Gewirz Student Center, opened in the fall of 1993, houses approximately 300 students. Priority for this housing is given to first-year students. The Gewirz Student Center offers a variety of apartment styles with one, two, and three bedrooms. Each resident has a private bedroom. The apartments are air conditioned and each contains a kitchen and bathroom (the three-bedroom apartments have two bathrooms). Some apartments include a separate living room. Also available are apartments designed for students with disabilities.

For those who will not reside on campus, the Office of Student Affairs maintains a listing of available apartments, houses, and rooms to rent. During the summer, the office also offers housing orientation sessions to help students find off-campus accommodations.

■ Student Activities

The Law Center publishes eight student-edited scholarly journals: *Georgetown Journal on Fighting Poverty*; *Georgetown Law Journal*; *Law Policy in International Business*; *Immigration Law Journal*; *American Criminal Law Review*, the official publication of the ABA criminal justice section; *Georgetown Journal of Legal Ethics*; *International Environmental Law Review*; and *Tax Lawyer*, the national publication of the ABA taxation section. The *Georgetown Law Weekly*, the school newspaper, is also printed under student direction. The Barristers' Council is responsible for the many appellate advocacy and trial practice programs, including intraschool and interschool competitions. Through the student bar association and student/faculty committees, students participate in the decision processes of the Law Center. There are over 40 student organizations and legal fraternities.

■ Financial Aid

➨ *tuition & fees—full-time, $18,995; part-time, $650/credit hour* ➨ *estimated additional expenses—$12,455 (room & board, books, transportation, and personal expenses)* ➨ *financial aid available; FAFSA and/or GAPSFAS and institutional application due March 1* ➨ *all GULC aid is need-based, awards combine federal & school loans & scholarships funds*

■ Career Services

Services include on-going counseling/consultation on job-search strategies, career decision-making and résumé writing assistance; interview skills training sessions; programs on law practice, opportunities in the legal profession, and trends in the legal job market; one of the largest on-campus interview programs in the country and off-campus interview opportunities; an extensive print and data resource center; and active current job listing resources.

Admission Profile Not Available

University of Georgia School of Law

Athens, GA 30602-6012   Phone: 706.542.7060

■ Introduction

The University of Georgia School of Law, established in 1859, is on the campus of the nation's first state-chartered university (1785). It is an excellent setting for the study of law with outstanding libraries and academic, cultural, social, and recreational opportunities. Located in Athens, the commercial and legal center for northeast Georgia, the campus is less than an hour from Atlanta. This location enables students to live and study in a university setting yet be in close proximity to one of the nation's outstanding metropolitan areas.

The School of Law is approved by the American Bar Association, is a member of the Association of American Law Schools, and has a chapter of the Order of the Coif.

■ Enrollment/Student Body

➻ *2,335 applicants*   ➻ *477 admitted first-year class 1993*
➻ *241 enrolled first-year class 1993*   ➻ *641 total full-time*
➻ *15% minority*   ➻ *43% women*

■ Faculty

➻ *52 total*   ➻ *39 full-time*   ➻ *13 part-time or adjunct*
➻ *10 women*   ➻ *4 minority*   ➻ *13 endowed chairs*

■ Library and Physical Facilities

➻ *456,000 volumes & equivalents*   ➻ *library hours: Mon.-Fri., 7:30 A.M.-MIDNIGHT; Sat. & Sun., 8:00 A.M.-MIDNIGHT*
➻ *LEXIS*   ➻ *NEXIS*   ➻ *WESTLAW*   ➻ *INFOTRAC*
➻ *9 full-time librarians*   ➻ *library seats 469*

The Law Library is the only library in the Southeast designated as a Specialized European Documentation Center by the European Community.

The university's main library with over 3 million volumes is contiguous. The Institute of Continuing Judicial Education is located in the school; the Institute of Continuing Legal Education is located nearby. The shops, restaurants, and businesses of downtown Athens are about two blocks away.

■ Curriculum

➻ *Academic Support Program, Legal Aid and Defender Clinic, Prosecutorial Clinic, Prisoner Legal Counseling Project, Public Interest Practicum*   ➻ *88 credits required to graduate*
➻ *degrees available: J.D./M.B.A.; J.D./Master of Historic Preservation*   ➻ *semesters, start in Aug.*
➻ *range of first-year class size—44-120*

The required first-year courses provide a basic foundation and are followed by a diverse offering of elective courses during the second and third years of full-time, day study.

Students are offered an outstanding clinical education in criminal and civil procedure. Certified third-year students are permitted to try cases in the civil and criminal courts and to appear before governmental administrative authorities.

International and Comparative Law—While the overall curriculum of the University of Georgia School of Law has gained a national reputation for high quality, the school's reputation as a center for International Law goes beyond national boundaries. The Dean Rusk Center for International and Comparative Law conducts research and policy analyses relating to laws that affect international trade and development. Georgia law students edit and publish the *Georgia Journal of International and Comparative Law*. Summer clerkships with British law firms provide unique educational opportunities as does the annual Brussels Seminar at the University of Brussels.

The School of Law has formal exchange agreements with the University of Regensberg (Germany), Southampton University (Great Britain), and the University of Brussels (Belgium).

Scholarly publications and Moot Court Activities—Georgia law students edit and publish three internationally circulated scholarly journals. The *Georgia Law Review*, the *Georgia Journal of International and Comparative Law*, and the *Journal of Intellectual Property Law*.

Moot Court teams successfully participate in numerous state, regional, and national events. In the last three years, Georgia moot court teams have won three national championships and one world championship.

■ Admission

➻ *Bachelor's degree required*   ➻ *application deadline—March 1*   ➻ *LSAT, LSDAS required*
➻ *median GPA—3.40*   ➻ *median LSAT score—163*
➻ *application fee—$30*

The School of Law seeks to enroll a talented, diverse student body. The Admissions Committee considers admission test scores and grade-point averages significant measures upon which to base admission decisions, but it also recognizes the importance of other components of the applicant's record. In reviewing an applicant's file, the committee members may take into consideration whether the applicant might contribute to the academic, cultural, ethnic, geographical, racial or socio-economic diversity of the Law School.

■ Expenses and Student Financial Aid

➻ *tuition & fees—full-time resident, $2,677; full-time nonresident, $7,221*   ➻ *estimated additional expenses—$7,000 min. (room, board, books, supplies, etc.)*   ➻ *scholarships available*
➻ *minority scholarships available*   ➻ *financial aid available; FAFSA, Free Application for Federal Student Aid required*

Fees include charges for health services, transportation services, and most campus athletic and cultural activities.

School of Law scholarships include Academic Merit Scholarships, such as Founders Scholarships (preference to minority applicants), Tuition Equalization Scholarships which waive the nonresident portion of tuition for nonresident students, and Academic Merit/Financial Need Scholarships. Applications for scholarships are not required for merit-based scholarships awarded by the School of Law.

Candidates are encouraged to complete admission application files by January 31 to ensure full consideration for all merit awards.

Candidates who may demonstrate financial need are encouraged to contact the University Office of Student Financial Aid regarding student loans and other student financial aid programs. Applications for Regents Opportunity Scholarships for minority and economically disadvantaged applicants are available in late spring.

The University of Georgia participates in several federally funded student loan programs including Perkins Loans, Stafford Loans, and Supplemental Loans for Students (SLS). The Law Access Loan (LAL) is also available.

Limited part-time employment may be available on- or off-campus; however, first-year law students are not encouraged to work.

■ Housing

Law students may reside in university residence halls and family housing units. Students desiring university housing are encouraged to make early application.

Most law students choose to live in nearby off-campus rental units. Ample housing opportunities are available in Athens at rates below those in typical metropolitan areas.

■ Student Activities

Students participate in School of Law governance through the Student Bar Association and by way of representation on faculty and administrative committees. Intramural sports are available through law school leagues.

Student interest organizations are active on campus. The Equal Justice Foundation provides financial assistance to University of Georgia law clerks serving the public interest.

■ Legal Career Services

The School of Law maintains a Legal Career Services Office to assist students and alumni with employment matters. Alumni and faculty members actively support the employment efforts of the students.

Services of the Legal Career Services Office range from coordinating on-campus interviews and career seminars to an outreach program including participation in one of the most successful off-campus interview consortium programs in the United States.

In the past five years, an average of greater than 92 percent of the graduates have reported successful placement within six months of graduation.

The average first-time bar passage rate for Georgia graduates exceeds 94 percent over the last several years.

Applicant Group for the 1993–1994 Academic Year

University of Georgia School of Law
This grid includes only applicants who earned 120-180 LSAT scores under standard administrations.

LSAT Score	3.75 +		3.50 - 3.74		3.25 - 3.49		3.00 - 3.24		2.75 - 2.99		2.50 - 2.74		Below 2.50		No GPA		Total	
	Apps	Adm	Apps	Adm	Apps	Adm	Apps	Adm	Apps	Adm	Apps	Adm	Apps	Adm	Apps	Adm	Apps	Adm
180 - 175	1	1	1	1	3	3	1	1	0	0	0	0	0	0	0	0	6	6
174 - 170	4	3	3	3	10	10	8	8	3	1	4	1	1	0	0	0	33	26
169 - 165	15	15	31	31	47	47	32	30	32	12	16	2	9	0	0	0	182	137
164 - 160	40	28	56	34	125	69	115	52	64	13	44	1	19	0	1	1	464	198
159 - 155	48	19	94	22	152	9	146	7	66	1	53	0	33	0	1	0	593	58
154 - 150	28	5	82	6	96	5	103	2	76	8	60	0	39	1	2	0	486	27
149 - 145	8	2	31	4	47	7	51	1	59	1	43	3	46	0	4	1	289	19
144 - 140	0	0	11	1	25	4	23	1	27	0	42	0	42	0	0	0	170	6
Below 140	0	0	2	0	5	0	11	0	12	0	15	0	32	0	0	0	77	0
No LSAT	0	0	0	0	0	0	0	0	0	0	0	0	0	0	35	0	35	0
Total	144	73	311	102	510	154	490	102	339	36	277	7	221	1	43	2	2335	477

Apps = Number of Applicants
Adm = Number Admitted

Georgia State University College of Law

P.O. Box 4049
Atlanta, GA 30302-4049

Phone: 404.651.2048

■ Introduction

Georgia State University College of Law is located in downtown Atlanta, the center of legal, financial, and governmental activities in the Southeast. This location provides easy access to federal, state, and local courts and agencies, the State Capitol, legislature, corporations, major law firms in the metropolitan area, and the library and other facilities of Georgia State University.

The College of Law began operation in 1982 and is fully accredited by the American Bar Association.

■ Enrollment/Student Body

➥ *2,859 applicants*   ➥ *457 admitted first-year class 1993*
➥ *195 enrolled first-year class 1993*   ➥ *378 total full-time*
➥ *244 total part-time*   ➥ *21% minority*
➥ *50% women*   ➥ *30 states & foreign countries represented*
➥ *98 undergraduate schools represented*

■ Faculty

➥ *41 total*   ➥ *37 full-time*   ➥ *4 part-time or adjunct*
➥ *16 women*   ➥ *5 minority*

■ Library and Physical Facilities

➥ *220,327 volumes & equivalents*   ➥ *library hours: Mon.-Fri., 7:00 A.M.-11:00 P.M.; Sat., 9:00 A.M.-9:00 P.M.; Sun., NOON-11:00 P.M.*   ➥ *LEXIS*   ➥ *NEXIS*
➥ *WESTLAW*   ➥ *DIALOG*   ➥ *OLLI*
➥ *6 full-time librarians*   ➥ *library seats 325*

Georgia State University College of Law is one of the leading law schools in the Southeast. Located on a 25-acre campus in the heart of downtown Atlanta, the College of Law building houses a moot courtroom equipped with state-of-the-art video technology and provides activities directed toward trial and appellate advocacy. Students have access to many other campus facilities including the athletic complex, which offers a variety of individual fitness opportunities and team sports.

■ Curriculum

➥ *Academic Enrichment Program*   ➥ *Summer Skills Program*   ➥ *90 total credits required to graduate*
➥ *202 courses available*   ➥ *degrees and combined degrees available: J.D.; J.D./M.B.A.*   ➥ *semesters, start in Aug.*
➥ *range of first-year class size—16-133*

Other: The College of Law offers both a full-time, six-semester program and a part-time, nine-semester program leading to the degree of Juris Doctor. In addition, speakers such as Supreme Court Justices Sandra Day O'Connor and Antonin Scalia, International Court Judge Stephen Schwebel, U.S. Court of Appeals Judge Leon Higgenbotham, Derrick Bell and others enrich our program. A six-day orientation program introduces first-year students to the study of law.

■ Special Programs

Tax Law Clinic—The Tax Law Clinic permits students to assist individual clients to prepare their cases for presentation before the Small Claims Division of U.S. Tax Court and before the Appeals Office of the Internal Revenue Service. Under appropriate supervision, students will provide advice in a wide range of matters arising in regard to the Internal Revenue Code. Students will interview clients, research legal issues, analyze facts, and prepare protests and petitions.

Externships—Externships are designed to tie theoretical knowledge to a practical base of experience in the profession. Externships involve actual participation in rendering legal services. Enrollment may be limited and may involve a selection process. Students interested in the externship program should contact the Lawyer Skills Development Office.

Trial Advocacy—Trial advocacy has several components. The first is the required second-year litigation course, which is offered in the spring semester. Second, after completing the second-year required course, students may take advanced advocacy seminars in the areas of civil and criminal litigation. Finally, students may become members of the Student Trial Lawyer Association (STLA) and the National Association of Criminal Defense Law Student Division. The STLA annually sponsors student advocate teams in the ATLA Trial Competition and the Georgia Intrastate Trial Competition. As a result of the impressive performance of our trial advocacy teams, Georgia State University's College of Law was identified as having one of the top 16 trial advocacy programs in the country and was invited to the 1989, 1990, 1991, 1992, and 1993 National Invitational Trial Competition Tournament of Champions. In 1989 and 1993, a GSU College of Law student was selected Best Advocate at the NITT competition. In 1990 our team finished fourth, and in 1992 and 1993 we placed second in the nation.

Moot Court—The Moot Court Society consists of second- and third-year students who have distinguished themselves in appellate advocacy and who are interested in achieving excellence in brief writing and oral advocacy. The society competes in numerous national and regional competitions. In addition, members prepare the case, problems and trial briefs for the appellate advocacy course competitions and serve as judges and brief graders in the Appellate Court competition. In its first 11 years, the College of Law has fielded teams that have won the Intrastate Competition, the regional NAAC and National Moot Court competitions, the 1988 National Championship in the National Moot Court Competition sponsored by the Association of the Bar of the City of New York, and the 1990 and 1992 Wagner Cup National Labor Law Competition.

■ Admission

➡ *Bachelor's degree from accredited college or university required* ➡ *application deadline—April 1, rolling admissions policy beginning in Jan., early application is encouraged* ➡ *LSAT, LSDAS required* ➡ *median GPA—3.12* ➡ *median LSAT score—159* ➡ *application fee—$10*

The College of Law of Georgia State University actively seeks to enroll a student body with diversity in educational, cultural, and racial backgrounds that will enrich the educational experience of the entire group.

Applicants are encouraged to visit the College of Law. Please make arrangements through the Admissions Office to tour the campus; talk with students, faculty and admissions staff; or attend a class.

■ Student Activities

The *Georgia State University Law Review* is published four times a year by students who have demonstrated outstanding writing and academic skills.

Student organizations include Activating Awareness for Choice and Equality, Association of Women Law Students, Black Law Students Association, Christian Legal Society, Delta Theta Phi Law Fraternity, Environmental Law Society, Federalist Society, International Law Society, Jewish Student Association, GSU Criminal Defense Lawyers Association, GSU Public Interest Law, Lesbian and Gay Law Student Association, National Lawyers Guild, Phi Delta Phi Law Fraternity, Phi Alpha Delta Law Fraternity, Student Trial Lawyers' Association, and Student Bar Association.

■ Expenses and Financial Aid

➡ *tuition & fees—full-time resident, $2,632/year; full-time nonresident, $7,500; part-time resident, $1,700; part-time nonresident, $4,734* ➡ *estimated additional expenses—$7,000 (room, board, books)* ➡ *minority scholarships available* ➡ *performance- and need-based scholarships available* ➡ *financial aid available—Fee Application for Federal Student Aid form preferred*

■ Career Services

The Career Planning Office offers a broad range of services including individual career counseling, educational programs about career options, workshops to assist in the development of job-search skills, networking programs, current job listing services, on-campus interviews, and job fairs. Students may begin using the Career Planning Office in November of the first year of law school, and may continue utilizing career planning services throughout their careers. Specific programs geared toward minority students are the Atlanta Bar Association Minority Clerkship Program and the Southeastern Minority Job Fair.

Applicant Group for the 1993–1994 Academic Year

Georgia State University College of Law
This grid includes only applicants who earned 120-180 LSAT scores under standard administrations.

LSAT Score	GPA 3.75 +		3.50 -3.74		3.25 - 3.49		3.00 - 3.24		2.75 - 2.99		2.50 - 2.74		2.25 - 2.49		2.00 - 2.24		Below 2.00		No GPA		Total	
	Apps	Adm	Apps	Adm	Apps	Adm	Apps	Adm	Apps	Adm	Apps	Adm	Apps	Adm	Apps	Adm	Apps	Adm	Apps	Adm	Apps	Adm
175 - 180	0	0	0	0	1	1	0	0	0	0	0	0	0	0	0	0	0	0	0	0	1	1
170 - 174	2	2	0	0	3	3	2	0	3	2	1	1	0	0	0	0	0	0	0	0	11	8
165 - 169	4	3	6	6	8	8	11	9	10	8	6	5	5	2	2	0	1	0	1	1	54	42
160 - 164	11	9	19	19	37	33	54	40	41	19	41	13	24	7	6	1	2	0	5	2	240	143
155 - 159	19	14	47	29	82	33	141	36	111	14	58	5	39	1	12	0	1	0	4	0	514	132
150 - 154	17	4	58	9	95	9	145	12	139	8	94	5	63	2	22	0	4	0	11	3	648	52
145 - 149	4	0	27	1	68	9	117	6	105	5	96	3	51	3	23	0	5	0	9	2	505	29
140 - 144	3	1	11	0	39	4	58	3	78	0	73	0	51	0	33	1	6	0	20	0	372	9
135 - 139	1	0	3	0	9	0	30	0	33	0	51	0	32	0	26	0	8	0	18	0	211	0
130 - 134	0	0	3	0	2	0	11	0	15	0	15	0	17	0	17	0	6	0	9	0	95	0
125 - 129	0	0	0	0	0	0	2	0	3	0	6	0	8	0	2	0	4	0	4	0	29	0
120 - 124	0	0	0	0	0	0	0	0	3	0	0	0	2	0	1	0	0	0	2	0	8	0
Total	61	33	174	64	344	100	571	106	541	56	441	32	292	15	144	2	37	0	83	8	2688	416

Apps = Number of Applicants
Adm = Number Admitted
Reflects 94% of the total applicant pool.

Golden Gate University School of Law

536 Mission Street
San Francisco, CA 94105

Phone: 415.442.6630

■ Introduction

Founded in 1901, Golden Gate University School of Law is located in the heart of San Francisco's legal and financial district. The law school is noted for integrating practical skills training with legal theory. Golden Gate has a distinguished faculty who share a strong commitment to both excellence in teaching and accessibility to students.

The school is accredited by the ABA and is a member of the AALS.

■ Enrollment/Student Body

➡ *2,851 fall applicants* ➡ *1,401 admitted fall first-year class 1993* ➡ *237 enrolled fall first-year class 1993*
➡ *527 total full-time* ➡ *213 total part-time*
➡ *26% minority* ➡ *50% women*
➡ *34 states & foreign countries represented*
➡ *249 undergraduate schools represented*

■ Faculty

➡ *109 total* ➡ *29 full-time* ➡ *80 part-time or adjunct*
➡ *33 women* ➡ *12 minority*

■ Library Facilities

➡ *200,000 total volumes & equivalents* ➡ *LEXIS*
➡ *WESTLAW* ➡ *CALI* ➡ *12 full-time librarians*
➡ *library seats 350*

■ Curriculum

➡ *86 total required credits* ➡ *122 courses available*
➡ *Academic Assistance Program*

Entering students are provided with an orientation that introduces them to study techniques as well as an overview of what the practice of law is like. Because writing is the lawyer's basic tool, the law school trains students to master the skills needed to draft a wide array of legal documents. The law school also provides students with additional instruction in legal analysis and exam-writing through its Academic Assistance Program.

■ Special Programs

Program Options—The law school offers both full-time and part-time programs. The full-time program normally involves three years of study; the part-time evening program takes four years. Golden Gate also offers mid-year admission, thus allowing students to begin law school in January.

Combined Degrees—The law school, in conjunction with the university's graduate programs in management, finance, taxation, accounting, and public administration, offers one of the most extensive combined-degree programs in the nation, which allow a student to pursue simultaneously a law degree and a master's degree in a related field.

Specialty Areas—The law school's curriculum offers students the opportunity to concentrate in one of many specialty areas, including corporate and commercial law, criminal law, entertainment law, environmental law, intellectual property law, labor and employment law, real estate development, or public-interest law.

Students may also earn Certificates of Specialization in International Law and Public Interest Law. Each certificate evidences completion of core courses and significant clinical or practical experience in the specialty area.

Each summer, Golden Gate offers courses focusing on Pacific Rim issues in Bangkok, Thailand, in cooperation with Chulalongkorn University. The law school also has a summer program housed at Europe's oldest university, the University of Bologna. Golden Gate graduates are eligible to participate in a student exchange program with the University of Paris at Nanterre.

Students who enroll in the Public Interest Law Program work with the Public Interest Clearinghouse, which places students with interest groups and agencies throughout the San Francisco Bay Area. The law school also offers a public interest loan forgiveness program for graduates who obtain employment in public-interest law.

The Environmental Law Program includes basic courses in Environmental Law, but also offers clinical opportunities and advanced seminars in such areas as Hazardous Site Liability, International Environmental Law, California Environmental Law, and Race, Poverty and the Environment.

The law school also houses the Graduate Program in Taxation, which offers an LL.M. in Taxation. Students who are working toward the J.D. and wish to concentrate in tax law may takes courses offered in the LL.M. program.

Advocacy Training—The law school offers an advocacy and dispute resolution curriculum that is one of the most comprehensive in the country. Its nationally-recognized litigation program trains students in every aspect of litigation, from the pre-trial thinking and planning stages, to the techniques of trial, to the appellate review of a case. Students with a serious interest in litigation may participate in trial advocacy and appellate advocacy competitions. Over the past several years, the law school's teams have won four regional championships in trial competitions and were semi-finalists in six others.

Besides learning courtroom tactics, Golden Gate students may learn techniques of mediation and arbitration in Alternative Dispute Resolution. Students also receive training in the skills of client counseling and negotiating.

Clinics and Externships—Clinical programs, both on-site and field placement, are an integral part of the curriculum at Golden Gate. Through these programs, students may earn academic credit while working closely with attorneys.

The law school houses two legal clinics. In the Women's Rights Clinic, students represent low-income women with employment-related problems. The Constitutional Law

Clinic, established in 1976 as part of the Western Center for Constitutional Rights, enables students to work on civil rights cases focusing on health care issues of institutionalized persons.

Students may also receive credit for participating in the Judicial Externship Program, which places students with judges on the California Supreme Court, federal district courts, and the California state appellate and superior courts.

■ Admission

➡ *Bachelor's degree required* ➡ *April 15 deadline for fall, Nov. 15 for midyear* ➡ *median GPA—3.14* ➡ *median LSAT score—158* ➡ *application fee—$40*

Admission is competitive. The Admission Committee considers applicants' undergraduate GPA, LSAT score, and information contained in their personal statement. The committee also weighs such factors as graduate work, social and economic background, and personal and employment accomplishments.

■ Minority Students

Applications from minority students and other underrepresented groups are encouraged and given special attention. Golden Gate participates in the CLEO Program and offers a summer Conditional Admissions Program designed to enhance the achievement of minority students. The law school works closely with minority student groups regarding issues such as admissions, academic assistance, and placement. In October 1993, the law school received the California Minority Counsel Program's Second Annual Law School Racial and Ethnic Diversity Commitment Award.

■ Student Activities and Scholarship

The law school has over fifteen student organizations, which range from groups representing minority students to groups focusing on specific areas of the law. In addition, a student editorial board publishes three issues of the *Golden Gate University Law Review* annually. In 1994, the law school began publishing the *Annual Survey of International and Comparative Law*.

■ Expenses and Financial Aid

➡ *tuition & fees—full-time, $14,554; part-time, $10,109* ➡ *estimated additional expenses—$10,000 (housing, transportation, insurance, books, food)* ➡ *financial aid available* ➡ *FAFSA, FAF, FAAP, Financial Aid Transcripts, and SAR due March 1 for priority*

Approximately 80 percent of the student body receives some form of financial aid. Golden Gate awards merit scholarships to many highly-qualified entering students. Last year, Merit Scholarships ranged in amount from $6,000 to full tuition. In addition, the law school participates in federally subsidized and private loan programs.

■ Placement

The Career Services Office maintains listings of summer, part-time, and permanent positions and organizes on- and off-campus recruiting programs.

Applicant Group for the 1993–1994 Academic Year

Golden Gate University School of Law
This grid includes only applicants who earned 120-180 LSAT scores under standard administrations.

LSAT Score	3.75 +		3.50 -3.74		3.25 - 3.49		3.00 - 3.24		2.75 - 2.99		2.50 - 2.74		2.25 - 2.49		2.00 - 2.24		Below 2.00		No GPA		Total	
	Apps	Adm	Apps	Adm	Apps	Adm	Apps	Adm	Apps	Adm	Apps	Adm	Apps	Adm	Apps	Adm	Apps	Adm	Apps	Adm	Apps	Adm
175 - 180	0	0	0	0	2	2	0	0	0	0	0	0	0	0	0	0	0	0	0	0	2	2
170 - 174	0	0	1	1	1	1	4	4	1	1	2	2	0	0	1	1	0	0	1	1	11	11
165 - 169	0	0	4	4	8	8	7	7	10	10	11	11	7	7	4	2	0	0	3	1	54	50
160 - 164	11	11	19	18	32	30	45	44	41	39	33	30	29	16	6	1	1	1	4	4	221	194
155 - 159	11	11	38	38	87	86	130	116	137	91	86	27	55	12	20	5	3	0	8	4	575	390
150 - 154	12	11	50	40	143	85	206	64	196	38	118	27	77	7	20	1	5	1	21	6	848	280
145 - 149	9	3	25	12	80	24	139	22	142	17	127	2	64	1	26	0	3	0	18	5	633	86
140 - 144	6	2	16	2	34	7	57	7	83	4	81	3	49	2	20	0	2	0	13	2	361	29
135 - 139	0	0	3	1	12	2	21	1	21	2	29	2	30	0	15	0	3	0	7	1	141	9
130 - 134	0	0	0	0	1	0	7	0	5	0	10	0	13	0	5	0	4	0	4	0	49	0
125 - 129	0	0	0	0	0	0	0	0	1	0	0	0	0	0	3	0	1	0	3	0	8	0
120 - 124	0	0	0	0	0	0	0	0	0	0	1	0	0	0	0	0	0	0	0	0	1	0
Total	49	38	156	116	400	245	616	265	637	202	498	104	324	45	120	10	22	2	82	24	2904	1051

Apps = Number of Applicants
Adm = Number Admitted
Reflects 94% of the total applicant pool.

Gonzaga University School of Law

Box 3528
Spokane, WA 99220

Phone: 509.328.4220
Phone: Toll-free: 800.572.9658 WA residents, 800.523.9712 Continental US

■ Introduction

Gonzaga University School of Law belongs to a long and distinguished tradition of humanistic, Catholic, and Jesuit education. It is an integral part of Gonzaga University, which was founded in 1887 and continues to maintain the tradition of academic excellence in education that is at the heart of the mission of the 450-year-old Jesuit order. The School of Law was established in 1912. The campus is located in Spokane, a four-season city with the Spokane River flowing through its center. The city of 170,000 serves as the regional hub of the Inland Northwest, a large area running from the Cascade Mountains in the west to the Rockies in the east. Canada is a mere 100 miles to the north.

Spokane is not only an economic hub for manufacturing, agriculture, and light industry, but it is also a recreational sports area abundant with lakes, mountains, and forests. In minutes you can get away from the city's robust, rapidly growing business community to the surrounding pine-covered hills, where there is an evergreen splendor unlike any place in America.

■ Enrollment/Student Body

➡ *1,919 applicants*   ➡ *738 admitted first-year class 1993*
➡ *194 enrolled first-year class 1993*   ➡ *541 total full-time*
➡ *15 total part-time*   ➡ *7% minority*   ➡ *38% women*
➡ *40 states & foreign countries represented*   ➡ *218 undergraduate schools represented*   ➡ *average age—27*

■ Faculty

➡ *43 total*   ➡ *33 full-time*   ➡ *10 part-time or adjunct*
➡ *12 women*

The faculty are committed to teaching excellence and are eager to develop student abilities through classroom and personal instruction—and they are accessible and approachable.

■ Library and Physical Facilities

➡ *196,150 volumes & equivalents*   ➡ *library hours: Mon.-Thurs., 8:00 A.M.-MIDNIGHT; Fri., 8:00 A.M.-9:00 P.M.; Sat., 9:00 A.M.-9:00 P.M.; Sun., 8:00 A.M.-MIDNIGHT*   ➡ *LEXIS*
➡ *NEXIS*   ➡ *WESTLAW*   ➡ *DIALOG, CARL*
➡ *5 full-time librarians*   ➡ *library seats 285*

Students also have access to campus facilities such as the Foley Center, a new 137,000 square foot high-technology library; the University Health and Counseling Centers; the Student Union; and the Martin Athletic Centre, complete with indoor running track, full-sized pool, state-of-the-art weight room, dance studio, basketball/volleyball courts, and racquetball courts.

■ Curriculum

➡ *Academic Support Program*   ➡ *90 credits required to graduate*   ➡ *75 courses available*   ➡ *degrees available: J.D./M.B.A.*   ➡ *semesters, start in Aug.*   ➡ *range of Legal Writing sections—15-20*

There is a deliberate and delicate balance to legal education at Gonzaga. The rigorous, full, and rounded curriculum focuses on legal analysis, problem solving, values, and ethics. Equally as important is the emphasis on practical experience to develop real-world lawyering skills. Beyond the required courses, students are free to tailor their studies to areas of interest.

The School of Law offers a favorable student-to-faculty ratio and an emphasis on positive rather than negative competition.

■ Special Programs

The first year of coursework is devoted to building a strong legal foundation for upper-division study. In order to ease the transition to the rigorous demands of law school, entering students may take advantage of the support offered through the student and attorney mentor programs, academic advisors, and special tutorials.

A joint program leading to the J.D./M.B.A. degree is offered to prepare students who anticipate careers in corporate law and other fields that require thorough knowledge of both business and the law. Application must be made to the School of Business as well as to the School of Law.

An added dimension to the legal education for many Gonzaga law students is the opportunity to practice law while in school through the award-winning clinical law program.

■ Admission

➡ *Bachelor's degree required for admission*   ➡ *application deadline—March 15*   ➡ *LSAT, LSDAS required*
➡ *median GPA—3.16*   ➡ *median LSAT score—154*
➡ *application fee—$30*

The School of Law endeavors to attract students with ambitious minds, professional motivation, and commitment to the highest ethics and values of the legal profession and to public service. A faculty committee reviews all applications. The consideration of applicants is not restricted to impersonal statistics. The enriching qualities of applicants such as work and life experiences, personal accomplishment, and opinions of others reflected in letters of recommendation will be considered.

The School of Law seeks to enroll a diverse student body to assure that the school and the legal profession are enriched through the participation of people from different cultural and ethnic backgrounds. Those individuals who desire diversity factors to be considered in their admission decision should include it in their application.

Students who have completed 45 semester credits or their equivalent or less and who are in good standing at another ABA law school may apply for admission to the School of Law with advanced standing.

Special Admission Program—The School of Law offers special acceptance to a limited number of applicants who do not meet regular admissions requirements, but whose application file suggests there may be potential for success beyond what the statistics would normally predict. There is no special application procedure for this program, and applicants will be considered automatically. Those accepted will be admitted to a special summer program, which will consist of 10 weeks commencing the summer before entrance into the first year. Students who are successful in the summer program will continue with their studies in the fall semester.

■ Student Activities

Students find it easy to become involved in a broad range of activities at the School of Law. Gonzaga is a major player in moot court competition through five moot court teams. The student-run *Gonzaga Law Review*, more than 28 years in existence, is circulated throughout the country. The award-winning Student Bar Association is a strong, active organization which encourages student involvement. There is also an opportunity to participate in intraschool moot court competition, two legal fraternities, and other numerous organizations and activities.

Law students, representing many cultural heritages, join together in the Multi-Cultural Law Caucus to provide a support network on campus and in the Spokane community for those students of diverse backgrounds.

■ Housing

The Gonzaga campus is in a residential area with housing within walking distance to the School of Law. Rental housing rates are reasonably priced compared to larger population centers.

■ Expenses and Financial Aid

➡ *tuition & fees—full-time, $13,175 (30 credits per year); part-time, $8,500 (20 credits per year)* ➡ *estimated additional expenses—$11,150 (books, $850; room and board, $6,400; personal, $2,950; transportation, $950)* ➡ *academic and need-based scholarships available* ➡ *minority scholarships available: Patricia Roberts Harris Fellowship* ➡ *financial aid available; FAFSA (needed for all types) due May 1* ➡ *loans available—Stafford, SLS, LAL*

Law school is a career investment. For the tuition, fees, and other costs incurred to attend Gonzaga University, each student is offered an opportunity for a quality legal education and a rewarding legal career. For those who need financial assistance to help fund this investment, Gonzaga University will assist in identifying and obtaining financial aid packages.

■ Career Services

The active Career Services Office is dedicated to assisting law students and alumni in planning careers and seeking employment throughout law school and in the course of their professional career. The size of the school allows the Career Services Director the opportunity to work individually with students and alumni in their job searches. Entering students are pleased to learn Gonzaga participates in federal and state work-study programs and provides interns to more than 200 Spokane law firms and numerous government agencies.

Applicant Group for the 1993–1994 Academic Year

Gonzaga University School of Law
This grid includes only applicants who earned 120-180 LSAT scores under standard administrations.

LSAT Score	3.75 +		3.50 -3.74		3.25 - 3.49		3.00 - 3.24		2.75 - 2.99		2.50 - 2.74		2.25 - 2.49		2.00 - 2.24		Below 2.00		No GPA		Total	
	Apps	Adm	Apps	Adm	Apps	Adm	Apps	Adm	Apps	Adm	Apps	Adm	Apps	Adm	Apps	Adm	Apps	Adm	Apps	Adm	Apps	Adm
175 - 180	0	0	0	0	0	0	0	0	0	0	0	0	0	0	0	0	0	0	0	0	0	0
170 - 174	0	0	2	2	0	0	2	2	0	0	3	2	0	0	0	0	0	0	0	0	7	6
165 - 169	2	2	1	1	4	4	9	9	7	7	2	2	3	3	3	3	0	0	0	0	31	31
160 - 164	4	4	7	6	12	12	22	22	17	15	9	9	8	5	2	0	1	1	0	0	82	74
155 - 159	12	11	34	34	38	37	73	72	69	56	31	20	28	8	7	1	3	0	2	0	297	239
150 - 154	5	5	36	34	89	73	138	89	107	40	72	16	38	8	9	1	3	0	6	3	503	269
145 - 149	7	5	31	18	89	21	110	19	99	12	65	8	29	1	16	0	1	0	2	0	449	84
140 - 144	2	0	18	5	26	2	47	1	47	3	46	3	20	2	8	0	3	0	1	0	218	16
135 - 139	2	0	2	0	7	0	18	0	17	0	25	1	11	0	5	0	1	0	3	0	91	1
130 - 134	0	0	1	0	2	0	3	0	7	0	6	0	7	0	3	0	1	0	1	0	31	0
125 - 129	0	0	0	0	0	0	0	0	0	0	2	0	0	0	0	0	1	0	1	0	5	0
120 - 124	0	0	0	0	0	0	0	0	0	0	0	0	0	0	0	0	0	0	0	0	0	0
Total	34	27	132	100	267	149	422	214	370	133	261	61	145	27	53	5	14	1	16	3	1714	720

Apps = Number of Applicants
Adm = Number Admitted
Reflects 95% of the total applicant pool.

Hamline University School of Law

1536 Hewitt Avenue
St. Paul, MN 55104

Phone: 612.641.2461 or 800.388.3688

■ Introduction

Hamline University School of Law is committed to providing personal, socially responsive, comprehensive legal education. Law students are afforded the intellectual and social advantages of participation in the larger community of Hamline University with its rich heritage dating back to 1854. The School of Law is the only private, university-affiliated law school in the state, and is a member of the Association of American Law Schools. The beautiful 30-acre Hamline campus is located in a residential neighborhood midway between the downtowns of St. Paul and Minneapolis. The Twin Cities of St. Paul and Minneapolis are frequently cited as two of the nations "most liveable" cities. Thirty-nine of the largest businesses in Fortune magazine are headquartered here, and the state capital is just minutes away from the campus. From the Tony Award-winning Guthrie Theatre, to the Hubert H. Humphrey Metrodome, home to the 1991 World Series Champion Minnesota Twins, to the 54 miles of scenic pathways linking lakes and parks, the Twin Cities offer something for everyone.

■ Enrollment/Student Body

➡ *1,586 applicants*   ➡ *665 admitted first-year class 1993*
➡ *226 enrolled first-year class 1993*   ➡ *603 total full-time*
➡ *28 average age first-year class 1993*   ➡ *10% minority*
➡ *45% women*   ➡ *44 states & foreign countries represented (including District of Columbia)*
➡ *185 undergraduate schools represented*

■ Faculty

➡ *29 full-time faculty*   ➡ *44 part-time or adjunct*
➡ *19 women*   ➡ *10 minority*   ➡ *5 legal writing instructors*

88 practicum mentor-attorneys bring the experience of their day-to-day practice into the educational program.

■ Library and Physical Facilities

➡ *204,000 volumes & equivalents*   ➡ *cooperative borrowing between local law libraries and local college libraries*
➡ *LEXIS*   ➡ *NEXIS*   ➡ *WESTLAW*   ➡ *DIALOG*
➡ *5 full-time librarians*   ➡ *library seats 360*
➡ *computerized catalog system which also searches the holdings of local university and reference libraries*

The School of Law is accessible to persons with disabilities and housed in a modern, award-winning law center.

■ Curriculum

➡ *Academic Support Program*   ➡ *88 units/credits required to graduate*   ➡ *120 courses available*   ➡ *combined degrees available: J.D./M.A.P.A. (Master of Arts in Public Administration); J.D./M.B.A. with the University of St. Thomas*
➡ *full-time, semesters, start in Aug.*
➡ *range of first-year class size—41-73*

➡ *first year flexible scheduling options, 3-year program, 2-1/2 with summer school*

To assist students with commitments outside of law school, three first-year scheduling options are offered. First-year students may select a traditional all-day schedule or may elect to block their classes in either the morning or the afternoon. First-year students may also choose to reduce their course load by dropping Criminal Law in the fall and Property in the spring. Students who do so are still considered full-time students by ABA standards. These courses can be taken the following summer or in the next year.

■ General Practice Clinic

The School of Law operates a law clinic that functions as a typical small, general practice law office. Supervised by clinical instructors, students handle their own case load, from client counseling through the litigation, settlement, or passage of laws favoring the client.

■ Practicum Program

Guided by a seasoned judge or attorney, students serve as interns in law offices, public agencies, and courtrooms in specialized areas such as children and the law, criminal work, corporate practice, administrative law, and public-interest practice.

■ Public Law

Extensive offerings in public law are available for those considering legislative, administrative, or public-interest careers.

■ Student Activities

The *Hamline Law Review* publishes articles by students, leading members of the academic community, and practicing attorneys.

The *Hamline Journal of Public Law and Policy* is a forum for public policy articles on state and federal legislative, executive, and administrative functions.

The Journal of Law and Religion has established an international reputation and publishes articles, colloquia, and essays of interest to the legal, ethical, and religious communities. The *Journal*, published twice yearly, is edited by faculty members and employs students as assistant editors.

Participation in **Moot Court** offers students the opportunity to develop and refine writing and speaking skills for academic credit with the assistance of faculty members as well as members of the bench and bar. Hamline's teams have won numerous awards.

Student organizations are numerous and include organizations representing specialized areas of law.

■ Admission

➡ *Bachelor's degree required*   ➡ *application deadline—May 15, rolling admission, early application preferred*
➡ *LSAT, LSDAS required*   ➡ *median GPA—3.15*
➡ *median LSAT score—155*   ➡ *application fee—$30*
➡ *summer conditional program, acceptance by performance*

All applications are reviewed by an admissions committee composed of faculty members, administrators and students. Hamline's admissions policy is designed to maintain and enhance the diversity, vigor, social concern, professional dedication and academic ability of the student body. Hamline is strongly committed to a student body diverse in its cultural, economic, racial and ethnic composition and actively pursues such diversity.

The School of Law strives to maintain a selection process that emphasizes a fair examination of each person as an individual, not merely as a set of credentials. In addition to the LSAT and undergraduate GPA, the committee gives significant weight to motivation, personal experiences, employment history, graduate education, maturity, letters of recommendation, and the ability to articulate one's interest in and suitability for the study of law.

At the discretion of the Admissions Committee, a limited number of students whose objective factors do not qualify them for entrance directly into the fall program are given the opportunity to demonstrate their ability and earn a position in the fall entering class by successfully completing summer course work. This Acceptance by Performance program serves as part of the admissions process, and participation in this program does not guarantee admission to Hamline as a degree candidate.

■ Expenses and Financial Aid

➡ *tuition & fees—$12,560*   ➡ *estimated additional expenses—$5,812-$6,584 (on-campus housing and meal plan)*
➡ *merit-based scholarships available*
➡ *minority scholarships available*
➡ *financial aid available—Free Application for Federal Student Aid (FAFSA) for needs analysis; no deadline*
➡ *Public Law Loan Forgiveness available*

■ Career Services

A wide variety of career-information programs and skills workshops are offered by our Career Services Office. Individualized counseling is also provided in areas such as interviewing, résumé writing, career assessment, and the development of job-search strategies.

The office maintains extensive job listings for part-time, summer, and full-time employment. Hamline's 2,000 plus alumni are located in 29 states, the District of Columbia, and several foreign countries.

Applicant Group for the 1993–1994 Academic Year

Hamline University School of Law
This grid includes only applicants who earned 120-180 LSAT scores under standard administrations.

LSAT Score	3.75 +		3.50 -3.74		3.25 - 3.49		3.00 - 3.24		2.75 - 2.99		2.50 - 2.74		2.25 - 2.49		2.00 - 2.24		Below 2.00		No GPA		Total	
	Apps	Adm	Apps	Adm	Apps	Adm	Apps	Adm	Apps	Adm	Apps	Adm	Apps	Adm	Apps	Adm	Apps	Adm	Apps	Adm	Apps	Adm
175 - 180	0	0	4	4	0	0	0	0	0	0	0	0	0	0	0	0	0	0	0	0	4	4
170 - 174	0	0	0	0	0	0	1	1	0	0	1	1	1	1	0	0	0	0	0	0	3	3
165 - 169	2	2	2	2	1	1	9	9	2	2	3	3	1	1	0	0	0	0	0	0	20	20
160 - 164	5	5	15	15	12	9	19	19	20	18	12	12	7	5	1	1	0	0	2	1	93	85
155 - 159	14	14	19	19	43	37	61	59	52	43	29	19	22	10	7	2	4	0	4	3	255	206
150 - 154	18	17	37	28	71	48	89	48	85	27	72	13	35	6	13	0	2	0	5	3	427	190
145 - 149	8	4	21	7	41	15	63	11	76	8	51	4	27	1	21	0	0	0	6	1	314	51
140 - 144	2	2	13	6	26	3	42	6	39	3	45	5	31	3	18	2	7	0	8	0	231	30
135 - 139	1	0	3	0	8	1	13	0	13	1	27	1	12	0	7	0	3	0	5	2	92	5
130 - 134	0	0	1	0	2	0	3	0	10	0	6	0	14	0	6	0	2	0	1	0	45	0
125 - 129	0	0	0	0	0	0	0	0	1	0	1	0	3	0	2	0	2	0	1	1	10	1
120 - 124	0	0	0	0	0	0	0	0	0	0	0	0	0	0	0	0	1	0	0	0	1	0
Total	50	44	115	81	204	114	300	153	298	102	247	59	153	27	75	5	21	0	32	11	1495	595

Apps = Number of Applicants
Adm = Number Admitted
Reflects 94% of the total applicant pool.
This grid includes those admitted through the summer conditional program.

Harvard University Law School

1563 Massachusetts Avenue
Cambridge, MA 02138

Phone: 617.495.3109

■ Introduction

Harvard Law School, established in 1817, is the oldest existing law school in the United States. It is located, along with most other parts of Harvard University, in Cambridge, Massachusetts. The school offers a diverse curriculum intended to provide comprehensive training for those who wish to become legal practitioners, as well as those interested in public service, law teaching, and legal scholarship. Through its faculty, students, and graduates, Harvard seeks to make substantial contributions toward solving the complex legal problems confronting our society.

■ Enrollment/Student Body

➤ *7,600 applicants* ➤ *831 admitted first-year class 1993*
➤ *553 enrolled first-year class 1993* ➤ *1,616 total full-time J.D.* ➤ *122 total LL.M.* ➤ *27% minority*
➤ *40% women* ➤ *50 states & 20 foreign countries represented (J.D.)* ➤ *60 foreign countries (LL.M.)*
➤ *300+ undergraduate schools represented*

■ Faculty

➤ *113 total* ➤ *80 full-time* ➤ *33 part-time or adjunct*
➤ *15 women* ➤ *10 minority*

■ Library & Physical Facilities

➤ *1,745,384 volumes & equivalents* ➤ *library hours: Mon.-Thurs., 8:30 A.M.-MIDNIGHT; Fri.-Sat., 8:30 A.M.-9:00 P.M.; Sun., NOON-MIDNIGHT* ➤ *LEXIS (home access avail.)* ➤ *NEXIS (home access avail.)*
➤ *WESTLAW (home access avail.)*
➤ *32 full-time librarians* ➤ *library seats 901*

The school occupies 18 buildings that include dormitories, dining facilities, classrooms and offices. Through the public access catalog, many online research systems are available. Included are DIALOG, RLIN, Vu/Text, Dow-Jones News/Retrieval, Legi-Slate, and Legal Resources Index.

■ Curriculum

➤ *Academic Support Program* ➤ *82 credits required to graduate* ➤ *217 courses available* ➤ *degrees available: J.D.; LL.M.; S.J.D.; J.D./M.B.A.; J.D./M.A.L.D.; J.D./M.P.P.; J.D./PhD. and numerous other concurrent degrees*
➤ *cross-registration possibilities with other Harvard graduate schools* ➤ *range of first-year class size—45-135*

Our basic aim is to train students to be lawyers. The emphasis is not on any particular type of law: the curriculum includes courses in civil liberties as well as corporate finance, international trade as well as criminal law, and taxation as well as legal services for the poor. Nor is the curriculum oriented toward mastering detail or teaching the law "as it is." Law reform, legal philosophy, the historical development of legal institutions—all of these subjects and many more are important fields of study for an educated

member of the profession. Since the law changes often and the problems lawyers face vary endlessly, it is more important to master the enduring principles of law, its methods of reasoning, and its process of development and change rather than the law as it is currently written.

The first-year curriculum is designed to give each student a thorough grounding in the basic intellectual processes of legal reasoning and analysis. It consists of criminal law, contracts, civil procedure, torts, property, a legal methods course including Ames moot court work, and an elective course during the second semester. Except for a required paper and a course in professional responsibility, the second and third years of the J.D. degree program are entirely elective.

■ Special Programs

Special research and study programs of particular interest to students in the J.D. program include: the Criminal Justice Institute, the East Asian Legal Studies Program, the Middle Eastern Studies Program, the Human Rights Program, the Program on International Financial Systems, the Program in Law and Economics, the Program on the Legal Profession and the Program on Negotiation.

■ Admission

➤ *Bachelor's degree from accredited college or university required*
➤ *rolling admission, early application preferred*
➤ *LSAT, LSDAS required* ➤ *application fees—$50/$65/$75*

A main goal of our selection process is to enroll the ablest student body possible. To do this, we try to understand each applicant's academic and personal achievements, and compare these achievements to those of all other applicants. In understanding these factors, we evaluate all information in each applicant's file including transcripts, extracurricular and community activities, work experience, personal background, letters of recommendation, personal statements, and LSAT scores. Background factors such as demonstrated societal, economic, educational, or personal disadvantage the candidate has overcome often help the committee to fully understand applicants' achievements.

Our admission standards are set only by the comparative quality of our applicants, not by an absolute minimum level of achievement. All completed applications receive full consideration for admission. We have no computational methods for making admissions decisions, no mechanical shortcuts, no substitutes for careful assessment and good judgment. We encourage all those who would like to study law at Harvard to apply. We actively encourage applications from minority groups, women, older candidates, and others who are well qualified, but who might not seek admission for financial, geographic, or other reasons.

Please see the applicant group section for further information about the selection process.

■ Student Activities

Law-related activities at Harvard Law School are diverse and numerous. They include 10 law student publications (*Harvard Law Review, Harvard Journal on Legislation, Harvard International Law Journal, Harvard Civil Rights-Civil Liberties Law Review, Harvard Environmental Law Review, Harvard Women's Law Journal, Harvard Journal of Law and Public Policy, Harvard Human Rights Journal, Harvard Blackletter Journal*, and *Harvard Journal of Law and Technology*) as well as the Board of Student Advisers (which administers the Ames moot court and alternative programs), the Legislative Research Bureau, International Law Society, Civil Liberties Union, and Student Bar Association. Massachusetts allows law students to represent the indigent of the Commonwealth in the district courts. There are three curricular-based organizations that represent indigent clients under this provision. They include the Criminal Justice Institute, the Legal Services Clinic, and the Immigration Clinic. In addition, there are five extracurricular student-practice organizations which allow students similar opportunities: the Harvard Legal Aid Bureau, Harvard Defenders, Prison Legal Assistance Project, Students for Public Interest Law, and the Harvard Mediation Program. Other activities are the *Law School Record* (America's oldest law school newspaper); Law School Forum; Yearbook; Drama Society; Harvard Black Law Students Association; Harvard Environmental Law Society; the Committee on Gay, Bisexual, and Lesbian Legal Issues; La Alianza; Native American Law Students Association; Asian American Law Students Association; Women's Law Association, and more than 35 other student organizations not mentioned above.

■ Expenses and Financial Aid

➡ *tuition & fees—full-time, $18,364* ➡ *estimated additional expenses—$12,056 (room, board, living expenses, books & supplies)* ➡ *scholarships & financial aid available*

All students who demonstrate financial need according to a combination of federal and institutional guidelines receive assistance. Our program includes the Low Income Protection Plan, which provides partial forgiveness of loans to graduates who pursue public interest and other low-paid law-related careers.

■ Career Services

Our placement office assists students in obtaining permanent, part-time, and summer positions. Recently the employment pattern at graduation has been: law firms, 58 percent; judicial clerkships, 26 percent; federal, state, and local government, 3 percent; legal services, 2 percent; and teaching, further education, corporations, and other positions, 11 percent. Sixty-five percent of each year's class locates in New York; Washington, DC; Massachusetts; or California; the remainder locates in about 35 other states plus two or three foreign countries. In the past few years, 97 percent of the graduates have accepted offers for employment or further education by the time of graduation.

Applicant Group for the 1993-1994 Academic Year

We do not provide a profile chart of applicants considered and admitted because it is based solely upon undergraduate GPA and LSAT scores. Our admissions process takes many factors besides college grades and LSAT scores into account, and is far too complex to be represented fairly or completely by a two-factor profile.

At no point on any objective scale of qualifications are the chances for admission to Harvard Law School 0 or 100 percent. A number of applicants with relatively low UGPAs or LSAT scores are offered admission each year while a significant proportion of candidates with very high grades and/or LSAT scores are not admitted.

University of Hawaii at Manoa—William S. Richardson School of Law

2515 Dole Street
Honolulu, HI 96822

Phone: 808.956.3000

■ Introduction

Established in 1973, the University of Hawaii School of
Law is located in Honolulu on the main campus of Hawaii's nine-campus system. As the only law school in the
state, its primary purpose is to equip degree candidates
for active, effective, and creative participation as lawyers
in both the private and public sectors. The school has
ABA accreditation and membership in AALS.

   Some unique and differentiating features of this law
school are: its small size and close interaction among faculty, students, and the Hawaii legal community; its
emphasis on and resources for environmental/ocean
law, Pacific-Asia legal systems, and elder law; its standing as perhaps the most racially and ethnically diverse
law school in the country; and its mandatory graduation
requirement of 60 hours of law-related community service.

■ Enrollment/Student Body

➡ *759 applicants*   ➡ *135 admitted first-year class 1993*
➡ *76 enrolled first-year class 1993*   ➡ *240 total full-time*
➡ *72% minority*   ➡ *48% women*   ➡ *23 states & foreign
countries represented*   ➡ *81 undergraduate schools represented*

The student body reflects Hawaii's diversity. Students
represent the following race/ethnic groups: African-
American, Caucasian, Chinese, Filipino, Hispanic,
Japanese, Korean, Native American, Native Hawaiian,
Micronesian, Samoan, Fijian, Laotian, and Vietnamese. A
number of students come from Japan, China, Guam, Sa-
moa, Yap, Palau, and Pohnpei.

■ Faculty

➡ *36 total*   ➡ *16 full-time*   ➡ *20 part-time or adjunct*
➡ *13 women*   ➡ *15 minority*

■ Library and Physical Facilities

➡ *230,593 volumes & equivalents*   ➡ *library hours:
Mon.-Thurs., 8:00 A.M.-11:00 P.M.; Fri., 8:00 A.M.-5:00 P.M.;
Sat., 9:00 A.M.-5:00 P.M.; Sun., NOON-9:00 P.M.*   ➡ *LEXIS*
➡ *NEXIS*   ➡ *WESTLAW*   ➡ *5 full-time librarians*
➡ *library seats 392*

The law school is housed in two buildings constructed in
1983—the library and a classroom/office structure.
The library contains a study carrel and locker for each
student and seminar/discussion rooms for study
groups.The classroom building houses a moot courtroom with video technology for support of clinical
education programs.

   The library's collection of American law includes extensive holdings of case reports, statutes, regulations,
legislative history materials, records and briefs, treatises,
restatements, law reviews, and specialized looseleaf publications. It also has basic sources of English law and is
commencing the development of a collection on East
Asian and Pacific Island jurisdictions.

Law students have full access to all facilities of the University, including the health, counseling and computing
centers, and athletic facilities.

■ Curriculum

➡ *89 credits required to graduate, 42 of which are nonelective*
➡ *approximately 80 courses available*   ➡ *degrees available:
J.D.; J.D./M.B.A.; J.D./M.A. Asian Studies; J.D./Masters in
Urban & Regional Planning*   ➡ *semesters, start in Aug.
(new students) and Jan. (transfers & visiting students)*
➡ *range of first-year class size—12-76*
➡ *six semesters of full-time residency*
➡ *other dual-degree programs can be arranged*

The J.D. program is a three-year program of full-time
day study. Full-time registration is defined as enrollment
for a minimum of 12 credits each semester. First-year students begin with a one-week orientation; the first-year
curriculum is entirely prescribed. All students must fulfill a pro bono requirement of 60 hours of law-related
community service in order to graduate.

■ Pacific-Asian Legal Studies

Because of Hawaii's location, population, culture, and
economic relationships, the law school faculty is developing a program in Pacific-Asian Legal Studies (PALS).
The program has the two-fold purpose of conducting
new research and enriching the J.D. curriculum. A number of faculty have expertise in Pacific/Asian research,
teaching, and consultation. Recent and occasional course
offerings in PALS have included Chinese Trade and Investment Law, Pacific Island Legal Systems, Korean Law,
Japanese Criminal Law, and Japanese Trade Law.

   The program benefits from a faculty exchange with the
Hiroshima, Japan, Law Faculty. A unique offering is the
opportunity for selected students to do a full semester
externship for academic credit with the court systems in
certain Pacific Island nations. Students may also arrange
a semester of study with certain law faculties in Asia
with prior approval.

■ Environmental/Ocean Law Programs

Students may focus their elective courses in the area of environmental law and earn the Certificate in Environmental
Law along with the J.D. degree. Emphasis is on fresh water
resources, oceans, coastal waters, and land use—all areas of
special interest to Hawaii and the Pacific.

   The University of Hawaii has unusually extensive programs in different types of marine research, and the law
faculty is equally interested in ocean law and policy. The
Law of the Sea Institute became formally affiliated with
the law school in 1981. It shares multidisciplinary interests in joint research and the development in the
curriculum of courses related to ocean law and to legal
concerns of the Pacific-Asian area. Law students may
elect to combine their J.D. studies with a university cer-

tificate program in Ocean Policy. The university also offers a certificate in Resource Management.

■ Admission

➡ *Bachelor's degree from an accredited college or university required* ➡ *application deadline—Feb. 16 (firm)*
➡ *LSAT, LSDAS required* ➡ *median GPA—3.42*
➡ *median LSAT score—160* ➡ *no application fee*

Admission is determined by an applicant's academic achievement, aptitude for the study of law, and professional promise. Preference is given to residents of Hawaii and to those with strong ties to or special interest in Hawaii or the Asia-Pacific region. Besides LSAT and undergraduate GPA and major, other factors that may be considered are: academic work beyond the bachelor's degree, work experience, writing ability, community service, class diversity, and unusual accomplishments.

Applications from students wishing to transfer, or from those wishing to visit for a semester or two, are considered on a space-available basis for both August and January admission.

■ Student Activities

Student editorial boards publish the *University of Hawaii Law Review* and the *Pacific-Asian Law Journal*, while other students participate in the moot court program, including national moot court competitions in international and environmental law. The 1993 Jessup International Moot Court Team placed first in the nation and second in international competition.

Other students are active in a variety of organizations within the school and the Honolulu community including: Advocates for Public Interest Law (APIL), the American Bar Association Student Division, American Inns of Court, Student Bar Association, Phi Delta Phi and Delta Theta Phi International Legal Fraternities, the Pacific Islands and Pacific-Asian Legal Studies Organizations, Association of Women Law Students, and Environmental Law Society. Student affinity groups include the Filipino Law Students Association and the *'Ahahui 'O Hawai'i*, an organization of Native Hawaiian law students.

■ Expenses and Financial Aid

➡ *tuition & fees—resident, $2,400; nonresident, $7,820 (1994-95 academic year)* ➡ *estimated minimum annual expenses—$8,000* ➡ *financial aid administered by Central University of Hawaii Financial Aid Services, deadline— March 1* ➡ *FAFSA required for financial aid*

■ Career Services

Career counseling and services are provided to students and alumni for part-time, summer clerk, or associate positions in both the public and private sectors. Placement emphasis is almost exclusively on Hawaii and the Asia/Pacific region, since about 95 percent of our graduates remain here. On-campus facilities are available for interviews. All large firms in Honolulu and many medium and small firms participate in the fall on-campus interview season for second-year students. Most recent graduating classes have had a 95-100 percent employment rate six months after graduation.

Applicant Group for the 1993-94 Academic Year

University of Hawaii—William S. Richardson School of Law
This grid includes only applicants who earned 120-180 LSAT scores under standard administrations in the 1991-1993 testing period.

LSAT Score	3.75 & Up		3.50 - 3.74		3.25 - 3.49		3.00 - 3.24		2.75 - 2.99		2.50 - 2.74		2.25 - 2.49		2.00 - 2.24		Below 2.00		No GPA		Totals	
	Apps	Adm	Apps	Adm	Apps	Adm	Apps	Adm	Apps	Adm	Apps	Adm	Apps	Adm	Apps	Adm	Apps	Adm	Apps	Adm	Apps	Adm
170- 180	1	1	2	2	3	3	2	2	1	1	0	0	0	0	0	0	0	0	0	0	9	9
165 - 169	2	2	2	2	3	3	3	3	2	0	4	1	1	0	1	0	0	0	0	0	18	11
160 - 164	4	4	15	15	21	20	21	10	13	6	9	1	5	0	0	0	0	0	0	0	88	56
155 - 159	9	7	23	10	28	4	33	9	14	1	11	1	3	0	2	0	0	0	0	0	123	32
150 - 154	13	4	23	6	35	5	32	3	35	1	14	0	11	0	2	0	0	0	3	0	168	19
145 - 149	4	1	5	0	21	0	25	0	21	0	18	0	11	0	1	0	1	0	0	0	107	1
140 - 144	5	0	5	0	8	0	19	0	14	0	15	0	8	0	4	0	0	0	0	0	78	0
Below 140	0	0	1	0	8	0	4	0	8	0	7	0	4	0	3	0	2	0	0	0	37	0
Total	38	19	76	35	127	35	139	27	108	9	78	3	43	0	13	0	3	0	3	0	628	128

Apps = Number of Applicants
Adm = Number Admitted
Figures reflect admission decisions as of 10/1/93 and approximately 95% of all completed applications. They do not include students admitted from the Pre-Admission Program nor those files that were left incomplete by applicants. Combined figures are for both residents and nonresidents.

Hofstra University School of Law

Hempstead, NY 11550   Phone: 516.463.5916

■ Introduction

The Hofstra University School of Law is accredited by the ABA and is a member of the AALS. As a national law school, Hofstra provides a legal education designed to give students fundamental professional training and to prepare them for practice in any jurisdiction. Accordingly, the academic program at Hofstra includes the demanding analytical discipline of Socratic classroom teaching, cooperative study group work, research and writing projects, trial practice experience, and contact with clients, practicing attorneys, legislators, and judges in clinical programs. As a relatively small school, Hofstra maintains considerable faculty/student contact and a strong sense of community.

■ Enrollment/Student Body

➨ *2,975 applicants*   ➨ *906 admitted first-year class 1993*
➨ *284 enrolled first-year class 1993*   ➨ *832 total full-time*
➨ *17% minority*   ➨ *40% women*
➨ *14 states & foreign countries represented*
➨ *106 undergraduate schools represented*

■ Faculty

➨ *67 total*   ➨ *42 full-time*   ➨ *25 part-time or adjunct*
➨ *12 women*   ➨ *2 minority*

One of Hofstra's greatest strengths is its faculty. The faculty are persons of academic distinction and many of them are recognized as national authorities in their fields. They make it a point to be accessible to students outside of the traditional classroom setting. There are frequent lectures and scholarly activities emanating from the 18 endowed chairs and distinguished professorships.

■ Library and Physical Facilities

➨ *395,000 volumes & equivalents*   ➨ *library hours:*
Mon.-Thurs., 8:00 A.M.-MIDNIGHT; Fri., 8:00 A.M.-9:00 P.M.;
Sat., 9:00 A.M.-5:00 P.M.; Sun., NOON-MIDNIGHT
➨ *LEXIS*   ➨ *NEXIS*   ➨ *WESTLAW*
➨ *8 full-time librarians*   ➨ *library seats 682*

■ Curriculum

➨ *Academic Support Program*   ➨ *85 credits required to graduate*   ➨ *degrees and combined degrees available: J.D.; J.D./M.B.A.*   ➨ *semesters, start in late Aug.*
➨ *range of first-year class size—25-30 (small section); 115-120 (large section)*

■ Special Programs

Each entering student at Hofstra is placed in one small section of fewer than 30 students in a substantive course during the first semester of their first year. This small section experience enables a closer relationship between students and faculty in a seminar-like environment.

Recognizing that legal writing and research are essential to competent lawyering, Hofstra had designed a required program that emphasizes individualized instruction in these skills. During the spring semester of their first year, students receive intensive instruction in legal research and writing. During the fall semester of their second year, students participate in the Appellate Advocacy Program, in which they receive instruction in persuasive writing and oral advocacy.

Each January, Hofstra students are able to select a three-credit course on trial techniques that is patterned on the program of the National Institute for Trial Advocacy. A carefully orchestrated sequence of exercises, covering every aspect of a trial from jury selection to closing arguments, builds the students' abilities so that they are able to conduct a full jury trial at the end of the course.

A courthouse of the United States District Court for the Eastern District of New York is located on the Hofstra campus. The court cooperates with the law school in various academic programs and offers the students additional educational and practical experiences.

Civil Externship Program—The Civil Externship Program provides students with opportunities to learn lawyering skills through placements in a variety of nonprofit organizations or government agencies. Depending upon the particular placement, students may engage in all phases of legal work, including interviewing clients and witnesses, drafting legal documents, negotiating with attorneys, conducting research, and preparing legal memoranda.

Criminal Externship Program—The Criminal Externship Program provides an opportunity for students to learn about all phases of criminal law practice through placements in such agencies as Nassau, Queens, and Kings County District Attorneys' offices and New York City, Nassau County, and Suffolk Legal Aid offices. Students work approximately 15 hours per week and may be exposed to a wide variety of experiences, including legal research and writing, case investigation, witness interviewing, and courtroom advocacy.

Criminal Justice Clinic—This program is a one-semester clinic in which students represent defendants in criminal cases in Nassau County District Court and in Hempstead and Mineola Village courts. Students represent clients in pretrial conferences, witness interviewing, motion and brief writing, case investigations, and trials—from jury selection through verdict. Additionally, students participate in a weekly seminar that focuses on developing lawyering and advocacy skills.

Judicial Externship Program—The Judicial Externship Program provides an opportunity for students to serve as apprentices to state and federal judges for a semester. As judicial externs, for approximately 15 hours per week, students do research, write memoranda, observe court proceedings, and discuss cases with their judge.

Environmental Law Clinic—This program provides an opportunity to work on current environmental issues with public interest law firms, state or local environmental agencies, and private practitioners engaged in pro bono work in the field.

Disabilities Law Clinic—The Disabilities Law Clinic is a new clinic that began handling cases in the fall of 1992. The clinic focuses principally on cases involving the Americans with Disabilities Act of 1990, transportation cases, public access cases, and employment discrimination cases. Students in the clinic represent individuals, and are responsible for handling cases on their own (with faculty supervision) as much as possible. Students interview clients and witnesses, prepare pleadings and discovery, appear before courts and administrative agencies, negotiate settlements, and, when necessary, try cases.

Housing Rights Clinic—Students handle a wide variety of housing cases for low-income clients, including defenses of eviction cases; actions by tenants against landlords challenging substandard conditions in their apartments; fair housing and exclusionary zoning cases; public utility shut-off cases; and work on behalf of community groups for housing rehabilitation. The course develops lawyering skills with special emphasis on litigation strategy, pretrial and trial preparation, and trial advocacy. Students will prepare and present their cases in state and federal courts.

Pro Bono Student Lawyers Project—The Pro Bono Student Lawyers Project places students with a variety of existing agencies, service organizations, law firms, and private practitioners. Students in the program volunteer their time without compensation or credit to work on pro bono cases.

Unemployment Action Center—The Unemployment Action Center (UAC) is a nonprofit, student-run corporation that offers free advice and representation to persons denied unemployment benefits. Hofstra Law School's UAC Chapter has approximately 100 student advocates, each of whom has taken at least one case. The Unemployment Action Center received the New York State Bar Association Law Student Pro Bono Award for 1992.

■ Admission

➡ *Bachelor's degree required for admission*
➡ *application deadline—April 15, modified rolling admission*
➡ *LSAT, LSDAS required* ➡ *median GPA—3.25*
➡ *application fee—$50*

■ Student Activities

Hofstra students publish two journals. The *Hofstra Law Review* enjoys national renown and an international circulation. The *Labor Law Journal* publishes scholarly articles on various aspects of labor and employment law. Other student organizations include ACCESS (Advancement of Challenged Citizens toward Equality and Self-Sufficiency), the Asian-Pacific American Law Students Association, the Black Law Students Association, Coming Out for Civil Rights, *Conscience* (the law school's student newspaper), the Democratic Law Students Association, the Environmental Law Society, the Jewish Law Students Association, the Latin Law Student Association, Law Fellows, MESH (Multicultural Environment for Students at Hofstra Law), the Moot Court Board, *Pocket Part* (the law school yearbook), the Public Justice Foundation, the Republican Law Students Association, the Student Bar Association, the Trial Advocacy Club, and the Unemployment Action Center.

■ Expenses and Financial Aid

➡ *tuition & fees—$16,740* ➡ *financial aid and scholarships available*

■ Career Services

The Office of Career Services provides a wide range of services to facilitate job placement. The Senior Assistant Dean for Career Services and the Director organize recruitment programs, conduct job development campaigns, teach résumé writing and interviewing techniques, provide career counseling to students and alumni, and maintain employment statistics.

Admission Profile Not Available

University of Houston Law Center

Houston, TX 77204-6391   Phone: 713.743.1070

■ Introduction

The University of Houston Law Center is located at the University of Houston. Located three miles south of downtown, the campus extends over 550 acres of wooded terrain. The state-assisted Law Center, located in the nation's sixth largest legal market, is noted throughout the South and Southwest not only for its excellence, but for its progressive and innovative approach to the teaching of law. The College of Law, the academic branch of the Law Center, is fully accredited by the American Bar Association and the American Association of Law Schools and has a chapter of the Order of the Coif, the national legal honorary scholastic society. The Law Center confers a J.D. degree as a first degree in law and a Masters of Law (LL.M.) degree to students pursuing work beyond the J.D. degree.

■ Enrollment/Student Body

➡ 2,778 applicants   ➡ 750 admitted first-year class 1993
➡ 310 enrolled first-year class 1993   ➡ 781 total full-time
➡ 238 total part-time   ➡ 19% minority
➡ 44% women   ➡ 109 undergraduate schools represented
➡ 119 students enrolled in LL.M. program

■ Faculty

➡ 113 total   ➡ 48 full-time   ➡ 65 part-time
➡ 21 women   ➡ 10 minority

■ Library and Physical Facilities

➡ 400,000 volumes & equivalents   ➡ 9 full time librarians
➡ LEXIS   ➡ WESTLAW   ➡ Computer-Based Legal
Instruction Center   ➡ Special Collections in International
Law with emphasis on Latin America, Admiralty, Tax, Labor,
Oil & Gas, and Mexican Law

■ Curriculum/Basic Program of Study

➡ 88 semester credits required to graduate
➡ Academic Enrichment Program   ➡ full-time class starts
early fall   ➡ part-time (evening) class starts early summer
➡ 130 courses available

The first-year curriculum at the Law Center is prescribed. Students are also required to complete a course in professional responsibility and one major piece of legal research and writing before graduation. Emphasis is placed on legal theory and the varying approaches to the law.

■ Special Programs

➡ concurrent degree programs: J.D./M.B.A.; J.D./M.A. in
History; J.D./M.P.H.; J.D./Ph.D. in Medical Humanities
➡ LL.M. degrees offered in Health Law, International Law,
Intellectual Property Law; Energy, Environmental, and
Natural Resources Law; and Tax Law

The University of Houston Law Center emphasizes current legal and administrative problems confronting the region and nation, including intellectual property law, environmental law, energy law, tax law, health law, and international law, with an emphasis on Latin America. In 1978, the Law Center joined with the University of Texas Medical Center in creating the Health Law & Policy Institute for research and instruction on interdisciplinary issues. The Law Center is also host to the Intellectual Property Law Institute, the Trial Advocacy Institute, the Environmental Liability Law Program, the Institute for Higher Education Law and Governance, and the International Law Institute. The Law Center operates the Mexican Legal Studies Program, an annual summer school in Mexico for students interested in the Mexican legal system , particularly as it applies to foreign investors seeking to do business in Mexico.

■ Clinical Programs and Trial Advocacy

The Law Center offers a wide variety of clinical course offerings. Students can choose among different areas of concentration, such as agency or judicial internships; health or environmental law; and criminal prosecution or defense. The Law Center houses the Legal Aid Clinic, which gives students clinic opportunities in providing legal services to the indigent. The Law Center also offers skills training in both civil and criminal trial and appellate advocacy. The Trial Advocacy Institute oversees the design and implementation of trial advocacy courses at the Law Center.

■ Activities

The Student Bar Association has input into every facet of student life at the Law Center. The SBA participates in the first-year orientation, organizes the annual charity Fun-Run, aids in the selection of student representatives to sit on various faculty committees, and presents student attitudes and views of development both within and outside the Law Center.

The Law Center features an extensive moot court program, active chapters of Phi Delta Phi, Phi Alpha Delta, and Delta Theta Phi, the leading legal fraternities, as well as the Law Review and the Houston Journal of International Law, two student-run scholarly publications.

Other student organizations include the Association of Women in Law, Black Law Students Association, Hispanic Law Students Association, Asian Law Students Association, Mandamus (Gay & Lesbian Student Organization), Health Law Organization, Admiralty Law Society, Intellectual Property Student Organization, and Environmental Law Society.

■ Student Body

The student body consists of approximately 1,100 persons from across the United States, although most students come from Texas and the Southwest. There is no provisional acceptance.

■ Admission

➠ *Bachelor's degree from an accredited university*
➠ *application deadline—Feb. 1* ➠ *LSAT, LSDAS required*
➠ *median GPA—3.30* ➠ *median LSAT score—159*
➠ *application fee—$50*

A completed application and LSDAS report must be furnished to the Law Center before February 1 to guarantee consideration for the following fall or summer semesters. Only new-scale LSAT scores will be accepted for consideration. Admission is based primarily on the applicant's test results and academic record. Multiple LSAT scores are averaged. Approximately 30 percent of students are admitted based on consideration of additional factors including background or career, graduate work, honors, ethnicity, extracurricular activities, employment, and a personal statement as requested on the application. The Law Center attempts to obtain broad diversity among students. All qualified applicants receive consideration for admission without regard to race, color, religion, national origin, sex, age, disability, sexual orientation, or veteran status.

■ Expenses and Financial Aid

➠ *tuition & fees—full-time resident, $4,500; nonresident, $7,300* ➠ *estimated additional expenses (room, board, and books)—$5,000* ➠ *merit scholarships available*
➠ *FAFSA for need analysis*

The Law Center forwards financial aid materials to applicants once they are accepted. The Student Financial Aid Liaison will assist accepted applicants with their questions. Once accepted, all applicants are automatically considered for merit scholarships.

■ Career Services

The Law Center's Office of Career Services actively assists students and graduates in legal career planning. The office annually hosts prospective employers in on-campus interview and recruiting programs for second- and third-year students seeking summer clerkships and permanent positions. The Office of Career Services receives notices of part-time and full-time positions available within the legal community, which are maintained for student review, and maintains a wide variety of resources such as legal directories, employers' résumés, and legal career planning publications.

Applicant Group for the 1993–1994 Academic Year

University of Houston Law Center
This grid includes only applicants who earned 120-180 LSAT scores under standard administrations.

LSAT	3.75+		3.50 - 3.74		3.25 - 3.49		3.00 - 3.24		2.75 - 2.99		2.50 - 2.74		2.25 - 2.49		2.00 - 2.24		Below 2.00		No GPA		Total	
	Apps	Adm	Apps	Adm	Apps	Adm	Apps	Adm	Apps	Adm	Apps	Adm	Apps	Adm	Apps	Adm	Apps	Adm	Apps	Adm	Apps	Adm
175 - 180	3	2	0	0	0	0	2	2	0	0	0	0	0	0	0	0	0	0	0	0	5	4
170 - 174	2	2	4	4	1	1	5	5	2	2	3	3	0	0	0	0	0	0	1	0	18	17
165 - 169	9	9	16	16	24	23	27	26	25	24	12	8	4	1	1	0	0	0	1	1	119	108
160 - 164	27	25	52	49	72	67	71	55	66	40	41	14	16	6	5	0	0	0	5	2	355	258
155 - 159	38	32	122	84	138	69	125	42	83	17	53	2	34	2	8	0	2	0	13	6	616	254
150 - 154	36	18	97	35	121	32	139	18	119	10	84	2	34	0	20	0	4	0	8	2	662	117
145 - 149	18	9	41	7	61	6	96	3	87	3	80	0	33	0	19	0	8	0	13	0	456	28
140 -144	5	1	12	1	32	1	54	2	56	0	49	1	43	0	14	0	4	0	12	1	281	7
135 - 139	0	0	6	0	14	0	14	0	21	0	30	0	21	0	8	0	2	0	7	0	123	0
130 - 134	0	0	0	0	3	0	5	0	8	0	10	0	14	0	7	0	3	0	3	0	53	0
125 - 129	0	0	0	0	0	0	1	0	2	0	5	0	3	0	1	0	1	0	1	0	14	0
120 - 124	0	0	0	0	0	0	0	0	1	0	1	0	0	0	1	0	0	0	0	0	3	0
Total	138	98	350	196	466	199	539	153	470	96	368	30	202	9	84	0	24	0	64	12	2705	793

Apps = Number of Applicants
Adm = Number Admitted
Reflects 96% of the total applicant pool.

Howard University School of Law

2900 Van Ness Street, NW
Washington, DC 20006

Phone: 202.806.8008

■ Introduction

Howard University, a coeducational, private institution in Washington, DC, was chartered by the U.S. Congress in 1867. Howard is a historically black institution that offers an educational experience of exceptional quality and value to students with high academic potential. Particular emphasis is placed on providing educational opportunities for promising African-Americans, other persons of color and those who have been historically underrepresented in the legal profession. The law school has a diverse student body and faculty. The main campus of Howard is located in northwest Washington. The law school is located on a separate 22-acre campus, also in northwest Washington, approximately three miles from the main campus. Howard University School of Law is fully approved by the American Bar Association and the Association of American Law Schools, and certifies its graduates for bar examination in all jurisdictions of the United States.

■ Enrollment

➡ *1,500 applicants*   ➡ *330 admitted first-year class 1993*
➡ *161 enrolled first-year class 1993*   ➡ *463 total full-time*
➡ *88% people of color*   ➡ *54% women*
➡ *55 states & foreign countries represented*
➡ *161 undergraduate schools represented*
➡ *42 different undergraduate majors represented*

■ Student Body

There are 453 students in the J.D. Program. They come from all parts of the United States, as well as Asia, Africa, Canada, and the Caribbean. Women comprise 54 percent of the student body, and minorities constitute 88 percent. The academic attrition rate is 5 percent. Attrition for other reasons is approximately another 5 percent.

■ Faculty

➡ *42 total*   ➡ *24 full-time*   ➡ *18 part-time or adjunct*
➡ *10 women*   ➡ *32 people of color*

■ Library & Physical Facilities

➡ *240,000 volumes & equivalents*   ➡ *library hours: Mon.-Thurs., 8:00 A.M.-MIDNIGHT; Fri.-Sun., 8:00 A.M.-9:00 P.M.*
➡ *LEXIS* ➡ *NEXIS* ➡ *WESTLAW* ➡ *EPIC*
➡ *DIALOG* ➡ *OCLC* ➡ *7 full-time librarian positions*
➡ *library seats 303*

The law library is both a working collection for law students and lawyers and a research institution for legal scholars. The civil rights archive contains briefs, working papers, and materials of the NAACP and other civil rights organizations, and has a collection that emphasizes civil and political rights. The library also has literature to support the study of legal problems of the poor. The computer lab has one computer per nine students ratio.

■ Curriculum

➡ *Academic Support Programs*   ➡ *Labor/EEO Clinic*
➡ *Civil Litigation Clinic*   ➡ *Criminal Justice Clinic*
➡ *Internship*   ➡ *88 credits required to graduate, with a cumulative weighted average of not less than 70*
➡ *residence in the last full year is also a requirement for graduation*   ➡ *degrees available: J.D.; J.D./M.B.A; M.C.J.*
➡ *range of first-year class size—25-50*

The curriculum leading to the first degree in law covers three academic years of two semesters each. Howard has no summer or evening program; it is a full-time day program. Experience has shown that beginning students must devote their entire time to their studies. During the first two years, emphasis is on the fundamental analytical concepts and skills of the law and the system by which it is administered; the functions required of a lawyer within a legal system based upon the common law. These courses afford rigorous training in the recognition of essential facts, in analysis and synthesis, and in the presentation of legal materials. Second-year courses also prepare students to apply the resources of the law to the resolution of contemporary problems studied during the third year. The curriculum in the third year provides diversified experience and a solid foundation for whatever specialization is desired. There is an emphasis on effective legal writing throughout the law school curriculum. Howard is firmly committed to producing lawyers who have mastered the art of effective written communication. Students wishing to participate in the Joint J.D./M.B.A program must be admitted both to the School of Law and the School of Business, one may use the law school application only to apply for the J.D./M.B.A. degree. Students interested in the M.C.J. program should make inquiry to the School of Law.

■ Special Programs

The School of Law has a strong commitment to human and civil rights, and many programs and activities in the school reflect that fact. The school also provides an opportunity for clinical experience in civil and criminal litigation and employment law. Other areas are either available or under active consideration.

■ Minority Programs

Howard University is a historically black institution, and has always had a strong, anti-discrimination policy. The School of Law, consistent with the mission and tradition of the university, believes in affirmative action both with regard to admissions and financial aid in order to ensure that all members of under-represented groups may have access to the legal profession.

■ Admission

➡ *Bachelor's degree from a college or university acceptable to the School of Law is required*
➡ *application deadline—April 30, rolling admissions used; early application preferred (Oct. 1)* ➡ *LSAT, LSDAS required*
➡ *median GPA—2.85* ➡ *median LSAT score—152*
➡ *application fee—$60* ➡ *letters of recommendation and undergraduate dean's survey should accompany application*

The large number of applications received for the available spaces in the first-year class has made the admissions process highly selective. The School of Law admits only full-time students for entrance in the fall. Applicants must take the LSAT, (and GMAT for the J.D./M.B.A.) and should arrange to take the LSAT no later than February of the year admission is sought to allow adequate processing time. Applicants must register with the LSDAS and must have obtained their college degrees before enrolling.

■ Student Activities

The *Howard Law Journal,* scheduled for publication three times a year, publishes legal materials of scholarly and professional interest. The national and international moot court teams sponsor intramural competitions and participate in competitions nationwide. *The Barrister,* the student newspaper, publishes several issues a year. The Student Bar Association (SBA) is the general student government organization. The Moot Court teams have won numerous honors. Other organizations represent students from diverse ethnic backgrounds, including, African-Americans, Latinos, Africans, Caribbean Islanders, and Asian-Pacific Islanders. Other activities include three legal fraternities, as well as organizations that address a range of student needs and interests, such as Organization of Women in Law, Project Outreach, the Progressive Law Students Association, and the Christian Fellowship. Other organizations are devoted to specific areas such as public-interest law, entertainment law, environmental law, and international law.

■ Expenses and Financial Aid

➡ *tuition & fees—full-time, $9,625; part-time, $535/credit*
➡ *additional expenses—$10,650 (room, board, & miscellaneous living expenses)* ➡ *merit scholarships are available*
➡ *need-based scholarships & grants available*
➡ *financial aid available; financial aid form due April 1*
➡ *extensive list of loans available*

■ Career Services

Howard affords its students varied career opportunities. Graduates work for courts; large and small law firms; federal, state, and local government agencies; public-interest organizations; and public and private corporations throughout the United States. The Career Services Office is an integral part of the law school. More than 250 recruiters from law firms, government agencies, and corporations visit the law school each year with offers of employment for promising students and graduates.

Applicant Group for the 1993–1994 Academic Year

Howard University School of Law

LSAT Score	GPA								
	3.75+	3.50 - 3.74	3.25 - 3.49	3.00 - 3.24	2.75 - 2.99	2.50 - 2.74	2.25 - 2.49	2.00 - 2.24	Below 2.00
175 - 180	■	■	■	■	■	■			
170 - 174	■	■	■	■	■	■			
165 - 169	■	■	■	■	■	■			
160 - 164	■	■	■	■	■	■			
155 - 159	■	■	■	■	■	■			
150 - 154	■	■	■	■	■	■			
145 - 149	▨	▨	▨	▨	▨	▨			
140 - 144									
135 - 139									
130 - 134									
125 - 129									
120 - 124									

■ Very Likely   ▨ Possible   ☐ Unlikely

University of Idaho College of Law

6th & Rayburn
Moscow, ID 83843

Phone: 208.885.6422

■ Introduction

The College of Law is located on the main campus of the University of Idaho in the city of Moscow, about 90 miles southeast of Spokane, Washington, and about 8 miles east of Pullman, Washington. The Moscow-Pullman community is the cultural center of a vast inland area of the Northwest covering parts of Idaho, Washington, and Oregon. This area is renowned for outstanding opportunities for outdoor sports and activities. Washington State University and the University of Idaho are only eight miles apart, and the two universities make their resources jointly available in many fields. The College of Law was established in 1909. It has been a member of the AALS since 1915 and has been on the approved list of the ABA since 1925.

■ Enrollment/Student Body

➡ 797 applicants   ➡ 247 admitted first-year class 1993
➡ 96 enrolled first-year class 1993   ➡ 293 total full-time
➡ 13% minority   ➡ 33% women
➡ 20 states & foreign countries represented
➡ 94 undergraduate schools represented

Students from Idaho constitute approximately 80 percent of the student body; the other 20 percent come from all regions of the United States. Although the total enrollment of the College of Law is relatively small (approximately 300), students typically represent over 90 different colleges and universities. Academic attrition is about 7 percent.

■ Faculty

➡ 22 total   ➡ 20 full-time   ➡ 2 part-time or adjunct
➡ 7 women   ➡ 1 minority

■ Library and Physical Facilities

➡ 146,000 volumes & equivalents   ➡ library hours:
Mon.-Thurs., 6:30 A.M.-11:00 P.M.; Fri.-Sat., 6:30 A.M.-9:30 P.M.;
Sun., 6:30 A.M.-11:00 P.M.   ➡ LEXIS   ➡ NEXIS
➡ WESTLAW   ➡ DIALOG   ➡ Online Legal Periodical
Indices   ➡ 4 full-time librarians   ➡ library seats 369

The College of Law occupies an air-conditioned building designed for its use and completed in 1973. It contains a courtroom, classrooms, offices for the clinical training program, and the law library. It is located across the street from the general library of the university.

The law library subscribes to CD-ROM libraries. Membership in the Western Library Network and the Inland Northwest Library Automation Network allows users to ascertain holdings of hundreds of libraries across the nation.

Law students have access to the other libraries of the University of Idaho, as well as to those of Washington State University.

■ Curriculum

➡ In-house Clinical Program   ➡ 88 credits required to graduate   ➡ 61 courses available   ➡ degree available: J.D.   ➡ semesters, start in Aug., Jan., & May (summer)
➡ externships

The school operates on a semester basis with six semesters and 88 semester credit hours required for the J.D. degree. A summer session is held for advanced students only, and the J.D. degree can be secured in five semesters and two summer sessions. The first-year curriculum is required and includes the traditional subjects of contracts, torts, procedure, property, criminal law, and an introduction to constitutional problems.

The focus is upon basic general principles widely applicable throughout the United States. Standard casebooks and other teaching materials are used, occasionally supplemented by references to the more localized problems of Idaho or the Northwest. No work is offered toward any degree other than the J.D.

■ Special Programs

The law school operates a variety of clinical programs. Law students in their third year may qualify as interns under the laws of Idaho and work in our in-house clinic. Interns are eligible to present cases in court under appropriate supervision. Interns may also receive limited credit for work performed in law offices and selected public agencies.

Externships are available, for limited credit, with the Supreme Court and Court of Appeals of Idaho, the United States Court of Appeals for the Ninth Circuit, the United States District Court for the District of Idaho, the Attorney General of Idaho, and the United States Attorney for the District of Idaho.

■ Admission

➡ Bachelor's degree required for admission
➡ application deadline—Feb. 1   ➡ LSAT, LSDAS required
➡ median GPA—3.25   ➡ median LSAT score—152
➡ application fee—$30

Applications are accepted beginning in September preceding the year in which enrollment is desired. Entering students are admitted only at the beginning of the fall semester. Applicants must submit LSAT scores and college transcripts for evaluation through LSDAS. Late fall application is recommended, and the deadline for being considered in the first wave of acceptances is Feb. 1. In making decisions, the Admissions Committee relies on both the LSAT and the college record, weighing scores slightly heavier.

■ Student Activities

Students publish the *Idaho Law Review*, which is devoted particularly to state and regional problems, although articles of general national interest do appear. An intramural moot court competition is held on a voluntary basis and, from winning teams, students are selected to participate in the National, International, and ABA Moot Court Teams. The Student Bar Association represents student interests, both educational and social, in many ways. From its ranks come elected student members who sit on various faculty/student committees. There are chapters of the Phi Alpha Delta, Delta Theta Phi, and Phi Delta Phi legal fraternities at the College of Law, as well as the American Bar Association Law Student Division, the Board of Student Advocates, the Christian Legal Society, the Environmental Law Society, the Federalist Society, the *Idaho Law Review*, the Idaho Women Lawyer's Student Chapter, the Idaho Trial Lawyers Association, the International Law Society, Law Students for Alternative Dispute Resolution, the Minority Law Student Association, the Student Bar Association, the Student Division of the Idaho State Bar's Corporate and Securities Section, the Public International Law Group, and the Law Student Spouse/Partner Association.

■ Expenses and Financial Aid

➡ *tuition & fees—resident, $2,300; nonresident, $6,810*
➡ *in-house & general achievement minority scholarships available* ➡ *outstanding achievement minority scholarships available* ➡ *financial aid available; University of Idaho Scholarship and Financial Aid Application required*
➡ *FAF due Feb. 14*

■ Career Services

The law school sponsors a variety of activities designed to facilitate students' career planning and assist in their employment search as summer clerks or for permanent positions. Facilities are available for on-campus interviews and the school is able to work with employers who cannot visit the school but have indicated a desire to recruit by mail. The majority of graduates find employment in Idaho, although Washington and Oregon continue to be popular locations. Graduates are also employed throughout the United States and several foreign countries. In recent years students have followed the national averages in finding employment in positions requiring bar membership or extensive legal training.

Applicant Group for the 1993–1994 Academic Year

University of Idaho College of Law
This grid includes only applicants who earned 120-180 LSAT scores under standard administrations.

LSAT Score	3.75 +		3.50 -3.74		3.25 - 3.49		3.00 - 3.24		2.75 - 2.99		2.50 - 2.74		2.25 - 2.49		2.00 - 2.24		Below 2.00		No GPA		Total	
	Apps	Adm	Apps	Adm	Apps	Adm	Apps	Adm	Apps	Adm	Apps	Adm	Apps	Adm	Apps	Adm	Apps	Adm	Apps	Adm	Apps	Adm
175 - 180	0	0	0	0	0	0	0	0	1	1	0	0	0	0	0	0	0	0	0	0	1	1
170 - 174	0	0	0	0	0	0	0	0	0	0	0	0	0	0	0	0	0	0	0	0	0	0
165 - 169	0	0	2	2	4	3	5	1	4	3	1	0	0	0	2	1	0	0	0	0	18	10
160 - 164	3	3	5	3	10	8	4	4	8	7	3	0	4	1	4	0	0	0	0	0	41	26
155 - 159	8	4	19	14	25	18	28	14	35	11	17	4	15	1	6	1	1	0	3	1	157	68
150 - 154	3	3	14	7	33	11	55	4	41	3	35	6	15	3	6	0	0	0	2	0	204	37
145 - 149	5	4	9	4	29	9	23	6	47	5	32	4	12	0	11	0	0	0	3	1	171	33
140 - 144	2	1	7	3	8	2	28	6	12	0	11	0	12	0	6	0	2	0	2	1	90	13
135 - 139	0	0	0	0	3	0	10	0	7	0	8	1	8	0	2	0	0	0	1	0	39	1
130 - 134	1	1	0	0	1	1	0	0	3	0	1	0	3	0	0	0	0	0	0	0	9	2
125 - 129	0	0	0	0	0	0	0	0	0	0	0	0	0	0	0	0	0	0	0	0	0	0
120 - 124	0	0	0	0	0	0	0	0	0	0	0	0	0	0	0	0	0	0	0	0	0	0
Total	22	16	56	33	113	52	153	35	158	30	108	15	69	5	37	2	3	0	11	3	730	191

Apps = Number of Applicants
Adm = Number Admitted
Reflects 92% of the total applicant pool.

University of Illinois College of Law

504 East Pennsylvania Avenue
Champaign, IL 61820

Phone: 217.244.6415

■ Introduction

Established nearly a century ago, the University of Illinois College of Law fosters excellence in legal education through a close community of faculty members and students, where teaching goes hand in hand with scholarship. The resources—intellectual, cultural, and recreational—of one of the world's largest and best universities are readily available to our law students, as is the appealing ambience of a university community. The college's comparatively low tuition costs, as well as the area's moderate living costs, make our program an outstanding value.

■ Enrollment/Student Body

➤ *2,159 applicants*   ➤ *205 enrolled first-year class 1993*
➤ *626 total full-time*   ➤ *22% minority*   ➤ *42% women*
➤ *24 states & foreign countries represented*
➤ *165 undergraduate schools represented*

■ Faculty

➤ *65 total*   ➤ *30 full-time*   ➤ *35 part-time*
➤ *15 women*   ➤ *3 minority*

■ Library and Physical Facilities

➤ *593,000 volumes & equivalents*   ➤ *LEXIS*
➤ *NEXIS*   ➤ *WESTLAW*   ➤ *6 full-time librarians*

In August 1993 the college completed a major addition and renovation which greatly increased the amount of space available for students.

The law library ranks fifth nationally in the number of titles held. The library has a substantial international collection and is one of the few American law libraries designated as a depository by the European Economic Community.

Directly across the street from the law school is one of the country's largest physical education buildings, with indoor and outdoor swimming pools, tennis courts, four gyms, weight and exercise equipment, archery, and ball courts of all kinds. The facility is free for students.

■ Curriculum

➤ *Academic Support Program*   ➤ *90 credits required to graduate*   ➤ *110 courses available*   ➤ *degrees and combined degrees available: J.D.; LL.M.; J.D./M.B.A.; J.D./M.D.; J.D./D.V.M.; J.D./M.A. in Labor & Industrial Relations; J.D./M.A. in Urban Planning; J.D./Master of Accounting; J.D./Master of Education; Doctor of Education*
➤ *semesters, start in Aug.*
➤ *range of first-year class size—65-70*

In the second and third years, courses vary in size. Seminar enrollment is limited to 12 students, and trial advocacy sections are limited to 20 students each. Independent studies—in which students work individually with faculty on research topics of special interest—are also offered.

■ Special Programs

International Legal Studies—Students pursuing international legal studies can choose from 13 international and comparative law courses, ranging from European Community law to international human rights law. Faculty members have long-standing international connections, and some collaborate with international scholars and legal experts to teach these courses.

Trial Advocacy Program—The college's trial advocacy program is especially popular, enrolling about three-quarters of the third-year class. The year-long program teaches the art of courtroom litigation and concludes with students conducting a day-long mock trial.

Environmental Law—The college has an active program of environmental and planning studies. Beyond the first-year course in property, the college offers courses in environmental law, natural resources, and land-use planning.

An innovative computer-based course called Metro-Apex offers a semester-long simulation of environmental controversies and legal disputes. Students adopt and enforce regulations and conduct full-scale administrative and judicial proceedings.

Taxation—Illinois offers one of the strongest tax curricula in the country, with core courses that address all aspects of tax practice and advanced offerings that integrate tax problems with other fields of law.

Skills Training— Classes in legal drafting, business planning, advanced bankruptcy, environmental management, estate planning, and tax practice challenge students to solve concrete problems and draft legal documents in a variety of fields. Courses on computer applications in the law and quantitative methods in legal decision-making familiarize students with sophisticated techniques necessary in today's law practice; these include computerized methods of document preparation and information retrieval, statistical analysis, the use of computer simulations in litigation, and the calculation of damage awards.

Offerings on alternative dispute resolution, the lawyer as negotiator, and collective bargaining and labor arbitration engage students in mock negotiations, arbitrations, and alternatives to traditional trials.

■ Admission

➤ *Bachelor's degree required*   ➤ *application deadline—March 15*   ➤ *rolling admissions, application by Jan. 15*
➤ *LSAT, LSDAS required*   ➤ *median GPA—3.40*
➤ *median LSAT score—161*   ➤ *application fee—$30*

In evaluating applications, the Admissions Committee places great weight on the undergraduate grade-point average and the Law School Admission Test score. A thorough admissions process, including individual review of all files by a faculty committee, attempts to identify students whose grades or scores appear to underpredict their performance in law school, as well as students whose admission would contribute to diversity at the College of Law. The committee also considers graduate work in other fields, employment experience, and demonstrated leadership ability. Applicants are not judged on the basis of in-state residency.

■ Student Activities

Students can write for the *University of Illinois Law Review* or for the *Elder Law Journal*, the only law journal in the country to concentrate on the legal problems of the elderly. Illinois students also write analyses of recent court decisions for the monthly *Illinois Bar Journal*.

Students interested in appellate advocacy can compete in any of ten moot court competitions and can gain practical experience through the client counseling and negotiation competitions.

The small size of the college allows students to become actively involved in the college's more than 30 student organizations.

■ Expenses and Financial Aid

➥ *tuition & fees—full-time resident, $5,010; full-time non-resident, $12,622* ➥ *estimated additional expenses—$7,296 average (room, board, books, transportation, personal)*
➥ *merit-based scholarships available*
➥ *FAFSA due by March 15*

Approximately 30 tuition and service fee waivers are available to African-American and Latino first-year students. Numerous graduate assistantships are available on-campus to second- and third-year students. Graduate assistants receive a tuition waiver plus a monthly stipend.

■ Career Services

The Office of Career Services works individually with students to help them decide which career choices are most attractive. Staff members arrange mock interviews with attorneys, assist with writing résumés and cover letters, and offer dozens of programs throughout the year. Faculty members counsel students on career goals, and attorneys regularly visit the college to discuss such topics as how to prepare for an interview or succeed as a summer associate.

Students participate in an active on-campus interviewing program and respond to requests for résumés from hundreds of employers nationwide. On average over the last five years, 95 percent of our graduates accepted positions within six months of completing the J.D.

Applicant Group for the 1993–1994 Academic Year

University of Illinois College of Law
This grid includes only applicants who earned 120-180 LSAT scores under standard administrations.

LSAT Score	GPA 3.75 +		3.50 -3.74		3.25 - 3.49		3.00 - 3.24		2.75 - 2.99		2.50 - 2.74		2.25 - 2.49		2.00 - 2.24		Below 2.00		No GPA		Total	
	Apps	Adm	Apps	Adm	Apps	Adm	Apps	Adm	Apps	Adm	Apps	Adm	Apps	Adm	Apps	Adm	Apps	Adm	Apps	Adm	Apps	Adm
175 - 180	3	3	1	0	4	4	2	1	0	0	0	0	0	0	0	0	0	0	0	0	10	8
170 - 174	6	5	6	6	14	11	9	3	6	1	1	0	0	0	0	0	0	0	0	0	42	26
165 - 169	29	29	45	44	41	34	47	22	24	4	9	4	2	0	0	0	0	0	1	0	198	137
160 - 164	54	53	95	81	120	78	84	29	43	7	18	1	7	0	1	0	0	0	3	1	425	250
155 - 159	59	20	112	29	128	17	112	15	42	2	28	1	11	3	4	0	2	0	4	0	502	87
150 - 154	27	3	71	13	84	2	65	6	62	9	40	2	11	1	6	0	2	0	4	1	372	37
145 - 149	15	1	23	6	50	4	54	7	36	0	27	1	9	0	10	0	1	0	6	0	231	19
140 - 144	1	1	12	1	18	1	34	1	35	0	29	0	23	0	9	0	0	0	8	0	169	4
135 - 139	1	0	2	0	4	0	10	0	6	0	20	0	14	0	6	0	3	0	6	0	72	0
130 - 134	0	0	0	0	0	0	2	0	0	0	4	0	3	0	8	0	2	0	2	0	21	0
125 - 129	0	0	0	0	0	0	0	0	1	0	0	0	3	0	0	0	0	0	1	0	5	0
120 - 124	0	0	0	0	0	0	0	0	0	0	0	0	0	0	0	0	0	0	0	0	0	0
Total	195	115	367	180	463	151	419	84	255	23	176	9	83	4	44	0	10	0	35	2	2047	568

Apps = Number of Applicants
Adm = Number Admitted
Reflects 96% of the total applicant pool.

Indiana University School of Law—Bloomington

Admissions Office, Law Building, Room 230
Bloomington, IN 47405-1001

Phone: 812.855.2704

■ Introduction

Founded in 1842, Indiana University School of Law—Bloomington, is located on the beautifully wooded campus of one of the nation's largest teaching and research universities. The presence of the university, including its world famous School of Music, offers students cultural opportunities available in few urban areas, while retaining the advantages of a small university town. The school is a charter member of the AALS and is approved by the ABA.

■ Enrollment/Student Body

- ➤ 1,925 applicants ➤ 684 admitted first-year class 1993
- ➤ 209 enrolled first-year class 1993 ➤ 614 total full-time
- ➤ 5 total part-time ➤ 20% minority ➤ 44% women
- ➤ 40 states & foreign countries represented
- ➤ 162 undergraduate schools represented

■ Faculty

- ➤ 54 total ➤ 35 full-time ➤ 19 part-time or adjunct
- ➤ 13 women ➤ 2 minority

■ Library and Physical Facilities

- ➤ 510,000 volumes & equivalents ➤ library hours: Mon.-Fri., 7:30 A.M.-MIDNIGHT; Sat., 8:00 A.M.-10:00 P.M.; Sun., 11:00 A.M.-MIDNIGHT ➤ LEXIS ➤ NEXIS
- ➤ WESTLAW ➤ DIALOG ➤ LEGISLATE
- ➤ WILSON-ON LINE ➤ 9 full-time librarians
- ➤ library seats 641

The law library's extensive collection is one of only ten in the nation to contain complete sets of records and briefs filed before the United States Supreme Court. It includes an exceptional collection in Anglo-American law and strong holdings in international and foreign law. Computer-assisted legal research systems and nonlaw databases, interactive video systems, and a computer center for student use are available.

■ Curriculum

- ➤ Academic Support Program ➤ 86 credits required to graduate ➤ 134 courses available ➤ degrees and combined degrees available: J.D.; J.D./M.B.A.; J.D./M.P.A.; J.D./M.S.E.S.; J.D./M.L.S.; LL.M.; M.C.L. ➤ fall semester starts in Aug. ➤ range of first-year class size—26-100

The curriculum does not emphasize the law of any state and its many offerings include traditional courses as well as specialized courses such as communications law, law and biomedical advance, immigration law, international business transactions, and environmental litigation. The school also offers intensive training in litigation. Students may also participate in clinics which enable them to deal with client problems under close faculty supervision.

The Legal Education Opportunity Program (LEOP) is a voluntary program designed to provide academic and peer support to selected law students. LEOP provides academic support through a series of voluntary workshops and classes. It provides peer support by introducing incoming law students to upper-class students who serve as guides through the rigors of the first year.

■ Joint-Degree Programs

Four formal joint J.D. and master's or doctoral degree programs are available with the School of Business, the School of Public and Environmental Affairs, and the School of Library and Information Science. Joint-degree programs in other disciplines may be individually designed.

■ London Law Consortium

The School of Law participates in a consortium with seven other law schools to offer a semester of study in London during the spring. Classes are held at the Florida State University London Study Center. Students are eligible to participate during their second or third year in law school, and, to date, all those wishing to participate have been able to do so.

■ Accelerated/Summer Program

By starting law school in the summer session and attending full summer sessions in the following two years, students may complete degree requirements in 27 months. Students who begin in the accelerated program are not required to continue with the program. Students who do not choose to begin their legal education in the accelerated program may enroll in summer-session courses following their first year.

■ Special Programs

The Center for the Study of Law and Society provides a forum for those students and faculty across the Bloomington campus interested in law-related research. Some of its research projects include transnational disputing, the role of courts, alternative dispute resolution, and the regulation of markets.

■ Admission

- ➤ Bachelor's degree required for admission
- ➤ application deadline—March 1 priority, rolling admission
- ➤ LSAT, LSDAS required ➤ median GPA—3.49
- ➤ median LSAT score—160 ➤ application fee—$35

Generally, the quality and size of the applicant pool forces the Admissions Committee to rely heavily on the undergraduate grade-point average and the LSAT score. However, numerical indicators are not the only considerations used in evaluating applications. The committee considers the quality of the applicant's undergraduate institution, level and rigor of course work, letters of recommendation (particularly from undergraduate or graduate faculty members), graduate work, employment during and after college, extracurricular activities, potential for service to the profession, educational diversity, and state of residence. Increasing the diversity of the student body, particularly with respect to minorities, is also important to the school.

■ Housing

Law students live both off campus and in graduate- or married-student campus housing. For information concerning campus housing contact Halls of Residence, 801 N. Jordan Ave., Bloomington, IN 47405-2107.

■ Student Activities

The *Indiana Law Journal* publishes articles by legal scholars, practitioners, jurists, and IU law students. Students edit the journal and publish it four times a year. Members are selected on the basis of academic achievement or through a writing competition. The *Federal Communications Law Journal* is the nation's oldest and largest communications law journal. A student-managed journal that publishes three times a year, the journal features articles of interest to those involved in federal communications law, telecommunications, intellectual property and information policy. The *Indiana Journal of Global Legal Studies* is a multidisciplinary journal that specializes in international and comparative law articles. The editorial board consists of practitioners and faculty from the law, business, and public policy schools.

In addition to the above journals, organizations common to most law schools such as moot court, international law society, volunteer legal aid, Student Bar Association, student newspaper, and legal fraternities are present. The student body is quite diverse, and there are many organizations that are very active. Along with clinics for which students receive academic credit, there are two clinics in which they may volunteer their time, and the school has a Public Interest Law Foundation to help fund pro bono activities of students during the summer.

■ Expenses and Financial Aid

➡ *tuition & fees—resident, $4,655; nonresident, $12,382*
➡ *estimated additional expenses—$9,000 includes room and board, books, supplies, and personal expenses*
➡ *fellowships available: scholastic and need-based*
➡ *minority fellowships available*
➡ *financial aid available; GAPSFAS for fellowships; FAFSA and FAC sheet for loan consideration*

■ Career Services

The Career Services Office actively assists with career planning and locating summer and permanent jobs. Typically, over 90 percent of each graduating class accepts employment within six months of graduation. Approximately one-half locate outside Indiana. Each year over 200 employers interview on-campus or at off-campus interview programs. Over 60 percent of each graduating class works in private law firms.

Applicant Group for the 1993–1994 Academic Year

Indiana University School of Law—Bloomington
This grid includes only applicants who earned 120-180 LSAT scores under standard administrations.

LSAT Score	3.75 +		3.50 -3.74		3.25 - 3.49		3.00 - 3.24		2.75 - 2.99		2.50 - 2.74		2.25 - 2.49		2.00 - 2.24		Below 2.00		No GPA		Total	
	Apps	Adm	Apps	Adm	Apps	Adm	Apps	Adm	Apps	Adm	Apps	Adm	Apps	Adm	Apps	Adm	Apps	Adm	Apps	Adm	Apps	Adm
175 - 180	0	0	1	1	1	1	0	0	0	0	0	0	0	0	0	0	0	0	0	0	2	2
170 - 174	3	3	2	2	4	4	3	3	4	3	2	0	0	0	0	0	0	0	0	0	18	15
165 - 169	16	16	18	18	27	27	35	32	16	8	11	6	1	1	1	0	0	0	0	0	125	108
160 - 164	43	43	67	66	98	82	85	43	30	8	12	1	13	2	3	0	1	0	0	0	352	245
155 - 159	44	28	106	58	149	46	106	13	55	3	36	4	18	2	3	0	1	0	1	0	519	154
150 - 154	31	18	61	20	82	6	82	12	57	8	29	0	13	1	8	1	0	0	4	0	369	66
145 - 149	12	2	26	7	51	9	60	9	45	8	20	3	8	1	7	0	5	0	3	0	237	39
140 - 144	3	1	8	2	12	3	29	5	26	2	26	2	17	2	5	0	1	0	3	0	130	17
135 - 139	0	0	2	0	5	0	12	0	7	0	12	0	6	0	9	0	2	0	2	0	57	0
130 - 134	0	0	0	0	1	0	4	1	4	0	7	1	2	0	6	0	1	0	0	0	25	2
125 - 129	1	0	0	0	0	0	0	0	0	0	1	0	0	0	0	0	0	0	0	0	2	0
120 - 124	0	0	0	0	0	0	0	0	0	0	0	0	0	0	0	0	1	0	0	0	1	0
Total	153	111	291	174	430	178	416	118	244	40	156	17	78	9	42	1	12	0	13	0	1835	648

Apps = Number of Applicants
Adm = Number Admitted
Reflects 95% of the total applicant pool.

Indiana University School of Law—Indianapolis

735 W. New York Street
Indianapolis, IN 46202

Phone: 317.274.2459

■ Introduction

The law school is located on the Indianapolis campus of Indiana University and Purdue University. This location is also home to most of the professional schools of Indiana University including the Schools of Medicine, Dentistry, Nursing, and Social Work. The law school is just minutes away from the state's courts, legislature, and major law firms, giving students opportunities not only to observe the legal process in action, but also to participate in that process as law clerks, judicial interns and legislative staff assistants. With nearly 800 students, the school is the largest in the state of Indiana and one of the few Big Ten law schools to offer the cultural, recreational, and professional advantages of an urban educational environment.

■ Enrollment/Student Body

➨ *1,392 applicants*   ➨ *432 admitted*
➨ *264 enrolled first-year class 1993*   ➨ *525 total full-time*
➨ *298 total part-time*   ➨ *11% minority*   ➨ *41% women*
➨ *26 states & foreign countries represented*
➨ *73 undergraduate schools represented*

■ Faculty

➨ *63 total*   ➨ *38 full-time*   ➨ *25 part-time or adjunct*
➨ *15 women*   ➨ *6 minority*

■ Library and Physical Facilities

➨ *410,000 volumes & equivalents*   ➨ *library hours:*
Mon.-Thurs., 8:00 A.M.-MIDNIGHT; Fri., 8:00 A.M.-11:00 P.M.;
Sat., 9:00 A.M.-7:00 P.M.   ➨ *LEXIS*   ➨ *NEXIS*
➨ *WESTLAW*   ➨ *25 full-time librarians*
➨ *library seats 412*

One of the largest in the nation, the library is a depository for the United States government and the United Nations publications. The library computer center features terminals from which students can conduct legal research.

■ Curriculum

➨ *Academic Support Program*   ➨ *90 credits required to graduate; of the 90 hours, 53 are in prescribed courses*
➨ *112 courses available, plus internships*
➨ *degrees available: J.D./M.B.A.; J.D./M.P.A.; J.D./M.H.A.*
➨ *semesters, start in Aug.*   ➨ *range of first-year class size: varies with the class, some as few as 30, others 70-90*

■ Academic Support Programs

Students are offered assistance through the Dean's Tutorial Society and the Tutorial Study Group. Supervised by a tenured faculty member, the tutorial society is staffed by academically distinguished students who offer assistance in case briefing, exam preparation, and through individual tutoring. The Tutorial Study Group meets for two hours each week under the direction of a faculty member and assists students with their legal writing and analytical skills.

■ Special Summer Program

Summer admission is offered to a select group of applicants who can benefit from a class emphasizing writing and analytical skills. Applicants who have either an LSAT score or GPA that is outside of the median range of accepted students, persons who are returning to school after several years outside of the classroom, and students for whom English is a second language may be considered for the summer program. Summer admittees earn two credits toward their J.D. degree, and continuation in the fall is not contingent upon performance in the summer program. There is no special application form for summer admission. All applicants who are not presumptively admitted are considered for the summer program.

■ Clinical Experiences

The law school offers several clinical programs: The Civil Practice Clinic allows students the opportunity to represent clients in a variety of cases, including housing, dissolution of marriage, support, consumer and administrative matters. In the Civil Practice Disability Clinic, students represent school-age children with special needs, as well as persons who are afflicted with the HIV virus, Alzheimer's disease, and AIDS. In the Criminal Defense Clinic, students represent clients in criminal cases involving a variety of misdemeanors or class D felony charges in the state of Indiana. A Federal Court internship program in which students work with federal judges is also operated each semester.

The law school has a Center for Law and Health. The center provides an environment for the study of the critical issues relating to health care. The center interprets health care regulations and conducts research on law reform issues both nationally and locally.

■ International Law

The law school offers several courses and seminars in the area of international law. Students can further cultivate their interest through participation in the professional journal, the *Indiana International and Comparative Law Review* and the International Law Society. Practical experience also can be gained through involvement in an internship in international law. Each year, the school sponsors a month-long China Summer Program, offered cooperatively with the East China Institute of Politics and Law in Shanghai. The program includes daily lectures in all major areas of Chinese law, instruction in the Chinese language, and visits to local courts and institutions.

■ Admission

➡ *LSAT, LSDAS required*   ➡ *median GPA—3.30*
➡ *median LSAT score—159*

The School of Law seeks to attain a culturally rich and diverse student body. To this end, admission decisions are based on a variety of factors. In addition to the LSAT and undergraduate GPA, the admissions committee considers, among other things, the undergraduate institution attended and its distribution of grades, the undergraduate major and grade performance from year to year, extracurricular activities and work responsibilities while in school, postgraduate experience, and proven ability to overcome adversity. Letters of recommendation and a short personal statement are also encouraged.

■ Student Activities

Students at the School of Law may participate in various activities, including the Student Bar Association, the Black Law Student Association, intramural and regional moot court, client counseling competitions, the student newspaper, legal fraternities, Women's Caucus, the *Indiana Law Review,* the *Indiana International and Comparative Law Review*, and the Dean's Tutorial Society. Students also serve as voting members on several faculty committees.

■ Expenses and Financial Aid

➡ *resident tuition & fees—full-time, $4,453; part-time, $3,017*   ➡ *nonresident tuition & fees—full-time, $11,588; part-time, $7,850*

Forty-four percent of the school's students receive financial aid. Scholarships are awarded on the basis of need and merit. Awards range from $1,000 to full tuition, regardless of residency status. While the law school does not grant fee waivers for applications, it will consider fee waivers for the LSAT.

■ Career Services and Bar Passage

The Career Services Office serves students interested in part-time, summer, and permanent employment. Services include, but are not limited to, inviting prospective employers to campus, staging mock interviews, a résumé review service, workshops, brown bag lunches with attorneys, judges and persons in alternative careers, and individual counseling sessions. The law school's graduates have an outstanding record of achievement on the Indiana Bar Examination—better than a 91 percent passage rate since the early 1970s.

Applicant Group for the 1993–1994 Academic Year

Indiana University School of Law—Indianapolis
This grid includes only applicants who earned 120-180 LSAT scores under standard administrations.

LSAT Score	3.75 +		3.50 -3.74		3.25 - 3.49		3.00 - 3.24		2.75 - 2.99		2.50 - 2.74		2.25 - 2.49		2.00 - 2.24		Below 2.00		No GPA		Total	
	Apps	Adm	Apps	Adm	Apps	Adm	Apps	Adm	Apps	Adm	Apps	Adm	Apps	Adm	Apps	Adm	Apps	Adm	Apps	Adm	Apps	Adm
175-180	0	0	1	1	0	0	0	0	0	0	0	0	0	0	0	0	0	0	0	0	1	1
170-174	2	2	0	0	0	0	1	1	1	1	0	0	0	0	1	1	0	0	0	0	5	5
165-169	3	3	4	4	4	4	7	7	4	4	5	5	2	1	1	1	0	0	0	0	30	29
160-164	10	10	19	19	24	23	25	25	16	16	5	2	10	5	5	1	1	0	1	1	116	102
155-159	15	15	41	41	57	50	74	49	38	17	20	6	11	3	6	1	1	0	4	4	267	186
150-154	20	12	36	15	59	9	78	10	54	8	40	5	22	3	5	2	2	1	3	0	319	65
145-149	9	1	17	1	40	6	49	10	48	12	35	6	10	2	8	2	5	0	4	0	225	40
140-144	1	0	8	0	17	2	36	0	37	3	36	5	12	1	9	1	1	0	9	1	166	13
135-139	0	0	1	0	1	0	14	1	13	0	13	0	6	0	12	0	1	0	5	0	66	1
130-134	0	0	0	0	0	0	2	0	2	0	5	0	2	0	4	0	1	0	1	0	17	0
125-129	0	0	0	0	0	0	0	0	1	0	1	0	3	0	1	0	0	0	1	0	7	0
120-124	0	0	0	0	0	0	1	0	0	0	0	0	0	0	0	0	0	0	0	0	1	0
Total	60	43	127	81	202	94	287	103	214	61	160	29	78	15	52	9	12	1	28	6	1220	442

Apps = Number of Applicants
Adm = Number Admitted
Reflects 94% of the total applicant pool.

Inter American University of Puerto Rico School of Law

P.O. Box 70351
San Juan, PR 00936-8351

Phone: 809.751.1912, exts. 2013, 2012

■ Introduction

The Inter American University School of Law is one of the 11 units of the Inter American University of Puerto Rico, a private nonprofit educational corporation accredited by the Middle States Association of Colleges and Secondary Schools, the Puerto Rico Council of Higher Education, and the Commonwealth of Puerto Rico Department of Education. The School of Law is approved by the ABA and is located in Santurce, part of San Juan, the capital city of Puerto Rico. Since its founding, the School of Law has successfully strived to meet the needs of the legal profession in particular, and Puerto Rico's society in general.

■ Enrollment/Student Body

➡ *1,060 applicants* ➡ *294 admitted first-year class 1993*
➡ *176 enrolled first-year class 1993* ➡ *77 total part-time*
➡ *99 first-year class 1993*

The student body comes mainly from Puerto Rico, although applicants from the mainland are encouraged to apply.

■ Faculty

➡ *38 total* ➡ *20 full-time* ➡ *18 part-time or adjunct*
➡ *9 women*

■ Library and Physical Facilities

➡ *160,098 volumes & equivalents* ➡ *100 library hours per week: Mon.-Fri., 7:30 A.M.-11:00 P.M.; Sat.-Sun. & holidays, 9:00 A.M.-10:00 P.M.* ➡ *LEXIS* ➡ *NEXIS*
➡ *DIALOG* ➡ *DOBIS/LUVEN* ➡ *MICRO JURIS*
➡ *9 full-time librarians* ➡ *library seats 329*

The Domingo Toledo Alamo Law School Library is a fully developed learning resources and audiovisual center, and contains two laboratories for computer-assisted legal research and learning.

Acquisitions, circulation, and cataloging functions are fully automated, and an on-line union catalog contains the resources of all the libraries of the university system.

In January 1990, the library signed a collaboration agreement to establish a consortium with the law school library of the Catholic University of Puerto Rico and the library of the Supreme Court of Puerto Rico, with the purpose of coordinating collection development and sharing its resources through an automated bibliographic network, interlibrary loans, and telecommunication services.

■ Curriculum

➡ *92 credits required to graduate* ➡ *158+ courses available for J.D.* ➡ *semesters, start in Aug. & Jan.*

The J.D. program covers three years in the day division and four years in the evening division. Candidates must complete a minimum of 92 credit hours with a GPA of not less than 2.0 to qualify for graduation.

Inter American University School of Law offers a three-week preparation course to be taken during the summer on a compulsory basis by students admitted to the school.

Students who enter law school must be willing to make a heavy commitment of time and energy. For its part, Inter American University is willing to provide the best possible professional education experience through the careful recruitment of a first-rate faculty, the development of a progressive curriculum, and a willingness to create new and exciting programs of clinical studies and research.

■ Admission

➡ *Bachelor's degree required* ➡ *application deadline—March 1* ➡ *LSAT required* ➡ *application fee—$25*
➡ *median GPA: 3.15 full-time; 3.18 part-time*
➡ *median LSAT score: 140 full-time; 139 part-time*

Proficiency in Spanish is essential in the program. Applicants must have a minimum grade index of 2.5, a medical certificate for students 21 years or younger, a police department certificate of good conduct, and appear for a personal interview, if required.

Candidates are required to take the Prueba de Admisión para Estudios Graduados (PAEG), The Aptitude Test for Graduate Education. Students should attain a 575 minimum score on this test. Application forms and other relevant information concerning the PAEG may be obtained from: Educational Testing Service, G.P.O. Box 1271, San Juan, PR 00936.

■ Housing

The university does not provide housing for law students. However, the areas surrounding the School of Law contain many private houses, apartments, and condominiums for rent.

■ Student Activities

The Inter American School of Law Review is the official publication of the School of Law. Leading articles are prepared by academicians, student members of *Law Review*, and practicing members of the profession. Its members work under the supervision of an editorial board of four students chosen on the basis of merit and dedication to the *Review*, and an academic advisor who is a faculty member appointed by the Dean.

Student organizations include the Student Council, an organization that represents the student body and participates in matters of administrative policy related to students' interests. Council representatives serve on various faculty committees, as well as the University Senate and the Board of Trustees; the Law Student Division of the American Bar Association; Phi Alpha Delta legal fraternity (composed not only of law students of the school, but also of distinguished, honorary members who are Supreme Court Justices, Federal District Court Judges, and other prominent attorneys); and the National Association of Law Students (which represents the three law schools of Puerto Rico and provides needed services to students, the legal profession, and the general community).

Guest speakers are invited to speak on topics of current concern in law and the social and behavioral sciences.The law review, *Revista Juridica de la Universidad Interamericana*, is written principally in Spanish by students, professors, and legal scholars on areas of current importance in the development of the law.

The Legal Aid Clinic Program of the Faculty is integrated with the Santurce Law Office through a combined effort of the U.S. Legal Service Corporation and Inter American University. Law students are provided with the opportunity to learn skills such as interviewing, negotiation and counselling, fact gathering and analysis, legal research and drafting, decision-making about alternative strategies, and preparation for trial and field practice. They also represent clients before administrative agencies and courts with the close supervision of the program's staff attorneys-professors, pursuant to rules of the Supreme Court of Puerto Rico. Students also gain practical experience by serving with Puerto Rico Legal Services, Inc.; San Juan Community Law Office, Inc.; Legal Aid Society of Puerto Rico; the district attorney's offices; and the Environmental Quality Board.

■ Expenses and Financial Aid

➡ *tuition & fees—full-time, $7,224; part-time, $5,504*
➡ *additional expenses (room & board, personal, books & supplies, transportation, and loan fees) full-time and part-time, $7,403* ➡ *scholarships available—State Student Incentive Grant Program, Legislature Educational Fund and merit (merit application due Aug. & Jan.)*
➡ *financial aid available; applications due—March 31*

The general university fee is $20 per semester. Students pay $25 to reserve a place in the class (after admission approval), $5 for the *Law Review*, and $10 per semester for student activities. There is a deferred-payment plan, and financial aid options include Federal Guaranteed Loan Program; Perkins Loan; Stafford; LAL; the Commonwealth Education Fund; the Students Incentive Grant program, and the College Work-Study Program. The university also has an Honor Scholarship program for law students based on academic accomplishment and financial need.

■ Career Services

The placement program's main purpose is to locate job opportunities for students and alumni, to orient students and alumni with regard to those job opportunities, and to advise prospective employees of placement services offered by the school.

The Dean of Students Office gives orientation and provides information concerning available graduate programs in Puerto Rico, the United States, and foreign countries. A collection of catalogues of law school graduate programs in the United States, Europe, and Canada is kept.

The Continuing Legal Education Program offers advanced courses and seminars concerning different fields of the law of interest to practicing lawyers as well as to the community in general.

Applicant Group for the 1993–1994 Academic Year

Inter American University of Puerto Rico School of Law
This grid includes only applicants who earned 120-180 LSAT scores under standard administrations.

LSAT Score	GPA 3.75 + Apps	Adm	3.50 -3.74 Apps	Adm	3.25 - 3.49 Apps	Adm	3.00 - 3.24 Apps	Adm	2.75 - 2.99 Apps	Adm	2.50 - 2.74 Apps	Adm	2.25 - 2.49 Apps	Adm	2.00 - 2.24 Apps	Adm	Total Apps	Adm
170 - 180	0	0	0	0	0	0	0	0	0	0	0	0	0	0	0	0	0	0
160 - 169	1	1	2	2	2	2	0	0	1	1	0	0	0	0	0	0	6	6
150 - 159	4	4	7	7	3	3	8	6	6	4	4	2	0	0	0	0	32	26
140 - 149	20	18	27	19	57	39	57	36	38	24	29	12	9	0	1	0	238	148
130 - 139	37	14	34	18	69	29	110	26	93	22	91	5	21	0	12	0	467	114
120 -129	7	0	13	0	22	0	37	0	37	0	57	0	9	0	5	0	187	0
Total	69	37	83	46	152	73	212	68	175	51	179	19	39	0	18	0	927	294

Apps = Number of Applicants
Adm = Number Admitted
Reflects 87% of the total applicant pool; 133 applicants were not included, as information concerning LSAT or GPA was not available.

University of Iowa College of Law

276 Boyd Law Building
Melrose at Byington Streets
Iowa City, IA 52242

Phone: 319.335.9071

■ Introduction

The College of Law was founded in 1865 and is the oldest law school west of the Mississippi River. It has been continuously approved by the ABA and is a charter member of the AALS. In 1967, the Iowa College of Law was among the first law schools to commit itself to take aggressive steps to encourage a stronger minority presence in legal education. Minority students constitute 23 percent of the student body of the College of Law. This is particularly noteworthy when it is considered that the state of Iowa has less than a 5 percent minority population. Iowa has hosted numerous summer institutes sponsored by the Council on Legal Education Opportunity (CLEO).

■ Student Body

- ➡ *1,814 applicants*   ➡ *498 admitted first-year class 1993*
- ➡ *233 enrolled first-year class 1993*   ➡ *660 total full-time*
- ➡ *23% minority*   ➡ *43% women*
- ➡ *41 states & foreign countries represented*
- ➡ *190 undergraduate schools represented*

■ Faculty

- ➡ *54 total*   ➡ *52 full-time*   ➡ *2 part-time or adjunct*
- ➡ *13 women*   ➡ *6 minority*

■ Library and Physical Facilities

- ➡ *727,308 volumes & equivalents*   ➡ *library open 108 hours per week*   ➡ *LEXIS*   ➡ *NEXIS*   ➡ *WESTLAW*
- ➡ *ILP*   ➡ *11 full-time librarians*   ➡ *library seats 666*
- ➡ *12 carrels in A/B room for audio/video playback & microfilm reading/printing*
- ➡ *2 CD-ROM workstations with numerous databases*
- ➡ *32-station LAN*   ➡ *380 individual study carrels*

The law building's central location on a bluff overlooking the Iowa River provides a professional enclave well suited to the college's intensive style of education, but with easy access to the academic, cultural, social, and recreational resources of the university.

■ Curriculum

- ➡ *Academic Support Program*   ➡ *90 semester-hours required to graduate*   ➡ *192 courses available*
- ➡ *degrees available: J.D.; J.D./M.B.A., (joint-program students enrolled in law and 13 other departments)*
- ➡ *semesters, start in Aug.*
- ➡ *range of first-year class size—28-120*
- ➡ *accelerated program begins in mid-May*   ➡ *graduate (LL.M.) program in International and Comparative Law*

■ Special Programs

Iowa is a leader among the nation's law schools in the development of a modern curriculum in which individual instruction in basic lawyer skills is integrated with the exploration of conceptual and institutional issues central to the legal process. The mainspring of this progressive curriculum is an ambitious writing program in which faculty-supervised writing exercises are provided in small classes each semester of a student's training. The lawyer-skills emphasis shifts from first-year concern with close analysis, research, precise expression, and advocacy to upper-class work on drafting, interviewing, counseling, negotiation, and litigation skills. The College of Law features a small-section program in the first year under which each student takes two courses in small sections of 30 or fewer. The first-year curriculum is required; thereafter, almost all courses are electives. The College of Law has a strong research orientation and students are encouraged to propose special projects in which they are interested.

■ Legal Clinic

Students who have completed the equivalent of three semesters (which may include a full summer session) toward their J.D. degrees (usually in excess of 37 credits) are eligible to participate in the College of Law's Legal Clinic Program. Students in the law school's in-house program work directly with faculty members on cases involving civil rights and liberties, statutory entitlements, criminal defense, and general representation in civil matters. Clinic interns participate fully in interviewing, fact investigation, negotiation, trials, and appellate proceedings. The clinic also administers specialized programs in representing farmers in financial distress and persons with HIV disease.

■ International Law

The College of Law offers a strong program of study in international law. In this era of accelerating global interdependence, virtually any lawyer may find herself or himself confronted by problems that require knowledge and understanding of international law and foreign legal systems. The study of international and comparative law provides unique insight into the nature of law and legal process and helps to establish the necessary theoretical foundations upon which superior lawyering skills depend.

■ Admission

- ➡ *Bachelor's degree from approved college or university required*   ➡ *application deadline—Feb. 1*
- ➡ *LSAT, LSDAS required*   ➡ *median GPA—3.49*
- ➡ *median LSAT score—159*   ➡ *application fee—$20*
- ➡ *foreign application fee—$30*

A faculty rule limits the college to no more than 30 percent nonresidents in the freshman class, so the resulting criteria for nonresidents are somewhat higher. Criteria other than the LSAT will be taken into account for applicants who demonstrate the inapplicability of the LSAT as a predictor of success for them. Included in this group are applicants from disadvantaged backgrounds as well as others.

Student Activities

Student-run cocurricular programs include the *Iowa Law Review*, the *Journal of Corporation Law*, the *Journal of Transnational Law and Contemporary Problems*, the Moot Court Board, Trial Advocacy, and Client Counseling. Other law student organizations are the American Bar Association Law Student Division, Equal Justice Foundation, National Lawyers Guild, Iowa Student Bar Association, the Iowa Society of International and Comparative Law, Environmental Law Society, Phi Delta Phi and Phi Alpha Delta (national law fraternities open to both men and women), the Black Law Students Association, the Chicano Hispanic Association for Legal Education, Asian American Law Student Association, Native American Law Student Association, National Lesbian and Gay Law Association, Community of Associated Nontraditional Age Law Students, and the Organization of Women Law Students and Staff.

Expenses and Financial Aid

➡ *tuition & fees—full-time resident, $3,624, nonresident, $10,190* ➡ *estimated additional expenses—$7,648 (health fee, books & supplies, room & board, personal, transportation)* ➡ *merit & need-based scholarships available* ➡ *minority scholarships available* ➡ *financial aid available*

The Law Opportunity Fellowship program provides financial and counseling services to students from economically and educationally disadvantaged backgrounds. Eligibility for financial aid is based on need established by completion of the Free Application for Federal Student Aid (FAFSA). FAFSA forms are available after January 1 and should be completed as soon as possible.

Career Services

Each year the Placement Office brings a variety of employers to campus from across the United States to conduct job interviews. During the 1991-92 academic year (the most recent year for which we have complete statistics) more than 225 employers visited the campus. Of those graduates reporting, 91 percent were placed within six months of graduation. Nearly all of our second-year students (and a good number of our first-year students) seek and find law-related employment for the summer. While most work as clerks in law firms throughout the country, some work as prosecuting interns for county attorney's offices across the state and others serve as research assistants to faculty members here at the law school. The Placement Office actively encourages students' career growth by sponsoring weekly programs that explore the various employment options available, from small- and large-firm practice, judicial clerkships, and prosecution careers to the areas of public-interest, government, and corporate legal counsel. The placement staff meets individually with all first-year students to make sure they get off to a good start.

Applicant Group for the 1993–1994 Academic Year

University of Iowa College of Law
This grid includes only applicants who earned 120-180 LSAT scores under standard administrations.

LSAT Score	3.75 +		3.50 -3.74		3.25 - 3.49		3.00 - 3.24		2.75 - 2.99		2.50 - 2.74		2.25 - 2.49		2.00 - 2.24		Below 2.00		No GPA		Total	
	Apps	Adm	Apps	Adm	Apps	Adm	Apps	Adm	Apps	Adm	Apps	Adm	Apps	Adm	Apps	Adm	Apps	Adm	Apps	Adm	Apps	Adm
175-180	1	1	1	1	1	1	0	0	0	0	0	0	0	0	0	0	0	0	0	0	3	3
170-174	2	2	5	5	3	3	1	1	1	0	1	0	1	1	0	0	0	0	1	0	15	12
165-169	24	23	18	15	22	14	26	11	5	3	2	0	3	0	1	0	0	0	1	1	102	67
160-164	39	39	74	59	67	34	52	18	23	3	15	0	6	0	2	0	0	0	2	0	280	153
155-159	56	27	81	38	86	28	72	15	43	9	28	2	11	2	5	0	0	0	7	1	389	122
150-154	27	10	69	23	67	11	64	7	44	3	25	3	19	1	12	0	0	0	8	1	335	59
145-149	18	4	26	7	38	10	35	3	38	3	34	1	21	0	10	0	3	0	8	1	231	29
140-144	14	4	8	2	24	1	33	0	25	1	30	1	25	0	14	0	3	0	10	1	186	10
135-139	0	0	3	0	8	0	15	1	18	0	34	0	20	0	8	0	2	0	5	0	113	1
130-134	0	0	0	0	0	0	3	0	6	0	12	0	13	0	7	0	4	0	5	0	50	0
125-129	0	0	0	0	0	0	1	0	2	0	1	0	3	0	2	0	2	0	2	0	13	0
120-124	0	0	0	0	0	0	0	0	0	0	0	0	0	0	0	0	2	0	0	0	2	0
Total	181	110	285	150	316	102	302	56	205	22	182	7	122	4	61	0	16	0	49	5	1719	456

Apps = Number of Applicants
Adm = Number Admitted
Reflects 95% of the total applicant pool.

The John Marshall School of Law

315 South Plymouth Court
Chicago, IL 60604

Phone: 312.987.1406

■ Introduction

The John Marshall School of Law is an independent
school founded in 1899 to provide a legal education to
academically qualified persons without consideration of
sex, sexual orientation, race, religion, color, national origin, ancestry, age, or physical handicap. The school is
located in downtown Chicago, across the street from the
federal court building and within easy walking distance
from the Civic Center, which houses most local courts. It
is approved by the ABA and is a member of the AALS.

■ Enrollment/Student Body

- 2,290 applicants   - 260 enrolled first-year class 1993
- 609 total full-time   - 372 total part-time
- 13% minority   - 34% women
- 28 states & foreign countries represented by first-year class
- 121 undergraduate schools represented by first-year class

Approximately 69 percent of the students are Illinois residents. Over 250 colleges and universities are represented
in the student body.

■ Faculty

- 188 total   - 54 full-time   - 136 part-time or adjunct
- 11 women   - 5 minority

■ Library and Physical Facilities

- 280,000 volumes & equivalents   - 900 audiovisual
tapes   - library hours: Mon.-Fri., 8:00 A.M.-11:00 P.M.;
Sat.-Sun., 9:00 A.M.-9:00 P.M.   - LEXIS   - NEXIS
- WESTLAW   - CALI, DIALOG
- 20 full-time librarians   - library seats 594

The library's Center for Computerized Legal Instruction includes eight LEXIS terminals, eight WESTLAW terminals,
and 17 PCs with CALI (Computer Assisted Legal Instruction) software. Seventeen PCs with WordPerfect software
are available in two word processing centers. Special arrangements with LEXIS and WESTLAW permit students to
access these services from their home computers.

■ Curriculum

- 90 semester hours required to graduate   - semesters,
start in Aug. & Jan.   - degrees available: J.D.;
J.D./M.B.A.; LL.M.   - range of first-year class size—10-50

The school has day and evening divisions, both requiring 90 semester hours to earn the J.D. degree. The
instruction, course content, and scholastic requirements
are identical in each division. Summer-term courses are
also offered. A joint J.D./M.B.A. degree program in cooperation with Rosary College is also offered.

■ Special Programs

The law school offers comprehensive professional skills
training. Three interrelated programs comprise this training: the Lawyering Skills Program, the Center for Advocacy, and the Clinical Law Externship Program. The
Legal Writing Program, formally known as Lawyering
Skills, consists of a four-semester required sequence of
courses taught in small sections, enabling faculty to
work with students individually. The Center for Advocacy serves John Marshall students by providing a
comprehensive and focused approach to attaining advocacy skills. The Clinical Law Externship Program places
students with approved federal, state, and local agencies, law firms, the judiciary, and other legal
organizations to gain practical experience outside the
classroom.

The Center for Informatics Law was established in 1983
to carry on legal research and policy analysis regarding
newly developing information and communications
technology. Courses offered include Information Law
and Policy, Computers and the Law, and Media Law and
the Right of Privacy. Qualified students may apply after
their first year of academic study to work for the center
as research assistants. The Center for Intellectual Property Law offers extensive programs in this rapidly
growing area of law. Courses in the J.D. program focus
on patent and trade secrets; trademark, unfair competition, and copyright law; computer and franchising law;
and entertainment law.

■ Admission

- B.A./B.S. required   - application deadline—April 1/
Oct. 1, rolling admission   - LSAT, LSDAS required
- median GPA—3.20   - median LSAT score—158
- application fee—$40

Students are admitted in August and January. Applications for August entrance may be filed between October
1 and April 15; for January entrance, between May 1 and
October 15. The LSAT score is evaluated together with
the cumulative grade-point average and other relevant
factors including difficulty of undergraduate program,
postgraduate experience, leadership potential, business
and professional background, and letters of recommendation. Applicants from minority and disadvantaged
groups will be given special consideration in cases
where their overall records are competitive with other
applicants. Applicants with a B average overall and an
LSAT score in the 74th percentile may be presumed to be
within the range for favorable consideration. A Summer
Conditional Program is offered to a limited number of
candidates whose qualifications do not meet the usual
standards, but whose discrepant predictors may be persuasive of probable success in law school. A special
minority program, the Legal Education Access Program,
is also offered during the fall semester. No separate application form is used for either of these programs.

■ Student Activities

The *John Marshall Law Review*, edited exclusively by students, publishes works on a broad range of current legal topics written by legal scholars, practitioners, and John Marshall law students. The *Software Law Journal* is an international law review focusing on law and policy with regard to software, databases, and information networks. It is managed by a student editorial board. The John Marshall Moot Court Council and Executive Board are the student organizations that coordinate the various moot court activities, including participation in over 20 national and international competitions. The law school sponsors a nationally respected moot court competition, the John Marshall National Moot Court Competition in Information Technology and Privacy. A new, national trial advocacy competition, cosponsored with the American Bar Association and focusing on criminal justice problems, is also held each spring at the law school. Many fraternal, ethnic, and legal-interest organizations reflect the broad variety of interests among John Marshall students.

■ Expenses and Financial Aid

➨ *tuition & fees—full-time, $13,200/year; part-time, $7,920*
➨ *estimated additional expenses—$12,370/year (books, $400; living expenses, $11,910; registration, $60)*
➨ *academic scholarships available* ➨ *academic minority scholarships available* ➨ *need-based financial aid available, JMLS financial aid form due May 1*
➨ *participates in Stafford, Supplemental Loan for Students, and Law Access Loan programs*

Tuition for the 1993-94 academic year is $440 per semester-hour. The regular day-division course load is 15 hours and the regular evening-division course load is 9-11 hours. Dean's scholarships and grants are awarded to entering students based upon academic achievement. Renewal of these awards is based on academic performance. All applicants for financial aid must file the Graduate and Professional School Financial Aid Service (GAPSFAS) form.

■ Career Services

The Career Services Office assists students and graduates in obtaining permanent employment and helps students find summer and part-time positions. The office also offers a two-semester program in professional/personal development. There is an active on-campus interviewing program throughout the year and many employers who do not interview on-campus do interview John Marshall students in their offices. Virtually all of the major Chicago law firms include John Marshall graduates among their associates and partners. In addition to private practice, John Marshall graduates can be found in government, corporate, and public-interest sectors. Some of our most recent graduates have taken positions with the U.S. Department of Justice and other agencies of the federal government, in accounting firms, and as judicial clerks in federal courts of appeal, U.S. district courts, and state supreme and appellate courts.

Applicant Group for the 1993–1994 Academic Year

The John Marshall School of Law
This grid includes only applicants who earned 120-180 LSAT scores under standard administrations.

LSAT Score	GPA 3.75 +		3.50 -3.74		3.25 - 3.49		3.00 - 3.24		2.75 - 2.99		2.50 - 2.74		2.25 - 2.49		2.00 - 2.24		Below 2.00		No GPA		Total	
	Apps	Adm	Apps	Adm	Apps	Adm	Apps	Adm	Apps	Adm	Apps	Adm	Apps	Adm	Apps	Adm	Apps	Adm	Apps	Adm	Apps	Adm
175-180	0	0	0	0	1	1	0	0	0	0	0	0	0	0	0	0	0	0	0	0	1	1
170-174	2	2	0	0	0	0	2	2	1	1	2	2	2	2	0	0	0	0	1	0	10	9
165-169	3	2	4	4	1	0	11	10	3	3	7	7	3	2	2	2	0	0	0	0	34	30
160-164	9	9	9	9	16	16	30	30	30	29	26	26	15	12	10	9	2	1	0	0	147	141
155-159	11	10	37	35	71	63	95	83	97	78	87	56	46	26	19	8	6	2	1	1	470	362
150-154	14	9	41	32	116	88	160	107	149	53	117	36	65	6	29	7	3	2	7	2	701	342
145-149	14	8	25	8	65	23	116	25	115	17	95	15	64	4	33	1	3	0	4	0	534	101
140-144	4	0	16	4	20	2	64	9	78	2	78	3	46	3	26	1	4	0	12	0	348	24
135-139	2	0	3	1	10	1	17	0	24	0	33	2	30	0	19	0	3	0	8	0	149	4
130-134	0	0	1	0	2	0	10	1	11	1	16	0	13	0	6	0	4	0	3	0	66	2
125-129	0	0	0	0	0	0	0	0	3	0	3	0	1	0	1	0	0	0	1	0	9	0
120-124	0	0	0	0	0	0	1	0	0	0	0	0	0	0	0	0	1	0	0	0	2	0
Total	59	40	136	93	302	194	506	267	511	184	464	147	285	55	145	28	26	5	37	3	2471	1016

Apps = Number of Applicants
Adm = Number Admitted
Reflects 93% of the total applicant pool.

University of Kansas School of Law

205 Green Hall
Lawrence, KS 66045

Phone: 913.864.4378

■ Introduction

The University of Kansas School of Law was founded in 1891, replacing a Department of Law that had existed since 1878. The School of Law is located in Lawrence, Kansas, 40 miles west of Kansas City and 25 miles east of Topeka, the state capital. The school is a charter member of the AALS and is fully accredited by the ABA.

■ Enrollment/Student Body

➟ *1,063 applicants*   ➟ *302 admitted first-year class 1993*
➟ *166 enrolled first-year class 1993*   ➟ *525 total full-time*
➟ *12% minority*   ➟ *43% women*
➟ *29 states & foreign countries represented*
➟ *80 undergraduate schools represented*

The student body consists of 82 percent Kansas residents. The nonresidents come from all parts of the country.

■ Faculty

➟ *39 total*   ➟ *29 full-time*   ➟ *10 part-time or adjunct*
➟ *10 women*   ➟ *3 minority*

■ Library and Physical Facilities

➟ *325,000 volumes & equivalents*   ➟ *library hours: Mon.-Thurs., 7:30 A.M.-11:00 P.M.; Fri., 7:30 A.M.-10:00 P.M.; Sat., 10:00 A.M.-5:00 P.M.; Sun., NOON-11:00 P.M.*
➟ *LEXIS*   ➟ *NEXIS*   ➟ *WESTLAW*   ➟ *DIALOG*
➟ *3 full-time librarians*   ➟ *library seats 353*

The law library has ample reading areas and individual study carrels and maintains a microcomputer laboratory for student use.

■ Curriculum

➟ *Academic Support Program*   ➟ *90 credits required to graduate*   ➟ *108 courses available*   ➟ *degrees available: J.D.; J.D./M.B.A.; J.D./M.P.A.; J.D./M.A. in Economics; J.D./M.S. in Urban Planning; J.D./M.S.W.; J.D./M.S. Health Services Administration; J.D./M.A. in Philosophy*
➟ *fall semester starts in Aug. and summer semester starts in May*
➟ *range of first-year class size—20-100*

Six semesters of full-time study are required for graduation. Two summer sessions of five weeks each are available. Students may begin their law studies in either the summer session or the fall semester. Students who begin in the summer and are continuously enrolled in summer sessions and regular semesters can graduate in 26 months. The summer program is also open to students with advanced standing at an accredited law school other than the University of Kansas.

The first-year curriculum is prescribed. All first-year students take one course in a small section of about 20 students. Second- and third-year students are required to take courses in commercial law, constitutional law, evidence, and legal profession. Each student must also complete a faculty-supervised writing project in the second or third year. Upper-class students can choose from a wide variety of elective courses, workshops, and clinical programs. Many third-year courses offer intensive training in planning and supervising legal transactions and drafting legal documents.

■ Special Programs

The Legal Aid Clinic is operated for the benefit of the Douglas County Legal Aid Society. Third-year law students represent low-income clients in actual civil cases under the supervision of clinical faculty and practicing attorneys in Lawrence. Students in the Criminal Justice Clinic assist prosecutors in virtually all phases of the criminal process, including criminal trials. Participants in the Defender Project counsel and perform legal services for indigent inmates of the U.S. Penitentiary at Leavenworth, the Kansas State Penitentiary, and Kansas Correctional Institution at Lansing.

The Judicial Clerkship Clinic provides an opportunity for students to serve as part-time law clerks for judges in a district court, the Kansas Court of Appeals, or a federal court. The Legislative Clinic sends a number of students to work as legislative interns to Kansas state legislators.

The school offers seven joint-degree programs. Each program allows a student to obtain two degrees in less time than it would normally take to earn them separately, generally four years.

■ Admission

➟ *Bachelor's degree required for admission*
➟ *application deadline—March 15*
➟ *LSAT, LSDAS required*   ➟ *median GPA—3.43*
➟ *median LSAT score—159*   ➟ *application fee—$40*

The application deadline is March 15 for both the summer session and the fall semester. The school encourages students to apply by February 1.

The Admissions Committee seeks to admit highly qualified students with diverse backgrounds. Admissions decisions are based on a variety of criteria. The committee considers and compares applicants' undergraduate coursework and grades, and LSAT scores as well as other factors, including race, ethnic background, employment or professional experience, undergraduate and graduate program of study, leadership in university and civic activities, unique individual qualities and achievements, and demonstrated ability to overcome cultural, financial, or other disadvantages. The committee also considers the applicant's state of residence; preference is given to Kansas residents. One letter of recommendation is required, two or three letters are encouraged. A personal statement is also required. Interviews are not part of the admissions process.

The School of Law is committed to the principle of providing access to the legal profession to men and women of all races, religions, ethnic backgrounds, and physical abilities. To that end, the School of Law engages in active recruitment of potential applicants with diverse backgrounds and characteristics, including those of minority race and ethnic background.

Admissions decisions are made from January through April. After the class is filled, a waiting list is established. Each applicant offered admission pays a $50 deposit which is refunded to the student at enrollment.

■ Student Activities

The *Kansas Law Review*, published four times annually, is edited by third-year students. The *Kansas Journal of Law and Public Policy* is edited by third-year students and is published twice annually. The Moot Court Council operates all phases of the Appellate Advocacy program and also has responsibility for the Moot Court competition. The Student Bar Association is responsible for most student activities. There are active chapters of Phi Alpha Delta and Phi Delta Phi legal fraternities, Black Law Students Association, Hispanic American Law Students Association, Native American Law Student Association, Pacific American Law Student Association, Women in Law, Christian Legal Society, International Law Society, American Trial Lawyers Association, and Order of the Coif.

■ Expenses and Financial Aid

➡ *tuition & fees—full-time resident, $2,928; nonresident, $6,996* ➡ *estimated additional expenses—$9,500 (books, room and board, transportation, and misc. expenses)* ➡ *merit-based scholarships available (generally first year only)* ➡ *minority scholarships available* ➡ *financial aid available: FAFSA Form—priority deadline March 1*

For more information: Office of Student Financial Aid, University of Kansas, 50 Strong Hall, Lawrence, KS 66045.

■ Career Services

The school has a full-time career services director and an aggressive placement program involving career counseling, a wide variety of workshops, and resource facilities for extensive legal and nontraditional job hunting research. Of the numerous placement opportunities available to law school graduates, law firms of all sizes attracted the highest percentage (55.9 percent) of those placed. By November 1, 1992, 74 percent of the 1992 class was employed, with one percent not looking for employment at that time. Students were placed in 16 states across the nation. The greatest percentage (70 percent) of those placed chose to remain in Kansas and the Kansas City metropolitan area.

Applicant Group for the 1993–1994 Academic Year

University of Kansas School of Law
This grid includes only applicants who earned 120-180 LSAT scores under standard administrations.

LSAT Score	3.75 +		3.50 -3.74		3.25 - 3.49		3.00 - 3.24		2.75 - 2.99		2.50 - 2.74		2.25 - 2.49		2.00 - 2.24		Below 2.00		No GPA		Total	
	Apps	Adm	Apps	Adm	Apps	Adm	Apps	Adm	Apps	Adm	Apps	Adm	Apps	Adm	Apps	Adm	Apps	Adm	Apps	Adm	Apps	Adm
175-180	2	2	1	1	0	0	1	1	0	0	0	0	0	0	0	0	0	0	0	0	4	4
170-174	2	2	1	1	4	4	3	3	2	0	0	0	0	0	0	0	0	0	0	0	12	10
165-169	8	8	6	4	15	11	9	8	2	0	11	3	3	0	0	0	0	0	0	0	54	34
160-164	18	16	29	28	32	31	36	19	21	4	9	2	5	0	1	0	0	0	0	0	151	100
155-159	28	21	47	31	76	24	61	18	31	4	15	2	15	1	2	0	1	0	1	1	277	102
150-154	13	5	41	7	47	5	69	5	35	1	20	1	15	1	4	0	0	0	3	0	247	25
145-149	14	2	12	1	14	3	47	4	30	0	16	0	9	0	5	0	1	0	7	0	155	10
140-144	3	0	2	0	12	1	9	0	12	2	13	0	9	0	2	0	2	0	2	0	66	3
135-139	1	0	0	0	3	0	4	0	6	0	6	1	4	0	4	0	0	0	3	0	31	1
130-134	0	0	0	0	0	0	1	0	3	0	2	0	3	0	5	0	0	0	0	0	14	0
125-129	0	0	0	0	0	0	0	0	0	0	0	0	0	0	1	0	0	0	0	0	1	0
120-124	0	0	0	0	0	0	0	0	0	0	0	0	0	0	0	0	0	0	0	0	0	0
Total	89	56	139	73	203	79	240	58	142	11	92	9	63	2	24	0	4	0	16	1	1012	289

Apps = Number of Applicants
Adm = Number Admitted
Reflects 95% of the total applicant pool.

University of Kentucky College of Law

Dean's Office
209 Law Building
Lexington, KY 40506-0048

Phone: 606.257.7938 for catalogs; 606.257.1678 for other inquiries

■ Introduction

The University of Kentucky College of Law is a medium-sized, state-supported law school located on the main campus of the university at Lexington. Lexington, a city of approximately 220,000, is the center of the Bluegrass horse farm region of Kentucky. The college was founded in 1908, has held membership in the AALS since 1912, and has been approved by the ABA since 1925. The faculty has wide experience in teaching, research, law practice, and government service and provides a student-faculty ratio of 19 to 1. By long tradition, the educational mission of the school has been to prepare its graduates for a full range of professional interests in law throughout the nation.

■ Enrollment/Student Body

➥ 1,195 applicants   ➥ 134 enrolled first-year class 1993
➥ 413 total full-time (356 residents; 57 nonresidents)
➥ 6% minority   ➥ 40% women
➥ 25 states & foreign countries represented
➥ 104 undergraduate schools represented

■ Faculty

➥ 48 total   ➥ 28 full-time   ➥ 20 part-time or adjunct
➥ 13 women   ➥ 2 minority

■ Library and Physical Facilities

➥ 328,730 volumes & equivalents   ➥ LEXIS
➥ NEXIS   ➥ WESTLAW   ➥ DIALOG
➥ library seats 392

The college is housed in a contemporary brick and marble building that provides all facilities for a complete program of legal education, including a large courtroom.

The law library contains one of the major legal collections in the southeast. The newest acquisition, a state-of-the-art, 50-station computer laboratory for students, was completed in fall 1993 and is located on the main floor of the library.

■ Curriculum

➥ Academic Support Program   ➥ 90 total credits required to graduate   ➥ 64 courses available
➥ degrees available: J.D.; J.D./M.B.A.; J.D./M.P.A.
➥ range of first-year class size—10-75

The college offers only a full-time program, designed to be completed over three academic years (six semesters) of residence. The first-year program is prescribed. In the second and third years, a full range of elective courses is offered in traditional and newly developing legal fields. After the first year, the only specific requirements are that each student take a course in professional ethics and complete one upper-class course that involves substantial writing.

■ Special Programs

The Mineral Law Center, established in 1983, concentrates on legal problems relating to coal and other minerals. It publishes the *Journal of Natural Resources and Environmental Law*, a journal devoted to mineral law and related issues. The center is a resource for the state and nation in matters of coal extraction, use, and environmental protection. The college provides second- and third-year students with opportunities for clinical experience in civil and criminal cases. Students are invited to participate in all seminars for the bench and bar sponsored by the college's Office of Continuing Legal Education. The college also hosts two lectureship series, bringing U.S. Supreme Court Justices and other national figures to speak to its students and the community.

■ Student Activities

The College of Law has a variety of cocurricular activities in which students may earn credit and which are an integral part of the instructional program. The *Kentucky Law Journal*, a quarterly containing articles by prominent national scholars, is the tenth oldest American law review and is edited entirely by a student editorial board.

Another journal, the *Journal of Natural Resources and Environmental Law*, focuses on articles about mineral, natural resources, and environmental law, and also offers its student staff an opportunity to work with lawyers of national stature.

The Moot Court Program consists of competitive appellate arguments by student teams; the successful team represents the college each year in the National Moot Court Competition. The college's teams have a history of excellence and have advanced to the national finals five times in the last seven years.

The Trial Advocacy Board teaches effective trial level advocacy through student competition; its members also are members of the local chapter of Inns of Court.

The Student Bar Association, affiliated with the Law Student Division of the ABA, serves as the student governing body, produces a student newspaper, and arranges weekly professional, cultural, and social programs.

The college has long had an Order of the Coif. Other organizations include the Women's Law Caucus, the Association of Black Law Students, the Christian Legal Society, the International Law Society, National Lawyers' Guild, The Federalist Society, Student Public Interest Law Foundation, and three legal fraternities.

■ Admission

➥ Bachelor's degree from accredited college or university required   ➥ application deadline—Mar. 1; admission decisions begin in Nov., continue weekly through spring
➥ LSAT, LSDAS required   ➥ median GPA—3.30
➥ median LSAT score—160   ➥ application fee—$25

Admission is considered and granted by the Faculty Admissions Committee. Each file is reviewed completely before any action is taken. The committee considers all the information in an applicant's file, including undergraduate grade record, the LSAT score, and other quantitative and nonquantitative factors indicative of aptitude for law study. The committee examines with particular care the grade average for the most recent semesters of undergraduate study, recommendations of faculty, the nature and difficulty of coursework attempted, undergraduate extracurricular activities, work experience, and postbaccalaureate experiences. The committee reviews the file of each applicant to determine whether there is evidence of both the capability and motivation to do successful law school work. The committee also considers factors that bear on the provision of adequate legal services to all segments of Kentucky. Each applicant is urged to read the full description of the admissions process contained in the law school bulletin and to provide full information about his or her intellectual and nonacademic achievements. The February LSAT is the last examination accepted by the Admissions Committee. Applicants are admitted for the fall term only.

■ Expenses and Financial Aid

➡ *1993-94 full-time tuition & fees—resident, $3,598; nonresident, $9,738*   ➡ *estimated additional expenses— $8,000 (books, room and board, misc.)*
➡ *minority scholarships available*
➡ *financial aid programs available; Federal Free Form due April 1 for all loan assistance and work-study*

Scholarships for the first year of study are merit-based and usually awarded to students whose academic records are exceptionally strong. The largest and most prestigious are the three-year, $20,000 awards to Bert Combs Scholars, chosen by an application and competition process.

For all other first-year student scholarship awards, no additional application is necessary. All students admitted to the College of Law are considered automatically by the Scholarships and Honors Committee on the basis of their admission files. Second- and third-year students must submit applications on the basis of merit and/or need.

Law students are also eligible for loan assistance with federal Perkins Loans, Stafford Loans, Supplemental Loans for Students, the College Work-Study program and private loan programs specifically for law students. Contact the university Student Financial Aid Office, 128 Funkhouser Building, University of Kentucky, Lexington, KY 40506-0054.

■ Career Services

UK Law students have access to hundreds of summer and permanent jobs nationwide through the College of Law's on-campus interviewing program and its participation in six off-campus interviewing conferences. The Southeastern Law Placement Consortium holds an annual conference in Atlanta that attracts government, corporate, and law firm employers from across the country. UK also participates in the Southeastern Law School Minority Job Fair, the Mid-South Law Placement Consortium, the NAPIL Public Interest Job Fair, the All-Kentucky Job Fair, the new Sci-Law Job Fair, and the Southeastern Public Interest Job Fair. Many local legal employers hire UK law students to work part-time during the school year. The College's Career Planning Office, run by an Associate Dean who formerly practiced law, also has initiated a computerized service to connect UK law students with employers in its region.

Applicants for the 1993–1994 Academic Year

University of Kentucky College of Law
This grid includes only applicants who earned 120-180 LSAT scores under standard administrations in the 1992-1993 testing year.

LSAT Score	3.75 +		3.50 - 3.74		3.25 - 3.49		3.00 - 3.24		2.75 - 2.99		2.50 - 2.74		2.25 - 2.49		Below 2.25		Total	
	Apps	Adm	Apps	Adm	Apps	Adm	Apps	Adm	Apps	Adm	Apps	Adm	Apps	Adm	Apps	Adm	Apps	Adm
165 & Above	4	4	10	10	11	11	14	14	11	10	8	7	2	2	2	2	62	60
160 - 164	13	13	26	25	27	24	33	33	23	19	11	8	9	3	3	1	145	126
155 - 159	23	15	49	26	59	20	65	18	55	5	21	0	15	0	3	0	290	84
150 - 154	20	6	41	4	64	4	71	1	57	2	31	0	11	1	4	0	299	18
145 - 149	11	2	27	0	39	2	53	2	28	1	31	2	14	1	4	0	207	10
140 - 144	3	1	5	1	12	0	23	1	26	1	20	0	16	0	3	0	108	4
Below 140	1	0	2	0	3	0	10	0	9	0	16	0	9	0	4	0	54	0
Total	75	41	160	66	215	61	269	69	209	38	138	17	76	7	23	3	1165	302

Apps = Number of Applicants
Adm = Number Admitted
The class enrolled had a median LSAT score of 160 and a median GPA of 3.30.

Lewis and Clark, Northwestern School of Law

10015 SW Terwilliger Blvd.
Portland, OR 97219

Phone: 503.768.6613

■ Introduction

Northwestern School of Law of Lewis and Clark College believes in a balanced approach to legal education that assures a solid theoretical foundation along with hands-on experience in practice. The campus is one of the most beautiful in the nation. Situated next to a state park, students are only a moment away from an extensive trail system used by joggers, walkers, and bicyclists. The law school is accredited by the ABA and AALS.

■ Enrollment/Student Body

➡ 2,574 applicants   ➡ 904 admitted first-year class 1993
➡ 246 enrolled first-year class 1993   ➡ 473 total full-time
➡ 216 total part-time   ➡ 15% minority
➡ 42% women   ➡ 34 states & foreign countries represented
➡ 230 undergraduate schools represented

The 680-700 students attending the law school represent a spectrum of ages, experiences, and priorities. Business executives, biologists interested in resources and environmental law, students of politics, musicians, school teachers—people from almost all of the analytical disciplines meet at the law school in a common pursuit. The atmosphere at the law school is one of mutual support during a time of academic challenge. Students and faculty can often be found discussing questions long after class has ended.

■ Faculty

➡ 100 total   ➡ 39 full-time   ➡ 61 part-time or adjunct
➡ 25 women   ➡ 2 minority

The full-time faculty were educated at the nation's most distinguished law schools. The faculty reflects a breadth of experience and interests that give depth and creative energy to their teaching. A number of faculty members have spent sabbaticals in recent years teaching in other countries; several have been Fulbright professors in such places as China, Greece, and Venezuela.

■ Library/Physical Facilities

➡ 325,000 volumes & equivalents   ➡ library hours: Mon.-Thurs., 7:00 A.M.-MIDNIGHT; Fri., 7:00 A.M.-10:00 P.M.;
Sat.-Sun., 9:00 A.M.-MIDNIGHT   ➡ LEXIS
➡ NEXIS   ➡ WESTLAW   ➡ 7 full-time librarians
➡ library seats 433

The materials and staff of the Paul Boley Law Library, the largest law library in the state, well exceed the standards set by the Association of American Law Schools. Our collection of more than 300,000 volumes is augmented by extensive microform materials and advanced computer retrieval systems.

Framed by majestic fir trees, the campus is composed of contemporary buildings with both classrooms and a large state park within a moment's walk from the library. Traditional student needs and those of individuals with disabilities are met through a variety of facilities.

■ Curriculum

➡ 86 units/credits required to graduate   ➡ 123 courses available   ➡ degrees available: J.D.; LL.M. in Environmental & Natural Resources Law   ➡ semesters, begin in Aug.   ➡ range of first-year class size—12-84
➡ Academic Support Program

The law school confers both the J.D. degree and a specialized LL.M. in Environmental and Natural Resources Law. To earn a J.D., a student must take a prescribed first-year set of courses. In the upper division, students must take a seminar, constitutional law, and professionalism and fulfill two writing requirements. Students choose between a three-year day program and a four-year evening program. Admission criteria, faculty, academic opportunities, and graduation requirements are the same for each. After the first year, students may select courses in either division as their scheduling requirements suggest.

■ Specific Special Programs

Environmental Law Certificate (B.F.): The faculty has established a certificate program to acknowledge the law school's nationally renowned concentration in Environmental and Natural Resource Law. The specialty is grounded in a core curriculum broad enough to allow students to prepare for careers in numerous areas of law practice.

Externships: Externships combine practical and scholarly components by placing the student in full-time work for a semester and then requiring a substantial research paper and attendance at a special seminar. Four types of externship are available—judicial, natural resources and environmental law, criminal, and general. Externs are placed in Oregon, throughout the United States, and in foreign countries.

International Business Law: The law school offers a selection of courses in international business law emphasizing the Pacific Rim. More than one-quarter of the full-time faculty have substantial international experience.

Moot Courts: Students may get moot court experience in mock trial, appellate advocacy, environmental law, international law, and client counseling. The school regularly competes at the regional and national levels.

Trial Advocacy: Students get the opportunity to try civil and criminal cases in front of local judges in the trial practice course offered each year. A criminal practice course deals solely with criminal trial work and is taught by a local trial judge.

■ Admission

➡ *Bachelor's degree required*   ➡ *application deadline—*
March 15, rolling admission   ➡ *LSAT, LSDAS required*
➡ *median GPA—3.20*   ➡ *median LSAT score—161*
➡ *application fee—$45*

Lewis and Clark affirmatively seeks a diverse student
body. The Admission Committee makes a serious effort to
consider each applicant as an individual. Factors such as
college, program, length of time since the degree was
obtained, experience, writing ability, and community activities are taken into consideration. Only those candidates
with excellent professional promise are admitted. Academic attrition is low, averaging 2 to 4 percent.

First-year students may begin only in the fall; there is
no provision for midyear admission.

■ Student Activities

These include the law review, *Environmental Law*, numerous speakers on campus, an endowed program that brings
an outstanding legal scholar to campus for lectures and
seminars, and a number of student organizations reflecting
the diverse make-up of the student body.

■ Expenses and Financial Aid

➡ *tuition & fees—full-time, $13,900; part-time, $9,650*
➡ *estimated additional expenses—$6,000 (books, rent, trans-
portation, living expenses)*   ➡ *scholarships available*
➡ *minority scholarships available*   ➡ *financial aid available:
FAF form application deadline—Feb. 15*

Approximately 40 percent of the students at Lewis and
Clark receive some scholarship support during their law
school career. The school annually awards Dean's Fellowships, Natural Resources Scholarships, Public Interest
Fellowships, and International Business Law Fellowships
for up to $9,000 apiece. In addition, loan money and work-
study funds are available. There is no separate application
procedure for scholarship funds. Scholarship consideration
is part of the admission process. Students are considered
on the basis of undergraduate record, LSAT score, activities, and writing ability.

Students interested in loans need to apply for financial
aid as early as possible and should not wait for an admission decision to begin the process.

■ Career Services

The Career Services Office gives seminars, maintains an
alumni network around the country to help with positions
after graduation, and hosts panels of working attorneys
who discuss with students specific areas of practice. There
are on-campus interviews each fall, and the career services
office assists students in finding clerking positions during
law school. Recent graduates have been placed in a wide
variety of desirable positions around the country.

Applicant Group for the 1993–1994 Academic Year

Lewis and Clark, Northwestern School of Law
This grid includes only applicants who earned 120–180 LSAT scores under standard administrations.

LSAT Score	3.75 +		3.50 -3.74		3.25 - 3.49		3.00 - 3.24		2.75 - 2.99		2.50 - 2.74		Below 2.50		No GPA		Total	
	Apps	Adm	Apps	Adm	Apps	Adm	Apps	Adm	Apps	Adm	Apps	Adm	Apps	Adm	Apps	Adm	Apps	Adm
175-180	0	0	2	2	2	2	3	3	1	1	2	2	1	1	2	1	13	12
170-174	1	1	7	7	6	6	9	9	3	3	4	4	2	1	1	1	33	32
165-169	4	14	25	23	29	29	34	34	26	25	18	16	16	10	2	2	164	153
160-164	35	35	77	73	94	77	101	76	58	35	40	20	32	4	8	5	445	325
155-159	31	22	95	66	129	52	159	42	109	24	53	4	31	2	10	2	617	214
150-154	22	7	72	15	122	16	146	12	100	8	55	7	40	1	10	1	567	67
145-149	10	1	30	4	51	4	68	5	64	5	56	2	34	0	8	1	321	22
140-144	2	0	11	1	19	2	20	2	32	2	34	0	32	0	7	0	157	7
Below 140	2	0	2	0	3	0	10	0	20	0	18	0	31	0	8	0	94	0
Total	117	80	321	191	455	188	550	183	413	103	280	55	219	19	56	13	2411	832

Apps = Number of Applicants
Adm = Number Admitted
Reflects 94% of the total applicant pool.

Louisiana State University Law Center

Baton Rouge, LA 70803

Phone: 504.388.8646

■ Introduction

The Louisiana State University Law Center was originally established as the Louisiana State University Law School in 1907, pursuant to an authorization contained in the university charter. In 1979, the Law Center was renamed the Paul M. Hebert Law Center of Louisiana State University. The Law Center holds membership in the AALS and is on the approved list of the ABA.

■ Enrollment/Student Body

➡ *1,234 applicants*   ➡ *479 admitted first-year class 1993*
➡ *284 enrolled first-year class 1993*   ➡ *743 total full-time*
➡ *7% minority*   ➡ *43% women*

■ Faculty

➡ *47 total*   ➡ *36 full-time*   ➡ *11 part-time*
➡ *4 women*   ➡ *2 minority*

■ Library and Physical Facilities

➡ *539,287 volumes & equivalents*   ➡ *library hours: Mon.-Fri., 7:00 A.M.-11:00 P.M.; Sat., 9:00 A.M.-5:00 P.M.; Sun., NOON-11:00 P.M.*   ➡ *LEXIS*   ➡ *NEXIS*
➡ *WESTLAW*   ➡ *DIALOG*   ➡ *STAIRS*
➡ *9 full-time librarians*   ➡ *library seats 565*

The Law Center Building, completed in October 1969, adds extensive facilities to the original Law Building dedicated in 1938. This complex provides classroom areas, seminar rooms, discussion rooms, and meeting areas as well as a practice court room. Special offices for student research and student activities such as the *Louisiana Law Review*, Appellate Advocacy Board, and Student Bar Association are included in the facility. The Law Library, housed in the complex, provides one of the most complete collections of Roman and modern civil law reports and materials in the country. Library resources include reading rooms, discussion rooms, study carrels, personal computers, and audiovisual facilities. Students also have access to other campus facilities including the Student Health Center, residential housing, and the Sports Recreational Complex.

■ Curriculum

➡ *97 units required to graduate*   ➡ *87 courses available*
➡ *degrees available: J.D.; J.D./M.P.A.; LL.M.; & M.C.L.*
➡ *semesters, start in Aug.*
➡ *range of first-year class size—75-80*

First-year students have a prescribed curriculum and thereafter students may choose a wide variety of electives in addition to the core of civil law courses. An orientation program and library tour introduces the first-year class to the study of law. The Law Center's dedication to the study of both the civil and the common law prepares its graduates to practice in any state and in some foreign countries. Students receive a unique insight with the comparison of the two legal systems. Seven semesters of resident study are required for the degree. In addition to its full-time law faculty, the LSU Law Center each semester invites a number of special lecturers, including practicing attorneys and legal scholars, to teach courses in which they are particularly distinguished. A number of faculty have law degrees from foreign countries. This serves to promote the study of international law and an understanding of the policies of foreign law.

■ Summer Session Abroad

The Law Center conducts a summer program in France at the University of Aix-Marseille III Law School, Aix-en-Provence, France. All classes of the six-week summer program are conducted in English and are designed to meet the requirements of the ABA and AALS.

■ Special Programs

A wide variety of courses affords each student the opportunity to participate in the preparation and trial of mock cases, both civil and criminal, and also to develop skill in legal negotiations and counseling. LSU sponsors and encourages student participation in national trial and appellate competitions through the school year.

In cooperation with the Center of Continuing Professional Development, the Law Center presents several seminars, institutes, and conferences for practicing lawyers.

The LSU Law Center admits candidates for the degrees of Master of Laws (LL.M.) and Master of Civil Law (M.C.L.). The program is highly selective and admits students with exceptional ability.

■ Admission

➡ *Bachelor's degree from accredited college or university required*   ➡ *application deadline—Feb. 1, rolling admissions, early application preferred*   ➡ *LSAT, LSDAS required*
➡ *median GPA—3.35*   ➡ *median LSAT score—156*
➡ *application fee—$25*

No specific prelaw curriculum is required for admission. Applicants are chosen mainly on the basis of the combination of their GPA and LSAT score. Applicants are advised to take the LSAT in October or no later than December prior to the year in which they seek admission to the Law Center. When the LSAT is repeated, the highest score received is used. The Law Center admits students only in the fall and only for full-time study. There are no night courses offered. Written recommendations are not required, and personal interviews are not encouraged. Because of the great number of applicants, only a few nonresidents are accepted. Transfer applications may be made, but only students who originally would be admissible to the Law Center and have excellent law school records are accepted.

Louisiana State University assures equal opportunity for all qualified persons without regard to race, color, religion, sex, national origin, age, disability, marital status, or veteran's status in the admission to, participation in, or employment in the programs and activities that the university operates.

■ Student Activities

The *Louisiana Law Review* was established to encourage high-quality legal scholarship in the student body, to contribute to the development of the law by scholarly criticism and analysis, and to serve the bar of Louisiana by comments and discussion of current cases and legal problems. It is edited by a board of student editors with faculty cooperation.

The Louisiana Chapter of the Order of the Coif, a national honorary law fraternity, was established in the Law Center in 1942. Election to the Order of the Coif is recognized as the highest honor a law student may receive.

Since a large number of graduates of the Law Center go directly into practice, the LSU Law Center has an extensive Trial Advocacy Program in which moot court training is offered both for trial work and in appellate argument.

All students in the Law Center are eligible to join the Student Bar Association. This association promotes and coordinates student activities within the Law Center and serves as an instructional medium for postgraduate bar association activities.

■ Expenses and Financial Aid

➡ *tuition & fees—full-time/semester resident students, $1,937, full-time/semester nonresident students, $4,247*
➡ *estimated additional expenses—$300/semester books*
➡ *performance & need-based scholarships available*
➡ *ACT form for need analysis due to financial aid office in March*

A number of loan funds are available to help deserving students who need financial assistance to continue their education. All such funds are subject to the policies and regulations authorized by the LSU Student Loan Fund Committee. Detailed information on all loan funds may be secured by contacting the Student Loan Section, LSU Office of Financial Aid and Scholarships, 202 Himes Hall, Baton Rouge, LA 70803.

■ Career Services

The Career Services Office of the Law Center provides job opportunities for students and graduates. It serves as a liaison between the numerous firms, businesses, and governmental agencies in providing on-campus interviews each year. This office offers a series of workshops and individual counseling to help meet the career needs of all students.

Applicant Group for the 1993–1994 Academic Year

Louisiana State University Law Center

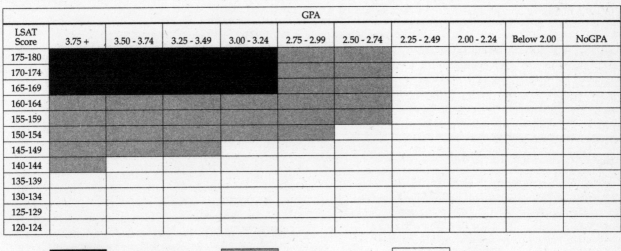

LSAT Score	GPA									
	3.75 +	3.50 - 3.74	3.25 - 3.49	3.00 - 3.24	2.75 - 2.99	2.50 - 2.74	2.25 - 2.49	2.00 - 2.24	Below 2.00	NoGPA
175-180	■	■	■	■	▨	▨				
170-174	■	■	■	■	▨	▨				
165-169	■	■	■	■	▨	▨				
160-164	▨	▨	▨	▨	▨	▨				
155-159	▨	▨	▨	▨	▨	▨				
150-154	▨	▨	▨	▨	▨	▨				
145-149	▨	▨	▨							
140-144	▨									
135-139										
130-134										
125-129										
120-124										

■ Good Possibility   ▨ Possible   ☐ Unlikely

University of Louisville School of Law

Louisville, KY 40292

Phone: 502.852.6364

■ Introduction

Founded in 1846, the University of Louisville School of Law is Kentucky's oldest law school and America's fifth oldest in continuous operation. Heir to the legacy of Justice Louis D. Brandeis, the school is distinguished by a rich history, national outreach, and profound dedication to public service. It is an integral part of the University of Louisville, a public institution and major research center founded in 1798. The metropolitan area, with a population of approximately one million, combines a gracious ambience of southern hospitality with cultural, aesthetic, and recreational attractions that have put Louisville on the "Places Rated Almanac" top ten list of most liveable American cities. Historic Churchill Downs, the acclaimed Kentucky Center for the Arts, the J.B. Speed Art Museum and the university's outstanding sports facilities are near the law school or within a few minutes drive.

■ Enrollment/Student Body

➡ *1,388 applicants* ➡ *383 admitted first-year class 1993*
➡ *142 enrolled first-year class 1993* ➡ *426 total full-time*
➡ *106 total part-time* ➡ *6% minority* ➡ *45% women*
➡ *27 states & foreign countries and 105 undergraduate schools represented in student body*

The School of Law promotes equal opportunity, geographical and cultural diversity, and a positive learning environment for all students.

■ Faculty

➡ *39 total* ➡ *28 full-time* ➡ *11 part-time or adjunct*
➡ *13 women (including 5 adjunct faculty)* ➡ *4 minority*

Based on full-time equivalency standards, the law school has an attractive faculty-student ratio of 1 to 18.5. Law faculty recently have acted as consultants to the Kentucky General Assembly, the U.S. Securities and Exchange Commission, the State Justice Institute, the U.S. Administrative Office of the Courts, and the constitutional drafting commissions of the former Soviet republics of Belarus and Kyrghystan.

■ Library and Physical Facilities

➡ *236,032 volumes & equivalents (4,300 serials)*
➡ *library hours: Mon.-Thurs., 8:00 A.M.-11:00 P.M.; Fri., 8:00 A.M.-6:00 P.M.; Sat., 9:00 A.M.-5:00 P.M.; Sun., 1:00 P.M.-11:00 P.M.* ➡ *LEXIS* ➡ *WESTLAW* ➡ *OCLC*
➡ *4 full-time librarians* ➡ *library seats 367*

The modern law library contains two computer rooms; OCLC, LEXIS and WESTLAW services; CD-ROM and interactive instructional workstations; and distance education (satellite and ground network) connections. The library also houses the Brandeis Rare Book Room and, by direction of Justice Brandeis, a collection of original Supreme Court briefs.

■ Curriculum

➡ *90 units/credits and public service component required for J.D. degree (3 years full time, 4 years part time)* ➡ *117 courses available, 4 internship programs; 8 moot court, mock trial and other professional skill competitions; law review and individual studies* ➡ *degrees available: J.D. and two combined degree (J.D./M.B.A. and J.D./M.Div.) programs*
➡ *semesters, start in Aug. and Jan.; summer term in May*
➡ *range of first-year class size—40-60 (in 3 sections)*

The law school full-time day division and part-time evening division share the same curriculum, faculty, and academic standards. After basic courses in the first year, students take "core" courses in doctrinal subjects, advanced research and writing, and professional responsibility. Students also may choose among a rich variety of specialized and interdisciplinary electives. The School of Law conducts an innovative summer enrichment program for selected, newly admitted students. A highly successful academic support office serves students throughout the year.

■ Special Programs

The School of Law contains a Center for Environmental Policy, which promotes interdisciplinary studies. National speakers present the annual Brandeis Lecture, Harlan Lecture, Petrilli Family Law Seminar, and Labor/Employment Law Institute. The school operates clinical internship programs in which upperclass students, with supervision, represent clients and appear in court. The school has active faculty and/or student international exchanges with law schools in England, France, Germany, Japan, and Australia.

■ Specific Special Programs

The M.B.A./J.D. program is offered jointly by the School of Law and the School of Business. Upon successful completion of the program, the student is awarded both the M.B.A. and J.D. degrees. The School of Law, in connection with the Louisville Presbyterian Theological Seminary, offers a double competency program leading to the degree of Master of Divinity (M.Div.) as well as the J.D.

■ Public Service Program

Reflecting the spirit of Justice Louis D. Brandeis, the School of Law is one of America's first five law schools to adopt public service as part of the prescribed course of study. Through this public-service work, students develop lawyering skills, serve their communities and establish professional values.

■ Admission

➡ *Baccalaureate degree (candidacy) required*
➡ *application deadline—Feb. 15* ➡ *rolling admission*
➡ *LSAT, LSDAS required* ➡ *median GPA—3.20*
➡ *median LSAT score—157* ➡ *application fee—$30*

The School of Law has no specific prelaw requirements but agrees with the suggestions on prelaw study contained in the first section of this handbook. Applicants are encouraged to complete their files no later than February 15. Later applications ordinarily will be considered only if space becomes available. In truly exceptional circumstances the School of Law may consider applicants who have taken the LSAT in June immediately preceding the fall semester of expected enrollment. Applicants with nontraditional credentials may be invited to a summer admission-by-performance program.

■ Expenses and Financial Aid

➡ *annual tuition & fees—full-time resident, $3,490; full-time nonresident, $9,630; part-time resident, $2,343; part-time nonresident, $6,438 (8 hours per semester)* ➡ *estimated additional expenses—$9,528 (includes full housing, board, books & supplies, transportation, and personal expenses)* ➡ *moderate cost housing available near university* ➡ *merit and need scholarships available* ➡ *financial aid approximately $320,000 in 1993-94* ➡ *FAF due April 1*

■ Publications and Student Activities

The School of Law publishes three student-edited periodicals with national or international circulation. The *Journal of Family Law*, the school's "law review," is published quarterly, including an internation edition. The *Journal of Law and Education* is published jointly by the law schools of the University of Louisville and the University of South Carolina. *The Brandeis Brief* is a magazine-style publication containing interdisciplinary articles in the Brandeis tradition and news of the law school.

The School of Law emphasizes professional skill programs. It participates in five different national moot court competitions, an international moot court program, a negotiations competition sponsored by the American Bar Association, a mock trial program sponsored by the American Bar Association, and a mock trial program sponsored by the Association of Trial Lawyers of America. All students are thoroughly trained in legal writing and oral argument in their first year, and they may participate in the intraschool Pirtle-Washer Competition.

Honor students are recognized by membership in the law school's Brandeis Society. The Society awards the prestigious Brandeis Medal to America's outstanding lawyers and jurists. Recipients have included Supreme Court Justices Sandra Day O'Connor and Harry Blackman, Senator Christopher Dodd, and civil rights attorney Morris Dees.

The Student Bar Association, affiliated with the Law Student Division of the American Bar Association, plays an important role in law school governance.

■ Career Opportunities

Graduates have enjoyed a higher Kentucky bar passage rate than the overall average, and they have been successful in other states as well. The most recent (1993) national survey of law graduates showed University of Louisville law students well above the national average in obtaining law employment within six months of graduation. Students are assisted by a "proactive" career services program enhanced by computer databases and headed by a full-time director with dual J.D. and M.B.A. degrees. The law school participates in, and occasionally hosts, regional job fairs and consortia.

Applicant Group for the 1993–1994 Academic Year

University of Louisville School of Law
This grid includes only applicants who earned 120-180 LSAT scores under standard administrations.

LSAT Score	3.75 +		3.50 -3.74		3.25 - 3.49		3.00 - 3.24		2.75 - 2.99		2.50 - 2.74		2.25 - 2.49		2.00 - 2.24		Below 2.00		No GPA		Total	
	Apps	Adm	Apps	Adm	Apps	Adm	Apps	Adm	Apps	Adm	Apps	Adm	Apps	Adm	Apps	Adm	Apps	Adm	Apps	Adm	Apps	Adm
175 - 180	0	0	0	0	0	0	0	0	0	0	0	0	0	0	0	0	0	0	0	0	0	0
170 - 174	1	1	1	1	3	3	0	0	1	1	2	2	1	0	0	0	0	0	0	0	9	8
165 - 169	2	2	4	4	6	6	5	5	7	7	2	2	1	0	1	0	0	0	1	1	29	27
160 - 164	3	3	5	5	14	14	21	21	21	18	14	9	10	6	5	2	0	0	0	0	93	78
155 - 159	14	14	36	33	45	36	64	40	55	21	33	8	18	6	3	0	0	0	2	0	270	158
150 - 154	19	13	55	24	85	12	99	11	79	9	44	2	22	1	8	0	0	0	4	0	415	72
145 - 149	10	2	24	1	49	1	66	6	56	1	33	1	15	1	9	0	0	0	3	0	265	13
140 - 144	1	0	7	0	15	1	32	0	34	0	32	1	19	0	9	0	0	0	2	0	151	2
135 - 139	1	0	0	0	3	0	12	0	7	0	16	0	9	0	8	0	1	0	2	0	59	0
130 - 134	0	0	1	0	1	0	1	0	5	0	1	0	7	0	2	0	1	0	0	0	19	0
125 - 129	0	0	0	0	0	0	1	0	0	0	0	0	1	0	0	0	0	0	0	0	2	0
120 - 124	0	0	0	0	0	0	1	0	0	0	0	0	0	0	1	0	0	0	0	0	2	0
Total	51	35	133	68	221	73	302	83	265	57	177	25	103	14	46	2	2	0	14	1	1314	358

Apps = Number of Applicants
Adm = Number Admitted
Reflects 95% of the total applicant pool.

Loyola University Chicago School of Law

One East Pearson Street
Chicago, IL 60611

Phone: 312.915.7170, 1.800.545.5744

■ Introduction

Loyola University Chicago is the second largest private institution of higher learning in Illinois. The School of Law is located on the Water Tower campus of the university, a few blocks north of the Chicago Loop. This campus adjoins Michigan Avenue at the historical Water Tower, a Chicago landmark, in approximately the center of the renowned "Magnificent Mile," a commercial center over which the John Hancock Center Towers. This location provides ready access to the state and federal courts and to the offices of most other institutions of federal, state, and local government as well as the cultural centers of Chicago. The school is a member of the AALS and is approved by the ABA.

■ Enrollment/Student Body

➡ *2,639 applicants*   ➡ *861 admitted first-year class 1993*
➡ *246 enrolled first-year class 1993*   ➡ *511 total full-time*
➡ *176 total part-time*   ➡ *18% minority*
➡ *52% women*   ➡ *38 states & foreign countries represented*
➡ *90 undergraduate schools represented*

■ Faculty

➡ *154 total*   ➡ *34 total full-time*   ➡ *120 total part-time or adjunct*   ➡ *57 women*   ➡ *6 minority*

■ Library and Physical Facilities

➡ *285,000 volumes & equivalents*   ➡ *library hours (including weekends and evenings)—99 hours per week*
➡ *LEXIS*   ➡ *NEXIS*   ➡ *WESTLAW*
➡ *7 full-time librarians*   ➡ *library seats 326*

■ Curriculum

➡ *Academic Support Program*   ➡ *86 units/credits required to graduate*   ➡ *101 courses available*   ➡ *degrees and combined available: J.D.; LL.M.; M.J.; J.D./M.B.A.; J.D./M.S.W.; J.S./M.A.; J.D./M.I.R.*   ➡ *semesters, start in Aug.*   ➡ *range of first-year class size—45-75*
➡ *first-year legal writing sections of 16 max.*

■ Foreign Study Programs

Since 1983 the School of Law has offered a program of international and comparative law courses at the Rome Center for Liberal Arts, the university's campus in Rome, Italy. Each summer, for approximately five weeks, law students from the United States and elsewhere can take one or more of the courses offered in Rome by members of the full-time Loyola law faculty.

In January 1989, Loyola inaugurated its London Advocacy Program in which eight students travel to London for approximately 15 days to become immersed in the world of the British barrister. In addition to a series of lectures and tours, law students accompany British barristers to courts and observe them as they conduct trials at London's renowned "Old Bailey."

The Institute for Health Law sponsors a summer course on comparative health law in conjunction with the McGill University Center for Medicine, Ethics, and Law. In alternate summers, the program is conducted at McGill University in Montreal, Canada.

■ Dual Degree Programs

The School of Law has dual-degree programs with Loyola's School of Social Work, the Graduate Program of the Department of Political Science, the Graduate School of Business, and the Institute of Human Resources and Industrial Relations. The dual-degree programs are structured to allow completion after four years.

■ Institute for Health Law

The Institute for Health Law was created in 1984, in recognition of the need for an academic forum to study the field of health law and to act as a vehicle to foster dialogue between the law and the health sciences. Based in a university with schools of medicine, dentistry, nursing, and social work, and a large urban medical center, the School of Law is in an ideal position to act as a catalyst to foster interdisciplinary evaluation of the expansive legal issues encountered by our health delivery systems.

The institute is the sponsor of the first Master of Jurisprudence in health law (M.H.) degree program in the country, a program designed to provide health professionals with an intensive overview of health-care law. In addition, the institute offers a health law LL.M. for attorneys who wish to specialize in this field. In the J.D. curriculum, the institute works with law faculty to ensure that the school's health law offerings are both comprehensive and timely. There are currently 18 health law courses taught in the law school.

Civitas ChildLaw Center—The Civitas ChildLaw Center was created to prepare law students to represent abused and neglected children. Each year only 10 Civitas Scholars are accepted from among students admitted to the Law School's entering class. Each scholar selected receives a $3,000 grant, renewable for three years, as well as summer financial internship support. In addition to a regular course of legal study, the selected Civitas scholars will have the opportunity to participate in a unique specialized curriculum, including extensive extern opportunities and "hands-on" internship experiences designed to create enhanced knowledge and practical skills needed for effective representation of children. This specialized academic/clinical curriculum will give the students first-hand experience in the physical, psychological, and emotional realities of child abuse.

As an integral component of the law school, the Center is able to draw on the full resources of Loyola University, including its schools of medicine, nursing, social work, and education, to educate students dedicated to using the law for children. The Center is the first of its kind at any American law school and is being referred to as a model for other law school-based child advocacy programs. At the conclusion of the three-year J.D. program, students will have been trained thoroughly to serve as skilled litigators and advocates for children.

■ Admission

➨ *Bachelor's degree required* ➨ *application deadline—April 1* ➨ *rolling admission, early application preferred* ➨ *LSAT, LSDAS required* ➨ *median GPA—3.24* ➨ *median LSAT score—160* ➨ *application fee—$40*

Factors other than LSAT scores and college grades are considered whenever the LSAT and the GPA are at or above acceptable levels. Such factors include work experience, specialized education, and other evidence of ability to contribute invaluable insight to law classes.

■ Student Activities

Students are encouraged to participate in cocurricular activities, especially after completion of the first year. *The Loyola Law Journal* is a quarterly professional journal edited by students who are selected on a competitive basis. Articles, comments, and notes on both state and federal developments in law are published. *The Loyola Consumer Law Reporter* is devoted to legal analyses of current issues affecting consumers. Students compete in many interschool and intraschool moot court competitions as well as the National Mock Trial Competitions.

All students are eligible to participate on the staff of the School of Law newspaper, *Blackacre*, which is published approximately eight times each year.

■ Expenses and Financial Aid

➨ *tuition & fees—full-time, $13,950; part-time, $10,460* ➨ *estimated additional expenses—$9,400 (books, rent, food, clothing, transportation)* ➨ *scholarships available: average $3,500; academic, public interest, ethnic, Law Journal, Consumer Law Reporter and The Bar Examiner* ➨ *minority scholarships available: black, Hispanic, and Italian* ➨ *financial aid available; FAF or GAPSFAS required, priority deadline—April 1*

■ Career Services

The Career Services Office assists students and alumni with career planning and employment selection.

A year-round on-campus employer interview and recruitment program provides employment opportunities for students. In addition, there is daily posting of employment opportunities for legal and nonlegal positions.

Seminars by practicing attorneys and alumni; résumé preparation, review and critique; interviewing techniques and strategies; individual counseling sessions; and job-search strategies are just some of the many programs for students and alumni administered by the Career Services Office.

An extensive resource center contains information on law firms, corporations, judicial clerkships, governmental agencies, legal service/public-interest programs, academic and fellowship opportunities. Bar information and general career resource files on all areas of practice are available to assist students in defining those areas of practice most suited to their goals and life styles.

The School of Law is a member of the National Association for Law Placement (NALP).

Applicant Group for the 1993–1994 Academic Year

Loyola University Chicago School of Law
This grid includes only applicants who earned 120-180 LSAT scores under standard administrations (reflects 96% of the total applicant pool).

LSAT Score	3.75 +		3.50 -3.74		3.25 - 3.49		3.00 - 3.24		2.75 - 2.99		2.50 - 2.74		2.25 - 2.49		2.00 - 2.24		Below 2.00		No GPA		Total	
	Apps	Adm	Apps	Adm	Apps	Adm	Apps	Adm	Apps	Adm	Apps	Adm	Apps	Adm	Apps	Adm	Apps	Adm	Apps	Adm	Apps	Adm
175 - 180	0	0	2	1	2	2	3	1	0	0	0	0	0	0	0	0	0	0	0	0	7	4
170 - 174	3	3	1	1	3	3	4	3	2	2	2	2	2	2	0	0	0	0	1	0	18	16
165 - 169	8	8	19	18	19	18	29	26	20	16	11	8	3	3	3	1	0	0	0	0	112	98
160 - 164	34	33	50	50	88	85	80	66	52	36	25	13	15	9	3	1	0	0	1	1	348	294
155 - 159	29	23	108	61	146	70	157	53	101	20	63	15	24	3	10	1	3	0	6	3	647	249
150 - 154	20	5	67	11	152	26	156	23	97	12	60	7	35	5	8	2	2	0	4	1	601	92
145 - 149	14	1	39	9	64	9	91	8	78	7	62	9	37	3	16	1	3	0	2	0	406	47
140 - 144	2	0	15	0	26	2	41	1	47	1	50	0	23	0	12	0	2	0	4	1	222	5
135 - 139	2	0	3	0	7	0	14	0	10	0	18	0	20	0	3	0	1	0	5	0	83	0
130 - 134	0	0	1	0	3	0	5	0	7	1	8	0	11	0	7	0	2	0	2	0	46	1
125 - 129	0	0	0	0	1	0	0	0	2	0	0	0	1	0	1	0	0	0	1	0	6	0
120 - 124	0	0	0	0	0	0	0	0	0	0	0	0	0	0	1	0	0	0	0	0	1	0
Total	112	73	305	151	511	215	580	181	416	95	299	54	172	25	63	6	13	0	26	6	2497	806

Apps = Number of Applicants
Adm = Number Admitted

Loyola Law School, Los Angeles, Loyola Marymount University

1441 W. Olympic Blvd.
Los Angeles, CA 90015

Phone: 213.736.1180

■ Introduction

Loyola Law School, established in 1920, is one of the oldest law schools in Southern California. The Law School has strong ties with the city of Los Angeles, one of the world's most important legal, political, and financial centers. Loyola is a member of the Order of the Coif and provides the highest standards of education and professional development in the context of the university's deeply held ethical and moral values. Recognized for the teaching excellence of its faculty, Loyola offers a comprehensive academic program with the opportunity for both in-depth scholarly development and intensive preparation for the practice of law.

■ Enrollment/Student Body

➡ *3,862 applicants*   ➡ *1,173 admitted first-year class 1993*
➡ *456 enrolled first-year class 1993*
➡ *1,025 total full-time*   ➡ *336 total part-time*
➡ *30% minority*   ➡ *44% women*
➡ *over 40 states & foreign countries represented*
➡ *over 100 undergraduate schools represented*

■ Library and Physical Facilities

➡ *340,456 volumes & equivalents*   ➡ *library hours: Mon.-Thurs., 7:00 A.M.-MIDNIGHT; Fri., 7:00 A.M.-8:30 P.M.; Sat., 9:00 A.M.-8:30 P.M.; Sun., 9:00 A.M.-MIDNIGHT*   ➡ *LEXIS*
➡ *NEXIS*   ➡ *WESTLAW*   ➡ *DIALOG, C.CALI*
➡ *11 full-time librarians*   ➡ *library seats 683*

Loyola's modern and dynamic campus was designed by the internationally renowned architect Frank Gehry. Encompassing an entire city block, the Law School occupies eight buildings, including a new parking structure, classrooms, courtrooms, advanced audio-visual and computer centers, dining facilities and offices. The "academical village" design with its many courtyards, plazas, rooftop terraces, and grassy knolls, has become the focal point for outdoor group study, social activities, and various participation sports. The William M. Rains Law Library features large reading areas, open stacks, individual study carrels, group-study areas, and extensive on-line and database resources. Large computer research and word-processing centers equipped with personal computers and laser printers are designated solely for student use. With one of the largest budgets in the nation and an aggressive schedule for expansion, Loyola is committed to maintaining one of the country's finest law libraries.

■ Faculty

➡ *96 total*   ➡ *57 full-time*   ➡ *39 part-time or adjunct*
➡ *21 women*   ➡ *12 minority*

■ Curriculum

Loyola's curriculum is designed to provide the knowledge and skills that will enable students to become excellent practicing lawyers. The curriculum integrates traditional instruction in legal doctrine and theory with a special commitment to innovative skills education. The first-year curriculum includes a rigorous grounding in basic subjects and includes an intensive course in legal writing, taught by the full-time faculty. The required upper-division curriculum includes Ethics, Counseling, and Negotiation, in which simulated negotiation and counseling exercises provide students with an opportunity to apply the principles of legal ethics in a practical context.

Because of its large faculty, the Law School has a wide variety of course offerings, ranging from comprehensive offerings in the traditional subjects to a wide variety of advanced courses in many areas, including environmental law, entertainment law, international law, and the protection of civil and constitutional rights.

The 87-unit course of study for the J.D. can be completed in three years by full-time day students, and in four years by part-time evening students. The day and evening programs have identical admission standards and academic requirements.

■ Special Programs

Loyola's extensive clinical program offers students an opportunity to explore the nature of the attorney-client relationship, experience the operation of legal institutions, and, particularly, to refine and enhance lawyering skills. In addition to an extensive program of clinical placements in courts, government, and legal service agencies throughout the region, the Law School supports an on-campus clinic, the Western Center for Disability Rights, which is nationally recognized for excellence in the representation of disabled persons.

The Law School offers a summer program in Central America that enables students to take courses in Costa Rica on international environmental law and the protection of human rights. The Central American program includes a variety of study trips to neighboring countries.

■ Admission

➡ *Baccalaureate degree required*   ➡ *application deadline—day, Feb. 1; evening, April 15*   ➡ *LSAT, LSDAS required*
➡ *median GPA—3.35*   ➡ *median LSAT score—161*
➡ *application fee—$50*

The Law School is nonsectarian and is committed to maintaining the diversity of its student population. Members of all religious, ethnic, and cultural groups are actively recruited and encouraged to apply. All applications are reviewed in their entirety and many factors, both academic and nonacademic, are considered. Applicants are encouraged to provide information about extracurricular activities and awards, educational history, cultural background, and other life experiences. Applicants are strongly urged to take the LSAT no later than the December administration. At least one academic letter of evaluation is recommended. Decisions are made on a rolling basis.

■ Student Activities

Three journals are published by Loyola students: the *Loyola of Los Angeles Law Review*; the *International and Comparative Law Journal*; and the *Entertainment Law Journal*. Membership on intramural and intermural moot court and trial advocacy teams is highly sought. Students can participate in student bar associations and the monthly newspaper, as well as in a number of student organizations including the Black Law Students Association, Asian-Pacific American Law Students Association, La Raza de Loyola, Christian Legal Society, Jewish Law Students Association, Lesbian and Gay Law Union, St. Thomas More Legal Honor Society, Phi Alpha Delta Professional Legal Fraternity, Phi Delta Phi Honor Fraternity, and the Women's Law Association.

■ Expenses and Financial Aid

➡ *tuition & fees—full-time, $16,604; part-time, $11,102*
➡ *scholarships available* ➡ *financial aid available; FAFSA forms due March 2*

Loyola offers a number of full- and partial-tuition scholarships to entering students based on academic achievement. Additional scholarship funds are set aside for continuing students who are in approximately the top 10 percent of their class at the end of the first year. Applicants should complete the FAFSA by March 2.

■ Career Services

The Office of Career Services provides a professional staff to counsel students and graduates and to assist them in job searches in a variety of ways. Many major national and regional firms recruited in the On-Campus Interviewing Program in 1993, and students and graduates are employed by the nation's most prestigious private and public legal institutions.

Applicant Group for the 1993–1994 Academic Year

Loyola Law School, Los Angeles, Loyola Marymount University
This grid includes only applicants who earned 120-180 LSAT scores under standard administrations in the 1992-1993 testing year.

	LSAT Score														
	120-142		143-148		149-153		154-157		158-162		163-169		170-180		Total	
GPA	Apps	Adm	Apps	Adm	Apps	Adm	Apps	Adm	Apps	Adm	Apps	Adm	Apps	Adm	Apps	Adm
3.75 & above	3	0	6	2	21	5	46	30	35	35	30	30	4	4	145	106
3.74-3.50	20	0	52	1	79	19	110	61	102	95	64	64	6	6	433	246
3.49-3.25	28	0	102	7	161	32	164	63	163	126	77	77	6	5	701	310
3.24-3.00	61	0	138	4	180	29	160	29	137	81	83	81	6	6	765	230
2.99-2.75	75	0	127	2	166	24	128	23	89	39	53	49	8	6	646	143
2.74-2.50	75	0	126	0	119	7	73	9	70	24	23	20	4	4	490	64
2.49-2.25	63	0	73	0	69	0	26	2	29	7	12	8	2	1	274	18
2.24-2.00	39	0	28	0	11	0	15	3	6	2	6	1	0	0	105	6
1.99 - 1.00	10	0	2	0	2	0	0	0	0	0	0	0	0	0	14	0
Pass/Fail CES	6	0	23	0	8	2	9	3	7	5	5	4	0	0	58	14
Total	380	0	677	16	816	118	731	223	638	414	353	334	36	32	3631	1137

Apps = Number of Applicants
Adm = Number Admitted
Represents 94% of the applicant pool.

Loyola University School of Law—New Orleans

7214 St. Charles Avenue
New Orleans, LA 70118

Phone: 504.861.5575

■ Introduction

The School of Law was established at Loyola University in 1914. It has been approved by the ABA since 1931 and has been a member of the AALS since 1934. The university is a member of the Southern Association of Colleges and Schools and is operated by the Jesuit Fathers of the Southern Province. The campus is located in uptown New Orleans approximately five miles from the historic French Quarter and the Central Business District.

■ Enrollment/Student Body

- *2,243 applicants* ➡ *621 admitted first-year class 1993*
- *255 enrolled first-year class 1993* ➡ *551 total full-time*
- *244 total part-time* ➡ *22% minority*
- *48% women* ➡ *36 states & foreign countries represented* ➡ *116 undergraduate schools represented*

■ Faculty

- *61 total* ➡ *31 full-time* ➡ *30 part-time or adjunct*
- *9 women* ➡ *10 minority*

■ Library and Physical Facilities

- *230,000 volumes & equivalents* ➡ *library hours: Mon.-Thurs., 7:30 A.M.-MIDNIGHT; Fri., 7:30 A.M.-9:00 P.M.; Sat., 10:00 A.M.-10:00 P.M.; Sun., 11:00 A.M.-11:00 P.M.*
- *LEXIS* ➡ *NEXIS* ➡ *WESTLAW* ➡ *DIALOG*
- *10 full-time librarians* ➡ *library seats 524*

In 1986, the School of Law moved to a new and larger facility on the Broadway Campus of Loyola University. Located approximately six blocks from the main campus, the facility houses all academic and research components of the School of Law, including the Gillis W. Long Law Poverty Center. The law school is designed to accommodate the needs of people with disabilities. Law students also have complete access to the facilities located on the main campus.

The library's collection of over 230,000 volumes supports the curriculum and research needs of the law school faculty and students. Its working collection contains legal authorities of international law, comparative law, and laws of individual foreign countries, as well as materials dealing with law-related subjects. In addition to conventional resources, the library has extensive computer facilities for students' use.

■ Curriculum

- *Academic Support Program* ➡ *90 credits required to graduate* ➡ *112 courses available* ➡ *degrees and combined degrees available: J.D./M.B.A.; J.D./M.A.—Religious Studies; J.D./M.A.—Communications; J.D./Master of Public Administration; J.D./Master of Urban and Regional Planning; J.D.* ➡ *semesters, start in Aug.*
- *range of first-year class size—40-100*

■ Special Programs

The State of Louisiana is governed in the area of private (property) law by the civil law tradition as found in the provisions of the Louisiana Civil Code. The common law tradition, however, is predominant throughout most of the United States. The School of Law offers both traditions. The full-time student may select either tradition while still maintaining sufficient flexibility to elect courses in the other. Such a system allows the student to study the private law by the comparative method. The part-time (evening) program offers the civil law tradition as found in the State of Louisiana.

In addition to the regular curriculum, each student entering the School of Law must accumulate a number of lawyering-skills points in order to graduate. Lawyering-skills points, including trial practice, client counseling, and negotiation and document drafting, may be earned by taking certain skills courses for which normal academic credit is given, by participating in other skills-related activities such as moot court and trial competitions, and by participating in short extracurricular courses that will be offered by the School of Law from time to time.

Full-time students are required to be in residence for a minimum of six full semesters. The normal time frame for part-time students is eight semesters and two summer sessions.

Loyola offers three summer-abroad programs. Courses are taught in five-week sessions in Cuernavaca, Mexico, Kyoto, Japan and Eastern Europe. All students, after completion of their freshman year, are permitted to enroll in summer school classes.

The School of Law has inaugurated a Law Clinic under special rules adopted by the Supreme Court of the State of Louisiana. Students chosen to participate in the senior-year program will be assigned cases, civil and criminal, and will be expected to prepare them for trial. Thereafter, they will actually participate in the trial process. Upper-division students also have an opportunity to serve as judicial clerks in the federal extern program sponsored in conjunction with the U. S. District Court for the Eastern District of Louisiana.

The Public Law Center represents a new departure in American legal education. The center takes legislative initiatives from the conceptual stage through research and drafting into the actual legislative process, then beyond into administrative rulemaking following the enactment of new statutes. In addition, the center offers a vital program of legislative and administrative assistance to community and public-interest groups, thereby providing access to two nonlitigation advocacy methodologies traditionally underutilized by the poor and disadvantaged interests of society.

■ Admission

➡ *Bachelor's degree required* ➡ *rolling admission, priority given to applications completed by April 1*
➡ *LSAT, LSDAS required* ➡ *median GPA—3.10*
➡ *median LSAT score—152* ➡ *application fee—$20*

■ Student Activities

The *Loyola Law Review* is published by a student editorial board and includes student work and articles written by specialists from the practicing bar, as well as from the academic community. Staff membership is based on scholarship and interest in legal writing.

The Moot Court Board, selected from prior years' competitions, is responsible for the Moot Court Program. Teams are entered each year in competitions.

The Student Bar Association is comprised of all students enrolled in the day and evening divisions of the law school. It provides a professional program for students and appoints members to attend faculty meetings and to sit on the student-faculty relations committee. The law school newspaper, *The Code*, is published by a student editorial board. Three legal fraternities, Delta Theta Phi, Phi Alpha Delta, and Phi Delta Phi have active chapters within the school. Other organizations include the A.P. Tureaud Chapter of BLSA, Spanish American Law Student Association, Association of Women Law Students, Communications Law Club, St. Thomas More Law Club, the Trial Advocacy Club, the Association of Trial Lawyers of America (ATLA), and the National Lawyers Guild.

■ Expenses and Financial Aid

➡ *tuition & fees—full-time, $14,663; part-time, $9,933*
➡ *estimated additional expenses—$6,550 (books, room and board, transportation, misc.)* ➡ *scholarships available: based on academic merit only* ➡ *minority scholarships available: based on academic merit only* ➡ *financial aid available; FAFSA analysis, no deadline, priority given to those applications completed by May 1*

■ Career Services

The School of Law Career Services Office offers a variety of services to both students and alumni. Staffed by the director and an assistant, the office maintains and operates a career-planning center, assists students in preparing résumés, videotapes mock interviews, and conducts seminars on career planning, employment opportunities, and interviewing techniques. The office actively solicits job opportunities for summer and school-term clerkships, as well as employment options for each year's graduating class.

Applicant Group for the 1993–1994 Academic Year

Loyola University School of Law—New Orleans
This grid includes only applicants who earned 120-180 LSAT scores under standard administrations.

LSAT Score	3.75 +		3.50 -3.74		3.25 - 3.49		3.00 - 3.24		2.75 - 2.99		2.50 - 2.74		2.25 - 2.49		2.00 - 2.24		Below 2.00		No GPA		Total	
	Apps	Adm	Apps	Adm	Apps	Adm	Apps	Adm	Apps	Adm	Apps	Adm	Apps	Adm	Apps	Adm	Apps	Adm	Apps	Adm	Apps	Adm
175 - 180	0	0	0	0	0	0	0	0	0	0	0	0	0	0	0	0	0	0	0	0	0	0
170 - 174	0	0	1	1	1	1	1	1	1	1	3	3	0	0	0	0	0	0	0	0	7	7
165 - 169	0	0	2	2	2	2	2	1	7	7	5	3	3	0	1	0	1	0	0	0	23	15
160 - 164	4	4	12	11	4	4	16	13	20	9	13	8	16	8	4	2	1	0	4	2	94	61
155 - 159	10	9	15	13	30	24	58	44	63	30	63	15	40	2	13	2	3	0	1	0	296	139
150 - 154	12	11	38	28	59	36	126	48	160	32	100	23	48	5	18	1	0	0	7	0	568	184
145 - 149	12	8	31	14	77	31	123	25	114	19	97	14	49	4	24	1	5	0	12	2	544	118
140 - 144	6	4	15	1	30	10	61	11	62	12	68	10	44	2	23	2	2	0	13	2	324	54
135 - 139	2	0	0	0	11	0	24	1	27	0	34	2	21	0	13	0	5	0	11	0	148	3
130 - 134	0	0	0	0	3	0	10	0	6	0	11	1	11	0	6	0	4	0	3	0	54	1
125 - 129	0	0	0	0	1	0	0	0	0	0	4	0	0	0	0	0	0	0	9	0	14	0
120 - 124	0	0	0	0	0	0	0	0	0	0	0	0	0	0	0	0	0	0	1	0	1	0
Total	46	36	114	70	218	108	421	144	460	110	398	79	232	21	102	8	21	0	61	6	2073	582

Apps = Number of Applicants
Adm = Number Admitted
Reflects 94% of the total applicant pool.

University of Maine School of Law

246 Deering Ave.
Portland, ME 04102

Phone: 207.780.4341

■ Introduction

The University of Maine School of Law is located in Portland, an attractive seacoast community. The city of Portland offers a variety of cultural and outdoor recreational opportunities; Boston is a two-hour drive from Portland. The School of Law is a collegial unit of the University of Southern Maine, which is part of the University of Maine system. A distinctive feature of the school is the close working relationship between students and faculty resulting from its small enrollment of approximately 260 students and a highly favorable faculty-to-student ratio of 1 to 16. The school is a charter member of the AALS and is fully approved by the ABA.

■ Enrollment/Student Body

- ➡ *947 applicants* ➡ *249 admitted first-year class 1993*
- ➡ *95 enrolled first-year class 1993* ➡ *263 total full-time*
- ➡ *6% minority* ➡ *49% women*
- ➡ *27 states & foreign countries represented*
- ➡ *98 undergraduate schools represented*

■ Faculty

- ➡ *23 total* ➡ *16 full-time* ➡ *7 part-time or adjunct*
- ➡ *5 women*

■ Library and Physical Facilities

- ➡ *280,000 volumes & equivalents* ➡ *library hours: Sun.-Thurs., 8:00 A.M.-11:00 P.M.; Fri., 8:00 A.M.-9:00 P.M.; Sat., 9:00 A.M.-8:00 P.M.* ➡ *LEXIS* ➡ *NEXIS*
- ➡ *4 full-time librarians*

■ Curriculum

- ➡ *Academic Support Program* ➡ *89 credits required to graduate* ➡ *96 courses available*
- ➡ *degrees available: J.D.* ➡ *semesters, start in Aug.*
- ➡ *range of first-year class size—90*

The first-year curriculum encompasses the basic legal subjects and is required of all students. The perspective of the curriculum is national. Classroom work is supplemented by programs in legal writing, drafting, advocacy, and clinical practice designed to promote professional skills. Before graduating, each student is required to prepare and submit a major research paper on a topic determined by the student in consultation with a faculty advisor. This independent-writing requirement, along with opportunities for independent studies or student-organized group studies, lends variety and flexibility to the program, enabling students to explore, in depth, topics of special interest that may not be treated in the regular curriculum.

■ Special Programs

Third-year students are permitted under special rules to appear before any state court in Maine, provided they are properly supervised in the law school clinic. Some third-year students may represent the state in prosecutors' offices in counties near Portland. The clinical practice courses are specifically designed to help the student further develop and refine skills in advocacy and negotiation. Specialized clinical programs are available in family, juvenile, and environmental law. The school has exchange programs with Dalhousie University, Halifax, Nova Scotia, and with University College, Galway, Ireland. The school's Marine Law Institute is devoted to research and educational activities focusing on the operation of marine resource law in the northeast coastal region. Law students participate in its activities as research assistants and take courses offered by its staff.

The law school coordinates volunteer opportunities for law students in various public interest endeavors, such as Court Appointed Special Advocates, Volunteer Lawyers Project, Maine Pre-Trial Services, and Pine Tree Legal Service's Family Law Project.

■ Admission

- ➡ *Bachelor's degree from an accredited college or university required* ➡ *application deadline—Feb. 15* ➡ *LSAT, LSDAS required* ➡ *median GPA—3.30*
- ➡ *median LSAT score—157* ➡ *application fee—$25*

■ Student Activities

Law students participate on many law school and university committees. The *Maine Law Review*, published twice a year by law students, concerns itself with national, regional, and state legal problems, with emphasis on matters of current interest. The *Ocean and Coastal Law*, published by the Law School's Marine Law Institute, includes student articles on marine resource, environmental, and ocean legal issues. The moot court program involves preparation of a formal brief upon an assigned legal issue and argument of the position orally before a moot court. In competitions with other law schools, the Maine Moot Court Team has won several national awards. The Student Bar Association performs the varied functions of student government. Students may also participate in active chapters of such organizations as the Black Law Students Association, Environmental Law Society, Federalist Society, International Law Society, Lesbian/Gay/Bisexual Law Caucus, Maine Association for Public Interest Law, Maine Law and Technology Association, National Lawyers Guild, Native American Law Students, and Women's Law Association.

■ Expenses and Financial Aid

➡ *tuition & fees—resident, $228/credit hour; nonresident, $452/credit hour* ➡ *annual fees—$154; room, board, books—$6,600* ➡ *need-based scholarships available* ➡ *minority scholarships available* ➡ *financial aid available* ➡ *FAFSA for need analysis due to College Scholarship Service by Feb. 14* ➡ *New England Board of Higher Education Compact tuition—$342 credit/hour*

Three trustee tuition waivers are available to assist in increasing the diversity of the student body.

■ Career Services

The Placement & Career Services Office provides a full range of services including counseling, career resource materials, and specific summer, full-time, and work/study job listings. The small enrollment of the law school ensures services tailored to meet the specific needs of students. In addition to individual counseling, a series of workshops and panel discussions with practitioners is held each year. Graduates practice from Florida to California, although most remain in New England and many choose to stay in Maine. The full-time placement officer is happy to provide further information to interested applicants.

Applicant Group for the 1993–1994 Academic Year

University of Maine School of Law
This grid includes only applicants who earned 120-180 LSAT scores under standard administrations.

LSAT Score	3.75 +		3.50 -3.74		3.25 - 3.49		3.00 - 3.24		2.75 - 2.99		2.50 - 2.74		2.25 - 2.49		2.00 - 2.24		Below 2.00		No GPA		Total	
	Apps	Adm	Apps	Adm	Apps	Adm	Apps	Adm	Apps	Adm	Apps	Adm	Apps	Adm	Apps	Adm	Apps	Adm	Apps	Adm	Apps	Adm
175 - 180	0	0	0	0	0	0	2	2	0	0	0	0	0	0	0	0	0	0	0	0	2	2
170 - 174	1	1	0	0	0	0	2	2	1	0	0	0	1	0	0	0	0	0	0	0	5	3
165 - 169	1	1	10	10	9	9	13	10	4	2	5	1	3	0	1	0	0	0	0	0	46	33
160 - 164	8	8	8	6	19	18	35	22	14	4	10	1	7	0	2	0	0	0	0	0	103	59
155 - 159	6	4	18	13	47	30	48	20	41	10	27	1	13	1	5	0	0	0	2	0	207	79
150 - 154	9	5	25	10	44	13	65	10	46	3	26	1	18	1	5	0	3	0	4	0	245	43
145 - 149	2	0	12	3	27	5	30	1	38	0	29	1	14	0	5	0	1	0	4	0	162	10
140 - 144	3	1	3	0	12	1	19	0	15	0	7	0	10	0	4	0	1	0	0	0	74	2
135 - 139	2	0	2	0	2	0	5	0	6	0	5	0	8	0	2	0	1	0	2	1	35	1
130 - 134	0	0	0	0	1	0	1	0	0	0	1	0	1	0	2	0	0	0	0	0	6	0
125 - 129	0	0	0	0	0	0	0	0	0	0	0	0	0	0	0	0	0	0	1	0	1	0
120 - 124	0	0	0	0	0	0	0	0	0	0	0	0	0	0	0	0	0	0	0	0	0	0
Total	32	20	78	42	161	76	220	67	165	19	110	5	75	2	26	0	6	0	13	1	886	232

Apps = Number of Applicants
Adm = Number Admitted
Reflects 94% of the total applicant pool.

Marquette University Law School

1103 W. Wisconsin Avenue
Milwaukee, WI 53233

Phone: 414.288.6767

■ Introduction

The Marquette University Law School offers a challenging program of study designed to maximize students' mastery of legal reasoning and analysis, to impart an understanding of the dynamics and theory of law, and to recognize the effect of law on society. The Law School, founded in 1892, is located on the campus of Marquette University, which is adjacent to downtown Milwaukee. The university, named for the renowned Jesuit explorer Father Pere Jacques Marquette and founded in 1881, has an enrollment of approximately 11,500. Marquette's urban location provides law students with exceptional opportunities to observe and become involved in the operation of our legal system within the community, law practices, administrative agencies, and the courts. The Milwaukee County Courthouse, housing over 37 branches of the state trial courts, is two blocks from the Law School; The United States District Court for the Eastern District of Wisconsin, where four federal judges preside (three of whom are Marquette law alumni), is located about one mile from the Law School. Milwaukee, a city of approximately 630,000, is known for its ethnic festivals, charming neighborhoods, cosmopolitan cuisine. Milwaukee is located 90 miles north of Chicago on the shores of Lake Michigan.

■ Enrollment/Student Body

➡ *1,330 applicants*   ➡ *500 admitted first-year class 1993*
➡ *169 enrolled first-year class 1993*   ➡ *495 total full-time*
➡ *5 total part-time*   ➡ *11% minority*   ➡ *44% women*
➡ *35 states & foreign countries represented*
➡ *157 undergraduate schools represented*

The Law School is actively committed to increasing diversity and encourages applications from members of groups historically disadvantaged in the U.S. and underrepresented in the legal profession.

■ Faculty

➡ *51 total*   ➡ *21 full-time*   ➡ *30 part-time or adjunct*
➡ *15 women*   ➡ *4 minority*

■ Library and Physical Facility

➡ *220,000 volumes & equivalents*   ➡ *library hours:*
Mon.-Thurs., 7:00 A.M.-MIDNIGHT; Fri., 7:00 A.M.-8:00 P.M.;
Sat., 9:00 A.M.-8:00 P.M.; Sun., 10:00 A.M.-MIDNIGHT
➡ *LEXIS*   ➡ *NEXIS*   ➡ *WESTLAW*   ➡ *DIALOG*
➡ *INFOTRAC*   ➡ *LEGALTRAC*   ➡ *CD-ROM*
➡ *MARTINDALE-HUBBEL*   ➡ *OCLC*
➡ *8 full-time librarians*   ➡ *library seats 308*

The Law School is located in Sensenbrenner Hall, an attractive, comfortable, four-story, air-conditioned building that houses faculty offices, classrooms, two courtrooms, and administrative offices. The Legal Research Center, a four-level facility of contemporary design, is connected to the Law School. The library's material operations are fully automated. Technical assistance for the law student computer lab is available during library hours. The law library is a federal document depository and is the largest legal research facility in southeastern Wisconsin. Law students have access to all Marquette University campus facilities, including both the health and recreation centers (RecPlex).

■ Curriculum

➡ *Academic Support Program*   ➡ *90 credits required to graduate*   ➡ *80 courses available*   ➡ *12 clinical*
➡ *degrees available: J.D.; J.D./M.B.A.; J.D./M.A. Pol. Sci.*
➡ *semesters, start in Aug.*
➡ *range of first-year class size—21-81*

The Law School curriculum is designed to develop a wide range of interests, knowledge, and skills, enabling graduates to adapt to the changing opportunities and demands of the legal profession. The curriculum provides instruction in all the traditional subjects basic to an understanding of the law, teaches students the craft as well as the theory of the law, develops research and writing expertise, and exposes students to other necessary lawyering skills. A week-long academic and general orientation is conducted for first-year students. The degree of Juris Doctor is conferred upon the successful completion of 90 semester hours of credit during the residence of at least six academic semesters. All students must complete an advanced writing requirement prior to graduation.

■ Special Programs

Our comprehensive trial-practice courses are an excellent complement to the curriculum and provide an exceptional opportunity for students to develop trial skills. Distinctive programs include the Legal Clinic for the Milwaukee Community, Prosecutor and Defender Clinics, Judicial Internships (Appellate and Trial), Municipal Ordinance Defense Clinic, and supervised fieldwork opportunities in specialized areas.

■ Admission

➡ *Bachelor's degree from accredited college or university required*   ➡ *application deadline—March 15, modified rolling admission, early application preferred*
➡ *LSAT, LSDAS required*   ➡ *median GPA—3.20*
➡ *median LSAT score—157*   ➡ *application fee—$35*

Review of completed applications begins in January and continues through the spring. All applications are read. Although the applicant's overall academic performance and LSAT score are principal considerations in the selection process, non-numeric factors play a significant part in the review. Personal accomplishments are highly valued by the Admissions Committee as are characteristics of diversity which contribute to the enrichment of the student community and the profession. Accepted applicants are required to submit an initial tuition deposit after April 1; a second deposit is required in June. Tuition deposits are applied to the fall semester's tuition. Applicants are welcome to visit the Law School (arrangements can be made through the Admission Office) or to contact the Office of Admissions with inquiries, but interviews are not part of the application process.

■ Diploma Admission

Since 1933, graduates of the Law School who otherwise qualify have been admitted to practice in all courts of Wisconsin without being required to take the Wisconsin Bar Examination. Marquette graduates are entitled to sit for bar examinations in any American jurisdiction.

■ Student Activities

The Law School publishes the *Marquette Law Review*, a scholarly legal journal, founded in 1916, edited and substantially written by law students, and the *Marquette Sports Law Journal*. All students have the opportunity to develop advocacy skills during the first year of law school. Law School Moot Court teams have won regional titles or championships in National Moot Court, Frederick Douglass, and National Labor Law competitions. Active law student organizations include the Association for Women in Law, Project Outreach, Black Law Student Association, Hispanic Law Student Association, Asian Law Students, Environmental Law Society, Jewish Law Student Society, Health Law Society, International Law Society, and the Student Bar Association.

■ Expenses and Financial Aid

➡ *tuition & fees—full-time, $12,600; part-time, $495/hr.*
➡ *estimated additional expenses—$9,000 (room & board, personal, medical)* ➡ *renewable scholarships available (performance & diversity tuition-based awards)*
➡ *renewable minority scholarships available (tuition-based awards, amount vary)* ➡ *financial aid available; FAFSA required—Federal Subsidized Stafford Loan, Federal Unsubsidized Stafford Loan, Federal Perkins, Federal Supplemental Loan for Students*

■ Career Services

The Office of Career Planning processes hundreds of listings of employment opportunities, coordinates campus interviews, and provides counseling assistance to students. Marquette law alumni are engaged in the practice of law in virtually every state and U.S. territory. In recent years over 90 percent of graduates have secured employment.

■ Housing

University apartments are located within two blocks of the Law School (1992-93 average rents $325-340/month). In addition to campus housing, ample and affordable housing is available throughout the city of Milwaukee and suburbs. Applications for university apartments may be obtained from the Law School Office of Admissions or the Office of Residence Life, Marquette University, Milwaukee WI 53233, Phone: 414.288.7208.

Applicant Group for the 1993–1994 Academic Year

Marquette University Law School

LSAT Score	GPA								
	3.75 +	3.50 - 3.74	3.25 - 3.49	3.00 - 3.24	2.75 - 2.99	2.50 - 2.74	2.25 - 2.49	2.00 - 2.24	Below 2.00
175-180	■	■	■	■	■	■			
170-174	■	■	■	■	■	■			
165-169	■	■	■	■	■	■			
160-164	■	■	■	■	■				
155-159	■	■	■	■	■				
150-154									
145-149									
140-144									
135-139									
130-134									
125-129									
120-124									

■ Good Possibility   ▒ Possible   ☐ Unlikely

University of Maryland School of Law

500 West Baltimore Street
Baltimore, MD 21201

Phone: 410.706.3492

■ Introduction

Facilitating an exciting mix of legal education and practice, the University of Maryland School of Law is an integral part of downtown Baltimore's legal and business community. Just a few blocks from the famous inner harbor and Oriole Park at Camden Yards, the law school is one of six professional schools of the University of Maryland at Baltimore. Our location within the Baltimore-Washington-Annapolis triangle affords students the full advantages of local, state, and national governments, as well as many law firms, agencies, and organizations of prominence. Maryland is a member of the AALS and has a chapter of the Order of the Coif.

■ Enrollment/Student Body

➤ *3,669 applicants first-year class 1993* ➤ *856 admitted first-year class 1993* ➤ *261 enrolled first-year class 1993* ➤ *604 total full-time day* ➤ *20 total part-time day, 230 total part-time evening* ➤ *30% minority* ➤ *50% women* ➤ *25% nonresident* ➤ *21 states represented first-year class 1993* ➤ *125 undergraduate schools represented first-year class 1993* ➤ *56 majors first-year class 1993* ➤ *age range—20-60 first-year class 1993*

■ Faculty

➤ *103 total* ➤ *50 full-time* ➤ *15 women* ➤ *7 minority* ➤ *53 adjunct* ➤ *faculty/student ratio—1:16*

■ Library and Physical Facilities

➤ *325,000 volumes & equivalents* ➤ *LEXIS* ➤ *NEXIS* ➤ *WESTLAW* ➤ *DIALOG* ➤ *7 full-time librarians* ➤ *4,200 serials, periodicals, and looseleaf services*

The School of Law comprises an unusual, attractive, and functional series of buildings surrounding two inner courtyards, one of which is the famous Westminster Burial Ground. Westminster Hall, adjacent to the law library, is designed to accommodate a variety of school and community activities, including formal lectures and the Westminster concert series. The Thurgood Marshall Law Library, the largest law library in the state of Maryland, occupies an attractive four-story facility adjacent to the School of Law.

■ Curriculum

➤ *Academic Support Program* ➤ *85 credits required to graduate* ➤ *J.D. degree available* ➤ *fall and spring semesters, summer session (evening classes only) open to students in good standing at any ABA-approved law school* ➤ *range of first-year class size—25-75* ➤ *3-year day, 4-year part-time day and evening programs* ➤ *160 elective courses available*

Each first-semester student is assigned to a fall-semester course with enrollment of 25 to 30, combining an introduction to legal institutions and processes, an

understanding of the skills necessary in the professional use of case law and legislation, and one of the traditional substantive courses. In addition to promoting close contact between professor and student and allowing for substantial research and writing experience, it also serves as a precursor to the live-client Legal Theory and Practice course required of full-time students in their second or third semester. Second- and third-year students take constitutional law and legal profession, and select a program of study from a wide range of courses, seminars, independent studies, simulations, clinics, and internships. Each student must produce at least one substantial paper based on extensive research.

■ Legal Theory and Practice

Maryland integrates traditional classroom study of legal theory with experiential learning through our Legal Theory and Practice courses. In connection with one of the traditional law school courses, day students undertake a number of carefully selected clinical practice experiences under close faculty supervision. Students meet regularly with their instructors to review the substantive, professional, ethical, and craft issues raised by their work and to explore the connections between what is taught in the classroom and the practice of law as they are experiencing it.

■ Clinical Law Program

Building on Legal Theory and Practice, students electing to enroll in the nationally recognized Clinical Law Program undertake primary responsibility for direct client service and begin the transition from law school to law practice; from learning to be a lawyer to being one. Maryland has made a significant commitment to clinical education and has one of the nation's finest facilities for clinical practice.

Practice in the clinic includes civil and criminal law matters and may include appearances before courts, administrative agencies, legislature, and other officials.

■ Dual Degrees and Interdisciplinary Study

➤ *dual degrees with Business Administration, Criminal Justice, Liberal Education, Marine/Environmental Sciences, Policy Sciences, Public Management, Social Work*

Supplementing the dual-degree programs, students are encouraged to explore the connection between law and other disciplines by enrolling in as many as nine credits in related graduate-level programs.

Maryland's interdisciplinary programs, including the Environmental Law Program, the Law and Health Care Program, and the Entrepreneurship Program, offer students the opportunity to work with lawyers and professionals in related disciplines toward the resolution of problems that transcend traditional disciplinary boundaries.

■ Admission

▶ *application deadline—Feb. 15*   ▶ *LSAT, LSDAS required*
▶ *median GPA—3.35*   ▶ *median LSAT score—160*
▶ *application fee—$40*

First-year students are admitted only for the fall. Applicants should file applications as early as possible after September 1 of the year preceding enrollment and prior to February 15. Later receipt of the application, the LSAT score, or LSDAS report may seriously prejudice the applicant's chances of acceptance. February 1994 LSAT scores will be considered on time for August 1994 admission. Applicants are welcome to visit the school, but interviews are not part of the admission process.

Admission decisions are made by a faculty committee. Although the undergraduate record and LSAT score(s) are determinative in many cases, the entire file of each applicant is reviewed and supplemental information is considered. Multiple test scores normally are averaged.

Supplemental information may be important where undergraduate grades and LSAT scores do not permit meaningful differentiation among applicants, or in unusual situations. Factors that can have a bearing include the undergraduate institution, the nature of the coursework, graduate education, employment, evidence of unusual motivation and maturity, and experience signifying interest in law or in making a significant contribution to the community. Residency may be a factor in close cases.

The School of Law has adopted an affirmative program aimed at increasing the number of qualified African American and other minority students.

■ Student Activities

Student Publications—*Business Lawyer* (a joint publication with the American Bar Association), *Maryland Journal of Contemporary Legal Issues, Maryland Journal of International Law and Trade, Maryland Law Review.*

Student Organizations—American Civil Liberties Union, Asian/Pacific American Law Student Association, Black Law Student Association, Business Law Society, Christian Legal Society, Criminal Law Association, Debate Society, Honor Board, International Law Society, Jewish Law Students Network, Latino Law Student Association, Maryland Environmental Interest Group, Maryland Public Interest Law Project, Moot Court Board, National Lawyers Guild, Phi Alpha Delta, Phi Delta Phi, *The Raven*, Returning Students Organization, Student Bar Association, Student Health Law Organization, Student Peer Advisors, Women's Bar Association.

■ Expenses and Financial Aid

▶ *tuition & fees—full-time resident, $7,502; full-time non-resident, $13,245; evening resident, $5,469; evening nonresident, $9,725*   ▶ *financial aid deadline—Feb.15; FAF (not GAPSFAS) and FAFSA required*
▶ *State of Maryland Loan Repayment Assistance for some public-interest employment*

■ Career Services

Preparation for the legal profession requires a dual approach—academic accomplishment and professional development. Career Services supports the latter by mediating between the classroom and the professional world. As of this writing, the class of 1992 was employed as follows: 38%, private law firms; 20%, judicial clerkships; 16%, public sector; 15% not responding/not employed; 8%, business/corporations; 2%, military; and 1%, academe.

Applicant Group for the 1993–1994 Academic Year

University of Maryland School of Law
Approximately 3,669 candidates applied for admission to Maryland's 1993 entering class. Figures in the chart below reflect 1993 admission decisions as of 6/1/93 for all applicants with an LSAT score on the 120-180 score scale (approximately 95% of all applicants).

| | LSAT Score | | | | | | | | | | | |
| | 151 & Below | | 152 - 154 | | 155- 157 | | 158 - 160 | | 161 - 163 | | 164 & Above | |
GPA	Apps	Adm	Apps	Adm	Apps	Adm	Apps	Adm	Apps	Adm	Apps	Adm
3.75 - 4.00	32	16	23	6	28	13	39	37	18	18	19	19
3.50 - 3.74	91	16	60	16	91	28	65	37	40	37	42	42
3.25 - 3.49	209	25	94	11	128	19	108	32	66	41	55	51
3.00 - 3.24	298	33	103	10	124	14	99	12	75	18	80	68
2.75 - 2.99	321	33	90	13	82	12	73	5	45	9	45	23
2.74 & Below	487	19	102	9	87	11	65	7	52	12	52	16
Total	1438	142	472	65	540	97	449	130	296	135	293	219

Apps = Number of Applicants
Adm = Number Admitted

McGeorge School of Law, University of the Pacific

3200 Fifth Avenue
Sacramento, CA 95817

Phone: 916.739.7105

■ Introduction

McGeorge School of Law of the University of the Pacific, located in Sacramento, California, prepares students for practice and public service in any state. Established in 1924, the school offers both full-time day and part-time evening programs as well as graduate law programs and a Summer Prelaw Program. McGeorge is a member of the AALS, is approved by the ABA and the State Bar of California, is registered by the Regents of the State of New York, and has a chapter of the Order of the Coif.

■ Enrollment/Student Body

➡ *3,122 applicants*   ➡ *1,272 admitted first-year class 1993*
➡ *437 enrolled first-year class 1993 (319 day, 118 evening)*
➡ *858 total full-time*   ➡ *401 total part-time*
➡ *15% minority*   ➡ *44% women*
➡ *42 states & foreign countries represented*
➡ *149 undergraduate schools represented*

The first-year day division class meets in three sections for most classes and twelve sections for the year-long Legal Process course. Part-time evening division students meet in one section with four sections for Legal Process. The student body has a rich diversity of educational and career backgrounds, age, talents and interests, marital and family circumstances, and cultural heritage.

■ Faculty

➡ *88 total*   ➡ *50 full-time*   ➡ *38 part-time or adjunct*
➡ *17 women*   ➡ *11 minority*

■ Library and Physical Facilities

➡ *385,000 volumes & equivalents*   ➡ *library hours: Sun.-Thurs., 8:00 A.M.-MIDNIGHT; Fri.-Sat., 8:00 A.M.-11:00 P.M.*
➡ *LEXIS*   ➡ *NEXIS*   ➡ *WESTLAW*   ➡ *DIALOG*
➡ *19 full-time library staff*   ➡ *library seats 545*

McGeorge's unique 21-acre law school campus in Sacramento is separate from the university's main campus in Stockton. The McGeorge campus includes a variety of classroom settings, the law library, the Courtroom of the Future, the Center for Advanced Study of Law and Policy, the Institute for Administrative Justice, model law offices and clinical facilities, the Student Center, student apartments, and recreational facilities.

McGeorge's law library provides spacious and well-lighted reading rooms with a variety of study carrels, tables, and group study rooms.

The library's LawLab provides terminals for computer-assisted legal instruction, word processing, desktop publishing, text-graphic scanning, and laser printing.

■ Curriculum

➡ *Academic Support Program*   ➡ *88 credits required to graduate*   ➡ *157 courses available*   ➡ *37 clinical offerings*
➡ *degrees available: J.D.; J.D./M.B.A.; LL.M. (Taxation, Business & Taxation, Transnational Business Practice)*
➡ *semesters, start in Aug.*
➡ *range of first-year class size—24-117*

Special areas of curricular strength include business, taxation, international business practice, land use, environmental and natural resources law, public-interest law, child, family, and elder law, and practice skills.

■ Special Programs

Graduate Programs lead to the Master of Laws (LL.M.) degree in Taxation, Business and Taxation, or Transnational Business Practice. A number of graduate courses are open to qualified J.D. candidates.

Joint degrees are available in cooperation with California State University, Sacramento.

A Summer Prelaw Program provides a five-week summer session for undergraduates.

■ Advocacy and Clinical Programs

An intensive Trial Preparation and Advocacy course involves each student with videotaped exercises in a courtroom setting of each phase of a trial and with preparing and trying a full-day mock jury trial.

More than 30 quite diverse clinics and internships are available, including the on-campus Community Legal Services Center where student attorneys, certified to practice under the supervision of an attorney, handle more than 800 cases each year.

■ International Programs

International programs encompass a rich variety of courses and activities. Faculty members experienced in international areas, extensive elective offerings, the Pacific International Law Society, *The Transnational Lawyer* journal, frequent speakers and guests, and the annual International Moot Court Competition are some of the resources available on the Sacramento campus. Summer programs for J.D. students include the London Institute on Comparative Litigation, the London Institute on International Business and Commercial Law, the Salzburg Institute on International Legal Studies, and the Budapest/Vienna Institute on East/West Commerce and Law. For law graduates, the Master of Laws in Transnational Business Practice provides opportunities for internship placements with private practitioners and companies in Europe and the Pacific Rim.

■ Admission

➡ *Bachelor's degree or senior standing from accredited college or university required* ➡ *application deadline— day division, May 1* ➡ *LSAT, LSDAS required* ➡ *median GPA—3.24* ➡ *median LSAT score—157* ➡ *application fee—$40*

Review of completed application files and notification of decisions begin early in each calendar year and continue throughout the spring months. Primary weight is given to the applicant's undergraduate record and LSAT results as the initial indication of academic potential. Where there are multiple LSAT results, the highest is accorded significant weight.

Additional information furnished by an applicant is useful concerning accomplishments, grade patterns or trends, employment and community experiences, cultural background, graduate work, or special talents and interests.

Applicants are encouraged to visit the school. Information can be obtained from the Admissions Office for a campus tour and class attendance.

■ Student Activities

Students are invited to enter a writing competition for positions on the *Pacific Law Journal* and *The Transnational Lawyer*. Student boards administer Moot Court Programs and the Community Legal Services Clinic. All students belong to the Student Bar Association. Many other student organizations representing special interests and social groups are active on campus.

■ Expenses and Financial Aid

➡ *tuition & fees—full-time, $15,114; part-time, $8,952* ➡ *estimated additional expenses—$13,910 (housing, food, books, utilities, transportation, personal expenses)* ➡ *both performance and need-based scholarships available* ➡ *minority scholarships available* ➡ *financial aid available*

■ Housing

McGeorge has 165 on-campus apartments, including efficiencies and one or two-bedroom units. Early application is advised. The Housing Office assists in locating off-campus accommodations which are readily available in Sacramento.

■ Career Services

The well-staffed Career Development Office offers a full range of counseling and resource services for students and alumni. Fall and spring interview seasons bring employers to campus, and other employers from throughout the country use the CDO facilities to solicit applications from McGeorge students. Among the services provided by CDO are résumé, job search, and interview workshops, a program of speakers with firsthand information about traditional and nontraditional law careers, and individual counseling about career paths.

Applicant Group for the 1993–1994 Academic Year

McGeorge School of Law, University of the Pacific
This grid includes only applicants who earned 120-180 LSAT scores under standard administrations.

LSAT Score	3.50 +		3.25 - 3.49		3.00 - 3.24		2.75 - 2.99		2.50 - 2.74		2.25 - 2.49		Below 2.25		No GPA		Total	
	Apps	Adm	Apps	Adm	Apps	Adm	Apps	Adm	Apps	Adm	Apps	Adm	Apps	Adm	Apps	Adm	Apps	Adm
165 - 180	11	10	15	13	16	14	21	17	15	7	6	1	3	2	1	1	88	65
155 - 164	159	151	191	181	225	200	194	133	126	49	74	22	26	6	11	4	1006	746
150 - 154	101	76	162	102	207	92	186	56	108	27	59	7	16	1	15	1	854	362
145 - 149	53	4	81	12	130	8	112	5	101	2	51	0	20	1	14	1	562	33
140 - 144	24	0	31	0	72	1	55	0	46	0	38	0	19	0	9	0	294	1
120 - 139	6	0	12	0	29	0	26	0	33	0	25	0	20	0	8	0	159	0
Total	354	241	492	308	679	315	594	211	429	85	253	30	104	10	58	7	2963	1207

Apps = Number of Applicants
Adm = Number Admitted
Reflects 96% of the total applicant pool.

Memphis State University—Cecil C. Humphreys School of Law

Law School Admissions Office
Memphis, TN 38152

Phone: 901.678.2073

■ Introduction

The School of Law, located on the Memphis State University campus, was established in 1962 and was accredited by the ABA in 1965. The school is conveniently located east of the downtown area of Memphis. With a population of over 900,000, Memphis provides an excellent location for local, state, and federal courts, and the various judicial administrative offices associated with them.

■ Enrollment/Student Body: 1993-94

➧ *1,371 applicants*   ➧ *397 admitted first-year class 1993*
➧ *166 enrolled first-year class 1993*   ➧ *399 total full-time*
➧ *24 total part-time*   ➧ *7% minority*   ➧ *39% women*
➧ *71 undergraduate schools represented*
➧ *21% nonresidents*   ➧ *average age, first-year class—26*

Preference in admission is given to resident applicants because of the school's primary responsibility to provide adequate opportunities for citizens of Tennessee to pursue a legal education.

■ Faculty

➧ *41 total*   ➧ *21 full-time*   ➧ *20 part-time or adjunct*
➧ *17 women*   ➧ *1 minority*

■ Library and Physical Facilities

➧ *245,334 volumes & equivalents*   ➧ *library hours: Mon.-Thurs., 7:00 A.M.-MIDNIGHT; Fri., 7:00 A.M.-10:30 P.M.; Sat., 9:00 A.M.-10:00 P.M.; Sun., 11:00 A.M.-MIDNIGHT*
➧ *LEXIS*   ➧ *NEXIS*   ➧ *WESTLAW*   ➧ *DIALOG*
➧ *5 full-time librarians*   ➧ *library seats 307*
➧ *library designated as a Federal Depository—2,686 serials*

■ Curriculum

➧ *Academic Support Program*   ➧ *90 credits required to graduate*   ➧ *80 courses available*   ➧ *degrees available: J.D.; J.D./M.B.A.*   ➧ *range of first-year class size—160-175*

The school offers a full-time day program on the semester system. Students normally graduate in three years, although summer classes are available and some students graduate after five semesters plus two summers. A total of 90 semester hours are required for graduation; 56 are required, and 34 are electives that may be chosen from a wide selection of elective courses, seminars, externships, law review or moot court participation, and independent research.

A part-time day program is available for up to 10 percent of the entering class. This program, unlike the full-time program, permits students to be employed more than 20 hours per week while attending law school.

The faculty-to-student ratio of 1:20 enables the faculty to take a personal interest in the welfare and education of our students. In addition, approximately 20 distinguished practicing attorneys offer upper-level elective courses and participate in the first-year legal research and writing program.

■ Special Programs

In cooperation with the College of Business and Economics, a joint J.D./M.B.A. program is available.

Upper-class law students are eligible to enroll in practice skills courses which are under the supervision of the full-time faculty. The General Sessions Clinic provides students with the opportunity to represent clients under the supervision of an attorney.

The school has an externship program in conjunction with four federal agencies: the United States Attorney's Office for the Western District of Tennessee, the Equal Employment Opportunity Commission, the National Labor Relations Board, and the U.S. Bankruptcy Court. These programs allow a limited number of students to earn two credit-hours by working in one of these agencies 10 hours a week for one semester.

■ Admission

➧ *Bachelor's degree required for admission*
➧ *application deadline—Feb. 1*   ➧ *LSAT, LSDAS required*
➧ *median GPA—3.20*   ➧ *median LSAT score—154*
➧ *application fee—$10*   ➧ *fall entrance only for first-year class*

A completed file includes application form, domicile certificate, application matching form, LSDAS report, dean's certification form, recommendation with waiver form, and personal statement. An applicant must have taken the LSAT within three years prior to enrollment, and must have utilized LSDAS. Students are admitted only in the fall semester.

Approximately 85 percent of admissions are based on a weighted combination of the LSAT score and the cumulative undergraduate GPA. Approximately 15 percent of the entering class will be selected by the Faculty Admission Committee through the subjective admission process. In this process, the committee takes into consideration nonquantifiable subjective factors, such as undergraduate institution, performance in "core" and "major" curriculum, public or community service, personal background, employment history, and performance in graduate school. Offers of acceptance are then extended to those applicants in the subjective pool whom the committee feels have the best chance of successfully competing in law school.

In an effort to increase the number of blacks admitted to law school in Tennessee, the Tennessee Preprofessional Program (TPP) is offered. TPP is a preparatory and developmental effort available to black Tennessee residents only. Students participate for two consecutive summers in an eight-week intensive development program. Students who successfully complete both summers, and who meet minimum requirements for admission, will be offered admission to the law school. Aside from TPP, the law school encourages applications from members of racial and ethnic groups who have been underrepresented in the legal profession. A student who has done acceptable work at a law school on the approved list of the ABA may be admitted to advanced standing under a transfer student program.

■ Student Activities

The Memphis State Law Review is written, edited, and published quarterly by a student staff with contributions made by legal specialists in various fields. Students also participate in national, regional, and intraschool moot court and mock trial activities. All students are members of the Student Bar Association, which organizes many social and law-related activities. There are also active chapters of the Black Law Students Association, legal fraternities, and other special-interest organizations.

■ Expenses and Financial Aid

➡ *full-time tuition & fees—resident, $2,962; nonresident, $7,504* ➡ *part-time tuition & fees—resident, $127/credit hour/ nonresident, $324/credit hour*
➡ *estimated additional expenses—$4,100, room & board; $600, books & supplies* ➡ *scholarships available*
➡ *minority scholarships available: Black Law Student Scholarships available to enrolled black students who are Tennessee residents* ➡ *financial aid available; Free Application for Federal Student Aid (FAFSA) required, priority deadline—April 1*

Financial aid is available in the form of scholarships, loans, and on-campus jobs. During 1993-94, 75 students received approximately $330,000 in scholarship awards. Scholarships may range from $500 to $8,000 for the academic year.

■ Career Services

The School of Law maintains the Career Services Office to assist students seeking part-time and summer employment, and alumni and graduates searching for full-time positions. The office provides students with information on employment searches, résumé writing, and interviewing skills.

The School of Law is a member of the Southeastern Law Placement Consortium, a group of 11 Southeastern law schools that sponsors a recruiting conference in Atlanta each October. The recruiting conferences provide second- and third-year students and judicial law clerks with the opportunity to interview with law firms from cities throughout the country, as well as with government agencies and corporations.

The law school is a founding member of the Southeastern Law Schools Minority Job Fair. The purpose of this Job Fair is to provide minority students with an additional opportunity to interview with law firms, public-interest and governmental employers, and corporations.

According to the 1992 graduating class employment survey, more than 89 percent of those graduates responding reported employment within nine months of graduation.

Applicant Group for the 1993–1994 Academic Year

Memphis State University—Cecil C. Humphreys School of Law
This grid includes only applicants who earned 120-180 LSAT scores under standard administrations.

LSAT Score	3.75 +		3.50 -3.74		3.25 - 3.49		3.00 - 3.24		2.75 - 2.99		2.50 - 2.74		2.25 - 2.49		2.00 - 2.24		Below 2.00		No GPA		Total	
	Apps	Adm	Apps	Adm	Apps	Adm	Apps	Adm	Apps	Adm	Apps	Adm	Apps	Adm	Apps	Adm	Apps	Adm	Apps	Adm	Apps	Adm
175 - 180	0	0	0	0	0	0	0	0	0	0	0	0	0	0	0	0	0	0	0	0	0	0
170 - 174	0	0	0	0	2	2	0	0	0	0	0	0	1	1	0	0	0	0	0	0	3	3
165 - 169	1	1	4	4	0	0	3	3	1	1	2	2	0	0	2	1	0	0	1	0	14	12
160 - 164	3	3	8	5	9	9	12	12	4	3	13	9	11	6	3	2	2	0	0	0	65	49
155 - 159	9	9	13	11	29	23	38	35	42	23	27	11	28	2	11	2	0	0	0	0	197	116
150 - 154	14	14	39	32	56	38	91	31	93	7	49	3	35	5	9	0	1	0	1	0	388	130
145 - 149	10	7	21	9	52	8	82	3	57	1	53	2	19	0	11	0	1	0	3	0	309	30
140 - 144	2	2	13	3	16	1	41	2	36	1	37	0	22	0	11	0	5	0	3	1	186	10
135 - 139	1	0	0	0	2	0	8	0	12	0	20	0	18	0	10	0	2	0	2	0	75	2
130 - 134	0	0	0	0	0	0	5	0	6	0	10	0	4	0	2	0	4	0	1	0	32	0
125 - 129	0	0	0	0	1	0	0	0	0	0	1	0	2	0	1	0	1	0	0	0	6	0
120 - 124	0	0	0	0	0	0	0	0	0	0	0	0	0	0	0	0	0	0	0	0	0	0
Total	40	36	98	64	167	81	280	86	251	36	212	29	140	14	60	5	16	0	11	1	1275	352

Apps = Number of Applicants
Adm = Number Admitted
Reflects 94% of the total applicant pool.

Mercer University—Walter F. George School of Law

Office of Admissions
Macon, GA 31207 — Phone: (toll-free) out-of-state, 800.MERCER-U, ext. 2605; in-state 800.342.0841, ext. 2605

■ Introduction

The Walter F. George School of Law of Mercer University is located in Macon, about 80 miles south of Atlanta. Founded in 1873, it is one of the oldest private law schools in the South. Named for a distinguished alumnus who served as a United States Senator for 36 years, the school became a member of AALS in 1923 and has been ABA-approved since 1925.

In 1987, George Woodruff bequeathed the school $15 million, making possible the curricular renaissance now enjoyed by Mercer law students. Two major initiatives were pursued as a result of Mr. Woodruff's beneficence: enrollment was reduced to approximately 400 students, and a new curriculum was put in place. The new curriculum emphasizes small classes, a progression in the course of study, and a unique sixth semester designed to facilitate the transition from student to lawyer.

■ Enrollment/Student Body

➦ 1,642 applicants ➦ 406 admitted first-year class 1993
➦ 155 enrolled first-year class 1993 ➦ 409 total full-time
➦ 1 total part-time ➦ 17% minority ➦ 41% women
➦ 31 states & foreign countries represented
➦ 121 undergraduate schools represented

■ Faculty

➦ 49 total ➦ 29 full-time ➦ 20 part-time or adjunct
➦ 9 women ➦ 2 minority

■ Library and Physical Facilities

➦ 252,000 volumes & equivalents ➦ library hours:
Mon.-Fri., 8:00 A.M.-11:00 P.M.; Sat., 9:00 A.M.-9:00 P.M.;
Sun., NOON-11:00 P.M. ➦ LEXIS ➦ NEXIS
➦ WESTLAW ➦ DIALOG ➦ 6 full-time librarians
➦ library seats 320 ➦ library keys provide 24-hour access

Mercer School of Law enjoys the use of one of the finest law buildings in the country. The library contains a computer learning center. The computer learning center offers 24-hour access to all legal research databases.

■ Admission

➦ Bachelor's degree required for admission
➦ application deadline—Apr. 1 ➦ LSAT, LSDAS required
➦ median GPA—3.10 ➦ median LSAT score—157
➦ application fee—$35 ➦ rolling admissions, early application preferred

The Admissions Committee weighs a wide range of factors, including LSAT score and undergraduate GPA. Letters of recommendation are required and are considered along with other evidence of nonacademic experiences. Other factors that influence the admission decision include: 1) undergraduate activities and honors; 2) work/military experience; 3) quality of the applicant's undergraduate institution; 4) postgraduate

work; 5) factors that indicate an unusual degree of motivation or maturity; and, 6) factors that would contribute to the overall diversity of the entering class.

■ Student Activities

The Mercer Law Review is the oldest and most widely circulated student-staffed legal journal in the state of Georgia.

In addition to the Student Bar Association, the law school has chapters of Phi Alpha Delta and Phi Delta Phi legal fraternities, Black Law Students Association, Hispanic Bar Association, Environmental Law Society, International Law Society, Christian Legal Society, Jewish Legal Society, and the Association of Women Law Students, as well as student chapters of the American Trial Lawyers Association and National Association of Criminal Defense Lawyers.

■ Curriculum

➦ Academic Support Program ➦ 88 credits required to graduate ➦ 106 courses available ➦ degrees available: J.D.; J.D./M.B.A. ➦ range of first-year class size—25-75

Mercer School of Law offers an innovative curriculum leading in an orderly fashion toward the practice of law. The Woodruff Program begins each year with an introductory week-long course exploring one role of the practicing lawyer as legal analyst and initiates the student into the law school routine of briefing and analyzing appellate case options. Introduction to Counseling, featuring the lawyer as problem-solver for the client, kicks off the second year. Introduction to Dispute Resolution launches the final year by teaching the lawyering skills of negotiation and mediation in the lawyer's roles as an advocate representing the client.

First-semester courses immerse the student in case-method study of the classic subjects of the common law. The focus broadens from case analysis to include constitutional and statutory analysis in the second semester. The middle semesters of legal study offer a wide array of electives along with required courses that ensure a thorough grounding in the core elements of the general practice of law. Students are required to select electives from three blocks of courses so that every Mercer graduate has the breadth of legal background to adapt to the changing demands of modern practice. Mercer offers enough small sections of a very popular Trial Practice Course, enabling each of our students to learn trial techniques through individual videotaped performances and one-on-one tape reviews with the professor.

One pervasive skill needed for law practice is the ability to write clearly and convincingly. In each year of law study students sharpen their powers of written persuasion. In the spring semester of the first year students take the basic course in Legal Writing, followed by a Legal Writing II in the second year, and a writing seminar on a topic of current interest in the final year.

The last semester of study offers students a unique opportunity to make the transition from law school to law practice. Most Mercer students sit for the Georgia bar examination in February of their third year. After the bar exam, an intensive 10-week session features advanced courses in a variety of practical lawyering skills such as negotiation, business planning, and advanced criminal trial techniques. Also during this session, a number of outstanding judges and lawyers offer Mercer students a variety of "Practice Electives," courses exploring particular areas of specialized practice. Noted lawyers are called upon to provide the benefit of their experience and perspective in a special pre-practice course titled Perspectives on Lawyering. The course of study at Mercer is a logical progression of preparation for the practice of law.

■ Special Programs

The Woodruff Program is one of the most innovative and exciting education programs available, and unlike special programs at other schools, it is offered to every Mercer student. A more complete description of the program is available from the Office of Admissions. The National Criminal Defense College sponsors summer practice institutes that bring several hundred criminal defense attorneys to Mercer from across the United States. Selected students are given the opportunity to meet, observe, and work with some of the most prominent criminal defense attorneys in the nation.

■ Expenses and Financial Aid

➡ *tuition & fees—$13,800*   ➡ *merit scholarships available*
➡ *minority scholarships available*
➡ *financial aid available; FAF due May 1*

The tuition rate is guaranteed to remain the same for students in good standing for three consecutive years. Tuition for the 1994 entering class will be set in May. For entering students, scholarships and loans are available to applicants with strong admissions credentials and demonstrated need. The school has its own scholarships and loan funds.

■ Career Services

Mercer Law School has an active placement office headed by the Assistant Dean for Career Services. Alumni and faculty members support students in their efforts to find satisfying employment. The office assists students in obtaining permanent, summer, and part-time employment.

Services of the office include arranging on-campus interviews with employers, career planning seminars, and off-campus interviewing consortia. Individual career counseling and résumé and cover letter writing workshops also comprise much of the work of the office. There is an extensive library of career resources available for student use.

The Class of 1992 reported 87 percent employed within six months of graduation. Members of the Class of 1993 who took the February Georgia Bar Examination passed the exam at a rate of over 98 percent.

Applicant Group for the 1993–1994 Academic Year

Mercer University—Walter F. George School of Law
This grid includes only applicants who earned 120-180 LSAT scores under standard administrations.

LSAT Score	3.75 +		3.50 -3.74		3.25 - 3.49		3.00 - 3.24		2.75 - 2.99		2.50 - 2.74		2.25 - 2.49		2.00 - 2.24		Below 2.00		No GPA		Total	
	Apps	Adm	Apps	Adm	Apps	Adm	Apps	Adm	Apps	Adm	Apps	Adm	Apps	Adm	Apps	Adm	Apps	Adm	Apps	Adm	Apps	Adm
175 - 180	0	0	0	0	0	0	0	0	0	0	0	0	0	0	0	0	0	0	0	0	0	0
170 - 174	0	0	0	0	0	0	0	0	1	1	0	0	0	0	0	0	0	0	0	0	1	1
165 - 169	1	1	0	0	3	3	7	7	7	7	3	3	3	2	2	1	0	0	0	0	26	24
160 - 164	1	1	5	5	9	9	19	17	22	15	18	15	10	4	3	0	1	1	0	0	88	67
155 - 159	9	8	12	12	36	35	68	58	61	28	62	11	29	3	6	2	2	0	0	0	285	157
150 - 154	13	13	31	22	64	20	107	16	89	5	74	2	43	3	15	4	0	0	3	0	439	85
145 - 149	5	2	30	6	41	4	100	6	90	4	76	6	33	1	15	0	3	0	2	0	395	29
140 - 144	2	0	10	1	22	2	41	0	56	3	54	2	34	1	9	0	3	0	3	1	234	10
135 - 139	0	0	0	0	12	0	14	0	16	0	22	0	19	0	11	0	3	0	4	0	101	0
130 - 134	0	0	0	0	1	0	1	0	4	0	8	0	7	0	2	0	1	0	1	0	25	0
125 - 129	1	0	0	0	0	0	1	0	2	0	0	0	1	0	0	0	1	0	0	0	6	0
120 - 124	0	0	0	0	0	0	1	0	1	0	0	0	0	0	0	0	0	0	0	0	2	0
Total	32	25	88	46	188	73	359	104	349	63	317	39	179	14	63	7	14	1	13	1	1602	373

Apps = Number of Applicants
Adm = Number Admitted
Reflects 96% of the total applicant pool.

University of Miami School of Law

P.O. Box 248087
Coral Gables, FL 33124-8087

Phone: 305.284.2523

■ Introduction

Established in 1926 in Coral Gables, Florida, the University of Miami School of Law is part of one of the largest private research universities in the United States. The school's location in a city of 40,000 south of Miami allows students to attend law school in a tranquil subtropical setting while gaining legal experience in the nearby international business center of Miami. The school is accredited by the American Bar Association and is a member of the Association of American Law Schools. The school has a chapter of the Order of the Coif, the legal profession's most prestigious scholastic honor society.

■ Enrollment/Student Body

➡ 3,251 applicants   ➡ 1,328 admitted first-year class 1993   ➡ 482 enrolled first-year class 1993
➡ 1,223 total full-time   ➡ 185 total part-time
➡ 23% minority   ➡ 42.4% women
➡ 70 states & foreign countries represented
➡ over 230 undergraduate schools represented
➡ 45% out-of-state residents

■ Faculty

➡ 138 total   ➡ 53 full-time   ➡ 85 part-time or adjunct
➡ 36 full-time women   ➡ 6 full-time minority

The quality of a University of Miami legal education is directly attributable to the faculty, whose expertise covers the wide spectrum of the law, from jurisprudence to the law of the sea, from labor law to land use, from legal ethics to the law of international sales, and from Latin American legal systems to British legal history.

■ Library and Physical Facilities

➡ 391,284 volumes & equivalents   ➡ library hours: Mon.-Thurs., 7:00 A.M.-12:30 A.M.; Fri., 7:00 A.M.-MIDNIGHT; Sat., 8:30 A.M.-MIDNIGHT; Sun., 8:30 A.M.-12:30 A.M.
➡ LEXIS   ➡ NEXIS   ➡ WESTLAW   ➡ LEGAL-TRAC   ➡ 43 full-time librarians   ➡ library seats 640

One of the best and largest in the South, the school's law library contains special collections in taxation, estate planning, ocean law, and foreign and international law, with special emphasis on Latin America and the Caribbean. The law library also provides an interactive video system for practicing trial skills and a room with 10 personal computers.

■ Curriculum

➡ 88 units required to graduate   ➡ 170+ courses, workshops, and seminars   ➡ degrees available: J.D. & LL.M.
➡ semesters, start in Aug.   ➡ range of first-year class size—130 day/80 evening divisions; one first-year class will be approximately 40 students; tutorial will be approximately 25 students

Students ordinarily satisfy the requirements for the J.D. degree in three academic years of full-time study. An evening program and summer sessions are also available. A combined degree program is not offered.

The school offers a graduate curriculum through which the degree of Master of Laws (LL.M.) is conferred. This program offers specialization in inter-American law, international law, ocean and coastal law, taxation, estate planning, or real property development.

Applicants to the LL.M. Program must have earned a J.D. degree or its equivalent from an accredited law school and demonstrated the capacity for graduate law work. The school also offers an LL.M. for foreign students.

■ Special Programs

The University of Miami School of Law, with studies in law and economics, law and the behavioral sciences, empirical research methods, and legal history, is a center for interdisciplinary as well as traditional research in law.

The school offers one of the most comprehensive and sophisticated skills-training programs in the nation. This unique model of clinical legal education integrates trial, pre-trial, and clinical experiences into one program, enabling students to more quickly develop the full range of effective trial advocacy skills. Directed by a full-time faculty member, more than 50 distinguished trial attorneys and judges, from both state and federal courts, assist with the trial and pre-trial courses and help to supervise the clinical placements.

The school also offers the London Summer Program, a five-week course of study at University College London. Courses in the 1994 program include Evidence, European Community Law, International Business Transactions, International Human Rights, and Lawyering in Different Societies.

The school is committed to increasing the representation of minorities in the legal profession and offers several innovative programs for admitting minority students. The James Weldon Johnson Summer Institute, held for 5 weeks before the fall semester, acquaints students with the discipline necessary to succeed in law school. The Professional Opportunities Program for Black Law Students, a coalition of local bar organizations, established attorneys, law firms, and the school, assists students in securing federal or judicial clerkships, summer associate positions, and internships, and provides a mentor program with attorneys.

■ Admission

➡ Bachelor's degree from a regionally accredited college or university required   ➡ application deadline—March 7
➡ LSAT, LSDAS required   ➡ median GPA—3.20
➡ median LSAT score—70th percentile
➡ nonrefundable application fee—$40
➡ rolling admissions, early application preferred

Admission to the school is highly competitive. LSAT scores and undergraduate averages are used in the selection process. Letters of recommendation are required. Also considered are the applicant's work and extracurricular history, special skills, and background. The school encourages members of minority groups to apply. Entering students are admitted only in the fall semester. Applicants are urged to apply for admission as early as possible after September 1. Applications received after March 7 will be considered on a space-available basis. No applications will be accepted after July 31. Transfer applications will be considered for students with excellent records who have completed at least, but no more than, one full year of work at an accredited law school.

Student Activities

The school's many student activities include governance groups; publications such as the *University of Miami Law Review*, *Inter-American Law Review*, *Yearbook of International Law* and *Entertainment and Sports Law Review*; and organizations such as the International Law Society, the Banking and Business Law Society, the Black Law Students Association, the Forum for Women and Law, the Gay People's Alliance, and the Hispanic Law Students Association.

The school runs one of the nation's largest mock trial competitions, involving over 200 experienced lawyers who coach some 100 students. The school is distinguished by winning the 1989 National Negotiation Competition and the State Moot Court championship for four consecutive years.

Expenses and Financial Aid

➡ *yearly tuition & fees—full-time, $17,310; part-time, $12,832* ➡ *estimated additional expenses—$8,350 min. (room, board, books) plus $4,900 (personal and transportation)* ➡ *merit and need-based scholarships available* ➡ *financial aid available; FAFSA form for need analysis due in Jan. or early Feb.*

Scholarship aid available through the school normally does not exceed the cost of tuition. Most scholarships are awarded on the basis of merit, although need is sometimes considered as well. All applicants are automatically considered for scholarship awards. Those admitted by February 1 are also considered for Reid Scholarships. Loan funds are available through the Law School Financial Aid Office. The priority deadline for all financial assistance is March 1.

Career Services

The Office of Law Career Services assists students in finding employment through a wide range of services and programs. Each year, on- and off-campus interviewing programs give students an opportunity to interview with approximately 525 national employers. Miami's alumni are located in every major metropolitan area and in several foreign countries, and practice in virtually all areas of traditional and nontraditional fields of law. Services provided through the Office include: The fall On-Campus Interview Program that attracts both local and national employers representing firms, corporations, government agencies, and public interest legal providers; the Southeastern Law Placement Consortium; Public Interest/Public Sector Career Week; Southeastern Minority Job Fair; National Association for Public Interest Law Fair; the Florida Bar Job Fair; listings of approximately 1,100 job postings for clerkships and associate positions; individual counseling sessions for students and alumni; workshops devoted to résumé-writing and interviewing skills; a resource library featuring national directories, periodicals, newspapers, and information on law firms, corporations, judicial clerkships, and government agencies; computerized programs through LEXIS and WESTLAW; 24-hour Placement Hotline; and alumni contact listings.

Admission Profile Not Available

University of Michigan Law School

Hutchins Hall
Ann Arbor, MI 48109-1215

Phone: 313.764.0537

■ Introduction

The University of Michigan Law School is located in Ann Arbor, a cosmopolitan city rich in cultural offerings and recreational opportunities. Established in 1859, the school is housed in magnificent Gothic buildings on the university's main campus. The school's faculty includes a diverse group of scholars, practitioners, judges, and educators, many of whom enjoy distinguished reputations in fields outside the law. Michigan's graduates are found in every state, in every major American city, and on every continent. Michigan is one of a few law schools whose graduates regularly go on to careers as law professors and legal scholars.

■ Enrollment/Student Body

➡ *4,703 applicants*   ➡ *381 enrolled first-year class 1993*
➡ *1,186 total full-time*   ➡ *23% minority*
➡ *43% women*   ➡ *82 states & foreign countries represented*
➡ *206 undergraduate schools represented*

The first-year class includes approximately 370 J.D. candidates who are joined each year by about 30 new graduate students, most of them young law faculty from a score of foreign countries. Students routinely come from all 50 states. In 1993, 37 percent of the first-year students were classified as Michigan residents.

■ Faculty

➡ *97 total*   ➡ *82 full-time*   ➡ *15 part-time or adjunct*
➡ *20 women*   ➡ *6 minority*

Michigan is the home of interdisciplinary legal scholarship and teaching. Even our clinical programs benefit from an interdisciplinary emphasis. For example, the legal work of the Child Advocacy Clinic utilizes the work of psychiatrists, social workers, and physicians; the Great Lakes Natural Resources Clinic coordinates its classes with the School of Natural Resources; and, the clinical program, Legal Assistance for Urban Communities, makes use of business organizational theories.

■ Library and Physical Facilities

➡ *750,000 volumes & equivalents*   ➡ *library hours: 8:00 A.M.-2:00 A.M. daily*   ➡ *LEXIS*   ➡ *NEXIS*
➡ *WESTLAW*   ➡ *LEXCALIBUR*
➡ *11 full-time librarians*   ➡ *library seats 868*

The Legal Research Library, with its magnificent three-story reading room, houses an exhaustive and outstanding collection of legal materials. Michigan's law library is an important center of research. Frequently, visitors from abroad find that Michigan's coverage of their native country is fuller and more accessible than at home. The Legal Research Library was joined in 1982 by a three-story, light-filled underground addition of striking contemporary design. LEXIS, WESTLAW, and Law School and university computing facilities are also readily available.

■ Curriculum

➡ *Academic Support Program*   ➡ *Minority Affairs Program*
➡ *83 credits required to graduate*   ➡ *93 courses available*
➡ *81 seminars*   ➡ *9 clinical offerings*
➡ *degrees available: J.D.; LL.M.; S.J.D.; J.D./M.B.A.; J.D./M.A.; Modern Middle Eastern & North African Studies; Natural Resources; World Politics; Public Policy Studies; Russian & East European Studies; J.D./PhD. in Economics*

The first-year program is designed to give all students mastery of the basic methods of legal analysis, and of the processes of reasoning used by lawyers, while introducing major areas of legal specialization. A small-section program emphasizes the importance of collegiality between faculty and students, as does the unusually large number of students hired as research assistants with the help of the William Cook endowment. The first-year curriculum is presented to four sections of first-year students. One section begins work in late May, and three start in the fall. One of these, the New Section, employs team teaching and looks at selected topics through an interdisciplinary approach. The Writing and Advocacy Programs afford another opportunity for small-group work. Every student has the option of taking at least one elective course during the first year. The second and third years are entirely elective, the only requirements being that each student elect before graduation one seminar and a course meeting the professional responsibility requirement.

In addition to the joint J.D. programs with other disciplines, other concurrent programs may be arranged. The Belfield-Bates Overseas Travel Fellowships provide funds for legal studies abroad or professional internships with international or governmental agencies or law firms. Externships provide individual students with advanced training in their areas of interest.

■ Clinical Opportunities

The Law School offers an extensive range of clinical opportunities to its students—two general clinical courses; the Child Advocacy Clinic; Criminal Appellate Practice; the Environmental Law Clinic; Women and the Law; the interdisciplinary Legal Assistance for Urban Communities Clinic; Legal Practice; and Law in a Public Health Crisis: The Response to AIDS. The Family Law Project, the Haitian Law Project, the Immigration Law Project, and the Unemployment Benefits Clinic are student-run organizations offering additional opportunities for counseling, courtroom experience and some credit.

■ Admission

➡ *Bachelor's degree required*   ➡ *application deadline—Feb. 15, modified rolling (strongest applications evaluated earliest)*
➡ *LSAT, LSDAS required*   ➡ *median GPA—3.67*
➡ *median LSAT score—168*   ➡ *application fee—$70*

Michigan seeks to form a class which comprises an exciting and productive mix of students who will enhance the educational experience for each other. Law School Admission Test scores and the quality of the applicant's educational experience (particularly the nature of and performance in course work) are relied on heavily. Serious regard also is given to one's promise of making a notable contribution to the class by way of a particular strength in one or more of the many attainments and characteristics examined in the application process. Selections among applicants are guided by the purpose of making the school a better and livelier place in which to learn, and improving its service to the profession and the public.

■ Student Activities

The *Michigan Law Review* covers significant research in all areas of law. *The Journal of Law Reform* focuses on the law as it has changed and as it ought to be, while the *Michigan Journal of International Law* concentrates on international and comparative law. A fourth journal, the *Michigan Journal of Gender and Society*, will begin publication soon. Students interested in combining oral argument with experience as writers of briefs may choose to enter the Campbell Moot Court Competition or the Philip C. Jessup International Moot Court Competition. The Law School Student Senate funds approximately 50 student organizations. Students enjoy speakers and social support through groups defined by religion, ethnicity, sexual orientation, age, or gender.

■ Expenses and Financial Aid

➻ *tuition & fees—resident $12,475; nonresident—$19,575*
➻ *estimated additional expenses—$11,090*
➻ *financial aid available; GAPSFAS and FAFSA forms required*

Virtually all financial aid is need-based and consists of a combination of loans and grants. The school's Financial Aid program is very substantial, drawing on a variety of Law School Scholarship and Loan Funds, as well as funds from the federal government and other external sources. Parental information is necessary in order to be considered·for grant aid. We endeavor to provide financial assistance to all full-time students seeking the J.D. degree who would be unable to meet the costs of their law school education if drawing only on their own and family resources. A few merit-based awards are made each year. A post-graduate debt forgiveness program assists law graduates in making job choices, including, but not limited to, public-interest positions in which salaries are typically lower than many alternatives.

■ Career Services

The Law School Placement Office at Michigan schedules more than 12,000 interviews each year with nearly 800 potential employers from all over the country. It also informs students of announcements of some 2,000 other employment opportunities with employers who do not visit the school. The Director of Public Interest works with students interested in employment in the public sector. The majority of Michigan graduates accept positions with private law firms. A substantial proportion accept judicial clerkships. Michigan graduates last year were offered positions in 47 states and the District of Columbia, as well as several foreign countries.

Applicant Group for the 1993–1994 Academic Year

University of Michigan Law School
This grid includes only applicants who earned 120-180 LSAT scores under standard administrations.

LSAT Score	3.75 +		3.50 -3.74		3.25 - 3.49		3.00 - 3.24		2.75 - 2.99		2.50 - 2.74		2.25 - 2.49		2.00 - 2.24		Below 2.00		No GPA		Total	
	Apps	Adm	Apps	Adm	Apps	Adm	Apps	Adm	Apps	Adm	Apps	Adm	Apps	Adm	Apps	Adm	Apps	Adm	Apps	Adm	Apps	Adm
175 - 180	39	39	36	31	29	22	16	7	3	2	0	0	1	0	0	0	0	0	0	0	124	101
170 - 174	138	133	139	118	86	37	50	16	15	2	4	0	1	0	0	0	0	0	5	3	438	309
165 - 169	231	150	358	145	202	45	104	14	34	3	20	1	4	0	3	0	0	0	6	1	962	359
160 - 164	262	43	340	43	256	25	125	15	43	5	23	2	7	0	0	0	0	0	10	1	1066	134
155 - 159	109	9	197	17	179	24	116	14	78	6	28	2	14	0	5	1	2	0	12	1	740	74
Below 155	63	0	161	12	223	7	196	7	166	1	115	3	79	0	33	0	11	0	43	0	1090	30
Total	842	374	1231	366	975	160	607	73	339	19	190	8	106	0	41	1	13	0	76	6	4420	1007

Apps = Number of Applicants
Adm = Number Admitted
Reflects 94% of the total applicant pool.

University of Minnesota Law School

229 19th Avenue South
Minneapolis, MN 55455

Phone: 612.625.5005

■ Introduction

The University of Minnesota Law School has entered its 105th year in vigorous health. The quality of Minnesota's faculty, the academic credentials of its students, and the caliber of its library collection and physical facilities are the strongest in the history of the school. This vitality is a result of thoughtful and forward-looking development of the school's century-old tradition of excellence in legal education. The law school provides a personal, collegial environment for the study of law; at the same time, students have access to the academic, professional, and cultural resources of the larger university, and the Twin Cities of St. Paul and Minneapolis, one of the most progressive and livable metropolitan communities in the country.

■ Enrollment/Student Body

➡ *2,336 applicants*   ➡ *635 admitted first-year class 1993*
➡ *270 enrolled first-year class 1993*   ➡ *810 total full-time*
➡ *15% minority*   ➡ *41% women*
➡ *43 states & foreign countries represented*
➡ *207 undergraduate schools represented*

■ Faculty

➡ *128 total*   ➡ *52 full-time*   ➡ *76 part-time or adjunct*
➡ *39 women*   ➡ *8 minority*

The faculty's wide-ranging expertise allows students to choose from a curriculum that offers traditional legal training as well as innovative clinical and computer-assisted programs.

■ Library and Physical Facilities

➡ *800,000 volumes & equivalents*   ➡ *library hours: open 365 days/year, 24 hours/day; staffed, Mon.-Fri., 8:00 A.M.-10:00 P.M.; Sat., 9:00 A.M.-6:00 P.M.; Sun., NOON-6:00 P.M.*
➡ *LEXIS*   ➡ *NEXIS*   ➡ *WESTLAW*   ➡ *LUMINA*
➡ *28 full-time librarians*   ➡ *library seats 900*

The award-winning Law Center on the west bank of the university's Minneapolis Campus, dedicated in 1978, remains a model for new law school complexes. The Law Library is the sixth largest academic law library in the United States and offers an exceptional international collection, comprehensive primary and secondary legal materials, and computerized connections to WESTLAW, LEXIS, and the entire University of Minnesota library system.

■ Curriculum

➡ *Academic Support Program*   ➡ *88 credits required to graduate*   ➡ *130 courses available*   ➡ *degrees available: J.D.; J.D./M.B.A.; J.D./M.P.A. (Public Affairs), joint degrees are available with most graduate programs*   ➡ *semesters, start in late Aug.*   ➡ *range of first-year class size—18-108*

The traditional Socratic teaching method appears in all three years of the J.D. curriculum. Tutorial seminars,

computer-assisted instruction, and clinical and simulated skills training are offered in various forms throughout a student's law school career. Students must fulfill a legal writing requirement in each of their three years and take one class in professional responsibility, but otherwise their second and third years are entirely elective. The first-year writing class and the various moot courts, journals, and writing seminars all provide students with small-group instruction, editing, and supervision.

■ Clinical Legal Education

The law school has developed one of the country's largest and most active clinical programs. Each year, over 160 students receive academic credit for participating in negotiations, client interviews, court appearances, and other case work supervised by clinic faculty. Clinic course offerings include antitrust, domestic abuse, appellate practice, civil litigation, federal taxation, criminal prosecution and defense, immigration, public-interest law, worker's compensation, social security disability, gender and the law, family law, and prisoner assistance in civil matters.

■ International Law

International programs are supported by a broad comparative and international law curriculum taught by Minnesota's own faculty experts on GATT, Public and Private International Law, and International Human Rights, and by visiting international scholars. This year, law professors and students from the People's Republic of China, Mexico, Poland, France, Germany, and Sweden are engaged in research, J.D., and graduate studies, and scholars from many other countries will visit for special programs. Summer sessions abroad in alternate years offer the study of comparative law at Lyon, France or Uppsala, Sweden. School-year study is possible in several countries for students possessing fluency in the language of the host institution.

■ Computer-Assisted Study and Research

The law school is home to and a founding member of CCALI, the Center for Computer-Assisted Legal Instruction, a consortium of more than 116 law schools, which develops computer-assisted exercises for legal education. Students complete these tutorials, drills, and simulation exercises as assignments or supplements for classroom instruction. The Law School computer lab provides student access to personal computers for CCALI exercises, computer-based legal research, and word-processing.

■ Admission

➡ *Bachelor's degree required*   ➡ *application deadline—March 1, rolling admissions, early application preferred*
➡ *LSAT, LSDAS required*   ➡ *median GPA—3.56*
➡ *median LSAT score—163*   ➡ *application fee—$30*

The Admissions Committee seeks to enroll 270 highly qualified, widely talented full-time students each fall. Roughly half of the class is selected on the basis of numerical indicators of potential success in law school. The other half of the class is drawn from a pool of similarly well-qualified applicants for whom numerical predictors, while high, are less determinative of the committee's decision. For this second group of applicants, the committee considers individual scholastic honors, extracurricular activities, personal statements, recommendations, work experience, unusual life experiences, and other factors that indicate a potential for success as a law student and lawyer. Minnesota is committed to equal educational opportunities for women and minorities and strongly encourages their applications. Applicants are encouraged to visit the Law School. Arrangements can be made through the Office of Admissions to sit in on a class, tour the Law Center, and meet with an admissions representative.

■ Student Activities

Members of the *Minnesota Law Review*, founded in 1917, *The Journal of Law and Inequality*, established in 1982, and *The Minnesota Journal of Global Trade*, established in 1991 analyze scholarly legal articles, refining their writing skills under close editorial supervision. Minnesota's moot court teams have built a strong record of success in regional and national competition. Extracurricular organizations focus on international human rights, minority concerns, public-interest law internships, environmental law, law and religion, and other areas.

■ Expenses and Financial Aid

➡ *tuition & fees—full-time resident, $7,029; nonresident, $12,949* ➡ *estimated additional expenses—$8,820* ➡ *scholarships available (performance and need-based)* ➡ *minority scholarships available (performance and need-based)* ➡ *financial aid available* ➡ *FAFSA form for need analysis should be filed before Feb. 15*

In recent years more than 85 percent of the student body has received financial aid, primarily in loans, but including scholarships, grants, and work-study programs. Forms are available from the Office of Student Financial Aid, 210 Fraser Hall, 106 Pleasant Street, S.E., University of Minnesota, Minneapolis, MN 55455.

■ Career Services

Our graduates are leaders in federal and state judiciary and government, academics, law practice, legal services, and business. In 1993-94, approximately 130 law firms, corporations, and governmental agencies from around the United States will interview on campus. In addition, more than 900 employers send notices for posting in the Career Planning and Placement Office. While a majority of graduates accept positions in the Midwest, the national composition of our student body is attractive to employees across the country. The Career Planning and Placement Office provides numerous career-planning seminars and services, and maintains a resource library.

Applicant Group for the 1993–1994 Academic Year

University of Minnesota Law School
This grid includes only applicants who earned 120-180 LSAT scores under standard administrations.

LSAT Score	3.75 +		3.50 -3.74		3.25 - 3.49		3.00 - 3.24		2.75 - 2.99		2.50 - 2.74		2.25 - 2.49		2.00 - 2.24		Below 2.00		No GPA		Total	
	Apps	Adm	Apps	Adm	Apps	Adm	Apps	Adm	Apps	Adm	Apps	Adm	Apps	Adm	Apps	Adm	Apps	Adm	Apps	Adm	Apps	Adm
175 - 180	1	1	5	4	3	3	1	1	2	2	0	0	1	0	0	0	0	0	0	0	13	11
170 - 174	11	10	13	10	14	12	19	13	3	3	3	1	3	0	1	0	0	0	1	1	68	50
165 - 169	47	33	67	39	61	37	48	24	20	2	11	2	3	1	0	0	0	0	3	1	260	139
160 - 164	87	53	138	66	151	36	86	9	40	3	28	0	10	0	3	0	0	0	4	0	547	167
155 - 159	80	31	135	19	140	13	101	5	61	1	30	3	7	0	4	0	0	0	8	1	566	73
150 - 154	42	5	91	8	73	3	58	6	51	5	23	1	14	0	6	0	0	0	4	0	362	28
145 - 149	8	0	30	1	37	4	38	7	31	2	21	0	12	0	8	0	0	0	9	1	194	15
140 - 144	5	0	8	0	18	0	24	1	19	1	14	1	13	0	6	0	1	0	8	0	116	3
135 - 139	0	0	0	0	3	0	9	0	7	0	14	0	8	0	2	0	1	0	4	0	48	0
130 - 134	0	0	0	0	1	0	0	0	4	0	5	0	2	0	6	0	1	0	2	0	21	0
125 - 129	0	0	0	0	1	0	1	0	0	0	1	0	2	0	0	0	0	0	0	0	5	0
120 - 124	0	0	0	0	0	0	0	0	0	0	0	0	1	0	0	0	0	0	0	0	1	0
Total	281	133	487	147	502	108	385	66	238	19	150	8	76	1	36	0	3	0	43	4	2201	486

Apps = Number of Applicants
Adm = Number Admitted
Reflects 94% of the total applicant pool.

The University of Mississippi School of Law

University, MS 38677   Phone: 601.232.7361

■ Introduction

Recognizing the need for formal law instruction in the state of Mississippi, the Legislature in 1854 established the Department of Law at The University of Mississippi. Over the years, the law department has evolved into today's modern Law Center. Located in Oxford, Mississippi, on the main campus of the University of Mississippi, the Law Center is housed in Lamar Hall, named in honor of the late Mississippian, L.Q.C. Lamar, former Associate Justice of the United States Supreme Court and first law professor at the university. Oxford, a small town of approximately 10,000 people, lies nestled in the quiet hills of North Mississippi, just 75 miles southeast of bustling Memphis, Tennessee, and 180 miles north of the state capital of Jackson.

The University of Mississippi is the fourth oldest state-supported law school in the nation. The School of Law is fully approved by the American Bar Association and is a long-standing member of the Association of American Law Schools.

■ Enrollment/Student Body

➨ *1,628 applicants*   ➨ *334 admitted first-year class 1993*
➨ *170 enrolled first-year class 1993*   ➨ *507 total full-time*
➨ *3 total part-time*   ➨ *10% minority*   ➨ *33% women*
➨ *24 states & foreign countries represented*
➨ *103 undergraduate schools represented*

■ Faculty

➨ *32 total*   ➨ *24 full-time*   ➨ *8 part-time or adjunct*
➨ *6 women*   ➨ *3 minority*

■ Library and Physical Facilities

➨ *260,000 volumes & equivalents*   ➨ *library hours: 115*
➨ *LEXIS*   ➨ *NEXIS*   ➨ *WESTLAW*   ➨ *DIALOG*
➨ *6 full-time librarians*   ➨ *library seats 335*

In August 1978, the law school moved into a new and modern five-story structure which contains, among many other features, five large classrooms with tiered seating and video capabilities, two fully-equipped Moot Court Rooms, office space for several auxiliary law programs and their staff, and individual faculty offices.

The law library collection consists of nearly 260,000 volumes, 119,000 of which are in microform equivalents. During 1989-90, the law library installed an on-line system, replacing the card catalog and other manual record-keeping systems. The law library also expanded onto an additional floor of the building, adding a microcomputer lab, additional seating at study carrels for students, and growth space for the library's collection.

■ Special Programs

The law school actively recruits minority students and has on staff an Assistant to the Dean for nority Affairs,

who provides counseling and support programs for minority students both before and after enrollment. At present, 36 minority students are pursuing a law degree.

■ Curriculum

➨ *Academic Support Program*   ➨ *90 credits required to graduate*   ➨ *93 courses available*   ➨ *degrees available: J.D.; J.D./M.B.A.*   ➨ *semesters, start in June and August*

■ Housing Intern Program

The University of Mississippi Housing Law Clinic is a vital part of the School of Law. The second- and third-year students enrolled in the clinic receive training in negotiation, drafting, counseling, and advocacy. They spend approximately 10 hours each week on the projects of the clinic and attending the classroom component of the program.

■ Admission

➨ *Bachelor's degree required for admission*
➨ *application deadline—March 1*   ➨ *LSAT, LSDAS required*
➨ *median GPA—3.30*   ➨ *median LSAT score—153*
➨ *application fee—$20*

Admission to law school is gained by committee approval based upon an applicant's credentials. These credentials include a satisfactory Law School Admission Test (LSAT) score and an acceptable academic record at the undergraduate level. A bachelor's degree from an accredited school is required before an applicant can register for law school.

There are no prelaw requisites. Every applicant must take the LSAT and subscribe to the LSDAS. An LSAT score obtained more than three years before application is not valid, and the applicant will be required to retake the test. Applications are available the September preceding admission, with the application deadline for both summer and fall enrollment being March 1. However, early application is encouraged. Applicants who file late risk being placed on a waiting list.

Although the LSAT and GPA are obviously the most important factors in the admissions process, other considerations are: (1) grade patterns and progression; (2) quality of undergraduate institution; (3) difficulty of major field of study; (4) number of years since bachelor's degree was earned; (5) job experience; (6) social, personal, or economic circumstances that may have affected college grades or performance on the LSAT or academic record; (7) nonacademic achievements; (8) letters of recommendation; and (9) residency.

■ Student Activities

The *Mississippi Law Journal* is edited and published by law students. Students also administer the Moot Court program. Membership in each is competitive with grade and writing requirements.

■ Expenses and Financial Aid

➡ *tuition & fees—full-time resident, $3,006; full-time non-resident, $6,268* ➡ *estimated additional expenses—$7,000 (books and living expenses)* ➡ *scholarships available* ➡ *minority scholarships available* ➡ *financial aid available; FAF due—March 1*

■ Career Services

A full-time Director of Career Services assists students in finding permanent, summer, or part-time employment. Seventy-five to 100 law firms and other prospective employers interview at the law school each year. The majority of graduating seniors are employed prior to graduation, with the remaining few being placed within six months of graduation. The law school is an active member of the National Association of Law Placement (NALP) and annually participates in the Mid-South Placement Consortium (Nashville), the Southeastern Public Interest Job Fair (Washington, DC), the National Public Interest Law Career Fair (Atlanta), and the Minority Job Fair (Atlanta).

Applicant Group for the 1993–1994 Academic Year

The University of Mississippi School of Law
This grid includes only applicants who earned 120-180 LSAT scores under standard administrations.

LSAT Score	3.75 +		3.50 -3.74		3.25 - 3.49		3.00 - 3.24		2.75 - 2.99		2.50 - 2.74		2.25 - 2.49		2.00 - 2.24		Below 2.00		No GPA		Total	
	Apps	Adm	Apps	Adm	Apps	Adm	Apps	Adm	Apps	Adm	Apps	Adm	Apps	Adm	Apps	Adm	Apps	Adm	Apps	Adm	Apps	Adm
175 - 180	0	0	0	0	0	0	0	0	0	0	0	0	0	0	0	0	0	0	0	0	0	0
170 - 174	0	0	0	0	1	1	0	0	2	0	1	1	0	0	0	0	0	0	0	0	4	2
165 - 169	1	1	3	3	2	2	2	1	3	2	6	3	2	0	1	0	1	0	0	0	21	12
160 - 164	6	6	10	9	15	12	15	13	22	8	18	4	9	0	5	1	1	0	1	1	102	54
155 - 159	11	10	31	29	58	33	68	15	51	9	47	6	26	1	7	0	2	0	2	1	303	104
150 - 154	18	16	60	27	73	15	108	23	94	10	58	2	36	0	16	0	7	0	1	0	471	93
145 - 149	18	9	34	14	53	4	78	10	67	4	54	4	20	1	6	1	2	0	3	1	335	48
140 - 144	3	1	19	2	25	2	33	2	34	0	32	0	26	0	10	0	5	0	6	1	193	8
135 - 139	2	1	3	0	7	1	11	0	11	0	11	0	10	0	11	0	2	0	5	0	73	2
130 - 134	0	0	0	0	1	0	4	0	7	0	4	0	5	0	2	0	1	0	1	0	25	0
125 - 129	0	0	0	0	1	0	1	0	3	0	2	0	4	0	0	0	0	0	0	0	11	0
120 - 124	0	0	0	0	0	0	0	0	0	0	0	0	1	0	0	0	0	0	0	0	1	0
Total	59	44	160	84	236	70	320	64	294	33	233	20	139	2	58	2	21	0	19	4	1539	323

Apps = Number of Applicants
Adm = Number Admitted
Reflects 95% of the total applicant pool.

Mississippi College School of Law

151 E. Griffith St.
Jackson, MS 39201

Phone: 601.353.3907

■ Introduction

Mississippi College School of Law is conveniently located in downtown Jackson, the state capital, and is within walking distance of the legislature, as well as all federal and state administrative agencies and courts. Jackson is the legal and commercial center of the state and has a metropolitan population of approximately 400,000. The main campus of Mississippi College, with an enrollment of more than 3,000 students, is located in Clinton, a suburb 12 miles west of Jackson. Mississippi College School of Law is fully accredited by the American Bar Association and is a member of the Association of American Law Schools.

■ Enrollment/Student Body

➡ *1,156 applicants*   ➡ *419 admitted first-year class 1993*
➡ *151 enrolled first-year class 1993*   ➡ *376 total full-time*
➡ *10% minority*   ➡ *38% women*
➡ *28 states & foreign countries represented*
➡ *110 undergraduate schools represented*

■ Faculty

➡ *35 total*   ➡ *17 full-time*   ➡ *18 part-time or adjunct*
➡ *6 women*   ➡ *1 minority*

■ Library and Physical Facilities

➡ *220,000 volumes & equivalents*   ➡ *library hours:*
Mon.-Thurs., 8:00 A.M.-MIDNIGHT; Fri., 8:00 A.M.-9:00 P.M.;
Sat., 9:00 A.M.-9:00 P.M.; Sun., 2:00 P.M.-10:00 P.M.
➡ *LEXIS*   ➡ *NEXIS*   ➡ *WESTLAW*   ➡ *DIALOG*
➡ *5 full-time librarians*   ➡ *library seats 207*

The Law Library is housed on the second and third floors of the facility in attractive space that makes generous use of natural light and affords pleasing views of the park-like law school grounds. Carpeted throughout, the library has separate rooms for individual and group study, typing, audiovisual equipment, microform use, and photocopying. A chief feature is the modern computer lab that provides computer-assisted legal instruction and word processing using both WordPerfect and Microsoft Word software. The library is a government depository and serves bench and bar, along with its students, by providing access to primary and secondary authority for legal research in federal and state law, in addition to selective foreign and international materials.

■ Curriculum

➡ *Academic Support Program*   ➡ *88 credits required to graduate*   ➡ *82 courses available*
➡ *degree available: J.D.*   ➡ *semesters, start in Aug.*
➡ *range of first-year class size—12-75*

Mississippi College School of Law is an institution that provides superior academic instruction with a curriculum that is national in focus. The school is operated on a semester basis. A beginning student must enter in the fall semester. A summer term is available to second- and third-year students who wish to accelerate and/or enrich their studies.

■ Special Programs

In order to assist students in choosing elective courses, four areas of concentration have been developed. These areas consist of general practice, commercial and corporate practice, government-related practice, and litigation practice. These groupings, however, are not intended to provide specialization during a student's first degree in law. Recognizing the importance of developing lawyering skills, Mississippi College School of Law has a curriculum that includes instruction in both theoretical and practical skills. Students have an opportunity to put into practice what they have learned in courses such as Pretrial Practice, Trial Practice, Counseling and Negotiation, Appellate Advocacy I and II, Legal Drafting, and Real Estate Transactions.

■ Minority Program

The law school offers a variety of programs to assist minority students: dedicated scholarships/stipends; mentoring by Jackson minority attorneys; writing/tutorial; Minority Interaction Placement in conjunction with the state bar; and CLEO participation. Minority students are strongly encouraged to apply and each applicant's entire record will be carefully considered.

■ Admission

➡ *Bachelor's degree required*   ➡ *application deadline—May 1*   ➡ *LSAT, LSDAS required*
➡ *median GPA—3.00*   ➡ *median LSAT score—153*
➡ *application fee—$20*

The admissions standards are set annually by the faculty. They are based on the college undergraduate grade-point average, the LSAT score, and personal and/or academic achievements or honors. A degree from an accredited four-year college or university is a prerequisite to admission. Every applicant must take the LSAT and subscribe to the LSDAS prior to being considered for admission. Applications should be accompanied by a Law School Application Matching Form found in the *LSAT/LSDAS Registration and Information Book*. The school makes admissions decisions without discrimination against any person on the basis of race, religion, sex, or national origin. A $20 application fee must accompany the application. The LSAT scores should reach the Admissions Office by May 1 for fall admission. When an applicant is accepted, a deposit of $100 is required to reserve a seat in the entering class. A second deposit of $200 must be received by July 1. Upon enrollment, these nonrefundable payments are credited to the applicant's tuition.

■ Student Activities

The *Mississippi College Law Review* is a legal journal edited and published by law students selected on the basis of scholarship and the ability to do creative, scholarly research and writing. The students write comments and notes on legal developments and significant cases and edit lead articles and book reviews written by professors, lawyers, judges, legislators, and other scholars. Membership on the *Law Review* staff is recognized as both an honor and a unique educational experience. Mississippi College School of Law also provides an appellate advocacy program administered by the Moot Court Board, composed of second- and third-year students. This required program provides students with instruction and practice in both brief writing and oral argument. The Law Student Bar Association (LSBA) is the organized student government of the law school. All students are members and are eligible to hold office in the association. Other student activities include: three national legal fraternity chapters, Phi Alpha Delta, Delta Theta Phi, and Phi Delta Phi; a student chapter of the Mississippi Trial Lawyers Association; the Women's Student Bar; Christian Legal Society; Black Law Students Association; the Law School Speakers Program; and Environmental Law Club.

■ Expenses and Financial Aid

➠ *tuition & fees—full-time, $10,050*
➠ *estimated additional expenses—$12,050 (room & board, $6,950; books, $700; travel, $1,900; personal, $2,500)*
➠ *performance-based scholarships available*
➠ *performance-based minority scholarships available*
➠ *financial aid available*
➠ *CSS financial aid form due May 1*
➠ *MS College financial aid application*

■ Career Services

The Dean of Student Services coordinates and assists in placement activities. In addition to the traditional on-campus interviews, the law school also sponsors regional interviews that enable students to interview in the employers' home city. Graduates are finding employment with major law firms, corporations, and government agencies throughout the United States, with a primary focus in the Southeast. Students have received clerkships with the United States Circuit Court of Appeals, United States District Courts, and the Supreme Courts of various states.

Applicant Group for the 1993–1994 Academic Year

Mississippi College School of Law

Highest LSAT	GPA 3.75+		3.50 - 3.74		3.25 - 3.49		3.00 - 3.24		2.75 - 2.99		2.50 -2.74		Below 2.50		No GPA		Total	
	Apps	Adm	Apps	Adm	Apps	Adm	Apps	Adm	Apps	Adm	Apps	Adm	Apps	Adm	Apps	Adm	Apps	Adm
175 - 180	0	0	0	0	0	0	0	0	0	0	0	0	0	0	0	0	0	0
170 - 174	0	0	0	0	1	1	2	2	0	0	0	0	0	0	0	0	3	3
165 - 169	0	0	0	0	0	0	0	0	1	1	0	0	1	0	0	0	2	1
160 - 164	2	2	7	7	4	4	5	5	7	7	6	4	19	6	1	1	51	36
155 - 159	4	4	11	11	14	14	27	27	36	32	39	26	36	10	0	0	167	124
150 - 154	11	11	20	20	46	40	64	48	89	49	55	8	56	2	0	0	341	178
145 - 149	9	9	13	8	38	14	62	12	49	4	56	2	43	0	0	0	270	49
140 - 144	2	0	11	0	14	0	14	0	31	0	33	0	32	0	0	0	137	0
Below 140	0	0	3	0	5	0	12	0	19	0	26	0	38	0	1	0	104	0
Total	28	26	65	46	122	73	186	94	232	93	215	40	225	18	2	1	1075	391

Apps = Number of Applicants
Adm = Number Admitted
Reflects 93% of the total applicant pool.

University of Missouri—Columbia School of Law

103 Hulston Hall
Columbia, MO 65211

Phone: 314.882.6042

■ Introduction

The University of Missouri (now called the University of Missouri—Columbia or Mizzou) was founded in 1839 and was the first state university established west of the Mississippi. The School of Law in Columbia was established in 1872. The faculty consists almost entirely of full-time teachers with prior experience in the practice of law. The school has an enviable history of service to the state and the nation. It is a charter member of the AALS and is fully accredited.

The new law building, completed in the fall of 1988, has tripled the space available to the law school and serves as a focal point of the Mizzou campus.

■ Enrollment/Student Body

➡ *1,100 applicants*   ➡ *350 admitted first-year class 1993*
➡ *160 enrolled first-year class 1993*   ➡ *455 total full-time*
➡ *8% minority*   ➡ *42% women*
➡ *34 states & foreign countries represented*
➡ *118 undergraduate schools represented*

■ Faculty

➡ *36 total*   ➡ *31 full-time*   ➡ *5 part-time or adjunct*
➡ *11 women*   ➡ *1 minority*

■ Library and Physical Facilities

➡ *275,000 volumes & equivalents*   ➡ *library hours:*
Mon.-Thurs., 8:00 A.M.-10:00 P.M. (building hours 7:30-MIDNIGHT); Fri.-Sat., 8:00 A.M.-6:00 P.M.; Sun.,
10:00 A.M.-10:00 P.M.   ➡ *LEXIS*   ➡ *NEXIS*
➡ *WESTLAW*   ➡ *DIALOG*   ➡ *INFOTRAC*
➡ *LUMIN/OCLC*   ➡ *6 full-time librarians*
➡ *library seats 465*   ➡ *22 private 3L study rooms*

The law library is a focal point to the new law building, with windows overlooking most of the campus. The library also includes a state-of-the-art computer lab with 20 individual work stations for word processing, database searching, and other uses.

■ Curriculum

➡ *89 credits required to graduate*   ➡ *90 courses available*
➡ *degree available: J.D.*   ➡ *semesters, start in Aug.*
➡ *usually admit 3-5 second-year transfer students*

The program of study leading to the J.D. degree consists of six semesters of study. There is one seven-week semester each summer.

The first-year curriculum is prescribed. A substantial portion of the second-year curriculum is also prescribed. There is writing instruction in each year of study. A student must complete the 89 semester hours with a minimum average of 70 on a 55 to 100 scale for graduation.

■ Special Programs

The School of Law has a new clinical program that includes four new courses: Clinical Skills, Family Violence and the Law, Family Violence Clinic, and Criminal Clinic.

Students participating in Family Violence Clinic will be responsible for the representation of indigent women seeking assistance in the filing of protective orders pursuant to the Missouri Adult Abuse Law. They will also represent the state at misdemeanor trials and preliminary hearings involving assaultive conduct.

Students in the criminal clinic will assume full responsibility for examination of the legal issues relevant to the court proceedings, interviewing witnesses, preparing for hearings, representing the state at hearings, and completing one research project during the course of the semester.

The School of Law participates in the London Law Consortium, in cooperation with the Universities of Kansas, Utah, Iowa, Arizona, Indiana, IIT Chicago-Kent, and Arizona State. A semester in London, each January through May, is available to second- and third-year law students in good standing. Academic facilities are located in the Bloomsbury district. The courses are taught by regular faculty from the participating American universities. Students also may enroll in classes taught by British professors.

The Center for the Study of Dispute Resolution is a unique feature of the law school. The center was created in 1984 to respond to the needs of lawyers and others to understand various methods of preventing and resolving disputes. To fulfill this goal, the center sponsors interdisciplinary research and conferences, and, through its own student editorial board, publishes the *Journal of Dispute Resolution*. The center provides national leadership in this rapidly developing area of the law.

■ Admission

➡ *Bachelor's degree required for admission*
➡ *rolling admission*   ➡ *preference given to applications before March 1*   ➡ *LSAT, LSDAS required*
➡ *median GPA—3.35*   ➡ *median LSAT score—158*
➡ *application fee—$25*
➡ *nonrefundable deposit to hold seat—$150*

A faculty committee reviews all applications. No one is automatically accepted or rejected. In many cases, factors other than GPA or LSAT score prove to be determinative. When the LSAT is repeated, the school will use an average of those scores for its evaluation. Qualifications of applicants with a disadvantaged background (cultural or economic) are specially evaluated.

Students should apply very early in the year. Applicants are encouraged to visit the School of Law. Arrangements can be made through the Admissions Office to attend a law class, meet with an admissions counselor, or tour the facilities.

■ Student Activities

The School of Law publishes the *Missouri Law Review*, a respected periodical, four times each year. The review contains articles written by legal specialists and by students. It is edited by a student editorial board. Law students become eligible to participate in the review after their first year in law school.

The School of Law also maintains a very active appellate advocacy program under the supervision of a specially selected student Board of Advocates. These programs are open to all law students. Students are involved in a wide variety of advocacy competitions.

The school has chapters of the Order of the Coif; the Order of Barristers; Student Bar Association; BLSA, Women's Law Association; and Phi Delta Phi, Phi Alpha Delta, and Delta Theta Phi legal fraternities. There are numerous other student organizations that encompass almost every aspect of social and academic life at the law school.

■ Expenses and Financial Aid

➡ *tuition & fees—residents, $6060; nonresidents, $11,500*
➡ *estimated additional expenses—$9,100 (books/supplies, room & board, personal expenses, and transportation)*
➡ *scholarships available: mostly academic, some need-based— usually range from $500/yr. to full tuition*
➡ *minority scholarships available: academic and need-based— usually range from $500/yr. to full tuition*
➡ *financial aid available: Stafford, Supplemental, Law Access, and university loan programs*
➡ *highly recommended that Free Application Form for Student Aid (FAFSA) be submitted by March 1*

Missouri residents are not charged tuition, but are charged fees.

Although it is necessary to apply for scholarships on an annual basis, scholarships are normally renewed each year for those students who have need and maintain academic achievement.

■ Career Services

The Career Services Office serves as a liaison between students and prospective employers. As many as 100 firms, businesses, government agencies, and judges interview on campus each year. Graduates find employment in the legal profession in Missouri and throughout the country, and the world.

The office focuses on providing resources for career planning and development. A series of workshops, seminars, and individual counseling sessions help students develop their career goals.

Applicant Group for the 1993–1994 Academic Year

University of Missouri—Columbia School of Law
This grid includes only applicants who earned 120-180 LSAT scores under standard administrations.

LSAT Score	GPA 3.75 +		3.50 -3.74		3.25 - 3.49		3.00 - 3.24		2.75 - 2.99		2.50 - 2.74		2.25 - 2.49		2.00 - 2.24		Below 2.00		No GPA		Total	
	Apps	Adm	Apps	Adm	Apps	Adm	Apps	Adm	Apps	Adm	Apps	Adm	Apps	Adm	Apps	Adm	Apps	Adm	Apps	Adm	Apps	Adm
175 - 180	1	0	0	0	0	0	0	0	0	0	0	0	0	0	0	0	0	0	0	0	1	0
170 - 174	1	1	2	2	2	2	0	0	1	1	0	0	1	1	0	0	0	0	0	0	7	7
165 - 169	4	4	9	9	5	5	5	5	5	5	6	5	2	2	1	0	0	0	0	0	37	35
160 - 164	17	15	15	14	23	21	37	36	18	12	12	2	5	0	0	0	0	0	1	0	128	100
155 - 159	29	29	26	25	56	45	47	19	27	0	17	2	20	1	3	0	2	0	2	2	229	123
150 - 154	17	16	32	15	52	6	53	2	37	1	29	3	12	1	2	0	1	1	0	0	235	45
145 - 149	7	1	14	2	22	1	30	1	34	5	22	3	7	1	7	0	0	0	3	0	146	14
140 - 144	0	0	6	0	11	1	15	1	17	1	25	1	8	0	6	0	3	0	3	0	94	4
135 - 139	2	0	0	0	3	0	7	0	8	0	10	0	8	0	5	0	4	0	7	0	54	0
130 - 134	0	0	0	0	0	0	2	0	2	0	3	0	2	0	4	0	1	0	1	0	15	0
125 - 129	0	0	0	0	1	0	0	0	2	0	3	0	2	0	0	0	0	0	1	0	9	0
120 - 124	0	0	0	0	0	0	0	0	0	0	0	0	1	0	1	0	0	0	0	0	2	0
Total	78	66	104	67	175	81	196	64	151	25	127	16	68	6	29	0	11	1	18	2	957	328

Apps = Number of Applicants
Adm = Number Admitted
Reflects 95% of the total applicant pool.

University of Missouri—Kansas City School of Law

5100 Rockhill Road
Kansas City, MO 64110

Phone: 816.235.1657

■ Introduction

The University of Missouri—Kansas City (UMKC) School of Law was initially founded in 1895 as the Kansas City School of Law. It merged with the University of Kansas City in 1938, and affiliated with the University of Missouri in 1963. The law school is fully accredited by the ABA and the AALS.

■ Enrollment/Student Body

➤ *933 applicants*   ➤ *420 admitted first-year class 1993*
➤ *159 enrolled first-year class 1993*   ➤ *460 total full-time*
➤ *6% minority*   ➤ *42% women*
➤ *28 states & foreign countries represented*
➤ *143 undergraduate schools represented*

■ Faculty

➤ *57 total*   ➤ *28 full-time*   ➤ *29 part-time or adjunct*
➤ *17 women*   ➤ *2 minority*

■ Library and Physical Facilities

➤ *245,000 volumes & equivalents*   ➤ *library hours: Mon.-Thurs., 7:30 A.M.-10:00 P.M.; Fri., 7:30 A.M.-5:00 P.M.; Sat., 9:00 A.M.-5:00 P.M.; Sun., NOON-10:00 P.M.*
➤ *LEXIS*   ➤ *NEXIS*   ➤ *WESTLAW*   ➤ *DIALOG*
➤ *5 full-time librarians*   ➤ *library seats 415*

The School of Law is housed on the UMKC campus, in a location that offers convenient access to downtown law offices, courts, and government agencies. The law building contains modern classrooms equipped with the latest audiovisual aids, ample seminar rooms, a large student lounge, and individual offices for student organizations. A Computer Media Center houses the microforms collection, nine LEXIS and eleven WESTLAW terminals, and a computer lab for student use.

A unique feature of the building is the placement of student study stations in office suites shared by faculty. These student stations include study carrels and double-occupancy student offices that are available to all second- and third-year students. This suite arrangement provides considerable study space and facilitates student-faculty interaction.

■ Curriculum

➤ *Academic Support Program*   ➤ *91 credits required to graduate*   ➤ *over 140 courses available*
➤ *degrees available: J.D.; J.D./M.B.A.; and LL.M. (Tax and General)*   ➤ *semesters, start in Aug.*
➤ *range of first-year class size—fewer than 60*

The first-year J.D. program is prescribed. First-year courses are taught in classes of fewer than 60 students each. Students take a year-long intensive course in Introduction to Law and Lawyering Processes that includes instruction in legal analysis, research, writing, and advocacy. Classes in this course are taught in groups of fewer

than 30, with weekly workshops of 15. The upper-level program includes seven additional required courses, as well as familiarity requirements in federal agency law and jurisprudence. Students must also complete an intensive research and writing project. Students may elect from a broad selection of elective courses, including approved non-law courses in other UMKC divisions. No class offered is larger than 80 students, and most are significantly smaller.

Courses at UMKC are taught in a variety of formats, but all have in common high-quality teaching and student-faculty interaction. Many of the substantive required and elective courses include problem-solving and skills components, and there are many smaller skills courses offered as well.

An academic enrichment program in the form of supervised, structured study groups is offered to all students. Additional opportunities, including a week-long summer program and weekly enrichment sessions, are available to special admissions students.

Students may graduate in two and one-half years by attending two summer sessions. An LL.M. degree is available, including a degree with a concentration in taxation. Many of the courses in the LL.M. program are available to J.D. candidates as electives. This rich assortment of course offerings provides flexibility in the choice of J.D. elective courses.

■ J.D./M.B.A. Dual-Degree Program

The School of Law has established a dual-degree program with the School of Business and Public Administration. The program allows students to earn a J.D. degree and a Master of Business Administration degree on an accelerated basis through cross-acceptance of some credit hours. Applicants to the program must satisfy the admission requirements of each school and, if admitted, may enroll in the first year of law school either before or after beginning M.B.A. courses.

■ Student Activities

UMKC's location in a metropolitan area provides abundant opportunities for student participation in clinical programs, including judicial clerkships, Legal Aid, Public Defender, and Death Penalty clinics. Missouri and Kansas Supreme Court rules permit senior law students to appear in court and before administrative tribunals on behalf of indigent persons.

Students write and edit a substantial portion of the *UMKC Law Review*, a scholarly legal journal, and also serve as assistant editors of the *Urban Lawyer*, published by the ABA Section of Local Government Law, and of the *Journal of the American Academy of Matrimonial Lawyers*.

All students develop skills in appellate advocacy through Introduction to Law, with further opportunity to participate in a sequenced upper-level program. UMKC also has an extensive trial advocacy program.

Both offer opportunities for participation in national competition. UMKC also participates in the ABA Negotiation and Client Counseling competitions, as well as several specialized moot court competitions. UMKC competition teams have won regional and national honors in each of the past several years.

The law school has an active Student Bar Association that is affiliated with the Law Student Division of the ABA. Students are represented at faculty and committee meetings, and play an important role in establishing school policy. Three national fraternities, Delta Theta Phi, Phi Alpha Delta, and Phi Delta Phi, have chapters at the school, as do BLSA, Association of Women Law Students, and other organizations that specialize in particular areas of interest.

■ Admission

➡ *Bachelor's degree from accredited school required; combined degree admission without undergraduate degree possible* ➡ *rolling admissions, early application preferred* ➡ *LSAT, LSDAS required* ➡ *median GPA—3.28* ➡ *median LSAT score—154* ➡ *application fee—$25*

Admission decisions have been based primarily on an index formula determined by combining an applicant's cumulative undergraduate grade-point average with the LSAT score. A candidate may also qualify for admission based on the school's desire to ensure that the entering class contains persons of diverse background who are qualified for law study.

Students may be admitted with a bachelor's degree from an approved institution, or, in appropriate cases, with 90 hours of acceptable academic work.

A $100 seat deposit fee is payable by April 1, or within 20 days of admission, whichever comes later. Applicants are encouraged to visit the school. Arrangements can be made through the Admissions Office to meet with students and faculty, or to visit a class or tour the law school.

■ Expenses and Financial Aid

➡ *full-time tuition & fees—resident, $6,281; nonresident, $12,133* ➡ *estimated additional expenses—$8,900 (room & board, transportation, medical and personal expenses)* ➡ *merit & need-based scholarships available* ➡ *merit & need-based minority scholarships available* ➡ *government loan program available through UMKC Financial Aid Office* ➡ *FFS, UMKC financial aid form, and financial aid transcripts required*

■ Career Services

The Career Services Office assists law students and graduates in exploring and defining career options through individual counseling, workshops, and seminars. Law firms, businesses, and government agencies interview students on campus for summer clerkships and post-graduate employment. Additionally, area law firms list available clerk and attorney positions with the office. In cooperation with area bar associations, a mentor program pairs first-year students with practicing attorneys. The Career Services Office also provides resources for career planning and development.

Applicant Group Applying for the 1993–1994 Academic Year

University of Missouri—Kansas City School of Law
This grid includes only applicants who earned 120-180 LSAT scores under standard administrations in the 1992-1993 testing year.

GPA	LSAT Score																		
	Below 140		140 - 144		145 - 149		150 - 154		155 - 159		160 - 164		165 - 169		170 - 174		175 - 180		Total
	Apps	Adm	Apps	Adm	Apps	Adm	Apps	Adm	Apps	Adm	Apps	Adm	Apps	Adm	Apps	Adm	Apps	Adm	Apps	Adm
3.75 +	0	0	2	0	9	5	23	23	25	24	10	10	3	3	0	0	0	0	72	65
3.50 - 3.74	1	0	4	0	8	3	34	33	18	17	13	13	2	2	0	0	0	0	80	68
3.25 - 3.49	2	0	13	0	20	0	56	51	54	54	18	17	4	4	1	1	0	0	168	127
3.00 - 3.24	7	0	13	0	28	2	75	20	63	47	20	19	5	5	0	0	0	0	211	93
2.75 - 2.99	5	1	15	0	22	4	37	6	33	13	13	9	3	3	0	0	0	0	128	36
Below 2.75	96	1	29	1	48	3	39	6	37	10	18	6	6	4	1	0	0	0	274	31
Total	111	2	76	1	135	17	264	139	230	165	92	74	23	21	2	1	0	0	933	420

Apps = Number of Applicants
Adm = Number Admitted

University of Montana School of Law

Missoula, MT 59812   Phone: 406.243.4311

■ Introduction

The University of Montana is located in Missoula, on the west slopes of the Rocky Mountains. Missoula is situated halfway between Yellowstone and Glacier National Parks and is surrounded by several of the largest designated wilderness areas in the continental United States. The city is known for its outdoor opportunities and quality of life.

The University of Montana School of Law was established in 1911. It has been accredited by the AALS since 1914 and by the ABA since 1923. As one of the smallest law schools in the nation, students enjoy a congenial academic, intellectual, and social environment. The law school serves as a legal center for the state.

■ Enrollment: First-Year Class

➡ *607 applicants*   ➡ *137 admitted first-year class 1993*
➡ *77 enrolled first-year class 1993*   ➡ *4% minority*
➡ *30% women*   ➡ *14 states, countries, and Indian tribes represented*   ➡ *37 undergraduate schools represented*

■ Faculty

➡ *27 total*   ➡ *18 full-time*   ➡ *9 part-time*   ➡ *9 women*

■ Library and Physical Facilities

➡ *123,853 volumes & equivalents*   ➡ *LEXIS*
➡ *WESTLAW*   ➡ *two computer labs*
➡ *computer research integrated with class assignments*

■ Curriculum

➡ *90 semester hours required to graduate*
➡ *65 courses available*   ➡ *degrees available: J.D.; J.D./M.P.A.*   ➡ *semesters, start in Sept.*

The University of Montana School of Law integrates theory and practice throughout its curriculum to instill entry level practice competence in its graduates. The law school's curriculum, teaching methodology and assessment techniques are designed to address the following components of a lawyer's work: (1) knowledge of the law; (2) the ability to apply legal rules to resolve problems; (3) ability to use lawyer skills (e.g., negotiation, client counseling); (4) perspective on the societal role and responsibility of lawyers; and (5) sensitivity to the dynamics of social and interpersonal interaction.

The school has created three distinctive programs to acquaint first-year students with the ways lawyers think and work: (1) the Introductory Program, (2) the Lawyer Skills Program, and (3) the Law Firm Program. In the introductory program, students are initiated into the legal culture by surveying legal history, the American legal system, the litigation process, legal writing, and legal analysis and jurisprudence. The law school is one of the few to introduce first-year students to the skills involved in dispute resolution, including client counseling, legal drafting, and oral argument. The innovative "law firm" program encourages students to cooperate and collaborate rather than compete as they begin to think and work as lawyers. From the beginning of law school, entering students belong to "law firms," groups of six students, called associates, directed by specially trained upper-class students.

The school has long emphasized performance in its curriculum. The school's four-semester legal writing program and three-year dispute resolution program represent a coherent and comprehensive approach to lawyer skills. Students master specific transactional skills such as planning an estate, drafting a contract, and creating a small business.

The upper division clinical training program provides students with a wide range of opportunities to earn required academic credit by working on actual cases under the supervision of faculty and practicing attorneys in Missoula. The clinical offerings include the Montana Defender Project, Natural Resource Clinic, Indian Law Clinic, Montana Legal Services Association, ASUM Legal Services, Missoula County Attorney's Office, Forest Service Clinic, and University of Montana Legal Counsel's Office.

■ Special Programs

The law school also offers students wishing to specialize several clusters of courses. Because of Montana's natural setting, many students enroll in the natural resource and environmental law courses. The school offers extensive course offerings in resource and environmental law, as well as natural resource clinics and the opportunity to participate as editors of the *Public Land Law Review*.

Montana is home to seven Indian reservations. The law school's Indian Law courses, Indian Law Clinic, and Native American Law Student Association provide opportunities for students to learn about and participate in the administration of justice for Montana's Native Americans.

The school also offers clusters of courses in the areas of business and tax (with emphasis on the problems of small businesses), public law, and individual and property rights.

■ Admission

➡ *application deadline—March 15, rolling admissions, early application preferred*   ➡ *LSAT, LSDAS required*
➡ *average GPA—above 3.20*   ➡ *median LSAT score—155*
➡ *application fee—$60*

A committee of the law faculty passes on all applications. Candidates must be of good moral character, have intellectual promise, and have a baccalaureate degree from an approved college or university prior to matriculation. As a state-assisted institution, the School of Law gives some preference in admissions to residents. The school seeks a diverse student body and welcomes applications from members of groups historically underrepresented in the legal profession.

The most important admissions criteria are the cumulative undergraduate GPA and the LSAT score. The admissions committee weighs such factors as writing ability; experience prior to application to law school, including graduate study, college attended, trend in grades, quality of work in difficult courses, ability to overcome economic or other disadvantage, and change in performance after an absence from college.

The school recognizes a commitment to providing full opportunities for the study of law and entry into the legal profession of qualified members of groups (notably racial and ethnic minorities) which have been victims of discrimination in various forms. This commitment is implemented by special recruitment and retention efforts.

If the LSAT is repeated, the average of the scores will be used in computing the applicant's prediction index. No test score achieved later than the February administration of the LSAT can be considered in decisions for the subsequent September.

■ Student Activities

All students are members of the Student Bar Association. Its programs contribute to the professional development and the social life of the student body. Clayberg Inn of Phi Delta Phi national law fraternity encourages scholarship, promotes fellowship, and fosters the ideals of the profession. The Women's Law Caucus is part of the SBA, and other organizations include a Christian Legal Society, a student chapter of the American Trial

Lawyers—Montana Trial Lawyers Association, the Environmental Law Group, the Native American Law Student Association, the Federalist Society and the University of Montana Public Interest Law Coalition. The *Montana Law Review* and the *Public Land Law Review* afford supplementary training in analyzing legal problems precisely and presenting legal issues cogently. The UMLS team placed first in the nation in the 1991-1992 American Trial Lawyers Association trial competition and first in the 1990-1991 American Bar Association Client Counseling Competition. The UMLS National Moot Court Competition teams have advanced from regional to the national finals nine times in the last 13 years.

■ Expenses and Financial Aid

➠ *tuition & fees—residents, $4,591; nonresidents, $9,292*
➠ *estimated additional expenses—$7,000 (room, board, books)* ➠ *performance and need-based scholarships available (primarily to second-and third-year students)*
➠ *file FAFSA financial aid applications by March 1*

■ Career Services

The School of Law maintains a career service to assist students in finding part-time and summer employment, and attorney positions upon graduation. The job placement rate for the 1991 class for the period not less than 18 months after graduation was 95 percent.

Admission Profile Not Available

University of Nebraska College of Law

Lincoln, NE 68583-0902

Phone: 402.472.2161

■ Introduction

The University of Nebraska College of Law is large enough to provide students with a diverse curriculum, yet small enough to ensure that students are not lost in a faceless crowd. The college was founded in 1888 and is accredited by both the AALS and the ABA. It is located on the East Campus of the University of Nebraska in Lincoln, a city of approximately 200,000, and the state capital.

■ Enrollment/Student Body

➡ *918 applicants*   ➡ *386 admitted first-year class 1993*
➡ *162 enrolled first-year class 1993*   ➡ *467 total full-time*
➡ *2 total part-time*   ➡ *11% minority*   ➡ *43% women*
➡ *22 states & foreign countries represented*
➡ *59 undergraduate schools represented*

■ Faculty

➡ *56 total*   ➡ *26 full-time*   ➡ *30 part-time*
➡ *15 women*   ➡ *4 minority*

■ Library and Physical Facilities

➡ *303,748 volumes & equivalents*   ➡ *library hours:*
Mon.-Fri., 7:30 A.M.-12:30 A.M.; Sat., 9:00 A.M.-10:00 P.M.;
Sun., NOON-12:30 A.M.   ➡ *LEXIS*   ➡ *NEXIS*
➡ *WESTLAW*   ➡ *DIALOG*   ➡ *5 full-time librarians*
➡ *library seats 301*

The law college building offers the best in modern facilities, all of which are accessible to the physically disabled. The college's courtroom addition features a fully equipped teaching courtroom and expanded facilities for the civil clinical program. The college's criminal clinic program is located in the Lancaster County Attorney's office.

The law library provides an excellent study atmosphere. Students have access to microform materials, audio and video cassettes, photocopying, and the LEXIS and WESTLAW computerized research systems. The law library has a student computer laboratory with personal computers and printers.

■ Curriculum

➡ *Academic Resource Program*   ➡ *96 credits required to graduate*   ➡ *90 courses available*   ➡ *degrees available:*
J.D.; M.L.S.; J.D./M.B.A.; J.D./M.P.A.; J.D./Ph.D. (Psychology); J.D./Econ.; J.D./Poli. Sci.; J.D./M.C.R.P; J.D./Ph.D. (Ed. Admin.); J.D./individually designed programs   ➡ *semesters, start in Aug.*   ➡ *range of first-year class size—27-86*

The academic year runs from late August to early May. A two-day orientation before the beginning of the fall semester introduces first-year students to the law school and the study of law. Although completing the requirements for a J.D. degree normally takes three years, it is possible to graduate in two and one-half years by attending summer school during two summers. The college offers no night classes and only rarely accepts part-time students. Students

receiving the J.D. degree are qualified to practice law in any state upon passage of that state's bar examination.

The first-year curriculum is 18 hours per semester and includes civil procedure, contracts, criminal law, legal process, legal writing, property, and torts. Courses in the second and third years are elective, with the exception of required courses in constitutional law, professional responsibility, and a research seminar. The curriculum encompasses a broad range of areas, from taxation and securities to Native American law, legal control of discrimination, and international transactions. The college offers many courses in the environmental and natural resource law areas including environmental law I and II, water law, oil & gas law and agricultural law. The average upper-class student takes 15 hours per semester.

Under faculty supervision, students in criminal clinic prosecute actual misdemeanor cases while students in civil clinic represent actual clients in civil cases.

The college's interdisciplinary program in Law and Psychology is recognized as one of the finest in the nation. Students can receive either a Ph.D. and J.D. after six years of study or an M.A. and J.D. after four years of study.

The college also participates in a number of other joint-degree programs, including Accounting (J.D./M.P.A.), Business Administration (J.D./M.B.A.), Economics (J.D./M.A.), Educational Administration (J.D./ Ph.D.), Political Science (J.D./M.A.), and Community and Regional Planning (J.D./M.C.R.P.).

■ Minority Programs

The college is committed to diversity in its student population. Minority students comprise approximately 11 percent of the 1993 entering class and 11 percent of the students at the college.

The college takes special care in evaluating applications from members of minority groups that have been underrepresented in the legal profession, and will waive the application fee upon demonstration of financial need. The college participates in the CLEO program and looks favorably upon candidates for admission who have successfully completed the program. The college offers entering minority students a two-day program to introduce the College of Law, the study of law, and fellow students.

The college provides an Academic Resource Program to assist first-year students in developing and improving fundamental skills such as note-taking, case briefing, outlining, analyzing, and exam-taking. The college also offers a skills seminar to focus on these skills. Participation in the seminar is by invitation.

■ Admission

➡ *Bachelor's degree from accredited institution required*
➡ *application deadline—March 1*   ➡ *rolling admission, early application preferred*   ➡ *LSAT, LSDAS required*
➡ *median GPA—3.40*   ➡ *median LSAT score—156*
➡ *application fee—$25*

The college starts reviewing applications in early January. Although an applicant's undergraduate GPA and LSAT score weigh heavily in the admission decision, substantial weight is also given to the quality of the applicant's undergraduate institution, course of study, personal statement, work experience, extracurricular activities, recommendations, and other background information supplied by the applicant. To visit a law class, meet with admission personnel or tour the Law College, call the Admissions Office. The College of Law has an annual open house in February.

Student Activities

The *Nebraska Law Review*, published by a student editorial board, publishes leading articles from well-known authorities in their fields, as well as student notes and comments. The Nebraska Transcript, published by students three times a year, provides information about the college to students, faculty, and alumni.

Other student activities or organizations include the National Moot Court Competition, Client Counseling Competition, National Trial Competition, Student Bar Association, Women's Law Caucus, Community Legal Education Project, Black Law Students Association, Civil Liberties Group, Equal Justice Foundation, Multi-Cultural Legal Society, Natural Resources Law Society, Christian Legal Society, Federalist Society, Association of Trial Lawyers of America, International Law Society,

Law Student Research Service, The Rutherford Institute, Volunteer Income Tax Assistance Program, and three national legal fraternities.

Expenses and Financial Aid

➡ *first-year tuition & fees—resident, $3,972; nonresident, $8,706* ➡ *estimated additional expenses—$6,225 (books, living expenses, transportation, personal)* ➡ *academic scholarships, need-based grants, and opportunity grants available* ➡ *FAFSA forms & College of Law need-based grant application forms for financial aid due March 1*

For the 1993-1994 academic year, resident tuition is $84 per hour, and nonresident tuition is $215.50 per hour. Fees total $474 per semester.

Residency may be established by residing in Nebraska for six months before the start of a semester or summer session and complying with the statutory requirements.

Career Services

The college operates its own career services office for students seeking full-time employment or summer clerkships. The office provides students with a variety of placement-related services and also organizes on-campus interviews by private law firms, governmental agencies, corporations, and other potential employers. As of December 1992, approximately 87 percent of the members of the class of 1992 were employed or were enrolled in advanced degree programs.

Applicant Group for the 1993–1994 Academic Year

University of Nebraska College of Law

GPA	LSAT Score							
	Below 144	145-149	150-154	155-159	160-164	165-169	170-174	175-180
3.75 + Above								
3.74 - 3.50								
3.49 - 3.25								
3.24 - 3.00								
2.99 - 2.75								
2.74 - 2.50								
Below 2.50								

☐ Unlikely   ☐ Fair   ■ Good   ■ Excellent

Includes all applicants

New England School of Law

154 Stuart Street
Boston, MA 02116

Phone: 617.451.0010

■ Introduction

New England School of Law was founded in 1908 as Portia Law School, the only school in the nation dedicated exclusively to the legal education of women. The institution became coeducational in 1934, but it has remained sensitive to the needs of those underrepresented in the legal profession. New England is fully accredited by the American Bar Association (ABA).

Boston is an ideal city in which to study law. Our school occupies a completely modern, downtown facility near Boston's government, business, and theater districts.

New England capitalizes on its advantageous location by providing an extensive clinical program and by utilizing members of the city's legal community as adjunct faculty and lecturers. The school has attracted a number of distinguished speakers through its Speakers Series and other events. Most notably, we welcomed United States Supreme Court Justice Sandra Day O'Connor on September 20, 1991, and United States Supreme Court Justice Harry A. Blackmun on March 11, 1993.

■ Enrollment/Student Body

→ *3,656 applicants*   → *1,338 admitted first-year class 1993*
→ *402 enrolled first-year class 1993*   → *640 total full-time*
→ *489 total part-time*   → *5% minority*   → *42% women*
→ *30 states & foreign countries represented*
→ *167 undergraduate schools represented*

■ Faculty

→ *103 total members*   → *40 full-time*
→ *63 part-time or adjunct*   → *24 women faculty*
→ *4 minority faculty*

■ Library and Physical Facilities

→ *242,000 volumes & equivalents*   → *library hours:*
Mon.-Fri., 8:00 A.M.-11:00 P.M.; Sat., 9:00 A.M.-10:00 P.M.;
Sun., 10:00 A.M.-11:00 P.M.   → *LEXIS*   → *NEXIS*
→ *WESTLAW*   → *DIALOG*   → *OCLC*   → *CALI*
→ *8 full-time librarians*   → *library seats 376*

The tri-level law library incorporates computerized legal research equipment, study carrels, typing space, and consultation and lounge areas. Offering the latest in technology, the library has an extensive audio and video collection, several trials presented on Interactive Videodisc, and two CD-ROM indexes to legal periodical literature.

■ Curriculum

→ *Academic Support Program*
→ *84 units/credits required to graduate*   → *98 courses available*
→ *J.D. degree offered*   → *semesters, start in Aug.*
→ *range of first-year class size—15-129*

As a national law school, New England's curriculum is designed to prepare graduates to practice in any jurisdiction in the United States. The school has both a day and evening division, each offering the J.D. degree. The day program requires 84 credit hours over three academic years. The work of the first year is prescribed. Second-year students are required to take criminal law and procedure, evidence, and professional responsibility. Remaining courses are elective.

The evening program requires 84 credit-hours over four academic years. The evening program curriculum is prescribed for the first and second years; the third and fourth years are elective.

In addition to its day and evening programs, New England offers a third program of study for persons whose child-care responsibilities permit only part-time study with more flexibility.

■ Special Programs

New England prides itself on the great variety of high quality clinical programs available to its students. The school offers 13 clinics and maintains its own fully equipped Clinical Law Office, in which supervised students handle actual cases. Besides its civil and criminal practice clinics, the school offers clinical programs in such diverse areas as health law, mental health law, immigration law, tax law, land use and environmental law, administrative law, prisoners' rights, and domestic violence.

■ Admission

→ *Bachelor's degree required for admission*
→ *application deadline—March 15*
→ *LSAT, LSDAS required*   → *median GPA—3.07*
→ *median LSAT score—152*   → *application fee—$45*

New England requires the LSAT, use of the LSDAS, and two letters of recommendation. This information, together with a completed application, must be received by the Admissions Office by March 15 (and preferably much earlier, since decisions are made on a rolling basis).

Like most law schools in desirable urban locations, New England receives applications from many more qualified individuals than it can accommodate. The Admissions Committee makes decisions to provide stability and diversity in the entering class. Factors that reflect stability are the GPA and the LSAT score. Factors weighted heavily for diversity include, but are not limited to, undergraduate major and institution, extracurricular activities and/or work experience, geographic distribution, minority status, gender, and exceptional characteristics.

■ Student Activities

Upper-class students are selected for membership on the *New England Law Review* on the basis of academic achievement or success in a writing competition. Our other scholarly journal, *The New England Journal of Criminal and Civil Confinement*, is the only student publication in the country devoted solely to this field. Our school participates in several moot court programs, including the National Moot Court, the Jessup (international law), the National Environmental Law, the F. Lee Bailey Moot Court, and National Tax Moot Court. In 1991 and 1992, New England teams won the Northeast Regional round of the National Trial Competition.

The Student Bar Association (SBA) is the school's student government, with members serving as student representatives on most faculty and law school committees. The SBA also sponsors a variety of social events, athletic competitions, and a Speaker's Forum. Other student organizations include the Computer Law Society, Environmental Law Society, International Law Society, Irish Law Society, Law Student Division of the ABA, Lesbian and Gay Caucus, Minority Students' Association, and the Women's Law Caucus.

Minority Programs

As part of fulfilling its continued pledge to those underrepresented in the legal profession, New England has developed a new recruitment program, funded additional allocations of financial aid, and established the Charles Hamilton Houston Enrichment Program (CHHEP). The CHHEP has three components that involve first-year students: the speaker series, the first-year discussion groups, and the academic support program.

Housing

New England does not operate any student housing facilities. Numerous privately owned apartment buildings are within walking and commuting distance of the school, and roommate referral listings are available in the Dean's office.

Expenses and Financial Aid

➡ *tuition & fees—full-time, $11,150; part-time, $8,400*
➡ *estimated additional expenses—books, $400; health insurance, $490; living expenses, $10,240*
➡ *scholarships available: NESL grant, Maclean grant, Arthur Getchell grants, Jacqueline Lloyd grants, Trustee Scholars*
➡ *minority scholarships available: Jacqueline Lloyd grant*
➡ *financial aid available*   ➡ *GAPSFAS form and New England School of Law Financial Aid Application required, due April 15*

The school participates in the Federal Perkins Loan and Federal Work-Study programs. Limited institutional employment, grants, and scholarships are also available to needy applicants, including the MacLean Grant for students from extremely disadvantaged backgrounds and the Jacqueline Lloyd grant for students from minority backgrounds.

Placement

The Law School maintains a Career Development and Placement Office to assist students and alumni in securing law-related employment both prior to and after graduation. The services provided by the office include individual and group career counseling, résumé preparation, maintenance of a career-resource library, and specific job listings for students and graduates. In addition, information is disseminated concerning summer internships, part-time and full-time employment, judicial clerkships, and graduate programs.

Respondents to the employment survey of the Class of 1992 indicated an overall employment rate of 84 percent. Of the employed graduates, 48 percent were working in private law practice.

Applicant Group for the 1993–1994 Academic Year

New England School of Law
This grid includes only applicants who earned 120-180 LSAT scores under standard administrations.

LSAT Score	GPA																			
	3.75 +		3.50 -3.74		3.25 - 3.49		3.00 - 3.24		2.75 - 2.99		2.50 - 2.74		2.25 - 2.49		2.00 - 2.24		Below 2.00		No GPA		Total	
	Apps	Adm	Apps	Adm	Apps	Adm	Apps	Adm	Apps	Adm	Apps	Adm	Apps	Adm	Apps	Adm	Apps	Adm	Apps	Adm	Apps	Adm
175 - 180	0	0	0	0	0	0	0	0	1	1	0	0	0	0	0	0	0	0	0	0	1	1
170 - 174	0	0	2	2	1	1	1	1	0	0	1	0	2	0	0	0	0	0	0	0	7	4
165 - 169	1	1	2	2	2	2	6	6	11	9	3	1	3	0	1	0	0	0	0	0	29	21
160 - 164	6	6	13	13	16	15	40	36	45	27	31	13	15	2	4	0	1	0	1	0	172	112
155 - 159	5	5	34	32	61	58	130	111	122	58	98	38	48	7	6	0	2	0	5	0	511	309
150 - 154	22	22	64	56	151	130	259	177	269	98	167	33	77	10	32	1	3	1	10	5	1054	533
145 - 149	14	10	49	23	122	44	195	55	221	24	144	8	72	7	28	0	5	0	12	6	862	177
140 - 144	6	4	28	9	47	9	104	5	134	5	92	1	64	3	27	1	9	0	8	2	519	39
135 - 139	3	0	4	0	13	0	36	1	39	2	40	0	35	0	18	0	3	0	7	0	198	3
130 - 134	0	0	0	0	6	0	3	0	13	0	18	0	19	0	9	0	3	0	3	0	74	0
125 - 129	0	0	0	0	0	0	2	0	0	0	4	0	4	0	4	0	1	0	2	0	17	0
120 - 124	0	0	0	0	0	0	0	0	0	0	0	0	1	0	0	0	0	0	1	0	2	0
Total	57	48	196	137	419	259	776	392	855	224	598	94	340	29	129	2	27	1	49	13	3446	1199

Apps = Number of Applicants
Adm = Number Admitted
Reflects 94% of the total applicant pool.

University of New Mexico School of Law

1117 Stanford N.E.
Albuquerque, NM 87131-1431

Phone: 506.277.2146

■ Introduction

The University of New Mexico is the state's major university with over 24,000 students. The law school, located on the north campus of the university in Albuquerque, is just minutes from the downtown area and 60 miles from Santa Fe, the state's capital. This proximity to local, state, and federal courts, key government offices, and law firms allows students opportunities to observe and participate in the practice of law. In their leisure, students have access to symphony, theater, the Santa Fe Opera, galleries, museums, and the beauty of outdoor New Mexico. The combination of Indian, Spanish, and Anglo cultures reflected in food, music, art, architecture, and local customs heightens Albuquerque's appeal.

The University of New Mexico School of Law is known for its small classes, easy student-faculty interaction, and innovative education and research. The School of Law has an 11:1 student-faculty ratio, one of the best in the country. This ratio allows the school to offer more courses with smaller enrollments.

The school offers a comprehensive curriculum and has special programs in natural resources law, American Indian law, and international transboundary law. It also has a legal education equal opportunity program that recruits and assists minority students and is a member of the Southwest CLEO consortium. It is a member of the AALS and is fully approved by the ABA.

■ Enrollment/Student Body

➡ *1,251 applicants*   ➡ *203 admitted first-year class 1993*
➡ *109 enrolled first-year class 1993*   ➡ *343 total full-time*
➡ *46% minority*   ➡ *56% women*
➡ *48 undergraduate schools represented in first-year class*

■ Faculty

➡ *48 total*   ➡ *29 full-time*   ➡ *19 part-time or adjunct*
➡ *16 women*   ➡ *8 minority*

■ Library and Physical Facilities

➡ *350,000 volumes & equivalents*   ➡ *library hours: Mon.-Thurs., 7:30 A.M.-MIDNIGHT; Fri., 7:30 A.M.-10:00 P.M.; Sat., 8:00 A.M.-10:00 P.M.; Sun., 10:00 A.M.-MIDNIGHT*
➡ *LEXIS*   ➡ *NEXIS*   ➡ *WESTLAW*   ➡ *Q/L*
➡ *DIALOG*   ➡ *4 full-time librarians*   ➡ *library seats 380*

The law school is housed in Bratton Hall. In addition to classrooms, seminar rooms, the moot courtroom, the library, and faculty and student organization offices, Bratton Hall also houses the Natural Resources Center, the American Indian Law Center, and the Law Practice Clinic.

The UNM Law Library is the primary New Mexico legal research center. The library includes comprehensive collections of British, federal, and state court reports, and annotations, session laws, current state and federal statutes, legal treatises, periodicals, encyclopedias, digests, administrative reports, and other classes of legal materials. Special collections are being developed in American Indian law, Mexican and Latin American law, and community land grant law.

Over 100 carrels are available to students and faculty engaged in on-going research. Pocket lounges and browsing areas, five audiovisual carrels, sound-proofed typing rooms, a conference room, photocopying room, and computer lab are available for students' use.

■ Curriculum

➡ *Academic Support Program*   ➡ *programs offered: Orientation, Mentor, Summer Academic Support/Academic Year Tutorials, Medical/Legal Professional Responsibility Day*
➡ *86 credits required to graduate*   ➡ *over 120 courses available*   ➡ *degrees available: J.D.; J.D./M.B.A.; J.D./M.P.A.; J.D./M.A. (Latin American Studies)*
➡ *semesters, start in Aug. & Jan. (15 weeks), May (clinic)*
➡ *range of first-year class size—16-55*

First-year students must take a full first-year curriculum, including basic courses in torts, contracts, civil procedure, property, and criminal law. Emphasis is also placed on the skills of advocacy; legal writing, oral argument, litigation, counseling, and negotiation. Second- and third-year courses are elective except for Ethics, Introduction to Constitutional Law, and a clinical program. Students normally complete the requirements for the J.D. degree in three academic years (six semesters).

Unlike most other law schools, UNM requires six credit hours of clinical work for graduation. In 1970, the New Mexico Supreme Court adopted a rule permitting students to practice before state courts. Today, the UNM Program in Clinical Law is regarded as one of the finest practical-lawyering programs in the country. The program is based at the school, but also has a branch in the Bernalillo County District Attorney's office. Students may elect to take a year-long clinical course, the Institute for Access to Justice, which focuses on the delivery of legal services to economically disadvantaged clients. The clinical program also operates an extern placement program. Students may elect assignment to a judge's office, the Public Defender's Office, federal and state administrative offices, and private practitioners.

■ Special Programs

Four research and training institutes are a part of the law school: the American Indian Law Center; the Institute of Public Law; the Natural Resources Center; and the International Transboundary Center. The American Indian Law Center is an independent institute devoted to strengthening Indian tribal government. It has worked closely with the Navajo, Pueblo, and other tribes to assist them in improving their judicial systems. The Institute of Public Law serves New Mexico and the Southwest in an advisory capacity and provides training programs and research for state and local governments. Recent activities by its centers include projects in bioethics, environmental clean-up, wildlife law, and mediation.

The Natural Resources Center plans and administers special academic programs in natural resources and policy and coordinates research activities and grant programs. Since 1961, the law school has published the *Natural Resources Journal*. The journal has led to the development of a special program at the law school. Students may earn a certificate showing concentration in this area of law. The International Transboundary Center is research-oriented and concerns itself with the management of natural resources complicated by political divisions.

The School of Law is a member of a consortium which offers six weeks of summer law study in Guanajuato, followed by an optional internship in a Mexico City law firm.

■ Admission

➠ *Bachelor's degree from an accredited college or university required*   ➠ *application deadline—Feb. 1*
➠ *LSAT, LSDAS required*   ➠ *median GPA—3.20*
➠ *median LSAT score—158*   ➠ *application fee—$30*
➠ *admittance fall semester only*
➠ *no deposit required of accepted applicants*

Applicants should take the LSAT no later than December before the year in which they wish to enroll.

A five-member committee reviews all applications from residents and all competitive applications from nonresidents. Substantial weight is given to the applicant's personal statement, prior work experience, extracurricular activities, recommendations, and to other background information supplied by the applicant.

The profile printed below does not make any distinction between residents and nonresidents, but applications from New Mexico residents are given a very decided preference.

■ Student Activities

Extracurricular activities include the *Natural Resources Journal*, the *New Mexico Law Review*, and several moot court and mock trial competitions. All law students are members of the university's Graduate Student Association and the Student Bar Association. Students may participate in more than 15 law-student organizations.

■ Expenses and Financial Aid

➠ *full-time tuition & fees—resident, $2,466/year; nonresident, $8,274/year*   ➠ *estimated additional expenses—room & board, $4,726; books & supplies, $595; transportation, $926; personal expenses, $1,816; childcare supplement for any number of dependents age 12 or under, $2,322*
➠ *grants available*   ➠ *Native American grants available*
➠ *financial aid available*   ➠ *UNM Supplemental Application due March 1 or ASAP after admission*

The law school awards a significant number of need-based grants to full-time students each year.

Applicant Group for the 1993–1994 Academic Year

University of New Mexico School of Law
This grid includes only applicants who earned 120-180 LSAT scores under standard administrations.

LSAT Score	GPA 3.75 +		3.50 -3.74		3.25 - 3.49		3.00 - 3.24		2.75 - 2.99		2.50 - 2.74		2.25 - 2.49		2.00 - 2.24		Below 2.00		No GPA		Total	
	Apps	Adm	Apps	Adm	Apps	Adm	Apps	Adm	Apps	Adm	Apps	Adm	Apps	Adm	Apps	Adm	Apps	Adm	Apps	Adm	Apps	Adm
175 - 180	0	0	0	0	0	0	0	0	0	0	0	0	0	0	0	0	0	0	0	0	0	0
170 - 174	1	1	2	2	2	2	1	1	1	0	2	1	2	1	0	0	0	0	0	0	11	8
165 - 169	2	2	7	6	11	7	6	4	7	0	3	0	3	1	1	0	0	0	1	0	41	20
160 - 164	10	9	15	10	25	7	32	11	25	6	11	1	8	0	4	0	1	0	2	0	133	44
155 - 159	13	9	26	10	48	12	56	10	39	6	23	3	21	1	6	0	2	0	7	2	241	53
150 - 154	13	4	30	5	70	12	71	5	48	6	33	1	22	1	4	0	0	0	5	0	296	34
145 - 149	3	1	12	2	33	1	43	4	46	5	34	4	22	0	12	1	0	0	6	0	211	18
140 - 144	2	1	5	1	18	1	21	2	30	1	30	5	21	2	9	0	6	0	1	0	143	13
135 - 139	1	0	0	0	3	1	14	1	7	1	16	0	6	0	5	0	0	0	4	0	56	3
130 - 134	0	0	1	0	3	0	0	0	3	0	1	0	5	0	2	0	2	0	2	0	19	0
125 - 129	0	0	1	0	0	0	0	0	2	0	3	0	5	0	2	0	0	0	1	0	14	0
120 - 124	0	0	0	0	0	0	0	0	0	0	0	0	0	0	0	0	0	0	0	0	0	0
Total	45	27	99	36	213	43	244	38	208	25	156	15	115	6	45	1	11	0	29	2	1165	193

Apps = Number of Applicants
Adm = Number Admitted
Reflects 93% of the total applicant pool.

City University of New York School of Law at Queens College

65-21 Main Street
Flushing, NY 11367

Phone: 718.575.4210

■ Introduction

CUNY School of Law at Queens College has a special emphasis on public service and public-interest law. The school is fully accredited by the American Bar Association. It is the only publicly funded law school in New York City.

The School of Law is a unit of the City University of New York, one of the largest and most distinguished university systems in the nation. Queens College, on whose campus the Law School is situated, is one of nine four-year colleges in the CUNY system.

■ Enrollment/Student Body

➡ *2,246 applicants* ➡ *413 admitted first-year class 1993*
➡ *153 enrolled first-year class 1993* ➡ *438 total full-time*
➡ *12 total part-time* ➡ *28% minority* ➡ *50% women*
➡ *29 states & foreign countries represented*
➡ *189 undergraduate schools represented*

The law school has been remarkably successful in recruiting the diverse, committed, and richly experienced student body that it has sought. The median age of matriculated students during 1992-93 was 30. Approximately 80 percent of enrolled students in 1992-93 were residents of New York State, and approximately one-third have attended one or more of the City University schools for undergraduate or graduate work. The academic credentials of our students run the full range of possible grades and scores. Where the traditional indicators are low, the applicants can demonstrate academic potential through nonstandard indicia and very strong work or life experiences that are relevant to the school's mission.

■ Faculty

➡ *55 total* ➡ *39 full-time* ➡ *16 part-time or adjunct*
➡ *24 women* ➡ *19 minority*

■ Library and Physical Facilities

➡ *210,620 volumes & equivalents* ➡ *library hours: Mon.-Thurs., 8:00 A.M.-6:00 P.M.; Fri., 8:00 A.M.-5:00 P.M.; closed Sat; Sun., 1:00 P.M.-9:00 P.M.* ➡ *LEXIS* ➡ *NEXIS*
➡ *WESTLAW* ➡ *DIALOG* ➡ *7 full-time librarians*
➡ *library seats 370*

The law school's permanent facility is unique in that it allocates space—Houses—for student use. Each pair of Houses, called a Section, comprises a suite of rooms. Two of these rooms are student work areas, with a desk, book shelves, and locking file drawers for each student. In addition, there are three faculty offices, a Section Library (with access to computer-assisted legal research databases), a secretarial/reception area, a pair of video-equipped interview rooms, and photocopy and wordprocessing equipment.

The library combines a substantial print collection with extensive microform holdings and widely accessible computer databases.

■ Curriculum

➡ *Academic Support Program* ➡ *92 credits required to graduate* ➡ *J.D. degree available* ➡ *semesters, start in Aug.* ➡ *range of first-year class size—20-150*

Our purpose is to create an educational program that honors students' aspirations toward a legal career built on a commitment to justice, fairness, and equality.

The overall theme of an integrated curriculum is especially reflected in our treatment of three areas that are given much heavier emphasis than has been traditional. These areas are legal theory, clinical education, and professional responsibility. The first three semesters consist almost entirely of required courses. The final three semesters allow the student to select from a number of elective courses, in a variety of doctrinal areas. In addition, in the final two semesters, the student is enrolled either in a concentration area (with classroom work and practice placement combined) or in a clinic (with virtually full-time live-client practice).

The school offers only a full-time day program.

■ Lawyering Seminars

Clinical work is comprehensively integrated into the course of study. Throughout the program students are organized into work units called Lawyering Seminars. These offices of 20 students provide a context for a series of simulated practice situations related to the substantive courses. Students spend half of their time at the Law School engaged in work in their Lawyering Seminars, and half of their time attending lectures. Each Lawyering Seminar is affiliated with a faculty member. Through the simulations, the students engage in a wide range of lawyering tasks; they draft documents, interview and counsel clients, engage in negotiations, and make arguments before trial and appellate courts, often reviewing their work with the Lawyering Seminar teachers and other faculty.

We believe that grappling with issues of professional responsibility is at the heart of public-interest practice, and that an awareness of personal and professional responsibility therefore should be integral to students' lawyering work.

■ Admission

➡ *Bachelor's degree from accredited college or university required* ➡ *application deadline—March 13*
➡ *LSAT, LSDAS required* ➡ *median GPA—3.00*
➡ *median LSAT score—150* ➡ *application fee—$35*
➡ *early application preferred*

We actively seek to recruit, retain, promote, and train students of all races, national origins, classes, and belief systems, without regard to gender or sexual preference.

We admit people based on several criteria. We look at academic performance and scores on the LSAT, and beyond these to other demonstrations of academic promise.

Assessment of academic ability alone does not dominate the admissions process. We try to assess some of the less tangible qualities that make an outstanding lawyer, including judgment, energy, initiative, and the ability to work both collaboratively and independently. We look for indications that the candidate has a special affinity for our particular program; people with a demonstrated commitment to the principles of justice, fairness, and equality in the legal process; people with a sensitivity to the diversity of society and the equal worth of each of its members; and people who manifest a regard for providing all groups the broadest participation in our public life.

Finally, we try to select a diverse group of students, genuinely representative of the remarkable diversity of the city the school serves.

The school's admissions process is described in detail in its application materials. In brief, all applications are read closely. The detailed personal statement that we require forms the core of most applications.

Recommendations, while not required, are also often a decisive part of the applicant's file. Applicants may be invited to come in and meet with members of the committee. Students who have questions about our program or who want to visit the law school are of course welcome to contact the Admissions Office for an informational interview with a member of the Admissions Office staff.

■ Expenses and Financial Aid

➡ *full-time tuition & fees—resident, $2,647/semester; non-resident; $3,887/semester* ➡ *estimated additional expenses—$8,300 (room & board, transportation, personal expenses, insurance)* ➡ *Law School Tuition Waivers available* ➡ *special CUNY form only (no cost to process) required for financial aid*

Perkins Loans (formerly NDSL) and college work-study funds are available, as are a limited number of tuition waivers. During 1992-93, approximately 66 percent of our students received tuition waivers ranging from $100 to $3,700 for the year or other financial assistance.

■ Career Services

The law school views the placement function as part of its academic program. Our placement program begins in the first year. We encourage students to reflect on the choices they make as they seek work and decide among employment opportunities. We also work actively to develop job opportunities during the year, during the summer, and after graduation. We have been aided by a continuing grant from the Revson Foundation that has helped to provide summer stipends for our law students working in public-interest placements during the summer. We also have a small but increasing loan forgiveness program.

Applicant Group for the 1993–1994 Academic Year

City of New York School of Law at Queens College
This grid includes only applicants who earned 120-180 LSAT scores under standard administrations.

LSAT Score	3.75 +		3.50 -3.74		3.25 - 3.49		3.00 - 3.24		2.75 - 2.99		2.50 - 2.74		2.25 - 2.49		2.00 - 2.24		Below 2.00		No GPA		Total	
	Apps	Adm	Apps	Adm	Apps	Adm	Apps	Adm	Apps	Adm	Apps	Adm	Apps	Adm	Apps	Adm	Apps	Adm	Apps	Adm	Apps	Adm
175 - 180	0	0	1	1	1	1	0	0	1	1	0	0	0	0	0	0	0	0	0	0	3	3
170 - 174	1	1	0	0	0	0	3	3	0	0	0	0	1	0	0	0	0	0	0	0	5	4
165 - 169	2	2	3	3	4	3	2	2	4	3	3	1	3	0	1	0	0	0	0	0	22	14
160 - 164	1	0	3	3	12	10	4	3	7	4	13	3	4	1	5	0	3	1	3	3	55	28
155 - 159	5	5	20	14	25	10	35	11	29	7	34	11	22	3	6	2	1	0	5	2	182	65
150 - 154	5	3	17	7	69	29	85	21	94	11	73	12	47	6	19	1	2	1	6	1	417	92
145 - 149	8	5	32	8	61	22	107	22	131	21	88	12	53	2	31	3	6	1	14	5	531	101
140 - 144	7	3	23	5	34	4	75	11	86	11	80	7	71	2	31	1	2	0	23	0	432	44
135 - 139	0	0	11	2	21	4	36	0	57	0	52	1	59	1	33	0	4	0	16	2	289	10
130 - 134	1	0	1	0	4	1	8	0	18	0	28	1	29	0	15	0	6	1	12	0	122	3
125 - 129	1	0	0	0	1	0	2	0	6	0	8	0	7	0	4	0	1	0	6	0	36	0
120 - 124	0	0	0	0	0	0	0	0	0	0	1	0	1	0	0	0	0	0	2	0	4	0
Total	31	19	111	43	232	84	357	73	433	58	380	48	297	15	145	7	25	4	87	13	2098	364

Apps = Number of Applicants
Adm = Number Admitted
Reflects 93% of the total applicant pool.

New York Law School

57 Worth Street
New York, NY 10013-2960

Phone: 212.431.2888

■ Introduction

The New York Law School has been an integral part of New York's legal community for over 100 years. Founded in 1891, the school's approach to law study combines practical perspective with theoretical analysis to produce a lawyer centered legal education. The school's central location and proximity to courts, government agencies, major law firms, corporations, and financial institutions provides invaluable educational and practical experiences for students. The Law School offers clerkship and externship opportunities in numerous law offices and government agencies within walking distance. The Law School is located in TriBeCa, one of the city's most colorful and dynamic communities and the home of film studios, art galleries, fine restaurants, and numerous other cultural and entertainment resources.

The school's success is reflected in the many leaders of the legal and business community who are New York Law School graduates. It offers a full-time day program, a part-time day program, and a part-time evening program. The New York Law School is a member of the Association of American Law Schools and is fully approved by the ABA and the New York State Board of Regents.

■ Enrollment/Student Body

➨ *3,944 applicants* ➨ *1,616 admitted first-year class 1993*
➨ *447 enrolled first-year class 1993* ➨ *890 total full-time*
➨ *479 total part-time* ➨ *22% minority* ➨ *40% women*
➨ *27 states & foreign countries represented*
➨ *177 undergraduate schools represented*
➨ *35 first-year students hold advanced degrees*

The student body reflects rich diversity and brings to the school a wide variety of experiences, talents, and viewpoints. New York Law School has a long-standing and continuing interest in enrolling students from varied backgrounds, including older students, minority students, women, career changers, and public servants. Students range in age from 21 to 65, with the average age of 25.

■ Faculty

➨ *150 total faculty* ➨ *49 full-time* ➨ *101 part-time or adjunct* ➨ *40 women* ➨ *7 minority*

The school's broad curriculum of more than 100 elective courses and seminars is taught by a distinguished faculty. Leading jurists and attorneys who work in nearby offices are members of the adjunct faculty and teach courses in their areas of practice and expertise. Collectively, the faculty offers exceptional breadth and depth in their backgrounds and professional interests.

■ Library and Physical Facilities

➨ *377,124 volumes & equivalents* ➨ *library hours: Mon.-Fri., 8:00 A.M.-11:00 P.M.; Sat. and Sun., 10:00 A.M.-10:00 P.M.*
➨ *LEXIS* ➨ *NEXIS* ➨ *WESTLAW* ➨ *OCLC*
➨ *RLIN* ➨ *13 full-time librarians* ➨ *library seats 592*

The Mendik Library houses the collection and reflects the latest developments in information technology. Designed to be a functional, comfortable environment in which to study, it features separate rooms for computer terminals, spacious study areas, and informal lounges. Of particular interest is the Communications Library, which is devoted to material related to the school's Media Law program. The Law School's facilities occupy a group of four connected buildings in Lower Manhattan. A new Student Center includes a cafeteria situated in a sky-lit atrium, student organization offices, bookstore, art gallery, and a spacious lounge area.

■ Curriculum and Special Programs

➨ *Academic Support Program* ➨ *86 units/credits required to graduate* ➨ *225 courses available*
➨ *degrees available: J.D./M.B.A.; J.D./M.P.A. with Baruch College (City University of New York); and Bachelor's/J.D. with Stevens Institute of Technology*
➨ *range of first-year class size—15-115*

The curriculum is designed primarily to prepare students to be effective, productive, and responsible members of the legal profession. The required curriculum comprises the entire first year and part of the second year to provide a foundation in legal reasoning and in areas of law that are considered indispensable building blocks of a legal education. In the second year and thereafter, students may design their programs with elective courses chosen from an extraordinarily rich array.

The Lawyering Skills Program—Elements such as legal analysis and legal writing, counseling, interviewing, negotiating, advocacy, planning, and strategizing form the core subject areas of the school's Lawyering Skills Program. This program integrates skills-related courses as part of the required first-year sequence and thereafter. The key elements of the Lawyering Skills Program include simulation courses such as Negotiating, Counseling, and Interviewing, Trial Advocacy, externships and judicial internships, practice workshops, and clinics.

The Externship and Judicial Internship Programs—These programs permit students to do actual lawyering work at outside placements.

Communications Media Center—In response to the explosive growth of new communication technologies, the Law School established a Communications Media Center in 1977. The center promotes education, discussion, research, and writing about mass communications law. The scope of the center's activities is broad, and the faculty involved offer a substantial number of related courses and extracurricular programs dealing with issues such as cable television franchising procedures, direct broadcast satellites, videotext services, racial discrimination in television, and the future of public broadcasting.

■ Clinical Program

The school has a tradition of a strong clinical program that permits students to do actual lawyering work, representing clients in clinics supervised by Law School faculty.

■ Admission

➤ *Bachelor's degree from accredited college or university required for admission* ➤ *application deadline—April 1* ➤ *rolling admissions, early application preferred* ➤ *LSAT, LSDAS required* ➤ *median GPA—3.00* ➤ *median LSAT score—154* ➤ *application fee—$50*

In the admission process a range of factors is taken into account, including the applicant's academic record and Law School Admission Test scores. The school seeks to admit students who, in addition to possessing strong academic credentials, also have demonstrated leadership ability, motivation, and a sense of service and responsibility to society. In evaluating applicants, excellence in a particular field of study, motivation, progression of grades, strength of undergraduate curriculum, work and community-service experience, graduate study in other disciplines, and extracurricular activities all are considered. Writing ability receives particular attention.

The school seeks to enroll a diverse student body made up of individuals who, through their backgrounds, experiences, perspectives, and ambitions, promise to enrich the law school community and, ultimately, the larger society.

■ Student Activities

There is a Moot Court Board with active participation in intermural competitions, as well as three scholarly publi-cations, edited and staffed by students, that are integral parts of the Law School's program—*New York Law School Law Review, New York Law School Journal of International and Comparative Law*, and *New York Law School Journal of Human Rights*. Students have established some 30 interest organizations as well.

■ Expenses and Financial Aid

➤ *tuition & fees—full-time, $16,670; part-time, $12,500* ➤ *average additional expenses—$6,800 (room, board, books)* ➤ *merit and need-based scholarships available* ➤ *minority scholarships available* ➤ *financial aid available (GAPSFAS form should be submitted by Jan. or early Feb.)*

New York Law School has established a program of financial aid to assist students in meeting the costs of a legal education. Financial assistance is available in the form of grants, scholarships, work-study awards, and loans. New York Law School awards scholarships on the basis of academic merit and financial need. Complete information may be obtained from the Office of Financial Aid.

■ Career Services

The Career Services Office provides an array of services, including individual career counseling; On-Campus Interview Programs; numerous career panels and workshops; alumni services and network/mentoring programs; law firm lists categorized by specialty areas and size; computerized legal employer databases; and information on summer, full-time, and part-time positions and alternative career opportunities.

Applicant Group for the 1993–1994 Academic Year

New York Law School
This grid includes only applicants who earned 120-180 LSAT scores under standard administrations.

LSAT Score	3.75 +		3.50 -3.74		3.25 - 3.49		3.00 - 3.24		2.75 - 2.99		2.50 - 2.74		2.25 - 2.49		2.00 - 2.24		Below 2.00		No GPA		Total	
	Apps	Adm	Apps	Adm	Apps	Adm	Apps	Adm	Apps	Adm	Apps	Adm	Apps	Adm	Apps	Adm	Apps	Adm	Apps	Adm	Apps	Adm
175 - 180	1	1	0	0	0	0	0	0	1	1	1	1	0	0	0	0	0	0	0	0	3	3
170 - 174	0	0	0	0	2	2	5	5	0	0	2	2	2	2	0	0	1	1	0	0	12	12
165 - 169	4	3	6	6	9	9	17	17	17	17	11	10	5	4	2	2	1	0	0	0	72	68
160 - 164	6	6	21	20	40	40	48	44	38	37	41	36	24	17	7	4	0	0	1	1	226	205
155 - 159	19	18	62	60	121	117	158	147	142	109	110	69	53	29	16	8	2	0	11	9	694	566
150 - 154	27	24	76	52	171	105	256	122	214	66	137	36	86	19	30	5	3	0	19	10	1019	439
145 - 149	21	9	46	13	105	27	191	39	171	33	118	19	94	7	41	7	5	0	21	10	813	164
140 - 144	7	0	27	2	51	4	99	5	107	6	92	3	71	1	33	1	7	0	21	3	515	25
135 - 139	2	0	9	0	22	0	33	0	49	0	51	0	51	0	24	0	8	0	13	0	262	0
130 - 134	0	0	0	0	5	0	8	0	16	0	20	0	25	0	15	0	4	0	7	0	100	0
125 - 129	0	0	1	0	1	0	4	0	5	0	8	0	6	0	3	0	3	0	3	0	34	0
120 - 124	0	0	0	0	1	0	0	0	0	0	0	0	1	0	1	0	0	0	1	0	4	0
Total	87	61	248	153	528	304	819	379	760	269	591	176	418	79	172	27	34	1	97	33	3754	1482

Apps = Number of Applicants
Adm = Number Admitted
Reflects 94% of the total applicant pool.

New York University School of Law

110 West Third Street
New York, NY 10012

Phone: 212.998.6060

■ Introduction

Founded in 1835, New York University School of Law is distinguished by traditions that grow out of its being the oldest law school in New York—once the nation's and now the world's economic and legal capital. The School of Law has a record of academic excellence and national scholarly influence extending back into the nineteenth century, and more than 100 years ago became one of the first law schools routinely to admit women and those from groups that were victims of discrimination in many other institutions.

In recent decades, New York University School has been a pioneer in such widely diverse areas as the clinical education programs for all interested students, programs to train lawyers for public service, and interdisciplinary colloquia taught by faculty members with both J.D.s and Ph.D.s in fields including jurisprudence, criminal law and criminology, legal history, and international legal studies.

These traditions remain vibrant today as the School of Law, located on the university's campus in Greenwich Village—a residential neighborhood with its own special traditions—continues to use its position in New York City advantageously to create an international paradigm for twenty-first century legal education of global justice grounded in solid sociological and jurisprudential training and reflected in sensitive professional service to the world's peoples.

■ Enrollment/Student Body

➡ 6,918 applicants   ➡ 430 enrolled first-year class 1993
➡ 1,299 total full-time   ➡ 23% minority
➡ 44% women   ➡ 69 states & foreign countries represented
➡ 219 undergraduate schools represented

■ Faculty

➡ 105 full-time faculty (38 women, 5 minority)
➡ 97 part-time or adjunct faculty (13 women, 4 minority)

■ Library and Physical Facilities

➡ 888,000 volumes & equivalents   ➡ 100 library hours per week   ➡ LEXIS   ➡ NEXIS   ➡ WESTLAW
➡ DIALOG   ➡ 17 full-time librarians

In addition to its classroom and clinical buildings, the School of Law owns two modern apartment buildings which provide housing for more than 900 people, including law students, their spouses, their partners, and their children.

■ Curriculum

➡ 82 credits required to graduate   ➡ 199 courses available beyond first year   ➡ degrees available: J.D./LL.M. in Taxation; J.D./M.A. (sociology, politics, history, philosophy, economics, French); J.D./M.B.A.; J.D./M.P.A. with Princeton or NYU; J.D./M.S.W.; J.D./M.U.P.; LL.M.; M.C.J.; J.S.D.
➡ semesters, start in Aug.
➡ range of first-year class size—18-112

NYU School of Law's Law Center includes the J.D. and graduate divisions, the Institute for Judicial Administration, the Center for International Studies, the Center for Research in Crime and Justice, the Arthur Garfield Hays Civil Liberties Program, the Program for the Study of Law, Philosophy and Social Theory, the Program on Philanthropy and the Law, and the Public Interest Center.

NYU's curriculum is distinguished by its strength in traditional areas of legal study, interdisciplinary study, and clinical education, and has long been committed to educating lawyers who will use their degrees to serve the public. The **Root-Tilden-Snow Program** and the **Public Interest Center**, with five full-time staff members, sponsor speakers, offer academic and career counseling, and administer summer internship, volunteer, and mentoring programs.

The interdisciplinary programs combine a resident faculty, distinguished visitors, and courses at entry through advanced levels. Students may elect a single course or pursue a joint J.D./M.A., which generally can be earned within the normal three-year period of law school.

The J.D. Program is enriched by the graduate program, which offers advanced degrees. Attorneys, law teachers, and judges from over 30 countries enroll each year in degree programs in corporations, international, tax, trade regulation, and individual specialties.

■ Admission

➡ baccalaureate degree or its foreign equivalent required
➡ application deadline—early action, Oct. 15; regular Feb. 1
➡ LSAT, LSDAS required   ➡ application fee—$65

The admissions process is highly selective. The Committee on Admissions selects candidates with the strongest combination of qualifications and the greatest potential to contribute to NYU and to the legal profession. The committee bases its decisions on intellectual potential, academic achievement, character, community involvement, and work experience.

New York University has one of the largest and most competitive applicant pools in the country; only about one in six of those who apply is admitted. An applicant's undergraduate record and LSAT, while important, are not the sole determinants for admission. No index or cut-off is used in reviewing applications. An applicant's transcripts are analyzed for breadth and depth of coursework, trend in grades, and rank; the competitiveness of the school and major are taken into account, as are special honors and awards.

A strong undergraduate record and LSAT are most important for those applying to law school directly after graduating from college. In all cases, however, other aspects of the application significantly influence the decision. Letters of recommendation, activities, and work experience are reviewed for evidence of significant nonacademic or professional achievement, and for qualities including rigor of thought, maturity, judgement, motivation, leadership, imagination, and social commitment.

Factors beyond the undergraduate record are particularly important for older applicants, for international students, for those who have experienced educational or socioeconomic disadvantage, and for those who have racial or ethnic identities that are underrepresented in the student body and the legal profession.

In making its decisions the committee aims to enroll an entering class of students with diverse experience, backgrounds, and points of view. Applicants are encouraged to provide information to help the committee reach thoughtful, informed decisions on their applications.

■ Student Activities

Student-edited publications are *New York University Law Review, Annual Survey of American Law, Environmental Law Journal, Journal of International Law and Politics*, and *New York University Review of Law and Social Change. The Commentator* is the law school newspaper.

There are more than 30 active student organizations in 1993-94, and in most years.

■ Expenses and Financial Aid

➡ *full-time tuition—$19,740* ➡ *an average amount of additional expenses—$12,600 (rent, food, utilities, personal expenses, books, and course expenses)*
➡ *scholarships available* ➡ *GAPSFAS form required for NYU aid* ➡ *FAFSA form required for federal aid*

The School of Law, on the basis of financial need, enables accepted students to enroll and remain in attendance. Approximately 38 percent of J.D. students receive need-based scholarships; approximately 84 percent receive some financial aid. In addition to providing aid based on need, the law school has special fellowships in several fields.

Loan Forgiveness Program—Graduates who work in lower-paying sectors of the law, such as public-interest or government service, may be helped by the law school in repaying loans. The program helps make up the difference between the amount eligible graduates can reasonably repay from their limited salaries and the total amount of their repayment obligation.

■ Career Services

NYU has an extensive placement program. Career planning for first-year students includes personal career counseling; workshops on all aspects of the search, specialty panels featuring speakers from all areas of practice, and a videotape mock interview program.

In 1992-93, more than 700 private law firms, public interest organizations, government agencies, corporations, and public accounting firms came to NYU to interview students. Two-thirds of these employers were from outside New York.

The Career Services Office sponsors recruitment programs in several cities, and, with area law schools, a public-service symposium and a recruiting conference for students of color.

Admission Profile Not Available

University of North Carolina School of Law

Campus Box 3380, 101 Van Hecke-Wettach Hall
Chapel Hill, NC 27599-3380

Phone: 919.962.5109

■ Introduction

The University of North Carolina, the first state university chartered in the United States, has offered degrees in law since 1845. The School of Law has been a member of the AALS since 1920 and has been an approved school since the ABA began its accreditation activities in 1923. The School of Law is one of the outstanding institutions in the United States, and the University of North Carolina is recognized as being among the nation's leaders in graduate and professional education. The school aims to provide quality legal education that will prepare students to practice successfully in any jurisdiction. Chapel Hill is a university community close to the metropolitan and industrial centers of Greensboro and Durham, the Research Triangle Park, and the state capital, Raleigh. The immediate area offers an attractive blend of an academic atmosphere in a cosmopolitan setting.

■ Enrollment/Student Body

➼ *3,113 applicants* ➼ *612 admitted first-year class 1993*
➼ *249 enrolled first-year class 1993* ➼ *704 total full-time*
➼ *14.9% minority* ➼ *44.6% women*
➼ *26 states & 2 foreign countries represented*
➼ *92 undergraduate schools represented*
➼ *11% 30 years or older in first-year class 1993*

■ Faculty

➼ *42 total* ➼ *31 full-time* ➼ *11 part-time*
➼ *10 women* ➼ *4 minority*

■ Library and Physical Facilities

➼ *360,000 volumes & equivalents* ➼ *library hours: Mon.-Fri., 7:30 A.M.-MIDNIGHT; Sat., 9:00 A.M.-9:00 P.M.; Sun., 10:00 A.M.-MIDNIGHT* ➼ *LEXIS* ➼ *NEXIS*
➼ *WESTLAW* ➼ *21 full-time library staff*
➼ *library seats 513*

The school occupies a contemporary complex within walking distance of residence halls, dining halls, athletic facilities, student union, and the main libraries. The law library, wholly contained within the complex, includes microforms, CD-ROM, interactive video, and other specialized items. Also included within the library wing is a microcomputer laboratory with 17 workstations, and an electronic resources learning center with 10 workstations to access computer-assisted legal research systems and CD-ROM libraries.

■ Admission

➼ *Bachelor's degree from accredited college or university required* ➼ *application deadline—Feb. 1*
➼ *LSAT, LSDAS required* ➼ *median GPA—3.48*
➼ *median LSAT score—162* ➼ *application fee—$55*

Admission is a competitive process, and applicants with the strongest records are given priority. A substantial majority of admission decisions are made on the basis of combining LSAT scores with undergraduate grades, with 50 percent weight placed on the undergraduate grade-point average. Other relevant factors also are considered in order to assure meaningful diversity in the entering class. Graduate school grades are not incorporated with undergraduate grades but are considered among the other factors. Letters of recommendation are required for all applicants. Admission decisions are made progressively from December into the late spring, and are controlled to ensure that all applications submitted by February 1 are given equal consideration.

Applicants are encouraged to visit the law school to attend a class and then tour the campus. Guided tours and self-guided tours are both available. Regular group sessions are conducted throughout the year. Personal meetings are also available typically in the fall.

■ Student Activities

The *North Carolina Law Review*, a professional journal edited by students, publishes articles, comments, and notes on national and local legal problems; the *N.C. Journal of International Law*, edited by students, performs a similar function in international matters. The Student Bar Association sponsors a full range of professional, athletic, and social events, a speakers program, minority recruitment, a legal research service for practicing lawyers, and participation in school governance. There is a complete Moot Court Program that is student operated and privately endowed. The school sponsors teams that compete nationally in moot court, client counseling, and international law. Students serve on most faculty committees. Other student organizations include the American Indian Law Students Association, Black Law Students Association, Christian Legal Society, Hispanic Law Students Association, Phi Alpha Delta, Women in Law, Second Careers in Law, and Public Interest Law Fellowships.

■ Expenses and Financial Aid

➼ *full-time tuition & fees—resident, $1,512; nonresident, $10,328* ➼ *estimated additional expenses—$5,824*
➼ *Chancellors Scholars Program scholarship available*
➼ *Minority Presence Scholarships available*
➼ *need-based scholarships available (FAF due March 1 to College Scholarship Service)*

Most scholarships are awarded based on a combination of need and merit. Admitted applicants are automatically considered for merit-based scholarships. A significant amount of scholarship funds are awarded to students who are members of a minority group.

Recipients of the Chancellors Scholars awards benefit from substantial financial support which generally includes full tuition and fees and a stipend toward living expenses. Awards are made only on a merit basis.

Financial aid sources available to law students include need-based sources. Some research assistance grants are available for second- and third-year students. Applications for scholarships and loans must be completed by March 1.

■ Housing

There are graduate dormitories near the law school for single students. University student family housing and private apartments are available. Information may be obtained by writing to the University Housing Office, Carr Building CB 5500, Chapel Hill, NC 27599-3380.

■ Placement

The Career Development and Services Office, with a full-time director and staff, assists students and alumni with summer and permanent positions. Interviews are held in the law school, and contact is maintained with law offices and agencies throughout the country.

In 1992-93, over 220 employers from throughout the United States and the District of Columbia interviewed on-campus; 1992 graduates are employed in 21 states, the District of Columbia, and one foreign country. Of those 1992 graduates reporting to the Placement Office, 86 percent had accepted employment by May 1993; 34 percent accepted employment outside of North Carolina. Fifty-four percent of 1992 graduates entered private practice, 6 percent accepted judicial clerkships, 6 percent entered business-related fields, 14 percent entered government practice, and 6 percent entered public-interest work.

■ Correspondence

Admissions Office, University of North Carolina, School of Law, Van Hecke-Wettach Hall CB 3380, Chapel Hill, NC 27599-3380. Phone: 919.962.5106.

Applicant Group for the 1993–1994 Academic Year

University of North Carolina School of Law
This grid includes only applicants who earned 120-180 LSAT scores under standard administrations.

LSAT Score	GPA																					
	3.75 +		3.50 -3.74		3.25 - 3.49		3.00 - 3.24		2.75 - 2.99		2.50 - 2.74		2.25 - 2.49		2.00 - 2.24		Below 2.00		No GPA		Total	
	Apps	Adm	Apps	Adm	Apps	Adm	Apps	Adm	Apps	Adm	Apps	Adm	Apps	Adm	Apps	Adm	Apps	Adm	Apps	Adm	Apps	Adm
175 - 180	3	3	6	6	5	5	5	4	0	0	1	0	0	0	0	0	0	0	0	0	20	18
170 - 174	24	24	24	23	26	23	18	9	8	2	6	0	1	0	0	0	0	0	0	0	107	81
165 - 169	51	50	88	59	112	54	72	11	31	6	11	0	6	0	1	0	0	0	1	1	373	181
160 - 164	124	82	178	53	200	38	129	9	65	3	33	1	18	2	3	0	2	0	2	1	754	189
155 - 159	92	23	164	18	177	11	131	7	73	4	42	3	18	1	6	0	1	0	4	0	708	67
150 - 154	31	1	86	6	115	5	101	10	59	6	26	0	21	0	7	0	0	0	5	0	451	28
145 - 149	15	1	34	3	55	4	59	5	41	1	41	0	17	1	8	0	1	0	3	0	274	15
140 - 144	4	0	9	1	26	2	24	0	37	1	25	0	18	0	9	0	4	0	7	0	163	4
135 - 139	3	0	4	0	7	0	15	0	11	0	11	0	11	0	8	0	2	0	2	0	74	0
130 - 134	0	0	2	0	2	0	2	0	4	0	6	0	6	0	5	0	1	0	2	0	30	0
125 - 129	0	0	0	0	0	0	2	0	1	0	2	0	2	0	0	0	0	0	0	0	7	0
120 - 124	0	0	0	0	0	0	0	0	0	0	1	0	1	0	0	0	0	0	0	0	2	0
Total	347	184	595	169	725	142	558	55	330	23	205	4	119	4	47	0	11	0	26	2	2963	583

Apps = Number of Applicants
Adm = Number Admitted
Reflects 95% of the total applicant pool.

North Carolina Central University School of Law

1512 South Alston Avenue
Durham, NC 27707

Phone: 919.560.6333

■ Introduction

The North Carolina Central University School of Law was established in 1939. The School of Law is located in Durham, which, along with Raleigh and Chapel Hill, forms North Carolina's thriving "Research Triangle." The school has been accredited by the American Bar Association since 1950.

North Carolina Central University (NCCU) was chartered in 1909 as a private institution and opened to students in July of 1910. In 1923, when the General Assembly of North Carolina appropriated funds for the purchase and maintenance of the school, the institution became the first state-supported liberal arts college for African-Americans in the United States. In July 1972, NCCU became one of the constituent institutions of the University of North Carolina system.

■ Enrollment/Student Body

➥ *1,320 applicants*   ➥ *160 admitted first-year class 1993*
➥ *94 enrolled first-year class 1993*   ➥ *224 total full-time*
➥ *82 total part-time*   ➥ *55% minority*   ➥ *57% women*

■ Faculty

➥ *25 total*   ➥ *20 full-time*   ➥ *5 part-time or adjunct*
➥ *10 women*   ➥ *14 minority*

■ Library and Physical Facilities

➥ *101,649 volumes & 493,453 pieces*   ➥ *library hours:*
Mon.-Thurs., 8:00 A.M.-MIDNIGHT; Fri., 8:00 A.M.-9:00 P.M.;
Sat., 10:00 A.M.-9:00 P.M.; Sun., 1:00 P.M.-10:00 P.M.   ➥
LEXIS   ➥ *NEXIS*   ➥ *WESTLAW*   ➥ *DIALOG*
➥ *5 full-time librarians*

■ Curriculum

➥ *Academic Support Program*   ➥ *88 credits required to*
graduate   ➥ *degrees available: J.D.; J.D./M.L.S.*
➥ *semesters, start in Aug.*
➥ *range of first-year class size—20-45*

■ Special Programs

The joint degree J.D./M.L.S. program allows students interested in a career in law librarianship to simultaneously pursue the J.D. degree and a masters degree in library and information sciences. Application to and acceptance by both the School of Law and the School of Library and Information Sciences are required. The degree of Juris Doctor is granted upon the completion of a minimum of 88 semester hours of required and elective courses. A total of 36 required and elective semester hours is required for the M.L.S.

The Clinical Program consists of courses in evidence and trial practice with mock trials and oral arguments involving outstanding trial lawyers, appellate lawyers, and jurists. Third-year students represent indigent clients in civil matters and misdemeanor criminal cases under the supervision of practicing attorneys connected with local legal service or district attorney offices.

The School of Law offers the only part-time evening law program in North Carolina. This four-year program offers a unique opportunity for motivated professionals to pursue a legal education while maintaining their current careers.

■ Admission

➥ *Bachelor's degree required for admission*
➥ *application deadline—April 15*   ➥ *rolling admissions*
➥ *LSAT, LSDAS required*   ➥ *application fee—$15*
➥ *median GPA—full-time program, 3.00; part-time program,*
3.19   ➥ *median LSAT score—full-time program 148; part-time program, 155*

North Carolina Central University School of Law welcomes students of all races to contribute to its diversity as it continues to pursue with vigor its historic mission of producing a substantial percentage of minority attorneys for the state and nation. The school gives considerable weight to the traditional criteria of the LSAT score and UGPA, but it also considers evidence that an applicant has demonstrated in other ways a likelihood of succeeding in the legal profession.

The School of Law seeks students who are more likely to contribute affirmatively to the learning of others by reason of their intellectual attainments, demonstrated emotional maturity and self-discipline, social background, or exceptional capacity to benefit from the school's educational program. For this reason, applicants are asked to provide full information about their intellectual attainments, their personal achievements, employment experience, and social background.

■ Student Activities

The *North Carolina Central Law Journal*, published semi-annually, is devoted to articles by legal scholars and to case notes and comments by students. Invitations to join the *Law Journal* are extended to students on the basis of academic achievement and writing ability.

The School of Law has a complete moot court and trial advocacy program. Intra- and interscholastic competitions provide students with an opportunity to write appellate briefs, participate in mock trials and appellate oral arguments, and counsel clients.

Student organizations at the School of Law include the Student Bar Association, Moot Court Board, American Bar Association/Law Students Division, Black Law Students Association, Women's Caucus, National Lawyers Guild and F.A.C.E.S. (Future Attorneys Challenging Elementary Students). There are chapters of three legal fraternities: Delta Theta Phi; Phi Alpha Delta; and Phi Delta Phi.

■ Expenses and Financial Aid

➤ *tuition & fees—$1,381; nonresident, $8,969*
➤ *part-time tuition & fees—resident, $1,340; nonresident;*
$8,928   ➤ *estimated additional expenses—$12,000 (books,*
supplies, living expenses)   ➤ *merit- and need-based scholar-*
ships available   ➤ *merit- and need-based minority*
scholarships available   ➤ *financial aid available*
➤ *application for Federal Student Aid (FAFSA) form for need*
analysis due by Feb. 1

■ Housing

There is a graduate dormitory near the law school for
single students. Information may be obtained by writing to the University Housing Director, North Carolina
Central University, P.O. Box 19382, Durham, N.C., 27707.

■ Career Services

The Placement Office offers a range of services to students and prospective employers. These services include
career counseling, interview preparation and résumé
writing workshops, firm and résumé referral banks, a
placement information booklet and resource library, and
an on-campus interview program. Graduates typically
find employment in judicial clerkships, government
agencies, law firms, legal service organizations and the
Judge Advocate General's Corps.

Admission Profile Not Available
Applicant should feel free to contact the Admission
Office for additional information.

University of North Dakota School of Law

Office of the Dean
Grand Forks, ND 58202

Phone: 701.777.2260

■ Introduction

The University of North Dakota School of Law was established in 1899, and has been a member of the AALS since 1910. In 1923, it was approved by the ABA; it is a fully accredited graduate professional school of the university awarding the J.D. degree. The School of Law is located on the main campus of the university in Grand Forks, a city of approximately 50,000, in the northeastern part of the state. The third largest city in the state, Grand Forks is a center of commerce for the Upper Great Plains, as well as a large legal community, including county, state, and federal trial courts.

■ Enrollment/Student Body

➡ *243 total full-time*

While a large percentage of the entering students are North Dakota residents, the School of Law enrolls students from all parts of the country.

■ Library and Physical Facilities

➡ *250,000 volumes & equivalents*

The Thormodsgard Law Library, constructed in 1973 as an addition to the classroom and office building, offers generous seating and study space on its four levels. The Baker Moot Court Room, completed in 1973, provides facilities for trial and appellate arguments, and is occasionally used by the North Dakota Supreme Court, United States Court of Appeals for the Eighth Circuit, United States District Court for the District of North Dakota, and other state and federal courts.

■ Curriculum

➡ *90 credits required to graduate*

The curriculum of the School of Law covers a period of three full academic years. All the work of the first year is prescribed. Courses in the second and third years are elective, except for the course in Professional Responsibility.

■ Special Programs

The size of the student body is ideally suited for close professional contact with the faculty. Students are given ample opportunity to participate in the governance of the school. Elected members of the Student Bar Association attend regularly scheduled faculty meetings and are active voting participants in most law school committees. Participation by students in the State Bar Association of North Dakota is encouraged, and students are eligible to serve on selected state bar committees.

The School of Law is committed to the principle that all students should have an opportunity to elect, as a portion of their educational development, clinical legal education. This is not intended to diminish the law school's responsibility for education in legal analysis and legal principles,

but adds an additional responsibility, providing experience in the application of analysis and theory.

The clinical program provides training in practical skills through simulation training and client representation. Under supervision, law students work with clients in cases, as permitted under the rule of the North Dakota Supreme Court. Training is received in such skills as interviewing, counseling, negotiating, fact gathering, and advocacy.

The school has an extensive Trial Advocacy Program, in which students learn trial skills in a simulated advocacy setting under the close supervision of experienced trial lawyers. Each student in this course is responsible, with one student advocate co-counsel, for the trial of at least one full civil or criminal case during the semester. This program has received the Emil Gumpert Award of the American College of Trial Lawyers for excellence in the teaching of trial advocacy.

During sessions of the state legislature, selected students serve as legislative interns at the state capital in Bismarck.

Central Legal Research, directed by an attorney under the supervision of the Dean, is housed in the School of Law. This bureau is the research arm for the criminal justice system of the State of North Dakota. Competitively hired students perform original legal research upon request for judges, prosecutors, court-appointed defense counsel, police, and others.

In 1982 the law school initiated two new foreign exchange programs, the Canadian-United States Legal Issues Program and the UND-University of Oslo Program. The Canadian-U.S. Program provides a forum for discussions and research of transboundary legal issues, particularly those unique to the upper midwest. The Norwegian program provides for exchange of students and faculty between these two fine law schools.

■ Admission

➡ *undergraduate degree from accredited college or university required*   ➡ *application deadline—April 1*   ➡ *late fee for applications after April 1*   ➡ *LSAT, LSDAS required*
➡ *median GPA—3.22*   ➡ *median LSAT score—152*

The School of Law has no specific undergraduate course prerequisites and agrees with the observations in the introduction to this guide. The school admits students only in August, and only for full-time study. Applications are available upon request. The policy of the faculty of the School of Law is to admit those applicants who, in the determination of the faculty, will be able to satisfactorily complete the law school program. The admissions committee utilizes the following criteria to achieve this goal: 1) LSAT score; 2) undergraduate GPA; 3) past performance in an academic environment; 4) past performance in activities that would tend to predict the applicant's ability to complete successfully the law school program; and, 5) other evidence relevant to predicted success and prospective professional responsibility. The total number of students admitted is, of course, limited by considerations involving space and faculty course load.

The law school does not have a nonresident quota; however, preference is given to residents.

Students who have begun the study of law in other accredited law schools may be admitted in exceptional circumstances to advanced standing, provided they have fulfilled the requirements for admission to the University of North Dakota School of Law. Ordinarily, no transfer credit will be allowed for more than two semesters of work completed elsewhere, nor will transfer credit be given for any courses in which an unsatisfactory or failing grade has been received. Moreover, admission may be conditioned upon meeting such additional requirements as the faculty may prescribe. No student will be admitted as a transfer student with advanced standing who is not eligible to continue as a student at his or her present law school.

■ Student Activities

The *North Dakota Law Review* and Agricultural Law Research program provide research and writing opportunities. Students also participate in various moot court activities, including regional and national competitions. Student organizations include the Law Women's Caucus, National Lawyers Guild, and an active Student Bar Association. The School of Law also has chapters of the Order of the Coif and Phi Alpha Delta, Delta Theta Phi, and Phi Delta Phi legal fraternities.

■ Expenses and Financial Aid

➥ *full-time tuition and fees—resident,$1,359/semester; nonresident, $3,367/semester (1993-94)* ➥ *scholarships available* ➥ *financial aid available*

The semester fees include student activity and university fees totaling $156 per semester, and cover payment for health services, the university center, campus publications, and drama and athletic events. Fees are subject to change without notice. Loan funds for all qualified students are available through the university Student Financial Aids Office, Twamley Hall.

■ Housing

The university's family housing facilities are open to law students. University residence halls are open to single law students. Inquiries should be directed to the Housing Office, Post Office Box 9029, University Station, Grand Forks, ND 58202.

Applicant Group for the 1993-94 Academic Year

University of North Dakota School of Law
This grid includes only applicants who earned 120-180 LSAT scores under standard administrations.

LSAT Score	3.75 + Apps	Adm	3.50 -3.74 Apps	Adm	3.25 - 3.49 Apps	Adm	3.00 - 3.24 Apps	Adm	2.75 - 2.99 Apps	Adm	2.50 - 2.74 Apps	Adm	2.25 - 2.49 Apps	Adm	2.00 - 2.24 Apps	Adm	Below 2.00 Apps	Adm	No GPA Apps	Adm	Total Apps	Adm
175 - 180	0	0	0	0	0	0	0	0	0	0	0	0	0	0	0	0	0	0	0	0	0	0
170 - 174	0	0	0	0	0	0	0	0	0	0	0	0	0	0	0	0	0	0	0	0	0	0
165 - 169	1	1	0	0	0	0	3	2	0	0	2	2	1	1	1	0	0	0	1	0	9	6
160 - 164	1	1	0	0	5	5	6	5	2	1	2	0	1	0	2	0	0	0	0	0	19	12
155 - 159	2	2	8	7	8	8	25	22	18	13	10	7	6	1	2	0	2	0	2	1	83	61
150 - 154	2	2	8	8	33	22	33	20	38	12	22	4	11	0	8	1	1	0	0	0	156	69
145 - 149	5	1	10	3	25	7	43	4	27	2	26	1	10	0	4	0	0	0	2	1	152	19
140 - 144	2	1	7	2	9	1	22	0	19	0	13	0	12	0	2	0	2	0	4	0	92	4
135 - 139	0	0	0	0	2	0	5	1	6	0	4	0	4	0	3	0	0	0	2	0	26	1
130 - 134	0	0	0	0	0	0	1	0	0	0	6	0	3	0	1	0	0	0	0	0	11	0
125 - 129	0	0	0	0	0	0	0	0	0	0	0	0	1	0	0	0	0	0	1	0	2	0
120 - 124	0	0	0	0	0	0	0	0	0	0	0	0	0	0	0	0	0	0	0	0	0	0
Total	13	8	33	20	82	43	138	54	110	28	85	14	49	2	23	1	5	0	12	2	550	172

Apps = Number of Applicants
Adm = Number Admitted
Reflects 95% of the total applicant pool.

Northeastern University School of Law

P.O. Box 728
Boston, MA 02117-0728

Phone: 617.373.2395

■ Introduction

Located in Boston, Massachusetts, Northeastern is a
small law school with a unique program combining rigorous academic study with practical legal work
experience and a strong tradition of public service.
While maintaining the highest academic standards, it enables students to learn the skills of actual practice across
a broad spectrum of the law. The cooperative legal education program ensures that no graduate will enter the
practice of law without having first spent half of his or
her second and third years as a full-time apprentice or legal assistant to cooperating employers, generally in
several diverse areas of legal practice. Through this program, students have an unusual opportunity to learn an
array of practical skills, to observe various approaches to
the practice of law, and to determine which areas of the
law interest them most. The law school is accredited by
the ABA and is a member of the AALS.

■ Enrollment/Student Body

➡ 3,037 applicants   ➡ 833 admitted first-year class 1993
➡ 209 enrolled first-year class 1993   ➡ 603 total full-time
➡ 21% minority   ➡ 56% women
➡ 43 states & foreign countries represented
➡ 190 undergraduate schools represented

■ Faculty

➡ 55 total   ➡ 31 full-time   ➡ 24 part-time or adjunct
➡ 23 women   ➡ 11 minority

■ Library and Physical Facilities

➡ 164,880 volumes & equivalents   ➡ library hours: Mon.-
Thurs., 8:00 A.M.-11:00 P.M.; Fri., 8:00 A.M.-6:00 P.M.; Sat.,
9:00 A.M.-11:00 P.M.; Sun., NOON-10:00 P.M.
➡ LEXIS   ➡ NEXIS   ➡ WESTLAW   ➡ DIALOG
➡ 7 full-time librarians and 2 paraprofessional staff
➡ library seats 291

■ Curriculum

➡ Academic Support Program   ➡ Legal Writing, Legal
Analysis, and Analytical Skills workshops   ➡ 99 credits
required to graduate   ➡ Public Interest graduation
requirement   ➡ 85-95 total courses available
➡ degrees available: J.D.; J.D./M.B.A.; J.D./M.S. in Accounting
➡ first-year class starts late Aug.
➡ range of first-year class size—50-100

■ Special Programs

The **Cooperative Legal Education Program** is an integral
part of each student's experience at Northeastern: academic credit is awarded for successful completion of
four quarters of legal "co-op" work. Students earn their
J.D. degree in the same time as their counterparts at
other law schools; however, they follow a continuous
two-year, nine-month program.

First-year students begin in late August and follow a
traditional full-time academic program for nine months
until the end of May. The second year starts in June. Half
the class undertakes work as full-time clerks for the summer quarter; the other half undertakes the first academic
period of the second year. At the end of the summer, the
sections exchange places. They continue this process of
alternating work and academic periods through the 24
months of the second and third years.

Students work for large and small firms, judges, government agencies, legal assistance and public defender
organizations, corporate law departments, unions, and
practically every type of legal practitioner. There are
over 750 participating employers throughout the United
States, including Alaska and Hawaii, and students occasionally work in foreign nations.

The cooperative program is not a way to "work your
way through law school." However, earnings from cooperative employment may somewhat reduce the net cost
of attending school during the second and third years.
Salaries range from a nominal amount to in excess of
$1,000 per week. Recent statistics show average earnings
of just over $375 per week. Last year the school provided
over $266,000 in funding to students engaged in public-
interest work and judicial internships.

The school offers clinical courses including: the Domestic Violence Advocacy Project, the Poverty Law and
Practice Program, the Criminal Advocacy Program, and
the Prisoner Rights Program.

The **Domestic Violence Advocacy Project**, which combines classroom instruction with supervised clinical
practice, is offered each quarter. There are openings for
eight students; places are allocated based on responses
to a questionnaire. The class meets for an average of
three hours each week. In addition, each student must
commit a minimum of 16 hours per week to the project.

The course integrates theory, substantive law and skills
training. The substantive law focus is on the Massachusetts Abuse Prevention Act, related areas of family law,
benefits, and the criminal process as it relates to domestic violence. Skills training focuses on interviewing,
counseling, and preparation and presentation of cases.

The **Poverty Law and Practice Program** combines classroom instruction with clinical practice under the
supervision of experienced clinical instructors. All
course and clinical work takes place at the Legal Services
Center in Jamaica Plain.

Classes include substantive training in poverty law in
the areas of landlord/tenant, family law, immigration,
AIDS, welfare and other public benefits, as well as skills
training in evidence, and preparation and presentation
of cases for trial and hearings. Students are expected to
work at least 16 hours per week assisting and representing clients at the Legal Services Center.

■ Admission

➡ *Bachelor's degree required*
➡ *application deadline—March 1*   ➡ *LSAT, LSDAS required*
➡ *median GPA—3.23*   ➡ *median LSAT score—159*
➡ *application fee—$55*

Northeastern operates a full-time day program only. Students are enrolled only in late August.

An applicant should ordinarily have undergraduate grades and LSAT scores in the 80th percentile or better. The Admission Committee recognizes that some very successful students are not adept at taking standardized multiple-choice tests, that the grading standards among undergraduate schools vary, and that all courses of undergraduate study are not equally demanding. In addition to attempting to assess a candidate's academic achievement to date, the committee considers other factors that indicate his or her potential. These include professional or work experience, extracurricular or community activities, and clear indications of unusual determination, motivation, and accomplishment.

■ Student Activities

Students are elected to serve as representatives on all standing committees within the school. Through the Black Law Students Association, Asian American Law Students Association and the Latina/o American Law Students Association, students work closely with the school in an effort to recruit minority students. Other student groups include the Environmental Law Forum; Critical Legal Theory Study Group; Women's Caucus; Lesbian, Gay, and Bisexual Caucus; the National Lawyers Guild; the Business Law Forum; Christian Legal Society; Jewish Law Student Association; Older/Non-Traditional and Re-Entry Law Student Caucus; the International Law Society; the Cooperative Income Sharing Program; the Coalition for the Public Interest; Moot Court Society; Parents in Law School Group; and the Student Bar Association.

■ Expenses and Financial Aid

➡ *full-time tuition & fees—$16,860*
➡ *estimated additional expenses—$10,500-11,500 (living expenses and books)*
➡ *limited merit- and need-based scholarships available*
➡ *FAF, FAFSA, Northeastern Graduate/Law Financial Aid Form, and Financial Aid Transcript (FAT) due March 1*

■ Career Services

The Office of Career Services assists students with all phases of the job-search process. Northeastern graduates are employed throughout the United States and abroad with private firms, government agencies, legal services and public defender organizations, the judiciary, labor unions and corporate law departments. In recent years, approximately 23 percent of NUSL graduates, almost twice the national average, began their legal careers as judicial clerks. Graduates of the School of Law have entered public-interest work at a rate nearly five times the national average. In addition, for the last five years, NUSL graduates have been among the 25 recipients nationwide to be awarded one of the prestigious Skadden Fellowships enabling them to pursue careers in public-interest law.

Applicant Group for the 1993–1994 Academic Year

Northeastern University School of Law
This grid includes only applicants who earned 120-180 LSAT scores under standard administrations.

LSAT Score	GPA 3.75 +		3.50 -3.74		3.25 - 3.49		3.00 - 3.24		2.75 - 2.99		2.50 - 2.74		2.25 - 2.49		2.00 - 2.24		Below 2.00		No GPA		Total	
	Apps	Adm	Apps	Adm	Apps	Adm	Apps	Adm	Apps	Adm	Apps	Adm	Apps	Adm	Apps	Adm	Apps	Adm	Apps	Adm	Apps	Adm
175 - 180	2	2	3	3	3	3	0	0	1	1	0	0	1	1	0	0	0	0	0	0	10	10
170 - 174	2	2	7	6	6	6	10	9	6	2	3	3	0	0	0	0	0	0	0	0	34	28
165 - 169	10	10	23	22	23	23	39	30	28	19	7	3	4	1	2	1	0	0	2	1	138	110
160 - 164	22	22	52	49	93	78	110	69	61	25	27	10	16	5	4	0	0	0	3	3	388	261
155 - 159	31	24	103	60	195	61	175	48	102	17	61	10	32	1	8	0	2	0	7	4	716	225
150 - 154	19	6	82	16	158	31	179	29	116	11	62	5	34	1	21	0	4	1	9	4	684	104
145 - 149	15	2	40	4	88	7	96	3	115	6	66	3	22	2	12	0	2	0	6	1	462	28
140 - 144	3	0	22	0	29	0	61	0	62	0	40	0	29	0	13	0	4	0	8	0	271	0
135 - 139	1	0	2	0	8	0	22	0	23	0	24	0	14	0	5	0	2	0	2	0	103	0
130 - 134	0	0	0	0	2	0	3	0	3	0	7	0	11	0	2	0	2	0	2	0	32	0
125 - 129	0	0	0	0	0	0	0	0	0	0	1	0	2	0	2	0	2	0	1	0	10	0
120 - 124	0	0	0	0	0	0	0	0	0	0	1	0	0	0	0	0	0	0	0	0	1	0
Total	105	68	334	160	605	209	697	188	517	81	299	34	165	11	69	1	18	1	40	13	2849	766

Apps = Number of Applicants
Adm = Number Admitted
Reflects 95% of the total applicant pool.

Northern Illinois University College of Law

DeKalb, IL 60115

Phone: 815.753.1420 or 815.753.9485

■ Introduction

The College of Law is located on the 546-acre main campus of NIU in DeKalb. The community of DeKalb, known as the "Barb City" because barbed wire was invented here, is conveniently located approximately 60 miles west of Chicago and 25 miles outside of the suburban area on the Illinois Research and Development Corridor. It is close enough to the Chicago metropolitan area to draw on its resources, yet retain its own college-town flavor—a safe and low-cost environment with a high quality of life.

The College of Law seeks to prepare its graduates not only for the traditional role of lawyers, but for the tasks we can now only speculate will be assumed by the law-trained.

■ Enrollment/Student Body

➡ *1,240 applicants*   ➡ *361 admitted first-year class 1993*
➡ *118 enrolled first-year class 1993*   ➡ *308 total full-time*
➡ *24% minority*   ➡ *41% women*
➡ *39 states & foreign countries represented*
➡ *60 undergraduate schools represented*

The current student body reflects broad geographic, cultural, and economic diversity. Though over 24,000 students currently attend N.I.U., the law school limits its enrollment to approximately 100 students per class.

■ Faculty

➡ *35 total*   ➡ *25 full-time*   ➡ *11 part-time or adjunct*
➡ *6 women*   ➡ *4 minority*

The school has a diverse and professionally distinguished faculty dedicated to teaching and scholarship.

■ Library and Physical Facilities

➡ *200,000 volumes & equivalents*   ➡ *LEXIS*   ➡ *WEST-LAW*   ➡ *Illinois State Legislative Information System (LIS)*

The College of Law is located at the center of campus in Swen Parson Hall, an impressive gothic building that combines the distinction of the traditional with the sleek lines of the modern in its architectural design. The classrooms are designed to maximize interaction between students and their professors. The law school provides an atmosphere of shared goals and achievement and a genuine sense of community. The David C. Shapiro Memorial Law Library provides one of the best ratios of library resources to students. The Founders Memorial Library, adjacent to the College of Law, contains more than 1.2 million volumes and an additional one million federal, state, and international governmental documents.

■ Curriculum

➡ *Academic Support Program*   ➡ *85 units/credits required to graduate*   ➡ *77 courses available*   ➡ *degrees available: J.D.; J.D./M.B.A.*   ➡ *semesters, start in Aug.*

The College of Law provides its students with the type of curriculum that will make them well-rounded legal professionals. The first year consists of required courses in civil procedure, constitutional law, contracts, criminal law, legal research, legal writing and advocacy, property, and torts. A second course in constitutional law in the second year and a course in legal ethics in the third year are required. Students select the remainder of the 85 hours required for graduation from a wide range of electives.

The law school recognizes that a rigorous analytical legal education taught from traditional materials can be enriched by a breadth of exposure, in all areas of the curriculum, to supervised training in the skills of law practice. Clinical lawyering skills programs offer students the opportunity to acquire essential techniques needed in pretrial and trial work through structured simulations in the classroom and professional experiences in a variety of legal settings. The Externship Program provides students with sound educational experience under the supervision of a practicing attorney, or as a law clerk for a judge.

■ Student Activities

The College of Law affords its students a wide variety of educationally and professionally oriented activities. Among these are the *Law Review*, a forum for the expression of serious legal scholarship, and *The Advocate*, a newspaper published by law students. Members of the Moot Court Society compete in the National, ABA, the all-Illinois, and the Chicago Bar Association Moot Courts; and the International Law Society participates in the Philip C. Jessup International Moot Court competition. Student organizations include the Student Bar Association, the Black Law Students Association, the Hispanic Law Students Association, the Women's Law Caucus, the Law Students Civil Rights Research Council, the Christian Legal Society, the Business Law Club, Delta Theta Phi, and Phi Alpha Delta. Many of these organizations provide peer-support programs.

■ Admission

➡ *B.S./B.A. required for admission*   ➡ *application deadline—May 1*   ➡ *rolling admission; early application preferred*   ➡ *LSAT, LSDAS required*
➡ *median GPA—3.00*   ➡ *median LSAT score—157*
➡ *application fee—$35*

The College of Law grants admission strictly on a competitive basis through an evaluation of an applicant's aptitude and professional promise. Prospective students are encouraged to visit. Such visits, however, will not play a role in the evaluation process. Admissions decisions are strictly based on what the applicant communicates in the application.

Two letters of recommendation and a personal statement must be included with the other necessary application materials. The applicant's undergraduate record and LSAT score are of principal importance to the Admissions Committee, but the committee is also interested in other factors such as an applicant's reasons for seeking admission, the applicant's school or community activities and accomplishments, employment background, and the applicant's ability to add diversity to the law school community.

■ Expenses and Financial Aid

➼ *full-time tuition & fees—resident; $4,207.20; nonresident, $6,511.20* ➼ *Dean's scholarships, Dean's grants, and Rhoten Smith Scholarship available*
➼ *work-study and loan programs available*
➼ *FAFSA for financial aid due March 1*

Persons who enter as nonresidents usually qualify as Illinois residents for their second and third years. After the first year, law students qualify for research assistantships. Admitted students are sent financial aid information.

■ Housing

Moderately priced housing is available both on-campus and off-campus. Neptune Hall, one block from the law school, designates its first floor just for law students.

Married and handicapped housing is also available on-campus. The law school floor is $3,276 per academic year depending on the meal plan chosen. Housing information is sent to admitted students.

■ Career Services

The College of Law Career Services Office provides a service for law students to improve awareness and provide assistance in the selection of suitable employment opportunities. The office refers qualified applicants to prospective employers and conducts on-campus interviews. The Career Services Office maintains listings of opportunities in the legal profession as well as information on judicial clerkships and fellowships.

The director of career services counsels and advises students on all phases of career and placement activity and provides assistance with résumé preparation, job-search strategy, and interviewing skills. A library of placement resources is maintained for both students and alumni.

■ Correspondence

Northern Illinois University, College of Law, DeKalb, IL 60115. Phone: 815.753.1420 or 800.892.3050 (IL Only).

Applicant Group for the 1993–1994 Academic Year

Northern Illinois University College of Law
This grid includes only applicants who earned 120-180 LSAT scores under standard administrations (reflects 93% of all applicants).

LSAT Score	GPA 3.75 +		3.50 - 3.74		3.25 - 3.49		3.00 - 3.24		2.75 - 2.99		2.50 - 2.74		2.25 - 2.49		2.00 - 2.24		Below 2.00		Total	
	Apps	Adm	Apps	Adm	Apps	Adm	Apps	Adm	Apps	Adm	Apps	Adm	Apps	Adm	Apps	Adm	Apps	Adm	Apps	Adm
175 - 180	0	0	0	0	0	0	0	0	0	0	0	0	0	0	0	0	0	0	0	0
170 - 174	0	0	0	0	0	0	0	0	0	0	1	1	0	0	1	1	0	0	2	2
165 - 169	1	1	4	3	2	2	1	1	6	6	5	5	4	4	2	2	1	0	26	24
160 - 164	4	4	3	3	9	9	21	20	16	14	7	7	8	6	3	2	0	0	71	65
155 - 159	6	6	21	20	39	33	45	34	60	33	44	24	21	8	6	3	1	0	243	161
150 - 154	3	1	19	8	51	14	72	6	74	10	59	3	36	2	8	2	5	0	327	46
145 - 149	5	0	10	2	31	4	60	9	46	6	38	2	19	2	12	0	2	0	223	25
140 - 144	1	1	7	0	9	1	29	3	34	0	34	2	17	0	8	0	6	0	145	7
135 - 139	1	0	2	0	4	0	13	2	18	1	23	0	10	1	4	1	5	0	80	5
130 - 134	0	0	0	0	0	0	1	0	5	0	6	0	5	0	5	0	4	0	26	0
125 - 129	1	0	0	0	0	0	0	0	1	0	1	0	1	0	0	0	0	0	4	0
120 - 124	0	0	0	0	0	0	0	0	0	0	0	0	1	0	0	0	0	0	1	0
Total	22	13	66	36	145	63	242	75	260	70	218	44	122	23	49	11	24	0	1148	335

Apps = Number of Applicants
Adm = Number Admitted

	App	Adm	
Applicants with 120-180 LSAT scores earned under standard administrations:	1,148	335	
Applicants with only 10-48 LSAT scores earned under standard administrations:	60	21	(not on grid)
Applicants with no LSAT or Nonstandard Administration LSAT:	32	5	(not on grid)
Total	1,240	361	

Northern Kentucky University—Salmon P. Chase College of Law

Office of Admissions
Nunn Dr.
Highland Heights, KY 41099

Phone: 606.572.6476

■ Introduction

The Salmon P. Chase College of Law of Northern Kentucky University, founded in 1893 in Cincinnati, Ohio, is located in Highland Heights, Kentucky, eight miles southeast of Cincinnati. The campus is situated on 300 acres of rolling countryside in the largest metropolitan area of any state university in Kentucky. The curriculum not only provides instruction aimed at developing competent legal practitioners, but also includes courses that will enable students to become especially proficient in certain areas of the law. Day and evening programs are offered. Apartment and traditional student housing is available on campus.

■ Enrollment/Student Body

➡ 1,003 applicants ➡ 291 admitted first-year class 1993
➡ 172 enrolled first-year class 1993 ➡ 275 total full-time
➡ 171 total part-time ➡ 10% minority
➡ 47% women ➡ 15 states & foreign countries represented
➡ 71 undergraduate schools represented

The College of Law is operated under the auspices of the Commonwealth of Kentucky; thus, some preference is given to Kentucky residents.

■ Faculty

➡ 47 total ➡ 20 full-time ➡ 27 part-time or adjunct
➡ 14 women ➡ 3 minority

The Chase College Foundation brings in outstanding legal scholars, judges, and practitioners to enrich the education of the student body.

■ Library and Physical Facilities

➡ 233,526 volumes & equivalents ➡ library hours: Mon.-Thurs., 8:00 A.M.-MIDNIGHT; Fri., 8:00 A.M.-10:00 P.M.; Sat., 9:00 A.M.-9:00 P.M.; Sun., NOON-10:00 P.M. ➡ extended hours during exams, shortened hours during academic breaks
➡ LEXIS ➡ NEXIS ➡ WESTLAW ➡ DIALOG
➡ 5 full-time librarians ➡ library seats 286

The extensive law library has a liberal borrowing policy and participates in interlibrary lending programs.

Students also have access to excellent recreational facilities at A.D. Albright Health Center on campus, including basketball and racquetball courts, Nautilus and other exercise equipment, indoor running track and pool, and sauna. University Center, including a cafeteria, snack bar, and bookstore, is near the College of Law.

■ Curriculum

➡ 90 credits required to graduate ➡ 83 courses available
➡ degrees available: J.D.; J.D./M.B.A. ➡ semesters, start in Aug. ➡ range of first-year class size—17-125

The program of study may be completed in three years for full-time students and four years for part-time students. A week-long course introduces first-year students to the study of law. Forty-one semester hours of coursework are prescribed. Students must also select 19 hours from a list of core courses. Two additional courses developing legal research and drafting skills are required. The remaining hours may be chosen from a broad offering of electives.

Informal academic support is available to all students. Students may earn credit for work as law clerks in federal courts.

■ Special Programs

The J.D./M.B.A. degree is designed for students who seek to expand their expertise in the increasingly dynamic and complex business area. Selected courses in the College of Law serve as electives for 9 of the 36 hours required for the M.B.A. degree while M.B.A. courses count for 14 of the 90 hours required in the J.D. program. Thus, the number of hours required to obtain the joint degree is less than the number required if each degree were pursued independently.

The College of Law operates a prestigious Moot Court Program, entering teams in the National Moot Court, Tri-School Moot Court, and other competitions. Degree credit may be earned for participation in this program.

The College of Law has established the Ohio Valley Environmental and Natural Resources Law Institute which will sponsor annually both an environmental law moot court competition and an environmental law symposium.

A course in Trial Advocacy based upon a national model allows students to practice and participate in every part of a trial. The course ends with its students conducting an entire civil and criminal trial including jury selection and jury deliberation.

■ Admission

➡ Bachelor's degree from accredited college or university required ➡ application deadline—March 1 ➡ priority application deadline—Feb. 1 ➡ LSAT, LSDAS required
➡ median GPA—3.31 ➡ median LSAT score—151
➡ application fee—$25 ➡ financial aid deadline—Feb. 1
➡ rolling admission, early application preferred

First-year students are admitted for the fall semester only. In measuring academic potential for admission, the Admissions Committee relies primarily on the applicant's undergraduate GPA and the applicant's performance on the LSAT. Each file is reviewed for motivational factors, which include rising trend in academic performance, college and/or course selection, graduate study, employment pressures, competence in another profession or vocation, significant changes in the LSAT, leadership ability, cultural or educational deprivation, and evidence of oral or written linguistic ability. The committee seeks diversity in the student body by considering, in no particular order, sex, age, minority status, and cultural or geographic background.

Persons in good academic standing at another ABA-accredited school may apply for admission as transfer students. Transfer determinations are based upon the quality of the applicant's performance at the other law school and the reason for the applicant's desire to transfer.

■ Student Activities

The *Northern Kentucky Law Review*, published by the students of the College of Law, devotes space to national and regional law problems. The Student Bar Association (SBA) sponsors many activities, including a student mentor program, as well as student-faculty mixers and other social events. The SBA also selects students to participate on several faculty committees. There are chapters of the Black American Law Students Association, Delta Theta Phi Law Fraternity, Phi Alpha Delta Law Fraternity, and the Law Student Division of the American Bar Association. Other groups at the College of Law include the Chase Trial Lawyers Association, Christian Legal Society, Environmental Law Society, International Law Society, and Women's Law Caucus. Additionally, the Kentucky Municipal Law Center, the Academy of Criminal Justice Sciences, and the Ohio Valley Environmental and Natural Resources Law Institute are housed in Nunn Hall.

■ Expenses and Financial Aid

➡ tuition & fees—resident, $147/sem. hr. (not to exceed $1,750/sem.); nonresident, $403/sem. hr. (not to exceed $4,820/sem.) ➡ estimated additional expenses—$1,800-5,396/sem., (books & supplies, room & board, transportation, personal) ➡ one-year & multiyear performance and need-based scholarships available ➡ one-year and multiyear performance and need-based minority scholarships available ➡ appropriate form for need analysis due to national processing organization in Jan.; form required may vary from year to year

Chase College of Law and Northern Kentucky University financial aid application forms are due February 1. The latter forms are available from the Financial Aid Office, Northern Kentucky University. Certain scholarships and stipends have been established specifically to aid students from Kentucky or designated counties in Ohio.

All tuition and fees are due and payable prior to the first day of classes.

■ Career Services

With the support of a Placement Advisory Board, made up of practitioners in Ohio and Kentucky, and a Student Placement Board, Chase has a strong program to assist students in planning their legal careers. This includes scheduling on-campus interviews, posting job notices from law firms throughout Kentucky and greater Cincinnati, holding career seminars and publishing a placement newsletter. Students participate in the All-Kentucky Legal Job Fair, a public-interest job fair, a federal job options program and the Minority Access Program. Reciprocal agreements with career services offices at other law schools assist those students who are looking for opportunities in different parts of the country. Chase alumni are employed in 45 states and throughout the world. Further, the Career Development Office houses a career opportunity library and provides access to several employment databases.

Applicant Group for the 1993–1994 Academic Year

Northern Kentucky University—Salmon P. Chase College of Law
This grid includes only applicants who earned 120-180 LSAT scores under standard administrations.

LSAT Score	3.75 +		3.50 -3.74		3.25 - 3.49		3.00 - 3.24		2.75 - 2.99		2.50 - 2.74		2.25 - 2.49		2.00 - 2.24		Below 2.00		No GPA		Total	
	Apps	Adm	Apps	Adm	Apps	Adm	Apps	Adm	Apps	Adm	Apps	Adm	Apps	Adm	Apps	Adm	Apps	Adm	Apps	Adm	Apps	Adm
175 - 180	0	0	0	0	0	0	0	0	0	0	0	0	0	0	0	0	0	0	0	0	0	0
170 - 174	0	0	0	0	1	1	1	0	1	1	0	0	0	0	0	0	0	0	0	0	3	2
165 - 169	1	1	0	0	1	1	1	0	6	5	0	0	1	0	0	0	1	0	0	0	11	7
160 - 164	4	3	3	2	4	3	3	3	6	4	3	1	4	2	4	0	0	0	1	0	32	18
155 - 159	9	7	19	16	13	7	26	17	27	14	29	11	11	0	4	2	0	0	2	0	140	74
150 - 154	11	9	34	23	51	27	70	28	66	7	34	2	25	2	8	4	1	0	6	3	306	105
145 - 149	6	3	23	18	46	12	53	5	56	4	33	6	24	2	7	0	2	0	1	0	251	50
140 - 144	3	2	5	3	15	1	34	3	26	3	26	2	18	1	5	0	1	0	2	0	135	15
135 - 139	2	2	0	0	2	1	11	3	9	2	14	2	9	1	8	0	1	0	3	2	59	13
130 - 134	0	0	1	1	2	0	3	1	1	0	1	0	8	2	2	0	0	0	1	0	19	4
125 - 129	0	0	0	0	1	0	1	0	0	0	0	0	0	0	0	0	1	0	0	0	3	0
120 - 124	0	0	0	0	0	0	1	0	0	0	0	0	0	0	0	0	0	0	0	0	1	0
Total	36	27	85	63	136	53	204	60	198	40	140	24	100	10	38	6	7	0	16	5	960	288

Apps = Number of Applicants
Adm = Number Admitted
Reflects 95% of the total applicant pool.

Northwestern University School of Law

357 East Chicago Avenue
Chicago, IL 60611

Phone: 312.503.8465

■ Introduction

Northwestern University School of Law offers students an outstanding education, magnificent lakefront facilities in the heart of one of the nation's most interesting cities, and membership in a scholarly community enriched by the accomplishments of its faculty and the achievements of its graduates.

Northwestern was founded in 1859 as a small law department and between 1873 and 1891 was called Union College of Law. In 1893 John Henry Wigmore joined the faculty, serving as dean for 28 years and setting the intellectual standard for the school that remains to this day.

■ Enrollment/Student Body

➡ 4,178 applicants ➡ 783 admitted first-year class 1993 ➡ 203 enrolled first-year class 1993 ➡ 612 total full-time ➡ no part-time program ➡ 25% minority ➡ 42% women ➡ 40 states & 10 foreign countries represented ➡ 178 colleges and universities represented

■ Faculty

➡ 111 total ➡ 54 full-time ➡ 57 part-time/adjunct ➡ 29 women (12 full-time, 17 part-time/adjunct) ➡ 10 minority (5 full-time, 5 part-time/adjunct)

The activities and varied academic interests of Northwestern's faculty complement and enrich their instruction and contribute to a high degree of innovation in both teaching and scholarship.

The faculty includes scholars with advanced degrees in economics, history, philosophy, and political science as well as law, it includes a former chairman of the United States Securities and Exchange Commission, a former deputy solicitor general of the United States, and individuals who have argued before the European Court of Human Rights. Among the faculty are men and women who began their law careers as judicial clerks in state supreme courts, US district courts, courts of appeals, and the Supreme Court of the United States, and they have devoted their energies since then to many different areas of the law in this country and abroad.

■ Library and Physical Facilities

➡ 556,743 volumes & equivalents ➡ library hours: Mon.-Thurs., 7:30 A.M.-MIDNIGHT; Fri., 7:30 A.M.-8:00 P.M.; Sat., 9:00 A.M.-8:00 P.M.; Sun., 9:00 A.M.-MIDNIGHT ➡ LEXIS ➡ NEXIS ➡ WESTLAW ➡ CCH Access ➡) DIALOG ➡ 12 full-time librarians ➡ library seats 750

Northwestern consists of a complex of three connected buildings. The original buildings, Levy Mayer Hall and the Elbert H. Gary Library, both completed in 1926, and Robert R. McCormick Hall and the Owen L. Coon Library, both completed in 1960, form a quadrangle around a garden area. An addition, the Arthur Rubloff Building,

was dedicated in 1984 and has doubled library space and greatly expanded student study and activity areas. It includes classrooms, a moot courtroom, offices, and an 800-seat university auditorium. The Rubloff Building also houses the national headquarters of the American Bar Association and the American Bar Foundation.

The current law library collection is known as one of the finest in the nation and includes outstanding collections in international, foreign, and Anglo-American law and rare books. An open-stack policy encourages student use of the collections.

■ Curriculum

➡ 86 credits required to graduate ➡ more than 130 courses available ➡ degrees available: J.D.; J.D./M.M.; J.D./Ph.D.; LL.M.; S.J.D ➡ semesters, begin in Aug. ➡ range of first-year class size—25-100 ➡ senior writing requirements for graduation ➡ clinical program available ➡ senior research program available

Northwestern offers a curriculum designed to develop fundamental legal skills rather than to merely impart knowledge of the legal rules applicable to one jurisdiction or region. The Senior Research Program enables third-year students to do individual research under the supervision of a professor, using library, field, and inter-disciplinary research methods. Students may receive up to 12 hours of credit during two semesters. Northwestern has made a firm commitment to quality clinical education by maintaining a fully funded clinical program with five full-time professors and eight staff attorneys. Clinic attorneys and students handle both civil and criminal cases and are intensively involved in juvenile court work.

■ Special Programs

The school offers two combined-degree programs in cooperation with other schools in the university: the J.D./Master of Management program with J.L. Kellogg Graduate School of Management and the J.D./Ph.D. in one of the social sciences with the Graduate School.

Law students may be able to work with the university-based Center for Urban Affairs and Policy Research, designed to bring together the work of various disciplines related to urban affairs and to apply research efforts to problems of urban society. A limited number of fellowships are awarded to second- and third-year law students for work with the center.

■ Student Activities

Northwestern offers a number of student activities that provide students with opportunities to practice their skills and gain experience in legal analysis, writing and research, and oral and written argument. Students at Northwestern are fortunate to have several scholarly journals available for research, writing, and editing: the *Northwestern University Law Review, Journal of Criminal*

Law and Criminology, and *Northwestern Journal of International Law & Business*. The First-year Moot Court Program, participation in which is required of all first-year students, trains students in preparing briefs and delivering oral arguments. The annual Julius Miner Moot Court competition, a voluntary second-year program, provides excellent practice in appellate advocacy. Each year law schools throughout the United States and in more than 30 foreign countries participate in the Philip C. Jessup International Law Moot Court competition. Northwestern teams have been among the most successful at the regional, national, and international level tournaments.

The Student Bar Association is the basic student governing group in which all students belong and whose activities and programs range from educational to recreational. The SBA voices the concerns of the student body in matters of curriculum and administration. Student groups and activities, most established under the aegis of the SBA, have grown out of student's concerns and interests and represent diverse political ideologies; multiple ethnic, minority, and religious affiliations; and far-ranging career focuses and public issues. There are more than 32 student organizations.

■ Admission

➠ *Bachelor's degree or its equivalent from accredited college or university required*   ➠ *application deadline—Feb. 1*
➠ *rolling admission; early completion of application encouraged*
➠ *LSAT, LSDAS required*   ➠ *application fee—$60 ($75 after Jan. 1)*   ➠ *two letters of recommendation required*
➠ *personal statement required*

Competition for admission is intense, but a Faculty Admission Committee individually reviews most applications, regardless of the LSAT score and the GPA, and bases its decision on a broad range of factors.

■ Expenses and Financial Aid

➠ *tuition & fees—$18,170*   ➠ *estimated additional expenses—$10,787 (room, board, books, transportation, personal)*   ➠ *merit- and need-based scholarships available*
➠ *minority scholarships available*   ➠ *GAPSFAS required*
➠ *Loan Repayment Assistance Program available*
➠ *deadline for financial aid application—March 15*

■ Housing

Two dormitories with dining and recreational facilities are close to the law school and are available to all students. Off-campus housing is easily accessible by public transportation.

■ Placement

Northwestern operates a full-range career counseling and placement service. The office schedules student interviews with employers, offers useful workshops, individual counseling, and other services to help students pursue their professional goals. Responding to increased student interest in international law, the school recently established a summer internship program that attempts to match students with law firms, international corporations, and government and public agencies abroad.

Admission Profile Not Available

University of Notre Dame Law School

P.O. Box 959
Notre Dame, IN 46556-0959

Phone: 219.631.6626, fax: 219.631.6371

■ Introduction

Notre Dame Law School is located on the university campus near South Bend, Indiana. Founded in 1869, it is the oldest law school under Catholic auspices in the United States. It is accredited by the AALS and the ABA.

Notre Dame is proud of its Christian tradition and of its prominent place as a national forum for debate and exploration in human values. Its law school stands in that tradition and in a tradition of academic excellence and humanistic legal education that has placed practicing lawyers throughout the nation and abroad—on the bench, in government, in business, and in service to the poor and disadvantaged. Its student body includes men and women of all races and creeds, from 200 colleges and universities, about half of whom are non-Catholic. The Law School is particularly conscious of its tradition of close faculty-student relationships and of the implications this has for the humanistic practice of law and for legal service to the community.

■ Enrollment/Student Body

➥ *175 enrolled first-year class 1993*　➥ *583 total full-time*
➥ *21% minority*　➥ *41% women*
➥ *200 undergraduate schools represented*

■ Faculty

➥ *35 full-time*　➥ *25 part-time or adjunct*

Faculty members have extensive experience in private practice and government service, and represent a broad spectrum of law schools and state bars.

■ Library and Physical Facilities

➥ *340,000 volumes & equivalents*　➥ *library hours: 24 hours/day, 7 days/week*　➥ *LEXIS*　➥ *NEXIS*
➥ *WESTLAW*　➥ *VUTEXT*　➥ *DIALOG*
➥ *20 full-time librarians*

The Law School is a handsome building with traditional Tudor Gothic exterior on the Notre Dame Campus. The collections and services of the recently refurbished Kresge Law Library are designed to support student learning and research through acquisition of information technologies and continuous implementation of new services. With permanent learning centers contributed by the major national legal databases, the library is a national leader in legal research techniques using automated technology.

■ Curriculum

➥ *Academic Support Program*　➥ *90 credits required to graduate*　➥ *degrees available: J.D.; J.D./M.B.A.; LL.M.; J.S.D., and other joint degrees*　➥ *semesters, begin in Aug.*

The school awards the J.D. degree after three years (six semesters) of full-time residential day study. The Law School curriculum has been revised to make it com-

pletely attuned to the needs of the competent and compassionate lawyer of today. A broad range of electives offers extensive interdisciplinary and specialized programs and clinical work that places students in supervised practice throughout northern Indiana and southern Michigan.

■ London Programs

The Notre Dame London Law Center (Concannon Program of International Law) is an integral part of the University of Notre Dame Law School. Founded in 1968, it provides the opportunity for American students to study law in the country that gave birth to common law. By providing an extensive array of international and comparative law courses, some taught by prominent British professors, the program serves the student with the strong interest in comparative and international law. But the program is not limited to those with such an interest. The course of studies is designed to further the education of all law students by availing them of an opportunity to observe the American legal system against the background of its common law origins, the laws and practices of other nations, and the law of nations.

All courses offered by the center are in strict conformity with the recommended standards of the Association of American Law Schools and the American Bar Association. The academic standards are fully equal to those of the home campus.

The Law School also offers a summer program in London. It is the oldest American summer law program conducted in London, with more than 100 students from over 50 different law schools. The curriculum emphasizes courses in the comparative and international law field taught largely by British faculty.

An LL.M. program in comparative and international law also is offered.

■ Admission

➥ *Bachelor's degree required for admission*　➥ *application deadline—April 1*　➥ *LSAT, LSDAS required*　➥ *application fee—$45*

Admissions result from recommendations by a faculty committee that considers each application individually. The faculty members and the Dean make their decisions based on the whole-person concept, including academic performance, work experiences, recommendations, extracurricular activities, activities evidencing concern for charitable and social improvements, and leadership qualities, as well as LSAT scores.

Special consideration is given to disadvantaged students, resulting in a significant representation of ethnic minority groups.

■ Student Activities

The school publishes *The Notre Dame Law Review, The Journal of Law, Ethics & Public Policy; The Journal of Legisla-*

tion, the only journal of legal philosophy in the nation, *The American Journal of Jurisprudence*, and *The Journal of College & University Law*. The school has a three-year moot court program; a mock trial program; a legal clinic; a student legislative drafting service that serves state legislators and members of the Congress; a student bar association; and chapters of the Women's Legal Forum, Hispanic American Law Association, the Christian Legal Society, the Black Law Students Association, and the Social Justice Forum and Asian Law Students Association.

The Legal Clinic operates civil and criminal legal aid programs in northern Indiana and southern Michigan. The Notre Dame Center for Civil and Human Rights operates an LL.M. and J.S.D. Program with emphasis on international human rights. It maintains an extensive library of civil rights-related materials. The Thomas J. White Center on Law and Government prepares students to serve as government lawyers. It publishes the *Journal of Law, Ethics and Public Policy*. The National Institute for Trial Advocacy, whose purpose is to contribute to the development of a competent, effective, and professionally responsible trial bar, is headquartered in the Law School. The Moot Court Program provides training and practice in appellate advocacy. Notre Dame Law School is a regular participant in The Philip C. Jessup International Moot Court Competition. The Trial Advocacy Program, offered as courses in the third year, involves students in the preparation and trial of a jury case.

■ Expenses and Financial Aid

➡ *tuition & fees—$16,400*   ➡ *scholarships available (need- and merit-based)*   ➡ *financial aid available; GAPSFAS and FAFSA form required*   ➡ *work-study available*

The Law School awards grants to disadvantaged students on the basis of need and demonstrated ability to perform satisfactorily in the Law School. The Judge Roger Kiley Fellowships, highly prestigious awards of national renown, are reserved for exceptional academic leaders.

■ Housing

Both men and women may live on the university campus, and the university provides apartments for married students with children. Single students interested in serving as resident assistants in the university dorms should contact the director of student affairs at the university.

■ Career Services

The Career Services Office is an integral part of the Law School. Many interviewers representing the full spectrum of lawyer job opportunities actively recruit at the office each year. A national network of Law School alumni assisting in job opportunities is coordinated through the Career Services Office.

Admission Profile Not Available

Nova University—Shepard Broad Law Center

3305 College Avenue
Fort Lauderdale, FL 33314

Phone: 305.452.6117

■ Introduction

Nova Law Center opened in 1974 as part of Nova University, a private, nonsectarian institution. The Law Center is accredited by the American Bar Association and is a member of the AALS. Goodwin Hall, our new building, is located just west of Fort Lauderdale. It is easily accessible from the airport and from all areas of Dade, Broward, and Palm Beach counties.

■ Faculty

➡ *86 total*   ➡ *39 full-time*   ➡ *47 part-time or adjunct*
➡ *20 women*   ➡ *9 minority*

Our faculty is committed to excellence in teaching and maintains an open-door policy for students. By limiting all first-year courses to sections of 45 or fewer students, they can offer each student individualized attention. Our faculty is relatively young and represents numerous practice fields. Their expertise is reflected in scholarly articles and texts as well as in their public service activities. Distinguished practicing attorneys join our full-time faculty, particularly for courses in our skills curriculum.

■ Library and Physical Facilities

➡ *261,307 volumes & equivalents*   ➡ *library hours: Mon.-Thurs., 7:45 A.M.-MIDNIGHT; Fri., 7:45 A.M.-10:00 P.M.; Sat., 9:00 A.M.-9:00 P.M.; Sun., 10:00 A.M.-MIDNIGHT*
➡ *LEXIS*   ➡ *NEXIS*   ➡ *WESTLAW*   ➡ *DIALOG*
➡ *8 full-time librarians*   ➡ *library seats 548*

The Law Center moved into a new building in July 1992. Surrounded by palm trees and adjoining a small campus lake, Goodwin Hall is within walking distance of university cafeteria, bookstore, dormitory, and apartment facilities.

Goodwin Hall is divided into two wings, which are connected by a spacious atrium. The atrium functions as a town hall—a place where students relax between classes, assemble for speakers, or listen to lunch-hour musical performances by students attending the university's high school.

The classroom/student activities wing includes the Civil Clinic, Disability Law Institute, and the Center for the Study of Youth Policy. There are 10 classroom and seminar rooms. Our courtrooms are used by students in trial advocacy classes, by National Institute for Trial Advocacy programs, and by state appellate court judges. All faculty offices are on the second floor of this wing.

The library's extensive holdings include special collections in tax, criminal law, law and popular culture, and international law. There are several LEXIS and WESTLAW computerized legal research terminals, and Computer Assisted Instruction is available for student use. Several publications are available on CD-ROM. The library is a depository for state, federal, and United Nations documents.

■ Curriculum

➡ *Academic Support Program*   ➡ *84 units/credits required to graduate*   ➡ *99 courses available*   ➡ *degrees available: J.D.; J.D./M.B.A.; J.D./M.S. (Psych.); J.D./M.U.R.P.*
➡ *range of first-year class size—22-45*

First-year students begin their studies in an intensive two-day orientation taught by members of the full-time faculty. Two upperclass offerings—Professional Responsibility and Constitutional Law II—and all first-year courses are required. Upperclass students can select from numerous electives, which include extensive skills offerings.

■ Special Programs

Our clinical programs are constantly augmented and expanded to include additional areas of the law. An in-house civil clinic allows students to represent indigent clients. Projects funded by external grants include representation for persons with AIDS and representation of children needing advocacy. External placements are available with agencies such as the SEC and IRS as well as with Legal Aid offices. Criminal clinic internships are available with state attorneys' and public defenders' offices throughout Florida.

Many Nova students participate in our highly acclaimed Judicial Internship Program. Our Legislative Internship Program, Guardian Ad Litem Program, and Individuals with Disabilities Project provide valuable academic experiences, and students in our Street Law Program introduce middle and high school students to the legal system.

By combining law studies with work in other disciplines, our students can complete requirements for the J.D./M.B.A., the J.D./M.S. (Psychology), or the J.D./M.U.R.P. in three or four calendar years.

Students enrolled in our part-time day program take a reduced load and complete their studies in four or five years. Part-time students must have superior credentials and compelling reasons for part-time status.

Students who attend two eight-week summer sessions can accelerate their graduation by one semester. As many as 20 courses are offered during the typical summer term.

■ Admissions

➡ *Bachelor's degree from accredited college or university required for admission*   ➡ *application deadline—March 1*
➡ *rolling admissions, applications after March 1 at extreme disadvantage*   ➡ *LSAT, LSDAS required*
➡ *median GPA—2.97*   ➡ *median LSAT score—151*
➡ *application fee—$45*

Each application is read by at least one member of the admissions committee. In passing upon applications, the committee reviews undergraduate grades, the LSAT score, and the writing sample. However, committee members also consider the applicant's personal statement, work experience, and letters of recommendation. While no single factor is determinative, applicants who fail to demonstrate academic promise on both the LSAT score and the GPA are unlikely to be offered admission.

Selected students who otherwise would be rejected may receive an opportunity to compete for admission by taking two three-credit courses during June and July. Summer Conditional Acceptance Program courses are taught by experienced full-time faculty members. Students earning at least a 2.5 average for the summer, with no grade lower than C, are admitted to the entering class.

The Law Center is committed to diversity in its student body. Approximately 45 percent of the 1993 entering class is female; over 31 percent are members of minority groups. Students range in age from 20 through 55.

Applicants are encouraged to visit the campus, either for an Admissions Open House or for a classroom visit. Alumni in many regions are available to answer applicant questions about the Nova experience.

■ Student Activities

The top 5 percent of the first-year class is invited to join the *Nova Law Review*, which is published three times each year. Symposium topics have dealt with issues as varied as Drug Testing, Hurricane Andrew, and Legal Humor.

The Moot Court Society sponsors the F. Lee Bailey Moot Court Competition. Mr. Bailey, an adjunct faculty member, works with teams from throughout the United States during this competition.

Students participate on faculty committees and with organizations such as ATLA, BLSA, JLSA, SALSA, and Florida Association for Women Lawyers. The Student Bar Association is particularly active, and there are several legal fraternities and Inns of Court chapters. Ad hoc groups are formed for various sports activities.

■ Expenses and Financial Aid

➠ *tuition & fees—full-time, $15,720; part-time, $13,270*
➠ *estimated additional expenses—$7,000-$12,000 (room, board, books, transportation)*
➠ *performance and need-based scholarships available*
➠ *minority performance and need-based scholarships available*
➠ *financial aid available (FAF form and Nova financial aid application required)*

A number of partial tuition waivers are available. These waivers are awarded on the basis of demonstrated financial need and academic merit and are primarily reserved for upperclass students. In addition to work-study opportunities, upperclass students are able to work as faculty research assistants at salaries that approximate those for law clerks.

■ Career Services

Our Career Services Office assists students and alumni with career counseling and the employment process. In addition to facilitating on-campus interviews and résumé distribution, the director coordinates career-option seminars and interviewing workshops. Although opportunities are available throughout the country, most alumni choose employment in Florida firms and government agencies.

Applicant Group for the 1993–1994 Academic Year

Nova University—Shepard Broad Law Center
This grid includes only applicants who earned 120-180 LSAT scores under standard administrations.

LSAT Score	3.75 +		3.50-3.74		3.25-3.49		3.00-3.24		2.75-2.99		2.50-2.74		2.25-2.49		2.00-2.24		Below 2.00		No GPA		Total	
	Apps	Adm	Apps	Adm	Apps	Adm	Apps	Adm	Apps	Adm	Apps	Adm	Apps	Adm	Apps	Adm	Apps	Adm	Apps	Adm	Apps	Adm
175-180	0	0	0	0	0	0	0	0	0	0	0	0	0	0	0	0	0	0	0	0	0	0
170-174	0	0	0	0	0	0	0	0	1	1	1	1	1	1	0	0	0	0	0	0	3	3
165-169	0	0	1	1	3	3	9	9	2	2	2	0	2	0	1	0	1	1	1	0	22	16
160-164	3	3	6	6	9	9	17	16	20	14	17	6	13	5	0	0	3	1	2	2	90	62
155-159	8	8	12	12	35	31	72	62	81	51	68	34	35	7	16	3	4	0	3	0	334	208
150-154	15	15	37	23	109	76	134	70	150	38	126	19	79	13	31	5	3	0	7	1	691	260
145-149	11	6	46	14	85	17	150	21	180	16	160	6	72	4	33	2	8	1	14	6	759	93
140-144	7	2	18	3	49	9	94	10	117	13	99	4	72	9	22	2	12	0	11	1	501	58
135-139	4	3	2	0	12	3	23	3	51	4	56	3	45	4	24	3	3	0	6	1	226	24
130-134	1	0	3	1	4	0	11	1	13	0	18	1	19	1	15	0	3	0	5	0	92	4
125-129	0	0	0	0	0	0	1	0	0	0	3	0	3	1	6	0	1	0	5	0	19	1
120-124	0	0	0	0	0	0	0	0	0	0	0	0	1	0	0	0	0	0	1	0	2	0
Total	49	37	125	60	306	148	511	192	615	139	550	79	342	45	148	15	38	3	55	11	2739	729

Apps = Number of Applicants
Adm = Number Admitted
Reflects 92% of the total applicant pool.

Ohio Northern University—Claude W. Pettit College of Law

525 S. Main Street
Ada, OH 45810

Phone: 419.772.2211

■ Introduction

Founded in 1885, the Claude W. Pettit College of Law of Ohio Northern University is fully accredited by the American Bar Association and is a member of both the Association of American Law Schools and the League of Ohio Law Schools.

The university of 2,900 students is small enough to provide individual attention to student needs, yet large enough to provide the amenities of a major research institution. The 280-acre campus is located in Ada, a small and picturesque college town in the midwest. Ada is approximately 70 to 90 miles from the Ohio cities of Dayton, Toledo, and Columbus, as well as Fort Wayne, Indiana.

■ Enrollment/Student Body

➡ *2,035 applicants*   ➡ *621 admitted first-year class 1993*
➡ *139 enrolled first-year class 1993*   ➡ *397 total full-time*
➡ *9% minority*   ➡ *30% women*
➡ *33 states & foreign countries represented*
➡ *246 undergraduate schools represented*

■ Faculty

➡ *41 total*   ➡ *26 full-time*   ➡ *15 part-time or adjunct*
➡ *8 women*

The faculty strives for excellence in both teaching and scholarship. All faculty members have practiced law, bringing a wealth of practical experience gained from law firms, corporate law departments, and government to the classroom. The faculty also maintains a high level of scholarly productivity and professional service.

Small classes and individual attention are the hallmarks of the college. First-year classes are generally limited to 50 or fewer students. Faculty maintain open-door policies to foster good communication with students.

■ Library and Physical Facilities

➡ *225,000 volumes & equivalents*   ➡ *library hours:*
Mon.-Fri., 8:00 A.M.-MIDNIGHT; Sat., 9:00 A.M.-MIDNIGHT;
Sun., 11:00 A.M.-MIDNIGHT   ➡ *LEXIS*   ➡ *NEXIS*
➡ *WESTLAW*   ➡ *4 full-time librarians*
➡ *library seats 300*

The College of Law is housed in Tilton Hall, a modern building containing classrooms, faculty and administrative offices, student organization offices, moot courtrooms, a student lounge, and the law library. The Taggart Law Library, a federal government depository, houses on-line card cataloguing and an excellent computer lab.

Law students also have access to the other campus facilities, including a wide variety of entertainment programs at the Freed Center for the Performing Arts and the athletic facilities in the recently expanded Sports Center.

■ Curriculum

➡ *Academic Support Program*   ➡ *full-time program*
➡ *87 credits required to graduate*   ➡ *80 courses available*
➡ *degrees available: J.D.; B.S./Pharmacy/J.D.; Pharm D.*
➡ *semesters, start in Aug.*   ➡ *average size of first-year class—45*

First-year courses include contracts, torts, property, civil procedure, criminal law, and legal writing and research. Courses required in the second and third years include Constitutional law, federal income taxation, evidence, business associations, corporations, legal profession, and trial advocacy.

Students may choose from over 67 elective courses, including advanced courses and seminars. Each student must complete a research paper in the second or third year under the supervision of a faculty member.

■ Special Programs

Pharmacy and Law—This cooperative venture involving the Colleges of Law and Pharmacy provides students with the opportunity to earn a joint degree and utilize the services of the Pharmacy-Law Institute. The Institute publishes *The Journal of Pharmacy & Law*; sponsors research and instructional programs; and conducts workshops, conferences, and seminars.

Clinical Education—The College of Law offers a variety of opportunities for experiential learning in its clinical education program. Clinics focusing on the problems of the economically disadvantaged and elderly are offered at its offices in Ada and nearby Lima. Students also participate in extern programs with judges' offices, legal aid societies, public defender offices, and prosecutors' offices.

Icelandic Exchange Program—The college shares an exchange program with the law school at the University of Iceland. Participating students travel to Iceland to experience its culture and legal system.

■ Admission

➡ *Bachelor's degree from accredited college or university required*   ➡ *no application deadline*   ➡ *rolling admission, early application preferred*   ➡ *LSAT, LSDAS required*
➡ *median GPA—3.00*   ➡ *median LSAT score—156*
➡ *application fee—$40*

While Ohio Northern gives most weight to the LSAT and undergraduate GPA, the Admissions Committee may consider other nonquantifiable factors such as candidates' undergraduate program and grade trends, completion of other graduate degrees, professional accomplishments, and socioeconomic or cultural barriers faced by the applicant. Letters of recommendation are not required, but letters from persons who have a basis to assess the candidate's intellectual ability, such as former professors or employers, will be considered by the committee.

Ohio Northern University is committed to a culturally and socially diverse student body. Applications from women, minority group members, and persons with disabilities are strongly encouraged. The College of Law is a contributing supporter of the Council on Legal Education Opportunity (CLEO) Program. The facilities of the College of Law are accessible to physically handicapped students.

Student Activities

Students can choose from a variety of extracurricular activities. The College of Law publishes the *Ohio Northern University Law Review*, a student-edited commentary on legal issues. Students also serve on the staff of the *Pharmacy-Law Journal* published by the Pharmacy-Law Institute.

Intraschool, regional, and national moot court competitions are open to all students. Ohio Northern University students participate in at least 10 national and regional moot court competitions each year.

Through the Student Bar Association, students participate in a variety of extracurricular activities such as the Environmental Law and International Law societies. Students volunteer their services through the Volunteer Income Tax Assistance program. Ohio Northern also has active chapters of BLSA (Black Law Students Association), LAW (Legal Association of Women), Christian Legal Society, and the Cardozo (Jewish) Law Student Association. Ohio Northern also offers membership in Phi Kappa Phi (national honorary society), the Willis Society (honorary society), Phi Alpha Delta, Delta Theta Phi, and Phi Delta Phi.

Expenses and Financial Aid

➡ *full-time tuition & fees—$16,960* ➡ *average additional expenses—$5,000 (books, living expenses, transportation)* ➡ *merit-based scholarships and need-based grants are available, renewable for second and third years* ➡ *financial aid available* ➡ *FAFSA preferred, FAF accepted for financial aid* ➡ *students who apply after March 15 may be disadvantaged in consideration for scholarship or grant aid*

Our Legal Scholar Program provides scholarship awards for students whose undergraduate records demonstrate academic excellence. The scholarship amounts range from $7,000 to $12,000 and are renewable provided the student remains in good academic standing. Additionally, substantial scholarships are awarded to students who excel in their first year of law school. Diversity awards, subject to the availability of funds, are also made available to selected students.

Career Services

Through individualized counseling, students and graduates obtain valuable guidance in obtaining summer jobs and permanent positions. The Office of Career Services assists in the application and interviewing processes; provides current listings of positions in law firms, governmental agencies, and corporations; and hosts on-campus interviews.

Applicant Group for the 1993–1994 Academic Year

Ohio Northern University—Claude W. Pettit College of Law

The Ohio State University College of Law

55 West 12th Avenue
Columbus, OH 43210

Phone: 614.292.8810

■ Introduction

➻ *founded 1891*   ➻ *charter member, AALS*
➻ *ABA-accredited since 1923*

The College of Law is located on the main campus of the Ohio State University, one of the largest comprehensive institutions of higher education in the world. In addition to being the state capital, Columbus is a commercial and cultural center which has expanded dramatically in the past decade. The curriculum and experiences of law students are enriched by the opportunities presented by interaction with the university, state government, the bar, the bench, and community organizations.

■ Enrollment/Student Body

➻ *total enrollment—660*   ➻ *first-year class size—225-230*
➻ *18% minority*   ➻ *45% women*
➻ *29 states and over 180 colleges and universities represented*

■ Faculty

➻ *37 full-time*   ➻ *20 part-time*   ➻ *9 women full-time*
➻ *6 minority full-time*   ➻ *student/full-time faculty ratio: 18:1*

■ Library and Physical Facilities

➻ *590,000 volumes & equivalents*   ➻ *LEXIS*
➻ *WESTLAW*   ➻ *12 other databases*   ➻ *9 full-time professional librarians*   ➻ *11 support staff*   ➻ *computer lab for student use*   ➻ *open stacks*   ➻ *carrels for 350*

Construction of a new addition and renovation of the existing building were completed in early 1993. The result is a state-of-the-art teaching and research facility that includes three comfortably furnished lounges for students. The building has an abundance of natural light which creates a bright and cheerful environment. Attractive landscaping and a covered colonnade invite students to spend time outdoors in good weather studying or just relaxing.

The law library, the largest in the state and the fourteenth largest in the nation, has an extensive research collection. The collection of foreign law materials is very strong, containing titles from over 100 jurisdictions, with particular strengths in legal literature from the Commonwealth countries, France, and Germany. The library is a partial government depository for federal documents.

The new library has a computer laboratory for students and comfortable study and seating space for all students. Students have immediate access to the vast collections housed in the university libraries.

■ Curriculum

➻ *summer program at University of Oxford*   ➻ *joint degrees available: J.D./M.B.A.; J.D./M.P.A.; J.D./M.H.A.; and others*   ➻ *summer courses for upper-level students*
➻ *88 semester hours required for J.D.*   ➻ *clinical programs*
➻ *legal writing*   ➻ *dispute resolution courses & journal*

The first-year curriculum is prescribed. Class size in most first-year courses is between 50 and 70 students; first-year students are also assigned to a small section of 25-30 students. Most of the second- and third-year curriculum is elective. The curriculum offers great depth in specialized areas such as tax, commercial, administrative, international, and criminal law. In addition, offerings extend beyond the traditional curriculum into areas such as legislation, legal history, natural resources, law and social sciences, alternative dispute resolution, and international trade relations.

■ Special Programs

The Summer Law Program at the University of Oxford permits upper-level students to take courses with faculty from both Oxford and the College of Law.

Ohio State has one of the oldest clinical programs in the country. Second-year students can enroll in courses that simulate litigation practice and procedure. Third-year students can enroll in civil, criminal, or dispute resolution clinics to represent clients under the close supervision of an attorney and a faculty member.

The college offers joint-degree programs in business administration, public administration, and health administration. In addition, students may earn joint degrees in individually designed programs.

During their second year, all students participate in the moot court program. Following that course, students may elect to compete for positions on teams the college places in national interschool competitions.

■ Activities

Students have played a major role in shaping the law school. The College of Law was established in 1891 in response to requests from Columbus law clerks for formal legal training. Students organized the *Ohio State Law Journal* and were instrumental in establishing the legal clinic, the *Ohio State Journal on Dispute Resolution*, and the Student Funded Fellowship Program. Students serve on all standing faculty committees. The Student Bar Association serves as the students' governing body, hosts social events and speakers throughout the year, and runs the bookstore for law students.

There are many student organizations, including three legal fraternities, Asian American Law Students Association, Black Law Students Association, Christian Legal Society, Environmental Law Association, Federalist Society, Feminist Law Caucus, Gay and Lesbian Caucus, Health Care Organization, Hispanic Law Students Association, International Law Society, a student newspaper, a Street Law Program, and a Volunteer Income Tax Assistance Program.

■ Admissions

➻ *Bachelor's degree required for admission*
➻ *application deadline—March 15*
➻ *LSAT, LSDAS required*   ➻ *median GPA—3.50*

➡ *median LSAT score—161* ➡ *application fee—$30*
➡ *early application encouraged* ➡ *rolling admission*

Each candidate's file is carefully reviewed. The most important factor is the candidate's academic potential which is usually best evidenced by the LSAT score and undergraduate transcript. Some factors believed relevant to success in law school may also be considered, such as: trend in academic performance; letters of recommendation addressing the candidate's intellectual potential; achievement in graduate school; caliber of the undergraduate college or university; unusually time-consuming extracurricular activities or work experience; and rigor of coursework selected. The college desires to enroll a diverse student body and, consistent with that objective, those from disadvantaged backgrounds, who have unusual or extensive work experience, or who have overcome significant or unusual obstacles to obtain an education are thought by the Admissions Committee to add diversity. For the same reason, the college has a longstanding affirmative action program. Applicants are encouraged to visit the college.

■ Expenses and Financial Aid

➡ *1993-94 tuition & fees—residents, $4,950; nonresidents $12,200* ➡ *estimated additional expenses—$7,700*
➡ *financial aid—mostly need-based, competition for merit-based awards is strong*
➡ *Free Application for Federal Student Aid (FAFSA) and OSU Supplemental Form required, March 1 deadline*
➡ *100 members of the entering class receive grants*

■ Housing

The university has dormitories for single graduate and professional students as well as married student housing units. The college provides assistance in locating off-campus housing. Columbus, a major metropolitan area, offers a wide variety of housing.

■ Placement

The placement office helps all students secure summer and permanent positions, and also helps second-and third-year students find part-time employment during the academic year. Under the supervision of a full-time director, the program provides a wide range of services including individual career counseling, computerized and manual job prospecting, résumé preparation, and interviewing techniques. The office runs the largest on-campus interview program in the state and posts hundreds of openings from employers who cannot visit the campus. Although national law firms constitute the largest category of employers in the on-campus interviewing program, opportunities to interview with employers from all levels of government and corporate legal departments are also available. Typically, between 85 and 90 percent of each class accept employment within nine months of graduation. Generally, 65 percent go into private practice and 15 percent into judicial clerkships, with the remainder divided among government work, corporate law, etc. Graduates are currently practicing in all 50 states, the District of Columbia, and more than a dozen foreign countries.

Applicant Group for the 1993–1994 Academic Year

The Ohio State University College of Law
This grid includes only applicants who earned 120-180 LSAT scores under standard administrations.

LSAT Score	3.75 +		3.50 -3.74		3.25 - 3.49		3.00 - 3.24		2.75 - 2.99		2.50 - 2.74		2.25 - 2.49		2.00 - 2.24		Below 2.00		No GPA		Total	
	Apps	Adm	Apps	Adm	Apps	Adm	Apps	Adm	Apps	Adm	Apps	Adm	Apps	Adm	Apps	Adm	Apps	Adm	Apps	Adm	Apps	Adm
175 - 180	1	1	1	1	1	1	0	0	0	0	0	0	0	0	0	0	0	0	0	0	3	3
170 - 174	5	5	6	6	2	2	7	6	3	3	1	0	1	0	0	0	0	0	0	0	25	22
165 - 169	18	16	25	25	25	20	22	22	17	10	4	1	4	2	1	0	0	0	0	0	116	96
160 - 164	51	44	62	55	75	51	64	28	27	7	16	1	3	0	0	0	0	0	0	0	298	186
155 - 159	45	22	93	45	117	26	83	17	41	5	22	0	10	1	2	0	2	0	3	3	418	119
150 - 154	34	7	88	10	74	7	76	6	47	5	31	4	15	3	6	0	1	0	2	1	374	43
145 - 149	9	4	31	1	48	7	69	10	35	2	39	11	15	1	4	0	0	0	2	2	252	38
140 - 144	3	0	13	3	24	2	33	6	22	0	24	1	11	0	8	0	1	0	6	0	145	12
135 - 139	3	0	3	1	11	0	10	0	11	0	17	0	13	0	7	0	0	0	3	0	78	1
130 - 134	0	0	2	0	0	0	1	0	5	0	11	0	3	0	7	0	1	0	1	0	31	0
125 - 129	0	0	0	0	0	0	1	0	2	0	1	0	0	0	0	0	1	0	0	0	5	0
120 - 124	0	0	0	0	0	0	0	0	0	0	0	0	0	0	1	0	0	0	0	0	1	0
Total	169	99	324	147	377	116	366	95	210	32	166	18	75	7	36	0	6	0	17	6	1746	520

Apps = Number of Applicants
Adm = Number Admitted
Reflects 96% of the total applicant pool.

University of Oklahoma College of Law

300 Timberdell Road
Norman, OK 73019

Phone: 405.325.4726

■ Introduction

The University of Oklahoma College of Law is located on the main campus of the university in Norman, a city of 80,000 in the Oklahoma City metropolitan area. The college was founded in 1909. The only state-supported law school in Oklahoma, it has been a member of the AALS since 1911 and ABA-approved since that list was first published in 1923. The Law Center, on the south campus of the University of Oklahoma, is within walking distance of dormitories, apartments, book exchange and recreational facilities.

■ Enrollment/Student Body

→ *983 applicants*   → *360 admitted first-year class 1993*
→ *213 enrolled first-year class 1993*   → *670 total full-time*
→ *10% minority*   → *40% women*
→ *24 states & foreign countries represented*
→ *66 undergraduate schools represented*

■ Faculty

→ *40 total*   → *32 full-time*   → *8 visiting or adjunct*
→ *7 women*   → *2 minority*

■ Library and Physical Facilities

→ *261,277 volumes & equivalents*   → *library hours: Mon.-Thurs., 7:30 A.M.-11:00 P.M.; Fri., 7:30 A.M.-8:00 P.M.; Sat., 8:00 A.M.-8:00 P.M.; Sun., 1:00 P.M.-11:00 P.M.*
→ *LEXIS*   → *NEXIS*   → *WESTLAW*
→ *7 full-time librarians*   → *library seats 355*

The law library features three computer labs (one for LEXIS and WESTLAW and two for word-processing and other computer activities), as well as a variety of automated indexes. Records for all materials in the law library are contained in OLIN (Oklahoma Information Network) which serves as the on-line catalog for the entire University of Oklahoma campus.

■ Curriculum

→ *Academic Support Program*   → *Summer Abroad Program, Oxford, England*   → *90 credits required to graduate*
→ *125 courses available*   → *degrees available: J.D.; J.D./M.B.A.; J.D./Master of Public Health; J.D./M.S. in Health Administration; J.D./M.S. in Environmental Mgmt.; J.D./M.S. in Occupational Health*   → *semesters, start in Aug. & Jan.*   → *summer session, starts mid-May*

Each fall, first-year students attend a one-day required orientation conducted on the Friday before classes begin on Monday. The first-year curriculum is prescribed. Students are assigned all of their first-year classes in one of four sections. Students are assigned a faculty advisor for their first year of law study.

■ Special Programs

The American Indian Law and Policy Center of the College of Law provides a resource on historic and contemporary matters relating to Native Americans. The center supports the work of the *American Indian Law Review* and the Native American Law Students Association.

The Oxford Summer Program in Law is cosponsored by the College of Law and the Department for Continuing Education of Oxford University. The program affords students an opportunity to live and study in stimulating and beautiful surroundings under the guidance of American and English legal educators.

The Enrichment Program brings outstanding individuals in law and public service to the school to speak on a variety of subjects.

The Jurist-in-Residence Program brings distinguished justices and judges to the College of Law as resident scholars providing instruction in the areas of criminal law, constitutional law, and trial techniques.

The International Law Professor-in-Residence appoints distinguished international visiting scholars.

The Clinical Legal Education Program is designed to provide law students an opportunity to prepare for the practice of law by working with actual clients with real legal problems. Clinical opportunities include the Cleveland County Legal Aid Office, the Criminal Defense Clinic, the Externship Clinic, the Prisoners' Rights Clinic, and the Judicial Clinic.

Students may receive course credit for participation in all clinical programs. Supervision of students is provided by the director and assistant director of the clinical legal education program.

■ Admission

→ *Bachelor's degree required*   → *application deadline—March 15*   → *rolling admission, fall semester only*
→ *LSAT, LSDAS required*   → *median GPA—3.28*
→ *median LSAT score—154*   → *application fee—$25*

A faculty committee reviews all applications. In evaluating an applicant, undergraduate grade-point average and the LSAT score are each given great weight. Consideration is also given to employment experience, achievements in graduate study, extracurricular activities, and other relevant factors. In evaluating grade-point averages, consideration is given to distinct trends or discrepancies among the applicant's grades, time commitments while attending, and other relevant factors.

The College of Law conducts a Special Admission by Performance Group program. Admission to this program is offered to a select group of about 30 students whose grade-point averages and LSAT scores do not meet the current standards for regular admission, but whose records reveal past performance affected by adverse circumstances or disadvantage and other factors, and whose records indicate possible future success. Factors considered by the Admissions Committee include, but are not limited to, social, cultural or physical handicaps, work necessity and experience, and minority status. Students in the program are required to complete six hours of summer coursework beginning in mid-May. Those successfully completing the program with a C- average (4.0 on a 12.0 scale) are offered regular admission to the entering class in the fall.

■ Student Activities

The *Oklahoma Law Review*, a quarterly publication, is a student publication that is scholarly in tone and gives expression to legal scholarship. Each issue has major articles by authorities in the field and sections written by the student members of the *Review* on significant topics and recent developments in the law.

The *American Indian Law Review*, published biannually, includes articles by authorities in the field; student-written sections; and addresses by noted speakers on Indian law, special recent developments in the area of Indian law, and recent federal developments of interest to tribal attorneys.

The Student Bar Association, affiliated with the Law Student Division of the American Bar Association, elects the Board of Governors to supervise activities and to present the students' viewpoints to the faculty and administration. Students sit as voting members on most of the College of Law faculty-administration committees. There are two legal fraternities and numerous student organizations.

The College of Law participates in several competitions including the National Moot Court, National Appellate Advocacy, National Trial Advocacy, American Client Counseling. Course credit may be earned for participation in these teams.

■ Expenses and Financial Aid

➤ *full-time tuition & fees—resident, $3,160; nonresident, $9,198* ➤ *estimated additional expenses—$7,800 (room & board, books)* ➤ *performance and need-based scholarships available* ➤ *Oklahoma State Regents Professional Study Grants* ➤ *financial aid available; FAFSA due by March 1 or no later than June 1*

■ Career Services

The Office of Legal Career Services is involved in a variety of activities designed to assist students seeking employment as summer clerks and attorneys. While the most visible activity sponsored by the college is its fall on-campus interview program, many students benefit from the office's collection of materials about legal employers and legal careers, available positions, and bar membership requirements.

Typically 98 percent of our graduating students accept positions within twelve months of graduation.

The College of Law participates in three Minority Job Fairs each year. They are held in Dallas and Chicago. We also sponsor a public interest job fair in Oklahoma and participate in the National Association of Public Interest Law job fair held annually in Washington, DC., and the newly formed Scilaw Job Fair held in Orlando each January.

Applicant Group for the 1993–1994 Academic Year

University of Oklahoma College of Law
This grid includes only applicants who earned 120-180 LSAT scores under standard administrations.

LSAT Score	GPA																					
	3.75 +		3.50 -3.74		3.25 - 3.49		3.00 - 3.24		2.75 - 2.99		2.50 - 2.74		2.25 - 2.49		2.00 - 2.24		Below 2.00		No GPA		Total	
	Apps	Adm	Apps	Adm	Apps	Adm	Apps	Adm	Apps	Adm	Apps	Adm	Apps	Adm	Apps	Adm	Apps	Adm	Apps	Adm	Apps	Adm
175 - 180	1	1	0	0	0	0	0	0	0	0	0	0	0	0	0	0	0	0	0	0	1	1
170 - 174	0	0	1	1	1	1	0	0	1	1	0	0	1	0	0	0	0	0	0	0	4	3
165 - 169	2	2	3	3	5	5	4	4	2	2	2	2	0	0	0	0	0	0	0	0	18	18
160 - 164	5	5	8	8	16	16	14	14	10	9	8	6	2	1	3	0	0	0	0	0	66	59
155 - 159	14	11	11	11	30	28	29	29	31	24	14	5	13	0	2	1	2	0	2	0	148	109
150 - 154	20	18	31	29	50	43	61	38	41	10	27	4	16	3	4	0	0	0	2	0	252	145
145 - 149	14	8	24	9	41	14	39	19	34	6	26	2	14	0	11	1	4	0	3	0	210	59
140 - 144	2	0	8	0	17	0	26	3	24	3	27	2	18	2	8	0	2	0	1	0	133	10
135 - 139	3	0	3	1	8	0	9	0	17	0	17	1	9	0	4	0	0	0	3	0	73	2
130 - 134	0	0	1	0	1	0	3	0	3	0	4	0	8	0	4	0	2	0	0	0	26	0
125 - 129	0	0	0	0	0	0	0	0	1	0	2	0	1	0	1	0	1	0	0	0	6	0
120 - 124	0	0	0	0	0	0	0	0	0	0	0	0	0	0	1	0	0	0	0	0	1	0
Total	61	45	90	62	169	107	185	107	164	55	127	22	82	6	38	2	11	0	11	0	938	406

Apps = Number of Applicants
Adm = Number Admitted
Reflects 95% of the total applicant pool.

Oklahoma City University School of Law

P.O. Box 61310
Oklahoma City, OK 73146-1310

Phone: 1.800.633.7242 or 405.521.5354

■ Introduction

Oklahoma City University School of Law is located within a metropolitan area of over 950,000, only minutes from several of Oklahoma's largest law firms, corporations, banks, city and state government agencies, and the federal courts. As part of Epworth University, it was the first law school founded in Oklahoma.

The School of Law is fully accredited by the American Bar Association, the Supreme Court of Oklahoma, and the Oklahoma Board of Bar Examiners.

■ Enrollment/Student Body

➡ *1,409 applicants* ➡ *707 admitted first-year class 1993*
➡ *237 enrolled first-year class 1993* ➡ *418 total full-time*
➡ *240 total part-time* ➡ *9.3% minority*
➡ *35% women* ➡ *38 states & foreign countries represented*
➡ *108 undergraduate schools represented*

■ Faculty

➡ *48 total* ➡ *27 full-time* ➡ *21 part-time or adjunct*
➡ *13 women* ➡ *4 minority*

■ Library and Physical Facilities

➡ *215,455 volumes & equivalents* ➡ *LEXIS*
➡ *NEXIS* ➡ *WESTLAW* ➡ *5 full-time librarians*

The law library is a member of CALI and subscribes to the Varalex Interactive Video Library. The law library subscribes to some of the West CD-Rom libraries and has four workstations. In addition, the law library offers student training and access to WESTLAW and LEXIS in the permanent learning center, plus access to the word processing computer lab.

■ Curriculum

➡ *90 credits required to graduate* ➡ *99 courses available*
➡ *degrees available: J.D.; J.D./M.B.A.; J.D./M. Div.*
➡ *semesters, start in Aug.*
➡ *range of first-year class size—25-80*

The School of Law has full J.D. programs during both the day and evening hours, requiring the completion of 90 semester hours. The school operates two 16-week semesters and one eight-week summer term. Day students may complete their degree requirements in two-and-a-half years, and evening students in four years by attending summer sessions.

All students take Civil Procedure, Constitutional Law, Contracts, Criminal Law, Criminal Procedure, Legal Research and Writing, Legal Profession, Property, Torts, and Evidence. The remaining 47 hours of work may be selected from electives and seminars. All upper-class students are required to complete a substantial written project.

The law school faculty consists of full-time and adjunct professors and seven to nine writing instructors. Full-time faculty members hail from many states and hold degrees from 27 different graduate or professional schools. Law de-

grees among faculty members represent a diversity of law schools, including the nation's most prestigious.

■ Special Programs

Three times each year, the student-edited *Law Review* is published. The School of Law also enters student teams in such interscholastic competitions as the National Moot Court Competition, the Philip C. Jessup International Moot Court Competition, the Benton Moot Court Competition, and the American Trial Lawyers Association Student Trial Advocacy Competition. OCU is gaining a national reputation for its performance in these competitions.

Most of the students selected for these teams are members of the Moot Court Board, an honors organization comprised of students selected for their skills in oral advocacy. The board sponsors an annual Intramural Moot Court Competition judged by 80 to 90 judges and lawyers from the Oklahoma City area.

Oklahoma has one of the most liberal policies toward limited licenses for legal interns. Students who have completed at least 50 hours are eligible, and those who qualify may appear in court under certain circumstances. In the fall of 1988, the School of Law opened the Native American Legal Resource Center, an institution which seeks to improve the quality of legal representation for individuals with problems in the field of Native American law. The center is designed to provide high quality basic and advanced training and resource support in varied areas of Native American law. It is also active in providing direct services to tribal court personnel and practitioners through its sponsorship of training seminars for judges, clerks, and other personnel of the Courts of Indian Offenses (CFR Courts), and continuing legal education programs for attorneys and others with an interest in this area of the law.

As a corollary to the center, the School of Law has also opened the Native American Legal Assistance Clinic, a for-credit clinical program currently operated in conjunction with Legal Aid of Western Oklahoma and Oklahoma Indian Legal Services. This clinic provides students with the opportunity for supervised hands-on experience in dealing with real-life problems in the field while receiving training for which academic credit is awarded.

■ Admission

➡ *Bachelor's degree required* ➡ *application deadline—Aug. 1*
➡ *LSAT, LSDAS required* ➡ *median GPA—3.03*
➡ *median LSAT score—150* ➡ *application fee—$35*

Admission decisions are determined by a faculty committee that considers each application separately. Many factors are considered, including academic performance, undergraduate institution and curriculum, advanced degrees, work experiences, background, activities, recommendations, and LSAT scores.

Regular students are admitted only in the fall term. Transcript evaluation by LSDAS is required, as are standard law school recommendation forms supplied by the School of Law.

The summer Alternate Admissions Program offers approximately 30 students who cannot meet ordinary admissions requirements for law school an opportunity to earn their way academically into regular fall admission.

■ Student Activities

Active student organizations include the *Law Review*, Moot Court Board, Federalist Society, Black American Law Students Association, Phi Alpha Delta, Phi Delta Phi, Iota Tau Tau, Native American Law Students Association, American Inns of Court, Merit Scholars, and the Trial Lawyers Association. The social year culminates in the annual spring dance and Gridiron (the Gridiron is a student roast of faculty and administrators).

■ Expenses and Financial Aid

➡ *tuition & fees—full-time, $10,850; part-time, $7,000*
➡ *estimated additional expenses—$3,630 (on campus housing, $825/semester; meal plan, $990/semester)*
➡ *scholarships available: Hatton Sumners & University Merit* ➡ *minority scholarships available*
➡ *financial aid available; FAF & ACT forms*

In addition to the nonrefundable $35 application fee, when accepted a student is required to pay a $250 nonrefundable tuition deposit, credited toward the first semester's tuition.

A number of scholarships for first-year and upper-class students are available. Both financial need and academic promise/performance are considered in awards. For example, the Hatton W. Sumners Scholarship Foundation offers up to five full scholarships each year to outstanding beginning students. These scholarships cover full tuition, books, fees, and a stipend for room and board. Minority applications are encouraged. The Kerr Foundation Scholarship Program provides scholarship assistance to upper-class students on the basis of academic performance, participation in school activities, exemplary character, and need. Other scholarships and various loan funds are also available. Students with need who are seeking financial aid should contact the Office of Financial Aid. The school accepts the Financial Aid Form (FAF) of the College Scholarship Service.

■ Career Services

The School of Law operates an Office of Career Services. The service assists students seeking employment or legal internship positions and graduates seeking positions.

All students have access to notices of job opportunities, campus interviews, and general placement information issued by Career Services. Registration with the office affords them individual attention and notification of opportunities available in their fields of interest.

Prospects for Admission

Oklahoma City University School of Law

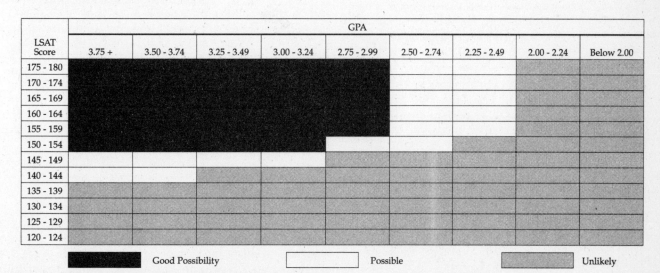

LSAT Score	GPA								
	3.75 +	3.50 - 3.74	3.25 - 3.49	3.00 - 3.24	2.75 - 2.99	2.50 - 2.74	2.25 - 2.49	2.00 - 2.24	Below 2.00
175 - 180									
170 - 174									
165 - 169									
160 - 164									
155 - 159									
150 - 154									
145 - 149									
140 - 144									
135 - 139									
130 - 134									
125 - 129									
120 - 124									

■ Good Possibility   □ Possible   ▨ Unlikely

University of Oregon School of Law

Office of Admissions, Room 201
Eugene, OR 97403-1221

Phone: 503.346.3846

■ Introduction

Eugene, Oregon is nestled in the southern Willamette Valley which is outlined by the Coast Range and the Pacific Ocean to the west and the Cascade mountain range to the east. Named by Sunset Magazine (October 1992) as one of the top five college towns in the west, Eugene is the home of an internationally-ranked research institution—the University of Oregon. The University of Oregon School of Law was founded in 1884 and continues to promote the joy of learning, creative scholarship, public service, ethics, and commitment to human diversity as well as providing a broad level of legal training for a wide variety of professional interests. The university, the surrounding community and the state offer students a wealth of cultural, social and athletic opportunities as well as the tools to prepare their lives for the future.

■ Enrollment/Student Body

➡ *1,835 applicants*   ➡ *482 admitted first-year class 1993*
➡ *149 enrolled first-year class 1993*   ➡ *410 total full-time*
➡ *14% minority*   ➡ *44% women*
➡ *164 undergraduate schools represented*

■ Faculty

➡ *40 total*   ➡ *29 full-time*   ➡ *11 part-time or adjunct*
➡ *10 women*   ➡ *4 minority*   ➡ *4 endowed professorships*

■ Library and Physical Facilities

➡ *290,400 volumes & equivalents*   ➡ *LEXIS*
➡ *NEXIS*   ➡ *WESTLAW*   ➡ *Janus*
➡ *6.9 full-time librarians*   ➡ *library seats 271*

The library's collection is accessed through Janus, an on-line catalog that is an important tool for researchers. The on-line Legal Resource Room in the law library contains 21 computer work stations which can be used to access information, information management, electronic communication, and word processing.

The Law Center's facilities include spacious classrooms, seminar rooms, a courtroom with videotape facilities, Student Bar Association office, student organization offices, *Oregon Law Review* and *Journal of Environmental Law and Litigation* (JELL) offices, offices for clinical programs, and a student lounge and courtyard.

■ Curriculum

➡ *Academic Support Program*   ➡ *85 credits required to graduate*   ➡ *80 courses available*   ➡ *degrees available: J.D.; J.D./M.B.A.; J.D./M.S.*   ➡ *semesters, start in Aug.*

The School of Law core curriculum emphasizes rigorous courses in all traditional legal subjects: civil procedure, contracts, criminal law, legal research and writing, legislative and administrative processes, property, and torts. The elective curriculum allows students to concentrate their studies in particular areas such as business and corporate law, international law, estate planning, taxation, litigation, constitutional law, and administrative law.

■ Academic Programs

The Business Law Program offers second- and third-year students an opportunity to receive a Business Law Statement of Completion or an Estate Planning Statement of Completion upon successfully completing a number of specific courses.

The School of Law and the Graduate School of Management offer a concurrent J.D./M.B.A. degree program; the School of Law and the Graduate School's Interdisciplinary Studies Program offer a concurrent J.D./M.S. with a specialty in environmental studies.

An intensive year-long research and writing program is required of all first-year students. Students present final oral arguments at the end of the second semester in a courtroom setting.

The location of the school in the natural resource laden Pacific Northwest has led to a strong emphasis in environmental law and ocean and coastal law offerings. Courses in water resources law, land use law, environment and pollution, ocean and coastal law, law of the sea, public land law, Indian law, and wildlife law give students insight into legal problems involved in these specific areas. Statements of completion offered in Environmental and Natural Resources and Ocean and Coastal Law give the school the distinction of being one of only a few schools in the nation to offer such programs.

The School of Law offers four clinical programs: Civil Practice, Criminal Defense, Prosecution, and Environmental Law.

The Academic Support Program is a voluntary program designed to address the academic needs of nontraditional law students. This nationally recognized program includes a two-week summer orientation and an academic year program designed to teach the principles that underlie first-year coursework, to develop research and writing skills, and to clarify the law school examination process. Particular emphasis is given to cross-cultural analysis of legal issues.

■ Admission

➡ *Bachelor's degree required*   ➡ *application deadline—April 1*   ➡ *LSAT, LSDAS required*   ➡ *rolling admissions*
➡ *median GPA—3.50*   ➡ *median LSAT score—160*
➡ *application fee—$50*

Over 1,800 applications were received for the 149 openings in the fall 1993 entering class. While the applicant's entire background is considered, numerical credentials are given considerable weight. Written recommendations and personal statements are highly encouraged. Entering students are accepted for admission in the fall only.

Applications from minorities and women are strongly encouraged. The school does not discriminate on the basis of race, color, religion, sex, age, handicap, national origin, marital status, veteran status, or sexual orientation.

■ Student Activities

The *Oregon Law Review* is published by a student editorial board and has been in continuous publication since 1921. The *Journal of Environmental Law and Litigation* (JELL) is published by students and focuses on current issues in environmental law. The Moot Court Board sponsors five in-house school competitions each year from which teams are selected to represent the school in regional and national competitions. The Student Bar Association represents the student body by serving on faculty committees and sponsoring numerous activities. Other organizations include Black Law Students Association; Christian Legal Society; FACT; Federalist Society; International Law Society; Jewish Law Students Association; Journal of Environmental Law & Litigation; Land Air Water; Lesbian & Gay Law Student Association; Minority Law Students Association; Monitor; National Lawyers Guild; Oregon Law Students' Public Interest Fund; Oregon Women Lawyers; Partners in Law, Lovers & Relatives Support; Peer Advising Board; People's Law School; Phi Alpha Delta; Phi Delta Phi; Sports Club; The Weekly Dissent, and the Women's Law Forum.

■ Expenses and Financial Aid

➧ *full-time tuition & fees—resident, $6,964/yr.; nonresident, $12,680/yr.* ➧ *estimated additional expenses—$6,740 (books, room & board, personal)*
➧ *academic and need-based scholarships available*
➧ *academic and need-based minority scholarships available*
➧ *financial aid available; FAFSA due March 1*

■ Career Services

The Career Services Office provides counseling, assistance with résumé preparation, job search strategy, and interviewing skills. It offers a library of career planning resources for use by student and alumni. More than 40 law firms, corporations, government organizations and public interest agencies interview students each year. Graduates have risen to prominent positions in the state and federal court systems, have served with distinction in state and national legislative and executive offices, and have distinguished themselves in private practice and in business.

Applicant Group for the 1993–1994 Academic Year

University of Oregon School of Law
This grid includes only applicants who earned 120-180 LSAT scores under standard administrations.

LSAT Score	GPA 3.75 +		3.50 -3.74		3.25 - 3.49		3.00 - 3.24		2.75 - 2.99		2.50 - 2.74		2.25 - 2.49		2.00 - 2.24		Below 2.00		No GPA		Total	
	Apps	Adm	Apps	Adm	Apps	Adm	Apps	Adm	Apps	Adm	Apps	Adm	Apps	Adm	Apps	Adm	Apps	Adm	Apps	Adm	Apps	Adm
175 - 180	1	1	0	0	1	1	2	2	1	0	1	0	0	0	0	0	0	0	0	0	6	4
170 - 174	3	3	2	2	3	2	8	6	5	1	3	1	1	0	0	0	0	0	0	0	25	15
165 - 169	4	4	18	18	31	31	30	12	17	5	14	2	7	2	3	0	0	0	1	1	125	75
160 - 164	21	21	55	53	82	71	78	25	48	12	24	3	14	1	1	0	1	0	3	3	327	189
155 - 159	23	21	72	51	105	18	107	6	76	3	37	1	21	0	5	0	0	0	4	0	450	100
150 - 154	18	14	53	28	93	7	101	4	73	1	42	2	25	2	8	0	1	0	6	0	420	58
145 - 149	6	3	21	8	39	1	45	1	45	1	35	0	16	0	6	0	1	0	4	0	218	14
140 - 144	3	1	9	1	12	2	19	1	21	0	16	1	12	0	4	0	2	0	2	0	100	6
135 - 139	0	0	3	0	2	0	5	0	6	0	8	1	4	0	3	0	1	0	3	0	35	1
130 - 134	0	0	0	0	1	0	0	0	1	0	1	0	3	0	0	0	0	0	1	0	7	0
125 - 129	0	0	0	0	2	0	0	0	0	0	1	0	0	0	1	0	0	0	1	0	5	0
120 - 124	0	0	0	0	0	0	0	0	0	0	0	0	0	0	0	0	0	0	0	0	0	0
Total	79	68	233	161	371	133	395	57	293	23	182	11	103	5	31	0	6	0	25	4	1718	462

Apps = Number of Applicants
Adm = Number Admitted
Reflects 94% of the total applicant pool.

Pace University School of Law

78 North Broadway
White Plains, NY 10603

Phone: 914.422.4210

■ Introduction

The Pace University School of Law, a division of a multi-campus university, is fully accredited by the ABA and is a member of the AALS. Located in White Plains, the County Seat of Westchester, the Law School provides convenient access to metropolitan New York, Connecticut, and New Jersey. In the county are the headquarters of some of the nation's largest corporations, as well as a growing legal community and county, state, and federal courts. This concentration and the law school's proximity to New York City have enabled Pace to attract highly qualified professors, speakers, and advisors.

The programs of the law school, including the J.D. and LL.M. in Environmental Law, are national in perspective and are based on the concept that rigorous standards and high quality teaching can coexist with an atmosphere congenial to learning and enjoyment. The aspirations of the students and faculty are high: to achieve national recognition and to reflect the range and level of varied resources of the metropolitan New York City area.

■ Enrollment/Student Body

➡ 3,017 applicants   ➡ 830 admitted first-year class 1993
➡ 232 enrolled first-year class 1993   ➡ 460 total full-time
➡ 334 total part-time   ➡ 46% women

■ Faculty

➡ 78 total   ➡ 49 full-time   ➡ 29 part-time
➡ 2 Emeritus in Residence   ➡ 15 women   ➡ 4 minority

■ Library and Physical Facilities

➡ 280,000 volumes & equivalents   ➡ library hours: Mon.-Thurs., 8:00 A.M.-MIDNIGHT; Fri., 8:00 A.M.-10:00 P.M.; Sat., 9:00 A.M.-9:00 P.M.; Sun., 11:00 A.M.-11:00 P.M.   ➡ LEXIS
➡ NEXIS   ➡ WESTLAW   ➡ DIALOG
➡ VUTEXT   ➡ EPIC   ➡ RLN   ➡ OCLC   ➡ PAL
➡ 8 full-time librarians   ➡ library seats 321

■ Curriculum

➡ Academic Support Program   ➡ 90 total credits required to graduate   ➡ 134 courses available
➡ degrees available: J.D.; J.D./M.B.A.; J.D./M.P.A.; LL.M. in Environmental Law   ➡ semesters, first-year begin mid Aug.
➡ range of first-year class size—278

■ Special Programs

Certificates in Environmental Law, Health Law and Policy, and International Trade Law are awarded when students complete a sequence of courses with specific GPAs in the applicable area. Clinics are available in the areas of appellate, environmental, and civil (health) litigation as well as criminal justice, as are advocacy courses and externships.

In conjunction with the Faculty of Laws, University of London, Pace law students may study in London. The program includes the opportunity for clinical internships with members of Parliament, law firms, and corporations.

Pace offers the opportunity to pursue the joint J.D./M.B.A. or joint J.D./M.P.A. degree programs. The programs are typically completed in four years of full-time study; evening study is also possible.

■ Admission

➡ Bachelor's degree required   ➡ application deadline—March 15   ➡ rolling admission
➡ LSAT, LSDAS required   ➡ median GPA—3.30
➡ median LSAT score—159   ➡ application fee—$50
➡ 2 letters of recommendation and a personal statement

The law school received over 3,017 applications for 1993 admission. It enrolls approximately 169 day and 110 evening students annually. Admission is therefore very competitive. The GPAs of the entering classes average around 3.30, and the mean LSAT score may be found around the 80th percentile. The GPA and LSAT are the most important criteria for admission. However, many additional factors (e.g., schools attended, grade progression, courses, experiences) are also considered.

Minority students are encouraged to identify themselves as such on the application, as they will then be considered for a special admissions program designed to encourage and increase minority representation in the school and profession.

A number of students who show academic promise (e.g., high GPAs and low LSATs or the reverse) are invited to enroll in the Summer Conditional Admission Program. If a student, upon completion of the two courses, receives a C+ (2.5) GPA with neither grade below a C, he/she is guaranteed admission to the entering fall class.

■ Activities

Students may participate in the writing, running, and production of three law journals: the *Pace Law Review*; the *Pace Environmental Law Review*; and the *Pace Journal of International and Comparative Law*. Other law student organizations at Pace include *Hearsay*, the student newspaper, the moot court board, the Pace Student Bar Association, the Women's Association of Law Students, the Minority Student Association, Entertainment and Sports Law, Labor and Employment Law, Environmental Law, and International Law Clubs, and other special-interest groups. Special activities such as workshops and speakers sponsored by these groups, as well as social events, enrich Pace's offerings.

In addition, Pace students compete in the Philip C. Jessup International Moot Court, the National Moot Court, the National Client Counseling Competitions, and the National Trial Competition. Pace University School of Law is continuing to host the annual National Environmental Law Moot Court Competition and Litigation

Skills Workshops. Students may also attend various Continuing Legal Education (CLE) programs.

■ Expenses and Financial Aid

➥ *tuition & fees—full-time, $16,130; part-time, $12,160*
➥ *estimated additional expenses—$9,395 (off-campus living allowance)*   ➥ *merit- and need-based scholarships available*
➥ *merit minority scholarships available*
➥ *financial aid available*   ➥ *FAFSA required by March 15*

■ Career Services

The school's reputation continues to grow and, over the course of the past 15 years, Pace has succeeded in firmly establishing itself in the legal marketplace. That success is due largely to the achievements of our graduates and continued employer satisfaction. Graduates of the school's early classes have achieved positions of prominence with a wide variety of employers. Pace graduates typically go on to careers with national, regional, and local law firms; government agencies; county prosecutors; and public interest organizations. Pace students are awarded federal and state judicial clerkships each year.

The Office of Career Development provides guidance and assistance to students as they engage in the search for legal employment. The office serves as a liaison between law students and legal employers. It solicits and identifies employment opportunities, develops and maintains resources for student use in their job search, and encourages employers to accept student résumés and to interview on campus. The office provides counseling on résumé and cover letter preparation, interviewing techniques and career options as well as advice on how best to conduct a job search. In an effort to provide students with information on the various legal career alternatives, the Office of Career Development arranges panel presentations, often with Pace graduates as speakers. Additional information is available to students through their participation in the office's Alumni Advisor Program. Students who are interested in learning more about particular areas of practice are matched with graduates who practice in those areas for counseling and mentoring purposes.

Admission Profile Not Available

University of Pennsylvania Law School

3400 Chestnut Street
Philadelphia, PA 19104

Phone: 215.898.7400

■ Introduction

The study of law at the University of Pennsylvania began in 1790 and the Law School was formally organized in 1852. The Law School is a charter member of the AALS and is on the approved list of the ABA. The university is a private institution. The Law School, located on the university campus, is convenient to the many places of cultural and historical interest in Philadelphia.

■ Enrollment/Student Body

➡ *3,565 applicants*   ➡ *995 admitted first-year class 1993*
➡ *238 enrolled first-year class 1993*   ➡ *710 total full-time*
➡ *21% minority*   ➡ *40% women*
➡ *42 states & foreign countries represented*
➡ *150 undergraduate schools represented*

The student body is a diverse group of J.D. candidates plus a number of full-time graduate students from the United States and abroad. In recent years, 47 percent of the J.D. candidates did not matriculate directly from undergraduate study; 8 percent possess other graduate or professional degrees.

■ Faculty

➡ *93 total*   ➡ *39 full-time*   ➡ *54 part-time or adjunct*
➡ *18 women*   ➡ *8 minority*

■ Libraries and Physical Facilities

➡ *540,000 volumes & equivalents*   ➡ *library hours: Mon.-Thurs., 8:00 A.M.-MIDNIGHT; Fri., 8:00 A.M.-10:00 P.M.; Sat., 9:00 A.M.-10:00 P.M.; Sun., 9:00 A.M.-MIDNIGHT*   ➡ *LEXIS*
➡ *NEXIS*   ➡ *WESTLAW*   ➡ *DIALOG*   ➡ *BRS*
➡ *VUTEXT*   ➡ *Dow Jones*   ➡ *14 full-time librarians*
➡ *library seats 525*

The Law School is a modern, self-contained complex of buildings. A new library adjacent to the Law School was completed in 1993. Law students also have ready access to the university's other libraries, which contain an additional three million books.

■ Curriculum

➡ *degrees available: J.D.; J.D./M.B.A.; J.D./M.S.W.; J.D./M.C.P.; J.D./M.A. Economics; J.D./M.A. Middle Eastern Studies; J.D./M.A. Public Policy; J.D./Ph. D. Philosophy; LL.M.; S.J.D.*

The Law School awards the J.D. degree upon the successful completion of three academic years. There are no summer or night classes. The school operates on the semester basis. The prescribed program of the first year includes courses based on statutory and administrative law, as well as the traditional common law courses. In a small group, each student receives individualized instruction in legal research and writing. In the second and third years the work is elective, with opportunity for in-depth work in particular areas, including nonclassroom study. Additionally, second- and third-year students are required to perform 35 hours of unpaid professional service each year. This public service is a graduation requirement. Under rules on the practice of law in the Commonwealth, students in the Law School's clinical programs are permitted to represent clients in a variety of judicial and administrative tribunals. All third-year students write a major senior research paper. The program of graduate study leads to the degree of Master of Laws (LL.M.) and Doctor of Juridical Science of Law (S.J.D.).

■ Special Programs

The Law School's sensitivity to the problems confronting contemporary society is reflected in its programs. Among these are four-year programs with the Department of City Planning, leading to the J.D. and Master of City Planning degrees; the Wharton School of Business Administration, leading to the J.D. and M.B.A. or J.D. and M.A./Ph.D. in Public Policy and Management; the Department of Economics leading to the J.D. and M.A. or, through a very rigorous program, a combined J.D./Ph.D.; the School of Social Work leading to the J.D. and Master of Social Work; and the Department of Philosophy leading to a J.D./Ph.D. in Philosophy. In conjunction with the university's Middle East Center, the Law School offers a program designed for law students who wish to focus their attention on legal issues arising in the Islamic Middle East. Through arrangements with the graduate faculty, well-qualified J.D. candidates may pursue a joint program in other law-related graduate disciplines. Selected students may spend one semester working and studying in externship programs away from the Law School. The Law School maintains a Legal Assistance Office where students represent clients under the supervision of experienced attorneys. A small-business clinic has been established in conjunction with the Wharton School.

■ Admission

➡ *Bachelor's degree from accredited institution required*
➡ *application deadline—Feb. 1*   ➡ *LSAT, LSDAS required*
➡ *median GPA—3.70*   ➡ *median LSAT score—165*
➡ *application fee—$60*

Admission is highly selective. The school lays prime emphasis upon overall undergraduate performance and LSAT score. It may also take into account maturity, extracurricular records, and other personal qualifications. Recommendations, preferably from former teachers, are required. Personal interviews are not required, but students contemplating law study are encouraged to visit the school. For the class that entered in August 1993, the average LSAT score was in the 94th percentile. There is a special program involving recruitment for members of minority groups. The deadline for admission and financial aid applications is February 1. The school admits students only in the fall and only for full-time study. The school accepts a number of transfer students each year from applicants with superior undergraduate and law school records.

■ Housing

Facilities for single and married students are available in the Graduate Towers and International House which are adjacent to the Law School. A wide range of off-campus facilities is also available. For information students may write to the Office of Graduate Housing, 3901 Locust Walk, Philadelphia, PA 19104.

■ Student Activities

The *University of Pennsylvania Law Review* is edited by a board of student editors. It dates from 1896 and is a lineal successor to the *American Law Register*, which originated in 1852. The Law School also publishes a *Journal of International Business Law* and the *Comparative Labor Law Journal*. There is a chapter of the Order of the Coif. Student representatives participate in the governance of the Law School by participating in committee and faculty meetings. There is a full program of moot court activities. Other activities include the National Lawyer's Guild, the Federalist Society, and the Environmental Law Group. There are organizations for women, black, Asian-American, Latino, and gay and lesbian students, and various professional interests.

■ Expenses and Financial Aid

➡ *tuition & fees—full-time, $19,767* ➡ *estimated additional expenses—$10,733* ➡ *scholarships available (Public Interest Scholarships)* ➡ *need-based grants available* ➡ *minority scholarships available* ➡ *financial aid available* ➡ *GAPSFAS required for need-based scholarships, as well as institutional application*

The school maintains a substantial program of both scholarship and loan aid based entirely on need. Over 75 percent of the student body receives some type of financial aid.

Entering students may apply for several Public Interest Scholarships. These cover two-thirds of tuition and fees for three years. Applicants are selected on the basis of previous work experience in the public sector and commitment to employment in the public sector after graduation. Applications for the scholarships are contained in our admission material.

The Law School has a loan forgiveness program to assist graduates in repaying law school debts if they choose to work in the public sector.

■ Career Services

The Career Planning and Placement Office is staffed by three professionals who assist law students in finding employment and counsel students and alumni on employment opportunities. We offer specialized counseling for public-interest work, first-year job searches, minority students' concerns, and judicial clerkships. About 70 percent of the Class of 1992 entered private practice and 19 percent held judicial clerkships.

Applicant Group for the 1993–1994 Academic Year

University of Pennsylvania Law School

| GPA | LSAT Percentiles | | | | | | | | | | | |
| | 60 & Below | | 61 - 80 | | 81 - 90 | | 91 - 95 | | 96 & Above | | Total | |
	Apps	Adm	Apps	Adm	Apps	Adm	Apps	Adm	Apps	Adm	Apps	Adm
3.75 - 4.00	42	6	80	4	144	58	165	131	159	151	590	350
3.50 - 3.74	94	7	165	8	245	47	316	188	238	199	1058	449
3.25 - 3.49	140	7	152	14	186	15	201	32	198	66	877	134
3.00 - 3.24	130	10	86	11	101	5	89	7	105	12	511	45
Below 3.00	233	1	98	7	66	5	51	3	55	1	503	17
Total	639	31	581	44	742	130	822	361	755	429	3539	995

Apps = Number of Applicants
Adm = Number Admitted
Figures reflect admission decisions as of 6/15/93, including all applicant groups. The profile reflects approximately 99% of all applications but does not include decisions for those on the Waiting List.

Pepperdine University School of Law

24255 Pacific Coast Highway
Malibu, CA 90263

Phone: 310.456.4631

■ Introduction

Pepperdine University School of Law is located in the Odell McConnell Law Center on the university's 830-acre Malibu campus in Los Angeles County. This campus is the site of Seaver College, the university's undergraduate school, and the School of Business and Management's Residential M.B.A. program. The natural beauty of the Malibu campus combines the majesty of the rugged Santa Monica Mountains with a breathtaking view of the Pacific Ocean. Known for its clean air and almost rural setting, Malibu is less than a half hour's drive from the heavily populated San Fernando Valley; the business and legal communities of Santa Monica, Westwood, and Century City, and the fast-growing Thousand Oaks/Conejo Valley areas in nearby Ventura County. It is less than a 45-minute drive from downtown Los Angeles.

The School of Law is approved by the ABA and is a member of the AALS. With half of its students coming from states other than California, the school has a national reputation for excellence. Pepperdine offers a unique opportunity for the student who wishes to pursue a legal education in an institution that stresses academic excellence while supporting Christian values. Pepperdine is an independent, private university with a long-standing relationship with churches of Christ.

■ Enrollment/Student Body

➡ *3,100 applicants*   ➡ *978 admitted first-year class 1993*
➡ *250 enrolled first-year class 1993*   ➡ *714 total full-time*
➡ *18% minority*   ➡ *44% women*
➡ *40 states & 2 foreign countries represented*
➡ *205 undergraduate schools represented*

The school actively recruits minority students.

■ Faculty

➡ *46 total*   ➡ *37 full-time*   ➡ *9 part-time or adjunct*
➡ *4 women*   ➡ *2 minority*

The opportunity for a personal relationship between faculty and students increases the effectiveness of the entire educational experience.

■ Library and Physical Facilities

➡ *235,000 volumes & equivalents*   ➡ *library hours: Mon.-Fri., 7:00 A.M.-MIDNIGHT; Sat., 10:00 A.M.-10:00 P.M.; Sun., NOON-MIDNIGHT*   ➡ *LEXIS*   ➡ *NEXIS*   ➡ *WESTLAW*
➡ *5 full-time librarians*   ➡ *library seats 500*

The Jerene Appleby Harnish Law Library maintains an on-line public catalog as well as on-line, CD-ROM, and book indexes to provide access to the monograph and serials collections. All first-year students receive extensive training in both the LEXIS/NEXIS and the WESTLAW computer-assisted legal research systems, administered through the library.

■ Curriculum

➡ *Academic Support Program*   ➡ *88 credits required to graduate*   ➡ *131 courses available*   ➡ *degrees available: J.D.; J.D./M.B.A.*   ➡ *semesters, start in Aug., Jan., May*

An eight-week summer session is available for interested continuing students. It is possible to accelerate graduation one semester by taking appropriate course loads for two summer sessions. During the summer session, classes are offered in the evenings to allow students employment opportunities during the day.

■ Special Programs

Through extensive clinical programs and the California State Bar Legal Intern Program, students engage in a wide variety of practical legal activities under the supervision of experienced attorneys. The faculties of the School of Law and the Pepperdine University School of Business and Management offer a four-year, combined-degree program in business administration, J.D./M.B.A.

■ Institute for Dispute Resolution

In 1986, the School of Law established the Institute for Dispute Resolution, recognizing the needs for effective, timely, and affordable justice. The most comprehensive dispute resolution program in the country, the institute's activities include academic programs, research, publications, national training and actual dispute resolution sources. In 1988, the institute began its unique certificate program, which recognizes students who complete special coursework in the dispute-resolution field. Through the institute, the School of Law has received national recognition as a leader in the field of dispute resolution.

■ London Program

In the fall semester of every academic year, the School of Law offers a limited selection of courses in London, England, with an emphasis on international law. Second- and third-year students are given the opportunity to take courses in London under the direction of Pepperdine faculty and London adjunct professors. Several students from other law schools also participate.

■ Student Activities

Students are involved in a number of challenging activities, such as publication of the *Pepperdine Law Review*. The school operates one of the finest moot court programs in the country, with Pepperdine students excelling in statewide and national competitions. There are also successful trial advocacy and client-counseling competitions. Student organizations and legal fraternities offer additional opportunities for activities centered around the profession of law.

■ Admission

➡ *four-year undergraduate degree required*   ➡ *application deadline—March 1*   ➡ *rolling admission*   ➡ *LSAT, LSDAS required*   ➡ *median GPA—3.20*   ➡ *median LSAT score—160*   ➡ *application fee—$40*

No specific prelaw curriculum is required. First-year students are admitted only in the fall. Applications should be received by March 1.

Pepperdine University does not discriminate on the basis of race, color, national or ethnic origin, religion, age, sex, handicap, or prior military service. Evaluation is based on GPA, LSAT score, personal references, and extracurricular activities. The GPA and LSAT scores provide the objective factors in the selection process. In addition, intangible and personal factors are weighed to ensure diversity among the student body and to meet institutional objectives. Admission is limited to those who show substantial promise of successfully completing the study of law.

A limited number of transfer students may be accepted each year. Transfer applicants must be in good academic standing (top 15 percent of class) at a law school approved by the ABA and holding membership in the AALS, and must complete their last 58 units in residence at Pepperdine.

■ Housing

A limited number of law students can be housed in the on-campus School of Law apartment complex, which is located directly across the street from the Law Center.

■ Expenses and Financial Aid

➡ *tuition & fees—full-time, $17,800; part-time, $655/unit*   ➡ *estimated additional expenses—$13,930 (room, & board, $8,181; books, $700; travel, $1,863; personal, $3,186)*   ➡ *merit and need-based scholarships available*   ➡ *minority academic scholarships available*   ➡ *financial aid available; FAFSA, FAF*

An active financial aid program provides over 85 percent of the student body with some type of financial assistance. Scholarship grants are available to students with outstanding academic credentials and to those with demonstrated financial need. The school's catalog contains loan and scholarship information. The deadline for students to complete applications for financial aid is April 15 of the entering year. Financial aid application packages are available January 15.

■ Career Services

Career planning services are available to students and alumni of the School of Law, which is a member of the National Association for Law Placement and participates in its annual employment survey of law graduates. The law school currently has alumni located in 49 states and 12 foreign countries; the largest concentration of 1992 alumni was located in California. Graduates have become affiliated with prestigious law firms, government agencies, and corporations in Southern California and throughout the country.

Applicant Group for the 1993–1994 Academic Year

Pepperdine University School of Law
This grid includes only applicants who earned 120-180 LSAT scores under standard administrations.

LSAT Score	3.75 +		3.50 -3.74		3.25 - 3.49		3.00 - 3.24		2.75 - 2.99		2.50 - 2.74		2.25 - 2.49		2.00 - 2.24		Below 2.00		No GPA		Total	
	Apps	Adm	Apps	Adm	Apps	Adm	Apps	Adm	Apps	Adm	Apps	Adm	Apps	Adm	Apps	Adm	Apps	Adm	Apps	Adm	Apps	Adm
175 - 180	1	1	0	0	1	1	0	0	0	0	0	0	0	0	0	0	0	0	0	0	2	2
170 - 174	3	3	3	3	5	5	4	4	2	1	1	1	1	1	0	0	0	0	0	0	19	18
165 - 169	21	20	24	23	21	20	19	18	18	16	4	3	3	1	3	1	0	0	1	0	114	102
160 - 164	32	32	54	51	81	77	72	66	62	59	31	25	11	2	3	0	0	0	6	4	352	316
155 - 159	33	24	107	74	155	96	164	85	133	54	76	18	31	7	12	1	0	0	15	7	726	366
150 - 154	32	4	104	20	173	27	181	24	163	18	97	5	53	2	11	1	1	0	16	0	831	101
145 - 149	7	0	35	4	87	2	141	7	114	1	94	2	43	0	17	0	1	0	13	0	552	16
140 - 144	5	0	13	0	32	0	68	1	65	0	58	0	41	1	12	1	4	0	8	0	306	3
135 - 139	0	0	2	0	8	0	15	0	18	0	27	0	25	0	8	0	1	0	4	0	108	0
130 - 134	0	0	0	0	3	0	3	0	5	0	11	0	10	0	5	0	3	0	0	0	40	0
125 - 129	1	0	0	0	0	0	1	0	2	0	2	0	0	0	1	0	0	0	1	0	8	0
120 - 124	0	0	0	0	0	0	0	0	0	0	0	0	1	0	1	0	0	0	1	0	3	0
Total	135	84	342	175	566	228	668	205	582	149	401	54	219	14	73	4	10	0	65	11	3061	924

Apps = Number of Applicants
Adm = Number Admitted
Reflects 95% of the total applicant pool.

University of Pittsburgh School of Law

3900 Forbes Avenue
Pittsburgh, PA 15260

Phone: 412.648.1412

■ Introduction

Tradition: Law teaching at the University of Pittsburgh began in 1843, making Pittsburgh one of the first universities in the United States to offer a legal education. **Reputation**: The University of Pittsburgh remains one of the finest law schools in the country, featuring a broad and varied curriculum, an internationally renowned, enthusiastic faculty, first-rate physical facilities, and a talented and heterogeneous student body. **Venue**: The School of Law is located in its own modern building on the university campus in Oakland, the cultural and educational center of the city of Pittsburgh. State and federal courts, major corporate headquarters, and hundreds of large and small law firms are located nearby in downtown Pittsburgh, minutes from the campus. The Oakland area is home to four colleges and universities, the seven-hospital University Health Center, scientific and high-tech research centers, museums, art galleries, and libraries. The university campus abuts a safe and attractive city park, and desirable and affordable residential areas are less than a mile away.

■ Enrollment/Student Body

➡ *1,844 applicants*   ➡ *732 admitted first-year class 1993*
➡ *245 enrolled first-year class 1993*   ➡ *684 total full-time*
➡ *13 total flex-time*   ➡ *12% minority*   ➡ *46% women*
➡ *40 states & foreign countries represented*
➡ *190 undergraduate schools represented*

■ Faculty

➡ *63 total*   ➡ *35 full-time*   ➡ *28 part-time or adjunct*
➡ *11 women*   ➡ *4 minority*

■ Library and Physical Facilities

➡ *265,000 volumes & equivalents*   ➡ *library hours: Mon.-Thurs., 8:00 A.M.-MIDNIGHT; Fri., 8:00 A.M.-11:00 P.M.; Sat., 9:00 A.M.-8:00 P.M.; Sun., NOON-MIDNIGHT*   ➡ *LEXIS*
➡ *NEXIS*   ➡ *WESTLAW*   ➡ *6 full-time librarians*
➡ *library seats 438*

Faculty offices ring the perimeter of the library. This encourages ease of interaction between students and faculty.

■ Curriculum

➡ *Academic Support Program*
➡ *88 credits required to graduate*   ➡ *128 courses available*
➡ *21 are seminars with limited enrollment (15 students)*
➡ *degrees available: J.D./M.P.A., Law and Urban and Public Administration; J.D./M.P.I.A., Law and International Affairs; J.D./M.U.R.P., Law and Urban and Regional Planning; J.D./M.B.A., Law and Business Administration; J.D./M.P.H., Law and Public Health; J.D./M.A., Law and Medical Ethics; J.D./M.S.I.A., Law and Industrial Management; J.D./M.S., Law and Public Management, Law and Arts Management*
➡ *range of first-year class size—10-80*

The first-year class is divided into three sections. For each section, one course is taught in a small class of fewer than 30 students. Upper-level students may enroll in seminars, limited to 15 students, where they complete a faculty-supervised writing project. The upper-level curriculum is extremely varied, and the courses have been grouped into 19 practice areas, permitting students to develop a specialization, if they choose.

■ Special Programs

Clinical Programs—Four specialized legal clinics and a wide range of externship positions offer students the opportunity to learn by handling actual cases under the supervision of experienced lawyers and the law faculty. In the interdisciplinary Child Abuse and Neglect Law Clinic, students represent parents and children involved in proceedings before the Pennsylvania juvenile courts. Participants receive training from members of the law faculty, as well as teachers from the School of Social Work, and the departments of Psychiatry, Psychology, and Pediatric Medicine. In the Criminal and Appellate Practice Clinic, students work with the local public defender.

The Corporate Counsel Clinic allows students to gain practical experience representing business clients by serving as legal advisers in the Management Game course at Carnegie Mellon University's Graduate School of Industrial Administration. Students in the Elder Law/Guardianship Clinic represent older individuals in guardianship proceedings before Pennsylvania courts.

The law school's externship program permits students to earn academic credit while working in public law offices, as clerks for one of the 25 federal and state judges, or with one of many institutions associated with the program.

Mellon Legal Writing Program—The Mellon Legal Writing Program provides academic support to minority students through intensive training in legal analysis and writing. The program has been so successful in enhancing the performance of minority students that it was expanded to include other underrepresented groups, including older students and students with disabilities.

Students in the Mellon program participate in a week-long orientation prior to the start of classes. Throughout the academic year, students receive close, individual attention in class meetings of only 10 to 12 people.

Receptions, class parties, and group projects are held to provide opportunities for Mellon Program students to develop friendships and mentoring relationships with minority attorneys.

International Law—In the law school's dynamic program in international law, 13 courses are offered by internationally respected faculty in addition to a course entitled French for Lawyers. Students participate in two annual international law moot court competitions, and the very active International Law Society sponsors a range of speakers and programs. Summer internships with international organizations in Geneva are available, as are opportunities to earn joint degrees with graduate programs in business and international studies. Students also have participated in internships with the international corporations headquartered in Pittsburgh, including Alcoa, Mellon Bank, PPG Industries, and Westinghouse.

The study of international law at the University of Pittsburgh is enhanced by active faculty exchange programs with the University of Augsburg (Germany) and by visiting faculty from various other non-U.S. law faculties. It also benefits from other respected international programs at the University of Pittsburgh, such as the Center for International Studies, identified by the Council on Learning as one of the exemplary programs in the country.

■ Admission

➡ *Bachelor's degree from accredited college or university required* ➡ *application deadline—March 1*
➡ *LSAT, LSDAS required* ➡ *median GPA—3.30*
➡ *median LSAT score—159* ➡ *application fee—$40*

This School of Law is committed to providing opportunities for individuals in all segments of society: minorities, women, older students, and students with disabilities.

Since some individuals do not score well on standardized tests, in accepting students we look at all factors and all information submitted to see if an individual has the potential and capacity to study law.

The law school offers a very small flex-time program for an extremely limited number of students whose outside obligations necessitate a more flexible program of study. All requirements for the J.D. degree must be completed within five years from the time of matriculation. There are no night classes.

■ Student Activities

The *Law Review* is a quarterly legal periodical published by second- and third-year law students. The *Journal of Law and Commerce* is a semiannual legal periodical focusing on commercial law.

There are many organizations at the law school that provide rewarding social and intellectual experiences.

■ Expenses and Financial Aid

➡ *full-time tuition & fees—resident, $9,964; nonresident, $15,158* ➡ *additional expenses (room, board, other living expenses)—$8,600* ➡ *scholarships available: need-based and academic* ➡ *minority scholarships available*
➡ *financial aid available; GAPSFAS required for law school awards, FAFSA required for loans*

■ Career Services

The Placement Office provides year-round assistance to the school's students and graduates. The office serves as a clearinghouse for information on summer, part-time, and permanent work with law firms, corporations, accounting firms, government agencies, judges, and other legal employers.

The Minority Student Employment Program provides second-year students with part-time work opportunities in several large law firms.

Applicant Group for the 1993–1994 Academic Year

University of Pittsburgh School of Law
This grid includes only applicants who earned 120-180 LSAT scores under standard administrations.

LSAT Score	3.75 +		3.50 -3.74		3.25 - 3.49		3.00 - 3.24		2.75 - 2.99		2.50 - 2.74		Below 2.50		No GPA		Total	
	Apps	Adm	Apps	Adm	Apps	Adm	Apps	Adm	Apps	Adm	Apps	Adm	Apps	Adm	Apps	Adm	Apps	Adm
165+	12	21	20	18	16	16	30	30	19	15	16	11	4	1	0	0	117	103
160 - 164	19	19	43	43	60	60	64	58	39	30	31	14	14	4	1	0	271	228
155 - 159	30	28	81	69	123	76	95	49	64	15	31	6	21	0	2	1	447	244
150 - 154	20	11	63	14	106	14	79	8	71	5	50	6	29	1	4	2	422	61
145 - 149	8	2	29	5	47	6	66	8	57	6	35	10	19	4	2	0	263	41
Below 145	2	0	13	3	29	1	30	4	46	4	49	4	56	0	10	0	245	16
Total	91	72	249	152	381	173	374	157	296	75	212	51	147	10	19	3	1765	693

Apps = Number of Applicants
Adm = Number Admitted
Reflects 96% of the total applicant pool.

Pontifical Catholic University of Puerto Rico, School of Law

Ponce, PR 00732   Phone: 809.841.2000 ext. 339 or 340

■ Introduction

The School of Law of the Pontifical Catholic University of Puerto Rico was founded in 1961. It is located within the main campus of the Pontifical Catholic University of Puerto Rico, on the southern part of the island in the historical city of Ponce, one of the most beautiful places in Puerto Rico.

The primary objective of the Pontifical Catholic University of Puerto Rico School of Law is the formation of lawyers imbued with a deep love and concern for their Catholic faith and steeped in the redeeming truths of Christian philosophy and ethics. The law school of the Pontifical Catholic University of Puerto Rico hopes to contribute to upholding the high ethical, cultural, and literary accomplishments of the Puerto Rican bar, which historically represents a tradition of moral austerity, intellectual achievement, and professional competence.

■ Enrollment/Student Body

➼ *420 total part-time & full-time students*
➼ *most students are from Puerto Rico*

■ Library and Physical Facilities

➼ *136,636 volumes of Puerto Rican, Hispanic, Anglo-American, and foreign legal publications*   ➼ *LEXIS*
➼ *NEXIS*   ➼ *WESTLAW*

The School of Law occupies the Spellman Building. Its location on the campus of Pontifical Catholic University of Puerto Rico enables the students to study related academic disciplines, to participate in the intellectual life, and to enjoy many other facilities of the university.

Among the materials in the library is a comprehensive and growing collection of legal treatises, tests, monographs, and periodicals, including the most important and recent publications in civil, common, and comparative law. Modern audiovisual equipment and computerized services are also available. The library is an authorized depository for United Nations documents as well as for United States documents. In addition, it offers the services of the computerized WESTLAW and LEXIS/NEXIS systems, which permit computer-assisted legal research.

■ Curriculum

➼ *94 credits required to graduate*   ➼ *degrees available: J.D.; J.D./M.B.A.*   ➼ *semester system*

The required subjects are Introduction to Law, Constitutional Law, Torts, Property Law, Legal Ethics and Professional Responsibility, Theology, Family Law, Successions and Donations, Penal Law, Criminal Procedure, Administrative Law, Obligations, Contracts, Notary Law, Civil Procedure, Evidence, Mortgages, Trial Practice, Legal Aid Clinic, Corporations, Mercantile Law, Negotiable Instruments, Federal Jurisdiction, Special Legal Proceedings, Computers and the Legal Profession, Analysis of Jurisprudence, Legal Document Workshop, and Legal Bibliography. The basic program covers three years in the day division or four years in the evening division.

The school curriculum includes a clinical program for third-year students. Pursuant to a rule approved by the Supreme Court of the Commonwealth of Puerto Rico in 1974, students practice trial advocacy under the supervision of law school professors in the superior and district courts and in administrative agencies.

The required credits for the joint degree are as follows: J.D. degree, 88 credits (82 required credits and 6 elective credits) and an additional 6 approved elective credits in the Graduate Program of the School of Business Administration, for a total of 94 credits; M.B.A. degree, 37 credits (31 required credits and 6 elective credits) and an additional 6 approved elective credits in J.D., for a total of 43 credits, plus four hours of Theology.

■ Admission

➼ *Bachelor's degree required for admission*
➼ *application deadline—May 15*   ➼ *LSAT required*
➼ *beginning students admitted in Aug.*

Application for admission is open to men and women of good character who have received a bachelor's degree from a qualified institution with substantive content or training and a 2.5 grade-point average. Students without a bachelor's degree are not admitted.

The required forms of application and all other information may be obtained upon request from the registrar of the law school and should be filed with all supporting documents before May 15 in order to ensure consideration. The School of Law admits beginning students in August for both the full-time and part-time programs.

Applicants are required to take both the LSAT and the Prueba de Admision para Estudios Graduados (PAEG).

Test scores are not the only factor considered. Besides the objective factors, there are many intangible and personal considerations, such as strong motivation, disadvantaged circumstances, evidence of improving performance, and relevant work experience. A personal interview of the applicant by a committee is essential before a decision is made. Applicants of both sexes and from all religious, racial, social, and ethnic backgrounds are encouraged to apply.

■ Student Activities

The law review, *Revista de Derecho Puertorriqueño*, is devoted to scholarly analysis and discussion of development of the law. It publishes student notes, comments, and surveys, as well as articles of outstanding quality submitted by attorneys, judges, and other members of the legal profession. We have a student council, a chapter of the National Association of Law Students of Puerto Rico, and an Association Pro Women's Rights. Local chapters of Phi Alpha Delta international law fraternity, the Delta Theta Phi law fraternity, and the Law Student Division of the ABA are also active and well organized in the law school.

■ Housing

Students live either in the university residences or in private housing. Inquiries concerning housing facilities should be addressed to the Housing Office, Pontifical Catholic University of Puerto Rico, Ponce, Puerto Rico 00732.

■ Expenses and Financial Aid

➡ *tuition & fees—$190/credit hour*
➡ *estimated additional expenses—$226.50/semester*
➡ *scholarships available*   ➡ *financial aid available*

There is a deferred plan for students who have financial difficulties at the time of registration. The university has made available for law students several full-tuition scholarships to be awarded on the basis of scholastic excellence and financial need. The university also has an office for loans and other types of financial aid for students.

Admission Profile Not Available

University of Puerto Rico School of Law

P.O. Box 23349, UPR Station
Rio Piedras, PR 00931   Phone: 809.764.1655

■ Introduction

The University of Puerto Rico School of Law was founded in 1913 at its present site on the University Campus at Rio Piedras, within the metropolitan area of San Juan. The School of Law has been accredited by the American Bar Association since 1945 and the University of Puerto Rico is accredited by the Middle States Colleges Association. In 1948, the school was approved by the Association of American Law Schools. It is also accredited by the Council on Higher Education and the Puerto Rico Supreme Court.

■ Enrollment/Student Body

➡ 664 applicants ➡ 167 admitted first-year class 1993
➡ 149 enrolled first-year class 1993 ➡ 253 total full-time
➡ 204 total part-time ➡ 47% women
➡ 2 states & foreign countries represented
➡ more than 20 undergraduate schools represented

■ Faculty

➡ 56 total ➡ 33 full-time ➡ 23 part-time or adjunct
➡ 7 women

■ Library and Physical Facilities

➡ 210,628 volumes & equivalents ➡ library hours: Mon.-Fri., 7:30 A.M.-11:45 P.M.; Sat. & Sun., 8:00 A.M.-10:15 P.M.
➡ LEXIS ➡ NEXIS ➡ WESTLAW ➡ DIALOG
➡ COMPUCLERK ➡ CUMPULEY ➡ LEGALTRAC
➡ 10 full-time librarians ➡ library seats 400

The law library is the largest law library in the Caribbean. Its collection reflects both the Romano-Germanic civil law and Anglo-American common law traditions. The law library is in the process of developing a comprehensive collection of legal materials from the Caribbean Basin including resources from Mexico, Central America, Venezuela, and Colombia, as well as the island jurisdictions. In addition to hard-copy and microform materials, the law library subscribes to a variety of computerized legal research services. The law library has been designated as a European Documentation Centre by the European Communities and is also a selective depository for US government documents.

■ Curriculum

➡ 92 credits required to graduate ➡ 124 courses available
➡ J.D. degree available ➡ semesters, start in Aug.
➡ range of first-year class size—10-50

The basic program covers three years in the day division and four years in the evening division. Seventy credits consist of required courses and 22 are elective. Students are required to take two seminars (two credit-hours each).

■ Special Programs

The curriculum includes a clinical program for third-year students. The Legal Aid Clinic handles upwards of 1,300 cases per year. Rules for the participation of students before the local courts were approved by the Puerto Rico Supreme Court in March 1974 and by the U.S. District Court in 1991.

The clinical program also includes the Project for the Legal Representation of Handicapped Persons, where second- and third-year students participate in administrative and judicial proceedings on behalf of clients with disabilities.

■ Student Exchange Programs

The law school has Student Exchange Programs with the University of Arizona College of Law and the University of Connecticut School of Law. Under these programs, the students will register at their home institution but will take a full course load at the host institution. The credits and grades earned during a single semester will be awarded by the home institution according to the standard procedure of the home law school.

The law school also sponsors the UPR Summer Law Program at the University of Barcelona, Spain (June 23 to July 31, 1994).

■ Admission

➡ Bachelor's degree from accredited college or university required ➡ application deadline—Feb. 16
➡ LSAT, LSDAS required ➡ median GPA—3.38
➡ median LSAT score—146 ➡ application fee—$15
➡ median PAEG—659

The admissions procedure is absolutely nondiscriminating. There is no preference toward undergraduates from the University of Puerto Rico, nor toward men or women.

The University of Puerto Rico School of Law does not have a minority group breakdown since approximately 98 percent of our students are Puerto Rican, which would be considered a minority in stateside institutions, but certainly not in Puerto Rico. Racial composition is highly mixed due to the historical circumstances of the island.

Applicants must take the LSAT and the Prueba de Admision para Estudios Graduados (PAEG) no later than February 16 of the year of application, and must complete their undergraduate degree before enrolling in the law school. The LSAT, the PAEG, and the graduating index are given the same weight.

The cases of applicants with disabilities, who, by reason of their disability cannot take the required aptitude tests, are considered individually by the Admissions Committee.

■ Expenses and Financial Aid

➡ *tuition & fees: full-time, $2,623; part-time, $1,713*
➡ *estimated additional expenses—$5,000 (books, room and board, transportation)* ➡ *performance and need-based scholarships available* ➡ *financial aid available*
➡ *FAF due April 15*

Resident law students pay tuition fees amounting to $75 per credit each semester. Nonresident students who are American citizens pay the same amount that would be required from Puerto Rican students if they were to study in the state from which the nonresidents come, thus establishing a reciprocity principle. Nonresident students who are not American citizens pay tuition fees amounting to $1,500 for each semester.

Regular fees for medical services amount to $105 for the first semester and $141 for the second semester, which includes summer. The medical fee for the summer session only is $42.

All financial aid for the University of Puerto Rico is administered by the Office of Financial Aid, Dean of Students, Rio Piedras Campus, University of Puerto Rico, San Juan, PR 00931. Each student is considered on his or her own merit and need. Awards are made only after an applicant has been admitted.

■ Career Services

Since 1981, the school has had an Office of Student Affairs under an assistant dean that offers a variety of services, including placement. The Placement Officer, with the aid of the Puerto Rico Bar Association, the Department of Justice, and other government agencies, helps students obtain part-time jobs, regular jobs, or scholarships.

The Office of Student Affairs has initiated a series of statistical studies on the school's graduates and will continue to do so. Among the school's alumni are the Governor of Puerto Rico, the Secretary of Justice, most cabinet members, and Puerto Rico Supreme Court justices, judges, and legislators.

Applicant Group for the 1993–1994 Academic Year

University of Puerto Rico School of Law
This grid includes only applicants who earned 120-180 LSAT scores under standard administrations.

LSAT Score	3.75 +		3.50 -3.74		3.25 - 3.49		3.00 - 3.24		2.75 - 2.99		2.50 - 2.74		2.25 - 2.49		2.00 - 2.24		Below 2.00		No GPA		Total	
	Apps	Adm	Apps	Adm	Apps	Adm	Apps	Adm	Apps	Adm	Apps	Adm	Apps	Adm	Apps	Adm	Apps	Adm	Apps	Adm	Apps	Adm
175 - 180	0	0	0	0	0	0	0	0	0	0	0	0	0	0	0	0	0	0	0	0	0	0
170 - 174	0	0	0	0	0	0	1	1	0	0	0	0	0	0	0	0	0	0	0	0	1	1
165 - 169	1	1	0	0	1	1	0	0	0	0	1	1	0	0	0	0	0	0	0	0	3	3
160 - 164	0	0	1	1	2	2	0	0	1	1	0	0	0	0	0	0	0	0	1	1	5	5
155 - 159	0	0	0	0	4	4	3	2	0	0	2	1	1	1	1	0	0	0	0	0	11	8
150 - 154	1	1	3	3	4	4	6	6	8	7	4	4	2	1	1	1	0	0	0	0	29	27
145 - 149	7	7	6	6	19	14	21	15	11	5	4	1	5	0	1	0	0	0	0	0	74	48
140 - 144	15	15	19	11	22	15	22	9	18	1	15	0	8	1	2	0	0	0	1	0	122	52
135 - 139	10	5	18	5	27	2	28	1	20	0	23	0	10	0	7	0	2	0	1	0	146	13
130 - 134	8	0	13	1	21	3	23	0	21	0	18	0	11	0	2	0	1	0	2	0	120	4
125 - 129	4	0	8	0	12	0	17	0	11	0	9	0	5	0	3	0	1	0	4	0	74	0
120 - 124	0	0	0	0	7	0	4	0	9	0	4	0	2	0	0	0	0	0	1	0	29	0
Total	46	29	68	27	119	45	125	34	99	14	80	7	44	3	17	1	6	0	10	1	614	161

Apps = Number of Applicants
Adm = Number Admitted
Reflects 99% of the total applicant pool.

Puget Sound/Seattle University School of Law

950 Broadway Plaza
Tacoma, WA 98402

Phone: 206.591.2252

■ Introduction

In the Pacific Northwest, midway between Seattle, Washington's largest city, and its state capital, Olympia, sits a four-building complex in downtown Tacoma. This is the home of the Puget Sound School of Law, which merges with Seattle University in August 1994. Housed with the law school are the Washington State Court of Appeals, the Pierce County Office of Assigned Counsel, the Federal Public Defender, and a number of private law firms.

Tacoma, a major Pacific Rim port city and part of the "gateway to Alaska," offers students a lively urban environment that represents an ideal setting for our brand of legal education—a student body from throughout the nation; a blend of traditional textbook and innovative hands-on legal education; the school that former Supreme Court Chief Justice Warren Burger over a decade ago termed "a remarkable experiment in legal education."

■ Enrollment/Student Body

➡ *1,969 applicants* ➡ *740 admitted first-year class 1993*
➡ *305 enrolled first-year class 1993* ➡ *719 total full-time*
➡ *148 total part-time* ➡ *15% minority* ➡ *46% women*
➡ *48 states & foreign countries represented*
➡ *245 undergraduate schools represented*

Puget Sound students range in age from 20 to 59. While their average age at entry is 27, about 30 percent choose to pursue legal studies directly after undergraduate school. The remainder come to us from an impressive array of professional careers. On average, they rank in the top quarter of their graduating class and their performance in the LSAT is in the 80th percentile. More than 15 percent already hold at least one advanced degree.

■ Faculty

➡ *65 total* ➡ *40 full-time* ➡ *25 adjunct*
➡ *25 women* ➡ *3 minority*

When the law faculty meet to decide on faculty selection, promotion, and tenure, they first consider teaching aptitude and performance. Against this backdrop, the professors' production of significant scholarship is impressive, earning them a place among the "top 50" law faculties in the nation (first/1989 and second/1992, *Faculty Scholarship Survey*).

■ Library

➡ *300,258 volumes & equivalents* ➡ *library hours:*
7:00 A.M.–MIDNIGHT, daily ➡ *LEXIS* ➡ *NEXIS*
➡ *WESTLAW* ➡ *DIALOG* ➡ *BRS*
➡ *WILSONLINE* ➡ *VuText* ➡ *10 other CD-ROM databases* ➡ *DATATIMES* ➡ *8 full-time librarians*
➡ *library seats 600*

The law library houses the largest private law collection in the Northwest. In addition, state-of-the-art computer facilities allow students and faculty to utilize the most modern legal research methods. Puget Sound was the first law school in the Northwest to install both WESTLAW and LEXIS terminals and today is known nationally as a leader in computerized legal research.

■ Curriculum

➡ *90 credits required to graduate* ➡ *125 courses offered each year* ➡ *J.D. degree* ➡ *semesters, start in late Aug.*
➡ *optional early start in July*
➡ *range of first-year class size—15-80*

In the first intensive year, the curriculum concentrates on the highly traditional and prescribed basic courses, and on an intensive, year-long course refining legal analysis and writing skills which the ABA has called "among the finest legal writing programs in the nation." The upper-level courses allow for choice, innovation, and diversity. Students may choose either a broad, balanced program of study, or focus on a particular area such as: Business, Corporate, and Tax Law (20 related courses plus clerkship opportunities with over 100 law firms, government agencies, and corporations in Western Washington); Law in the Public Sector (40 course offerings); or Environmental Law (12 courses plus internships with the Port of Seattle, Sierra Club Legal Defense Fund, U.S. Environmental Protection Agency, and Washington Environmental Council, among others).

■ Academic Resource Center

The law school's Academic Resource Center offers a range of academic support services designed to maximize every student's success. Workshops and seminars for new students emphasize self-evaluation techniques and support-group strategies. Representative programs include the following workshops: Effective Study Techniques; How To Outline; Preparing For Exams; and Organizing Your Time. The center is staffed by a full-time director (a J.D. graduate) and second- and third-year law students who serve as advisors and teaching assistants.

■ Expanded Scheduling

One of the most distinctive and popular features of the academic program is what we term "expanded scheduling." Puget Sound, unlike any other school in the region, offers courses from 8:00 A.M. to 10:00 P.M., all year, for all students. At entry, students have the option of completing first-year studies over nine, twelve, or fifteen months. They may commence their studies in the summer or in the fall.

■ Admission

➡ *Bachelor's degree from an accredited college or university*
➡ *application deadline—April 1* ➡ *application fee—$50*
➡ *rolling admissions, early application preferred*
➡ *LSAT, LSDAS required* ➡ *typed personal statement and two letters of recommendation required*
➡ *median GPA—3.3* ➡ *median LSAT score—159*

The Faculty Admission Committee places primary emphasis on three factors: 1) LSAT scores; 2) undergraduate academic performance; and 3) personal accomplishments.

Each applicant file is reviewed individually by a minimum of two evaluators. Personal achievements weigh heavily in each admission decision.

Candidates for admission are advised to apply as early as possible and complete their files no later than April 1. A very few spaces in the class are held for persons taking the February and June LSATs.

The law school is committed to a wholly nondiscriminatory admission policy and philosophy.

■ Alternative Admission

A select group of applicants is admitted each year through an alternative-admission program established by the law school based on recognition that traditional admission criteria are, in some cases, inadequate predictors of success in law school and the legal profession. The majority of individuals considered for this program are members of historically disadvantaged groups or are persons with physical disabilities. Enrollment is strictly limited to 10 percent of the entering class.

■ Student Activities

A partial listing of student organizations illustrates the scope of interests held by law students: Alaska Student Bar Association; Asian/Pacific Islander Law Student Association; Black Law Student Association; Christian Legal Fellowship; Entertainment/Sports Law Association; Environmental Law Society; Inn of Court; International Law Society; Latino Law Student Association; Law Partners; Law Review; Moot Court; Puget Sound Law Foundation; Student Bar Association; and Women's Law Caucus.

■ Expenses and Financial Aid

➡ *tuition & fees—$13,800*   ➡ *additional expenses—$9,480 (books, room, board, and living expenses)*
➡ *performance and/or need-based scholarships available*
➡ *minority scholarships available*

Well over 80 percent of the student body receives some form of financial assistance. A full 30 percent of students receive law school-funded scholarships or merit grants which total over $1 million per year. Information on scholarships, grants, loans, and employment opportunities is mailed to all applicants.

■ Career Services

Well over 80 percent of law students have been employed in at least one law firm, legal agency, or other law-related position prior to graduation. Many have held two or three such jobs in order to strengthen and diversify their resumes. Puget Sound alumni/ae are employed throughout the U.S. and in 19 foreign countries. Recently compiled employment statistics reveal that our graduates are engaged in: private practice/55 percent; government service/15 percent; business & industry/11 percent; judicial service/10 percent; public interest law/3 percent; academics/3 percent; and advanced studies/3 percent.

Applicant Group for the 1993–1994 Academic Year

Puget Sound/Seattle University Law School

LSAT Score	GPA									
	3.75 +	3.50 - 3.74	3.25 - 3.49	3.00 - 3.24	2.75 - 2.99	2.50 - 2.74	2.25 - 2.49	2.00 - 2.24	Below 2.00	No GPA
175 - 180	L	L	L	L	P	P	U	U	U	L
170 - 174	L	L	L	L	P	P	U	U	U	L
165 - 169	L	L	L	L	P	P	U	U	U	L
160 - 164	L	L	L	L	P	P	U	U	U	L
155 - 159	L	L	P	P	U	U	U	U	U	P
150 - 154	P	P	U	U	U	U	U	U	U	U
145 - 149	U	U	U	U	U	U	U	U	U	U
140 - 144	U	U	U	U	U	U	U	U	U	U
135 - 139	U	U	U	U	U	U	U	U	U	U
130 - 134	U	U	U	U	U	U	U	U	U	U
125 - 129	U	U	U	U	U	U	U	U	U	U
120 - 124	U	U	U	U	U	U	U	U	U	U

L = Likely
P = Possible
U = Unlikely
Of applicants in the Unlikely category, about one in 20 candidates was admitted to the Alternative Admission Program.

Quinnipiac College School of Law

303 University Avenue
Bridgeport, CT 06604-5770

Phone: 203.576.4048

■ Introduction

In the spring of 1992, Bridgeport Law School became affiliated with Quinnipiac College, in Hamden, Connecticut. Now officially Quinnipiac College School of Law, the school is entering a new era in its professional history. A new Law Center consisting of four buildings will be constructed on the Quinnipiac College campus and it is expected that students who enter the law school in the fall of 1994 will complete their second and third years of legal studies at the new facility. The law school, which is provisionally accredited, will be eligible for full accreditation once it moves to the new premises.

Hamden, where students will spend their second and third years, is just 25 miles northeast of Bridgeport and about eight miles from metropolitan New Haven. From that location, students will continue to have easy access to the area's diverse resources. With its beautifully landscaped grounds, Quinnipiac is considered one of the most ideally situated and attractive college campuses in New England.

Bridgeport, located in Fairfield County, is Connecticut's largest city. Its urban setting is easily accessible by train, bus, or car. Only 75 minutes north of New York City and three hours south of Boston, Fairfield County is at the heart of one of the nation's largest concentrations of corporate headquarters and banking institutions. The area offers many excellent employment and residential opportunities as well as extensive cultural and recreational facilities.

■ Enrollment/Student Body

➡ 2,068 applicants   ➡ 937 admitted first-year class 1993
➡ 254 enrolled first-year class 1993   ➡ 531 total full-time
➡ 177 total part-time   ➡ 10% minority
➡ 32% women   ➡ 22 states & foreign countries represented
➡ 155 undergraduate schools represented

Traditionally, the first-year fall class consists of about 225 students taught in four sections, three day and one evening. The law school enrolls 225 students in the fall and 40 students in January.

■ Faculty

➡ 65 total   ➡ 35 full-time   ➡ 30 part-time or adjunct
➡ 20 women   ➡ 5 minority

Although the fundamental strength of the law school lies in the faculty's dedication to academic excellence, the rigors of its programs are tempered by the personal attention and individual regard that students receive. Indeed, the care with which members of the faculty demonstrate their interest in each student's progress and success is a distinguishing characteristic of Quinnipiac School of Law.

In addition to teaching, members of the faculty devote considerable attention to scholarly research. Before joining the faculty, many enjoyed successful legal careers in a variety of areas including corporate, governmental, tax, and general practice.

■ Library and Physical Facilities

➡ 278,000 volumes & equivalents   ➡ library hours: Mon.-Thurs., 8:30 A.M.-11:00 P.M.; Fri.-Sat., 8:30 A.M.-9:00 P.M.; Sun., 10:00 A.M.-11:00 P.M.   ➡ LEXIS   ➡ NEXIS
➡ WESTLAW   ➡ DIALOG   ➡ 6 full-time librarians
➡ library seats 400

Students enjoy free and ample access to the on-line research terminals as well as to the library's IBM PCs.

■ Curriculum

➡ 86 total units/credits required to graduate   ➡ 115 courses available   ➡ J.D. degree available (upon completion of 6 full-time or 8 part-time semesters)   ➡ semesters, start in Aug. & Jan.   ➡ range of first-year class size—15-65

Full-time students are admitted in the fall(day only), while part-time students are admitted in the fall and in the spring.

The first and second year curriculum is traditional and prescribed. There is flexibility within the electives scheme to allow students to fashion their own programs of concentration.

A Quinnipiac Law education offers the opportunity to be either a generalist or specialist. Concentrations include business and tax law, healthcare law, public-interest law, and litigation. The J.D./M.B.A. degree program is also available.

■ Special Programs

A total of eight clinical and internship programs are available to full-time day students after completion of their sixth semester. These programs represent tangible work experience to employers and often provide an important service to the community.

The three clinical programs are civil, tax, and criminal justice. The five internship programs are Corporate Counsel, Municipal Counsel, Public Interest, Legislative, and Judicial.

An Academic Support Program and a writing program are made available to students of the law school.

■ Admission

➡ Bachelor's degree required   ➡ LSAT, LSDAS required
➡ median GPA—3.00   ➡ median LSAT score—155
➡ application fee—$40   ➡ rolling admission, early application preferred   ➡ Pre-Admission Summer Program

Admission is based on a variety of factors—undergraduate scholastic record, scores on the Law School Admission Test, and other evidence such as advanced degrees, employment, experience, and extracurricular activities. Although the best indicator for performance in law school is past performance, this may be rebutted in certain cases when factors in the background of an individual, such as economic, cultural, and physical considerations, indicate that past performance may not be a reliable guide.

In the Pre-Admission Summer Program, students not admitted through the regular admissions process attend a small seven-week session taught by a full-time faculty member, applying normal standards to assess students' performances. Students who attain a grade of C or better are admitted to the regular part-time program. The offering of the Pre-Admission Summer Program is determined on a year-to-year basis. The law school also participates in CLEO.

Admission decisions are made by a faculty admissions committee which reviews every application. The law school places special emphasis on minority recruitment. Application fee waivers are available.

■ Student Activities

The *Quinnipiac Law Review* publishes two to four times a year. The journal is organized and edited by a board of student editors under the guidance of faculty advisors.

The *Connecticut Probate Law Journal* is the result of a cooperative effort with the Connecticut Probate Assembly that chose Quinnipiac, from the three law schools in the state, to produce it.

The Moot Court Board organizes an annual intramural moot court competition for entry onto the Board. The Moot Court Board edits briefs and supervises its own members as they participate in regional and national competitions. During the fall 1993 semester, the Mock Trial Society competed in the National Association of Criminal Defense Lawyers Cathy G. Bennett Criminal Trial Competition, and won two of three Best Advocate awards.

Quinnipiac has a very active Student Bar Association, and students publish their own newspaper titled *Common Pleas*. The law school has local chapters of three international professional law fraternities: Delta Theta Phi; Phi Delta Phi and Phi Alpha Delta. In addition, it has chapters of BALSA, SALSA, Jewish Law Students' Association, and Law Women's Association.

■ Expenses and Financial Aid

➠ *tuition & fees—full-time $13,200; part-time, $550/credit*
➠ *estimated additional expenses—campus identification fee, $25; Student Bar Association fee, $75; student fee, $90*
➠ *academic and need-based merit awards available*
➠ *academic and need-based merit awards available for minorities*
➠ *FAFSA & Quinnipiac Financial Aid application required*
➠ *work/study program*

Room and board fees are available through the University. At the present time, approximately 80 percent of the student body receives some form of financial aid.

■ Housing

Housing is available on campus. There is also ample nonuniversity housing in the area. The Admissions Office assists in the off-campus housing process.

■ Career Services

The office assists students in writing résumés and letters of application, in interviewing techniques, and in other employment-related questions. It sponsors an extensive on-campus recruitment program for summer internships as well as for permanent jobs, and also career symposia to expose students to more diverse areas of work and to apprise them of employment trends.

Placement statistics attest to the success of the law school's students in the contemporary job market. A number of the law school's alumni are judicial clerks, Justice Department attorneys, and associates in prestigious metropolitan firms.

Applicant Group for the 1993–1994 Academic Year

Quinnipiac College School of Law
This grid includes only applicants who earned 120-180 LSAT scores under standard administrations (91% of the total applicant pool).

LSAT Score	3.75 +		3.50 -3.74		3.25 - 3.49		3.00 - 3.24		2.75 - 2.99		2.50 - 2.74		2.25 - 2.49		2.00 - 2.24		Below 2.00		No GPA		Total	
	Apps	Adm	Apps	Adm	Apps	Adm	Apps	Adm	Apps	Adm	Apps	Adm	Apps	Adm	Apps	Adm	Apps	Adm	Apps	Adm	Apps	Adm
175 - 180	0	0	0	0	0	0	0	0	0	0	0	0	0	0	0	0	0	0	0	0	0	0
170 - 174	0	0	0	0	0	0	1	1	0	0	0	0	0	0	0	0	0	0	0	0	1	1
165 - 169	1	1	2	2	2	2	1	1	2	1	1	1	2	1	1	1	1	0	0	0	13	10
160 - 164	4	4	3	3	4	4	10	10	15	14	11	10	10	9	2	1	2	0	1	1	62	56
155 - 159	9	9	16	15	19	18	37	31	43	40	47	41	27	24	8	4	2	1	7	3	215	186
150 - 154	5	5	26	23	48	42	119	102	131	98	121	80	68	30	26	9	2	1	19	11	565	401
145 - 149	10	4	22	7	68	22	131	38	150	40	94	16	61	7	18	0	4	0	22	5	580	139
140 - 144	4	0	16	1	30	2	50	3	73	2	54	3	49	0	27	0	7	0	16	0	326	11
135 - 139	1	0	6	0	11	0	14	1	26	1	20	0	20	0	18	0	3	0	12	0	131	2
130 - 134	0	0	2	1	2	0	2	0	10	0	9	0	15	0	6	1	3	0	6	0	55	2
125 - 129	0	0	0	0	0	0	3	0	0	0	1	0	2	0	2	0	0	0	1	0	9	0
120 - 124	0	0	0	0	0	0	0	0	0	0	1	0	0	0	0	0	0	0	0	0	1	0
Total	34	23	93	52	184	90	368	187	450	196	359	151	254	71	108	16	24	2	84	20	1958	808

Apps = Number of Applicants
Adm = Number Admitted

Regent University School of Law

1000 Centerville Turnpike
Virginia Beach, VA 23464-5041

Phone: 804.523.7444

■ Introduction

The School of Law at Regent University, formerly CBN University, opened in 1986 and is the successor to the O. W. Coburn School of Law at Oral Roberts University. Regent University is a graduate-level institution affiliated with the Christian Broadcasting Network, Inc., a multifaceted television ministry that broadcasts Christian and family-oriented programming in the United States and in 58 foreign countries.

Regent University is located on a beautiful 200-acre campus in Virginia Beach, which is famed for its 28 miles of ocean and bay beaches. It is within an hour's drive from historic Yorktown, Jamestown, and Colonial Williamsburg and within four hours of Washington, DC, the Blue Ridge Mountains, and North Carolina's Outer Banks.

The foremost objective of the School of Law at Regent University is to train professional lawyers to participate effectively in the private and public sectors of this nation. The School of Law is unique, however, in that its curriculum is taught in the context of a historical and Biblical foundation and framework. Students learn not only the current status and trends of the law, but they also learn the historical and Biblical foundations for our Anglo-American legal system.

Regent University School of Law has been approved by the American Bar Association since 1989. Graduates are eligible to take the bar examination in all 50 states and the District of Columbia.

■ Enrollment/Student Body

➡ *500 applicants* ➡ *190 admitted first-year class 1993*
➡ *135 enrolled first-year class 1993* ➡ *325 total full-time*
➡ *5% minority* ➡ *27% women*
➡ *35 states & foreign countries represented*
➡ *118 undergraduate schools represented*

■ Faculty

➡ *25 total* ➡ *13 full-time* ➡ *12 part-time or adjunct*
➡ *4 women* ➡ *2 minority*

Adjunct faculty includes judges, private practitioners, and public prosecutors.

■ Library and Physical Facilities

➡ *280,000 volumes & equivalents* ➡ *library hours: Mon.-Fri., 7:30 A.M.-MIDNIGHT; Sat., 8:00 A.M.-MIDNIGHT*
➡ *LEXIS* ➡ *NEXIS* ➡ *WESTLAW* ➡ *DIALOG*
➡ *INFOTRAC* ➡ *LEGALTRAC*
➡ *4 full-time librarians* ➡ *library seats 200*

Construction of the new Law and Justice Center was completed in the fall of 1993. The center is next door to the 150,000-square-foot university library which houses the law library on the third floor. The law library contains all the materials necessary for training students for the practice of law plus significant materials for advanced research in public policy and law.

■ Curriculum

➡ *90 total units/credits required to graduate*
➡ *75 courses available* ➡ *degrees available: J.D.; J.D./M.B.A.; J.D./M.A. in Government; J.D./M.A. in Management* ➡ *semesters, start in Aug.*
➡ *range of first-year class size—65-75*

The law school admits a limited number of students on a provisional basis. These students are assigned advisors and are required to meet periodically with their advisors for assistance.

A two-day Legal Study Skills Workshop has been incorporated into the new student orientation program. Topics covered include class preparation, case briefing, outlining, and study habits.

At the heart of the School of Law curriculum are the common law courses. The foundational course for the initial year of study is The Common Law. This course includes a historical survey of the Biblical foundations and principles in the Anglo-American common law and an examination of these foundations and principles in light of current legal issues.

The second- and third-year curricula include such basic law courses as Business Associations, Constitutional Law, Secured Transactions, Taxation, Evidence, and Professional Responsibility. In these two years students discover the law governing the administration of justice in the nation.

During each of the three years, students receive training in professional skills designed to equip them for entrance into the legal profession. This preparation includes a law-practice requirement which may be fulfilled by taking either Trial Practice or Negotiations.

■ Externship Opportunities

In addition to the regular course offerings, students have the opportunity to receive academic credit through legal externships. A standing extern program has been established with the local US Attorney's Office and students often seek approval for externships with judges, prosecutors, and public defenders. Students interested in public-interest law can arrange an externship with the American Center for Law and Justice, a not-for-profit public interest law firm dedicated to defending the religious and civil liberties of Americans. Opportunities are also available for students to work with local attorneys providing legal services to the poor.

■ Admission

➡ *Bachelor's degree required for admission*
➡ *application deadline—April 1* ➡ *LSAT, LSDAS required*
➡ *median GPA—3.00* ➡ *median LSAT score—153*
➡ *application fee—$30*

The law school admission committee assesses the qualifications of each applicant by examining his or her undergraduate record, LSAT score, any graduate study or work experience, the applicant's statement of goals, three recommendations and, in most cases, two personal interviews. The committee further determines if the educational experience at Regent University will meet a mutually shared goal discerned by the committee and the student. A student must be willing to receive a legal education in accordance with the university's Statement of Faith.

The law school admits a limited number of second-year transfer students who are in good academic standing at their current law school. All transfer students are required to take The Common Law and Constitutional Law I and II at Regent University.

■ Student Activities

The College of Law and Government publishes the *Journal of Christian Jurisprudence*, which was previously published by the O. W. Coburn School of Law. The journal features articles giving a Biblical perspective on legal as well as public policy-related issues. The latest volume focused on the unalienable rights and the Bill of Rights.

The *Regent University Law Review* provides a forum for a Christian perspective on law in a traditional legal periodical. Student editors and staff members, chosen on the basis of academic achievement and writing ability, gain valuable experience by writing and editing the *Law Review* under the guidance of the law faculty.

In addition to an active student bar association, law students are involved in other organizations including the Grotius International Law Society, the Christian Legal Society, the ABA/Law Student Division, and Women In Law. Law students also are involved in the university-wide Council of Graduate Students and New Generation Christian Fellowship.

■ Expenses and Financial Aid

➡ *full-time tuition & fees—$10,000*
➡ *estimated additional expenses—$550 (books and supplies)*
➡ *scholarships available (performance and need-based, as well as several institutionally funded scholarships and grants, and several named and endowed scholarships)*
➡ *financial aid application—July 15*

■ Career Services

The law school at Regent University has developed a three-year placement strategy. The program includes self-assessment, a general investigation of career opportunities, and a specific career search. Workshops are conducted to assist students with résumé writing, interviews, and career selection.

The Law Career Services Department offers both on-campus interviewing and a Non-Visiting Employers Program. Regent law students also participate in the Virginia law schools public interest and spring recruitment job fairs. For 1993-94, selected students will receive grants from the Virginia Law Foundation for summer clerkships with public-interest organizations. The career services program has a national focus, with its graduates employed in the legal profession in a variety of capacities including judicial clerks, criminal prosecutors, public-interest attorneys, corporate counsel, and as partners and associates in firms across the nation.

Applicant Group for the 1993–1994 Academic Year

Regent University School of Law
This grid includes only applicants who earned 120-180 LSAT scores under standard administrations (90% of all applicants).

LSAT Score	3.75 +		3.50 - 3.74		3.25 - 3.49		3.00 - 3.24		2.75 - 2.99		2.50 - 2.74		2.25 - 2.49		2.00 - 2.24		Below 2.00		No GPA		Total	
	Apps	Adm	Apps	Adm	Apps	Adm	Apps	Adm	Apps	Adm	Apps	Adm	Apps	Adm	Apps	Adm	Apps	Adm	Apps	Adm	Apps	Adm
175 - 180	0	0	1	1	0	0	0	0	0	0	0	0	0	0	0	0	0	0	0	0	1	1
170 - 174	0	0	0	0	0	0	1	1	0	0	0	0	0	0	0	0	0	0	0	0	1	1
165 - 169	1	1	3	3	0	0	1	1	1	1	1	1	0	0	0	0	0	0	0	0	7	7
160 - 164	4	4	8	7	0	0	1	1	4	4	0	0	0	0	0	0	0	0	0	0	17	16
155 - 159	2	2	9	8	4	3	8	7	7	7	9	7	5	3	4	3	0	0	0	0	48	40
150 - 154	8	6	8	7	8	6	18	15	18	12	11	4	8	2	6	0	3	0	1	1	89	53
145 - 149	3	2	10	8	18	10	21	12	39	9	14	2	14	2	4	1	3	0	0	0	126	46
140 - 144	3	1	9	1	9	2	11	0	22	1	15	1	9	0	9	0	1	0	0	0	88	6
135 - 139	0	0	3	0	2	0	8	0	11	0	8	0	6	0	5	0	3	0	0	0	46	0
130 - 134	0	0	1	0	0	0	0	0	2	0	1	0	5	0	4	0	0	0	0	0	13	0
125 - 129	0	0	0	0	0	0	0	0	1	0	0	0	1	0	0	0	0	0	0	0	2	0
120 - 124	0	0	0	0	0	0	0	0	1	0	0	0	0	0	0	0	0	0	1	0	2	0
Total	21	16	52	35	41	21	69	37	106	34	59	15	48	7	32	4	10	0	2	1	440	170

Apps = Number of Applicants
Adm = Number Admitted

University of Richmond—T.C. Williams School of Law

University of Richmond, VA 23173   Phone: 804.289.8189

■ Introduction

The University of Richmond School of Law, founded in 1870, enjoys an established reputation for preparing its graduates for legal careers throughout the US. Accredited by the ABA and a member of the AALS, its J.D. qualifies graduates to seek admission to the bar of all 50 states and the District of Columbia.

Situated on the university's beautiful suburban campus, the law school community thrives on the stimulation found only in such an academic setting. Yet, the campus is within a 20-minute drive of Richmond's pulsating legal community.

■ Enrollment/Student Body

➡ *1,875 applicants*   ➡ *502 admitted first-year class 1993*
➡ *163 enrolled first-year class 1993*   ➡ *456 total full-time*
➡ *1 total part-time*   ➡ *22% minority*   ➡ *50% women*
➡ *44 states & foreign countries represented*
➡ *175 undergraduate schools represented*

■ Faculty

➡ *87 total*   ➡ *23 full-time*   ➡ *64 part-time or adjunct*
➡ *41 women*   ➡ *10 minority*

■ Library and Physical Facilities

➡ *215,320 volumes & equivalents*   ➡ *library hours: 105 per week—Mon.-Thurs., 8:30 A.M.-MIDNIGHT; Fri., 7:30 A.M.-9:00 P.M.; Sat., 9:00 A.M.-9:00 P.M.; Sun., 10:00 A.M.-MIDNIGHT*
➡ *LEXIS*   ➡ *NEXIS*   ➡ *WESTLAW*   ➡ *DIALOG*
➡ *VuText*   ➡ *VA Legislative Bill Service*
➡ *5 full-time librarians*   ➡ *library seats 601*

The law school building provides technically equipped classrooms, seminar rooms, a state-of-the-art law library, a magnificent courtroom, faculty offices, administrative offices, lounges, and offices for student organizations.

Every student is assigned to a study carrel in our expansive law library. Each carrel consists of a desk with a sliding tray for a laptop computer and a secure storage area allowing students ready access to books and notes. These carrels soon will be linked via students' personal computers to a school-wide computer system giving instant access to the electronic age in law.

■ Curriculum

➡ *clinical programs offered*   ➡ *86 units/credits required to graduate*   ➡ *111 total courses available*
➡ *degrees available: J.D.; J.D./M.B.A.; J.D./M.U.R.P.; J.D./M.H.A.; J.D./M.B.A.*   ➡ *semesters, start in Aug.*
➡ *range of first-year class size—75-80*

Courses in environmental law, contracts, torts, criminal law, procedure, property, and constitutional law comprise the first-year curriculum. Required upper-level courses include professional responsibility and a third-year writing seminar. Elective courses in a variety of areas are available to satisfy each student's interests.

In addition, all students complete a program in legal reasoning, writing, research, and fundamental lawyering skills and values. In mock law offices, students interview and counsel clients, negotiate simulated transactions, and resolve legal disputes through trial and appeal.

■ International Program

In addition to an on-campus curriculum, students may participate in our popular Summer Program in International Law in Cambridge, England. For more than 17 years, our law students have been taught by some of the world's most renowned teachers of international law from the Cambridge faculty, giving students a basic understanding of international law and trade.

■ Special Programs

Several dual-degree programs are offered that allow students to earn the J.D. degree as well as a master's degree in a related discipline. Students can reduce the time and cost associated with obtaining two degrees while enjoying the study of two fields of interest. Dual-degree programs are available in Business Administration, Health Administration, Social Work, and Urban Studies and Planning.

The law school operates the Youth Advocacy Clinic in which qualified third-year law students represent clients. This clinic is staffed by a teaching, practicing attorney who works together with students to represent juveniles in both civil and criminal judicial proceedings. Students receive assistance in developing trial strategies and guidance in courtroom procedure while handling several court cases each semester.

The Law School also arranges exciting clinical placements for academic credit in the nearby courts and law offices. Among the opportunities available are positions in various Commonwealth, city, and county attorneys' offices; the Virginia Attorney General's Office; the US Attorney's Office; the ACLU; environmental organizations; and the Alternative Dispute Resolution Center.

■ Student Activities

A student board publishes *The University of Richmond Law Review* on a quarterly basis. The *Law Review* presents scholarly articles by professors, judges, attorneys, and students on matters of current interest in the law.

Richmond's moot court activities allow students to test their research, brief-writing, trial, and appellate advocacy skills. Students participate in intraschool tournaments that lead to membership on the Moot Court Board and on teams that represent the law school in regional and national competitions.

The Client Counseling and Negotiation Board organizes intra- and interschool competitions. It most recently hosted the National Environmental Negotiation Competition, which was attended by teams from schools throughout the country.

Other student organizations playing a vital role in the law school community include the Student Bar Association, the Law Student Division of the ABA, the Public Interest Law Association, the Black Law Students Association, the Women's Law Association, and the Multi-Ethnic Law Students Association.

■ Admission

➡ *B.S./B.A. degree required for admission*
➡ *application deadline—Jan. 15*
➡ *LSAT, LSDAS required* ➡ *median GPA—3.23*
➡ *median LSAT score—161* ➡ *application fee—$35*

Applications are reviewed beginning in late January. All decisions are released by May 15. The undergraduate GPA and LSAT are two important items considered by the admissions committee, although the committee is also interested in extracurricular and community-service activities and employment experience. The law school provides an equal educational opportunity without regard to race, color, national origin, age, sex, sexual orientation, handicap, or religion.

Applicants who apply and complete their admissions files with our office before January 1 (including all support documentation) will be eligible to participate in the Richmond Applicant Video Essay (RAVE) program. RAVE allows selected applicants to personalize their files by providing a videotaped interview to be viewed by the admissions committee. Applicants will be selected in early January and will receive detailed instructions at that time. Admission conferences are available in November, December, and January. Although these conferences do not impact on the committee's decision, they are invaluable in providing information and answering questions.

■ Expenses and Financial Aid

➡ *tuition & fees—full-time, $14,040; part-time, $695/credit hour* ➡ *estimated additional expenses—books, $700; room & board, $4,500; personal expenses, $1,350*
➡ *merit and need-based scholarships available*
➡ *minority scholarships available*
➡ *financial aid available; FAF form due Feb. 25*

■ Career Services

Our Career Services Office is responsible for bringing students and legal employers together. Over 85 percent of our recent classes were employed within nine months after receiving their diplomas.

In addition to reviewing résumés, counseling students, and arranging for on-campus interviews, our office conducts many innovative marketing campaigns. We were the first law school in the country to send videotaped interviews to law firms. Students identify geographic areas in which they are most interested; we then contact employers from these areas with information about the law school, its curriculum, and student résumés.

Applicant Group for the 1993–1994 Academic Year

University of Richmond—T.C. Williams School of Law
This grid includes only applicants who earned 120-180 LSAT scores under standard administrations.

LSAT Score	GPA																					
	3.75 +		3.50 -3.74		3.25 - 3.49		3.00 - 3.24		2.75 - 2.99		2.50 - 2.74		2.25 - 2.49		2.00 - 2.24		Below 2.00		No GPA		Total	
	Apps	Adm	Apps	Adm	Apps	Adm	Apps	Adm	Apps	Adm	Apps	Adm	Apps	Adm	Apps	Adm	Apps	Adm	Apps	Adm	Apps	Adm
175 - 180	0	0	0	0	0	0	1	1	0	0	0	0	0	0	0	0	0	0	0	0	1	1
170 - 174	0	0	1	0	2	2	6	6	4	4	0	0	0	0	0	0	0	0	0	0	13	12
165 - 169	2	2	6	5	16	16	22	21	11	11	6	2	4	3	0	0	0	0	0	0	67	60
160 - 164	5	5	26	26	50	49	69	67	48	25	26	5	16	4	4	4	0	0	1	1	245	182
155 - 159	16	10	55	33	96	44	129	43	77	15	47	11	21	5	4	0	2	0	1	0	448	161
150 - 154	13	1	53	6	109	11	93	5	101	8	63	4	31	3	16	0	2	0	2	0	483	38
145 - 149	5	0	21	2	45	5	67	2	54	6	62	7	29	2	15	0	4	0	6	2	308	26
140 - 144	0	0	9	1	16	0	22	3	30	0	24	1	23	1	6	0	1	0	2	1	133	7
135 - 139	1	0	2	0	6	0	12	0	13	0	5	0	10	0	6	0	2	0	6	0	63	0
130 - 134	0	0	1	0	1	0	2	0	9	0	2	0	6	0	3	0	1	0	1	0	26	0
125 - 129	0	0	0	0	0	0	1	0	3	0	0	0	1	0	1	0	1	0	0	0	7	0
120 - 124	0	0	0	0	0	0	0	0	1	0	0	0	1	0	0	0	0	0	0	0	2	0
Total	42	18	174	73	341	127	424	148	351	69	235	30	142	18	55	0	13	0	19	4	1796	487

Apps = Number of Applicants
Adm = Number Admitted
Reflects 96% of the total applicant pool.

Rutgers—The State University—School of Law—Camden

406 Penn Street
Camden, NJ 08102

Phone: 609.225.6102

■ Introduction

Set against a center-city Philadelphia backdrop, Rutgers University's thriving urban campus in Camden is a handsome blend of converted Victorian buildings and newly constructed facilities. The School of Law shares the spacious campus mall with two undergraduate colleges, the Graduate School, and the School of Business. A member of the Association of American Law Schools, the school is included on the list of approved schools of the American Bar Association.

■ Enrollment/Student Body

➥ *2,318 applicants* ➥ *710 admitted first-year class 1993*
➥ *222 enrolled first-year class 1993* ➥ *584 total full-time*
➥ *137 total part-time* ➥ *29% minority*
➥ *45% women* ➥ *31 states & foreign countries represented* ➥ *230 undergraduate schools represented*

■ Faculty

➥ *37 full-time* ➥ *60 part-time or adjunct*
➥ *20 women* ➥ *6 minority*

The law school faculty is engaged in a dynamic program of scholarship, teaching, and service to the bar and community. The faculty is ranked among the 20 most accomplished producers of scholarly articles in eminent journals. Faculty scholarship has been cited by numerous courts, including the New Jersey and United States Supreme Courts. Faculty members also serve as consultants and reporters for the American Bar Association, the American Law Institute, and several federal and state commissions, and are counsel in important public-interest litigation.

■ Library and Physical Facilities

➥ *450,000 volumes & equivalents* ➥ *library hours: Mon.-Thurs., 8:00 A.M.-MIDNIGHT; Fri., 8:00 A.M.-10:00 P.M.; Sat., 9:00 A.M.-5:00 P.M.; Sun., 10:00 A.M.-MIDNIGHT*
➥ *LEXIS* ➥ *NEXIS* ➥ *WESTLAW*
➥ *7 full-time librarians* ➥ *library seats 450*

Noted for its extensive collection of East European legal materials, the law library, with its especially broad holdings in government documents and legal periodicals, ranks among the top 25 in the country. Students receive extensive training in the use of computers in legal research. A major renovation to the building for additional library space is currently under construction.

■ Curriculum

➥ *Academic Support Program* ➥ *Tax Honors Program*
➥ *International and Comparative Law Honors Program*
➥ *84 credits required to graduate* ➥ *150 courses available*
➥ *degrees available: J.D./M.B.A.; J.D./M.A. (Pol. Sci.); J.D./M.C.R.P. (Urban Planning)*
➥ *semesters, start in Aug. & Jan.*

The full-time program requires six semesters; the part-time evening program is completed in eight semesters, plus one summer session. Both programs are subject to the same admission and academic standards, and are taught by the same faculty. First-year required courses include Civil Procedure, Contracts, Torts, and Legal Research and Writing the first semester, followed by Constitutional Law, Criminal Law, Property, and Moot Court the second semester. After the core curriculum is completed, students select their own courses. One seminar and courses in both Professional Responsibility and Introduction to Federal Income Taxation must be included for graduation.

The general curriculum prepares students for work in any jurisdiction of the United States.

■ Special Programs

Formal honors programs for concentrations in taxation and international law are available. The law school, in conjunction with the Society for the Reform of Criminal Law, also publishes a refereed scholarly journal devoted to international and comparative criminal law, *The Criminal Law Forum*. The international and comparative law program also encompasses a faculty and student exchange program with the University of Graz, Austria.

Joint-degree programs are offered in Urban Planning, Political Science, and Business Administration. Upon approval by the faculty, students may also pursue ad hoc joint-degree programs within Rutgers University or other institutions, leading to the award of the Juris Doctor and a Master's or Doctoral Degree.

The Externship Program furnishes third-year students an opportunity to work 12 to 15 hours a week in various federal and state judicial chambers, public agencies, or public-interest organizations. Students in the clinical program represent low income elderly clients and small businesses.

The student-directed *Rutgers Law Journal* offers in-depth training in independent research and analysis of current legal problems. One issue of the journal each year is devoted to a symposium on state constitutional law.

The extensive Moot Court Programs provide trial experience before panels of judges and practicing attorneys.

■ Admission

➥ *Baccalaureate degree required for admission*
➥ *application deadline—March 1*
➥ *LSAT, LSDAS required* ➥ *median GPA—3.22*
➥ *median LSAT score—157* ➥ *application fee—$40*

Entering class size ranges between 200 and 250. Those students who matriculated in fall 1993, under the regular admissions process, had a mean LSAT of 160, with a 3.2 undergraduate average. The school also has a special admissions program that applies a greater range of criteria. A few places are available for applicants for advanced standing; transfer students may be admitted at the beginning of either semester only upon completion of one full year of law study.

▪ Student Activities

Among the numerous student organizations are ALIANZA (the Hispanic Students Association), Asian/Pacific American Law Students Association (APALSA), Association for Public Interest Law (APIL), Black Law Students Association (BLSA), Brehon Law Society (Irish students association), Christian Legal Society, Community Outreach Group, Democrats Society, Environmental Law Students Association, Federalist Society, Francis Deak International Law Society, Gay-Bar, Human Rights Group, Italian-American Law Students Organization (ITALSO), Jewish Law Students Association (JLSA), Law Journal (publishes the *Rutgers Law Journal*), Phi Alpha Delta law fraternity (PAD), the Public Interest Research Group (PIRG), and the Women's Law Caucus.

In addition, there are active intramural programs in various sports for men and women. The gymnasium offers recreational swimming, tennis, racquetball, squash and basketball.

▪ Expenses and Financial Aid

➥ *full-time tuition & fees—resident, $7,233.50; nonresident, $10,638* ➥ *part-time tuition—resident, $264.25 per credit; nonresident, $407.75 per credit* ➥ *student fee—$156.35 per semester* ➥ *scholarships available* ➥ *minority scholarships available* ➥ *financial aid available; FAFSA form due March 1 for full consideration*

In the 1992-1993 academic year, over $5.7 million was distributed to students in the law school through fellowships, grants, loans, and employment. The average financial aid package was about $11,000, with 75 percent of all law students receiving some form of assistance. The largest program was the Stafford Loan Program, providing over $3.0 million to some 442 students.

▪ Housing

An air-conditioned and carpeted residence hall, with 12 two-bedroom and 50 four-bedroom apartments, opened in 1986. Four students share each furnished unit consisting of a living room, kitchen and dining area, and bathroom. This year, leases that include utilities are $2,900 for nine months, and $3,500 for a year. There also are abundant housing opportunities in the nearby suburbs or in Philadelphia, made more convenient by an excellent transportation system. In addition, first-year students are invited to attend a Housing Opportunity Day sponsored by the Student Bar Association.

▪ Career Services

The Career Services office has five staff members, as well as computer databases and numerous publications available to assist students in achieving their career goals. Each year, nearly 200 national and regional law firms and agencies interview second- and third-year students for summer and permanent employment through on-campus recruiting programs, job fairs, and a consortium of Delaware Valley law schools. In recent years, over 90 percent of each graduating class has been employed within nine months after commencement. Members of the recent graduating classes have accepted employment in many states—from the East Coast to California and abroad.

Applicant Group for the 1993–1994 Academic Year

Rutgers The State University—School of Law—Camden
This grid includes only applicants who earned 120-180 LSAT scores under standard administrations.

LSAT Score	3.75 +		3.50 -3.74		3.25 - 3.49		3.00 - 3.24		2.75 - 2.99		2.50 - 2.74		2.25 - 2.49		2.00 - 2.24		Below 2.00		No GPA		Total	
	Apps	Adm	Apps	Adm	Apps	Adm	Apps	Adm	Apps	Adm	Apps	Adm	Apps	Adm	Apps	Adm	Apps	Adm	Apps	Adm	Apps	Adm
175 - 180	2	2	0	0	0	0	1	1	0	0	0	0	0	0	0	0	0	0	0	0	3	3
170 - 174	1	1	3	3	3	3	3	3	2	2	6	5	1	1	1	1	0	0	0	0	20	19
165 - 169	9	9	9	9	15	15	12	12	14	11	9	8	2	2	1	1	0	0	0	0	71	67
160 - 164	14	14	35	35	35	34	57	55	45	37	29	19	16	11	6	1	1	0	5	2	243	208
155 - 159	28	28	59	48	103	66	102	51	72	16	40	7	15	4	7	1	3	1	7	2	436	224
150 - 154	16	10	59	14	89	12	110	20	93	16	61	6	29	6	11	1	2	0	5	2	475	86
145 - 149	14	3	46	7	59	14	102	17	98	16	53	4	40	0	14	0	7	0	9	2	442	63
140 - 144	6	0	10	2	39	3	54	4	75	0	54	0	46	0	17	0	4	0	9	0	314	9
135 - 139	2	0	5	0	11	0	23	0	25	0	27	0	24	0	9	0	7	0	5	0	138	0
130 - 134	0	0	1	0	3	0	4	0	12	0	15	0	16	0	8	0	2	0	6	0	67	0
125 - 129	0	0	0	0	0	0	1	0	5	0	2	0	2	0	1	0	3	0	0	0	14	0
120 - 124	0	0	0	0	0	0	0	0	0	0	0	0	2	0	1	0	0	0	1	0	4	0
Total	92	67	227	118	357	147	469	163	441	98	296	48	193	24	76	5	29	1	47	8	2227	679

Apps = Number of Applicants
Adm = Number Admitted
Reflects 96% of the total applicant pool.

Rutgers University School of Law—Newark

S.I. Newhouse Center for Law & Justice
15 Washington Street
Newark, NJ 07102

Phone: 201.648.5557

■ Introduction

The Rutgers School of Law—Newark is the oldest law school in New Jersey. The School of Law is accredited by the American Bar Association and registered by the Board of Regents of New York. It has a chapter of the Order of the Coif.

The School of Law is located on the urban campus of Rutgers University in Newark. The social, cultural, vocational, and education opportunities of the New York-Newark area combine to provide a fitting location for the study of law.

Qualities that typify the Rutgers School of Law—Newark include its informal atmosphere, its nationally recognized faculty, a comparatively favorable tuition, a public-interest focus, and a very diverse student body. Almost 80 percent of the students are New Jersey residents, but all parts of the country are represented.

■ Enrollment/Student Body

➡ *2,864 applicants*   ➡ *651 admitted first-year class 1993*
➡ *242 enrolled first-year class 1993*   ➡ *527 total full-time*
➡ *247 total part-time*   ➡ *31% minority*
➡ *46% women*   ➡ *15 states & foreign countries represented*
➡ *146 undergraduate schools represented*

New Jersey residents receive no preference except in admission from the waiting list.

■ Faculty

➡ *35 full-time*   ➡ *45 part-time or adjunct*   ➡ *8 women*
➡ *5 minority*   ➡ *8 full-time clinical staff*

■ Library and Physical Facilities

➡ *392,796 volumes & equivalents*   ➡ *library hours: Mon.-Fri., 8:00 A.M.-MIDNIGHT; Sat., 9:00 A.M.-MIDNIGHT; Sun., NOON-MIDNIGHT*   ➡ *LEXIS*   ➡ *NEXIS*
➡ *WESTLAW*   ➡ *9 full-time librarians*
➡ *13 support staff*   ➡ *library seats 394*

The Justice Henry Ackerson Library has an extensive collection of primary and secondary legal materials and associated finding tools for the federal law of the United States and the law of all fifty states, international law, and the law of England. The library is a depository for federal and New Jersey government publications. A training program in WESTLAW and LEXIS automated legal research programs is offered to each student as part of the course in Legal Research and Writing I & II.

■ Curriculum

➡ *Academic Support Program*   ➡ *84 credits required to graduate*   ➡ *research and teaching assistantships*
➡ *55 courses available*   ➡ *degrees available: J.D./M.A., Criminal Justice; J.D./M.C.R.P.; J.D./M.A. Pol. Sci.; J.D./Ph.D. Philosophy*   ➡ *semesters, start in Aug.*

Following the required courses, the law school allows the student substantial freedom in the selection of courses and seminars. During the four upper-class terms, approximately 200 class and seminar hours are available to satisfy the 53 credit-hours required.

Second- and third-year clinics include the Urban Legal Clinic, Constitutional Litigation Clinic, Women's Rights Clinic, Environmental Law Clinic, and Animal Rights Clinic.

Only limited summer courses are available. The first-year curriculum is prescribed except for one enrichment elective; the second and third years are fully elective.

A part-time program permits students to earn a J.D. degree in the evening over a four or four-and-one-half year period. Evening summer classes are available and are necessary for those students who wish to complete their program in four years. The summer after the first year is required.

The law school permits limited cross-registration with other Rutgers graduate programs, such as business, social work, sociology, economics, and political science. Law students may enroll in certain courses in these graduate schools and receive up to nine credits toward the law degree.

With permission, upper-class students may engage in independent research projects under the supervision of a member of the faculty and may earn credit for work in the chambers of federal and state judges.

■ Admission

➡ *B.A. required for admission—in exceptional cases, 3/4 of B.A. acceptable*   ➡ *application deadline—March 1*
➡ *LSAT, LSDAS required*   ➡ *median GPA—3.39*
➡ *median LSAT score—161*   ➡ *application fee—$40*

While factors other than undergraduate GPAs and LSAT scores are given significant weight in admissions decisions, applicants should be aware that approximately 11 applications are received for each seat. The mean scores of the classes entering in the last five years under the regular admissions program have been around a 3.4 GPA and the 88th percentile LSAT ranges.

There is a Minority Student Admission Program for minority and disadvantaged applicants. Minorities include Black/African, Asian, Hispanic, and Native Americans. Disadvantaged applicants include nonminorities who grew up as members of low-income families with a history of poverty or who can demonstrate that for other reasons they are educationally disadvantaged. The mean scores of persons entering under the Minority Student Program were around the 44th percentile range (LSAT), and 3.0 (GPA). Inquiries concerning this program should be directed to the Dean of the Minority Student Program.

LSAT scores older than three years from date of application to law school are not accepted. Applications received after March 1 have little prospect of favorable action. Applicants whose files do not contain all required documentation by June 1 will be denied admission. First-year students are accepted for classes commencing in the fall only. Transfer and visiting student applications are also accepted for the spring term, but only students with excellent law school records are accepted at any time.

Personal interviews are not a part of the admissions process, and applicants are requested not to seek them. Periodically during the academic year, the Director of Admissions conducts group meetings to answer questions of general interest and to explain admissions procedures. Any interested person should call the Office of Admissions to make an appointment for one of these meetings.

■ Student Activities

Publications—Students contribute to the *Rutgers Law Review*, the *Rutgers Journal of Computers, Technology and the Law*, and the *Women's Rights Law Reporter*.

Organizations—The variety of student-run organizations reflects the varied professional, political, social, and community interests of the student body. There are approximately 24 such organizations.

■ Expenses and Financial Aid

➡ *full-time tuition & fees—resident, $7,249; nonresident, $10,653* ➡ *part-time tuition & fees—resident, $264.25 per credit hour, plus student fee of $166/semester; nonresident, $407.75 per credit hour, plus student fee of $166/semester* ➡ *estimated additional expenses—$12,000-$14,000 (living expenses, books, travel, miscellaneous)* ➡ *need-based scholarships available*

➡ *Graduate Law Fellowship (1-year tuition)* ➡ *merit scholarships* ➡ *minority scholarships available* ➡ *Ralph Bunche Fellowships (full tuition and stipend)* ➡ *financial aid available; FAFSA and Rutgers Institutional Form (FA005) due March 1*

The school administers an aid program for students in the school that integrates scholarships, loans, and college work-study into a total program based upon the student's financial needs within the limits of the funds available. In most cases, students are expected to provide for most of their personal living expenses.

■ Housing

An eight-story university apartment complex offers 22 two-bedroom units and 66 four-bedroom units, as well as 10 apartments for married students of the graduate schools of Rutgers University in Newark. Other accommodations are available in the vicinity of the school, as well as in nearby suburban areas and New York City. Public transportation is readily available.

■ Career Services

The Office of Career Services provides information, job hunting, strategy training (including interview workshops and résumé review), and contacts, both direct (through on-campus interviews, résumé collection and job postings), and indirect (through lists, directories and alumnae/i records).

In the past several years, over 85 percent of the graduates seeking law placement have obtained law-related jobs within six months of graduation.

Applicant Group for the 1993–1994 Academic Year

Rutgers University School of Law—Newark
This grid includes only applicants who earned 120-180 LSAT scores under standard administrations.

LSAT Score	GPA																					
	3.75 +		3.50 -3.74		3.25 - 3.49		3.00 - 3.24		2.75 - 2.99		2.50 - 2.74		2.25 - 2.49		2.00 - 2.24		Below 2.00		No GPA		Total	
	Apps	Adm	Apps	Adm	Apps	Adm	Apps	Adm	Apps	Adm	Apps	Adm	Apps	Adm	Apps	Adm	Apps	Adm	Apps	Adm	Apps	Adm
175 - 180	0	0	0	0	1	1	1	1	0	0	1	0	0	0	0	0	0	0	0	0	3	2
170 - 174	2	2	6	5	3	3	2	2	5	5	4	3	0	0	0	0	0	0	1	1	23	21
165 - 169	15	15	21	21	24	21	25	23	16	14	13	9	1	1	0	0	0	0	1	1	116	105
160 - 164	19	18	47	44	73	69	62	51	41	18	26	11	7	1	4	0	0	0	5	3	284	215
155 - 159	20	18	74	49	109	38	93	17	69	10	36	2	24	1	10	0	1	1	6	2	442	138
150 - 154	22	6	51	8	104	12	129	25	87	7	55	2	29	2	14	0	2	0	10	3	503	65
145 - 149	8	3	37	1	72	6	106	16	97	12	75	6	38	0	25	0	3	0	25	1	486	45
140 - 144	11	0	14	4	33	2	70	7	80	5	77	2	61	2	29	0	9	0	18	0	402	22
135 - 139	3	0	14	2	25	1	33	1	53	0	41	0	45	0	33	0	6	0	13	0	266	4
130 - 134	0	0	0	0	4	0	8	0	21	0	18	0	32	0	16	0	8	0	7	0	114	0
125 - 129	0	0	1	0	1	0	5	0	3	0	6	0	1	0	3	0	3	0	1	0	24	0
120 - 124	0	0	0	0	0	0	0	0	0	0	1	0	1	0	0	0	0	0	1	0	3	0
Total	100	62	265	134	449	153	534	143	472	71	353	35	239	7	134	0	32	1	88	11	2666	617

Apps = Number of Applicants
Adm = Number Admitted
Reflects 96% of the total applicant pool.

St. John's University School of Law

8000 Utopia Parkway
Jamaica, NY 11439

Phone: 718.990.6611

■ Introduction

St. John's University School of Law is a forceful presence
and an integral part of the New York metropolitan area.
It imparts to its students training and competency in the
basic skills and techniques of the legal profession, a
grasp of the history and the system of common law, and
a familiarity with important statutes and decisions in
federal and state jurisdictions, including the state of
New York. The School of Law is located on the Queens
Campus of St. John's University. Situated on almost 100
rolling acres in a residential area of New York City, the
campus boasts a spectacular view of the Manhattan sky-
line. St. John's School of Law is approved by the ABA
and is a member of the AALS.

■ Enrollment/Student Body

➡ 3,590 applicants   ➡ 992 admitted first-year class 1993
➡ 305 enrolled first-year class 1993   ➡ 867 total full-time
➡ 312 total part-time   ➡ 14% minority
➡ 40% women   ➡ 117 undergraduate schools represented
in 1993 entering class

■ Faculty

➡ 63 total   ➡ 50 full-time   ➡ 13 part-time or adjunct
➡ 14 full-time women   ➡ 7 full-time minority

■ Library and Physical Facilities

➡ 408,738 volumes & equivalents   ➡ library hours: Mon.,-
Fri., 8:30 A.M.-MIDNIGHT; Sat.-Sun., 10:00 A.M.-11:00 P.M.
➡ LEXIS   ➡ NEXIS   ➡ WESTLAW   ➡ DIALOG
➡ 7 full-time librarians   ➡ library seats 607

The showpiece of the law school building is its beautiful
state-of-the-art law library. It contains a 22-terminal computer classroom, a 30-terminal computer laboratory, and
nine study rooms for student conferences. The library occupies approximately 60,000 square feet on five of the
seven building levels. It has been designated a depository library for U.S. government documents.

■ Curriculum

➡ Academic Support Program
➡ 85 credits required to graduate   ➡ 126 courses available
➡ degrees available: J.D.; B.A./B.S. & J.D.; J.D./M.A. Gov't.
& Politics; M.B.A./J.D.   ➡ semesters, start in Aug. & Jan.

■ Special Programs

An elective clinical program is available to second- and
third-year full-time students.

In the Civil Clinical Seminar, students work 12 hours
per week in (1) a legal services office assisting lawyers
who provide legal representation to the poor in a variety
of civil matters; or (2) a public service or governmental
agency such as the United States Attorney's Office, the

Securities and Exchange Commission, and the New York
Legal Aid Society.

In the Criminal Clinical Seminar, students work 12
hours per week in a District Attorney's office, a Legal
Aid office, or in the law department of the Supreme
Court or Criminal Court.

In the Judicial Clinical Seminar, students work 12 hours
per week in the federal, state, or city court system.

The Estate Administration Clinical Component is offered in conjunction with the elective Estate
Administration. Participants assist the Surrogate in
nearby counties and receive practical insight into the
functioning of the Surrogate's Court, which is responsible for the judicial administering of decedent's estates.

■ Live Client—In-School Clinic

Beginning with the fall 1993, this in-school, live client
clinic will enable students to represent actual clients in
real cases under the close supervision of a faculty member. The clinic is designed to reproduce the experience of
a beginning associate in a small litigation law firm. Students will actually interview clients, draft pleadings and
litigation papers, perform legal research, participate in
discovery proceedings, prepare for trial, engage in settlement negotiations and try cases, while honing skills such
as decision-making and office management. The three-
credit per semester clinic will be open to second- and
third-year students who must enroll for a full academic
year and devote a minimum of 12 hours per week.

■ Special Diversity Admissions Program

The law school sponsors a special educational program
for individuals who have suffered the effects of discrimination, chronic financial hardship, and/or other social,
educational, or physical disadvantages to such an extent
that their undergraduate performance or LSAT score
would not otherwise warrant unconditional acceptance
into the entering class. This program, which is available
at no charge to the participants, consists of a substantial
course taught and graded according to the same qualitative standard applied to all first-year courses, as well as
a legal writing course. The program enables individuals
whose LSAT score and/or grade-point average are not
reliable predictors of their success to demonstrate that
they have the ability to succeed in the study of law.

■ Admission Standards

➡ Bachelor's degree required   ➡ application deadlines—
March 1 & Oct. 1   ➡ LSAT, LSDAS required
➡ average GPA—3.20   ➡ average LSAT score—158
➡ application fee—$50

■ Student Activities

Publications:—*St. John's Law Review, The Catholic Lawyer, Journal of Legal Commentary, International Law Review of the New York State Bar Association, American Bankruptcy Institute Law Review.*

Mock Trial and Appellate Activities—Moot Court, Criminal Law Institute, Civil Trial Institute.

Specialized Legal Activities—The Student Bar Association, Admiralty Law Society, Women's Law Association, Bankruptcy Law Society, Environmental Law Club, Entertainment and Sports Club, International Law Society, Intellectual Property, Labor and Employment Club, Real Property Club, and Client Counseling Competition. The School also maintains chapters in two legal societies, Phi Delta, Phi and Phi Alpha Delta and the Black, Asian and Latino Law Students Association.

■ Expenses and Financial Aid

➡ *tuition & fees—full-time, $15,500; part-time, $11,650*
➡ *scholarships available: St. Thomas More, University Scholarships and Law School Scholarships*
➡ *diversity minority scholarships available*
➡ *financial aid available; FAFSA & FAF by April 1*

Although there are no dormitory facilities at St. John's, many students find suitable living accommodations in the vicinity of the university. A housing service for all St. John's students is provided by the university's Office of Student Life. In addition, the law school Admissions Office coordinates a housing network for law school students. Students with housing needs are invited to contact the housing network coordinator in the law school Admissions Office for assistance and information. Average housing costs run approximately $500 per month.

■ Career Services

The Office of Career Development, supervised by the Assistant Dean, provides an array of services to students and alumni, including résumé and cover letter critiquing, mock interview coaching, career and job opening newsletters, lists of prospective employers, interview programs, and career education panels. Students in the class of 1992 have obtained employment in many areas of the legal profession, including the largest New York law firms and smaller firms throughout the metropolitan area and elsewhere.

Alumni of the School of Law are currently practicing in all states and territories of the United States. Many have achieved positions of prominence in executive and legislative branches of the government, as members of the judiciary, and in both private and corporate practice. The governors of New York and the U.S. Virgin Islands, a former governor of California, and the chairman of the Democratic party are graduates of St. John's.

Applicant Group for the 1993–1994 Academic Year

St. John's University School of Law
This grid includes only applicants who earned 120-180 LSAT scores under standard administrations.

LSAT Score	3.75 +		3.50 -3.74		3.25 - 3.49		3.00 - 3.24		2.75 - 2.99		2.50 - 2.74		2.25 - 2.49		Below 2.50		No GPA		Total	
	Apps	Adm	Apps	Adm	Apps	Adm	Apps	Adm	Apps	Adm	Apps	Adm	Apps	Adm	Apps	Adm	Apps	Adm	Apps	Adm
175 - 180	0	0	1	1	1	1	2	2	0	0	0	0	0	0	0	0	0	0	4	4
170 - 174	2	2	3	3	2	2	2	2	2	2	1	1	0	0	0	0	1	1	13	13
165 - 169	8	8	10	10	18	18	20	19	17	17	8	8	3	2	4	2	0	0	88	84
160 - 164	16	16	30	30	59	58	73	69	55	55	36	34	11	7	4	0	2	1	286	270
155 - 159	35	29	87	70	143	116	162	131	102	59	84	49	39	15	11	5	8	5	671	479
150 - 154	41	11	104	18	221	43	225	43	177	22	120	20	66	10	31	3	15	5	1000	175
Below 150	44	2	128	1	201	3	368	4	344	4	274	4	184	2	139	0	73	1	1732	21
Total	146	68	363	133	645	241	852	270	697	159	523	116	303	36	166	10	99	13	3794	1046

Apps = Number of Applicants
Adm = Number Admitted
Reflects 94% of the total applicant pool.

Saint Louis University School of Law

3700 Lindell Blvd.
St. Louis, MO 63108

Phone: 314.658.2800

■ Introduction

At Saint Louis University School of Law, you will find a
unique character and atmosphere that are the result of a
number of factors, including Jesuit institutional traditions and goals, the law faculty and students, and the
quality of life in a thriving midwestern city. The School
of Law is known for its open and friendly atmosphere,
for the rapport among students and between students
and faculty, and for its inviting physical plant. It is located on the main campus of Saint Louis University in
midtown. The campus is just a block from the Fox Theatre and Powell Symphony Hall, just minutes from St.
Louis Union Station, the Arch, the riverfront, and downtown. There is a wide choice of affordable rental housing
for students in the neighborhoods around the university.
St. Louis offers the amenities of urban living without the
inconveniences and high costs normally associated with
living in a major metropolitan area.

■ Enrollment/Student Body

➡ *1,391 applicants* ➡ *571 admitted first-year class 1993*
➡ *259 enrolled first-year class 1993* ➡ *559 total full-time*
➡ *267 total part-time* ➡ *18% minority first-year class 1993*
➡ *44% women* ➡ *39 states & foreign countries represented*
➡ *125 undergraduate schools represented*

■ Faculty

➡ *59 total* ➡ *44 full-time* ➡ *15 part-time or adjunct*
➡ *7 women* ➡ *4 minority*

The offices of individual faculty members are located in
the law library, and all classrooms, administrative offices, and clinical facilities are housed within this same
building complex for convenience and collegiality.

■ Library and Physical Facilities

➡ *400,000 volumes & equivalents* ➡ *library hours: Mon.-*
Thurs., 9:00 A.M.-MIDNIGHT; Fri., 8:00 A.M.-11:00 P.M.; Sat.,
9:00 A.M.-8:00 P.M.; Sun., 10:00 A.M.-MIDNIGHT
➡ *LEXIS* ➡ *NEXIS* ➡ *WESTLAW* ➡ *DIALOG*
➡ *9 full-time librarians* ➡ *library seats 437*

■ Curriculum

➡ *Academic Support Program* ➡ *88 credits required to*
graduate ➡ *100+ courses available* ➡ *degrees available:*
J.D.; J.D./M.B.A.; J.D./M.H.A.; J.D./M.U.A.; J.D./M.S.W.;
others as requested ➡ *semesters, start in Aug.*
➡ *range of first-year class size—30-90*

A cumulative grade-point average (GPA) of 2.0 is required to earn the J.D. degree. The part-time program of
legal education involves the same degree of academic
quality and rigor, and the same admissions standards in
evaluating applicants, as the full-time program. The
same faculty members are involved in teaching both the
full- and part-time programs.

The school has gained national recognition in the areas
of health law, lawyering skills, employment law, and international law.

■ Special Programs

The Center for Health Law Studies—The Center's fac-
ulty work closely with Saint Louis University's School of
Medicine, School of Nursing, School of Allied Health
Professions, Graduate Department of Hospital and
Health Care Administration, and the Medical Center.

The school's health law program is unique in that there
are eight full-time faculty members teaching in the
health law area. Its endowed library collection in health
law provides an outstanding research facility. Many special programs are offered throughout the year to bring
students information about the many opportunities in
health law. Saint Louis University health law alumni are
particularly helpful in this area.

The Center for International and Comparative Law—
The strength of the international law program at Saint
Louis University School of Law is a result of the combination of curricular and extracurricular offerings, permanent
and visiting faculty, and a strong library collection.

The school also has developed cooperative agreements
with Sichuan University in Chengdu, People's Republic
of China, and the University of Warsaw.

To complement the course offerings in international
law, the school has a number of special study opportunities in European countries. Through the Brussels
Seminar and the Ruhr University Exchange Program, the
school offers its qualified students four to five weeks of
high quality instruction in Europe, at no charge for tuition and accommodations.

The Center for Employment Law—The center offers interested students an opportunity to specialize in the
subject of the employment relationship as a unifying
thread for their study of law.

■ Admission

➡ *Bachelor's degree required* ➡ *preferential application*
deadline—March 1 ➡ *LSAT, LSDAS required*
➡ *median GPA—3.30* ➡ *median LSAT score—156*
➡ *application fee—$30*

Factors considered by the committee in addition to the
GPA and LSAT score are strength of the undergraduate
program, work experience, any extraordinary circumstances that may have affected a student's performance
in college, and motivation.

There are 175 spaces available for full-time students
and 75 spaces available for part-time students in the fall
entering class.

The admissions committee is composed of the Assistant Dean for Admissions, four faculty members, and
three law students. The committee uses an admission index in preliminary evaluations of applicants. With the

exception of those applications whose index falls in a clearly defined upper or lower percentile and whose application is reviewed by the Assistant Dean and the faculty committee chair, the committee reviews the entire application of each applicant. No action is taken without the consensus of the committee.

The School of Law is committed to increasing the number of minorities in the legal profession. Accordingly, the School of Law actively seeks applications from qualified minorities.

A special admissions program is conducted each summer at the School of Law. The Summer Institute is designed to identify students who have suffered the effects of cultural or racial discrimination, cultural deprivation, or economic or other disadvantages to such an extent that their undergraduate work or performance on standardized tests is affected.

■ Student Activities

Student organizations play a vital role in meeting the many special interests of the student body. Programs and publications sponsored by these organizations add considerable depth to the overall program.

■ Expenses and Financial Aid

➠ tuition & fees—full-time, $13,520; part-time, $10,100
➠ estimated additional expenses—$7,500 (includes room & board)   ➠ academic merit scholarships available
➠ minority scholarships available: merit & need-based
➠ financial aid available; FAFSA or GAPSFAS required

The majority of law students receive some form of financial assistance. Most awards are need-based, with the exception of the academic scholarships and grants administered directly by the School of Law.

■ Career Services

The Career Planning and Placement Office is designed to assist students, alumni, and employers. Students and alumni are welcome to utilize the services of the office throughout their academic and legal careers. These services include career counseling, assistance in developing résumés and letters, access to job postings, an alumni job bulletin, assistance in the job search in other geographic areas, and on-campus interviews for current students. The office houses a career library which has information on a wide range of employers and career choices, including government job bulletins, books and brochures on a variety of practice areas and placement bulletins from law schools throughout the United States. The office lists positions for student clerks, summer positions, full-time positions for recent graduates, and positions for attorneys with experience. In order to assist students in finding additional information about employers, the LEXIS, NEXIS, and WESTLAW computer research services are also available in the Career Library.

The distribution of graduates by types of employment is comparable to that of many law schools. Approximately 70 percent of the graduates enter private practice. Within six months of graduation, 91 percent of the class is employed, with salaries ranging from $20,000 to $70,000. Although there are alumni practicing in all 50 states and several foreign countries, the majority are practicing in the midwest region, especially in the states of Illinois and Missouri.

Applicant Group for the 1993–1994 Academic Year

Saint Louis University School of Law

LSAT Score	GPA						
	3.75 +	3.50 - 3.74	3.25 - 3.49	3.00 - 3.24	2.75 - 2.99	2.50 - 2.74	Below 2.50
175 - 180	Likely	Likely	Likely	Likely	Likely	Likely	Likely
170 - 174	Likely	Likely	Likely	Likely	Likely	Likely	Likely
165 - 169	Likely	Likely	Likely	Likely	Likely	Likely	Likely
160 - 164	Likely	Likely	Likely	Likely	Possible	Possible	Possible
155 - 159	Likely	Likely	Possible	Possible	Possible	Possible	Possible
150 - 154	Possible	Possible	Possible	Possible	Possible	Possible	Possible
145 - 149	Possible	Possible	Possible	Unlikely	Unlikely	Unlikely	Unlikely
140 - 144	Possible	Unlikely	Unlikely	Unlikely	Unlikely	Unlikely	Unlikely
135 - 139	Unlikely	Unlikely	Unlikely	Unlikely	Unlikely	Unlikely	Unlikely
130 - 134	Unlikely	Unlikely	Unlikely	Unlikely	Unlikely	Unlikely	Unlikely
125 - 129	Unlikely	Unlikely	Unlikely	Unlikely	Unlikely	Unlikely	Unlikely
120 - 124	Unlikely	Unlikely	Unlikely	Unlikely	Unlikely	Unlikely	Unlikely

Likely   Possible   Unlikely

St. Mary's University School of Law

One Camino Santa Maria
San Antonio, TX 78228-8601

Phone: 210.436.3424

■ Introduction

St. Mary's University School of Law, founded in San Antonio, Texas in 1927, is maintaining its strength as an institution that offers a solid curriculum of traditional legal studies and teaches its students the practical skills and habits of mind that enable them to become effective advocates. As part of a Catholic institution founded by the Society of Mary (Marianists), the mission of the law school is to give its students the knowledge and attributes of mind and character essential to the effective rendition of public service, while developing new methodologies to prepare students for the practice of law in a changing world.

■ Enrollment/Student Body

➡ *2,114 applicants*   ➡ *815 admitted first-year class 1993*
➡ *260 enrolled first-year class 1993*   ➡ *746 total full-time*
➡ *24% minority*   ➡ *47% women*
➡ *27 states & foreign countries represented*
➡ *93 undergraduate schools represented*

■ Faculty

➡ *69 total*   ➡ *35 full-time*   ➡ *34 part-time or adjunct*
➡ *15 women*   ➡ *9 minority*

■ Library and Physical Facilities

➡ *267,700 volumes & equivalents*   ➡ *library hours: Mon.-Thurs., 7:00 A.M.-MIDNIGHT; Fri., 7:00 A.M.-10:00 P.M.; Sat., 9:00 A.M.-10:00 P.M.; Sun., 10:00 A.M.-MIDNIGHT*
➡ *LEXIS*   ➡ *NEXIS*   ➡ *WESTLAW*   ➡ *DIALOG*
➡ *8 full-time librarians*   ➡ *library seats 446*

The Sarita Kennedy East Law Library is a modern, recently constructed, award-winning building. The collection includes legal documents from the United Nations that provide access to American, British, Canadian, and International law.

■ Curriculum

➡ *Academic Support Program*   ➡ *90 credits required to graduate*   ➡ *145 courses available*
➡ *degrees available: J.D.; J.D./M.B.A.; J.D./M.P.A.; J.D./EC.; J.D./IR; J.D./TH*   ➡ *semesters, start in Aug.*
➡ *range of first-year class size—85*

Required first-year courses are Constitutional Law, Contracts, Criminal Law, Legal Research and Writing, Procedure I, Property, and Torts. In addition to other electives, all students must take the following required courses: Professional Responsibility; Evidence; Procedure II & III; and one course chosen from Jurisprudence, American Legal History, Legal Philosophy, or Law and Economics, and complete one research paper. Procedure I & II (Texas) is only required of those planning to take the Texas bar examination.

■ Clinical Legal Education

The Poverty Law Clinic operates through two projects—The Homelessness Project and the Women, Children & Elderly Project. The clinic introduces students to the skills and responsibilities of lawyering through supervised representation of low-income, including homeless, clients in four areas: family law, public benefits, landlord-tenant, and wills and probate. The Capital Punishment Clinic, in conjunction with the Texas Resource Center, provides representation for death-row inmates in postconviction proceedings. It consists of seminar training in constitutional and procedural law governing postconviction and death penalty litigation, and closely supervised field work.

The Immigration Clinic engages students in representing indigent people from other nations who are seeking asylum in the United States. A Human Rights Clinic will be added to expand the advocacy in the international area.

The Juvenile Justice Clinic is a cooperative program between St. Mary's and the Community Law Center of San Antonio. The program is designed to provide legal representation to young people brought before the juvenile courts.

■ International Law

The St. Mary's Institute on World Legal Problems is conducted at the University of Innsbruck in Austria during July and August. The program is designed to provide law students with a broader understanding of global issues and the role that law can play in their peaceful resolution. Professor Laurence Tribe of Harvard Law School taught at the 1990 Institute. Other Distinguished Visiting Lecturers have included the Hon. William H. Rehnquist, Chief Justice of the United States, during the 1991 Institute, the Hon. Antonin Scalia (1992 Institute) and the Hon. John Paul Stevens (1993 Institute), Associate Justices of the Supreme Court of the United States. In 1994, the Hon. William H. Rehnquist will return for a second engagement as Distinguished Visiting Lecturer.

■ Judicial Internships

St. Mary's students are eligible to apply for an internship with the Supreme Court of Texas, where they work under the supervision of a justice, preparing memoranda and making oral presentations in conferences with the Court. Similar programs exist with the Texas Court of Criminal Appeals and with the Texas Court of Appeals, both located in Austin, Texas.

■ Center for International Legal Studies

The Center International Legal Studies was established as part of the law school's strategic plan for the development of a strong concentration in international and comparative law, particularly the law of the Americas. The center's Foreign Visiting Scholars program has attracted legal scholars from several other nations, including Nigeria, Russia, and Mexico.

■ Admission Standards

➡ *Bachelor's degree required* ➡ *application deadline—March 1* ➡ *LSAT, LSDAS required* ➡ *median GPA—3.00* ➡ *median LSAT score—154* ➡ *application fee—$45*

St. Mary's goal is to create an intellectually stimulating student body comprised of persons with diverse backgrounds who share a desire for academic excellence and accomplishment in the practice of law. In addition to academic ability, we seek evidence of qualities such as leadership ability, maturity, community organization skills, knowledge of other languages and cultures, a history of overcoming disadvantage, public-interest accomplishments, or success in a previous career. Participants in the CLEO program are especially encouraged to apply. A faculty committee reviews all applications. No one is automatically rejected. All files are read.

■ Student Activities

Student organizations include the *St. Mary's Law Journal*; Hispanic Law Students Association; Women's Law Association; Christian Legal Society; St. Thomas More Society; Jewish Law Students Association; Family Law Association; Federalist Society; American Civil Liberties Union Committee; William S. Sessions American Inns of Court; International Law Association; Aggie Bar; Black Allied Law Students Association; Environmental Law Society; Criminal Law Association; Harlan Society; Board of Advocates; Student Bar Association; Law Student Division, San Antonio Bar; Arts, Sports, & Entertainment Law Student Association; Asian-Pacific American Law Students Association (APALSA); Delta Alpha Delta;

Delta Theta Phi; Phi Alpha Delta; Phi Delta Phi; Public Interest Law Association (PILA); and Society of Legal Entrepreneurs (SOLE).

■ Expenses and Financial Aid

➡ *tuition & fees—$420/credit hr.* ➡ *student service fee—$64* ➡ *University Center fee—$20* ➡ *parking fee—$30* ➡ *performance and need-based scholarships available* ➡ *donated funds may be earmarked for minority scholarships* ➡ *financial aid available; financial aid forms must be filed with the University Office of Financial Assistance between Jan. 1 and April 1 of the year for which student is enrolling*

■ Career Services

The Office of Career Services is under the direction of an associate dean with 10 years of recruiting experience on a hiring committee in a major law firm. The mission of the office is to provide personal, individualized assistance to all students as they seek employment during and after law school. Confidential strategy sessions provide a unique opportunity for students to develop a personal plan to assess and meet their career goals. The office publishes a weekly job newsletter for students, and a monthly job newsletter for graduates. The office's Student Résumé Center offers an extensive and up-to-date library of career resources and directories of attorneys, as well as computer terminals with employer databases to help students direct and begin their careers in legal and nontraditional positions. A diverse and active alumni association offers mentors and career programs throughout the year.

Ninety percent of the class of 1992 reported employment within six months following graduation, a figure slightly better than national statistics.

Applicant Group for the 1993–1994 Academic Year

St. Mary's University School of Law
This chart is to be used as a general guide only. Nonnumerical factors are strongly considered for all applicants.

LSAT Score	3.75 +		3.50 - 3.74		3.25 - 3.49		3.00 - 3.24		2.75 - 2.99		2.50 - 2.74		Below 2.50		No GPA		Total	
	Apps	Adm	Apps	Adm	Apps	Adm	Apps	Adm	Apps	Adm	Apps	Adm	Apps	Adm	Apps	Adm	Apps	Adm
175 - 180	0	0	0	0	0	0	0	0	0	0	0	0	0	0	0	0	0	0
170 - 174	0	0	0	0	0	0	3	1	0	0	0	0	0	0	0	0	3	1
165 - 169	3	0	4	0	7	0	8	2	9	1	9	2	7	1	1	0	48	6
160 - 164	5	0	8	0	11	0	28	6	33	6	26	7	25	5	0	0	136	24
155 - 159	14	3	29	5	46	5	78	19	83	14	74	19	49	6	0	0	373	71
150 - 154	16	1	41	8	75	6	134	27	121	25	89	21	87	8	0	0	563	96
145 - 149	12	3	24	3	58	7	68	7	95	12	102	3	83	3	0	0	442	38
140 - 144	3	1	11	1	32	0	49	1	51	1	71	4	61	0	2	0	280	8
Below 140	2	0	7	1	10	0	25	2	39	1	26	0	57	0	0	0	166	4
Total	55	8	124	18	239	18	393	65	431	60	397	56	369	23	3	0	2011	248

Apps = Number of Applicants
Adm = Number Admitted
Reflects 84% of the applicant pool.

St. Thomas University School of Law

16400 NW 32 Avenue
Miami, FL 33054

Phone: 305.623.2310

■ Introduction

St. Thomas University, formerly Biscayne College, was founded in 1961, by the Order of Augustinians. St. Thomas University School of Law, the only Catholic law school in the southeastern United States, was granted provisional approval by the House of Delegates of the American Bar Association in February 1988. Students who graduate from St. Thomas University School of Law are entitled to the same recognition accorded to students and graduates of fully approved ABA law schools.

St. Thomas University is located on a 140-acre campus in northwest suburban Miami. Fifteen miles southeast in downtown Miami stands the new federal courthouse, the location of the United States District Court for the Southern District of Florida. State trial and appellate courts are several blocks away. Approximately 20 miles to the north of the law school is the city of Ft. Lauderdale, another venue for state trial and appellate courts.

■ Enrollment/Student Body

➡ *2,043 applicants*   ➡ *640 admitted first-year class 1993*
➡ *186 enrolled first-year class 1993*   ➡ *478 total full-time*
➡ *32% minority*   ➡ *36% women*
➡ *21 states & foreign countries represented*
➡ *79 undergraduate schools represented*

■ Faculty

➡ *60 total*   ➡ *29 full-time*   ➡ *31 part-time or adjunct*
➡ *21 women*   ➡ *11 minority*

■ Library and Physical Facilities

➡ *213,489 volumes & equivalents*   ➡ *library hours: Mon.-Thurs., 8:00 A.M.-MIDNIGHT; Fri., 8:00 A.M.-10:00 P.M.; Sat., 9:00 A.M.-10:00 P.M.; Sun, 9:00 A.M.-MIDNIGHT*   ➡ *LEXIS*
➡ *NEXIS*   ➡ *WESTLAW*   ➡ *DIALOG*
➡ *7 full-time librarians, 10 full-time support staff*
➡ *library seats 304-study rooms available*
➡ *computer lab and other locations with 60+ PCs & printers*

Students are provided with unlimited opportunities to use on-line full text computer-assisted legal retrieval systems. Personal computers are available for student use and the library has over 200 software packages, including word processing, database management, and spread sheet programs.

■ Curriculum

➡ *Academic Support Program*   ➡ *90 credits required to graduate*   ➡ *over 100 courses available*
➡ *J.D. degree available*   ➡ *semesters, start in Aug.*

The curriculum of the School of Law covers a period of three academic years. The first-year curriculum is fully prescribed, while the second-year curriculum is partially prescribed, with third-year courses being electives.

■ Clinical Legal Education Programs

St. Thomas University School of Law has three Clinical Legal Education Programs: the Field Placement Clinic, the Immigration Clinic, and the Appellate Litigation Clinic. Each clinic is a year-long program for which third-year students receive eight hours of credits. The classroom component for each clinic is two hours per week.

The Field Placement Clinic involves 20 students working as interns in public defender, states attorneys, city and county attorneys, and Legal Aid Agency offices. Supervising attorneys are assigned by the offices involved and general supervision, including a classroom component, is provided by a full-time, tenure-track professor. Many students in this clinic are allowed to try cases or participate in trials by the supervising attorneys.

The Immigration Clinic, partially funded by a federal grant, has offices in the School of Law, and all fieldwork is supervised by a full-time, tenure-track professor and a clinical assistant professor. Indigent immigrants incarcerated at a federal facility in Dade County are represented in deportation and exclusion hearings and in other immigration matters.

The 15 students enrolled in the **Appellate Litigation Clinic**, which also has offices at the law school, represent indigents in appellate cases before courts of appeals under the supervision of a tenure-track faculty member. The students brief and argue the cases on appeal.

The Peter T. Fay American Inn of Court at St. Thomas, the first of its kind in South Florida, is one of intense professional interaction among distinguished members of the local bench and bar and student members.

Street Law is a two-hour-per-week course in which law students teach local high school students, in areas of the law of practical importance in the daily lives of community members. Selected topics include consumer, housing, and constitutional law, as well as criminal law and procedure.

The **St. Thomas Public Service Fellowship Program**, sponsored by the Florida Bar Foundation Interest on Trust Accounts program, places selected law students in various public service agencies where they provide legal assistance to indigents under the supervision and direction of attorneys working in the agencies involved. The fellows are paid for their work and receive no course credit.

Legal Assistance Wednesday, L.A.W., is a pro bono program sponsored by St. Thomas University School of Law and Greater Bethel A.M.E. Church, with additional support from the Florida Bar Foundation. Every Wednesday, students and attorneys volunteer their time to provide legal assistance and representation to the poor.

■ Admission

➡ *Bachelor's degree required*
➡ *application deadline—April 30, early application preferred*
➡ *LSAT, LSDAS required*   ➡ *median GPA—2.92*
➡ *median LSAT score—152*   ➡ *application fee—$40*

Applicants must possess a bachelor's degree from a regionally accredited college or university. While no particular program of prelaw study is required, the undergraduate transcript should reflect a strong aptitude for study in a challenging academic field. The School of Law does not discriminate on the basis of sex, age, race, color, disability, religion, or national origin in its educational programs, admission policies, employment policies, financial aid, or other school-administered programs. The School of Law is committed to a policy of enhancing the diversity of its student body and encouraging applications for admission from members of all minority groups.

In determining which applicants will be accepted for admission, the Admissions Committee will look for both demonstrated academic ability and diversity of background. Consideration will be given to a variety of factors beyond the Law School Admission Test score and the undergraduate grade-point average. Those factors include work experience, honors or awards, extracurricular activities, strong letters of recommendation from instructors or others familiar with the applicant's academic abilities, and ethnic diversity.

■ Student Activities

The *St. Thomas Law Review* is a scholarly journal edited and managed by students of the School of Law. The *St. Thomas Law Review* publishes articles, submitted by students, faculty and members of the Bench and Bar. Membership is based on superior academic credentials and writing abilities.

The Student Bar Association is active in matters concerning law students and in selecting representative student members to serve on faculty committees. Numerous student organizations are active on campus, and students publish the newspaper, *Opinio Juris*.

■ Expenses and Financial Aid

➡ *full-time tuition and fees—$13,980*
➡ *estimated additional expenses—$13,135 (books & supplies, $1,400; room & board, $6,500; transportation, $2,200; personal expenses, $3,035)* ➡ *scholarships available*
➡ *minority scholarships available (diversity, among other criteria, determines eligibility)*
➡ *financial aid available; FAFSA due March 1 (priority)*

The awarding of financial aid is administered by the University Financial Aid Office. Inquiries regarding financial aid programs should be directed to the University Financial Aid Office, St. Thomas University, 16400 N.W. 32nd Avenue, Miami, FL 33054, or call 305.628.6547.

■ Career Services

The Office of Career Services offers career counseling, employability skills training, and placement assistance to students and alumni. Career and personal development workshops are scheduled regularly and the office maintains a Career Services Library for students' use. Employers from the legal, government, and corporate sectors are invited on campus during the fall and spring semesters to conduct recruitment interviews with students. Contact the Assistant Dean of Career Services for more information, 305.623.2350.

Applicant Group for the 1993–1994 Academic Year

St. Thomas University School of Law
This grid includes only applicants who earned 120-180 LSAT scores under standard administrations.

LSAT Score	3.75 +		3.50 -3.74		3.25 - 3.49		3.00 - 3.24		2.75 - 2.99		2.50 - 2.74		2.25 - 2.49		2.00 - 2.24		Below 2.00		No GPA		Total	
	Apps	Adm	Apps	Adm	Apps	Adm	Apps	Adm	Apps	Adm	Apps	Adm	Apps	Adm	Apps	Adm	Apps	Adm	Apps	Adm	Apps	Adm
175 - 180	0	0	0	0	0	0	0	0	0	0	0	0	0	0	0	0	0	0	0	0	0	0
170 - 174	0	0	0	0	0	0	0	0	0	0	0	0	0	0	0	0	0	0	0	0	0	0
165 - 169	0	0	0	0	0	0	0	0	1	1	1	1	0	0	2	2	0	0	0	0	4	4
160 - 164	1	1	3	3	3	2	8	8	7	7	5	4	6	5	4	3	3	0	0	0	40	33
155 - 159	3	3	4	3	14	13	29	27	35	31	36	33	23	16	14	5	1	0	0	0	159	131
150 - 154	5	5	9	9	40	40	79	69	120	91	109	66	68	13	26	1	2	0	4	1	462	295
145 - 149	11	10	25	21	59	24	109	19	138	8	133	11	56	3	24	0	4	0	14	1	573	97
140 - 144	6	2	19	1	37	2	58	7	87	4	80	5	60	4	21	0	6	0	9	0	383	25
135 - 139	2	1	5	0	5	0	15	1	42	0	42	0	32	0	21	0	6	0	11	0	181	2
130 - 134	0	0	3	0	2	0	6	0	15	0	13	0	15	0	14	0	1	0	3	0	72	0
125 - 129	0	0	0	0	0	0	1	0	0	0	3	0	2	0	3	0	0	0	5	0	14	0
120 - 124	0	0	0	0	0	0	0	0	0	0	0	0	1	0	0	0	1	0	0	0	2	0
Total	28	22	68	37	160	81	305	131	445	142	422	120	263	41	129	11	24	0	46	2	1890	587

Apps = Number of Applicants
Adm = Number Admitted
Reflects 93% of the total applicant pool.

University of San Diego School of Law

5998 Alcala Park
San Diego, CA 92110

Phone: 619.260.4528

■ Introduction

The University of San Diego School of Law, founded in 1954, is centrally located to the city's downtown area. The campus, a superb 180-acre site, overlooks Mission Bay and San Diego's spectacular shoreline. The graceful Spanish Renaissance architecture and year-round gentle climate make this a lovely place to live and study. As part of a private, values-based university, the law school is committed to develop an educational environment that encourages concern with larger issues of social justice.

The law school is a member of the AALS and is accredited by the ABA.

■ Enrollment/Student Body

➥ 3,671 applicants   ➥ 1,138 admitted first-year class 1993
➥ 337 enrolled first-year class 1993
➥ 757 total full-time   ➥ 315 total part-time
➥ 18% minority   ➥ 42% women
➥ 37 states & foreign countries represented first-year class 1993
➥ 120 undergraduate schools represented first-year class 1993

■ Faculty

➥ 114 total   ➥ 67 full-time   ➥ 47 part-time or adjunct
➥ 36 women   ➥ 9 minority

■ Library and Physical Facilities

➥ over 320,000 volumes & equivalents   ➥ library hours:
Sun.-Thurs., 8:00 A.M.-MIDNIGHT; Fri.-Sat., 8:00 A.M.-10:00 P.M.
➥ LEXIS   ➥ NEXIS   ➥ WESTLAW   ➥ DIALOG
➥ 8 full-time librarians   ➥ library seats 600

■ Curriculum

➥ Academic Support Program   ➥ 85 credits required to graduate   ➥ over 150 total courses available
➥ degrees available: J.D.; J.D./M.B.A.; J.D./MIB; J.D./M.A. (Graduate Programs: General LL.M.; LL.M. in Taxation; Masters in Comparative Law)   ➥ semesters, start in Aug.
➥ range of first-year class size—20-85

Students in the day division normally require six semesters to complete the J.D., while evening-division students normally complete it in eight semesters plus one summer session. Attendance at two summer sessions may accelerate graduation by one semester. The first-year curriculum is prescribed in both divisions. Curricula beyond the first year include both required and elective courses. First-year students are encouraged to get a head start in their legal education by beginning law school the summer before their first year. There are many small classes, including a legal research and writing program with a student faculty ratio of 18:1; and an academic support program for eligible students.

All students attend an intensive one-day orientation program sponsored by the Student Body Association at the start of school.

■ Special Programs

Institute on International and Comparative Law—The School of Law, in cooperation with five foreign schools, sponsors the Institute on International and Comparative Law. The Institute conducts summer law study programs in England, France, Ireland, Mexico, Poland and Russia. The programs introduce American law students to foreign law and legal institutions and provide intensive study during four- to six-week sessions.

Clinical Education Program—The School of Law Clinical Education Program is recognized as one of the most extensive and successful in the nation. The law school received the Emil Gumpert Award from the American College of Trial Lawyers for excellence in trial advocacy training.

The clinical programs provide students with the opportunity to learn lawyering skills and to apply knowledge by representing clients in actual cases. Students represent actual clients with problems in consumer, housing, family, administrative, mental health, environmental, immigration, criminal, and juvenile law, and a variety of other areas.

The Public Interest Law Clinic and Child Advocacy Clinics offer research and advocacy opportunities for upper-division students.

Alumni Advisor Program—Sponsored by the Law Alumni Association and coordinated by the Office of Development and Alumni Relations, this program is offered to first-year students. It pairs students with graduates of similar legal interest. The practitioners meet with their student advisees and provide counseling on course selection and the realities of legal practice.

Pro Bono Legal Advocates—Pro Bono Legal Advocates was formed to promote the values of charity, service and selflessness in the USD Student Bar, assist members of the bar in donating their talents and time to the community, and promote diversity in the bar. Pro bono legal work is done by attorneys, without compensation, for clients who cannot afford a lawyer.

■ Admission

➥ Bachelor's degree from an accredited college or university required for admission   ➥ priority application deadline—Feb. 1   ➥ rolling admission, early application preferred
➥ LSAT, LSDAS required   ➥ median GPA—3.25
➥ median LSAT score—160   ➥ application fee—$35

While the applicant's LSAT score and undergraduate GPA are important elements in the admission process, other factors also are considered. The goal of the Admissions Committee is to admit those applicants most likely to be successful in law school.

■ Student Activities

The *San Diego Law Review* is a legal journal containing articles that address major issues in law written by students, professors, and legal practitioners. Each annual volume contains four issues. The *California Regulatory Law Reporter* is a quarterly journal published by the Center for Public Interest Law. It is the only journal in the nation that covers activities of 70 state agencies and 25 public interest organizations. The *Journal of Contemporary Legal Issues* is a semiannual national publication that examines contemporary legal, political, and social issues.

The Moot Court Board coordinates various appellate advocacy competitions where students act as attorneys for fictitious clients involved in contemporary legal disputes. The USD Moot Court Board also competes against other law schools at various competitions in the national level. The success of the national teams in recent years has established the USD Moot Court Program as one of the best in the nation. The law school also holds Trial Advocacy Competitions open to all continuing law students. Participants for Mock Trial teams are selected by instructors of trial advocacy classes.

Student organizations include the Black Law Students Association, La Raza, Asian-Pacific American Law Students Association, Women's Law Caucus, International Law Forum, Comparative Law Forum, National Lawyers Guild, ACLU, Environmental Law Society, Phi Alpha Delta, Phi Delta Phi, Native American Association, Christian Legal Society, Delta Theta Phi, Federalist Society, GALSA, and Jewish Student Association.

Law students automatically become members of the Student Bar Association, which is active in law school affairs and provides impetus to develop new programs. The students also publish a newspaper, *Motions.*

■ Expenses and Financial Aid

➠ *tuition & fees—full-time, $16,480; part-time, $11,690* ➠ *estimated additional expenses—$7,585 (room, board, books)* ➠ *scholarships available: entering merit awards; academic achievement scholarships; private scholarships* ➠ *minority scholarships available: Dean's Outstanding Scholar awards; diversity scholarships* ➠ *financial aid available; FAFSA form for need analysis due March 2*

■ Career Services

The Career Services Office is available to all students for assistance with career planning and the development of employment opportunities. Students may make appointments with a member of the Career Services staff to review their résumés and discuss job-search strategies and career options. The office maintains current job listings for full- and part-time law clerk and attorney positions from employers nationwide. The Career Services library consists of over 200 employer directories, periodicals, newsletters, judicial clerkship manuals, and many other career resources.

Applicant Group for the 1993–1994 Academic Year

University of San Diego School of Law

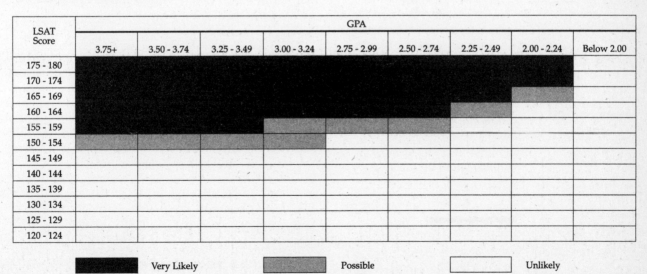

LSAT Score	GPA								
	3.75+	3.50 - 3.74	3.25 - 3.49	3.00 - 3.24	2.75 - 2.99	2.50 - 2.74	2.25 - 2.49	2.00 - 2.24	Below 2.00
175 - 180									
170 - 174									
165 - 169									
160 - 164									
155 - 159									
150 - 154									
145 - 149									
140 - 144									
135 - 139									
130 - 134									
125 - 129									
120 - 124									

■ Very Likely ■ Possible □ Unlikely

University of San Francisco School of Law

2130 Fulton Street
San Francisco, CA 94117-1080

Phone: 415.666.6544

■ Introduction

The University of San Francisco School of Law is situated on a 51-acre residential campus adjacent to Golden Gate Park and a short distance from downtown San Francisco. Its graduates play leading roles on the bench and in the bar of the San Francisco Bay Area and in over 40 states and 20 foreign countries. The university was founded by the Jesuit fathers in 1855. The law school dates from 1912 and is located in its own modern building, which was constructed in 1962.

The school's close proximity to the San Francisco Civic Center makes it convenient for students to engage in clerkships with the federal and state courts. San Francisco, the concentrated center for legal activity in the western United States, includes numerous administrative clerking opportunities. The school is fully accredited by the ABA and is a member of the AALS.

■ Enrollment/Student Body

➤ 3,100 applicants   ➤ 936 admitted first-year class 1993
➤ 241 enrolled first-year class 1993   ➤ 529 total full-time
➤ 130 total part-time   ➤ 25% minority
➤ 50% women   ➤ 25 states & foreign countries represented
➤ 89 undergraduate schools represented

At the time of admission the median age of the day and evening students is 24. Students in the two divisions merge into an integral unit of organizations for mutual activities.

■ Faculty

➤ 91 total   ➤ 26 full-time   ➤ 65 part-time
➤ 17 women   ➤ 13 minority

The school draws from the best of the Bay Area and from the finest lawyers in the area to their area of expertise. The faculty is further supplemented by visiting faculty from throughout the United States, Europe, and China.

Upper-class moot court teams participate in major national, regional, and state competitions.

The Student Bar Association is responsible for student activities and liaison with the faculty and administration. Students participate directly in the school's governance through voting representation at faculty meetings and on faculty committees.

■ Library and Physical Facilities

➤ 246,962 volumes & equivalents   ➤ 100 library hours per week   ➤ LEXIS   ➤ NEXIS   ➤ WESTLAW
➤ DIALOG   ➤ INNOPAC automated library system
➤ 6 full-time librarians   ➤ 6 library support staff
➤ library seats 315   ➤ student computer lab

The law school and law library are self-contained in a modern three-story structure. The library's collection includes over 234,900 volumes of Anglo-American legal materials in print and microformat. A student computer center, group-study conference rooms, and copier facilities are also located in the law library.

■ Admission

➤ B.A./B.S. required for admission   ➤ application deadline—Feb. 1 (priority)   ➤ LSAT, LSDAS required
➤ median GPA—3.17   ➤ median LSAT score—159
➤ application fee—$40

The School of Law does not discriminate on the basis of sex, race, color, creed, age, handicap, or national origin. Beginning students are admitted only in the fall semester, and applicants must present a baccalaureate degree prior to registration. No application is considered until all supporting documents have been received. The admission committee employs a rolling admissions procedure. The committee strives to bring together an entering class that represents a variety of social, educational, geographical, and cultural backgrounds. Students from economically disadvantaged backgrounds are encouraged to apply through the Special Admission Program.

■ Curriculum

➤ Academic Support Program   ➤ 86 units/credits required to graduate   ➤ degrees available: J.D.; J.D./M.B.A.
➤ semesters, start in Aug. & Jan.
➤ summer session starts in June
➤ range of first-year class size—day, 85; evening, 60

The first-year program begins with a four-day orientation program featuring a "minicourse," seminars, and a practice exam. The first-year curriculum includes the traditional curriculum plus Moot Court. The upper-class curriculum permits students to pursue their particular areas of interest.

■ Clinical Education—Law Clinic

The in-house Law Clinic gives students an alternative to learning law in a classroom. The clinic accepts cases in the following areas: criminal, civil (with an emphasis on civil rights issues), and refugee and international human rights, while students are supervised by four full-time professors. Students work shoulder-to-shoulder with their clinic supervisors in meeting with clients, taking depositions, writing briefs, and making court appearances. In addition, all clinic participants meet in a weekly briefing session where they discuss current cases and share ideas, strategies, and "war stories."

■ Additional Clinical Opportunities

Consistent with its commitment to practical training, the School of Law offers opportunities for students to experience actual law practice while in law school. Students may obtain practical experience outside the law school. Many students earn a semester's academic credit by clerking for the courts. Students may also receive academic credit by clerking for governmental agencies, state and federal courts, public interest law firms, corporate legal departments, and private firms.

The School of Law pioneered and now directs a program in "Street Law." Under the program, students from five Bay Area law schools receive academic credit for teaching a course on the basics of our legal system to pupils in local high schools.

■ Student Activities

➡ *University of San Francisco Law Review*
➡ *University of San Francisco Maritime Law Journal*
➡ *The FORUM, student newspaper* ➡ *over 20 professional, social, and academic student organizations under the auspices of the Student Bar Association*

■ Intensive Advocacy Program

A two-week Intensive Advocacy Program is offered each summer. This unique program provides outstanding training in both pretrial and trial skills. The program features over 80 hours of lecture, demonstration, and practice workshops. At the conclusion of the program each student will conduct a jury trial. The faculty for the program will be made up of over 100 distinguished judges, practitioners, and professors from around the United States.

■ International Law and Study Abroad

The school offers an extensive list of courses in International Law. The faculty exchange program offers students the opportunity to study with faculty visiting USF from Irish, Czech, and Chinese universities. Summer study abroad programs are available in both Ireland and the Czech Republic.

The Asian Pacific Legal Studies program at the University of San Francisco School of Law is unique among Bay Area Law Schools and is one of only a few Asian law programs currently offered in the United States. The program has four components: curriculum, research and publication, academic exchange, and community outreach.

■ Expenses and Financial Aid

➡ *tuition & fees—full-time, $15,800; part-time, $567/unit*
➡ *$9,300 average additional expenses (housing, board, books, misc. for 9 months)* ➡ *scholarships available* ➡ *financial aid available (grants and low-interest subsidized loans)*

■ Career Services

The Career Services Office facilitates the job search process for law school students and alumni. The office features a complete resource library, including in-depth dossiers on legal employers, and an aggressive placement program. Workshops, individual counseling, and panel presentations enable students to discern which areas of practice and types of employers best suit their individual career goals. In addition to listings for externships, part-time, permanent, and summer employment with law firms, corporations, accounting firms, governmental agencies, the judiciary, and other legal employers, USF also features fall and spring on-campus interview programs. Students are encouraged to consider employment in public interest law and may join the Public Interest Law Program sponsored by the Public Interest Clearinghouse. The law school is a member of the National Association for Law Placement.

Applicant Group for the 1993–1994 Academic Year

University of San Francisco School of Law

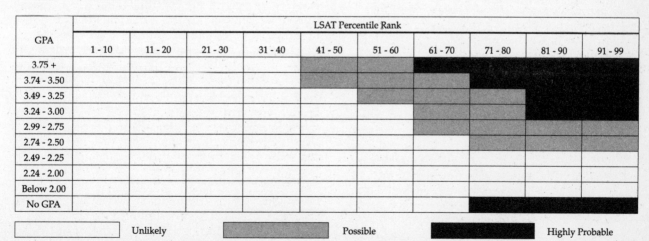

GPA	LSAT Percentile Rank									
	1 - 10	11 - 20	21 - 30	31 - 40	41 - 50	51 - 60	61 - 70	71 - 80	81 - 90	91 - 99
3.75 +										
3.74 - 3.50										
3.49 - 3.25										
3.24 - 3.00										
2.99 - 2.75										
2.74 - 2.50										
2.49 - 2.25										
2.24 - 2.00										
Below 2.00										
No GPA										

☐ Unlikely   ▩ Possible   ■ Highly Probable

Santa Clara University School of Law

500 El Camino Real
Santa Clara, CA 95053

Phone: 408.554.4800

■ Introduction

Santa Clara University School of Law is located 46 miles from San Francisco, near the southern tip of San Francisco Bay. It is situated on the university campus, which was founded by the Jesuit fathers in 1851 and which surrounds the Mission of Santa Clara de Asis, the eighth of California's original 21 missions. The School of Law was added to the Santa Clara College in 1912 when the college became a university. The school is approved by the ABA and is a member of the AALS. For more than 140 years, Santa Clara has fostered an exceptional academic program based on the Jesuit tradition. Located adjacent to San Jose and situated in the midst of one of the nation's greatest concentrations of high technology industry, internationally known as Silicon Valley, the law school has established a curriculum that addresses the fundamental demands of law practice and the evolving needs of society.

■ Enrollment/Student Body

➡ *3,750 applicants first-year class 1993*
➡ *1,014 admitted first-year class 1993*
➡ *286 enrolled first-year class 1993* ➡ *678 total full-time*
➡ *205 total part-time* ➡ *33% minority* ➡ *50% women*
➡ *23 states & foreign countries represented*
➡ *100 undergraduate schools represented*

Santa Clara is consistently among the top law schools nationwide in terms of ethnic diversity.

■ Faculty

➡ *53 total* ➡ *34 full-time* ➡ *19 part-time*
➡ *15 women* ➡ *6 minority*

■ Library and Physical Facilities

➡ *209,624 volumes & equivalents* ➡ *library hours: Mon.-Fri., 8:00 A.M.-MIDNIGHT; Sat., 9:00 A.M.-8:00 P.M.; Sun., 10:00 A.M.-MIDNIGHT (hours extended during exam periods)*
➡ *LEXIS* ➡ *NEXIS* ➡ *WESTLAW*
➡ *OSCAR (on-line catalog)* ➡ *17 full-time librarians*
➡ *library seats 419*

The School of Law is on the 103-acre university campus. Towering palm trees, spacious lawns, and extensive flower gardens surround the Heafey Law Library. A new moot courtroom provides a setting for advocacy training and activities of the Edwin A. Heafey, Jr. Center for Trial and Appellate Advocacy. Other facilities include Bergin Hall faculty office building, Bannan Hall classroom building and Law House where law career services and alumni offices are located. Students also have access to other campus facilities including computer laboratories, Cowell Student Health Center, Benson Memorial Center, and Leavey Activities Center with its pool, basketball, volleyball and racquetball courts, steam room and sauna.

■ Curriculum

➡ *Academic Success Program* ➡ *full-time and part-time programs* ➡ *86 semester-units required to graduate*
➡ *138 courses available* ➡ *degrees available: J.D.; J.D./M.B.A.* ➡ *semesters, start in Aug.*

A week-long academic program and social orientation introduces first-year students to the study of law. The first-year curriculum is prescribed. The legal research and writing course includes a unique full-month program in the middle of the first year. The Academic Success Program has been used as a model academic assistance program by Law School Admission Services. All students of color are encouraged to participate in a special Pre-Law Orientation, a First-Year Program, an Upper-Division Program, and an Introduction to the Bar Program. The J.D./M.B.A. Combined Degree Program offers students the opportunity to earn both degrees in 3 1/2 to 4 years. This means a savings in both time and tuition fees.

■ International Law

The Institute of International and Comparative Law sponsors summer law study programs in Budapest, Hungary; Strasbourg, France; Geneva, Switzerland; Oxford, England; Hong Kong; Singapore; Seoul, Korea; Bangkok, Thailand; and Tokyo, Japan. Each of these programs is unique because it strives for maximum integration of the students into the host institution and culture. All of the programs, with the exception of Oxford, offer internships with law offices, corporations, or groups particularly suited to give students on-site observation and participation in areas of international law.

■ Special Programs

Students concerned with social issues and public service can receive a certificate in public-interest law through the Public Interest Law Program. The Public Interest Endowment funds a limited number of scholarships, summer work fellowships, and income-supplement grants for graduates. Students may also enroll in selected graduate counseling courses for credit.

The Santa Clara University Law Clinic allows students to practice law under the supervision of an experienced attorney. Students participate in all phases of a case from the initial client interview through the trial.

A clinical consortium in disability law enables students to provide legal services to persons with disabilities. Students also have the opportunity to earn credit for work as law clerks with public agencies such as the district attorney or public defender, with legal aid offices, or with private law offices. Students may also work as judges' clerks in appellate courts including the California Supreme Court or trial courts including the United States District Court and local superior and municipal courts.

■ Computer and High-Technology Law

Santa Clara has capitalized on its Silicon Valley location by establishing a specialized curriculum that emphasizes computer and high-technology law. Thirteen courses in the curriculum focus on high technology issues including patents, copyrights, biotechnology, and technology licensing.

■ Student Activities

The school's quarterly, *Santa Clara Law Review*, is published by a student editorial board. It includes comments contributed by students as well as experts in various legal fields. The *Computer and High Technology Law Journal* provides a practical resource for high technology industry and the corresponding legal community. Through the Student Bar Association and student-faculty committees, students participate in the decision processes of the law school. Student organizations include Asian/Pacific Law Students, Black Law Students, La Raza Law Students, Middle Eastern Law Students, Native American Law Students, Women in Law, Environmental Law Society, International Law Society, Phi Alpha Delta, Public Interest Law Foundation, and other law-related groups.

■ Admissions

➡ *Baccalaureate degree from accredited college or university required* ➡ *application deadline—March 1*
➡ *rolling admissions, early application preferred*
➡ *LSAT, LSDAS required* ➡ *median GPA—3.32*
➡ *median LSAT score—159* ➡ *application fee—$40*

A faculty committee reviews all applications. No one is automatically accepted or rejected. In many cases factors other than GPA and LSAT score prove to be determinative. When the LSAT is repeated, the highest score received is used. Recognizing the critical need for persons from underrepresented groups to gain access to the legal profession, the School of Law has adopted a policy for special admission. Applicants may request special consideration because of race, disadvantaged background, or other factors. Over 37 percent of the entering class is composed of students of color and 57 percent are women. Applicants are encouraged to visit the School of Law. Arrangements can be made through the Admissions Office to attend a law class, meet with an admission counselor, or tour the campus.

■ Expenses and Financial Aid

➡ *tuition & fees—$15,540, full-time; $11,298, part-time*
➡ *estimated additional expenses—$8,000 minimum (room, board, books)* ➡ *academic and need-based scholarships available* ➡ *public interest scholarships, summer fellowships, and income supplement grants* ➡ *FAFSA form and FAF for need analysis should be completed in Jan. or early Feb.*
➡ *financial aid counselor available for individual counseling*

■ Career Services

The Career Services Office serves as a liaison between students and prospective employers. Firms, businesses, and government agencies interview on campus each year. Graduates find employment in the legal profession throughout the 50 states. Office services include individual career counseling and a series of workshops in job-search strategies. Strong alumni support assists students in all stages of their career exploration and development.

Applicant Group for the 1993–1994 Academic Year

Santa Clara University School of Law

LSAT Score	GPA								
	3.75 +	3.50 - 3.74	3.25 - 3.49	3.00 - 3.24	2.75 - 2.99	2.50 - 2.74	2.25 - 2.49	2.00 - 2.24	Below 2.00
175 - 180									
170 - 174									
165 - 169									
160 - 164									
155 - 159									
150 - 154									
145 - 149									
140 - 144									
135 - 139									
130 - 134									
125 - 129									
120 - 124									

Good Possibility   Possible   Unlikely

Seton Hall University School of Law

Office of Admissions
1 Newark Center
Newark, NJ 07102-5210

Phone: 201.642.8747

■ Introduction

Seton Hall University School of Law is among the largest law schools in the country. Founded in 1951, the school is on the approved list of the ABA and is a member of the AALS. The School of Law is located in Newark, the largest city in New Jersey, and is conveniently situated in the center of the city's business and legal community.

Our law students are within walking distance of federal, appellate, state, and county courts, the Gateway Complex, and the Legal and Communications Tower. Efficient transportation options provide easy access to many suburban communities and New York City.

■ Enrollment/Student Body

➡ 2,854 applicants   ➡ 1,162 admitted first-year class 1993
➡ 454 enrolled first-year class 1993   ➡ 996 total full-time
➡ 379 total part-time   ➡ 20% minority
➡ 45% women   ➡ 17 states represented in first-year class
➡ 155 undergraduate schools represented in first-year class

Day-division applications numbered 2,257 for 320 seats, and evening-division applications numbered 597 for 90 seats. Women comprise 45 percent of the 1993 first-year class, while minority matriculants comprise 16 percent.

■ Faculty

➡ 148 total   ➡ 51 full-time   ➡ 97 part-time or adjunct
➡ 46 women   ➡ 16 minority

■ Library and Physical Facilities

➡ 315,595 volumes & equivalents   ➡ library hours: Mon.-Fri., 8:00 A.M.-11:45 P.M.; Sat., 9:00 A.M.-10:00 P.M.; Sun., 10:00 A.M.-10:00 P.M.   ➡ LEXIS   ➡ NEXIS
➡ WESTLAW   ➡ DIALOG   ➡ 11 professional librarians
➡ 15 library assistants   ➡ library seats 600

■ Curriculum

➡ Academic Support Program   ➡ 85 credits required to graduate   ➡ 176 courses available   ➡ degrees available: J.D.; J.D./M.B.A.   ➡ semesters, start in Sept. first-year only

The program emphasizes humanistic principles and encourages their synthesis with knowledge of the law and professional responsibility. The law school is committed to in-depth training in legal writing and research.

The school year is conducted on a two-semester basis. The day division requires three years; the evening division normally requires four.

■ Special Programs

Clinics—Seton Hall Law School is committed to clinical education and is at its forefront. The 21 years of service performed by the law school's clinics was recently recognized by Congress and the President in the form of a $5.4 million grant. With this grant, the school has created the Center for Social Justice, a clinical legal education center that serves as a national model. The school's litigation clinics presently represent more than 3,000 disadvantaged and underrepresented clients each year in a wide range of litigation such as housing and shelter, consumer protection, family law, public entitlement, juvenile justice, disability law, immigration, and inmate advocacy. A transactional clinic represents community groups providing affordable housing to those in need.

Judicial Internships—The law school also offers judicial internships with justices of the New Jersey Supreme Court; judges of the New Jersey Appellate Division, Chancery and Law Courts, the Third Circuit Court of Appeals, the U.S. District Courts, and the U.S. Bankruptcy Courts. There are internship programs with the Environmental Protection Agency, the Office of the U.S. Trustee for Bankruptcy, and the Internal Revenue Service.

Journals—The law school offers students an opportunity to advance legal scholarship through four student journals—*The Seton Hall Law Review, Seton Hall Legislative Journal, Seton Hall Constitutional Law Journal*, and the *Seton Hall Sports Law Journal*.

Foreign Study—Each summer the law school cosponsors, with the Universities of Parma and Milan, a course of international studies for American law students in Milan, Genoa, and Parma, Italy. The law school hosts students from the University of Milan Law School.

M.B.A./J.D. Program—Students may be admitted to the joint M.B.A./J.D. program during the first year of their law school career. The M.B.A. degree consists of 60 credits, and a maximum of 12 credits may be applied to both degree requirements. The LSAT and GMAT examinations are both required.

LEO Institute—The Monsignor Thomas Fahy Legal Education Opportunities (LEO) Institute provides an intense, summer-long classroom experience for educationally disadvantaged students.

Moot Court Program—Students represent the law school in the National Moot Court Competition as well as in 14 interschool competitions focusing on specific areas of law.

■ Admission

➡ B.A./B.S. required   ➡ application deadline—April 1
➡ LSAT, LSDAS required   ➡ median GPA—3.16
➡ median LSAT score—155   ➡ application fee—$45

All applicants for admission as beginning law students are required to hold a bachelor's degree from a regionally accredited four-year institution by the time of matriculation. The LSAT is also required for all prospective applicants, with the exception of those applicants who are blind or who have physical disabilities that can be medically certified.

The law school recognizes the desirability of bringing together an entering class of diverse cultural, social, and educational backgrounds. Candidates are expected to demonstrate sufficient academic achievement in a rigorous undergraduate and/or graduate major and communicate that they possess the aptitude for the successful pursuit of the demanding three- or four-year professional degree program. Nonquantifiable indicators of success in law school may surface in one's demonstrated skills. These skills can be reflected in things such as the employment record, meaningful community endeavors, and unusual cocurricular service projects of a candidate.

Applicants from disadvantaged groups, regardless of race, religion, age, sex, or national origin, may wish to inquire into the Monsignor Thomas Fahy Legal Education Opportunities Institute (LEO Institute).

Acceptances are processed for candidates as early as December. Subsequent decisions are processed regularly through June. A $500 tuition deposit is required by April 15. A second tuition deposit of $1,000 is due by June 15.

■ Student Activities

Student organizations flourish at Seton Hall. Many are related to specific areas of practice; others related to student governance and student representation on faculty standing committees. International law fraternities have chapters here. Several organizations, including the St. Thomas More Society, are committed to community service. Many other groups represent a wide range of professional interests, religious commitments, and cultural identities found among an enormously diverse student population.

The law school is also very involved in encouraging the study of law and the pursuit of legal careers among college and high school students, through the Mentor and Pre-Legal programs.

■ Expenses and Financial Aid

➡ *tuition & fees—full-time, $15,870; part-time, $11,638 ($529/credit hour)* ➡ *recommended budget including tuition—full-time, $29,995; part-time, $25,620* ➡ *merit and need-based scholarships available* ➡ *merit, need-based, and geography-specific minority scholarships available* ➡ *FAFSA due May 15th* ➡ *financial aid pamphlet available*

In 1993-94, over $1.7 million was allocated from the law center's financial resources to approximately 55 percent of the student body. The average student loan was approximately $14,000. From all sources, approximately 1,000 students received over $18 million in aid and loans.

■ Career Services

Seton Hall School of Law maintains a Career Development Office staffed by one full-time and two part-time counselors who assist students in defining their career objectives and goals and establishing contact with employers. Every fall, law firm, corporate, public-interest and government employers conduct interviews through the school's On-Campus Interview Program. The placement ratio for 1992 graduates was 93 percent.

Applicant Group for the 1993–1994 Academic Year

Seton Hall University School of Law
This grid includes only applicants who earned 120-180 LSAT scores under standard administrations.

LSAT Score	GPA																				
	3.75 +		3.50 -3.74		3.25 - 3.49		3.00 - 3.24		2.75 - 2.99		2.50 - 2.74		2.25 - 2.49		2.00 - 2.24		Below 2.00		No GPA		Total	
	Apps	Adm	Apps	Adm	Apps	Adm	Apps	Adm	Apps	Adm	Apps	Adm	Apps	Adm	Apps	Adm	Apps	Adm	Apps	Adm	Apps	Adm
175 - 180	0	0	0	0	1	1	0	0	0	0	1	1	0	0	0	0	0	0	1	0	3	2
170 - 174	0	0	1	1	3	2	0	0	4	3	2	2	0	0	0	0	0	0	0	0	10	8
165 - 169	4	4	7	7	5	4	13	13	11	11	6	6	4	2	2	2	0	0	0	0	52	49
160 - 164	11	9	13	12	35	32	34	34	27	24	19	17	7	6	2	1	0	0	3	2	151	137
155 - 159	24	24	54	50	98	93	100	93	77	57	45	30	27	12	10	2	6	1	0	0	441	362
150 - 154	23	19	70	54	142	94	163	83	109	38	85	20	37	5	11	1	3	0	5	2	648	316
145 - 149	12	5	52	10	82	19	135	19	109	18	85	11	49	5	20	2	4	0	8	4	556	93
140 - 144	8	0	22	1	42	6	85	9	85	9	73	10	44	4	29	0	6	1	7	2	401	42
135 - 139	3	0	11	1	21	1	34	3	29	0	40	3	54	1	33	0	6	0	7	1	238	10
130 - 134	0	0	0	0	4	0	8	0	18	0	17	1	35	0	13	0	5	0	3	0	103	1
125 - 129	0	0	1	0	0	0	5	0	3	0	6	0	0	0	5	0	3	0	1	0	24	0
120 - 124	0	0	0	0	0	0	0	0	1	0	1	0	1	0	0	0	0	0	0	0	3	0
Total	85	61	231	136	433	252	577	254	473	160	380	101	258	35	125	8	33	2	35	11	2630	1020

Apps = Number of Applicants
Adm = Number Admitted
Reflects 95% of the total applicant pool.

University of South Carolina School of Law

Columbia, SC 29208

Phone: 803.777.6605

■ Introduction

The University of South Carolina School of Law, established in 1867, is located in Columbia, South Carolina. Situated in the state capital in the center of the state, there is easy access to the mountains and to the coast. The school is within close proximity of state and federal courts, government agencies, the State Capitol, and large law firms. The School of Law is fully accredited by the American Bar Association and has been a member of the Association of American Law Schools since 1924.

■ Enrollment/Student Body

➽ 1,714 applicants　➽ 400 admitted first-year class 1993　➽ 240 enrolled first-year class 1993　➽ 765 total full-time　➽ 10% minority　➽ 39% women　➽ 13 states & foreign countries represented　➽ 81 undergraduate schools represented　➽ 85% residents of South Carolina

■ Faculty

➽ 69 total　➽ 44 full-time　➽ 25 part-time or adjunct　➽ 9 women　➽ 3 minority

■ Library and Physical Facilities

➽ 326,000 volumes & equivalents　➽ library hours: open 111 hours per week under regular schedule; Mon.-Thurs.,7:00 A.M.-MIDNIGHT; Fri.,7:00 A.M.-10:00 P.M.; Sat.,9:00 A.M.-10:00 P.M.; Sun., 9:00 A.M.-MIDNIGHT　➽ LEXIS　➽ NEXIS　➽ WESTLAW　➽ DIALOG　➽ RLIN　➽ OCLC　➽ USCAN (online card catalog)　➽ 5.5 full-time librarians　➽ library seats 645　➽ South Carolina Legal History Collection is housed in the School of Law Library

Closed carrels are available for assignment to students for year-long use.

■ Curriculum

➽ Academic Support Program　➽ 91 total units/credits required to graduate　➽ 121 courses available　➽ joint degree programs: J.D./Masters Business Administration; J.D./Masters Criminal Justice; J.D./Masters Public Administration; J.D./Masters International Business; J.D./Masters Employee Personnel Relations; J.D./Master of Accountancy; J.D./Master of Arts in Economics　➽ two semesters, begin in Aug. and Jan.　➽ one summer session　➽ beginning students admitted for fall semester only　➽ range of first-year class size—20-80

Transfer students are accepted in limited numbers.

■ Special Programs

Clinical Legal Education Program. Under special court rule, third-year law students in South Carolina may represent clients and appear in court when enrolled in a clinical legal education course. The clinical education program offers courses designed to develop lawyering skills. The program, through the use of simulation techniques, offers training in trial advocacy, negotiation, settlement, interviewing, and counseling. Clinics include domestic relations, criminal defense, appellate practice, employment discrimination, social security, and bankruptcy.

■ Admissions

➽ Bachelor's degree from an accredited college or university required for admission　➽ application deadline—Feb. 15, 1994　➽ fall admission only　➽ transfer application deadline—May 1, 1994　➽ LSAT, LSDAS required　➽ median GPA—3.20　➽ median LSAT score—157　➽ application fee—SC resident, $25; non-SC resident, $35　➽ state-supported institution, admission standards are higher for non-residents of South Carolina　➽ candidates who want to be considered for merit scholarships must complete their applications by February 1, 1994

The Faculty Committee on Admissions reviews applications to the School of Law. Factors considered include LSAT, GPA, degree-granting institution, major, work and/or military experience, extracurricular activities, letters of recommendation, and the personal statement. When multiple LSAT scores are presented, the average of the scores is used.

The fall 1993 entering class was 11 percent minority, 47 percent women, and 86 percent South Carolina residents.

Visits to the Office of Admissions and the School of Law to discuss specific questions and concerns are welcomed.

■ Student Activities

Order of the Coif—National legal honorary society which recognizes outstanding student academic achievement.

Order of Wig and Robe—Local legal scholastic organization organized in 1935.

South Carolina Law Review—Published quarterly and contains articles by distinguished scholars, members of the bar, and students.

South Carolina Environmental Law Journal—Published regularly by students of the School of Law. Each issue, containing articles written by attorneys, professors, and professionals in the field, provides updates on current developments in environmental law.

Real Property, Probate, and Trust Journal—The School of Law serves as the host affiliate for this ABA journal.

Pro Bono Program—Directed by a student board, the Pro Bono Program offers students an opportunity to be involved in activities such as income tax assistance, legal research, and teaching law-related courses to juveniles. On May 1, 1991, former President Bush named the Pro Bono Program the 444th "Daily Point of Light" for its outstanding contribution to community service through volunteer action.

Moot Court—Teams are sponsored in the National, International, American Bar Association, and Labor Law Moot Court competitions and National Trial Competition.

Other student organizations include the Student Bar Association, which is the student government for the School of Law, the Black Law Student Association, the Association of Women Law Students, the Christian Legal Society, and the Environmental Law Society.

■ Expenses and Financial Aid

➡ *full-time tuition & fees—SC resident, $4970 per year; non-SC resident; $10,546 per year*
➡ *average amount of additional expenses—$8,000 (rent, transportation, utilities, books, food, misc.)*
➡ *scholarships available (merit-based full- and half-tuition scholarships, need-based scholarships)*
➡ *minority scholarships available (merit-based full- and half-tuition scholarships)* ➡ *financial aid available*
➡ *priority deadline for applications for federal student loan programs—April 15*
➡ *Application for Federal Student Aid (AFSA) required*

Candidates who want to be considered for merit scholarships should complete their application to the School of Law by February 1.

■ Office of Career Services

The Office of Career Services serves as liaison between students and legal employers and offers services to equip students with the skills and information necessary for a successful employment search. Services available include individual counseling, résumé writing, and interviewing seminars, on-campus interviews, participation in job fairs including the Southeastern Law Placement Consortium in Atlanta, GA; the South Atlantic Recruiting Conference in Washington, DC; the Southeastern Minority Job Fair; and the Southeastern Public Interest Job Fair.

Applicant Group for the 1993–1994 Academic Year

University of South Carolina School of Law
This grid includes only applicants who earned 120-180 LSAT scores under standard administrations.

LSAT Score	3.75 +		3.50 -3.74		3.25 - 3.49		3.00 - 3.24		2.75 - 2.99		2.50 - 2.74		2.25 - 2.49		2.00 - 2.24		Below 2.00		No GPA		Total	
	Apps	Adm	Apps	Adm	Apps	Adm	Apps	Adm	Apps	Adm	Apps	Adm	Apps	Adm	Apps	Adm	Apps	Adm	Apps	Adm	Apps	Adm
175 - 180	1	1	0	0	0	0	0	0	0	0	0	0	0	0	0	0	0	0	0	0	1	1
170 - 174	2	2	2	2	3	3	0	0	0	0	1	1	2	2	0	0	0	0	0	0	10	10
165 - 169	6	5	11	11	11	11	7	7	8	8	2	1	3	1	1	0	0	0	0	0	49	44
160 - 164	15	15	22	20	44	44	50	37	29	10	14	2	10	1	5	2	2	0	2	1	193	132
155 - 159	26	26	52	43	84	38	115	30	58	8	37	4	18	0	10	1	2	0	2	1	404	151
150 - 154	15	6	57	18	81	9	91	10	78	5	44	2	31	4	12	1	3	1	2	0	414	56
145 - 149	6	1	27	6	50	4	62	4	65	7	44	8	19	1	12	1	5	0	7	0	297	32
140 - 144	2	2	10	1	14	1	19	1	38	0	31	1	9	0	20	2	6	0	5	0	154	8
135 - 139	1	0	3	0	7	0	8	1	14	1	9	0	11	0	9	0	1	0	1	0	64	2
130 - 134	0	0	1	0	3	0	2	0	4	0	7	0	6	0	3	0	1	0	3	0	30	0
125 - 129	0	0	0	0	0	0	0	0	2	0	1	0	1	0	1	0	2	0	0	0	7	0
120 - 124	0	0	0	0	0	0	0	0	0	0	1	0	1	0	0	0	0	0	0	0	2	0
Total	74	58	185	101	297	110	354	90	296	39	191	19	111	9	73	7	22	1	22	2	1625	436

Apps = Number of Applicants
Adm = Number Admitted
Reflects 95% of the total applicant pool.

University of South Dakota School of Law

Admissions/Office of the Dean
414 E. Clark
Vermillion, SD 57069-2390

Phone: 605.677.5443

■ Introduction

The School of Law, located on the university campus in Vermillion, is noted for its contributions in training distinguished leaders for the bench, the bar, and the lawmaking bodies of the state and region. Founded in 1901, the school is accredited by both the ABA and the AALS.

Approximately 225 students are enrolled at USD School of Law, with a total university population of over 7,700. The city of Vermillion, with a population of only 9,800, provides a small-town atmosphere for students, faculty, and staff.

■ Enrollment/Student Body

➡ *613 applicants*   ➡ *172 admitted first-year class 1993*
➡ *77 enrolled first-year class 1993*   ➡ *218 total full-time*
➡ *3% minority*   ➡ *41% women*
➡ *18 states & foreign countries represented*
➡ *41 undergraduate schools represented*

■ Faculty

➡ *18 total*   ➡ *16 full-time*   ➡ *2 part-time or adjunct*
➡ *4 women*

Excellent student-faculty ratio fosters a close relationship between students and teaching faculty.

■ Library and Physical Facilities

➡ *155,717 volumes & equivalents*   ➡ *library hours: Mon.-Thurs., 7:30 A.M.-MIDNIGHT; Fri., 7:30 A.M.-7:00 P.M.; Sat., 10:00 A.M.-5:00 P.M.; Sun., NOON-10:00 P.M.*
➡ *LEXIS*   ➡ *NEXIS*   ➡ *WESTLAW*   ➡ *DIALOG*
➡ *SDLN*   ➡ *6 full-time librarians*   ➡ *library seats 223*
➡ *approx. 85 computer-assisted legal instruction exercises*

The law school has been housed in its present facility since 1981. It contains three classrooms, three seminar rooms, a student computer room, a spacious student lounge, offices for faculty, administration, and student organizations, and a teaching courtroom with judges' chambers and an audiovisual control room. The courtroom doubles as an assembly hall and can accommodate the entire student body.

The library occupies a substantial portion of all three floors of the facility, and provides study carrels for students and group study space. Many library functions are automated providing easy access to the library's own collection and to the collection of more than 30 other libraries in South Dakota and 18 other law libraries in the region.

■ Curriculum

➡ *90 credits required to graduate*   ➡ *75 courses available*
➡ *degrees available: J.D.; J.D./Masters offered in 10 areas including Bus., Educ., Arts & Science and Agriculture*
➡ *semesters, start in Aug.*
➡ *range of first-year class size—75*

There is a three-semester core curriculum and three semesters of advanced studies. Ninety semester credits are required for the J.D. degree. The first-year curriculum is required of all students. In the second and third years, electives are available in addition to required courses. An optional skills training semester is available for 15 credit hours during the spring semester. Also, during the summer a clinical externship program is offered for 7 credit hours. Clinical interns learn by doing under the close supervision of a supervising attorney and the clinical law director. Skills training is also available to second- and third-year students in the trial techniques course, negotiations, and other courses, each of which utilizes to the fullest extent the audiovisual capabilities of the law school.

The excellent student-to-faculty ratio fosters a close relationship between students and a teaching faculty of 16 full-time and two part-time teachers.

■ Special Programs

The school has joint programs with other departments of the graduate school, with joint degrees available in accounting, business administration, history, English, psychology, education, political science/public administration, and economics. Students may transfer nine hours of approved interdisciplinary course work for J.D. credit. For students not enrolled in a joint-degree program, up to six interdisciplinary credits may be applied toward the 90-credit J.D. requirement.

Various paid summer legal internships both within and outside of South Dakota are available in both private firms and public agencies. The South Dakota Supreme Court has adopted a student-practice rule that allows students who have completed their second year to represent clients in court under the supervision of a member of the bar.

■ Admission Standards

➡ *Bachelor's degree required*   ➡ *preferred application deadline—March 1*   ➡ *rolling admission, early application preferred*   ➡ *LSAT, LSDAS required*
➡ *median GPA—3.24*   ➡ *median LSAT score—156*
➡ *application fee—(first time applications only)*
➡ *application form, 2 letters of recommendation, personal statement required*

Accepted students are required to pay a $50 nonrefundable deposit to reserve a position in the entering first-year class, and to submit two photographs and an official transcript reflecting their undergraduate degree.

Students who do not meet regular admission criteria may be invited to participate in the Summer Screening Program. Program participants are enrolled in two non-credit law school courses during a five-week summer session. Up to 10 students who receive the highest cumulative grade-point average while maintaining a grade of 70 or better in both courses are offered admission to the entering first-year class. The program provides a valuable proving ground for applicants whose abilities are not accurately reflected in past undergraduate or LSAT performance.

USD School of Law is committed to providing full opportunity for the study of law and entry into the profession by qualified members or groups (notably racial and ethnic minorities, including Native Americans) that have been victims of discrimination in various forms.

Transfer students may apply for admission with advanced standing only if they are in good standing and eligible to return to the transferor law school.

Foreign students who attended undergraduate programs in which English was not the dominant language must also submit a TOEFL score as part of their application package.

■ Student Activities

The *South Dakota Law Review* presents articles by second- and third-year students, lawyers, judges, and professors. Participation in moot court, client counseling, and negotiation is encouraged, and competitions in all activities are held at the intramural, regional, and national levels.

The school is active in the Law Student Division of the ABA. Two legal fraternities—Delta Theta Phi and Phi Alpha Delta—are active at the school. Other organizations with chapters at the school include Women in Law, the Native American Law Students Association, the Christian Legal Society, the Law Caucus, and the Environmental Law Society.

■ Expenses and Financial Aid

➡ *tuition & fees—full-time resident, $3,610*
➡ *estimated additional expenses—$3,500 (books, room & board)*
➡ *academic performance and need-based scholarships available*
➡ *minority scholarships available*   ➡ *financial aid available; FAFSA needs analysis must be submitted through central University Financial Aid Office*

Scholarships are awarded to more than 25 percent of the student body.

A limited number of teaching assistantships are available for academically qualified second- and third-year students. A research service provided by the McKusick Law Library for practicing attorneys also provides employment opportunities for several law students during the academic year.

Student loans are available through the university's Office of Student Financial Aids (605.677.5446). Special scholarship opportunities are available for minority students. For additional information about such programs, applicants should contact Minority Student Financial Aids Coordinator, 14 Slagle Hall, USD, 414 E. Clark, St., Vermillion, SD 57069-2390 (605.677.5446).

■ Career Services

The placement opportunities for third-year law students have been excellent both in South Dakota, the surrounding areas and throughout the United States. Over one-third of the graduates of the school practice law outside of South Dakota. The law school also has an active program to place first- and second-year students in summer internship programs with law firms.

Applicant Group for the 1993–1994 Academic Year

University of South Dakota School of Law
This grid includes only applicants who earned 120-180 LSAT scores under standard administrations. It does **not** includes students admitted through the Summer Screening Program.

LSAT Score	3.75 +		3.50 -3.74		3.25 - 3.49		3.00 - 3.24		2.75 - 2.99		2.50 - 2.74		2.25 - 2.49		2.00 - 2.24		Below 2.00		No GPA		Total	
	Apps	Adm	Apps	Adm	Apps	Adm	Apps	Adm	Apps	Adm	Apps	Adm	Apps	Adm	Apps	Adm	Apps	Adm	Apps	Adm	Apps	Adm
175 - 180	0	0	0	0	0	0	0	0	0	0	0	0	0	0	0	0	0	0	0	0	0	0
170 - 174	0	0	0	0	0	0	0	0	0	0	0	0	0	0	0	0	0	0	0	0	0	0
165 - 169	2	1	1	1	1	0	2	1	4	3	5	5	0	0	1	0	0	0	0	0	16	11
160 - 164	6	4	1	1	6	5	7	5	3	0	2	0	5	0	1	0	0	0	0	0	31	15
155 - 159	9	9	17	13	17	11	35	26	19	4	21	5	12	2	2	0	1	0	1	0	134	70
150 - 154	6	4	22	15	27	13	47	16	33	9	21	1	11	0	5	0	0	0	1	0	173	58
145 - 149	5	1	20	3	19	3	26	1	22	1	15	0	7	0	3	0	1	0	3	0	121	9
140 - 144	8	0	5	0	10	0	14	0	6	0	11	1	11	0	4	0	2	0	1	0	72	1
135 - 139	0	0	0	0	2	0	2	0	6	0	6	0	2	0	2	0	1	0	2	0	23	0
130 - 134	0	0	0	0	1	0	1	0	1	0	1	0	0	0	1	0	0	0	0	0	5	0
125 - 129	0	0	0	0	0	0	0	0	1	0	0	0	2	0	0	0	1	0	0	0	4	0
120 - 124	0	0	0	0	0	0	0	0	0	0	0	0	0	0	0	0	0	0	0	0	0	0
Total	36	19	66	33	83	32	134	49	95	17	82	12	50	2	19	0	6	0	8	0	579	164

Apps = Number of Applicants
Adm = Number Admitted

South Texas College of Law

1303 San Jacinto Street
Houston, TX 77002-7000

Phone: 713.646.1810

■ Introduction

South Texas College of Law is a private, nonprofit, independent educational institution located in downtown Houston. Founded in 1923, South Texas is the oldest law school in the metropolitan area and one of the larger private law schools in the nation. South Texas offers both full-time and part-time study leading to the Doctor of Jurisprudence degree, and is accredited by the ABA.

■ Enrollment/Student Body

➡ *2,619 applicants* ➡ *1,067 admitted first-year class 1993*
➡ *464 enrolled first-year class 1993* ➡ *854 total full-time*
➡ *462 total part-time* ➡ *18% minority*
➡ *40% women* ➡ *29 states & foreign countries represented*
➡ *271 undergraduate schools represented*

The student-to-faculty ratio at South Texas is approximately 24 to 1. The approximate median age of students is 29. Many South Texas students are pursuing law as a second career or to complement their current employment.

■ Faculty

➡ *89 total* ➡ *54 full-time* ➡ *35 part-time or adjunct*
➡ *23 women* ➡ *5 minority*

■ Library and Physical Facilities

➡ *290,000 volumes & equivalents* ➡ *library hours: Mon.-Thurs., 7:30 A.M.-MIDNIGHT; Fri., 7:30 A.M.-10:00 P.M.; Sat., 8:30 A.M.-7:00 P.M.; Sun., 10:00 A.M.-10:00 P.M.* ➡ *LEXIS*
➡ *NEXIS* ➡ *WESTLAW* ➡ *DIALOG*
➡ *Vu/Text* ➡ *Epic* ➡ *CompuServe*
➡ *9 full-time librarians* ➡ *library seats 594*

Located in the law school complex are the hearing rooms and chambers of the First and Fourteenth Texas Courts of Appeals (intermediate appellate tribunals with both civil and criminal jurisdiction), making South Texas the only American law school to house two appellate courts on a permanent basis.

Also housed in the complex is the law library, which is committed to new information technology. Library users enjoy access to a variety of on-line databases; interactive video; CD-ROM and laserdisc databases; a modern computer center; and one of the most advanced audiovisual departments in the country.

■ Curriculum

➡ *Academic Support Program* ➡ *90 credits required to graduate* ➡ *143 courses available*
➡ *J.D. degree available* ➡ *semesters, start in Aug. and Jan.*
➡ *range of first-year class size—20-80*

The curriculum at South Texas College of Law combines classroom instruction with simulated and clinical courses and cocurricular activities. The full-time program requires a minimum of 90 weeks of study and

the part-time program requires a minimum of 120 weeks of study.

South Texas operates a unified class scheduling system, whereby students may select convenient class times rather than having to choose between day and evening divisions. To accommodate part-time working students, a complete curriculum of classes is scheduled after 5:30 P.M. A few classes also are scheduled on Saturday mornings.

■ Special Programs

South Texas administers an academic support program for students who are referred by the Admissions Committee, legal-writing instructors, and the Associate Dean for Academic Affairs. This highly successful program assists students in their first 30 hours of course work through individual and small-group tutorial sessions and weekly reviews of study techniques, such as taking class notes, outlining, briefing cases, and reviewing for examinations. Participants are tutored by advanced students selected on a merit basis. Student participation is voluntary but strongly encouraged for those who are eligible. The program is augmented by periodic seminars covering similar topics, which are open to all interested students.

South Texas provides students with practical legal experience through on-campus clinics in disability entitlement, mediation, and capital-punishment appeals. In each of these clinics, students work on actual cases under the direction of a faculty member. Externships provide practical hands-on experience through placements in prosecutors' offices, state and federal government agencies, and with members of the state and federal judiciary, both at the trial and appellate level.

■ Admission Standards

➡ *Bachelor's degree required* ➡ *application deadline—fall, March 15; spring, Oct. 1* ➡ *LSAT, LSDAS required*
➡ *median GPA—3.00* ➡ *median LSAT score—155*
➡ *application fee—$40*

Beginning and transfer students are admitted for the fall and spring terms, and early application is encouraged. Students are admitted primarily on the basis of their LSAT score and undergraduate grade-point average. A significant percentage of each class, however, is selected on the basis of other factors, such as exceptional personal or academic achievement (not necessarily demonstrated in academic or testing assessments); letters of recommendation; work, community service, or life experiences; leadership potential; a history of overcoming adversity and hardship; and a talent for communicating effectively. Every attempt is made to evaluate each applicant as an individual, a prospective student, and a future professional.

South Texas College of Law does not discriminate on the basis of sex, sexual orientation, age, race, color, religion, national or ethnic origin, or disability in administration of its educational policies, admissions policies, scholarships and loan programs, and other school-administered programs. South Texas gives special consideration to applications from members of minority groups to help ensure a diverse student body.

■ Student Activities

The *South Texas Law Review* is a scholarly periodical published and edited by a staff of law school students selected for membership on the basis of outstanding scholarship or writing ability. In addition, South Texas students edit and publish the *Corporate Counsel Review* on behalf of the Corporate Counsel Section of the State Bar of Texas, and *Currents*, a journal of international trade law, which focuses on the latest legislation, treaties, cases, and trends affecting international trade.

Each year, South Texas is represented by student teams at various state, national, and international moot court competitions, as well as mock trial, client counseling, and negotiation and settlement competitions. Since 1980, South Texas teams have earned an unmatched record, winning various national and state championships and numerous individual honors.

The Student Bar Association is the general organization for all students. The college has a local honor society, the Order of the Lytae; a chapter of the National Order of Barristers; three legal fraternities; and numerous special-interest student organizations.

■ Expenses and Financial Aid

➡ *tuition & fees—full-time, $12,600; part-time, $8,600*
➡ *estimated additional expenses—$11,380 (room and board, books, transportation, and other personal expenses)*

➡ *academic merit and financial need scholarships available*
➡ *financial aid available; FAFSA form for need analysis due to central processor in Feb. or early March for fall, and July or early Aug. for spring*

The college offers a deferred tuition payment program. In addition, various financial aid programs are available. Depending on the circumstances, students at South Texas may be eligible for Tuition Equalization Grants and State Student Incentive Grants for Texas residents, Stafford Loans, Supplemental Loans for Students, the Law Student Loan, the Law Access Loan, the Texas College Access Loan, and college work-study. South Texas also offers an expanding variety of merit and need-based scholarships, tuition waivers, grants, and emergency loans. A number of scholarships and grants are targeted toward members of minority groups. Deadlines for these assistance programs vary. Interested applicants may contact the Office of Scholarships and Financial Aid at the college.

■ Career Services

The Career Development Office at South Texas assists students in obtaining full-time or part-time employment and aids graduating seniors and alumni in obtaining permanent employment. While no law school can assure students or graduates of employment, the Career Development Office has expanded its activities each year on behalf of South Texas constituents, with favorable results. The Career Development Office provides professional seminars, counseling, and referrals to assist students and graduates in marketing themselves to potential employers. In addition, the Career Development Office sponsors a mentor program, whereby students can meet informally with alumni to network and learn more about the legal profession.

Applicant Group for the 1993–1994 Academic Year

South Texas College of Law

GPA	Below 135		135 - 139		140 - 144		145 - 149		150 - 154		155 - 159		160 - 164		165 - 169		170 - 174		175 - 180		Total	
	Apps	Adm	Apps	Adm	Apps	Adm	Apps	Adm	Apps	Adm	Apps	Adm	Apps	Adm	Apps	Adm	Apps	Adm	Apps	Adm	Apps	Adm
3.75 - 4.00	1	0	1	0	2	2	8	3	14	14	6	6	2	2	1	1	0	0	0	0	35	28
3.50 - 3.74	1	0	8	0	16	8	20	3	42	35	30	30	8	6	1	1	1	1	0	0	127	84
3.25 - 3.49	3	0	13	0	27	2	55	7	74	55	44	42	17	17	10	10	0	0	0	0	243	133
3.00 - 3.24	7	0	12	0	48	8	91	20	109	65	83	83	25	25	7	7	0	0	0	0	382	208
2.75 - 2.99	11	0	26	0	57	6	81	14	127	73	79	75	30	30	10	10	0	0	0	0	421	208
2.50 - 2.74	20	0	30	0	59	3	97	9	97	28	64	56	21	20	8	8	0	0	0	0	396	124
2.25 - 2.49	19	0	31	1	41	1	52	3	50	9	40	26	14	13	2	2	0	0	0	0	249	55
2.00 - 2.24	5	0	22	0	19	0	25	1	22	3	16	2	5	4	3	1	0	0	0	0	117	11
No GPA	7	0	9	0	12	0	13	0	8	0	2	0	2	1	2	0	1	1	0	0	56	2
Total	74	0	152	1	281	30	442	60	543	282	364	320	124	118	44	40	2	2	0	0	2026	853

Apps = Number of Applicants
Adm = Number Admitted

University of Southern California Law Center

Director of Admissions
USC Law Center
University Park, CA 90089-0071

Phone: 213.740.7331

■ Introduction

The Law Center of the University of Southern California is a nationally oriented, private institution offering an innovative program focusing on the law as an expression of social values and as an instrument for implementing social goals. The Law Center is small and informal, boasting an unusually advantageous student/faculty ratio of better than 15:1. Instruction is both highly theoretical and highly practical, emphasizing in various courses both a critical understanding of how law functions in society and a practical knowledge of how lawyers function within the legal system. The Law Center has achieved national recognition both for its innovative, interdisciplinary-oriented young faculty and for its leadership in clinical education.

The Law Center's location on the main campus of the University of Southern California, University Park, facilitates access to instruction in law-related disciplines. University Park is located five miles from the center of Los Angeles, a dynamic city which itself is the core of an internationally important region.

Fully accredited nationwide, the Law Center has been a member of the AALS since 1907, and was included in the first group of schools to be accredited by the ABA.

■ Enrollment/Student Body

➡ *3,464 applicants*   ➡ *200-210 enrolled first-year class*
➡ *600 full-time*   ➡ *30% minority*
➡ *42% women*   ➡ *25 states represented*
➡ *100 undergraduate schools represented*

Typically, the size of the entering class is between 195 and 200 students, divided for first-year instructional purposes into two, three, or four sections.

■ Faculty

➡ *48 full-time*   ➡ *28 part-time or adjunct*

■ Library and Physical Facilities

➡ *330,000 volumes & equivalents*   ➡ *LEXIS*
➡ *WESTLAW*   ➡ *21 full-time library staff*

Recently completed construction on a major addition to the Law Center building provides student lounge space with food service, additional classrooms, a modern trial courtroom, two new computer classrooms, and office space for additional faculty. The law library occupies two floors of the five-story structure. It has an excellent, service-oriented professional staff. The library collection includes a substantial number of interdisciplinary materials, reflecting the Law Center's commitment to this aspect of legal education.

■ Curriculum

➡ *Academic Support Program*   ➡ *88 credits required to graduate*   ➡ *joint degrees offered*

The Law Center operates on a semester basis, and admits only full-time students. The first-year curriculum consists of required courses; the remaining two years are elective, enabling students to concentrate on subjects of special interest. The composition and interest of the faculty allow several areas of law to be especially well represented. Numerous courses are offered by faculty experts in international law, corporations and business-government relationships, bioethics, civil rights and liberties, and judicial administration. The Law Center curriculum draws upon several related disciplines such as philosophy, linguistics, economics, psychology, sociology, international relations, and urban planning to provide an integrated approach to legal study.

■ Special Programs

Dual Degrees—The Law Center maintains dual-degree programs with the Graduate School of Business Administration, the Department of Economics, the School of Philosophy, the School of Public Administration, the School of Urban and Regional Planning, the School of Social Work, the School of Religion, the Annenberg School of Communications, and the School of International Relations. These programs enable qualified students to earn a law degree and the appropriate Master's degree. The Law Center also maintains a dual-degree program with the California Institute of Technology, enabling students to receive a J.D. from USC and a Ph.D. in Social Science from Cal Tech, or to complete the requirements for the Graduate Certificate in the USC Program for the Study of Women and Men in Society.

Legal Clinics—The Poverty and Public Interest Law Clinic and Post-Conviction Justice Clinic, taught by faculty members with substantial practical experience, enable students to gain valuable advocacy skills and learn first-hand about access to justice and poverty law issues by representing real clients. In addition, the school arranges placements for academic credit with federal and state court judges, and numerous government and public interest law offices.

■ Admission

➡ *Bachelor's degree from accredited college required*
➡ *application deadline—Feb. 1; early application encouraged*
➡ *median GPA—3.50*   ➡ *median LSAT score—164 (93rd percentile)*   ➡ *application fee—$60*

Students applying for admission should take the LSAT no later than the December administration. Admissions decisions are made on the basis of the student's academic record, LSAT score, personal statement, and letters of recommendation. The Admissions Committee gives primary consideration to outstanding academic and professional promise and to qualities which will enhance the diversity of the student body. Applicants are strongly urged to submit at least one academic recommendation letter.

The committee focuses on the student's college grades, academic major, selection of courses, and significant scholarly achievements. The Law Center does not require applicants to take any specific college courses of study. Whatever the discipline, the student should concentrate on developing strong writing and analytic skills.

■ Student Activities

The school's *Law Review* has one of the largest circulations in the nation. Students also publish the *Southern California Interdisciplinary Law Journal*, *Major Tax Planning*, and the *Review of Law and Women's Studies*. The Moot Court competition sends participants to national and state competitions; recently the final rounds at the Law Center have been judged by justices of the U.S. Supreme Court. The Order of the Coif, the national legal scholastic honor society, has a local chapter at the school.

Public service activities abound. The Public Interest Law Foundation provides financial assistance for summer and postgraduate public-service employment and volunteer opportunities. The school provides annual awards to students who excel in public and community service, and who author the best essay on a social-justice topic.

Asian, African-American, and Chicano law students are represented by associations. Other student organizations include international and entertainment law societies, chapters of major legal fraternities, a Women's Law Association, Gay and Lesbian Law Union, Christian Legal Society, Jewish Law Students, and chapters of the ACLU and Federalist Society.

■ Expenses and Financial Aid

➡ *1993-94 tuition—$9,578/semester*

A significant financial commitment is made each year to assist worthy applicants so that they may attend. No student should refrain from applying because of financial need.

To assist in the partial payment of educational loans, the Law Center offers funds to graduates who accept employment with low-paying public interest organizations.

For more information, please call Mary Bingham, Director of Financial Aid at 213.740.7331.

■ Housing

University housing is available for law students in various university dormitories and apartments.

■ Career Services

The Law Center maintains a career services office to assist students and alumni in securing professional employment. The office provides three basic services: arranging on-campus interviews by legal employers, placing students in summer and part-time jobs; and, maintaining a file and monthly newsletter for alumni seeking a change of employment. In addition, programs designed to provide guidance concerning career selection are offered during the year. The career services office maintains a public interest and government employment directory listing all available positions. Each year, several hundred private firms, government agencies, public interest agencies, and corporations from throughout the country come to the Law Center to interview students for summer and permanent employment. Historically, approximately 90 percent of each graduating class has found employment.

Applicant Group for the 1993–1994 Academic Year

University of Southern California Law Center
This grid includes only applicants who earned 120-180 LSAT scores under standard administrations.

LSAT Score	GPA 3.75 +		3.50 -3.74		3.25 - 3.49		3.00 - 3.24		2.75 - 2.99		Below 2.75		No GPA		Total	
	Apps	Adm	Apps	Adm	Apps	Adm	Apps	Adm	Apps	Adm	Apps	Adm	Apps	Adm	Apps	Adm
175 - 180	3	3	5	5	5	5	3	3	2	2	3	0	0	0	21	18
170 - 174	8	8	19	19	25	25	20	19	9	4	4	1	0	0	85	76
165 - 169	49	49	86	85	98	92	68	57	29	3	17	4	4	1	351	291
160 - 164	84	76	171	139	177	68	126	21	54	8	47	1	11	1	670	314
155 - 159	75	17	148	17	209	28	139	16	86	9	83	3	12	0	752	90
150 - 154	37	3	98	7	137	8	135	8	118	3	98	3	17	0	640	32
Below 150	16	0	60	1	104	1	158	1	150	0	241	0	35	0	764	3
Total	272	156	587	273	755	227	649	125	448	29	935	12	79	2	3283	824

Apps = Number of Applicants
Adm = Number Admitted
Reflects 95% of the total applicant pool.

Southern Illinois University School of Law

Lesar Law Building
Carbondale, IL 62901

Phone: 618.453.8767

■ Introduction

Southern Illinois University School of Law is located in Carbondale, a community of 27,000 people in the hilly, wooded Ozark area of Illinois. Carbondale's quality of life has recently been rated as number one among all small cities in Illinois. The School of Law is one of nine colleges of Southern Illinois University-Carbondale, a comprehensive state university with a total student enrollment of 24,000. The school is fully accredited by the ABA and is a member of the Association of American Law Schools.

■ Enrollment/Student Body

➤ *1,162 applicants* ➤ *362 admitted first-year class 1993*
➤ *127 enrolled first-year class 1993* ➤ *344 total full-time*
➤ *11% minority* ➤ *41% women*
➤ *20 states & foreign countries represented*
➤ *40 undergraduate schools represented*

■ Faculty

➤ *33 total* ➤ *25 full-time* ➤ *8 part-time or adjunct*
➤ *10 women* ➤ *3 minority*

■ Library and Physical Facilities

➤ *301,526 volumes & equivalents* ➤ *library hours: Mon.-Thurs., 8:00 A.M.-9:00 P.M.; Fri., 8:00 A.M.-6:00 P.M.; Sat., 1:00 P.M.-5:00 P.M.; Sun., 1:00 P.M.-9:00 P.M.* ➤ *LEXIS*
➤ *NEXIS* ➤ *WESTLAW* ➤ *DIALOG*
➤ *LEGALTRAC* ➤ *7 full-time librarians*
➤ *library seats 407*

The law library's professional staff provides a wide range of services to patrons. The on-line public catalog provides immediate and detailed information about the monographs and journals available in the library collection. A LAN-based computer lab provides access to computer-assisted research systems, both legal (e.g., WESTLAW, LEXIS) and nonlegal, as well as computer-aided instruction, word processing, and other applications software. Ample seating in a variety of settings, including tables, unreserved carrels, and locked carrels for research assistants and seminar students, help make the library an activity center of the law school. All facilities are fully accessible to individuals with disabilities. Students have 24-hour keyed access to the library and other facilities.

■ Curriculum

➤ *Academic Support Program* ➤ *90 credits required to graduate* ➤ *83 courses available* ➤ *degrees available: J.D.; J.D./M.D.; J.D./M.B.A.; J.D./M.Acct.; J.D./M.P.A.*
➤ *semesters, start in Aug.* ➤ *range of first-year class size—20-65*

All students have a uniform first-year curriculum. A broad range of courses and seminars is offered in the second and third years. Throughout the curriculum the faculty emphasize the inculcation of professional skills such as writing, oral argumentation, drafting documents, interviewing, negotiating, and counseling.

■ Special Programs

The school's clinical program enables senior law students to have various "real-life" experiences with clients and the legal system under the supervision of clinical faculty members, judges, and licensed attorneys. The Elderly Clinic provides direct legal assistance to persons over 60 years of age in the 13 southernmost counties of Illinois. Students may participate in an externship program in which they obtain academic credit while working with the state's attorney, public defender, Illinois Attorney General's office, and other approved legal offices as well as federal and state judges. The ADR Clinic allows students to learn more about alternative dispute resolution techniques and participate with clients in some of the processes. An elderly mediation service is one of the practical applications for the ADR Clinic student.

Concurrent J.D./Masters Degree programs (M.B.A., M.P.A., M. Acct.) are offered in conjunction with the Graduate School. An innovative six-year program offered in cooperation with the School of Medicine permits selected students to concurrently obtain J.D. and M.D. degrees. The school has a very strong health law curriculum, featuring five courses in this specialty.

The school provides a comprehensive legal argumentation program, sponsoring teams that compete in the National Moot Court, ABA Moot Court, all-Illinois Moot Court, and Philip C. Jessup International Moot Court competitions. SIU law students have enjoyed success in these competitions.

Environmental law is a prominent specialty in the law school's curriculum, with six elective courses as well as a National Environment Law Moot Court team.

As part of its mission to emphasize leadership skills, the law school sponsors an active public speakers' program focusing on important national and regional issues. In addition, the school sponsors a major symposium each year bringing a large number of prominent legal educators to Carbondale. Recent symposia have addressed gender bias in legal education (1989), the legal ramifications of the Persian Gulf Crisis (1990), the Bill of Rights (1991), and Justice Oliver Wendell Holmes (1993).

■ Admission

➤ *Bachelor's degree required* ➤ *rolling admission, early application (before Feb. 1) recommended*
➤ *LSAT, LSDAS required* ➤ *median GPA—3.30*
➤ *median LSAT score—156* ➤ *application fee—$25*

Admission decisions are based on a number of factors, the LSAT score and undergraduate GPA being most prominent. Multiple LSAT scores are averaged. There is no formal cutoff for either the LSAT score or GPAs. Other factors considered by the Admissions Committee include trends in academic performance, writing ability, leadership and maturity, letters of recommendation, employment or community service experience, and obstacles imposed by racial, religious, ethnic, gender, or disability discrimination. The admissions committee actively recruits minority students, and the law school supports CLEO.

■ Student Activities

The school publishes the *SIU Law Journal*, which provides editorial and writing experience for a number of upper-class students. Students with a particular interest in health law can also publish articles in *The Journal of Legal Medicine*.

All students automatically belong to the Student Bar Association. The SBA schedules lectures and social affairs, provides services to its members, and serves as a channel of communication between students and faculty. Students play an active role in law school governance, serving on most faculty committees. Other student organizations include Phi Alpha Delta, the International Law Society, the Women's Law Forum, the Environmental Law Society, the Black Law Student Association, Lesbian and Gay Law Students, the Rutherford Institute, Phi Delta Phi, the Law School Democrats, the Law School Republicans, the Nontraditional Students, the Law and Medicine Society, the Christian Legal Society, the Peer Support Network, and law student divisions of the Illinois State Bar Association and the ABA.

■ Expenses and Financial Aid

➡ *full-time tuition & fees—resident, $3,594/yr.; nonresident, $9,186/yr.*   ➡ *estimated additional expenses—$7,686 (books & supplies, room & board, transportation & misc.)*

➡ *partial tuition-waiver scholarships available*
➡ *minority Dean's Fellowships available*
➡ *financial aid available; Free Application for Federal Student Aid (FAFSA) need form is preferred*

Student loans, work-study opportunities, and most other forms of financial aid are administered by the university's Financial Aid Office. Information concerning loans and financial aid procedures may be obtained from the Financial Aid Office, Woody Hall, Southern Illinois University-Carbondale.

A relatively large number of research assistantships are available to qualified upper-class students. Approximately one quarter of the upper-class students hold research assistantships.

■ Career Services

Under the direction of an assistant dean, the Career Development Office provides services for both enrolled students and alumni. Students have the opportunity to participate in a variety of regional and national job fairs and career conferences throughout the year. Other programs and services provided include individual career counseling, an on-campus interview program, a research pool service, and career workshops. Special panel presentations that cover a variety of career and employment topics are offered during Law Week in February.

The Career Development Office provides a job listing service, subscribes to a variety of job newsletters, publishes a biweekly job vacancy bulletin, and exchanges job bulletins with other law schools. The career library contains diverse career materials including firm résumés, corporate brochures, and directories.

Applicant Group for the 1993–1994 Academic Year

Southern Illinois University School of Law
This grid includes only applicants who earned 120-180 LSAT scores under standard administrations.

LSAT Score	3.75 +		3.50 -3.74		3.25 - 3.49		3.00 - 3.24		2.75 - 2.99		2.50 - 2.74		2.25 - 2.49		2.00 - 2.24		Below 2.00		No GPA		Total	
	Apps	Adm	Apps	Adm	Apps	Adm	Apps	Adm	Apps	Adm	Apps	Adm	Apps	Adm	Apps	Adm	Apps	Adm	Apps	Adm	Apps	Adm
175 - 180	0	0	0	0	0	0	0	0	0	0	0	0	0	0	0	0	0	0	0	0	0	0
170 - 174	0	0	0	0	1	1	0	0	0	0	0	0	0	0	0	0	0	0	0	0	1	1
165 - 169	1	1	2	2	3	3	4	4	2	2	3	3	0	0	0	0	0	0	0	0	15	15
160 - 164	5	5	10	10	16	16	13	13	11	10	12	8	7	3	2	1	0	0	1	1	77	67
155 - 159	13	13	32	32	47	46	45	41	31	15	39	10	17	6	3	0	1	0	2	1	230	164
150 - 154	11	8	26	17	62	24	65	2	68	5	36	3	25	1	4	0	2	0	1	0	300	60
145 - 149	8	1	16	3	34	6	58	2	44	3	23	1	14	2	6	0	1	0	5	0	209	18
140 - 144	3	1	9	1	17	3	30	0	30	2	29	2	15	0	8	0	3	0	5	0	149	9
135 - 139	2	0	2	0	4	0	10	0	15	0	18	0	13	0	9	0	6	0	3	0	82	0
130 - 134	0	0	1	0	0	0	0	0	4	0	6	0	8	0	3	0	1	0	4	0	27	0
125 - 129	1	0	0	0	0	0	0	0	2	0	1	0	3	0	0	0	0	0	1	0	8	0
120 - 124	0	0	0	0	0	0	0	0	0	0	0	0	2	0	1	0	0	0	0	0	3	0
Total	44	29	98	65	184	99	225	62	207	37	167	27	104	12	36	1	14	0	22	2	1101	334

Apps = Number of Applicants
Adm = Number Admitted
Reflects 95% of the total applicant pool.

Southern Methodist University School of Law

Director of Admissions
Dallas, TX 75275-0116

Phone: 214.768.2550

■ Introduction

The SMU School of Law has established a 70-year history of leadership and excellence in legal education. The law school currently leads with curricular innovations in first-year studies, an emphasis on international law in a global economy, and a community-wide commitment to public service. Located in Dallas, a major urban center, the law school offers students a historic and dynamic learning partnership with local lawyers and legal employers. For these and other reasons, the law school attracts the highest caliber of students and faculty from across the country and abroad. The law school is a member of the AALS and is accredited by the ABA.

■ Enrollment/Student Body

➡ *1,838 applicants* ➡ *698 admitted first-year class 1993*
➡ *256 enrolled first-year class 1993* ➡ *721 total full-time J.D.s* ➡ *20% minority* ➡ *43% women* ➡ *38 states & 6 foreign countries & the District of Columbia represented*
➡ *234 undergraduate schools represented in all classes*

■ Faculty

➡ *41 total* ➡ *39 full-time* ➡ *2 part-time or adjunct*
➡ *11 women* ➡ *6 minority*

■ Library and Physical Facilities

➡ *440,199 volumes & equivalents* ➡ *computer center with WESTLAW and LEXIS* ➡ *8 full-time librarians*
➡ *library seats 700*

The law school occupies the northwest corner of campus and is situated in a quadrangle. Florence and Storey Halls contain classrooms, hearing/court rooms, student lockers, and faculty/administrative offices. Collins Hall, currently under renovation, will open in the Fall of 1994 and contain expanded career services offices, student organizations offices, student lounges and study areas, and state-of-the-art seminar classrooms. Underwood Law Library contains two large classrooms, a student lobby, and ample carrels and study space.

Students have access to other campus facilities outside the law school quad. Graduate student housing is available as well as a computer center, a wellness/athletic center, and a health and counseling center. For "culture" buffs, there are frequent music, theater, and art productions in connection with the renowned Meadows School of the Arts.

■ Curriculum

➡ *Academic Support Program* ➡ *90 credits required to graduate* ➡ *113 total courses available*
➡ *degrees available: J.D.; J.D./M.B.A.; J.D./M.A. in Economics; LL.M.; LL.M. (Taxation); LL.M. (International and Comparative, for foreign attorneys only)*
➡ *range of first-year class size—16-90*
➡ *part-time evening program for LL.M. Tax*

A two-day orientation program introduces new students to their legal education. First-year students take required courses, including civil procedure, contracts, legal research and writing, torts, property, constitutional law, criminal law and procedure, and lawyering. Lawyering, an innovative course for first-year students, uses simulated case files to introduce the roles and tasks of lawyers to students. Students interview and counsel mock "clients," develop facts through interviews, negotiate settlements, and participate in an oral advocacy exercise. Both legal research and writing and lawyering are taught by faculty members or adjuncts in small groups of 16-18 students.

In the second and third years, students choose from a broad range of elective courses. The other requirements for graduation are professional responsibility and two writing units, one of which must be in a third-year edited writing seminar. All students are required to complete 30 hours of public service prior to graduation. Placements are arranged through the law school at local public interest agencies and governmental entities.

Overseas Study: SMU sponsors an overseas summer program at Oxford University. Students who have completed their first year are eligible to apply for the program.

Legal Clinics: The school has several clinical programs that provide students with the opportunity to earn academic credit while engaging in the actual practice of law. Each clinical program is under the supervision of a director and a full-time staff of practicing attorneys. The clinics serve clients from Dallas County in civil, criminal, immigration, and tax cases.

Public Service Opportunities: Students interested in public service or pro bono opportunities will find them available at SMU. The faculty is committed to providing 30 hours of public service every two years. Likewise, students in their second and third years are required to complete 30 hours of pro bono assistance in legal settings. Curricular offerings, such as Civil Rights Legislation and First Amendment and Mass Media, are course complements to the requirement. SMU has a loan repayment assistance program for eligible graduates working in nonprofit or government service.

■ Admission Standards

➡ *Bachelor's degree required* ➡ *application deadline—March 1* ➡ *rolling admission beginning in December*
➡ *LSAT, LSDAS required* ➡ *median GPA—3.18*
➡ *median LSAT score—159* ➡ *application fee—$45*

Applicants must show the ability to handle a rigorous intellectual challenge, a capacity to acquire lawyering skills, and the potential for success as a law student and lawyer. In deciding whether an applicant meets these standards, the Admissions Committee relies heavily on the LSAT and undergraduate grades. The index score provided by Law Services weights the LSAT slightly heavier than the GPA. The personal statement is of great importance in the application package. Letters of recommendation, extracurricular activities, work experience, and other maturing experiences are also considered.

The Admissions Committee welcomes applications from those who, because of their backgrounds, will bring to the school different perspectives, including those from minority groups traditionally underrepresented in the legal community. The School of Law is committed to a policy of nondiscrimination based on sex, age, race, color, religious creed, sexual orientation, or national origin.

■ Student Activities

The Law School publishes the *SMU Law Review* and the *Journal of Air Law and Commerce*, student-edited scholarly journals. The American Bar Association's *The International Lawyer* is edited at the school through a program involving faculty and qualified students. Editorial staffs are selected on the basis of scholarship and through a writing competition conducted each year.

Through the Student Bar Association and student/faculty committees, students participate in the decision processes of the school. Other student activities and organizations include: Asian American Law Students Association; Black Law Students Association; Hispanic American Law Students Association; Jewish Law Students Association; Christian Legal Society; Women in Law; Moot Court Board and teams; mock trial teams;

The Barristers (a service organization); and the Tutorial Program. The school also has three legal fraternities.

■ Expenses and Financial Aid

➡ *full-time tuition & fees—$17,372*   ➡ *estimated additional expenses—$6,914 (room & board, $4,940; books, $930; misc., $1,544)*   ➡ *merit scholarships available including several full tuition and fees plus stipend* ➡ *diversity scholarships based on performance and need available* ➡ *financial aid available; FAF preferred by Feb. 28; scholarship deadlines vary*

■ Career Services

The Office of Career Services aids each law student in his or her career planning through various means. Students are provided with individual counseling, seminars, workshops, and groups conducted or organized by the director. Students have the opportunity to interview with national law firms and other legal employers through on-campus interviewing and to participate in multi-school job fairs, including Texas-in-Washington and minority job fairs.

SMU students are very successful in their search for permanent positions. Ninety percent of the class of 1992 reported employment within six months following graduation. The vast majority of graduates begin their legal practice in Texas, but a significant minority opt for positions across the United States.

Applicant Group for the 1993–1994 Academic Year

Southern Methodist University School of Law
This grid includes only applicants who earned 120-180 LSAT scores under standard administrations.

LSAT Score	3.75 +		3.50 -3.74		3.25 - 3.49		3.00 - 3.24		2.75 - 2.99		2.50 - 2.74		2.25 - 2.49		2.00 - 2.24		Below 2.00		No GPA		Total	
	Apps	Adm	Apps	Adm	Apps	Adm	Apps	Adm	Apps	Adm	Apps	Adm	Apps	Adm	Apps	Adm	Apps	Adm	Apps	Adm	Apps	Adm
175-180	1	1	2	2	0	0	0	0	0	0	1	1	0	0	0	0	0	0	0	0	4	4
170-174	1	1	2	2	2	2	5	5	0	0	0	0	0	0	0	0	0	0	0	0	10	10
165-169	15	15	11	11	13	13	20	17	11	10	9	9	3	2	1	1	0	0	0	0	83	78
160-164	21	20	31	30	37	36	57	54	41	33	21	12	10	6	1	0	0	0	1	1	220	192
155-159	28	26	75	58	92	70	112	72	62	20	40	5	18	0	5	0	0	0	6	3	438	254
150-154	23	5	52	15	75	17	120	17	84	16	59	2	20	2	8	0	2	0	7	2	450	76
145-149	9	4	29	8	44	7	55	8	70	9	51	4	28	1	9	0	4	0	4	1	303	42
140-144	1	0	9	1	18	0	30	0	37	0	40	0	22	0	3	0	3	0	6	1	169	2
135-139	0	0	1	0	6	0	6	0	9	0	15	0	12	0	8	0	0	0	4	1	61	1
130-134	0	0	0	0	2	0	1	0	2	0	4	0	5	0	2	0	0	0	1	0	17	0
125-129	0	0	0	0	1	0	0	0	2	0	0	0	1	0	2	0	0	0	1	0	7	0
120-124	0	0	0	0	0	0	0	0	0	0	0	0	0	0	1	0	0	0	0	0	1	0
Total	99	72	212	127	290	145	406	173	318	88	240	33	119	11	40	1	9	0	30	9	1763	659

Apps = Number of Applicants
Adm = Number Admitted
Reflects 95% of the total applicant pool.

Southern University Law Center

Admissions Office
P.O. Box 9294, Southern Branch Post Office
Baton Rouge, LA 70813

Phone: 504.771.5340 or 800.537.1135

■ Introduction

In September 1947, the Southern University School of Law was officially opened. Accredited by the American Bar Association, the Supreme Court of Louisiana, and the Southern Association of Colleges and Secondary Schools, the Law Center maintains a high standard of professional education. It is fully approved by the Veterans Administration for the training of eligible veterans. The Southern University Law Center adheres to the principle of equal opportunity without regard to race, sex, color, creed, national origin, age, handicap, or marital status.

■ Enrollment/Student Body

➡ *960 applicants*   ➡ *191 admitted first-year class 1993*
➡ *120 enrolled first-year class 1993*   ➡ *339 total full-time*
➡ *58% minority*   ➡ *38% women*
➡ *22 states & foreign countries represented*
➡ *59 undergraduate schools represented*

■ Faculty

➡ *37 total*   ➡ *28 full-time*   ➡ *9 part-time or adjunct*
➡ *9 women*   ➡ *24 minority*

■ Library and Physical Facilities

➡ *339,763 volumes & equivalents*   ➡ *library hours: Mon.-Thurs., 7:30 A.M.-MIDNIGHT; Fri., 7:30 A.M.-5:00 P.M.; Sat., 9:00 A.M.-5:00 P.M.; Sun., 2:00 P.M.-10:00 P.M.*   ➡ *LEXIS*
➡ *NEXIS*   ➡ *WESTLAW*   ➡ *DIALOG*
➡ *Legal Trac*   ➡ *13 full-time librarians*   ➡ *library seats 265*

The Law Center building is located on the parent campus of the Southern University system. A $4 million expansion and improvement program is currently underway. Plans call for a complete renovation of the adjoining old university library building. The new facility will give the Law Center a total area of approximately 80,000 square feet.

Special arrangements have been made with the Louisiana State University Library, which has one of the largest collections of Anglo-American and civil law materials in the South, to make its resources available for research purposes through the Southern University Law Library.

Training sessions are conducted each semester by library staff to assist students in the proper utilization of the WESTLAW system.

■ Curriculum

➡ *Academic Support Program*   ➡ *Pre-Law Success offered*
➡ *96 credits required to graduate*   ➡ *81 courses available*
➡ *fall semester—Aug.-Dec.*   ➡ *spring semester—Jan.-May*   ➡ *summer session—June-July*

The program of study is designed to give students a comprehensive knowledge of both the civil law and common law. While emphasis is given to the substantive and procedural law of Louisiana with its French and Spanish origins, Anglo-American law is strongly integrated into the curriculum.

Fundamental differences in method and approach and the results reached in the two systems are analyzed.

The civil law system of Louisiana offers the law student a unique educational opportunity. The program of instruction examines the historical background of the civil law system and its development in the Anglo-American setting.

Students are trained in the art of advocacy, legal research, and the sources and social purposes of legal principles. Techniques to discipline the students' minds in legal reasoning are an integral part of the educational objectives of the Law Center. Students are instructed in the ethics of the legal profession and the professional responsibility of the lawyer to society.

The three-year curriculum is based upon the standard professional courses usually given in member schools of the AALS. The curriculum requires a full six semesters of residence. Any study undertaken in a summer session shall not count toward residence requirements. Electives have been integrated as part of the curriculum, and students are required to take courses specified for the respective years.

■ Admission

➡ *Bachelor's degree required*   ➡ *application deadline—March 31*   ➡ *LSAT, LSDAS required*
➡ *median GPA—2.62*   ➡ *median LSAT score—145*
➡ *no application fee*

The Law Center does not prescribe any prelegal courses but strongly recommends a foundation in such courses as English, Speech, Political Science, History, Economics, Psychology, Logic, Mathematics and Analytical Courses, and Science.

Students beginning the study of law are admitted only in the fall semester. The Law Center operates a full-time day program. Applicants are advised to take the LSAT prior to the February test date of the expected year of enrollment. Under no circumstances will a score received on the test administered more than three years prior to the anticipated date of acceptance be considered. All applications for admission are reviewed by a special committee. Though many variables are taken into consideration for admission, primary emphasis is given to the undergraduate grade-point average and scores from the LSAT. Work experience and past pursuits are also reviewed.

Completed application forms, in addition to two letters of recommendation and two copies of official transcripts, should be filed with the Admissions Office during the fall semester prior to the year in which admission is sought.

■ Housing

Dormitory accommodations are available for law students. All students desiring to live in campus housing are required to submit an application to the Housing Office, in addition to a security deposit of $50. Applications should be made to the Director of Housing, Southern University, as early as possible.

■ Student Activities

Students with advanced standing are eligible to enroll in the Clinical Education Program, which allows students to handle cases under the direct supervision of a full-time faculty member of the Law Center.

The *Southern University Law Review* is a scholarly periodical published semiannually under the auspices of the Southern University Law Center. Editorial administration and managerial responsibilities are handled by the student members of the *Law Review* staff with guidance from a faculty advisor. Candidacy for law review membership is offered to the top 15 percent of the first-year class on the basis of the student's academic achievement. However, actual membership is conditional on the submissions by each candidate, or other interested students, of a manuscript deemed by the editorial board to be publishable. *Law Review* membership provides eligible students with a wealth of experience in legal research and writing.

■ Other Student Organizations

➡ *Moot Court board*   ➡ *Student Bar Association*
➡ *Law Student Division, ABA*   ➡ *Black Law Students Association*   ➡ *Delta Theta Phi Law Fraternity*
➡ *Phi Alpha Delta Law Fraternity, International*
➡ *Women in Law*

The purposes of the Student Bar Association are to promote the general welfare of the Law Center, encourage among its members high scholarship, and cultivate rapport and cooperation among the students, faculty, and members of the legal profession.

■ Expenses and Financial Aid

➡ *full-time tuition & fees—resident, $3,088; nonresident, $3,088+ $3,200*   ➡ *estimated additional expenses—$6,900 (books, lodging, food, transportation, misc.)*
➡ *merit and need-based scholarships available*
➡ *limited merit and need-based minority scholarships available*
➡ *financial aid available; financial aid transcripts from other schools, copy of previous signed tax return, and financial aid verification data required Student Aid Report (SAR)*
➡ *all forms due April 15*

A limited number of direct stipends and jobs are available. Direct stipends are awarded on the basis of the applicant's academic standing and demonstrated financial need. Applications for stipends should be directed to the Financial Aid Committee, Southern University Law Center. Short-term loans to meet emergency needs are available from the Law Center loan fund. All students are expected to pay the required fees on the day of registration.

■ Career Services

A placement office has been established in the Law Center to assist students and alumni in obtaining meaningful employment opportunities. Information on part-time employment before graduation is available through this office. Assistance is also given in job-seeking skills and interviewing techniques.

Applicant Group for the 1993–1994 Academic Year

Southern University Law Center
This grid includes only applicants who earned 120-180 LSAT scores under standard administrations.

LSAT Score	3.75 +		3.50 -3.74		3.25 - 3.49		3.00 - 3.24		2.75 - 2.99		2.50 - 2.74		2.25 - 2.49		2.00 - 2.24		Below 2.00		No GPA		Total	
	Apps	Adm	Apps	Adm	Apps	Adm	Apps	Adm	Apps	Adm	Apps	Adm	Apps	Adm	Apps	Adm	Apps	Adm	Apps	Adm	Apps	Adm
175 - 180	0	0	0	0	0	0	0	0	0	0	0	0	0	0	0	0	0	0	0	0	0	0
170 - 174	0	0	0	0	0	0	0	0	0	0	0	0	0	0	1	1	0	0	0	0	1	1
165 - 169	0	0	0	0	0	0	0	0	0	0	0	0	0	0	0	0	0	0	0	0	0	0
160 - 164	0	0	0	0	0	0	1	0	3	0	1	0	1	1	1	0	1	0	0	0	8	2
155 - 159	0	0	0	0	2	2	1	0	8	0	10	1	7	3	4	1	1	1	0	0	33	8
150 - 154	1	0	2	2	6	1	16	5	40	5	30	6	35	7	14	2	4	1	0	0	148	29
145 - 149	4	2	8	3	19	2	30	4	42	5	54	11	35	6	22	5	2	1	9	6	225	45
140 - 144	1	0	6	1	23	8	29	6	48	10	76	19	59	10	31	5	4	0	11	4	288	63
135 - 139	3	0	0	0	8	1	22	3	31	2	52	4	41	3	31	4	13	1	10	0	211	18
130 - 134	1	0	2	0	4	0	13	0	14	0	24	2	21	1	18	0	9	0	13	0	119	3
125 - 129	1	0	1	0	2	0	0	0	2	0	10	0	5	0	4	0	3	0	7	0	35	0
120 - 124	0	0	0	0	0	0	1	0	1	0	0	0	0	0	3	0	2	0	0	0	7	0
Total	11	2	19	6	64	14	113	18	189	22	257	43	204	31	129	18	39	5	50	10	1075	169

Apps = Number of Applicants
Adm = Number Admitted
Reflects 96% of the total applicant pool.

Southwestern University School of Law

675 South Westmoreland Avenue
Los Angeles, CA 90005-3992

Phone: 213.738.6717

■ Introduction

The only law school with four courses of study leading to the J.D. degree, Southwestern University School of Law offers traditional full-time and part-time programs as well as a unique two-year alternative curriculum. Southwestern is an innovative, urban legal center located among Los Angeles' major law firms, corporate headquarters, and Superior Court, just a short distance from the other courts and government offices in the downtown district. Many public officials, as well as numerous members of the California judiciary, are among the outstanding Southwestern graduates who practice law throughout the US and abroad. Southwestern was founded in 1911 as an independent, nonprofit, nonsectarian institution, is approved by the ABA, and holds membership in the AALS.

■ Enrollment/Student Body

→ *3,003 applicants*   → *1,332 admitted first-year class 1993*
→ *410 enrolled first-year class 1993*   → *811 total full-time*
→ *338 total part-time*   → *24% minority*   → *50% women*
→ *290 undergraduate schools represented*

Southwestern students come from virtually every state as well as from a dozen foreign countries. More than two-thirds have prior work experience or have already completed advanced degrees in such diverse disciplines as accounting, business, chemistry, engineering, international relations, medicine, and urban planning.

■ Faculty

→ *78 total*   → *48 full-time*   → *30 part-time or adjunct*
→ *19 women faculty*   → *12 minority faculty*

The full-time faculty brings to the classroom an average of seven years of law practice and 13 years of law teaching experience, and includes several nationally recognized experts on the law. The distinguished judicial officers and practicing attorneys on the adjunct faculty offer courses in a number of legal specialties.

■ Library and Physical Facilities

→ *340,000 volumes & equivalents*   → *over 100 weekly library hours include: Mon.-Thurs., 7:00 A.M.-MIDNIGHT; Fri., 7:00 A.M.-9:00 P.M.; Sat., 9:00 A.M.-6:00 P.M.; Sun., 10:00 A.M.-11:00 P.M. (open until 2:00 A.M. during reading and exam periods)*   → *library seats 376*   → *LEXIS*   → *NEXIS*
→ *WESTLAW*   → *RLIN*   → *WILSONLINE*
→ *LEGALTRAC*   → *one of the most extensive multimedia legal collections in Southern California*   → *7 full-time librarians*   → *state and federal government depository*

The library also features computer labs, group-study rooms, and CALI stations, as well as special collections on constitutional law, entertainment law, environmental law, international law and taxation.

■ Curriculum

→ *Academic Support Program*   → *87 units/credits required to graduate*   → *130 courses available*   → *J.D. degree*
→ *semesters, begin mid-Aug. (Jul. for SCALE program)*
→ *range of first-year class size—19-100*
→ *8-week on-campus summer session*
→ *Foreign Summer Law Programs in Argentina & Canada*

Southwestern's four courses of study include a three-year, full-time day division; a four-year, part-time evening division; a four-year, part-time day division known as PLEAS (Part-time Legal Education Alternative at Southwestern), designed to accommodate students with child-care responsibilities; and an intensive, two-calendar-year alternative program known as SCALE (Southwestern's Conceptual Approach to Legal Education).

The required curriculum for students in the day, evening, and PLEAS divisions includes 20 courses ranging from Business Organizations to Torts. More than 100 elective courses and over 100 different externships are offered.

Legal Research and Writing is required of all first-year students. Students must also fulfill an advanced writing requirement later in their course of studies.

■ SCALE Program

SCALE, introduced in 1974, is an alternative, innovative legal education course of study offered exclusively at Southwestern. Its two calendar years of instruction are equivalent to three full academic years in a traditional J.D. curriculum. The program design presents the law as an integrated whole rather than as a series of discrete courses, incorporating instruction in lawyering skills throughout. In the second year, the classroom functions as a "teaching law office" using simulated client files as the primary instructional vehicle. SCALE students also undertake off-campus externships to acquaint them with the working life of the lawyer and judge.

■ Student Support Network

An extensive network of faculty, administrators, students, and alumni provides individual counseling and guidance through the Academic Support Program, Helpnet, the Tutorial Program, the Student Mentor Program, and the Alumni Mentor Program.

■ Public Interest Involvement

A member school of the National Association for Public Interest Law, Southwestern encourages students to pursue public-interest service through special scholarship funds, a Loan Forgiveness Program for new graduates involved in public-interest careers, several summer grants for students working with public-service agencies, student volunteer work with local schools and community organizations, and a variety of externships.

Expenses and Financial Aid

➡ *tuition & fees—$16,240 (SCALE program, $21,190); part-time, $10,322*   ➡ *estimated additional expenses—housing, food, transportation, $1,400/month; books and supplies, $425-$625/year*   ➡ *financial aid available*
➡ *financial aid application, FAFSA, financial aid transcripts, due June 1*   ➡ *Federal Work/Study funds available*

Two special scholarship funds, the Paul W. Wildman Scholarship Program and the John J. Schumacher Minority Leadership Scholarship Program, have been established to provide up to full-tuition renewable scholarships to members of the entering class who demonstrate exceptional academic and leadership potential.

Career Services

The career planning and placement program at Southwestern helps prepare students to succeed in a changing legal job market. The office helps students identify and evaluate their career options and goals, learn about available practice areas, and prepare for and conduct a successful job search. Individual and small-group sessions on résumé writing, interview techniques, and job-search strategies are conducted. Special panel presentations, seminars, and individual mock interview sessions featuring alumni and other attorneys representing a variety of law practice and legal specialization options are also offered. In addition, the Placement Office sponsors intensive on- and off-campus interview programs with prospective employers and maintains comprehensive job listings from around the US and several foreign countries.

Admission

➡ *Bachelor's degree required for admission*
➡ *application deadline—June 30 (May 30 for SCALE)*
➡ *LSAT, LSDAS required*   ➡ *application fee—$50*
➡ *rolling admissions, early application advised*

Southwestern does not require a particular prelaw major or curriculum. Primary emphasis is placed upon GPA and LSAT scores earned within the past three-year period. Applicants with GPAs of 3.15 and LSAT scores in the 70th percentile have a good chance of acceptance, although these are not minimum standards for all cases. Each applicant's file is also assessed in such areas as nonacademic work, motivation, recommendations, and diversity.

Student Activities

Southwestern has one of the most active and successful interscholastic moot court programs in the country, with teams participating in 14 competitions a year. The *Southwestern University Law Review* and the *Southwestern Journal of Law and Trade in the Americas* feature scholarly articles and commentary on current legal issues contributed by noted jurists, attorneys, academicians, and students. The law review and journal staffs also coordinate Distinguished Lecture Series and symposia on campus.

A five-time ABA regional award winner and National Student Bar Association award winner, Southwestern's Student Bar Association sponsors student welfare programs and community outreach projects. There are also over 30 on-campus student organizations including three legal fraternities; minority, cultural, and religious groups; and a variety of associations concerned with specific areas of law.

Applicant Group for the 1993–1994 Academic Year

	LAW SCHOOL ADMISSION TEST SCORE										
GPA	120-124	125-129	130-134	135-139	140-144	145-149	150-154	155-159	160-169	170-180	TOTAL
3.75+	0/0	0/0	0/0	0/0	3/0	9/6	18/18	18/18	20/20	0/0	68/62
3.50 - 3.74	0/0	1/0	2/0	5/0	15/0	39/16	63/55	44/44	19/17	0/0	188/132
3.25 - 3.49	1/0	0/0	4/0	6/0	33/3	91/25	167/144	112/107	46/46	1/0	461/325
3.00 - 3.24	0/0	1/0	4/0	16/0	71/1	138/33	202/166	132/129	55/55	2/2	621/386
2.75 - 2.99	0/0	2/0	7/0	33/0	77/1	135/14	183/112	109/90	55/55	4/4	605/276
2.50 - 2.74	0/0	2/0	7/0	30/0	74/1	105/1	136/31	85/31	35/19	1/1	475/84
2.25 - 2.49	1/0	1/0	12/0	26/0	53/1	66/0	70/4	36/5	22/6	0/0	287/16
2.00 - 2.24	1/0	2/0	4/0	18/0	19/0	29/0	24/0	13/3	8/3	0/0	118/6
Below 2.00	0/0	0/0	2/0	6/0	4/0	7/0	4/0	3/0	2/0	0/0	28/0
No GPA	0/0	0/0	1/0	4/0	14/0	19/2	10/4	5/5	1/1	0/0	54/12
TOTAL	3/0	9/0	43/0	144/0	363/7	638/97	877/534	557/432	263/222	8/7	2905/1299

Southwestern University School of Law
In each box, the figure to the left of the slash represents applicants, while the figure to the right of the slash represents acceptances for that particular combination of LSAT score and GPA.

The above figures are reflective of applicants with an LSAT taken using the 120-180 score scale. This represents 94% of all fall '93 admissions decisions.

Stanford University Law School

Office of Admissions
Stanford, CA 94305-8610

Phone: 415.723.4985

■ Introduction

Stanford Law School is a privately funded institution dedicated to professional and graduate education and to the advancement of legal knowledge. Part of world-renowned Stanford University, it is located on Stanford's 6,109-acre campus, 35 miles south of San Francisco, California. The Law School admitted its first students in 1893 and granted its first LL.B. degree in 1901.

The school is small and intimate, enabling students to pursue personalized courses of study. In addition to providing a top-flight education, Stanford strives to maintain an environment in which diverse students feel welcome and respect one another's backgrounds and views.

■ Enrollment/Student Body

➦ *5,246 applicants*   ➦ *464 admitted first-year class 1993*
➦ *180 enrolled first-year class 1993*   ➦ *536 total full-time*
➦ *36% minority*   ➦ *47% women*
➦ *50 states & foreign countries represented*
➦ *127 undergraduate schools represented*

■ Faculty

➦ *52 total*   ➦ *45 full-time faculty; includes 7 emeriti*
➦ *59 visiting and lecturers*   ➦ *10 women*   ➦ *6 minority*

■ Library and Physical Facilities

➦ *414,000 volumes & equivalents*   ➦ *library hours: Mon.-Thurs., 8:00 A.M.-MIDNIGHT; Fri., 8:00 A.M.-5:00 P.M.; Sat., 9:00 A.M.-5:00 P.M.; Sun., 10:00 A.M.-MIDNIGHT*
➦ *LEXIS*   ➦ *NEXIS*   ➦ *WESTLAW*
➦ *numerous other on-line research systems available*
➦ *9 full-time librarians*   ➦ *386 assignable library carrels*

Robert Crown Law Library is one of this nation's most efficient and comfortable legal-research facilities. Features include a computer-assisted research center, on-line catalogs, open stacks, and rooms for conferences and joint work. The law library resources are augmented by the interdisciplinary 6.4-million volume Stanford University collections.

■ Curriculum

➦ *86 units/credits required to graduate*   ➦ *course listings available in current school bulletin*   ➦ *semesters, start in Aug.*
➦ *range of first-year class size—10-60*

Stanford Law School offers a day curriculum leading to the Doctor of Jurisprudence (J.D.) or one of three other degrees. The J.D., the basic professional law degree, normally requires three years of full-time study. The first-year curriculum allows two to four elective courses. Each first-year student also participates in a small class section in research and legal writing. The second and third years are fully elective.

The Law School offers concentrations in business law, comparative and international law, environmental and natural resources law, "lawyering for social change" and other areas of public-interest law, litigation and alternative methods of dispute resolution, Constitutional law, law and economics, public policy and administration, law and technology, health law and policy, and legal theory and history. Law students may also take relevant courses in other university departments.

■ Special Programs

Stanford is a leader in the use of simulated clinical instruction and in the integration of the substantive study of law and legal institutions with actual practice. Working under close faculty supervision, students undertake the roles and responsibilities of practicing lawyers through simulated exercises in the classroom and, in some instances, through experience with clients in administrative and judicial proceedings. Some of this work takes place at the East Palo Alto Community Law Project, a neighborhood legal clinic serving largely low-income clients. About one-third of students spend their fourth or fifth term of school in approved, supervised off-campus externships.

Joint-degree programs have been established at Stanford with the Graduate School of Business and with the departments of economics, history, and political science, and may be arranged with other departments, including communications, Latin American studies, sociology, and health services administration. Joint-degree programs have also been established with the Woodrow Wilson School of Public and International Affairs at Princeton University (J.D./M.P.A.) and with the Johns Hopkins School of Advanced International Studies (J.D./M.A.).

Some J.D. students spend their third year on intensive research training, working under the supervision of two professors on one or more projects and, where relevant, coursework.

■ Admission

➦ *B.A. required for admission*   ➦ *application deadline—March 1*   ➦ *rolling admissions*
➦ *LSAT, LSDAS required*   ➦ *median GPA—3.78*
➦ *median LSAT score—167*   ➦ *application fee—$65*

Admission to Stanford Law School is based primarily upon superior academic achievement and potential to contribute to the development of the law. Competition is severe: the 180 members of the Class of 1996 were selected from among 5,246 applicants. The largest part of each class is drawn from the upper 5 percent of their undergraduate colleges and the upper 5 percent of the LSAT pool.

In evaluating individual files, the faculty considers both the record of undergraduate and graduate education and the applicant's nonacademic experience, talents, and aspirations.

Recent classes included many persons who have chosen to study law in order to enhance their contribution to fields like finance, academics, computer and natural sciences, medicine, the arts, and government. Because of its strong belief in the value of diversity, the school especially encourages applications from African Americans, Mexican Americans, American Indians, and Puerto Ricans, as well as others whose ethnic and social background provide additional dimensions that will enhance the school's program.

Applications must be postmarked after September 15 and before March 1 to meet the application deadline.

■ Student Activities

Thirty student organizations enrich the law school experience. Opportunities for scholarly work are provided through *Stanford Law Review*; *Stanford Journal of International Law*; *Stanford Law & Policy Review*; and *Stanford Environmental Law Journal*. Courtroom skills are developed in moot court. Other student-run activities include the newspaper (*Stanford Law Journal*), orientation committee, and Stanford Law Students Association.

Students who are female, Asian, Black, Latino, Native American, Christian, Jewish, Roman Catholic, older, bisexual, gay, or lesbian will all find groups with their particular concerns. Other organizations focus on business law, criminal law, entertainment law, environmental law, international law, the J.D./M.B.A. program, law and technology, and public-interest law. Local affiliates of the Federalist Society and National Lawyers Guild are also present.

■ Expenses and Financial Aid

➨ *1993-94 full-time tuition & fees—$20,186*
➨ *estimated additional expenses (housing and misc.)—single students, $9,700; married students, $17,800*
➨ *scholarships awarded on the basis of financial need*
➨ *financial aid available; GAPSFAS and FAFSA forms required*

The purpose of student financial aid is to assist students who would otherwise be unable to pursue a legal education at Stanford. Approximately 73 percent of the student body receives tuition fellowship or loan assistance.

Stanford law students planning public service careers may obtain Public Service Fellowships for their second and third years of school. The school also offers grants to students who dedicate a law school summer to qualified public-service work. And for graduates who take low-paying public interest jobs and have substantial educational debt, the school has a loan relief program—Public Interest Loan Repayment Assistance Program (LRAP).

■ Career Services

The Office of Career Services helps students find both permanent employment following graduation and part-time and summer employment during law school. Over 275 employers representing 450 offices from throughout the country participate in the spring and fall on-campus interview programs. The office also offers counseling and information on traditional and nontraditional careers and employers. The school encourages students to consider public-interest and public-sector employment, and assists students to secure such positions.

A survey of students graduating in the Class of 1992 showed the following employment patterns: law firm associates, 52 percent; judicial clerks, 24 percent; nonlaw, public interest, government, or law teaching, 17 percent; business firms, 4 percent.

Applicant Group for the 1993–1994 Academic Year

Stanford University Law School
This grid includes only applicants who earned 120-180 LSAT scores under standard administrations.

LSAT Score	3.75 +		3.50 -3.74		3.25 - 3.49		3.00 - 3.24		2.75 - 2.99		2.50 - 2.74		2.25 - 2.49		2.00 - 2.24		Below 2.00		No GPA		Total	
	Apps	Adm	Apps	Adm	Apps	Adm	Apps	Adm	Apps	Adm	Apps	Adm	Apps	Adm	Apps	Adm	Apps	Adm	Apps	Adm	Apps	Adm
175-180	88	48	56	12	39	1	19	0	3	0	2	0	1	0	0	0	0	0	1	1	209	62
170-174	174	84	193	18	103	5	46	3	9	0	5	0	6	0	2	0	0	0	5	1	543	111
165-169	304	104	382	31	245	15	117	6	37	0	18	1	7	0	2	0	0	0	14	2	1126	159
160-164	304	20	363	28	266	14	132	5	54	0	17	1	7	1	1	0	0	0	17	1	1161	70
155-159	114	7	206	3	182	2	86	0	55	0	27	0	19	0	8	0	1	0	16	1	714	13
150-154	48	0	98	0	122	0	110	0	59	0	30	0	17	0	4	0	2	0	28	0	518	0
145-149	15	0	41	0	71	0	59	0	39	0	26	0	21	0	6	0	1	0	20	0	299	0
140-144	10	0	18	0	29	0	32	0	31	0	13	0	13	0	8	0	3	0	12	0	169	0
135-139	2	0	4	0	12	0	10	0	12	0	13	0	12	0	4	0	0	0	7	0	76	0
130-134	0	0	0	0	2	0	5	0	5	0	4	0	8	0	2	0	1	0	2	0	29	0
125-129	0	0	1	0	1	0	0	0	1	0	4	0	0	0	1	0	0	0	1	0	9	0
120-124	0	0	0	0	0	0	0	0	0	0	1	0	0	0	0	0	0	0	1	0	2	0
Total	1059	263	1362	92	1072	37	616	14	305	0	160	2	111	1	38	0	8	0	124	6	4855	415

Apps = Number of Applicants
Adm = Number Admitted
Reflects 93% of the total applicant pool.

Stetson University College of Law

1401 61st Street South
St. Petersburg, FL 33707

Phone: 813.345.1121, ext. 214

■ Introduction

Stetson University College of Law, founded in 1900, is Florida's oldest law school. For more than half a century it was located in DeLand, Florida, on the main campus of Stetson University. In 1954, it was relocated on its own campus in St. Petersburg, Florida. The present campus is only a few miles from downtown St. Petersburg, Tampa, and Clearwater, a metropolitan area in which many educational opportunities are afforded because of the heavy concentration of law firms and courts. The College of Law is approved by the ABA and became a member of the AALS in 1931.

It is the policy of the Stetson University College of Law not to discriminate on the basis of sex, age, handicap, race, color, religion, or national or ethnic origin in its admissions policies. The school is particularly proud of its long history of providing an education to the physically handicapped.

■ Enrollment/Student Body

➡ *2,209 applicants*   ➡ *593 admitted first-year class 1993*
➡ *217 enrolled first-year class 1993*   ➡ *648 total full-time*
➡ *17% minority*   ➡ *52% women*
➡ *41 states & foreign countries represented*
➡ *184 undergraduate schools represented*

The number of applicants, admitted and enrolled in the 1993 first-year class represent the spring, summer and fall entering classes.

■ Faculty

➡ *83 total*   ➡ *35 full-time*   ➡ *48 part-time or adjunct*
➡ *18 women*   ➡ *4 minority*

■ Library and Physical Facilities

➡ *316,000 volumes & equivalents*   ➡ *library hours: Mon.-Thurs., 7:00 A.M.-MIDNIGHT; Fri., 7:00 A.M.-10:00 P.M.; Sat., 9:00 A.M.-10:00 P.M.; Sun., 9:00 A.M.-MIDNIGHT*
➡ *LEXIS*   ➡ *NEXIS*   ➡ *WESTLAW*
➡ *7 full-time librarians*   ➡ *library seats 304*

The physical plant of the college is located on an 18-acre campus. Adapted from an early type of Spanish architecture featuring a central plaza with palm trees, fountains, and massive arcades after the plan of ancient monasteries, it is nevertheless utilitarian in every educational particular. The college has three model courtroom/classrooms, two of which are used by state courts and administrative boards for periodic sessions which students are usually invited to attend.

■ Curriculum

➡ *Academic Support Program*   ➡ *88 credits required to graduate*   ➡ *125 courses available*   ➡ *degrees available: J.D.; J.D./M.B.A.*   ➡ *semester system, new classes enroll in Jan., May, and Aug.*   *curriculum for first 3 semesters is prescribed*   ➡ *range of first-year class size—30-70*

The college offers a course of instruction planned to equip the graduate for effective service in those areas in which the fundamental knowledge and skills of a lawyer are required. Effort is made to give students a broad perspective of the role of the lawyer and the law in a changing society and an understanding of how they, as future community leaders, will be responsible for improving the law and for bringing about desirable social change.

■ Special Programs

The Public Defender Clinic at Stetson is well known and widely emulated. In its inception, it was supported by the National Legal Aid and Defenders Association and the Ford Foundation as one of three model programs in the country. In 1971, the integration rule of the Florida Bar was amended to permit students to study and participate in the criminal legal process from the prosecution's viewpoint. The college then established a Prosecution Clinic in conjunction with the Office of the State Attorney, Sixth Judicial Circuit of Florida. A few years later, the Office of the United States Attorney for the Middle District of Florida joined this clinic. The college conducts a Civil Clinic in cooperation with Gulf Coast Legal Services, Inc., and a Labor Law Clinic in cooperation with the National Labor Relations Board and the Florida Public Employee Relations Commission. Among the many activities of the college's Labor-Management Dispute Resolution Center is the coordination of numerous educational programs focusing on labor law. In the Elder Law Clinic, students represent elderly clients who meet federal guidelines, in all phases of civil practice.

■ Expenses and Financial Aid

➡ *full-time tuition & fees—$16,585*   ➡ *estimated additional expenses—$10,000 (room, board, and expenses of a single student living on campus)*   ➡ *academic merit awards available for entering students and currently enrolled students*   ➡ *diversity-based scholarships in varying amounts available for minority students*   ➡ *financial aid available; FAFSA forms, deadlines are the same as application deadlines*

Stetson has a level tuition plan. Whatever tuition rate is in effect when a new student matriculates is maintained throughout that student's three years of law school.

■ Career Services

The College of Law maintains an active placement office to assist students in obtaining employment information and scheduling employment interviews. Placement surveys are conducted on each graduating class, and the results provide up-to-date information regarding the percentage of responding graduates who have obtained employment in legal positions and the average starting salary for such positions. Stetson College of Law is a member of the National Association for Law Placement.

Applicant Group for the 1993–1994

Stetson University College of Law
This grid includes only applicants who earned 120-180 LSAT scores under standard administrations.

LSAT Score	GPA																					
	3.75 +		3.50 -3.74		3.25 - 3.49		3.00 - 3.24		2.75 - 2.99		2.50 - 2.74		2.25 - 2.49		2.00 - 2.24		Below 2.00		No GPA		Total	
	Apps	Adm	Apps	Adm	Apps	Adm	Apps	Adm	Apps	Adm	Apps	Adm	Apps	Adm	Apps	Adm	Apps	Adm	Apps	Adm	Apps	Adm
175 - 180	0	0	0	0	1	1	0	0	0	0	0	0	1	1	0	0	0	0	0	0	2	2
170 - 174	0	0	0	0	0	0	1	1	1	0	2	2	0	0	0	0	0	0	0	0	4	3
165 - 169	2	1	1	1	7	7	12	11	5	5	8	5	2	0	0	0	1	0	0	0	38	30
160 - 164	6	6	23	21	21	19	30	29	25	15	24	8	11	1	2	0	2	0	2	1	146	100
155 - 159	16	14	32	26	65	58	93	46	76	14	50	2	34	1	12	0	2	0	2	0	382	161
150 - 154	19	13	48	26	93	26	103	13	94	9	71	2	37	2	18	0	1	0	4	2	488	93
145 - 149	13	3	39	6	63	4	81	10	113	7	53	0	39	1	10	0	4	0	5	1	420	32
140 - 144	5	1	13	1	31	0	51	5	54	0	41	1	29	2	5	0	3	0	5	0	237	10
135 - 139	3	1	3	1	8	0	9	0	27	1	20	1	12	0	9	0	2	0	3	1	96	5
130 - 134	0	0	2	1	1	0	2	0	7	0	7	0	16	0	3	0	0	0	1	0	39	1
125 - 129	0	0	0	0	0	0	2	0	0	0	1	0	0	0	4	0	1	0	1	0	9	0
120 - 124	0	0	0	0	0	0	0	0	0	0	0	0	0	0	1	0	0	0	1	0	2	0
Total	64	39	161	83	290	115	384	115	402	51	277	21	181	8	64	0	16	0	24	5	1863	437

Apps = Number of Applicants
Adm = Number Admitted
Reflects 94% of the total applicant pool.

Suffolk University Law School

41 Temple Street
Boston, MA 02114

Phone: 617.573.8144

■ Introduction

Established in 1906, the Law School is located in the heart of historic Boston and is a short distance from New England's largest legal center. The Law School is approved by the American Bar Association and is a member of the Association of American Law Schools.

At Suffolk University Law School you will find a consistent emphasis on academic excellence in educating lawyers and advancing the profession. The curriculum builds upon a strong core of substantive courses that provide extensive exposure to all fundamental areas of the law.

The school's downtown Boston location allows it to draw upon outstanding leaders from the legal community as distinguished lecturers and adjunct faculty.

■ Enrollment/Student Body

➡ *3,200 applicants*   ➡ *1,130 admitted first-year class 1993*
➡ *520 enrolled first-year class 1993*   ➡ *990 total full-time*
➡ *650 total part-time*   ➡ *13% minority*   ➡ *52% women*
➡ *47 states & foreign countries represented*
➡ *340 undergraduate schools represented*

■ Faculty

➡ *130 total*   ➡ *70 full-time*   ➡ *60 part-time or adjunct*
➡ *34 women*   ➡ *5 minority*

■ Library and Physical Facilities

➡ *300,000 volumes & equivalents*   ➡ *library hours:*
Mon.-Fri., 8:00 A.M.-11:00 P.M.; Sat. & Sun., 9:00 A.M.-11:00 P.M.
➡ *LEXIS*   ➡ *NEXIS*   ➡ *WESTLAW*   ➡ *DIALOG*
➡ *10 full-time librarians*   ➡ *library seats 655*

■ Curriculum

➡ *Academic Support Program*
➡ *84 credits required to graduate*   ➡ *158 courses available*
➡ *degrees available: J.D.; J.D./M.B.A; J.D./M.P.A.;*
J.D./International Economics

■ Special Programs

One of the key components of Suffolk's first-year curriculum is the Legal Practice Skills Program. Each year, 10 full-time, highly qualified instructors teach small (18-20) groups of first-year students the basics of legal research and writing. Computerized research, preparation of legal and brief memoranda, brief writing, and oral argumentation are emphasized as this program evolves through the entire first year.

Clinical legal education is an area of primary interest at Suffolk University Law School.

Suffolk Voluntary Defenders—This program consists of a field and classroom component; students receive thorough training in trial practice skills in their second year, and in their third year represent indigent adult and juvenile criminal defendants in the Massachusetts District Courts. Students witness the criminal justice system first-hand throughout all phases of the District Court process,

including arraignments, bail hearings, suppression and discovery hearings, negotiations, trials, and sentencing, while providing a valuable service to clients.

The Prosecutor Program—Students in their final year are assigned to a court in proximity to Suffolk Law School where they work under the supervision of an assistant district attorney. They learn how a criminal case progresses through the judicial system from the arrest stage through the trial and appeal. Court appearances are supplemented by weekly classes in the law school.

Suffolk University Legal Assistance Bureau (SU-LAB)—This civil clinical program is designed for students in their final year. It has two components—the Family Law Unit and the Housing Law Unit, both located in a law office setting. In the Family Law Unit, the students generally represent clients seeking a divorce in the probate courts of Suffolk and Middlesex counties; students in the Housing Law Unit typically represent tenants in summary process proceedings in the Boston Housing Court.

S.U. Clinica Legal—This program provides legal assistance in housing cases to indigent tenants in Chelsea, Massachusetts. The program is staffed by second- and third-year students, fluent in Spanish or an Asian language, who can provide legal representation to the growing Latin and Asian population. The students assume full responsibility for their cases.

Battered Women's Advocacy Program (BWAP)—Similar to other clinical programs, BWAP combines classroom lectures/discussions with actual client representation under the supervision of an attorney working in the area. The majority of clients are women who seek protection from abusive spouses or partners, but all victims of domestic violence are represented. Students staff a "crisis line" at the Law School to give legal advice to domestic violence victims so that they may understand and pursue their civil and criminal remedies. Students appear in court under Supreme Judicial Court Rule 3:03, which provides for them to represent clients without compensation in both civil and criminal cases.

Legal Internship Program—Students are provided opportunities to work for government or nonprofit agencies and must perform 90 hours of uncompensated legal service for the agency as well as satisfy a classroom component. Students may make unsolicited inquiries to agencies that have not sought student assistance or may refer to listings of placement opportunities provided by the Suffolk Placement Office.

Simulation and Trial Advocacy Programs—Suffolk University Law School has long been known for graduating outstanding trial lawyers. Our new trial classroom was designed as a modern trial courtroom housed with the latest video equipment so that students may review their performance as trial counsel. Interactive videodisc and computer programs are available to students for learning about the application of evidence in the trial context.

■ Admission

➤ *B.A/B.S degree required for admission*
➤ *application deadline—March 1*   ➤ *LSAT, LSDAS required*
➤ *median GPA—3.30*   ➤ *median LSAT score—158*
➤ *application fee—$50*

Admission to the Law School is highly competitive. Applicants must possess a bachelor's degree from an accredited college or university prior to registration. Both a dean's recommendation and a letter of recommendation are required.

Candidates applying for admission must take the LSAT no later than February. The Admission Committee does not use a minimum cutoff system in its evaluation of an applicant's LSAT score or GPA. The subjective review includes analysis of class rank, grade trends, year of graduation, range as well as depth of courses, and extracurricular activities. Work experience since graduation is evaluated on the basis of achievement since college, maturity, and responsibility. Applicants are required to submit a personal statement discussing the subjective factors that they feel are particularly important to a review of their application.

The review of completed files begins early in November. While the application deadline is March 1, it is clearly to the applicant's advantage to complete his or her file early.

A student who has maintained a satisfactory academic record at another accredited law school and who meets the admission requirements of Suffolk University Law School may apply for admission as a transfer student. Students applying for transfer must do so by June 5.

Admitted applicants reserve a place by paying a two-part deposit totaling $500. No payment is required before April 15.

■ Student Activities

Academically distinguished law students edit and publish the *Suffolk University Law Review* and *Transnational Law Review*. Other publications include *The Advocate*, an alumni/ae-student magazine, and *Dicta*, the Law School newspaper.

Participation in the Moot Court Program is compulsory for first-year students; upper-class students may participate in a voluntary Moot Court Program or the school's national or international Moot Court teams.

Numerous student organizations are active on campus and play a vital role in meeting the many special interests of students.

■ Expenses and Financial Aid

➤ *1993-94 tuition & fees—full-time, $14,340; part-time, $10,756*   ➤ *estimated additional expenses—books and supplies, $850; health insurance, $510*   ➤ *scholarships available*   ➤ *David J. Sargent Fellowship available*
➤ *need and merit-based financial aid available; FAFSA, GAPSFAS, Suffolk Financial Aid Application, financial aid transcripts, tax returns, & W-2 forms (students & parents, if applicable) required by March 4*

■ Placement

A professional staff oversees numerous services and programs designed to benefit students and alumni/ae. These services include assisting students in securing part-time, summer, and permanent employment. Assistance is also provided for students seeking volunteer and work-study positions. A special feature of the service is an alumni network of over 13,000 Suffolk University Law School Graduates.

Applicant Group for the 1993–1994 Academic Year

Suffolk University Law School

LSAT Score	GPA								
	3.75 +	3.50 - 3.74	3.25 - 3.49	3.00 - 3.24	2.75 - 2.99	2.50 - 2.74	2.25 - 2.49	2.00 - 2.24	Below 2.00
175 - 180									
170 - 174									
165 - 169									
160 - 164									
155 - 159									
150 -154									
145 - 149									
140 - 144									
135 - 139									
130 - 134									
125 - 129									
120 - 124									

■ Good Possibility   □ Possible   ▨ Unlikely

Syracuse University College of Law

Office of Admissions and Financial Aid, Suite 212
Syracuse, NY 13244

Phone: 315.443.1962

■ Introduction

The Syracuse University College of Law is located on the 200-acre Syracuse University campus, which overlooks the scenic upstate city of Syracuse, New York. The college was established in 1895 as the fourth of the now 21 schools, colleges, and major academic units comprising Syracuse University.

The College of Law prepares students for the effective representation of clients in any jurisdiction and for the purpose of shaping the future of American society. The college is a charter member of the AALS and is fully approved by the ABA.

■ Enrollment/Student Body

➤ 2,720 applicants ➤ 1,077 admitted first-year class 1993
➤ 294 enrolled first-year class 1993 ➤ 797 total full-time
➤ 13 total part-time ➤ 30% minority ➤ 43% women
➤ 38 states & 6 foreign countries represented
➤ 180 undergraduate schools represented
➤ average age at entry—25
➤ 13% earned advanced degrees prior to the study of law

■ Faculty

➤ 75 total ➤ 41 full-time ➤ 34 part-time or adjunct
➤ 18 women ➤ 6 minority

■ Library and Physical Facilities

➤ 318,772 volumes & equivalents ➤ LEXIS
➤ WESTLAW ➤ 7 full-time librarians
➤ library seats 531

■ Curriculum

➤ Academic Support Program ➤ Legal Education
Opportunity (LEO) Program ➤ 87 credits required to
graduate ➤ degrees available: J.D.; J.D./M.B.A.;
J.D./M.P.A.; J.D./M.S.; J.D./M.A.; J.D./Ph.D.; LL.M.

The law curriculum is taught by a full-time faculty and by occasional adjunct faculty members from the bench and practicing bar. The curriculum is designed to offer both broad exposure to the various topics of substantive law and an orderly, in-depth study of a specific area of law. Of the 87 credits required for the J.D. degree, slightly more than one-third are devoted to the required first-year curriculum. After the first year, students will have three course requirements: the second half of constitutional law; professional responsibility; and a two-semester writing requirement, usually completed in the third year. The curriculum offers a broad range of opportunities for advanced and special-interest study, in addition to courses in the more traditional areas of the law. Students may also take as many as six credits toward the J.D. degree in university graduate courses outside the College of Law.

■ Special Programs

Clinical Programs—The College of Law is committed to extensive clinical legal education. Students enrolled in a clinic represent clients in actual legal matters. Diverse clinical opportunities include: the Criminal Law Clinic; the Public Interest Law Firm; the Housing and Finance Clinic and the Civil Law Clinic. Under the supervision of a member of the faculty, students appear in court and develop the skills of client interviewing, counseling, drafting of pleadings, case planning and strategy development, written and oral advocacy, and negotiation.

International Legal Studies—The International Legal Studies Program allows students to concentrate in public and private international law. Cocurricular activities for students interested in international issues include moot court competitions, the International Law Society, and the *Syracuse Journal of International Law and Commerce*. The college offers a summer program of study in London, which permits a limited number of students to gain clinical legal experience in an international setting.

Interdisciplinary Legal Education—The College of Law has long been committed to the concept of interdisciplinary legal education. Within the College of Law, courses are offered that stress the interrelationships between the law and other disciplines. For students desiring to combine their study of law with in-depth graduate study in other disciplines, formal joint-degree programs are offered in public administration, business administration, accounting, public communications, international relations, and environmental science. Other joint-degree programs are designed to fit special career objectives. Joint-degree programs are structured for students to earn both degrees in substantially less time than required to earn each degree separately.

The Law, Technology and Management (LT&M) Program—This program emphasizes interdisciplinary and applied approaches to the study of commercial development of new technologies. Graduate students with backgrounds in law, management, engineering and other technical fields work together in cross-disciplinary teams on projects involving various aspects of new technology development. The LT&M Program involves studying intellectual property and licensing, patents and copyrights, tax consequences of new technology business, and business-management techniques.

■ Admission

➤ Bachelor's degree required ➤ application deadline—
April 1 ➤ rolling admissions, early application encouraged
➤ LSAT, LSDAS required ➤ median GPA—3.20
➤ median LSAT score—155 ➤ application fee—$40

The experience of Syracuse reveals that undergraduate grades and LSAT scores are reliable measures, in most cases, for predicting probable success in law study. Thus, an index combining grades and test scores becomes a factor in most admission decisions. However, recognizing that numerical indicators are not always the best predictors of success in law school—even when considered in combination with other factors—the college admits a limited number of students each year through its Legal Education Opportunity (LEO) Program. A goal of the LEO program is the admission of persons who may have been deprived of equal education opportunities for reasons of race, gender, poverty, or other factors beyond their control.

■ Student Activities

The *Syracuse Law Review* is an intense legal research and writing program for its student editors and a national forum for scholars who contribute to it. Four issues are published annually. The college also publishes the *Syracuse Journal of International Law and Commerce*, a scholarly journal devoted to international law.

A moot court program is offered to give students an understanding of the appellate process and experience in oral advocacy. An extensive intramural competition is conducted each year and outstanding students are selected to represent the college in numerous national and international competitions.

The Law Student Senate, an affiliate of the Law Student Division of the ABA, is the governing body with regard to all student extracurricular activities. Other student organizations represent the varied interests of Syracuse law students.

■ Expenses and Financial Aid

➡ *full-time tuition & fees—$17,348*
➡ *estimated additional expenses—$10,000 (room, board, books, and personal)* ➡ *combination need/merit scholarships available* ➡ *financial aid available; FAFSA/FAF and Syracuse internal application due March 1, FAFSA/FAF also due to CSS by Jan. 31*

The College of Law offers a financial aid program that awards combinations of tuition grants, work-study, and loans, primarily on the basis of financial need. Scholarships and fellowships are also awarded to students of outstanding academic promise. Approximately 70 percent of the student body receive some form of financial aid.

■ Career Services

The Career Services Office takes pride in the personal treatment it offers to students and graduates. The professional staff carefully guides students through résumé drafting and interviewing, formulating an appropriate career objective, and determining an effective job search strategy. The graduates of Syracuse Law have succeeded in acquiring post-bar pass employment in percentages consistently over 92 percent for the past several years.

Applicant Group for the 1993–1994 Academic Year

Syracuse University College of Law
This grid includes only applicants who earned 120-180 LSAT scores under standard administrations.

LSAT Score	GPA																					
	3.75 +		3.50 -3.74		3.25 - 3.49		3.00 - 3.24		2.75 - 2.99		2.50 - 2.74		2.25 - 2.49		2.00 - 2.24		Below 2.00		No GPA		Total	
	Apps	Adm	Apps	Adm	Apps	Adm	Apps	Adm	Apps	Adm	Apps	Adm	Apps	Adm	Apps	Adm	Apps	Adm	Apps	Adm	Apps	Adm
175 - 180	1	1	0	0	1	1	1	1	0	0	0	0	0	0	0	0	0	0	0	0	3	3
170 - 174	0	0	3	3	1	1	4	4	1	1	2	2	3	3	0	0	0	0	0	0	14	14
165 - 169	3	3	13	12	10	10	15	14	16	16	3	3	5	3	0	0	2	1	0	0	67	62
160 - 164	12	12	23	23	41	41	58	57	50	40	28	9	14	1	2	0	1	0	2	1	231	184
155 - 159	25	23	79	74	155	131	171	96	131	38	59	10	21	5	8	1	1	1	4	3	654	382
150 - 154	23	22	84	65	148	55	177	34	142	25	80	16	44	5	18	3	5	1	5	2	726	228
145 - 149	8	5	46	14	91	14	112	23	110	14	58	7	24	2	14	1	2	0	15	5	480	85
140 - 144	4	3	21	7	32	10	58	10	58	7	43	2	30	1	15	2	2	0	2	1	265	43
135 - 139	2	0	2	0	7	0	26	3	21	2	30	1	12	1	12	0	6	0	11	0	129	7
130 - 134	0	0	0	0	2	0	1	0	5	2	3	0	8	0	9	0	3	1	4	0	35	3
125 - 129	0	0	1	0	0	0	2	0	0	0	1	0	3	0	1	0	1	0	0	0	9	0
120 - 124	0	0	0	0	0	0	0	0	0	0	0	0	1	0	0	0	0	0	0	0	1	0
Total	78	69	272	198	488	263	625	242	534	145	307	50	165	21	79	7	23	4	43	12	2614	1011

Apps = Number of Applicants
Adm = Number Admitted
Reflects 96% of the total applicant pool.

Temple University School of Law

1719 North Broad Street
Philadelphia, PA 19122

Phone: 215.204.8925

■ Introduction

Established in 1895, Temple University School of Law is an urban law school with a national reputation for excellence in academics and clinical education. The law school is situated in north-central Philadelphia on the 90-acre main campus of Temple University, a state-related university. Philadelphia is a city rich in tradition and in tune with the future. It offers something for everyone—history, music, art, theater, sports, and entertainment. For the legal scholar, Philadelphia is also home to the US Court of Appeals for the Third Circuit, the US District Court for the Eastern District of Pennsylvania, the Pennsylvania Supreme Court, state appellate and trial courts, and federal, state, and municipal agencies.

■ Student Body

➡ *3,698 applicants*   ➡ *1,037 admitted first-year class 1993*
➡ *396 enrolled first-year class 1993*   ➡ *883 total full-time*
➡ *391 total part-time*   ➡ *18% minority*
➡ *44% women*   ➡ *51 states & foreign countries represented*
➡ *290 undergraduate schools represented*

■ Faculty

➡ *190 total*   ➡ *59 full-time*   ➡ *131 part-time or adjunct*
➡ *59 women*   ➡ *31 minority*

■ Curriculum

➡ *83 units required to graduate*   ➡ *182 courses available*
➡ *degrees available: J.D. and J.D./M.B.A.*   ➡ *semesters, start in Aug.*   ➡ *range of first-year class size—10-100*

A Temple legal education combines the practical and the theoretical and gives graduates the tools they need to practice in diverse settings and to provide leadership for their communities.

In 1993, Temple was the only law school awarded the prestigious E. Smythe Gambrell Professionalism Award by the American Bar Association. The Gambrell Award acknowledges the success of Temple's innovative advocacy course, known as the "Integrated Program," which combines the teaching of trial advocacy, evidence, and professional responsibility. In the spring of 1994, Temple began its LL.M. in Trial Advocacy, the first master's program in the country designed to train practicing trial lawyers in the art of trial advocacy.

Temple's reputation for superior training in business and tax law has been recognized by a three-year, $750,000 grant from the United States Department of Education to introduce an experimental program called the "Integrated Transactional Representation Program." This program combines the teaching of business-related courses and professional responsibility with clinical experience representing nonprofit, grass-roots citizens' groups and families in crisis seeking mediation. The clinical program supplements a challenging and diverse business law curriculum that gives students the opportunity to explore topics as diverse as antitrust, tax planning, bankruptcy, real estate finance, sports law, and environmental law.

Public services is a Temple tradition. Students provide legal services to the community through the clinical program. Temple's outreach to the community also includes the Temple Legal Aid Office, located in the law school building, and the Temple Law, Education and Participation Program (LEAP), which implements programs designed to teach educators and community leaders to work with children in developing their knowledge of the law. Public-interest careers are supported by the Student Public Interest Network, which provides grants for summer internships in public service, and the Loan Repayment Assistance Program, which helps to defray the cost of educational loan repayments for Temple graduates in public-interest jobs.

Students interested in environmental law, health care law, criminal law, international or comparative law, or civil rights law can also explore these specialties at Temple.

■ International Law

Recognizing that an international experience is best gained by actually living, learning, and working abroad, the law school established a semester-abroad program in Tokyo, Japan, in the spring of 1994. No other law school in the country offers a semester-abroad program outside of London. The curriculum includes a mix of standard law courses and specialty law courses focusing on comparative, Japanese, and Asian legal studies. Internships in Japanese law firms and corporations are also available to some students. In establishing the Japan program, Temple is capitalizing on its strengths in international law: a distinguished international law faculty; a diverse curriculum in international and comparative law; the opportunity for summer study in Rome, Athens, and Tel Aviv; a longstanding program that offers the Master of Laws (LL.M.) to international students holding foreign law degrees; and active student organizations, such as the *International Law Journal* and the International Law Society.

■ Library and Physical Facilities

➡ *438,743 volumes & equivalents*   ➡ *library hours: Mon.-Thurs., 8:00 A.M.-11:00 P.M.; Fri., 8:00 A.M.-10:00 P.M.; Sat., 9:00 A.M.-5:00 P.M.; Sun., 1:00 P.M.-10:00 P.M.*
➡ *LEXIS*   ➡ *NEXIS*   ➡ *WESTLAW*
➡ *RLN, INNOVAC, DIALOG, CALI*
➡ *11 full-time librarians*   ➡ *library seats 730*

The law library collection is one of the largest in the country. Computer research laboratories provide access to word processing, legal research databases, the library card catalog and serials system, and Internet. Large classrooms are equipped with the latest in video and audio technology. Two mock trial practice rooms are furnished with judicial benches and jury boxes, and a large moot courtroom provides space for competitions.

■ Activities

Students are an integral part of policy-making and governance at the law school. The Student Bar Association (SBA) is the umbrella organization that oversees over 30 student groups. Student publications include *Temple Law Review*, the *Temple Environmental Law & Technology Journal*, the *Temple International and Comparative Law Journal*, and the *Temple Political & Civil Rights Law Review*. Students who excel in trial advocacy and brief writing may participate in the Moot Court Honor Society, the Barrister's Society, and the National Trial Competition Team. Other active student organizations include the Asian American Law Student Association, the Black Law Students Association, the Indian Law Students Association, the Latino Law Students Association, and the Women's Law Caucus.

■ Career Planning

Just as many aspiring law students choose Temple, so do employers deciding to hire. According to the responses of 97 percent of its members, the 1992 graduating class had a 94 percent employment rate nine months after graduation. The Career Planning Office administers several interview programs each year, including Four-In-One Recruitment, an award-winning national interviewing program, On-Campus Interviewing, the Philadelphia Area Minority Interviewing Program, Public Interest Job Fairs, and recruiting days in New York and Washington, DC. The career planning staff provides one-on-one counseling, publishes a weekly newsletter, sponsors workshops and programs on job-search skills, and maintains the Career Planning Resources Center.

■ Admission

➼ *Bachelor's degree from accredited college or university required*   ➼ *application deadline—Mar. 1*
➼ *LSAT, LSDAS required*   ➼ *median GPA—3.33*
➼ *median LSAT score—157*   ➼ *application fee—$50*
➼ *rolling admissions, early application preferred*

All applicants are ranked on an index designed to evaluate an applicant's undergraduate grade-point average and average LSAT score. Scholastic achievement is weighed equally with the LSAT. At the discretion of the faculty Admissions Committee, applications may be considered through the Sp.A.C.E. Program. The Sp.A.C.E. Program was established by the faculty for two reasons: the School of Law's concern that an overreliance on the LSAT, or any other abstract measuring factor, could create an unhealthy rigidity in the composition of the law school class; and a faculty commitment to a policy that seeks to correct minority and other imbalances in the legal profession. The task of the Sp.A.C.E. Program is to recruit candidates who have an outstanding performance record and an exceptional aptitude for the study and practice of law, not necessarily reflected by those factors that compose the applicant's index.

■ Expenses and Financial Aid

➼ *full-time tuition & fees—resident, $7,178; nonresident, $13,300*   ➼ *part-time tuition & fees—resident, $5,742; nonresident, $10,640*   ➼ *estimated additional expenses—$10,000 min. (fees, room, board, books)*
➼ *scholarships and grants available*
➼ *FAFSA need analysis form due April 1*

Applicant Group for the 1993–1994 Academic Year

Temple University School of Law
This grid includes only applicants who earned 120-180 LSAT scores under standard administrations.

LSAT Score	3.75 +		3.50 -3.74		3.25 - 3.49		3.00 - 3.24		2.75 - 2.99		2.50 - 2.74		2.25 - 2.49		2.00 - 2.24		Below 2.00		No GPA		Total	
	Apps	Adm	Apps	Adm	Apps	Adm	Apps	Adm	Apps	Adm	Apps	Adm	Apps	Adm	Apps	Adm	Apps	Adm	Apps	Adm	Apps	Adm
175 - 180	0	0	0	0	1	1	2	1	0	0	0	0	0	0	0	0	0	0	0	0	3	2
170 - 174	2	2	3	3	4	4	6	5	5	3	6	4	4	2	1	0	0	0	0	0	31	23
165 - 169	9	8	15	14	16	14	19	13	17	7	9	3	2	0	3	2	0	0	2	1	92	62
160 - 164	17	16	40	38	65	58	83	47	52	18	43	13	18	2	3	0	0	0	3	1	324	193
155 - 159	34	33	103	89	198	111	168	54	107	20	86	16	31	3	7	0	2	0	7	1	743	327
150 - 154	35	31	105	58	177	53	206	38	166	36	100	13	64	10	14	0	2	0	9	1	878	240
145 - 149	15	2	59	23	116	26	143	25	135	17	95	9	68	3	17	0	4	0	8	0	660	105
140 - 144	9	3	25	4	56	10	78	6	89	8	87	3	52	1	23	0	3	0	10	0	432	35
Below 140	1	0	11	1	20	0	40	0	63	0	65	1	58	0	32	0	13	0	15	0	318	2
Total	122	95	361	230	653	277	749	189	634	109	491	62	297	21	100	2	24	0	54	4	3481	989

Apps = Number of Applicants
Adm = Number Admitted
Reflects 95% of the total applicant pool.

University of Tennessee College of Law

Admissions Office
Knoxville, TN 37996-1800

Phone: 615.974.4131

■ Introduction

The University of Tennessee College of Law is located on the main campus of the university at Knoxville, in a major metropolitan area. Knoxville is in eastern Tennessee, near the foothills of the Great Smoky Mountains, half a day's drive from Atlanta, Georgia, and Nashville, the state capital. The College of Law, established in 1890, is a charter member of the AALS, and is ABA-approved.

■ Enrollment/Student Body

➡ *total enrollment—472*   ➡ *10% minority*
➡ *44% women*   ➡ *65 undergraduate schools represented*

Traditionally, Tennessee residents account for approximately 80 percent of the student body. While an appropriate proportion of out-of-state applications is sought, the College of Law will continue to give priority to Tennessee residents.

■ Library and Physical Facilities

➡ *345,000 volumes & equivalents*   ➡ *LEXIS*
➡ *WESTLAW*   ➡ *INFOTRAC*   ➡ *15 full-time staff*
➡ *ready access to the vast collection of the University of Tennessee main library system*

The physical facilities include the law library, classrooms, two courtrooms, faculty and administrative offices, a student lounge, and the University of Tennessee Legal Clinic. Nearby are residence and dining halls, the main library, the university student center, athletic facilities, and downtown Knoxville.

■ Curriculum

➡ *89 credits required to graduate*   ➡ *degrees available: J.D.;J.D./M.B.A; J.D./M.P.A.*   ➡ *semesters, start in Aug.*

The basic program of study requires the completion of six semesters of resident study for the J.D. degree. Entering students are admitted only in the fall. The College of Law offers a summer term of courses for students who have completed their first year of law study, including students in good standing at other law schools. By completing a sufficient number of hours in two summer terms, a student may accelerate completion of the program by one semester.

Upper-class students may take a limited number of law-related courses in other graduate departments in the university for credit toward the J.D. degree. The dual-degree program permits students to receive the J.D. degree and a M.B.A. or M.P.A. in a shorter period than would normally be required if the degrees were sought separately.

■ Special Programs

The University of Tennessee Legal Clinic, established in 1947, has long been recognized as one of a small group of outstanding legal clinics in the United States. Under the supervision of the clinic faculty, students obtain invaluable practical experience representing actual clients in state and federal court.

■ Student Activities

Students publish the *Tennessee Law Review* quarterly. Members of the editorial board of the *Law Review* are selected each year from the second-year class on the basis of scholarship and writing ability. The Student Bar Association, an affiliate of the ABA, affords students opportunities for participation in a variety of activities, including speaker programs and student government. The national honor fraternity, Order of the Coif, and two leading professional fraternities—Phi Delta Phi and Phi Alpha Delta, have local chapters. Other student professional activities include Law Women, the Black Law Students Association, the Environmental Law Association, the East Tennessee Lawyers Guild, the Christian Legal Society, Tennessee Association for Public Interest Law, and student chapters of the Association of Trial Lawyers of America and the Tennessee Trial Lawyers Association.

Twice in recent years, Tennessee teams have distinguished themselves by winning the National Moot Court Competition. Teams have also competed successfully in regional and national competitions in fields including International Law, Tax Law, Labor Law, Trial Advocacy and Intellectual Property Law, as well as the Frederick Douglass Moot Court Competition. The college also sponsors its own intramural moot court competition, the Advocates' Prize, in which students in the final round argue before distinguished judges from state and federal courts, as well as an intramural trial competition.

■ Admission

➡ *Bachelor's degree from accredited four-year institution required.*   ➡ *application deadline—Feb. 1*
➡ *application fee—$15*

Applications should be filed as soon after October 1 as possible for admission to the following fall's entering class. It is strongly recommended that the LSAT be taken no later than December. Upon acceptance, a seat deposit may be required.

Admission to the College of Law is competitive. In making selections, the Admissions Committee places substantial emphasis upon traditional indicators of performance, undergraduate GPA and LSAT score. When an applicant retakes the LSAT, the scores will be averaged. Normally, the committee will not consider LSAT scores that are more than five years old. In come cases, the committee will consider other factors such as an improvement in undergraduate grades; strength of the undergraduate institute attended; circumstances that may have affected an applicant's UGPA or LSAT score; economic, social or cultural background, or success in overcoming social or economic disadvantages; community service; and extracurricular activities.

The College of Law also recognizes its obligation to assure meaningful access to a legal education to qualified applicants who are members of groups that have been historically underrepresented in the legal profession. Special consideration may be given to members of such groups whose applications indicate a reasonably high probability of success. The College of Law encourages applications from such students. The successful completion of the Council on Legal Education Opportunity (CLEO) summer institute and similar programs also may be considered by the Admissions Committee.

■ Expenses and Financial Aid

➥ *full time tuition & fees—residents $3,092 nonresidents, $7,716*   ➥ *scholarships available (academic promise and/or demonstrated need)*   ➥ *minority scholarships available:* ➥ *financial aid available; Perkins loans, Stafford loans, Supplemental Loan for Students, Federal Loan Program, Law Access, Law Loans, work-study*

University fees are set by the Board of Trustees and are subject to change without notice. Students who wish to receive priority consideration for need-based scholarships must complete the Free Application for Federal Student Aid (FAFSA) by February 14. There is no application form to complete for merit-based scholarships, as eligible students are automatically considered.

■ Housing

For information on university apartments, contact the Office of Rental Properties, 474 South Stadium Hall, The University of Tennessee, Knoxville, TN 37996. For information on university residence halls, contact the Housing Office, 405 Student Services Building, The University of Tennessee, Knoxville, TN 37996.

■ Career Services

The College of Law maintains a Career Services Office with a full-time director and staff whose sole responsibilities are to assist students and alumni in placement matters. Services of the office range from coordinating on-campus interviews and career seminars to participation in two of the most successful off-campus interview consortia in the United States.

Though many graduates choose to remain in Tennessee, increasing numbers seek and obtain opportunities outside the region, in firms and government agencies in locations from New York and Washington to Texas and California. Many students, frequently as many as 10 percent of those graduating in the spring, secure prestigious clerkships with federal and state judges. In the past three years, roughly 90 percent of the graduates of the College of Law have reported successful legal placement within nine months of graduation.

Applicant Group for the 1993–1994 Academic Year

University of Tennessee College of Law
This grid includes only applicants who earned 120-180 LSAT scores under standard administrations.

LSAT Score	3.75 +		3.50 -3.74		3.25 - 3.49		3.00 - 3.24		2.75 - 2.99		2.50 - 2.74		2.25 - 2.49		2.00 - 2.24		Below 2.00		No GPA		Total	
	Apps	Adm	Apps	Adm	Apps	Adm	Apps	Adm	Apps	Adm	Apps	Adm	Apps	Adm	Apps	Adm	Apps	Adm	Apps	Adm	Apps	Adm
175 - 180	0	0	0	0	0	0	0	0	0	0	0	0	0	0	0	0	0	0	0	0	0	0
170 - 174	0	0	2	2	2	2	1	1	1	1	0	0	0	0	0	0	0	0	0	0	6	6
165 - 169	5	5	7	7	6	5	7	7	8	8	2	2	2	0	1	0	0	0	1	0	39	34
160 - 164	12	12	24	23	32	30	35	22	22	11	19	5	4	0	3	0	0	0	0	0	151	103
155 - 159	22	21	38	28	60	27	67	15	41	4	23	5	17	1	2	0	2	0	1	0	273	101
150 - 154	24	16	57	12	72	10	61	6	51	6	29	3	21	6	8	1	0	0	3	0	326	60
145 - 149	18	4	21	2	42	5	51	2	36	0	24	2	11	1	8	0	1	0	2	1	214	17
140 - 144	4	1	16	2	18	0	27	3	28	1	28	2	11	0	6	0	3	0	4	0	145	9
135 - 139	3	0	2	0	5	0	6	0	7	0	13	1	8	0	0	0	3	0	1	0	48	1
130 - 134	0	0	1	0	1	0	1	0	3	0	7	0	4	0	3	0	0	0	1	0	21	0
125 - 129	0	0	0	0	0	0	2	0	0	0	0	0	1	0	1	0	0	0	0	0	4	0
120 - 124	0	0	0	0	0	0	0	0	0	0	1	0	0	0	0	0	0	0	0	0	1	0
Total	88	59	168	76	238	79	258	56	197	31	146	20	79	8	32	1	9	0	13	1	1228	331

Apps = Number of Applicants
Adm = Number Admitted
Reflects 94% of the total applicant pool.

The University of Texas School of Law

Post Office Box 149105
Austin, TX 78714-9105

Phone: 512.471.3207

■ Introduction

The School of Law is located on the University of Texas campus in Austin, the state capital. This location provides ready access to the state legislature, the Supreme Court of Texas, federal trial and appellate courts, offices of state and federal agencies, and the library and other facilities of the University of Texas campus. Long recognized as having a distinguished faculty and educational program, the law school has been a member of the AALS since 1907, and is fully accredited.

Austin is situated in the hill country of Texas, allowing for easy access to lakes and wilderness areas. The University of Texas plays an important role in this city of 550,000 and many of the entertainment and cultural activities cater to the student population.

■ Enrollment/Student Body

➼ *4,000 applicants*   ➼ *523 enrolled first-year class 1993*
➼ *1,487 total full-time*   ➼ *23.5% minority*
➼ *42% women*   ➼ *150 undergraduate schools represented*
➼ *nonresident enrollment limited to 20%*

■ Library and Physical Facilities

➼ *850,000 volumes & equivalents*   ➼ *18 full-time librarians*

Recent additions and alterations to the law school complex have made it one of the most attractive and spacious educational facilities of any law school in the nation. Eight large classrooms, numerous seminar rooms, and spacious student lounge areas provide an attractive setting for law study. Federal and state courts hold trial and appellate cases in the moot courtroom on a regular basis. The Tarlton Law Library is the fifth largest in the nation. Open stacks and the most modern computer and audiovisual equipment available make the library facilities accessible to students, scholars, and practicing lawyers.

■ Curriculum

➼ *86 credits required to graduate*   ➼ *various joint-degree programs offered*   ➼ *semesters, start the last week of Aug.*

All first-year students (except those in the Extended First-Year Program for parents of small children and disabled students) are required to take a full course load of 15 hours per week in contracts, property, torts, civil procedure, criminal law, constitutional law, brief writing and oral advocacy, and legal research and writing. After the first year, the only required courses are professional responsibility, advanced constitutional law, and a writing and research seminar. The student may design his or her course of study from an array of course offerings in many fields of law. These offerings include interdisciplinary and advanced public and private law courses. There is also a large summer program enabling the student to complete degree requirements in less than three years.

The school awards a Master of Laws (LL.M) degree for foreign law school graduates. The law school offers three joint-degree programs: J.D./Master of Public Administration with the LBJ School of Public Affairs; J.D./Master in Business Administration with the Graduate School of Business; and J.D./Master of Arts in Latin American Studies. Each of the joint-degree programs can be completed within four years.

■ Special Programs

The school offers clinical education courses for credit in such fields as capital punishment, children's rights, criminal defense, elder law, juvenile justice, and mental health. Internships are available to qualified students with the Texas Supreme Court, the Texas Court of Criminal Appeals, and the Third Court of Appeals. The law school also has an extensive trial advocacy program.

■ Admission

➼ *application deadline—Feb. 1*   ➼ *median GPA—3.50*
➼ *median LSAT score—163*   ➼ *application fee—$50*

To be eligible for admission, an applicant must hold a baccalaureate degree from an accredited college or university and must have a competitive grade-point average and LSAT score. In 1993, only one of every three resident applicants was offered admission, and one of seven nonresident applicants was offered admission. Minority students are actively recruited, and a special financial aid program has been established to support their attendance. Special facilities are available for students who have disabilities. A partially refundable $200 tuition deposit is required from an applicant who is offered admission.

The law school accepts a limited number of transfer students who have completed the first year curriculum at an accredited law school, and who have compiled a superior academic record at their original law school.

■ Student Activities

The School of Law offers many student-administered, cocurricular activities that enhance the law students' regular studies. Student-edited journals include: *American Journal of Criminal Law; Hispanic Law Journal ; The Review of Litigation ; Texas Environmental Law Journal ; Texas Intellectual Property Law Journal ; Texas International Law Journal ; Texas Journal of Women and the Law ;* and *Texas Law Review* . Other activities include the Legal Research Board, whose members research actual legal problems for practicing attorneys; the Student Bar Association, which includes the entire student body and promotes student social and professional activities; the Women's Law Caucus; the Chicano Law Students Association; the Thurgood Marshall Legal Society; the Teaching Quizmaster Program, in which qualified senior students teach the first-year courses in legal research and writing; the Board of Advocates, which administers the mock trial and moot court programs; and chapters of legal fraternities. The Mock Trial and Moot Court Program consists of eight voluntary intramural competitions involving both trial and appellate advocacy and 17 interscholastic competitions. The following competitions are also offered: Alternative Dispute Resolution; Client Counseling; Negotiations; and Voir Dire. Interscholastic teams consistently achieve a high degree of success in competition and have won several national championships.

■ Expenses and Financial Aid

➡ *full-time tuition & fees—resident, $4,440; nonresident, $8,640*   ➡ *scholarships available*
➡ *three-year scholarships to qualified minority students*

A limited number of scholarships are awarded to first-year students on the basis of performance in undergraduate studies, academic promise in the study of law, and financial need. The prestigious Rice Scholarship is designed to support eight outstanding law students with full tuition and fees for all three years of law school. Scholarships and research assistantships are available for second- and third-year students. The law school administers several short and long-term loan funds for students with financial need, and the university offers substantial federally funded loan programs. Information on these programs is given in the Law School Application/Bulletin.

■ Housing

The law school is within 25 minutes by car of almost any point in Austin, and good housing is available within walking distance. Arrangements must be made by the student. For information concerning university dormitories, write to: The University of Texas Housing Division, Kinsolving Dormitory, Austin, TX 78712, or call 512.471.3136.

■ Career Services

Each year, the law school's active placement service arranges interviews with approximately 300 employers throughout the country, including law firms, judges, corporations, and government agencies. The service is available to students and alumni seeking part-time jobs, summer clerkships, and full-time employment. Generally, 83 percent of each graduating class has secured employment prior to graduation, and most of the remaining graduates are employed within six months after graduation. Information available on the 1993 graduating class indicates that 85 percent of the class has secured employment.

Applicant Group for the 1993–1994 Academic Year

The University of Texas School of Law
This grid includes only applicants who earned 120-180 LSAT scores under standard administrations.

LSAT Score	3.75 +		3.50 -3.74		3.25 - 3.49		3.00 - 3.24		2.75 - 2.99		2.50 - 2.74		2.25 - 2.49		2.00 - 2.24		Below 2.00		No GPA		Total	
	Apps	Adm	Apps	Adm	Apps	Adm	Apps	Adm	Apps	Adm	Apps	Adm	Apps	Adm	Apps	Adm	Apps	Adm	Apps	Adm	Apps	Adm
175 - 180	13	13	10	10	11	9	8	7	2	0	1	0	0	0	0	0	0	0	1	0	46	39
170 - 174	44	44	48	40	23	16	38	23	12	6	4	0	3	1	1	0	0	0	2	0	175	130
165 - 169	107	84	167	96	141	56	76	18	34	10	20	3	6	1	0	0	0	0	3	2	554	270
160 - 164	182	88	261	93	231	49	143	30	70	12	37	2	15	1	3	0	0	0	8	2	950	277
155 - 159	128	41	186	35	193	27	152	15	73	3	35	1	18	0	7	0	0	0	9	2	801	124
150 - 154	62	10	113	14	126	10	138	8	82	1	36	0	16	0	12	0	0	0	10	0	595	43
145 - 149	18	3	51	2	61	2	61	0	54	0	40	1	25	0	13	0	3	0	10	1	336	9
140 - 144	5	1	22	0	29	0	36	0	42	0	44	0	23	0	7	0	1	0	8	1	217	2
135 - 139	2	0	5	0	11	0	17	0	21	0	20	0	15	0	8	0	1	0	6	0	106	0
130 - 134	0	0	1	0	2	0	2	0	5	0	3	0	3	0	8	0	2	0	3	0	29	0
125 - 129	0	0	1	0	0	0	1	0	1	0	3	0	1	0	2	0	0	0	0	0	9	0
120 - 124	0	0	0	0	0	0	0	0	0	0	0	0	1	0	0	0	0	0	0	0	1	0
Total	561	284	865	290	828	169	672	101	396	32	243	7	126	3	61	0	7	0	60	8	3819	894

Apps = Number of Applicants
Adm = Number Admitted
Reflects 95% of the total applicant pool.

Texas Southern University—Thurgood Marshall School of Law

Office of Admissions
3100 Cleburne Avenue
Houston, TX 77004

Phone: 713.527.7114

■ Introduction

The Thurgood Marshall School of Law, a state institution founded in 1947, seeks to provide a legal education and an opportunity to excel to students from a wide range of backgrounds, including those who otherwise would not have an opportunity for legal training. The law school is accredited by the ABA. The student body is truly multiethnic and multicultural. The law school is housed in a tri-level structure and is located just outside downtown Houston. Campus housing is available in the form of modern apartments for single and married students. The school makes extensive use of legal facilities in Houston through its clinical programs.

■ Enrollment/Student Body

➼ *1,628 applicants* ➼ *428 admitted first-year class 1993*
➼ *230 enrolled first-year class 1993* ➼ *650 total full-time*
➼ *77% minority* ➼ *43% women*
➼ *27 states & foreign countries represented*
➼ *114 undergraduate schools represented*

A majority of the students are from Texas, but all parts of the country are represented. Approximately 52 percent of the students are black, 22 percent Chicano, 20 percent Caucasian, and 4 percent Asian and native American. The median age range is about 25 to 35 years.

■ Faculty

➼ *45 total* ➼ *31 full-time* ➼ *14 part-time or adjunct*
➼ *9 women* ➼ *38 minority*

■ Library and Physical Facilities

➼ *300,000 volumes & equivalents* ➼ *library hours: Mon.-Fri., 7:00 A.M.-MIDNIGHT; Sat.-Sun., 9:00 A.M.-MIDNIGHT*
➼ *LEXIS* ➼ *NEXIS* ➼ *WESTLAW* ➼ *DIALOG*
➼ *5 full-time librarians* ➼ *library seats 335*

Students receive individual and/or group orientation and intensive training in the use of the library. The law school has recently undergone approximately $3 million dollars in renovations, expanding the available space from 16,000 to 32,000 square feet.

■ Curriculum

➼ *Academic Support Program* ➼ *Moot Court, Law Review & Legal Clinics offered* ➼ *90 credits required to graduate*
➼ *74 courses available* ➼ *J.D. degree available*
➼ *semesters, start in Aug.*
➼ *range of first-year class size—230-260*

Upon entry to the School of Law, all students in the first-year class are required to attend a week-long orientation program. Attention is given to examanship, briefing cases, outlining, and an overview of law school life and expectations.

The law school offers a three-year, full-time J.D. program. The minimum course load is 12 hours. Required courses for the first year are Case Analysis and Legal Writing, Civil Procedure, Property, Contracts, Torts, Appellate Litigation, and Criminal Law. Second-year students must take Constitutional Law, Evidence, Criminal Procedure, Trial Simulation, Business Associations, Commercial Law, Basic Federal Taxation, Professional Responsibility, and Wills and Trusts. Third-year students are required to take Federal Jurisdiction and Procedure, a seminar/independent research project, and Texas Practice. The remaining hours required to complete the degree may be selected from a number of areas of interest.

The law school operates a full-time, in-house clinic in which students work under the supervision of faculty and adjunct faculty members. Internships are available with the Harris County District Attorney's Office, the Federal Magistrates, Gulf Coast Legal Foundation, the Federal Bankruptcy Court, the Harris County Attorney's Office, the Internal Revenue Service, and the U.S. District Court. The school operates a number of clinics, including Homeless Advocacy, Immigration, Aids, and Elderly. A judicial externship with state and federal judges is available to academically outstanding third-year students. The summer session offers a different series of related courses each year. A six-week summer pre-enrollment (L.E.A.P) program, by invitation, and a tutorial program for all first-year classes are provided.

■ Admission

➼ *Baccalaureate degree required* ➼ *LSAT, LSDAS required* ➼ *median GPA—2.73* ➼ *median LSAT score—145* ➼ *application fee—$40*

The GPA and LSAT (or average LSAT if attempted more than once on same scale) are factored into a formula which places more weight on the LSAT. The number derived, "the index," is used to determine an applicant's initial competitiveness.

No particular undergraduate major is preferred, but the school looks for applicants with broad backgrounds in the social sciences, natural sciences, humanities, and business sciences. Admission decisions are based primarily on the applicant's motivation and intellectual capacity, undergraduate GPA, and LSAT scores. Newly admitted students must send two seat deposits ($150 upon acceptance and $100 in June), which are refundable upon matriculation. The law school makes special efforts to recruit members of minority groups. Transfer applications are accepted; students must submit a transcript and letter from the dean of their former law school stating that they are in good standing. All newly admitted students must submit an official transcript from the baccalaureate degree-granting institution as well as all law schools attended. No application will be evaluated by the Admissions Committee until the LSDAS report has been received. In order to ensure complete review, applications must be received by the Office of Admissions no later than April 1, although there is no official deadline. Entering students are admitted only in August (fall semester). Students are notified of acceptance after the Admissions Committee has reviewed the complete file. Early completion of applications is encouraged. Admission decisions are made on a rolling basis.

■ Student Activities

Numerous law school organizations are active on campus. A student board edits the *Thurgood Marshall Law Review.* Moot court competitions are held in trial and appellate work, labor law, and client counseling.

■ Expenses and Financial Aid

➡ *full-time tuition—resident, $120/sem. hr.; nonresident, $210/sem. hr.* ➡ *estimated additional expenses per semester—fees, $250; books & supplies, $275; parking, $25* ➡ *law school & university scholarships available* ➡ *numerous minority scholarships available* ➡ *financial aid available; GAPSFAS form due May 1*

About 90 percent of the students receive some form of aid. The law school administers its own scholarship program, which is competitive. Scholarships are awarded on the basis of both need and merit, and may range up to full tuition. The university also offers additional scholarship aid, and the law school and the university offer loan assistance. Ten to fifteen percent of the students hold assistantships. The aid application deadline is May 1.

The scholarship program makes several awards (approximately 40) each year. The awards have enabled out-of-state residents to qualify for resident-tuition rates. In addition, a number of law students each year qualify for the federal work study and loan programs. Additional limited scholarship aid is available to students after they have completed a year of law study. An applicant in need of other financial assistance should make arrangements for financial aid through the Director of Financial Aid, Thurgood Marshall School of Law, Texas Southern University, 3100 Cleburne Ave., Houston, TX 77004.

■ Career Services

The law school employs a full-time placement officer. Graduates are placed primarily with law firms, federal and state agencies, legal services, judges, and businesses. The Office of Placement and Career Development also conducts a major national effort to encourage legal employers in every major city in the United States to recruit Texas Southern University—Thurgood Marshall School of Law graduates.

Applicant Group for the 1993–1994 Academic Year

Texas Southern University—Thurgood Marshall School of Law
This grid includes only applicants who earned 120-180 LSAT scores under standard administrations.

LSAT Score	3.75 +		3.50 -3.74		3.25 - 3.49		3.00 - 3.24		2.75 - 2.99		2.50 - 2.74		2.25 - 2.49		2.00 - 2.24		Below 2.00		No GPA		Total	
	Apps	Adm	Apps	Adm	Apps	Adm	Apps	Adm	Apps	Adm	Apps	Adm	Apps	Adm	Apps	Adm	Apps	Adm	Apps	Adm	Apps	Adm
175 - 180	0	0	0	0	0	0	0	0	0	0	0	0	0	0	0	0	0	0	0	0	0	0
170 - 174	0	0	0	0	0	0	0	0	0	0	0	0	0	0	0	0	0	0	0	0	0	0
165 - 169	0	0	0	0	0	0	0	0	0	0	0	0	0	0	0	0	0	0	0	0	0	0
160 - 164	1	1	0	0	0	0	3	3	5	5	1	1	3	3	1	1	0	0	0	0	14	14
155 - 159	0	0	1	1	3	3	4	4	8	7	11	10	7	6	3	2	0	0	1	1	38	34
150 - 154	1	1	5	4	14	14	20	15	41	31	38	27	35	18	21	12	2	1	4	2	181	125
145 - 149	1	1	7	4	20	10	41	22	64	21	74	37	50	29	18	12	6	0	13	2	294	138
140 - 144	2	2	12	9	28	16	42	15	67	26	83	20	71	17	41	2	14	0	14	0	374	107
135 - 139	2	1	6	4	12	3	41	4	55	3	71	6	71	3	46	3	16	2	13	0	333	29
130 - 134	0	0	4	1	6	0	18	0	31	4	35	0	40	1	23	0	13	0	7	0	177	6
125 - 129	1	0	1	0	2	0	6	1	9	0	9	0	11	0	8	0	6	0	6	0	59	1
120 - 124	0	0	0	0	0	0	1	0	2	0	0	0	2	0	6	0	2	0	0	0	13	0
Total	8	6	36	23	85	46	176	64	282	97	322	101	290	77	167	32	59	3	58	5	1483	454

Apps = Number of Applicants
Adm = Number Admitted
Reflects 94% of the total applicant pool.

Texas Tech University School of Law

Box 40004
Lubbock, TX 79409

Phone: 806.742.3791

■ Introduction

The School of Law, which accepted its first class in 1967, is located on the main campus of Texas Tech University in Lubbock. It is fully accredited, having received approval from the Supreme Court of Texas and the ABA and membership in the AALS at the earliest dates possible under the rules of those organizations. As a result, its graduates are eligible for admission to practice in any state in the nation, and many are engaged in practice throughout the United States. In 1974, a chapter of the Order of the Coif, the national legal honorary society, was established at the School of Law.

■ Enrollment/Student Body

➡ *1,483 applicants*   ➡ *518 admitted first-year class 1993*
➡ *217 enrolled first-year class 1993*   ➡ *627 total full-time*
➡ *17% minority*   ➡ *37.4% women*
➡ *68 undergraduate schools represented*

■ Faculty

➡ *36 total*   ➡ *23 full-time*   ➡ *13 part-time or adjunct*
➡ *8 women*   ➡ *5 minority*

■ Library and Physical Facilities

➡ *250,000 volumes & equivalents*   ➡ *library hours: Mon.-Thurs., 7:30 A.M.-MIDNIGHT; Fri., 7:30 A.M.-6:00 P.M.; Sat., NOON-6:00 P.M.; Sun., 2:00 P.M.-MIDNIGHT*   ➡ *LEXIS*
➡ *NEXIS*   ➡ *WESTLAW*   ➡ *5 full-time librarians*
➡ *library seats 475*

The law school is housed in a beautiful and functional building designed to comfortably accommodate a student body of about 600 and a full-time faculty of 29. The recent renovation of the law library added 12,000 square feet of stack and study space. Two hundred fifty study carrels housing 500 students are equipped with 250 PCs offering access to WESTLAW and LEXIS, as well as to the library's online catalog. Word processing capabilities are also provided. Student organizations occupy spacious offices on the third floor. Two other notable features of the building are the beautiful and functional courtroom where the Texas Court of Appeals sits each year, and the Forum which serves as a student lounge and the site of various law school social functions. As a result of the remodeling, the building now complies with ADA standards.

■ Curriculum

➡ *Academic Support Program*   ➡ *90 semester hours required to graduate*   ➡ *degrees available: J.D.; J.D./M.B.A.; J.D./M.P.A.; J.D./AG. ECON*
➡ *semesters, start in Aug. & Jan.*   ➡ *range of first-year class size—60-70*   ➡ *summer sessions available*

The program of study is planned to equip the student to practice law as advocate, counselor, judge, or law teacher. At the same time, recognition is given to the use of law training as a stepping-stone to a career in government, politics, or business. All of the courses in the first year and some of the courses in the advanced years are required. The remainder of the courses are electives.

■ Special Programs

In addition to the basic program of study for the J.D. degree, qualified students may elect to pursue one of three joint-degree programs: the J.D./Master of Business Administration; the J.D./Master of Public Administration; and the J.D./Master of Science in Agricultural Economics. The joint-degree programs allow a student to complete the requirements for both degrees in less than four academic years instead of the five required if both degrees were pursued separately.

The School of Law offers opportunities to practice various lawyering skills in courses such as trial advocacy, appellate advocacy, arbitration, skills development, and others.

In recognition of the lack of representation of minority groups in the legal profession, the School of Law participates actively in programs designed to increase the number of minority group lawyers.

■ Admission

➡ *Bachelor's degree from accredited college or university required*   ➡ *application deadline—Feb. 1*
➡ *LSAT, LSDAS required*   ➡ *median GPA—3.28*
➡ *median LSAT score—157*   ➡ *application fee—$40*
➡ *rolling admissions, early application preferred*

Written recommendations are not required, but in borderline cases may prove helpful. Anyone filing an application after February 1 will be at a disadvantage in competing for the limited number of places available. Accepted applicants must pay a nonrefundable $50 deposit to hold a place in the entering class, and in June must pay one-half of their tuition and fees for the fall semester.

Admissions decisions are made by the Admissions Committee and are based on an evaluation of the LSAT score, the quality of the undergraduate course work and performance, and other criteria including background and employment experience, graduate work, and evidence of leadership qualities in campus and community activities. The LSAT score and the undergraduate GPA are weighted about equally.

Applicants are admitted for entrance in the fall with the exception of 20 to 25 who are admitted to commence their studies in June. The summer admittees are selected from a group of applicants whose LSAT scores are below the 40th percentile and who are residents of Texas. By carrying a limited number of hours of law courses during the nine-week summer program, the students are able to take a reduced course load over the remainder of the first year. All students admitted, however, including those admitted for summer entrance, are admitted for full-time study only.

■ Student Activities

In addition to activities available to all students of the university, there are many extracurricular activities provided for the law student.

The *Texas Tech Law Review*, published four times a year, consists of articles written by students and leading jurists, practitioners, and faculty. Membership is based on academic qualification.

The Board of Barristers supervises and conducts an extensive moot court program, in which the student develops skills in brief writing and in the art of oral advocacy. The school enters teams in interschool competition in mock trial, moot court, client counseling, and negotiation.

The Legal Research Board is a student organization that offers attorneys a service similar to that of a briefing staff. The board methodically researches requested legal topics and then compiles the information in a memorandum of law.

The Student Bar Association is the focal point for many student activities, both professional and social. The SBA cooperates closely with the faculty in bringing speakers and programs to the law school. In addition, the SBA sponsors numerous student social events.

The legal fraternities at the school sponsor professional and social functions. They admit both men and women to membership.

■ Expenses and Financial Aid

➡ *full-time tuition & fees—$4,388* ➡ *average additional expenses—$8,450 (room and board, books, transportation, personal expenses)* ➡ *merit, minority, and need-based scholarships available* ➡ *FAFSA, financial aid transcripts, and loan applications required for financial aid*

More than 80 scholarships are available, ranging in value from $1,000 to a full scholarship. Long-term educational loan funds are available through the Office of the Director of Financial Aid, and short-term loans are available through the Law School Foundation.

■ Housing

A variety of housing convenient to the campus is available for single and married students. Information on campus housing may be obtained from the Housing Office, Texas Tech University.

■ Career Services

The Placement Office of the School of Law is under the direction of the assistant dean. Graduates of the law school find employment in every area of practice in the public and private sectors. Historically, a significant majority of graduates are employed within six months of graduation. The law school is a member of the National Association of Law Placement, which provides information on opportunities for placement nationally to students.

Applicant Group for the 1993–1994 Academic Year

Texas Tech University School of Law
This grid includes only applicants who earned 120-180 LSAT scores under standard administrations.

LSAT Score	3.75 +		3.50 - 3.74		3.25 - 3.49		3.00 - 3.24		2.75 - 2.99		2.50 - 2.74		2.25 - 2.49		2.00 - 2.24		Below 2.00		No GPA		Total	
	Apps	Adm	Apps	Adm	Apps	Adm	Apps	Adm	Apps	Adm	Apps	Adm	Apps	Adm	Apps	Adm	Apps	Adm	Apps	Adm	Apps	Adm
175 - 180	0	0	0	0	0	0	0	0	0	0	1	0	0	0	0	0	0	0	0	0	1	0
170 - 174	0	0	0	0	1	1	0	0	0	0	0	0	1	1	0	0	0	0	2	1	4	3
165 - 169	2	2	8	8	7	6	9	9	10	8	5	3	3	1	1	1	0	0	0	0	45	38
160 - 164	14	14	21	20	21	21	34	33	30	25	17	9	12	4	3	0	0	0	0	0	152	126
155 - 159	23	22	60	58	58	54	75	51	44	17	41	5	17	0	5	0	0	0	0	0	323	207
150 - 154	32	24	35	27	64	18	90	18	76	14	57	5	22	0	5	0	2	0	0	0	383	106
138 - 149	5	3	39	9	57	6	97	4	87	2	83	0	60	1	22	0	9	0	4	0	463	25
137 - 120	0	0	3	0	3	0	3	0	9	0	5	0	7	0	8	0	1	0	1	0	40	0
Total	76	65	166	122	211	106	308	115	256	66	209	22	122	7	44	1	12	0	7	1	1411	505

Apps = Number of Applicants
Adm = Number Admitted

Thomas M. Cooley Law School

217 S. Capitol Avenue
Post Office Box 13038
Lansing, MI 48901

Phone: 517.371.5140

■ Introduction

America's leader in part-time, year-round legal education, Thomas M. Cooley Law School was established in 1972 in Lansing, Michigan by former Supreme Court Chief Justice Thomas E. Brennan and a group of dedicated lawyers and judges.

Named for Michigan's renowned Judge Cooley, the school is committed to open admissions, practical scholarship, and uncompromising professionalism. The American Bar Association approved Thomas Cooley Law School in 1975.

As an independent, graduate college, Thomas Cooley enjoys the reputation of a tough law school, run by experienced lawyers and judges. Its faculty, students, and alumni take pride in the school's close contacts with the bench and bar.

The *Thomas M. Cooley Law Review* has received national recognition for promoting the use of plain English lawsuit papers.

■ Enrollment/Student Body

➤ *2,377 applicants for Sept. 1993 class*   ➤ *1,987 accepted*
➤ *285 matriculated first-year class 1993*   ➤ *110 full-time*
➤ *1,513 total part-time*   ➤ *8% minority*   ➤ *30% women*

Of Thomas Cooley's diverse student body, 75 percent hail from out-of-state and 12 percent hold advanced degrees. The median age of entering students is 26.

As a result of the rolling admissions method used at Thomas Cooley, 1,022 of the applicants accepted for the 1993 class enrolled in a future class.

■ Faculty

➤ *51 full-time*   ➤ *over 100 part-time or adjunct*
➤ *16 women*   ➤ *5 minority*

■ Library and Physical Facilities

➤ *305,000 volumes & equivalents*   ➤ *library is open 111 hours per week, including weekends*   ➤ *LEXIS*
➤ *NEXIS*   ➤ *WESTLAW*   ➤ *9 full-time librarians*
➤ *library seats 500*

Cooley's technologically advanced research facility is designed to meet the research needs of today's law student. The library features a large computer lab, two electronic classrooms for computer-assisted legal instruction and Innopac, a state-of-the-art integrated automated library system.

Occupying nearly 65,000 square feet and five levels, the library collection includes the standard state and federal materials. Primary research materials from every state are maintained and updated. Nearby, the State Law Library and the general libraries of the city of Lansing, state of Michigan, Lansing Community College, and Michigan State University are available to Thomas Cooley students.

■ Curriculum

➤ *90 credits required to graduate*   ➤ *J.D. degree available*
➤ *three terms per year, beginning Jan., May, and Sept.*

Thomas Cooley Law School is organized on a 12-month academic year, consisting of three full 15-week terms of school. Each term meets the definition of a full semester. Like the terms of the English Courts of Common Law, Thomas Cooley's three academic terms are designated Hilary Term (January to April), Trinity Term (May to August), and Michaelmas Term (September to December).

Thomas Cooley students typically attend classes only 10 hours per week. Many are employed full-time. Still, they graduate in three years or less. Some prefer to be full-time students and graduate in as little as 28 months. Classes are offered in the morning, afternoon, and evening.

Thomas Cooley's catalog lists 26 required and over 100 elective courses. Before graduating, every Thomas Cooley student argues a case before a real judge in a real courtroom.

■ Special Programs

The Sixty-Plus Law Center, Thomas Cooley's award-winning clinic for elderly citizens, permits students to earn academic credit while representing real clients.

Directed studies, trial workshops, law review, and moot court programs enrich the curriculum. Because Thomas Cooley has a national student body, civil and criminal practice courses for New York, New Jersey, Pennsylvania, Florida, Indiana, Arizona, Texas, Wisconsin, and Illinois are offered.

■ Admission

➤ *Bachelor's degree required*   ➤ *rolling admissions*
➤ *LSAT, LSDAS required*   ➤ *application fee—$100*
➤ *median LSAT score—149 (29, old scale)*
➤ *$25 nonrefundable enrollment fee upon acceptance*

The admissions office uses a simple index (15 times undergraduate grade-point average [UGPA] + LSAT) to determine admissibility. All applicants within an index of 180 or more are virtually assured of acceptance.

Candidates otherwise qualified may be rejected for specific negative factors, such as previous dismissal, criminal record, and the like. Morning, afternoon, and evening divisions are organized in September, January, and May, respectively. There are 240 seats available in each new class. New students who cannot be accommodated in the class of their choice are carried forward to the next available class. Students with index scores below 180 are usually urged to retake the LSAT. (Applicants with the old two-digit LSAT [prior to June 1991], will use the old formula to calculate index: UGPA x 10 + LSAT = 50).

Student Activities

All students are members of the Student Bar Association, and chapters of two national legal fraternities have been established. In addition, students publish a newspaper, operate the Scholastic Review Board for student grade appeals, supervise the Student Tutorial Service, edit and publish *The Thomas M. Cooley Law Review*, and conduct an active intramural sports program.

The Thomas M. Cooley Law Review focuses upon legal questions of significance to state governments, state court jurists, and state public policy matters. The *Review* prepares and publishes three issues per year. Each issue features articles written by practicing attorneys, judges, and professors; casenotes and comments written by Thomas Cooley students; and distinguished briefs argued before the Michigan Supreme Court.

The school has an internship program with various state administrative agencies under which students are compensated to work a maximum of 20 hours per week.

There are 32 clubs and organizations for students. They include the International Law Society, Women's Law Alliance, Black Law Students Association, Christian Legal Society, the Environmental Law Society, and Jewish Law Caucus.

Expenses and Financial Aid

➤ *tuition & fees—full-time/part-time, $425/per credit hour*
➤ *estimated additional expenses—$15,215 (room and board, books, personal, transportation)* ➤ *honors, need-based, academic standing, and special-factor scholarships available*
➤ *Martin Luther King and Rosa Parks minority scholarships available* ➤ *financial aid available*

Because Thomas Cooley Law School seeks to attract top students and reward academic excellence, the Board of Directors has established a unique Honors Scholarship Program, based entirely on a student's entering credentials and his/her academic performance in law school. The chart below shows the percent of Thomas Cooley tuition awarded to first- and second-term honors scholars based on their admission index (multiply UGPA by 15 and add LSAT score to determine the index):

Index	Scholarship
219 or above	100 percent
218	90 percent
217	80 percent
216	70 percent
215	60 percent
213 & 214	50 percent
211 & 212	40 percent
209 & 210	30 percent
207 & 208	20 percent
205 & 206	10 percent

In the third and subsequent terms, all Thomas Cooley students who maintain a cumulative GPA of 3.0 or better are eligible for tuition scholarships ranging from 10 percent for a GPA of 3.0 to 100 percent for a GPA of 3.9.

Honors scholarships are applicable only to offset future tuition at Thomas Cooley Law School and are not redeemable in money. Many Cooley students qualify for State of Michigan tuition grants. More than 80 percent receive guaranteed student loans. Five to 10 percent are awarded work-study funds.

Housing

The law school does not operate residence facilities. There is an ample supply of living accommodations available nearby in all price ranges.

Career Services

The Placement and Student Services Office provides a wide variety of services to students and graduates of the law school. Job postings (updated weekly) provide listings for full-time positions in both in and out of state, as well as listings for legally related part-time work in the greater Lansing area. Reciprocal agreements with law school placement offices in other parts of the country are maintained for those students and graduates who wish to practice in other states. Workshops and seminars, focusing on topics ranging from interviewing skills to business etiquette, are open to all students. Services for students and alumni include the Thomas Cooley Placement Hotline, a 24-hour recording of the most recent week's listings. The office also maintains a credential file system for graduates, utilized by employers who wish the Placement Office to supply résumés of interested candidates.

Applicant Group for the 1993–1994 Academic Year

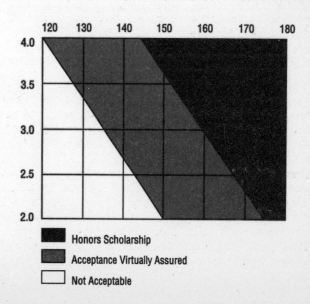

- Honors Scholarship
- Acceptance Virtually Assured
- Not Acceptable

The University of Toledo College of Law

2801 West Bancroft Street
Toledo, OH 43606

Phone: 419.537.4131

■ Introduction

The University of Toledo is a state university of 25,000 students, conveniently located on the western edge of Toledo, Ohio, in one of the city's nicest residential areas.

The College of Law, located on the main campus of the University of Toledo, is accredited by the ABA and is a member of the AALS and the League of Ohio Law Schools. It has been training lawyers since 1906 and in 1984 was awarded a chapter of the Order of the Coif. Toledo, at the western end of Lake Erie, is within an hour's drive of Ann Arbor and Detroit, Michigan.

■ Enrollment/Student Body

➡ *1,250 applicants*   ➡ *571 admitted first-year class 1993*
➡ *232 enrolled first-year class 1993*   ➡ *447 total full-time*
➡ *183 total part-time*   ➡ *10% minority*   ➡ *39% women*
➡ *25 states and foreign countries represented*
➡ *200 undergraduate schools represented*

The college seeks a diverse student body. Approximately 40 percent of the entering students come from outside Ohio. The day-division entering class ranges from 160 to 170; evening, from 50 to 60.

■ Faculty

➡ *58 total*   ➡ *36 full-time*   ➡ *22 part-time or adjunct*
➡ *9 women*   ➡ *2 minority*

The full-time faculty hold law degrees from some of the most outstanding universities in the country. Many have advanced law degrees.

While legal scholarship is important and many faculty members have national reputations for scholarship, the College of Law places a high priority on effective teaching and accessibility to students.

■ Library and Physical Facilities

➡ *260,000 volumes & equivalents*   ➡ *library hours: Mon.-Fri., 7:30 A.M.-MIDNIGHT; Sat.-Sun., 9:00 A.M.-MIDNIGHT*
➡ *LEXIS*   ➡ *NEXIS*   ➡ *WESTLAW*
➡ *14 full-time librarians*   ➡ *library seats 540*

The spacious, modern Law Center includes tiered classrooms, a striking student lounge, moot courtroom, law office classroom, and amphitheater auditorium.

The law library contains eight group study rooms, videotaping facilities, and several microcomputers and printers for use by law students.

■ Curriculum

➡ *Academic Support Program*   ➡ *87 credits required to graduate*   ➡ *150 courses available*   ➡ *degrees available: J.D.; J.D./M.B.A.*   ➡ *semesters, start in Aug.*
➡ *range of first-year class size—20-55*

Both a full-time day and a part-time evening program are available. The first-year curriculum is prescribed.

Prior to graduation, all students are required to complete the course in Legal Ethics and a perspective course, as well as a scholarly paper within the context of a seminar.

■ Special Programs

The college was a pioneer in clinical legal education. Under a rule of the Ohio Supreme Court, upperclass students appear in court under close faculty supervision in both civil and criminal cases and represent indigents in civil cases in cooperation with the Toledo Legal Aid Society.

The college has a long-standing interest in international legal studies.

■ The Legal Institute of the Great Lakes

The Institute supports research, special studies and conferences on legal issues of greater than ordinary import to the Great Lakes Region of the United States and Canada. The Institute sponsors a course of study on Law and the Great Lakes which integrates major topical areas including environmental law, natural resources law, transportation law, agricultural law, commercial and corporate law, and international and comparative Canadian law. It publishes a newsletter prepared with student assistance and generates research projects using students as primary researchers.

■ Admission

➡ *Bachelor's degree from an accredited college or university required*   ➡ *application deadline—full time, March 15; part-time, May 15*   ➡ *LSAT, LSDAS required*
➡ *median GPA—3.10*   ➡ *median LSAT score—157*
➡ *application fee—$30*

Candidates should expect stiff but not impossible competition. Grades and LSAT scores are the most important determinants of admission. Evidence showing that the GPA and LSAT score understate an applicant's ability is carefully considered. Letters of recommendation are important.

Prospective students are encouraged to visit the College of Law and sit in on classes. Appointments can be made through the Admission Office.

■ Student Activities

The *University of Toledo Law Review* is published four times a year by students selected on the basis of scholarship. Students may also qualify by submitting a publishable article. Training and practice in brief writing and oral argument beyond the required appellate advocacy course are obtained in the Charles Fornoff Intramural Moot Court Competition and in several national and regional competitions. Client counseling and trial practice programs are also stressed. All students are members of the Student Bar Association. The Black Law Students Association, Business Law Society, Environmental Law Society, Federalist Society, Health Care Law Association, Hispanic Law Student Association, International Law Society, Sports Law

Association, and the Women Law Students Association are active student organizations.

■ Expenses and Financial Aid

➡ *full time tuition & fees—$5,350, resident; $10,280, nonresident*   ➡ *part-time tuition & fees—$4,012, resident; $7,709, nonresident*   ➡ *estimated additional expenses— $10,220 (room, board, books, personal expenses, transportation)*   ➡ *merit and merit/need-based scholarships available:*   ➡ *financial aid available; need analysis form due to Financial Aid Office by April 1*

Under the terms of an agreement entered into by the states of Ohio and Michigan, residents of Monroe County, Michigan, who are attending the University of Toledo are treated as in-state residents for tuition purposes. Although the university has no housing for law students, housing near the university is plentiful. Newly admitted students desiring assistance in obtaining housing receive help from the Student Bar Association and the University's Off-Campus Living Office.

■ Career Services

The College places top priority on providing comprehensive career planning and placement for its students and graduates. The office assists students through workshops, videotapes, and counseling, and provides guest speakers on legal career options.

As a result of both on- and off-campus interviews, second- and third-year students in 1992-93 accepted summer or attorney positions in all major cities of Ohio and Michigan plus Anchorage, Baltimore, Chicago, District of Columbia, Indianapolis, Memphis, New York City, Philadelphia, Rochester, Sacramento, and Tallahassee.

The College's Judicial Clerkship Program places graduates as clerks with federal courts of appeals and district courts, and with state trial and appellate courts around the country. Second- and third-year students have the opportunity to participate in internships in federal and Ohio appellate courts.

College of Law graduates take the bar examination in many states. The college's first-time takers of the Ohio Bar Examination consistently pass the exam with scores above the state's average.

Applicant Group for the 1993–1994 Academic Year

The University of Toledo College of Law
Graph reflects admission decisions as of 9/1/93.

GPA	\multicolumn{9}{c}{LSAT (10) Percentile Intervals}
	0-20	21-30	31-40	41-50	51-60	61-70	71-80	81-90	91-99
3.75 Above					Possible	Highly Likely	Highly Likely	Highly Likely	Highly Likely
3.74 3.50					Possible	Highly Likely	Highly Likely	Highly Likely	Highly Likely
3.49 3.25					Possible	Highly Likely	Highly Likely	Highly Likely	Highly Likely
3.24 3.00					Possible	Highly Likely	Highly Likely	Highly Likely	Highly Likely
2.99 2.75					Possible	Highly Likely	Highly Likely	Highly Likely	Highly Likely
2.74 2.50									
2.49 2.25									
2.24 2.00									
Below 2.00									

■ Highly Likely   ▨ Possible   ☐ Unlikely

Touro College—Jacob D. Fuchsberg Law Center

300 Nassau Road
Huntington, NY 11743

Phone: 516.421.2244, ext. 313

■ Introduction

The Jacob D. Fuchsberg Law Center is a component of Touro College, which was established under Jewish auspices. The college derives its name from Judah and Isaac Touro, leaders of Colonial America, whose commitment to academic excellence and to the Jewish heritage represent the ideals upon which Touro College bases its mission.

Touro College is fully approved by the Middle States Association of Colleges and Schools. The Law Center is fully accredited by the American Bar Association.

The Law Center is located in Huntington, Long Island, a residential community near the western boundary of Suffolk County, one of the most rapidly expanding and developing areas of New York State. The school enjoys the many benefits of a suburban campus in close proximity to New York City.

■ Enrollment/Student Body

➡ *2,196 applicants* ➡ *797 admitted first-year class 1993*
➡ *286 enrolled first-year class 1993* ➡ *539 total full-time*
➡ *325 total part-time* ➡ *22% minority* ➡ *42% women* ➡ *11 states & foreign countries represented in first-year class 1993* ➡ *109 undergraduate schools represented in first-year class 1993* ➡ *average age in the full-time class is 25* ➡ *average age in part-time class is 31*

The law school has a diverse student body. Students range in age from 21 to 71. The fall 1993 entering class consisted of 181 full-time students and 105 part-time students, of which 42 percent are women and 28 percent are persons of color.

■ Faculty

➡ *65 total* ➡ *41 full-time*
➡ *24 part-time and adjunct (varies by year)*
➡ *15 women* ➡ *3 minority*

■ Library & Physical Facilities

➡ *310,000 volumes & equivalents* ➡ *library hours: Mon.-Thurs., 8:00 A.M.-11:45 P.M.; Fri., 8:00 A.M.-2:45 P.M.; Sat., closed; Sun., 9:00 A.M.-11:45 P.M.* ➡ *LEXIS* ➡ *NEXIS* ➡ *WESTLAW* ➡ *DIALOG* ➡ *OCLC* ➡ *AUTO-CITE* ➡ *6 full-time librarians* ➡ *library seats 580*

In addition to case law and statutes for all state and federal jurisdictions, the library has an impressive collection of important English, American, and foreign legal works.

In observance of the Jewish Sabbath, the law library closes early on Friday, and remains closed on Saturday. Resource-sharing arrangements are available with nearby law libraries.

■ Curriculum

➡ *Academic Support Program* ➡ *Professional Development Program* ➡ *Writing Clinic* ➡ *87 credits required to graduate* ➡ *107 courses available (not offered every semester)* ➡ *J.D. degree available* ➡ *fall semester begins mid-Aug.; spring semester begins early-Jan.* ➡ *range of first-year class size—17-80*

The Law Center operates on a semester system. Students enrolled in the J.D. program may study full-time for three years or part-time for four years. Part-time students may attend classes either during the day or evening. The first-year curriculum is required. A number of required courses extend into the second year for full-time students and into the third year for part-time students. In addition, every student must, before graduation, satisfy the Public-Interest Law Perspective, the Perspective requirement, the course in Professional Responsibility, and comply with the writing requirement. The upper-class curriculum includes electives in litigation, business, taxation, real estate, commercial law, criminal law, the law of administrative agencies, health law, international law, public interest, civil rights, family law, and a full range of clinical offerings.

■ Special Programs

The Institute of Local and Suburban Law—The Institute of Local and Suburban Law is dedicated to the research of local and suburban problems and education in the areas of municipal law, environmental law, and their interrelationship with state and federal law.

Legal Education Access Program—The Legal Education Access Program represents a committed effort by the Law Center to offset barriers to success that often are experienced by students of color at a predominately white law school.

LEAP is comprised of several key components, including a three-week summer program; group discussions; a mentor program; and individual counseling and assistance for all participants.

The Housing Rights Project—The Housing Rights Project is an on-campus legal services program designed to offer students the opportunity to obtain hands-on experience by volunteering their time to provide representation for low-income clients in housing-related proceedings. This program is a collaborative effort between the Jacob D. Fuchsberg Law Center and the Nassau/Suffolk Law Services Committee, Inc.

Institute of Jewish Law—The Institute of Jewish Law is concerned with research, scholarship, publication, and courses in Jewish Law.

Moscow Summer Program—A four-week program focused on Russia's legal system in transition. Coursework is enhanced by supplemental lectures and tours.

■ Admission

➡ *Bachelor's degree from accredited college/university required* ➡ *application deadline—May 1* ➡ *early application preferred, rolling admission* ➡ *LSAT, LSDAS required* ➡ *median GPA—2.80* ➡ *median LSAT score—152* ➡ *application fee—$40* ➡ *personal statement required*

Students are admitted to the first-year full-time and part-time day and evening class for the fall semester of each academic year. Transfer students may be admitted to either fall or spring semesters. The admissions process is selective. It seeks to identify those applicants who evidence an ability to pursue the study of law successfully and to make a significant contribution to the educational program and diversity of the law school.

The principal criteria used in the admissions process are the cumulative grade-point average and the LSAT score. The selection process, however, recognizes that other factors, such as major and course selection, graduate study, personal qualities of character, integrity and good citizenship, and professional experience after college, may also be indicators of potential.

The effect of a long delay between college and proposed entry to law school is, of course, taken into consideration. Letters of recommendation from those with direct personal knowledge of the intellectual capacity of an applicant can contribute to the admission decision.

The Law Center does not and will not discriminate against any applicant for admission because of race, color, religion, sex, national origin, age, marital status, financial status, or physical disability.

Applicants are always welcome to visit the campus. The Admissions Office is open weekdays throughout the year. Visitors should make advance arrangements by contacting the Admissions Office. Inquiries may be addressed to the Director of Admissions.

■ Student Activities

Students may participate in various activities outside the classroom that offer opportunities for academic and social growth. Key among these are the *Touro Law Review*, the *Touro Journal of Transnational Law*, the *Journal of the Suffolk Academy of Law*, and the Moot Court Board. In ad-dition to the Student Bar Association—which supports social and academic activities for all Touro students—there are 19 professional and social organizations open to students, including national law fraternities, minority student associations, and specialized law societies.

■ Expenses and Financial Aid

➡ *tuition & fees—full-time, $14,470; part-time, $11,770*
➡ *estimated additional expenses (approximate cost of books and supplies in the first year)—$500*   ➡ *scholarships available: Dean's Fellow Award, Merit Scholarship, Siben Fellowship, Incentive Award*   ➡ *financial aid available; FAFSA and GAPSFAS due June 1, March 1 strongly preferred*

The Law Center provides access to educational loans such as the Stafford Loans, Supplemental Loan Service, and the New York Tuition Assistance Program. There is also a College Work Study Program. Institutional aid includes the Touro Grant Program, Merit Scholarships, Tuition Incentive Awards, and Full-Tuition Scholarships through the Dean's Fellow Program. Financial need does not affect, in any way, admission decisions.

■ Career Services

The Office of Career Planning and Counseling functions as a career center, offering a variety of services to students and employers. Workshops and individual counseling on résumé preparation, interviewing techniques, job searching, and career options are provided. Employers participate in on-campus interviews, information seminars, and career panels. The resources of the placement library assist students in their efforts to secure employment upon graduation, and part-time and full-time employment during the school year and summer.

Admission Profile Not Available

Tulane University Law School

Joseph Merrick Jones Hall
New Orleans, LA 70118

Phone: 504.865.5930, fax: 504.865.6710

■ Introduction

Tulane Law School, established in 1847, provides comprehensive legal training in the common law, in all federal subjects, and in the civil law. Students choose the courses in which they enroll and have the opportunity to pursue comparative education in two legal systems. Tulane's location in a picturesque residential neighborhood of New Orleans provides ready access to the downtown activities of the U.S. Court of Appeals for the Fifth Circuit, the Louisiana Supreme Court, and lower federal and state civil and criminal courts. In addition to cultural events at Tulane University, students enjoy the advantages of city life and many aspects of traditional New Orleans including the annual Mardi Gras celebration.

■ Enrollment/Student Body

➧ *3,866 applicants*   ➧ *1,203 admitted first-year class 1993*
➧ *338 enrolled first-year class 1993*   ➧ *1,001 total full-time*
➧ *22% minority*   ➧ *43% women*
➧ *52 states & foreign countries represented*
➧ *225 undergraduate schools represented*

■ Faculty

➧ *96 total*   ➧ *48 full-time*   ➧ *48 part-time or adjunct*
➧ *22 women*   ➧ *6 minority*

Assistant or associate deans oversee admissions and financial aid, student life, minority student concerns, and the full-service Office of Career Services.

■ Library and Physical Facilities

➧ *474,000 volumes & equivalents*   ➧ *library hours: Mon.-Thurs., 7:30 A.M.-MIDNIGHT; Sat.-Sun., 9:00 A.M.-MIDNIGHT*
➧ *LEXIS*   ➧ *NEXIS*   ➧ *WESTLAW*   ➧ *DIALOG*
➧ *EELS*   ➧ *ORBIT*   ➧ *QUICKLAW*   ➧ *VUTEXT*
➧ *DATATIMES*   ➧ *INTERNET*   ➧ *MARC*
➧ *WILSONDISC*   ➧ *INFOTRAC*   ➧ *CALI*
➧ *several cataloging systems*   ➧ *10 full-time librarians*
➧ *library seats 438*   ➧ *9 CD-ROM Players*

The law library has both national and international collections. Located directly across from the Law School is the university's Howard-Tilton Library, housing over one million volumes.

Construction has begun on the Law School's new building, due to be completed in the summer of 1994. The floor plan will ensure that faculty offices are well integrated with classrooms and other student spaces.

On-campus housing is available, as is plentiful and nearby off-campus housing.

■ Curriculum

➧ *Academic Support Program*   ➧ *88 credits required to graduate*   ➧ *175 courses available*   ➧ *degrees available: J.D.; J.D./M.B.A.; JD./M.H.A.;J .D./M.A.; J.D./M.S.P.H.;*

➧ *LL.M.; M.C.L., S.J.D.*   ➧ *semesters, start in Aug.*
➧ *range of first-year class size—40-100*

Six semesters in residence, at least a C average, and fulfillment of a 20-hour community service obligation are required for graduation from the J.D. degree program. The first-year curriculum, including a moot court argument, is required. Thereafter, all courses are elective. Many courses are taught in multiple sections to allow for smaller classes, and faculty members teach seminars in their fields of specialty.

The Legal Analysis course is a voluntary, invitational program during the first semester in which students work closely with faculty and senior fellows on writing and analysis skills.

■ Special Programs

Among the strengths for which the school is known are international and comparative law, admiralty and maritime law, and environmental law. The school offers four "concentration" programs which allow J.D. students to receive a certificate of completion of successful studies in (a) European Legal Practice, (b) Environmental Law, (c) Maritime Law, or (d) Sports Law. Tulane's Eason-Weinmann Center for Comparative Law and its Maritime Law Center add depth to the curriculum.

The annual Tulane Tax Institute and Corporate Law Institute, and the biennial Admiralty Law Institute, are recognized for their excellence. Tulane conducts a summer school in New Orleans and offers summer-study programs abroad in: England, Israel, The Netherlands, Canada, France, Italy, Germany, and Greece. All summer programs are open to law students enrolled at Tulane or other accredited law schools.

■ Clinical Programs

The school offers eight different live clinical programs: civil, criminal, juvenile, immigration, environmental, appellate, legislative advocacy, and administrative advocacy. In addition, there is a very active simulated Trial Advocacy program, and selected third-year students may do externships with federal and state judges. The school was the first to institute a mandatory pro bono program, requiring that each student complete at least 20 hours of community-service work prior to graduation.

■ Joint-Degree and Graduate Programs

Joint-degree programs are offered in conjunction with Tulane's Freeman School of Business, (J.D./M.B.A.), School of Public Health and Tropical Medicine, (J.D./M.H.A. or M.P.H.), and Graduate School (J.D./M.A.), in a variety of fields including Latin American Studies and International Affairs. At the graduate level, the Law School offers a general LL.M. program, LL.M. programs in Admiralty and in Energy and Environmental Law, the LL.M. with specialization in international trade and finance, the M.C.L. with specialization in European legal practice, and the S.J.D.

■ Admission

➧ *Bachelor's degree from accredited univerisity or college required; strong candidates who have completed 3/4 of work toward undergraduate degree are also considered*
➧ *application deadline—May 1; application by end of Feb. strongly recommended* ➧ *rolling admissions, early application preferred* ➧ *LSAT, LSDAS required*
➧ *median GPA—3.30* ➧ *median LSAT score—160*
➧ *application fee—$45*

Competition is keen, and a combination of the objective factors, the LSAT score and the UGPA, is relied upon heavily. In the case of multiple LSAT scores, the school looks at the highest score. However, Tulane seeks to individualize the admissions process by also considering subjective factors such as grade trends, course load, undergraduate school, nonacademic activities, the student's background and experience, and the writing sample. A special admissions program exists for students from disadvantaged backgrounds.

The Law School receives applications for admission starting October 1 and begins to announce decisions after December 1.

■ Student Activities

Credit may be earned for work on the student-edited *Tulane Law Review*, *Tulane Maritime Law Journal*, or for participation in the several moot court appellate and trial competitions. Other journals include *Tulane Environmental Journal*, the *Journal of Law & Sexuality*, the *Tulane*

European and Civil Law Forum, and the new *Journal of International and Comparative Law*. The Law School has a chapter of the Order of the Coif. Over 20 student organizations are represented at Tulane including Tulane Law Women, Black Law Students Association, La Alianza, Asian Law Student Organization, Environmental Law Society, and several legal fraternities. The Tulane Public Interest Law Foundation raises funds, matched by the Law School, to support as many as 45 students each summer in public-interest fellowships with a variety of organizations.

■ Expenses and Financial Aid

➧ *1993-94 full-time tuition & fees $19,085*
➧ *estimated additional expenses—$9,830 (room, board, health, books, transportation, misc.)* ➧ *scholarships available; student must demonstrate need, after which scholarship size is indexed according to merit*
➧ *financial aid available; FAFSA due Feb. 15, preliminary financial aid form due at time of application for admission*

■ Career Services

The Office of Career Services at the Law School assists both students and alumni in finding employment in the legal profession. The office is staffed by a full-time director, assistant, counselor, and support staff. A large placement library is available to students, as well as a full range of counseling services. Tulane participates in several job fairs across the country, and over 150 employers interview students on campus.

The office has taken a proactive stance in assisting students with their job searches, with the result that Tulane graduates find law-related employment throughout the United States.

Applicant Group for the 1993–1994 Academic Year

Tulane University Law School

LSAT Score	GPA									
	3.75 +	3.50 - 3.74	3.25 - 3.49	3.00 - 3.24	2.75 - 2.99	2.50 - 2.74	2.25 - 2.49	2.00 - 2.24	Below 2.00	No GPA
175 - 180										
170 - 174										
165 - 169										
160 - 164										
155 - 159										
150 - 154										
145 - 149										
140 - 144										
135 - 139										
130 - 134										
125 - 129										
120 - 124										

■ Excellent   ■ Good   ▢ Fair   ▢ Unlikely

University of Tulsa College of Law

3120 East Fourth Place
Tulsa, OK 74104

Phone: 918.631.2709

■ Introduction

The College of Law, a private, nonsectarian institution, with an enrollment of about 655 students, is located on the main campus of the University of Tulsa about two miles from downtown Tulsa, providing the benefits of a quiet, residential campus and an active urban center. Tulsa is a flourishing city of approximately 725,000 located in the northeast quarter in the green country of Oklahoma, with lakes and hills nearby.

The college is accredited by the ABA and the AALS. The university is accredited through the doctoral level and consists of five colleges and a graduate school.

■ Enrollment/Student Body

➡ 1,478 applicants ➡ 601 admitted first-year class 1993
➡ 216 enrolled first-year class 1993 ➡ 456 total full-time
➡ 172 total part-time ➡ 12% minority
➡ 35% women ➡ 45 states & foreign countries represented
➡ 175 undergraduate schools represented

Approximately 55 percent of the first-year class is from out of state. Typically, an entering class represents students from about 35 states and 120 colleges and universities.

■ Faculty

➡ 56 total ➡ 37 full-time (includes one full-time chair)
➡ 19 part-time or adjunct ➡ 15 women ➡ 6 minority

■ Library and Physical Facilities

➡ 260,000 volumes & equivalents ➡ library hours: Mon.-Fri., 7:30 A.M.-MIDNIGHT; Sat., 9:00 A.M.-10:00 P.M.; Sun., 9:00 A.M.-MIDNIGHT ➡ LEXIS ➡ NEXIS
➡ WESTLAW ➡ DIALOG ➡ Legal Track (periodical index) ➡ Wilson Disk (periodical index)
➡ 7 full-time librarians ➡ 8 full-time support staff
➡ library seats 493

The College of Law occupies John Rogers Hall, which provides commodious facilities for the library, classes, seminars, model courtroom, faculty, admissions, placement, and other support services.

The library presently contains specialized collections in energy law and policy and Native American law. Computer labs for word processing, computer-assisted legal instruction, and other law-related database searching also are available.

■ Curriculum

➡ Academic Support Program ➡ minority support group
➡ 88 credits required to graduate ➡ 75 courses available
➡ degrees offered: J.D.; J.D./M.A. in History, Modern Letters, Industrial/Organizational Psychology; J.D./M.S. in Geosciences, Biological Sciences, Anthropology; J.D./M.B.A.; J.D./Master of Accountancy; J.D./Master of Taxation

The college is on a semester system. The full-time program typically takes three academic years. The first two semesters are devoted to required courses; thereafter, although some required, sequential courses are in the curriculum, a student is relatively free to select courses in areas of interest.

A part-time evening program is also available. Completion of this program generally takes four academic years. Both programs require successful completion of 88 credit hours.

Classes are offered during the summer in both divisions. The summer program consists of one eight-week and two four-week sessions.

The first-year curriculum is required. Legal Authorities is taught in concentrated form to entering students during the week preceding the beginning of other courses.

To assist in curriculum planning, the faculty has defined the following three areas of concentration:

Corporate Practice—This area covers courses which are basic to a corporate or corporate-related practice, including those courses concerning business structures, governmental control of business, taxes, financing, and planning.

Energy Law and Policy—Energy, natural resources, and environmental law subjects are integrated into a comprehensive area of concentration designed to give students both theoretical and practical exposure to the field of energy and environmental law.

General Practice—These courses cover a wide range of subjects including procedure (both civil and criminal), basic corporate law, commercial law, evidence, federal income taxation, administrative law, and decedents' estates and trusts.

■ Special Programs

Through the Oklahoma Bar's Legal Internship Program, students who have completed 50 hours and certain prerequisites may be granted a limited license to practice law under the supervision of a practicing attorney. The College of Law, in cooperation with both state and federal courts located in Tulsa, also offers a Judicial Internship Program wherein students work in the court system.

New additions to our special programs are our legal clinics which give students an opportunity to handle actual cases and develop professional skills under the close supervision of faculty supervisors.

The National Energy Law and Policy Institute offers students an opportunity to develop expertise in natural resource areas of critical importance.

The Native American Law Certificate program is designed for students interested in Native American Law issues. The certificate studies include coursework, research, and practical experiences in externships with tribal entities. The John W. Shleppey Indian Law and History Collection, housed at the university, supports a major center for the study of Indian law and history. It is one of the country's finest collections in these areas.

In the summer of 1993 we sponsored a summer institute which took faculty and students from the University of Tulsa College of Law to Comenius University in Bratislava, Slovakia to engage in a four-week set of classes and seminars.

■ Admission

➡ *B.A. or B.S. degree required*   ➡ *application deadline—Jan. 15 (for full consideration on scholarship awards)*
➡ *LSAT, LSDAS required*   ➡ *median GPA—3.00*
➡ *median LSAT score—155*   ➡ *application fee—$30*

Application may be made by anyone who will be, by the time of enrollment, a graduate of a regionally accredited college. No applicant will be required to make a final decision on an offer prior to April 1. There is no firm application cutoff date; however, early applications are preferable. Tulsa is committed to an affirmative action program. Special care is taken in evaluating applications from members of minority groups traditionally not well represented in the profession.

■ Student Activities

The *Tulsa Law Journal*, edited by students, is published four times per year. The *Energy Law Journal*, The *Tulsa Journal of Comparative and International Law*, and the Natural Resources Law Monograph Series are also produced. Student competitions include national and international moot court, national trial advocacy, negotiations, and client counseling. The Negotiation Team placed first in the regional competition (fall 1993) and will be going to the National Competition. The University of Tulsa's Student Bar Association has been named the outstanding chapter in the United States by the American Bar Association. Presentation of the award was made during the SBA convention in New York City, August 1993. The student newspaper, *Baculus*, has achieved national recognition also for the efforts of its law school journalists. Student groups include: Native American Law Organization; Black Law Students Association; Tulsa International Law Society; Board of Advocates; Christian Legal Society; Volunteer Income Tax Assistance; Oklahoma Trial Lawyers Association; Rutherford Institute; Women's Law Caucus; American Civil Liberties Union; Environmental and Natural Resources Society; Law and Medicine Society; the Forum; Communications, Entertainment and Sports Law Club; and three national legal fraternities.

■ Housing

Housing is available both in dormitories and university apartments. Accommodations are available in nonuniversity facilities at reasonable cost.

■ Expenses and Financial Aid

➡ *tuition & fees—full-time, $12,450 part-time, $8,715*
➡ *estimated additional expenses—on-campus, $6,140; off-campus, $8,050 (room and board, transportation, books and supplies)*   ➡ *merit scholarships available*   ➡ *financial aid available*   ➡ *FAF, FFS, GAPSFAS, or USAF accepted*

Tuition and fees are the same for resident and nonresident students.

■ Career Services

The law school's Career Services Office has a full-time director. Individual interviews are with law firms, corporations, and governmental agencies. Counseling services and a career services library including direct referrals to part-time, full-time, summer, and career positions are available.

Our graduates are employed in all 50 states, the District of Columbia, and several foreign countries.

Prospects for Admission

University of Tulsa College of Law

GPA	LSAT Score						
	120-147	147-151	151-153	153-157	157-163	163-170	170-180
3.75 + Above			Possible	Likely	Likely	Likely	Likely
3.74 3.50			Possible	Likely	Likely	Likely	Likely
3.49 3.25				Likely	Likely	Likely	Likely
3.24 3.00				Possible	Likely	Likely	Likely
2.99 2.75					Possible	Likely	Likely
2.74 2.50					Possible	Likely	Likely
2.49 2.25						Possible	Likely
2.24 2.00							Possible

Unlikely*   Possible   Likely

* Individual accomplishments crucial

This chart is to be used as a general guide in determining the chances for admittance.

University of Utah College of Law

Admissions Office
Salt Lake City, UT 84112

Phone: 801.581.7479

■ Introduction

The University of Utah College of Law, approved by the ABA and a member of AALS, is situated in the foothills of the picturesque Wasatch Mountain Range of the Rocky Mountains, and is a five-minute drive from downtown Salt Lake City, the seat of federal, state, and local governmental bodies. The College of Law is nationally recognized for its academic reputation, innovative curriculum and favorable faculty/student ratio. There is a prevailing sense of community among students fostered by a faculty and administration that is friendly, open and service oriented. A comprehensive student survey administered last year confirmed that College of Law students have a high level of satisfaction with virtually every facet of their law school experience.

■ Enrollment/Student Body

➤ *900 applicants* ➤ *305 admitted first-year class 1993*
➤ *124 enrolled first-year class 1993* ➤ *366 total full-time*
➤ *14% minority* ➤ *43% women*
➤ *43 states & 15 foreign countries represented*
➤ *85 undergraduate schools represented*

■ Faculty

➤ *55 total* ➤ *27 full-time* ➤ *28 part-time or adjunct*
➤ *8 women* ➤ *4 minority*

■ Library and Physical Facilities

➤ *264,000 volumes & equivalents* ➤ *library hours: Mon.-Thurs., 7:00 A.M.-11:00 P.M.; Fri., 7:00 A.M.-8:00 P.M.; Sat., 9:00 A.M.-8:00 P.M.; Sun., 11:00 A.M.-11:00 P.M.* ➤ *LEXIS*
➤ *NEXIS* ➤ *WESTLAW* ➤ *VuText*
➤ *Utah Capitol Hill Services* ➤ *Utah Courts Information Xchange* ➤ *PACER* ➤ *7 full-time librarians; 5 of the full-time librarians hold law degrees* ➤ *library seats 381*

The law center is located in the lower portion of the beautifully landscaped 1,500-acre University of Utah campus, which also serves as the site of the official state arboretum. The recently remodeled law building provides first-year students with their own study hall and personal carrels, houses two student computing labs and other computer support and has classrooms equipped with state-of-the-art video-computer projection equipment. Advanced students are provided a personal study carrel in the adjacent law library building, which is a modern, spacious facility with functional compact shelving to house its collection and the latest technological equipment and library research services.

■ Curriculum

➤ *Academic Support Program* ➤ *88 credits required to graduate* ➤ *111 courses available* ➤ *degrees available: J.D.; J.D./M.B.A.; J.D./M.P.A.; LL.M. (Environmental Law)*
➤ *semesters, start in Aug.* ➤ *full-time, day program; 10-week summer term* ➤ *range of first-year class size—10-65*

The innovative curriculum is designed to allow more efficient and rational sequencing of legal education that responds to the evolving legal, social and ethical needs of our society. The entering students are first offered an intensive four-day Introduction to Law course before they begin the required first-year curriculum. Second-year students select from a variety of foundational Cornerstone courses. In the third year, students may take year-long intensive Capstone courses that provide the opportunity for in-depth study, research, and practicum in a focused area of law. In addition, students may select from more than 50 advanced courses and seminars, a variety of clinical and skills courses, and numerous cocurricular opportunities. The curriculum is geared to prepare students to practice in any state.

■ Special Programs

The Center for Energy, Public Lands, and Environmental Law provides opportunities for J.D. candidates to engage in energy, public lands, environmental, and natural resource academic courses and related law activities while at Utah. Regular courses offered include Natural Resource Law, Oil & Gas, Mining & Minerals, Water Law, Public Land Use, and Environmental Law. The law school offers a specialized LL.M. degree in energy and environmental law.

The clinical programs offer both live and simulated opportunities for students to assume the lawyering role. In the Civil Clinic and the Criminal Clinic, students directly represent clients, investigate cases, and appear in court. In the Judicial Clinic, students act as clerks to judges, researching issues and drafting opinions in pending cases. The Judicial Extern Program allows students to spend a semester away from the school working as full-time clerks for certain courts.

■ Admission Standards

➤ *Bachelor's degree required* ➤ *application deadline—Feb. 1*
➤ *rolling admission, early application (Nov. 15-Jan. 15) preferred*
➤ *LSAT, LSDAS required* ➤ *median GPA—3.55*
➤ *median LSAT score—161* ➤ *application fee-$25-40*
➤ *begin fall only*

No applicant is accepted or rejected without a member of the Admission Committee having first fully considered the entire application. The Personal Statement should expand on the applicant's biographic and academic background and motivations for seeking a legal education. The College of Law makes a special effort to attract nontraditional students from diverse cultural, educational, economic and ethnic backgrounds. Each applicant is evaluated for the contribution that person can make to the student body or the legal profession, in addition to evidence of demonstrated high academic ability. Members of minority, racial or ethnic groups, women and persons with disabilities are encouraged to apply.

Qualified candidates may be invited to participate in the Academic Support Program.

■ Student Activities

The *Utah Law Review*, the *Journal of Contemporary Law*, and *Journal of Energy, Natural Resources, and Environmental Law* are professional journals edited and published by students.

Student organizations include the Student Bar Association, the Women's Law Caucus, Natural Resources Law Forum, the Moot Court Society, the Minority Law Caucus, the International Law Society, Health Law Coalition, Law Students for the Arts, the Federalist Society, the Gay & Lesbian Law Student Alliance, Native American Law Student Association, and the Public Interest Law Organization.

■ Expenses and Financial Aid

➧ *tuition & fees—$3,853/yr., resident; $8,529/yr., nonresident*
➧ *need-based & merit scholarships available*
➧ *minority scholarships available: Minority Law Caucus Scholarship, Immigration & refugee Scholarship, need & merit-based scholarships*
➧ *financial aid available; Free Application for Federal Student Aid (FAFSA) due Feb. 15, may submit after Jan. 1*

Students who wish to apply for need-based scholarships or long-term loans such as Perkins Loans (formerly NDSL), Stafford Loans (formerly GSL), or others, must submit a FAFSA and should contact the Financial Aid Office, 105 SSB, University of Utah, Salt Lake City, UT 84112, (801) 581-6211. The deadline for submitting a FAFSA to begin the application process for financial aid is February 15. The law school also has an endowed Loan Forgiveness Program for qualified graduates who practice in the public sector.

■ Career Services

The College of Law and its graduates have access to one of the most technologically advanced Legal Career Services programs in the country. The LCS office transmits information to prospective employers, both on and off campus. The LCS office also offer personal counseling, maintains a resource library and sponsor numerous seminars throughout the year.

Applicant Group for the 1993–1994 Academic Year

University of Utah College of Law
This grid includes only applicants who earned 120-180 LSAT scores under standard administrations.

LSAT Score	GPA 3.75 +		3.50 -3.74		3.25 - 3.49		3.00 - 3.24		2.75 - 2.99		2.50 - 2.74		2.25 - 2.49		2.00 - 2.24		Below 2.00		No GPA		Total	
	Apps	Adm	Apps	Adm	Apps	Adm	Apps	Adm	Apps	Adm	Apps	Adm	Apps	Adm	Apps	Adm	Apps	Adm	Apps	Adm	Apps	Adm
175 - 180	0	0	0	0	0	0	1	1	0	0	0	0	0	0	0	0	0	0	0	0	1	1
170 - 174	1	1	5	4	3	2	3	3	2	2	0	0	0	0	0	0	0	0	0	0	14	12
165 - 169	7	6	11	11	5	4	9	7	5	3	1	0	2	0	1	1	0	0	1	1	42	33
160 - 164	18	18	33	29	45	31	30	8	15	5	7	2	7	0	3	0	0	0	0	0	158	93
155 - 159	25	21	46	25	51	14	39	7	36	6	10	2	7	1	4	0	0	0	1	0	219	76
150 - 154	21	16	28	7	38	7	40	4	27	4	17	1	7	0	5	0	0	0	4	2	187	41
145 - 149	3	1	12	4	23	3	26	0	20	1	17	2	7	0	7	0	0	0	2	1	117	12
140 - 144	2	1	7	3	7	0	13	2	8	0	6	2	7	2	2	0	1	0	2	0	55	10
135 - 139	0	0	0	0	1	0	4	0	7	0	7	0	0	0	1	0	0	0	2	0	22	0
130 - 134	0	0	0	0	2	0	1	0	1	0	3	0	1	0	2	0	0	0	1	0	11	0
125 - 129	0	0	0	0	0	0	0	0	0	0	1	0	1	0	0	0	0	0	1	0	3	0
120 - 124	0	0	0	0	0	0	0	0	0	0	0	0	0	0	0	0	0	0	1	0	1	0
Total	77	64	142	83	175	61	166	32	121	21	69	9	39	3	25	1	1	0	15	4	830	278

Apps = Number of Applicants
Adm = Number Admitted
Reflects 94% of the total applicant pool.

Valparaiso University School of Law

Wesemann Hall
Valparaiso, IN 46383

Phone: 800.262.0656 or 219.465.7829

■ Introduction

Founded in 1879, Valparaiso University School of Law is accredited by the American Bar Association and the Association of American Law Schools. Located in Valparaiso, Indiana, 55 miles southeast of Chicago and 15 miles from the Indiana Dunes National Lakeshore, Valparaiso University is a private university affiliated with the Lutheran Church. The School of Law seeks to challenge and assist students with realizing intellectual abilities and talents. The diversity and scholarship of the faculty offer students traditional lectures in the Socratic method and a strong skills-oriented clinical program.

■ Enrollment/Student Body

- ➡ *1,126 applicants*   ➡ *521 admitted first-year class 1993*
- ➡ *175 enrolled first-year class 1993*   ➡ *501 total full-time*
- ➡ *38 total part-time*   ➡ *18.5% minority*   ➡ *45% women*
- ➡ *40 states & foreign countries represented*
- ➡ *180 undergraduate schools represented*

■ Faculty

- ➡ *42 total*   ➡ *25 full-time*   ➡ *17 part-time or adjunct*
- ➡ *11 women*   ➡ *2 minority*

Faculty members have completed graduate and professional studies at institutions throughout the world. While teaching is the primary and most important function of faculty members, they continuously engage in scholarly research and writing, as reflected in the numerous publications in professional law reviews, journals, and texts. Several faculty members maintain an active role in the practice of law.

■ Library and Physical Facilities

- ➡ *214,600 volumes & equivalents*   ➡ *library hours: Mon.-Fri., 8:00 A.M.-MIDNIGHT; Sat.-Sun., 9:00 A.M.-MIDNIGHT*
- ➡ *LEXIS*   ➡ *NEXIS*   ➡ *WESTLAW*   ➡ *DIALOG*
- ➡ *Vutext*   ➡ *Datatimes*   ➡ *QLSystems*
- ➡ *5 full-time librarians*   ➡ *library seats 304*

Included in the law library collection are both hard book and microfilm format. Individual and group study carrels are available for student use.

■ Curriculum

- ➡ *90 credits required to graduate*   ➡ *85 courses available*
- ➡ *J.D. degree available*   ➡ *semesters, start in Aug.*
- ➡ *range of first-year class size—60-100*

Five distinct elements of legal education make up the curriculum: legal analysis, practical training, legal theory, writing and research, and professional responsibility. Designed with a national scope preparing students for practice in any part of the country, the first-year curriculum is enhanced with three main objectives: to provide a solid foundation in the substantive areas of the law; to assist

with the mastery of the base methods of legal analysis and of the processes of reasoning used by lawyers; and to introduce students to the major areas of specialization, including civil or criminal litigation, taxation, international law, environmental law, comparative law, business and commercial law, and public law.

A 20-hour commitment of pro bono legal service required of all students for graduation meets the needs of expanding legal service to the poor and provides law students with valuable practical experience and contacts within the legal community.

A part-time day program allows students to extend their legal education from the normal three-year period to five years, enrolling in five to eleven credit-hours per semester.

■ Special Programs

Legal Internship Programs —These allow students to develop and enhance professional skills by working closely with faculty, attorneys, and judges on actual cases, client representation, and legal proceedings. Indiana court rules allow third-year students to represent indigent clients or state or local governmental agencies in court. Legal Services Clinic students participate in all stages of representation from interview to trial/hearings on issues of divorce, landlord/tenant, and public entitlements. Civil Criminal Law Clinic students represent indigents involved in the criminal justice system; the nature of the caseload varies but may include trial-level cases, appeals, and post-conviction proceedings. With Current Representation, faculty members invite students to perform work in connection with legal representation provided by the faculty member. Seven extern programs are available to third-year students: Federal Judge Externship, U.S. Attorney Externship, Bankruptcy Externship, U.S. Environmental Protection Agency, Region V Externship, and the County Prosecutors Externship, the Local Rules Externship and the State Judge Externship .

Summer Study Abroad—Valparaiso's interests in international and comparative law are enhanced with Summer Study Abroad Programs in Cambridge, England and Ningbo, China. Participating law students attend classes led by Valparaiso's professors, distinguished alumni, and guest lecturers from the host communities.

■ Admission Standards

- ➡ *Bachelor's degree from accredited college or university required*   ➡ *application deadline—April 15*
- ➡ *rolling admission*   ➡ *LSAT, LSDAS required*
- ➡ *median GPA—3.30*   ➡ *median LSAT score—155*
- ➡ *application fee—$30*

The commitment to student-centered education is expressed in the admission policy. While the LSAT and GPA weigh heavily in determining the applicant's academic ability, the Admissions Committee also considers nonquantifiable factors.

Minorities are strongly encouraged to apply and are eligible for a special admissions program designed to encourage and increase minority enrollment.

Valparaiso offers a voluntary Academic Support Program for select students identified by the committee; this includes a summer preparatory program and tutorial sessions during the semester.

■ Student Activities

The *Valparaiso University Law Review* is published four times per year by a student editorial board selected on the basis of academic achievement and quality writing skills. The *Review* covers significant research in all areas of law. Students interested in enhancing advocacy skills may join the National Moot Court Competition, Client Counseling Competition, Mock Trial Competition, Negotiation Competition, Philip C. Jessup International Moot Court Competition, or the Giles Sutherland Rich Patent Law Competition.

The Student Bar Association conducts professional programs and social activities, and funds more than 20 student organizations, including the American Association of Trial Lawyers, Black Law Students Association, Hispanic Law Students Association, Christian Legal Society, Jewish Law Student Association, International Law Society, Midwest Environmental Law Caucus, Women Law Students Association, Patent Law Student Association, Law Spouses Association, and the *Forum* (student newspaper). Students participate in academic, literary, musical, social, and athletic events including intramural sports.

■ Expenses and Financial Aid

➠ *tuition & fees—full-time, $13,710; part-time, $7,610; 1993-94 Guaranteed Tuition Program, $14,780*
➠ *estimated additional expenses—$$7,230 (room, board, & books)* ➠ *scholarships available* ➠ *minority scholarships available* ➠ *public-service grants & financial aid available*

Approximately one-quarter of the first-year students were awarded scholarships and about two-thirds received assistance through university law grants and loan programs. To assist students to pursue careers in public service, Valparaiso established a Loan Repayment Assistance Program; students may receive scholarships for summer employment and grants for securing positions with public-service employers upon graduation.

Valparaiso offers a **Guaranteed Tuition Program** that guarantees entering students the same tuition for three years; this program protects students against tuition increases that will occur in the second and third years of law school.

■ Career Services

Career Services offers career planning and counseling services including résumé/cover-letter preparation and state bar examination information as well as placement assistance; maintains an extensive resource library and the on-campus interview program; and participates in regional and national job fairs. In recent years more than 88 percent of graduates have found law-related employment within six months of passing a bar. Alumni practice in 48 states and abroad.

Applicant Group for the 1993–1994 Academic Year

Valparaiso University School of Law
These projections are based on applications and decisions during the 1992-1993 year.

LSAT Score	GPA								
	3.75 +	3.50 - 3.74	3.25 - 3.49	3.00 - 3.24	2.75 - 2.99	2.50 - 2.74	2.25 - 2.49	2.00 - 2.24	Below 2.00
175 - 180	A	A	A	A	A	A	P	P	U
170 - 174	A	A	A	A	A	A	P	P	U
165 - 169	A	A	A	A	A	A	P	U	U
160 - 164	A	A	A	A	P	P	P	U	U
155 - 159	A	A	A	A	P	P	P	U	U
150 - 154	A	A	A	A	P	P	U	U	U
145 - 149	P	P	P	U	U	P	U	U	U
140 - 144	P	P	U	U	P	U	U	U	U
135 - 139	U	U	U	P	U	U	U	U	U
130 - 134	U	U	U	U	U	U	U	U	U
125 - 129	U	U	U	U	U	U	U	U	U
120 - 124	U	U	U	U	U	U	U	U	U

A = Acceptance Likely
P = Acceptance Possible
U = Acceptance Unlikely

Vanderbilt University School of Law

Admissions Office
Nashville, TN 37240

Phone: 615.322.6452

■ Introduction

Vanderbilt is an independent, privately endowed university founded in Nashville in 1873 by Commodore Cornelius Vanderbilt. The School of Law occupies a corner of the university's 305-acre campus. About 540 of Vanderbilt University's 8,600 students attend the law school, which is one of the 10 schools of the university. In its students, faculty, and educational approach, Vanderbilt is a nationally oriented law school with a reputation for excellence. It is a member of the AALS and is approved by the ABA.

Nashville, the state capital of Tennessee, has a metropolitan population of about one million, and is the location of the executive and legislative branches of the state government. State trial and appellate courts and the U.S. District Court, Middle Tennessee District, are located here.

■ Enrollment/Student Body

➧ *2,800 applicants* ➧ *650 admitted first-year class 1993*
➧ *187 enrolled first-year class 1993* ➧ *550 total full-time*
➧ *21% minority* ➧ *39% women*
➧ *48 states & foreign countries represented*
➧ *203 undergraduate schools represented*

■ Faculty

➧ *75 total* ➧ *33 full-time* ➧ *42 part-time or adjunct*
➧ *18 women* ➧ *5 minority*

■ Library and Physical Facilities

➧ *329,060 volumes & equivalents* ➧ *library hours: Mon.-Sun., 7:30 A.M.-1:00 A.M.* ➧ *LEXIS* ➧ *NEXIS*
➧ *WESTLAW* ➧ *INFOTRAC* ➧ *CD-based systems*
➧ *8 full-time librarians* ➧ *library seats 431*

The School of Law and law library are housed in a well-designed modern building located near university activity centers, and accessible to people who are disabled. In addition to the full range of traditional printed, microform, and on-line legal materials, the library performs extensive reference services, and trains students in legal bibliography. All other university libraries, containing more than one million volumes, are also available to law students.

■ Curriculum

➧ *88 credits required to graduate* ➧ *123 courses available*
➧ *degrees available: J.D./M.Div.; J.D./M.B.A.; J.D./M.P.P.; J.D./M.T.S.; J.D./M.A.; J.D./PhD.* ➧ *semesters, start in Aug.* ➧ *range of first-year class size—30-90*

A student may take up to six credit-hours of work toward the J.D. degree in nonlaw courses offered by other departments of the university. All work is done under the honor system. The faculty-to-student ratio, 1 to 17, is excellent. The open-door policy and extensive faculty-student contact are traditions at Vanderbilt. First-year students are assigned in groups of 30 to a faculty member who supervises a legal-writing and research program during the first semester in conjunction with the constitutional law or contracts course.

■ Special Programs

Clinical programs offer law students the opportunity to obtain academic credit while actively participating in aspects of the actual practice of law. Through cooperative arrangements with Legal Services of Nashville, Inc., the District Attorney's Office, the Public Defender's Office of Nashville-Davidson County, and the juvenile court, students perform a number of legal services under the supervision of licensed attorneys.

Transnational Legal Studies Program—The Transnational Legal Studies Program coordinates courses and extracurricular activities to serve two general purposes. First, it provides an opportunity for those interested in specializing in either public or private international legal work to prepare effectively for such a career. Second, it permits students who do not have a career interest in international legal practice to gain some contact with the field as part of their broader legal endeavors, either by means of selected course work or by participation in one or more of the extracurricular activities associated with the program.

Courses in the transnational program include Admiralty, Comparative Law, Conflict of Law, Foreign Relations Law of the United States, Immigration Law and Policy, Intellectual Property in International Trade, Internation Civil Litigation, International Commercial Transactions, International Law, Latin American Legal Systems, Law of Developing Countries, United States Taxation of Transnational Operations, Soviet Law, and seminars in selected international problems.

Students interested in concentration in transnational studies should also examine offerings in the areas of economics, international business, and political science in the Graduate School and in Owen Graduate School of Management.

■ Admission

➧ *Bachelor's degree from an accredited college or university required* ➧ *application deadline—Feb. 1*
➧ *LSAT, LSDAS required* ➧ *median GPA—3.62*
➧ *median LSAT score—164* ➧ *application fee—$50*

Students are selected on the basis of the quality of their undergraduate academic and extracurricular records, considered together with the LSAT results and letters of recommendation. The selection committee also takes into account any elements in the applicant's background that are likely to add depth and perspective to the law school student body or which indicate promise of leadership in the legal profession.

The faculty places great emphasis on the development during the college years of the abilities to read and comprehend accurately, thoroughly, and rapidly; to speak and write clearly and correctly; to think precisely; and to analyze complex situations and weigh and appraise their several elements. A broad cultural background is also important. Since law touches life at every point, every subject in the college curriculum may bear on a lawyer's work.

The entering class is limited to approximately 180 students. The school strictly adheres to a racially nondiscriminatory policy in its admissions process. Each application is reviewed on an individual basis, and no applicant is rejected solely because of a single quantitative predictor.

■ Student Activities

Extracurricular activities constitute an integral part of the instruction program. The school publishes two nationally recognized legal periodicals, the *Vanderbilt Law Review* and the *Vanderbilt Journal of Transnational Law*. In addition, the Vanderbilt Moot Court Board administers a moot court program of brief writing and oral argument available to students in both the first and second years. Vanderbilt enters teams in two national appellate advocacy competitions. The Vanderbilt Bar Association (VBA), official student organization of the law school, is affiliated with the Law Student Division of the ABA. The VBA publishes a newspaper and involves itself in a variety of activities, both professional and social. Active student organizations welcome members interested in

the legal issues of health care, intellectual property, the environment, labor, crime, and litigation. Special interest groups include BLSA, ALSA, women students, Amnesty International, Christians, Jews, gays and lesbians, and legal fraternities.

■ Expenses and Financial Aid

➡ *full-time tuition & fees—$17,750*
➡ *estimated additional expenses—$11,125 (housing, food, books, travel, misc.)* ➡ *need-based & merit scholarships available*
➡ *need-based minority scholarships available*
➡ *financial aid available, GAPSFAS and FAFSA due March 1*

A substantial amount of scholarship aid is available for entering students. Most scholarships are awarded on the basis of need, and a significant amount of scholarship funds have been awarded to minority group students.

■ Career Services

The school maintains its own career services office with a full-time director and staff. In addition to working with students, the office also assists alumni with relocation. Over the past two years graduates have located in 35 states. Approximately 300 employers visit the campus each year to conduct interviews.

Admission Profile Not Available

Vermont Law School

Chelsea Street
South Royalton, VT 05068

Phone: 800.227.1395 or 802.763.8303

■ Introduction

In an era when the dominant focus of legal education
has been law and economics, Vermont Law School has
emphasized training students for public service. The informal atmosphere of a beautiful rural setting and a real
sense of community underlie the learning environment.
Nearby Dartmouth College complements the law
school's social and cultural offerings.

■ Enrollment/Student Body

➡ 2,128 applicants   ➡ 734 admitted first-year class 1993
➡ 163 enrolled first-year class 1993   ➡ 483 total full-time
➡ 9% minority   ➡ 49% women
➡ 48 states & foreign countries represented
➡ 235 undergraduate schools represented

Vermont Law School students bring with them a remarkable
diversity of experience and backgrounds. Ninety percent
come from outside of Vermont. The average age of the entering class is 26, although ages range from 21 to over 50 years.
  Minority Student Information—Vermont Law School
is committed to a culturally and socially diverse student
body. Applications from women and minorities are encouraged. The most recent entering class consisted of 48
percent women and 10 percent students of color. The
school is a contributing supporter of the Council on Legal Education Opportunity (CLEO) Program.

■ Faculty

➡ 53 total   ➡ 31 full-time   ➡ 22 part-time or adjunct
➡ 18 women   ➡ 2 minority

Vermont Law School attracts faculty who are committed
to teaching and scholarship. Their professional involvement extends beyond teaching to include writing,
research (frequently with student assistance), and service
to the community.

■ Library and Physical Facilities

➡ 175,000 volumes & equivalents   ➡ library hours: Mon.-
Fri., 8:00 A.M.-MIDNIGHT; Sat.-Sun., 9:00 A.M.-MIDNIGHT
➡ LEXIS   ➡ NEXIS   ➡ WESTLAW   ➡ DIALOG
➡ 5 full-time librarians   ➡ library seats 350
➡ member, New England Law Library Consortium
➡ access to Dartmouth College Library

Opened in 1991, the 33,000 square-foot Cornell Library
houses all primary sources needed for student research.
The library subscribes to some 1,065 periodicals and features an exceptionally fine environmental law collection.
It also serves as a selective depository for United States
government documents. Situated in a National Historic
District along Vermont's scenic White River, the school's
eight-acre campus is an integrated complex of 11 renovated turn-of-the-century buildings and a modern
library and community center. School-owned housing is

limited, but ample private accommodations are available
in the surrounding community.

■ Curriculum

➡ Academic Support Program   ➡ 84 credits required to
graduate   ➡ 88 courses available   ➡ degrees available:
J.D.; M.S.L.; J.D./M.S.L.   ➡ summer session available (31
courses)   ➡ range of first-year class size—20-83

The academic program provides students with an understanding of the nature and function of law in society. A
wide variety of electives, a rich seminar program, clinical programs, and opportunities for supervised
independent research are also available.
  Environmental Law Center—Vermont Law School's Environmental Law Center is recognized internationally as
a preeminent center for the study of environmental law
and policy. The Environmental Law Center offers a one-
year program leading to a Master of Studies in Law
(M.S.L.) degree based upon a multidisciplinary curriculum of law, science, policy, and economics, and a joint
J.D.-M.S.L. degree program that can be completed in
three academic years and two summers. The center offers over 50 environmental courses, sponsors
conferences and research, and is the site of such special
projects as the Institute for Sustainable Communities,
The National Center for Comparative Risk, the Superfund Commission, and the Superfund Project.
  General Practice Program—The optional General Practice Program has classes structured to operate as a law
firm, with professors in the role of senior partners. Because
it teaches the range of skills generally required of new associates in most types of legal environments, the program is
also valuable to students who ultimately plan to specialize.
  Special Programs—The **Semester in Practice Program** allows students to participate in a full-credit, supervised
clinical program in a legal environment outside the law
school. Students currently work throughout the Northeast,
including New York, Boston, and Washington, DC. In the
Legislation Clinic, students work under the direction of a
legislative committee chair on research and drafting projects
directly related to legislation pending before the Vermont
General Assembly. Students working with the **South Royalton Legal Clinic** develop legal skills while providing legal
assistance to low-income clients. The **Dispute Resolution
Project** introduces students to nonlitigious approaches to
dispute resolution, such as arbitration, mediation, and negotiation. Through the **Law School Exchange Program** with
the University of Connecticut School of Law, Franklin Pierce
Law Center, Hastings College of the Law, New York Law
School, and the University of Puget Sound School of Law,
students may spend a semester at a participating institution.

■ Admission

➡ Bachelor's degree or equivalent required for admission
➡ application deadline—Feb. 15   ➡ LSAT, LSDAS required

▶ *median GPA—3.20* ▶ *median LSAT score—159*
▶ *application fee—$50* ▶ *admission to fall term only*

The school seeks candidates who will bring diverse perspectives and talents to the law school community and the community-at-large. Successful applicants demonstrate substantial ability, motivation, life experience, and unique personal attributes. The two most important admission criteria are the undergraduate record and the LSAT score. The LSAT score is normally weighted more than the GPA. A high LSAT score might offset a weak academic record if the academic work was undertaken some time ago. However, even a strong LSAT score will not compensate for recent marginal academic performance in college. Although there are no minimum scores or grades required, performance well below average is rarely competitive. Multiple LSAT scores are averaged. The LSAT writing sample is used in borderline cases. The undergraduate record is considered from a number of perspectives: quality of the undergraduate institution; nature and rigor of the curriculum; performance compared with applicants from the same institution; grade trend from freshman to senior years; and length of time intervening between undergraduate degree and law school application. For a significant number of applicants, the application essay is decisive in determining admissibility. The school responds favorably to community and college involvement and work experience, and is committed to attracting people traditionally underrepresented in the legal profession.

■ Student Activities

A community-oriented and active student body supports more than 30 official organizations. A few are: *Vermont Law Review*; Vermont Legal Research Group; Environmental Law Society; Association of Trial Lawyers of America; *Forum* (student newspaper); Federalist Society; National Lawyers Guild; Jazz Ensemble; several minority student groups; and Women's Group. Student organizations and the law school sponsor a full range of social, cultural, and academic events. Students also field several intercollegiate and intramural athletic teams.

■ Expenses and Financial Aid

▶ *full-time tuition & fees—$15,114*
▶ *$10,891 average additional expenses* ▶ *merit scholarships, grants, and fellowships (primarily need-based)* ▶ *need-based minority scholarships* ▶ *private, government, and school-funded loans* ▶ *Vermont Law School Financial Aid Application, FAFSA, and GAPSFAS required by Feb. 15 for full consideration*

Combinations of loans, tuition grants, and work-study employment are used to meet demonstrated financial need. About 85 percent of the student body receives some form of assistance.

■ Career Services

The school provides a broad range of counseling and placement services and aggressively pursues employment opportunities throughout the country. Over 1,500 positions with employers nationwide were listed during 1992. In response to employer requests, the office forwarded nearly 3,000 student résumés to 255 employers in 40 states. The school also provides opportunities for students to interview with legal employers on campus.

Applicant Group for the 1993–1994 Academic Year

Vermont Law School
This grid includes only applicants who earned 120-180 LSAT scores under standard administrations.

LSAT Score	3.75 +		3.50 -3.74		3.25 - 3.49		3.00 - 3.24		2.75 - 2.99		2.50 - 2.74		2.25 - 2.49		2.00 - 2.24		Below 2.00		No GPA		Total	
	Apps	Adm	Apps	Adm	Apps	Adm	Apps	Adm	Apps	Adm	Apps	Adm	Apps	Adm	Apps	Adm	Apps	Adm	Apps	Adm	Apps	Adm
175 - 180	0	0	1	1	2	2	1	1	0	0	0	0	0	0	0	0	0	0	0	0	4	4
170 - 174	0	0	3	3	1	0	3	3	5	4	3	0	3	0	0	0	0	0	0	0	18	10
165 - 169	7	7	15	15	18	18	20	19	16	9	9	6	11	5	3	1	1	0	0	0	100	80
160 - 164	18	18	32	31	42	38	66	55	58	39	39	22	23	10	3	0	0	0	5	5	286	218
155 - 159	13	12	47	40	97	67	125	66	105	36	69	21	33	4	6	1	1	0	5	2	501	249
150 - 154	11	7	55	18	101	24	149	34	117	11	74	7	43	4	21	2	2	2	7	2	580	111
145 - 149	9	2	24	4	52	5	70	2	79	3	56	2	29	0	13	0	2	0	5	0	339	18
140 - 144	2	1	8	2	9	0	32	1	34	1	23	0	29	1	9	0	2	0	3	2	151	8
135 - 139	1	0	2	0	4	0	12	0	6	0	11	0	10	0	3	0	2	0	2	0	53	0
130 - 134	0	0	0	0	2	0	2	0	0	0	2	0	9	1	2	0	0	0	2	0	19	1
125 - 129	0	0	0	0	0	0	0	0	1	0	1	0	0	0	0	0	0	0	0	0	2	0
120 - 124	0	0	0	0	0	0	0	0	0	0	0	0	0	0	0	0	0	0	0	0	0	0
Total	61	47	187	114	328	154	480	181	421	103	287	58	190	25	60	4	10	2	29	11	2053	699

Apps = Number of Applicants
Adm = Number Admitted
Reflects 95% of the total applicant pool.

Villanova University School of Law

299 North Spring Mill Road
Villanova, PA 19085

Phone: 215.645.7010

■ Introduction

The School of Law, opened in 1953, is approved by the American Bar Association and is a member of the Association of American Law Schools. Students are graduates of more then 200 colleges and universities; many have significant work experience outside of law.

The curriculum is responsive to the needs of modern law practice on local, regional, national and global bases. Courses are designed to teach the rules of law and their application; to demonstrate how lawyers analyze legal issues and express arguments and conclusions; to inculcate the skills of the counselor, advocate and decision maker, and to explore the ethical and moral dimensions of law practice and professional conduct.

Few law schools are located in a more beautiful and convenient environment. Although the school is in a tranquil suburban setting, the advantages of Philadelphia are 20 minutes by railroad with frequent commuter service.

■ Enrollment/Student Body

➡ *1,745 applicants*   ➡ *700 admitted first-year class 1993*
➡ *228 enrolled first-year class 1993*   ➡ *675 total full-time*
➡ *15% minority*   ➡ *47% women*
➡ *35 states & foreign countries represented*
➡ *192 undergraduate schools represented*

■ Faculty

➡ *74 total*   ➡ *37 full-time*   ➡ *37 part-time or adjunct*
➡ *10 women*   ➡ *3 minority*

■ Library and Physical Facilities

➡ *420,000 volumes & equivalents*   ➡ *library hours: 110 hours/wk., including 24 hour access for VU law students*
➡ *LEXIS*   ➡ *NEXIS*   ➡ *WESTLAW*   ➡ *DIALOG*
➡ *10 full-time librarians*   ➡ *library seats 445*

The library contains microform materials and readers, reading rooms, group study rooms, a computer laboratory, personal computers, photocopying equipment, and numerous individual study carrels. The library is an officially designated depository for United States government documents. Students also have access to the other university libraries and the many excellent libraries in the Philadelphia area.

The law school building also contains classrooms, including one equipped for study of law and computers; a moot courtroom; student lounges; faculty and administrative offices; and dining facilities.

■ Curriculum

➡ *Academic Support Program*   ➡ *87 credits required to graduate*   ➡ *151 courses available*   ➡ *degrees available: J.D.;J.D./M.B.A.;J.D./Ph.D.*   ➡ *semesters, start in Aug.*

■ Joint J.D./M.B.A. Program

The Villanova University School of Law and College of Commerce and Finance offer a joint program permitting simultaneous study for both the Law and Master of Business Administration degrees. The College of Commerce and Finance is one of the few colleges of business in the United States whose Department of Accountancy and Master of Business Administration program have been approved by the American Assembly of Collegiate Schools of Business.

Credit is given in the program for certain courses by both the School of Law and the College of Commerce and Finance. Business courses may be taken in far less time, perhaps as little as three years, than it would take to obtain the degrees separately.

■ Joint J.D./Ph.D. Program in Law & Psychology

Villanova Law School, in cooperation with Hahnemann University Graduate School, offers an integrated program in Law and Psychology leading to a Juris Doctor from Villanova and a Ph.D. in clinical psychology from Hahnemann. The clinical psychology component is fully accredited by the American Psychological Association.

The Program has three major purposes: 1) to produce lawyer-psychologists who can participate in the development of more databased mental health policy in the legislature and the courts; 2) to develop scientist-practitioners who will produce legally sophisticated social science research to assist the legal system in making better, more empirically based decisions; and 3) to educate highly trained clinicians who can contribute to the advancement of forensic psychology in such areas as criminal law, domestic relations, and civil commitment.

■ Special Programs

The clinical program in juvenile justice involves third-year students in the representation of indigent juvenile defendants in the Delaware County juvenile court. Clinical experience also is available through Delaware County Community Legal Services and in the law school's Tax Clinic. Additional clinical experiences are available in some seminars.

In addition to traditional courses, students may: represent actual clients; receive training in practical lawyers' skills such as trial practice, appellate advocacy, drafting, interviewing, counseling and negotiation; do research and write, closely supervised by a faculty member, in seminars and directed research. Many of these courses are in small classes.

■ Admission

➡ *Bachelor's degree required*   ➡ *application deadline— Jan. 31*   ➡ *rolling admissions, most decisions made after application deadline*   ➡ *LSAT, LSDAS required*
➡ *median GPA—3.41*   ➡ *median LSAT score—160*
➡ *application fee—$75*

■ Student Activities

The *Villanova Law Review* is a scholarly journal prepared and edited by law students. Members of the *Review* are selected on the basis of academic rank at the end of the first or second year of law studies. Students not selected on the basis of academic rank can enter an open writing competition. Successful competitors earn positions on the *Review* equivalent to those achieved by academic rank selection.

The *Villanova Environmental Law Journal* is a scholarly journal prepared and edited by law students. The *Journal* publishes both student and outside articles dealing with environmental issues. Students are selected for membership on the *Journal* by an open writing competition.

The Moot Court Board recognizes students with outstanding writing and advocacy skills. Members participate in at least one Moot Court competition each year and assist in administering the Reimel Moot Court Competition.

Other student organizations include: Asian-Pacific American Law Students, Black Law Students Association, Catholic Law Students, Christian Legal Society, Civil Rights Law Society, Corporate Law Society, Court Jesters, Criminal Law Society, *The Docket*, Environmental Law Society, Family Law Society, Health Law Society, Intellectual Property Protection Society, International Law Society, Jewish Law Students Association, Latin American Law Student Association, National Italian-American Bar Association Justian Society, Phi Delta Phi, Public Interest Law Society,Rugby Club, Sports and Entertainment Law Society, *Sports and Entertainment Law Forum*, Tax Law Society, Women's Law Caucus.

■ Expenses and Financial Aid

➨ *full time tuition & fees—$15,620* ➨ *estimated additional expenses—$11,820 (room, board, books, and living expenses for off-campus students)* ➨ *academic scholarships and disadvantaged student scholarships available* ➨ *financial aid available; FAFSA priority deadline is March 1*

■ Career Services

An active, full-time career services office is available for career reference, research, counseling, communication instruction, and employment information. On-campus interviews with prospective legal employers are scheduled for second- and third-year students. Part-time jobs are also listed for second- and third-year students seeking employment during the school year. Graduates are employed in private law firms, corporations, public services, governmental agencies, judicial clerkships, and other law-related occupations.

Applicant Group for the 1993–1994 Academic Year

Villanova University School of Law

LSAT Score	GPA 3.75 + Apps	Adm	3.50 - 3.74 Apps	Adm	3.25 - 3.49 Apps	Adm	3.00 - 3.24 Apps	Adm	2.75 - 2.99 Apps	Adm	2.50 - 2.74 Apps	Adm	Below 2.50 Apps	Adm	Total Apps	Adm
175 - 180	1	1	1	1	1	1	0	0	0	0	0	0	0	0	3	3
170 - 174	1	1	1	1	3	3	7	7	3	3	4	2	3	0	22	17
165 - 169	3	3	15	15	17	17	21	21	17	15	13	7	4	0	90	78
162 - 164	9	9	23	23	32	31	42	41	11	8	8	3	4	0	129	115
159 - 161	20	20	38	38	62	62	43	25	29	18	11	1	5	0	208	164
156 - 158	19	19	50	49	70	35	54	1	31	0	11	0	11	0	246	104
153 - 155	17	13	48	26	59	11	65	2	30	0	18	0	5	0	242	52
150 - 152	12	4	30	4	42	2	46	0	32	0	20	0	11	0	193	10
140 - 149	8	0	34	0	56	0	53	0	49	0	38	0	24	0	262	0
130 - 139	0	0	0	0	7	0	8	0	5	0	5	0	8	0	33	0
120 - 129	0	0	0	0	0	0	1	0	0	0	1	0	0	0	20	0

Apps = Number of Applicants
Adm = Number Admitted

University of Virginia School of Law

Admissions Office
Charlottesville, VA 22901

Phone: 804.924.7351

■ Introduction

The University of Virginia School of Law is a state-sup-ported law school located in Charlottesville, 120 miles southwest of Washington, DC. Among the original schools contemplated in Mr. Jefferson's plan for the organization of the University of Virginia, the law school was established upon the opening of the University in 1825, and has been an integral part of the University since that date.

■ Enrollment/Student Body

➡ 5,049 applicants   ➡ 980 admitted first-year class 1993
➡ 380 enrolled first-year class 1993   ➡ 1,148 total full-time
➡ 15% minority   ➡ 38% women   ➡ 54 states & foreign countries represented   ➡ 231 undergraduate schools represented   ➡ 55% residents   ➡ 45% nonresidents

■ Faculty

➡ 107 total   ➡ 55 full-time   ➡ 52 part-time or adjunct
➡ 16 women   ➡ 4 minority

■ Library and Physical Facilities

➡ 700,000 volumes & equivalents   ➡ library hours: Mon.-Sat., 8:00 A.M.-MIDNIGHT; Sun, 10:00 A.M.-MIDNIGHT
➡ LEXIS   ➡ NEXIS   ➡ WESTLAW
➡ 11 full-time librarians   ➡ library seats 662

The law building, completed in 1979, is a modern facility which houses a library, classrooms, faculty and student organization offices, an auditorium, and the Center for Oceans Law and Policy.

■ Curriculum

➡ Academic Support Program   ➡ 86 credits required to graduate   ➡ 165 courses available   ➡ degrees available: J.D.; LL.M.; S.J.D.; J.D./M.B.A.; J.D./M.A.; J.D./M.P.; J.D./M.S.   ➡ semesters, start in Aug.
➡ range of first-year class size—32-128

The first-year curriculum is arranged so that each entering student takes one of five courses in the first semester in a class of only 32 students. This "small section" concept, plus numerous second- and third-year electives, seminars, and individual research projects, assures the student a great deal of contact and interaction with the faculty.

The first-semester curriculum of torts, contracts, civil procedure, criminal law, and legal writing is required of all students. Property, constitutional law, and also legal writing are required in the spring semester of the first year. The only other required course is Professional Responsibility. A wide selection of electives can be chosen; these are outlined in the law school catalog.

■ Special Programs

The law school offers combined degree programs with the Department of Economics, the Department of History, the Department of Sociology, the Graduate School of Business Administration, the School of Architecture in Urban and Environmental Planning, the Department of Environmental Sciences in Marine Affairs, the School of Commerce in Accounting, the Department of Philosophy, and the Department of Government and Foreign Affairs. A student not enrolled in one of these programs may also take up to 12 credit hours of graduate courses in other schools and departments of the university.

In addition, the school offers opportunities for clinical experience under the direction of a clinical director and also offers interdisciplinary courses in law and medicine, law and economics, and law and social science.

■ Admission

➡ Bachelor's degree from accredited college or university required   ➡ application deadline—Jan. 15
➡ LSAT, LSDAS required   ➡ median GPA—3.60
➡ median LSAT score—164   ➡ application fee—$40

The Admissions Committee believes that absolute standards based on a combination of LSAT score and grade-point average (GPA) cannot be the sole criteria for selection. The committee recognizes that the real meaning of GPA will vary with such factors as quality of the institution attended, rigor of courses selected, and degree of grade inflation. The committee considers an array of elements in addition to the essential LSAT and GPA, with a view toward assembling a diverse class while arriving at a fair appraisal of the individual applicant.

Although it is difficult to predict the action on an individual application, the LSAT and GPA are the primary determinants for the committee; usually about 80 percent total weight is accorded these two factors. However, there are other elements taken into account: for example, the maturing effect of some years away from formal education; trends in academic performance versus solid but unexceptional work; employment during the undergraduate years; significant personal achievement in extracurricular work at college or in a work or military situation; and/or unusual prior training, background, or ethnicity, which promises a contribution to the law school community. Economic, social, or educational obstacles successfully overcome by an applicant have contributed to favorable consideration.

It is clear, though, that unless an applicant has a high LSAT score and strong GPA, the chances of admission are severely reduced. Each year, the committee chooses a few applicants whose GPA and LSAT are lower than the prevailing averages, but who present other impressive credentials for admission, and rejects some whose performance on these two predictors is quite high.

The charts provided below track the selection process during the 1993 admissions year. In reviewing these charts, it is important to note that, since the new 120-180 LSAT score scale replaced the old 10-48 scale as of June, 1991, most 1993 applicants to Virginia (around 95 percent) presented scores and Admission Indices based on the 120-

180 scale. Consequently, these charts project actions taken on approximately 95 percent of our 1993 applicant pool. It is also important to keep in mind that students admitted under the affirmative action minority program described below are included in the analysis. To interpret the charts, one must understand the Admission Index. This number results from combining LSAT score(s) with the undergraduate GPA for each applicant, using weights for each chosen by this school. The formula used at Virginia for applicants with test scores on the 120-180 scale is (4.1590 X UGPA) + (.240 X LSAT) + (2.0) = Index. Thus, an applicant with a 3.62 UGPA and a 168 LSAT would receive a 57 Admissions Index, while a 3.17 UGPA and a 158 LSAT would produce a 53 Admissions Index. The index provides the law school with a convenient method for simultaneously reviewing LSAT score(s) and undergraduate GPAs.

The 380 students who entered the first year of law study in August 1993 were selected from a total of 5,049 applicants from 632 different colleges and universities. There were 209 Virginia residents, while the remaining 171 came from 34 different states, Canada, the District of Columbia, Hong Kong, Kenya, Lebanon, and the United Kingdom. There were 147 women and 42 black students.

The primary focus of minority recruitment at the University of Virginia is on black applicants. Members of other minority groups are given special attention by the Admissions Committee.

■ Student Activities

Popular student activities include *Virginia Law Review*, *Virginia Journal of International Law*, *Virginia Journal of*

Law and Politics, *Virginia Journal of Natural Resources Law*, *Virginia Tax Review*, *Virginia Journal of Social Policy & the Law*, moot court competitions, Black Law Student Association, Legal Assistance Society, Environmental Forum and the Post Conviction Assistance Project, First-Year Council, Student Peer Advisors, Students United to Promote Racial Awareness, Virginia Health Law Forum, and Virginia Law Women.

■ Expenses and Financial Aid

➡ *full time tuition and fees—residents, $7,570; nonresidents, $15,678*   ➡ *estimated additional expenses—$9,260 (room, board, books)*   ➡ *need-based scholarships available*   ➡ *financial aid available*   ➡ *FAF and FAFSA form for need analysis due to College Scholarship Service in Jan. or early Feb.*

■ Career Services

The School of Law expends considerable time and effort to assist students seeking employment. Despite a tightening job market, 82 percent of the Class of 1993 reported to the Placement Office that they obtained permanent jobs, and more than 95 percent of the second-year class has reported they have obtained summer clerkships, primarily through Placement Office services. An examination of these jobs reveals a remarkable diversity in both geography and type of employment. For example, in the graduation class of 1992, the graduates reporting jobs were employed in 35 states and the District of Columbia. Sixty-one graduates took jobs in Virginia, 52 in Washington, DC, 45 in New York, 19 in California, 15 in Texas, 14 in Pennsylvania, 11 in North Carolina, and 10 each in Georgia and Illinois.

Profile of the Entering Class—Fall 1993

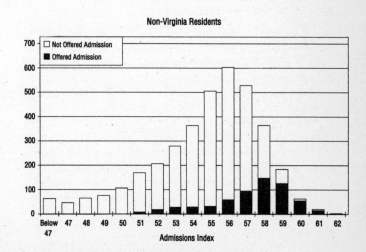

Wake Forest University School of Law

P.O. Box 7206
Reynolda Station
Winston-Salem, NC 27109

■ Introduction

The Wake Forest University School of Law, established in 1894, is a member of AALS and is ABA-approved. Wake Forest is located in Winston-Salem, North Carolina, a city of 150,000 and a center for recreation, education, and the arts.

The philosophy at Wake Forest law school embodies meaningful promises for the future. The school's undertaking embraces seven principal commitments. They are: 1) To maintain a school of the right size that begins with a first-year class of 160 students comprised of four sections of 40 students each. 2) To develop and retain a faculty strong in teaching, strong in experience, and strong in current scholarly writing. 3) To assure that students are taught substantive law and research skills through maximum use of leading-edge technology. 4) To continue the school's emphasis on dispute resolution and the development of litigation skills through instruction, competition, and comprehensive clinical practice. 5) To bridge the chasm between law and management communities by an enhanced curriculum, the sharing of resources, and collaborative instruction. 6) To seek to provide placement opportunities for our students and graduates that match their potential. 7) To teach the transcendence of ethics and to inculcate in graduates the importance of doing good while doing well throughout their professional lives.

Our goal is to graduate students who are not only eligible to practice law but qualified as well.

■ Enrollment/Student Body

➡ *1,897 applicants*   ➡ *464 admitted first-year class 1993*
➡ *165 enrolled first-year class 1993*   ➡ *465 total full-time*
➡ *8% minority*   ➡ *39% women*
➡ *37 states and foreign countries represented*
➡ *175 undergraduate school represented*

■ Faculty

➡ *67 total*   ➡ *34 full-time*   ➡ *33 adjunct*   ➡ *15 women*
➡ *4 minority*   ➡ *30 supervising clinical attorneys*

■ Library and Physical Facilities

➡ *250,000 volumes & equivalents*   ➡ *108 library hours per week*   ➡ *LEXIS*   ➡ *NEXIS*   ➡ *WESTLAW*
➡ *DIALOG*   ➡ *EPIC*   ➡ *ACES*   ➡ *Dow Jones*
➡ *6 full-time librarians*   ➡ *library seats 568*

The law school occupies the Worrell Professional Center for Law and Management which was dedicated on April 3, 1993, by Justice Sandra Day O'Connor. This 178,000-square-foot, state-of-the-art facility, houses the law school and the School of Management.

■ Curriculum

➡ *89 units/credits required to graduate*   ➡ *100 courses available*   ➡ *degrees available: J.D. & J.D./M.B.A.*

➡ *semesters, start in Aug. & Jan.*
➡ *first-year class size—approx. 40*

Three academic years are divided into two semesters of 15 weeks each. A solid core of first-year courses is required, with strong emphasis on legal research and writing. Advanced elective courses are offered in specialty areas such as securities regulation, taxation, corporations, and environmental law.

■ Special Programs

The law school offers two clinical programs. The first is a third-year program of academic instruction, skills training, and live client representation, and is a cooperative venture of the bench, bar, and law school. Clinical students participate in an integrated program of both civil and criminal law practice. They are placed with supervising attorneys in the following areas: private practice, legal aid, the United States Attorney, district attorney, National Labor Relations Board, or corporate general counsel. The classroom component includes interviewing, counseling, negotiation, and discovery. The second clinical program is an in-house legal clinic for the elderly operating as an interdisciplinary element in the Sticht Center for the Aging.

The joint J.D./M.B.A. degree program permits the student to obtain both degrees in four years.

■ Computer Instruction and Services

Wake Forest provides a wide range of computer services to students, faculty, and staff, and ranks among the top five law schools nationally for computers per student.

The Computerized Legal Research and Instruction Center contains 53 microcomputers, laser printers, and programs that allow students to access WESTLAW and LEXIS, use word processing and other legal software, and access computer-assisted legal research instruction programs.

■ Admission

➡ *Bachelor's degree from accredited college or university required*   ➡ *application deadline—March 15*
➡ *rolling admission, early application preferred (particularly for scholarship consideration)*   ➡ *LSAT, LSDAS required*
➡ *median GPA—3.31*   ➡ *median LSAT score—162*
➡ *application fee—$50*

First-year students are admitted in the fall semester and only for full-time study. One academic recommendation and a Dean's certification are required in addition to the other application materials, and the file must be completed by April 15. Applicants are advised of their status by May 15.

The LSAT score and the undergraduate GPA are combined into an index computed by LSDAS. For multiple LSAT scores, the index is based on the average of all tests; however, the school will consider all scores. All files are reviewed on a case-by-case basis. The school considers a number of subjective factors indicating intellectual capacity, character, motivation, and maturity with the objective of selecting those most likely to succeed in law study and in the legal profession and also those who would contribute to the diversity essential to a rich educational experience.

The School of Law is committed to providing access to men and women of all races, religions, ethnic backgrounds, and physical abilities. Special scholarships and grants are available to qualified minority applicants. Inquiries should be addressed to the Director of Admissions and Financial Aid of the Law School.

Applicants admitted for the entering class in 1994 are required to pay a $300 nonrefundable deposit by April 1, and an interim tuition deposit on July 1 (both fees are applicable toward tuition and fee charges).

Personal interviews are not required, but may be arranged upon request. Individual applicants or groups are encouraged to visit the campus.

Transfer students who meet law school admission requirements are accepted on a space-available basis after the successful completion of one year at an AALS or ABA-approved law school.

■ Student Activities

All students are members of the Student Bar Association, which has an important place in the life of the law school. A number of other organizations allow students to pursue a variety of interests.

The *Wake Forest Law Review* is a recognized scholastic journal. Selection to the *Law Review* is based on academic performance or demonstrated writing and academic ability.

The Moot Court Board and Student Trial Bar assist in the administration of the school's strong trial and appellate advocacy program through various intramural and intercollegiate competitions.

■ Expenses and Financial Aid

➡ *tuition & fees—$14,200* ➡ *estimated living expenses—$5,000-$7,000* ➡ *merit and need-based scholarships available* ➡ *minority scholarships available* ➡ *GAPSFAS, Federal Needs Analysis, due May 1*

Approximately 78 percent of the students receive financial assistance from scholarships, loans, work-study funds, and assistantships.

■ Placement

The Placement Program increases graduates' opportunities to reach their full professional potential, opportunities the law school believes it owes to its students.

The Placement Office conducts workshops in résumé preparation, interviewing techniques, and career planning to help prepare students to find employment.

Firms and corporations who cannot send a representative to the campus may request résumés and invite students to interview. These services are provided for those seeking permanent employment, and for summer work, clerkships, and part-time employment.

The Placement Office encourages employers to notify the director of openings for experienced attorneys. Placement maintains a list of Law School graduates seeking a change in employment. A listing of opportunities is mailed to these graduates each month.

Applicant Group for the 1993–1994 Academic Year

Wake Forest University School of Law
This grid includes only applicants who earned 120-180 LSAT scores under standard administrations in the 1992-1993 testing year.

LSAT Score	3.75 +		3.50 - 3.74		3.25 - 3.49		3.00 - 3.24		2.75 - 2.99		2.50 - 2.74		2.00 - 2.49		Below 2.00		Total	
	Apps	Adm	Apps	Adm	Apps	Adm	Apps	Adm	Apps	Adm	Apps	Adm	Apps	Adm	Apps	Adm	Apps	Adm
175 - 180	1	1	0	0	1	1	1	0	0	0	1	0	0	0	0	0	4	2
170 - 174	3	3	1	1	4	4	3	2	3	3	2	2	1	0	0	0	17	15
165 - 169	8	8	12	11	30	29	29	26	24	13	6	4	9	2	0	0	118	93
160 - 164	25	25	36	35	86	85	106	55	57	18	28	7	14	1	0	0	352	226
155 - 159	27	16	73	35	122	27	126	4	76	6	46	4	30	2	3	0	503	94
150 - 154	14	0	64	2	95	3	91	4	56	4	38	5	30	1	0	0	388	19
145 - 149	6	0	19	0	34	3	45	2	34	1	38	1	19	1	2	0	197	8
140 - 144	3	0	6	1	25	1	14	0	23	0	23	0	21	0	3	0	118	2
135 - 139	1	0	3	1	4	0	9	0	8	0	4	0	13	0	2	0	44	1
130 - 134	0	0	0	0	1	0	0	0	3	0	5	0	6	0	0	0	15	0
125 - 129	0	0	0	0	0	0	0	0	2	0	0	0	1	0	0	0	3	0
Total	88	53	214	86	402	153	424	93	286	45	191	23	144	7	10	0	1759	460

Apps = Number of Applicants
Adm = Number Admitted
Reflects 92% of the total applicant pool.
Accepted applicants with 10-48 LSAT scores had a median LSAT of 40 and a median GPA of 3.18.

Washburn University School of Law

1700 College
Topeka, KS 66621

Phone: 913.231.1185 (out-of-state), 800.332.0291 (in-state)

■ Introduction

Washburn University began as Lincoln College in 1865 and became Washburn College in 1868. The School of Law opened its doors in 1903, and in 1905 became one of the early members of the Association of American Law Schools. In 1923, Washburn was among the first law schools to be fully accredited by the American Bar Association. Washburn University today is an urban university serving 6,600 students. It is located in Topeka, the capital city of Kansas, about 60 miles west of Kansas City.

■ Enrollment/Student Body

➡ *974 applicants*   ➡ *343 admitted first-year class 1993*
➡ *148 enrolled first-year class 1993*   ➡ *425 total full-time*
➡ *16% minority*   ➡ *44% women*
➡ *45 states & foreign countries represented*
➡ *172 undergraduate schools represented*

■ Faculty

➡ *59 total*   ➡ *27 full-time*   ➡ *32 part-time or adjunct*
➡ *18 women*   ➡ *6 minority*

■ Library and Physical Facilities

➡ *250,467 volumes & equivalents*   ➡ *library hours: Mon.-Thurs., 7:30 A.M.-11:00 P.M., Fri., 7:30 A.M.-9:00 P.M., Sat., 8:00 A.M.-8:00 P.M.; Sun., NOON-11:00 P.M.*   ➡ *LEXIS*
➡ *NEXIS*   ➡ *WESTLAW*   ➡ *INTERNET*
➡ *DIALOG*   ➡ *Dow Jones*   ➡ *7 full-time librarians*
➡ *library seats 346*   ➡ *30-station computer lab*

Library highlights include a 30-station microcomputer lab, addition of 75 individual study carrels equipped for laptop microcomputer use, group study rooms, lounge seating areas, and a richly furbished special collections room. The law building has a barrier-free design. Washburn's clinical program, one of the first in the nation, is housed in an attached model law office. A beautiful moot courtroom is regularly used for administrative law hearings and occasional sittings by the Kansas Supreme Court and the US Tenth Circuit Court of Appeals.

The law library has a national reputation for leadership in the use of new information technologies. Each law student receives a password for accessing LEXIS, WESTLAW, Internet, and E-mail from home or school. A local area network provides convenient access to CD-ROM indexes, computer-assisted learning exercises, and computer software.

The library collection has had over a decade of vigorous growth, ranking in the top quarter of all law school libraries for new titles added since 1979. A strong law-related videotape collection is used to supplement classroom instruction. Specialized research facilities include US and Kansas government document depositories, a local public document room for the US Nuclear Regulatory Commission, and a satellite reference center for the Kansas Patent Depository Library.

Law students have access to the 200,000-volume Kansas Supreme Court Law Library. Membership in the Mid-America Law School Library Consortium provides ready access to catalogs and resources of 18 other academic law libraries in 7 midwestern states. The Internet enables researchers to search hundreds of on-line catalogs and information files worldwide.

■ Curriculum

➡ *Academic Support Program*   ➡ *90 credits required to graduate*   ➡ *121 courses available*   ➡ *semesters, begin in Aug. and Jan.*   ➡ *range of first-year class size—25-80*
➡ *two six-week summer sessions*

Students may begin their study in either the fall or spring semester. The first-year curriculum is prescribed. To complete the upper-level program, students must meet distributional requirements in six areas of study plus writing and oral presentational requirements.

■ Certificate Programs

A Certificate in Law and Mental Health is awarded jointly by Washburn and the world-renowned Menninger Foundation psychiatric center to students who graduate with 96 credit hours and receive a B average in at least 15 hours of credit in the Mental Health Law area. Students participate in a colloquium with psychiatric residents at Menninger and represent clients in mental disability cases in the Washburn Law Clinic.

A Certificate in Tax Law is awarded to students graduating with 96 credit hours who achieve a B average in at least 15 hours of credit in the Tax Law area.

■ Special Programs

Washburn has gained national recognition through its Law Clinic, a general practice firm of senior law students representing indigent clients. The clinic experience includes direct client representation in a wide range of civil and criminal litigation.

Valuable academic and work opportunities are provided by the state legislature, state executive offices, state and federal district courts, state supreme court, court of appeals, bankruptcy court, and state and federal agencies.

Washburn sponsors a six-credit-hour, six-week program abroad each summer. Washburn faculty team teach classes with faculty members from the host school.

The Rural Law Center focuses teaching and research on aspects of the law affecting the rural environment.

■ Admission

➡ *Bachelor's degree from accredited college or university*
➡ *application deadline—fall, March 15; spring, Sept. 15*
➡ *LSAT, LSDAS required*   ➡ *median GPA—3.27*
➡ *median LSAT score—154*   ➡ *application fee—$30*

Significant factors that the Admissions Committee considers are the LSAT score and grade-point average. There is no automatic cutoff for LSAT score or GPA. Other factors which are evaluated are work experience, graduate work, cultural background, extracurricular activities, and the need for diversity in the student body. Late applications are accepted but applicants may be at a disadvantage. Admitted applicants pay a $100 admission deposit which applies toward tuition when the student enrolls. Applicants are encouraged to visit the school and attend a law class.

■ **Student Activities**

Students are selected to membership on the Board of Editors of the *Washburn Law Journal* on the basis of class rank or performance in a writing competition.

Washburn has assumed editorial responsibility for publication of the *Family Law Quarterly* of the American Bar Association's Family Law Section. The *Quarterly* provides a second editorial experience for Washburn students.

The Washburn Student Bar Association directs student affairs, sponsoring a wide variety of educational and social activities. Students participate in Moot Court, Client Counseling, Negotiations, and Trial Advocacy competitions. There are more than 20 active student organizations, including three law fraternities, Asian, Hispanic-American, and Black Law Student Associations, Women's Legal Forum, and societies for students interested in Environmental, International, and Public Interest Law.

■ **Expenses and Financial Aid**

➡ *full time tuition—residents, $4,844 ($173 per credit hour); nonresidents, $7,000 (250 per credit hour)* ➡ *books and supplies—$600* ➡ *performance and need-based scholarships available* ➡ *GAPSFAS form required for need-based scholarships, Free Application for Federal Student Aid required for loans ·* ➡ *financial aid forms due with admission application*

Scholarships may be awarded on a combination of academic performance and need. Diversity is considered as a factor in making scholarship awards. In recognition of its efforts to diversify its faculty and student body, the US Department of Education has awarded Patricia Roberts Harris Fellowships to Washburn in three of the last four years. Washburn received three new fellowships for 1992-93. These fellowships provide full tuition and a substantial stipend for living expenses. Second- and third-year students appreciate the availability of research-assistant positions within the law school and the abundance of law-related jobs in Topeka.

Housing costs vary, but are quite reasonable. Dormitory room and board—$3,160 per year. University apartments for families, 1 bedroom—$175. Most students live in apartments in the residential areas surrounding the campus.

■ **Career Services**

Washburn provides students and alumni with professional career-planning services. Programs emphasize assessment of career goals, exploration of varied applications of a legal education, and support for the transition into the professional marketplace. Extensive resources are available regarding local, regional, national, and international legal employment in the public and private sectors, graduate and foreign study, and judicial clerkships.

Washburn graduates' employment experiences are consistent with national law placement averages within one year of graduation. Alumni are located in every state in the nation and several foreign countries.

Applicant Group for the 1993–1994 Academic Year

Washburn University School of Law

LSAT	3.75 & UP	3.50 - 3.74	3.25 - 3.49	3.00 - 3.24	2.75 - 2.99	2.50 - 2.74	2.25 - 2.49	< 2.25	Totals
175 - 180	0/0	0/0	0/0	0/0	0/0	0/0	0/0	0/0	0/0
170 - 174	0/0	0/0	0/0	0/0	0/0	0/0	0/0	0/0	0/0
165 - 169	3/3	0/0	3/3	1/1	2/2	4/2	0/0	1/0	14/11
160 - 184	4/4	7/7	9/9	14/12	5/4	12/4	8/1	2/0	61/41
155 - 159	13/13	16/14	31/31	33/30	41/14	23/7	21/3	4/1	182/113
150 - 154	10/10	17/13	42/37	75/36	63/10	40/2	19/1	9/0	275/109
145 - 149	11/11	13/7	38/11	60/17	45/1	32/1	11/2	12/0	222/50
140 - 144	2/1	4/1	21/6	23/6	20/2	13/1	11/0	10/0	104/17
< 140	1/0	1/0	6/0	11/0	21/1	13/0	11/0	10/0	74/1
Totals	44/42	58/42	150/97	217/102	197/34	137/17	81/7	48/1	932/342

Undergraduate GPA

Applicants/Admitted

This chart is to be used for general information only. Nonnumerical factors are weighed heavily in all admission decisions and students are encouraged to refer to the above narrative description of the admission process.

University of Washington School of Law

316 Condon Hall
1100 N.E. Campus Parkway
Seattle, WA 98105

Phone: 206.543.4078

■ Introduction

Established in 1899, the School of Law is part of the main campus of the University of Washington, approximately four miles from downtown Seattle. The university, the largest single campus institution in the western United States, with an enrollment of 33,500 students, offers nearly every discipline for study. The School of Law has 44 full-time faculty members and about 500 students. Because of the favorable student-to-faculty ratio, classes are generally small, with frequent opportunities for student-teacher contacts. Each first-year student is usually in at least one class of 30 or fewer students, in addition to the Basic Legal Skills course. The school is a member of the AALS, is approved by the ABA, and has a chapter of the Order of the Coif.

■ Enrollment/Student Body

- ➡ 2,600 applicants ➡ 511 admitted first-year class 1993
- ➡ 148 enrolled first-year class 1993 ➡ 478 total full-time
- ➡ 39% minority ➡ 46% women
- ➡ 20 states & foreign countries represented
- ➡ 80 undergraduate schools represented

■ Faculty

- ➡ 69 total ➡ 44 full-time ➡ 25 part-time or adjunct
- ➡ 14 women ➡ 5 minority

■ Library and Physical Facilities

- ➡ 450,000 volumes & equivalents ➡ library hours: Mon.-Thurs., 8:00 A.M.-10:00 P.M.; Fri., 8:00 A.M.-6:00 P.M.; Sat., 10:00 A.M.-6:00 P.M.; Sun., NOON-6:00 P.M. ➡ LEXIS
- ➡ NEXIS ➡ WESTLAW ➡ DIALOG
- ➡ DATATIMES ➡ 12 full-time librarians
- ➡ library seats 454

■ Curriculum

- ➡ 135 quarter credits required to graduate ➡ 115 total courses available;full-time day program only ➡ degrees available: J.D./M.B.A.; J.D./International Studies; LL.M. in Asian Law, Law and Marine Affairs, International Environmental Law, and Law of Sustainable International Development ➡ quarters, begin in Oct.
- ➡ range of first-year class size—30-120

The first-year curriculum is prescribed. After that, except for an analytical writing requirement and a class in professional responsibility, all courses in the second and third years are elective. In addition to traditional courses and seminars, advanced students may participate in a civil, criminal, mediation, family law, immigration, or affordable housing clinic, or in courses in trial advocacy. Judicial, legislative, agency, and public interest externships are available. Students must also perform 60 hours of public service legal work.

Students are encouraged to rely on their initiative and to develop their own powers of perception. Classroom discussion in which students participate fully is one means used to assist this development. Independent research projects, either in the context of a seminar or through individual study under faculty supervision, are also emphasized. Although it is a state law school, Washington state law is not emphasized unduly. Graduates of the school are prepared to practice law anywhere in the United States or in other common law countries.

■ Special Programs

Students studying for the J.D. program may take courses in any of the LL.M. programs during the second and third years. The UW also offers a master's degree in Law Librarianship.

■ Admission Standards

- ➡ Bachelor's degree required ➡ application deadline—Jan. 15; applicants must take the LSAT no later than Dec.
- ➡ decisions made from Jan. 15 to April 1
- ➡ LSAT, LSDAS required ➡ median GPA—3.63
- ➡ application fee—$50 ➡ median LSAT score—163; multiple LSAT scores are averaged

In selecting the entering class, the law school does not make all of its admission decisions solely on the basis of predicted academic performance. Important academic objectives are furthered by classes comprised of students having talents and skills derived from diverse backgrounds believed to be relevant to a rich and effective study of law.

Over 36 percent of the incoming class consists of students of color, for whom the school provides student, faculty, and professional mentoring programs.

■ Student Activities

The *Washington Law Review* and *Pacific Rim Law Journal* are edited and published by students. In 1991 the Jessup International Law Moot Court team won the national championship.

Through the Student Bar Association and student/faculty committees, students participate in the decision processes of the law school. Student organizations include the Law Women's Caucus; Minority Law Students Association; Environmental Law Society; International Law Society; Christian Legal Society; National Lawyer's Guild; Law, Science and Technology Group; Lesbian and Gay Legal Society; Phi Alpha Delta; ABA Student Division; Federalist Society and Public Interest Project.

■ Expenses and Financial Aid

➡ *full-time tuition & fees—$4,000; resident; $10,000; nonresident* ➡ *estimated additional expenses—$10,835 (books, $800; room & board, $7,000; transportation, $750; insurance, $585; personal, $1,700)*
➡ *need-based scholarships available*
➡ *financial aid available; FAFSA due Feb. 28*

■ Career Services

The Career Services Office serves as a liaison between students and prospective employers. Firms, agencies, and other potential employers are invited to interview at the school and to list job openings in the regularly published placement bulletin. About 80 percent of the graduates choose to remain in Washington state.

Admission Statistics of the 1993 Entering Class

University of Washington School of Law
This grid includes 100% of all applications reviewed with scores on the 120-180 score scale.

GPA Range	Average LSAT Score															
	120 - 153		154 - 156		157 - 159		160 - 162		163 - 165		166 - 168		169 - 180		Total	
	Apps	Adm	Apps	Adm	Apps	Adm	Apps	Adm	Apps	Adm	Apps	Adm	Apps	Adm	Apps	Adm
3.75 & Above	33	5	17	2	48	9	59	27	51	42	33	32	35	35	276	152
3.50 - 3.74	77	7	70	9	111	12	105	11	98	34	51	39	48	47	560	159
3.25 - 3.49	148	5	89	7	95	9	111	9	111	7	63	24	48	43	665	104
3.00 - 3.24	100	4	56	5	68	5	67	5	39	3	40	1	25	12	395	35
2.75 - 2.99	119	4	33	4	36	4	39	2	27	1	13	0	15	2	282	17
2.50 - 2.74	69	1	15	0	16	2	15	3	12	1	6	0	4	0	137	7
Below 2.50	74	2	7	0	11	0	8	0	1	0	2	0	4	0	107	2
LSAT only	26	2	4	0	1	0	1	0	1	0	0	0	0	0	33	2
Total	646	30	291	27	386	41	405	57	340	88	208	96	179	139	2455	478

Apps = Number of Applicants
Adm = Number Admitted
In cases where an applicant presented multiple LSAT scores, the average score was used.

This information is presented to give applicants some idea of the likelihood of admission. It should be noted, however, that these data can and do change from year to year. In addition, there is some latitude within each category, so that a person presenting credentials at the upper limits of one cell might have an excellent chance for admission, while another applicant at the lower limits might only have a marginal chance. For these reasons, this chart should be used as an approximate gauge of the likelihood of admission and **not** as a guarantee.

Washington and Lee University School of Law

Lewis Hall
Lexington, VA 24450

Phone: 703.463.8503

■ Introduction

Washington and Lee University School of Law is a private institution located in Lexington, Virginia, approximately 175 miles southwest of Washington, DC, in the Blue Ridge Mountains. Founded in 1849, the school is a member of the AALS and is fully accredited by the ABA.

As a small, selective private law school, Washington and Lee takes pride in offering a nationally oriented legal education that is professionally rigorous and intellectually challenging. The size of the school is carefully controlled to achieve a generous faculty-to-student ratio and a closely-knit community of students and faculty, in which the opportunity for informal contact and collaboration in ongoing research enhances the educational process. The school seeks to limit its total enrollment to 360 students; there are 36 regular faculty members and 12 adjunct members.

■ Enrollment/Student Body

➤ *1,551 applicants*   ➤ *431 admitted first-year class 1993*
➤ *125 enrolled first-year class 1993*   ➤ *360 total full-time*
➤ *16% minority*   ➤ *40% women*
➤ *45 states & foreign countries represented*
➤ *173 undergraduate schools represented*

■ Faculty

➤ *48 total*   ➤ *36 full-time*   ➤ *12 part-time or adjunct*
➤ *8 women*   ➤ *2 minority*

■ Library and Physical Facilities

➤ *297,000 volumes & equivalents*   ➤ *library open 24 hours a day, 7 days a week, year-round*   ➤ *LEXIS*
➤ *NEXIS*   ➤ *WESTLAW*   ➤ *7 full-time librarians*
➤ *library seats 400*

The School of Law is located on the campus of Washington and Lee University in Lewis Hall, originally built in 1976 and expanded in 1991 with the addition of the Lewis F. Powell, Jr. Archives, which house the Supreme Court and professional papers of retired Supreme Court Justice Powell, a graduate of the University's college and law school. Each student is provided his or her own study carrel or office space in Lewis Hall. Training in the use of all online research services is provided to all first-year students. Students have access to the library collection on an open-stack basis. The school makes extensive use of state-of-the-art video and computer technology in classroom settings and in trial advocacy training.

■ Curriculum

➤ *Academic Support Program*   ➤ *85 credits required to graduate*   ➤ *101 courses available (excluding all clinical programs and journals, which do carry academic credit)*
➤ *J.D. degree available*   ➤ *range of first-year class size—19-60*   ➤ *average class size after first year—28*

■ Special Programs

Second- and third-year law students may elect to participate in a number of clinical or specialized practice programs offered by the School of Law, including the Legal Aid Society, providing legal services to indigent civil clients; the Western State Hospital Legal Aid Society, providing legal services to residents of a state mental hospital; the Alderson Legal Assistance Program, providing legal services to inmates of a major federal institution for female offenders; and the Public Defender Program, providing legal services to indigent persons charged with crimes. In the U.S. Attorney's Program, students participate in prosecutorial trial work in the federal court system. The Judicial Clerkship Program provides opportunities to clerk for trial or appellate judges in the Virginia court system.

The International Environmental Law Program was founded with a grant from the Creswell Foundation, and provides students with an opportunity to participate in a year-long program of seminars, directed research, and summer internships in the field of international environmental law. Governmental organizations, corporations, or public-interest entities submit project proposals; program participants select the project and entity of their choice. Last year, students worked for the Natural Resources Defense Council, the government of Hungary, the Community Nutrition Institute, for public-interest groups concerned with development in the Arctic, and in environmental issues dealing with human rights, among others.

The Virginia Capital Case Clearinghouse was established to provide research and litigation support to attorneys appointed to represent persons charged with capital crimes, or who are pursuing appeals of cases in which the death penalty has been imposed. Students pursue in-depth research into developments in current death-penalty law and assist with the preparation of pleadings, legal memoranda, and briefs in ongoing cases. Students write and edit the *Capital Case Digest*, a journal dealing with the complex and important area of capital sentencing.

■ Admission

➤ *undergraduate degree required for admission*
➤ *application deadline—Feb. 1*   ➤ *applications received after Feb. 1 will be considered but cannot be guaranteed a response by April 1*   ➤ *LSAT, LSDAS required*
➤ *median GPA—3.47*   ➤ *median LSAT score—163*
➤ *application fee—$40*

Students enter the School of Law only in the fall semester, which begins in late August. There is no part-time program.

Although the LSAT score and undergraduate grade-point average are important factors considered by the Admissions Committee, other, more subjective factors, such as trends in grades, the rigor of an applicant's academic program, achievement in extracurricular or community service activities, work experience, and evaluations from professors are a significant part of an admissions decision. An applicant may request an interview with a member of the Admissions Committee. Applicants are encouraged to visit the school to sit in on classes, tour the facility, and talk with students and faculty if it is convenient for them to do so.

The School of Law actively seeks a diversified student body whose members are of different religious, racial, ethnic, economic, and geographic backgrounds. Applications from persons considering a change in career are encouraged.

■ Student Activities

The *Washington and Lee Law Review*, managed and published by students, is a quarterly journal for scholarly discussion of important legal problems. A variety of moot court and advocacy competitions, both intra- and inter-school, provide students with opportunities to hone advocacy, counseling, negotiation, and trial skills.

All students are members of the Student Bar Association, which represents students in the ongoing affairs of the school and sponsors professional programs and social activities. Law students also participate in University intramural sports, drama, music, and political programs. The Black Law Student Association, Women Law Student Association, the National Lawyers Guild, the Federalist Society, the Environmental Law Forum, the International Law Society, and three national professional fraternities all present programs addressing matters of special concern to their members.

■ Expenses and Financial Aid

➤ *full-time tuition—$13,600*   ➤ *full-time fees—$191*
➤ *estimated additional expenses—$6,500 (room, board, books, misc. expenses)*   ➤ *need- and merit-based scholarships available*   ➤ *merit-based research fellowships available*
➤ *FAFSA required for financial aid*

■ Housing Opportunities

On-campus housing is available in the Woods Creek Apartments, adjacent to the law school. The law school provides an off-campus housing referral service to interested students.

■ Career Services

The Placement Office acts as a liaison between law students and legal employers. Workshops, brown-bag lunches, and panel presentations focus on special topics or skills, but individual counseling with personal attention to each student is the hallmark of the placement effort. An active alumni network is in place to assist students. In recent years, approximately 65 percent of graduates have entered the private practice of law immediately following graduation. Twenty percent serve judicial clerkships. Other graduates go into business-related employment, including corporate law staffs, banks, and accounting firms; take positions in various federal, state, or local governmental agencies; serve in public-interest law, or in the JAG Corps; and some pursue advanced law degrees. Graduates are employed throughout the country; in the last three years, students have accepted employment in 44 states and seven foreign countries. About 95 percent report employment within six months of graduation.

Profile of Applications and Acceptances—Fall 1993

Washington and Lee University School of Law

GPA	LSAT Percentile																		
	0 - 10		11 - 20		21 - 30		31 - 40		41 - 50		51 - 60		61 - 70		71 - 80		81 - 90		91 - 100	
	Apps	Adm	Apps	Adm	Apps	Adm	Apps	Adm	Apps	Adm	Apps	Adm	Apps	Adm	Apps	Adm	Apps	Adm	Apps	Adm
3.75 - 4.00	1	0	2	0	1	0	6	0	5	0	7	2	25	6	21	11	33	32	32	32
3.50 - 3.74	1	0	7	0	3	0	15	1	17	4	22	4	45	8	41	19	52	43	42	38
3.25 - 3.49	2	0	13	0	10	0	28	1	24	0	31	2	46	1	62	2	77	20	65	60
3.00 - 3.24	6	0	8	0	6	1	32	0	19	0	29	2	45	2	35	1	72	4	65	54
2.75 - 2.99	8	0	12	0	9	1	25	4	7	0	16	1	34	0	30	2	34	3	45	29
2.50 - 2.74	7	0	10	1	11	1	23	4	12	2	9	0	16	1	25	0	18	3	22	13
2.25 - 2.49	9	0	9	1	10	0	9	2	5	1	7	0	3	0	6	1	9	1	6	6
2.00 - 2.24	5	0	3	0	2	0	5	0	4	0	3	0	3	1	4	0	5	0	2	2
Below 2.00	1	0	2	0	1	0	0	0	0	0	1	0	0	0	0	0	0	0	0	0

Apps = Number of Applicants
Adm = Number Admitted
This profile includes minority applicants.

Washington University School of Law

Box 1120
One Brookings Drive
St. Louis, MO 63130

Phone: 314.935.4525

■ Introduction

Founded in 1867, Washington University School of Law is the oldest private law school in continuous operation west of the Mississippi River. A charter member of the AALS and approved by the ABA, the school was one of the first accredited law schools to graduate women. The law school is located on the beautiful and serene 169-acre Hilltop Campus bordered by Forest Park, the site of the 1904 World's Fair, and the lovely suburban communities of Clayton and University City.

■ Enrollment/Student Body

➡ *1,878 applicants*   ➡ *853 admitted first-year class 1993*
➡ *210 enrolled first-year class 1993*   ➡ *650 total full-time*
➡ *13% minority*   ➡ *42% women*
➡ *35 states & 1 foreign country represented*
➡ *121 undergraduate schools represented*

The law school has a national approach to legal education and attracts students from throughout the United States and several foreign countries. The wide variety of undergraduate academic disciplines enriches the Socratic method of teaching.

■ Faculty

➡ *86 total*   ➡ *38 full-time*   ➡ *48 part-time or adjunct*
➡ *11 women*   ➡ *2 minority*

■ Library and Physical Facilities

➡ *475,544 volumes & equivalents*   ➡ *library hours: Mon.-Thurs., 7:00 A.M.-1:00 A.M.; Fri., 7:00 A.M.-MIDNIGHT; Sat., 9:00 A.M.-MIDNIGHT; Sun., 9:00 A.M.-1:00 A.M.*   ➡ *LEXIS*
➡ *NEXIS*   ➡ *WESTLAW*   ➡ *Congressional Information System*   ➡ *LEGI-SLATE*   ➡ *assorted CD ROMs*
➡ *6 full-time librarians*   ➡ *library seats 310*

■ Curriculum

➡ *85 credits required to graduate*   ➡ *82 courses available*
➡ *degrees available: J.D./Asian studies; J.D./M.B.A.; J.D./M.A.-Econ.; J.D./M.A.-Pol.Sci.; J.D./M.H.A.; J.D./M.S.W.; J.D./M.A. or M.S.-Environmental Policy*

A three-year, full-time course of study leads to the J.D. degree. The prescribed first-year courses are sectioned to ensure individualized instruction. In addition, all first-year students participate in a year-long legal research and writing program. Coursework in the second and third years is chosen by the student. A Congressional Clinic and a Federal Administrative Agency Clinic offered in the spring semester of the third year allow a small group of students to work in Washington, DC, with individual members of Congress, congressional committees, and federal agencies. Other areas of strength include urban studies, taxation, criminal, international, corporate, labor, Asian, and Soviet law.

■ Special Programs

➡ *Congressional Clinic (Washington DC)—spring sem., 3rd yr.*
➡ *7 joint-degree programs available*

The School of Law offers a Masters degree (LL.M.) in Taxation. Combined-study programs exist between the Law School and School of Social Work (J.D./M.S.W), the Health Administration Department of the School of Medicine (J.D./M.H.A.), the School of Business (J.D./M.B.A.), and the Department of Economics (J.D./M.S.Ec.), and Political Science (J.D./M.A.). The School of Law has recently established two new joint-degree programs. The first is with the Asian Studies department (J.D./M.A.). The second, and most recent, is with the Department of Engineering and Policy of the School of Engineering and Applied Science. This degree (J.D./M.S. or M.A.) places an emphasis on environmental law and policy.

Additional combined-degree programs are available by arrangement with other departments.

■ Admission

➡ *Bachelor's degree required*   ➡ *application deadline—March 1*   ➡ *LSAT, LSDAS required*
➡ *median GPA—3.20*   ➡ *mean LSAT score—160*
➡ *application fee—$50*

Applications for the following fall are accepted any time after September 15 until March 1. The Admissions Committee informs applicants of their status between March 1 and April 1. Decisions on transfer applications are made in midsummer and considered only if the student has an outstanding record at another AALS-ABA approved school.

Admission decisions are based on a wide range of factors, including undergraduate record, the Law School Admissions Test score, and personal statement. Letters of recommendation are encouraged but not required, and should be limited to no more than three. Applicants are also advised to visit the law school; arrangements can be made by contacting the Admissions Office.

In general, a reasonable prediction of academic ability can be based on undergraduate performance, the LSAT score, and writing sample.

The committee makes a conscientious effort to examine the more personal variables which have a real impact on the quality of life and the quality of education in this institution, such as energy, motivation, self-discipline, and character. Insight into these variables is derived from careful examination of the undergraduate record, personal statement, résumé, and/or letters of recommendation, and other items in the applicant's file.

■ Housing

The university has no housing for graduate students. A wide range of private housing is available near the School of Law. For housing information, students should contact the University Housing Office.

■ Student Activities

The School of Law publishes two student-edited law review periodicals, the *Law Quarterly* and the *Journal of Urban and Contemporary Law*. A very active moot court program, mock trial competition, and competitions in negotiation and client counseling are available. Law students participate in a variety of other programs, including the Women's Law Caucus, the Pro Bono Law Association, the Black Law Students Association, and the Student Bar Association. The student body is self-regulated through the Law School Honor Council. Students are eligible for election to the Order of the Coif. Students also serve on many joint committees with faculty members.

■ Affirmative Action Requirement

One of the first women to receive a degree from an American law school graduated from Washington University in 1871. The school successfully continues to recruit outstanding women, although admission decisions are made on a nondiscriminatory basis. Women with exceptional academic records are encouraged to apply for an Olin Fellowship, which provides full tuition and some stipends for eight women pursuing graduate degrees at Washington University. Application deadline for this award is February 1. The environment for minority students is excellent at Washington University. Minority students have been actively involved in both law review publications, moot court, mock trial competitions, legal fraternities, student government, and other academic and extracurricular activities.

■ Expenses and Financial Aid

➡ *tuition & fees—$17,750 (1993-94)* ➡ *estimated additional expenses—$8,000 (housing, food, etc.)*
➡ *scholarships available: Scholars in Law, Minority Scholars in Law, Buder Scholarship (for Native Americans), Farmer Scholarship (for African Americans)*
➡ *minority scholarships available*
➡ *financial aid available; FAFSA due March 1*

Most student aid is in the form of government and privately sponsored loans. One-third of the students receive some scholarship assistance; two-thirds receive loans. (Virtually all those receiving scholarships also receive loans.) Financially needy applicants whose credentials indicate a likelihood of exceptional academic achievement receive preferential treatment in the awarding of scholarships. The school also has some merit scholarships that are awarded to entering students with exceptional credentials without regard to financial need.

■ Career Services

An aggressive and efficient Career Services Office serves both students and employers. For the class of 1991, 60 percent accepted positions outside metropolitan St. Louis, 69 percent entered private practice, and 26 percent found positions in the public sector. Others are employed in corporate legal departments, accounting firms, banks, and commercial businesses.

Applicant Group for the 1993–1994 Academic Year

Washington University School of Law
This grid includes only applicants who earned 120-180 LSAT scores under standard administrations.

LSAT Score	3.75 +		3.50 -3.74		3.25 - 3.49		3.00 - 3.24		2.75 - 2.99		2.50 - 2.74		2.25 - 2.49		2.00 - 2.24		Below 2.00		No GPA		Total	
	Apps	Adm	Apps	Adm	Apps	Adm	Apps	Adm	Apps	Adm	Apps	Adm	Apps	Adm	Apps	Adm	Apps	Adm	Apps	Adm	Apps	Adm
175 - 180	0	0	0	0	4	4	4	4	0	0	0	0	0	0	0	0	0	0	0	0	8	8
170 - 174	8	8	6	6	10	8	7	7	3	3	2	2	1	0	0	0	1	1	0	0	38	35
165 - 169	20	20	19	19	22	22	35	35	21	21	8	5	4	3	0	0	0	0	0	0	129	125
160 - 164	37	33	80	78	95	92	91	76	41	23	28	17	8	3	2	0	0	0	1	1	383	323
155 - 159	38	31	96	76	137	67	136	25	66	5	29	10	7	2	3	0	2	0	5	3	519	219
150 - 154	22	4	72	14	87	3	71	9	56	10	15	4	13	2	8	2	1	0	2	1	347	49
145 - 149	7	0	23	1	46	7	43	8	35	6	25	3	7	0	7	0	0	0	3	0	196	25
140 - 144	1	0	7	0	13	1	21	0	25	1	23	0	9	0	3	0	2	0	5	0	109	2
135 - 139	0	0	2	0	4	0	8	0	7	0	5	0	5	0	2	0	3	0	3	0	39	0
130 - 134	0	0	2	0	1	0	2	0	5	0	2	0	4	0	2	0	0	0	0	0	18	0
125 - 129	1	0	0	0	0	0	0	0	0	0	4	0	0	0	0	0	0	0	0	0	5	0
120 - 124	0	0	0	0	0	0	0	0	0	0	0	0	0	0	0	0	0	0	0	0	0	0
Total	134	96	307	194	419	204	418	164	259	69	141	41	58	10	27	2	9	1	19	5	1791	786

Apps = Number of Applicants
Adm = Number Admitted
Reflects 96% of the total applicant pool.

Wayne State University Law School

Admissions Office, 468 W. Ferry Mall
Detroit, MI 48202

Phone: 313.577.3937

■ Introduction

Wayne State University Law School was established in 1927, is accredited by the ABA, is a member of the AALS, and has a chapter of the Order of the Coif, the national honor society of the legal profession.

The Law School is a flagship unit of Wayne State University, a major metropolitan research university, located in the Detroit Cultural Center. The Law School's three-building complex is situated at the north end of the university's campus, which covers 185 beautifully land-scaped acres and is highlighted by famous Yamasaki-designed buildings.

■ Enrollment/Student Body

- ➻ *1,623 applicants*   ➻ *504 admitted first-year class 1993*
- ➻ *234 enrolled first-year class 1993*   ➻ *510 total full-time*
- ➻ *190 total part-time*   ➻ *13% minority*   ➻ *48% women*
- ➻ *13 states & foreign countries represented*
- ➻ *99 undergraduate schools represented*   ➻ *age range—20-54*

Approximately 700 students are enrolled in the J.D. program, including individuals from diverse racial, ethnic and socioeconomic backgrounds. Student life, both social and academic, is unusually friendly.

When compared with graduates of other law schools, Wayne State law graduates consistently have the highest or the second highest passing rate on the Michigan Bar Examination.

■ Faculty

- ➻ *66 total*   ➻ *32 full-time*   ➻ *34 part-time or adjunct*
- ➻ *7 women*   ➻ *2 minority*

The members of the full-time faculty are committed to teaching, research, and publishing yet remain accessible to students. One-fourth of the faculty are elected members of the American Law Institute. Many are nationally or internationally recognized experts in their fields of specialization.

Judges and attorneys prominent in specific areas of law, and professors from the United States and other countries serve as adjunct faculty and visiting professors.

■ The Arthur Neef Law Library

- ➻ *415,000 volumes & equivalents*   ➻ *library hours: Mon.-Thurs., 8:00 A.M.-11:00 P.M.; Fri., 8:00 A.M.-9:00 P.M.; Sat., 9:00 A.M.-9:00 P.M.; Sun., 11:00 A.M.-11:00 P.M.; exam periods until MIDNIGHT*   ➻ *24 hours a day off-site access*
- ➻ *LEXIS*   ➻ *NEXIS*   ➻ *WESTLAW*
- ➻ *5 full-time librarians (3 hold J.D. degrees)*
- ➻ *library seats 456*   ➻ *32-station computer lab*
- ✱➻ *31st largest accredited law library*

■ Curriculum

- ➻ *Academic Support Program (Summer Institute)*   ➻ *86 credits required to graduate*   ➻ *103 total courses available*
- ➻ *degrees available: J.D.; J.D./M.A. History; J.D./M.A.*

Public Policy; J.D./M.B.A.—other disciplines by special arrangement   ➻ *semesters, start in Aug.*
➻ *range of first-year class size—25-80*

The first-year curriculum includes the required basic courses: civil procedure, contracts, criminal law, property, torts, and legal research and writing.

The legal research and writing course is one of the best in the nation. The research and writing proficiency of Wayne State law students is highly valued by law firms and other employers. The course is taught by full-time instructors, who are attorneys with experience in the courts, legal practice, and teaching.

Upper-class students are required to take a semester each of constitutional law and professional responsibility. Other courses may be chosen from a broad and diverse range of elective courses, seminars, and skills training classes.

The Law School offers LL.M. programs in the areas of taxation, labor law, and corporate planning

■ Admission

- ➻ *Bachelor's degree required*   ➻ *application deadline—March 15*   ➻ *rolling admission*   ➻ *LSAT, LSDAS required*   ➻ *median GPA—3.35*   ➻ *median LSAT score—158 & 38*   ➻ *application fee—$20*

Most of the class is admitted strictly on the basis of superior undergraduate GPA and LSAT scores. Others are admitted on the basis of academic credentials and other discretionary factors.

Transfer applications may be made, but only students from ABA-approved law schools with excellent academic credentials will be accepted.

■ Minority Students and Other Special Programs

Wayne State Law School has a commitment to enroll a diverse student body and maintains an affirmative action admissions policy for minority group members. Our goal is to assure that every individual we admit has the potential to be successful at our law school.

Minority students admitted to Wayne State Law School have a high graduation and bar passage rate. Qualified minority students are considered for the Kenneth Cockrel, Wade McCree, Patricia Roberts Harris, and Law Alumni Scholarships/Fellowship.

The Supportive Services Program, under the full-time supervision of an Assistant Dean, offers academic and related support to all students. The Summer Institute Program allows entering students to complete Torts, a first-year required course, prior to the beginning of the regular academic year.

■ Student Activities

The *Wayne Law Review*, a scholarly legal journal with nationwide circulation, is published by upper-class law students selected on the basis of their superior academic achievement and/or writing ability.

The Wayne Moot Court Program enjoys national recognition and is affiliated with the Order of the Barristers, a national honorary organization.

The Student Trial Advocacy Program (STAP) provides basic instruction in evidence and the techniques of trial advocacy.

Many students work in the Free Legal Aid Clinic representing indigent clients in court under attorney supervision. Students in the Criminal Appellate Practice Program, in cooperation with the Michigan State Appellate Defender Office, prepare briefs and other pleadings for indigent clients with pending felony appeals.

Second- and third-year students may intern on a part-time basis for distinguished judges and in a variety of governmental and nonprofit agencies.

The Student Board of Governors plays a significant role in the decision-making process of the school and also sponsors social activities for law students. Other student organizations include the Black Law Students Association, Hispanic Law Student Association, Jewish Law Students Association, Federalist Society, Women's Law Caucus, National Lawyers' Guild, Environmental Law Society, International Law Society, Student Recruiters organization, ABA Law Student Division, and legal fraternities.

■ Study Abroad

Each year a Wayne State Law Student is selected for the Freeman Fellowship to support study during a summer session at the Academy of International Law at the Hague, The Netherlands.

The Law School has a student exchange program with the School of Law of the University of Warwick, England for six weeks of study during the summer.

Wayne State Law students may also study one semester abroad through participation in the London Law Programme.

■ Intellectual Property Law Institute (I.P.L.I.)

The I.P.L.I. offers an exceptional and rich curriculum for law students and lawyers in such areas of intellectual property as patents, copyrights, trademarks, trade secrets, computers and related technology, communications and media, entertainment, technology transfer, trade regulation, and the arts.

■ Expenses and Financial Aid

➡ *full-time tuition & fees—resident, $5,750; nonresident, $12,440* ➡ *part-time tuition and fees—resident, $3,132; nonresident, $6,700* ➡ *estimated additional expenses— $13,969 (books, room & board, transportation, miscellaneous expenses)* ➡ *merit- and need-based scholarships available* ➡ *merit- and need-based minority scholarships* ➡ *financial aid available* ➡ *FAFSA priority date—April 23*

Applicant Group for the 1993–1994

Wayne State University LawSchool
This grid includes only applicants who earned 120-180 LSAT scores under standard administrations.

LSAT Score	3.75 +		3.50 -3.74		3.25 - 3.49		3.00 - 3.24		2.75 - 2.99		2.50 - 2.74		2.25 - 2.49		2.00 - 2.24		Below 2.00		No GPA		Total	
	Apps	Adm	Apps	Adm	Apps	Adm	Apps	Adm	Apps	Adm	Apps	Adm	Apps	Adm	Apps	Adm	Apps	Adm	Apps	Adm	Apps	Adm
175 - 180	1	1	0	0	0	0	1	1	1	1	0	0	0	0	0	0	0	0	0	0	3	3
170 - 174	2	2	6	6	0	0	1	1	4	4	1	1	0	0	1	0	0	0	0	0	15	14
165 - 169	4	4	11	11	9	9	13	13	12	11	12	5	1	0	2	0	0	0	0	0	64	53
160 - 164	12	12	33	33	46	46	37	35	20	10	10	4	10	1	2	1	0	0	3	3	173	145
155 - 159	16	16	53	52	67	60	72	29	57	4	29	2	11	0	5	0	0	0	2	1	312	164
150 - 154	17	15	40	22	70	19	82	7	79	7	33	2	19	1	10	1	1	0	3	0	354	74
145 - 149	10	0	16	6	54	6	54	5	53	2	35	0	31	0	7	0	1	0	11	2	272	21
140 - 144	3	0	7	0	29	0	25	0	36	0	40	0	17	0	15	0	1	0	10	0	183	0
135 - 139	1	0	3	0	5	0	14	0	15	0	13	0	19	0	14	0	6	0	6	0	96	0
130 - 134	0	0	0	0	1	0	1	0	5	0	7	0	5	0	7	0	3	0	6	0	35	0
125 - 129	0	0	0	0	0	0	1	0	3	0	1	0	2	0	1	0	1	0	2	0	11	0
120 - 124	0	0	0	0	0	0	0	0	0	0	1	0	1	0	1	0	0	0	3	0	6	0
Total	66	50	169	130	281	140	301	91	285	39	182	14	116	2	65	2	13	0	46	6	1524	474

Apps = Number of Applicants
Adm = Number Admitted
Reflects 94% of the total applicant pool.

West Virginia University College of Law

P.O. Box 6130
Morgantown, WV 26506-6130

Phone: 304.293.5304

■ Introduction

The College of Law was established in 1878 and is the oldest professional school at West Virginia University. The university is located in Morgantown, West Virginia, a community of 50,000, and is easily accessible by interstate highways, commercial airlines, and bus services. The College of Law has been a member of the AALS since 1914 and was fully accredited by the ABA in 1923. The college has had a chapter of the Order of the Coif since 1925.

Since its founding in 1867, West Virginia University has become the center of graduate and professional education, research, and extension programs in West Virginia. The university's rural setting makes for an ideal learning environment for its 20,000 full-time students.

The College of Law has established itself as a national leader in legal issues relating to the development and production of energy resources. The college is the host institution for the Eastern Mineral Law Foundation, Inc., which annually publishes the National Coal Issue of the *West Virginia Law Review* and sponsors conferences and continuing legal education seminars on legal issues in mineral law.

West Virginia University provides a full range of both athletic and cultural facilities. The Personal Rapid Transit System (PRT) provides convenient, modern transportation among the university's three campuses.

■ Enrollment/Student Body

➡ *452 total full-time*   ➡ *16 total part-time*
➡ *8% minority*   ➡ *46% women*

■ Faculty

➡ *26 full-time*   ➡ *12 part-time or adjunct*

■ Library and Physical Facilities

➡ *198,400 volumes & equivalents*   ➡ *LEXIS*
➡ *WESTLAW*   ➡ *CALI*   ➡ *3 full-time librarians*
➡ *library seats 296*

The three-floor library features open stacks, group study rooms, study carrels, a rare book room, labs for word processing and computer-assisted legal instruction, and terminals to access legal research databases and the campus-wide, on-line catalog. A Co-op Day Care Center is located at the Law Center.

■ Curriculum

➡ *90 credits required to graduate*
➡ *degrees available: J.D.; J.D./M.B.A.; J.D./M.P.A.*

The first-year curriculum is required. The second- and third-year programs offer a number of course options and possibilities for concentration. No summer programs are regularly scheduled. The college does accept a limited number of transfer students only after the first year. The college has long stressed advocacy training, and each student completes the trial of a mock suit before a jury prior to graduation.

Students have the option of attending the College of Law on a part-time basis during the day along with full-time students. There is not a separate nighttime track.

■ Student Activities

Candidates for the *West Virginia Law Review* are selected on the basis of performance during their first year in law school and a writing competition.

An active Moot Court Program is conducted at the law school under the supervision of the Moot Court Board. Members competed in five interscholastic regional and national moot court competitions last year.

The Student Bar Association is the student government of the school. It is administered by elected representatives from each class, along with officers elected by the entire student body. All law school organizations have a representative on the council in order to foster a greater feeling of community among all law students.

The college hosts several other organizations representing the varied interests of students.

■ Opportunities for Minority Students

The opportunities available to minority students at the College of Law evolve from our institution's commitment to promote an academic environment comprised of student representation from all segments of society.

This commitment is furthered by the financial aid that is made available to our minority students. First of all, the Board of Trustees makes available full tuition and fees scholarships. Second, there is the W.E.B. Dubois Fellowship that provides full tuition, fees, and a yearly living stipend to qualified African-American professional or graduate students. Third, the Mountain State Bar Association, an African-American–founded professional association, provides available funds in the form of fellowships to African-American students. Finally, the contributions from our alumni have contributed significantly to the total amount of money made available to minority students so they may finance their education.

Additional opportunities for minority students involve the academic support provided by our student-initiated Student/Faculty Academic Assistance Program and the social and professional support provided by our Black Law Students Association (BLSA).

Our Book Loan Program, which provides free textbooks and other materials for all of our members, is a popular feature of BLSA's support to our students. It cuts down on expenditures that would ordinarily be between $200 and $300 a semester.

The academic assistance program offers students an opportunity to become paired with a member of our faculty during their entire law school experience.

The most recent feature available to minority students who are considering law as a career is our **Bridging The**

Gap Program. The program involves seminars on the LSAT; information on joint-degree programs, financial aid, career planning, and legal research and writing; mock law school classes, and opportunities to speak with minority attorneys about issues and concerns.

■ Placement

The Meredith Career Services Center actively assists students and alumni in securing employment, including employment in nontraditional legal careers such as: legal aid societies, business, insurance companies, and government agencies.

■ Admission

➡ *Baccalaureate degree from regionally accredited college or university required* ➡ *application deadline—Feb. 15* ➡ *LSAT required* ➡ *application fee—$40*

No specific prelaw curriculum is required for admission. The college subscribes to the suggestions on prelaw study in this handbook with an additional admonition that at least one year of accounting may be helpful.

In addition, undergraduate grades and performance on the LSAT are carefully and objectively evaluated and compared against that of all other applicants. Applicants must arrange for the timely submission of at least one recommendation from a college professor. Preference is given to West Virginia residents. The College of Law receives many more applications for admission than it has been able to accommodate.

Applications are accepted beginning in September of each year for the class to be admitted in the following August. As soon as applicant files can be completed, they will be notified of the final decision. Those accepted are required to make a deposit of $100 against tuition and fees within a designated period, but not before April 1.

■ Expenses and Financial Aid

➡ *full-time tuition & fees—residents, $3,786; nonresidents, $9,346* ➡ *estimated expenses for books and supplies— $800* ➡ *living allowance for 9 months—$6,285* ➡ *estimated budget: residents, $10,900; nonresident, $16,500* ➡ *Free Application for Federal Student Aid (FAFSA), Law School Datasheet due by March 1* ➡ *Scholarship application due by April 1*

Applicants for admission can seek financial assistance by contacting Candi Hostutler, Financial Aid Counselor, P.O. Box 6130, Morgantown, WV 26506-6130, phone: 304.293.5302.

Note: It is suggested that students apply for financial aid assistance before being accepted.

■ Housing

The University Housing Office (304.293.3621) provides information concerning university-owned housing, including dormitories and apartments. Off-campus, privately owned housing information may be obtained by calling the main campus (304.293.5613). The university maintains 361 furnished and unfurnished apartments for graduate students, married students, faculty, and staff. There is usually a waiting list for apartments, so application should be made as early as possible. Listings for privately owned rentals change daily.

Admitted students are urged to visit Morgantown during the summer prior to registration to secure housing.

Applicant Group for the 1993–1994 Academic Year

West Virginia University College of Law
This grid includes only applicants who earned 120-180 LSAT scores under standard administrations.

LSAT Score	3.75 +		3.50 -3.74		3.25 - 3.49		3.00 - 3.24		2.75 - 2.99		2.50 - 2.74		2.25 - 2.49		2.00 - 2.24		Below 2.00		No GPA		Total	
	Apps	Adm	Apps	Adm	Apps	Adm	Apps	Adm	Apps	Adm	Apps	Adm	Apps	Adm	Apps	Adm	Apps	Adm	Apps	Adm	Apps	Adm
175 - 180	0	0	0	0	0	0	0	0	0	0	0	0	0	0	0	0	0	0	0	0	0	0
170 - 174	0	0	0	0	0	0	0	0	0	0	0	0	0	0	0	0	0	0	0	0	0	0
165 - 169	1	1	3	3	0	0	2	2	2	1	4	2	1	1	0	0	0	0	0	0	13	10
160 - 164	4	4	7	7	6	5	10	7	12	7	11	7	5	2	1	1	1	1	0	0	57	41
155 - 159	17	17	21	15	31	13	40	25	30	8	19	5	7	2	6	3	1	0	1	0	173	88
150 - 154	14	11	38	19	57	17	73	17	47	9	33	3	11	3	5	1	0	0	1	0	279	80
145 - 149	5	2	23	3	42	7	59	2	40	4	28	6	7	0	1	0	3	1	4	0	212	25
140 - 144	2	0	6	1	24	1	22	0	22	1	20	0	11	0	8	0	1	0	1	0	117	3
135 - 139	0	0	0	0	1	0	12	0	8	0	10	0	7	0	2	0	1	0	1	0	42	0
130 - 134	0	0	0	0	0	0	2	0	2	0	4	0	4	0	1	0	1	0	0	0	14	0
125 - 129	0	0	0	0	0	0	0	0	0	0	0	0	1	0	0	0	0	0	0	0	1	0
120 - 124	0	0	0	0	0	0	0	0	0	0	0	0	0	0	0	0	0	0	0	0	0	0
Total	43	35	98	48	161	43	220	53	163	30	129	23	54	8	24	5	8	2	8	0	908	247

Apps = Number of Applicants
Adm = Number Admitted
Reflects 96% of the total applicant pool.

Western New England College School of Law

1215 Wilbraham Road
Springfield, MA 01119-2689

Phone: 413.782.1406

■ Introduction

Western New England College School of Law is centrally located in the Northeast. Springfield offers distinguished museums, a symphony, major recreational activities, and the Basketball Hall of Fame. Springfield is a city of approximately 157,000 residents, 19 percent of whom are African American, and 17 percent of whom are Hispanic. Along with the cultural opportunities available in Springfield, the nearby Five Colleges —Amherst, Hampshire, Mount Holyoke, Smith Colleges, and the University of Massachusetts—contribute to the recreational and cultural activities in the Pioneer Valley.

■ Enrollment/Student Body

➼ *2,089 applicants*   ➼ *789 admitted first-year class 1993*
➼ *251 enrolled first-year class 1993*   ➼ *482 total full-time*
➼ *293 total part-time*   ➼ *8% minority*   ➼ *48% women*

■ Faculty

➼ *59 total*   ➼ *29 full-time*   ➼ *30 part-time or adjunct*
➼ *14 women*   ➼ *3 minority*

Our faculty members come from varied backgrounds and all share a love of teaching. They take pride in their ability to engage students in rigorous law study without the rancor and bitter competitiveness that may characterize other legal educations. Our faculty encourages cooperation among students in the learning process and among each other.

■ Library and Physical Facilities

➼ *301,000 volumes & equivalents*   ➼ *library hours: Mon.-Thurs., 8:00 A.M.-MIDNIGHT; Fri., 8:00 A.M.-10:00 P.M.; Sat., 9:00 A.M.-9:00 P.M.; Sun., 10:00 A.M.-11:00 P.M.*
➼ *LEXIS*   ➼ *NEXIS*   ➼ *WESTLAW*   ➼ *MEDIS*
➼ *DIALOG*   ➼ *OCLC*   ➼ *7 full-time librarians*
➼ *library seats 397*   ➼ *participant in New England Law Library Consortium—access to 13 academic & 2 private law libraries in New England*

The law school building was designed and constructed in 1978 and houses the law library, classrooms, a moot courtroom, and administrative offices. The law school building is located on Western New England College's 94-acre campus and is in a residential neighborhood. In September 1993, the college opened the Healthful Living Center to promote the physical well-being of its students. The center includes a basketball court; a four-lane indoor track; two weight rooms; four indoor tennis courts; an eight-lane swimming pool; two racquetball/handball courts; and two squash courts. Additionally, the center houses an all-purpose room with cushioned floors for aerobics and dance classes and a classroom for health-related workshops and seminars.

■ Curriculum

➼ *88 units/credits required to graduate*   ➼ *84 total courses available in 1993-94*   ➼ *6 clinics available*   ➼ *first-year class size range—full-time, 75-100; part-time, 60-80*

Our Legal Education Assistance Program (LEAP) is an optional tutorial program and is offered in the fall term to first-year students whose applications for admission suggest that they might benefit from additional academic support. A second academic assistance program is available to all first-year students who get two or more grades below 70 in the December exams.

Our first-year courses are taught using the Socratic Method. All required courses, both day and evening, are taught by full-time, tenure-track faculty members. Some of the upper-level courses are taught through classroom discussion of judicial decisions and statutes. Others are taught through simulations in which students perform the roles of lawyers in life-like situations and through clinics where students represent actual clients.

■ Special Programs

Clinical Courses—These enable students to work with actual clients under the supervision of faculty and members of the legal community. We currently offer six clinical courses. Students in the Criminal Law Clinic are appointed special assistant district attorneys who represent the Commonwealth in pretrial and plea negotiations, motions, and trials. They also meet regularly to discuss their cases and increase their understanding of their professional and ethical obligations. Other clinical programs include the Civil Law Clinic, where students represent clients before the Massachusetts Commission Against Discrimination; the Disability Law Clinic; the Consumer Protection Clinic; and the Legal Services Clinic, where students work with Western Massachusetts Legal Services to interview and counsel clients.

Part-time Day and Evening Programs—Western New England College has a long-standing commitment to educating the part-time, evening law student. Evening students come to the law school mostly from the Springfield, Hartford, and Albany, NY areas. The average age for the part-time evening division is 30, and students range in age 21 to 54. Evening law students spend approximately 30 hours per week studying and attending classes. First-year classes meet on Monday, Wednesday, and Thursday from 6:30 P.M.-9:15 P.M., with an additional hour for Lawyering Process either before or after Wednesday classes. The program takes four years including one or two summers, or four and one-half years without summer courses. Our part-time day program is similar to our part-time evening program, but is limited to students who have primary care responsibilities for children or other dependents.

■ Admission

➡ *B.A., B.S. required* ➡ *preferred deadline—March 1*
➡ *rolling admission* ➡ *LSAT, LSDAS required*
➡ *median GPA—3.08* ➡ *median LSAT score—153*
➡ *application fee—$35*
➡ *TOEFL preferred for foreign-educated applicants*

All facets of the application are carefully considered, including racial, gender, physical, language, education, social, and economic obstacles overcome in the applicant's pursuit of higher education.

■ Expenses and Financial Aid

➡ *1993-94 tuition—full-time, $11,775; part-time, $8,830*
➡ *estimated additional first-year educational expenses—books, $525; fees, $510* ➡ *Merit, O'Connor, Sullivan, Sheehan scholarships available (Merit is renewable annually provided student remains in top 25% of class)*
➡ *Diversity, Vera scholarships available to incoming students of color at the discretion of the Admissions Committee (Diversity is renewable annually)*
➡ *free application for Federal Student Aid required*

Application fee waivers are granted upon completion of the law school's fee waiver application form and demonstration that payment of the $35 fee would constitute a heavy burden. Fee waivers may be obtained by calling the Office of Admissions, 413.782.1406.

■ Student Activities

The law school's *Law Review* is published by a student editorial board with faculty supervision. Students sit on faculty committees such as the Admissions Committee and the Academic Standards Committee, and two students attend regular faculty meetings. Student organizations include the Multi-Cultural Law Students Association, which incorporates all students of color and organizes a mentorship program for current students with the Springfield-based Concerned Lawyers of Color; the Environment Law Coalition, which cosponsors the Law School's National Environmental Moot Court team; the Jewish Law Students Association; the Law Rugby Club; and the Women's Law Association, which brought Sarah Weddington, attorney for Jane Roe, to campus in 1992. Other groups include the Phi Alpha Delta fraternity, a chapter of the American Bar Association's Law Student Division, the newspaper *Lex Brevis*, and a yearbook.

■ Career Services

Individual attention to each student is important at Western New England College School of Law, and counseling is an important function of Career Services. Students discuss potential career paths and employment application strategies, and review job application materials with a professional counselor. During the on-campus interview program, students interview with some of the most prestigious employers in Western Massachusetts and Connecticut. There are over 4,400 alumni employed in 45 states, US Territories, Canada, Europe, and Asia. They are employed in diverse occupations as well, including top law firms in New York and Boston, Hartford Insurance Companies, the Springfield Urban League, the Massachusetts Commission Against Discrimination, state and district court judgeships, many public defender's and district attorney's offices, and numerous small firms.

Applicant Group for the 1993–1994 Academic Year

Western New England College School of Law
This grid includes only applicants who earned 120-180 LSAT scores under standard administrations.

LSAT Score	3.75 +		3.50 -3.74		3.25 - 3.49		3.00 - 3.24		2.75 - 2.99		2.50 - 2.74		2.25 - 2.49		2.00 - 2.24		Below 2.00		No GPA		Total	
	Apps	Adm	Apps	Adm	Apps	Adm	Apps	Adm	Apps	Adm	Apps	Adm	Apps	Adm	Apps	Adm	Apps	Adm	Apps	Adm	Apps	Adm
175 - 180	0	0	0	0	0	0	0	0	0	0	0	0	0	0	0	0	0	0	0	0	0	0
170 - 174	0	0	1	1	1	1	1	1	1	1	0	0	0	0	0	0	0	0	0	0	4	4
165 - 169	3	3	2	2	3	3	5	4	2	1	1	1	2	2	2	1	1	1	1	1	22	19
160 - 164	4	4	7	7	14	13	12	10	20	19	10	9	9	7	3	2	0	0	0	0	79	71
155 - 159	10	10	28	25	35	33	79	70	66	56	56	41	18	8	6	3	0	0	1	1	299	247
150 - 154	13	12	39	34	101	81	155	103	126	34	105	22	40	7	12	2	3	1	3	1	597	297
145 - 149	9	6	31	17	84	30	128	19	125	8	86	2	39	1	13	1	3	0	9	1	527	85
140 - 144	5	2	22	4	28	6	58	10	62	3	65	3	32	3	18	0	4	0	3	0	297	31
135 - 139	3	0	4	0	13	1	19	0	24	0	19	0	24	0	8	0	2	0	7	0	123	1
130 - 134	0	0	0	0	4	0	2	0	10	0	10	0	7	0	6	0	0	0	1	0	40	0
125 - 129	0	0	0	0	0	0	0	0	0	0	1	0	2	0	0	0	0	0	1	0	4	0
120 - 124	0	0	0	0	0	0	0	0	0	0	0	0	0	0	0	0	0	0	0	0	0	0
Total	47	37	134	90	283	168	459	217	436	122	353	78	173	28	68	9	13	2	26	4	1992	755

Apps = Number of Applicants
Adm = Number Admitted
Reflects 94% of the total applicant pool.

Whittier College School of Law

5353 West Third Street
Los Angeles, CA 90020

Phone: 1.800.808.8188 or 213.938.3621, ext. 123, 128

■ Introduction

Whittier College is a nationally recognized, independent college of arts and sciences founded in 1887 in Whittier, California. The School of Law, located in Los Angeles, was established in 1975.

The Whittier tradition of concern for students as individuals is reflected in admissions practices, a close student-to-faculty ratio (approximately 24 to 1), small classes, and continuous student counseling and placement services.

Located in the residential Hollywood-Wilshire area of Los Angeles on a spacious five-acre site, the gracious Tudor-style building with its sweeping lawns and central open courtyard is a local landmark. Proximity to state and federal courts, law offices from downtown Los Angeles to Century City, libraries, and the cultural activities of metropolitan Los Angeles enrich the experiences and opportunities of law students. Affiliation with Whittier College ensures a continuing commitment to academic excellence and individual attention.

Whittier Law School is fully accredited by the ABA and is a member of the AALS.

■ Enrollment/Student Body

➡ *2,750 applicants* ➡ *1,016 admitted first-year class 1993*
➡ *247 enrolled first-year class 1993* ➡ *429 total full-time*
➡ *240 total part-time* ➡ *28% minority* ➡ *40% women*
➡ *41 states & 2 foreign countries represented*
➡ *107 undergraduate schools represented* ➡ *40% nonresident*

■ Faculty

➡ *40 total* ➡ *28 full-time* ➡ *12 part-time or adjunct*
➡ *8 women* ➡ *1 minority*

The full-time faculty is drawn from law schools throughout the country so that the school's perspective will be a national one, preparing students to pursue legal careers anywhere in the United States.

Faculty members recognize that their teaching obligation includes considerable interaction with students. The unique building provides a noninstitutional atmosphere conducive to this interaction.

■ Library and Physical Facilities

➡ *230,000 volumes & equivalents* ➡ *library hours: Mon.-Fri., 7:30 A.M.-11:30 P.M.; Sat.-Sun., 10:00 A.M.-11:30 P.M.*
➡ *LEXIS* ➡ *NEXIS* ➡ *WESTLAW* ➡ *DIALOG*
➡ *7 full-time librarians* ➡ *library seats 270*

The library is a rapidly growing legal research collection and serves as a state and federal depository. The Student Computer Center, located in the Law School Library, is available to students free of charge. The center houses computer hardware and a variety of software to aid students with computer-assisted instruction and legal research.

The law school also offers free, on-site parking.

■ Curriculum

➡ *Academic Support Program* ➡ *87 credits required to graduate* ➡ *68 courses available* ➡ *J.D. degree available*
➡ *semesters, start in Aug., Jan. & June*
➡ *range of first-year class size—65-75*

Typically, the J.D. will be completed in three years of full-time study; for part-time students, four years, including three summer sessions, will be necessary.

Part-time students generally attend classes three evenings a week. Standards for admission and retention are identical for all students, and the full-time faculty serve both day and evening programs.

Required courses total 38 of the 87 units needed to graduate. The remainder of the requirement is met from a wide variety of elective courses reflecting the diversity of careers and activities of modern lawyers.

■ Special Programs

Whittier Law School offers a variety of externships with trial and appellate judges and government agencies. Students perform lawyering tasks and apply their academic studies to real client cases, gaining valuable insights into the operation of legal institutions. They also develop a better understanding of the legal and socioeconomic problems common in the practice of law.

The externship program is coordinated by a full-time, tenured professor who assures that students receive significant legal experience in interviewing and counseling clients, negotiating, participation in alternative dispute resolutions, drafting documents, or litigating in administrative hearings and trials.

In conjunction with the externship, a one-unit course, "Lawyering Skills," provides students with a forum for discussing externship experiences.

■ Admission

➡ *Bachelor's degree generally required*
➡ *application deadline—March 15* ➡ *rolling admissions, early application preferred* ➡ *LSAT, LSDAS required*
➡ *median GPA—3.00* ➡ *median LSAT score—155*
➡ *application fee—$50* ➡ *Summer Performance Program*

In rare instances, an applicant will be admitted as a special student without a baccalaureate degree upon showing an unusually high LSAT score, excellence in college work completed, a statement of personal factors indicating maturity, and capacity for legal studies and professional achievement.

Consistent with Whittier Law School's tradition of concern for students as individuals, no magic numbers are used to determine admissions decisions. In addition to the objective criteria of the LSAT score and the undergraduate GPA, subjective factors such as undergraduate school, course of study, graduate work, social and economic background, and personal accomplishments are considered. Thus, objective criteria are balanced with subjective factors. Applicants are encouraged to discuss these factors in their written personal statements.

Summer Performance—Whittier permits a select group of applicants to be admitted based upon their performance during an eight-week, full-time Summer Performance Admission Program. Applicants are chosen from those individuals who have not demonstrated aptitude for the study of law according to the traditional criteria of LSAT scores and undergraduate GPA, but whom the faculty believes should be given an opportunity to perform based on other factors. Successful completion of this summer work will result in regular admission for the fall semester.

■ Student Activities

The law school's location in the center of one of America's busiest and most diverse legal communities affords many opportunities for law-related experiences as students pursue their legal education.

The *Whittier Law Review*, published by a board of student editors selected from among those with superior academic records in the law school, is open to all students on the basis of a writing competition. The *Review* stresses the highest standards of legal scholarship in preparing notes and articles of significance to the legal community.

Moot court competition offers the opportunity to develop skills in written and oral advocacy. Students who perform well are invited to the Moot Court Honors Board. Members compete in school, regional, state, and national competitions.

The Student Bar Association is an independent student organization with officers elected by fellow students. Its activities include a speakers' program, publication of the student newspaper, various social functions, and participation in student-faculty committees for school governance.

Other student organizations represent the numerous and varied interests of Whittier law students.

■ Expenses and Financial Aid

➡ *tuition & fees—full-time, $15,960; part-time, $9,576*
➡ *estimated additional expenses—$12,425 (books & supplies, room & board, personal & transportation)*
➡ *scholarships available; need-based and merit-based*
➡ *minority scholarships available: diversity*
➡ *financial aid available, FAFSA required*

The law school offers several alternatives for financial assistance, including loan programs, scholarships, and employment opportunities.

After notification of admission, applicants will receive detailed information and instructions on applying for financial aid.

■ Career Services

Whittier College School of Law provides assistance to students and alumni in obtaining clerkships and attorney positions. The Office of Placement and Career Planning offers seminars and individual counseling on résumé writing, interviewing techniques, and career planning. Services are provided to help locate and place students in clerkship positions with private attorneys and companies, judges, and governmental agencies. The office hosts on-campus interviews for permanent attorney positions by firms and agencies. Individual guidance is given which is tailored to the student's and graduate's special needs and areas of legal interest.

Applicant Group for the 1993–1994 Academic Year

Whittier College School of Law
This grid includes only applicants who earned 120-180 LSAT scores under standard administrations.

LSAT Score	3.75 +		3.50 -3.74		3.25 - 3.49		3.00 - 3.24		2.75 - 2.99		2.50 - 2.74		2.25 - 2.49		2.00 - 2.24		Below 2.00		No GPA		Total	
	Apps	Adm	Apps	Adm	Apps	Adm	Apps	Adm	Apps	Adm	Apps	Adm	Apps	Adm	Apps	Adm	Apps	Adm	Apps	Adm	Apps	Adm
175 - 180	0	0	0	0	1	1	0	0	0	0	0	0	1	1	0	0	0	0	0	0	2	2
170 - 174	0	0	0	0	0	0	1	1	1	1	0	0	1	1	0	0	0	0	0	0	3	3
165 - 169	0	0	2	2	1	1	5	4	2	2	4	4	1	1	2	2	0	0	0	0	17	16
160 - 164	1	1	5	5	8	8	14	12	21	20	16	14	13	10	5	3	0	0	2	2	85	75
155 - 159	8	8	17	16	48	47	69	60	81	73	61	48	44	25	23	9	3	0	4	1	358	287
150 - 154	11	11	26	25	103	97	135	115	168	112	137	57	78	23	23	5	2	0	8	4	691	449
145 - 149	5	4	34	24	84	44	156	47	162	34	130	15	95	3	38	2	4	0	18	2	726	175
140 - 144	4	2	19	3	33	6	92	6	86	5	100	2	65	2	22	1	7	0	15	2	443	29
135 - 139	0	0	4	0	11	1	25	1	39	0	44	0	44	0	20	0	2	0	7	0	196	2
130 - 134	0	0	1	0	3	0	8	0	15	1	15	0	15	0	15	0	3	0	6	0	81	1
125 - 129	0	0	1	0	0	0	1	0	2	0	5	0	0	0	3	0	0	0	1	0	13	0
120 - 124	0	0	0	0	0	0	0	0	0	0	0	0	1	1	1	0	0	0	2	0	4	0
Total	29	26	109	75	292	205	506	246	577	248	512	140	358	66	152	22	21	0	63	11	2619	1039

Apps = Number of Applicants
Adm = Number Admitted
Reflects 94% of the total applicant pool.

Widener University School of Law

P.O. Box 7474, Wilmington, DE 19803
3800 Vartan Way, Harrisburg, PA 17110-9450 ,

Phone: 302.477.2162
Phone: 717.541.3903

■ Introduction

Widener University School of Law strives to produce the highest level of legal education and professional development to meet the needs of society and the legal profession. Widener is recognized for the teaching excellence of its faculty. Its comprehensive educational program makes available the opportunity to prepare intensively for legal practice through professional skills courses and through research and study in more traditional academic areas.

Our two branches—one in Wilmington, DE, and one in Harrisburg, PA—form one of the largest law schools in the nation. Widener's size means resources are available to offer: an extensive curriculum; a distinguished, diverse faculty; modern facilities; fully automated law libraries; and state-of-the-art technology.

■ Enrollment/Student Body

➡ *4,127 applicants*   ➡ *1,513 admitted first-year class 1993*
➡ *679 enrolled first-year class 1993*   ➡ *1,505 total full-time*
➡ *688 total part-time*   ➡ *8% minority*   ➡ *41% women*
➡ *25 states & foreign countries represented*
➡ *228 undergraduate schools represented*

■ Faculty

➡ *206 total*   ➡ *96 full-time*   ➡ *110 part-time or adjunct*
➡ *50 women*   ➡ *9 minority*

The full-time faculty bring the broadest possible range of interests, expertise, and accomplishments. Many have served as clerks to notable judges and justices, and most have substantial legal practice experience. Many faculty members are actively engaged in professional activities that enhance the educational environment. A large percentage are female.

■ Library and Physical Facilities

➡ *480,500 volumes & equivalents*   ➡ *LEXIS*
➡ *NEXIS*   ➡ *WESTLAW*   ➡ *DIALOG*
➡ *17 full-time librarians*

The combined libraries of the two campuses house one of the most significant legal collections in the region. The collection in Delaware focuses on tax, corporation, and health law, and the collection in Harrisburg focuses on public law, which includes administrative, legislative, constitutional, and regulatory law. The library's resources include legal and nonlegal computer databases, a rapidly growing collection of audio- and videotapes, and a sizeable microform collection. The library is a selective depository for U.S. government documents.

There are large personal computer laboratories available to students on both campuses. All students are instructed in LEXIS and WESTLAW. Classrooms and moot court rooms are linked to videotaping equipment, and the two campuses are linked by teleconference equipment.

■ Curriculum

➡ *Academic Support Program*   ➡ *87 credits required to graduate*   ➡ *229 courses available*   ➡ *degrees available: J.D.; J.D./M.B.A.; J.D./Psy.D.; LL.M.*   ➡ *summer school*   ➡ *range of first-year class size—25-120*
➡ *day and evening programs*

The law school offers two programs leading to the J.D. degree—a three-year day program and an evening program of four years; each requires the completion of 87 hours of credit. Day and evening programs are available on both campuses.

■ Special Programs and Institutes

Widener was a leader in developing professional skills courses and curricula in the early 1980s. The law school operates in-house clinics in the following areas: bankruptcy, civil (elder law, family law, and landlord-tenant), environmental, housing, tax, and energy law. In these clinics, students represent clients in a supervised setting.

A large number of supervised externships and judicial clerkships that permit students to work as neophyte lawyers in nonprofit corporations, with the state government, or with a federal or state judge are also available.

A second part of the Professional Skills Program is the Trial Advocacy Institute. That institute promotes and develops student trial practice skills through development of numerous courses and programs that focus on teaching trial advocacy.

An extensive moot court program that prepares students to compete in regional and national interschool competitions exists on both campuses. Moot court teams from Widener reached the ABA National Appellate Advocacy final round in the past two academic years.

The school's Health Law Institute provides research, policy analysis, specialty education, and service to law students, health lawyers, and health-care professionals. The institute's program takes advantage of the considerable expertise of the school's faculty in such areas as the rights of the elderly, professional liability, regulation of the health-care industry, and long-term care.

The School of Law's graduate program grants an LL.M. degree in Corporate Law and Finance. A joint J.D./M.B.A. degree is offered in cooperation with the Widener School of Management and Applied Economics. The J.D./Psy.D. Program is offered in cooperation with the Widener University Institute for Graduate Clinical Psychology, and requires six years of study.

■ International Law Programs

Widener offers the opportunity to study international and comparative law courses while living abroad in Paris, Geneva, or Nairobi. Out law school conducts summer programs in Switzerland and Kenya. The Geneva International Law Institute, held at the University of Geneva, specializes in International Trade Law. The Nairobi International Law Institute at the University of Nairobi specializes in International Environmental Law. Widener also operates a semester-abroad exchange program with the University of Paris-Nanterre that focuses on European Community Law.

■ Student Activities

The students at the Delaware campus publish the *Delaware Journal of Corporate Law*, as well as a new journal that will consist of one symposium issue each year. The students at the Harrisburg campus, publish the *Widener Journal of Public Law*.

Numerous cocurricular and extracurricular activities provide opportunities designed to enrich the law school experience on both campuses.

■ Admission

➡ *baccalaureate degree required*   ➡ *application deadline—May 15*   ➡ *rolling admissions*   ➡ *LSAT, LSDAS required*   ➡ *median GPA—3.10*   ➡ *median LSAT score for standard admission—154*   ➡ *application fee—$60*

While there are no fixed admission criteria, great weight is given to the applicant's LSAT score and undergraduate grade-point average. Other materials considered for admission include graduate degrees, writing sample, extracurricular activities, and community activities.

The law school actively seeks to diversify the student body.

Widener conducts a Trial Admission Program (TAP) in the summer on both campuses for a small number of carefully selected applicants who show promise of success in law studies despite a relatively low score on one of the two principal measures used for admission.

Interested persons are invited to visit either branch of the school.

■ Expenses and Financial Aid

➡ *tuition & fees—full-time, $14,200; part-time, $10,650*
➡ *estimated additional expenses—$9,950 (living expenses and books)*   ➡ *Widener Achievement Scholarships available for qualified majority and minority applicants*
➡ *financial aid available; FAFSA required for need analysis*
➡ *on-campus housing available in Delaware*
➡ *housing available adjacent to campus in both locations*

■ Career Planning and Placement

The Career Planning and Placement Office actively provides career counseling and placement opportunities on both campuses. The office's programs, services, and guidance assist students as they formulate and realize professional, educational, and career goals. This office conducts on-campus interviewing programs at both campuses. Graduates are employed by large, medium, and small law firms; corporations; nonprofit corporations; governmental agencies; and the judiciary.

Admission Profile Not Available

Willamette University College of Law

900 State Street
Salem, OR 97301

Phone: 503.370.6282

■ Introduction

In 1883, Willamette University established the first law school in the Pacific Northwest, Willamette University College of Law. Today, it remains one of the smallest and most intellectually intimate law schools in the West. In its 110-year history, more than 3,500 alumni have benefitted from a program of legal education that is traditional in content and approach.

Willamette University is located in Salem, Oregon's capital city, 45 minutes from Portland. The peaceful 57-acre campus is situated adjacent to the state capitol and courts. A city of 110,000, Salem is "small town" in feel. It is bordered by pastures, farmland, and vineyards. The Cascade Mountains and Pacific Ocean are about a one-hour drive. Seattle is four hours north; San Francisco is eleven hours south.

The College of Law is accredited by the American Bar Association and is a member of the Association of American Law Schools.

■ Enrollment/Student Body

➡ 1,219 applicants   ➡ 493 admitted first-year class 1993
➡ 182 enrolled first-year class 1993   ➡ 484 total full-time
➡ 12% minority   ➡ 38% women

■ Faculty

➡ 39 total   ➡ 29 full-time   ➡ 10 part-time or adjunct
➡ 9 women   ➡ 1 minority

■ Library and Physical Facilities

➡ 244,000 volumes & equivalents   ➡ library hours: 24-hour access to library   ➡ LEXIS   ➡ NEXIS
➡ WESTLAW   ➡ CALI   ➡ 5 full-time librarians
➡ library seats 500

Enlarged and rededicated in 1992, the Truman Wesley Collins Legal Center is the newest facility for legal education in the Northwest. It contains nine modern, comfortable classrooms, a state-of-the-art courtroom, three student lounges, and faculty and administrative offices.

An open and spacious three-story law library anchors the northeast wing of the Collins Center. It is an outstanding research facility to which students have 24-hour access. In addition to numerous study tables and individual study carrels, the law library includes conference rooms, video rooms, and two computer labs with 24 IBM-compatible workstations. Noteworthy are the library's tax law and international law collections. The Oregon Supreme Court Library and the Hatfield Library, Willamette's undergraduate library, are two blocks away.

All facilities of Willamette University are also available for law student use, including the Sparks Physical Education and Recreation Center and Bishop Student Health Center.

■ Admission

➡ B.A. required for admission   ➡ application deadline—April 1   ➡ LSAT, LSDAS required   ➡ median GPA—3.20
➡ median LSAT score—157   ➡ application fee—$40

More than 75 percent of the first-year class are graduates of institutions outside Oregon. Graduates of California schools constitute 23 percent of the entering class. Most applicants intend to practice in the West, chiefly Oregon or Washington. The first-year enrollment is 165 and only full-time study is permitted.

The Committee on Admission convenes in mid-February to begin reviewing applications. The strength of the candidate's LSAT score and GPA are weighed heavily.

■ Ethnic Student Programs

Willamette encourages applications from students interested in building a diverse community of attorneys to help meet the future needs of our region.

Ethnic student trustee scholarships are available to those demonstrating academic success and leadership in their college or community. Students participate in the Multicultural Law Student Association, Black Law Student Association, and the Minority Affairs Committee. M.A.C. and M.L.S.A. cosponsor a first-year tutorial program.

The Oregon State Bar Affirmative Action Program provides ethnic law students with opportunities for support and professional development. These include an honors clerking program, a mentor program, and scholarship and loan programs. For more information, contact the Office of Admission or the Oregon State Bar, 503.620.0222.

■ Curriculum

➡ Academic Support Program   ➡ 88 units/credits required to graduate   ➡ 95 total courses available
➡ degrees available: J.D.; J.D./M.M.   ➡ semesters, start in Aug.   ➡ range of first-year class size—165-180

Willamette's first-year curriculum is prescribed. It includes civil procedure, contracts, property, torts, constitutional law, criminal law, dispute resolution, and legal research and writing. Courses in alternative dispute resolution enrich the student's practical application of lawyering skills. One clinical opportunity is available.

Each first-year student is guaranteed two classes of fewer than 30, enabling a degree of classroom interaction unmatched by any law school in the region. Relationships among faculty and students are friendly and collaborative. Nevertheless, because of the critical relationship that rank-in-class and grades have in the employment process, the academic environment remains competitive.

■ Special Programs

Each summer, a small group of students travels to the East China Institute of Politics and Law in Shanghai. Chinese legal theory is examined in detail and students participate in several field experiences. They also meet with lawyers, officials, and academics involved in international trade and investment.

Together with the Atkinson Graduate School of Management, the College of Law offers a joint-degree program leading to the awarding of the Doctor of Jurisprudence (J.D.) and the Master of Management (M.M.) in four years. Candidates must apply to each school separately. Contact the Atkinson Graduate School of Management, 503.370.6440.

Each year, several conferences are sponsored by the College of Law, and a dispute resolution conference and a tax conference are annual events.

■ Placement and Bar Passage

Despite national and regional economic pressures facing the Class of 1992, 88 percent were employed within one year of graduation, most in the West. Of this number, 74 percent were employed in private practice. About 26 percent were in government positions, including 6 graduates holding judicial clerkships.

The small size of the entering class enables the Director of Career Services to work individually with students, preparing each for the rigors of the job search. A well-developed, on-campus program brings a variety of prospective employers to Willamette, principally from Oregon and Washington. Most graduates pursue careers in tax, commercial, international, labor, and criminal law, as well as government service.

In 1992, 88 percent of College of Law graduates passed the Oregon state bar examination on their first attempt.

■ Expenses, Financial Aid, and Scholarships

➤ *$12,800 full-time tuition and fees* ➤ *average additional expenses—books,$1,000; room & board, $6,650; misc., $1,615* ➤ *merit scholarships available* ➤ *merit minority scholarships available* ➤ *FAFSA due by Feb. 1* ➤ *merit- and need-based loans available*

An enviable endowment of $80 million supports Willamette University, ranking it among the most financially stable institutions in the Pacific Northwest. Not only are its facilities among the best, but its tuition is among the least expensive of the 16 private law schools in the West.

More than 25 percent of the first-year class are merit scholarship recipients. The average scholarship award is $7,400. Merit scholarships are automatically renewed each year so long as students maintain a GPA of 2.00. About 80 percent of the first- year class are recipients of student loans.

The cost of living in Salem is less than most major cities in the West. There is no sales tax in Oregon.

■ Housing

First-year students secure rental housing in Salem in an average of two days. The average rental range for a one-bedroom apartment is $350 to $400 a month. Limited on-campus housing is available to single students in Lee House, a residence hall located near the Collins Legal Center. About 10 percent of the first-year class makes the 45-minute commute from southwest Portland.

■ Interviews and Tours

Candidates desiring an informational interview and tour of the Truman Wesley Collins Legal Center should make arrangements to meet with the Director of Admission. Please call 503.370.6282.

Applicant Group for the 1993–1994 Academic Year

Willamette University College of Law

LSAT Score	GPA								
	3.75+	3.50 - 3.74	3.25 - 3.49	3.00 - 3.24	2.75 - 2.99	2.50 - 2.74	2.25 - 2.49	2.00 - 2.24	Below 2.00
175 - 180	■	■	■	■	▨	▨			
170 - 174	■	■	■	■	▨	▨			
165 - 169	■	■	■	■	▨	▨			
160 - 164	■	■	■	■					
155 - 159	■	■	▨	▨					
150 - 154	▨	▨	▨						
145 - 149									
140 - 144									
135 - 139									
130 - 134									
125 - 129									
120 - 124									

■ Likely   ▨ Possible   □ Unlikely

College of William and Mary—Marshall-Wythe School of Law

Law Admissions
P.O. Box 8795
Williamsburg, VA 23187-8795

Phone: 804.221.3785

■ Introduction

William and Mary's Marshall-Wythe School of Law is located in historic Williamsburg in the tidewater area of Virginia, within easy reach of the metropolitan areas of Norfolk, Richmond, and Washington, DC. Its origin dates from 1779, when George Wythe was appointed professor of law, making the College of William and Mary America's first educational institution to offer instruction in law. The school is named for Wythe and John Marshall, Wythe's most renowned student and later Chief Justice of the United States. It is accredited by the ABA, is a member of the AALS, is registered by the New York State Department of Education, and has a chapter of the Order of the Coif.

■ Enrollment/Student Body

➡ 3,417 applicants ➡ 702 admitted first-year class 1993
➡ 178 enrolled first-year class 1993 ➡ 564 total full-time
➡ 14% minority ➡ 43% women
➡ 37 states, D.C. & foreign countries represented
➡ 164 undergraduate schools represented

■ Faculty

➡ 50 total ➡ 27 full-time ➡ 23 part-time or adjunct
➡ 12 women ➡ 5 minority

■ Library and Physical Facilities

➡ 300,000 volumes & equivalents ➡ library hours: Mon.-Thurs., 7:30 A.M.-1:30 A.M.; Fri., 7:30 A.M.-12:30 A.M.; Sat., 8:30 A.M.-12:30 A.M.; Sun., 8:30 A.M.-1:30 P.M. ➡ LEXIS
➡ NEXIS ➡ WESTLAW ➡ DIALOG
➡ Virginia Legislative Service ➡ 7 full-time librarians
➡ library seats 430

The law school's modern facility is located adjacent to the National Center for State Courts, and includes an experimental moot courtroom designed and equipped to allow testing of innovative approaches to the conduct of judicial proceedings. A new apartment complex for graduate students is located adjacent to the law school. The law library's collection provides a strong combination of primary and secondary sources. Students may also access several legal and nonlegal databases from 34 computer terminals as well as other information sources from the CD-ROM network, and may freely use the 25 additional personal computers in the library's computer lab. The law library has more than 400 seats, including a combination of carrels, tables, audio-visual seating, and lounge furniture. Law students also have access to Swem Library, which houses the general college collections. Both libraries serve as federal document depositories.

■ Curriculum

➡ Academic Support Program ➡ 90 credits required to graduate ➡ 97 courses available ➡ degrees available: J.D; J.D./M.B.A.; J.D./M.P.P.; J.D./M.A. (American Studies); LL.M. ➡ semesters, begin in Aug. and Jan.

■ Special Programs

Successful completion of 90 semester credit hours of law studies and 90 weeks of residence is required. The first-year curriculum is prescribed and consists of studies in contracts, constitutional law, torts, civil procedure, property, and legal skills. Prior to graduation, students must take criminal law and a second year of legal skills which includes professional ethics. The school's legal skills program was the winner of the 1991 American Bar Association's Gambrell Award for excellence in professional training. Fully accredited summer sessions are offered in Williamsburg, The University of Exeter in Devonshire, England, The University of Madrid in Spain, The University of Adelaide in Australia, and in Amsterdam, The Netherlands. Marshall-Wythe also offers a LL.M. in the American Legal System for foreign students and a LL.M. in Taxation.

The law school provides a wide variety of clinical opportunities, including: the Legal Aid Clinic, the US Attorney Practice Clinic, Attorney General Practice Clinic, the Virginia Court of Appeals Clinic, and the Post-Conviction Assistance Project. In addition, second- and third-year students are able to work in a variety of legal settings, such as private firms, public law offices, and legal clinics.

The curriculum is enriched by The Institute of Bill of Rights Law, a privately funded organization. The institute's central focus is scholarship and education on freedom of speech and of the press, with interests also in legal history, legal writing, and professional responsibility.

The Marshall-Wythe School of Law is committed to providing opportunities for the study of law and entry into the legal profession to qualified racial and ethnic minority students, and students who, because of economic circumstances, may have been denied access to advantageous educational experiences. This commitment includes a special concern for determining the potential of these applicants through the admission process and special recruitment efforts. Special interest organizations include the Black Law Students Association and the Mary and William Feminist Law Society. The physical facilities are barrier-free.

■ Admission

➡ Bachelor's degree from accredited college or university
➡ application deadline—March 1
➡ LSAT, LSDAS required ➡ median GPA—3.34
➡ median LSAT score—93rd percentile
➡ application fee—$30

Applicants must take the LSAT and complete their college degree prior to enrolling in the law school. Transcript evaluation by LSDAS is required. Two written recommendations are required, one of which must be from a college professor or dean. Applications, which will be processed upon completion of three years of academic work, are available the September preceding admission. Personal interviews will be granted upon request. February 1 is the deadline for completing the registration process with LSDAS. Admission to the Marshall-Wythe School of Law is offered to those applicants who, in the opinion of the faculty admission committee, will make the most significant contribution to society as members of the legal profession. Factors such as general academic ability based on undergraduate work, capacity for the study of law based on the LSAT, work experience, and other personal qualities are considered.

■ Student Activities

The *William and Mary Law Review* is published four times yearly and, in addition to carrying articles by nationally-noted legal scholars, provides opportunity for publication of student case comments and notes. The *Administrative Law Review*, the quarterly journal of the ABA Section on Administrative Law and Regulatory Practice, is edited by a staff of William and Mary students. The *William and Mary Bill of Rights Journal* is a student publication devoted to student research and analysis of contemporary Bill of Rights issues. The *Journal of Bankruptcy Law & Practice* is published six times each year in cooperation with the Warren, Gorham & Lamont publishing company. Students prepare bankruptcy law surveys for publication under the direction of a faculty member. The Moot Court Program provides opportunity for experience in appellate briefing and argument on an intramural level and in national competition. The School of Law offers a wide variety of other extracurricular activities.

■ Expenses and Financial Aid

➡ *full-time tuition & fees—resident, $5,340; nonresident, $13,530* ➡ *estimated additional expenses—living allowance, $8,900; books, $800* ➡ *merit- and need-based scholarships available* ➡ *minority scholarships available as one factor in achieving diversity* ➡ *financial aid available; FAF due Feb. 1*

■ Career Services

Employers from 35 states and the District of Columbia conducted on-campus interviews during 1992. Over 1,000 additional nonvisiting employers from all 50 states and the District of Columbia contacted the Law School to recruit our students. William and Mary students participate in 11 off-campus job fairs with a national employer base, including specialized programs for intellectual property law, public interest and government positions, and small regional firms. The law school offers five funding programs to assist students who want to work in low-paying or nonpaying public-service positions during the academic year and the summer. The class of 1992 reported employment in virtually all areas of the country. Thirty-eight percent remained in Virginia, the other 62 percent accepted positions in 26 states and the District of Columbia.

Applicant Group for the 1993–1994 Academic Year

College of William and Mary—Marshall-Wythe School of Law
This grid includes only applicants who earned 120-180 LSAT scores under standard administrations.

LSAT Score	3.75 +		3.50 -3.74		3.25 - 3.49		3.00 - 3.24		2.75 - 2.99		2.50 - 2.74		2.25 - 2.49		2.00 - 2.24		Below 2.00		No GPA		Total	
	Apps	Adm	Apps	Adm	Apps	Adm	Apps	Adm	Apps	Adm	Apps	Adm	Apps	Adm	Apps	Adm	Apps	Adm	Apps	Adm	Apps	Adm
175 - 180	4	4	3	3	5	4	6	5	1	1	1	0	1	1	0	0	0	0	0	0	21	18
170 - 174	9	9	21	21	30	29	23	18	15	10	5	0	2	0	1	0	0	0	0	0	106	87
165 - 169	47	45	80	75	111	88	98	45	35	8	18	5	5	2	0	0	0	0	0	0	394	268
160 - 164	95	50	195	76	247	58	128	8	68	5	32	1	17	0	3	0	0	0	3	0	788	198
155 - 159	62	8	127	10	210	9	147	4	90	4	47	7	18	1	11	1	2	0	2	0	716	44
150 - 154	30	2	89	7	121	6	120	12	88	4	57	5	24	1	10	0	1	0	6	0	546	37
145 - 149	17	2	40	2	99	3	89	2	63	1	66	2	31	0	5	0	1	0	1	0	412	12
140 - 144	4	0	17	0	22	1	32	0	37	0	27	0	22	0	9	0	2	0	3	0	175	1
135 - 139	0	0	2	0	4	0	9	0	16	0	13	0	11	0	3	0	2	0	4	0	64	0
130 - 134	0	0	1	0	2	0	0	0	5	0	2	0	4	0	0	0	0	0	1	0	15	0
125 - 129	0	0	1	0	0	0	1	0	2	0	1	0	2	0	3	0	0	0	0	0	10	0
120 - 124	0	0	0	0	0	0	0	0	0	0	0	0	0	0	0	0	1	0	1	0	2	0
Total	268	120	576	194	851	198	653	94	420	33	269	20	137	5	45	1	9	0	21	0	3249	665

Apps = Number of Applicants
Adm = Number Admitted
Reflects 95% of the total applicant pool.

William Mitchell College of Law

Admissions Office
875 Summit Avenue
St. Paul, MN 55105

Phone: 612.290.6329

■ Introduction

William Mitchell College of Law is the largest law school
in Minnesota. It focuses on practical and theoretical skills
in addition to its strong traditional academic curriculum.
It is the only flexible program in the upper Midwest for
law students who choose to work full- or part-time while
pursuing a law degree. We also offer a full-time program.

Among the college's 6,500 alumni/ae are these distinguished members of the judiciary: Warren E. Burger, '31,
retired Chief Justice of the United States; Douglas K. Am-
dahl, '51, retired Chief Justice of the Minnesota Supreme
Court; Peter Popovich, '47, retired Chief Justice of the
Minnesota Supreme Court; Esther Tomljanovich, '55,
and Rosalie Wahl, '67, justices on the Minnesota Supreme Court.

The college is accredited by the ABA, is a member of
the Association of American Law Schools, and is approved by the U.S. Veterans Administration.

■ Enrollment/Student Body

➡ *327 enrolled first-year class 1993* ➡ *508 total full-time*
➡ *622 total part-time* ➡ *12% minority* ➡ *47% women*

William Mitchell is committed to correcting the historical
problem of too few minority persons in the legal profession. We work to facilitate the admission of minority
students and have minority-oriented organizations, curriculum, and academic support.

■ Faculty

➡ *35 full-time faculty* ➡ *65 part-time or adjunct*

The excellent full-time and part-time faculty bring their experience to the classroom in areas of special interest. Their
expertise is particularly valuable in the areas of instruction
relating to practical application of law such as legal writing and trial practice skills.

■ Library and Physical Facilities

➡ *200,000 volumes & equivalents* ➡ *LEXIS*
➡ *WESTLAW* ➡ *17 full-time librarians*

Our campus, located in St. Paul, Minnesota, provides
space for classrooms, seminar rooms, moot courtrooms,
the Law Clinic, library and study areas, a student lounge,
and offices for student organizations. Students also have
access to materials from other law libraries in the Twin Cities and, through the MINITEX interlibrary loan network,
to libraries throughout the United States and Canada. Students are trained to use on-line computer terminals for
legal research.

■ Curriculum

➡ *Academic Support Program*
➡ *86 credits required to graduate*

William Mitchell offers 3, 3-1/2, and 4-year programs of afternoon and evening classes leading to a J.D. degree.

Students in the full-time program take 12 to 15 hours of
classroom instruction per week over a three-year period.
Students in the four-year part-time program take a maximum of 11 hours of classroom instruction per week over
a period of four years, allowing them to work up to full-
time while attending school. The required courses and
number of electives that can be taken are the same under
all of the programs. All students must complete their degree requirements within six academic years of their
original matriculation.

The college is not committed to any single system or
method of instruction. The case method involves the
study and analysis of selected cases, as well as classroom
discussion of the rules of law established or illustrated
by the cases. The problem method, seminars, written assignments, and simulated exercises are employed in
certain courses. The use of videotapes and computers
adds another learning dimension.

The curriculum has a broad national focus, and elective
courses enable advanced students to specialize.

■ Special Programs

The William Mitchell Law Clinic results in a graduate who is
ready to immediately begin to practice law. This is distinguished from one who needs to learn how to practice. Since
its beginning in 1972, the Law Clinic has become a nationally
recognized leader in trial advocacy teaching methods and
clinical education. In 1981, the college received the prestigious Emil Gumpert Award for excellence in the teaching of
trial advocacy. Students are eligible to participate in any of a
broad range of clinical courses. The clinics are taught by full-
time professors and supervisory attorneys.

The Legal Writing Program has been singled out for
praise by the American Bar Association and the Association of American Law Schools as an excellent legal
writing program. One of the strengths of the program is
the 13 to 1 student-faculty ratio.

The Child Care Center meets the needs of our students
who must have child care available at more flexible
times than traditional child care facilities. The center is
on campus.

■ Admission

➡ *Bachelor's degree required for admission*
➡ *application deadline—May 1* ➡ *LSAT required*
➡ *application fee—$35*

Admission decisions are based upon academic factors
such as the applicant's LSAT score and undergraduate
GPA, as well as non-academic factors such as work record,

writing ability, economic or educational disadvantage, and handicap. The college does not require any particular area of undergraduate study, but does prefer applicants with strong written communication and analytical skills. William Mitchell College of Law admits students of either sex and of any race, color, religion, national or ethnic origin, and sexual preference.

■ Expenses and Financial Aid

➡ *tuition & fees—four year program, $9,340; three-year program, $12,870* ➡ *estimated additional expenses— books, $500 per year* ➡ *need-based scholarships available* ➡ *financial aid available—Stafford loans, Perkins loans, LAL, SLS, and SELF loans*

The Warren E. Burger Entrance Scholarship is awarded annually.

■ Housing

The college maintains no dormitories or housing facilities, but the college's location in an urban residential area assures students of the availability of private apartment housing. A monthly Housing Bulletin is published by the Student Service Office.

■ Career Services

William Mitchell graduates are highly employable. We attract a special kind of student: motivated, industrious, mature, and serious about a legal education. Many William Mitchell students hold full- or part-time jobs while in school and have valuable work experience to offer the employer. Also, because we combine practical skills with actual legal experience, our students have related experience to offer the employer. We provide a complete career services office with a full-time Assistant Dean and staff, on-campus interviews, a computerized résumé search service, career counseling, programs, publications, and job postings.

According to a recent survey of our graduates, 88 percent of those responding were satisfactorily employed within six to nine months after graduation; 47 percent of those were in private practice; 22 percent were in business and corporations; 24 percent were in government, including judicial clerkships; and the rest were in graduate school, teaching, or the military.

Applicant Group for the 1993–1994 Academic Year

William Mitchell College of Law
This grid includes only applicants who earned 120-180 LSAT scores under standard administrations.

LSAT Score	3.75 +		3.50 -3.74		3.25 - 3.49		3.00 - 3.24		2.75 - 2.99		2.50 - 2.74		2.25 - 2.49		2.00 - 2.24		Below 2.00		No GPA		Total	
	Apps	Adm	Apps	Adm	Apps	Adm	Apps	Adm	Apps	Adm	Apps	Adm	Apps	Adm	Apps	Adm	Apps	Adm	Apps	Adm	Apps	Adm
175 - 180	0	0	2	2	0	0	0	0	0	0	0	0	0	0	0	0	0	0	0	0	2	2
170 - 174	0	0	0	0	1	1	1	1	1	1	2	2	0	0	0	0	0	0	0	0	5	5
165 - 169	3	3	5	5	8	8	9	6	6	5	5	4	3	3	1	1	0	0	0	0	40	35
160 - 164	6	5	7	6	25	24	28	24	21	16	12	8	5	2	2	0	0	0	1	0	107	85
155 - 159	18	5	31	26	47	42	58	42	43	22	26	10	14	6	6	2	0	0	3	1	246	166
150 - 154	20	19	37	34	57	39	79	33	69	13	56	16	19	2	9	1	2	1	6	1	354	159
145 - 149	12	11	26	17	53	16	61	23	64	18	35	8	32	5	13	1	2	0	3	1	301	100
140 - 144	1	1	13	10	27	9	41	18	33	7	31	5	29	6	17	0	4	0	4	2	200	58
135 - 139	1	0	3	2	3	1	17	4	17	1	21	5	7	0	5	0	1	0	2	0	77	13
130 - 134	0	0	1	0	3	0	3	0	4	0	7	0	8	0	3	0	1	0	1	0	31	0
125 - 129	0	0	0	0	0	0	2	0	0	0	2	0	2	0	1	0	0	0	0	0	7	0
120 - 124	0	0	0	0	0	0	0	0	0	0	0	0	0	0	0	0	0	0	0	0	0	0
Total	61	54	125	102	224	140	299	151	258	83	197	58	119	24	57	5	10	1	20	5	1370	623

Apps = Number of Applicants
Adm = Number Admitted
Reflects 94% of the total applicant pool.

University of Wisconsin Law School

975 Bascom Mall
Madison, WI 53706

Phone: 608.262.5914

■ Introduction

The University of Wisconsin Law School is a part of one of the world's largest, most honored, and most diversified universities. In Madison, a particularly interesting and livable city of just under 200,000, the school is located in the center of the main campus, close to downtown and the state capital. The school pioneered the belief that the law must be studied in action, as it relates to society, not as a self-contained system. Close connections with other departments and facilities of the university and research and service projects with state and federal governments have given concrete meaning to this law-in-action emphasis and have enriched the school's whole program. The school has a national reputation, is a charter member of the AALS, and is ABA-approved.

■ Enrollment/Student Body

➡ 2,735 applicants   ➡ 698 admitted first-year class 1993
➡ 285 enrolled first-year class 1993   ➡ 869 total full-time
➡ 50 total part-time   ➡ 16% minority   ➡ 44% women
➡ 26 states & foreign countries represented in first-year class
➡ 111 undergraduate schools represented in first-year class
➡ loss of first-year students due to academic failure runs less than 2%

■ Faculty

➡ 47 total, all full-time   ➡ 9 women   ➡ 7 minority

■ Library and Physical Facilities

➡ 400,000 volumes & equivalents   ➡ library hours: Mon.-Thur., 7:45 A.M.-MIDNIGHT; Fri., 7:45 A.M.-11:00 P.M.; Sat., 9:00 A.M.-9:00 P.M.; Sun., 9:00 A.M.-MIDNIGHT   ➡ LEXIS
➡ NEXIS   ➡ WESTLAW   ➡ DIALOG
➡ 10+ full-time librarians   ➡ library seats 550

The library's print collections are strong in all areas of US state and federal law, international law, and the law of select foreign jurisdictions and support research and document requests from practitioners and legal scholars throughout the world. These print collections are complemented with distributed access to online legal information from virtually anywhere in the library through a combination of LANs, computer labs, and an innovative computer lap-top check-out program. Additionally, the library's online catalog ties into a campus rich in library resources, including the 5 million volumes located in the nearby main campus library and Historical Society Library.

■ Curriculum

➡ Academic Support Program   ➡ 90 credits required to graduate   ➡ semesters, start in Aug.
➡ range of first-year class size—20-89

The first semester runs from late August to shortly before Christmas; the second, from January to May. A total of 13 weeks of summer school is available each year, making it possible for a student to complete credit and residence requirements in roughly two years. Summer school is available for advanced students only, including students in good standing at other law schools. The first-year curriculum consists of required courses plus one limited elective choice. A broad selection of elective courses and seminars is available in the second and third years. Students who wish admission to the state bar of Wisconsin without bar examination must elect some advanced courses in traditional areas. In addition to the J.D., research-oriented LL.M. and S.J.D. programs are available on an individual basis. There are formalized joint-degree programs in: Law and Public Administration; Law and Library and Information Services; Law and Ibero-American Studies, Law and Environmental Studies; Law and Business Masters Degree, Ph.D. in Philosophy, and Ph.D. in Sociology.

■ Special Programs

Eight clinical programs provide a variety of opportunities including public-interest work, administrative and environmental law practices, judicial clerkships, legal services to institutionalized persons, representation of indigent defendants, and advocacy for disadvantaged persons.

■ Admission

➡ Bachelor's degree from accredited college or university required   ➡ application deadline—Feb. 1
➡ LSAT, LSDAS required   ➡ median GPA—3.40
➡ median LSAT score—161   ➡ application fee—$35

The Law School has no specific undergraduate course prerequisites and agrees with the suggestions in the introduction of this handbook. Although most students attend on a full-time basis, part-time attendance opportunities are available to those admitted students who cannot or do not wish to attend full-time. It is faculty policy to encourage women and members of minority and disadvantaged groups to apply for admission. An active program for recruitment, admission, and financial aid for minority and disadvantaged students is important to the school. Applications are available the October preceding admission. Written recommendations are welcomed but not required; interviews are not part of the admissions process. A carefully prepared personal statement reflecting consideration of our admissions criteria is often very helpful to the Admissions Committee. An application deadline of February 1 is enforced. No statement of intention to enroll is required until after April 1. College grades and LSAT score are significant, but many other factors are considered. Large numbers of applications from highly qualified Wisconsin residents have forced Wisconsin's only state-supported law school to reserve approximately 70 to 80 percent of the available places for Wisconsin residents, with the result that criteria are somewhat higher for non-residents. In recent years, the Law School has been able eventually to offer acceptance to about one of every three Wisconsin residents who apply and about one of every seven nonresidents.

Transfer applications may be made, but only students with excellent law school records can be accepted. The deadline for transfer applicants for fall admission is June 1, but a decision cannot be expected until the full year's law school record is available.

■ Student Activities

In addition to the myriad of university activities, there are many activities especially for law students. The *Wisconsin Law Review*, edited by students, devotes substantial space to national and international problems and Wisconsin law. Written by both professionals in the field and law students, the student-edited *Wisconsin International Law Journal*, *Women's Law Journal*, and *Multi-Cultural Law Journal* offer articles of scholarly and practical interest in various areas of law. The Student Bar Association operates a bookstore, sponsors activities, and nominates students for such student/faculty committees as curriculum, tenure, and admissions.

■ Expenses and Financial Aid

➡ *full-time tuition and fees—residents, $4,348; nonresidents, $11,334*

Scholarship grants are awarded to students on the basis of need, as determined through application to the Campus Office of Student Financial Services. Scholarship money is limited, and will not meet the student's total needs. Entering students must apply for financial aid no later than March 1, and, therefore, should not wait until acceptance to apply. The Law School participates in Free Application for Federal Student Aid and will not accept GAPSFAS applications. Loan funds from government and private sources to law students in 1993-94 amounted to approximately $4,500,000. The Law School has an emergency short-term loan fund available for qualified students.

■ Career Services

The school operates a full-time Career Services Office to assist students and alumni seeking summer, part-time, or permanent employment. Most graduates have found employment within a few months of graduation. About 65 percent remain in Wisconsin. About 60 percent of the graduates enter private practice, and 20 percent enter government service. The average annual starting salary for the class of 1992 was over $41,500.

Applicant Group for the 1993–1994 Academic Year

University of Wisconsin Law School
This grid includes only applicants who earned 120-180 LSAT scores under standard administrations.

LSAT Score	3.75 +		3.50 -3.74		3.25 - 3.49		3.00 - 3.24		2.75 - 2.99		2.50 - 2.74		2.25 - 2.49		2.00 - 2.24		Below 2.00		No GPA		Total	
	Apps	Adm	Apps	Adm	Apps	Adm	Apps	Adm	Apps	Adm	Apps	Adm	Apps	Adm	Apps	Adm	Apps	Adm	Apps	Adm	Apps	Adm
175-180	1	1	3	3	1	1	3	2	1	1	0	0	0	0	0	0	0	0	0	0	9	8
170-174	8	8	17	17	15	15	9	7	4	1	3	2	2	1	0	0	0	0	1	1	59	52
165-169	33	32	61	58	52	44	37	25	22	10	16	6	4	0	1	0	0	0	1	1	227	176
160-164	65	56	131	82	161	63	111	31	48	11	32	3	9	1	3	0	0	0	4	2	564	249
155-159	55	17	152	28	171	25	126	6	76	7	36	3	11	1	4	1	0	0	8	3	639	91
150-154	32	4	90	13	103	4	99	10	76	10	45	5	24	3	6	0	1	0	8	1	484	50
145-149	14	2	33	4	53	6	64	11	56	5	40	1	17	1	6	1	2	0	9	0	294	31
140-144	5	1	16	0	27	2	40	1	45	1	31	2	24	0	8	0	1	0	10	0	207	7
135-139	2	0	3	0	9	0	10	0	16	0	12	0	13	0	2	0	1	0	2	0	70	0
130-134	0	0	2	0	0	0	1	0	1	0	4	0	4	0	8	0	2	0	5	0	27	0
125-129	0	0	0	0	0	0	2	0	0	0	0	0	2	0	0	0	1	0	0	0	5	0
120-124	0	0	0	0	0	0	0	0	0	0	0	0	1	0	1	0	1	0	0	0	3	0
Total	215	121	508	205	592	160	502	93	345	46	219	22	111	7	39	2	9	0	48	8	2588	664

Apps = Number of Applicants
Adm = Number Admitted
Reflects 95% of the total applicant pool.

University of Wyoming College of Law

Post Office Box 3035
Laramie, WY 82071-3035

Phone: 307.766.6416

■ Introduction

The College of Law is located on the campus of the University of Wyoming in Laramie. The university, the only four-year institution of higher learning in Wyoming, comprises eight colleges, a graduate school, and several organized research units. The university has a student body of 10,000 in Laramie.

The College of Law, founded in 1920, is a member of the AALS and is accredited by the ABA. The college has approximately 220 students, a faculty of 14 full-time teachers, and several lecturers. The small student body and the excellent student-to-faculty ratio make possible a congenial atmosphere and a great amount of informal communication between students and faculty.

Laramie is a town of 25,000 located in the southeastern part of Wyoming at an altitude of 7,200 feet, on the high plains between two mountain ranges. Laramie's proximity to the mountains provides a variety of recreational activities including skiing, backpacking, rock climbing, hiking, camping, fishing, and hunting.

■ Enrollment/Student Body

- ➥ 829 applicants ➥ 188 admitted first-year class 1993
- ➥ 79 enrolled first-year class 1993 ➥ 222 total full-time
- ➥ 6% minority ➥ 45% women
- ➥ 28 states & foreign countries represented
- ➥ 70 undergraduate schools represented

■ Faculty

- ➥ 17 total ➥ 14 full-time ➥ 3 part-time or adjunct
- ➥ 5 women

■ Library and Physical Facilities

- ➥ 174,000 volumes & equivalents ➥ library hours: Mon.-Thurs., 7:30 A.M.-11:00 P.M.; Fri., 7:30 A.M.-6:00 P.M.; Sat., 9:00 A.M.-5:00 P.M.; Sun., 10:00 A.M.-11:00 P.M. ➥ LEXIS
- ➥ NEXIS ➥ WESTLAW ➥ INFOTRAC
- ➥ 3 full-time librarians ➥ library seats 181

The College of Law first occupied its new building in 1977. The facility provides ample classroom, library, and student study space, and furnishes a pleasant environment for study. A new three-story library addition was completed in the fall of 1993. This addition doubled the existing square footage of the law library. All law students are trained in computerized legal research, as well as in traditional research methods.

■ Curriculum

- ➥ Academic Support Program ➥ 88 credits required to graduate ➥ 60 courses available ➥ degrees available: J.D.; J.D./M.B.A.; J.D./M.P.A. ➥ semesters, start in Aug.
- ➥ range of first-year class size—20-80

The first year consists entirely of required courses. During the second year, students must take additional required courses including evidence, professional responsibility, and a second semester of constitutional law and civil procedure. Students must also complete an advanced writing requirement prior to graduation. As a condition of graduation from the College of Law, all students must successfully complete at least two of the following three courses: administrative law; business organizations; and trusts and estates. In addition, all students must successfully complete at least one of the following three courses: creditors' rights, income taxation, or secured transactions.

In both the second and third years, practical legal training is available through courses in legal research, legal skills and problems, trial practice, and clinical work. The college has no summer session; however, graduation may be accelerated one semester by summer work at other accredited law schools.

■ Special Programs

The College of Law has a strong program of elective courses in natural resources law. Courses are regularly offered in environmental law, hazardous waste and water pollution, oil and gas, mining law, public land resources, water rights, and mineral taxation. Other electives include coverage of trial and appellate practice, corporate taxation, estate planning, corporate and commercial law, administrative and regulatory law, consumer law, and Indian law.

Students may obtain practical experience and receive academic credit for work in three clinical programs: (1) a defender aid program in which students brief and argue criminal appeals on behalf of indigent persons and assist penitentiary inmates in postconviction cases; (2) a prosecution assistance program in which students work directly with prosecuting attorneys and the United States Attorney in criminal cases; and, (3) a legal services program in which students provide legal assistance to economically disadvantaged persons. All clinical programs operate under faculty supervision.

■ Admission Standards

- ➥ Bachelor's degree from accredited college or university
- ➥ application deadline—April 1
- ➥ early application preferred ➥ early review of applications begins in late February ➥ LSAT, LSDAS required
- ➥ median GPA—3.40 ➥ median LSAT score—157
- ➥ application fee—$35

The College of Law restricts the entering class to 80. Approximately 55 of these students are Wyoming residents, and 25 are nonresidents. In recent years, about 85 percent of the entering class have successfully completed law study and received the J.D. degree. The school does not discriminate on the basis of race, sex, or age in making admissions decisions.

Students are admitted only for the fall semester. The college begins to accept applications in October for the class entering the following August. The entering class is selected from applications completed and on file by April 1. Applications are accepted after April 1, but only to fill vacancies that occur in the class initially selected. To meet the April 1 deadline, applicants should take the LSAT no later than February and should subscribe to LSDAS and arrange for forwarding of official transcripts no later than mid-January.

As a general rule, applicants must have received an undergraduate degree prior to registration. In very exceptional cases, a candidate without an undergraduate degree who possesses extraordinary experience and training may be admitted.

Written recommendations are not required. Selection of the entering class is based primarily on LSAT score and undergraduate grade-point average. As a limited number of places are assigned to nonresidents, out-of-state applicants who do not have a 3.25 grade average on a 4.0 scale and an LSAT score in the 67th percentile have little chance of serious consideration. However, a lower grade-point average or LSAT score may be offset by a higher LSAT score or grade average.

■ Student Activities

The College of Law publishes the *Land and Water Law Review*, a student-edited journal devoted to legal problems of natural resources, environmental issues, questions of Wyoming jurisprudence, and legal topics of general interest.

Student professional organizations include Potter Law Club, which provides student government and social activities and affiliation with the Law Student Division of the ABA, three legal fraternities, Christian Legal Society,

Hispanic Bar Association, Minority Law Student Association, Natural Resources Law Forum, Women's Law Forum, and the Wyoming Trial Lawyers Association. Students represent the college each year in the National Moot Court Competition, National Environmental Law Moot Court Competition, National Client Counseling Competition, ATLA National Student Trial Advocacy Competition, and the Natural Resources Law Moot Court Competition. Student organizations include two law school honoraries: the Order of the Coif, and the Order of the Barrister.

■ Expenses and Financial Aid

➤ *tuition & fees—resident, $3,328; nonresident, $7,396*
➤ *estimated additional expenses—$6,500 (room, board, books)* ➤ *academic and need-based scholarships available*
➤ *Minority Graduate Assistantship Program*
➤ *financial aid available, FAF form for need analysis due to College Board in Jan. or early Feb.*
➤ *College of Law Scholarship Application due June 1*

■ Career Services

The placement service, under the direction of the Career Services Director, coordinates job placement for law students and recent graduates who seek permanent or summer employment; disseminates information to potential employers; collects résumés and employer information; and arranges interviews and conferences. Advice is given on the various opportunities for legal employment, résumé preparation, job interview dynamics, and techniques for obtaining employment.

Applicant Group for the 1993–1994 Academic Year

University of Wyoming College of Law
This grid includes only applicants who earned 120-180 LSAT scores under standard administrations in the 1992-93 testing year.

LSAT Score	3.75 +		3.50 - 3.74		3.25 - 3.49		3.00 - 3.24		2.75 - 2.99		2.50 - 2.74		2.25 - 2.49		2.00 - 2.24		No GPA		Total	
	Apps	Adm	Apps	Adm	Apps	Adm	Apps	Adm	Apps	Adm	Apps	Adm	Apps	Adm	Apps	Adm	Apps	Adm	Apps	Adm
175 - 180	0	0	0	0	0	0	0	0	0	0	0	0	0	0	0	0	0	0	0	0
170 - 174	1	1	1	1	0	0	1	1	1	1	0	0	0	0	0	0	0	0	4	4
165 - 169	0	0	3	2	1	1	3	3	3	3	5	4	1	0	0	0	0	0	16	13
160 - 164	4	4	8	8	14	13	19	11	10	5	4	1	6	0	1	0	1	1	67	43
155 - 159	8	8	17	17	37	23	48	15	39	4	23	4	15	4	0	0	2	0	189	75
150 - 154	5	4	30	14	31	2	59	4	31	3	28	0	21	0	3	0	3	0	211	27
145 - 149	2	0	19	4	26	0	39	3	30	2	19	1	13	0	3	0	5	0	156	10
140 - 144	0	0	8	0	5	0	10	0	18	0	13	0	8	0	1	0	1	0	64	0
135 - 139	0	0	0	0	1	1	5	1	10	0	6	0	4	0	0	0	4	0	30	2
130 - 134	0	0	0	0	0	0	0	0	1	0	1	0	0	0	0	0	0	0	2	0
120 - 129	0	0	0	0	0	0	0	0	1	0	1	0	0	0	0	0	0	0	2	0
Total	20	17	86	46	115	40	184	38	144	18	100	10	68	4	8	0	16	1	741	174

Apps = Number of Applicants
Adm = Number Admitted
Reflects 90% of the total applicant pool.

Yale Law School

P.O. Box 208215
New Haven, CT 06520-8215

■ Introduction

Yale Law School is an extraordinary community in which to study law. Our unmatched faculty-to-student ratio allows us to offer a vast array of courses, an average class size of under 20 students, and countless opportunities for independent research, writing, and student-organized seminars. Easy student-faculty interaction and institutional flexibility are hallmarks of the school. Law students have access to scholars in all of Yale's departments, to the university's nine-million-volume library system, and to its cultural, social, intellectual, and athletic activities. At the same time, Yale Law School has ties to the city of New Haven, a small, lively urban center with the attractions and problems of an American city. New Haven has two of the finest repertory theaters in the country, commercial theaters that bring in touring shows and performers, several first-rate museums, and the best pizza in America. Students are involved with New Haven's less prosperous side through the legal services organization.

■ Enrollment/Student Body

➥ 4,947 applicants   ➥ 342 admitted first-year class 1993 (including previously deferred)
➥ 181 enrolled first-year class of 1993
➥ 612 total full-time   ➥ 25% minority   ➥ 43% women
➥ 68 states & foreign countries represented (1992-1993)
➥ 189 undergraduate schools represented (1992-1993)

The vitality of Yale Law School depends as much on the knowledge, experience, and expertise of the students as it does on the faculty, the library, the university, or the alumni. The school selects its students from applicants with the highest academic qualifications in the country; within this group, it seeks diversity of background and experience. Most of the international students in the school are enrolled in the LL.M program. The Law School welcomes older students and students with disabilities.

■ Faculty

➥ 100 total   ➥ 46 full-time   ➥ 54 part-time or adjunct
➥ 9 women full-time   ➥ 6 minority full-time

The law school faculty is as broad-ranging in its interests and expertise as it is distinguished. It includes prominent scholars of economics, philosophy, and psychoanalysis, as well as leading specialists in every area of law. Approximately 50 full-time professors are joined each year by visiting lecturers, adjunct professors from other parts of the university, and practicing lawyers who assist the full-time clinical faculty as tutors in the clinical program. In addition, dozens of guest lecturers from around the world help to make Yale Law School a vibrant intellectual community.

■ Library and Physical Facilities

➥ 850,000 volumes & equivalents   ➥ library hours: 24 hours a day, 7 days a week during academic year
➥ LEXIS   ➥ NEXIS   ➥ WESTLAW   ➥ DIALOG
➥ 16 full-time librarians   ➥ library seats 380

The Sterling Law Buildings occupy one city block at the heart of Yale University and close to downtown New Haven. Constructed in 1929-31, they were modeled on the idea of the English Inns of Court. Classrooms, offices, the law library and the international law library, two student computer labs, dormitory rooms for about 150 law students, a day-care center, and the dining hall surround a pleasant courtyard.

■ Curriculum

➥ 82 credits required to graduate   ➥ 146 courses available
➥ degrees available: J.D./M.P.A.; M.S.L.; LL.M.; J.S.D.; J.D.; J.D./M.P.P.M.; J.D./M.A.; J.D./P.H.D.; J.D./M.D.; J.D./M.E.S.; J.D./M.F.S.; J.D./M.DIV.   ➥ semesters, start in Aug.   ➥ range of first-year class size—15-90

In the fall semester, all first-year students take classes in constitutional law, contracts, procedure, and torts. After the first term, the only required course is criminal law. A supervised analytic paper, a substantial paper, and attendance at a series of lectures on professional responsibility are also required. For the first term, all grades are credit/fail. After that, grades are honors, pass, low pass, and fail, with credit/fail options.

■ Special Programs

Yale Law School sees the study of law as interrelated with other intellectual disciplines and with practical experience. The Law School encourages special programs, including joint-degree opportunities with many other departments at Yale and with some other universities, intensive semester experiences outside the law school, work with state legislative committees drafting legislation and preparing reports, and work with local organizations such as schools, human rights, and civil rights agencies under the aegis of student-run programs.

■ Transfer Students and Advanced Degrees

Yale Law School welcomes applications for transfer. Students who wish to transfer may be granted residence and academic credit for up to two semesters of study. Transfer students must do at least two years of work at Yale Law School.

In addition to the J.D., Yale Law School offers an LL.M degree, for those who are interested in teaching law. The Master of Studies in Law degree (M.S.L.) is a one-year program designed for professionals in other fields who desire an intensive introduction to the law.

■ Admission

➥ *Bachelor's degree from accredited college or university required*
➥ *application deadline—Feb. 15*
➥ *LSAT, LSDAS required*   ➥ *median GPA—3.82*
➥ *median LSAT score—171*   ➥ *application fee—$60*

The admissions process at Yale Law School is an intensely competitive one in which the totality of available information about the applicant is taken into account. No one element is decisive. The competition is stiff; nevertheless, we encourage all those who desire to be a part of the Yale Law School community to submit applications. Each application file is first read by the Dean or Director of Admissions. A group of the most highly rated files is then considered by faculty file readers. On the basis of the faculty ratings we admit candidates and establish a waiting list. Use of the waiting list varies from year to year; the list is not ranked until offers are to be made from the list. A number of waiting-list candidates are held for consideration through registration day. Faculty file readers' ratings are based on their own criteria, and the relative weight to be given to experience versus academic achievement is within each file reader's discretion. A 250-word essay, on a subject of your choice, is required. Personal statements of any length are welcome. Two letters of recommendation are required; additional letters are welcome. The Law School begins to issue decisions in late February. Minority applicants are evaluated in the same fashion as and along with nonminority applicants. Applicants are encouraged to bring to our attention aspects of their personal background and other special characteristics that they believe to be pertinent.

■ Student Activities

Yale Law students are very active outside the classroom. In any given year, as many as 40-50 student organizations may be active. Included in that group are seven student-run journals.

■ Expenses and Financial Aid

➥ *$19,780 full-time tuition & fees*
➥ *average amount of additional expenses—$9,880 (room & board, books, and personal expenses)*
➥ *need-based scholarships available for all eligible students*
➥ *financial aid available*   ➥ *Loan Forgiveness Program (COAP)*   ➥ *GAPSFAS form required*   ➥ *FAFSA required*

Financial aid is awarded solely on the basis of need. Admissions decisions are made before and independently of financial aid decisions. Approximately 70 percent of the student body now receives some form of financial assistance; about 40 percent receive loans only. A financial aid award consists of a portion in gift and a portion in loan; typically the higher the total financial need, the higher the proportion of gift.

■ Career Services

Yale Law School graduates occupy positions of leadership in a tremendous range of endeavors. The Career Development Office, staffed by five full-time employees and one part-time public interest counselor, helps students explore the unparalleled diversity of opportunities they face.

Applicant Group for the 1993–1994 Academic Year

Yale Law School

Undergraduate GPA	Average LSAT Score on the 120 - 180* Scale													
	Below 154		155 - 159		160 -164		165 -169		170 - 174		175 - 180		Total	
	Apps	Adm	Apps	Adm	Apps	Adm	Apps	Adm	Apps	Adm	Apps	Adm	Apps	Adm
3.75+	77	1	126	3	315	16	397	42	249	98	116	63	1280	222
3.50 - 3.74	157	0	195	3	328	14	395	17	205	21	69	9	1349	64
3.25 - 3.49	194	0	135	0	220	3	208	2	88	2	33	1	878	8
3.00 - 3.24	145	0	59	0	91	0	93	1	50	0	18	1	456	2
Below 3.00	297	0	73	0	51	0	38	0	17	0	4	0	480	0
No GPA	70	0	19	1	11	0	12	1	8	0	2	2	122	5
Total	940	1	607	7	1016	33	1143	63	617	121	242	76	4565	301*

Apps = Number of Applicants
Adm = Number Admitted
*Because only applicants with scores on the 120-180 scale are included above, the grid includes only 92% of applicants and 88% of admitted applicants. Total applicants for the fall of 1993 were 4948; total admitted applicants, 342.

Appendix A: Canadian Member Law Schools

University of Alberta
Faculty of Law
Edmonton, Alberta
CANADA T6G 2H5

University of British Columbia
Faculty of Law
1822 East Mall
Vancouver, British Columbia
CANADA V6T 1Z1

University of Calgary
Faculty of Law
Calgary, Alberta
CANADA T2N 1N4

Dalhousie Law School
6061 University Avenue
Halifax, Nova Scotia
CANADA B3H 4H9

University of Manitoba
Faculty of Law
Winnipeg, Manitoba
CANADA R3T 2N2

McGill University
Faculty of Law
3644 Peel
Montreal, Quebec
CANADA H3A 1W9

University of New Brunswick
Faculty of Law
P.O. Box 4400
Fredericton, New Brunswick
CANADA E3B 5A3

University of Ottawa
Faculty of Law
57 Louis Pasteur
P.O. Box 450
Station A
Ottawa, Ontario
CANADA K1N 6N5

Queen's University
Faculty of Law
Kingston, Ontario
CANADA K7L 3N6

University of Saskatchewan
College of Law
Saskatoon, Saskatchewan
CANADA S7N 0W0

University of Toronto
Faculty of Law
78 Queen's Park
Toronto, Ontario
CANADA M5S 2C5

University of Victoria
Faculty of Law
P.O. Box 2400
Victoria, British Columbia
CANADA V8W 3H7

University of Western Ontario
Faculty of Law
London, Ontario
CANADA N6A 3K7

University of Windsor
Faculty of Law
Windsor, Ontario
CANADA N9B 3P4

York University
Osgoode Hall Law School
4700 Keele Street
North York, Ontario
CANADA M3J 1P3

Appendix B: U.S. Law Schools Not Approved by the ABA

Alabama

Jones School of Law
5345 Atlanta Highway
Montgomery, AL 36109

California

American College of Law
401 South Brea Boulevard
Brea, CA 92621

CAL Northern School of Law
2525 Dominic Drive
Chico, CA 95928

California Pacific School of Law
1600 Truxton Avenue
Suite 100
Bakersfield, CA 93301

California Southern Law School
3775 Elizabeth Street
Riverside, CA 92506

Central California College
School of Law
925 "N" Street #110
Fresno, CA 93721

Empire College
3033 Cleveland Avenue
Suite 102
Santa Rosa, CA 95401-2185

Glendale University
College of Law
220 North Glendale Avenue
Glendale, CA 91206

Humphreys College of Law
6650 Inglewood Avenue
Stockton, CA 95207

John F. Kennedy University
School of Law
547 Ygnacio Valley Road
Walnut Creek, CA 94596

University of LaVerne
College of Law

Encino Campus
5445 Balboa Boulevard
Encino, CA 91316

University of LaVerne
College of Law
1950 3rd Street
LaVerne, CA 91750

Lincoln Law School of Sacramento
3140 J Street
Box 160328
Sacramento, CA 95816

Lincoln University
The Law School
2160 Lundy Avenue
San Jose, CA 95131

Monterey College of Law
498 Pearl Street
Monterey, CA 93940

New College of California
Law School
50 Fell Street
San Francisco, CA 94102

University of Northern California
Lorenzo Patino School of Law
816 H Street, Suite 108
Sacramento, CA 95814

Oakland College of Law
436 14th Street
Suite 411
Oakland, CA 94612-2703

Peninsula University
Law School
436 Dell Avenue
Mountain View, CA 94043

San Francisco Law School
20 Haight Street
San Francisco, CA 94102

San Joaquin College of Law
3385 East Shields Avenue
Fresno, CA 93726

Santa Barbara College of Law
911 Tremonto Road
Santa Barbara, CA 93103

Simon Greenleaf School of Law
3855 East LaPalma Avenue
Anaheim, CA 92807

Southern California
College of Law
595 West Lambert Road
Brea, CA 92621

Ventura College of Law
4475 Market Street
Ventura, CA 93003

University of West Los Angeles
12201 Washington Place
Los Angeles, CA 90066

Western State University—Irvine
16485 Laguna Canyon Road
Irvine, CA 92718

Western State University—Fullerton
College of Law
1111 North State College Boulevard
Fullerton, CA 92631

Western State University—San Diego
College of Law
2121 San Diego Avenue
San Diego, CA 92110

Massachusetts

Massachusetts School of Law
500 Federal Street
Andover, MA 01810

Southern New England School of Law
874 Purchase Street
New Bedford, MA 02740

Rhode Island

Roger Williams University
School of Law
One Old Ferry Road
Bristol, RI 02809

Appendix C: LSAC Statement of Good Admission Practices

Introduction

This Statement of Good Admission Practices is designed to focus attention on principles that should guide law school admission programs. No attempt has been made to develop "legislative" guidelines, because no absolute rules apply to every situation. The statement is intended to improve the admission process in law schools and to promote fairness for all participants.

General Principles

1. The primary purpose of the law school admission process is to serve law school applicants, law schools, and the legal profession by making informed judgments about those who seek legal education. The responsibility that role carries with it demands the highest standards of professional conduct.

2. Law school admission professionals should avoid impropriety and the appearance of impropriety, as well as any conflict of interest or the appearance of conflict. They should not accept anything for themselves or the law school or pursue any activity that might compromise or seem to compromise their integrity or that of the admission process.

3. Law schools should strive to achieve and maintain the highest standards of accuracy and candor in the development and publication of print and other materials designed to inform or influence applicants. A law school should provide any applicant or potential applicant with information and data that will enable the applicant to assess his or her prospects for successfully (1) seeking admission to that school, (2) financing his or her education at that school, (3) completing the educational program at that school, and (4) seeking employment with degree from that school. If statistics are provided regarding admissions, financial aid, and placement, law schools should provide the most current information and should present it in an easily understood form. Significant errors of fact, as well as errors of omission, should be corrected promptly and prominently.

4. Law schools should establish application procedures that inform applicants of relevant criteria, processes, and deadlines, respect the confidentiality of student records and admission data, and provide for timely notification of admission decisions. Law schools should also ensure that all parties concerned with the admission process are familiar with and observe relevant laws, accreditation standards, and institutional guidelines, including the *Cautionary Policies Concerning LSAT Scores and Related Services* developed by Law School Admission Council/Law School Admission Services (Law Services).

5. In making admission decisions, law schools should give special consideration to applicants who are members of cultural, ethnic, or racial groups that have not had adequate opportunities to develop and demonstrate potential for academic achievement and would not otherwise be meaningfully represented in the entering class. Schools should also make reasonable accommodations to the special needs of disabled applicants. Law schools should make a special effort to provide the information noted in Number 3 above to those applicants who are members of minority groups or who are disabled.

Admission Policy

1. Law schools should develop coherent and consistent admission policies. The admission policies should serve law school applicants by clearly setting forth the criteria on which admission decisions are made and the manner in which the criteria will be applied.

Law schools should develop and promulgate concise and coherent admission policies designed both to regularize the admission process and to inform fully prospective applicants and prelaw advisors of the means used to select new law students. The policies should include consideration of the various criteria and processes used to make admission decisions, such as the Law School Admission Test (LSAT), prior academic performance, professional and other work experiences, equal opportunity considerations, disabled status, geographical diversity, letters of recommendation, personal statements, and personal interviews, if required. These and other considerations related to a law school's institutional mission or objectives may result in a preference for certain applicants. Each law school's admission policies should be adequately disclosed to all prospective applicants at the outset of the admission process.

Scores obtained on the LSAT and undergraduate grade point averages are factors by which applicants are judged by virtually all law schools. Law schools should ensure that all application materials accurately describe the manner in which LSAT scores, prior academic performance, and other factors are used in the admission process.

The LSAT is designed to measure some, but certainly not all, of the mental and academic abilities that are needed for successful law study. Within limits, it provides a reasonable assessment of these factors. LSAT scores provide at best a partial measure of an applicant's ability and should be considered in relation to the total range of information available about a prospective law student. Thus, the LSAT score should be used as only one of several criteria for evaluation and should not be given undue weight.

Use of cut-off LSAT scores below which no candidate will be considered is explicitly discouraged in the Law Services Cautionary Policies. However, a particular law school may discover evidence that applicants scoring below a certain point have substantial difficulty in performing satisfactorily in its program of studies. Based on that evidence, the law school may rationally choose to implement a policy of discouraging applications with LSAT scores below a certain point. Should a law school make that determination, applicants should be informed of that fact.

Similar considerations govern the evaluation of the applicant's prior academic record. Undergraduate grades are a significant indicator of potential success in law school. In addition to being one measure of academic ability, a strong scholastic record may indicate perseverance, organization, and motivation, all important factors which have few direct measures. There are, of course, measures of intellectual ability other than the cumulative grade point average. Unusual creativity, exceptional research skills, analytical prowess, and other factors may not be reflected on a candidate's college transcript.

In evaluating the academic record, law schools may choose to consider factors such as grade inflation, the age of the grades, discrepancies among the applicant's grades, the quality of the college attended, difficulty of course work, and time commitments while attending college.

Law schools may also take into consideration additional factors when choosing among various law school candidates. Letters of recommendation often have a significant impact on admission decisions. Some schools believe that letters of recommendation are usually more candid when the subject of the letter waives access to them and recommend that applicants limit their rights to inspect this portion of their admission files. However, waiver of access to letters of recommendation or of any part of the student's record should not be made a mandatory prerequisite to admission. The Buckley Amendment specifically mandates that U.S. law schools must not require such a waiver.

As with members of cultural, ethnic, and racial groups, law schools should also recognize the importance of providing equal educational opportunity for disabled individuals. Sometimes the applicant's disability may prevent the assembly of a complete admission file. For example, some applicants can take the LSAT only under special conditions, making it difficult to interpret their test scores. Others may seek to have certain admission requirements waived entirely. In these circumstances, law schools can properly give weight to the disabled applicant's demonstrated ability to overcome obstacles in building a record of academic and professional performance.

Admission of applicants from a wide variety of academic, cultural, ethnic, and racial backgrounds, and the resulting diversity, enhances and enriches the educational experience of all students and faculty.

It is proper to prefer students who have taken courses such as those that develop skills in both written and oral communications, develop analytical and problem-solving skills, or promote familiarity with the humanities and social sciences to understand the human condition and the social context in which legal problems arise. The decision to prefer either a classical liberal arts education or a more narrowly focused one should rest within the sound discretion of the law school.

2. Law schools that accept transfer applications should state clearly the application procedures for transfer applicants and inform them of all relevant deadlines, necessary documents and records, courses accepted for credit, and, to the extent possible, course equivalency.

Recruitment and Promotion

1. Law schools are responsible for all people they involve in admission, promotional, and recruitment activities (including graduates, students, and faculty), and for educating them about the principles of good practice outlined in this Statement, as well as all relevant laws, accreditation standards, and institutional policies. Law schools that use admission management firms or consulting firms are responsible for assuring that these firms adhere to sound admission practices.

The oversight role entrusted to law schools includes supervision of all personnel involved in the admission process. Law school personnel, students, and graduates who represent the law school at recruitment and other promotional activities should be informed of current law school programs and activities. They should be knowledgeable about the academic and financial requirements of attending the law school, and they should honestly and forthrightly respond to inquiries.

Professional recruiting organizations, though not formally affiliated with law schools, nonetheless are part of the admission process when they are engaged by law schools. Law schools engaging outside services are responsible for ensuring the integrity and the accuracy of the work performed for them. For example, errors or misleading statements appearing in recruitment brochures and law school catalogs may not be ascribed to the company performing the service. Law schools cannot abdicate the responsibility for accuracy by shifting blame to third parties.

2. Admissions publications should contain an accurate and current admission calendar and information about financial aid opportunities and requirements.

In addition to containing a complete listing of all relevant admission and financial aid deadlines, admission material should also convey accurate information about optimum dates, if any, for submitting admission materials. Among the items that might usefully be included are: dates for taking the Law School Admission Test; dates for submission of financial aid applications, including the best time for submission of materials to a financial aid need analysis service, if used; and the most useful date for submission of letters of recommendation. This information is particularly useful when law schools begin to make admission decisions prior to the deadline date for receipt of application materials under a "rolling" admission system.

Law schools should notify applicants about deadlines for financial aid applications and the criteria used in awarding aid. To the extent reasonably practicable, law schools should disclose how parental income will affect the financial aid determination. Similarly, the availability of need-based and of merit-based aid should be disclosed.

3. Law school admission professionals should be forthright and accurate in providing information about their institutions. Law school publications and any statements submitted for publication should contain current and accurate descriptions and representations of law school programs, campus life, and the surrounding community. Law schools should provide accurate, candid, and comprehensive information with respect to the law school opportunities sought by students and available to them.

Law school recruitment activities, e.g., law school forums, prelaw days, caravans, and law school fairs, provide an opportunity for law school representatives to engage in personal contact with applicants. In many instances, these activities are not only the first, but often the only direct contact applicants have with law schools until registration. In all of these instances, law school representatives should conduct themselves in a professional manner. Representatives attending these activities have an obligation to familiarize themselves with all aspects of the admission process at their respective schools. Recruitment activities should not include unreasonable and unfounded comparisons with other law schools.

4. Law schools should provide prelaw advisors and other educational and career counselors with accurate and appropriate information to assist them in counseling applicants about law school opportunities.

Issues of law school recruitment and enrollment require the cooperative efforts of college and university personnel working with law school admission counselors. Prelaw colleagues and other college counselors daily encounter students who are or may be interested in pursuing legal education. To serve the undergraduate population effectively, law schools should keep interested prelaw advisors, minority and other counselors informed of their admission requirements and institutional programs.

Application Procedures

1. Law schools should promptly notify applicants of admission decisions.

2. Law schools should respect the confidential nature of information received about applicants.

While a policy of openness and accessibility should form the basis for all communications with law school applicants, law schools should be scrupulous in maintaining the privacy of applicants. Without the expressed consent of the applicant involved and the author of the material in question, admission information relating to an applicant, such as LSAT scores, prior academic record, letters of recommendation, and dean's reports, should not be released to persons other than admission decision makers, the candidate and others with a legitimate interest in the admission process. This restriction would not prevent schools from sharing information that is not in a personally identifiable form, but even in this case, law schools should take care that the information is released with appropriate discretion.

From time to time, information about law school applicants at a particular law school is provided by Law Services. Information contained in many of these periodic reports is also confidential and should not be released to persons outside of the admission process, except as required by law.

3. A law school application should state clearly what information is being sought. The application should also state the applicant's obligation to provide accurate, current, and complete information. Further, the application should define the consequences of providing false, misleading, or incomplete information.

If the law school believes that false or misleading information has been provided by an applicant, that allegation should be submitted to the LSAC Misconduct and Irregularities in the Admission Process Panel for investigation. Then, if misconduct is found, all law schools to which the applicant has applied, or may apply, will be notified.

4. Except under early decision plans, law schools should not require applicants or other persons to indicate the order of applicants' law school preferences.

Law schools should allow applicants the freedom to explore as many opportunities to pursue legal education as possible. To preserve applicant options, law schools should not base admission decisions on the order of applicants' law school preferences, unless the school has established an early decision plan. An early decision plan is one under which an applicant and a law school mutually agree at the point of application that the applicant will be given an admission decision at a date earlier than usual in return for the applicant's commitment, at that date, to attend the school and withdraw all applications pending at other law schools, and not initiate new applications.

5. Except under early decision plans, law schools should permit applicants to choose among offers of admission as well as offers of scholarships, grants, and loans without penalty until April 1. Admitted applicants who have submitted a timely financial aid application should not be required to commit to enroll until notified of financial aid awards that are within the control of the law school.

6. No law school has an obligation to maintain an offer of admission if it discovers that the applicant has accepted an offer at another institution. Except under early decision plans, law schools should not suggest that acceptance of their offer of admission creates a moral or legal obligation to register at that school. Every accepted applicant should be free to deal with all law schools and to accept an offer from one of them even though a deposit has been paid to another school. To provide applicants with an uncoerced choice among various law schools, no excessive fee should be required solely to maintain a place in the class. Law schools should give applicants sufficient warning and ample time before withdrawing offers.

7. Law schools should maintain a waiting list of reasonable length and only for a reasonable length of time.

Law schools using waiting lists should ensure that the lists are of reasonable length and that final decisions about applicants placed on the waiting lists are made and communicated to the applicant as soon as possible.

Index